THE CHARLT

BASEBALL CARD

PRICE GUIDE

THIRD EDITION

published under agreement by

P. M. Fiocca, Publisher
ST. CATHARINES, ONTARIO

W. K. Cross, Publisher
TORONTO, ONTARIO ❖ BIRMINGHAM, MICHIGAN

Canadian Cataloguing in Publication Data

The National Library of Canada has catalogued this publication as follows:

Main entry under title:

The Charlton Canadian baseball card price guide

Annual.
1st ed.(1992)-
On cover: "Cards from 1912..."
ISSN 1188-6447
ISBN 0-88968-172-4 (1998)

1. Baseball cards - Prices - Canada - Periodicals.
2. Baseball cards - Collectors and collecting - Canada - Periodicals. I. Title: Baseball card price guide.

GV875.3.C5 769'.49796357'097105 C93-030190-0

Printed in Canada
in the Province of Ontario

Editorial Office
103 Lakeshore Road, Suite 202
St. Catharines, Ontario L2N 2T6
Tel: (905) 646-7744 1-800-408-0352
Fax: (905) 646-0995
website: www.trajan.com
Email: office@trajan.com

Editorial Office
2040 Yonge Street, Suite 208
Toronto, Ontario M4S 1Z9
Tel: (416) 488-1418 1-800-442-6042
Fax: (416) 488-4656 1-800-442-1542
website: www.charltonpress.com
email: chpress@charltonpress.com

EDITORIAL

Project Editor	Richard Scott	Production Co-ordinator	Jan Coles
Associate Editor	Baron Bedesky	Production Team	Cheryl Venneri
Advertising Sales	Paul Starrs		Mary-Anne Leftley
Publisher	Paul M. Fiocca		Sylvie Tremblay
			Lisa Grünwald
			Jim Szeplaki

ACKNOWLEDGEMENTS TO THE THIRD EDITION

The Charlton Press and Trajan Publishing Corporation wish to thank all of those who have in the past helped and assisted with the Charlton Canadian Baseball Card Price Guide.

COLLECTOR CONTRIBUTORS

Steve Rimbault, John Mele, Robert and Ceka Butt, Steven Singer, John Wessel, John Doolittle, Angelo Savelli, George Gray, Bob Boin, Mark Lee, Eric Beamish, Peter Semerak, Terry Brunt, Joe Herries, André Archambault, Joe Marco.

INSTITUTIONAL CONTRIBUTORS

Mike Monson, Pacific Trading Cards; **Marty Appel and Kevin Crux,** Topps Chewing Gum; **Jeff Morris,** Pinnacle Brands; **Kevin Watters,** Donruss Trading Cards; **Terry Melia,** Upper Deck Company; **Doug Drotman,** Fleer/SkyBox.

CONTRIBUTING RETAIL DEALERS

Joseph E. Filion, Cartomania; **Andrew Kossman**, Action Coin & Card; **Harvey Goldfarb,** A.J. Cards; **Léandre Normand,** Promodium; **Mike & Mary Drandzyk**, Kitchener Coin Shop; **Hans-Lee Tan**, Game Breakers; **Brad Norris-Jones**, MVP Sports; **David Chu,** Toronto Sportscards; **Bruce Romaniuk,** Triple C Auctions; **Gary Gagen,** Let's Collect; **John Brenner,** Lookin' For Heroes; **George Kumagai,** Major Leagues; **Frank Leardi,** Frank Leardi Sports Cards; **Jason Martin,** Martin's Sports Cards; **Bruce Lounsbury,** Bozley's Cards & Collectables; **Doug Scott,** Maple Leaf Cards & Videos; **Daniel May,** The Sports Connection; **Kevin Lawr,** Niagara Sports Cards; **Mike Dean,** Strictly Singles Sportscards; **Ken Tallman,** Select Sportscards; **Mel McNulty,** Kingston All Sports II.

CORRECTIONS

The publisher welcomes information for future editions, from interested collectors, manufacturers and retail dealers concerning any aspect of the listings in this book.

TABLE OF CONTENTS

Chapter 4: Minor League Team Issues

Chapter 5: Alphabetical Index

Chapter 6: Canadian-born Players

INTRODUCTION

This price guide offers the Canadian baseball card collector the most comprehensive guide to Canadian-issued cards and Canadian-born players. Whether you are a novice collector or a seasoned pro, this book will be an invaluable aid and source of reference.

Everyone is a collector of something. People collect things for a variety of reasons: for investment purposes, the joy of the hunt, for sentimental reasons, or just for the thrill of owning something rare or limited.

Those just starting out will soon discover that collecting sports cards can become an addictive pastime that has many variations, whatever its theme.

Deciding what to collect is a totally personal choice. It's impossible to collect everything. Collectors should focus on a particular era, player, team, company, or issue year. They may focus on a certain types of card, such as All-Stars, highlight, MVP, rookie, insert, parallel or superstar cards.

In this book, you will find complete checklists and pricing for Canadian issues 1912 to present. Chapter 1 details the pre-sixties era while Chapter 2 deals with post-sixties issues. All sets in these two chapters are sorted in chronological order.

The Canadian team-issues are listed in Chapters 3 (Major Leagues) and 4 (Minor Leagues). American-produced minor league team sets which were issued at the Canadian ballparks are also listed in this book.

In Chapter 5 you will find an alphabetical index to the first four chapters. You'll find this index a great cross-reference to finding individual items in this book.

The Canadian-born players' checklist is found in Chapter 6. This checklist lists every card and parallel card for all Canadian-born big league stars.

PRICING IN THIS CATALOGUE

The purpose of this catalogue is to give accurate, up-to-date retail prices for baseball cards. These individual market results are drawn from both dealer and collector activity and are averaged to reflect the current marketplace. Regional price differences will occur due to team and player popularity across the country. The early cards in mint condition, especially those issued before the Second World War, will command premiums of two or three times NRMT prices.

A necessary word of caution. No catalogue can or should propose to be a fixed price list. Except in the case of newly issued cards (where the published price is actually a manufacturer's suggested retail price), collector interest, rarity factors and other vagaries of the hobby invariably dictate true retail values.

This catalogue then, should be considered as a guide, indicating current retail prices possible for the collector and dealer alike to use as a starting point for a buy/sell transaction.

Those who take a little more time than average to read a price guide probably understand there is structure and order that is consistent throughout. For example, if a Frank Thomas card is worth more than a Juan Gonzalez card in one set, the Thomas card should be worth more than the Gonzalez in every baseball set.

This is one way to help keep better track of the monstrous volume of product out there. It helps the price guide editors, it helps the dealers and it helps the collectors.

A tendency that has become more evident than ever is sellers settling on even or round numbers for a selling price on their items. Fifty cents, $1.00, $2.00, $5.00, $50.00, those are numbers mostly commonly defaulted to when a seller is asked to state his price. Price guides should reflect this accordingly.

With the exception of complete annual guides such as this one, individual card listings from regular sets have been shortened to an extent in the hobby publications. There is no need to chart whether certain minor stars have gone up from eight cents to 12 cents from one month to the next. And many long-time collectors have no interest in knowing if a certain card has gone up from .50 cents to .75 cents either.

Just the same, newer collectors, whether they are adults or kids may be interested and fascinated by following even the smallest change in price. It is one way they will better understand the market until they progress to the higher stage of hobby consciousness achieved by many others.

THE MARKET

Like all businesses, the value of baseball cards is determined by the law of supply and demand. The supply of available cards is less than the quantity produced because a certain percentage of cards are thrown away or destroyed. Not all purchasers of baseball cards are serious collectors intent on preserving the quality of their cards. People are now aware of the potential appreciation in value of mint condition sports cards.

The supply is almost impossible to determine since private companies are not required by law to divulge information on the quantity of cards they produce. Variations in supply have gradually been noted over the years.

Several factors determine the demand of any given card: the number of cards produced, the popularity of the player depicted on the card, the age of the card, the condition of the card and the card's over-all attractiveness.

Rookie cards consistently demand a higher value, even for common players. Long-time hobby people or collecting purists may cringe, but speculation is an integral and unavoidable aspect of the hobby. Every industry or business is rife with it. Rookie cards continue to be an important aspect of this.

It is a well-known phenomenon that rookie cards garner

much hype and attention. However, nine times out of 10, the player does not fulfill the lofty expectations assigned to him and his card values will decline. For every Ken Griffey, Jr., there are plenty of Brien Taylors and Todd Van Poppels.

Promotional and community issues are primarily of regional interest only. Non-standard size cards and those produced by small manufacturers tend to be sold at a higher price as complete sets. But still, a diehard collector will buy almost anything.

The demand for cards will vary regionally across the nation. Human nature dictates that cards depicting local or hometown players and teams will demand a higher price locally than in other regions.

Although one would think that a complete set would cost more than the total price of the individual cards, this is usually not the case. This trend began with the growing interest among collectors in individual player cards, specifically rookie, star, and superstar cards. Because the same quantity of each card in a series was produced, it became more difficult to complete a set because of the shortage of certain individual player cards. With the decreased demand for sets, dealers were more inclined to let a set go at a lower price in order to get rid of a large stock of less desirable cards. The older cards, however, still sell better individually because the sets are very difficult to complete.

Simple economics have more to do with establishing a real value for sports cards than collectors often realize.

A case in point is the nagging issue of new cards, especially inserts, starting at a very high book value only to drop substantially after only a few months or even weeks. News like this is hardly conducive to promoting new sports card sales.

Unfortunately, too many hobbyists have interpreted this trend as a sign something is wrong with the hobby. If the shoe was on the other foot, and prices started low only to go up significantly in price, interest in the product, and ultimately sales, would increase substantially.

Well this is exactly what happened back in the late 1980s and early 1990s. People warmed to the allure of prices increasing on a weekly or even daily basis. Suddenly large numbers of people became a sports card dealer or "investor. "

There is no one simple reason why new cards decline in price soon after release but a pretty convincing argument can be made to back up the following theories though.

Of all potential sports card consumers, some have more disposable income than others. If a certain expensive card or product is released, the first ones to buy are often the wealthiest. One of reason why the more successful dealers today are turning a profit is they may have assembled a reliable group of "clients," collectors they know have no financial worries. These clients remain loyal to a dealer who takes care of their needs promptly, without going beyond ethical bounds and flagrantly overcharging.

BUYING AND SELLING CARDS

Several avenues are available as sources for buying, selling, or trading individual cards and sets.

Naturally, like any business person, you want to sell your cards for the highest possible price and purchase them at the lowest possible price. Using this price guide as a reference, you will have to shop around to become familiar with pricing differences among the various sources. The sports card market is not as liquid as the stock market and a certain degree of patience is necessary to sell your cards at what you think is a fair price.

It's a good idea to keep abreast of the changing market by regularly reading the several monthly sports card periodicals available. These publications are very useful in keeping up-to-date on pricing fluctuations, collectors' personal advertisements and the dates and locations of shows, auctions, and conventions. Canadian Sportscard Collector is the only Canadian national publication available.

Shows and conventions offer you the best opportunity to shop around and meet a wide range of dealers and collectors assembled under one roof. Not only do you have a huge selection of older cards to choose from, but you may also buy unopened product by the single pack or by the box.

Whether you are at the twice annual Sportscard Expo in Toronto, or any other show for that matter, to spend $20 or $20,000, it is best to plan your approach. How you approach the show depends largely on what you are looking for and how much you want to spend.

Traditionally, early in a show is pivotal for the serious collector. If you are looking for pre-war vintage items, this is when you will likely do business. If you wait until the weekend, the good stuff is picked over.

Early is also a good time to browse. The crowd is usually small enough that you can get a good look at the different items each dealer has. You may find items you never knew existed. If you are at a large show, it will take a while to get a good look at what everybody has. Don't be afraid to bring a notebook and write down some of the good items you find. It will be the only way to remember where you saw it.

You may also find a corporate presence at a show. The earlier you visit the booths, the more likely you are to get good promo cards. Also, the corporate people are not as busy early on as they are later. You, as a collector, could get the opportunity to talk to some of the inside people at your favourite card companies.

It's also not a bad idea to make note of the show's autograph guests, so you can time your visit to the event around any autograph guests you will want to meet.

If you are looking for new product, it may pay to buy these items later in the show. Soon enough, dealer price wars are well underway. Though you may get a better deal if you wait until the last minute, product is more plentiful earlier on.

The best deals in wax are found with products one or more years old. Many dealers may be trying to clear out inventory, and you will find more $5 to $20 boxes of cards than you will know what to do with.

If you like cheap wax and cheap hand collected sets, later in a show can be a gold mine. Dealers are preparing to pack up from the show. They are tired, and may want to take back as little as possible. Complete sets can be found for as little as two to five dollars. There may not be a great investment potential in the purchase, but who cares? They are fun sets and they were cheap.

If you have certain sets or boxes you are looking for, be sure to make a want list, and jot down prices as you make your first round of the show. Again, we can't tell you how important lists and role books can be in doing a big show. If you are filling in holes in old sets, lists are a given, and you may want to try a time when you know the crowd has thinned out. To fill a want list, you will need to take time to look for what you need. It can be hard in a crowd.

You may wish to maximize your profit by selling your cards on your own. You may advertise in a local newspaper or sports periodical or rent a booth space at a card show if you have a large collection to sell. But before you set out, take into consideration the time you must invest, advertising costs, miscellaneous expenses, your sales ability, and your knowledge of card collecting. These factors will all dictate your success.

For the collector who enjoys assembling a collection slowly, piece by piece, foil packs are usually available at your local convenience store.

If you are in a hurry to make a transaction, or you don't want the hassle of selling your cards yourself, you may choose a dealer as a source. Dealers are in touch with an extensive network of collectors and suppliers and are more knowledgeable at identifying potential buyers for your cards, or locating the owners of elusive cards. You must be fully aware, however, that a dealer has to cover expenses, and his primary reason for setting up shop is to make a profit. Dealers will pay anywhere from 10% to 75% of the book value depending on demand (measured as the time it takes the dealer to sell the item). You may also arrange for a dealer to accept your cards on consignment. This assures you that he will attempt to obtain the highest possible price, since he will charge a percentage of the sale price as his fee.

Direct mail is another source for obtaining cards. If you choose this route, it would be wise to start off buying small quantities of cards until you become accustomed with the quality of cards purchased unseen. This also gives one a chance to build up a rapport and trust with a mail-order dealer before engaging in larger purchases.

CARD CARE

In order to ensure the continued appreciation in value of your cards, you must keep card handling to a minimum. It is highly recommended that you obtain suitable storage containers to preserve the condition of your delicate cards. Items such as sleeves, boxes and binder sheets are commercially available in specific sizes in which to safely store your prized collectibles.

Card sleeves are handy for displaying single cards. Sleeves are made of various materials, ranging from pliable polypropylene and polyethylene, to a stiffer mylar, to hard acrylic and Plexiglass.

Specially designed cardboard boxes enable you to store hundreds of cards and also facilitate transportation or storage. Try to use boxes with flat bottoms as boxes with bottom flaps can damage your cards. Since some cardboard boxes may contain an element of acid, you may wish to insert your cards into individual sleeves before placing them in boxes. As an added precaution, take care not to place your valuable cards at either end of the box.

Plastic three-ring binder sheets with pockets are a popular means of holding and displaying cards. Make certain that the pockets will hold your cards snugly but not tightly, as some sheets are designed to hold a specific size of card. Sheets made of polyvinyl chloride (PVC) are less flexible and more transparent, but contain certain oils which may, after long periods of time, damage your cards. PVC may be detected by its customary vinyl odour, whereas polypropylene and polyethylene are odourless.

Needless to say, mint condition cards do not have foreign substances applied to them. Adding glue, tape, protective coating, or writing; removing tabs; applying elastic bands to stacks of cards; or using photograph corners to store cards in a scrap album are all taboo.

Extreme environmental conditions will, in time, adversely affect the condition of your cards. Prolonged direct sunlight will remove the gloss from cards and fade their colours. High humidity or extreme changes in humidity will result in gradual deterioration and warping, while excessive heat will increase the rate of decomposition.

It's not necessary to handle cards with gloves or tongs, just be aware of the adverse affects of mishandling and take a realistic approach to preserving the condition of your cards.

CARD GRADING

Grading any collectable item is always a subjective decision, but grading is the most important characteristic the collector must understand for condition determines the price catagory.

The main criteria for judging the condition of a card are centering, corner wear, creases, alterations, and surface wear.

THE CONDITION OF THE CARD MUST BE DETERMINED BEFORE A CARD CAN BE PRICED.

CENTERING

Centering is one defect beyond the control of the card purchaser. Whereas a mint card is one which is in the same condition as when issued, poor centering will devalue this card before it is even packaged. A well centred card has opposing borders of equal width. However, width differences in adjacent borders are acceptable. The degree of centering varies from perfectly centered to blatantly miscut.

Centred: The card image is perfectly centred within the borders.

Slightly Off-centred: One border width is barely smaller than its opposite border.

Off-centred: One border width is noticeably larger than the opposite border.

Badly Off-centred: A border is barely perceptible on one side of the card.

Miscut: The card is cut so badly that one border is missing, and the opposite border shows part of the adjacent card.

CORNER WEAR

The degree of rounding and fraying (paper layer separation) of the corners on cards decreases the value. Corner wear may be expressed in the following degrees: sharp corners, slight fraying, slightly rounded, rounded corners, and badly rounded corners.

CREASES

Creases range in severity from light to heavy.

Light Crease: This crease is barely perceptible. It is not as serious if the crease is on the back of the card.

Medium Crease: This crease is noticeable, but is not the length of the card or deep enough to break the surface of the card.

Heavy Crease: The crease breaks through the card surface.

SURFACE WEAR

Cards that are mishandled or handled too often will show signs of surface wear. Prolonged direct exposure to sunlight will remove the gloss and cause discolouration to the surface of the card. Warping or banding will also cause surface wear.

CONDITION GUIDE

The following eight categories are commonly used to describe the condition of a card:

MINT (MT): A card containing no defects. The picture is in focus, the borders are even, the corners are sharp, the edges are smooth, the surface contains no creases and has its orignal gloss, and there are no printing defects.

NEAR MINT (NRMT): A card with one of the very slight defects previously mentioned. This would include printer's lines or spots.

EXCELLENT-MINT (EX-MT): A card with two or three very slight defects.

EXCELLENT (EX): A card with only a few minor defects; such as, stains or marks on the back of the card, loss of gloss, and only slight rounding, off-centring, or creasing.

VERY GOOD (VG): A card displaying one major or several minor defects which are noticeable but not serious; such as, some corner rounding, loss of surface gloss, off-centred or discoloured borders, minor creases, or the picture being slightly out of focus.

GOOD (G): A card showing the results of much handling, with two or three major defects. Common major flaws include deceptive trimming, badly off-centred borders showing signs of browning, and a higher degree of corner rounding and layering, creasing, scuffing of the card face, and edge notching.

FAIR (F): A card with one serious defect or several major defects. Serious defects include writing on the front, miscutting, large holes, noticeable trimming, heavy creases, and tears.

POOR (P): A card with two or more serious defects. If it has any value at all, it would only be as a filler until a replacement card is found.

MISHANDLING DEFECTS

Poor handling habits and improper storage of cards will cause several other defects. Common flaws include tape or paste marks, pin holes, tears, fuzzy or worn edges, rubber band marks, smoke stains, writing, and removal of perforated tabs or coupons. Improper manufacturer packaging may also cause gum staining.

PRINTING

Poor centering, poor printing, creasing, cutting, packaging or just poor quality control can result in a card coming from the manufacturer in any condition but mint.

ALTERATIONS

Buyers must take special care to ensure that cards have not been trimmed or touched-up in an attempt to improve their condition.

Trimming: This is an attempt to remove rounding, fraying, and uneven border defects by cutting away parts of the card. The safest way to check this suspicion is to measure the card with a ruler.

Touch-up: This is an attempt to enhance faded areas on a card by covering up obvious defects with the use of some sort of colouring device.

Food, Glorious Food!

Canada's food and regional baseball card sets are untapped gold mines in the hobby

By Baron Bedesky

Canadian regional and food issue baseball cards are not a Johnny-come-lately to the sports card market. There are a number of fascinating and relatively inexpensive sets to collect dating back to World War II.

Actually, there are a number of sets that pre-date World War II but they qualify more as "vintage" cards, and while they are not unattractive or undesirable, they often carry "vintage" prices.

During the mid 1940s, a series of black and white photos were issued by radio stations in the Montreal area. Entitled "Parade Sportive" or "Paul Stuart" photos, they are best known for featuring hockey players. However, several baseball players were also featured on these photos, most from the Montreal Royals, the top farm team of the Brooklyn Dodgers at the time. While there are few household names in the lot, they are attractive and often available at card shows for as little as five dollars a piece, not bad for a 50-year-old piece of Canadian baseball nostalgia.

The province of Québec remained the baseball hotbed of Canada for many years, helping explain why two other baseball issues originated from this province in the early 1950s. The newspaper *La Patrie* issued a series of colour photos in their publication, very similar to their popular hockey photos. The baseball players are mostly from the Québec Provincial League, a semi-pro loop that thrived at the time. While most of the names have long since faded into obscurity, a few like Don Hoak, Jim Gilliam and Québec native Georges Maranda went on to make their mark in the big leagues. These are difficult to find because the newspaper stock on which they were printed has not held up well over the years. Considering their scarcity, they are a bargain at 10-20 dollars a piece.

Laval Dairies, again a familiar name with collectors because of their hockey card issues from the same time, released a 114-card set in 1952 focusing on players from the Provincial League. Now these are extremely difficult to find. Many veteran collectors from the province of Québec are not even familiar with them. Again, they are available for a relatively low price (around 25 dollars each), probably because of the obscure player content and because so little is known about them. These black and white smaller sized cards are on cardboard stock and feature a sprinkling of players who made it to "the show", including Hector Lopez and Humberto Robinson.

Other sets from the 1950s include the 1950 World Wide Gum set, the 1952 Parkhurst issue and the 1953 Canadian Exhibits. Some Major League stars were included in these sets, especially in the Canadian Exhibits but many minor league players from teams in Montreal, Ottawa, and Toronto were also included.

In 1962, Post cereal released an extensive set on the back side of cereal boxes. Consisting of 200 cards, many of which were short printed, most of the Major League stars were included, such as Mickey Mantle, Roger Maris, Willie Mays, Hank Aaron, Sandy Koufax and a young Carl Yastrzemski. It is no easy task finding these in near mint shape, as kids everywhere cut them out of the cereal boxes with their trusty scissors and often then glued them somewhere.

Most hockey collectors are familiar with the four popular series of Shirriff coins. The 1962 Shirriff baseball coin set is not quite as well known. Its sheer size makes it a tough venture to complete. There are 200 coins in all, many of which feature Hall-of-Famers. At three to five bucks for a common, you can get a good start on putting a set together without spending wads of cash.

We now enter a scary era so hang on tight. It is the ominous void of 1963 to 1982, a period in which few if any Canadian specialty baseball cards were produced. Undoubtedly, this can be partly explained by O-Pee-Chee releasing an annual set in Canada from 1965 onward. Also, all Canadian minor league teams had disappeared and moved elsewhere by the mid 1960s. Even the debut of Major League baseball in Montreal in 1969 did little to spur new card releases for several years.

One exception is an Expo postcard set released in 1974 by Weston bakeries. A popular issue for many years after its release, this 10-card set included Ken Singleton, Tim Foli and the immortal John Boccabella. Some collectors are turned off by the airbrushing of the logos, but it remains a colourful and inexpensive set chronicling some of those early Expo favourites.

1982 marked a turning point of sorts for Canadian baseball food and regional cards. By now, Canada had a second Major League team, even though they were lousy. And minor league baseball was slowly returning to north of the border. Enthusiasm and interest in Major League baseball was at an all-time high.

A 24-card Expos set was released in Québec with Hygrade Luncheon Meats. Featuring French text, rounded corners, and the Hygrade logo in the top right hand corner, notable players include Tim Raines, Gary Carter, Andre Dawson and Jeff Reardon. A word of caution, however. While unopened packages of baseball cards from the early 1980s are rapidly appreciating in value, the market for unopened packages of Hygrade Luncheon Meat cards remains inexplicably slow.

Zellers released another Expo set the same year featuring players giving instructional tips. The cards were issued in three-card panels with perforations for easy separation. Each panel had three different poses of players demonstrating proper baseball technique such as Tim Raines on sliding, and Andre Dawson illustrating a proper batting stroke. Collectors were never keen on the instructional aspect of these cards and they never have been exceedingly popular.

1984 witnessed the release of the first annual Blue Jay Fire Safety set. Nobody ever expected these sets to be as popular as they have been over the past 10 years. That first set featured a lot of mediocre players from a mediocre team and figured to be a one-shot deal. Along the way, however, the Blue Jays became more and more competitive and increasingly popular with their fans, and the card boom was just in its infancy. The set was eagerly awaited for every year.

They are all characterized by their thorough player content including not only star players but also fringe pitchers and third string catchers as well as coaches. These are complete team sets in every sense of the word.

There is some confusion about sets from the later years as they are marked on the reverse "Not for resale," apparently in an effort to curb activity and profiting on the secondary market. While some dealers are wary of the warning, many others pay the suggestion little heed.

As the 1980s progressed, many more food sets were launched, many of which featured the Expos and the Blue Jays. The companies responsible included Stuart's Baked Goods, General Mills, Ault Foods, Provigo, Quaker Oats, Hostess and Ben's Bread.

Andre Dawson

These thin-stock colour cards were released as part of a promotion for Hygrade Luncheon Meats in 1982. Consisting of 24 cards featuring the Montreal Expos, they were the first Canadian baseball food issue to be released in several years.

Scott Sanderson

As the 1980s progressed, more and more baseball food issues were hitting the grocery store shelves. Stuart issued this conventional-sized 30-card set in 1983 which, again, featured the Expos.

CHAPTER ONE

BASEBALL ISSUES 1912 TO 1953

1912 IMPERIAL TOBACCO

GAUNT

Pitcher Gaunt, who is with the Baltimore club in the International League is a development from the college campus and just through his initial year in organized base ball. Last year he worked in 11 games mostly as a substitute and is only credited with a single victory. He batted .067 but looks to be of the promising kind.

BASEBALL SERIES. NO 69

These cards were issued by Imperial Tobacco in 1912 as premiums in packs of Black Cat, Sweet Caporal and other brand-name cigarettes. The 90-card set is Canada's first known issue of baseball cards and features players from the International League (formerly known as the Eastern League). The wood-grain borders make it difficult to find cards in NRMT to mint condition.

Card Size: 1 1/2" x 2 5/8"
Face: Sepia, wood-grain border; name
Back: Black and white; name, number, résumé
Imprint: None
ACC No.: C46

Complete Set (90 cards):		**1,250.00**	**2,500.00**	**4,500.00**
Common Player:		**15.00**	**30.00**	**50.00**

	No.	Player	VG	EX	NRMT
☐	1	William O'Hara, Tor.	50.00	150.00	300.00
☐	2	James McGinley, Tor.	25.00	50.00	100.00
☐	3	Frenchy LeClaire, Mtl.	15.00	30.00	50.00
☐	4	John White, Buffalo	15.00	30.00	50.00
☐	5	James Murray, Buffalo	15.00	30.00	50.00
☐	6	Joe Ward, Rochester	15.00	30.00	50.00
☐	7	Whitey Alperman, Rochester	15.00	30.00	50.00
☐	8	Natty Nattress, Mtl.	15.00	30.00	50.00
☐	9	Fred Sline, Providence	15.00	30.00	50.00
☐	10	Royal Rock, Bal.	15.00	30.00	50.00
☐	11	Ray Demmitt, Mtl.	15.00	30.00	50.00
☐	12	Butch Schmidt, Bal.	15.00	30.00	50.00
☐	13	Samuel Frock, Bal.	15.00	30.00	50.00
☐	14	Fred Burchell, Mtl.	15.00	30.00	50.00
☐	15	Jack Kelley	15.00	30.00	50.00
☐	16	Frank Barberich, Mtl.	15.00	30.00	50.00
☐	17	Frank Corridon, Buffalo	15.00	30.00	50.00
☐	18	Doc Adkins, Bal.	15.00	30.00	50.00
☐	19	Jack Dunn, Mgr., Bal.	15.00	30.00	50.00
☐	20	James Walsh, Bal.	15.00	30.00	50.00
☐	21	Charles Hanford, Mtl., Error	15.00	30.00	50.00
☐	22	Dick Rudolph, Tor.	15.00	30.00	50.00
☐	23	Curt Elston, Providence	15.00	30.00	50.00
☐	24	Sutton, Mtl.	15.00	30.00	50.00
☐	25	Charlie French, Mtl.	15.00	30.00	50.00
☐	26	J. Ganzel, Mgr., Rochester	15.00	30.00	50.00
☐	27	Joe Kelley, Mgr.	90.00	175.00	325.00
☐	28	Benny Meyer, Jersey City	15.00	30.00	50.00
☐	29	George Schirm, Buffalo	15.00	30.00	50.00
☐	30	William Purtell, Mtl.	15.00	30.00	50.00
☐	31	Bayard Sharpe, Buffalo	15.00	30.00	50.00
☐	32	Tony Smith, Tor.	15.00	30.00	50.00
☐	33	John Lush, Tor.	15.00	30.00	50.00
☐	34	William Collins, Newark	15.00	30.00	50.00
☐	35	Art Phelan, Providence	15.00	30.00	50.00
☐	36	Edward Phelps, Tor.	15.00	30.00	50.00
☐	37	Rube Vickers, Bal.	15.00	30.00	50.00
☐	38	Cy Seymour, Newark	15.00	30.00	50.00
☐	39	Shadow Carroll, Mtl.	15.00	30.00	50.00
☐	40	Jake Gettman, Bal.	15.00	30.00	50.00
☐	41	Luther Taylor, Mtl.	15.00	30.00	50.00
☐	42	Walter Justis, Jersey City	15.00	30.00	50.00
☐	43	Robert Fisher, Newark	15.00	30.00	50.00
☐	44	Freddy Parent, Bal.	15.00	30.00	50.00
☐	45	James Dygert, Bal.	15.00	30.00	50.00
☐	46	John Butler, Jersey City	15.00	30.00	50.00
☐	47	Fred Mitchell, Buffalo	15.00	30.00	50.00
☐	48	Heinie Batch, Rochester	15.00	30.00	50.00
☐	49	Michael Corcoran, Bal.	15.00	30.00	50.00
☐	50	Edward Doescher,Jersey City	15.00	30.00	50.00
☐	51	Wheeler, Jersey City	15.00	30.00	50.00
☐	52	Elijah Jones, Rochester	15.00	30.00	50.00
☐	53	Fred Truesdale, Buffalo	15.00	30.00	50.00
☐	54	Fred Beebe, Buffalo	15.00	30.00	50.00
☐	55	Lewis Brockett, Buffalo	15.00	30.00	50.00
☐	56	Wells, Jersey City	15.00	30.00	50.00
☐	57	Lewis McAllister, Bal.	15.00	30.00	50.00
☐	58	Ralph Stroud, Buffalo	15.00	30.00	50.00
☐	59	Manser, Rochester	15.00	30.00	50.00
☐	60	Ducky Holmes, Rochester	15.00	30.00	50.00
☐	61	Rube Dessau, Rochester	15.00	30.00	50.00
☐	62	Fred Jacklitsch, Rochester	15.00	30.00	50.00
☐	63	Graham, Tor.	15.00	30.00	50.00
☐	64	Noah Henline, Bal.	15.00	30.00	50.00
☐	65	Chick Gandil, Mtl.	65.00	125.00	200.00
☐	66	Tom Hughes, Rochester	15.00	30.00	50.00
☐	67	Joseph Delahanty, Tor.	15.00	30.00	50.00
☐	68	Pierce, Mtl.	15.00	30.00	50.00
☐	69	Gaunt, Bal.	15.00	30.00	50.00
☐	70	Edward Fitzpatrick, Tor.	15.00	30.00	50.00
☐	71	Wyatt Lee, Newark	15.00	30.00	50.00
☐	72	John Kissinger, Jersey City	15.00	30.00	50.00
☐	73	William Malarkey, Buffalo	15.00	30.00	50.00
☐	74	William Byers, Bal.	15.00	30.00	50.00
☐	75	George Simmons, Rochester	15.00	30.00	50.00
☐	76	Daniel Moeller, Rochester	15.00	30.00	50.00
☐	77	Joseph McGinnity, Newark	90.00	175.00	300.00
☐	78	Alex Hardy, Mtl.	15.00	30.00	50.00
☐	79	Bob Holmes, Newark	15.00	30.00	50.00
☐	80	William Baxter, Buffalo	15.00	30.00	50.00
☐	81	Edward Spencer, Rochester	15.00	30.00	50.00
☐	82	Bradley Kocher, Tor.	15.00	30.00	50.00
☐	83	Robert Shaw, Tor.	15.00	30.00	50.00
☐	84	Joseph Yeager, Mtl.	15.00	30.00	50.00
☐	85	Carlo, Newark	15.00	30.00	50.00
☐	86	William Abstein, Jersey City	15.00	30.00	50.00
☐	87	Tim Jordan, Tor.	15.00	30.00	50.00
☐	88	Dick Breen, Jersey City	15.00	30.00	50.00
☐	89	Tom McCarty, Newark	15.00	30.00	50.00
☐	90	Ed Curtis, Tor.	50.00	100.00	300.00

1921 NEILSON'S

Issued in Neilson's chocolate bars during 1921, this set was printed on both paper and cardboard stocks. The designs are identical on the two stocks but the cardboard cards are unnumbered and command a slight premium over the paper cards. The prices below are for the paper issue.

Card Size: 2 1/2" x 3 1/2"

Face: Paper: Name, number, position, team Cardboard: Name, position, team

Back: Paper: Neilson's in large serif type, Advertisement Cardboard: Neilson's in normal type, Advertisement

Imprint: NEILSON'S

ACC No.: V61

	No.	Player	VG	EX	NRMT
		Complete Set. (120 cards):	**4,000.00**	**8,000.00**	**14,000.00**
		Common Player:	**20.00**	**40.00**	**70.00**
☐	1	George H. Burns, Cle.	25.00	50.00	100.00
☐	2	John Tobin, St.L.B	20.00	40.00	70.00
☐	3	J.T. Zachary, Wsh.	20.00	40.00	70.00
☐	4	L. (Bullet Joe) Bush, Bos.	30.00	60.00	100.00
☐	5	Lu Blue, Det.	20.00	40.00	70.00
☐	6	C. (Tilly) Walker, Phi.A	20.00	40.00	70.00
☐	7	Carl Mays, NYY.	30.00	60.00	100.00
☐	8	L. (Goose) Goslin, Wsh.	75.00	150.00	250.00
☐	9	Eddie Rommel, Phi.A	20.00	40.00	70.00
☐	10	C. Robertson, Chi.-A.L.	20.00	40.00	70.00
☐	11	Ralph Perkins, Phi.A	20.00	40.00	70.00
☐	12	Joe Sewell, Cle.	65.00	125.00	200.00
☐	13	Harry Hooper, Chi.-A.L.	65.00	125.00	200.00
☐	14	Red Faber, Chi.-A.L.	65.00	125.00	200.00
☐	15	Bibb Falk, Chi.-A.L.	20.00	40.00	70.00
☐	16	George Uhle, Cle.	20.00	40.00	70.00
☐	17	Emory Rigney, Det.	20.00	40.00	70.00
☐	18	George Dauss, Det.	20.00	40.00	70.00
☐	19	Herman Pillette, Cin.	20.00	40.00	70.00
☐	20	Wally Schang, NYY.	20.00	40.00	70.00
☐	21	Lawrence Woodall, Det.	20.00	40.00	70.00
☐	22	Steve O'Neill, Cle.	20.00	40.00	70.00
☐	23	Edmund Miller, Wsh.	20.00	40.00	70.00
☐	24	Sylvester Johnson, Det.	20.00	40.00	70.00
☐	25	Henry Severeid, St.L.B	20.00	40.00	70.00
☐	26	Dave Danforth, Chi.-A.L.	20.00	40.00	70.00
☐	27	Harry Heilmann, Det.	45.00	90.00	150.00
☐	28	Bert Cole, Det.	20.00	40.00	70.00
☐	29	Eddie Collins, Chi.-A.L.	45.00	90.00	150.00
☐	30	Ty Cobb, Mgr., Det.	750.00	1,500.00	2,500.00
☐	31	Bill Wambsganss,	30.00	60.00	100.00
☐	32	George Sisler, St.L.B	45.00	90.00	150.00
☐	33	Bobby Veach, Det.	20.00	40.00	70.00
☐	34	Earl Sheely, Chi.-A.L.	20.00	40.00	70.00
☐	35	Pat Collins, St.L.B	20.00	40.00	70.00
☐	36	Frank Davis, St.L.B	20.00	40.00	70.00
☐	37	Babe Ruth, NYY.	1,000.00	2,000.00	3,500.00
☐	38	Bryan Harris	20.00	40.00	70.00
☐	39	Bob Shawkey, NYY.	30.00	60.00	100.00
☐	40	Urban Shocker, St.L.B	20.00	40.00	70.00
☐	41	Martin McManus, St.L.B	20.00	40.00	70.00
☐	42	Clarke Pittenger, Bos.RS	20.00	40.00	70.00
☐	43	Deacon Jones, Det.	20.00	40.00	70.00
☐	44	Waite Hoyt, NYY.	65.00	125.00	200.00
☐	45	Johnny Mostil, Chi.-A.L.	20.00	40.00	70.00
☐	46	Mike Menosky, Bos.	20.00	40.00	70.00
☐	47	Walter Johnson, Wsh.	300.00	600.00	1,000.00
☐	48	Wally Pipp, NYY.	30.00	60.00	100.00
☐	49	Walter Gerber, St.L.B	20.00	40.00	70.00
☐	50	Ed Gharrity, Wsh.	20.00	40.00	70.00
☐	51	Frank Ellerbe, Wsh.	20.00	40.00	70.00
☐	52	Kenneth Williams, St.L.B	30.00	60.00	100.00
☐	53	Joe Hauser, Phi.A	20.00	40.00	70.00
☐	54	Carson Bigbee, Pgh.	20.00	40.00	70.00
☐	55	Emil (Irish) Meusel, Pha.	20.00	40.00	70.00
☐	56	Milton Stock, Stl..	20.00	40.00	70.00
☐	57	Wilbur Cooper, Pgh.	20.00	40.00	70.00
☐	58	Tommy Griffith, Bkn.	20.00	40.00	70.00
☐	59	C. (Shovel) Hodge, Chi.-A.L.	20.00	40.00	70.00
☐	60	E. (Bubbles) Hargrave, Cin.	20.00	40.00	70.00
☐	61	Russell Wrightstone, Pha.	20.00	40.00	70.00
☐	62	Frank Frisch, NYG.	60.00	120.00	200.00
☐	63	Jack Peters	20.00	40.00	70.00
☐	64	Dutch Reuther	20.00	40.00	70.00
☐	65	Bill Doak, Stl.	20.00	40.00	70.00
☐	66	Marty Callaghan, Chi.-N.L.	20.00	40.00	70.00
☐	67	Sammy Bohne, Cin.	20.00	40.00	70.00
☐	68	Earl Hamilton, Pgh.	20.00	40.00	70.00
☐	69	G. C. Alexander, Chi.-N.L.	90.00	175.00	300.00
☐	70	George J. Burns, NYG.	20.00	40.00	70.00
☐	71	Max Carey, Pgh.	45.00	90.00	150.00
☐	72	Adolfo Luque, Cin.	20.00	40.00	70.00
☐	73	Walt Barbare, Bos.B	20.00	40.00	70.00
☐	74	Vic Aldridge, Chi.-N.L.	20.00	40.00	70.00
☐	75	Jack Smith, Stl.	20.00	40.00	70.00
☐	76	Bob O'Farrell, Chi.-N.L.	20.00	40.00	70.00
☐	77	Pete Donohue, Cin.	20.00	40.00	70.00
☐	78	Ralph Pinelli, Det.	20.00	40.00	70.00
☐	79	Eddie Roush, Cin.	50.00	100.00	175.00
☐	80	Norman Boeckel, Bos.B	20.00	40.00	70.00
☐	81	Rogers Hornsby, Stl.	200.00	400.00	750.00
☐	82	George Toporcer, Stl.	20.00	40.00	70.00
☐	83	Ivy Wingo, Cin.	20.00	40.00	70.00
☐	84	Virgil Cheeves, Chi.-N.L.	20.00	40.00	70.00
☐	85	Verne Clemons, Stl.	20.00	40.00	70.00
☐	86	Lawrence Miller, Bos.	20.00	40.00	70.00
☐	87	John Kelleher, Chi.-N.L.	20.00	40.00	70.00
☐	88	Heinie Groh, Cin.	20.00	40.00	70.00
☐	89	Burleigh Grimes, Bkn.	45.00	90.00	150.00
☐	90	Rabbit Maranville, Pgh.	45.00	90.00	150.00
☐	91	Babe Adams, Pgh.	30.00	60.00	100.00
☐	92	Lee King, NYG.	20.00	40.00	70.00
☐	93	Art Nehf, NYG.	20.00	40.00	70.00
☐	94	Frank Snyder, NYG.	20.00	40.00	70.00
☐	95	Raymond Powell, Bos.B	20.00	40.00	70.00
☐	96	Wilbert (Bill) Hubbell, Pha.	20.00	40.00	70.00
☐	97	Leon Cadore, Bkn.	20.00	40.00	70.00
☐	98	Joe Oeschger, Bos.B	20.00	40.00	70.00
☐	99	Jake Daubert, Cin.	20.00	40.00	70.00
☐	100	Bill Sherdel, Stl.	20.00	40.00	70.00
☐	101	Hank DeBerry, Cle.	20.00	40.00	70.00
☐	102	John Lavan, Stl.	20.00	40.00	70.00
☐	103	Jesse Haines, Stl.	40.00	75.00	125.00
☐	104	J. (Goldie) Rapp, NYG.	20.00	40.00	70.00
☐	105	O. Ray Grimes, Chi.-N.L.	20.00	40.00	70.00

	No.	Player	VG	EX	NRMT
☐	106	Ross Youngs, NYG.	45.00	90.00	150.00
☐	107	Art Fletcher, Pha.	20.00	40.00	70.00
☐	108	Clyde Barnhart, Pgh.	20.00	40.00	70.00
☐	109	Louis (Pat) Duncan, Cin.	20.00	40.00	70.00
☐	110	Charlie Hollocher, Chi.-N.L.	20.00	40.00	70.00
☐	111	Horace Ford, Bos.B	20.00	40.00	70.00
☐	112	Bill Cunningham, NYG.	20.00	40.00	70.00
☐	113	Walter Schmidt, Pgh.	20.00	40.00	70.00
☐	114	Joe Schultz, Stl.	20.00	40.00	70.00
☐	115	John Morrison, Pgh.	20.00	40.00	70.00
☐	116	James Caveney, Cin.	20.00	40.00	70.00
☐	117	Zack Wheat, Bkn.	45.00	90.00	150.00
☐	118	Fred (Cy) Williams, Pha.	30.00	60.00	100.00
☐	119	George Kelly, NYG.	45.00	90.00	150.00
☐	120	Jimmy Ring, Pha.	25.00	50.00	100.00

1922 WILLIAM PATERSON

This set was offered as a premium in packages of caramel candy and was issued in Brantford, Ontario. There are slight size variations in these cards due to variances when the cards were trimmed at the printer.

Card Size: 2" x 3 1/4"
Face: Sepia; name, number, team, card number
Back: Blank
Imprint: Wm. Paterson, Limited Brantford, Canada
ACC No.: V89

	No.	Player	VG	EX	NRMT
		Complete Set (50 cards):	**3,000.00**	**6,000.00**	**11,000.00**
		Common Player:	**30.00**	**60.00**	**100.00**
☐	1	Edd Roush, Cin.	50.00	100.00	300.00
	2	Unknown			
☐	3	Del Gainer, Stl.	30.00	60.00	100.00
☐	4	George Sisler, St.L.B	75.00	150.00	250.00
☐	5	Joe Bush, NYY.	50.00	100.00	175.00
☐	6	Joe Oeschger, Bos.B	30.00	60.00	100.00
☐	7	Willie Kamm, Chi.-A.L.	30.00	60.00	100.00
☐	8	John Watson, Bos.B	30.00	60.00	100.00
☐	9	Adolfo Luque, Cin.	30.00	60.00	100.00
☐	10	Miller Huggins, Mgr., NYY.	50.00	100.00	175.00
☐	11	Wally Schang, NYY.	30.00	60.00	100.00
	12	Unknown			
☐	13	Tris Speaker, Mgr., Cle.	125.00	250.00	450.00
☐	14	Hugh McQuillen, NYG.	30.00	60.00	100.00
☐	15	George Kelly, NYG.	75.00	150.00	250.00
☐	16	Ray Schalk, Chi.-A.L.	75.00	150.00	250.00
☐	17	Sam Jones, NYY.	30.00	60.00	100.00
☐	18	Grover Alexander, Chi.-N.L.	125.00	250.00	450.00
☐	19	Bob Meusel, NYY.	30.00	60.00	100.00
☐	20	Emil Meusel, NYG.	30.00	60.00	100.00
☐	21	Rogers Hornsby, Stl.	125.00	350.00	600.00
☐	22	Harry Heilmann, Det.	65.00	125.00	200.00
☐	23	Heinie Groh, NYG.	30.00	60.00	100.00
☐	24	Frankie Frisch, NYG.	75.00	150.00	250.00
☐	25	Babe Ruth, NYY.	1,250.00	2,500.00	4,500.00
☐	26	Jack Bentley, NYG.	30.00	60.00	100.00
	27	Unknown			
☐	28	Max Carey, Pgh.	65.00	125.00	200.00
☐	29	Chick Fewster, Bos.	30.00	60.00	100.00
☐	30	Cy Williams, Pha.	50.00	100.00	175.00
☐	31	Burleigh Grimes, Bkn.	75.00	150.00	250.00
☐	32	Waite Hoyt, NYY.	60.00	120.00	200.00
☐	33	Frank Snyder, NYG.	30.00	60.00	100.00
☐	34	Clyde Milan, Mgr., Wsh.	30.00	60.00	100.00
☐	35	Eddie Collins, Chi.-A.L.	90.00	175.00	300.00
☐	36	Travis Jackson, NYG.	30.00	60.00	100.00
☐	37	Ken Williams, St.L.B	50.00	100.00	175.00
☐	38	Dave Bancroft, NYG.	30.00	60.00	100.00
☐	39	Joe McNally, NYA	30.00	60.00	100.00
☐	40	John McGraw, Mgr., NYG.	100.00	200.00	350.00
☐	41	Art Nehf, NYG.	30.00	60.00	100.00
☐	42	Rabbit Maranville, Pgh.	75.00	150.00	250.00
☐	43	Charlie Grimm, Pgh.	30.00	60.00	100.00
☐	44	Joe Judge, Wsh.	30.00	60.00	100.00
☐	45	Wally Pipp, NYY.	50.00	100.00	175.00
☐	46	Ty Cobb, Det.	600.00	1,200.00	2,000.00
☐	47	Walter Johnson, Wsh.	225.00	450.00	800.00
☐	48	Jake Daubert, Cin.	50.00	100.00	175.00
☐	49	Zack Wheat, Bkn.	60.00	120.00	200.00
☐	50	Herb Pennock, Bos.	50.00	100.00	250.00

1923 MAPLE CRISPETTE

This set was issued by Maple Crispette Co. Ltd. of Montreal in their candy bars about 1923. On the backs of the premium cards is an offer for different prizes that can be obtained by sending all 30 cards (1 to 30) of assorted baseball or hockey players to Maple Crispette. Card number 15 was the short print card that made it difficult to win the prize offered. Only one copy is known to exist. Set price includes 29 cards.

Card Size: 1 3/8" x 2 1/4"
Face: Black and white; name, number
Back: Black and white; offer
Imprint: Maple Crispette Co. Ltd., Montreal
ACC No.: V117

	No.	Player	VG	EX	NRMT
		Complete Set (29 cards):	**2,500.00**	**5,000.00**	**9,000.00**
		Common Player:	**20.00**	**40.00**	**75.00**
☐	1	J. Barnes, NYG.	50.00	100.00	225.00
☐	2	Harold Traynor, Pgh.	75.00	150.00	250.00
☐	3	Ray Schalk, Chi.-A.L.	25.00	50.00	100.00
☐	4	Eddie Collins, Chi.-A.L.	125.00	250.00	400.00
☐	5	Lee Fohl, Mgr., St.L.B	20.00	40.00	75.00
☐	6	Howard Summa, Cle.	20.00	40.00	75.00
☐	7	Waite Hoyt, NYY.	75.00	150.00	250.00
☐	8	Babe Ruth, NYY.	1,500.00	3,000.00	5,000.00
☐	9	Cozy Dolan, NYG.	20.00	40.00	75.00
☐	10	Johnny Bassler, Det.	20.00	40.00	75.00
☐	11	George Dauss, Det.	20.00	40.00	75.00
☐	12	Joe Sewell, Cle.	75.00	150.00	250.00
☐	13	Syl Johnson, Det.	20.00	40.00	75.00
☐	14	Ivy Wingo, Cin.	20.00	40.00	75.00
☐	15	Casey Stengel, Pgh.			Very Rare
☐	16	Arnold Statz, Chi.-N.L.	20.00	40.00	75.00
☐	17	Emil Meusel, NYG.	20.00	40.00	75.00
☐	18	Bill Jacobson, St.L.B	20.00	40.00	75.00
☐	19	Jim Bottomley, Stl.	90.00	175.00	300.00
☐	20	Sammy Bohne, Cin. , Error	20.00	40.00	75.00
☐	21	Bucky Harris, Wsh.	20.00	40.00	75.00
☐	22	Ty Cobb, Mgr., Det.	750.00	1,500.00	2,500.00
☐	23	Roger Peckinpaugh, Wsh.	20.00	40.00	75.00

☐	24	Muddy Ruel, Wsh.	20.00	40.00	75.00
☐	25	Bill McKechnie, Mgr., Pgh.	50.00	100.00	175.00
☐	26	Riggs Stephenson, Cle.	20.00	40.00	75.00
☐	27	Herb Pennock, NYY. , Error	50.00	100.00	175.00
☐	28	Edd Roush, Cin. , Error	75.00	150.00	250.00
☐	29	Bill Wambsganss, Cle.	20.00	40.00	75.00
☐	30	Walter Johnson, Wsh.	300.00	600.00	1,200.00

1923 NEILSON'S

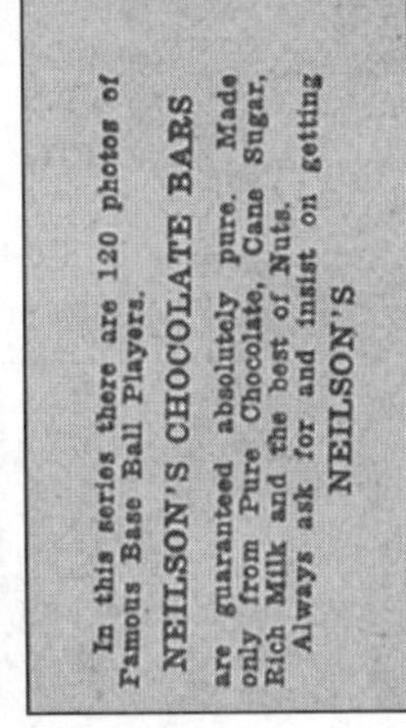

A previously unknown set that is similar in design to an American issue (W572 strip cards) released in 1923. The backs of these cards are printed, this being the big difference as the American set is blank. The Canadian issue has Neilson's chocolate clearly indicated on the back with the number of cards noted at 120. The cards are unnumbered and are listed here alphabetically. It is believed only 50 baseball cards exist. Too little maket activity has occured to price these, thought it is believed the Ruth cards is worth several thousand dollars alone.

Card Size: 1 5/16: x 2 1/2"
Face: Black and white or sepia tone; name
Back: Black and white; advertisement
Imprint: Neilson's Chocolate
Complete Set (50 cards)

	Player
☐	Eddie Ainsmith
☐	Grover Alexander, Chi.-N.L.
☐	Johnny Bassler
☐	Leon Cadore, Bkn.
☐	Virgil Cheeves
☐	Dave Danforth, Chi.-A.L.
☐	Jacob E. Daubert, Cin.
☐	Hank Buberry, Cle.
☐	Lou Devormer
☐	James Dykes
☐	Bibb Falk, Chi.-A.L.
☐	Frank Frisch, NYG.
☐	Henry Gowdy
☐	Stanley Harris
☐	Joe Hauser, Phi.A
☐	Harry Heilmann, Det.
☐	Walter Henline
☐	Charles J. Hollocher, Chi.-N.L.
☐	Waite Hoyt, NYY.
☐	Walter Johnson, Wsh.
☐	Joe Judge
☐	George Kelly, NYG.
☐	Lee King, NYG.
☐	George Leverette
☐	Walter J. (Rabbit) Maranville
☐	Richard W. (Rube) Marquard
☐	George Mogridge
☐	Roliene Naylor
☐	Steve O'Neill, Cle.
☐	Frank Parkinson
☐	Ralph Perkins
☐	Eddie (Edwin) Rommel, Phi.A
☐	Eddie Roush
☐	George Herman (Babe) Ruth, NYY.
☐	Wally Schang, NYY.
☐	Walter Schmidt, Pgh.
☐	Joe Schultz, Stl.
☐	Earl Sheely, Chi.-A.L.
☐	Will Sherdel, Stl.
☐	Urban Shocker, St.L.B
☐	George Sisler, St.L.B
☐	Earl Smith
☐	Bill Southworth
☐	Milton Stock
☐	Bartie Walker
☐	Clarence Walker, Phi.A

1923 WILLARDS CHOCOLATE

Issued by Willards Chocolate Company in 1923, this 180-card set is unnumbered. The set is listed here in alphabetical order. The words "Photo By International" appear in the lower left corner of the face of the card.

Card Size: 2" x 3 1/4"
Face: Sepia; Player's name in script
Back: Blank
Imprint: PHOTO BY INTERNATIONAL
ACC No.: V100

Complete Set (180 cards):		**5,000.00**	**10,000.00**	**18,000.00**
Common Player:		**20.00**	**40.00**	**75.00**
	Player	**VG**	**EX**	**NRMT**
☐	Charles Adams, Pgh.	30.00	60.00	150.00
☐	Grover C. Alexander, Chi.-N.L.	100.00	200.00	400.00
☐	J. P. Austin, Mgr., St.L.B	20.00	40.00	75.00
☐	James C. Bagby, Pgh.	20.00	40.00	75.00
☐	J. Franklin Baker, NYY.	75.00	150.00	275.00
☐	David J. Bancroft, NYG.	75.00	150.00	275.00
☐	Turner Barber, Bkn.	20.00	40.00	75.00
☐	Jesse L. Barnes, NYG.	20.00	40.00	75.00
☐	John L. Bassler, Det.	20.00	40.00	75.00
☐	Luzerne A. Blue, Det.	20.00	40.00	75.00
☐	Norman D. Boeckel, Bos.B	20.00	40.00	75.00
☐	Frank L. Brazill, Pha.A	20.00	40.00	75.00
☐	George H. Burns, Bos.	20.00	40.00	75.00
☐	George J. Burns, Cin.	20.00	40.00	75.00
☐	Leon Cadore, Bkn.	20.00	40.00	75.00
☐	Max Carey, Pgh.	75.00	150.00	275.00
☐	Harold G. Carlson, Pgh.	20.00	40.00	75.00

☐	L. R. Christenbury, Bos.B	20.00	40.00	75.00
☐	Verne J. Clemons, Stl.	20.00	40.00	75.00
☐	Tyrus R. Cobb, Mgr., Det.	500.00	1,000.000	1,750.00
☐	Albert Cole, Det.	20.00	40.00	75.00
☐	John F. Collins, Bos.	20.00	40.00	75.00
☐	Stanley Coveleski, Cle.	75.00	150.00	275.00
☐	Walton E. Cruise, Bos.B	20.00	40.00	75.00
☐	George W. Cutshaw, Det.	20.00	40.00	75.00
☐	Jacob E. Daubert, Cin.	30.00	60.00	100.00
☐	George Dauss, Det.	20.00	40.00	75.00
☐	Frank T. Davis, St.L.B	20.00	40.00	75.00
☐	Charles A. Deal, Chi.-N.L.	20.00	40.00	75.00
☐	William L. Doak, Stl.	20.00	40.00	75.00
☐	W. E. Donovan, Mgr., Pha.	20.00	40.00	75.00
☐	Hugh Duffy, Mgr., Bos.	75.00	150.00	275.00
☐	James A. Dugan, NYY.	30.00	60.00	100.00
☐	Louis B. Duncan, Cin.	20.00	40.00	75.00
☐	James Dykes, Pha.A	30.00	60.00	100.00
☐	H. J. Ehmke, Bos. RS	30.00	60.00	100.00
☐	Francis R. Ellerbe, St.L.B	20.00	40.00	75.00
☐	Eric G. Erickson, Wsh.	20.00	40.00	75.00
☐	J. J. Evers, Mgr., Chi.-A.L.	75.00	150.00	275.00
☐	Urban C. Faber, Chi.-A.L.	75.00	150.00	275.00
☐	Bibb A. Falk, Chi.-A.L.	20.00	40.00	75.00
☐	Max Flack, Stl.	20.00	40.00	75.00
☐	Leo Fohl, Mgr., St.L.B	20.00	40.00	75.00
☐	Jacques F. Fournier, Bkn.	20.00	40.00	75.00
☐	Frank F. Frisch, NYG.	90.00	175.00	300.00
☐	C. E. Galloway, Pha.A	20.00	40.00	75.00
☐	William L. Gardner, Cle.	20.00	40.00	75.00
☐	Edward P. Gharrity, Wsh.	20.00	40.00	75.00
☐	George Gibson, Mgr., Pgh.	20.00	40.00	75.00
☐	W. J. Gleason, Mgr., Chi.-A.L.	45.00	90.00	150.00
☐	William P. Gleason, St.L.A	30.00	60.00	100.00
☐	Henry M. Gowdy, Bos.B	20.00	40.00	75.00
☐	Ivy M. Griffin, Pha.A	20.00	40.00	75.00
☐	Thomas Griffith, Bkn.	70.00	140.00	250.00
☐	Burleigh A. Grimes, Bkn.	75.00	150.00	275.00
☐	Charles J. Grimm, Pgh.	30.00	60.00	100.00
☐	Jesse J. Haines, Stl.	75.00	150.00	275.00
☐	Stanley R. Harris, Wsh.	60.00	120.00	200.00
☐	William M. Harris, Cin.	20.00	40.00	75.00
☐	Robert K. Hasty, Pha.A	20.00	40.00	75.00
☐	Harry E. Heilmann, Det.	90.00	175.00	300.00
☐	Walter J. Henline, Pha.	20.00	40.00	75.00
☐	Walter M. Holke, Pha.	20.00	40.00	75.00
☐	Charles J. Hollocher, Chi.-N.L.	20.00	40.00	75.00
☐	Harry B. Hooper, Chi.-A.L.	75.00	150.00	275.00
☐	Rogers Hornsby, Stl.	150.00	300.00	500.00
☐	Waite C. Hoyt, NYY.	75.00	150.00	275.00
☐	Miller Huggins, Mgr., NYY.	90.00	175.00	300.00
☐	William C. Jacobson, St.L.B	20.00	40.00	75.00
☐	Charles D. Jamieson, Cle.	20.00	40.00	75.00
☐	Ernest Johnson, Chi.-A.L.	20.00	40.00	75.00
☐	Walter P. Johnson, Wsh.	200.00	400.00	750.00
☐	James H. Johnston, Bkn.	20.00	40.00	75.00
☐	Robert W. Jones, Det.	20.00	40.00	75.00
☐	Samuel Pond Jones, NYY.	20.00	40.00	75.00
☐	Joseph I. Judge, Wsh.	20.00	40.00	75.00
☐	James W. Keenan,Pha.	20.00	40.00	75.00
☐	George L. Kelly, NYG.	75.00	150.00	275.00
☐	Peter J. Kilduff, Bkn.	20.00	40.00	75.00
☐	W. Killefer, Mgr., Chi.-N.L.	20.00	40.00	75.00
☐	Edward Lee King, NYG.	20.00	40.00	75.00
☐	Raymond Kolp, St.L.B	20.00	40.00	75.00
☐	John Lavan, Stl.	20.00	40.00	75.00
☐	Harry L. Leibold, Bos.	20.00	40.00	75.00
☐	C. Mack, Mgr., Pha.A	125.00	250.00	400.00
☐	John W. Mails, Cle.	20.00	40.00	75.00
☐	Walter J. Maranville, Pgh.	75.00	150.00	275.00
☐	R. W. Marquard, Bos.B	75.00	150.00	275.00
☐	Carl W. Mays, NYY.	30.00	60.00	100.00
☐	G. F. McBride, Mgr., Wsh.	20.00	40.00	75.00
☐	H. M. McClellan, Chi.-A.L.	20.00	40.00	75.00
☐	J. J. McGraw, Mgr., NYG.	90.00	175.00	300.00
☐	Austin B. McHenry, Stl.	20.00	40.00	75.00
☐	John McInnis, Bos.B	20.00	40.00	75.00
☐	D. McWeeny, Chi.-A.L.	20.00	40.00	75.00
☐	Michael Menosky, Bos.	20.00	40.00	75.00
☐	Emil F. Meusel, NYG.	30.00	60.00	100.00
☐	Robert Meusel, NYY.	30.00	60.00	100.00
☐	Henry W. Meyers	20.00	40.00	75.00
☐	Jesse C. Milan, Mgr., Wsh.	20.00	40.00	75.00
☐	Edmund J. Miller, Pha.A	20.00	40.00	75.00
☐	Elmer Miller, Bos.	20.00	40.00	75.00
☐	L. Otto Miller, Bkn.	20.00	40.00	75.00
☐	John K. Milus	20.00	40.00	75.00
☐	Fred Mitchell, Mgr., Bos.B	20.00	40.00	75.00
☐	George Mogridge, Wsh. a	20.00	40.00	75.00
☐	Patrick J. Moran, Mgr., Cin.	20.00	40.00	75.00
☐	John D. Morrison, Pgh.	20.00	40.00	75.00
☐	John A. Mostil, Chi.-A.L.	20.00	40.00	75.00
☐	Clarence F. Mueller, Stl.	20.00	40.00	75.00
☐	A. Earle Neale, Cin.	60.00	120.00	200.00
☐	Joseph Oeschger, Bos.B	20.00	40.00	75.00
☐	Robert A. O'Farrell, Chi.-N.L.	20.00	40.00	75.00
☐	John C. Oldham, Det.	20.00	40.00	75.00
☐	Ivan M. Olson, Bkn.	20.00	40.00	75.00
☐	George M. O'Neil, Bos.B	20.00	40.00	75.00
☐	Stephen F. O'Neill, Cle.	20.00	40.00	75.00
☐	Frank J. Parkinson, Pha.	20.00	40.00	75.00
☐	George H. Paskert, Cin.	20.00	40.00	75.00
☐	Roger T. Peckinpaugh, Wsh.	30.00	60.00	100.00
☐	Herbert J. Pennock, NYY.	75.00	150.00	275.00
☐	Ralph Perkins, Pha.A	20.00	40.00	75.00
☐	Edward J. Pfeffer, Stl.	20.00	40.00	75.00
☐	Walter C. Pipp, NYY.	60.00	120.00	200.00
☐	C. Elmer Ponder, Chi.-N.L.	20.00	40.00	75.00
☐	Raymond R. Powell, Bos.B	20.00	40.00	75.00
☐	Derrill B. Pratt, Det.	20.00	40.00	75.00
☐	Joseph Rapp, Pha.	20.00	40.00	75.00
☐	John W. Rawlings, Pgh.	20.00	40.00	75.00
☐	Ed. C. Rice, Wsh. , Error	75.00	150.00	275.00
☐	W. Rickey, Mgr., St. L.C	100.00	200.00	350.00
☐	James J. Ring, Pha.	20.00	40.00	75.00
☐	Eppa Rixey, Cin.	75.00	150.00	275.00
☐	Davis A. Robertson, NYG.	20.00	40.00	75.00
☐	Edwin Rommel, Pha.A	30.00	60.00	100.00
☐	Edd J. Roush, Cin.	75.00	150.00	275.00
☐	Herold Ruel, Wsh.	20.00	40.00	75.00
☐	Allen Russell, Wsh.	20.00	40.00	75.00
☐	George H. Ruth, NYY.	1,000.00	2,000.00	3,500.00
☐	Wilfred P.D. Ryan, NYG.	20.00	40.00	75.00
☐	Harry F. Sallee, NYG.	20.00	40.00	75.00
☐	Walter H. Schang, NYY.	20.00	40.00	75.00
☐	R. H. Schmandt, Bkn.	20.00	40.00	75.00
☐	Everett Scott, NYY.	20.00	40.00	75.00
☐	Henry Severeid, St.L.B	20.00	40.00	75.00
☐	Joseph W. Sewell, Cle.	75.00	150.00	275.00
☐	Howard S. Shanks, Bos.	20.00	40.00	75.00
☐	Earl H. Sheely, Chi.-A.L.	20.00	40.00	75.00
☐	Ralph Shinners, NYG.	20.00	40.00	75.00
☐	Urban J. Shocker, St.L.B	30.00	60.00	100.00
☐	George H. Sisler, St.L.B	90.00	175.00	300.00
☐	Earl L. Smith, Wsh.	20.00	40.00	75.00
☐	Earl S. Smith, NYG.	20.00	40.00	75.00
☐	George A. Smith, Bkn.	20.00	40.00	75.00
☐	John W. Smith, Cin.	20.00	40.00	75.00

☐	T. E. Speaker, Mgr., Cle.	100.00	200.00	350.00
☐	Arnold Statz, Chi.-N.L.	20.00	40.00	75.00
☐	J. R. Stephenson, Cle.	50.00	60.00	100.00
☐	Milton J. Stock, Stl.	20.00	40.00	75.00
☐	John L. Sullivan, Chi.-N.L.	20.00	40.00	75.00
☐	H. E. Thormahlen, Bos.	20.00	40.00	75.00
☐	James A. Tierney, Pgh.	20.00	40.00	75.00
☐	John T. Tobin, St.L.B	20.00	40.00	75.00
☐	James L. Vaughn, Chi.-N.L.	20.00	40.00	75.00
☐	Robert H. Veach, Det.	20.00	40.00	75.00
☐	Clarence W. Walker, Pha.A	20.00	40.00	75.00
☐	Aaron L. Ward, NYY.	20.00	40.00	75.00
☐	Zachary D. Wheat, Bkn.	75.00	150.00	275.00
☐	George B. Whitted, Bkn.	20.00	40.00	75.00
☐	Irvin K. Wilhelm, Mgr., Pha.	20.00	40.00	75.00
☐	R. H. Wilkinson, Chi.-A.L.	20.00	40.00	75.00
☐	Fred Williams, Pha.	30.00	60.00	100.00
☐	Kenneth R. Williams, St.L.B	30.00	60.00	100.00
☐	Samuel M. Wilson, Pgh.	20.00	40.00	75.00
☐	Ivey B. Wingo, Cin.	20.00	40.00	75.00
☐	Lawton W. Witt, NYY.	20.00	40.00	75.00
☐	Joe Wood, Cle.	30.00	60.00	100.00
☐	C. E. Yaryan, Chi.-A.L.	20.00	40.00	75.00
☐	Ralph S. Young, Pha.A	20.00	40.00	75.00
☐	Ross Youngs, NYG.	65.00	125.00	275.00

1933 WORLD WIDE GUM

World Wide Gum, Goudey's Canadian subsidiary, issued this 94-card set in 1933. Its design was based on the Goudey set of the same year and it incorporated 94 of the players from the 240 American Goudey set.

Almost identical in design, the Canadian set was issued with English and French backs. There is a 20% to 30% premium for bilingual cards. There appear to be fewer Canadian sets being completed by collectors, and the American version seems to be more in demand. Prices below are for the English variations.

Card Size: 2 3/8" x 2 7/8"

Face: Four colour; name

Back: English: Green on card stock; name, number, résumé, Bilingual: Same as above

Imprint: WORLD WIDE GUM CO., LTD. MONTREAL Printed in Canada

ACC No.: V353

Complete English Set (94 cards):	**7,500.00**	**15,000.00**	**28,000.00**
Complete Bilingual Set (94 cards):	**10,000.00**	**20,000.00**	**35,000.00**
Common Player (English):	**30.00**	**60.00**	**100.00**
Common Player (Bilingual):	**40.00**	**75.00**	**125.00**

	No.	Player	VG	EX	NRMT
☐ ☐	1	Benny Bengough, St.L.B	300.00	750.00	1,500.00
☐ ☐	2	Dazzy Vance, Stl.	175.00	350.00	600.00
☐ ☐	3	Hugh Critz, NYG.	30.00	60.00	100.00
☐ ☐	4	H. (Heinie) Schuble, Det.	30.00	60.00	100.00
☐ ☐	5	Babe Herman, Chi.-N.L.	45.00	90.00	150.00
☐ ☐	6	Jimmy Dykes, Chi.-A.L.	45.00	90.00	150.00
☐ ☐	7	Ted Lyons, Chi.-A.L.	90.00	125.00	300.00
☐ ☐	8	Roy Johnson, Bos.	30.00	60.00	100.00
☐ ☐	9	Dave Harris, Wsh.	30.00	60.00	100.00
☐ ☐	10	Glenn Myatt, Cle.	30.00	60.00	100.00
☐ ☐	11	Billy Rogell, Det.	30.00	60.00	100.00
☐ ☐	12	George Pipgras, NYY.	30.00	60.00	100.00
☐ ☐	13	L. Thompson, Bkn.	30.00	60.00	100.00
☐ ☐	14	Henry Johnson, Bos.	30.00	60.00	100.00
☐ ☐	15	Victor Sorrell, Det.	30.00	60.00	100.00
☐ ☐	16	George Blaeholder	30.00	60.00	100.00
☐ ☐	17	Watson Clark, Bkn.	30.00	60.00	100.00
☐ ☐	18	Muddy Ruel, St.L.B	30.00	60.00	100.00
☐ ☐	19	Bill Dickey, NYY.	175.00	350.00	650.00
☐ ☐	20	Bill Terry, Mgr., NYG.	125.00	250.00	400.00
☐ ☐	21	Phil Collins, Pha.	30.00	60.00	100.00
☐ ☐	22	Pie Traynor, Pgh.	125.00	250.00	400.00
☐ ☐	23	Kiki Cuyler, Chi.-N.L.	125.00	250.00	400.00
☐ ☐	24	Horace Ford, Bos.B	30.00	60.00	100.00
☐ ☐	25	Paul Waner, Pgh.	175.00	350.00	600.00
☐ ☐	26	Chalmer Cissell, Cle.	30.00	60.00	100.00
☐ ☐	27	George Connally, Cle.	30.00	60.00	100.00
☐ ☐	28	Dick Bartell, Pha.	30.00	60.00	100.00
☐ ☐	29	Jimmie Foxx, Pha.A	300.00	600.00	1,000.00
☐ ☐	30	Frank Hogan, Bos.B	30.00	60.00	100.00
☐ ☐	31	Tony Lazzeri, NYY.	90.00	175.00	300.00
☐ ☐	32	Bud Clancy, Bkn.	30.00	60.00	100.00
☐ ☐	33	Ralph Kress, Chi.-A.L.	30.00	60.00	100.00
☐ ☐	34	Bob O'Farrell, Stl.	30.00	60.00	100.00
☐ ☐	35	Al Simmons, Chi.-A.L.	150.00	300.00	500.00
☐ ☐	36	Tommy Thevenow, Pgh.	30.00	60.00	100.00
☐ ☐	37	Jimmie Wilson, Stl.	30.00	60.00	100.00
☐ ☐	38	Fred Brickell, Pha.	30.00	60.00	100.00
☐ ☐	39	Mark Koenig, Chi.-N.L.	30.00	60.00	100.00
☐ ☐	40	Taylor Douthit, Cin.	30.00	60.00	100.00
☐ ☐	41	Gus Mancuso, NYG.	30.00	60.00	100.00
☐ ☐	42	Eddie Collins, Pha.A	90.00	175.00	300.00
☐ ☐	43	L. Fonseca, Mgr., Chi.-A.L.	30.00	60.00	100.00
☐ ☐	44	Jim Bottomley, Cin.	90.00	175.00	300.00
☐ ☐	45	Larry Benton, Cin.	30.00	60.00	100.00
☐ ☐	46	Ethan Allen, Stl.	30.00	60.00	100.00
☐ ☐	47	Heinie Manush, Wsh.	100.00	200.00	350.00
☐ ☐	48	M. McManus, Mgr., Bos.	30.00	60.00	100.00
☐ ☐	49	Frank Frisch, Mgr., Stl.	150.00	300.00	500.00
☐ ☐	50	Ed Brandt, Bos.B	30.00	60.00	100.00
☐ ☐	51	C. Grimm, Mgr., Chi.-N.L.	45.00	90.00	150.00
☐ ☐	52	Andy Cohen, NYG.	30.00	60.00	100.00
☐ ☐	53	Jack Quinn, Cin.	30.00	60.00	100.00
☐ ☐	54	Urban Faber, Chi.-A.L.	75.00	150.00	250.00
☐ ☐	55	Lou Gehrig, NYY.	1,750.00	3,500.00	6,500.00
☐ ☐	56	John Welch, Bos.	30.00	60.00	100.00
☐ ☐	57	Bill Walker, Stl.	30.00	60.00	100.00
☐ ☐	58	Lefty O'Doul, Bkn.	50.00	100.00	175.00
☐ ☐	59	Bing Miller, Pha.A	30.00	60.00	100.00
☐ ☐	60	Waite Hoyt, Pha.A	90.00	175.00	300.00
☐ ☐	61	Max Bishop, Pha.A	30.00	60.00	100.00
☐ ☐	62	Pepper Martin, Stl.	50.00	100.00	175.00
☐ ☐	63	Joe Cronin, Mgr., Wsh.	125.00	250.00	400.00
☐ ☐	64	Burleigh Grimes, Chi.-N.L.	125.00	250.00	450.00
☐ ☐	65	Milt Gaston, Chi.-A.L.	30.00	60.00	100.00
☐ ☐	66	George Grantham, Cin.	30.00	60.00	100.00
☐ ☐	67	Guy Bush, Chi.-N.L.	30.00	60.00	100.00
☐ ☐	68	Willie Kamm, Cle.	30.00	60.00	100.00
☐ ☐	69	Mickey Cochrane, Pha.A	175.00	350.00	600.00
☐ ☐	70	Adam Comorosky, Pgh.	30.00	60.00	100.00
☐ ☐	71	Alvin Crowder, Wsh.	30.00	60.00	100.00
☐ ☐	72	Willis Hudlin, Cle.	30.00	60.00	100.00
☐ ☐	73	E. (Doc) Farrell, NYY.	30.00	60.00	100.00
☐ ☐	74	Leo Durocher, Cin.	90.00	175.00	300.00
☐ ☐	75	Walter Stewart, Wsh.	30.00	60.00	100.00
☐ ☐	76	George Walberg,Pha.A	30.00	60.00	100.00
☐ ☐	77	Glenn Wright, Bkn.	30.00	60.00	100.00
☐ ☐	78	Buddy Myer, Wsh.	30.00	60.00	100.00

☐ ☐ 79	Zack Taylor, Chi.-N.L.	30.00	60.00	100.00
☐ ☐ 80	Babe Ruth, NYY.	2,500.00	5,000.00	9,000.00
☐ ☐ 81	Jake Flowers, Bkn.	30.00	60.00	100.00
☐ ☐ 82	Ray Kolp, Cin.	30.00	60.00	100.00
☐ ☐ 83	Oswald Bluege, Wsh.	30.00	60.00	100.00
☐ ☐ 84	Moe Berg, Wsh.	65.00	125.00	200.00
☐ ☐ 85	J. Foxx, Pha.A , Error	250.00	500.00	900.00
☐ ☐ 86	Sammy Byrd, NYY.	30.00	60.00	100.00
☐ ☐ 87	Danny MacFayden, NYY.	30.00	60.00	100.00
☐ ☐ 88	Joe Judge, Bkn.	30.00	60.00	100.00
☐ ☐ 89	Joe Sewell, NYY.	90.00	175.00	300.00
☐ ☐ 90	Lloyd Waner, Pgh.	90.00	175.00	300.00
☐ ☐ 91	Luke Sewell, Wsh.	30.00	60.00	100.00
☐ ☐ 92	Leo Mangum, Bos.B	30.00	60.00	100.00
☐ ☐ 93	Babe Ruth, NYY.	3,000.00	6,000.00	10,000.00
☐ ☐ 94	Al Spohrer, Bos.B	50.00	100.00	250.00

1934 WORLD WIDE GUM

World Wide used the Goudey American designs of 1933 and 1934 for their 96-card set of 1934. Cards numbered from 1 to 48 have the 1933 Goudey American design and those numbered from 49 to 96 have the Goudey design of 1934.

Like the World Wide cards of 1933, the backs of the 1934 issue have two variations. One is English only and the other is English and French. The bilingual cards have a 20 to 30% premium over the English-only cards. Prices below are for the English variations.

Card Size: 2 3/8" x 2 7/8"
Face: Four colour; name
Back: English: Green on card stock; name, number, team, résumé,
Bilingual: Same as above
Imprint: WORLD WIDE GUM CO., LTD. MONTREAL Printed in Canada.
ACC No.: V354

Complete English Set (96 cards):	**6,000.00**	**12,000.00**	**20,000.00**
Complete Bilingual Set (96 cards):	**7,500.00**	**15,000.00**	**25,000.00**
Common Player (English):	**30.00**	**60.00**	**100.00**
Common Player (Bilingual):	**40.00**	**75.00**	**125.00**

No.	Player	VG	EX	NRMT
☐ ☐ 1	R. Hornsby, Mgr., St.L.B.	300.00	600.00	1,200.00
☐ ☐ 2	Ed Morgan, Bos.	25.00	50.00	100.00
☐ ☐ 3	Valentine Picinich, Pgh.	25.00	50.00	100.00
☐ ☐ 4	Rabbit Maranville, Bos.B	90.00	175.00	300.00
☐ ☐ 5	Flint Rhem, Stl.	25.00	50.00	100.00
☐ ☐ 6	James Elliott, Pha.	25.00	50.00	100.00
☐ ☐ 7	Fred (Red) Lucas, Pgh.	25.00	50.00	100.00
☐ ☐ 8	Frederick Marberry, Det.	25.00	50.00	100.00
☐ ☐ 9	Clifton Heathcote, Pha.	25.00	50.00	100.00
☐ ☐ 10	Barney Friberg, Bos.	25.00	50.00	100.00
☐ ☐ 11	Elwood English, Chi.-N.L.	25.00	50.00	100.00
☐ ☐ 12	Carl Reynolds, Bos.	25.00	50.00	100.00
☐ ☐ 13	Ray Benge, Bkn.	25.00	50.00	100.00
☐ ☐ 14	Ben Cantwell, Bos.B	25.00	50.00	100.00
☐ ☐ 15	Bump Hadley, St.L.B	25.00	50.00	100.00
☐ ☐ 16	Herb Pennock, Bos.	90.00	175.00	300.00
☐ ☐ 17	Freddie Lindstrom, Pgh.	90.00	175.00	300.00
☐ ☐ 18	Sam Rice, Cle.	90.00	175.00	300.00
☐ ☐ 19	Fred Frankhouse, Bos.B	25.00	50.00	100.00
☐ ☐ 20	F. Fitzsimmons, NYG.	25.00	50.00	100.00
☐ ☐ 21	Earle Combs, NYY.	100.00	200.00	350.00
☐ ☐ 22	George Uhle, NYY.	25.00	50.00	100.00
☐ ☐ 23	Richard Coffman, St.L.B	25.00	50.00	100.00
☐ ☐ 24	Travis Jackson, NYG.	100.00	200.00	350.00
☐ ☐ 25	Robert Burke, Wsh.	25.00	50.00	100.00
☐ ☐ 26	Randy Moore, Bos.B	25.00	50.00	100.00
☐ ☐ 27	Heinie Sand, Pha.	25.00	50.00	100.00
☐ ☐ 28	G. Herman (Babe) Ruth, NYY.	2,500.00	5,000.00	9,000.00
☐ ☐ 29	Tris Speaker, Pha.A	150.00	300.00	550.00
☐ ☐ 30	Pat Malone, Chi.-N.L.	25.00	50.00	100.00
☐ ☐ 31	Sam Jones, Chi.-A.L.	25.00	50.00	100.00
☐ ☐ 32	Eppa Rixey, Cin.	90.00	75.00	300.00
☐ ☐ 33	Pete Scott, Pgh.	25.00	50.00	100.00
☐ ☐ 34	Pete Jablonowski, NYY.	25.00	50.00	100.00
☐ ☐ 35	Clyde Manion, Cin.	25.00	50.00	100.00
☐ ☐ 36	Dibrell Williams, Pha.A	25.00	50.00	100.00
☐ ☐ 37	Glenn Spencer, NYG.	25.00	50.00	100.00
☐ ☐ 38	Ray Kremer, Pgh.	25.00	50.00	100.00
☐ ☐ 39	Phil Todt, Pha.A	25.00	50.00	100.00
☐ ☐ 40	Russell Rollings, Bos.B	25.00	50.00	100.00
☐ ☐ 41	Earl Clark, St.L.B	25.00	50.00	100.00
☐ ☐ 42	Jesse Petty, Chi.-N.L.	25.00	50.00	100.00
☐ ☐ 43	Frank O'Rouke, St.L.B	25.00	50.00	100.00
☐ ☐ 44	Jesse Haines, Stl.	90.00	175.00	300.00
☐ ☐ 45	Horace Lisenbee, Bos.	25.00	50.00	100.00
☐ ☐ 46	Owen Carroll, Bkn.	25.00	50.00	100.00
☐ ☐ 47	Tom Zachary, Bos.B	25.00	50.00	100.00
☐ ☐ 48	Charles Ruffing, NYY.	90.00	175.00	300.00
☐ ☐ 49	Ray Benge, Bkn.	25.00	50.00	100.00
☐ ☐ 50	Woody English, Chi.-N.L.	25.00	50.00	100.00
☐ ☐ 51	Ben Chapman, NYY.	25.00	50.00	100.00
☐ ☐ 52	Joe Kuhel, Wsh.	25.00	50.00	100.00
☐ ☐ 53	Bill Terry, Mgr., NYG.	150.00	300.00	500.00
☐ ☐ 54	Lefty Grove, Bos.	175.00	325.00	550.00
☐ ☐ 55	Jay (Dizzy) Dean, Stl.	300.00	600.00	1,100.00
☐ ☐ 56	Chuck Klein, Chi.-N.L.	90.00	175.00	300.00
☐ ☐ 57	Charlie Gehringer, Det.	100.00	200.00	350.00
☐ ☐ 58	Jimmie Foxx, Pha.A	300.00	600.00	1,000.00
☐ ☐ 59	G. (Mickey) Cochrane, Mgr, Det.	150.00	300.00	550.00
☐ ☐ 60	Willie Kamm, Cle.	25.00	50.00	100.00
☐ ☐ 61	C. Grimm, Mgr., Chi.-N.L.	25.00	50.00	100.00
☐ ☐ 62	Ed Brandt, Bos.B	25.00	50.00	100.00
☐ ☐ 63	Tony Piet, Cin.	25.00	50.00	100.00
☐ ☐ 64	Frank Frisch, Mgr., Stl.	125.00	250.00	450.00
☐ ☐ 65	Alvin Crowder, Wsh.	25.00	50.00	100.00
☐ ☐ 66	Frank Hogan	25.00	50.00	100.00
☐ ☐ 67	Paul Waner, Pgh.	90.00	175.00	300.00
☐ ☐ 68	Heinie Manush, Wsh.	90.00	175.00	300.00
☐ ☐ 69	Leo Durocher, Stl.	100.00	200.00	350.00
☐ ☐ 70	Floyd Vaughan, Pgh.	115.00	225.00	400.00
☐ ☐ 71	Carl Hubbell, NYG.	100.00	200.00	350.00
☐ ☐ 72	Hugh Critz, NYG.	25.00	50.00	100.00
☐ ☐ 73	Blondy Ryan, NYG.	25.00	50.00	100.00
☐ ☐ 74	Roger Cramer, Pha.A	25.00	50.00	100.00
☐ ☐ 75	Baxter Jordan, Bos.B	25.00	50.00	100.00
☐ ☐ 76	Ed Coleman, Pha.A	25.00	50.00	100.00
☐ ☐ 77	Julius Solters, Bos.	25.00	50.00	100.00
☐ ☐ 78	Chick Hafey, Cin.	90.00	175.00	300.00
☐ ☐ 79	Larry French, Pgh.	25.00	50.00	100.00
☐ ☐ 80	Don Hurst, Pha.	25.00	50.00	100.00
☐ ☐ 81	Gerald Walker, Det.	25.00	50.00	100.00
☐ ☐ 82	Ernie Lombardi, Cin.	90.00	175.00	300.00
☐ ☐ 83	Huck Betts, Bos.B	25.00	50.00	100.00
☐ ☐ 84	Luke Appling, Chi.-A.L.	90.00	175.00	300.00
☐ ☐ 85	John Frederick, Bkn.	25.00	50.00	100.00
☐ ☐ 86	Fred Walker, NYY.	25.00	50.00	100.00

	No.	Player			
☐ ☐	87	Tommy Bridges, Det.	25.00	50.00	100.00
☐ ☐	88	Dick Porter, Cle.	25.00	50.00	100.00
☐ ☐	89	John Stone, Wsh.	25.00	50.00	100.00
☐ ☐	90	Tex Carleton, Stl.	25.00	50.00	100.00
☐ ☐	91	Joe Stripp, Bkn.	25.00	50.00	100.00
☐ ☐	92	Lou Gehrig, NYY.	1,750.00	3,500.00	6,5000.00
☐ ☐	93	G. Earnshaw, Chi.-A.L.	25.00	50.00	100.00
☐ ☐	94	Oscar Melillo, St.L.B	25.00	50.00	100.00
☐ ☐	95	Oral Hildebrand, Cle.	25.00	50.00	100.00
☐ ☐	96	John Allen, NYY.	50.00	100.00	250.00

1936 WORLD WIDE GUM

This set of 135 cards is numbered on the bottom left corner of the face. The player's name appears to the right of the number. The DiMaggio and Gehrig cards are the most sought after.

Card Size: 2 3/8" x 2 7/8"
Face: Black and white; name, number
Back: Black on card stock; name, number, résumé, bilingual
Imprint: World Wide Gum Co. Ltd. Granby, Que. Printed in Canada
ACC No.: V355

Complete Set (135 cards):			**7,000.00**	**14,000.00**	**26,000.00**
Common Player:			**35.00**	**70.00**	**120.00**

	No.	Player	VG	EX	NRMT
☐	1	J. Dykes, Mgr., Chi.-A.L.	40.00	75.00	150.00
☐	2	Paul Waner, Pgh.	100.00	200.00	350.00
☐	3	Cy Blanton, Pgh.	35.00	70.00	120.00
☐	4	Sam Leslie, NYG.	35.00	70.00	120.00
☐	5	J. Louis Vergez, Pha.	35.00	70.00	120.00
☐	6	Arky Vaughan, Pgh.	100.00	200.00	350.00
☐	7	Bill Terry, Mgr., NYG.	115.00	225.00	400.00
☐	8	Joe Moore, NYG.	35.00	70.00	120.00
☐	9	Gus Mancuso, NYG.	35.00	70.00	120.00
☐	10	F. (Firpo) Marberry, NYG.	35.00	70.00	120.00
☐	11	George Selkirk, NYY.	35.00	70.00	120.00
☐	12	Spud Davis, Stl.	35.00	70.00	120.00
☐	13	Chuck Klein, Chi.-N.L.	75.00	150.00	250.00
☐	14	Freddie Fitzsimmons, NYG.	35.00	70.00	120.00
☐	15	Bill DeLancey, Stl.	35.00	70.00	120.00
☐	16	Billy Herman, Chi.-N.L.	75.00	150.00	275.00
☐	17	George Davis, Bos.B	35.00	70.00	120.00
☐	18	Ripper Collins, Chi.-N.L., Error	45.00	90.00	150.00
☐	19	Dizzy Dean, Stl.	150.00	300.00	500.00
☐	20	Roy Parmelee, Stl.	35.00	70.00	120.00
☐	21	Vic Sorrell, Det.	35.00	70.00	120.00
☐	22	Harry Danning, NYG.	35.00	70.00	120.00
☐	23	Hal Schumacher, NYG.	35.00	70.00	120.00
☐	24	Cy Perkins, Det.	35.00	70.00	120.00
☐	25	Speedy (Leo) Durocher	125.00	250.00	400.00
☐	26	Glenn Myatt, Det.	35.00	70.00	120.00
☐	27	Bob Seeds, NewarkB	35.00	70.00	120.00
☐	28	Jimmy Ripple, NYG.	35.00	70.00	120.00
☐	29	Al Schacht, Wsh.	35.00	70.00	120.00
☐	30	Pete Fox, Det.	35.00	70.00	120.00
☐	31	Del Baker, Mgr., Det.	35.00	70.00	120.00
☐	32	Flea Clifton, Det.	35.00	70.00	120.00
☐	33	Tommy Bridges, Det.	35.00	70.00	120.00
☐	34	Bill Dickey, NYY.	150.00	300.00	550.00
☐	35	Wally Berger, Bos.B	35.00	70.00	120.00
☐	36	Slick Castleman, NYG.	35.00	70.00	120.00
☐	37	Dick Bartell, NYG.	35.00	70.00	120.00
☐	38	Red Rolfe, NYY.	35.00	70.00	120.00
☐	39	Waite Hoyt, Pha.A	90.00	175.00	300.00
☐	40	Wes Ferrell, Bos.	35.00	70.00	120.00
☐	41	Hank Greenberg, Det.	150.00	300.00	550.00
☐	42	Charlie Gehringer, Det.	90.00	175.00	300.00
☐	43	Goose Goslin, Det.	90.00	175.00	300.00
☐	44	Schoolboy Rowe, Det.	35.00	70.00	120.00
☐	45	M. Cochrane, Mgr., Det.	150.00	300.00	500.00
☐	46	Joe Cronin, Mgr., Bos.	125.00	250.00	400.00
☐	47	Jimmie Foxx, Bos.	150.00	300.00	500.00
☐	48	Gerald (Gee) Walker, Det.	35.00	70.00	120.00
☐	49	Charley Gelbert, Stl.	35.00	70.00	120.00
☐	50	Ray Hayworth, Det.	35.00	70.00	120.00
☐	51	Joe DiMaggio, NYY.	2,000.00	4,000.00	7,000.00
☐	52	Billy Rogell, Det.	35.00	70.00	120.00
☐	53	Joe McCarthy, Mgr., NYY.	75.00	150.00	250.00
☐	54	Phil Cavarretta, Chi.-N.L.	35.00	70.00	120.00
☐	55	Kiki Cuyler, Cin.	90.00	175.00	300.00
☐	56	Lefty Gomez, NYY.	125.00	250.00	400.00
☐	57	Gabby Hartnett, Chi.-N.L.	90.00	175.00	300.00
☐	58	Johnny Marcum, Bos.	35.00	70.00	120.00
☐	59	Burgess Whitehead, NYG.	35.00	70.00	120.00
☐	60	Earl Whitehill, Wsh.	35.00	70.00	120.00
☐	61	Bucky Walters, Pha.	35.00	70.00	120.00
☐	62	Luke Sewell, Chi.-A.L.	35.00	70.00	120.00
☐	63	Joe Kuhel, Wsh.	35.00	70.00	120.00
☐	64	Lou Finney, Pha.A	35.00	70.00	120.00
☐	65	Freddie Lindstrom, Bkn.	90.00	175.00	300.00
☐	66	Paul Derringer, Cin.	35.00	70.00	120.00
☐	67	Steve O'Neill, Mgr., Cle.	35.00	70.00	120.00
☐	68	Mule Haas, Chi.-A.L.	35.00	70.00	120.00
☐	69	Freck Owen	35.00	70.00	120.00
☐	70	Wild Bill Hallahan, Stl.	35.00	70.00	120.00
☐	71	Bill Urbanski, Bos.B	35.00	70.00	120.00
☐	72	Danny Taylor, Bkn.	35.00	70.00	120.00
☐	73	Heinie Manush, Bos.	125.00	250.00	400.00
☐	74	Jo-Jo White, Det.	35.00	70.00	120.00
☐	75	Joe Medwick, Stl.	90.00	175.00	300.00
☐	76	Joe Vosmik, Cle.	35.00	70.00	120.00
☐	77	Al Simmons, Det.	90.00	175.00	300.00
☐	78	S. Shaughnessy, Pha.A	35.00	70.00	120.00
☐	79	Harry Smythe, Bkn.	35.00	70.00	120.00
☐	80	Bennie Tate, Chi.-N.L.	35.00	70.00	120.00
☐	81	Billy Rhiel, Det.	35.00	70.00	120.00
☐	82	Lauri Myllykangas	35.00	70.00	120.00
☐	83	Ben Sankey, Pgh.	35.00	70.00	120.00
☐	84	Lou Polli, St.L.B	35.00	70.00	120.00
☐	85	Jim Bottomley, St.L.B	90.00	175.00	300.00
☐	86	William Watson Clark, Bkn.	35.00	70.00	120.00
☐	87	Ossie Bluege, Wsh.	35.00	70.00	120.00
☐	88	Lefty Grove, Bos.	175.00	300.00	500.00
☐	89	C. Grimm, Mgr., Chi.-N.L.	35.00	70.00	120.00
☐	90	Ben Chapman, NYY.	35.00	70.00	120.00
☐	91	Frank Crosetti, NYY.	65.00	125.00	200.00
☐	92	John Pomorski, Chi.-A.L.	35.00	70.00	120.00
☐	93	Jesse Haines, Stl.	90.00	175.00	300.00
☐	94	Chick Hafey, Cin.	90.00	175.00	300.00
☐	95	Tony Piet, Chi.-A.L.	35.00	70.00	120.00
☐	96	Lou Gehrig, NYY.	1,500.00	3,000.00	5,000.00
☐	97	Bill Jurges, Chi.-N.L.	35.00	70.00	120.00
☐	98	Smead Jolley, Bos.	35.00	70.00	120.00
☐	99	Jimmie Wilson, Mgr., Pha.	35.00	70.00	120.00
☐	100	L. Warneke, Chi.-N.L.	35.00	70.00	120.00
☐	101	Vito Tamulis, NYY.	35.00	70.00	120.00

	No.	Player	VG	EX	NRMT
☐	102	Charles Ruffing, NYY.	35.00	70.00	120.00
☐	103	Earl Grace, Pha.	35.00	70.00	120.00
☐	104	Roxie Lawson, Det.	35.00	70.00	120.00
☐	105	Stan Hack, Chi.-N.L.	35.00	70.00	120.00
☐	106	August Galan, Chi.-N.L.	35.00	70.00	120.00
☐	107	Frank Frisch, Mgr., Stl.	90.00	175.00	300.00
☐	108	B. McKechnie, Mgr., Bos.B	90.00	175.00	300.00
☐	109	Bill Lee, Chi.-N.L.	35.00	70.00	120.00
☐	110	Connie Mack, Mgr., Pha.A	125.00	250.00	400.00
☐	111	Frank Reiber, Det.	35.00	70.00	120.00
☐	112	Zeke Bonura, Chi.-A.L.	35.00	70.00	120.00
☐	113	Luke Appling, Chi.-A.L.	90.00	175.00	300.00
☐	114	Monte Pearson, NYY.	35.00	70.00	120.00
☐	115	Bob O'Farrell, Stl.	35.00	70.00	120.00
☐	116	Marvin Duke	35.00	70.00	120.00
☐	117	Paul Florence, NYG.	35.00	70.00	120.00
☐	118	John Berly, Pha.	35.00	70.00	120.00
☐	119	Tom Oliver, Bos.	35.00	70.00	120.00
☐	120	Norman Kies	35.00	70.00	120.00
☐	121	Hal King	35.00	70.00	120.00
☐	122	Tom Abernathy	35.00	70.00	120.00
☐	123	Phil Hensiek, Wsh.	35.00	70.00	120.00
☐	124	Roy Schalk, NYY.	90.00	175.00	300.00
☐	125	Paul Dunlap	35.00	70.00	120.00
☐	126	Benny Bates	35.00	70.00	120.00
☐	127	George Puccinelli, Pha.A	35.00	70.00	120.00
☐	128	Stevie Stevenson	35.00	70.00	120.00
☐	129	R. Maranville, Mgr., Mtl.R	75.00	150.00	250.00
☐	130	Bucky Harris, Mgr., Wsh.	75.00	150.00	250.00
☐	131	A. Raymond (Al) Lopez, Bos.	75.00	150.00	250.00
☐	132	Buddy Myer, Wsh.	35.00	70.00	120.00
☐	133	Cliff Bolton, Wsh.	35.00	70.00	120.00
☐	134	Estel Crabtree, Stl.	35.00	70.00	120.00
☐	135	Philip Weintraub, NYY.	35.00	70.00	120.00

1937 O-PEE-CHEE BATTER-UPS

The set consists of 40 black and white die-cut cards, numbered A101 to A140, and marks the first time O-Pee-Chee produced baseball cards in Canada. Cards without the top die cut have little or no value. Only cards that have not been popped up can have NRMT to mint status.

Card Size: 2 3/8" x 2 7/8"
Face: Black and white; name, number, position, bilingual
Back: Black on card stock; name, number, résumé, bilingual
Imprint: None
ACC No.: V300

	No.	Player	VG	EX	NRMT
		Complete Set (40 cards):	**3,500.00**	**7,000.00**	**13,000.00**
		Common Player:	**30.00**	**60.00**	**100.00**
☐	101	John Lewis, Wsh.	30.00	60.00	100.00
☐	102	J. Hayes, Chi.-A.L. , Error	30.00	60.00	100.00
☐	103	Earl Averill, Cle.	60.00	120.00	200.00
☐	104	H. Clift, St.L.B , Error	30.00	60.00	100.00
☐	105	Beau Bell, St.L.B	30.00	60.00	100.00
☐	106	Jimmie Fox, Bos.	175.00	350.00	600.00
☐	107	Hank Greenberg, Det.,	150.00	300.00	550.00
☐	108	George Selkirk, NYY.	45.00	90.00	150.00
☐	109	Wally Moses, Pha.A	30.00	60.00	100.00
☐	110	Gerald (Gee) Walker, Det.	30.00	60.00	100.00
☐	111	Goose Goslin, Det.	65.00	125.00	200.00
☐	112	Charlie Gehringer, Det.	100.00	200.00	350.00
☐	113	Hal Trosky, Cle.	30.00	60.00	100.00
☐	114	Buddy Myer, Wsh.	30.00	60.00	100.00
☐	115	Luke Appling, Chi.-A.L.	60.00	120.00	200.00
☐	116	Zeke Bonura, Chi.-A.L.	30.00	60.00	100.00
☐	117	Tony Lazzeri, NYY.	65.00	125.00	200.00
☐	118	Joe DiMaggio, NYY.	1,800.00	3,500.00	6,000.00
☐	119	Bill Dickey, NYY.	150.00	300.00	550.00
☐	120	Bob Feller, Cle.	350.00	700.00	1,200.00
☐	121	Harry Kelley, Pha.A	45.00	90.00	150.00
☐	122	Johnny Allen, Cle.	30.00	60.00	100.00
☐	123	Bob Johnson, Pha.A	30.00	60.00	100.00
☐	124	Joe Cronin, Mgr., Bos.	75.00	150.00	250.00
☐	125	Rip Radcliff, Chi.-A.L.	30.00	60.00	100.00
☐	126	Cecil Travis, Wsh.	30.00	60.00	100.00
☐	127	Joe Kuhel, Wsh.	30.00	60.00	100.00
☐	128	Odell Hale, Cle.	30.00	60.00	100.00
☐	129	Sammy West, St.L.B	30.00	60.00	100.00
☐	130	Ben Chapman, Wsh.	30.00	60.00	100.00
☐	131	Monte Pearson, NYY.	30.00	60.00	100.00
☐	132	Rick Ferrell, Bos.	60.00	120.00	200.00
☐	133	Tommy Bridges, Det.	30.00	60.00	100.00
☐	134	Schoolboy Rowe, Det.	30.00	60.00	100.00
☐	135	Vernon Kennedy, Chi.-A.L.	30.00	60.00	100.00
☐	136	Red Ruffing, NYY.	75.00	150.00	250.00
☐	137	Lefty Grove, Bos.	150.00	300.00	500.00
☐	138	Wes Ferrell, Bos.	30.00	60.00	100.00
☐	139	Buck Newsom, Wsh.	30.00	60.00	100.00
☐	140	Rogers Hornsby, St.L.B	200.00	450.00	900.00

1939 WORLD WIDE GUM

SERIES A

The World Wide wax box of 1939 contained 100 packages of gum and 25 cards. If the consumer purchased four pieces of gum at one time, the store keeper might offer a card, or the customer could choose a card of his choice. The card size was designed to stand upright at the end of the box for display purposes. The paper premiums are unnumbered and listed here in alphabetical order.

Card Size: 4" x 5 3/4"
Face: Sepia on cream coloured paper stock, cream border; facsimile autograph
Back: Brown; "How To Play" baseball tips
Imprint: Lithograph in Canada (Lawson Printing, Montreal)
ACC No.: V351

	No.	Player	VG	EX	NRMT
		Complete Set :	**1,000.00**	**2,000.00**	**3,500.00**
		Common Player:	**25.00**	**45.00**	**75.00**
☐	1	Morris Arnovich, Pha.	25.00	45.00	75.00
☐	2	Sam Bell, Mtl.R	25.00	45.00	75.00
☐	3	Zeke Bonura, NYG.	25.00	45.00	75.00
☐	4	Earl Caldwell, Tor.	25.00	45.00	75.00
☐	5	Flea Clifton (Minor League)	25.00	45.00	75.00
☐	6	Frank Crosetti, NYY.	35.00	70.00	125.00
☐	7	Harry Danning, NYG.	25.00	45.00	75.00
☐	8	J. H. (Dizzy) Dean, Chi.-N.L.	115.00	225.00	400.00
☐	9	Emile De Jonghe, Tor.	25.00	45.00	75.00
☐	10	Paul Derringer, Cin.R	25.00	45.00	75.00
☐	11	Joe DiMaggio, NYY.	350.00	700.00	1,200.00
☐	12	Vince DiMaggio, K.C. A.A.	45.00	90.00	150.00
☐	13	Charles Gehringer, Det.	90.00	175.00	300.00
☐	14	Gene Hasson, Ath.	25.00	45.00	75.00
☐	15	Tom Henrich, NYY.	35.00	70.00	125.00

	No.	Player	VG	EX	NRMT
☐	16	Fred Hutchinson, Det.	35.00	70.00	125.00
☐	17	Phil Marchildon, Tor/Ath	60.00	120.00	200.00
☐	18	Mike Meola, Tor. I.L.	25.00	45.00	75.00
☐	19	Arnold Mosey (Minor League)	25.00	45.00	75.00
☐	20	Frank Pytlak, Cle.	25.00	45.00	75.00
☐	21	Frank Reiber (Minor League)	25.00	45.00	75.00
☐	22	Lee Rogers, Mtl.R, I.L.	25.00	45.00	75.00
☐	23	Cecil Travis, Senators	35.00	70.00	125.00
☐	24	Hal Trosky, Cle.	35.00	70.00	125.00
☐	25	Ted Williams, Bos.	350.00	700.00	1,250.00

SERIES B

Toward the end of the year Series A premiums ran short. Without reprinting World Wide called on Goudey, the parent company, to supply what premiums it might have in surplus from its inventory. Goudey supplied its "Diamond Stars Gum" premium. The Goudey premium cards were longer by 7/16" than the Canadian premium cards. World Wide Gum had Lawson, its printer, trim the paper card to the required 5 3/4" size, removing the top and bottom cream border. The cards are unnumbered and are arranged here in alphabetical order. The prices for this set are based on those of the Goudey set, since American cards were simply trimmed for the Canadian market.

Card Size: Regular - 4" x 6 3/16"
Trimmed - 4" x 5 3/4"
Face: Sepia on cream coloured paper stock; facsimile autograph
Back: Brown; "How to Play" baseball tips
Imprint: DIAMOND STARS GUM Mfg'd By The Goudey Gum Co.
ACC No.: R303-A

Complete Set (22 cards):			**450.00**	**900.00**	**1,500.00**
Common Player:			**12.50**	**25.00**	**40.00**
	No.	**Player**	**VG**	**EX**	**NRMT**
☐	1	Earle Averill, Det.	25.00	50.00	100.00
☐	2	Zeke Bonura, NYG.	12.50	25.00	40.00
☐	3	Mace Brown, Pgh.	12.50	25.00	40.00
☐	4	George Case, Senators	12.50	25.00	40.00
☐	5	Ben Chapman, Cle.	20.00	35.00	60.00
☐	6	Joe Cronin, Chi.RS	30.00	60.00	100.00
☐	7	Bill Dickey, NYY.	35.00	70.00	125.00
☐	8	Jimmy Foxx, Bos.	50.00	100.00	175.00
☐	9	Charles Gehringer, Det.	30.00	50.00	100.00
☐	10	Billy Herman, Chi.-N.L.	12.50	25.00	40.00
☐	11	Frank Higgins, Det.	12.50	25.00	40.00
☐	12	Fred Hutchinson, Det.	12.50	25.00	40.00
☐	13	Mike Kreevich, Chi.-A.L.	12.50	25.00	40.00
☐	14	Ernie Lombardi	25.00	45.00	75.00
☐	15	Gus Mancuso, Chi.-N.L.	12.50	25.00	40.00
☐	16	Eric McNair, Chi.-A.L.	12.50	25.00	40.00
☐	17	Mel Ott, NYG.	45.00	90.00	150.00
☐	18	Al Simmons, Atl.	30.00	60.00	100.00
☐	19	James Tabor, Bos.	12.50	25.00	40.00
☐	20	Joe Vosmik, Bos.	12.50	25.00	40.00
☐	21	Lon Warneke, St.L.	12.50	25.00	40.00
☐	22	Ted Williams, Bos.	150.00	300.00	500.00

1950 WORLD WIDE GUM

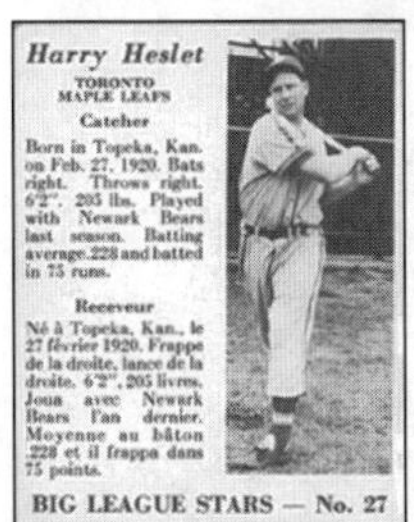

BIG LEAGUE STARS

This 48-card set was the final issue by World Wide Gum. The cards are printed in blue ink on one side only and are on heavy cardboard. International League Players are illustrated.

Card Size: 2 5/8" x 3 1/4"
Face: Blue; name, number, position, team, résumé, bilingual
Back: Blank
Imprint: None
ACC No.: V362

Complete Set (48 cards):			**1,000.00**	**2,000.00**	**3,500.00**
Common Player:			**20.00**	**35.00**	**65.00**
	No.	**Player**	**VG**	**EX**	**NRMT**
☐	1	Rocky Bridges, Mtl.	30.00	60.00	120.00
☐	2	Chuck Connors, Mtl.	175.00	350.00	600.00
☐	3	Jake Wade, Buffalo	20.00	35.00	65.00
☐	4	Al Cihocki, Bal.	20.00	35.00	65.00
☐	5	John Simmons,	20.00	35.00	65.00
☐	6	Frank Trechock, Buffalo	20.00	35.00	65.00
☐	7	Steve Lembo, Mtl.	20.00	35.00	65.00
☐	8	Johnny Welaj, Tor.	20.00	35.00	65.00
☐	9	Seymour Block, Buffalo	20.00	35.00	65.00
☐	10	Pat McGlothin, Mtl.	20.00	35.00	65.00
☐	11	Bryan Stephens, Bal.	20.00	35.00	65.00
☐	12	Clarence Podbielan, Mtl.	25.00	50.00	85.00
☐	13	Clem Hausmann, Buffalo	20.00	35.00	65.00
☐	14	Turk Lown, Mtl.	30.00	60.00	100.00
☐	15	Joe Payne, Bal.	20.00	35.00	65.00
☐	16	Coaker Triplett, Buffalo	20.00	35.00	65.00
☐	17	Nick Strincevich, Tor.	20.00	35.00	65.00
☐	18	Charlie Thompson, Mtl.	20.00	35.00	65.00
☐	19	Eric Silverman, Buffalo	20.00	35.00	65.00
☐	20	George Schmees, Mtl.	20.00	35.00	65.00
☐	21	George Binks, Buffalo	25.00	50.00	85.00
☐	22	Gino Cimoli, Mtl.	30.00	60.00	110.00
☐	23	Marty Tabacheck, Buffalo	20.00	35.00	65.00
☐	24	Al Gionfriddo, Mtl.	40.00	75.00	125.00
☐	25	Ronnie Lee, Mtl.	20.00	35.00	65.00
☐	26	Clyde King, Mtl.	30.00	60.00	110.00
☐	27	Harry Heslet, Tor.	20.00	35.00	65.00
☐	28	Jerry Scala, Buffalo	20.00	35.00	65.00
☐	29	Boris Woyt, Bal.	20.00	35.00	65.00
☐	30	Jack Collum, Rochester	25.00	50.00	85.00
☐	31	Chet Laabs, Jersey City	20.00	35.00	65.00
☐	32	Carden Gillenwater, Syc.	20.00	35.00	65.00
☐	33	Irving Medlinger, Bal.	20.00	35.00	65.00
☐	34	Toby Atwell, Mtl.	25.00	50.00	85.00
☐	35	Charlie Marshall, Rochester	20.00	35.00	65.00
☐	36	John (Jackie) Mayo, Tor.	20.00	35.00	65.00
☐	37	Gene Markland, Buffalo	20.00	35.00	65.00
☐	38	Russ Kerns, Bal.	20.00	35.00	65.00
☐	39	Jim Prendergast, Syc.	20.00	35.00	65.00
☐	40	Lou Welaj, Mtl.	20.00	35.00	65.00
☐	41	Clyde Kluttz, Bal.	30.00	60.00	100.00
☐	42	Bill Glynn, Tor.	20.00	35.00	65.00
☐	43	Don Richmond, Rochester	20.00	35.00	65.00
☐	44	Hank Biasetti, Buffalo	20.00	35.00	65.00
☐	45	Tom Lasorda, Mtl.	150.00	300.00	500.00
☐	46	Joseph Albert Roberge, Tor.	20.00	35.00	65.00
☐	47	George Byarn, Bal.	20.00	35.00	65.00
☐	48	Dutch Mele, Syc.	25.00	50.00	110.00

1950 PALM DAIRIES

Early 1950's Palm Daries Dixie cup lids. We have no pricing information on this set.

Card Size:
Face:
Back:
Imprint:
Complete Set (12 cards):

No.	Player
☐ 1	Richie Ashburn, Pha.
☐ 2	Sidney Gordon, Pgh.
☐ 3	William (Billy) Hoeft, Det.
☐ 4	Jackie Jensen, Bos.
☐ 5	Gil McDougald, NYY.
☐ 6	Minnie Minoso, Chi.-A.L.
☐ 7	Daniel (Danny) O'Connell, Milwaukee Braves
☐ 8	Melvin (Dusty) Parnell, Bos.
☐ 9	Preacher Roe, Brooklin Dodgers
☐ 10	Albert Schoendienst, Stl.
☐ 11	Enos Slaughter, Stl.
☐ 12	Gene Woodling, NYY.

1952 LAVAL DAIRY

This 114-card set was issued by Laval Dairies of Quebec. The ink on the cards has a greenish tint and there are size variations in the cards due to trimming variance at the printer. Ten of these cards have price premiums, as these players made it to the major leagues.

Card Size: 1 5/8" x 2 1/2"
Face: Black and white with green tint; name, number, team, date of birth
Back: Blank
Imprint: Provincial League 1952

		VG	EX	NRMT
Complete Set (114 cards):		**500.00**	**1,000.00**	**1,800.00**
Common Card:		**7.50**	**15.00**	**30.00**
No.	**Player**	**VG**	**EX**	**NRMT**
☐ 1	Georges McQuinn	7.50	15.00	30.00
☐ 2	Cliff Statham	7.50	15.00	30.00
☐ 3	Frank Wilson	7.50	15.00	30.00
☐ 4	Frank Neiri	7.50	15.00	30.00
☐ 5	Georges Maranda	10.00	20.00	30.00
☐ 6	Dick Gorderio	7.50	15.00	30.00
☐ 7	Roger McCardell	7.50	15.00	30.00
☐ 8	Joseph Janiak	7.50	15.00	30.00
☐ 9	Herbert Shankman	7.50	15.00	30.00
☐ 10	Joe Subbiondo	7.50	15.00	30.00
☐ 11	Jack Brenner	7.50	15.00	30.00
☐ 12	Donald Buchanan	7.50	15.00	30.00
☐ 13	Robert Smith	7.50	15.00	30.00
☐ 14	Raymond Lague	7.50	15.00	30.00
☐ 15	Mike Fandozzi	7.50	15.00	30.00
☐ 16	Dick Moler	7.50	15.00	30.00
☐ 17	Edward "Angie" Bazydlo	7.50	15.00	30.00
☐ 18	Danny Mazurek	7.50	15.00	30.00
☐ 19	Edwin Charles	7.50	15.00	30.00
☐ 20	Jack Mullaney	10.00	20.00	35.00
☐ 21	Bob Bolan	7.50	15.00	30.00
☐ 22	Bob Long	7.50	15.00	30.00
☐ 23	Cleo Lewright	7.50	15.00	30.00
☐ 24	Herb Taylor	7.50	15.00	30.00
☐ 25	Frank Gaeta	7.50	15.00	30.00
☐ 26	Bill Truitt	7.50	15.00	30.00
☐ 27	Jean Prats	7.50	15.00	30.00
☐ 28	Tex Taylor	7.50	15.00	30.00
☐ 29	Ronnie Delbianco	7.50	15.00	30.00
☐ 30	Joe Dilorenzo	7.50	15.00	30.00
☐ 31	John Paszek	7.50	15.00	30.00
☐ 32	Ken Suess	7.50	15.00	30.00
☐ 33	Harry Sims	7.50	15.00	30.00
☐ 34	William Jackson	7.50	15.00	30.00
☐ 35	Jerry Mayers	7.50	15.00	30.00
☐ 36	Gordon Maltzberger	10.00	15.00	30.00
☐ 37	Gerry Cabana	7.50	15.00	30.00
☐ 38	Gary Rutkay	7.50	15.00	30.00
☐ 39	Ken Hatcher	7.50	15.00	30.00
☐ 40	Vincent Cosenza	7.50	15.00	30.00
☐ 41	Edward Yaeger	7.50	15.00	30.00
☐ 42	Jimmy Orr	7.50	15.00	30.00
☐ 43	John Dimartino	7.50	15.00	30.00
☐ 44	Len Wisnaski	7.50	15.00	30.00
☐ 45	Pete Caniglia	7.50	15.00	30.00
☐ 46	Guy Coleman	7.50	15.00	30.00
☐ 47	Herb Fleischer	7.50	15.00	30.00
☐ 48	Charles Yahrling	7.50	15.00	30.00
☐ 49	Roger Bedard	7.50	15.00	30.00
☐ 50	Al Barillari	7.50	15.00	30.00
☐ 51	Hugh Mulcahy	7.50	15.00	30.00
☐ 52	Vincent Canepa	7.50	15.00	30.00
☐ 53	Bob Loranger	7.50	15.00	30.00
☐ 54	Georges Carpentier	7.50	15.00	30.00
☐ 55	Bill Hamilton	7.50	15.00	30.00
☐ 56	Hector Lopez	12.00	25.00	40.00
☐ 57	Joe Taylor	7.50	15.00	30.00
☐ 58	Alonso Brathwaite	7.50	15.00	30.00
☐ 59	Carl McQuillen	7.50	15.00	30.00
☐ 60	Robert Trice	7.50	15.00	30.00
☐ 61	John Dworak	7.50	15.00	30.00
☐ 62	Lou Pinkston	7.50	15.00	30.00
☐ 63	William Shannon	7.50	15.00	30.00
☐ 64	Stanley Watychowics	7.50	15.00	30.00
☐ 65	Roger Herbert	7.50	15.00	30.00
☐ 66	Troy Spencer	7.50	15.00	30.00
☐ 67	Johnny Rohan	7.50	15.00	30.00
☐ 68	John Sosh	7.50	15.00	30.00
☐ 69	Ramon Mason	7.50	15.00	30.00
☐ 70	Tom Smith	7.50	15.00	30.00
☐ 71	Douglas McBean	7.50	15.00	30.00
☐ 72	Bill Babik	7.50	15.00	30.00
☐ 73	Dante Cozzi	7.50	15.00	30.00
☐ 74	Melvil Doxtator	7.50	15.00	30.00
☐ 75	William Gilray	7.50	15.00	30.00
☐ 76	Armando Diaz	7.50	15.00	30.00
☐ 77	Ackroyd Smith	7.50	15.00	30.00
☐ 78	Germain Pizarro	7.50	15.00	30.00
☐ 79	James "Jim" Heap	7.50	15.00	30.00
☐ 80	Herbert B. Crompton	7.50	15.00	30.00
☐ 81	Howard J. Bodell	7.50	15.00	30.00
☐ 82	Andre Schreiber	7.50	15.00	30.00
☐ 83	John Wingo	7.50	15.00	30.00
☐ 84	Salvatore "Sol" Arduini	7.50	15.00	30.00
☐ 85	Fred Paccito	7.50	15.00	30.00
☐ 86	Aaron Osofsky	7.50	15.00	30.00
☐ 87	Jack Digrace	7.50	15.00	30.00
☐ 88	Alfonzo "Chico" Gerard	7.50	15.00	30.00
☐ 89	Manuel Trabous	7.50	15.00	30.00
☐ 90	Tom Barnes	7.50	15.00	30.00
☐ 91	Humberto Robinson	10.00	20.00	30.00
☐ 92	Jack Bukowatz	7.50	15.00	30.00
☐ 93	Marco Mainini	7.50	15.00	30.00
☐ 94	Claude St. Vincent	7.50	15.00	30.00
☐ 95	Fernand Brousseau	7.50	15.00	30.00
☐ 96	John Malangone	7.50	15.00	30.00
☐ 97	Pierre Nantel	7.50	15.00	30.00
☐ 98	Donald Stevens	7.50	15.00	30.00
☐ 99	Jim Prappas	7.50	15.00	30.00

	No.	Player	VG	EX	NRMT
☐	100	Richard Fitzgerald	7.50	15.00	30.00
☐	101	Yves Aubin	7.50	15.00	30.00
☐	102	Frank Novosel	7.50	15.00	30.00
☐	103	Tony Campos	7.50	15.00	30.00
☐	104	Gelso Oviedo	7.50	15.00	30.00
☐	105	July Becker	7.50	15.00	30.00
☐	106	Aurelio Ala	7.50	15.00	30.00
☐	107	Orlando Andux	7.50	15.00	30.00
☐	108	Tom Hackett	7.50	15.00	30.00
☐	109	Guillaume Vargas	7.50	15.00	30.00
☐	110	Francisco Salfran	7.50	15.00	30.00
☐	111	Jean-Marc Blais	7.50	15.00	30.00
☐	112	Vince Pizzitola	7.50	15.00	30.00
☐	113	John Olsen	7.50	15.00	30.00
☐	114	Jacques Monette	7.50	15.00	30.00

1952 PARKHURST

This set appears to be Parkhurst's only venture into baseball cards. However the American card catalogue number V338-1 seems to indicate the possibility of another.

Card Size: 2" x 2 1/2"
Face: Black and white
Back: Red on card stock; number, position, résumé, "Hey Kids?"
Imprint: None

			VG	EX	NRMT
		Complete Set (100 cards):	**750.00**	**1,500.00**	**2,500.00**
		Common Player:	**7.50**	**15.00**	**25.00**
	No.	**Player**	**VG**	**EX**	**NRMT**
☐	1	Joe Becker, Mgr., Tor.	12.50	25.00	50.00
☐	2	Aaron "Ernie" Silverman, Tor.	7.50	15.00	25.00
☐	3	"Bobby" Rhawn, Tor.	7.50	15.00	25.00
☐	4	Russell "Russ" Bars, Tor.	7.50	15.00	25.00
☐	5	William Jennings, Tor.	7.50	15.00	25.00
☐	6	Grover B. Bowers, Tor.	7.50	15.00	25.00
☐	7	Victor "Vic" Lombardi, Tor.	10.00	20.00	35.00
☐	8	Billy DeMars, Tor.	12.00	25.00	40.00
☐	9	Frank Colman, Tor.	7.50	15.00	25.00
☐	10	Charles Grant, Tor.	7.50	15.00	25.00
☐	11	Irving Medlinger, Tor.	7.50	15.00	25.00
☐	12	Burke McLaughlin, Tor.	7.50	15.00	25.00
☐	13	James Lewis "Lew" Morton, Tor.	7.50	15.00	25.00
☐	14	C.H. "Red" Barrett, Tor.	7.50	15.00	25.00
☐	15	Leon Ray Foulk, Tor.	7.50	15.00	25.00
☐	16	Neill Rawlings Sheridan, Tor.	7.50	15.00	25.00
☐	17	Ferrell "Andy" Anderson, Tor.	7.50	15.00	25.00
☐	18	Raymond E. "Ray" Shore, Tor.	7.50	15.00	25.00
☐	19	Duke Markell, Tor.	7.50	15.00	25.00
☐	20	Robert L. Balcena, Tor.	7.50	15.00	25.00
☐	21	Wilmer Fields, Tor.	7.50	15.00	25.00
☐	22	Charles White, Jr., Tor.	7.50	15.00	25.00
☐	23	Gerald Fahr, Tor.	7.50	15.00	25.00
☐	24	Jose Carreo Bracho, Tor.	7.50	15.00	25.00
☐	25	Edward Stevens, Tor.	10.00	20.00	35.00
☐	26	The Maple Leaf Stadium	15.00	30.00	55.00
		POINTERS/QUIZ QUESTIONS			
☐	27	Throwing Home	4.00	8.00	15.00
☐	28	Regulation Baseball Diamond	4.00	8.00	15.00
☐	29	Gripping The Bat	4.00	8.00	15.00
☐	30	Hiding Kind of Pitch	4.00	8.00	15.00
☐	31	Catcher's Stance	4.00	8.00	15.00
☐	32	Quiz Question	4.00	8.00	15.00
☐	33	Finger and Arm Exercises	4.00	8.00	15.00
☐	34	First Baseman	4.00	8.00	15.00
☐	35	Pitcher's Stance	4.00	8.00	15.00
☐	36	Swinging Bats	4.00	8.00	15.00
☐	37	Quiz Question	4.00	8.00	15.00
☐	38	Watch The Ball	4.00	8.00	15.00
☐	39	Quiz Question	4.00	8.00	15.00
☐	40	Quiz Question	4.00	8.00	15.00
☐	41	How To Bunt	4.00	8.00	15.00
☐	42	Wrist Snap	4.00	8.00	15.00
☐	43	Pitching Practice	4.00	8.00	15.00
☐	44	Stealing Bases	4.00	8.00	15.00
☐	45	Pitching 1	4.00	8.00	15.00
☐	46	Pitching 2	4.00	8.00	15.00
☐	47	Signals	4.00	8.00	15.00
☐	48	Regulation Baseballs	4.00	8.00	15.00
☐	49	Albert R. Ronning, Mtl.	7.50	15.00	25.00
☐	50	William Charles Glane, Mtl.	7.50	15.00	25.00
☐	51	William Clark Samson, Mtl.	7.50	15.00	25.00
☐	52	Charles Lemoine Thompson, Mtl.	7.50	15.00	25.00
☐	53	Ezra Mac "Pat" McGlothin, Mtl.	7.50	15.00	25.00
☐	54	Forrest V. Jacobs, Mtl.	10.00	20.00	35.00
☐	55	Arthur G. Fabbro, Mtl.	7.50	15.00	25.00
☐	56	James Robert Hughes, Mtl.	10.00	20.00	35.00
☐	57	Donald Albert Hoak, Mtl.	20.00	40.00	65.00
☐	58	Tom Lasorda, Mtl.	90.00	175.00	300.00
☐	59	Gilbert Wade Mills, Mtl.	7.50	15.00	25.00
☐	60	Malcolm Francis Mallette, Mtl.	7.50	15.00	25.00
☐	61	Glenn R. "Spike" Nelson, Mtl.	10.00	20.00	35.00
☐	62	John Earl Simmons, Mtl.	7.50	15.00	25.00
☐	63	R.S. "Alex" Alexander, Mtl.	7.50	15.00	25.00
☐	64	Dan Bankhead, Mtl.	15.00	25.00	40.00
☐	65	Solomon Hampton Coleman, Mtl	7.50	15.00	25.00
☐	66	Walter Emmons Alston, Mgr., Mtl.	50.00	100.00	175.00
☐	67	Walter Anthony Fiala, Mtl.	7.50	15.00	25.00
☐	68	James Gilliam, Mtl.	20.00	40.00	75.00
☐	69	James Edward Pendleton, Mtl.	12.00	25.00	40.00
☐	70	Gino Nicholas Cimoli, Mtl.	12.00	25.00	40.00
☐	71	Carmen Louis Mauro, Mtl.	7.50	15.00	25.00
☐	72	Walter J. Moryn, Mtl.	12.00	25.00	40.00
☐	73	James K. Romano, Mtl.	7.50	15.00	25.00
☐	74	Rollin Joseph Lutz, Mtl.	7.50	15.00	25.00
☐	75	Edward Jack Roebuck, Mtl.	12.00	25.00	40.00
☐	76	John Podres, Mtl.	25.00	50.00	85.00
☐	77	Walter "Walt" Ed. Novick, Ott.	7.50	15.00	25.00
☐	78	"Lefty" Vincent Leo Gohl, Ott.	7.50	15.00	25.00
☐	79	Thomas "Tom" Daniel Kirk, Ott.	7.50	15.00	25.00
☐	80	Robert "Bob" J. Betz, Ott.	7.50	15.00	25.00
☐	81	William "Bill"Hockenbury, Ott.	7.50	15.00	25.00
☐	82	Albert William Rubeling, Ott.	7.50	15.00	25.00
☐	83	Julius Neal Watlington, Ott.	7.50	15.00	25.00
☐	84	Frank Joseph Fanovich, Ott.	7.50	15.00	25.00
☐	85	Hank Foiles, Ott.	12.00	25.00	40.00
☐	86	Lou Limmer, Ott.	7.50	15.00	25.00
☐	87	Edward "Ed" Hrabcsak, Ott.	7.50	15.00	25.00
☐	88	R. "Bob" Clayton Gardner, Ott.	7.50	15.00	25.00
☐	89	John "Johnnie" Metkovich, Ott	7.50	15.00	25.00
☐	90	Jean-Pierre "Frenchie" Roy, Ott.	10.00	20.00	35.00
☐	91	Frank Skaff, Mgr., Ott.	7.50	15.00	25.00
☐	92	Harry C. Desert, Ott.	7.50	15.00	25.00
☐	93	Stanley "Stan" Edward Jok, Ott.	7.50	15.00	25.00
☐	94	Leo Russel "Russ" Swingle, Ott.	7.50	15.00	25.00
☐	95	Robert "Bob" J. Wellman, Ott.	7.50	15.00	25.00
☐	96	John Clements Conway, Ott.	7.50	15.00	25.00
☐	97	George Robert Moskovich, Ott.	7.50	15.00	25.00
☐	98	Charles Bishop, Ott.	7.50	15.00	25.00
☐	99	Joseph Murray, Ott.	7.50	15.00	25.00
☐	100	Mike Kume, Ott.	12.50	25.00	50.00

1953 EXHIBITS

This 64-card set was printed in the United States and bears various type styles for the players names on the face. The cards are on heavy cardboard and come in a number of different colours.

Card Size: 3 1/4" x 5 1/4"
Face: Purple, brown or blue, borderless; name, number
Back: Blank
Imprint: An Exhibit Card MADE IN U.S.A. or None

Complete Set (64 cards):		**500.00**	**1,000.00**	**1,800.00**
Common Player (1-32):		**3.50**	**7.00**	**12.00**
Common Player (33-64):		**2.50**	**5.00**	**8.00**

No.	Player	VG	EX	NRMT
☐ 1	Preacher Roe, Bkn.	6.00	12.00	20.00
☐ 2	Luke Easter, Cle.	6.00	12.00	20.00
☐ 3	Gene Bearden, Chi.-A.L.	3.50	7.00	12.00
☐ 4	Chico Carrasquel, Chi.-A.L.	3.50	7.00	12.00
☐ 5	Vic Raschi, NYY.	4.00	8.00	15.00
☐ 6	Monty Irvin, NYG.	7.50	15.00	25.00
☐ 7	Henry Sauer, Chi.-N.L.	3.50	7.00	12.00
☐ 8	Ralph Branca, Bkn.	4.00	8.00	15.00
☐ 9	Eddie Stanky, Stl.	4.00	8.00	15.00
☐ 10	Sam Jethroe, Bos.B	3.50	7.00	12.00
☐ 11	Larry Doby, Cle.	7.50	15.00	25.00
☐ 12	Hal Newhouser, Det.	7.50	15.00	25.00
☐ 13	Gil Hodges, Bkn.	15.00	30.00	50.00
☐ 14	Harry Brecheen, St.L.B	3.50	7.00	12.00
☐ 15	Ed Lopat, NYY.	4.00	8.00	15.00
☐ 16	Don Newcombe, Bkn.	7.50	15.00	25.00
☐ 17	Bob Feller, Cle.	20.00	40.00	65.00
☐ 18	Tommy Holmes, Bkn.	3.50	7.00	12.00
☐ 19	Jackie Robinson, Bkn.	60.00	120.00	200.00
☐ 20	Roy Campanella, Bkn.	40.00	80.00	140.00
☐ 21	Harold "Peewee" Reese, Bkn.	20.00	35.00	60.00
☐ 22	Ralph Kiner, Pit.	15.00	30.00	50.00
☐ 23	Dom DiMaggio, Bos.	6.00	12.00	20.00
☐ 24	Bobby Doerr, Bos.	9.00	18.00	30.00
☐ 25	Phil Rizzuto, NYY.	20.00	35.00	60.00
☐ 26	Bob Elliott, St.L.B	3.50	7.00	12.00
☐ 27	Tommy Henrich, NYY.	4.00	8.00	15.00
☐ 28	Joe DiMaggio, NYY.	125.00	250.00	400.00
☐ 29	Harry Lowery, Stl.	3.50	7.00	12.00
☐ 30	Ted Williams, Bos.	75.00	150.00	250.00
☐ 31	Bob Lemon, Cle.	10.00	20.00	35.00
☐ 32	Warren Spahn, Mil.	18.00	35.00	60.00
☐ 33	Don Hoak, Bkn.	4.00	8.00	15.00
☐ 34	Bob Alexander, Bal.	2.50	5.00	8.00
☐ 35	John Simmons, Mtl.	2.50	5.00	8.00
☐ 36	Steve Lembo, Bkn.	2.50	5.00	8.00
☐ 37	Norman Larker, Mtl.	3.00	6.00	100.00
☐ 38	Bob Ludwick, Mtl.	2.50	5.00	8.00
☐ 39	Walt Moryn, Bkn.	3.00	6.00	10.00
☐ 40	Charlie Thompson, Bkn.	2.50	5.00	8.00
☐ 41	Ed Roebuck, Bkn.	3.00	6.00	10.00
☐ 42	Rose,Mtl.	2.50	5.00	8.00
☐ 43	Edmundo Amoros, Bkn.	4.00	8.00	15.00
☐ 44	Bob Milliken, Bkn.	2.50	5.00	8.00
☐ 45	Arthur Fabbro, Mtl.	2.50	5.00	8.00
☐ 46	Forrest Jacobs, Phi.	2.50	5.00	8.00
☐ 47	Carmen Mauro, Bkn.	2.50	5.00	8.00
☐ 48	Walter Fiala, Mtl.	2.50	5.00	8.00
☐ 49	Rocky Nelson, Bkn.	2.50	5.00	8.00
☐ 50	Tom Lasorda, Bkn.	35.00	70.00	125.00
☐ 51	Ronnie Lee, Mtl.	2.50	5.00	8.00
☐ 52	Hampton Coleman, Mtl.	2.50	5.00	8.00
☐ 53	Frank Marchio, Mtl.	2.50	5.00	8.00
☐ 54	William Samson, Mtl.	2.50	5.00	8.00
☐ 55	Gil Mills, Mtl.	2.50	5.00	8.00
☐ 56	Al Ronning, Mtl.	2.50	5.00	8.00
☐ 57	Stan Musial, Stl.	35.00	70.00	125.00
☐ 58	Walker Cooper, Mil.	2.50	5.00	8.00
☐ 59	Mickey Vernon, Wsh.	4.00	8.00	15.00
☐ 60	Del Ennis, Pha.	2.50	5.00	8.00
☐ 61	Walter Alston, Mgr., Bkn.	15.00	30.00	50.00
☐ 62	Dick Sisler, Stl.	2.50	5.00	8.00
☐ 63	Billy Goodman, Bos.	3.50	7.00	12.00
☐ 64	Alex Kellner, Pha.	3.00	6.00	15.00

CHAPTER TWO

BASEBALL ISSUES 1960 TO 1997

1960 O-PEE-CHEE TATTOOS

The tattoo of this set was printed in reverse on the inside of the Tattoo Bubble Gum wrapper. The transfer was applied by moistening a spot on the skin. The labels and tattoos are unnumbered and are listed here alphabetically.

Wrapper Size: 1 9/16" x 3 1/2"
Face: Yellow, red, black and white on green background
Back: Red, blue and green; unnumbered
Imprint: O-PEE-CHEE CO., LTD., LONDON, CANADA MADE IN CANADA PRINTED IN CANADA

Complete Set (96 cards):		**1,200.00**	**2,000.00**
Common Player:		**6.00**	**10.00**
	Player	**EX**	**NRMT**
☐	Hank Aaron, Mil.	65.00	110.00
☐	Bob Allison, Wsh.	6.00	10.00
☐	John Antonelli, S.F.	6.00	10.00
☐	Richie Ashburn, Chi.-N.L.	18.00	30.00
☐	Ernie Banks, Chi.-N.L.	35.00	60.00
☐	Yogi Berra, NYY.	50.00	85.00
☐	Lew Burdette, Mil.	6.00	10.00
☐	Orlando Cepeda, S.F.	12.00	20.00
☐	Rocky Colavito, Det.	15.00	25.00
☐	Joe Cunningham, Stl.	6.00	10.00
☐	Bud Daley, K.C.	6.00	10.00
☐	Don Drysdale, L.A.	30.00	50.00
☐	Ryne Duren, NYY.	6.00	10.00
☐	Roy Face, Pgh.	6.00	10.00
☐	Whitey Ford, NYY.	35.00	60.00
☐	Nellie Fox, Chi.-A.L.	18.00	30.00
☐	Tito Francona, Cle.	6.00	10.00
☐	Gene Freese, Chi.-A.L.	6.00	10.00
☐	Jim Gilliam, L.A.	6.00	10.00
☐	Dick Groat, Pgh.	6.00	10.00
☐	Ray Herbert, K.C.	6.00	10.00
☐	Glen Hobbie, Chi.-N.L.	6.00	10.00
☐	Jackie Jensen, Bos.	6.00	10.00
☐	Sam Jones, S.F.	6.00	10.00
☐	Al Kaline, Det.	30.00	50.00
☐	Harmon Killebrew, Wsh.	30.00	50.00
☐	Harvey Kuenn, Cle., Error	9.00	15.00
☐	Frank Lary, Det.	6.00	10.00
☐	Vernon Law, Pgh.	6.00	10.00
☐	Frank Malzone, Bos.	6.00	10.00
☐	Mickey Mantle, NYY.	200.00	350.00
☐	Roger Maris, NYY.	35.00	60.00
☐	Eddie Mathews, Mil.	30.00	50.00
☐	Willie Mays, S.F.	65.00	110.00
☐	Cal McLish, Cin.	6.00	10.00
☐	Wally Moon, L.A.	6.00	10.00
☐	Walt Moryn, Chi.-N.L.	6.00	10.00
☐	Don Mossi, Det.	6.00	10.00
☐	Stan Musial, Stl.	50.00	90.00
☐	Charlie Neal, L.A.	6.00	10.00
☐	Don Newcombe, Cin.	9.00	15.00
☐	Milt Pappas, Bal.	6.00	10.00
☐	Camilo Pascual, Wsh.	6.00	10.00
☐	Billy Pierce, Chi.-A.L., Error	6.00	10.00
☐	Robin Roberts, Pha.	20.00	35.00
☐	Frank Robinson, Cin.	32.00	55.00
☐	Pete Runnels, Bos.	6.00	10.00
☐	Herb Score, Chi.-A.L.	9.00	15.00
☐	Warren Spahn, Mil.	30.00	50.00
☐	Johnny Temple, Cle.	6.00	10.00
☐	Gus Triandos, Bal.	6.00	10.00
☐	Jerry Walker, Bal.	6.00	10.00
☐	Bill White, Stl.	9.00	15.00
☐	Gene Woodling, Bal.	6.00	10.00
☐	Early Wynn, Chi.-A.L.	25.00	40.00

TEAM LOGOS

☐	Baltimore Orioles	6.00	10.00
☐	Boston Red Sox	6.00	10.00
☐	Chicago Cubs	6.00	10.00
☐	Chicago White Sox	6.00	10.00
☐	Cincinnati Reds	6.00	10.00
☐	Cleveland Indians	6.00	10.00
☐	Detroit Tigers	6.00	10.00
☐	Kansas City Athletics	6.00	10.00
☐	Los Angeles Dodgers	6.00	10.00
☐	Milwaukee Braves	6.00	10.00
☐	New York Yankees	6.00	10.00
☐	Philadelphia Phillies	6.00	10.00
☐	Pittsburgh Pirates	6.00	10.00
☐	St. Louis Cardinals	6.00	10.00
☐	San Francisco Giants	6.00	10.00
☐	Washington Senators	6.00	10.00

FACSIMILE AUTOGRAPHS

☐	Richie Ashburn, Chi.-N.L.	9.00	15.00
☐	Rocky Colavito, Det.	7.00	12.00
☐	Roy Face, Pgh.	6.00	10.00
☐	Jackie Jensen, Bos.	6.00	10.00
☐	Harmon Killebrew, Wsh.	13.00	22.00
☐	Mickey Mantle, NYY.	90.00	150.00
☐	Willie Mays, S.F.	30.00	50.00
☐	Stan Musial, Stl.	25.00	40.00
☐	Billy Pierce, Chi.-A.L.	6.00	10.00
☐	Jerry Walker, Bal.	6.00	10.00

IN ACTION

☐	Batter (Left Handed)	6.00	10.00
☐	Batter (Right Handed)	6.00	10.00
☐	Circus Catch	6.00	10.00
☐	Double Play	6.00	10.00
☐	The Final Word	6.00	10.00
☐	Grand Slam Homer	6.00	10.00
☐	Great Catch	6.00	10.00
☐	Out At First	6.00	10.00
☐	Out At Home	6.00	10.00
☐	Pitcher (Left Handed)	6.00	10.00
☐	Pitcher (Right Handed)	6.00	10.00
☐	Pitcher (Right Handed)	6.00	10.00
☐	Run-Down	6.00	10.00
☐	Stolen Base	6.00	10.00
☐	Twisting Foul	6.00	10.00

1962 POST CEREAL

1962 PROMOTIONAL CARDS

Inserted in Life magazine during 1962 as a promotional card for Post "200 Top Stars" cards. The cards were offered on the back of Post cereal boxes.

Card Size: 3 1/2" x 2 1/2"
Face: Four colour; number, position, resumé, Post logo
Back: Black and red on card stock; promotional message, Post logo
Imprint: Post
Complete Set No.: 2

	No.	Player	EX	NRMT
☐	5	Mickey Mantle	150.00	250.00
☐	6	Roger Maris	60.00	100.0

1962 REGULAR ISSUE

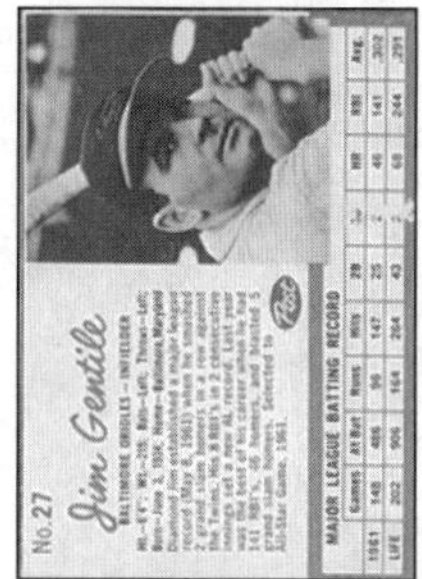

Carried on the backs of cereal boxes, these cards had to be cut out of the boxes. The care with which this was done will greatly affect the price. Many cards are available in differing degrees of scarcity depending on which brand and box size of cereal the card was issued on. Prices are based on VG and EX-MT grades. Near mint cards command a premium.

Card Size: 3 1/2" x 2 1/2"
Face: Four colour; number, position, resumé, bilingual
Back: Blank
Imprint: None

Complete Set (200 cards):			**1,800.00**	**3,000.00**
Common Player:			**3.50**	**6.00**

	No.	Player	VG	EX-MT
☐	1	Bill Skowron, NYY.	6.00	15.00
☐	2	Bobby Richardson, NYY.	6.00	10.00
☐	3	Cletis Boyer, NYY.	3.50	6.00
☐	4	Tony Kubek, NYY.	7.00	12.00
☐	5	Mickey Mantle, NYY. Error (153 hits)	180.00	300.00
☐	5	Mickey Mantle, NYY. (163 hits)	150.00	250.00
☐	6	Roger Maris, NYY.	60.00	100.00
☐	7	Yogi Berra, NYY. (*)	50.00	90.00
☐	8	Elston Howard, NYY.	6.00	10.00
☐	9	Whitey Ford, NYY. (L.A.)	35.00	60.00
☐	9A	Whitey Ford, L.A. (NYY.)	30.00	50.00
☐	10	Ralph Terry, NYY. (*)	25.00	40.00
☐	11	John Blanchard, NYY.	3.50	6.00
☐	12	Luis Arroyo, NYY.	3.50	6.00
☐	13	Bill Stafford, NYY.	3.50	6.00
☐	14	Norm Cash, Det.	3.50	6.00
☐	15	Jake Wood, Det.	3.50	6.00
☐	16	Steve Boros, Det.	3.50	6.00
☐	17	Chico Fernandez, Det.	3.50	6.00
☐	18	Bill Bruton, Det.	3.50	6.00
☐	19	Rocky Colavito, Det.	9.00	15.00
☐	20	Al Kaline, Det. (*)	30.00	55.00
☐	21	Dick Brown, Det. (*)	20.00	35.00
☐	22	Frank Lary, Det. (*)	18.00	30.00
☐	23	Don Mossi, Det.	3.50	6.00
☐	24	Phil Regan, Det.	3.50	6.00
☐	25	Charlie Maxwell, Det.	3.50	6.00
☐	26	Jim Bunning, Bal.	10.00	18.00
☐	27	Jim Gentile, Bal.	3.50	6.00
☐	28	Marv Breeding, Bal.	3.50	6.00
☐	29	Brooks Robinson, Bal.	25.00	45.00
☐	30	Ron Hansen, Bal.	3.50	6.00
☐	31	Jackie Brandt, Bal.	3.50	6.00
☐	32	Dick Williams, Bal. (*)	25.00	40.00
☐	33	Gus Triandos, Bal.	3.50	6.00
☐	34	Milt Pappas, Bal.	3.50	6.00
☐	35	Hoyt Wilhelm, Bal. (*)	30.00	50.00
☐	36	Chuck Estrada, Bal. (*)	25.00	40.00
☐	37	Vic Power, Cle.	3.50	6.00
☐	38	Johnny Temple, Cle.	3.50	6.00
☐	39	Bubba Phillips, Cle. (*)	20.00	35.00
☐	40	Tito Francona, Cle. (*)	18.00	30.00
☐	41	Willie Kirkland, Cle.	3.50	6.00
☐	42	John Romano, Cle. (*)	20.00	35.00
☐	43	Jim Perry, Cle.	3.50	6.00
☐	44	Woodie Held, Cle.	3.50	6.00
☐	45	Chuck Essegian, Cle.	3.50	6.00
☐	46	Roy Sievers, Chi.-A.L.	3.50	6.00
☐	47	Nellie Fox, Chi.-A.L.	10.00	18.00
☐	48	Al Smith, Chi.-A.L.	3.50	6.00
☐	49	Luis Aparicio, Chi.-A.L. (*)	30.00	55.00
☐	50	Jim Landis, Chi.-A.L.	3.50	6.00
☐	51	Minnie Minoso, Chi.-A.L. (*)	25.00	40.00
☐	52	Andy Carey, Chi.-A.L. (*)	25.00	40.00
☐	53	Sherman Lollar, Chi.-A.L.	3.50	6.00
☐	54	Billy Pierce, Chi.-A.L.	3.50	6.00
☐	55	Early Wynn, Chi.-A.L.	13.00	22.00
☐	56	Chuck Schilling, Bos.	3.50	6.00
☐	57	Pete Runnels, Bos.	3.50	6.00
☐	58	Frank Malzone, Bos.	3.50	6.00
☐	59	Don Buddin, Bos.	3.50	6.00
☐	60	Gary Geiger, Bos.	3.50	6.00
☐	61	Carl Yastrzemski, Bos.	40.00	70.00
☐	62	Jackie Jensen, Bos.	30.00	50.00
☐	63	Jim Pagliaroni, Bos. (*)	3.50	6.00
☐	64	Don Schwall, Bos. (*)	18.00	30.00
☐	65	Dale Long, Wsh.	3.50	6.00
☐	66	Chuck Cottier, Wsh.	3.50	6.00
☐	67	Billy Klaus, Wsh.	3.50	6.00
☐	68	Coot Veal, Wsh. (*)	15.00	25.00
☐	69	Marty Keough, Wsh.	3.50	6.00
☐	70	Willie Tasby, Wsh. (*)	30.00	50.00
☐	71	Gene Woodling, Wsh.	3.50	6.00
☐	72	Gene Green, Wsh.	3.50	6.00
☐	73	Dick Donovan, Wsh.	3.50	6.00
☐	74	Steve Bilko, LA.	3.50	6.00
☐	75	Rocky Bridges, LA. (*)	20.00	35.00
☐	76	Eddie Yost, LA.	3.50	6.00
☐	77	Leon Wagner, LA. (*)	25.00	40.00
☐	78	Albie Pearson, LA. (*)	20.00	35.00
☐	79	Ken Hunt, LA.	3.50	6.00
☐	80	Earl Averill, LA.	3.50	6.00
☐	81	Ryne Duren, LA.	3.50	6.00
☐	82	Ted Kluszewski, LA.	9.00	15.00
☐	83	Bob Allison, Min.	3.50	6.00
☐	84	Billy Martin, Min.	9.00	15.00
☐	85	Harmon Killebrew, Min. (*)	35.00	60.00
☐	86	Zoilo Versalles, Min.	3.50	6.00
☐	87	Lenny Green, Min. (*)	25.00	40.00
☐	88	Bill Tuttle, Min.	3.50	6.00
☐	89	Jim Lemon, Min.	3.50	6.00
☐	90	Earl Battey, Min.	3.50	6.00
☐	91	Camilo Pascual, Min.	3.50	6.00
☐	92	Norm Siebern, KC.A	3.50	6.00
☐	93	Jerry Lumpe, KC.A	3.50	6.00
☐	94	Dick Howser, KC.A (*)	20.00	35.00
☐	95	Gene Stephens, KC.A	3.50	6.00
☐	96	Leo Posada, KC.A	3.50	6.00
☐	97	Joe Pignatano, KC.A	3.50	6.00
☐	98	Jim Archer, KC.A	3.50	6.00
☐	99	Haywood Sullivan, KC.A (*)	25.00	40.00
☐	100	Art Ditmar, KC.A	3.50	6.00
☐	101	Gil Hodges, L.A.	13.00	22.00
☐	102	Charlie Neal, L.A.	3.50	6.00
☐	103	Daryl Spencer, L.A.	3.50	6.00
☐	104	Maury Wills, L.A.	9.00	15.00
☐	105	Tommy Davis, L.A. (*)	18.00	30.00
☐	106	Willie Davis, L.A.	3.75	7.50
☐	107	John Roseboro, L.A.	3.50	6.00
☐	108	John Podres, L.A.	20.00	35.00
☐	109	Sandy Koufax, L.A.	35.00	60.00

☐	110	Don Drysdale, L.A.	18.00	30.00
☐	111	Larry Sherry, L.A. (*)	25.00	45.00
☐	112	Jim Gilliam, L.A. (*)	30.00	50.00
☐	113	Norm Larker, L.A.	3.50	6.00
☐	114	Duke Snider, L.A.	25.00	40.00
☐	115	Stan Williams, L.A.	3.50	6.00
☐	116	Gordy Coleman, Cin.	3.50	6.00
☐	117	Don Blasingame, Cin. (*)	25.00	40.00
☐	118	Gene Freese, Cin. (*)	15.00	25.00
☐	119	Ed Kasko, Cin.	3.50	6.00
☐	120	Gus Bell, Cin.	3.50	6.00
☐	121	Vada Pinson, Cin.	6.00	10.00
☐	122	Frank Robinson, Cin.	18.00	30.00
☐	123	Bob Purkey, Cin. (*)	25.00	40.00
☐	124	Joey Jay, Cin.	3.50	6.00
☐	125	Jim Brosnan, Cin.	3.50	6.00
☐	126	Jim O'Toole, Cin.	3.50	6.00
☐	127	Jerry Lynch, Cin.	3.50	6.00
☐	128	Wally Post, Cin. (*)	50.00	80.00
☐	129	Ken Hunt, Cin.	3.50	6.00
☐	130	Jerry Zimmerman, Cin.	3.50	6.00
☐	131	Willie McCovey, S.F.	18.00	30.00
☐	132	Jose Pagan, S.F.	3.50	6.00
☐	133	Felipe Alou, S.F.	9.00	15.00
☐	134	Jim Davenport, S.F.	3.50	6.00
☐	135	Harvey Kuenn, S.F.	3.50	6.00
☐	136	Orlando Cepeda, S.F.	9.00	15.00
☐	137	Ed Bailey, S.F. (*)	25.00	40.00
☐	138	Sam Jones, S.F. (*)	28.00	45.00
☐	139	Mike McCormick, S.F.	3.50	6.00
☐	140	Juan Marichal, S.F.	18.00	30.00
☐	141	Jack Sanford, S.F.	3.50	6.00
☐	142	Willie Mays, S.F.	45.00	75.00
☐	143	Stu Miller, S.F.	3.50	6.00
☐	144	Joe Amalfitano, S.F. (*)	30.00	50.00
☐	145	Joe Adcock, Mil.-N.L.	3.50	6.00
☐	146	Frank Bolling, Mil.-N.L.	3.50	6.00
☐	147	Ed Mathews, Mil.-N.L.	18.00	28.00
☐	148	Roy McMillan, Mil.-N.L.	3.50	6.00
☐	149	Hank Aaron, Mil.-N.L.	45.00	75.00
☐	150	Gino Cimoli, Mil.-N.L.	3.50	6.00
☐	151	Frank Thomas, Mil.-N.L.	3.50	6.00
☐	152	Joe Torre, Mil.-N.L.	9.00	15.00
☐	153	Lew Burdette, Mil.-N.L. (*)	18.00	30.00
☐	154	Bob Buhl, Mil.-N.L.	3.50	6.00
☐	155	Carlton Willey, Mil.-N.L.	3.50	6.00
☐	156	Lee Maye, Mil.-N.L.	3.50	6.00
☐	157	Al Spangler, Mil.-N.L.	3.50	6.00
☐	158	Bill White, Stl.	6.00	10.00
☐	159	Ken Boyer, Stl. (*)	30.00	50.00
☐	160	Joe Cunningham, Stl.	3.50	6.00
☐	161	Carl Warwick, Stl. (*)	20.00	35.00
☐	162	Carl Sawatski, Stl.	3.50	6.00
☐	163	Lindy McDaniel, Stl.	3.50	6.00
☐	164	Ernie Broglio, Stl.	3.50	6.00
☐	165	Larry Jackson, Stl.	3.50	6.00
☐	166	Curt Flood, Stl.	6.00	10.00
☐	167	Curt Simmons, Stl.	20.00	35.00
☐	168	Alex Grammas, Stl.	3.50	6.00
☐	169	Dick Stuart, Pgh.	3.50	6.00
☐	170	Bill Mazeroski, Pgh. (*)	25.00	40.00
☐	171	Don Hoak, Pgh.	3.50	6.00
☐	172	Dick Groat, Pgh. (*)	30.00	50.00
☐	173	Roberto Clemente, Pgh.	50.00	90.00
☐	174	Bob Skinner, Pgh.	3.50	6.00
☐	175	Bill Virdon, Pgh.	3.50	6.00
☐	176	Smoky Burgess, Pgh. (*)	20.00	35.00
☐	177	Elroy Face, Pgh. (*)	30.00	50.00
☐	178	Bob Friend, Pgh.	3.50	6.00
☐	179	Vernon Law, Pgh.	3.50	6.00
☐	180	Harvey Haddix, Pgh.	3.50	6.00
☐	181	Hal Smith, Pgh. (*)	30.00	50.00
☐	182	Ed Bouchee, Chi.-N.L. (*)	20.00	35.00
☐	183	Don Zimmer, Chi.-N.L.	6.00	10.00
☐	184	Ron Santo, Chi.-N.L.	9.00	15.00
☐	185	Andre Rodgers, Chi.-N.L.	3.50	6.00
☐	186	Richie Ashburn, Chi.-N.L.	10.00	18.00
☐	187	George Altman, Chi.-N.L.	3.50	6.00
☐	188	Ernie Banks, Chi.-N.L.	25.00	40.00
☐	189	Sam Taylor, Chi.-N.L. (*)	18.00	30.00
☐	190	Don Elston, Chi.-N.L.	3.50	6.00
☐	191.	Jerry Kindall, Chi.-N.L.	3.50	6.00
☐	192	Pancho Herrera, Pha.	3.50	6.00
☐	193	Tony Taylor, Pha.	3.50	6.00
☐	194	Ruben Amaro, Pha.	3.50	6.00
☐	195	Don Demeter, Pha. (*)	20.00	35.00
☐	196	Bobby Gene Smith, Pha.	3.50	6.00
☐	197	Clay Dalrymple, Pha.	3.50	6.00
☐	198	Robin Roberts, Pha.	15.00	25.00
☐	199	Art Mahaffey, Pha.	3.50	6.00
☐	200	John Buzhardt, Pha.	4.00	10.00

Tips on Grading Post Cards

The 1962 Post Cereal set may be the toughest baseball set to grade. Because most of these cards were hand-cut from boxes of cereal, the majority will have some problem.

A NRMT card will have 75% or more of its blue border showing. A sharp photo and a nice square cut around the border is a must.

An EX card will have 50% of its border. Cuts will still be decent, although not totally square. Corners may have slight rounding. No creases should be apparent. Even if a card would normally grade NRMT, if the photo is fuzzy or "washed out" in appearance, the card will grade EX.

Most Post Cereal cards will grade G/VG. This grade is characterized by poor cuts, creases, etc.

One other factor that contributed to low grade cards in this set is a common border. To cut a perfect card from a six card box panel will always leave the other five cards without parts of their border.

1962 SHIRRIFF COINS

Issued in Shirriff's potato chips, this 221-coin set has a four-colour player's portrait inserted in a plastic disc. The U.S. Salada version of this set contains 221 coins. the following numbers are not found in the Canadian version: 2, 4, 6, 11, 18, 26, 30, 60, 66, 70, 73, 79, 84, 89, 104, 116, 121, 148, 162, 171, 179

Coin Size: 1 3/4" Diameter
Face: Four colour insert; name, number, position, team
Back: One of six colours; black, light blue, royal blue, orange, red or white mould plastic; bilingual
Imprint: MADE IN U.S.A.

Complete Set (200 coins):			**750.00**	**1,350.00**
Common Player:			**2.50**	**4.00**
	No.	**Player**	**EX**	**NRMT**
☐	1	Jim Gentile, Bal.	2.50	4.00
	2	Not issued		
☐	3	Chico Fernandez, Det.	2.50	4.00
	4	Not issued		
☐	5	Woodie Held, Cle.	2.50	4.00
	6	Not issued		
☐	7	Ken Aspromonte, Cle.	2.50	4.00
☐	8	Whitey Ford, NNY.	13.00	22.00
☐	9	Jim Lemon, Min.	2.50	4.00
☐	10	Billy Klaus, Pha.	2.50	4.00
	11	Not issued		
☐	12	Nellie Fox, Chi.-A.L.	7.00	12.00
☐	13	Jim Bunning, Det.	7.00	12.00
☐	14	Frank Malzone, Bos.	2.50	4.00
☐	15	Tito Francona, Cle.	2.50	4.00
☐	16	Bobby Del Greco, Oak.	2.50	4.00

	No.	Player		
☐	17	Steve Bilko, Cal.	2.50	4.00
	18	Not issued		
☐	19	Earl Battey, Min.	2.50	4.00
☐	20	Chuck Cottier, Wash.	2.50	4.00
☐	21	Willie Tasby, Wash.	2.50	4.00
☐	22	Bob Allison, Min.	2.50	4.00
☐	23	Roger Maris, NNY.	25.00	40.00
☐	24	Earl Averill, LA.A	2.50	4.00
☐	25	Jerry Lumpe, Oak.	2.50	4.00
	26	Not issued		
☐	27	Carl Yastrzemski, Bos.	20.00	35.00
☐	28	Rocky Colavito, Det.	6.00	10.00
☐	29	Al Smith, Chi.-A.L.	2.50	4.00
	30	Not issued		
☐	31	Dick Howser, Oak.	3.25	6.50
☐	32	Jim Perry, Cle.	2.50	4.00
☐	33	Yogi Berra, NNY.	18.00	28.00
☐	34	Ken Hamlin, Wash.	2.50	4.00
☐	35	Dale Long, Wash.	2.50	4.00
☐	36	Harmon Killebrew, Min.	15.00	25.00
☐	37	Dick Brown, Det.	2.50	4.00
☐	38	Gary Geiger, Bos.	2.50	4.00
☐	39	Minnie Minoso, Stl.	6.00	10.00
☐	40	Brooks Robinson, Bal.	18.00	28.00
☐	41	Mickey Mantle, NNY.	85.00	140.00
☐	42	Bennie Daniels, Wash.	2.50	4.00
☐	43	Billy Martin, Min.	6.00	10.00
☐	44	Vic Power, Cle.	2.50	4.00
☐	45	Joe Pignatano, Oak.	2.50	4.00
☐	46	Ryne Duren, LA.A	2.50	4.00
☐	47	Pete Runnels, Bos.	2.50	4.00
☐	48	Dick Williams, Bal.	3.50	6.00
☐	49	Jim Landis, Chi.-A.L.	2.50	4.00
☐	50	Steve Boros, Det.	2.50	4.00
☐	51	Zoilo Versalles, Min.	2.50	4.00
☐	52	Johnny Temple, Bal.	2.50	4.00
☐	53	Jackie Brandt, Bal.	2.50	4.00
☐	54	Joe McClain, Wsh.	2.50	4.00
☐	55	Sherm Lollar, Chi.-A.L.	2.50	4.00
☐	56	Gene Stephens, K.C.	2.50	4.00
☐	57	Leon Wagner, Cal.	2.50	4.00
☐	58	Frank Lary, Det.	2.50	4.00
☐	59	Bill Skowron, NNY.	2.50	4.00
	60	Not issued		
☐	61	Willie Kirkland, Cle.	2.50	4.00
☐	62	Leo Posada, Oak.	2.50	4.00
☐	63	Albie Pearson, Cal.	2.50	4.00
☐	64	Bobby Richardson, NNY.	4.50	8.00
☐	65	Marv Breeding, Bal.	2.50	4.00
	66	Not issued		
☐	67	Al Kaline, Det.	15.00	25.00
☐	68	Don Buddin, Hou.C	2.50	4.00
☐	69	Lenny Green, Min.	2.50	4.00
	70	Not issued		
☐	71	Luis Aparicio, Chi.-A.L.	9.00	15.00
☐	72	Norm Cash, Det.	2.50	4.00
	73	Not issued		
☐	74	Bubba Phillips, Cle.	2.50	4.00
☐	75	James Archer, K.C.	2.50	4.00
☐	76	Ken Hunt, LA.A	2.50	4.00
☐	77	Ralph Terry, NNY.	2.50	4.00
☐	78	Camilo Pascual, Min.	2.50	4.00
	79	Not issued		
☐	80	Clete Boyer, NNY.	2.50	4.00
☐	81	Jim Pagliaroni, Bos.	2.50	4.00
☐	82	Gene Leek, L.A.	2.50	4.00
☐	83	Jake Wood, Det.	2.50	4.00
☐	84	Not issued		
☐	85	Norm Siebern, Oak.	2.50	4.00
☐	86	Andy Carey, NYY.	2.50	4.00
☐	87	Bill Tuttle, Min.	2.50	4.00
☐	88	Jimmy Piersall, Wsh.	4.50	8.00
	89	Not issued		
☐	90	Chuck Stobbs, Min.	2.50	4.00
☐	91	Ken McBride, LA.A	2.50	4.00
☐	92	Bill Bruton, Det.	2.50	4.00
☐	93	Gus Triandos, Bal.	2.50	4.00
☐	94	John Romano, Cle.	2.50	4.00
☐	95	Elston Howard, NYY.	4.50	8.00
☐	96	Gene Woodling, Wsh.	2.50	4.00
☐	97	Early Wynn, Chi.-A.L.	10.00	18.00
☐	98	Milt Pappas, Bal.	2.50	4.00
☐	99	Bill Monbouquette, Bos.	2.50	4.00
☐	100	Wayne Causey, Oak.	2.50	4.00
☐	101	Don Elston, Chi.-N.L.	2.50	4.00
☐	102	Charlie Neal, NYM.	2.50	4.00
☐	103	Don Blasingame, Cin.	2.50	4.00
	104	Not issued		
☐	105	Wes Covington, Pha.	2.50	4.00
☐	106	Chuck Hiller, S.F.	2.50	4.00
☐	107	Don Hoak, Chi.-N.L.	2.50	4.00
☐	108	Bob Lillis, Hou.C	2.50	4.00
☐	109	Sandy Koufax, LA.D	25.00	40.00
☐	110	Gordy Coleman, Cin.	2.50	4.00
☐	111	Ed Mathews, Atl., Error	13.00	22.00
☐	112	Art Mahaffey, Pha.	2.50	4.00
☐	113	Ed Bailey, S.F.	2.50	4.00
☐	114	Smoky Burgess, Pgh.	2.50	4.00
☐	115	Bill White, Stl.	3.50	6.00
	116	Not issued		
☐	117	Bob Buhl, Atl.	2.50	4.00
☐	118	Vada Pinson, Cin.	3.50	6.00
☐	119	Carl Sawatski, Stl.	2.50	4.00
☐	120	Dick Stuart, Pgh.	2.50	4.00
	121	Not issued		
☐	122	Pancho Herrera, Pha.	2.50	4.00
☐	123	Don Zimmer, NYM.	3.50	6.00
☐	124	Wally Moon, LA.D	2.50	4.00
☐	125	Joe Adcock, Atl.	2.50	4.00
☐	126	Joey Jay, Cin.	2.50	4.00
☐	127	Maury Wills, L.A.	4.50	8.00
☐	128	George Altman, Chi.-N.L.	2.50	4.00
☐	129	John Buzhardt, Chi.-A.L.	2.50	4.00
☐	130	Felipe Alou, S.F.	4.50	8.00
☐	131	Bill Mazeroski, Pgh.	6.00	10.00
☐	132	Ernie Broglio, Stl.	2.50	4.00
☐	133	Johnny Roseboro, L.A.	2.50	4.00
☐	134	Mike McCormick, S.F.	2.50	4.00
☐	135	Chuck Smith, Chi.-A.L.	2.50	4.00
☐	136	Ron Santo, Chi.-N.L.	4.50	8.00
☐	137	Gene Freese, Cin.	2.50	4.00
☐	138	Dick Groat, Pgh.	2.50	4.00
☐	139	Curt Flood, Stl.	4.50	8.00
☐	140	Frank Bolling, Mil.	2.50	4.00
☐	141	Clay Dalrymple, Pha.	2.50	4.00
☐	142	Willie McCovey, S.F.	15.00	25.00
☐	143	Bob Skinner, Pgh.	2.50	4.00
☐	144	Lindy McDaniel, Stl.	2.50	4.00
☐	145	Glen Hobbie, Chi.-N.L.	2.50	4.00
☐	146	Gil Hodges, NYM.	10.00	18.00
☐	147	Eddie Kasko, Cin.	2.50	4.00
	148	Not issued		
☐	149	Willie Mays, S.F.	40.00	65.00
☐	150	Bob Clemente, Pgh.	45.00	70.00
☐	151	Red Schoendienst, Stl.	7.00	12.00
☐	152	Joe Torre, Atl.	4.50	8.00
☐	153	Bob Purkey, Cin.	2.50	4.00
☐	154	Tommy Davis, L.A.	2.50	4.00

	No.	Player	EX	NRMT
☐	155	Andre Rogers, Chi.-N.L.	2.50	4.00
☐	156	Tony Taylor, Pha.	2.50	4.00
☐	157	Bob Friend, Pgh.	2.50	4.00
☐	158	Gus Bell, NYM.	2.50	4.00
☐	159	Roy McMillan, Atl.	2.50	4.00
☐	160	Carl Warwick, Stl.	2.50	4.00
☐	161	Willie Davis, L.A.	2.50	4.00
	162	Not issued		
☐	163	Ruben Amaro, Pha.	2.50	4.00
☐	164	Sam Taylor, Chi.-N.L.	2.50	4.00
☐	165	Frank Robinson, Cin.	18.00	28.00
☐	166	Lew Burdette, Atl., Error	2.50	4.00
☐	167	Ken Boyer, Stl.	3.50	6.00
☐	168	Bill Virdon, Pgh.	2.50	4.00
☐	169	Jim Davenport, S.F.	2.50	4.00
☐	170	Don Demeter, Pha.	2.50	4.00
	171	Not issued		
☐	172	Johnny Podres, L.A.	3.50	6.00
☐	173	Joe Cunningham, Chi.-A.L.	2.50	4.00
☐	174	Elroy Face, Pgh., Error	2.50	4.00
☐	175	Orlando Cepeda, S.F.	6.00	10.00
☐	176	Bobby Gene Smith, NYM.	2.50	4.00
☐	177	Ernie Banks, Chi.-N.L.	18.00	28.00
☐	178	Daryl Spencer, L.A.	2.50	4.00
	179	Not issued		
☐	180	Henry Aaron, Mil.	35.00	60.00
☐	181	Hobie Landrith, NYM.	2.50	4.00
☐	182	Ed Bressoud, Bos.	2.50	4.00
☐	183	Felix Mantilla, NYM.	2.50	4.00
☐	184	Dick Farrell, Hou.	2.50	4.00
☐	185	Bob Miller, NYM.	2.50	4.00
☐	186	Don Taussig, Hou.	2.50	4.00
☐	187	Pumpsie Green, Bos.	2.50	4.00
☐	188	Bobby Shantz, Hou.	2.50	4.00
☐	189	Roger Craig, NYM.	4.50	8.00
☐	190	Hal Smith, Hou.	2.50	4.00
☐	191	Johnny Edwards, Cin.	2.50	4.00
☐	192	John DeMerit, NYM.	2.50	4.00
☐	193	Joe Amalfitano, Hou.	2.50	4.00
☐	194	Norm Larker, Hou.	2.50	4.00
☐	195	Al Heist, Hou.	2.50	4.00
☐	196	Al Spangler, Hou.	2.50	4.00
☐	197	Alex Grammas, Stl.	2.50	4.00
☐	198	Jerry Lynch, Cin.	2.50	4.00
☐	199	Jim McKnight, Chi.-N.L.	2.50	4.00
☐	200	Jose Pagan, S.F., Error	2.50	4.00
☐	201	Jim Gilliam, L.A.	4.50	8.00
☐	202	Art Ditmar, Oak.	2.50	4.00
☐	203	Bud Daley, NYY.	2.50	4.00
☐	204	John Callison, Pha.	2.50	4.00
☐	205	Stu Miller, S.F.	2.50	4.00
☐	206	Russ Snyder, Bal.	2.50	4.00
☐	207	Billy Williams, Chi.-N.L.	13.00	22.00
☐	208	Walt Bond, Cle.	2.50	4.00
☐	209	Joe Koppe, LA.	2.50	4.00
☐	210	Don Schwall, Bos.	2.50	4.00
☐	211	Billy Gardner, NYY.	2.50	4.00
☐	212	Chuck Estrada, Bal.	2.50	4.00
☐	213	Gary Bell, Cle.	2.50	4.00
☐	214	Floyd Robinson, Chi.-A.L.	2.50	4.00
☐	215	Duke Snider, L.A.	18.00	30.00
☐	216	Lee Maye, Mil.	2.50	4.00
☐	217	Howie Bedell, Atl.	2.50	4.00
☐	218	Bob Will, Chi.-N.L.	2.50	4.00
☐	219	Dallas Green, Pha.	4.50	8.00
☐	220	Carroll Hardy, Bos.	2.50	4.00
☐	221	Danny O'Connell, Wsh.	2.50	4.00

1965 O-PEE-CHEE

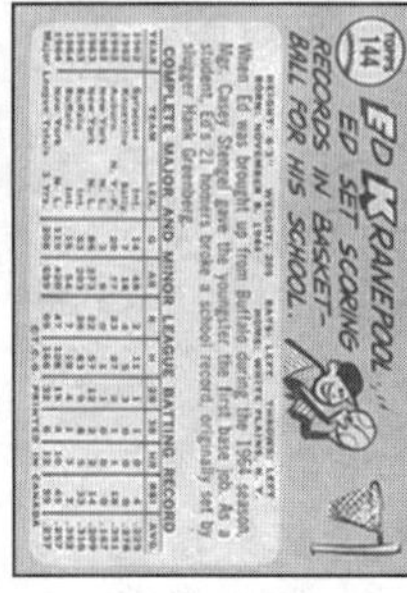

This set comprises the first 283 cards of the 598-card Topps set. High condition Canadian sets of this year are worth more than the sum of the individual cards in the set. With the exception of the 1937 Batters Up, this was the first time O-Pee-Chee produced baseball cards in Canada

O-Pee-Chee produces its baseball cards under the Topps Major League License and this is the reason for the great similarity between the sets.

Card Size: 2 1/2" x 3 1/2"

Face: Four colour, white border; name, position, team

Back: Blue and black on card stock; name, number, r,sum,, cartoon

Imprint: T.C.G. PRINTED IN CANADA

Complete Set (283 cards):			**1,300.00**	**2,600.00**
Common Player (1-196):			**1.75**	**3.50**
Common Player (197-283):			**4.00**	**8.00**
	No.	**Player**	**EX**	**NRMT**
☐	1	LL: E. Howard/ T. Oliva/ B. Robinson	17.50	35.00
☐	2	LL: H. Aaron/ B. Clemente/ R. Carty	15.00	30.00
☐	3	LL: H. Killebrew/ M. Mantle/ B. Powell	30.00	60.00
☐	4	LL: J. Callison/ O. Cepeda/ J. Ray Hart/ W. Mays / B. Williams	8.00	16.00
☐	5	LL: H. Killebrew/ M. Mantle/ B. Robinson / D. Stuart	30.00	60.00
☐	6	LL: K. Boyer/ W. Mays/ R. Santo	8.00	16.00
☐	7	LL: D. Chance/ J. Horlen	2.50	5.00
☐	8	LL: D. Drysdale/ S. Koufax	15.00	30.00
☐	9	LL: W. Bunker/ Chance/ G. Peters/ J. Pizarro / D. Wickersham	2.50	5.00
☐	10	LL: L. Jackson/ J. Marichal/ R. Sadeck	3.50	7.00
☐	11	LL: D. Chance/ A. Downing/ C. Pascual	2.50	5.00
☐	12	LL: D. Drysdale/ B. Gibson/ B. Veale	7.50	15.00
☐	13	Pedro Ramos, NYY.	1.75	3.50
☐	14	Len Gabrielson, Chi.-N.L.	1.75	3.50
☐	15	Robin Roberts, Bal.	7.50	15.00
☐	**16**	**Joe Morgan, Hou., RC**	**57.50**	**115.00**
☐	17	Johnny Romano, Chi.-A.L.	1.75	3.50
☐	18	Bill McCool, Cin.	1.75	3.50
☐	19	Gates Brown, Det.	1.75	3.50
☐	20	Jim Bunning, Pha.	7.50	15.00
☐	21	Don Blasingame, Wsh.	1.75	3.50
☐	22	Charley Smith, NYM	1.75	3.50
☐	23	Bob Tiefenauer, Mil.	1.75	3.50
☐	24	Twins Team	3.50	7.00
☐	25	Al McBean, Pgh.	1.75	3.50
☐	26	Bobby Knoop, Cal.	1.75	3.50
☐	27	Dick Bertell, Chi.-N.L.	1.75	3.50
☐	28	Barney Schultz, Stl.	1.75	3.50
☐	29	Felix Mantilla, Bos.	1.75	3.50
☐	30	Jim Bouton, NYY.	4.00	8.00
☐	31	Mike White, Hou.	1.75	3.50
☐	32	Herman Franks	1.75	3.50
☐	33	Jackie Brandt, Bal.	1.75	3.50
☐	34	Cal Koonce, Chi.-N.L.	1.75	3.50
☐	35	Ed Charles, K.C.	1.75	3.50

☐	**36**	**Bobby Wine, Phi., RC**	**1.75**	**3.50**
☐	**37**	**Fred Gladding, Det., RC**	**1.75**	**3.50**
☐	38	Jim King, Wsh.	1.75	3.50
☐	39	Gerry Arrigo, Cin.	1.75	3.50
☐	40	Frank Howard, Wsh.	3.50	7.00
☐	41	Chi.-A.L.: Bruce Howard/ Marv Staehle	1.75	3.50
☐	42	Earl Wilson, Bos.	1.75	3.50
☐	43	Mike Shannon, Stl.	1.75	3.50
☐	**44**	**Wade Blasingame, Mil., RC**	**1.75**	**3.50**
☐	45	Roy McMillan, NYM.	1.75	3.50
☐	46	Bob Lee, Cal.	1.75	3.50
☐	**47**	**Tommy Harper, Cin., RC**	**3.00**	**6.00**
☐	48	Claude Raymond, Hou.	2.50	5.00
☐	49	Bal.: Curt Blefary/ John Miller	1.75	3.50
☐	50	Juan Marichal, S.F.	7.50	15.00
☐	51	Billy Bryan, K.C.	1.75	3.50
☐	52	Ed Roebuck, Pha.	1.75	3.50
☐	53	Dick McAuliffe, Det.	1.75	3.50
☐	54	Joe Gibbon, Pgh.	1.75	3.50
☐	55	Tony Conigliaro, Bos.	9.00	18.00
☐	56	Ron Kline, Wsh.	1.75	3.50
☐	57	Cardinals Team	2.50	5.00
☐	**58**	**Fred Talbot, Chi.-A.L., RC**	**1.75**	**3.50**
☐	59	Nate Oliver, L.A.	1.75	3.50
☐	60	Jim O'Toole, Cin.	1.75	3.50
☐	61	Chris Cannizzaro, NYM.	1.75	3.50
☐	62	Jim Kaat, Min.	3.00	6.00
☐	63	Ty Cline, Min.	1.75	3.50
☐	64	Lew Burdette, Chi.-N.L., Error	1.75	3.50
☐	65	Tony Kubek, NYY.	4.00	8.00
☐	66	Bill Rigney, NYM.	1.75	3.50
☐	67	Harvey Haddix, Bal.	1.75	3.50
☐	68	Del Crandall, Pgh.	1.75	3.50
☐	69	Bill Virdon, Pgh.	1.75	3.50
☐	70	Bill Skowron, Chi.-A.L.	1.75	3.50
☐	71	John O'Donoghue, K.C.	1.75	3.50
☐	72	Tony Gonzalez, Pha.	1.75	3.50
☐	**73**	**Dennis Ribant, NYM., RC**	**1.75**	**3.50**
☐	**74**	**Rico Petrocelli, Bos., RC**	**7.50**	**15.00**
☐	75	Deron Johnson, Cin.	1.75	3.50
☐	**76**	**Sam McDowell, Cle., RC**	**4.00**	**8.00**
☐	77	Doug Camilli, Wsh.	1.75	3.50
☐	78	Dal Maxvill, Stl.	1.75	3.50
☐	79	Checklist 1st Series (1 - 88)	10.00	20.00
☐	**80**	**Turk Farrell, Hou., RC**	**1.75**	**3.50**
☐	81	Don Buford, Chi.-A.L.	1.75	3.50
☐	82	Atl.: Santos Alomar/ John Braun	2.50	5.00
☐	83	George Thomas, Det.	1.75	3.50
☐	84	Ron Herbel, S.F.	1.75	3.50
☐	**85**	**Willie Smith, Cal., RC**	**1.75**	**3.50**
☐	**86**	**Les Narum, Wash., RC**	**1.75**	**3.50**
☐	87	Nelson Mathews	1.75	3.50
☐	88	Jack Lamabe, Bos.	1.75	3.50
☐	89	Mike Hershberger, K.C.	1.75	3.50
☐	90	Rich Rollins, Min.,	1.75	3.50
☐	91	Cubs Team	2.50	5.00
☐	92	Dick Howser, Cle.	1.75	3.50
☐	**93**	**Jack Fisher, NYM., RC**	**1.75**	**3.50**
☐	94	Charlie Lau, Bal.	1.75	3.50
☐	95	Bill Mazeroski, Pgh.	3.50	7.00
☐	96	Sonny Siebert, Cle.	1.75	3.50
☐	97	Pedro Gonzalez, NYY.	1.75	3.50
☐	98	Bob Miller, L.A.	1.75	3.50
☐	99	Gil Hodges, NYM.	2.50	5.00
☐	**100**	**Ken Boyer, Stl.**	**1.75**	**3.50**
☐	101	Fred Newman, Cal.	1.75	3.50
☐	102	Steve Boros, Cin.	1.75	3.50
☐	103	Harvey Kuenn, S.F.	1.75	3.50
☐	104	Checklist 2nd Series (89 - 176)	10.00	20.00
☐	105	Chico Salmon, Cle.	1.75	3.50
☐	106	Gene Oliver, Min.	1.75	3.50
☐	107	Pha.: Pat Corrales/ Costen Shockley	1.75	3.50
☐	108	Don Mincher, Min.	1.75	3.50
☐	109	Walt Bond, Hou.	1.75	3.50
☐	110	Ron Santo, Chi.-N.L.	3.507.00	
☐	111	Lee Thomas, Bos.	1.75	3.50
☐	**112**	**Derrell Griffith, L.A., RC**	**1.75**	**3.50**
☐	113	Steve Barber, Bal.	1.75	3.50
☐	114	Jim Hickman, NYM.	1.75	3.50
☐	115	Bobby Richardson, NYY.	3.00	6.00
☐	116	Stl.: Dave Dowling/ Bob Tolan	1.75	3.50
☐	117	Wes Stock, K.C.	1.75	3.50
☐	**118**	**Hal Lanier, S.F., RC**	**1.75**	**3.50**
☐	119	John Kennedy, L.A.	1.75	3.50
☐	120	Frank Robinson, Cin.	25.00	50.00
☐	121	Gene Alley, Pgh.	1.75	3.50
☐	122	Bill Pleis, Min.	1.75	3.50
☐	123	Frank Thomas, Pha.	1.75	3.50
☐	124	Tom Satriano, Cal.	1.75	3.50
☐	**125**	**Juan Pizarro, Chi.-A.L.**	**1.75**	**3.50**
☐	126	Dodgers Team	4.00	8.00
☐	127	Frank Lary, NYM.	1.75	3.50
☐	128	Vic Davalillo, Cle.	1.75	3.50
☐	129	Bennie Daniels, Wsh.	1.75	3.50
☐	130	Al Kaline, Det.	25.00	50.00
☐	131	Johnny Keane	1.75	3.50
☐	132	WS-Game 1: Cards Take Opener	5.00	10.00
☐	133	WS-Game 2: Stottlemyre Wins	5.00	10.00
☐	134	WS-Game 3: Mantle's Clutch HR	55.00	110.00
☐	135	WS-Game 4: Boyer's Grand Slam	5.00	10.00
☐	136	WS-Game 5: 10th Inning Triumph	5.00	10.00
☐	137	WS-Game 6: Wins Again	5.00	10.00
☐	138	WS-Game 7: Gibson Wins Finale	9.00	18.00
☐	139	WS-Summary: The Cards Celebrate	6.00	12.00
☐	**140**	**Dean Chance, Cal., RC**	**2.50**	**5.00**
☐	141	Charlie James, Cin.	1.75	3.50
☐	142	Bill Monbouquette, Bos.	1.75	3.50
☐	143	Pgh.: John Gelnar/ Jerry May	1.75	3.50
☐	144	Ed Kranepool, NYM.	1.75	3.50
☐	**145**	**Luis Tiant, Cle., RC**	**12.50**	**25.00**
☐	146	Ron Hansen, Chi.-A.L.	1.75	3.50
☐	147	Dennis Bennett, Bos.	1.75	3.50
☐	148	Willie Kirkland, Wsh.	1.75	3.50
☐	149	Wayne Schurr, Chi.-N.L.	1.75	3.50
☐	150	Brooks Robinson, Bal.	25.00	50.00
☐	151	Athletics Team	2.50	5.00
☐	**152**	**Phil Ortega, Wsh., RC**	**1.75**	**3.50**
☐	153	Norm Cash, Det.	1.75	3.50
☐	154	Bob Humphreys, Chi.-N.L.	1.75	3.50
☐	155	Roger Maris, NYY.	35.00	70.00
☐	156	Bob Sadowski, Mil.	1.75	3.50
☐	**157**	**Zoilo Versalles, Min.**	**1.75**	**3.50**
☐	158	Dick Sisler, Stl.	1.75	3.50
☐	159	Jim Duffalo, S.F.	1.75	3.50
☐	160	Bob Clemente, Pgh.	87.50	175.00
☐	161	Frank Baumann, Chi.-N.L.	1.75	3.50
☐	162	Russ Nixon, Bos.	1.75	3.50
☐	163	John Briggs, Pha.	1.75	3.50
☐	164	Al Spangler, Hou.	1.75	3.50
☐	165	Dick Ellsworth, Chi.-N.L.	1.75	3.50
☐	166	Cle.: Tommie Agee/ George Culver	1.75	3.50
☐	167	Bill Wakefield, NYM.	1.75	3.50
☐	168	Dick Green, K.C.	1.75	3.50
☐	169	Dave Vineyard, Bal.	1.75	3.50
☐	170	Hank Aaron, Mil.	62.50	125.00
☐	171	Jim Roland, Min.	1.75	3.50
☐	172	Jim Piersall, Cal.	2.50	5.00
☐	173	Tigers Team	2.50	5.00

	No.	Player		
□	174	Joey Jay, Cin.	1.75	3.50
□	175	Bob Aspromonte, Hou.	1.75	3.50
□	176	Willie McCovey, S.F.	15.00	30.00
□	177	Pete Mikkelsen, NYY.	1.75	3.50
□	178	Dalton Jones, Bos.	1.75	3.50
□	179	Hal Woodeshick, Hou.	1.75	3.50
□	180	Bob Allison, Min.	1.75	3.50
□	181	Wsh.: Don Loun/ Joe McCabe	1.75	3.50
□	182	Mike de la. Hoz, Mil.	1.75	3.50
□	183	Dave Nicholson, Chi.-A.L.	1.75	3.50
□	184	John Boozer, Pha.	1.75	3.50
□	185	Max Alvis, Cle.	1.75	3.50
□	186	Billy Cowan, NYM.	1.75	3.50
□	187	Casey Stengel, Bos.	12.50	25.00
□	188	Sam Bowens, Bal.	1.75	3.50
□	189	Checklist 3rd Series (177 - 264)	10.00	20.00
□	190	Bill White, Stl.	2.50	5.00
□	191	Phil Regan, Det.	1.75	3.50
□	192	Jim Coker, Cin.	1.75	3.50
□	193	Gaylord Perry, S.F.	12.50	25.00
□	194	Ana.: Bill Kelso/ Rick Reichardt	1.75	3.50
□	**195**	**Bob Veale, Pgh., RC**	**1.75**	**3.50**
□	196	Ron Fairly, L.A.	1.75	3.50
□	197	Diego Segui, K.C.	4.00	8.00
□	198	Smoky Burgess, Chi.-A.L.	4.00	8.00
□	**199**	**Bob Heffner, Bos., RC**	**4.00**	**8.00**
□	200	Joe Torre, Mil.	7.50	15.00
□	201	Min.: Cesar Tovar/ Sandy Valdespino	4.00	8.00
□	202	Leo Burke, Chi.-N.L.	4.00	8.00
□	203	Dallas Green, Wsh.	4.00	8.00
□	204	Russ Snyder, Bal.	4.00	8.00
□	**205**	**Warren Spahn, NYM., RC**	**30.00**	**60.00**
□	206	Willie Horton, Det.	4.00	8.00
□	207	Pete Rose, Cin.	132.50	265.00
□	208	Tommy John, Chi.-A.L.	6.00	12.00
□	209	Pirates Team	4.00	8.00
□	210	Jim Fregosi, Cal.	4.00	8.00
□	211	Steve Ridzik, Wsh.	4.00	8.00
□	212	Ron Brand, Hou.	4.00	8.00
□	213	Jim Davenport, S.F.	4.00	8.00
□	214	Bob Purkey, Stl.	4.00	8.00
□	215	Pete Ward, Chi.-A.L.	5.00	10.00
□	216	Al Worthington, Min.	4.00	8.00
□	217	Walt Alston, Stl.	7.50	15.00
□	218	Dick Schofield, Pgh.	4.00	8.00
□	219	Bob Meyer, K.C.	4.00	8.00
□	220	Billy Williams, Chi.-N.L.	10.00	20.00
□	221	John Tsitouris, Cin.	4.00	8.00
□	222	Bob Tillman, Bos.	4.00	8.00
□	223	Dan Osinski, Mil.	4.00	8.00
□	224	Bob Chance, Wsh.	4.00	8.00
□	225	Bo Belinsky, Pha.	4.00	8.00
□	226	NYY.: Jake Gibbs/ Elvio Jimenez	4.00	8.00
□	227	Bobby Klaus, NYM.	4.00	8.00
□	228	Jack Sanford, S.F.	4.00	8.00
□	229	Lu Clinton, Cal.	4.00	8.00
□	230	Ray Sadecki, Stl.	4.00	8.00
□	231	Jerry Adair, Bal.	4.00	8.00
□	**232**	**Steve Blass, Pgh, RC**	**6.00**	**12.00**
□	233	Don Zimmer, Wsh.	4.00	8.00
□	234	White Sox Team	6.00	12.00
□	235	Chuck Hinton, Cle.	4.00	8.00
□	**236**	**Dennis McLain, Det.,RC**	**25.00**	**50.00**
□	237	Bernie Allen, Min.	4.00	8.00
□	238	Joe Moeller, L.A.	4.00	8.00
□	239	Doc Edwards, K.C.	4.00	8.00
□	240	Bob Bruce, Hou.	4.00	8.00
□	241	Mack Jones, Mil.	4.00	8.00
□	242	George Brunet, Cal.	4.00	8.00
□	243	Cin.: Ted Davidson/Tommy Helms	4.00	8.00
□	244	Lindy McDaniel, Chi.-N.L.	4.00	8.00
□	245	Joe Pepitone, NYY.	6.00	12.00
□	246	Tom Butters, Pgh.	4.00	8.00
□	247	Wally Moon, L.A.	4.00	8.00
□	248	Gus Triandos, Pha.	4.00	8.00
□	249	Dave McNally, Bal.	4.00	8.00
□	250	Willie Mays, S.F.	92.50	185.00
□	251	Billy Herman, Pgh.	4.00	8.00
□	252	Pete Richert, Wsh.	4.00	8.00
□	253	Danny Cater, Chi.-A.L.	4.00	8.00
□	254	Roland Sheldon, NYY.	4.00	8.00
□	255	Camilo Pascual, Min.	4.00	8.00
□	256	Tito Francona, Stl.	4.00	8.00
□	257	Jim Wynn, Hou.	4.00	8.00
□	258	Larry Bearnarth, NYM.	4.00	8.00
□	259	Det.: Jim Northrup/ Ray Oyler	4.00	8.00
□	260	Don Drysdale, L.A.	20.00	40.00
□	261	Duke Carmel, NYY.	4.00	8.00
□	262	Bud Daley, NYY.	4.00	8.00
□	263	Marty Keough, Cin.	4.00	8.00
□	264	Bob Buhl, Chi.-N.L.	4.00	8.00
□	265	Jim Pagliaroni, Pit.	4.00	8.00
□	**266**	**Bert Campaneris, K.C., RC**	**9.00**	**18.00**
□	267	Senators Team	6.00	12.00
□	268	Ken McBride, Cal.	4.00	8.00
□	269	Frank Bolling, Mil.	4.00	8.00
□	270	Milt Pappas, Bal.	4.00	8.00
□	271	Don Wert, Det.	4.00	8.00
□	272	Chuck Schilling, Bos.	4.00	8.00
□	273	Checklist 4th Series (265 - 352)	14.00	28.00
□	**274**	**Lum Harris, Wsh.,**	**4.00**	**8.00**
□	275	Dick Groat, Stl.	4.00	8.00
□	**276**	**Hoyt Wilhelm, Chi.-A.L.**	**9.00**	**18.00**
□	277	Johnny Lewis, NYM.	4.00	8.00
□	278	Ken Retzer, Wsh.	4.00	8.00
□	279	Dick Tracewski, L.A.	4.00	8.00
□	280	Dick Stuart, Pha.	4.00	8.00
□	281	Bill Stafford, NYY.	4.00	8.00
□	**282**	**S.F.: D. Estelle/ Masanori Murakami, RC**	**30.00**	**60.00**
□	283	Fred Whitfield, Cle.	4.00	8.00

1966 O-PEE-CHEE

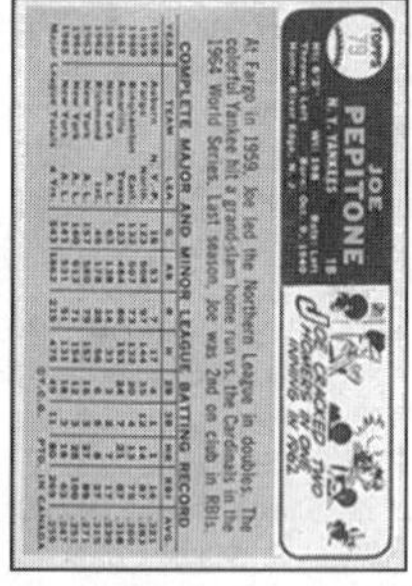

This set comprises the first 196 cards of the 598-card Topps set of 1966. It is numbered on the back, together with the player's statistics, a brief write-up and a small cartoon.

Card Size: 2 1/2" x 3 1/2"

Face: Four colour, white border; name, position, team

Back: Peach and black on card stock; name, number, team, résumé trivia

Imprint: ©T.C.G. PTD. IN CANADA

Complete Set (196 cards):	**900.00**	**1,800.00**
Common Player (1-109):	**1.50**	**3.00**

		EX	NRMT
Common Player (110-196):		**6.00**	**12.00**
No.	**Player**	**EX**	**NRMT**
1	Willie Mays, S.F.	112.50	225.00
2	Ted Abernathy, Chi.-N.L.	1.50	3.00
3	Sam Mele, Mgr., Min.	1.50	3.00
4	Ray Culp, Pha.	1.50	3.00
5	Jim Fregosi, Cal.	1.50	3.00
6	Chuck Schilling, Bos.	1.50	3.00
7	Tracy Stallard, Stl.	1.50	3.00
8	Floyd Robinson, Chi.-A.L.	1.50	3.00
9	Clete Boyer, NYY.	1.50	3.00
10	Tony Cloninger, Atl.	1.50	3.00
11	Wsh.: Brant Alyea/ Pete Craig	1.50	3.00
12	**John Tsitouris, Cin.**	**1.50**	**3.00**
13	Lou Johnson, L.A.	1.50	3.00
14	Norm Siebern, Bal.	1.50	3.00
15	Vern Law, Pgh.	1.50	3.00
16	Larry Brown, Cle.	1.50	3.00
17	Johnny Stephenson, NYM.	1.50	3.00
18	Roland Sheldon, K.C.	1.50	3.00
19	Giants Team	2.50	5.00
20	Willie Horton, Det.	1.50	3.00
21	Don Nottebart, Hou.	1.50	3.00
22	**Joe Nossek, Min.**	**1.50**	**3.00**
23	Jack Sanford, Cal.	1.50	3.00
24	**Don Kessinger, Chi.-N.L., RC**	**2.50**	**5.00**
25	Pete Ward, Chi.-A.L.	2.50	5.00
26	Ray Sadecki, Stl.	1.50	3.00
27	Bal.: Andy Etchebarren/ Darold Knowles	1.50	3.00
28	Phil Niekro, Atl.	15.00	30.00
29	Mike Brumley, Wsh.	1.50	3.00
30	Pete Rose, Cin.	30.00	60.00
31	Jack Cullen, NYY.	1.50	3.00
32	**Adolfo Phillips, Phi., RC**	**1.50**	**3.00**
33	Jim Pagliaroni, Pgh.	1.50	3.00
34	Checklist 1st Series (1 - 88)	7.50	15.00
35	Ron Swoboda, NYM.	1.50	3.00
36	Jim Hunter, K.C.	15.00	30.00
37	Billy Herman, Mgr., Bos.	1.50	3.00
38	Ron Nischwitz, Det.	1.50	3.00
39	Ken Henderson, S.F.	1.50	3.00
40	Jim Grant, Min.	1.50	3.00
41	**Don LeJohn, L.A., RC**	**1.50**	**3.00**
42	Aubrey Gatewood, Cal.	1.50	3.00
43	Don Landrum, S.F.	1.50	3.00
44	Cle.: Bill Davis/ Tom Kelley	1.50	3.00
45	Jim Gentile, Hou.	1.50	3.00
46	Howie Koplitz, Wsh.	1.50	3.00
47	J.C. Martin, Chi.-A.L.	1.50	3.00
48	Paul Blair, Bal.	1.50	3.00
49	Woody Woodward, Atl.	1.50	3.00
50	Mickey Mantle, NYY.	162.50	325.00
51	**Gordon Richardson, NYM., RC**	**1.50**	**3.00**
52	Johnny Callison/ Wes Covington	1.50	3.00
53	Bob Duliba, Bos.	1.50	3.00
54	Jose Pagan, Pgh.	1.50	3.00
55	Ken Harrelson, K.C.	1.50	3.00
56	**Sandy Valdespino, Min., RC**	**1.50**	**3.00**
57	Jim Lefebvre, L.A.	1.50	3.00
58	Dave Wickersham, Det.	1.50	3.00
59	Reds Team	2.50	5.00
60	Curt Flood, Stl.	2.50	5.00
61	Bob Bolin, S.F.	1.50	3.00
62	Merritt Ranew, Cal.	1.50	3.00
63	Jim Stewart, Chi.-N.L.	1.50	3.00
64	Bob Bruce, Hou.	1.50	3.00
65	Leon Wagner, Cle.	1.50	3.00
66	Al Weis, Chi.-A.L.	1.50	3.00
67	NYM.: Cleon Jones; Dick Selma	1.50	3.00
68	Hal Reniff, NYY.	1.50	3.00
69	Ken Hamlin, Wsh.	1.50	3.00
70	Carl Yastrzemski, Bos.	20.00	40.00
71	**Frank Carpin, Pgh., RC**	**1.50**	**3.00**
72	Tony Perez, Cin.	17.50	35.00
73	Jerry Zimmerman, Min.	1.50	3.00
74	Don Mossi, K.C.	1.50	3.00
75	Tommy Davis, L.A.	1.50	3.00
76	Red Schoendienst, Stl.	3.50	7.00
77	Johnny Orsino, Wsh.	1.50	3.00
78	Frank Linzy, S.F.	1.50	3.00
79	Joe Pepitone, NYY.	2.50	5.00
80	Richie Allen, Pha.	3.00	6.00
81	**Ray Oyler, Det., RC**	**1.50**	**3.00**
82	Bob Hendley, Chi.-N.L	1.50	3.00
83	Albie Pearson, Cal.	1.50	3.00
84	Atl.:Jim Beauchamp/ Dick Kelley	1.50	3.00
85	Eddie Fisher, Chi.-A.L.	1.50	3.00
86	John Bateman, Hou.	1.50	3.00
87	Dan Napoleon, NYM.	1.50	3.00
88	Fred Whitfield, Cle.	1.50	3.00
89	**Ted Davidson, Cin., RC**	**1.50**	**3.00**
90	Luis Aparicio, Bal.	5.00	10.00
91	Bob Uecker, Pha.	7.50	15.00
92	Yankees Team	7.50	15.00
93	Jim Lonborg, Bos.	1.50	3.00
94	Matty Alou, Pgh.	1.50	3.00
95	Pete Richert, Wsh.	1.50	3.00
96	Felipe Alou, Atl.	3.50	7.00
97	**Jim Merritt, Min., RC**	**1.50**	**3.00**
98	Don Demeter, Det.	1.50	3.00
99	Willie Stargell/ Donn Clendenon	5.00	10.00
100	Sandy Koufax, L.A.	62.50	125.00
101	Checklist 2nd Series (89 - 176), Error	7.50	15.00
102	Ed Kirkpatrick, Cal.	1.50	3.00
103	Dick Groat, Stl.	1.50	3.00
104	Alex Johnson, Pha.	1.50	3.00
105	Milt Pappas, Bal.	1.50	3.00
106	Rusty Staub, Hou.	4.00	8.00
107	Larry Stahl/ Ron Tompkins	1.50	3.00
108	Bobby Klaus, NYM.	1.50	3.00
109	**Ralph Terry, K.C.**	**1.50**	**3.00**
110	Ernie Banks, Chi.-N.L.	22.50	45.00
111	Gary Peters, Chi.-A.L.	2.00	4.00
112	Manny Mota, Pgh.	2.00	4.00
113	Hank Aguirre, Det.	2.00	4.00
114	**Jim Gosger, Bos., RC**	**2.00**	**4.00**
115	**Warren Spahn, S.F.**	**2.00**	**4.00**
116	Walt Alston, Mgr., L.A.	4.00	8.00
117	**Jake Gibbs, NYY., RC**	**2.00**	**4.00**
118	Mike McCormick, Wsh.	2.00	4.00
119	**Art Shamsky, Cin., RC**	**2.00**	**4.00**
120	Harmon Killebrew, Min.	12.50	25.00
121	Ray Herbert, Pha.	2.00	4.00
122	Joe Gaines, Hou.	2.00	4.00
123	Pgh.: Frank Bork/ Jerry May	2.00	4.00
124	Tug McGraw, NYM.	3.00	6.00
125	Lou Brock, Stl.	15.00	30.00
126	**Jim Palmer, Bal., RC**	**87.50**	**175.00**
127	Ken Berry, Chi.-A.L.	2.00	4.00
128	Jim Landis, Cle.	2.00	4.00
129	Jack Kralick, Cle.	2.00	4.00
130	Joe Torre, Atl.	4.00	8.00
131	Angels Team	3.00	6.00
132	Orlando Cepeda, S.F.	5.00	10.00
133	Don McMahon, Cle.	2.00	4.00
134	Wes Parker, L.A.	2.00	4.00
135	Dave Morehead, Bos.	2.00	4.00
136	Woodie Held, Bal.	2.00	4.00

	No.	Player	EX	NRMT
☐	**137**	**Pat Corrales, Stl., RC**	**2.00**	**4.00**
☐	**138**	**Roger Repoz, NYY., RC**	**2.00**	**4.00**
☐	139	Chi.: Byron Browne/ Don Young	2.00	4.00
☐	140	Jim Maloney, Cin.	2.00	4.00
☐	141	Tom McCraw, Chi.-A.L.	2.00	4.00
☐	**142**	**Don Dennis, Stl., RC**	**2.00**	**4.00**
☐	143	Jose Tartabull, K.C.	2.00	4.00
☐	144	Don Schwall, Pgh.	2.00	4.00
☐	145	Bill Freehan, Det.	2.00	4.00
☐	146	George Altman, Chi.-N.L.	2.00	4.00
☐	147	Lum Harris, Wsh.	2.00	4.00
☐	148	Bob Johnson, Bal.	2.00	4.00
☐	149	Dick Nen, Wsh.	2.00	4.00
☐	150	Rocky Colavito, Cle.	6.00	12.00
☐	**151**	**Gary Wagner, Pha., RC**	**2.00**	**4.00**
☐	152	Frank Malzone, Cal.	2.00	4.00
☐	153	Rico Carty, Atl.	2.00	4.00
☐	154	Chuck Hiller, NYM.	2.00	4.00
☐	155	Marcelino Lopez, Cal.	2.00	4.00
☐	156	S.F.: Dick Schofield/ Hal Lanier	2.00	4.00
☐	157	Rene Lachemann, K.C.	2.00	4.00
☐	158	Jim Brewer, L.A.	2.00	4.00
☐	159	Chico Ruiz, Cin.	2.00	4.00
☐	160	Whitey Ford, NYY.	20.00	40.00
☐	161	Jerry Lumpe, Det.	2.00	4.00
☐	162	Lee Maye, Hou.	2.00	4.00
☐	163	Tito Francona, Stl.	2.00	4.00
☐	164	Chi.-A.L.: Tommie Agee/ M. Staehle	2.00	4.00
☐	165	Don Lock, Wsh.	2.00	4.00
☐	**166**	**Chris Krug, Chi.-N.L., RC**	**2.00**	**4.00**
☐	167	Boog Powell, Bal.	4.00	8.00
☐	168	Dan Osinski, Atl.	2.00	4.00
☐	169	Duke Sims, Cle.	2.00	4.00
☐	170	Cookie Rojas, Pha.	2.00	4.00
☐	171	Nick Willhite, L.A.	2.00	4.00
☐	172	Mets Team, 10th Place National League	3.00	6.00
☐	173	Al Spangler, Cal.	2.00	4.00
☐	174	Ron Taylor, Hou.	3.00	6.00
☐	175	Bert Campaneris, K.C.	3.00	6.00
☐	176	Jim Davenport, S.F.	2.00	4.00
☐	177	Hector Lopez, NYY.	2.00	4.00
☐	178	Bob Tillman, Bos.	2.00	4.00
☐	179	Dennis Aust/ Bob Tolan	2.00	4.00
☐	180	Vada Pinson, Cin.	2.00	4.00
☐	181	Al Worthington, Min.	2.00	4.00
☐	182	Jerry Lynch, Pgh.	2.00	4.00
☐	183	Checklist 3rd Series (177 - 264)	9.00	18.00
☐	184	Denis Menke, Atl.	2.00	4.00
☐	185	Bob Buhl, Chi.-N.L.	2.00	4.00
☐	186	Ruben Amaro, NYY.	2.00	4.00
☐	187	Chuck Dressen, Mgr., Det.	2.00	4.00
☐	188	Al Luplow, NYM.	2.00	4.00
☐	189	John Roseboro, L.A.	2.00	4.00
☐	190	Jimmie Hall, Min.	2.00	4.00
☐	**191**	**Darrell Sutherland, NYM., RC**	**2.00**	**4.00**
☐	192	Vic Power, Cal.	2.00	4.00
☐	193	Dave McNally, Bal.	2.00	4.00
☐	194	Senators Team	3.00	6.00
☐	**195**	**Joe Morgan, Hou., RC**	**12.50**	**25.00**
☐	196	Don Pavletich, Cin.	2.00	4.00

1967 O-PEE-CHEE

This set comprises the first 196 cards of the 609-card Topps issue of the same year. The Canadian and corresponding Topps cards are identical, except the imprint on the back of the Canadian issue reads "Printed in Canada."

Card Size: 2 1/2" x 3 1/2"

Face: Four colour, white border; name, position, team, facsimile autograph

Back: Green and black on card stock; name, number, résumé, player trivia

Imprint: © T.C.G. PRINTED IN CANADA

Complete Set (196 cards):			**750.00**	**1,500.00**
Common Player (1-109):			**1.50**	**2.75**
Common Player (110-196):			**1.75**	**3.50**
	No.	**Player**	**EX**	**NRMT**
☐	1	Bal.: F. Robinson/ H. Bauer, Mgr./ B. Robinson	20.00	40.00
☐	2	Jack Hamilton, NYM.	1.50	2.75
☐	3	Duke Sims, Cle.	1.50	2.75
☐	4	Hal Lanier, S.F.	1.50	2.75
☐	5	Whitey Ford, NYY.	15.00	30.00
☐	6	Dick Simpson, Cin.	1.50	2.75
☐	7	Don McMahon, Bos.	1.50	2.75
☐	8	Chuck Harrison, Hou.	1.50	2.75
☐	9	Ron Hansen, Chi.-A.L.	1.50	2.75
☐	10	Matty Alou, Pgh.	1.50	2.75
☐	**11**	**Barry Moore, Wsh., RC**	**1.50**	**2.75**
☐	12	L.A.: Jim Campanis; Bill Singer	1.50	2.75
☐	13	Joe Sparma, Det.	1.50	2.75
☐	14	Phil Linz, Pha.	1.50	2.75
☐	15	Earl Battey, Min.	1.50	2.75
☐	16	Bill Hands, Chi.-N.L.	1.50	2.75
☐	17	Jim Gosger, K.C.	1.50	2.75
☐	18	Gene Oliver, Atl.	1.50	2.75
☐	19	Jim McGlothlin, Cal.	1.50	2.75
☐	20	Orlando Cepeda, Stl.	2.50	5.00
☐	21	Dave Bristol, Mgr., Cin.	1.50	2.75
☐	22	Gene Brabender, Bal.	1.50	2.75
☐	23	Larry Elliot, NYM.	1.50	2.75
☐	24	Bob Allen, Cle.	1.50	2.75
☐	**25**	**Elston Howard, NYY., RC**	**2.50**	**5.00**
☐	26	Bob Priddy, S.F.	1.50	2.75
☐	27	Bob Saverine, Wsh.	1.50	2.75
☐	28	Barry Latman, Hou.	1.50	2.75
☐	29	Tom McCraw, Chi.-A.L.	1.50	2.75
☐	30	Al Kaline, Det.	12.50	25.00
☐	31	Jim Brewer, L.A.	1.50	2.75
☐	32	Bob Bailey, L.A.	1.50	2.75
☐	33	Oak.: **Sal Bando (RC)**/ Randy Schwartz	3.00	6.00
☐	34	Peter Cimino, Cal.	1.50	2.75
☐	35	Rico Carty, Atl.	1.50	2.75
☐	36	Bob Tillman, Bos.	1.50	2.75
☐	37	Rick Wise, Pha.	1.50	2.75
☐	38	Bob Johnson, Bal.	1.50	2.75

	No.	Card		
☐	39	Curt Simmons, Chi.-N.L.	1.50	2.75
☐	**40**	**Rick Reichardt, Cal., RC**	**1.50**	**2.75**
☐	41	Joe Hoerner, Stl.	1.50	2.75
☐	42	New York Mets	6.00	12.00
☐	43	Chico Salmon, Cle.	1.50	2.75
☐	44	Joe Nuxhall, Cin.	1.50	2.75
☐	45	Roger Maris, Stl.	25.00	50.00
☐	46	Lindy McDaniel, S.F.	1.50	2.75
☐	47	Ken McMullen, Wsh.	1.50	2.75
☐	48	Bill Freehan, Det.	1.50	2.75
☐	49	Roy Face, Pgh.	1.50	2.75
☐	50	Tony Oliva, Min.	2.00	4.00
☐	51	Hou.: Dave Adlesh/ Wes Bales	1.50	2.75
☐	52	Dennis Higgins, Chi.-A.L.	1.50	2.75
☐	53	Clay Dalrymple, Pha.	1.50	2.75
☐	54	Dick Green, K.C.	1.50	2.75
☐	55	Don Drysdale, L.A.	12.50	25.00
☐	56	Jose Tartabull, Bos.	1.50	2.75
☐	**57**	**Pat Jarvis, Atl., RC**	**1.50**	**2.75**
☐	58	Paul Schaal, Cal.	1.50	2.75
☐	59	Ralph Terry, NYM.	1.50	2.75
☐	60	Luis Aparicio, Bal.	6.00	12.00
☐	61	Gordy Coleman, Cin.	1.50	2.75
☐	62	Checklist 1st Series (1 - 109)	7.50	15.00
☐	63	Lou Brock/ Curt Flood	7.50	15.00
☐	64	Fred Valentine, Wsh.	1.50	2.75
☐	65	Tom Haller, S.F.	1.50	2.75
☐	66	Manny Mota, Pgh.	1.50	2.75
☐	67	Ken Berry, Chi.-A.L.	1.50	2.75
☐	68	Bob Buhl, Chi.-A.L.	1.50	2.75
☐	69	Vic Davalillo, Cle.	1.50	2.75
☐	70	Ron Santo, Chi.-N.L.	2.50	5.00
☐	71	Camilo Pascual, Wsh.	1.50	2.75
☐	72	Det.: George Korince/ John Matchick	2.00	4.00
☐	73	Rusty Staub, Hou.	4.00	8.00
☐	74	Wes Stock, K.C.	1.50	2.75
☐	75	George Scott, Bos.	1.50	2.75
☐	**76**	**Jim Barbieri, L.A., RC**	**1.50**	**2.75**
☐	**77**	**Dooley Womack, NYY., RC**	**1.50**	**2.75**
☐	78	Pat Corrales, Stl.	1.50	2.75
☐	79	Bubba Morton, Cal.	1.50	2.75
☐	80	Jim Maloney, Cin.	1.50	2.75
☐	81	Eddie Stanky, Mgr., Chi.-A.L.	1.50	2.75
☐	82	Steve Barber, Bal.	1.50	2.75
☐	83	Ollie Brown, S.F.	1.50	2.75
☐	84	Tommie Sisk, Pgh.	1.50	2.75
☐	85	Johnny Callison, Pha.	1.50	2.75
☐	86	Mike McCormick, Wsh.	1.50	2.75
☐	87	George Altman, Chi.-A.L.	1.50	2.75
☐	88	Mickey Lolich, Det.	2.50	5.00
☐	**89**	**Felix Millan, Atl., RC**	**1.50**	**2.75**
☐	**90**	**Jim Nash, K.C., RC**	**1.50**	**2.75**
☐	91	Johnny Lewis, NYM.	1.50	2.75
☐	92	Ray Washburn, Stl.	1.50	2.75
☐	93	N.Y.: Stan Bahnsen/ Bobby Murcer	1.50	2.75
☐	94	Ron Fairly, L.A.	1.50	2.75
☐	95	Sonny Siebert, Cle.	1.50	2.75
☐	96	Art Shamsky, Cin.	1.50	2.75
☐	97	Mike Cuellar, Hou.	1.50	2.75
☐	98	Rich Rollins, Min.	1.50	2.75
☐	99	Lee Stange, Bos.	1.50	2.75
☐	100	Frank Robinson, Bal.	12.50	25.00
☐	101	Ken Johnson, Atl.	1.50	2.75
☐	102	Philadelphia Phillies	2.50	5.00
☐	103	CL: Mickey Mantle, NYY.	12.50	25.00
☐	**104**	**Minnie Rojas, Cal., RC**	**1.50**	**2.75**
☐	105	Ken Boyer, NYM.	1.50	2.75
☐	106	Randy Hundley, Chi.-N.L.	1.50	2.75
☐	**107**	**Joel Horlen, Chi.-A.L., RC**	**1.50**	**2.75**
☐	108	Alex Johnson, Stl.	1.50	2.75
☐	109	Rocky Colavito; Leon Wagner	3.00	6.00
☐	110	Jack Aker, K.C.	1.75	3.50
☐	111	John Kennedy, L.A.	1.75	3.50
☐	112	Dave Wickersham, Det.	1.75	3.50
☐	113	Dave Nicholson, Atl.	1.75	3.50
☐	114	Jack Baldschun, Cin.	1.75	3.50
☐	**115**	**Paul Casanova, Wsh., RC**	**1.75**	**3.50**
☐	116	Herman Franks, Mgr., S.F.	1.75	3.50
☐	117	Darrell Brandon, Bos.	1.75	3.50
☐	118	Bernie Allen, Wsh.	1.75	3.50
☐	119	Wade Blasingame, Atl.	1.75	3.50
☐	120	Floyd Robinson, Cin.	1.75	3.50
☐	121	Ed Bressoud, NYM.	1.75	3.50
☐	122	George Brunet, Cal.	1.75	3.50
☐	123	Pgh.: Jim Price/ Luke Walker	1.75	3.50
☐	124	Jim Stewart, Chi.-N.L.	1.75	3.50
☐	125	Moe Drabowsky, Bal.	1.75	3.50
☐	126	Tony Taylor, Pha.	1.75	3.50
☐	127	John O'Donoghue, Cle.	1.75	3.50
☐	128	Ed Spiezio, Stl.	1.75	3.50
☐	129	Phil Roof, K.C.	1.75	3.50
☐	130	Phil Regan, L.A.	1.75	3.50
☐	131	New York Yankees	6.00	12.00
☐	**132**	**Ozzie Virgil, S.F., RC**	**1.75**	**3.50**
☐	133	Ron Kline, Min.	1.75	3.50
☐	134	Gates Brown, Det.	1.75	3.50
☐	135	Deron Johnson, Cin.	1.75	3.50
☐	136	Carroll Sembera, Hou.	1.75	3.50
☐	137	Min.: Ron Clark/ Jim Ollom	1.75	3.50
☐	**138**	**Dick Kelley, Atl., RC**	**1.75**	**3.50**
☐	139	Dalton Jones, Bos.	1.75	3.50
☐	**140**	**Willie Stargell, Pit., RC**	**15.00**	**30.00**
☐	**141**	**John Miller, Bal., RC**	**1.75**	**3.50**
☐	142	Jackie Brandt, Pha.	1.75	3.50
☐	143	Pete Ward; Don Buford	2.50	5.00
☐	144	Bill Hepler, NYM.	1.75	3.50
☐	145	Larry Brown, Cle.	1.75	3.50
☐	**146**	**Steve Carlton, St.L., RC**	**62.50**	**125.00**
☐	147	Tom Egan, Cal.	1.75	3.50
☐	148	Adolfo Phillips, Chi.-N.L.	1.75	3.50
☐	149	Joe Moeller, L.A.	1.75	3.50
☐	150	Mickey Mantle, NYY.	225.00	450.00
☐	151	WS-Game 1: Moe Mows Down 11	3.50	7.00
☐	152	WS-Game 2: Palmer Blanks Dodgers	6.00	12.00
☐	153	WS-Game 3: Blair's Homer Defeats L.A.	3.50	7.00
☐	154	WS-Game 4: Orioles Win 4th Straight	3.50	7.00
☐	155	WS: The Winners Celebrate	3.50	7.00
☐	156	Ron Herbel, S.F.	1.75	3.50
☐	157	Danny Cater, K.C.	1.75	3.50
☐	158	Jimmie Coker, Cin., Error	1.75	3.50
☐	**159**	**Bruce Howard, Chi.-A.L., RC**	**1.75**	**3.50**
☐	160	Willie Davis, L.A.	1.75	3.50
☐	161	Dick Williams, Mgr., Bos.	2.50	5.00
☐	162	Billy O'Dell, Pgh.	1.75	3.50
☐	163	Vic Roznovsky, Bal.	1.75	3.50
☐	164	Dwight Siebler, Min.	1.75	3.50
☐	**165**	**Cleon Jones, NYM., RC**	**1.75**	**3.50**
☐	166	Ed Mathews, Hou.	12.50	25.00
☐	167	Wsh.: Joe Coleman/ Tim Cullen	1.75	3.50
☐	168	Ray Culp, Chi.-N.L.	1.75	3.50
☐	169	Horace Clarke, NYY.	1.75	3.50
☐	170	Dick McAuliffe, Det.	1.75	3.50
☐	171	Calvin Koonce, Chi.-N.L.	1.75	3.50
☐	172	Bill Heath, Hou.	1.75	3.50
☐	173	St. Louis Cardinals	3.50	7.00
☐	174	Dick Radatz, Cle.	1.75	3.50
☐	175	Bobby Knoop, Cal.	1.75	3.50
☐	176	Sammy Ellis, Cin.	1.75	3.50

	No.	Player	EX	NRMT
☐	177	Tito Fuentes, S.F.	1.75	3.50
☐	178	John Buzhardt, Chi.-A.L.	1.75	3.50
☐	179	Atl.: Charles Vaughan/ Cecil Upshaw	1.75	3.50
☐	**180**	**Curt Blefary, Bal., RC**	**1.75**	**3.50**
☐	181	Terry Fox, Pha.	1.75	3.50
☐	182	Ed Charles, K.C.	1.75	3.50
☐	183	Jim Pagliaroni, Pgh.	1.75	3.50
☐	184	George Thomas, Bos.	1.75	3.50
☐	**185**	**Ken Holtzman, Chi.-N.L., RC**	**3.50**	**7.00**
☐	186	Ed Kranepool; Ron Swoboda	1.75	3.50
☐	187	Pedro Ramos, Pha.	1.75	3.50
☐	188	Ken Harrelson, Wsh.	1.75	3.50
☐	189	Chuck Hinton, Cle.	1.75	3.50
☐	190	Turk Farrell, Hou.	1.75	3.50
☐	191	CL: Willie Mays, S.F.	9.00	18.00
☐	192	Fred Gladding, Det.	1.75	3.50
☐	193	Jose Cardenal, Cal.	1.75	3.50
☐	194	Bob Allison, Min.	1.75	3.50
☐	195	Al Jackson, Stl.	1.75	3.50
☐	196	Johnny Romano, Stl.	1.75	5.00

1968 O-PEE-CHEE

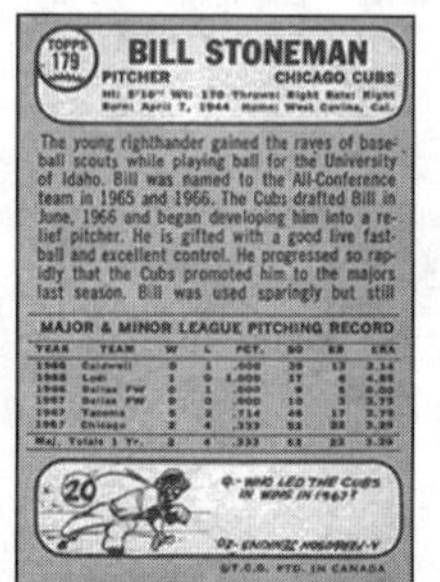

This set is identical to the first 196 cards in the Topps 598-card set for 1968, except for the imprint "Printed in Canada" on the backs of the Canadian cards. This set contains the key Nolan Ryan rookie card.

Card Size: 2 1/2" x 3 1/2"
Face: Four colour, brown border; name, position, team
Back: Brown on card stock; name, number, résumé, quiz
Imprint: © T.C.G. PTD. IN CANADA

Complete Set (196 cards):			**1,350.00**	**2,700.00**
Common Player:			**1.50**	**2.75**

	No.	Player	EX	NRMT
☐	1	LL: M. Alou/ R. Clemente/ T. Gonzalez	20.00	40.00
☐	2	LL: A. Kaline,/ F. Robinson/ C. Yastrzemski	10.00	20.00
☐	3	LL: H. Aaron/ O. Cepeda/ R. Clemente	12.50	25.00
☐	4	LL: H. Killebrew/ F. Robinson/ C. Yastrzemski	10.00	20.00
☐	5	LL: H. Aaron/ W. McCovey/ R. Santo/ J. Wynn	6.00	12.00
☐	6	LL: F. Howard/ H. Killebrew/ C. Yastrzemski	6.00	12.00
☐	7	LL: J. Bunning/ P. Niekro/ C. Short	4.00	8.00
☐	8	LL: J. Horlen/ G. Peters/ S. Siebert	2.50	5.00
☐	9	LL: J. Bunning/ F. Jenkins/ M. McCormick / C. Osteen	4.00	8.00
☐	10	LL: D. Chance/ Jim Lonborg/ E. Wilson	2.50	54.00
☐	11	LL: J. Bunning/ F. Jenkins/ G. Perry	4.00	8.00
☐	12	LL: D. Chance/ Jim Lonborg/ S. McDowell	2.50	5.00
☐	**13**	**Chuck Hartenstein, Chi.-N.L., RC**	**1.50**	**2.75**
☐	14	Jerry McNertney, Chi.-A.L.	1.50	2.75
☐	15	Ron Hunt, S.F.	1.50	2.75
☐	16	Cle.: Lou Piniella/ Richie Scheinblum	1.50	2.75
☐	17	Dick Hall, Pha.	1.50	2.75
☐	18	Mike Hershberger, Oak.	1.50	2.75
☐	19	Juan Pizarro, Pgh.	1.50	2.75
☐	20	Brooks Robinson, Bal.	17.50	35.00
☐	21	Ron Davis, Hou.	1.50	2.75
☐	**22**	**Pat Dobson, Det., RC**	**1.50**	**2.75**
☐	23	Chico Cardenas, Cin.	1.50	2.75
☐	24	Bobby Locke, Cal.	1.50	2.75
☐	25	Julian Javier, Stl.	1.50	2.75
☐	26	Darrell Brandon, Bos.	1.50	2.75
☐	27	Gil Hodges, NYM.	2.50	5.00
☐	28	Ted Uhlaender, Min.	1.50	2.75
☐	29	Joe Verbanic, NYY.	1.50	2.75
☐	30	Joe Torre, Atl.	2.50	5.00
☐	31	Ed Stroud, Wsh.	1.50	2.75
☐	32	Joe Gibbon, S.F.	1.50	2.75
☐	33	Pete Ward, Chi.-A.L.	2.00	4.00
☐	34	Al Ferrara, L.A.	1.50	2.75
☐	35	Steve Hargan, Cle.	1.50	2.75
☐	36	Pgh.: Bob Moose/ Bob Robertson	1.50	2.75
☐	37	Billy Williams, Chi.-N.L.	6.00	12.00
☐	38	Tony Pierce, Oak.	1.50	2.75
☐	39	Cookie Rojas, Pha., E	1.50	2.75
☐	40	Denny McLain, Det.	6.00	12.00
☐	41	Julio Gotay, Hou.	1.50	2.75
☐	42	Larry Haney, Bal.	1.50	2.75
☐	43	Gary Bell, Bos.	1.50	2.75
☐	44	Frank Kostro, Min.	1.50	2.75
☐	45	Tom Seaver, NYM., E	45.00	90.00
☐	46	Dave Ricketts, Stl., E	1.50	2.75
☐	47	Ralph Houk, Mgr., NYY.	2.50	5.00
☐	48	Ted Davidson, Chi.-N.L.	1.50	2.75
☐	49	Ed Brinkman, Wsh.	1.50	2.75
☐	50	Willie Mays, S.F.	55.00	110.00
☐	51	Bob Locker, Chi.-A.L.	1.50	2.75
☐	**52**	**Hawk Taylor, Cal., RC**	**1.50**	**2.75**
☐	53	Gene Alley, Pgh., E	1.50	2.75
☐	54	Stan Williams, Cle.	1.50	2.75
☐	55	Felipe Alou, Atl.	3.00	6.00
☐	56	Bal.: Dave Leonhard/ Dave May	1.50	2.75
☐	57	Dan Schneider, Hou.	1.50	2.75
☐	58	Ed Mathews, Det.	12.00	24.00
☐	59	Don Lock, Pha.	1.50	2.75
☐	60	Ken Holtzman, Chi.-N.L.	1.50	2.75
☐	**61**	**Reggie Smith, Bos., RC**	**1.50**	**2.75**
☐	62	Chuck Dobson, Oak.	1.37	2.75
☐	**63**	**Dick Kenworthy, Chi.-A.L., RC**	**1.50**	**2.75**
☐	64	Jim Merritt, Min.	1.50	2.75
☐	65	John Roseboro, Min.	1.50	2.75
☐	66	Casey Cox, Wsh.	1.50	2.75
☐	67	CL: Jim Kaat, Min.	6.00	12.00
☐	**68**	**Ron Willis, St.L., RC**	**1.50**	**2.75**
☐	69	Tom Tresh, NYY.	1.50	2.75
☐	70	Bob Veale, Pit., E	1.50	2.75
☐	71	Vern Fuller, Cle.	1.50	2.75
☐	72	Tommy John, Chi.-N.L., E	2.00	4.00
☐	73	Jim Hart, S.F.	1.50	2.75
☐	74	Milt Pappas, Cin.	1.50	2.75
☐	75	Don Mincher, Cal.	1.50	2.75
☐	76	Atl.: Jim Britton/ Ron Reed	1.50	2.75
☐	**77**	**Don Wilson, Hou., RC**	**1.50**	**2.75**
☐	**78**	**Jim Northrup, Det., RC**	**1.50**	**2.75**
☐	**79**	**Ted Kubiak, Oak., RC**	**1.50**	**2.75**
☐	80	Rod Carew, Min.	45.00	90.00
☐	81	Larry Jackson, Pha.	1.50	2.75
☐	82	Sam Bowens, Wsh.	1.50	2.75
☐	83	John Stephenson, Chi.-N.L.	1.50	2.75
☐	**84**	**Bob Tolan, Stl.**	**1.50**	**2.75**
☐	85	Gaylord Perry, S.F., E	7.00	14.00
☐	86	Willie Stargell, Pgh.	4.50	9.00
☐	87	Dick Williams, Mgr.,	1.50	2.75
☐	88	Phil Regan, L.A.	1.50	2.75

89	Jake Gibbs, NYY.	1.50	2.75
90	Vada Pinson, Cin.	1.50	2.75
91	**Jim Ollom, Min., RC, E**	**1.37**	**2.75**
92	Ed Kranepool, NYM.	1.50	2.75
93	Tony Cloninger, Atl.	1.50	2.75
94	Lee Maye, Cle.	1.50	2.75
95	Bob Aspromonte, Hou.	1.50	2.75
96	Wsh.: Frank Coggins/ Dick Nold	1.50	2.75
97	Tom Phoebus, Bal.	1.50	2.75
98	Gary Sutherland, Pha.	1.50	2.75
99	Rocky Colavito, L.A.	3.00	6.00
100	**Bob Gibson, Stl., RC**	**17.50**	**35.00**
101	Glenn Beckert, Chi.-N.L.	1.50	2.75
102	Jose Cardenal, Cle.	1.50	2.75
103	**Don Sutton, L.A., RC**	**5.00**	**10.00**
104	Dick Dietz, S.F.	1.50	2.75
105	Al Downing, NYY.	1.50	2.75
106	Dalton Jones, Bos.	1.50	2.75
107	CL: Juan Marichal, S.F.	6.00	12.00
108	Don Pavletich, Cin.	1.50	2.75
109	Bert Campaneris, Oak.	1.50	2.75
110	Hank Aaron, Atl.	50.00	100.00
111	Rich Reese, Min.	1.50	2.75
112	Woodie Fryman, Pha.	1.50	2.75
113	Det.: Tom Matchick/ Daryl Patterson	1.50	2.75
114	Ron Swoboda, NYM.	1.50	2.75
115	Sam McDowell, Cle.	1.50	2.75
116	Ken McMullen, Wsh.	1.50	2.75
117	Larry Jaster, Stl.	1.50	2.75
118	Mark Belanger, Bal.	1.50	2.75
119	Ted Savage, Chi.-N.L.	1.50	2.75
120	Mel Stottlemyre, NYY.	1.50	2.75
121	Jimmie Hall, Cal.	1.50	2.75
122	Gene Mauch, Mgr., Pha.	1.50	2.75
123	Jose Santiago, Bos.	1.50	2.75
124	Nate Oliver, S.F., E	1.50	2.75
125	Joe Horlen, Chi.-A.L.	1.50	2.75
126	**Bob Etheridge, S.F., RC**	**1.50**	**2.75**
127	Paul Lindblad, Oak.	1.50	2.75
128	Hou.: Tom Dukes/ Alonzo Harris	1.50	2.75
129	Mickey Stanley, Det.	1.50	2.75
130	Tony Perez, Cin.	3.50	7.00
131	Frank Bertaina, Wsh.	1.50	2.75
132	Bud Harrelson, NYM.	1.50	2.75
133	Fred Whitfield, Cin.	1.50	2.75
134	Pat Jarvis, Atl.	1.50	2.75
135	Paul Blair, Bal.	1.50	2.75
136	Randy Hundley, Chi.-N.L.	1.50	2.75
137	Twins Team	2.50	5.00
138	Ruben Amaro, NYY.	1.50	2.75
139	Chris Short, Pha.	1.50	2.75
140	Tony Conigliaro, Bos.	3.50	7.00
141	Dal Maxvill, Stl.	1.50	2.75
142	Chi.-A.L.: Buddy Bradford; Bill Voss	1.50	2.75
143	Pete Cimino, Cal.	1.50	2.75
144	Joe Morgan, Hou.	9.00	18.00
145	Don Drysdale, L.A.	9.00	18.00
146	Sal Bando, Oak.	2.00	4.00
147	Frank Linzy, S.F.	1.50	2.75
148	Dave Bristol, Mgr., Cin.	1.50	2.75
149	Bob Saverine, Wsh.	1.50	2.75
150	Bob Clemente, Pgh.	55.00	110.00
151	WS-Game 1: Brock Socks 4-Hits	7.50	15.00
152	WS-Game 2: Yaz Smashes Two Homers, E	7.50	15.00
153	WS-Game 3: Briles Cools Off Boston	3.00	6.00
154	WS-Game 4: Gibson Hurls Shutout!	7.50	15.00
155	WS-Game 5: Lonborg Wins Again!	3.00	6.00
156	WS-Game 6: Petrocelli Socks Two Homers	3.00	6.00
157	WS-Game 7: St. Louis Wins It!	3.00	6.00
158	WS-Summary: The Cardinals Celebrate	3.00	6.00
159	Don Kessinger, Chi.-N.L.	1.50	2.75
160	Earl Wilson, Det.	1.50	2.75
161	Norm Miller, Hou.	1.50	2.75
162	Hal Gibson/ Mike Torrez	1.50	2.75
163	Gene Brabender, Bal.	1.50	2.75
164	Ramon Webster, Oak.	1.50	2.75
165	Tony Oliva, Min.	2.00	4.00
166	Claude Raymond, Atl.	2.00	4.00
167	Elston Howard, Bos.	2.00	4.00
168	Dodgers Team	2.50	5.00
169	Bob Bolin, S.F.	1.50	2.75
170	Jim Fregosi, Cal.	1.50	2.75
171	Don Nottebart, Cin.	1.50	2.75
172	Walt Williams, Chi.-A.L.	1.50	2.75
173	John Boozer, Phi.	1.50	2.75
174	Bob Tillman, Atl.	1.50	2.75
175	Maury Wills, Pgh.	2.50	5.00
176	Bob Allen, Cle.	1.50	2.75
177	**NYM.: J. Koosman, RC/ N. Ryan, RC**	**800.00**	**1,600.00**
178	Don Wert, Det.	1.50	2.75
179	**Bill Stoneman, Chi.-N.L., RC**	**1.50**	**2.75**
180	Curt Flood, Stl.	2.00	4.00
181	Jerry Zimmerman, Min.	1.50	2.75
182	**Dave Giusti, Hou., RC**	**1.50**	**2.75**
183	Bob Kennedy, Mgr., Oak.	1.50	2.75
184	Lou Johnson, Chi.-N.L.	1.50	2.75
185	Tom Haller, L.A.	1.50	2.75
186	Eddie Watt, Bal.	1.50	2.75
187	**Sonny Jackson, Atl., RC**	**1.50**	**2.75**
188	Cap Peterson, Wsh.	1.50	2.75
189	**Bill Landis, Bos., RC**	**1.50**	**2.75**
190	Bill White, Pha.	2.00	4.00
191	**Dan Frisella, NYM. RC**	**1.50**	**2.75**
192	CL: Carl Yastrzemski, Bos.	6.00	12.00
193	Jack Hamilton, Cal.	1.50	2.75
194	Don Buford, Bal.	1.50	2.75
195	Joe Pepitone, NYY.	2.00	4.00
196	**Gary Nolan, Cin., RC**	**1.50**	**2.75**

1968 POSTER INSERTS

This set was inserted into O-Pee-Chee wax packs in 1968. The Canadian set is numbered differently than the Topps issue. The Canadian poster set is quite rare and was issued one year later than the Topps equivalent.

Poster Size: 4 7/8" x 6 7/8"

Face: Four colour, white border; name, position, team

Back: Blank

Imprint: © T.C.G. PTD. IN CANADA

Insert Set (32 posters):		**150.00**	**300.00**
Common Player:		**2.50**	**5.00**
No.	**Player**	**EX**	**NRMT**
1	Brooks Robinson, Bal.	6.00	12.00
2	Bert Campaneris, K.C.	2.50	5.00
3	Carl Yastrzemski, Bos.	6.00	12.00
4	Bob Clemente, Pgh.	20.00	40.00
5	Cleon Jones, NYM.	2.50	5.00
6	Don Drysdale, L.A.	5.00	10.00
7	Orlando Cepeda, Stl.	4.00	8.00
8	Hank Aaron, Alt.	10.00	20.00
9	Tommie Agee, NYM.	2.50	5.00
10	Boog Powell, Bal.	3.50	7.00
11	Mickey Mantle, NYY.	35.00	70.00
12	Chico Cardenas, Cin.	2.50	5.00
13	John Callison, Pha.	2.50	5.00
14	Frank Howard, Wsh.	2.50	5.00
15	Willie Mays, S.F.	10.00	20.00
16	Sam McDowell, Cle.	2.50	5.00
17	Al Kaline, Det.	6.00	12.00
18	Juan Marichal, S.F.	5.00	10.00

	No.	Player	EX	NRMT
☐	19	Denny McLain, Det.	3.50	7.00
☐	20	Matty Alou, Atl.	2.50	5.00
☐	21	Felipe Alou, Atl.	6.00	12.00
☐	22	Joe Pepitone, NYY.	2.50	5.00
☐	23	Leon Wagner, Cle.	2.50	5.00
☐	24	Bobby Knoop, Cal.	2.50	5.00
☐	25	Tony Oliva, Min.	3.50	7.00
☐	26	Joe Torre, Atl.	3.50	7.00
☐	27	Ron Santo, Chi.-N.L.	3.50	7.00
☐	28	Willie McCovey, S.F.	5.00	10.00
☐	29	Frank Robinson, Bal.	6.00	12.00
☐	30	Ron Hunt, L.A.	2.50	5.00
☐	31	Harmon Killebrew, Min.	5.00	10.00
☐	32	Joe Morgan	5.00	10.00

1969 O-PEE-CHEE

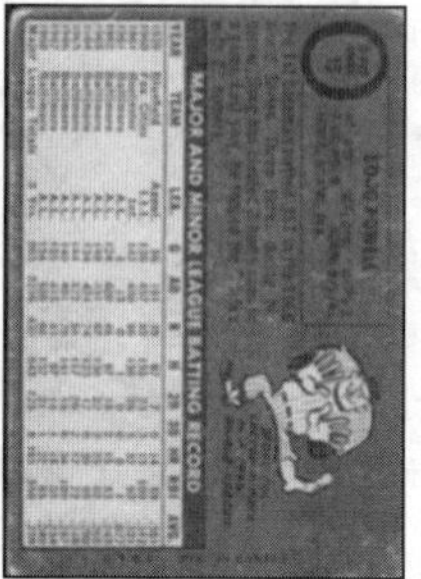

This set is identical in design to the first 218 cards in the 664-card Topps set of the same year, except the imprint "Ptd. in Canada" appears on the backs of the cards.

Card Size: 2 1/2" x 3 1/2"
Face: Four colour, white border; name, position, team
Back: Pink and black on card stock; number, résumé, cartoon
Imprint: © T.C.G. PTD. IN CANADA

Complete Set (218 cards):			**450.00**	**900.00**
Common Player:			**1.25**	**2.50**

	No.	Player	EX	NRMT
☐	1	LL: C. Yastrzemski/ D. Cater/ T. Oliva, Min.	12.50	25.00
☐	2	LL: P. Rose/ M. Alou/ F. Alou	5.00	10.00
☐	3	LL: K. Harrelson/ F. Howard/ J. Northrup	2.00	4.00
☐	4	LL: W. McCovey/ R. Santo/ B. Williams	4.50	9.00
☐	5	LL: F. Howard/ W. Horton/ K. Harrelson	2.00	4.00
☐	6	LL: W. McCovey/ R. Allen/ E. Banks.	4.50	9.00
☐	7	LL: L. Tiant,/ S. McDowell/ D. McNally	2.00	4.00
☐	8	LL: B. Gibson/ B. Bolin/ B. Veale	3.00	6.00
☐	9	LL: D. McLain/ D. McNally/ L. Tiant / M. Stottlemyre	2.00	4.00
☐	10	LL: J. Marichal/ B. Gibson/ F. Jenkins	6.00	12.00
☐	11	LL: S. McDowell/ D. McLain/ L. Tiant	2.00	4.00
☐	12	LL: B. Gibson/ F. Jenkins,/ B. Singer	6.00	12.00
☐	13	Mickey Stanley, Det.	1.25	2.50
☐	14	Al McBean, S.D.	1.25	2.50
☐	15	Boog Powell, Bal.	2.00	4.00
☐	16	SFG.: Cesar Gutierrez/ Rich Robertson	1.25	2.50
☐	17	Mike Marshall, Sea.	2.00	4.00
☐	18	Dick Schofield, Stl.	1.25	2.50
☐	19	Ken Suarez, Cle.	1.25	2.50
☐	20	Ernie Banks, Chi.-N.L.	15.00	30.00
☐	21	Jose Santiago, Bos.	1.25	2.50
☐	22	Jesus Alou, Mtl.	1.25	2.50
☐	23	Lew Krausse, Oak.	1.25	2.50
☐	24	Walt Alston, Mgr., L.A.	2.50	5.00
☐	25	Roy White, NYY.	1.25	2.50
☐	26	Clay Carroll, Cin.	1.25	2.50
☐	27	Bernie Allen, Wsh.	1.25	2.50
☐	28	Mike Ryan, Pha.	1.25	2.50
☐	29	Dave Morehead, K.C.	1.25	2.50
☐	30	Bob Allison, Min.	1.25	2.50
☐	**31**	**NYM.: Gary Gentry/ Amos Otis (RCs)**	**2.00**	**4.00**
☐	32	Sammy Ellis, L.A.	1.25	2.50
☐	33	Wayne Causey, Atl.	1.25	2.50
☐	34	Gary Peters, Chi.-A.L.	1.25	2.50
☐	35	Joe Morgan, Hou.	9.00	18.00
☐	**36**	**Luke Walker, Pgh., RC**	**1.25**	**2.50**
☐	37	Curt Motton, Bal.	1.25	2.50
☐	38	Zoilo Versalles, S.D.	1.25	2.50
☐	39	Dick Hughes, Stl.	1.25	2.50
☐	40	Mayo Smith, Mgr., Det.	1.25	2.50
☐	41	Bob Barton, S.F.	1.25	2.50
☐	42	Tommy Harper, Sea.	1.25	2.50
☐	43	Joe Niekro, Chi.-N.L.	1.25	2.50
☐	44	Danny Cater, Oak.	1.25	2.50
☐	45	Maury Wills, Mtl.	2.00	4.00
☐	46	Fritz Peterson, NYY.	1.25	2.50
☐	47	Paul Popovich, L.A.	1.25	2.50
☐	48	Brant Alyea, Wsh.	1.25	2.50
☐	49	K.C.: Steve Jones/ Eliseo Rodriguez	1.25	2.50
☐	50	Robeto Clemente, Pgh.	40.00	80.00
☐	51	Woodie Fryman, Pha.	1.25	2.50
☐	52	Mike Andrews, Bos.	1.25	2.50
☐	53	Sonny Jackson, Atl.	1.25	2.50
☐	54	Cisco Carlos, Chi.-A.L.	1.25	2.50
☐	55	Jerry Grote, NYM.	1.25	2.50
☐	56	Rich Reese, Min.	1.25	2.50
☐	57	CL: Denny McLain, Det.	5.50	11.00
☐	58	Fred Gladding, Hou.	1.25	2.50
☐	59	Jay Johnstone, Cal.	1.25	2.50
☐	60	Nelson Briles, Stl.	1.25	2.50
☐	61	Jimmie Hall, Cle.	1.25	2.50
☐	62	Chico Salmon, Sea.	1.25	2.50
☐	63	Jim Hickman, Chi.-N.L.	1.25	2.50
☐	64	Bill Monbouquette, S.F.	1.25	2.50
☐	65	Willie Davis, L.A.	1.25	2.50
☐	66	Bal.: Mike Adamson/ Merv Rettenmund	1.25	2.50
☐	67	Bill Stoneman, Mtl.	1.25	2.50
☐	68	Dave Duncan, Oak.	1.25	2.50
☐	69	Steve Hamilton, NYY.	1.25	2.50
☐	**70**	**Tommy Helms, Cin., RC**	**1.25**	**2.50**
☐	71	Steve Whitaker, K.C..	1.25	2.50
☐	72	Ron Taylor, NYM.	2.00	4.00
☐	73	Johnny Briggs, Pha.	1.25	2.50
☐	74	Preston Gomez, Mgr., S.D.	1.25	2.50
☐	75	Luis Aparicio, Chi.-A.L.	3.00	6.00
☐	76	Norm Miller, Hou.	1.25	2.50
☐	77	Ron Perranoski, Min.	1.25	2.50
☐	78	Tom Satriano, Cal.	1.25	2.50
☐	79	Milt Pappas, Atl.	1.25	2.50
☐	80	Norm Cash, Det.	1.25	2.50
☐	81	Mel Queen, Cin.	1.25	2.50
☐	82	Pgh.: Rich Hebner/ Al Oliver	7.50	15.00
☐	83	Mike Ferraro, Sea.	1.25	2.50
☐	84	Bob Humphreys, Wsh.	1.25	2.50
☐	85	Lou Brock, Stl.	15.00	30.00
☐	86	Pete Richert, Bal.	1.25	2.50
☐	87	Horace Clarke, NYY.	1.25	2.50
☐	88	Rich Nye, Chi.-N.L.	1.25	2.50
☐	89	Russ Gibson, Bos.	1.25	2.50
☐	90	Jerry Koosman, NYM.	1.25	2.50
☐	91	Al Dark, Mgr., Cle.	1.25	2.50
☐	92	Jack Billingham, Mtl.	1.25	2.50
☐	93	Joe Foy, K.C.	1.25	2.50
☐	94	Hank Aguirre, L.A.	1.25	2.50
☐	95	Johnny Bench, Cin.	37.50	75.00

No.	Card		
☐ 96	Denver Lemaster, Hou.	1.25	2.50
☐ **97**	**Buddy Bradford, Chi.-A.L., RC**	**1.25**	**2.50**
☐ 98	Dave Giusti, S.D.	1.25	2.50
☐ 99	Min.: Danny Morris/ Graig Nettles	12.50	25.00
☐ 100	Hank Aaron, Atl.	30.00	60.00
☐ **101**	**Daryl Patterson, Det., RC**	**1.25**	**2.50**
☐ 102	Jim Davenport, S.F.	1.25	2.50
☐ 103	Roger Repoz, Cal.	1.25	2.50
☐ 104	Steve Blass, Pgh.	1.25	2.50
☐ 105	Rick Monday, Oak.	1.25	2.50
☐ 106	Jim Hannan, Wsh.	1.25	2.50
☐ 107	CL.: Bob Gibson	5.50	11.00
☐ 108	Tony Taylor, Pha.	1.25	2.50
☐ 109	Jim Lonborg, Bos.	1.25	2.50
☐ 110	Mike Shannon, Stl.	1.25	2.50
☐ **111**	**John Morris, Sea., RC**	**1.25**	**2.50**
☐ 112	J.C. Martin, NYM.	1.25	2.50
☐ **113**	**Dave May, Bal., RC**	**1.25**	**2.50**
☐ 114	NYY.: Alan Closter/ John Cumberland	1.25	2.50
☐ 115	Bill Hands, Chi.-N.L.	1.25	2.50
☐ 116	Chuck Harrison, K.C.	1.25	2.50
☐ 117	Jim Fairey, Mtl.	1.25	2.50
☐ 118	Stan Williams, Cle.	1.25	2.50
☐ 119	Doug Rader, Hou.	1.25	2.50
☐ 120	Pete Rose, Cin.	20.00	40.00
☐ **121**	**Joe Grzenda, Min., RC**	**1.25**	**2.50**
☐ 122	Ron Fairly, L.A.	1.25	2.50
☐ 123	Wilbur Wood, Chi.-A.L.	1.25	2.50
☐ 124	Hank Bauer, Mgr., Oak.	1.25	2.50
☐ 125	Ray Sadecki, S.F.	1.25	2.50
☐ 126	Dick Tracewski, Det.	1.25	2.50
☐ 127	Kevin Collins, NYM.	1.25	2.50
☐ 128	Tommie Aaron, Atl.	1.25	2.50
☐ 129	Bill McCool, S.D.	1.25	2.50
☐ 130	Carl Yastrzemski, Bos.	15.00	30.00
☐ 131	Chris Cannizzaro, Pgh.	1.25	2.50
☐ 132	Dave Baldwin, Wsh.	1.25	2.50
☐ 133	Johnny Callison, Pha.	1.25	2.50
☐ 134	Jim Weaver, Cal.	1.25	2.50
☐ 135	Tommy Davis, Sea.	1.25	2.50
☐ 136	Steve Huntz/ Mike Torrez	1.25	2.50
☐ 137	Wally Bunker, K.C.	1.25	2.50
☐ 138	John Bateman, Mtl.	1.25	2.50
☐ 139	Andy Kosco, L.A.	1.25	2.50
☐ 140	Jim Lefebvre, L.A.	1.25	2.50
☐ 141	Bill Dillman, Bal.	1.25	2.50
☐ 142	Woody Woodward, Cin.	1.25	2.50
☐ 143	Joe Nossek, Oak.	1.25	2.50
☐ 144	Bob Hendley, NYM.	1.25	2.50
☐ 145	Max Alvis, Cle.	1.25	2.50
☐ 146	Jim Perry, Min.	1.25	2.50
☐ 147	Leo Durocher, Mgr., Chi.-N.L.	3.00	6.00
☐ 148	Lee Stange, Bos.	1.25	2.50
☐ 149	Ollie Brown, S.D.	1.25	2.50
☐ 150	Denny McLain, Det.	2.00	4.00
☐ 151	Clay Dalrymple, Pha.	1.25	2.50
☐ 152	Tommie Sisk, Pgh.	1.25	2.50
☐ 153	Ed Brinkman, Wsh.	1.25	2.50
☐ **154**	**Jim Britton, Atl., RC**	**1.25**	**2.50**
☐ 155	Pete Ward, Chi.-A.L.	2.00	4.00
☐ 156	Hou.: Hal Gibson/ Leon McFadden	1.25	2.50
☐ 157	Bob Rodgers, Cal.	1.25	2.50
☐ 158	Joe Gibbon, S.F.	1.25	2.50
☐ 159	Jerry Adair, K.C.	1.25	2.00
☐ 160	Vada Pinson, Stl.	1.25	2.50
☐ 161	John Purdin, L.A.	1.25	2.50
☐ 162	WS-Game 1: Gibson Sets New Record 17	6.00	12.00
☐ 163	WS-Game 2: Tiger Homers Deck The Cards	2.50	5.00
☐ 164	WS-Game 3: McCarver's Homer Puts St. Louis Ahead	6.00	12.00
☐ 165	WS-Game 4: Brock's Lead-Off HR Starts Cards' Romp	6.00	12.00
☐ 166	WS-Game 5: Kaline's Hit Sparks Tiger Rally	6.00	12.00
☐ 167	WS-Game 6: Tiger 10-Run Inning	2.50	5.00
☐ 168	WS-Game 7: Lolich Outduels Gibson	6.00	12.00
☐ 169	WS: Tigers Celebrate Their Victory	2.50	5.00
☐ 170	Frank Howard, Wsh.	2.00	4.00
☐ 171	Glenn Beckert, Chi.-N.L.	1.25	2.50
☐ **172**	**Jerry Stephenson, Bos., RC**	**1.25**	**2.50**
☐ 173	Chi.-A.L.: Bob Christian/ Gerry Nyman	1.25	2.50
☐ 174	Grant Jackson, Pha.	1.25	2.50
☐ 175	Jim Bunning, Pgh.	4.00	8.00
☐ 176	Joe Azcue, Cle.	1.25	2.50
☐ 177	Ron Reed, Atl.	1.25	2.50
☐ 178	Ray Oyler, Sea.	1.25	2.50
☐ 179	Don Pavletich, Chi.-A.L.	1.25	2.50
☐ 180	Willie Horton, Det.	1.25	2.50
☐ 181	Mel Nelson, Stl.	1.25	2.50
☐ 182	Bill Rigney, Mgr., Cal.	1.25	2.50
☐ 183	Don Shaw, Mtl.	1.25	2.50
☐ 184	Roberto Pena, S.D.	1.25	2.50
☐ 185	Tom Phoebus, Bal.	1.25	2.50
☐ 186	John Edwards, Hou.	1.25	2.50
☐ 187	Leon Wagner, Cin.	1.25	2.50
☐ 188	Rick Wise, Pha.	1.25	2.50
☐ 189	Bos.: Joe Lahoud/ John Thibdeau	1.25	2.50
☐ 190	Willie Mays, S.F.	40.00	80.00
☐ 191	Lindy McDaniel, NYY.	1.25	2.50
☐ 192	Jose Pagan, Pgh.	1.25	2.50
☐ 193	Don Cardwell, NYM.	1.25	2.50
☐ 194	Ted Uhlaender, Min.	1.25	2.50
☐ 195	John Odom, Oak.	1.25	2.50
☐ 196	Lum Harris, Mgr., Atl.	1.25	2.50
☐ 197	Dick Selma, S.D.	1.25	2.50
☐ 198	Willie Smith, Chi.-N.L.	1.25	2.50
☐ 199	Jim French, Wsh.	1.25	2.50
☐ 200	Bob Gibson, Stl.	11.00	22.00
☐ 201	Russ Snyder, Cle.	1.25	2.50
☐ 202	Don Wilson, Hou.	1.25	2.50
☐ 203	Dave Johnson, Bal.	1.25	2.50
☐ 204	Jack Hiatt, S.F.	1.25	2.50
☐ 205	Rick Reichardt, Cal.	1.25	2.50
☐ 206	Pha.: Larry Hisle/ Barry Lersch	1.25	2.50
☐ 207	Roy Face, Det.	1.25	2.50
☐ 208	Donn Clendenon, Mtl.	1.25	2.50
☐ 209	Larry Haney, Sea.	1.25	2.50
☐ 210	Felix Millan, Atl.	1.25	2.50
☐ 211	Galen Cisco, K.C.	1.25	2.50
☐ 212	Tom Tresh, NYY.	1.25	2.50
☐ 213	Gerry Arrigo, Cin.	1.25	2.50
☐ 214	Checklist 3rd Series (219 - 327)	5.00	11.00
☐ 215	Rico Petrocelli, Bos.	1.25	2.50
☐ 216	Don Sutton, L.A.	4.50	9.00
☐ 217	John Donaldson, Oak.	1.25	2.50
☐ 218	John Roseboro, Min.	1.25	4.00

DECKLE EDGE

This 24-card set is unnumbered and is listed here in alphabetical order. Each of the light-weight, cardboard, deckle-edge cards bears a facsimile signature.

Card Size: 2 1/8" x 3 1/8"
Face: Black and white; facsimile autograph
Back: Blank
Imprint: None

Insert Set (24 cards):		**62.50**	**125.00**
Common Player:		**1.50**	**3.00**

No.	Player	EX	NRMT
☐ 1	Rich Allen, Pha.	1.50	3.00
☐ 2	Lius Aparicio, Chi.-A.L.	3.00	6.00
☐ 3	Rodney Carew, Min.	6.00	12.00
☐ 4	Roberto Clemente, Pgh.	12.50	25.00
☐ 5	Curt Flood, Stl.	2.50	5.00
☐ 6	Bill Freehan, Det.	1.50	3.00
☐ 7	Robert Gibson, Stl.	1.50	3.00
☐ 8	Tom Haller, L.A.	1.50	3.00
☐ 9	Ken Harrelson, Bos.	1.50	3.00
☐ 10	Tommy Helms, Cin.	1.50	3.00
☐ 11	Willie Horton, Det.	1.50	3.00
☐ 12	Frank Howard, Wsh.	2.50	5.00
☐ 13	Juan Marichal, S.F.	3.50	7.00
☐ 14	Willie Mays, S.F.	12.50	25.00
☐ 15	Willie McCovey, S.F.	1.50	3.00
☐ 16	Denny McLain, Det.	2.50	5.00
☐ 17	John "Boog" Powell, Bal.	2.50	5.00
☐ 18	Brooks Robinson, Bal.	6.00	12.00
☐ 19	Ronald Santo, Chi.-N.L.	1.50	3.00
☐ 20	Rusty Staub, Mtl.	3.00	6.00
☐ 21	Mel Stottlemyre, NYY.	1.50	3.00
☐ 22	Luis Tiant, Cle.	1.50	3.00
☐ 23	Maurice Wills, Mtl.	2.50	5.00
☐ 24	Carl Yastrzemski, Bos.	5.00	10.00

1970 O-PEE-CHEE

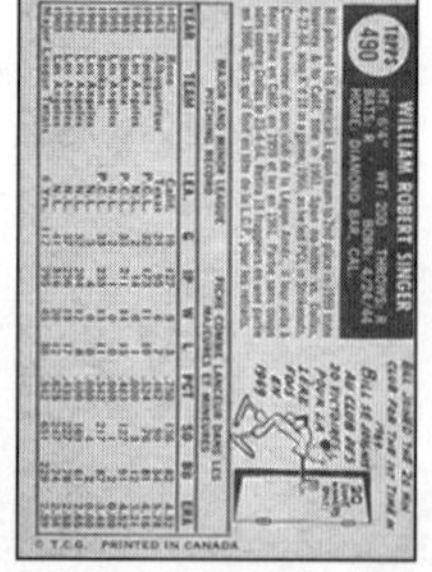

The cards in this set are identical to the first 546 cards in the 720-card Topps set for 1970. The Canadian cards can be distinguished from the Topps issue by the imprint "© T.C.G. PRINTED IN CANADA." In the Canadian issue, high-number commons are often difficult to find, particularly in higher grades.

Card Size: 2 1/2" x 3 1/2"
Face: Four colour, grey border; name, position, team
Back: Yellow and blue on card stock; name, number, résumé, bilingual, cartoon
Imprint: © T.C.G. PRINTED IN CANADA

Complete Set (546 cards):		**1,000.00**	**2,000.00**
Common Player (1 - 263):		**1.00**	**2.00**
Common Player (264 - 449):		**1.25**	**2.50**
Common Player (450 - 546):		**1.65**	**3.25**

No.	Player	EX	NRMT
☐ 1	World Champions: New York Mets	15.00	30.00
☐ 2	Diego Segui, Sea.	1.00	2.00
☐ 3	Darrel Chaney, Cin.	1.00	2.00
☐ 4	Tom Egan, Cal.	1.00	2.00
☐ 5	Wes Parker, L.A.	1.00	2.00
☐ 6	Grant Jackson, Pha.	1.00	2.00
☐ 7	Cle.: Gary Boyd/ Russ Nagelson	1.00	2.00
☐ **8**	**Jose Martinez, Pgh. RC**	**1.00**	**2.00**
☐ 9	Checklist 1st Series (1-132)	10.00	20.00
☐ 10	Carl Yastrzemski, Bos.	12.00	24.00
☐ 11	Nate Colbert, S.D.	1.00	2.00
☐ 12	John Hiller, Det.	1.50	3.00
☐ 13	Jack Hiatt, S.F.	1.00	2.00
☐ **14**	**Hank Allen, Wash., RC**	**1.00**	**2.00**
☐ 15	Larry Dierker, Hou.	1.00	2.00
☐ 16	Charlie Metro, Mgr., K.C.	1.00	2.00
☐ 17	Hoyt Wilhelm, Atl.	2.50	5.00
☐ 18	Rusty Staub (Mtl.)	3.00	6.00
☐ 19	John Boccabella, Mtl.	1.00	2.00
☐ 20	Dave McNally, Bal.	1.00	2.00
☐ **21**	**Oak.: Vida Blue/ Gene Tenace, RC**	**8.50**	**17.00**
☐ 22	Ray Washburn, Cin.	1.00	2.00
☐ 23	Bill Robinson, NYY.	1.00	2.00
☐ 24	Dick Selma, Pha.	1.00	2.00
☐ 25	Cesar Tovar, Min.	1.00	2.00
☐ 26	Tug McGraw, NYM.	1.00	2.00
☐ 27	Chuck Hinton, Cle.	1.00	2.00
☐ 28	Billy Wilson, Pha.	1.00	2.00
☐ 29	Sandy Alomar, Cal.	1.00	2.00
☐ 30	Matty Alou, Pgh.	1.00	2.00
☐ 31	Marty Pattin, Sea.	1.00	2.00
☐ 32	Harry Walker, Mgr., Hou.	1.00	2.00
☐ 33	Don Wert, Det.	1.00	2.00
☐ 34	Willie Crawford, L.A.	1.00	2.00
☐ 35	Joe Horlen, Chi.-A.L.	1.00	2.00
☐ 36	Cin.: Danny Breeden/ Bernie Carbo	1.00	2.00
☐ 37	Dick Drago, K.C.	1.00	2.00
☐ 38	Mack Jones, Mtl.	1.00	2.00
☐ **39**	**Mike Nagy, Bos., RC**	**1.00**	**2.00**
☐ 40	Rich Allen, Stl.	1.50	3.00
☐ 41	George Lauzerique, Oak.	1.00	2.00
☐ 42	Tito Fuentes, S.F.	1.00	2.00
☐ 43	Jack Aker, NYY.	1.00	2.00
☐ 44	Roberto Pena, S.D.	1.00	2.00
☐ 45	Dave Johnson, Bal.	1.00	2.00
☐ **46**	**Ken Rudolph, Chi.-N.L., RC**	**1.00**	**2.00**
☐ 47	Bob Miller, Min.	1.00	2.00
☐ 48	Gil Garrido, Atl.	1.00	2.00
☐ **49**	**Tim Cullen, Wash., RC**	**1.00**	**2.00**
☐ 50	Tommie Agee, NYM.	1.00	2.00
☐ **51**	**Bob Christian, Chi.-A.L., RC**	**1.00**	**2.00**
☐ 52	Bruce Dal Canton, Pgh.	1.00	2.00
☐ 53	John Kennedy, Sea.	1.00	2.00
☐ 54	Jeff Torborg, L.A.	1.00	2.00
☐ 55	John Odom, Oak.	1.00	2.00
☐ 56	Pha.: Joe Lis/ Scott Reid	1.00	2.00
☐ 57	Pat Kelly, K.C.	1.00	2.00

	#	Card		
☐	58	Dave Marshall, S.F.	1.00	2.00
☐	59	Dick Ellsworth, Cle.	1.00	2.00
☐	60	Jim Wynn, Hou.	1.00	2.00
☐	61	LL: P. Rose/ Roberto Clemente/ C. Jones	7.50	15.00
☐	62	LL: R. Carew/ R. Smith/ T. Oliva	2.50	5.00
☐	63	LL: W. McCovey/ R. Santo/ T. Perez	2.50	5.00
☐	64	LL: H. Killebrew/ B. Powell/ R. Jackson	4.50	9.00
☐	65	LL: W. McCovey/ H. Aaron/ L. May	4.50	9.00
☐	66	LL: H. Killebrew/ F. Howard/ R. Jackson	4.50	9.00
☐	67	LL: J. Marichal/ Steve Carlton/ B. Gibson	4.00	8.00
☐	68	LL: D. Bosman/ J. Palmer/ M. Cuellar	2.50	5.00
☐	69	LL: T. Seaver,/ P. Niekro/ F. Jenkins, / J. Marichal	4.00	8.00
☐	70	LL: D. McLain/ M. Cuellar/ D. Boswell / D. McNally/ J. Perry/ M. Stottlemyre	2.00	4.00
☐	71	LL: F. Jenkins/ B. Gibson/ B. Singer	4.00	8.00
☐	72	LL: S. McDowell/ M. Lolich/ A. Messersmith	2.00	4.00
☐	73	Wayne Granger, Cin.	1.00	2.00
☐	74	Ana.: Greg Washburn/ Wally Wolf	1.00	2.00
☐	75	Jim Kaat, Min.	1.50	3.00
☐	76	Carl Taylor, Stl.	1.00	2.00
☐	77	Frank Linzy, S.F.	1.00	2.00
☐	78	Joe Lahoud, Bos.	1.00	2.00
☐	79	Clay Kirby, S.D.	1.00	2.00
☐	80	Don Kessinger, Chi.-N.L.	1.00	2.00
☐	81	Dave May, Bal.	1.00	2.00
☐	82	Frank Fernandez, NYY.	1.00	2.00
☐	83	Don Cardwell, NYM.	1.00	2.00
☐	84	Paul Casanova, Wsh.	1.00	2.00
☐	85	Max Alvis, Cle.	1.00	2.00
☐	86	Lum Harris, Mgr., Atl.	1.00	2.00
☐	**87**	**Steve Renko, Mtl., RC**	**1.00**	**2.00**
☐	88	Sea.: Miguel Fuentes/ Dick Baney	1.00	2.00
☐	89	Juan Rios, K.C.	1.00	2.00
☐	90	Tim McCarver, Pha.	1.50	3.00
☐	91	Rich Morales, Chi.-A.L.	1.00	2.00
☐	92	George Culver, Stl.	1.00	2.00
☐	93	Rick Renick, Min.	1.00	2.00
☐	94	Fred Patek, Pgh.	1.00	2.00
☐	95	Earl Wilson, Det.	1.00	2.00
☐	96	Leron Lee/ Jerry Reuss	2.00	4.00
☐	97	Joe Moeller, L.A.	1.00	2.00
☐	98	Gates Brown, Det.	1.00	2.00
☐	**99**	**Bobby Pfeil, NYM., RC**	**1.00**	**2.00**
☐	100	Mel Stottlemyre, NYY.	1.00	2.00
☐	101	Bobby Floyd, Bal.	1.00	2.00
☐	102	Joe Rudi, Oak.	1.00	2.00
☐	103	Frank Reberger, S.D.	1.00	2.00
☐	104	Gerry Moses, Bos.	1.00	2.00
☐	105	Tony Gonzalez, Atl.	1.00	2.00
☐	106	Darold Knowles, Wsh.	1.00	2.00
☐	107	Bobby Etheridge, S.F.	1.00	2.00
☐	108	Tom Burgmeier, K.C.	1.00	2.00
☐	109	Mtl.: Garry Jestadt/ Carl Morton	1.00	2.00
☐	110	Bob Moose, Pgh.	1.00	2.00
☐	111	Mike Hegan, Sea.	1.00	2.00
☐	112	Dave Nelson, Cle.	1.00	2.00
☐	113	Jim Ray, Hou.	1.00	2.00
☐	114	Gene Michael, NYY.	1.00	2.00
☐	115	Alex Johnson, Cin.	1.00	2.00
☐	116	Sparky Lyle, Bos.	1.00	2.00
☐	**117**	**Don Young, Chi.-N.L., RC**	**1.00**	**2.00**
☐	118	George Mitterwald, Min.	1.00	2.00
☐	**119**	**Chuck Taylor, Stl., RC**	**1.00**	**2.00**
☐	120	Sal Bando, Oak.	1.00	2.00
☐	121	Bal.: Fred Beene/ Terry Crowley	1.00	2.00
☐	122	George Stone, Atl.	1.00	2.00
☐	123	Don Gutteridge, Mgr., Chi.-A.L.	1.00	2.00
☐	124	Larry Jaster, Mtl.	1.00	2.00
☐	125	Deron Johnson, Pha.	1.00	2.00
☐	126	Marty Martinez, Hou.	1.00	2.00
☐	127	Joe Coleman, Wsh.	1.00	2.00
☐	128	Checklist 2nd Series (133-263)	5.00	10.00
☐	129	Jimmie Price, Det.	1.00	2.00
☐	130	Ollie Brown, S.D.	1.00	2.00
☐	131	L.A.: Ray Lamb/ Bob Stinson	1.00	2.00
☐	132	Jim McGlothlin, Cal.	1.00	2.00
☐	133	Clay Carroll, Cin.	1.00	2.00
☐	**134**	**Danny Walton, Sea., RC**	**1.00**	**2.00**
☐	135	Dick Dietz, S.F.	1.00	2.00
☐	136	Steve Hargan, Cle.	1.00	2.00
☐	137	Art Shamsky, NYM.	1.00	2.00
☐	138	Joe Foy, NYM.	1.00	2.00
☐	139	Rich Nye, Stl.	1.00	2.00
☐	140	Reggie Jackson, Oak.	50.00	100.00
☐	141	Pgh.: Dave Cash/ Johnny Jeter	1.00	2.00
☐	142	Fritz Peterson, NYY.	1.00	2.00
☐	143	Phil Gagliano, Stl.	1.00	2.00
☐	144	Ray Culp, Bos.	1.00	2.00
☐	145	Rico Carty, Atl.	1.00	2.00
☐	146	Danny Murphy, Chi.-A.L.	1.00	2.00
☐	**147**	**Angel Hermoso, Mon., RC**	**1.00**	**2.00**
☐	148	Earl Weaver, Mgr., Bal.	3.75	7.50
☐	**149**	**Billy Champion, Phi., RC**	**1.00**	**2.00**
☐	150	Harmon Killebrew, Min.	7.00	14.00
☐	151	Dave Roberts, S.D.	1.00	2.00
☐	**152**	**Ike Brown, Det., RC**	**1.00**	**2.00**
☐	153	Gary Gentry, NYM.	1.00	2.00
☐	154	Wsh.: Jim Miles/ Jan Dukes	1.00	2.00
☐	155	Denis Menke, Hou.	1.00	2.00
☐	156	Eddie Fisher, Cal.	1.00	2.00
☐	157	Manny Mota, L.A.	1.50	3.00
☐	158	Jerry McNertney, Sea.	1.00	2.00
☐	159	Tommy Helms, Cin.	1.00	2.00
☐	160	Phil Niekro, Atl.	4.00	8.00
☐	161	Richie Scheinblum, Cle.	1.00	2.00
☐	**162**	**Jerry Johnson, St.L., RC**	**1.00**	**2.00**
☐	163	Syd O'Brien, Bos.	1.00	2.00
☐	164	Ty Cline, Mtl.	1.00	2.00
☐	165	Ed Kirkpatrick, K.C.	1.00	2.00
☐	166	Al Oliver, Pgh.	2.00	4.00
☐	167	Bill Burbach, NYY.	1.00	2.00
☐	**168**	**Dave Watkins, Phi., RC**	**1.00**	**2.00**
☐	169	Tom Hall, Min.	1.00	2.00
☐	170	Billy Williams, Chi.-N.L.	3.50	7.00
☐	171	Jim Nash, Atl.	1.00	2.00
☐	172	Atl.: Garry Hill/ Ralph Garr	1.00	2.00
☐	173	Jim Hicks, Cal.	1.00	2.00
☐	174	Ted Sizemore, L.A.	1.00	2.00
☐	175	Dick Bosman, Wsh.	1.00	2.00
☐	176	Jim Hart, S.F.	1.00	2.00
☐	177	Jim Northrup, Det.	1.00	2.00
☐	178	Denny Lemaster, Hou.	1.00	2.00
☐	179	Ivan Murrell, S.D.	1.00	2.00
☐	180	Tommy John, Chi.-A.L.	2.00	4.00
☐	181	Sparky Anderson, Mgr., Cin.	2.50	5.00
☐	182	Dick Hall, Bal.	1.00	2.00
☐	183	Jerry Grote, NYM.	1.00	2.00
☐	184	Ray Fosse, Cle.	1.00	2.00
☐	185	Don Mincher, Sea.	1.00	2.00
☐	186	Rick Joseph, Pha.	1.00	2.00
☐	187	Mike Hedlund, K.C.	1.00	2.00
☐	188	Manny Sanguillen, Pgh.	1.00	2.00
☐	189	NYY.: Thurman Munson/ Dave McDonald	37.50	75.00
☐	190	Joe Torre, Stl.	2.00	4.00
☐	191	Vicente Romo, Bos.	1.00	2.00
☐	192	Jim Qualls, Chi.-N.L.	1.00	2.00
☐	193	Mike Wegener, Mtl.	1.00	2.00

	No.	Player		
☐	194	Chuck Manuel, Min.	1.00	2.00
☐	195	NLCS-Game 1: Seaver Wins Opener!	10.00	20.00
☐	196	NLCS-Game 2: Mets Show Muscle!	2.50	5.00
☐	197	NLCS-Game 3: Ryan Saves The Day!	22.50	45.00
☐	198	Mets Celebrate: We're Number One!	12.00	24.00
☐	199	ALCS-Game 1: Orioles Win A Squeaker!	2.50	5.00
☐	200	ALCS-Game 2: Powell Scores Winning Run!	2.50	5.00
☐	201	ALCS-Game 3: Birds Wrap It Up!	2.50	5.00
☐	202	Orioles Celebrate: Sweep Twins In Three!	2.50	5.00
☐	203	Rudy May, Cal.	1.00	2.00
☐	204	Len Gabrielson, L.A.	1.00	2.00
☐	205	Bert Campaneris, Oak.	1.00	2.00
☐	206	Clete Boyer, Atl.	1.00	2.00
☐	207	Det.: Norman McRae/ Bob Reed	1.00	2.00
☐	208	Fred Gladding, Hou.	1.00	2.00
☐	209	Ken Suarez, Cle.	1.00	2.00
☐	210	Juan Marichal, S.F.	3.00	6.00
☐	211	Ted Williams, Mgr., Wsh.	9.00	18.00
☐	212	Al Santorini, S.D.	1.00	2.00
☐	213	Andy Etchebarren, Bal.	1.00	2.00
☐	214	Ken Boswell, NYM.	1.00	2.00
☐	215	Reggie Smith, Bos.	1.00	2.00
☐	216	Chuck Hartenstein, Pgh.	1.00	2.00
☐	217	Ron Hansen, Chi.-A.L.	1.00	2.00
☐	218	Ron Stone, Pha.	1.00	2.00
☐	219	Jerry Kenney, NYY.	1.00	2.00
☐	220	Steve Carlton, Stl.	12.50	25.00
☐	221	Ron Brand, Mtl.	1.00	2.00
☐	222	Jim Rooker, K.C.	1.00	2.00
☐	223	Nate Oliver, Chi.-N.L.	1.00	2.00
☐	224	Steve Barber, Sea.	1.00	2.00
☐	225	Lee May, Cin.	1.00	2.00
☐	226	Ron Perranoski, Min.	1.00	2.00
☐	**227**	**Hou.: John Mayberry/ Bob Watkins (RCs)**	**2.00**	**4.00**
☐	228	Aurelio Rodriguez, Cal.	1.00	2.00
☐	229	Rich Robertson, S.F.	1.00	2.00
☐	230	Brooks Robinson, Bal.	10.00	20.00
☐	231	Luis Tiant, Min.	1.00	2.00
☐	232	Bob Didier, Atl.	1.00	2.00
☐	233	Lew Krausse, Oak.	1.00	2.00
☐	234	Tommy Dean, S.D.	1.00	2.00
☐	235	Mike Epstein, Wsh.	1.00	2.00
☐	236	Bob Veale, Pgh.	1.00	2.00
☐	237	Russ Gibson, Bos.	1.00	2.00
☐	238	Jose Laboy, Mtl.	1.00	2.00
☐	239	Ken Berry, Chi.-A.L.	1.00	2.00
☐	240	Fergie Jenkins, Chi.-N.L.	6.00	12.00
☐	241	K.C.: Al Fitzmorris/ Scott Northey	1.00	2.00
☐	242	Walter Alston, Mgr., L.A.	2.00	4.00
☐	243	Joe Sparma, Mtl.	1.00	2.00
☐	244	Checklist 3rd Series (264 - 372)	5.00	10.00
☐	245	Leo Cardenas, Min.	1.00	2.00
☐	246	Jim McAndrew, NYM.	1.00	2.00
☐	247	Lou Klimchock, Cle.	1.00	2.00
☐	248	Jesus Alou, Hou.	1.00	2.00
☐	249	Bob Locker, Sea.	1.00	2.00
☐	250	Willie McCovey, S.F.	7.50	15.00
☐	251	Dick Schofield, Bos.	1.00	2.00
☐	**252**	**Lowell Palmer, Phi., RC**	**1.00**	**2.00**
☐	253	Ron Woods, NYY.	1.00	2.00
☐	254	Camilo Pascual, Cin.	1.00	2.00
☐	**255**	**Jim Spencer, Cal., RC**	**1.00**	**2.00**
☐	256	Vic Davalillo, Stl.	1.00	2.00
☐	257	Dennis Higgins, Cle.	1.00	2.00
☐	258	Paul Popovich, Chi.-N.L.	1.00	2.00
☐	259	Tommie Reynolds, Oak.	1.00	2.00
☐	260	Claude Osteen, L.A.	1.00	2.00
☐	261	Curt Motton, Bal.	1.00	2.00
☐	262	S.D.: Jerry Morales/ Jim Williams	1.00	2.00

	No.	Player		
☐	263	Duane Josephson, Chi.-A.L.	1.00	2.00
☐	264	Rich Hebner, Pgh.	1.00	2.00
☐	265	Randy Hundley, Chi.-N.L.	1.25	2.50
☐	266	Wally Bunker, K.C.	1.25	2.50
☐	267	Min.: Herman Hill/ Paul Ratliff	1.25	2.50
☐	268	Claude Raymond, Mtl.	2.00	4.00
☐	269	Cesar Gutierrez, Det.	1.25	2.50
☐	270	Chris Short, Pha.	1.25	2.50
☐	271	Greg Goossen, Sea.	1.25	2.50
☐	272	Hector Torres, Hou.	1.25	2.50
☐	273	Ralph Houk, Mgr., NYY.	2.00	4.00
☐	274	Gerry Arrigo, Chi.-A.L.	1.25	2.50
☐	275	Duke Sims, Cle.	1.25	2.50
☐	276	Ron Hunt, S.F.	1.25	2.50
☐	**277**	**Paul Doyle, Cal., RC**	**1.25**	**2.50**
☐	278	Tommie Aaron, Atl.	1.25	2.50
☐	**279**	**Bill Lee, Bos., RC**	**3.00**	**6.00**
☐	280	Donn Clendenon, NYM.	1.25	2.50
☐	281	Casey Cox, Wsh.	1.25	2.50
☐	**282**	**Steve Huntz, St.L., RC**	**1.25**	**2.50**
☐	**283**	**Angel Bravo, Cin., RC**	**1.25**	**2.50**
☐	284	Jack Baldschun, S.D.	1.25	2.50
☐	285	Paul Blair, Bal.	1.25	2.50
☐	286	L.A.: Jack Jenkins/ Bill Buckner	4.50	9.00
☐	287	Fred Talbot, Oak.	1.25	2.50
☐	288	Larry Hisle, Pha.	1.25	2.50
☐	289	Gene Brabender, Sea.	1.25	2.50
☐	290	Rod Carew, Min.	15.00	30.00
☐	291	Leo Durocher, Mgr., Chi.-N.L.	2.50	5.00
☐	**292**	**Eddie Leon, Cle., RC**	**1.25**	**2.50**
☐	293	Bob Bailey, Mtl.	1.25	2.50
☐	294	Jose Azcue, Cal.	1.25	2.50
☐	295	Cecil Upshaw, Atl.	1.25	2.50
☐	296	Woody Woodward, Cin.	1.25	2.50
☐	297	Curt Blefary, NYY.	1.25	2.50
☐	298	Ken Henderson, S.F.	1.25	2.50
☐	299	Buddy Bradford, Chi.-A.L.	1.25	2.50
☐	300	Tom Seaver, NYM.	32.50	65.00
☐	301	Chico Salmon, Bal.	1.25	2.50
☐	302	Jeff James, Pha.	1.25	2.50
☐	303	Brant Alyea, Wsh.	1.25	2.50
☐	**304**	**Bill Russell, L.A., RC**	**4.00**	**8.00**
☐	305	WS-Game 1: Buford Belts Leadoff Homer!	2.50	5.00
☐	306	WS-Game 2: Clendenon's Hr Breaks Ice!	2.50	5.00
☐	307	WS-Game 3: Agee's Catch Saves The Day!	2.50	5.00
☐	308	WS-Game 4: Martin's Bunt Ends Deadlock!	2.50	5.00
☐	309	WS-Game 5: Koosman Shuts The Door!	2.50	5.00
☐	310	Mets Whoop It Up!	5.00	10.00
☐	311	Dick Green, Oak.	1.25	2.50
☐	312	Mike Torrez, Stl.	1.25	2.50
☐	313	Mayo Smith, Mgr., Det.	1.25	2.50
☐	314	Bill McCool, S.D.	1.25	2.50
☐	315	Luis Aparicio, Chi.-A.L.	2.50	54.00
☐	316	Skip Guinn, Hou.	1.25	2.50
☐	317	Bos.: Billy Conigliario; Luis Alvarado	1.25	2.50
☐	318	Willie Smith, Chi.-N.L.	1.25	2.50
☐	319	Clayton Dalrymple, Bal.	1.25	2.50
☐	320	Jim Maloney, Cin.	1.25	2.50
☐	321	Lou Piniella, K.C.	1.25	2.50
☐	322	Luke Walker, Pgh.	1.25	2.50
☐	323	Wayne Comer, Sea.	1.25	2.50
☐	324	Tony Taylor, Pha.	1.25	2.50
☐	325	Dave Boswell, Min.	1.25	2.50
☐	**326**	**Bill Voss, Cal., RC**	**1.25**	**2.50**
☐	**327**	**Hal King, Atl., RC**	**1.25**	**2.50**
☐	328	George Brunet, Wsh.	1.25	2.50
☐	329	Chris Cannizzaro, S.D.	1.25	2.50
☐	330	Lou Brock, Stl.	7.50	15.00
☐	331	Chuck Dobson, Oak.	1.25	2.50

	No.	Player		
☐	332	Bobby Wine, Mtl.	1.25	2.50
☐	333	Bobby Murcer, NYY.	1.25	2.50
☐	334	Phil Regan, Chi.-N.L.	1.25	2.50
☐	335	Bill Freehan, Det.	1.25	2.50
☐	336	Del Unser, Wsh.	1.25	2.50
☐	337	Mike McCormick, S.F.	1.25	2.50
☐	338	Paul Schaal, K.C.	1.25	2.50
☐	339	Johnny Edwards, Hou.	1.25	2.50
☐	340	Tony Conigliaro, Bos.	2.50	5.00
☐	341	Bill Sudakis, L.A.	1.25	2.50
☐	342	Wilbur Wood, Chi.-A.L.	1.25	2.50
☐	343	Checklist 4th Series (373 - 459)	5.00	10.00
☐	344	Marcelino Lopez, Bal.	1.25	2.50
☐	345	Al Ferrara, S.D.	1.25	2.50
☐	346	Red Schoendienst, Mgr., Stl.	2.00	4.00
☐	347	Russ Snyder, Cle.	1.25	2.50
☐	348	NYM.: Mike Jorgensen/ Jesse Hudson	1.25	2.50
☐	349	Steve Hamilton, NYY.	1.25	2.50
☐	350	Roberto Clemente, Pgh.	50.00	100.00
☐	351	Tom Murphy, Cal.	1.25	2.50
☐	352	Bob Barton, S.D.	1.25	2.50
☐	353	Stan Williams, Min.	1.25	2.50
☐	354	Amos Otis, K.C.	1.25	2.50
☐	355	Doug Rader, Hou.	1.25	2.50
☐	356	Fred Lasher, Det.	1.25	2.50
☐	357	Bob Burda, S.F.	1.25	2.50
☐	**358**	**Pedro Borbon, Cin., RC**	**1.25**	**2.50**
☐	359	Phil Roof, Sea.	1.25	2.50
☐	360	Curt Flood, Pha.	2.00	4.00
☐	361	Ray Jarvis, Bos.	1.25	2.50
☐	362	Joe Hague, Stl.	1.25	2.50
☐	**363**	**Tom Shopay, Bal., RC**	**1.25**	**2.50**
☐	364	Dan McGinn, Mtl.	1.25	2.50
☐	365	Zoilo Versalles, Wsh.	1.25	2.50
☐	366	Barry Moore, Cle.	1.25	2.50
☐	367	Mike Lum, Atl.	1.25	2.50
☐	368	Ed Herrmann, Chi.-A.L.	1.25	2.50
☐	369	Alan Foster, L.A.	1.25	2.50
☐	370	Tommy Harper, Sea.	1.25	2.50
☐	**371**	**Rod Gasper, NYM., RC**	**1.25**	**2.50**
☐	372	Dave Giusti, Pgh.	1.25	2.50
☐	373	Roy White, NYY.	1.25	2.50
☐	374	Tommie Sisk, S.D.	1.25	2.50
☐	375	Johnny Callison, Chi.-N.L.	1.25	2.50
☐	376	Lefty Phillips, Mgr., Cal.	1.25	2.50
☐	377	Bill Butler, K.C.	1.25	2.50
☐	378	Jim Davenport, S.F.	1.25	2.50
☐	**379**	**Tom Tischinski, Min., RC**	**1.25**	**2.50**
☐	380	Tony Perez, Cin.	2.50	5.00
☐	381	Oak.: Bobby Brooks/ Mike Olivo	1.25	2.50
☐	**382**	**Jack DiLauro, Hou., RC**	**1.25**	**2.50**
☐	383	Mickey Stanley, Det.	1.25	2.50
☐	384	Gary Neibauer, Atl.	1.25	2.50
☐	385	George Scott, Bos.	1.25	2.50
☐	386	Bill Dillman, Stl.	1.25	2.50
☐	387	Baltimore Orioles	2.50	5.00
☐	**388**	**Byron Browne, Pha., RC**	**1.25**	**2.50**
☐	389	Jim Shellenback, Wsh.	1.25	2.50
☐	390	Willie Davis, L.A.	1.25	2.50
☐	391	Larry Brown, Cle.	1.25	2.50
☐	392	Walt Hriniak, S.D.	1.25	2.50
☐	393	John Gelnar, Sea.	1.25	2.50
☐	394	Gil Hodges, Mgr., NYM.	2.50	5.00
☐	395	Walt Williams, Chi.-A.L.	1.25	2.50
☐	396	Steve Blass, Pgh.	1.25	2.50
☐	397	Roger Repoz, Cal.	1.25	2.50
☐	398	Bill Stoneman, Mtl.	1.25	2.50
☐	399	New York Yankees	2.00	4.00
☐	400	Denny McLain, Det.	2.00	4.00
☐	401	S.F.: John Harrell/ Bernie Williams	1.25	2.50
☐	402	Ellie Rodriguez, K.C.	1.25	2.50
☐	403	Jim Bunning, Pha.	3.50	7.00
☐	404	Rich Reese, Min.	1.25	2.50
☐	405	Bill Hands, Chi.-N.L.	1.25	2.50
☐	406	Mike Andrews, Bos.	1.25	2.50
☐	407	Bob Watson, Hou.	1.25	2.50
☐	408	Paul Lindblad, Oak.	1.25	2.50
☐	409	Bob Tolan, Cin.	1.25	2.50
☐	410	Boog Powell, Bal.	2.00	4.00
☐	411	Los Angeles Dodgers	2.00	4.00
☐	412	Larry Burchart, Cle.	1.25	2.50
☐	413	Sonny Jackson, Atl.	1.25	2.50
☐	**414**	**Paul Edmondson, Chi.-A.L., RC**	**1.25**	**2.50**
☐	415	Julian Javier, Stl.	1.25	2.50
☐	416	Joe Verbanic, NYY.	1.25	2.50
☐	417	John Bateman, Mtl.	1.25	2.50
☐	418	John Donaldson, Sea.	1.25	2.50
☐	419	Ron Taylor, NYM.	2.00	4.00
☐	420	Ken McMullen, Wsh.	1.25	2.50
☐	421	Pat Dobson, S.D.	1.25	2.50
☐	422	Kansas City Royals	2.00	4.00
☐	423	Jerry May, Pgh.	1.25	2.50
☐	424	Mike Kilkenny, Det.	2.00	4.00
☐	425	Bobby Bonds, S.F.	2.50	5.00
☐	426	Bill Rigney, Mgr., Min.	1.25	2.50
☐	427	Fred Norman, L.A.	1.25	2.50
☐	428	Don Buford, Bal.	1.25	2.50
☐	429	Chi.: Randy Bobb/ Jim Cosman	1.25	2.50
☐	430	Andy Messersmith, Cal.	1.25	2.50
☐	431	Ron Swoboda, NYM.	1.25	2.50
☐	432	Checklist 5th Series (460 - 546)	5.00	10.00
☐	**433**	**Ron Bryant, S.F., RC**	**1.25**	**2.50**
☐	434	Felipe Alou, Oak.	2.50	5.00
☐	435	Nelson Briles, Stl.	1.25	2.50
☐	436	Philadelphia Phillies	2.00	4.00
☐	437	Danny Cater, NYY.	1.25	2.50
☐	438	Pat Jarvis, Atl.	1.25	2.50
☐	439	Lee Maye, Wsh.	1.25	2.50
☐	440	Bill Mazeroski, Pgh.	2.00	4.00
☐	441	John O'Donoghue, Sea.	1.25	2.50
☐	442	Gene Mauch, Mgr., Mtl.	1.25	2.50
☐	443	Al Jackson, Cin.	1.25	2.50
☐	444	Chi.-A.L.: Billy Farmer/ John Matias	1.25	2.50
☐	445	Vada Pinson, Cle.	1.25	2.50
☐	**446**	**Billy Grabarkewitz, L.A., RC**	**1.25**	**2.50**
☐	447	Lee Stange, Bos.	1.25	2.50
☐	448	Houston Astros	2.50	4.00
☐	449	Jim Palmer, Bal.	12.00	24.00
☐	450	N.L.: Willie McCovey, S.F.	5.00	10.00
☐	451	A.L.: Boog Powell, Bal.	2.00	4.00
☐	452	N.L.: Felix Millan, Atl.	1.25	2.50
☐	453	A.L.: Rod Carew, Min.	6.00	12.00
☐	454	N.L.: Ron Santo, Chi.-N.L.	1.25	2.50
☐	455	A.L: Brooks Robinson, Bal.	4.00	8.00
☐	456	N.L.: Don Kessinger, Chi.-N.L.	1.25	2.50
☐	457	A.L.: Rico Petrocelli, Bos.	1.25	2.50
☐	458	N.L.: Pete Rose, Cin.	10.00	20.00
☐	459	A.L.: Reggie Jackson, Oak.	11.00	22.00
☐	460	N.L.: Matty Alou, Pgh.	1.75	3.25
☐	461	A.L.: Carl Yastrzemski, Bos.	7.50	15.00
☐	462	N.L.: Hank Aaron, Atl.	12.00	24.00
☐	463	A.L.: Frank Robinson, Bal.	5.00	10.00
☐	464	N.L.: Johnny Bench, Cin.	10.00	20.00
☐	465	A.L.: Bill Freehan, Det.	1.75	3.25
☐	466	N.L.: Juan Marichal, S.F.	2.50	5.00
☐	467	A.L.: Denny McLain, Det.	1.75	3.25
☐	468	N.L.: Jerry Koosman, NYM.	1.75	3.25
☐	469	A.L.: Sam McDowell, Cle.	1.75	3.25

	No.	Player	EX	NRMT
☐	470	Willie Stargell, Pgh.	7.50	15.00
☐	471	Chris Zachary, K.C.	1.75	3.25
☐	472	Atlanta Braves	2.50	5.00
☐	473	Don Bryant, Sea.	1.75	3.25
☐	474	Dick Kelley, S.D.	1.75	3.25
☐	475	Dick McAuliffe, Det.	1.75	3.25
☐	476	Don Shaw, Mtl.	1.75	3.25
☐	477	Bal.: Al Severinson/ Roger Freed	1.75	3.25
☐	478	Bob Heise, S.F.	1.75	3.25
☐	**479**	**Dick Woodson, Min., RC**	**1.75**	**3.25**
☐	480	Glenn Beckert, Chi.-N.L.	1.75	3.25
☐	481	Jose Tartabull, Oak.	1.75	3.25
☐	**482**	**Tom Hilgendorf, Stl., RC**	**1.75**	**3.25**
☐	**483**	**Gail Hopkins, Chi.-A.L., RC**	**1.75**	**3.25**
☐	484	Gary Nolan, Cin.	1.75	3.25
☐	485	Jay Johnstone, Cal.	1.75	3.25
☐	486	Terry Harmon, Pha.	1.75	3.25
☐	487	Cisco Carlos, Wsh.	1.75	3.25
☐	488	J.C. Martin, NYM.	1.75	3.25
☐	489	Eddie Kasko, Mgr., Bos.	1.75	3.25
☐	490	Bill Singer, L.A.	1.75	3.25
☐	491	Graig Nettles, Cle.	2.50	5.00
☐	492	Hou.: Keith Lampard/ Scipio Spinks	1.75	3.25
☐	493	Lindy McDaniel, NYY.	1.75	3.25
☐	494	Larry Stahl, S.D.	1.75	3.25
☐	495	Dave Morehead, K.C.	1.75	3.25
☐	496	Steve Whitaker, S.F.	1.75	3.25
☐	497	Eddie Watt, Bal.	1.75	3.25
☐	498	Al Weis, NYM.	1.75	3.25
☐	499	Skip Lockwood, Sea.	1.75	3.25
☐	500	Hank Aaron, Atl.	45.00	90.00
☐	501	Chicago White Sox	2.50	5.00
☐	502	Rollie Fingers, Oak.	7.50	15.00
☐	503	Dal Maxvill, Stl.	1.75	3.25
☐	504	Don Pavletich, Bos.	1.75	3.25
☐	505	Ken Holtzman, Chi.-N.L.	1.75	3.25
☐	506	Ed Stroud, Wsh.	1.75	3.25
☐	507	Pat Corrales, Cin.	1.75	3.25
☐	508	Joe Niekro, Det.	1.75	3.25
☐	509	Montreal Expos	2.50	5.00
☐	510	Tony Oliva, Min.	2.50	5.00
☐	511	Joe Hoerner, Pha.	1.75	3.25
☐	**512**	**Billy Harris, K.C., RC**	**1.75**	**3.25**
☐	513	Preston Gomez, Mgr., S.D.	1.75	3.25
☐	**514**	**Steve Hovley, Sea., RC**	**1.75**	**3.25**
☐	515	Don Wilson, Hou.	1.75	3.25
☐	516	NYY.: John Ellis/ Jim Lyttle	1.75	3.25
☐	517	Joe Gibbon, Pgh.	1.75	3.25
☐	518	Bill Melton, Chi.-A.L.	1.75	3.25
☐	519	Don McMahon, S.F.	1.75	3.25
☐	520	Willie Horton, Det.	1.75	3.25
☐	521	Cal Koonce, NYM.	1.75	3.25
☐	522	California Angels	2.50	5.00
☐	523	Jose Pena, L.A.	1.75	3.25
☐	524	Alvin Dark, Mgr., Cle.	1.75	3.25
☐	525	Jerry Adair, K.C.	1.75	3.25
☐	526	Ron Herbel, S.D.	1.75	3.25
☐	527	Don Bosch, Mtl.	1.75	3.25
☐	528	Elrod Hendricks, Bal.	1.75	3.25
☐	529	Bob Aspromonte, Atl.	1.75	3.25
☐	530	Bob Gibson, Stl.	10.00	20.00
☐	531	Ron Clark, Oak.	1.75	3.25
☐	532	Danny Murtaugh, Mgr., Pgh.	1.75	3.25
☐	**533**	**Buzz Stephen, Sea., RC**	**1.75**	**3.25**
☐	534	Minesota Twins	2.50	5.00
☐	535	Andy Kosco, L.A.	1.75	3.25
☐	536	Mike Kekich, NYY.	1.75	3.25
☐	537	Joe Morgan, Hou.	7.50	15.00
☐	538	Bob Humphreys, Wsh.	1.75	3.25
☐	539	Pha.: Dennis Doyle/ Larry Bowa (R)	2.50	5.00
☐	540	Gary Peters, Bos.	1.75	3.25
☐	541	Bill Heath, Chi.-N.L.	1.75	3.25
☐	542	CheckList 6th Series (547 - 633)	6.00	12.00
☐	543	Clyde Wright, Cal.	1.75	3.25
☐	544	Cincinnati Reds	2.50	5.00
☐	545	Ken Harrelson, Cle.	1.75	3.25
☐	546	Ron Reed, Atl.	1.75	5.00

1970 O-PEE-CHEE BOOKLETS

This set consists of 24 booklets. Inserted in the wax packs of 1970, these booklets are identical to the Topps issue of the same year. The booklets give the player's autobiography in comic-book form.

Booklet Size: 2 1/2" x 3 1/2"
Face: Four colour on paper stock; name, number
Back: Four colour; checklist
Imprint: © T.C.G. PRINTED IN U.S.A.

Insert Set (24 booklets):			**25.00**	**50.00**
Common Player:			**1.00**	**2.00**
	No.	**Player**	**EX**	**NRMT**
☐	1	Mike Cueller, Bos.	1.00	2.00
☐	2	Rico Petrocelli, Bos.	1.00	2.00
☐	3	Jay Johnstone, Cal.	1.00	2.00
☐	4	Walt Williams, Chi.-A.L.	1.00	2.00
☐	5	Vada Pinson, Cle.	1.00	2.00
☐	6	Bill Freehan, Det.	1.00	2.00
☐	7	Wall Bunker, K.C.	1.00	2.00
☐	8	Tony Oliva, Min.	1.50	3.00
☐	9	Bobby Murcer, NYY.	1.00	2.00
☐	10	Reggie Jackson, Oak.	3.50	7.00
☐	11	Tommy Harper, Mil.	1.00	2.00
☐	12	Mike Epstein, Wsh.	1.00	2.00
☐	13	Orlando Cepeda, Atl.	1.50	3.00
☐	14	Ernie Banks, Chi.-N.L.	2.25	4.50
☐	15	Pete Rose, Cin.	3.50	7.00
☐	16	Denis Menke, Hou.	1.00	2.00
☐	17	Bill Singer, L.A.	1.00	2.00
☐	18	Rusty Staub, Mtl.	2.00	4.00
☐	19	Cleon Jones, NYM.	1.00	2.00
☐	20	Deron Johnson, Pha.	1.00	2.00
☐	21	Bob Moose, Pgh.	1.00	2.00
☐	22	Bob Gibson, Stl.	2.25	4.50
☐	23	Al Ferrara, S.D.	1.00	2.00
☐	24	Willie Mays, S.F.	5.00	10.00

1971 O-PEE-CHEE

This set is identical in number of cards and design to the 752 cards in the Topps set of the same year, but the cards bear the imprint "© T.C.G. PRINTED IN CANADA." It is difficult to find these cards of this set in NRMT to Mint condition due to the black borders that often peeled or chipped during the original trimming process at the printer. Accurate centering is also a problem. Because of these factors, cards in the higher grades often command substantial premiums over cards of lower grades.

Card Size: 2 1/2" x 3 1/2"

Face: Four colour, black border; name, position, team, facsimile autograph

Back: Yellow and black on card stock; name, number, resume, bilingual

Imprint: © T.C.G. PRINTED IN CANADA*

Complete Set (752 cards):	**1,500.00**	**3,000.00**
Common Player (1 - 393):	**1.25**	**2.50**
Common Player (394 - 523):	**1.75**	**3.75**
Common Player (524 - 643):	**3.25**	**6.50**
Common Player (644 - 752):	**6.00**	**12.00**

	No.	Player	EX	NRMT
☐	1	World Champions: Baltimore Orioles	12.50	25.00
☐	2	Dock Ellis, Pgh.	1.25	2.50
☐	3	Dick McAuliffe, Det.	1.25	2.50
☐	4	Vic Davalillo, Stl.	1.25	2.50
☐	5	Thurman Munson, NYY.	15.00	30.00
☐	6	Ed Spiezio, S.D.	1.25	2.50
☐	**7**	**Jim Holt, Min., RC**	**1.25**	**2.50**
☐	8	Mike McQueen, Atl.	1.25	2.50
☐	9	George Scott, Bos.	1.25	2.50
☐	10	Claude Osteen, L.A.	1.25	2.50
☐	**11**	**Elliott Maddox, Wsh., RC**	**1.25**	**2.50**
☐	12	Johnny Callison, Chi.-N.L.	1.25	2.50
☐	13	Chi.-A.L.: Charlie Brinkman/ Dick Moloney	1.25	2.50
☐	**14**	**Dave Concepcion, Cin., RC**	**12.50**	**25.00**
☐	15	Andy Messersmith, Cal.	1.25	2.50
☐	**16**	**Ken Singleton, NYM., RC**	**3.00**	**6.00**
☐	17	Bill Sorrell, K.C.	1.25	2.50
☐	18	Norm Miller, Hou.	1.25	2.50
☐	**19**	**Skip Pitlock, S.F., RC**	**1.25**	**2.50**
☐	20	Reggie Jackson, Oak.	22.50	45.00
☐	21	Dan McGinn, Mtl.	1.25	2.50
☐	22	Phil Roof, Mil.	1.25	2.50
☐	23	Oscar Gamble, Pha.	1.25	2.50
☐	**24**	**Rich Hand, Cle., RC**	**1.25**	**2.50**
☐	25	Clarence Gaston, S.D.	1.25	2.50
☐	**26**	**Bert Blyleven, Min., RC**	**5.00**	**10.00**
☐	27	Pgh.: Fred Cambria/ Gene Clines	1.25	2.50
☐	28	Ron Klimkowski, NYY.	1.25	2.50
☐	29	Don Buford, Bal.	1.25	2.50
☐	30	Phil Niekro, Atl.	3.50	7.00
☐	31	John Bateman, Mtl.	1.25	2.50
☐	**32**	**Jerry DeVanon, Stl. (Bal.), RC**	**1.25**	**2.50**
☐	33	Del Unser, Wsh.	1.25	2.50
☐	**34**	**Sandy Vance, L.A., RC**	**1.25**	**2.50**
☐	35	Lou Piniella, K.C.	1.25	2.50
☐	36	Dean Chance, NYM.	1.25	2.50
☐	**37**	**Rich McKinney, Chi.-A.L., RC**	**1.25**	**2.50**
☐	**38**	**Jim Colborn, Chi.-N.L., RC**	**1.25**	**2.50**
☐	39	Det.: Lerrin LaGrow/ Gene Lamont	1.25	2.50
☐	40	Lee May, Cin.	1.25	2.50
☐	**41**	**Rick Austin, Cle., RC**	**1.25**	**2.50**
☐	42	Boots Day, Mtl.	1.25	2.50
☐	43	Steve Kealey, Cal.	1.25	2.50
☐	44	Johnny Edwards, Hou.	1.25	2.50
☐	45	Jim Hunter, Oak.	5.50	11.00
☐	46	Dave Campbell, S.D.	1.25	2.50
☐	**47**	**Johnny Jeter, Pgh., RC**	**1.25**	**2.50**
☐	48	Dave Baldwin, Mil.	1.25	2.50
☐	49	Don Money, Pha.	1.25	2.50
☐	50	Willie McCovey, S.F.	7.50	15.00
☐	51	Steve Kline, NYY.	1.25	2.50
☐	52	Cal.: Oscar Brown/ Earl Williams	1.25	2.50
☐	53	Paul Blair, Bal.	1.25	2.50
☐	54	1st Series Checklist (1-132)	3.50	7.00
☐	55	Steve Carlton, Stl.	12.50	25.00
☐	56	Duane Josephson, Chi.-A.L.	1.25	2.50
☐	**57**	**Von Joshua, L.A., RC**	**1.25**	**2.50**
☐	58	Bill Lee, Bos.	2.00	4.00
☐	59	Gene Mauch, Mgr., Mtl.	1.25	2.50
☐	60	Dick Bosman, Wsh.	1.25	2.50
☐	61	LL: A. Johnson/ C. Yastrzemski/ T. Oliva	2.50	5.00
☐	62	LL: R. Carty/ Joe Torre/ M. Sanguillen	2.00	4.00
☐	63	LL: F. Howard,/ T.Conigliario/ B. Powell	2.00	4.00
☐	64	LL: J. Bench/ Tony Perez/ B. Williams	4.00	8.00
☐	65	LL: F. Howard/ Harmon Killebrew/ C. Yastrzemski	3.50	7.00
☐	66	LL: J. Bench/ B. Williams/ T. Perez	4.00	8.00
☐	67	LL: D. Segui/ J. Palmer/ C. Wright	3.00	6.00
☐	68	LL: T. Seaver/ W. Simpson/ L. Walker	3.00	6.00
☐	69	LL: M. Cuellar/ D. McNally/ J. Perry	2.00	4.00
☐	70	LL: B. Gibson/ G. Perry/ F. Jenkins	5.00	10.00
☐	71	LL: S. McDowell/ M. Lolich/ B. Johnson	2.00	4.00
☐	72	LL: T. Seaver/ B. Gibson/ F. Jenkins	5.00	10.00
☐	73	George Brunet, Stl.	1.25	2.50
☐	74	Min.: Pete Hamm/ Jim Nettles	1.25	2.50
☐	75	Gary Nolan, Cin.	1.25	2.50
☐	76	Ted Savage, Mil.	1.25	2.50
☐	**77**	**Mike Compton, Pha., RC**	**1.25**	**2.50**
☐	78	Jim Spencer, Cal.	1.25	2.50
☐	79	Wade Blasingame, Hou.	1.25	2.50
☐	80	Bill Melton, Chi.-A.L.	1.25	2.50
☐	81	Felix Millan, Atl.	1.25	2.50
☐	82	Casey Cox, Wsh.	1.25	2.50
☐	83	NYM.: Tim Foli/ Randy Bobb	1.25	2.50
☐	**84**	**Marcel Lachemann, Oak., RC**	**1.25**	**2.50**
☐	85	Billy Grabarkewitz, L.A.	1.25	2.50
☐	86	Mike Kilkenny, Det.	2.00	4.00
☐	**87**	**Jack Heidemann, Cle., RC**	**1.25**	**2.50**
☐	88	Hal King, Atl.	1.25	2.50
☐	89	Ken Brett, Bos.	1.25	2.50
☐	90	Joe Pepitone, Chi.-N.L.	1.25	2.50
☐	91	Bob Lemon, Mgr., K.C.	2.00	4.00
☐	92	Fred Wenz, Pha.	1.25	2.50
☐	93	Wsh.: Norm McRae/ Denny Riddleberger	1.25	2.50
☐	**94**	**Don Hahn, Mon., RC**	**1.25**	**2.50**
☐	95	Luis Tiant, Min.	1.25	2.50
☐	96	Joe Hague, Stl.	1.25	2.50
☐	97	Floyd Wicker, Mil.	1.25	2.50
☐	**98**	**Joe Decker, Chi.-N.L., RC**	**1.25**	**2.50**
☐	99	Mark Belanger, Bal.	1.25	2.50
☐	100	Pete Rose, Cin.	22.50	45.00
☐	101	Les Cain, Det.	1.25	2.50

	No.	Player		
☐	102	Hou.: Ken Forsch/ Larry Howard	1.25	2.50
☐	**103**	**Rich Severson, K.C., RC**	**1.25**	**2.50**
☐	104	Dan Frisella, NYM.	1.25	2.50
☐	105	Tony Conigliaro, Cal.	2.00	4.00
☐	106	Tom Dukes, S.D.	1.25	2.50
☐	**107**	**Roy Foster, Cle., RC**	**1.25**	**2.50**
☐	**108**	**John Cumberland, S.F., RC**	**1.25**	**2.50**
☐	109	Steve Hovley, Oak.	1.25	2.50
☐	110	Bill Mazeroski, Pgh.	2.00	4.00
☐	111	NYY.: Loyd Colson/ Bobby Mitchell	1.25	2.50
☐	112	Manny Mota, L.A.	1.25	2.50
☐	113	Jerry Crider, Chi.-A.L.	1.25	2.50
☐	**114**	**Billy Conigliaro, Bos., RC**	**1.25**	**2.50**
☐	115	Donn Clendenon, NYM.	1.25	2.50
☐	116	Ken Sanders, Mil.	1.25	2.50
☐	**117**	**Ted Simmons, Stl., RC**	**7.50**	**15.00**
☐	118	Cookie Rojas, K.C.	1.25	2.50
☐	119	Frank Lucchesi, Mgr., Pha.	1.25	2.50
☐	120	Willie Horton, Det.	1.25	2.50
☐	121	Chi.-N.L.: Jim Dunegan/ Roe Skidmore	1.25	2.50
☐	122	Eddie Watt, Bal.	1.25	2.50
☐	123	2nd Series Checklist (133-263)	3.50	7.00
☐	**124**	**Don Gullett, Cin., RC**	**1.25**	**2.50**
☐	125	Ray Fosse, Cle.	1.25	2.50
☐	126	Danny Coombs, S.D.	1.25	2.50
☐	**127**	**Danny Thompson, Min., RC**	**1.25**	**2.50**
☐	128	Frank Johnson, S.F.	1.25	2.50
☐	129	Aurelio Monteagudo, K.C.	1.25	2.50
☐	130	Denis Menke, Hou.	1.25	2.50
☐	131	Curt Blefary, NYY.	1.25	2.50
☐	132	Jose Laboy, Mtl.	1.25	2.50
☐	133	Mickey Lolich, Det.	1.25	2.50
☐	134	Jose Arcia, S.D.	1.25	2.50
☐	135	Rick Monday, Oak.	1.25	2.50
☐	136	Duffy Dyer, NYM.	1.25	2.50
☐	137	Marcelino Lopez, Bal.	1.25	2.50
☐	138	Pha.: Joe Lis/ Willie Montanez	1.25	2.50
☐	139	Paul Casanova, Wsh.	1.25	2.50
☐	140	Gaylord Perry, S.F.	6.00	12.00
☐	141	Frank Quilici, Min.	1.25	2.50
☐	142	Mack Jones, Mtl.	1.25	2.50
☐	143	Steve Blass, Pgh.	1.25	2.50
☐	144	Jackie Hernandez, K.C. (S.D.)	1.25	2.50
☐	145	Bill Singer, L.A.	1.25	2.50
☐	146	Ralph Houk, Mgr., NYY.	1.25	2.50
☐	147	Bob Priddy, Atl.	1.25	2.50
☐	148	John Mayberry, Hou.	1.25	2.50
☐	149	Mike Hershberger, Mil.	1.25	2.50
☐	150	Sam McDowell, Cle.	1.25	2.50
☐	151	Tommy Davis, Chi.-N.L. (Oak.)	1.25	2.50
☐	152	Ana.: Lloyd Allen/ Winston Llenas	1.25	2.50
☐	153	Gary Ross, S.D.	1.25	2.50
☐	154	Cesar Gutierrez, Det.	1.25	2.50
☐	155	Ken Henderson, S.F.	1.25	2.50
☐	156	Bart Johnson, Chi.-A.L.	1.25	2.50
☐	157	Bob Bailey, Mtl.	1.25	2.50
☐	158	Jerry Reuss, Stl.	1.25	2.50
☐	159	Jarvis Tatum, Bos.	1.25	2.50
☐	160	Tom Seaver, NYM.	15.00	30.00
☐	161	Ron Hunt, Mtl.	1.25	2.50
☐	162	Jack Billingham, Hou.	1.25	2.50
☐	163	Buck Martinez, K.C.	1.25	2.50
☐	164	Cin.: Frank Duffy/ Milt Wilcox	1.25	2.50
☐	165	Cesar Tovar, Min.	1.25	2.50
☐	166	Joe Hoerner, Pha.	1.25	2.50
☐	**167**	**Tom Grieve, Wsh., RC**	**2.00**	**4.00**
☐	168	Bruce Dal Canton, Pgh.	1.25	2.50
☐	169	Ed Herrmann, Chi.-A.L.	1.25	2.50
☐	170	Mike Cuellar, Bal.	1.25	2.50
☐	171	Bobby Wine, Mtl.	1.25	2.50
☐	172	Duke Sims, Chi.-N.L. (L.A.)	1.25	2.50
☐	173	Gil Garrido, Atl.	1.25	2.50
☐	**174**	**Dave LaRoche, Cal., RC**	**1.25**	**2.50**
☐	175	Jim Hickman, Chi.-N.L.	1.25	2.50
☐	176	Box.: Bob Montgomery/ Doug Griffin	1.25	2.50
☐	177	Hal McRae, Cin.	1.25	2.50
☐	178	Dave Duncan, Oak.	1.25	2.50
☐	179	Mike Corkins, S.D.	1.25	2.50
☐	180	Al Kaline, Det.	12.50	25.00
☐	181	Hal Lanier, S.F.	1.25	2.50
☐	182	Al Downing, Mil. (L.A.)	1.25	2.50
☐	183	Gil Hodges, Mgr., NYM.	2.00	4.00
☐	184	Stan Bahnsen, NYY.	1.25	2.50
☐	185	Julian Javier, Stl.	1.25	2.50
☐	**186**	**Bob Spence, Chi.-A.L., RC**	**1.25**	**2.50**
☐	187	Ted Abernathy, K.C.	1.25	2.50
☐	188	L.A.: Bob Valentine/ Mike Strahler	1.25	2.50
☐	189	George Mitterwald, Min.	1.25	2.50
☐	190	Bob Tolan, Cin.	1.25	2.50
☐	191	Mike Andrews, Chi.-A.L. (Chi.-A.L.)	1.25	2.50
☐	192	Billy Wilson, Pha.	1.25	2.50
☐	**193**	**Bob Grich, Bal., RC**	**2.00**	**4.00**
☐	194	Mike Lum, Atl.	1.25	2.50
☐	195	Game 1: Powell Muscles Twins!	2.50	5.00
☐	196	Game 2: McNally Makes It Two Straight!	2.50	5.00
☐	197	Game 3: Palmer Mows 'Em Down!	3.50	7.00
☐	198	Orioles Celebrate: A Team Effort!	2.50	5.00
☐	199	Game 1: Cline Pinch-Triple Decides It!	2.50	5.00
☐	200	Game 2: Tolan Scores For Third Time!	2.50	5.00
☐	201	Game 3: Cline Scores Winning Run!	2.50	5.00
☐	202	Claude Raymond, Mtl.	2.00	4.00
☐	**203**	**Larry Gura, Chi.-N.L., RC**	**1.25**	**2.50**
☐	204	Mil.: Bernie Smith/ George Kopacz	1.25	2.50
☐	205	Gerry Moses, Cal.	1.25	2.50
☐	206	3rd Series Checklist (264 - 393)	3.50	7.00
☐	207	Alan Foster, Cle. (Cle.)	1.25	2.50
☐	208	Billy Martin, Mgr., Det.	2.00	4.00
☐	209	Steve Renko, Mtl.	1.25	2.50
☐	210	Rod Carew, Min.	15.00	30.00
☐	**211**	**Phil Hennigan, Cle., RC**	**1.25**	**2.50**
☐	212	Rich Hebner, Pgh.	1.25	2.50
☐	213	Frank Baker, NYY.	1.25	2.50
☐	214	Al Ferrara, S.D.	1.25	2.50
☐	215	Diego Segui, Oak.	1.25	2.50
☐	216	Reggie Cleveland/ Luis Melendez	2.00	4.00
☐	217	Ed Stroud, Wsh.	1.25	2.50
☐	218	Tony Cloninger, Cin.	1.25	2.50
☐	219	Elrod Hendricks, Bal.	1.25	2.50
☐	220	Ron Santo, Chi.-N.L.	2.00	4.00
☐	221	Dave Morehead, K.C.	1.25	2.50
☐	222	Bob Watson, Hou.	1.25	2.50
☐	223	Cecil Upshaw, Atl.	1.25	2.50
☐	**224**	**Alan Gallagher, S.F., RC**	**1.25**	**2.50**
☐	225	Gary Peters, Bos.	1.25	2.50
☐	226	Bill Russell, L.A.	1.25	2.50
☐	227	Floyd Weaver, Chi.-A.L.	1.25	2.50
☐	228	Wayne Garrett, NYM.	1.25	2.50
☐	229	Jim Hannan, Det.	1.25	2.50
☐	230	Willie Stargell, Pgh.	6.00	12.00
☐	231	Cle.: Vince Colbert/ John Lowenstein	1.25	2.50
☐	**232**	**John Strohmayer, Mtl., RC**	**1.25**	**2.50**
☐	233	Larry Bowa, Pha.	1.25	2.50
☐	**234**	**Jim Lyttle, NYY., RC**	**1.25**	**2.50**
☐	235	Nate Colbert, S.D.	1.25	2.50
☐	236	Bob Humphreys, Mil.	1.25	2.50
☐	**237**	**Cesar Cedeno, Hou., RC**	**2.00**	**4.00**
☐	238	Chuck Dobson, Oak.	1.25	2.50
☐	239	Red Schoendienst, Mgr., Stl.	2.00	4.00

	No.	Card		
☐	240	Clyde Wright, Cal.	1.25	2.50
☐	241	Dave Nelson, Wsh.	1.25	2.50
☐	242	Jim Ray, Hou.	1.25	2.50
☐	243	Carlos May, Chi.-A.L.	1.25	2.50
☐	244	Bob Tillman, Atl.	1.25	2.50
☐	245	Jim Kaat, Min.	1.25	2.50
☐	246	Tony Taylor, Pha.	1.25	2.50
☐	247	K.C.: Jerry Cram/ Paul Splittorff	1.25	2.50
☐	**248**	**Hoyt Wilhelm, Atl., RC**	**3.00**	**6.00**
☐	249	Chico Salmon, Bal.	1.25	2.50
☐	250	Johnny Bench, Cin.	15.00	30.00
☐	251	Frank Reberger, S.F.	1.25	2.50
☐	252	Eddie Leon, Cle.	1.25	2.50
☐	253	Bill Sudakis, L.A.	1.25	2.50
☐	254	Cal Koonce, Bos.	1.25	2.50
☐	**255**	**Bob Robertson, Pgh., RC**	**1.25**	**2.50**
☐	256	Tony Gonzalez, Cal.	1.25	2.50
☐	257	Nelson Briles, Stl.	1.25	2.50
☐	258	Dick Green, Oak.	1.25	2.50
☐	259	Dave Marshall, NYM.	1.25	2.50
☐	260	Tommy Harper, Mil.	1.25	2.50
☐	261	Darold Knowles, Wsh.	1.25	2.50
☐	262	S.D.: Jim Williams/ Dave Robinson	1.25	2.50
☐	**263**	**John Ellis, NYY., RC**	**1.25**	**2.50**
☐	264	Joe Morgan, Hou.	6.00	12.00
☐	265	Jim Northrup, Det.	1.25	2.50
☐	266	Bill Stoneman, Mtl.	1.25	2.50
☐	267	Rich Morales, Chi.-A.L.	1.25	2.50
☐	268	Philadelphia Phillies	2.00	4.00
☐	269	Gail Hopkins, K.C.	1.25	2.50
☐	270	Rico Carty, Atl.	1.25	2.50
☐	271	Bill Zepp, Min.	1.25	2.50
☐	272	Tommy Helms, Cin.	1.25	2.50
☐	273	Pete Richert, Bal.	1.25	2.50
☐	274	Ron Slocum, S.D.	1.25	2.50
☐	275	Vada Pinson, Cle.	1.25	2.50
☐	276	S.F.: Mike Davison/ George Foster	5.00	10.00
☐	**277**	**Gary Waslewski, NYY., RC**	**1.25**	**2.50**
☐	278	Jerry Grote, NYM.	1.25	2.50
☐	279	Lefty Phillips, Mgr., Cal.	1.25	2.50
☐	280	Fergie Jenkins, Chi.-N.L.	6.00	12.00
☐	281	Danny Walton, Mil.	1.25	2.50
☐	282	Jose Pagan, Pgh.	1.25	2.50
☐	283	Dick Such, Wsh.	1.25	2.50
☐	284	Jim Gosger, Mtl.	1.25	2.50
☐	285	Sal Bando, Oak.	1.25	2.50
☐	286	Jerry McNertney, Stl.	1.25	2.50
☐	287	Mike Fiore, Bos.	1.25	2.50
☐	288	Joe Moeller, L.A.	1.25	2.50
☐	289	Rusty Staub, Mtl.	3.50	7.00
☐	290	Tony Oliva, Min.	2.00	4.00
☐	291	George Culver, Hou.	1.25	2.50
☐	292	Jay Johnstone, Chi.-A.L.	1.25	2.50
☐	293	Pat Corrales, Cin.	1.25	2.50
☐	**294**	**Steve Dunning, Cle., RC**	**1.25**	**2.50**
☐	295	Bobby Bonds, S.F.	2.00	4.00
☐	296	Tom Timmermann, Det.	1.25	2.50
☐	297	Johnny Briggs, Pha.	1.25	2.50
☐	**298**	**Jim Nelson, Pgh., RC**	**1.25**	**2.50**
☐	299	Ed Kirkpatrick, K.C.	1.25	2.50
☐	300	Brooks Robinson, Bal.	15.00	30.00
☐	301	Earl Wilson, S.D.	1.25	2.50
☐	302	Phil Gagliano, Bos.	1.25	2.50
☐	303	Lindy McDaniel, NYY.	1.25	2.50
☐	304	Ron Brand, Mtl.	1.25	2.50
☐	305	Reggie Smith, Bos.	1.25	2.50
☐	306	Jim Nash, Atl.	1.25	2.50
☐	307	Don Wert, Wsh.	1.25	2.50
☐	308	St. Louis Cardinals	2.00	4.00
☐	309	Dick Ellsworth, Mil.	1.25	2.50
☐	310	Tommie Agee, NYM.	1.25	2.50
☐	311	Lee Stange, Chi.-A.L.	1.25	2.50
☐	312	Harry Walker, Mgr., Hou.	1.25	2.50
☐	313	Tom Hall, Min.	1.25	2.50
☐	314	Jeff Torborg, L.A.	1.25	2.50
☐	315	Ron Fairly, Mtl.	1.25	2.50
☐	**316**	**Fred Scherman, Det., RC**	**1.25**	**2.50**
☐	317	Oak.: Jim Driscoll/ Angel Mangual	1.25	2.50
☐	318	Rudy May, Cal.	1.25	2.50
☐	319	Ty Cline, Cin.	1.25	2.50
☐	320	Dave McNally, Bal.	1.25	2.50
☐	321	Tom Matchick, K.C.	1.25	2.50
☐	**322**	**Jim Beauchamp, Stl., RC**	**1.25**	**2.50**
☐	323	Billy Champion, Pha.	1.25	2.50
☐	324	Graig Nettles, Cle.	2.00	4.00
☐	325	Juan Marichal, S.F.	3.00	6.00
☐	326	Richie Scheinblum, Wsh.	1.25	2.50
☐	327	WS-Game 1: Powell Homers!	2.50	5.00
☐	328	WS-Game 2: Buford Goes 2-For 4!	2.50	5.00
☐	329	WS-Game 3: F. Robinson Shows Muscle!	2.50	5.00
☐	330	WS-Game 4: Reds Stay Alive!	2.50	5.00
☐	331	WS-Game 5: B.Robinson Commits Robbery!	5.00	10.00
☐	332	Celebration!: Convincing Performance!	2.50	5.00
☐	333	Clay Kirby, S.D.	1.25	2.50
☐	334	Roberto Pena, Mil.	1.25	2.50
☐	335	Jerry Koosman, NYM.	1.25	2.50
☐	336	Detroit Tigers	2.00	4.00
☐	337	Jesus Alou, Hou.	1.25	2.50
☐	338	Gene Tenace, Oak.	1.25	2.50
☐	339	Wayne Simpson, Cin.	1.25	2.50
☐	340	Rico Petrocelli, Bos.	1.25	2.50
☐	**341**	**Steve Garvey, L.A., RC**	**20.00**	**40.00**
☐	342	Frank Tepedino, NYY.	1.25	2.50
☐	343	Pgh.: Ed Acosta/ Milt May	1.25	2.50
☐	344	Ellie Rodriguez, K.C.	1.25	2.50
☐	345	Joe Horlen, Chi.-A.L.	1.25	2.50
☐	346	Lum Harris, Mgr., Atl.	1.25	2.50
☐	347	Ted Uhlaender, Cle.	1.25	2.50
☐	348	Fred Norman, Stl.	1.25	2.50
☐	349	Rich Reese, Min.	1.25	2.50
☐	350	Billy Williams, Chi.-N.L.	3.50	7.00
☐	351	Jim Shellenback, Wsh.	1.25	2.50
☐	**352**	**Denny Doyle, Pha., RC**	**1.25**	**2.50**
☐	353	Carl Taylor, Mil.	1.25	2.50
☐	354	Don McMahon, S.F.	1.25	2.50
☐	355	Bud Harrelson, NYM.	1.25	2.50
☐	356	Bob Locker, Oak.	1.25	2.50
☐	357	Cincinnati Reds	3.00	6.00
☐	358	Danny Cater, NYY.	1.25	2.50
☐	359	Ron Reed, Atl.	1.25	2.50
☐	360	Jim Fregosi, Cal.	1.25	2.50
☐	361	Don Sutton, L.A.	5.00	10.00
☐	362	Bal.: Mike Adamson/ Roger Freed	1.25	2.50
☐	363	Mike Nagy, Bos.	1.25	2.50
☐	364	Tommy Dean, S.D.	1.25	2.50
☐	365	Bob Johnson, Pgh.	1.25	2.50
☐	366	Ron Stone, Pha.	1.25	2.50
☐	367	Dalton Jones, Det.	1.25	2.50
☐	368	Bob Veale, Pgh.	1.25	2.50
☐	369	4th Series Checklist (394 - 523)	3.50	7.00
☐	370	Joe Torre, Stl.	2.00	4.00
☐	371	Jack Hiatt, Hou.	1.25	2.50
☐	372	Lew Krausse, Mil.	1.25	2.50
☐	373	Tom McCraw, Chi.-A.L.	1.25	2.50
☐	374	Clete Boyer, Atl.	1.25	2.50
☐	375	Steve Hargan, Cle.	1.25	2.50
☐	376	Mtl.: Clyde Mashore/ Ernie McAnally	1.25	2.50
☐	377	Greg Garrett, Cin.	1.25	2.50

	No.	Player		
☐	378	Tito Fuentes, S.F.	1.25	2.50
☐	379	Wayne Granger, Cin.	1.25	2.50
☐	380	Ted Williams, Mgr., Wsh.	10.00	20.00
☐	381	Fred Gladding, Hou.	1.25	2.50
☐	382	Jake Gibbs, NYY.	1.25	2.50
☐	383	Rod Gaspar, S.D.	1.25	2.50
☐	384	Rollie Fingers, Oak.	6.00	12.00
☐	385	Maury Wills, L.A.	2.00	4.00
☐	386	Boston Red Sox	2.00	4.00
☐	387	Ron Herbel, Atl.	1.25	2.50
☐	388	Al Oliver, Pgh.	1.25	2.50
☐	389	Ed Brinkman, Det.	1.25	2.50
☐	390	Glenn Beckert, Chi.-N.L.	1.25	2.50
☐	391	Min.: Steve Brye/ Cotton Nash	1.25	2.50
☐	392	Grant Jackson, Bal.	1.25	2.50
☐	**393**	**Merv Rettenmund, Bal., RC**	**1.25**	**2.50**
☐	394	Clay Carroll, Cin.	2.00	3.75
☐	395	Roy White, NYY.	2.00	3.75
☐	396	Dick Schofield, Stl.	2.00	3.75
☐	397	Alvin Dark, Mgr., Cle.	2.00	3.75
☐	398	Howie Reed, Mtl.	2.00	3.75
☐	399	Jim French, Wsh.	2.00	3.75
☐	400	Hank Aaron, Atl.	42.50	85.00
☐	401	Tom Murphy, Cal.	2.00	3.75
☐	402	Los Angeles Dodgers	2.50	5.00
☐	403	Joe Coleman, Det.	2.00	3.75
☐	404	Hou.: Buddy Harris/ Roger Metzger	2.00	3.75
☐	405	Leo Cardenas, Min.	2.00	3.75
☐	406	Ray Sadecki, NYM.	2.00	3.75
☐	407	Joe Rudi, Oak.	2.00	3.75
☐	408	Rafael Robles, S.D.	2.00	3.75
☐	409	Don Pavletich, Bos.	2.00	3.75
☐	410	Ken Holtzman, Chi.-N.L.	2.00	3.75
☐	411	George Spriggs, K.C.	2.00	3.75
☐	412	Jerry Johnson, S.F.	2.00	3.75
☐	413	Pat Kelly, Chi.-A.L.	2.00	3.75
☐	414	Woodie Fryman, Pha.	2.00	3.75
☐	415	Mike Hegan, Mil.	2.00	3.75
☐	416	Gene Alley, Pgh.	2.00	3.75
☐	417	Dick Hall, Bal.	2.00	3.75
☐	418	Adolfo Phillips, Mtl.	2.00	3.75
☐	419	Ron Hansen, NYY.	2.00	3.75
☐	420	Jim Merritt, Cin.	2.00	3.75
☐	421	John Stephenson, Cal.	2.00	3.75
☐	422	Frank Bertaina, Stl.	2.00	3.75
☐	423	Det.: Dennis Saunders/ Tim Marting	2.00	3.75
☐	**424**	**Roberto Rodriguez, Chi.-N.L., RC**	**2.00**	**3.75**
☐	425	Doug Rader, Hou.	2.00	3.75
☐	426	Chris Cannizzaro, S.D.	2.00	3.75
☐	427	Bernie Allen, Wsh.	2.00	3.75
☐	428	Jim McAndrew, NYM.	2.00	3.75
☐	429	Chuck Hinton, Cle.	2.00	3.75
☐	430	Wes Parker, L.A.	2.00	3.75
☐	431	Tom Burgmeier, K.C.	2.00	3.75
☐	432	Bob Didier, Atl.	2.00	3.75
☐	433	Skip Lockwood, Mil.	2.00	3.75
☐	434	Gary Sutherland, Mtl.	2.00	3.75
☐	435	Jose Cardenal, Stl.	2.00	3.75
☐	436	Wilbur Wood, Chi.-A.L.	2.00	3.75
☐	437	Danny Murtaugh, Mgr., Pgh.	2.00	3.75
☐	438	Mike McCormick, NYY.	2.00	3.75
☐	439	Pha.: Greg Luzinski/ Scott Reid	3.00	6.00
☐	440	Bert Campaneris, Oak.	2.00	3.75
☐	441	Milt Pappas, Chi.-N.L.	2.00	3.75
☐	442	California Angels	2.50	5.00
☐	443	Rich Robertson, S.F.	2.00	3.75
☐	444	Jimmie Price, Det.	2.00	3.75
☐	445	Art Shamsky, NYM.	2.00	3.75
☐	446	Bobby Bolin, Bos.	2.00	3.75
☐	**447**	**Cesar Geronimo, Hou., RC**	**2.00**	**3.75**
☐	448	Dave Roberts, S.D.	2.00	3.75
☐	449	Brant Alyea, Min.	2.00	3.75
☐	450	Bob Gibson, Stl	12.50	25.00
☐	451	Joe Keough, K.C.	2.00	3.75
☐	452	John Boccabella, Mtl.	2.00	3.75
☐	453	Terry Crowley, Bal.	2.00	3.75
☐	454	Mike Paul, Cle.	2.00	3.75
☐	455	Don Kessinger, Chi.-N.L.	2.00	3.75
☐	456	Bob Meyer, Mil.	2.00	3.75
☐	457	Willie Smith, Cin.	2.00	3.75
☐	458	Chi.-A.L.: Ron Lolich/ Dave Lemonds	2.00	3.75
☐	459	Jim Lefebvre, L.A.	2.00	3.75
☐	460	Fritz Peterson, NYY.	2.00	3.75
☐	461	Jim Hart, S.F.	2.00	3.75
☐	462	Washington Senators	2.50	5.00
☐	**463**	**Tom Kelley, Atl., RC**	**2.00**	**3.75**
☐	464	Aurelio Rodriguez, Det.	2.00	3.75
☐	465	Tim McCarver, Pha.	2.50	5.00
☐	466	Ken Berry, Cal.	2.00	3.75
☐	467	Al Santorini, S.D.	2.00	3.75
☐	468	Frank Fernandez, Oak.	2.00	3.75
☐	469	Bob Aspromonte, NYM.	2.00	3.75
☐	470	Bob Oliver, K.C.	2.00	3.75
☐	471	Tom Griffin, Hou.	2.00	3.75
☐	472	Ken Rudolph, Chi.-N.L.	2.00	3.75
☐	473	Gary Wagner, Bos.	2.00	3.75
☐	474	Jim Fairey, Mtl.	2.00	3.75
☐	475	Ron Perranoski, Min.	2.00	3.75
☐	476	Dal Maxvill, Stl.	2.00	3.75
☐	477	Earl Weaver, Mgr., Bal.	4.00	8.00
☐	**478**	**Bernie Carbo, Cin., RC**	**2.00**	**3.75**
☐	479	Dennis Higgins, Cle.	2.00	3.75
☐	480	Manny Sanguillen, Pgh.	2.00	3.75
☐	481	Daryl Patterson, Det.	2.00	3.75
☐	482	San Diego Padres	2.50	5.00
☐	483	Gene Michael, NYY.	2.00	3.75
☐	484	Don Wilson, Hou.	2.00	3.75
☐	485	Ken McMullen, Cal.	2.00	3.75
☐	486	Steve Huntz, S.F.	2.00	3.75
☐	487	Paul Schaal, K.C.	2.00	3.75
☐	488	Jerry Stephenson, L.A.	2.00	3.75
☐	**489**	**Luis Alvarado, Chi.-A.L., RC**	**2.00**	**3.75**
☐	490	Deron Johnson, Pha.	2.00	3.75
☐	491	Jim Hardin, Bal.	2.00	3.75
☐	492	Ken Boswell, NYM.	2.00	3.75
☐	493	Dave May, Mil.	2.00	3.75
☐	494	Atl.: Ralph Garr/ Rick Kester	2.00	3.75
☐	495	Felipe Alou, Oak.	3.00	6.00
☐	496	Woody Woodward, Cin.	2.00	3.75
☐	**497**	**Horacio Pina, Wsh., RC**	**2.00**	**3.75**
☐	498	John Kennedy, Bos.	2.00	3.75
☐	499	5th Series Checklist (524 - 643)	4.00	8.00
☐	500	Jim Perry, Min.	2.00	3.75
☐	501	Andy Etchebarren, Bal.	2.00	3.75
☐	502	Chicago Cubs	3.00	6.00
☐	503	Gates Brown, Det.	2.00	3.75
☐	**504**	**Ken Wright, K.C., RC**	**2.00**	**3.75**
☐	505	Ollie Brown, S.D.	2.00	3.75
☐	506	Bobby Knoop, Chi.-A.L.	2.00	3.75
☐	507	George Stone, Atl.	2.00	3.75
☐	508	Roger Repoz, Cal.	2.00	3.75
☐	509	Jim Grant, Pgh.	2.00	3.75
☐	510	Ken Harrelson, Cle.	2.00	3.75
☐	511	Chris Short, Pha.	2.00	3.75
☐	512	Bos.: Dick Mills/ Mike Garman	2.00	3.75
☐	513	Nolan Ryan, NYM.	200.00	400.00
☐	514	Ron Woods, NYY.	2.00	3.75
☐	515	Carl Morton, Mtl.	2.00	3.75

	#	Card		
☐	516	Ted Kubiak, Mil.	2.00	3.75
☐	517	Charlie Fox, Mgr., S.F.	2.00	3.75
☐	518	Joe Grzenda, Wsh.	2.00	3.75
☐	519	Willie Crawford, L.A.	2.00	3.75
☐	520	Tommy John, Chi.-A.L.	2.50	5.00
☐	**521**	**Leron Lee, Stl., RC**	**2.00**	**3.75**
☐	522	Minnesota Twins	2.50	5.00
☐	523	John Odom, Oak.	2.00	3.75
☐	524	Mickey Stanley, Det.	3.25	6.50
☐	525	Ernie Banks, Chi.-N.L.	42.50	85.00
☐	526	Ray Jarvis, Cal.	3.25	6.50
☐	527	Cleon Jones, NYM.	3.25	6.50
☐	528	Wally Bunker, K.C.	3.25	6.50
☐	529	Bill Buckner/ Enzo Hernandez/ Marty Perez	4.00	8.00
☐	530	Carl Yastrzemski, Bos.	32.50	65.00
☐	531	Mike Torrez, Stl.	3.25	6.50
☐	532	Bill Rigney, Mgr., Min.	3.25	6.50
☐	533	Mike Ryan, Pha.	3.25	6.50
☐	534	Luke Walker, Pgh.	3.25	6.50
☐	535	Curt Flood, Stl.	4.00	8.00
☐	536	Claude Raymond, Mtl.	4.00	8.00
☐	537	Tom Egan, Chi.-A.L.	3.25	6.50
☐	538	Angel Bravo, Cin.	3.25	6.50
☐	539	Larry Brown, Cle.	3.25	6.50
☐	540	Larry Dierker, Hou.	3.25	6.50
☐	541	Bob Burda, Stl.	3.25	6.50
☐	542	Bob Miller, Chi.-N.L.	3.25	6.50
☐	543	New York Yankees	4.50	9.00
☐	**544**	**Vida Blue, Oak., RC**	**6.00**	**12.00**
☐	545	Dick Dietz, S.F.	3.25	6.50
☐	546	John Matias, K.C.	3.25	6.50
☐	547	Pat Dobson, Bal.	3.25	6.50
☐	548	Don Mason, S.D.	3.25	6.50
☐	549	Jim Brewer, L.A.	3.25	6.50
☐	550	Harmon Killebrew, Min.	20.00	40.00
☐	551	Frank Linzy, Stl.	3.25	6.50
☐	552	Buddy Bradford, Cle.	3.25	6.50
☐	553	Kevin Collins, Det.	3.25	6.50
☐	554	Lowell Palmer, Pha.	3.25	6.50
☐	555	Walt Williams, Chi.-A.L.	3.25	6.50
☐	556	Jim McGlothlin, Cin.	3.25	6.50
☐	557	Tom Satriano, Bos.	3.25	6.50
☐	558	Hector Torres, Chi.-N.L.	3.25	6.50
☐	559	Terry Cox/ Bill Gogolewski/ Gary Jones	3.25	6.50
☐	560	Rusty Staub, Mtl.	6.00	12.00
☐	561	Syd O'Brien, Cal.	3.25	6.50
☐	562	Dave Giusti, Pgh.	3.25	6.50
☐	563	San Francisco Giants	4.50	9.00
☐	**564**	**Al Fitzmorris, K.C., RC**	**3.25**	**6.50**
☐	565	Jim Wynn, Hou.	3.25	6.50
☐	566	Tim Cullen, Wsh.	3.25	6.50
☐	567	Walt Alston, Mgr., L.A.	5.00	10.00
☐	568	Sal Campisi, Min.	3.25	6.50
☐	569	Ivan Murrell, S.D.	3.25	6.50
☐	570	Jim Palmer, Bal.	25.00	50.00
☐	571	Ted Sizemore, Stl.	3.25	6.50
☐	572	Jerry Kenney, NYY.	3.25	6.50
☐	573	Ed Kranepool, NYM.	3.25	6.50
☐	574	Jim Bunning, Pha.	6.00	12.00
☐	575	Bill Freehan, Det.	3.25	6.50
☐	576	Chi.-N.L.: B. Davis/A. Garrett/ G. Jestadt	3.25	6.50
☐	577	Jim Lonborg, Bos.	3.25	6.50
☐	578	Eddie Kasko, Mgr., Bos.	3.25	6.50
☐	579	Marty Pattin, Mil.	3.25	6.50
☐	580	Tony Perez, Cin.	12.50	25.00
☐	581	Roger Nelson, K.C.	3.25	6.50
☐	582	Dave Cash, Pgh.	3.25	6.50
☐	**583**	**Ron Cook, Hou., RC**	**3.25**	**6.50**
☐	584	Cleveland Indians	4.50	9.00
☐	585	Willie Davis, L.A.	3.25	6.50
☐	586	Dick Woodson, Min.	3.25	6.50
☐	587	Sonny Jackson, Atl.	3.25	6.50
☐	**588**	**Tom Bradley, Chi.-A.L., RC**	**3.25**	**6.50**
☐	589	Bob Barton, S.D.	3.25	6.50
☐	590	Alex Johnson, Cal.	3.25	6.50
☐	**591**	**Jackie Brown, Wsh., RC**	**3.25**	**6.50**
☐	592	Randy Hundley, Chi.-N.L.	3.25	6.50
☐	593	Jack Aker, NYY.	3.25	6.50
☐	594	Bob Chlupsa/ Bob Stinson/ Al Hrabosky	4.50	9.00
☐	595	Dave Johnson, Bal.	3.25	6.50
☐	**596**	**Mike Jorgensen, NYM., RC**	**3.25**	**6.50**
☐	597	Ken Suarez, Cle.	3.25	6.50
☐	598	Rick Wise, Pha.	3.25	6.50
☐	599	Norm Cash, Det.	3.25	6.50
☐	600	Willie Mays, S.F.	75.00	150.00
☐	601	Ken Tatum, Bos.	3.25	6.50
☐	602	Marty Martinez, Hou.	3.25	6.50
☐	603	Pittsburgh Pirates	4.50	9.00
☐	604	John Gelnar, Mil.	3.25	6.50
☐	605	Orlando Cepeda, Atl.	4.50	9.00
☐	606	Chuck Taylor, Stl.	3.25	6.50
☐	**607**	**Paul Ratliff, Min., RC**	**3.25**	**6.50**
☐	608	Mike Wegener, Mtl.	3.25	6.50
☐	609	Leo Durocher, Mgr., Chi.-N.L.	5.00	10.00
☐	610	Amos Otis, K.C.	3.25	6.50
☐	611	Tom Phoebus, S.D.	3.25	6.50
☐	612	Cle.: Lou Camilli/ Ted Ford/ Steve Mingori	3.25	6.50
☐	613	Pedro Borbon, Cin.	3.25	6.50
☐	614	Billy Cowan, Cal.	3.25	6.50
☐	615	Mel Stottlemyre, NYY.	3.25	6.50
☐	616	Larry Hisle, Pha.	3.25	6.50
☐	617	Clay Dalrymple, Bal.	3.25	6.50
☐	618	Tug McGraw, NYM.	3.25	6.50
☐	619	6th Series Checklist (644 - 752)	7.50	15.00
☐	620	Frank Howard, Wsh.	3.25	6.50
☐	621	Ron Bryant, S.F.	3.25	6.50
☐	622	Joe Lahoud, Bos.	3.25	6.50
☐	623	Pat Jarvis, Atl.	3.25	6.50
☐	624	Oakland Athletics	4.50	9.00
☐	625	Lou Brock, Stl.	25.00	50.00
☐	626	Freddie Patek, K.C.	3.25	6.50
☐	627	Steve Hamilton, S.F.	3.25	6.50
☐	628	John Bateman, Mtl.	3.25	6.50
☐	629	John Hiller, Det.	5.00	10.00
☐	630	Roberto Clemente, Pgh.	75.00	150.00
☐	631	Eddie Fisher, Cal.	3.25	6.50
☐	632	Darrel Chaney, Cin.	3.25	6.50
☐	633	Bobby Brooks/ Pete Koegel/ Scott Northey	3.25	6.50
☐	634	Phil Regan, Chi.-N.L.	3.25	6.50
☐	635	Bob Murcer, NYY.	3.25	6.50
☐	636	Denny Lemaster, Hou.	3.25	6.50
☐	637	Dave Bristol, Mgr., Mil.	3.25	6.50
☐	638	Stan Williams, Min.	3.25	6.50
☐	639	Tom Haller, L.A.	3.25	6.50
☐	640	Frank Robinson, Bal.	32.50	65.00
☐	641	New York Mets	9.00	18.00
☐	642	Jim Roland, Oak.	3.25	6.50
☐	643	Rick Reichardt, Chi.-A.L.	3.25	6.50
☐	644	Jim Stewart, Cin. (*)	9.00	18.00
☐	645	Jim Maloney, Cal. (*)	9.00	18.00
☐	646	Bobby Floyd, K.C. (*)	9.00	18.00
☐	647	Juan Pizarro, Chi.-N.L.	6.00	12.00
☐	648	NYM.: R.Folkers/ T.Martinez/ J.Matlack	12.50	25.00
☐	649	Sparky Lyle, Bos. (*)	9.00	18.00
☐	650	Rich Allen, L.A. (*)	20.00	40.00
☐	651	Jerry Robertson, NYM. (*)	9.00	18.00
☐	652	Atlanta Braves	9.00	18.00
☐	653	Russ Snyder, Mil. (*)	9.00	18.00

	No.	Player	EX	NRMT
☐	654	Don Shaw, Stl. (*)	9.00	18.00
☐	655	Mike Epstein, Wsh. (*)	9.00	18.00
☐	**656**	**Gerry Nyman, S.D., RC**	**6.00**	**12.00**
☐	657	Jose Azcue, Cal.	6.00	12.00
☐	658	Paul Lindblad, Oak. (*)	9.00	18.00
☐	659	Byron Browne, Pha. (*)	9.00	18.00
☐	660	Ray Culp, Bos.	6.00	12.00
☐	661	Chuck Tanner, Mgr., Chi.-A.L. (*)	9.00	18.00
☐	662	Mike Hedlund, K.C. (*)	9.00	18.00
☐	**663**	**Marv Staehle, Atl., RC**	**6.00**	**12.00**
☐	664	A. Reynolds/ B. Reynolds/ K. Reynolds (*)	9.00	18.00
☐	665	Ron Swoboda, Mtl. (*)	9.00	18.00
☐	666	Gene Brabender, Cal. (*)	9.00	18.00
☐	667	Pete Ward, NYY.	7.50	15.00
☐	668	Gary Neibauer, Atl.	6.00	12.00
☐	669	Ike Brown, Det. (*)	9.00	18.00
☐	670	Bill Hands, Chi.-N.L.	6.00	12.00
☐	671	Bill Voss, Mil. (*)	9.00	18.00
☐	**672**	**Ed Crosby, Stl., RC** (*)	**9.00**	**18.00**
☐	**673**	**Gerry Janeski, Wsh., RC** (*)	**9.00**	**18.00**
☐	674	Montréal Expos	10.00	20.00
☐	675	Dave Boswell, Min.	6.00	12.00
☐	676	Tommie Reynolds, Cal.	6.00	12.00
☐	677	Jack DiLauro, Hou. (*)	9.00	18.00
☐	678	George Thomas, Bos.	6.00	12.00
☐	679	Don O'Riley, K.C.	6.00	12.00
☐	680	Don Mincher, Oak. (*)	9.00	18.00
☐	681	Bill Butler, K.C.	6.00	12.00
☐	682	Terry Harmon, Pha.	6.00	12.00
☐	683	Bill Burbach, NYY. (*)	9.00	18.00
☐	684	Curt Motton, Bal.	6.00	12.00
☐	685	Moe Drabowsky, Stl.	6.00	12.00
☐	686	Chico Ruiz, Cal. (*)	9.00	18.00
☐	687	Ron Taylor, NYM.	12.50	25.00
☐	688	Sparky Anderson, Mgr., Cin. (*)	30.00	60.00
☐	**689**	**Frank Baker, Cle., RC**	**6.00**	**12.00**
☐	690	Bob Moose, Pgh.	6.00	12.00
☐	691	Bob Heise, S.F.	6.00	12.00
☐	692	Hal Haydel/ R.Moret/ Wayne Twitchell (*)	9.00	18.00
☐	693	Jose Pena, L.A. (*)	9.00	18.00
☐	694	Rick Renick, Min. (*)	9.00	18.00
☐	695	Joe Niekro, Det.	6.00	12.00
☐	**696**	**Jerry Morales, S.D., RC**	**6.00**	**12.00**
☐	697	Rickey Clark, Cal. (*)	9.00	18.00
☐	698	Milwaukee Brewers	20.00	40.00
☐	699	Jim Britton, Mtl.	6.00	12.00
☐	700	Boog Powell, Bal.	22.50	45.00
☐	701	Bob Garibaldi, K.C.	6.00	12.00
☐	**702**	**Milt Ramirez, Stl., RC**	**6.00**	**12.00**
☐	703	Mike Kekich, NYY.	6.00	12.00
☐	704	J.C. Martin, Chi.-N.L. (*)	9.00	18.00
☐	705	Dick Selma, Pha. (*)	9.00	18.00
☐	706	Joe Foy, Wsh. (*)	9.00	18.00
☐	707	Fred Lasher, Cal.	6.00	12.00
☐	**708**	**Russ Nagelson, Det., RC** (*)	**9.00**	**18.00**
☐	**709**	**D. Baker/ D.Baylor,/ Tom Paciorek, RC (*)**	**75.00**	**150.00**
☐	710	Sonny Siebert, Bos.	6.00	12.00
☐	711	Larry Stahl, S.D. (*)	9.00	18.00
☐	712	Jose Martinez, Pgh.	6.00	12.00
☐	713	Mike Marshall, Mtl. (*)	11.00	22.00
☐	714	Dick Williams, Mgr., Oak. (*)	9.00	18.00
☐	715	Horace Clarke, NYY. (*)	9.00	18.00
☐	**716**	**Dave Leonhard, Bal., RC**	**6.00**	**12.00**
☐	717	Tommie Aaron, Atl. (*)	9.00	18.00
☐	**718**	**Billy Wynne, Cal., RC**	**6.00**	**12.00**
☐	719	Jerry May, K.C. (*)	9.00	18.00
☐	720	Matty Alou, Stl.	6.00	12.00
☐	721	John Morris, Mil.	6.00	12.00
☐	722	Houston Astros	20.00	40.00
☐	723	Vicente Romo, Chi.-A.L. (*)	9.00	18.00
☐	724	Tom Tischinski, Min. (*)	9.00	18.00
☐	725	Gary Gentry, NYM. (*)	9.00	18.00
☐	726	Paul Popovich, Chi.-N.L.	6.00	12.00
☐	**727**	**Ray Lamb, Cle., RC** (*)	**9.00**	**18.00**
☐	728	W. Redmond,/ K. Lampard/ B. Williams	6.00	12.00
☐	**729**	**Dick Billings, Wsh., RC**	**6.00**	**12.00**
☐	730	Jim Rooker, K.C.	6.00	12.00
☐	731	Jim Qualls, Cin. (*)	9.00	18.00
☐	**732**	**Bob Reed, Det., RC**	**6.00**	**12.00**
☐	733	Lee Maye, Chi.-A.L. (*)	9.00	18.00
☐	734	Rob Gardner, NYY. (*)	9.00	18.00
☐	735	Mike Shannon, Stl. (*)	9.00	18.00
☐	736	Mel Queen, Cal. (*)	9.00	18.00
☐	737	Preston Gomez, Mgr., S.D. (*)	9.00	18.00
☐	738	Russ Gibson, S.F. (*)	9.00	18.00
☐	**739**	**Barry Lersch, Pha., RC** (*)	**9.00**	**18.00**
☐	740	Luis Aparicio, Bos.	25.00	50.00
☐	741	Skip Guinn, Hou.	6.00	12.00
☐	742	Kansas City Royals	10.00	20.00
☐	743	John O'Donoghue, Mtl. (*)	9.00	18.00
☐	744	Chuck Manuel, Min. (*)	9.00	18.00
☐	745	Sandy Alomar, Cal. (*)	9.00	18.00
☐	746	Andy Kosco, Mil.	6.00	12.00
☐	747	Al Severinsen/ Scipio Spinks/ Baylor Moore	6.00	12.00
☐	748	John Purdin, Chi.-A.L.	6.00	12.00
☐	**749**	**Ken Szotkiewicz, Det., RC**	**3.00**	**12.00**
☐	750	Denny McLain, Wsh.	12.50	25.00
☐	751	Al Weis, NYM. (*)	9.00	18.00
☐	752	Dick Drago, K.C.	6.00	12.00

1972 O-PEE-CHEE

This set is identical to the first 525 cards in the 878-card Topps set of the same year, but the O-Pee-Chee imprint reads "T.C.G. PRINTED IN CANDA."

Card Size: 2 1/2" x 3 1/2"

Face: Four colour, white border; name, team

Back: Rust and black on card stock; name, number, position, résumé, bilingual

Imprint: * or ** © O.P.C. PRINTED IN CANADA

Complete Set (525 cards):	**800.00**	**1,600.00**
Common Player (1 - 132):	**.50**	**1.00**
Common Player (133 - 263):	**.75**	**1.50**
Common Player (264 - 394):	**1.00**	**2.00**
Common Player (395 - 525):	**1.25**	**2.50**

	No.	Player	EX	NRMT
☐	1	World Champions: Pittsburgh Pirates	6.00	12.00
☐	2	Ray Culp, Bos.	.50	1.00
☐	3	Bob Tolan, Cin.	.50	1.00
☐	4	Checklist: 1st Series (1 - 132)	1.50	3.00
☐	5	John Bateman, Mtl.	.50	1.00
☐	6	Fred Scherman, Det.	.50	1.00
☐	7	Enzo Hernandez, S.D.	.50	1.00

	No.	Card		
☐	8	Ron Swoboda, NYY.	.50	1.00
☐	9	Stan Williams, Stl.	.50	1.00
☐	10	Amos Otis, K.C.	.50	1.00
☐	11	Bobby Valentine, L.A.	.50	1.00
☐	12	Jose Cardenal, Mil.	.50	1.00
☐	13	Joe Grzenda, Stl.	.50	1.00
☐	14	Pha.: P.Koegel/ M. Anderson/ W. Twitchell	.50	1.00
☐	15	Walt Williams, Chi.-A.L.	.50	1.00
☐	16	Mike Jorgensen, NYM.	.50	1.00
☐	17	Dave Duncan, Oak.	.50	1.00
☐	18	Juan Pizarro, Chi.-N.L.	.50	1.00
☐	19	Billy Cowan, Cal.	.50	1.00
☐	20	Don Wilson, Hou.	.50	1.00
☐	21	Atlanta Braves	1.00	2.00
☐	22	Rob Gardner, NYY.	.50	1.00
☐	23	Ted Kubiak, Tex.	.50	1.00
☐	24	Ted Ford, Cle.	.50	1.00
☐	25	Bill Singer, L.A.	.50	1.00
☐	26	Andy Etchebarren, Bal.	.50	1.00
☐	27	Bob Johnson, Pgh.	.50	1.00
☐	28	Min.: Bob Gebhard/ Steve Brye/ Hal Haydel	.50	1.00
☐	**29**	**Bill Bonham, Chi.-N.L., RC**	**.50**	**1.00**
☐	30	Rico Petrocelli, Bos.	.50	1.00
☐	31	Cleon Jones, NYM.	.50	1.00
☐	32	In Action: Cleon Jones, NYM.	.50	1.00
☐	33	Billy Martin, Mgr., Det.	2.50	5.00
☐	34	In Action: Billy Martin, Mgr., Det.	1.00	2.00
☐	35	Jerry Johnson, S.F.	.50	1.00
☐	36	In Action: Jerry Johnson, S.F.	.50	1.00
☐	37	Carl Yastrzemski, Bos.	9.00	18.00
☐	38	In Action: Carl Yastrzemski, Bos.	5.00	10.00
☐	39	Bob Barton, S.D.	.50	1.00
☐	40	In Action: Bob Barton, S.D.	.50	1.00
☐	41	Tommy Davis, Oak.	.50	1.00
☐	42	In Action: Tommy Davis, Oak.	.50	1.00
☐	43	Rick Wise, Pha.	.50	1.00
☐	44	In Action: Rick Wise, Pha.	.50	1.00
☐	45	Glenn Beckert, Chi.-N.L.	.50	1.00
☐	46	In Action: Glenn Beckert, Chi.-N.L.	.50	1.00
☐	47	John Ellis, NYY.	.50	1.00
☐	48	In Action: John Ellis, NYY.	.50	1.00
☐	49	Willie Mays, S.F.	17.50	35.00
☐	50	In Action: Willie Mays, S.F.	9.00	18.00
☐	51	Harmon Killebrew, Min.	4.50	9.00
☐	52	In Action: Harmon Killebrew, Min.	2.50	5.00
☐	53	Bud Harrelson, NYM.	.50	1.00
☐	54	In Action: Bud Harrelson, NYM.	.50	1.00
☐	55	Clyde Wright, Cal.	.50	1.00
☐	**56**	**Rich Chiles, Hou., RC**	**.50**	**1.00**
☐	57	Bob Oliver, K.C.	.50	1.00
☐	58	Ernie McAnally, Mtl.	.50	1.00
☐	**59**	**Fred Stanley, Cle., RC**	**.50**	**1.00**
☐	60	Manny Sanguillen, Pgh.	.50	1.00
☐	61	Chi.-N.L.: B. Hooton/ G. Hiser/ E. Stephenson	1.00	2.00
☐	62	Angel Mangual, Oak.	.50	1.00
☐	63	Duke Sims, L.A.	.50	1.00
☐	**64**	**Pete Broberg, Tex., RC**	**.50**	**1.00**
☐	65	Cesar Cedeno, Hou.	1.00	2.00
☐	**66**	**Ray Corbin, Min., RC**	**.50**	**1.00**
☐	67	Red Schoendienst, Mgr., Stl.	1.25	2.50
☐	**68**	**Jim York, K.C., RC**	**.50**	**1.00**
☐	69	Roger Freed, Pha.	.50	1.00
☐	70	Mike Cuellar, Bal.	.50	1.00
☐	71	California Angels	1.00	2.00
☐	72	Bruce Kison, Pgh.	.50	1.00
☐	73	Steve Huntz, Chi.-A.L.	.50	1.00
☐	74	Cecil Upshaw, Atl.	.50	1.00
☐	75	Bert Campaneris, Oak.	.50	1.00
☐	**76**	**Don Carrithers, S.F., RC**	**.50**	**1.00**
☐	**77**	**Ron Theobald, Mil., RC**	**.50**	**1.00**
☐	**78**	**Steve Arlin, S.D., RC**	**.50**	**1.00**
☐	**79**	**Bos.: C. Cooper/ C. Fisk/ M. Garman, RC**	**50.00**	**100.00**
☐	80	Tony Perez, Cin.	1.25	2.50
☐	81	Mike Hedlund, K.C.	.50	1.00
☐	82	Ron Woods, Mtl.	.50	1.00
☐	83	Dalton Jones, Det.	.50	1.00
☐	84	Vince Colbert, Cle.	.50	1.00
☐	85	LL: J. Torre/ R. Garr/ G. Beckert	1.00	2.00
☐	86	LL: T. Oliva/ B. Murcer/ M. Rettenmund	1.00	2.00
☐	87	LL: J. Torre/ W. Stargell/ H. Aaron	2.50	5.00
☐	88	LL: H. Killebrew/ F. Robinson/ Reggie Smith	2.00	4.00
☐	89	LL: W. Stargell/ H. Aaron/ L. May	2.50	5.00
☐	90	LL: B. Melton/ N. Cash/ R. Jackson	2.00	4.00
☐	91	LL: T. Seaver/ D. Roberts/ D. Wilson	2.0.0	4.00
☐	92	LL: V. Blue/ W. Wood/ J. Palmer	2.00	4.00
☐	93	LL: F. Jenkins/ S. Carlton/ A. Downing / T. Seaver	2.50	5.00
☐	94	LL: M. Lolich/ V. Blue/ W. Wood	1.00	2.00
☐	95	LL: T. Seaver/ F. Jenkins/ B. Stoneman	2.50	5.00
☐	96	LL: M. Lolich/ V. Blue/ J. Coleman	1.00	2.00
☐	97	Tom Kelley, Atl.	.50	1.00
☐	98	Chuck Tanner, Mgr., Chi.-A.L.	.50	1.00
☐	**99**	**Ross Grimsley, Cin., RC**	**.50**	**1.00**
☐	100	Frank Robinson, Bal.	6.00	12.00
☐	101	Hou.: Bill Greif/ J.R. Richard/ Ray Busse	1.00	2.00
☐	**102**	**Lloyd Allen, Cal., RC**	**1.50**	**3.00**
☐	103	Checklist: 2nd Series (133 - 263)	1.50	3.00
☐	**104**	**Toby Harrah, Tex., RC**	**.50**	**1.00**
☐	105	Gary Gentry, NYM.	.50	1.00
☐	106	Milwaukee Brewers	1.00	2.00
☐	**107**	**Jose Cruz, Stl., RC**	**1.50**	**3.00**
☐	108	Gary Waslewski, NYY.	.50	1.00
☐	109	Jerry May, K.C.	.50	1.00
☐	110	Ron Hunt, Mtl.	.50	1.00
☐	111	Jim Grant, Oak.	.50	1.00
☐	112	Greg Luzinski, Pha.	.50	1.00
☐	113	Rogelio Moret, Bos.	.50	1.00
☐	114	Bill Buckner, L.A.	.50	1.00
☐	115	Jim Fregosi, Cal.	.50	1.00
☐	**116**	**Ed Farmer, Cle. RC**	**.50**	**1.00**
☐	**117**	**Cleo James, Chi.-N.L., RC**	**.50**	**1.00**
☐	118	Skip Lockwood, Mil.	.50	1.00
☐	**119**	**Marty Perez, Atl., RC**	**.50**	**1.00**
☐	120	Bill Freehan, Det.	.50	1.00
☐	121	Ed Sprague, Cin.	.50	1.00
☐	**122**	**Larry Biittner, Tex., RC**	**.50**	**1.00**
☐	**123**	**Ed Acosta, S.D.**	**.50**	**1.00**
☐	124	NYY.: A. Closter/ R. Torres/ R. Hambright	.50	1.00
☐	125	Dave Cash, Pgh.	.50	1.00
☐	126	Bart Johnson, Chi.-A.L.	.50	1.00
☐	127	Duffy Dyer, NYM.	.50	1.00
☐	128	Eddie Watt, Bal.	.50	1.00
☐	129	Charlie Fox, Mgr., S.F.	.50	1.00
☐	130	Bob Gibson, Stl.	6.00	12.00
☐	**131**	**Jim Nettles, Min.**	**.50**	**1.00**
☐	132	Joe Morgan, Hou.	4.00	8.00
☐	133	Joe Keough, K.C.	.75	1.50
☐	134	Carl Morton, Mtl.	.75	1.50
☐	135	Vada Pinson, Cal.	.75	1.50
☐	136	Darrel Chaney, Cin.	.75	1.50
☐	137	Dick Williams, Mgr., Oak.	.75	1.50
☐	138	Mike Kekich, NYY.	.75	1.50
☐	139	Tim McCarver, Pha.	1.50	3.00
☐	140	Pat Dobson, Bal.	.75	1.50
☐	141	NYM.: Buzz Capra/ Leroy Stanton/ Jon Matlack	.75	1.50
☐	142	Chris Chambliss, Cle.	2.0	4.00
☐	143	Garry Jestadt, S.D.	.75	1.50
☐	144	Marty Pattin, Bos.	.75	1.50

	No.	Player		
☐	145	Don Kessinger, Chi.-N.L.	.75	1.50
☐	146	Steve Kealey, Chi.-A.L.	.75	1.50
☐	**147**	**Dave Kingman, S.F., RC**	**3.25**	**6.50**
☐	148	Dick Billings, Tex.	.75	1.50
☐	149	Gary Neibauer, Atl.	.75	1.50
☐	150	Norm Cash, Det.	.75	1.50
☐	151	Jim Brewer, L.A.	.75	1.50
☐	152	Gene Clines, Pgh.	.75	1.50
☐	**153**	**Rick Auerbach, Mil., RC**	**.75**	**1.50**
☐	154	Ted Simmons, Stl.	1.50	3.00
☐	155	Larry Dierker, Hou.	.75	1.50
☐	156	Minnesota Twins	1.50	3.00
☐	157	Don Gullett, Cin.	.75	1.50
☐	158	Jerry Kenney, NYY.	.75	1.50
☐	159	John Boccabella, Mtl.	.75	1.50
☐	160	Andy Messersmith, Cal.	.75	1.50
☐	161	Brock Davis, Mil.	.75	1.50
☐	162	Mil.: J. Bell/ D. Porter. /B.Reynolds, Error	1.50	3.000
☐	163	Tug McGraw, NYM.	.75	1.50
☐	164	In Action: Tug McGraw, NYM.	.75	1.50
☐	**165**	**Chris Speier, S.F., RC**	**1.50**	**3.00**
☐	166	In Action: Chris Speier, S.F.	1.00	2.00
☐	167	Deron Johnson, Pha.	.75	1.50
☐	168	In Action: Deron Johnson, Pha.	.75	1.50
☐	169	Vida Blue, Oak.	1.50	3.00
☐	170	In Action: Vida Blue, Oak.	1.00	2.00
☐	171	Darrell Evans, Atl.	.75	1.50
☐	172	In Action: Darrell Evans, Atl.	.75	1.50
☐	173	Clay Kirby, S.D.	.75	1.50
☐	174	In Action: Clay Kirby, S.D.	.75	1.50
☐	175	Tom Haller, Det.	.75	1.50
☐	176	In Action: Tom Haller, Det.	.75	1.50
☐	177	Paul Schaal, K.C.	.75	1.50
☐	178	In Action: Paul Schaal, K.C.	.75	1.50
☐	179	Dock Ellis, Pgh.	.75	1.50
☐	180	In Action: Dock Ellis, Pgh.	.75	1.50
☐	181	Ed Kranepool, NYM.	.75	1.50
☐	182	In Action: Ed Kranepool, NYM.	.75	1.50
☐	183	Bill Melton, Chi.-A.L.	.75	1.50
☐	184	In Action: Bill Melton, Chi.-A.L.	.75	1.50
☐	185	Ron Bryant, S.F.	.75	1.50
☐	186	In Action: Ron Bryant, S.F.	.75	1.50
☐	187	Gates Brown, Det.	.75	1.50
☐	188	Frank Lucchesi, Mgr., Pha.	.75	1.50
☐	189	Gene Tenace, Oak.	.75	1.50
☐	190	Dave Giusti, Pgh.	.75	1.50
☐	**191**	**Jeff Burroughs, Tex., RC**	**1.50**	**3.00**
☐	192	Chicago Cubs	2.00	4.00
☐	**193**	**Kurt Bevacqua, Cle., RC**	**.75**	**1.50**
☐	194	Fred Norman, S.D.	.75	1.50
☐	195	Orlando Cepeda, Atl.	1.50	3.00
☐	196	Mel Queen, Cal.	.75	1.50
☐	197	Johnny Briggs, Mil.	.75	1.50
☐	**198**	**L.A.: C. Hough/ B. O'Brien/ M. Strahler, RC**	**3.25**	**6.50**
☐	199	Mike Fiore, Bos.	.75	1.50
☐	200	Lou Brock, Stl.	5.00	10.00
☐	201	Phil Roof, Min.	.75	1.50
☐	202	Scipio Spinks, Hou.	.75	1.50
☐	**203**	**Ron Blomberg, NYY., RC**	**.75**	**1.50**
☐	204	Tommy Helms, Hou.	.75	1.50
☐	205	Dick Drago, K.C.	.75	1.50
☐	206	Dal Maxvill, Stl.	.75	1.50
☐	207	Tom Egan, Chi.-A.L.	.75	1.50
☐	208	Milt Pappas, Chi.-N.L.	.75	1.50
☐	209	Joe Rudi, Oak.	.75	1.50
☐	210	Denny McLain, Tex.	1.25	2.50
☐	211	Gary Sutherland, Mtl.	.75	1.50
☐	212	Grant Jackson, Bal.	.75	1.50
☐	213	Ana.: Billy Parker/ Art Kusnyer/ Tom Silverio	.75	1.50
☐	214	Mike McQueen, Atl.	.75	1.50
☐	215	Alex Johnson, Cle.	.75	1.50
☐	216	Joe Niekro, Det.	.75	1.50
☐	217	Roger Metzger, Hou.	.75	1.50
☐	218	Eddie Kasko, Mgr., Bos.	.75	1.50
☐	**219**	**Rennie Stennett, Pgh., RC**	**.75**	**1.50**
☐	220	Jim Perry, Min.	.75	1.50
☐	221	National League: Bucs Champs!	1.50	3.00
☐	222	American League: Orioles Champs!	1.50	3.00
☐	223	WS-Game 1: Pittsburgh at Baltimore	1.50	3.00
☐	224	WS-Game 2: Pittsburgh at Baltimore	1.50	3.00
☐	225	WS-Game 3: Baltimore at Pittsburgh	1.50	3.00
☐	226	WS-Game 4: Baltimore at Pittsburgh	4.50	9.00
☐	227	WS-Game 5: Baltimore at Pittsburgh	1.50	3.00
☐	228	WS-Game 6: Pittsburgh at Baltimore	1.50	3.00
☐	229	WS-Game 7: Pittsburgh at Baltimore	1.50	3.00
☐	230	On Top of the World! Pittsburgh Pirates	1.50	3.00
☐	231	Casey Cox, Tex.	.75	1.50
☐	232	S.F.: Chris Arnold/ Jim Barr/ Dave Rader	.75	1.50
☐	233	Jay Johnstone, Chi.-A.L.	.75	1.50
☐	234	Ron Taylor, Mtl.	1.50	3.00
☐	235	Merv Rettenmund, Bal.	.75	1.50
☐	236	Jim McGlothlin, Cin.	.75	1.50
☐	237	New York Yankees	1.50	3.00
☐	238	Leron Lee, S.D.	.75	1.50
☐	239	Tom Timmerman, Det.	.75	1.50
☐	240	Rich Allen, Chi.-A.L.	.75	1.50
☐	241	Rollie Fingers, Oak.	4.25	8.50
☐	242	Don Mincher, Tex.	.75	1.50
☐	243	Frank Linzy, Stl.	.75	1.50
☐	**244**	**Steve Braun, Min., RC**	**.75**	**1.50**
☐	245	Tommie Agee, NYM.	.75	1.50
☐	246	Tom Burgmeier, K.C.	.75	1.50
☐	247	Milt May, Pgh.	.75	1.50
☐	248	Tom Bradley, Chi.-A.L.	.75	1.50
☐	249	Harry Walker, Mgr., Hou.	.75	1.50
☐	250	Boog Powell, Bal.	1.50	3.00
☐	251	Checklist: 3rd Series (264-394)	2.00	4.00
☐	252	Ken Reynolds, Pha.	.75	1.50
☐	253	Sandy Alomar, Cal.	.75	1.50
☐	254	Boots Day, Mtl.	.75	1.50
☐	255	Jim Lonborg, Mil.	.75	1.50
☐	256	George Foster, Cin.	1.50	3.00
☐	257	Det.: Jim Foor/ Tim Hosley/ Paul Jata	.75	1.50
☐	258	Randy Hundley, Chi.-N.L.	.75	1.50
☐	259	Sparky Lyle, Bos.	.75	1.50
☐	260	Ralph Garr, Atl.	.75	1.50
☐	261	Steve Mingori, Cle.	.75	1.50
☐	262	San Diego Padres	1.50	3.00
☐	263	Felipe Alou, NYY.	2.00	4.00
☐	264	Tommy John, L.A.	2.00	4.00
☐	265	Wes Parker, L.A.	1.00	2.00
☐	266	Bobby Bolin, Bos.	1.00	2.00
☐	267	Dave Concepcion, Cin.	2.00	4.00
☐	268	Oak.: Dwain Anderson/ Chris Floethe	1.00	2.00
☐	269	Don Hahn, NYM.	1.00	2.00
☐	270	Jim Palmer, Bal.	7.50	15.00
☐	271	Ken Rudolph, Chi.-N.L.	1.00	2.00
☐	272	Mickey Rivers, Cal., RC	1.00	2.00
☐	273	Bobby Floyd, K.C.	1.00	2.00
☐	274	Al Severinsen, S.D.	1.00	2.00
☐	275	Cesar Tovar, Min.	1.00	2.00
☐	276	Gene Mauch, Mgr., Mtl.	1.00	2.00
☐	277	Elliott Maddox, Tex.	1.00	2.00
☐	278	Dennis Higgins, Stl.	1.00	2.00
☐	279	Larry Brown, Oak.	1.00	2.00
☐	280	Willie McCovey, S.F.	5.00	10.00
☐	**281**	**Bill Parsons, Mil., RC**	**1.00**	**2.00**
☐	282	Houston Astros	2.00	4.00

	No.	Player		
☐	283	Darrell Brandon, Pha.	1.00	2.00
☐	284	Ike Brown, Det.	1.00	2.00
☐	285	Gaylord Perry, Cle.	5.00	10.00
☐	286	Gene Alley, Pgh.	1.00	2.00
☐	287	Jim Hardin, NYY.	1.00	2.00
☐	288	Johnny Jeter, S.D.	1.00	2.00
☐	289	Syd O'Brien, Cal.	1.00	2.00
☐	290	Sonny Siebert, Bos.	1.00	2.00
☐	291	Hal McRae, Cin.	1.00	2.00
☐	292	In Action: Hal McRae, Cin.	1.00	2.00
☐	293	Danny Frisella, NYM.	1.00	2.00
☐	294	In Action: Danny Frisella, NYM.	1.00	2.00
☐	295	Dick Dietz, S.F.	1.00	2.00
☐	296	In Action: Dick Dietz, L.A.	1.00	2.00
☐	297	Claude Osteen, L.A.	1.00	2.00
☐	298	In Action: Claude Osteen, L.A.	1.00	2.00
☐	299	Hank Aaron, Atl.	30.00	60.00
☐	300	In Action: Hank Aaron, Atl.	18.00	35.00
☐	301	George Mitterwald, Min.	1.00	2.00
☐	302	In Action: George Mitterwald, Min.	1.00	2.00
☐	303	Joe Pepitone, Chi.-N.L.	1.00	2.00
☐	304	In Action: Joe Pepitone, Chi.-N.L.	1.00	2.00
☐	305	Ken Boswell, NYM.	1.00	2.00
☐	306	In Action: Ken Boswell, NYM.	1.00	2.00
☐	307	Steve Renko, Mtl.	1.00	2.00
☐	308	In Action: Steve Renko, Mtl.	1.00	2.00
☐	309	Roberto Clemente, Pgh.	35.00	70.00
☐	310	In Action: Roberto Clemente, Pgh.	18.00	35.00
☐	311	Clay Carroll, Cin.	1.00	2.00
☐	312	In Action: Clay Carroll, Cin.	1.00	2.00
☐	313	Luis Aparicio, Bos.	3.00	6.00
☐	314	In Action: Luis Aparicio, Bos.	1.50	3.00
☐	315	Paul Splittorff, K.C.	1.00	2.00
☐	316	Stl.: J. Bibby/ J. Roque/ S. Guzman	1.00	2.00
☐	317	Rich Hand, Tex.	1.00	2.00
☐	318	Sonny Jackson, Atl.	1.00	2.00
☐	319	Aurelio Rodriguez, Det.	1.00	2.00
☐	320	Steve Blass, Pgh.	1.00	2.00
☐	321	Joe Lahoud, Mil.	1.00	2.00
☐	322	Jose Pena, L.A.	1.00	2.00
☐	323	Earl Weaver, Mgr., Bal.	3.00	6.00
☐	324	Mike Ryan, Pha.	1.00	2.00
☐	325	Mel Stottlemyre, NYY.	1.00	2.00
☐	326	Pat Kelly, Chi.-A.L.	1.00	2.00
☐	**327**	**Steve Stone, S.F., RC**	**1.50**	**3.00**
☐	328	Boston Red Sox	2.00	4.00
☐	329	Roy Foster, Tex.	1.00	2.00
☐	330	Jim Hunter, Oak.	3.50	7.00
☐	**331**	**Stan Swanson, Mtl., RC**	**1.00**	**2.00**
☐	332	Buck Martinez, K.C.	1.00	2.00
☐	333	Steve Barber, Atl.	1.00	2.00
☐	334	Tex.: Bill Fahey/ Jim Mason/ Tom Ragland	1.00	2.00
☐	335	Bill Hands, Chi.-N.L.	1.00	2.00
☐	336	Marty Martinez, Stl.	1.00	2.00
☐	337	Mike Kilkenny, Det.	1.75	3.50
☐	338	Bob Grich, Bal.	1.50	3.00
☐	339	Ron Cook, Hou.	1.00	2.00
☐	340	Roy White, NYY.	1.00	2.00
☐	341	Joe Torre, Stl. (Youth)	1.50	3.00
☐	342	Wilbur Wood, Chi.-A.L. (Youth)	1.00	2.00
☐	343	Willie Stargell, Pgh. (Youth)	3.00	6.00
☐	344	Dave McNally, Bal. (Youth)	1.00	2.00
☐	345	Rick Wise, Pha. (Youth)	1.00	2.00
☐	346	Jim Fregosi, NYM. (Youth)	1.00	2.00
☐	347	Tom Seaver, NYM. (Youth)	4.00	8.00
☐	348	Sal Bando, Oak. (Youth)	1.00	2.00
☐	349	Al Fitzmorris, K.C.,	1.00	2.00
☐	350	Frank Howard, Tex.	1.00	2.00
☐	351	Atl.: Tom House/ Rick Kester/ Jimmy Britton	1.00	2.00
☐	352	Dave LaRoche, Min.	1.00	2.00
☐	353	Art Shamsky, Stl.	1.00	2.00
☐	354	Tom Murphy, Cal.	1.00	2.00
☐	355	Bob Watson, Hou.	1.00	2.00
☐	356	Gerry Moses, Cle.	1.00	2.00
☐	357	Woodie Fryman, Pha.	1.00	2.00
☐	358	Sparky Anderson, Mgr., Cin.	2.00	4.00
☐	359	Don Pavletich, Mil.	1.00	2.00
☐	360	Dave Roberts, Hou.	1.00	2.00
☐	361	Mike Andrews, Chi.-A.L.	1.00	2.00
☐	362	New York Mets	2.00	4.00
☐	363	Ron Klimkowski, Oak.	1.00	2.00
☐	364	Johnny Callison, Chi.-N.L.	1.00	2.00
☐	365	Dick Bosman, Tex.	1.00	2.00
☐	**366**	**Jimmy Rosario, S.F., RC**	**1.00**	**2.00**
☐	367	Ron Perranoski, Det.	1.00	2.00
☐	368	Danny Thompson, Min.	1.00	2.00
☐	369	Jim Lefebvre, L.A.	1.00	2.00
☐	370	Don Buford, Bal.	1.00	2.00
☐	371	Denny Lemaster, Mtl.	1.00	2.00
☐	372	K.C.: Lance Clemons/ Monty Montgomery	1.00	2.00
☐	373	John Mayberry, K.C.	1.00	2.00
☐	374	Jack Heidemann, Cle.	1.00	2.00
☐	**375**	**Reggie Cleveland, Stl.**	**1.75**	**3.50**
☐	376	Andy Kosco, Mil.	1.25	2.50
☐	377	Terry Harmon, Pha.	1.25	2.50
☐	378	Checklist: 4th Series (395 - 525)	2.50	5.00
☐	379	Ken Berry, Cal.	1.25	2.50
☐	380	Earl Williams, Atl.	1.25	2.50
☐	381	Chicago White Sox	2.00	4.00
☐	382	Joe Gibbon, Cin.	1.25	2.50
☐	383	Brant Alyea, Oak.	1.25	2.50
☐	384	Dave Campbell, S.D.	1.25	2.50
☐	385	Mickey Stanley, Det.	1.25	2.50
☐	386	Jim Colborn, Mil.	1.25	2.50
☐	387	Horace Clarke, NYY.	1.25	2.50
☐	**388**	**Charlie Williams, NYM., RC**	**1.25**	**2.50**
☐	389	Bill Rigney, Mgr., Min.	1.25	2.50
☐	390	Willie Davis, L.A.	1.25	2.50
☐	391	Ken Sanders, Mil.	1.25	2.50
☐	**392**	**Pgh.: Fred Cambria/ Richie Zisk (RCs)**	**2.00**	**4.00**
☐	393	Curt Motton, Mil.	1.25	2.50
☐	394	Ken Forsch, Hou.	1.25	2.50
☐	395	Matty Alou, Stl.	1.25	2.50
☐	396	Paul Lindblad, Tex.	1.25	2.50
☐	397	Philadelphia Phillies	2.00	4.00
☐	398	Larry Hisle, L.A.	1.25	2.50
☐	399	Milt Wilcox, Cle.	1.25	2.50
☐	400	Tony Oliva, Min.	2.00	4.00
☐	401	Jim Nash, Atl.	1.25	2.50
☐	402	Bobby Heise, Mil.	1.25	2.50
☐	403	John Cumberland, S.F.	1.25	2.50
☐	404	Jeff Torborg, Cal.	1.25	2.50
☐	405	Ron Fairly, Mtl.	1.25	2.50
☐	**406**	**George Hendrick, Oak., RC**	**1.25**	**2.50**
☐	407	Chuck Taylor, NYM.	1.25	2.50
☐	408	Jim Northrup, Det.	1.25	2.50
☐	409	Frank Baker, NYY.	1.25	2.50
☐	410	Fergie Jenkins, Chi.-N.L.	6.00	12.00
☐	411	Bob Montgomery, Bos.	1.25	2.50
☐	412	Dick Kelley, S.D.	1.25	2.50
☐	413	Chi.-A.L.: Don Eddy/ Dave Lemonds	1.25	2.50
☐	414	Bob Miller, Pgh.	1.25	2.50
☐	415	Cookie Rojas, K.C.	1.25	2.50
☐	416	Johnny Edwards, Hou.	1.25	2.50
☐	417	Tom Hall, Cin.	1.25	2.50
☐	418	Tom Shopay, Bal.	1.25	2.50
☐	419	Jim Spencer, Cal.	1.25	2.50
☐	420	Steve Carlton, Pha.	15.00	30.00

☐	421	Ellie Rodriguez, Mil.	1.25	2.50
☐	422	Ray Lamb, Cle.	1.25	2.50
☐	423	Oscar Gamble, Pha.	1.25	2.50
☐	424	Bill Gogolewski, Tex.	1.25	2.50
☐	425	Ken Singleton, NYM.	2.00	4.00
☐	426	In Action: Ken Singleton, NYM.	1.25	2.50
☐	427	Tito Fuentes, S.F.	1.25	2.50
☐	428	In Action: Tito Fuentes, S.F.	1.25	2.50
☐	429	Bob Robertson, Pgh.	1.25	2.50
☐	430	In Action: Bob Robertson, Pgh.	1.25	2.50
☐	431	Cito Gaston, S.D.	1.25	2.50
☐	432	In Action: Cito Gaston, S.D.	1.25	2.50
☐	433	Johnny Bench, Cin.	20.00	40.00
☐	434	In Action: Johnny Bench, Cin.	12.00	24.00
☐	435	Reggie Jackson, Oak.	22.50	45.00
☐	436	In Action: Reggie Jackson, Oak.	13.50	27.00
☐	437	Maury Wills, L.A.	2.50	5.00
☐	438	In Action: Maury Wills, L.A.	1.25	2.50
☐	439	Billy Williams, Chi.-N.L.	4.00	8.00
☐	440	In Action: Billy Williams, Chi.-N.L.	2.50	5.00
☐	441	Thurman Munson, NYY.	10.00	20.00
☐	442	In Action: Thurman Munson, NYY.	6.00	12.00
☐	443	Ken Henderson, S.F.	1.25	2.50
☐	444	In Action: Ken Henderson, S.F.	1.25	2.50
☐	445	Tom Seaver, NYM.	25.00	50.00
☐	446	In Action: Tom Seaver, NYM.	15.00	30.00
☐	447	Willie Stargell, Pgh.	5.00	10.00
☐	448	In Action: Willie Stargell, Pgh.	3.00	6.00
☐	449	Bob Lemon, Mgr., K.C.	2.00	4.00
☐	450	Mickey Lolich, Det.	1.25	2.50
☐	451	Tony LaRussa, Atl.	2.50	5.00
☐	452	Ed Herrmann, Chi.-A.L.	1.25	2.50
☐	453	Berry Lersch, Pha.	1.25	2.50
☐	454	Oakland A's	2.00	4.00
☐	455	Tommy Harper, Bos.	1.25	2.50
☐	456	Mark Belanger, Bal.	1.25	2.50
☐	457	S.D.: Darcy Fast/ Derrel Thomas/ Mike Ivie	1.25	2.50
☐	458	Aurelio Monteagudo, K.C.	1.25	2.50
☐	459	Rick Renick, Min.	1.25	2.50
☐	460	Al Downing, L.A.	1.25	2.50
☐	461	Tim Cullen, Oak.	1.25	2.50
☐	462	Rickey Clark, Cal.	1.25	2.50
☐	463	Bernie Carbo, Cin.	1.25	2.50
☐	464	Jim Roland, Oak.	1.25	2.50
☐	465	HL: Gil Hodges, Mgr., NYM.	2.00	4.00
☐	466	Norm Miller, Hou.	1.25	2.50
☐	467	Steve Kline, NYY.	1.25	2.50
☐	468	Richie Scheinblum, K.C.	1.25	2.50
☐	469	Ron Herbel, Atl.	1.25	2.50
☐	470	Ray Fosse, Cle.	1.25	2.50
☐	471	Luke Walker, Pgh.	1.25	2.50
☐	472	Phil Gagliano, Bos.	1.25	2.50
☐	473	Dan McGinn, Mtl.	1.25	2.50
☐	474	Bal.: D. Baylor/ R. Harrison/ J. Oates	10.00	20.00
☐	475	Gary Nolan, Cin.	1.25	2.50
☐	**476**	**Lee Richard, Chi.-A.L., RC**	**1.25**	**2.50**
☐	477	Tom Phoebus, S.D.	1.25	2.50
☐	478	Checklist: 5th Series (526 - 656)	2.50	5.00
☐	479	Don Shaw, Stl.	1.25	2.50
☐	480	Lee May, Hou.	1.25	2.50
☐	481	Billy Conigliaro, Mil.	1.25	2.50
☐	482	Joe Hoerner, Pha.	1.25	2.50
☐	483	Ken Suarez, Tex.	1.25	2.50
☐	484	Lum Harris, Mgr., Atl.	1.25	2.50
☐	485	Phil Regan, Chi.-N.L.	1.25	2.50
☐	486	John Lowenstein, Cle.	1.25	2.50
☐	487	Detroit Tigers	2.00	4.00
☐	488	Mike Nagy, Bos.	1.25	2.50
☐	489	Mtl.: Terry Humphrey/ Keith Lampard	1.25	2.50
☐	490	Dave McNally, Bal.	1.25	2.50
☐	491	Lou Piniella, K.C. (Youth)	1.25	2.50
☐	492	Mel Stottlemyre, NYY. (Youth)	1.25	2.50
☐	493	Bob Bailey, Mtl. (Youth)	1.25	2.50
☐	494	Willie Horton, Det. (Youth)	1.25	2.50
☐	495	Bill Melton, Chi.-A.L. (Youth)	1.25	2.50
☐	496	Bud Harrelson, NYM. (Youth)	1.25	2.50
☐	497	Jim Perry, Min. (Youth)	1.25	2.50
☐	498	Brooks Robinson, Bal. (Youth)	1.25	2.50
☐	499	Vicente Romo, Chi.-A.L.	1.25	2.50
☐	500	Joe Torre, Stl.	2.00	4.00
☐	501	Pete Hamm, Min.	1.25	2.50
☐	502	Jackie Hernandez, Pgh.	1.25	2.50
☐	503	Gary Peters, Bos.	1.25	2.50
☐	504	Ed Spiezio, S.D.	1.25	2.50
☐	505	Mike Marshall, Mtl.	2.00	4.00
☐	506	Cle.: Terry Ley/ Jim Moyer/ Dick Tidrow	1.25	2.50
☐	507	Fred Gladding, Hou.	1.25	2.50
☐	508	Ellie Hendricks, Bal.	1.25	2.50
☐	509	Don McMahon, S.F.	1.25	2.50
☐	510	Ted Williams, Mgr., Tex.	7.50	15.00
☐	511	Tony Taylor, Det.	1.25	2.50
☐	512	Paul Popovich, Chi.-N.L.	1.25	2.50
☐	513	Lindy McDaniel, NYY.	1.25	2.50
☐	514	Ted Sizemore, Stl.	1.25	2.50
☐	515	Bert Blyleven, Min.	2.50	5.00
☐	516	Oscar Brown, Atl.	1.25	2.50
☐	517	Ken Brett, Mil.	1.25	2.50
☐	518	Wayne Garrett, NYM.	1.25	2.50
☐	519	Ted Abernathy, K.C.	1.25	2.50
☐	520	Larry Bowa, Pha.	2.00	4.00
☐	521	Alan Foster, Cal.	1.25	2.50
☐	522	Los Angeles Dodgers	2.00	4.00
☐	523	Chuck Dobson, Oak.	1.25	2.50
☐	524	Cin.: Ed Armbrister/ Mel Behney	1.25	2.50
☐	525	Carlos May, Chi.-A.L.	1.25	4.00

1972 PRO STAR PROMOTIONS

Postcard Size: 3 1/2" x 5 1/2"
Face: Four colour; name, league name
Back: Blank
Imprint: COPYRIGHT PRO STAR PROMOTIONS INC.

Complete Set (36 cards):		**150.00**	**300.00**
	Player	**EX**	**NRMT**
☐	Hank Aaron, Atl.	15.00	30.00
☐	Bob Bailey, Mtl.	3.50	7.50
☐	Johnny Bench, Cin.	10.00	20.00
☐	Vida Blue, Oak.	6.00	12.00
☐	John Boccabella, Mtl.	3.50	7.50
☐	Roberto Clemente, Pgh.	17.50	35.00

	Player	EX	NRMT
☐	Boots Day, Mtl.	3.50	7.50
☐	Jim Fairey, Mtl.	3.50	7.50
☐	Tim Foli, Mtl.	3.50	7.50
☐	Ron Hunt, Mtl.	3.50	7.50
☐	Reggie Jackson, Oak.	9.00	18.00
☐	Fergie Jenkins, Chi.-N.L.	7.50	15.00
☐	Mike Jorgenson, Mtl.	3.50	7.50
☐	Al Kaline, Det.	9.00	18.00
☐	Harmon Killebrew, Min.	10.00	20.00
☐	Mickey Lolich, Det.	6.00	12.00
☐	Juan Marichal, NYG.	7.50	15.00
☐	Wille Mays, NYG.	15.00	30.00
☐	Ernie McAnnally	3.50	7.00
☐	William McCovey, NYG.	10.00	20.00
☐	Dave McNally, Bal.	4.00	8.00
☐	Bill Melton, Chi.-A.L.	3.50	7.50
☐	Carl Morton, Mtl.	3.50	7.50
☐	Bobby Murcer, NNY.	6.00	12.00
☐	Fritz Peterson, NNY.	3.50	7.50
☐	Boog Powell, Bal.	6.00	12.00
☐	Steve Renko, Mtl.	3.50	7.50
☐	Merv Rettenmund, Bal.	3.50	7.50
☐	Brooks Robinson, Bal.	10.00	20.00
☐	Frank Robinson, NYD.	10.00	20.00
☐	Pete Rose, Cin.	10.00	20.00
☐	Tom Seaver, NYM.	10.00	20.00
☐	Ken Singleton, Mtl.	6.00	12.00
☐	Willie Stargell, Pgh.	9.00	18.00
☐	Bill Stoneman, Mtl.	3.50	7.50
☐	Joe Torre, St.	7.50	15.00
☐	Checklist	5.00	10.00

1972 PRO STAR PROMOTIONS POSTERS

Listed alphabetically
Poster Size:
Face: Four colour; name, league name
Back: Blank
Imprint: COPYRIGHT PRO STAR PROMOTIONS INC.

	No.	Player	EX	NRMT
		Complete Set (12 posters):	**175.00**	**350.00**
☐	1	Hank Aaron, Atl.	30.00	60.00
☐	2	Vida Blue, Oak.	12.00	25.00
☐	3	Roberto Clemente, Pgh.	35.00	70.00
☐	4	Ron Hunt, Mtl.	7.50	15.00
☐	5	Fergie Jenkins, Chi.-N.L.	15.00	30.00
☐	6	Willie Mays, S.F.	30.00	60.00
☐	7	Juan Marichal, S.F.	15.00	30.00
☐	8	Boog Powell, Bal.	12.00	25.00
☐	9	Frank Robinson, L.A.	20.00	40.00
☐	10	Pete Rose, Cin.	20.00	40.00
☐	11	Willie Stargell, Pgh.	17.50	35.00
☐	12	Bill Stoneman, Mtl.	7.50	15.00

1972 - 73 DIMANCHE / DERNIERE HEURE

1972 ISSUES

These photos were inserted in Derniere magazine. Three holes were punched on the left side to allow for storage in a binder. This set of photographs included hockey, baseball, football and soccer players, as well as those in wrestling, boxing, car racing and golf. Only the baseball photos are listed here.

Stamp Size: 8" x 10"
Face: Four colour, white border, name, jersey number, position, resume, French
Back: Blank
Imprint: DIMANCHE / DERNIERE HEURE

	No.	Player
☐	1	Bob Bailey
☐	2	John Boccabella
☐	3	Boots Day
☐	4	Ron Fairly
☐	5	Tim Foli
☐	6	Barry Foote
☐	7	Terry Humphrey
☐	8	Ron Hunt
☐	9	Mike Jorgensen
☐	11	Gene Mauch, Manager
☐	12	Ernie McAnally
☐	13	Steve Renko
☐	14	Ken Singleton
☐	15	Bill Stoneman
☐	16	Mike Torrez
☐	17	Bobby Wine
☐	18	Ron Woods

1973 ISSUES

Stamp Size: 8" x 10"
Face: Four colour, white border, name, jersey number, position, resume, French
Back:Blank
Imprint: DIMANCHE / DERNIERE HEURE

	No.	Player
☐	1	Coco Laboy
☐	2	Rusty Staub

1973 O-PEE-CHEE

Card Size: 2 1/2" x 3 1/2"
Face: Four colour, white border; name, position, team
Back: Gold and black on card stock; name, number, résumé, player trivia, bilingual
Imprint: * © O.P.C. PRINTED IN CANADA

	No.	Player	EX	NRMT
		Complete Set (660 cards):	**550.00**	**1,100.00**
		Common Player (1 - 264):	**.50**	**1.00**
		Common Player (265 - 396):	**.75**	**1.25**
		Common Player (397 - 528):	**1.00**	**2.00**
		Common Player (529 - 660):	**2.50**	**5.00**
☐	1	LL: Hank Aaron/ Willie Mays/ Babe Ruth	22.50	55.00
☐	2	Rich Hebner, Pgh.	.50	1.00
☐	3	Jim Lonborg, Pha.	.50	1.00
☐	4	John Milner, NYM.	.50	1.00
☐	5	Ed Brinkman, Det.	.50	1.00
☐	**6**	**Mac Scarce, Pha., RC**	**.50**	**1.00**
☐	7	Texas Rangers	1.00	2.00
☐	8	Tom Hall, Cin.	.50	1.00
☐	9	Johnny Oates, Bal.	1.50	3.00
☐	10	Don Sutton, L.A.	2.00	4.00
☐	11	Chris Chambliss, Cle.	.50	1.00
☐	12	S.D.: Manager: D. Zimmer Coaches: D. Garcia / J. Podres; Bob Skinner/ W. Wietelmann	.50	1.00
☐	13	George Hendrick, Oak.	.50	1.00

☐ 14	Sonny Siebert, Bos.	.50	1.00
☐ 15	Ralph Garr, Atl.	.50	1.00
☐ 16	Steve Braun, Min.	.50	1.00
☐ 17	Fred Gladding, Hou.	.50	1.00
☐ 18	Leroy Stanton, Cal.	.50	1.00
☐ 19	Tim Foli, Mtl.	.50	1.00
☐ 20	Stan Bahnsen, Chi.-A.L.	.50	1.00
☐ 21	Randy Hundley, Chi.-N.L.	.50	1.00
☐ 22	Ted Abernathy, K.C.	.50	1.00
☐ 23	Dave Kingman, S.F.	1.00	2.00
☐ 24	Al Santorini, Stl.	.50	1.00
☐ 25	Roy White, NYY.	.50	1.00
☐ 26	Pittsburgh Pirates	1.00	2.00
☐ 27	Bill Gogolewski, Tex.	.50	1.00
☐ 28	Hal McRae, Cin.	.50	1.00
☐ 29	Tony Taylor, Det.	.50	1.00
☐ 30	Tug McGraw, NYM.	.50	1.00
☐ **31**	**All-Star Rookie: Buddy Bell, Cle., RC**	**2.00**	**4.00**
☐ 32	Fred Norman, S.D.	.50	1.00
☐ **33**	**Jim Breazeale, Atl., RC**	**.50**	**1.00**
☐ 34	Pat Dobson, Bal.	.50	1.00
☐ 35	Willie Davis, L.A.	.50	1.00
☐ 36	Steve Barber, Cal.	.50	1.00
☐ 37	Bill Robinson, Pha.	.50	1.00
☐ 38	Mike Epstein, Oak.	.50	1.00
☐ 39	Dave Roberts, Hou.	.50	1.00
☐ 40	Reggie Smith, Bos.	.50	1.00
☐ **41**	**Tom Walker, Mtl., RC**	**.50**	**1.00**
☐ 42	Mike Andrews, Chi.-A.L.	.50	1.00
☐ **43**	**Randy Moffitt, S.F., RC**	**.50**	**1.00**
☐ 44	Rick Monday, Chi.-N.L.	.50	1.00
☐ 45	Ellie Rodriguez, Mil.	.50	1.00
☐ 46	Lindy McDaniel, NYY.	.50	1.00
☐ 47	Luis Melendez, Stl.	.50	1.00
☐ 48	Paul Splittorff, K.C.	.50	1.00
☐ 49	Min.: Manager: F. Quilici Coaches: V. Morgan / B. Rodgers; R. Rowe/ A. Worthington	.50	1.00
☐ 50	Roberto Clemente, Pgh.	37.50	75.00
☐ **51**	**Chuck Seelbach, Det., RC**	**.50**	**1.00**
☐ 52	Denis Menke, Cin.	.50	1.00
☐ 53	Steve Dunning, Cle.	.50	1.00
☐ 54	Checklist 1 (1 - 132)	1.00	2.00
☐ 55	Don Matlack, NYM.	.50	1.00
☐ 56	Merv Rettenmund, Bal.	.50	1.00
☐ 57	Derrel Thomas, S.D.	.50	1.00
☐ 58	Mike Paul, Tex.	.50	1.00
☐ **59**	**Steve Yeager, L.A., RC**	**1.00**	**2.00**
☐ 60	Ken Holtzman, Oak.	.50	1.00
☐ 61	LL: B. Williams/ Rod Carew	1.50	3.00
☐ 62	LL: J. Bench/ Dick Allen	1.25	2.50
☐ 63	LL: J. Bench/ D. Allen	1.25	2.50
☐ 64	LL: L. Brock/ B. Campaneris	1.25	2.50
☐ 65	LL: S. Carlton/ L. Tiant	1.25	2.50
☐ 66	LL: S. Carlton/ G. Perry/ W. Wood	1.50	3.00
☐ 67	LL: S. Carlton/ Nolan Ryan	22.50	45.00
☐ 68	LL: C. Carroll/ S. Lyle	1.00	2.00
☐ 69	Phil Gagliano, Bos.	.50	1.00
☐ 70	Milt Pappas, Chi.-N.L.	.50	1.00
☐ 71	Johnny Briggs, Mil.	.50	1.00
☐ 72	Ron Reed, Atl.	.50	1.00
☐ 73	Ed Herrmann, Chi.-A.L.	.50	1.00
☐ 74	Billy Champion, Mil.	.50	1.00
☐ 75	Vada Pinson, Cal.	.50	1.00
☐ 76	Doug Rader, Hou.	.50	1.00
☐ 77	Mike Torrez, Mtl.	.50	1.00
☐ 78	Richie Scheinblum, K.C.	.50	1.00
☐ **79**	**Jim Willoughby, S.F., RC**	**.50**	**1.00**
☐ 80	Tony Oliva, Min.	1.00	2.00
☐ 81	Chi.: Manager: W. Lockman Coaches: H. Aguirre / E. Banks/ L. Jansen/ P. Reiser	1.50	3.00
☐ 82	Fritz Peterson, NYY.	.50	1.00
☐ 83	Leron Lee, S.D.	.50	1.00
☐ 84	Rollie Fingers, Oak.	3.50	7.00
☐ 85	Ted Simmons, Stl.	1.00	2.00
☐ 86	Tom McCraw, Cle.	.50	1.00
☐ 87	Ken Boswell, NYM.	.50	1.00
☐ 88	Mickey Stanley, Det.	.50	1.00
☐ 89	Jack Billingham, Cin.	.50	1.00
☐ 90	Brooks Robinson, Bal.	6.00	12.00
☐ 91	Los Angeles Dodgers	1.00	2.00
☐ 92	Jerry Bell, Mil.	.50	1.00
☐ 93	Jesus Alou, Hou.	.50	1.00
☐ 94	Dick Billings, Tex.	.50	1.00
☐ 95	Steve Blass, Pgh.	.50	1.00
☐ 96	Doug Griffin, Bos.	.50	1.00
☐ 97	Willie Montanez, Pha.	.50	1.00
☐ 98	Dick Woodson, Min.	.50	1.00
☐ 99	Carl Taylor, K.C.	.50	1.00
☐ 100	Hank Aaron, Atl.	22.50	45.00
☐ 101	Ken Henderson, S.F.	.50	1.00
☐ 102	Rudy May, Cal.	.50	1.00
☐ **103**	**Celerino Sanchez, NYY., RC**	**.50**	**1.00**
☐ 104	Reggie Cleveland, Stl.	1.00	2.00
☐ 105	Carlos May, Chi.-A.L.	.50	1.00
☐ 106	Terry Humphrey, Mtl.	.50	1.00
☐ 107	Phil Hennigan, NYM.	.50	1.00
☐ 108	Bill Russell, L.A.	.50	1.00
☐ 109	Doyle Alexander, Bal.	.50	1.00
☐ 110	Bob Watson, Hou.	.50	1.00
☐ 111	Dave Nelson, Tex.	.50	1.00
☐ 112	Gary Ross, S.D.	.50	1.00
☐ 113	Jerry Grote, NYM.	.50	1.00
☐ **114**	**Lynn McGlothen, Bos., RC**	**.50**	**1.00**
☐ 115	Ron Santo, Chi.-N.L.	1.00	2.00
☐ 116	NNY.: Manager: R. Houk Coaches: J. Hegan / E. Howard/ D. Howser/ J. Turner	.50	1.00
☐ 117	Ramon Hernandez, Pgh.	.50	1.00
☐ 118	John Mayberry, K.C.	.50	1.00
☐ 119	Larry Bowa, Pha.	.50	1.00
☐ 120	Joe Coleman, Det.	.50	1.00
☐ 121	Dave Rader, S.F.	.50	1.00
☐ 122	Jim Strickland, Min.	.50	1.00
☐ 123	Sandy Alomar, Cal.	.50	1.00
☐ 124	Jim Hardin, Atl.	.50	1.00
☐ 125	Ron Fairly, Mtl.	.50	1.00
☐ 126	Jim Brewer, L.A.	.50	1.00
☐ 127	Milwaukee Brewers	1.00	2.00
☐ 128	Ted Sizemore, Stl.	.50	1.00
☐ 129	Terry Forster, Chi.-A.L.	.50	1.00
☐ 130	Pete Rose, Cin.	15.00	30.00
☐ 131	Bos.: Manager: E. Kasko; Coaches: D. Camilli / D. Lenhardt/ E. Popowski; L. Stange	.50	1.00
☐ 132	Matty Alou, NYY.	.50	1.00
☐ 133	All-Star Rookie: Dave Roberts, S.D.	.50	1.00
☐ 134	Milt Wilcox, Cle.	.50	1.00
☐ 135	Lee May, Hou.	.50	1.00
☐ 136	Bal.: Manager: E. Weaver; Coaches: G. Bamberger / J. Frey/ B. Hunter/ G. Staller	1.75	3.50
☐ 137	Jim Beauchamp, NYM.	.50	1.00
☐ 138	Horacio Pina, Tex.	.50	1.00
☐ **139**	**Carmen Fanzone, Chi.-N.L., RC**	**.50**	**1.00**
☐ 140	Lou Piniella, K.C.	.50	1.00
☐ 141	Bruce Kison, Pgh.	.50	1.00
☐ 142	Thurman Munson, NYY.	4.25	8.50
☐ 143	John Curtis, Bos.	.50	1.00
☐ 144	Marty Perez, Atl.	.50	1.00
☐ 145	Bobby Bonds, S.F.	1.00	2.00
☐ 146	Woodie Fryman, Det.	.50	1.00

	No.	Card		
☐	147	Mike Anderson, Pha.	.50	1.00
☐	**148**	**Dave Goltz, Min., RC**	**.50**	**1.00**
☐	149	Ron Hunt, Mtl.	.50	1.00
☐	150	Wilbur Wood, Chi.-A.L.	.50	1.00
☐	151	Wes Parker, L.A.	.50	1.00
☐	152	Dave May, Mil.	.50	1.00
☐	153	Al Hrabosky, Stl.	.50	1.00
☐	154	Jeff Torborg, Cal.	.50	1.00
☐	155	Sal Bando, Oak.	.50	1.00
☐	156	Cesar Geronimo, Cin.	.50	1.00
☐	157	Denny Riddleberger, Cle.	.50	1.00
☐	158	Houston Astros	1.00	2.00
☐	159	Clarence Gaston, S.D.	.50	1.00
☐	160	Jim Palmer, Bal.	6.00	12.00
☐	161	Ted Martinez, NYM.	.50	1.00
☐	162	Pete Broberg, Tex.	.50	1.00
☐	163	Vic Davalillo, Pgh.	.50	1.00
☐	164	Monty Montgomery, K.C.	.50	1.00
☐	165	Luis Aparicio, Bos.	1.50	3.00
☐	166	Terry Harmon, Pha.	.50	1.00
☐	167	Steve Stone, S.F.	.50	1.00
☐	168	Jim Northrup, Det.	.50	1.00
☐	**169**	**Ron Schueler, Atl., RC**	**.50**	**1.00**
☐	170	Harmon Killebrew, Min.	3.75	7.50
☐	171	Bernie Carbo, Stl.	.50	1.00
☐	172	Steve Kline, NYY.	.50	1.00
☐	173	Hal Breeden, Mtl.	.50	1.00
☐	**174**	**Rich Gossage, Chi.-A.L., RC**	**6.00**	**12.00**
☐	175	Frank Robinson, Cal.	5.00	10.00
☐	176	Chuck Taylor, Mil.	.50	1.00
☐	**177**	**Bill Plummer, Cin., RC**	**.50**	**1.00**
☐	**178**	**Don Rose, Cal., RC**	**.50**	**1.00**
☐	179	Oak.: Manager: D. Williams; Coaches: J. Adair / V. Hoscheit/ I. Noren/ W. Stock	.50	1.00
☐	180	Fergie Jenkins, Chi.-N.L.	4.75	8.50
☐	**181**	**ASR: Jack Brohamer, Cle., RC**	**.50**	**1.00**
☐	**182**	**Mike Caldwell, S.D., RC**	**.50**	**1.00**
☐	183	Don Buford, Bal.	.50	1.00
☐	184	Jerry Koosman, NYM.	.50	1.00
☐	185	Jim Wynn, Hou.	.50	1.00
☐	186	Bill Fahey, Tex.	.50	1.00
☐	187	Luke Walker, Pgh.	.50	1.00
☐	188	Cookie Rojas, K.C.	.50	1.00
☐	189	Greg Luzinski, Pha.	.50	1.00
☐	190	Bob Gibson, Stl.	6.00	12.00
☐	191	Detroit Tigers	1.00	2.00
☐	192	Pat Jarvis, Atl.	.50	1.00
☐	193	Carlton Fisk, Bos.	7.50	15.00
☐	**194**	**Jorge Orta, Chi.-A.L., RC**	**.50**	**1.00**
☐	195	Clay Carroll, Cin.	.50	1.00
☐	196	Ken McMullen, L.A.	.50	1.00
☐	**197**	**Ed Goodson, S.F., RC**	**.50**	**1.00**
☐	198	Horace Clarke, NYY.	.50	1.00
☐	199	Bert Blyleven, Min.	1.00	2.00
☐	200	Billy Williams, Chi.-N.L.	2.00	4.00
☐	201	A.L.: Hendrick Scores Winning Run	1.00	2.00
☐	202	N.L.: Foster's Run Decides It	1.00	2.00
☐	203	WS-Game 1: Tenace The Menace	1.00	2.00
☐	204	WS-Game 2: A's Make It Two Straight	1.00	2.00
☐	205	WS-Game 3: Reds Win Squeaker	1.00	2.00
☐	206	WS-Game 4: Tenace Singles In Ninth	1.00	2.00
☐	207	WS-Game 5: Odom Out At Plate	1.00	2.00
☐	208	WS-Game 6: Reds' Slugging Ties Series	4.00	8.00
☐	209	WS-Game 7: Campy Starts Winning Rally	1.00	2.00
☐	210	A's Win!: World Champions	1.00	2.00
☐	211	Balor Moore, Mtl.	.50	1.00
☐	212	Joe Lahoud, Mil.	.50	1.00
☐	213	Steve Garvey, L.A.	4.00	8.00
☐	**214**	**Dave Hamilton, Oak., RC**	**.50**	**1.00**
☐	215	Dusty Baker, Atl.	.50	1.00
☐	216	Toby Harrah, Tex.	1.00	2.00
☐	217	Don Wilson, Hou.	.50	1.00
☐	218	Aurelio Rodriguez, Det.	.50	1.00
☐	219	St. Louis Cardinals	1.00	2.00
☐	220	Nolan Ryan	75.00	150.00
☐	221	Fred Kendall, S.D.	.50	1.00
☐	222	Rob Gardner, Oak.	.50	1.00
☐	223	Bud Harrelson, NYM.	.50	1.00
☐	224	Bill Lee, Bos.	.50	1.00
☐	225	Al Oliver, Pgh.	.50	1.00
☐	226	Ray Fosse, Cle.	.50	1.00
☐	227	Wayne Twitchell, Pha.	.50	1.00
☐	228	Bobby Darwin, Min.	.50	1.00
☐	229	Roric Harrison, Bal.	.50	1.00
☐	230	Joe Morgan, Cin.	4.00	8.00
☐	231	Bill Parsons, Mil.	.50	1.00
☐	232	Ken Singleton, Mtl.	.50	1.00
☐	233	Ed Kirkpatrick, K.C.	.50	1.00
☐	**234**	**Bill North, Oak., RC**	**.50**	**1.00**
☐	235	Jim Hunter, Oak.	2.00	4.00
☐	236	Tito Fuentes, S.F.	.50	1.00
☐	237	Atl.: Manager: E. Mathews; Coaches: L. Burdette / J. Busby/ R. Hartsfield/ K. Silvestri	1.00	2.00
☐	**238**	**Tony Muser, Chi.-A.L., RC**	**.50**	**1.00**
☐	239	Pete Richert, L.A.	.50	1.00
☐	240	Bobby Murcer, NYY.	.50	1.00
☐	241	ASR: Dwain Anderson, Stl.	.50	1.00
☐	242	George Culver, Hou.	.50	1.00
☐	243	California Angels	1.00	2.00
☐	244	Ed Acosta, S.D.	.50	1.00
☐	245	Carl Yastrzemski, Bos.	9.00	18.00
☐	246	Ken Sanders, Pha.	.50	1.00
☐	247	Del Unser, Cle.	.50	1.00
☐	248	Jerry Johnson, S.F.	.50	1.00
☐	249	Larry Biittner, Tex.	.50	1.00
☐	250	Manny Sanguillen, Pgh.	.50	1.00
☐	251	Roger Nelson, K.C.	.50	1.00
☐	252	S.F.: Manager: C. Fox; Coaches: J. Amalfitano / A. Gilbert/ D. McMahon/ J. McNamara	.50	1.00
☐	253	Mark Belanger, Bal.	.50	1.00
☐	254	Bill Stoneman, Mtl.	.50	1.00
☐	255	Reggie Jackson, Oak.	12.50	25.00
☐	256	Chris Zachary, Det.	.50	1.00
☐	257	NYM.: Manager: Y. Berra; Coaches: R. McMillan / J. Pignatano/ R. Walker/ E. Yost	1.25	2.50
☐	258	Tommy John, L.A.	1.00	2.00
☐	259	Jim Holt, Min.	.50	1.00
☐	260	Gary Nolan, Cin.	.50	1.00
☐	261	Pat Kelly, Chi.-A.L.	.50	1.00
☐	262	Jack Aker, Chi.-N.L.	.50	1.00
☐	263	George Scott, Mil.	.50	1.00
☐	264	Checklist 2 (133 - 264)	1.00	2.00
☐	265	Gene Michael, NYY.	.75	1.25
☐	266	Mike Lum, Atl.	.75	1.25
☐	267	Lloyd Allen, Cal.	.75	1.25
☐	268	Jerry Morales, S.D.	.75	1.25
☐	269	Tim McCarver, Stl.	1.00	2.00
☐	270	Luis Tiant, Bos.	.75	1.25
☐	271	Tom Hutton, Pha.	.75	1.25
☐	272	Ed Farmer, Cle.	.75	1.25
☐	273	Chris Speier, S.F.	.75	1.25
☐	274	Darold Knowles, Oak.	.75	1.25
☐	275	Tony Perez, Cin.	1.50	3.00
☐	276	Joe Lovitto, Tex.	.75	1.25
☐	277	Bob Miller, Pgh.	.75	1.25
☐	278	Baltimore Orioles	1.25	2.50
☐	279	Mike Strahler, Cal.	.75	1.25
☐	280	Al Kaline, Det.	5.00	10.00

	No.	Player		
☐	281	Mike Jorgensen, Mtl.	.75	1.25
☐	282	Steve Hovley, K.C.	.75	1.25
☐	283	Ray Sadecki, NYM.	.75	1.25
☐	**284**	**Glenn Borgmann, Min., RC**	**.75**	**1.25**
☐	285	Don Kessinger, Chi.-N.L.	.75	1.25
☐	286	Frank Linzy, Mil.	.75	1.25
☐	287	Eddie Leon, Chi.-A.L.	.75	1.25
☐	288	Gary Gentry, Atl.	.75	1.25
☐	289	Bob Oliver, Cal.	.75	1.25
☐	290	Cesar Cedeno, Hou.	.75	1.25
☐	291	Rogelio Moret, Bos.	.75	1.25
☐	292	Jose Cruz, Stl.	.75	1.25
☐	293	Bernie Allen, NYY.	.75	1.25
☐	294	Steve Arlin, S.D.	.75	1.25
☐	295	Bert Campaneris, Oak.	.75	1.25
☐	296	Cin.: Manager: S. Anderson; Coaches: A. Grammas / T. Kluszeski/ G. Scherger/ L. Shepard	1.50	3.00
☐	297	Walt Williams, Cle.	.75	1.25
☐	298	Ron Bryant, S.F.	.75	1.25
☐	299	Ted Ford, Tex.	.75	1.25
☐	300	Steve Carlton, Pha.	9.00	18.00
☐	301	Billy Grabarkewitz, Cal.	.75	1.25
☐	302	Terry Crowley, Bal.	.75	1.25
☐	303	Nelson Briles, Pgh.	.75	1.25
☐	304	Duke Sims, Det.	.75	1.25
☐	305	Willie Mays, NYM.	30.00	60.00
☐	306	Tom Burgmeier, K.C.	.75	1.25
☐	307	Boots Day, Mtl.	.75	1.25
☐	308	Skip Lockwood, Mil.	.75	1.25
☐	309	Paul Popovich, Chi.-N.L.	.75	1.25
☐	310	Dick Allen, Chi.-A.L	.75	1.25
☐	311	Joe Decker, Min.	.75	1.25
☐	312	Oscar Brown, Atl.	.75	1.25
☐	313	Jim Ray, Hou.	.75	1.25
☐	314	Ron Swoboda, NYY.	.75	1.25
☐	315	John Odom, Oak.	.75	1.25
☐	316	San Diego Padres	1.25	2.50
☐	317	Danny Cater, Bos.	.75	1.25
☐	318	Jim McGlothlin, Cin.	.75	1.25
☐	319	Jim Spencer, Cal.	.75	1.25
☐	320	Lou Brock, Stl.	4.25	8.50
☐	321	Rich Hinton, Tex.	.75	1.25
☐	**322**	**Garry Maddox, S.F., RC**	**1.50**	**3.00**
☐	323	Det.: Manager: B. Martin; Coaches: A. Fowler / J. Schultz Jr./ C. Silvera/ D. Tracewski	1.50	3.00
☐	324	Al Downing, L.A.	.75	1.25
☐	325	Boog Powell, Bal.	1.25	2.50
☐	326	Darrell Brandon, Pha.	.75	1.25
☐	327	John Lowenstein, Cle.	.75	1.25
☐	328	Bill Bonham, Chi.-N.L.	.75	1.25
☐	329	Ed Kranepool, NYM.	.75	1.25
☐	330	Rod Carew, Min.	6.00	12.00
☐	331	Carl Morton, Mtl.	.75	1.25
☐	**332**	**John Felske, Mil., RC**	**.75**	**1.25**
☐	333	Gene Clines, Pgh.	.75	1.25
☐	334	Freddie Patek, K.C.	.75	1.25
☐	335	Bob Tolan, Cin.	.75	1.25
☐	336	Tom Bradley, S.F.	.75	1.25
☐	337	Dave Duncan, Oak.	.75	1.25
☐	338	Checklist 3 (265 - 396)	1.25	2.50
☐	339	Dick Tidrow, Cle.	.75	1.25
☐	340	Nate Colbert, S.D.	.75	1.25
☐	341	Jim Palmer, Bal. (Youth)	1.00	2.00
☐	342	Sam McDowell, S.F. (Youth)	.75	1.25
☐	343	Bobby Murcer, NYY. (Youth)	.75	1.25
☐	344	James Hunter, Oak. (Youth)	1.00	2.00
☐	345	Chris Speier, S.F. (Youth)	.75	1.25
☐	346	Gaylord Perry, Cin. (Youth)	1.00	2.00
☐	347	Kansas City Royals	1.25	2.50
☐	348	Rennie Stennett, Pgh.	.75	1.25
☐	349	Dick McAuliffe, Det.	.75	1.25
☐	350	Tom Seaver	12.50	25.00
☐	351	Jimmy Stewart, Hou.	.75	1.25
☐	**352**	**Don Stanhouse, Tex., RC**	**.75**	**1.25**
☐	353	Steve Brye, Min.	.75	1.25
☐	354	Billy Parker, Cal.	.75	1.25
☐	355	Mike Marshall, Mtl.	.75	1.25
☐	356	Chi.: Manager: C. Tanner; Coaches: J. Lonnett / J. Mahoney/ A. Monchak/ J. Sain	.75	1.25
☐	357	Ross Grimsley, Cin.	.75	1.25
☐	358	Jim Nettles, Min.	.75	1.25
☐	359	Cecil Upshaw, Atl.	.75	1.25
☐	360	Joe Rudi, Oak.	.75	1.25
☐	361	Fran Healy, S.F.	.75	1.25
☐	362	Eddie Watt, Bal.	.75	1.25
☐	363	Jackie Hernandez, Pgh.	.75	1.25
☐	364	Rick Wise, Stl.	.75	1.25
☐	365	Rico Petrocelli, Bos.	.75	1.25
☐	366	Brock Davis, Mil.	.75	1.25
☐	367	Burt Hooton, Chi.-N.L.	.75	1.25
☐	368	Bill Buckner, L.A.	.75	1.25
☐	369	Lerrin LaGrow, Det.	.75	1.25
☐	370	Willie Stargell, Pgh.	3.75	7.50
☐	371	Mike Kekich, NYY.	.75	1.25
☐	372	Oscar Gamble, Cle.	.75	1.25
☐	373	Clyde Wright, Cal.	.75	1.25
☐	374	Darrell Evans, Atl.	.75	1.25
☐	375	Larry Dierker, Hou.	.75	1.25
☐	376	Frank Duffy, Cle.	.75	1.25
☐	377	Mtl.: Mgr.: G. Mauch; Coaches: D. Bristol / L. Doby/ C. McLish/ J. Zimmerman	1.25	2.50
☐	378	Lenny Randle, Tex.	.75	1.25
☐	**379**	**Cy Acosta, Chi.-A.L., RC**	**.75**	**1.25**
☐	380	Johnny Bench, Cin.	8.00	16.00
☐	381	Vicente Romo, S.D.	.75	1.25
☐	382	Mike Hegan, Oak.	.75	1.25
☐	383	Diego Segui, Stl.	.75	1.25
☐	384	Don Baylor, Bal.	.75	1.25
☐	385	Jim Perry, Min.	.75	1.25
☐	386	Don Money, Mil.	.75	1.25
☐	387	Jim Barr, S.F.	.75	1.25
☐	388	Ben Oglivie, Bos.	.75	1.25
☐	389	New York Mets	1.25	2.50
☐	390	Mickey Lolich, Det.	1.25	2.50
☐	**391**	**Lee Lacy, L.A., RC**	**.75**	**1.25**
☐	392	Dick Drago, K.C.	.75	1.25
☐	393	Jose Cardenal, Chi.-N.L.	.75	1.25
☐	394	Sparky Lyle, NYY.	.75	1.25
☐	395	Roger Metzger, Hou.	.75	1.25
☐	396	Grant Jackson, Bal.	.75	1.25
☐	397	Dave Cash, Pgh.	1.00	2.00
☐	398	Rich Hand, Tex.	1.00	2.00
☐	399	George Foster, Cin.	20.00	4.00
☐	400	Gaylord Perry, Cle.	3.75	8.50
☐	401	Clyde Mashore, Mtl.	1.00	2.00
☐	402	Jack Hiatt, Cal.	1.00	2.00
☐	403	Sonny Jackson, Atl.	1.00	2.00
☐	404	Chuck Brinkman, Chi.-A.L.	1.00	2.00
☐	405	Cesar Tovar, Pha.	1.00	2.00
☐	406	Paul Lindblad, Oak.	1.00	2.00
☐	407	Felix Millan, NYM.	1.00	2.00
☐	408	Jim Colborn, Mil.	1.00	2.00
☐	409	Ivan Murrell, S.D.	1.00	2.00
☐	410	Willie McCovey, S.F.	4.50	9.00
☐	411	Ray Corbin, Min.	1.00	2.00
☐	412	Manny Mota, L.A.	1.00	2.00

	No.	Card		
☐	413	Tom Timmermann, Det.	1.00	2.00
☐	414	Ken Rudolph, Chi.-N.L.	1.00	2.00
☐	415	Marty Pattin, Bos.	1.00	2.00
☐	416	Paul Schaal, K.C.	1.00	2.00
☐	417	Scipio Spinks, Stl.	1.00	2.00
☐	418	Bobby Grich, Bal.	1.00	2.00
☐	419	Casey Cox, NYY.	1.00	2.00
☐	420	Tommie Agee, Hou.	1.00	2.00
☐	421	Cal.: Manager: B. Winkles; Coaches: T. Morgan / S. Parker/ J. Reese/ J. Roseboro	1.00	2.00
☐	422	Bob Robertson, Pgh.	1.00	2.00
☐	423	Johnny Jeter, Chi.-A.L.	1.00	2.00
☐	424	Denny Doyle, Pha.	1.00	2.00
☐	425	Alex Johnson, Cle.	1.00	2.00
☐	426	Dave LaRoche, Chi.-N.L.	1.00	2.00
☐	427	Rick Auerbach, Mil.	1.00	2.00
☐	428	Wayne Simpson, K.C.	1.00	2.00
☐	429	Jim Fairey, Mtl.	1.00	2.00
☐	430	Vida Blue, Oak.	2.00	4.00
☐	431	Gerry Moses, NYY.	1.00	2.00
☐	432	Dan Frisella, Atl.	1.00	2.00
☐	433	Willie Horton, Det.	1.00	2.00
☐	434	San Francisco Giants	2.00	4.00
☐	435	Rico Carty, Tex.	1.00	2.00
☐	436	Jim McAndrew, NYM.	1.00	2.00
☐	437	John Kennedy, Bos.	1.00	2.00
☐	438	Enzo Hernandez, S.D.	1.00	2.00
☐	439	Eddie Fisher, Chi.-A.L.	1.00	2.00
☐	440	Glenn Beckert, Chi.-N.L.	1.00	2.00
☐	441	Gail Hopkins, K.C.	1.00	2.00
☐	442	Dick Dietz, L.A.	1.00	2.00
☐	443	Danny Thompson, Min.	1.00	2.00
☐	444	Ken Brett, Pha.	1.00	2.00
☐	445	Ken Berry, Cal.	1.00	2.00
☐	446	Jerry Reuss, Hou.	1.00	2.00
☐	447	Joe Hague, Cin.	1.00	2.00
☐	448	John Hiller, Det.	2.50	5.00
	449	Cle.: Manager: K. Aspromonte; Coaches: R. Colavito / J. Lutz/ W. Spahn	2.00	4.00
☐	450	Joe Torre, Stl.	2.50	5.00
☐	**451**	**John Vukovich, Mil., RC**	**1.00**	**2.00**
☐	452	Paul Casanova, Atl.	1.00	2.00
☐	453	Checklist 4 (397 - 528)	2.00	4.00
☐	454	Tom Haller, Pha.	1.00	2.00
☐	455	Bill Melton, Chi.-A.L.	1.00	2.00
☐	456	Dick Green, Oak.	1.00	2.00
☐	457	John Strohmayer, Mtl.	1.00	2.00
☐	458	Jim Mason, Tex.	1.00	2.00
☐	**459**	**Jimmy Howarth, S.F., RC**	**1.00**	**2.00**
☐	460	Bill Freehan, Det.	1.00	2.00
☐	461	Mike Corkins, S.D.	1.00	2.00
☐	462	Ron Blomberg, NYY.	1.00	2.00
☐	463	Ken Tatum, Bos.	1.00	2.00
☐	464	Chicago Cubs	2.00	4.00
☐	465	Dave Giusti, Pgh.	1.00	2.00
☐	466	Jose Arcia, K.C.	1.00	2.00
☐	467	Mike Ryan, Pha.	1.00	2.00
☐	468	Tom Griffin, Hou.	1.00	2.00
☐	**469**	**Danny Monzon, Min., RC**	**1.00**	**2.00**
☐	470	Mike Cuellar, Bal.	1.00	2.00
☐	471	Hit Leader: Ty Cobb	6.00	12.00
☐	472	Grand Slam Leader: Lou Gehrig	11.00	22.00
☐	473	Total Base Leader: Hank Aaron	7.50	15.00
☐	474	R.B.I. Leader: Babe Ruth	12.50	25.00
☐	475	Batting Leader: Ty Cobb	6.00	12.00
☐	476	Shutout Leader: Walter Johnson	4.00	8.00
☐	477	Victory Leader: Cy Young	4.00	8.00
☐	478	Strikeout Leader: Walter Johnson	4.00	8.00
☐	479	Hal Lanier, NYY.	1.00	2.00
☐	480	Juan Marichal, S.F.	3.50	7.00
☐	481	Chicago White Sox.	2.00	4.00
☐	**482**	**Rick Reuschel, Chi.-N.L., RC**	**2.00**	**4.00**
☐	483	Dal Maxvill, Oak.	1.00	2.00
☐	484	Ernie McAnally, Mtl.	1.00	2.00
☐	485	Norm Cash, Det.	1.00	2.00
☐	486	Pha.: Manager: D. Ozark; Coaches: C. Beringer / B. DeMars/ R. Rippelmeyer/ B. Wine	1.00	2.00
☐	487	Bruce Dal Canton, K.C.	1.00	2.00
☐	488	Dave Campbell, S.D.	1.00	2.00
☐	489	Jeff Burroughs, Tex.	1.00	2.00
☐	490	Claude Osteen, L.A.	1.00	2.00
☐	491	Bob Montgomery, Bos.	1.00	2.00
☐	492	Pedro Borbon, Cin.	1.00	2.00
☐	493	Duffy Dyer, NYM.	1.00	2.00
☐	494	Rich Morales, Chi.-A.L.	1.00	2.00
☐	495	Tommy Helms, Hou.	1.00	2.00
☐	496	Ray Lamb, Cle.	1.00	2.00
☐	497	Stl.: Manager: R. Schoendienst; Coaches: V. Benson / G. Kissell/ B. Schultz	2.00	4.00
☐	498	Graig Nettles, NYY.	2.00	4.00
☐	499	Bob Moose, Pgh.	1.00	2.00
☐	500	Oakland A's	2.00	4.00
☐	501	Larry Gura, Chi.-N.L.	1.00	2.00
☐	502	Bobby Valentine, Cal.	1.00	2.00
☐	503	Phil Niekro, Atl.	3.50	7.00
☐	504	Earl Williams, Bal.	1.00	2.00
☐	505	Bob Bailey, Mtl.	1.00	2.00
☐	506	Bart Johnson, Chi.-A.L.	1.00	2.00
☐	507	Darrel Chaney, Cin.	1.00	2.00
☐	508	Gates Brown, Det.	1.00	2.00
☐	509	Jim Nash, Pha.	1.00	2.00
☐	510	Amos Otis, K.C.	1.00	2.00
☐	511	Sam McDowell, S.F.	1.00	2.00
☐	512	Dalton Jones, Tex.	1.00	2.00
☐	513	Dave Marshall, S.D.	1.00	2.00
☐	514	Jerry Kenney, Cle.	1.00	2.00
☐	515	Andy Messersmith, L.A.	1.00	2.00
☐	516	Danny Walton, Min.	1.00	2.00
☐	517	Pgh.: Manager: B. Virdon; Coaches: D. Leppert / B. Mazeroski/ D. Ricketts/ M. Wright	2.00	4.00
☐	518	Bob Veale, Bos.	1.00	2.00
☐	519	John Edwards, Hou.	1.00	2.00
☐	520	Mel Stottlemyre, NYY.	1.00	2.00
☐	521	Atlanta Braves	2.00	4.00
☐	522	Leo Cardenas, Cal.	1.00	2.00
☐	523	Wayne Granger, Stl.	1.00	2.00
☐	524	Gene Tenace, Oak.	1.00	2.00
☐	525	Jim Fregosi, NYM.	1.00	2.00
☐	526	Ollie Brown, Mil.	1.00	2.00
☐	527	Dan McGinn, Chi.-N.L.	1.00	2.00
☐	528	Paul Blair, Bal.	1.00	2.00
☐	529	Milt May, Pgh.	2.50	5.00
☐	530	Jim Kaat, Min.	4.00	8.00
☐	531	Ron Woods, Mtl.	2.50	5.00
☐	532	Steve Mingori, Cle.	2.50	5.00
☐	533	Larry Stahl, Cin.	2.50	5.00
☐	534	Dave Lemonds, Chi.-A.L.	2.50	5.00
☐	535	John Callison, NYY.	2.50	5.00
☐	536	Philadelphia Phillies	4.00	8.00
☐	**537**	**Bill Slayback, Det., RC**	**2.50**	**5.00**
☐	538	Jim Hart, S.F.	2.50	5.00
☐	539	Tom Murphy, K.C.	2.50	5.00
☐	540	Cleon Jones, NYM.	2.50	5.00
☐	541	Bob Bolin, Bos.	2.50	5.00
☐	542	Pat Corrales, S.D.	2.50	5.00
☐	543	Alan Foster, Cal.	2.50	5.00
☐	544	Von Joshua, L.A.	2.50	5.00
☐	545	Orlando Cepeda, Oak.	5.00	10.00

	No.	Player	EX	NRMT
☐	546	Jim York, Hou.	2.50	5.00
☐	547	Bobby Heise, Mil.	2.50	5.00
☐	**548**	**Don Durham, Stl., RC**	**2.50**	**5.00**
☐	549	Tex.: Manager: W. Herzog; Coaches: C. Estrada / C. Hiller/ J. Moore	2.50	5.00
☐	550	Dave Johnson, Atl.	2.50	5.00
☐	551	Mike Kilkenny, Cle.	4.00	8.00
☐	552	J.C. Martin, Chi.-N.L.	2.50	5.00
☐	553	Mickey Scott, Bal.	2.50	5.00
☐	554	Dave Concepcion, Cin.	4.00	8.00
☐	555	Bill Hands, Min.	2.50	5.00
☐	556	New York Yankees	4.00	8.00
☐	557	Bernie Williams, S.F.	2.50	5.00
☐	558	Jerry May, K.C.	2.50	5.00
☐	559	Barry Lersch, Pha.	2.50	5.00
☐	560	Frank Howard, Det.	2.50	5.00
☐	**561**	**Jim Geddes, Chi.-A.L., RC**	**2.50**	**5.00**
☐	562	Wayne Garrett, NYM.	2.50	5.00
☐	563	Larry Haney, Oak.	2.50	5.00
☐	**564**	**Mike Thompson, Tex., RC**	**2.50**	**5.00**
☐	565	Jim Hickman, Chi.-N.L.	2.50	5.00
☐	566	Lew Krausse, Bos.	2.50	5.00
☐	567	Bob Fenwick, Stl.	2.50	5.00
☐	568	Ray Newman, Mil.	2.50	5.00
☐	569	L.A.: Manager: W. Alston; Coaches: R. Adams / M. Basgall/ J. Gilliam/ T. Lasorda	7.50	15.00
☐	570	Bill Singer, Cal.	2.50	5.00
☐	571	Rusty Torres, Cle.	2.50	5.00
☐	572	Gary Sutherland, Hou.	2.50	5.00
☐	573	Fred Beene, NYY.	2.50	5.00
☐	574	Bob Didier, Atl.	2.50	5.00
☐	575	Dock Ellis, Pgh.	2.50	5.00
☐	576	Montréal Expos	5.00	10.00
☐	**577**	**Eric Soderholm, Min., RC**	**2.50**	**5.00**
☐	578	Ken Wright, K.C.	2.50	5.00
☐	579	Tom Grieve, Tex.	2.50	5.00
☐	580	Joe Pepitone, Chi.-N.L.	2.50	5.00
☐	581	Steve Kealey, Chi.-A.L.	2.50	5.00
☐	582	Darrell Porter, Mil.	2.50	5.00
☐	583	Bill Greif, S.D.	2.50	5.00
☐	584	Chris Arnold, S.F.	2.50	5.00
☐	585	Joe Niekro, Det.	2.50	5.00
☐	586	Bill Sudakis, NYM.	2.50	5.00
☐	587	Rich McKinney, Oak.	2.50	5.00
☐	588	Checklist 5 (529 - 660)	20.00	40.00
☐	589	Ken Forsch, Hou.	2.50	5.00
☐	590	Deron Johnson, Pha.	2.50	5.00
☐	591	Mike Hedlund, K.C.	2.50	5.00
☐	592	John Boccabella, Mtl.	2.50	5.00
☐	593	K.C.: Manager: J. McKeon; Coaches: G. Cisco / H. Dunlop/ C. Lau	2.50	5.00
☐	**594**	**Vic Harris, Tex., RC**	**2.50**	**5.00**
☐	595	Don Gullett, Cin.	2.50	5.00
☐	596	Boston Red Sox	4.00	8.00
☐	597	Mickey Rivers, Cal.	2.50	5.00
☐	598	Phil Roof, Min.	2.50	5.00
☐	599	Ed Crosby, Stl.	2.50	5.00
☐	600	Dave McNally, Bal.	2.50	5.00
☐	601	S. Robles/ G. Pena/ R. Stelmaszek	2.50	5.00
☐	602	M. Behney/ R. Garcia/ D. Rau	2.50	5.00
☐	603	T. Hughes/ B. McNulty/ K. Reitz	2.50	5.00
☐	604	J. Jefferson/ D. O'Toole/ B. Strampe	2.50	5.00
☐	605	E. Cabell/ P. Bourque/ G. Marquez	2.50	5.00
☐	606	G. Matthews/ T. Paciorek/ J. Roque	5.00	10.00
☐	607	P. Frias/ R. Busse/ M.Guerrero	2.50	5.00
☐	608	S. Busby/ D. Colpaert/ G. Medich	2.50	5.00
☐	609	L. Blanks/ P. Garcia,/ D. Lopes	4.00	8.00
☐	610	J. Freeman/ C. Hough/ H. Webb	4.00	8.00
☐	611	R. Coggins/ J. Wohlford/ R. Zisk	2.50	5.00
☐	612	S. Lawson/ B. Reynolds/ B. Strom	2.50	5.00
☐	613	B. Boone/ M. Ivie/ S. Jutze	17.50	35.00
☐	614	A. Bumbry/ D. Evans/ C. Spikes	14.00	28.00
☐	615	R. Cey/ J. Hilton/ M. Schmidt	225.00	450.00
☐	616	N. Angelini/ S. Blateric/ M. Garman	2.50	5.00
☐	617	Rich Chiles, NYM.	2.50	5.00
☐	618	Andy Etchebarren, Bal.	2.50	5.00
☐	619	Billy Wilson, Pha.	2.50	5.00
☐	620	Tommy Harper, Bos.	2.50	5.00
☐	621	Joe Ferguson, L.A.	2.50	5.00
☐	622	Larry Hisle, Min.	2.50	5.00
☐	623	Steve Renko, Mtl.	2.50	5.00
☐	624	Hou.: Manager: L. Durocher; Coaches: P. Gomez / G. Hatton/ H. Kittle/ J. Owens	4.00	8.00
☐	625	Angel Mangual, Oak.	2.50	5.00
☐	626	Bob Barton, Cin.	2.50	5.00
☐	627	Luis Alvarado, Chi.-A.L.	2.50	5.00
☐	628	Jim Slaton, Mil.	2.50	5.00
☐	629	Cleveland Indians	4.00	8.00
☐	630	Denny McLain, Atl.	4.00	8.00
☐	631	Tom Matchick, Bal.	2.50	5.00
☐	632	Dick Selma, Pha.	2.50	5.00
☐	633	Ike Brown, Det.	2.50	5.00
☐	634	Alan Closter, NYY.	2.50	5.00
☐	635	Gene Alley, Pgh.	2.50	5.00
☐	636	Rickey Clark, Cal.	2.50	5.00
☐	637	Norm Miller, Hou.	2.50	5.00
☐	638	Ken Reynolds, Min.	2.50	5.00
☐	639	Willie Crawford, L.A.	2.50	5.00
☐	640	Dick Bosman, Tex.	2.50	5.00
☐	641	Cincinnati Reds	6.00	12.00
☐	642	Jose Laboy, Mtl.	2.50	5.00
☐	643	Al Fitzmorris, K.C.	2.50	5.00
☐	644	Jack Heidemann, Cle.	2.50	5.00
☐	645	Bob Locker, Chi.-N.L.	2.50	5.00
☐	646	Mil.: Manager: D. Crandall; Coaches: H. Kuenn / J. Nossek/ B. Shaw/ J. Walton	2.50	5.00
☐	647	George Stone, NYM.	2.50	5.00
☐	648	Tom Egan, Chi.-A.L.	2.50	5.00
☐	649	Rich Folkers, Stl.	2.50	5.00
☐	650	Felipe Alou, NYY.	4.00	8.00
☐	651	Don Carrithers, S.F.	2.50	5.00
☐	652	Ted Kubiak, Oak.	2.50	5.00
☐	653	Joe Hoerner, Atl.	2.50	5.00
☐	654	Minnesota Twins	4.00	8.00
☐	655	Clay Kirby, S.D.	2.50	5.00
☐	656	John Ellis, Cle.	2.50	5.00
☐	657	Bob Johnson, Pgh.	2.50	5.00
☐	658	Elliott Maddox, Tex.	2.50	5.00
☐	659	Jose Pagan, Pha.	2.50	5.00
☐	660	Fred Scherman, Det.	2.50	8.00

TEAM CHECKLISTS

Card Size: 2 1/2" x 3 1/2"
Face: Red, yellow and white, blue border; autographs
Back: Black, orange border on card stock; unnumbered
Imprint: **O.P.C. PRINTED IN CANADA

Insert Set (24 cards):			**30.00**	**60.00**
Common Team Card:				

	No.	Player	EX	NRMT
☐	1	Atlanta Braves	1.50	3.00
☐	2	Baltimore Orioles	1.50	3.00
☐	3	Boston Red Sox	1.50	3.00
☐	4	California Angels	1.50	3.00
☐	5	Chicago Cubs	1.50	3.00
☐	6	Chicago White Sox	1.50	3.00
☐	7	Cincinnati Reds	2.50	5.00
☐	8	Cleveland Indians	1.50	3.00
☐	9	Detroit Tigers	1.50	3.00

☐	10	Houston Astros	1.50	3.00
☐	11	Kansas City Royals	1.50	3.00
☐	12	Los Angeles Dodgers	1.50	3.00
☐	13	Milwaukee Brewers	1.50	3.00
☐	14	Minnesota Twins	1.50	3.00
☐	15	Montréal Expos	2.50	5.00
☐	16	New York Mets	1.50	3.00
☐	17	New York Yankees	1.50	3.00
☐	18	Oakland A's	2.50	5.00
☐	19	Philadelphia Phillies	1.50	3.00
☐	20	Pittsburgh Pirates	1.50	3.00
☐	21	St. Louis Cardinals	1.50	3.00
☐	22	San Diego Padres	1.50	3.00
☐	23	San Francisco Giants	1.50	3.00
☐	24	Texas Rangers	1.50	3.00

1974 O-PEE-CHEE

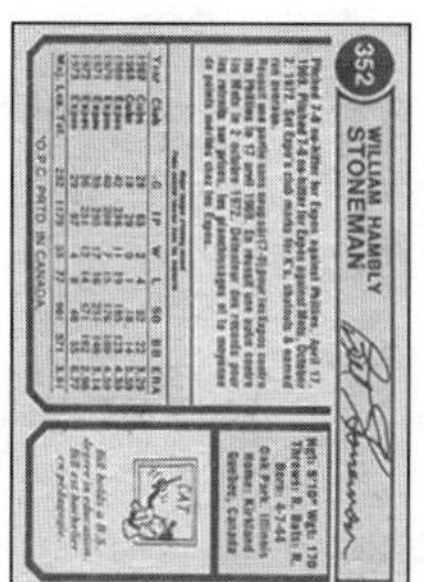

This 660-card set is identical to the Topps issue, with three exceptions. In the Canadian set, cards 7, 8 and 9 feature Hank Aaron. These three cards in the Topps set picture Jim Hunter, George Theodore and Mickey Lolich, respectively. The Canadian set is scarcer in the higher grades and is thought to be short printed.

Card Size: 2 1/2" x 3 1/2"
Face: Four colour, white border; name, position, team
Back: Yellow and black on card stock; name, number, facsimile autograph, resume, player trivia, bilingual
Imprint: © O.P.C. PRTD. IN CANADA

Complete Set (660 cards):			**475.00**	**950.00**
Common Player:			**.50**	**1.00**
	No.	**Player**	**EX**	**NRMT**
☐	1	Hank Aaron, Atl.	30.00	60.00
☐	2	Hank Aaron Special: 1954 to 1957	5.00	10.00
☐	3	Hank Aaron Special: 1958 to 1959	5.00	10.00
☐	4	Hank Aaron Special: 1960 to 1961	5.00	10.00
☐	5	Hank Aaron Special: 1962 to 1963	5.00	10.00
☐	6	Hank Aaron Special: 1964 to 1965	5.00	10.00
☐	7	Hank Aaron Special: 1966 to 1967	5.00	10.00
☐	8	Hank Aaron Special: 1968 to 1969	5.00	10.00
☐	9	Hank Aaron Special: 1970 to 1973	5.00	10.00
☐	10	Johnny Bench, Cin.	12.00	24.00
☐	11	Jim Bibby, Tex.	.50	1.00
☐	12	Dave May, Mil.	.50	1.00
☐	13	Tom Hilgendorf, Cle.	.50	1.00
☐	14	Paul Popovich, Chi.-N.L.	.50	1.00
☐	15	Joe Torre, Stl.	1.00	2.00
☐	16	Baltimore Orioles	1.00	2.00
☐	**17**	**Doug Bird, K.C., RC**	**.50**	**1.00**
☐	**18**	**Gary Thomasson, S.F., RC**	**.50**	**1.00**
☐	19	Gerry Moses, NYY.	.50	1.00
☐	20	Nolan Ryan, Cal.	60.00	120.00
☐	**21**	**Bob Gallagher, Hou., RC**	**.50**	**1.00**
☐	22	Cy Acosta, Chi.-A.L.	.50	1.00
☐	**23**	**Craig Robinson, Pha., RC**	**.50**	**1.00**
☐	24	John Hiller, Det.	1.25	2.50
☐	25	Ken Singleton, Mtl.	.50	1.00
☐	**26**	**Bill Campbell, Min., RC**	**.50**	**1.00**
☐	27	George Scott, Mil.	.50	1.00
☐	28	Manny Sanguillen, Pgh.	.50	1.00
☐	29	Phil Niekro, Atl.	1.50	3.00
☐	30	Bobby Bonds, S.F.	.50	1.00
☐	31	Hou.: Manager: P. Gomez; Coaches: R. Craig / H. Kittle/ G. Hatton/ B. Lillis	.50	1.00
☐	**32**	**John Grubb, S.D., RC**	**.50**	**1.00**
☐	33	Don Newhauser, Bos.	.50	1.00
☐	34	Andy Kosco, Cin.	.50	1.00
☐	35	Gaylord Perry, Cle.	3.00	6.00
☐	36	St. Louis Cardinals	1.00	2.00
☐	**37**	**Dave Sells, Cal., RC**	**.50**	**1.00**
☐	38	Don Kessinger, Chi.-N.L.	.50	1.00
☐	39	Ken Suarez, Tex.	.50	1.00
☐	40	Jim Palmer, Bal.	5.00	10.00
☐	41	Bobby Floyd, K.C.	.50	1.00
☐	42	Claude Osteen, L.A.	.50	1.00
☐	43	Jim Wynn, Hou.	.50	1.00
☐	44	Mel Stottlemyre, NYY.	.50	1.00
☐	45	Dave Johnson, Atl.	.50	1.00
☐	46	Pat Kelly, Chi.-A.L.	.50	1.00
☐	**47**	**Dick Ruthven, Pha., RC**	**.50**	**1.00**
☐	**48**	**Dick Sharon, Det., RC**	**.50**	**1.00**
☐	49	Steve Renko, Mtl.	.50	1.00
☐	50	Rod Carew, Min.	5.00	10.00
☐	51	Bobby Heise, Stl.	.50	1.00
☐	52	Al Oliver, Pgh.	.50	1.00
☐	53	Fred Kendall, S.D.	.50	1.00
☐	**54**	**Elias Sosa, S.F., RC**	**.50**	**1.00**
☐	55	Frank Robinson, Cal.	5.00	10.00
☐	56	New York Mets	1.00	2.00
☐	57	Darold Knowles, Oak.	.50	1.00
☐	58	Charlie Spikes, Cle.	.50	1.00
☐	59	Ross Grimsley, Cin.	.50	1.00
☐	60	Lou Brock, Stl.	5.00	10.00
☐	61	Luis Aparicio, Bos.	1.50	3.00
☐	62	Bob Locker, Chi.-N.L.	.50	1.00
☐	63	Bill Sudakis, Tex.	.50	1.00
☐	64	Doug Rau, L.A.	.50	1.00
☐	65	Amos Otis, K.C.	.50	1.00
☐	66	Sparky Lyle, NYY.	.50	1.00
☐	67	Tommy Helms, Hou.	.50	1.00
☐	68	Grant Jackson, Bal.	.50	1.00
☐	69	Del Unser, Pha.	.50	1.00
☐	70	Dick Allen, Chi.-A.L.	.50	1.00
☐	71	Danny Frisella, Atl.	.50	1.00
☐	72	Aurelio Rodriguez, Det.	.50	1.00
☐	73	Mike Marshall, Mtl.	.50	1.00
☐	74	Minnesota Twins	1.00	2.00
☐	75	Jim Colborn, Mil.	.50	1.00
☐	76	Mickey Rivers, Cal.	.50	1.00
☐	**77**	**Rich Troedson, S.D., RC**	**.50**	**1.00**
☐	78	S.F.: Manager: C. Fox; Coaches: J. McNamara / J. Amalfitano/ A. Gilbert/ D. McMahon	.50	1.00
☐	79	Gene Tenace, Oak.	.50	1.00
☐	80	Tom Seaver, NYM.	12.00	24.00
☐	81	Frank Duffy, Cle.	.50	1.00
☐	82	Dave Giusti, Pgh.	.50	1.00
☐	83	Orlando Cepeda, Bos.	1.00	2.00
☐	84	Rick Wise, Bos.	.50	1.00
☐	85	Joe Morgan, Cin.	4.00	8.00
☐	86	Joe Ferguson, L.A.	.50	1.00
☐	87	Fergie Jenkins, Tex.	3.25	6.50
☐	88	Freddie Patek, K.C.	.50	1.00
☐	89	Jackie Brown, Tex.	.50	1.00
☐	90	Bobby Murcer, NYY.	.50	1.00

	No.	Player		
☐	91	Ken Forsch, Hou.	.50	1.00
☐	92	Paul Blair, Bal.	.50	1.00
☐	**93**	**Rod Gilbreath, Atl., RC**	**.50**	**1.00**
☐	94	Detroit Tigers	1.00	2.00
☐	95	Steve Carlton, Pha.	6.50	13.00
☐	**96**	**Jerry Hairston, Chi.-A.L., RC**	**.50**	**1.00**
☐	97	Bob Bailey, Mtl.	.50	1.00
☐	98	Bert Blyleven, Min.	1.00	2.00
☐	**99**	**George Theodore, NYM., RC**	**.50**	**1.00**
☐	100	Willie Stargell, Pgh.	3.50	7.00
☐	101	Bobby Valentine, Cal.	.50	1.00
☐	102	Bill Greif, S.D.	.50	1.00
☐	103	Sal Bando, Oak.	.50	1.00
☐	104	Ron Bryant, S.F.	.50	1.00
☐	105	Carlton Fisk, Bos.	10.00	20.00
☐	**106**	**Harry Parker, NYM., RC**	**.50**	**1.00**
☐	107	Alex Johnson, Tex.	.50	1.00
☐	108	Al Hrabosky, Stl.	.50	1.00
☐	109	Bob Grich, Bal.	.50	1.00
☐	110	Billy Williams, Chi.-N.L.	1.75	3.50
☐	111	Clay Carroll, Cin.	.50	1.00
☐	112	Dave Lopes, L.A.	.50	1.00
☐	113	Dick Drago, Bos.	.50	1.00
☐	114	California Angels	1.00	2.00
☐	115	Willie Horton, Det.	.50	1.00
☐	116	Jerry Reuss, Pgh.	.50	1.00
☐	117	Ron Blomberg, NYY.	.50	1.00
☐	118	Bill Lee, Bos.	.50	1.00
☐	119	Pha.: Mgr.: D. Ozark; Coaches: R. Ripplemeyer / B. Wine/ C. Beringer/ B. DeMars	.50	1.00
☐	120	Wilbur Wood, Chi.-A.L.	.50	1.00
☐	**121**	**Larry Lintz, Mtl., RC**	**.50**	**1.00**
☐	122	Jim Holt, Min.	.50	1.00
☐	123	Nelson Briles, Pgh.	.50	1.00
☐	**124**	**Bob Coluccio, Mil., RC**	**.50**	**1.00**
☐	125	Nate Colbert, S.D.	.50	1.00
☐	126	Checklist 1 (1 - 132)	1.00	2.00
☐	127	Tom Paciorek, L.A.	.50	1.00
☐	128	John Ellis, Cle.	.50	1.00
☐	129	Chris Speier, S.F.	.50	1.00
☐	130	Reggie Jackson, Oak.	15.00	30.00
☐	131	Bob Boone, Pha.	1.00	2.00
☐	132	Felix Millan, NYM.	.50	1.00
☐	**133**	**David Clyde, Tex., RC**	**.50**	**1.00**
☐	134	Denis Menke, Cin.	.50	1.00
☐	135	Roy White, NYY.	.50	1.00
☐	136	Rick Reuschel, Chi.-N.L.	.50	1.00
☐	137	Al Bumbry, Bal.	.50	1.00
☐	138	Ed Brinkman, Det.	.50	1.00
☐	139	Aurelio Monteagudo, Cal.	.50	1.00
☐	140	Darrell Evans, Atl.	.50	1.00
☐	141	Pat Bourque, Oak.	.50	1.00
☐	142	Pedro Garcia, Mil.	.50	1.00
☐	143	Dick Woodson, Min.	.50	1.00
☐	144	L.A.: Manager: W. Alston; Coaches: T. Lasorda / J. Gilliam/ R. Adams/ M. Basgall	1.50	3.00
☐	145	Dock Ellis, Pgh.	.50	1.00
☐	146	Ron Fairly, Mtl.	.50	1.00
☐	147	Bart Johnson, Chi.-A.L.	.50	1.00
☐	148	Dave Hilton, S.D.	.50	1.00
☐	149	Mac Scarce, Pha.	.50	1.00
☐	150	John Mayberry, K.C.	.50	1.00
☐	151	Diego Segui, Stl.	.50	1.00
☐	152	Oscar Gamble, Cle.	.50	1.00
☐	153	Jon Matlack, NYM.	.50	1.00
☐	154	Houston Astros	1.00	2.00
☐	155	Bert Campaneris, Oak.	.50	1.00
☐	156	Randy Moffitt, S.F.	.50	1.00
☐	157	Vic Harris, Chi.-N.L.	.50	1.00
☐	158	Jack Billingham, Cin.	.50	1.00
☐	159	Jim Ray Hart, NYY.	.50	1.00
☐	160	Brooks Robinson, Bal.	6.00	12.00
☐	**161**	**Ray Burris, Chi.-N.L., RC**	**.50**	**1.00**
☐	162	Bill Freehan, Det.	.50	1.00
☐	163	Ken Berry, Mil.	.50	1.00
☐	**164**	**Tom House, Atl., RC**	**.50**	**1.00**
☐	165	Willie Davis, L.A.	.50	1.00
☐	166	Mickey Lolich, Det.	.50	1.00
☐	167	Luis Tiant, Bos.	.50	1.00
☐	168	Danny Thompson, Min.	.50	1.00
☐	**169**	**Steve Rogers, Mtl., RC**	**1.00**	**2.00**
☐	170	Bill Melton, Chi.-A.L.	.50	1.00
☐	**171**	**Eduardo Rodriguez, Mil., RC**	**.50**	**1.00**
☐	172	Gene Clines, Pgh.	.50	1.00
☐	**173**	**Randy Jones, S.D., RC**	**.50**	**1.00**
☐	174	Bill Robinson, Pha.	.50	1.00
☐	175	Reggie Cleveland, Stl.	1.00	2.00
☐	176	John Lowenstein, Cle.	.50	1.00
☐	177	Dave Roberts, Hou.	.50	1.00
☐	178	Garry Maddox, S.F.	.50	1.00
☐	179	NYM.: Manager: Y. Berra; Coaches: R. Walker / E. Yost/ R. McMillan/ J. Pignatano	1.25	2.50
☐	180	Ken Holtzman, Oak.	.50	1.00
☐	181	Cesar Geronimo, Cin.	.50	1.00
☐	182	Lindy McDaniel, NYY.	.50	1.00
☐	183	Johnny Oates, Atl.	.50	1.00
☐	184	Texas Rangers	1.00	2.00
☐	185	Jose Cardenal, Chi.-N.L.	.50	1.00
☐	186	Fred Scherman, Det.	.50	1.00
☐	187	Don Baylor, Bal.	.50	1.00
☐	**188**	**Rudi Meoli, Cal., RC**	**.50**	**1.00**
☐	189	Jim Brewer, L.A.	.50	1.00
☐	190	Tony Oliva, Min.	1.00	2.00
☐	191	Al Fitzmorris, K.C.	.50	1.00
☐	**192**	**Mario Guerrero, Bos., RC**	**.50**	**1.00**
☐	193	Tom Walker, Mtl.	.50	1.00
☐	194	Darrell Porter, Mil.	.50	1.00
☐	195	Carlos May, Chi.-A.L.	.50	1.00
☐	196	Jim Hunter, Oak.	3.25	6.50
☐	197	Vicente Romo, S.D.	.50	1.00
☐	198	Dave Cash, Pha.	.50	1.00
☐	199	Mike Kekich, Cle.	.50	1.00
☐	200	Cesar Cedeno, Hou.	.50	1.00
☐	201	LL: R. Carew/ P. Rose	4.25	8.50
☐	202	LL: R. Jackson/ W. Stargell	3.75	7.50
☐	203	LL: R. Jackson/ W. Stargell	3.75	7.50
☐	204	LL: T. Harper/ L. Brock	1.25	2.50
☐	205	LL: W. Wood/ R. Bryant	1.00	2.00
☐	206	LL: J. Palmer/ T. Seaver	3.75	7.50
☐	207	LL: N. Ryan/ T. Seaver	15.00	30.00
☐	208	LL: J. Hiller/ M. Marshall	1.00	2.00
☐	209	Ted Sizemore, Stl.	.50	1.00
☐	210	Bill Singer, Cal.	.50	1.00
☐	211	Chicago Cubs	1.00	2.00
☐	212	Rollie Fingers, Oak.	3.00	6.00
☐	213	Dave Rader, S.F.	.50	1.00
☐	214	Billy Grabarkewitz, Pha.	.50	1.00
☐	215	Al Kaline, Det.	5.00	10.00
☐	216	Ray Sadecki, NYM.	.50	1.00
☐	217	Tim Foli, Mtl.	.50	1.00
☐	218	Johnny Briggs, Mil.	.50	1.00
☐	219	Doug Griffin, Bos.	.50	1.00
☐	220	Don Sutton, L.A.	2.00	4.00
☐	221	Chi.-A.L.: Mgr.: C. Tanner; Coaches: J. Mahoney / A. Monchak/ J. Sain/ J. Lonnett	.50	1.00
☐	222	Ramon Hernandez, Pgh.	.50	1.00
☐	223	Jeff Burroughs, Tex.	.50	1.00
☐	224	Roger Metzger, Hou.	.50	1.00

☐	225	Paul Splittorff, K.C.	.50	1.00
☐	226	San Diego Padres	1.00	2.00
☐	227	Mike Lum, Atl.	.50	1.00
☐	228	Ted Kubiak, Oak.	.50	1.00
☐	229	Fritz Peterson, NYY.	.50	1.00
☐	230	Tony Perez, Cin.	1.00	2.00
☐	231	Dick Tidrow, Cle.	.50	1.00
☐	232	Steve Brye, Min.	.50	1.00
☐	233	Jim Barr, S.F.	.50	1.00
☐	234	John Milner, NYM.	.50	1.00
☐	235	Dave McNally, Bal.	.50	1.00
☐	236	Stl.: Manager: R. Schoendienst; Coaches: B. Schultz / G. Kissell/ J. Lewis/ V. Benson	1.25	2.50
☐	237	Ken Brett, Pgh.	.50	1.00
☐	238	Fran Healy, K.C.	.50	1.00
☐	239	Bill Russell, L.A.	.50	1.00
☐	240	Joe Coleman, Det.	.50	1.00
☐	241	Glenn Beckert, S.D.	.50	1.00
☐	242	Bill Gogolewski, Tex.	.50	1.00
☐	243	Bob Oliver, Cal.	.50	1.00
☐	244	Carl Morton, Atl.	.50	1.00
☐	245	Cleon Jones, NYM.	.50	1.00
☐	246	Oakland A's	1.00	2.00
☐	247	Rick Miller, Bos.	.50	1.00
☐	248	Tom Hall, Cin.	.50	1.00
☐	249	George Mitterwald, Min.	.50	1.00
☐	250	Willie McCovey, S.D.	4.50	9.00
☐	251	Graig Nettles, NYY.	.50	1.00
☐	**252**	**Dave Parker, Pgh., RC**	**6.00**	**12.00**
☐	253	John Boccabella, Mtl.	.50	1.00
☐	254	Stan Bahnsen, Chi.-A.L.	.50	1.00
☐	255	Larry Bowa, Pha.	.50	1.00
☐	256	Tom Griffin, Hou.	.50	1.00
☐	257	Buddy Bell, Cle.	.50	1.00
☐	258	Jerry Morales, Chi.-N.L.	.50	1.00
☐	259	Bob Reynolds, Bal.	.50	1.00
☐	260	Ted Simmons, Stl.	.50	1.00
☐	261	Jerry Bell, Mil.	.50	1.00
☐	262	Ed Kirkpatrick, K.C.	.50	1.00
☐	263	Checklist 2 (133 - 264)	1.00	2.00
☐	264	Joe Rudi, Oak.	.50	1.00
☐	265	Tug McGraw, NYM.	.50	1.00
☐	266	Jim Northrup, Det.	.50	1.00
☐	267	Andy Messersmith, L.A.	.50	1.00
☐	268	Tom Grieve, Tex.	.50	1.00
☐	269	Bob Johnson, Cle.	.50	1.00
☐	270	Ron Santo, Chi.-N.L.	1.00	2.00
☐	271	Bill Hands, Min.	.50	1.00
☐	272	Paul Casanova, Atl.	.50	1.00
☐	273	Checklist 3 (265-396)	1.00	2.00
☐	274	Fred Beene, NYY.	.50	1.00
☐	275	Ron Hunt, Mtl.	.50	1.00
☐	276	Cal.: Mgr.: B. Winkles; Coaches: J. Roseboro / T. Morgan/ J. Reese/ S. Parker	.50	1.00
☐	277	Gary Nolan, Cin.	.50	1.00
☐	278	Cookie Rojas, K.C.	.50	1.00
☐	**279**	**Jim Crawford, Hou., RC**	**.50**	**1.00**
☐	280	Carl Yastrzemski, Bos.	6.00	12.00
☐	281	San Francisco Giants	1.00	2.00
☐	282	Doyle Alexander, Bal.	.50	1.00
☐	283	Mike Schmidt, Pha.	50.00	100.00
☐	284	Dave Duncan, Cle.	.50	1.00
☐	285	Reggie Smith, Stl.	.50	1.00
☐	286	Tony Muser, Chi.-A.L.	.50	1.00
☐	287	Clay Kirby, Cin.	.50	1.00
☐	**288**	**Gorman Thomas, Mil., RC**	**1.50**	**3.00**
☐	289	Rick Auerbach, L.A.	.50	1.00
☐	290	Vida Blue, Oak.	1.00	2.00
☐	291	Don Hahn, NYM.	.50	1.00

☐	292	Chuck Seelbach, Det.	.50	1.00
☐	293	Milt May, Hou.	.50	1.00
☐	**294**	**Steve Foucault, Tex., RC**	**.50**	**1.00**
☐	295	Rick Monday, Chi.-N.L.	.50	1.00
☐	296	Ray Corbin, Min.	.50	1.00
☐	297	Hal Breeden, Mtl.	.50	1.00
☐	298	Roric Harrison, Atl.	.50	1.00
☐	299	Gene Michael, NYY.	.50	1.00
☐	300	Pete Rose, Cin.	12.50	25.00
☐	301	Bob Montgomery, Bos.	.50	1.00
☐	302	Rudy May, Cal.	.50	1.00
☐	303	George Hendrick, Cle.	.50	1.00
☐	304	Don Wilson, Hou.	.50	1.00
☐	305	Tito Fuentes, S.F.	.50	1.00
☐	306	Bal.: Manager: E. Weaver; Coaches: J. Frey / G. Bamberger/ B. Hunter/ G. Staller	1.50	3.00
☐	307	Luis Melendez, Stl.	.50	1.00
☐	308	Bruce Dal Canton, K.C.	.50	1.00
☐	309	Dave Roberts, S.D.	.50	1.00
☐	**310**	**Terry Forster, Chi.-A.L., RC**	**.50**	**1.00**
☐	311	Jerry Grote, NYM.	.50	1.00
☐	312	Deron Johnson, Oak.	.50	1.00
☐	313	Barry Lersch, Pha.	.50	1.00
☐	314	Milwaukee Brewers	1.00	2.00
☐	315	Ron Cey, L.A.	.50	1.00
☐	316	Jim Perry, Det.	.50	1.00
☐	317	Richie Zisk, Pgh.	.50	1.00
☐	318	Jim Merritt, Tex.	.50	1.00
☐	319	Randy Hundley, Chi.-N.L.	.50	1.00
☐	320	Dusty Baker, Atl.	.50	1.00
☐	321	Steve Braun, Min.	.50	1.00
☐	322	Ernie McAnally, Mtl.	.50	1.00
☐	323	Richie Scheinblum, Cal.	.50	1.00
☐	324	Steve Kline, NYY.	.50	1.00
☐	325	Tommy Harper, Bos.	.50	1.00
☐	326	Cin.: Manager: S. Anderson; Coaches: L. Shepard / G. Scherger/ A. Grammas/ T. Kluszewski	1.00	2.00
☐	327	Tom Timmermann, Cle.	.50	1.00
☐	**328**	**Skip Jutze, Hou., RC**	**.50**	**1.00**
☐	329	Mark Belanger, Bal.	.50	1.00
☐	330	Juan Marichal, S.F.	2.00	4.00
☐	331	AS: C. Fisk/ J. Bench	4.25	8.50
☐	332	AS: D. Allen/ H. Aaron	4.25	8.50
☐	333	AS: R. Carew/ J. Morgan	2.00	4.00
☐	334	AS: B. Robinson/ R. Santo	1.50	3.00
☐	335	AS: B. Campaneris/ C. Speier	1.00	2.00
☐	336	AS: B. Murcer/ P. Rose	1.75	3.50
☐	337	AS: A. Otis/ C. Cedeno	1.00	2.00
☐	338	AS: R. Jackson/ B. Williams	4.25	8.50
☐	339	AS: J. Hunter/ R. Wise	1.50	3.00
☐	340	Thurman Munson, NYY.	4.25	8.50
☐	**341**	**Dan Driessen, Cin., RC**	**.50**	**1.00**
☐	342	Jim Lonborg, Pha.	.50	1.00
☐	343	Kansas City Royals	1.00	2.00
☐	344	Mike Caldwell, S.F.	.50	1.00
☐	345	Bill North, Oak.	.50	1.00
☐	346	Ron Reed, Atl.	.50	1.00
☐	347	Sandy Alomar, Cal.	.50	1.00
☐	348	Pete Richert, L.A.	.50	1.00
☐	349	John Vukovich, Mil.	.50	1.00
☐	350	Bob Gibson, Stl.	4.25	8.50
☐	351	Dwight Evans, Bos.	1.00	2.00
☐	352	Bill Stoneman, Mtl.	.50	1.00
☐	**353**	**Rich Coggins, Bal., RC**	**.50**	**1.00**
☐	354	Chi.: Mgr: W. Lockman; Coaches: J.C. Martin / H. Aguirre/ Al. Spangler/ J. Marshall	.50	1.00
☐	355	Dave Nelson, Tex.	.50	1.00
☐	356	Jerry Koosman, NYM.	.50	1.00
☐	357	Buddy Bradford, Chi.-A.L.	.50	1.00

	No.	Player		
☐	358	Dal Maxvill, Pgh.	.50	1.00
☐	359	Brent Strom, Cle.	.50	1.00
☐	360	Greg Luzinski, Pha.	.50	1.00
☐	361	Don Carrithers, S.F.	.50	1.00
☐	362	Hal King, Cin.	.50	1.00
☐	363	New York Yankees	1.00	2.00
☐	364	Cito Gaston, S.D.	.50	1.00
☐	365	Steve Busby, K.C.	.50	1.00
☐	366	Larry Hisle, Min.	.50	1.00
☐	367	Norm Cash, Det.	.50	1.00
☐	368	Manny Mota, L.A.	.50	1.00
☐	369	Paul Lindblad, Oak.	.50	1.00
☐	370	Bob Watson, Hou.	.50	1.00
☐	371	Jim Slaton, Mil.	.50	1.00
☐	372	Ken Reitz, Stl.	.50	1.00
☐	373	John Curtis, Bos.	.50	1.00
☐	374	Marty Perez, Atl.	.50	1.00
☐	375	Earl Williams, Bal.	.50	1.00
☐	376	Jorge Orta, Chi.-A.L.	.50	1.00
☐	377	Ron Woods, Mtl.	.50	1.00
☐	378	Burt Hooton, Chi.-N.L.	.50	1.00
☐	379	Tex.: Manager: B. Martin; Coaches: A. Fowler / F. Lucchesi/ J. Moore/ C. Silvera	1.25	2.50
☐	380	Bud Harrelson, NYM.	.50	1.00
☐	381	Charlie Sands, Cal.	.50	1.00
☐	382	Bob Moose, Pgh.	.50	1.00
☐	383	Philadelphia Phillies	1.00	2.00
☐	384	Chris Chambliss, Cle.	.50	1.00
☐	385	Don Gullett, Cin.	.50	1.00
☐	386	Gary Matthews, S.F.	.50	1.00
☐	387	Rich Morales, S.D.	.50	1.00
☐	388	Phil Roof, Min.	.50	1.00
☐	389	Gates Brown, Det.	.50	1.00
☐	390	Lou Piniella, NYY.	.50	1.00
☐	391	Billy Champion, Mil.	.50	1.00
☐	392	Dick Green, Oak.	.50	1.00
☐	393	Orlando Pena, Stl.	.50	1.00
☐	394	Ken Henderson, Chi.-A.L.	.50	1.00
☐	395	Doug Rader, Hou.	.50	1.00
☐	396	Tommy Davis, Bal.	.50	1.00
☐	397	George Stone, NYM.	.50	1.00
☐	398	Duke Sims, NYY.	.50	1.00
☐	399	Mike Paul, Chi.-N.L.	.50	1.00
☐	400	Harmon Killebrew, Min.	4.00	8.00
☐	401	Elliott Maddox, Tex.	.50	1.00
☐	402	Jim Rooker, Pgh.	.50	1.00
☐	403	Bos.: Mgr.: D. Johnson; Coaches: E. Popowski / L.Stange/ D. Zimmer/ D. Bryant	.50	1.00
☐	404	Jim Howarth, S.F.	.50	1.00
☐	405	Ellie Rodriguez, Cal.	.50	1.00
☐	406	Steve Arlin, S.D.	.50	1.00
☐	407	Jim Wohlford, K.C.	.50	1.00
☐	408	Charlie Hough, L.A.	.50	1.00
☐	409	Ike Brown, Det.	.50	1.00
☐	410	Pedro Borbon, Cin.	.50	1.00
☐	411	Frank Baker, Bal.	.50	1.00
☐	412	Chuck Taylor, Mtl.	.50	1.00
☐	413	Don Money, Mil.	.50	1.00
☐	414	Checklist 4	1.00	2.00
☐	415	Gary Gentry, Atl.	.50	1.00
☐	416	Chicago White Sox	1.00	2.00
☐	417	Rich Folkers, Stl.	.50	1.00
☐	418	Walt Williams, Cle.	.50	1.00
☐	419	Wayne Twitchell, Pha.	.50	1.00
☐	420	Ray Fosse, Oak.	.50	1.00
☐	**421**	**Dan Fife, Min., RC**	**.50**	**1.00**
☐	422	Gonzalo Marquez, Chi.-N.L.	.50	1.00
☐	423	Fred Stanley, NYY.	.50	1.00
☐	424	Jim Beauchamp, NYM.	.50	1.00
☐	425	Pete Broberg, Tex.	.50	1.00
☐	426	Rennie Stennett, Pgh.	.50	1.00
☐	427	Bobby Bolin, Bos.	.50	1.00
☐	428	Gary Sutherland, Hou.	.50	1.00
☐	**429**	**Dick Lange, Cal., RC**	**.50**	**1.00**
☐	430	Matty Alou, S.D.	.50	1.00
☐	**431**	**Gene Garber, K.C., RC**	**1.00**	**2.00**
☐	432	Chris Arnold, S.F.	.50	1.00
☐	433	Lerrin LaGrow, Det.	.50	1.00
☐	434	Ken McMullen, L.A.	.50	1.00
☐	435	Dave Concepcion, Cin.	1.00	2.00
☐	**436**	**Don Hood, Bal., RC**	**.50**	**1.00**
☐	437	Jim Lyttle, Mtl.	.50	1.00
☐	438	Ed Herrmann, Chi.-A.L.	.50	1.00
☐	439	Norm Miller, Atl.	.50	1.00
☐	440	Jim Kaat, Chi.-A.L.	1.00	2.00
☐	**441**	**Tom Ragland, Cle., RC**	**.50**	**1.00**
☐	442	Alan Foster, Stl.	.50	1.00
☐	443	Tom Hutton, Pha.	.50	1.00
☐	444	Vic Davalillo, Oak.	.50	1.00
☐	445	George Medich, NYY.	.50	1.00
☐	446	Len Randle, Tex.	.50	1.00
☐	447	Min.: Manager: F. Quilici; Coaches: V. Morgan / B. Rodgers/ R. Rowe	.50	1.00
☐	**448**	**Ron Hodges, NYM., RC**	**.50**	**1.00**
☐	449	Tom McCraw, Cal.	.50	1.00
☐	450	Rich Hebner, Pgh.	.50	1.00
☐	451	Tommy John, L.A.	1.00	2.00
☐	**452**	**Gene Hiser, Chi.-N.L., RC**	**.50**	**1.00**
☐	453	Balor Moore, Mtl.	.50	1.00
☐	454	Kurt Bevacqua, Pgh.	.50	1.00
☐	455	Tom Bradley, S.F.	.50	1.00
☐	**456**	**Dave Winfield, S.D., RC**	**87.50**	**175.00**
☐	**457**	**Chuck Goggin, Atl., RC**	**.50**	**1.00**
☐	458	Jim Ray, Hou.	.50	1.00
☐	459	Cincinnati Reds	1.50	3.00
☐	460	Boog Powell, Bal.	1.00	2.00
☐	461	John Odom, Oak.	.50	1.00
☐	462	Luis Alvarado, Chi.-A.L.	.50	1.00
☐	463	Pat Dobson, NYY.	.50	1.00
☐	464	Jose Cruz, Stl.	.50	1.00
☐	465	Dick Bosman, Cle.	.50	1.00
☐	466	Dick Billings, Tex.	.50	1.00
☐	**467**	**Winston Llenas, Cal., RC**	**.50**	**1.00**
☐	**468**	**Pepe Frias, Mtl., RC**	**.50**	**1.00**
☐	469	Joe Decker, Min.	.50	1.00
☐	470	A.L.: A's: 3 Games Orioles: 2 Games	5.00	10.00
☐	471	N.L.: Mets: 3 Games Reds: 2 Games	1.00	2.00
☐	472	WS-Game 1: Oakland 2, New York 1	1.00	2.00
☐	473	WS-Game 2: New York 10, Oakland 7	5.00	10.00
☐	474	WS-Game 3: Oakland 3, New York 2	1.00	2.00
☐	475	WS-Game 4: New York 6, Oakland 1	1.00	2.00
☐	476	WS-Game 5: New York 2, Oakland 0	1.00	2.00
☐	477	WS-Game 6: Oakland 3, New York 1	5.00	10.00
☐	478	WS-Game 7: Oakland 5, New York 2	1.00	2.00
☐	479	A's Celebrate: Win 2nd Consecutive Champ.	1.00	2.00
☐	480	Willie Crawford, L.A.	.50	1.00
☐	**481**	**Jerry Terrell, Min., RC**	**.50**	**1.00**
☐	482	Bob Didier, Det.	.50	1.00
☐	483	Atlanta Braves	1.00	2.00
☐	484	Carmen Fanzone, Chi.-N.L.	.50	1.00
☐	485	Felipe Alou, Mtl.	1.50	3.00
☐	486	Steve Stone, Chi.-N.L..	.50	1.00
☐	487	Ted Martinez, NYM.	.50	1.00
☐	488	Andy Etchebarren, Bal.	.50	1.00
☐	489	Pgh.: Manager: D. Murtaugh; Coaches: D. Osborn / D. Leppert/ B. Mazeroski/ B. Skinner	.50	1.00
☐	490	Vada Pinson, Cal.	.50	1.00
☐	491	Roger Nelson, Cin.	.50	1.00

	No.	Card		
☐	**492**	**Mike Rogodzinski, Pha., RC**	**.50**	**1.00**
☐	493	Joe Hoerner, K.C.	.50	1.00
☐	494	Ed Goodson, S.F.	.50	1.00
☐	495	Dick McAuliffe, Bos.	.50	1.00
☐	496	Tom Murphy, Stl.	.50	1.00
☐	**497**	**Bobby Mitchell, Mil., RC**	**.50**	**1.00**
☐	498	Pat Corrales, S.D.	.50	1.00
☐	499	Rusty Torres, Cle.	.50	1.00
☐	500	Lee May, Hou.	.50	1.00
☐	501	Eddie Leon, Chi.-A.L.	.50	1.00
☐	502	Dave LaRoche, Chi.-N.L.	.50	1.00
☐	503	Eric Soderholm, Min.	.50	1.00
☐	504	Joe Niekro, Atl.	.50	1.00
☐	505	Bill Buckner, L.A.	.50	1.00
☐	506	Ed Farmer, Det.	.50	1.00
☐	507	Larry Stahl, Cin.	.50	1.00
☐	508	Montréal Expos	1.50	3.00
☐	509	Jesse Jefferson, Bal.	.50	1.00
☐	510	Wayne Garrett, NYM.	.50	1.00
☐	511	Toby Harrah, Tex.	.50	1.00
☐	512	Joe Lahoud, Cal.	.50	1.00
☐	**513**	**Jim Campanis, Pgh., RC**	**.50**	**1.00**
☐	514	Paul Schaal, K.C.	.50	1.00
☐	515	Willie Montanez, Pha.	.50	1.00
☐	516	Horacio Pina, Chi.-N.L.	.50	1.00
☐	517	Mike Hegan, NYY.	.50	1.00
☐	518	Derrel Thomas, S.D.	.50	1.00
☐	**519**	**Bill Sharp, Chi.-A.L., RC**	**.50**	**1.00**
☐	520	Tim McCarver, Stl.	.50	1.00
☐	521	Cle.: Manager: K. Aspromonte; Coaches: C. Bryant / T. Pacheco	.50	1.00
☐	**522**	**J.R. Richard, Hou., RC**	**2.00**	**4.00**
☐	523	Cecil Cooper, Bos.	.50	1.00
☐	524	Bill Plummer, Cin.	.50	1.00
☐	525	Clyde Wright, Mil.	.50	1.00
☐	526	Frank Tepedino, Atl.	.50	1.00
☐	527	Bobby Darwin, Min.	.50	1.00
☐	528	Bill Bonham, Chi.-N.L.	.50	1.00
☐	529	Horace Clarke, NYY.	.50	1.00
☐	530	Mickey Stanley, Det.	.50	1.00
☐	531	Mtl.: Manager: G. Mauch; Coaches: D. Bristol / C. McLish/ L. Doby/ J. Zimmerman	1.00	2.00
☐	532	Skip Lockwood, Cal.	.50	1.00
☐	**533**	**Mike Phillips, S.F., RC**	**.50**	**1.00**
☐	534	Eddie Watt, Bal.	.50	1.00
☐	535	Bob Tolan, S.D.	.50	1.00
☐	536	Duffy Dyer, NYM.	.50	1.00
☐	537	Steve Mingori, K.C.	.50	1.00
☐	538	Cesar Tovar, Pha.	.50	1.00
☐	539	Lloyd Allen, Tex.	.50	1.00
☐	540	Bob Robertson, Pgh.	.50	1.00
☐	541	Cleveland Indians	1.00	2.00
☐	542	Rich Gossage, Chi.-A.L.	1.50	3.00
☐	543	Danny Cater, Bos.	.50	1.00
☐	544	Ron Schueler, Atl.	.50	1.00
☐	545	Billy Conigliaro, Oak.	.50	1.00
☐	546	Mike Corkins, S.D.	.50	1.00
☐	547	Glenn Borgmann, Min.	.50	1.00
☐	548	Sonny Siebert, Stl.	.50	1.00
☐	549	Mike Jorgensen, Mtl.	.50	1.00
☐	550	Sam McDowell, NYY.	.50	1.00
☐	551	Von Joshua, L.A.	.50	1.00
☐	552	Denny Doyle, Cal.	.50	1.00
☐	553	Jim Willoughby, S.F.	.50	1.00
☐	**554**	**Tim Johnson, Mil., RC**	**1.50**	**3.00**
☐	555	Woodie Fryman, Det.	.50	1.00
☐	556	Dave Campbell, Hou.	.50	1.00
☐	557	Jim McGlothlin, Chi.-A.L.	.50	1.00
☐	558	Bill Fahey, Tex.	.50	1.00
☐	559	Darrel Chaney, Cin.	.50	1.00
☐	560	Mike Cuellar, Bal.	.50	1.00
☐	561	Ed Kranepool, NYM.	.50	1.00
☐	562	Jack Aker, Chi.-N.L.	.50	1.00
☐	563	Hal McRae, K.C.	.50	1.00
☐	564	Mike Ryan, Pha.	.50	1.00
☐	565	Milt Wilcox, Cle.	.50	1.00
☐	566	Jackie Hernandez, Pgh.	.50	1.00
☐	567	Boston Red Sox	1.00	2.00
☐	568	Mike Torrez, Mtl.	.50	1.00
☐	569	Rick Dempsey, NYY.	.50	1.00
☐	570	Ralph Garr, Atl.	.50	1.00
☐	571	Rich Hand, Cal.	.50	1.00
☐	572	Enzo Hernandez, S.D.	.50	1.00
☐	**573**	**Mike Adams, Min., RC**	**.50**	**1.00**
☐	574	Bill Parsons, Mil.	.50	1.00
☐	575	Steve Garvey, L.A.	1.50	3.00
☐	576	Scipio Spinks, Stl.	.50	1.00
☐	**577**	**Mike Sadek, S.F., RC**	**.50**	**1.00**
☐	578	Ralph Houk, Mgr., Det.	.50	1.00
☐	579	Cecil Upshaw, Hou.	.50	1.00
☐	580	Jim Spencer, Tex.	.50	1.00
☐	581	Fred Norman, Cin.	.50	1.00
☐	**582**	**Bucky Dent, Chi.-A.L., RC**	**1.00**	**2.00**
☐	583	Marty Pattin, K.C.	.50	1.00
☐	584	Ken Rudolph, Chi.-N.L.	.50	1.00
☐	585	Merv Rettenmund, Bal.	.50	1.00
☐	586	Jack Brohamer, Cle.	.50	1.00
☐	**587**	**Larry Christenson, Pha., RC**	**.50**	**1.00**
☐	588	Hal Lanier, NYY.	.50	1.00
☐	589	Boots Day, Mtl.	.50	1.00
☐	590	Rogelio Moret, Bos.	.50	1.00
☐	591	Sonny Jackson, Atl.	.50	1.00
☐	**592**	**Ed Bane, Min., RC**	**.50**	**1.00**
☐	593	Steve Yeager, L.A.	.50	1.00
☐	594	Leroy Stanton, Cal.	.50	1.00
☐	595	Steve Blass, Pgh.	.50	1.00
☐	596	W. Garland/ F.Holdsworth/ M. Littell/ D. Pole	1.00	2.00
☐	597	D. Chalk/ J. Gamble/ P. MacKanin/ M. Trillo	1.00	2.00
☐	598	D. Augustine/ K. Griffey/ S. Ontiveros / J. Tyrone	10.00	20.00
☐	599	D. Freisleben/ R. Diorio/ F. Riccelli / G. Shanahan	.50	1.00
☐	600	R. Cash/ J. Cox/ B. Madlock/ R. Saunders	2.75	5.50
☐	601	E. Armbrister/ R. Bladt/ B. Downing / B. McBride	1.25	2.50
☐	602	G. Abbott/ R. Henninger/ C. Swan/ D. Vossler	.50	1.00
☐	603	B. Foote/ T. Lundstedt/ C. Moore/ S. Robles	.50	1.00
☐	604	T. Hughes/ J. Knox/ A. Thornton/ F. White	3.00	6.00
☐	605	V. Albury/ K. Frailing/ K. Kobel/ F. Tanana	2.75	5.50
☐	606	J. Fuller/ W. Howard/ T. Smith/ O. Velez	.50	1.00
☐	607	L. Foster/ T. Heintzelman,/ D. Rosello / F. Taveras	.50	1.00
☐	608	B. Apodaco/ D. Baney/ John D'Acquisto / M. Wallace	.50	1.00
☐	609	Rico Petrocelli, Bos.	.50	1.00
☐	610	Dave Kingman, S.F.	1.25	2.50
☐	611	Rick Stelmaszek, Cal.	.50	1.00
☐	612	Luke Walker, Pgh.	.50	1.00
☐	613	Dan Monzon, Min.	.50	1.00
☐	**614**	**Adrian Devine, Atl., RC**	**.50**	**1.00**
☐	615	Johnny Jeter, Chi.-A.L.	.50	1.00
☐	616	Larry Gura, Chi.-N.L.	.50	1.00
☐	617	Ted Ford, Cle.	.50	1.00
☐	618	Jim Mason, Tex.	.50	1.00
☐	619	Mike Anderson, Pha.	.50	1.00
☐	620	Al Downing, L.A.	.50	1.00
☐	621	Bernie Carbo, Bos.	.50	1.00
☐	622	Phil Gagliano, Cin.	.50	1.00

	No.	Player	EX	NRMT
☐	623	Celerino Sanchez, NYY.	.50	1.00
☐	624	Bob Miller, NYM.	.50	1.00
☐	625	Ollie Brown, Cal.	.50	1.00
☐	626	Pittsburgh Pirates	1.00	2.00
☐	627	Carl Taylor, K.C.	.50	1.00
☐	628	Ivan Murrell, S.D.	.50	1.00
☐	629	Rusty Staub, NYM.	1.50	3.00
☐	630	Tommie Agee, Stl.	.50	1.00
☐	631	Steve Barber, Mil.	.50	1.00
☐	632	George Culver, Pha.	.50	1.00
☐	633	Dave Hamilton, Oak.	.50	1.00
☐	634	Atl.: Manager: E. Mathews; Coaches: H. Starrette / C. Ryan/ J. Busby/ K. Silvestri	1.25	2.50
☐	635	John Edwards, Hou.	.50	1.00
☐	636	Dave Goltz, Min.	.50	1.00
☐	637	Checklist 5	1.00	2.00
☐	638	Ken Sanders, Cle.	.50	1.00
☐	639	Joe Lovitto, Tex.	.50	1.00
☐	640	Milt Pappas, Chi.-N.L.	.50	1.00
☐	641	Chuck Brinkman, Chi.-A.L.	.50	1.00
☐	642	Terry Harmon, Pha.	.50	1.00
☐	643	Los Angeles Dodgers	1.00	2.00
☐	644	Wayne Granger, NYY.	.50	1.00
☐	645	Ken Boswell, NYM.	.50	1.00
☐	646	George Foster, Cin.	.50	1.00
☐	**647**	**Juan Beniquez, Bos., RC**	**.50**	**1.00**
☐	648	Terry Crowley, Bal.	.50	1.00
☐	**649**	**Fernando Gonzalez, Pgh., RC**	**.50**	**1.00**
☐	650	Mike Epstein, Cal.	.50	1.00
☐	651	Leron Lee, S.D.	.50	1.00
☐	652	Gail Hopkins, K.C.	.50	1.00
☐	653	Bob Stinson, Mtl.	.50	1.00
☐	654	Jesus Alou, Oak.	.50	1.00
☐	**655**	**Mike Tyson, Stl., RC**	**.50**	**1.00**
☐	**656**	**Adrian Garrett, Chi.-N.L., RC**	**.50**	**1.00**
☐	657	Jim Shellenback, Tex.	.50	1.00
☐	658	Lee Lacy, L.A.	.50	1.00
☐	659	Joe Lis, Min.	.50	1.00
☐	660	Larry Dierker, Hou.	.50	1.50

1974 TEAM CHECKLISTS

Card Size: 2 1/2" x 3 1/2"
Face: Green, yellow and black, red border; team, autographs
Back: Black and yellow on card stock; unnumbered
Imprint: **O.P.C. PRINTED IN CANADA

Insert Set (24 cards):			**15.00**	**30.00**
Common Team Card:				

	No.	Player	EX	NRMT
☐	1	Atanta Braves	.75	1.50
☐	2	Baltimore Orioles	.75	1.50
☐	3	Boston Red Sox	.75	1.50
☐	4	California Angels	.75	1.50
☐	5	Chicago Cubs	.75	1.50
☐	6	Chicago White Sox	.75	1.50
☐	7	Cincinnati Reds	1.25	2.50
☐	8	Cleveland Indians	.75	1.50
☐	9	Detroit Tigers	.75	1.50
☐	10	Houston Astros	.75	1.50
☐	11	Kansas City Royals	.75	1.50
☐	12	Los Angeles Dodgers	.75	1.50
☐	13	Milwaukee Brewers	.75	1.50
☐	14	Minnesota Twins	.75	1.50
☐	15	Montréal Expos	.75	1.50
☐	16	New York Mets	1.25	2.50
☐	17	New York Yankees	.75	1.50
☐	18	Oakland A's	1.25	2.50
☐	19	Philadelphia Phillies	.75	1.50
☐	20	Pittsburgh Pirates	.75	1.50
☐	21	St. Louis Cardinals	.75	1.50
☐	22	San Diego Padres	.75	1.50
☐	23	San Francisco Giants	.75	1.50
☐	24	Texas Rangers	.75	1.50

1975 O-PEE-CHEE

This 660-card set is identical in the number of cards and design to the Topps set for 1975, but the imprint reads "O.P.C. PTD. IN CANADA." It is hard to find in NRMT or mint condition due to the coloured borders. This set is one of the most popular of all O-Pee-Chee baseball issues.

Card Size: 2 1/2" x 3 1/2"
Face: Four colour, coloured border; name, position, team, Facsimile autograph
Back: Green and red on card stock; name, number, position, résumé, trivia, bilingual
Imprint: O.P.C. PTD. IN CANADA

Complete Set (660 cards):			**475.00**	**950.00**
Common Player:			**.35**	**.75**

	No.	Player	EX	NRMT
☐	1	HL: N.L. All Star: H. Aaron, Atl.	20.00	40.00
☐	2	HL: Lou Brock, Stl.	1.00	2.00
☐	3	HL: Bob Gibson, Stl.	1.00	2.00
☐	4	HL: Al Kaline, Det.	1.00	2.00
☐	5	HL: Nolan Ryan, Cal.	20.00	40.00
☐	6	HL: Mike Marshall, L.A.	.75	1.50
☐	7	HL: Steve Busby/ Dick Bosman/ Nolan Ryan	7.50	15.00
☐	8	Rogelio Moret, Bos.	.35	.75
☐	9	Frank Tepedino, Atl.	.35	.75
☐	10	Willie Davis, Mtl.	.35	.75
☐	11	Bill Melton, Chi.-A.L.	.35	.75
☐	12	David Clyde, Tex.	.35	.75
☐	**13**	**Gene Locklear, S.D., RC**	**.35**	**.75**
☐	14	Milt Wilcox, Cle.	.35	.75
☐	15	Jose Cardenal, Chi.-N.L.	.35	.75
☐	16	Frank Tanana, Cal.	.75	1.50
☐	17	Dave Concepcion, Cin.	.75	1.50
☐	18	Detroit Tigers: Ralph Houk, Mgr.	.35	.75
☐	19	Jerry Koosman, NYM.	.35	.75
☐	20	Thurman Munson, NYY.	3.25	6.50
☐	21	Rollie Fingers, Oak.	2.25	4.50
☐	22	Dave Cash, Pha.	.35	.75
☐	23	Bill Russell, L.A.	.35	.75
☐	24	Al Fitzmorris, K.C.	.35	.75
☐	25	Lee May, Hou.	.35	.75
☐	26	Dave McNally, Bal.	.35	.75
☐	27	Ken Reitz, Stl.	.35	.75
☐	28	Tom Murphy, Mil.	.35	.75
☐	29	Dave Parker, Pgh.	1.75	3.50
☐	30	Bert Blyleven, Min.	.75	1.50
☐	31	Dave Rader, S.F.	.35	.75
☐	32	Reggie Cleveland, Bos.	.75	1.50
☐	33	Dusty Baker, Atl.	.35	.75
☐	34	Steve Renko, Mtl.	.35	.75

	No.	Player		
☐	35	Ron Santo, Chi.-A.L.	.35	.75
☐	36	Joe Lovitto, Tex.	.35	.75
☐	37	Dave Freisleben, S.D.	.35	.75
☐	38	Buddy Bell, Cle.	.35	.75
☐	39	Andy Thornton	.35	.75
☐	40	Bill Singer, Cal.	.35	.75
☐	41	Cesar Geronimo, Cin.	.35	.75
☐	42	Joe Coleman, Det.	.35	.75
☐	43	Cleon Jones, NYM.	.35	.75
☐	44	Pat Dobson, NYY.	.35	.75
☐	45	Joe Rudi, Oak.	.35	.75
☐	46	Pha.: Danny Ozark, Mgr.	.35	.75
☐	47	Tommy John, L.A.	.75	1.50
☐	48	Freddie Patek, K.C.	.35	.75
☐	49	Larry Dierker, Hou.	.35	.75
☐	50	AS: Brooks Robinson, Bal.	4.25	8.50
☐	**51**	**Bob Forsch, St.L., RC**	**.35**	**.75**
☐	52	Darrell Porter, Mil.	.35	.75
☐	53	Dave Giusti, Pgh.	.35	.75
☐	54	Eric Soderholm, Min.	.35	.75
☐	55	Bobby Bonds, NYY.	.75	1.50
☐	56	Rick Wise, Bos.	.35	.75
☐	57	Dave Johnson, Atl.	.35	.75
☐	58	Chuck Taylor, Mtl.	.35	.75
☐	59	Ken Henderson, Chi.-A.L.	.35	.75
☐	60	Fergie Jenkins, Tex.	2.50	5.00
☐	61	Dave Winfield, S.D.	32.50	65.00
☐	62	Fritz Peterson, Cle.	.35	.75
☐	**63**	**Steve Swisher, Chi.-N.L., RC**	**.35**	**.75**
☐	64	Dave Chalk, Cal.	.35	.75
☐	65	Don Gullett, Cin.	.35	.75
☐	66	Willie Horton, Det.	.35	.75
☐	67	Tug McGraw, NYM.	.35	.75
☐	68	Ron Blomberg, NYY.	.35	.75
☐	69	John Odom, Oak.	.35	.75
☐	70	Mike Schmidt, Pha.	40.00	80.00
☐	71	Charlie Hough, L.A.	.35	.75
☐	72	K.C.: Jack McKeon, Mgr.	.35	.75
☐	73	J.R. Richard, Hou.	.35	.75
☐	74	Mark Belanger, Bal.	.35	.75
☐	75	Ted Simmons, Stl.	.35	.75
☐	76	Ed Sprague, Mil.	.35	.75
☐	77	Richie Zisk, Pgh.	.35	.75
☐	78	Ray Corbin, Min.	.35	.75
☐	79	Gary Matthews, S.F.	.35	.75
☐	80	AS: Carlton Fisk, Bos.	6.00	12.00
☐	81	Ron Reed, Atl.	.35	.75
☐	82	Pat Kelly, Chi.-A.L.	.35	.75
☐	83	Jim Merritt, Tex.	.35	.75
☐	84	Enzo Hernandez, S.D.	.35	.75
☐	85	Bill Bonham, Chi.-N.L.	.35	.75
☐	86	Joe Lis, Cle.	.35	.75
☐	87	George Foster, Cin.	.35	.75
☐	88	Tom Egan, Cal.	.35	.75
☐	89	Jim Ray, Det.	.35	.75
☐	90	Rusty Staub, NYM.	1.00	2.00
☐	91	Dick Green, Oak.	.35	.75
☐	92	Cecil Upshaw, NYY.	.35	.75
☐	93	Dave Lopes, L.A.	.35	.75
☐	94	Jim Lonborg, Pha.	.35	.75
☐	95	John Mayberry, K.C.	.35	.75
☐	**96**	**Mike Cosgrove, Hou., RC**	**.35**	**.75**
☐	97	Earl Williams, Bal.	.35	.75
☐	98	Rich Folkers, Stl.	.35	.75
☐	99	Mike Hegan, Mil.	.35	.75
☐	100	Willie Stargell, Pgh.	2.50	5.00
☐	101	Mtl.: Gene Mauch, Mgr.	.35	.75
☐	102	Joe Decker, Min.	.35	.75
☐	103	Rick Miller, Bos.	.35	.75
☐	104	Bill Madlock, Chi.-N.L.	.75	1.50
☐	105	Buzz Capra, Atl.	.35	.75
☐	**106**	**Mike Hargrove, Tex., RC**	**2.00**	**4.00**
☐	107	Jim Barr, S.F.	.35	.75
☐	108	Tom Hall, Cin.	.35	.75
☐	109	George Hendrick, Cle.	.35	.75
☐	110	Wilbur Wood, Chi.-A.L.	.35	.75
☐	111	Wayne Garrett, NYM.	.35	.75
☐	112	Larry Hardy, S.D.	.35	.75
☐	113	Elliott Maddox, NYY.	.35	.75
☐	114	Dick Lange, Cal.	.35	.75
☐	115	Joe Ferguson, L.A.	.35	.75
☐	116	Lerrin LaGrow, Det.	.35	.75
☐	117	Bal.: Earl Weaver, Mgr.	1.00	2.00
☐	118	Mike Anderson, Pha.	.35	.75
☐	119	Tommy Helms, Hou.	.35	.75
☐	120	Steve Busby, K.C.	.35	.75
☐	121	Bill North, Oak.	.35	.75
☐	122	Al Hrabosky, Stl.	.35	.75
☐	123	Johnny Briggs, Mil.	.35	.75
☐	124	Jerry Reuss, Pgh.	.35	.75
☐	125	Ken Singleton, Mtl.	.35	.75
☐	126	Checklist 1 (1 - 132)	.75	1.50
☐	127	Glenn Borgmann, Min.	.35	.75
☐	128	Bill Lee, Bos.	.35	.75
☐	129	Rick Monday, Chi.-N.L.	.35	.75
☐	130	Phil Niekro, Atl.	1.25	2.50
☐	131	Toby Harrah, Tex.	.35	.75
☐	132	Randy Moffitt, S.F.	.35	.75
☐	133	Dan Driessen, Cin.	.35	.75
☐	134	Ron Hodges, NYM.	.35	.75
☐	135	Charlie Spikes, Cle.	.35	.75
☐	136	Jim Mason, NYY.	.35	.75
☐	137	Terry Forster, Chi.-A.L.	.35	.75
☐	138	Del Unser, Pha.	.35	.75
☐	139	Horacio Pina, Cal.	.35	.75
☐	140	N.L. All Star: Steve Garvey, L.A.	2.50	5.00
☐	141	Mickey Stanley, Det.	.35	.75
☐	142	Bob Reynolds, Bal.	.35	.75
☐	**143**	**Cliff Johnson, Hou. RC**	**.35**	**.75**
☐	144	Jim Wohlford, K.C.	.35	.75
☐	145	Ken Holtzman, Oak.	.35	.75
☐	146	S.D.: John McNamara, Mgr.	.35	.75
☐	147	Pedro Garcia, Mil.	.35	.75
☐	148	Jim Rooker, Pgh.	.35	.75
☐	149	Tim Foli, Mtl.	.35	.75
☐	150	Bob Gibson, Stl.	3.75	7.50
☐	151	Steve Brye, Min.	.35	.75
☐	152	Mario Guerrero, Bos.	.35	.75
☐	153	Rick Reuschel, Chi.-N.L.	.35	.75
☐	154	Mike Lum, Atl.	.35	.75
☐	155	Jim Bibby, Tex.	.35	.75
☐	156	Dave Kingman, S.F.	.75	1.50
☐	157	Pedro Borbon, Cin.	.35	.75
☐	158	Jerry Grote, NYM.	.35	.75
☐	159	Steve Arlin, Cle.	.35	.75
☐	160	Graig Nettles, NYY.	.35	.75
☐	161	Stan Bahnsen, Chi.-A.L.	.35	.75
☐	162	Willie Montanez, Pha.	.35	.75
☐	163	Jim Brewer, L.A.	.35	.75
☐	164	Mickey Rivers, Cal.	.35	.75
☐	165	Doug Rader, Hou.	.35	.75
☐	166	Woodie Fryman, Det.	.35	.75
☐	167	Rich Coggins, Bal.	.35	.75
☐	168	Bill Greif, S.D.	.35	.75
☐	169	Cookie Rojas, K.C.	.35	.75
☐	170	AS: Bert Campaneris, Oak.	.35	.75
☐	171	Ed Kirkpatrick, Pgh.	.35	.75
☐	172	Bos.: Darrell Johnson, Mgr.	.35	.75

	No.	Player		
☐	173	Steve Rogers, Mtl.	.35	.75
☐	174	Bake McBride, Stl.	.35	.75
☐	175	Don Money, Mil.	.35	.75
☐	176	Burt Hooton, Chi.-N.L.	.35	.75
☐	**177**	**Vic Correll, Atl. RC**	**.35**	**.75**
☐	178	Cesar Tovar, Tex.	.35	.75
☐	179	Tom Bradley, S.F.	.35	.75
☐	180	AS: Joe Morgan, Cin.	3.75	7.50
☐	181	Fred Beene, Cle.	.35	.75
☐	182	Don Hahn, NYM.	.35	.75
☐	183	Mel Stottlemyre, NYY.	.35	.75
☐	184	Jorge Orta, Chi.-A.L.	.35	.75
☐	185	Steve Carlton, Pha.	4.50	9.00
☐	186	Willie Crawford, L.A.	.35	.75
☐	187	Denny Doyle, Cal.	.35	.75
☐	188	Tom Griffin, Hou.	.35	.75
☐	189	1951-MVPs: Yogi Berra, Roy Campanella	1.50	3.00
☐	190	1952-MVPs: Bobby Shantz, Hank Sauer	.75	1.50
☐	191	1953-MVPs: Roy Campanella, Al Rosen	1.00	2.00
☐	192	1951-MVPs: Yogi Berra Willie Mays	2.75	5.50
☐	193	1955-MVPs: Yogi Berra, Roy Campanella	1.50	3.00
☐	194	1956-MVPs: Mickey Mantle, Don Newcombe	9.00	18.00
☐	195	1957-MVPs: Mickey Mantle, Hank Aaron	15.00	30.00
☐	196	1958-MVPs: Jackie Jensen, Ernie Banks	1.00	2.00
☐	197	1959-MVPs: Nellie Fox, Ernie Banks	1.50	3.00
☐	198	1960-MVPs: Dick Groat, Roger Maris	1.00	2.00
☐	199	1961-MVPs: Roger Maris, Frank Robinson	1.50	3.00
☐	200	1962-MVPs: Mickey Mantle, Maury Wills	9.00	18.00
☐	201	1963-MVPs: Elston Howard, Sandy Koufax	1.00	2.00
☐	202	1964-MVPs: Brooks Robinson, Ken Boyer	1.00	2.00
☐	203	1965-MVPs: Zoilo Versailles, Willie Mays	1.00	2.00
☐	204	1966-MVPs: Frank Robinson, Bob Clemente	4.00	8.00
☐	205	1967-MVPs: Carl Yastrzemski, Orlando Cepeda	1.00	2.00
☐	206	1968-MVPs: Denny McLain, Bob Gibson	1.00	2.00
☐	207	1969-MVPs: Harmon Killebrew, Willie McCovey	1.50	3.00
☐	208	1970-MVPs: Boog Powell, Johnny Bench	1.00	2.00
☐	209	1971-MVPs: Vida Blue, Joe Torre	.75	1.50
☐	210	1972-MVPs: Rich Allen, Johnny Bench	1.00	2.00
☐	211	1973-MVPs: Reggie Jackson, Pete Rose	4.00	8.00
☐	212	1974-MVPs: Jeff Burroughs, Steve Garvey	.75	1.50
☐	213	Oscar Gamble, Cle.	.35	.75
☐	214	Harry Parker, NYM.	.35	.75
☐	215	Bobby Valentine, Cal.	.35	.75
☐	216	S.F.: Wes Westrum, Mgr.	.35	.75
☐	217	Lou Piniella, NYY.	.35	.75
☐	218	Jerry Johnson, Hou.	.35	.75
☐	219	Ed Herrmann, Chi.-A.L.	.35	.75
☐	220	Don Sutton, L.A.	1.50	3.00
☐	221	Aurelio Rodriguez, Det., Error	.35	.75
☐	**222**	**Dan Spillner, S.D., RC**	**.35**	**.75**
☐	**223**	**Robin Yount, RC**	**62.50**	**125.00**
☐	224	Ramon Hernandez, Pgh.	.35	.75
☐	225	Bob Grich, Bal.	.35	.75
☐	226	Bill Campbell, Min.	.35	.75
☐	227	Bob Watson, Hou.	.35	.75
☐	**228**	**George Brett, K.C., RC**	**137.50**	**275.00**
☐	**229**	**Barry Foote, RC**	**.35**	**.75**
☐	230	Jim Hunter, NYY.	1.50	3.00
☐	231	Mike Tyson, Stl.	.35	.75
☐	232	Diego Segui, Bos.	.35	.75
☐	233	Billy Grabarkewitz, Chi.-N.L.	.35	.75
☐	234	Tom Grieve, Tex.	.35	.75
☐	235	Jack Billingham, Cin.	.35	.75
☐	236	Cal.: Dick Williams, Mgr.	.35	.75
☐	237	Carl Morton, Atl.	.35	.75
☐	238	Dave Duncan, Cle.	.35	.75
☐	239	George Stone, NYM.	.35	.75
☐	240	Garry Maddox, S.F.	.35	.75
☐	241	Dick Tidrow, NYY.	.35	.75
☐	242	Jay Johnstone, Pha.	.35	.75
☐	243	Jim Kaat, Chi.-A.L.	.35	.75
☐	244	Bill Buckner, L.A.	.35	.75
☐	245	Mickey Lolich, Det.	.35	.75
☐	246	Stl.: Red Schoendienst, Mgr.	.75	1.50
☐	**247**	**Enos Cabell, Bal., RC**	**.35**	**.75**
☐	248	Randy Jones, S.D.	.35	.75
☐	249	Danny Thompson, Min.	.35	.75
☐	250	Ken Brett, Pgh.	.35	.75
☐	251	Fran Healy, K.C.	.35	.75
☐	252	Fred Scherman, Hou.	.35	.75
☐	253	Jesus Alou, Oak.	.35	.75
☐	254	Mike Torrez, Mtl.	.35	.75
☐	255	Dwight Evans, Bos.	.35	.75
☐	256	Billy Champion, Mil.	.35	.75
☐	257	Checklist 2 (133 - 264)	.75	1.50
☐	258	Dave LaRoche, Chi.-N.L.	.35	.75
☐	259	Len Randle, Tex.	.35	.75
☐	260	AS: Johnny Bench, Cin.	9.00	18.00
☐	**261**	**Andy Hassler, Cal., RC**	**.35**	**.75**
☐	**262**	**Rowland Office, Atl., RC**	**.35**	**.75**
☐	263	Jim Perry, Cle.	.35	.75
☐	264	John Milner, NYM.	.35	.75
☐	265	Ron Bryant, S.F.	.35	.75
☐	266	Sandy Alomar, NYY.	.35	.75
☐	267	Dick Ruthven, Pha.	.35	.75
☐	268	Hal McRae, K.C.	.35	.75
☐	269	Doug Rau, L.A.	.35	.75
☐	270	Ron Fairly, Mtl.	.35	.75
☐	271	Gerry Moses, Det.	.35	.75
☐	272	Lynn McGlothen, Stl.	.35	.75
☐	273	Steve Braun, Min.	.35	.75
☐	274	Vicente Romo, S.D.	.35	.75
☐	275	Paul Blair, Bal.	.35	.75
☐	276	Chi.: Chuck Tanner, Mgr.	.35	.75
☐	**277**	**Frank Taveras, Pgh., RC**	**.35**	**.75**
☐	278	Paul Lindblad, Oak.	.35	.75
☐	279	Milt May, Hou.	.35	.75
☐	280	Carl Yastrzemski, Bos.	4.50	9.00
☐	281	Jim Slaton, Mil.	.35	.75
☐	282	Jerry Morales, Chi.-N.L.	.35	.75
☐	283	Steve Foucault, Tex.	.35	.75
☐	284	Ken Griffey, Cin.	2.25	5.50
☐	285	Ellie Rodriguez, Cal.	.35	.75
☐	286	Mike Jorgensen, Mtl.	.35	.75
☐	287	Roric Harrison, Atl.	.35	.75
☐	**288**	**Bruce Ellingsen, Cle., RC**	**.35**	**.75**
☐	289	Ken Rudolph, Stl.	.35	.75
☐	290	Jon Matlack, NYM.	.35	.75
☐	291	Bill Sudakis, NYY.	.35	.75
☐	292	Ron Schueler, Pha.	.35	.75
☐	293	Dick Sahron, Det.	.35	.75
☐	**294**	**Geoff Zahn, L.A., RC**	**.35**	**.75**
☐	295	Vada Pinson, K.C.	.35	.75
☐	296	Alan Foster, Stl.	.35	.75
☐	**297**	**Craig Kusick, RC**	**.35**	**.75**
☐	298	Johnny Grubb, S.D.	.35	.75
☐	299	Bucky Dent, Chi.-A.L.	.35	.75
☐	300	Reggie Jackson	14.00	28.00
☐	301	Dave Roberts, Hou.	.35	.75
☐	302	Rick Burleson, Bos.	.35	.75
☐	303	Grant Jackson, Bal.	.35	.75
☐	304	Pgh.: Danny Murtaugh, Mgr.	.35	.75
☐	305	Jim Colborn, Mil.	.35	.75
☐	306	LL: Rod Carew/ Ralph Garr	1.00	2.00
☐	307	LL: Dick Allen/ Mike Schmidt	1.00	2.00
☐	308	LL: Jeff Burroughs/ Johnny Bench	1.00	2.00
☐	309	LL: Bill North/ Lou Brock	1.00	2.00
☐	310	LL: J. Hunter/ F. Jenkins		

	No.	Player		
		/ A. Messersmith/ P. Niekro	1.50	3.00
☐	311	LL: Jim Hunter/ Buzz Capra	1.00	2.00
☐	312	LL: Nolan Ryan/ Steve Carlton	14.00	28.00
☐	313	LL: Terry Forster/ Mike Marshall	.75	1.50
☐	314	Buck Martinez, K.C.	.35	.75
☐	315	Don Kessinger, Chi.-N.L.	.35	.75
☐	316	Jackie Brown, Tex.	.35	.75
☐	317	Joe Lahoud, Cal.	.35	.75
☐	318	Ernie McAnally, Mtl.	.35	.75
☐	319	Johnny Oates, Atl.	.35	.75
☐	320	AS: Pete Rose, Cin.	12.50	25.00
☐	321	Rudy May, NYY.	.35	.75
☐	322	Ed Goodson, S.F.	.35	.75
☐	323	Fred Holdsworth, Det.	.35	.75
☐	324	Ed Kranepool, NYM.	.35	.75
☐	325	Tony Oliva, Min.	.75	1.50
☐	326	Wayne Twitchell, Pha.	.35	.75
☐	327	Jerry Hairston, Chi.-A.L.	.35	.75
☐	328	Sonny Siebert, Stl.	.35	.75
☐	329	Ted Kubiak, Oak.	.35	.75
☐	330	Mike Marshall, L.A.	.35	.75
☐	331	Cle.: Frank Robinson, Mgr.	1.50	3.00
☐	332	Fred Kendall, S.D.	.35	.75
☐	333	Dick Drago, Bos.	.35	.75
☐	334	Greg Gross, Hou.	.35	.75
☐	335	Jim Palmer, Bal.	3.75	7.50
☐	336	Rennie Stennett, Pgh.	.35	.75
☐	337	Kevin Kobel, Mil.	.35	.75
☐	338	Rick Stelmaszek, Chi.-N.L.	.35	.75
☐	339	Jim Fregosi, Tex.	.35	.75
☐	340	Paul Splittorff, K.C.	.35	.75
☐	341	Hal Breeden, Mtl.	.35	.75
☐	342	Leroy Stanton, Cal.	.35	.75
☐	343	Danny Frisella, S.D.	.35	.75
☐	344	Ben Oglivie, Det.	.35	.75
☐	345	Clay Carroll, Cin.	.35	.75
☐	346	Bobby Darwin, Min.	.35	.75
☐	347	Mike Caldwell, S.F.	.35	.75
☐	348	Tony Muser, Chi.-A.L.	.35	.75
☐	349	Ray Sadecki, Stl.	.35	.75
☐	350	AS: Bobby Murcer, S.F.	.35	.75
☐	351	Bob Boone, Pha.	.75	1.50
☐	352	Darold Knowles, Chi.-N.L.	.35	.75
☐	353	Luis Melendez, Stl.	.35	.75
☐	354	Dick Bosman, Cle.	.35	.75
☐	355	Chris Cannizzaro, S.D.	.35	.75
☐	356	Rico Petrocelli, Bos.	.35	.75
☐	357	Ken Forsch, Hou.	.35	.75
☐	358	Al Bumbry, Bal.	.35	.75
☐	359	Paul Popovich, Pgh.	.35	.75
☐	360	George Scott, Mil.	.35	.75
☐	361	L.A.: Walter Alston, Mgr.	.75	1.50
☐	362	Steve Hargan, Tex.	.35	.75
☐	363	Carmen Fanzone, Chi.-N.L.	.35	.75
☐	364	Doug Bird, K.C.	.35	.75
☐	365	Bob Bailey, Mtl.	.35	.75
☐	366	Ken Sanders, Cal.	.35	.75
☐	367	Craig Robinson, Atl.	.35	.75
☐	368	Vic Albury, Min.	.35	.75
☐	369	Merv Rettenmund, Cin.	.35	.75
☐	370	Tom Seaver	9.00	18.00
☐	371	Gates Brown, Det.	.35	.75
☐	372	John D'Acquisto, S.F.	.35	.75
☐	373	Bill Sharp, Chi.-A.L.	.35	.75
☐	374	Eddie Watt, Pha.	.35	.75
☐	375	Roy White, NYY.	.35	.75
☐	376	Steve Yeager, L.A.	.35	.75
☐	377	Tom Hilgendorf, Cle.	.35	.75
☐	378	Derrel Thomas, S.D.	.35	.75
☐	379	Bernie Carbo, Bos.	.35	.75
☐	380	Sal Bando, Oak.	.35	.75
☐	381	John Curtis, Stl.	.35	.75
☐	382	Don Baylor, Bal.	.35	.75
☐	383	Jim York, Hou.	.35	.75
☐	384	Mil.: Del Crandall, Mgr.	.35	.75
☐	385	Dock Ellis, Pgh.	.35	.75
☐	386	Checklist 3 (265 - 396)	.75	1.50
☐	387	Jim Spencer, Tex.	.35	.75
☐	388	Steve Stone, Chi.-N.L.	.35	.75
☐	**389**	**Tony Solaita, K.C., RC**	**.35**	**.75**
☐	390	Ron Cey, L.A.	.35	.75
☐	**391**	**Don DeMola, Mtl., RC**	**.35**	**.75**
☐	**392**	**Bruce Bochte, Cal., RC**	**.35**	**.75**
☐	393	Gary Gentry, Atl.	.35	.75
☐	**394**	**Larvell Blanks, Atl., RC**	**.35**	**.75**
☐	395	Bud Harrelson, NYM.	.35	.75
☐	396	Fred Norman, Cin.	.35	.75
☐	397	Bill Freehan, Det.	.35	.75
☐	398	Elias Sosa, Stl.	.35	.75
☐	399	Terry Harmon, Pha.	.35	.75
☐	400	AS: Dick Allen, Chi.-A.L.	.35	.75
☐	**401**	**Mike Wallace, NYY., RC**	**.35**	**.75**
☐	402	Bob Tolan, S.D.	.35	.75
☐	**403**	**Tom Buskey, Cle., RC**	**.35**	**.75**
☐	404	Ted Sizemore, Stl.	.35	.75
☐	**405**	**John Montague, Mtl., RC**	**.35**	**.75**
☐	406	Bob Gallagher, NYM.	.35	.75
☐	**407**	**Herb Washington, Oak., RC**	**.75**	**1.50**
☐	408	Clyde Wright, Mil.	.35	.75
☐	409	Bob Robertson, Pgh.	.35	.75
☐	410	Mike Cuellar, Bal., Error	.35	.75
☐	411	George Mitterwald, Chi.-N.L.	.35	.75
☐	412	Bill Hands, Tex.	.35	.75
☐	413	Marty Pattin, K.C.	.35	.75
☐	414	Manny Mota, L.A.	.35	.75
☐	415	John Hiller, Det.	1.00	2.00
☐	416	Larry Lintz, Mtl.	.35	.75
☐	417	Skip Lockwood, Cal.	.35	.75
☐	418	Leo Foster, Atl.	.35	.75
☐	419	Dave Goltz, Min.	.35	.75
☐	420	AS: Larry Bowa, Pha.	.35	.75
☐	421	NYM.: Yogi Berra, Mgr.	1.00	2.00
☐	422	Brian Downing	.35	.75
☐	423	Clay Kirby, Cin.	.35	.75
☐	424	John Lowenstein, Cle.	.35	.75
☐	425	Tito Fuentes, S.F.	.35	.75
☐	426	George Medich, NYY.	.35	.75
☐	427	Clarence Gaston, Atl.	.35	.75
☐	428	Dave Hamilton, Oak.	.35	.75
☐	**429**	**Jim Dwyer, Stl., RC**	**.35**	**.75**
☐	430	Luis Tiant, Bos.	.35	.75
☐	431	Rod Gilbreath, Atl.	.35	.75
☐	432	Ken Berry, Mil.	.35	.75
☐	**433**	**Larry Demery, Pgh., RC**	**.35**	**.75**
☐	434	Bob Locker, Chi.-N.L.	.35	.75
☐	435	Dave Nelson, Tex.	.35	.75
☐	**436**	**Ken Frailing, Chi.-N.L., RC**	**.35**	**.75**
☐	**437**	**Al Cowens, K.C., RC**	**.35**	**.75**
☐	438	Don Carrithers, Mtl.	.35	.75
☐	439	Ed Brinkman, Det.	.35	.75
☐	440	AS: Andy Messersmith, L.A.	.35	.75
☐	441	Bobby Heise, Cal.	.35	.75
☐	**442**	**Maximino Leon, Atl., RC**	**.35**	**.75**
☐	443	Min.: Frank Quillici, Mgr.	.35	.75
☐	444	Gene Garber, Pha.	.35	.75
☐	445	Felix Millan, NYM.	.35	.75
☐	446	Bart Johnson, Chi.-A.L.	.35	.75
☐	447	Terry Crowley, Cin.	.35	.75

	No.	Player		
☐	448	Frank Duffy, Cle.	.35	.75
☐	449	Charlie Williams, S.F.	.35	.75
☐	450	Willie McCovey, S.D.	3.00	6.00
☐	451	Rick Dempsey, NYY.	.35	.75
☐	452	Angel Mangual, Oak.	.35	.75
☐	453	Claude Osteen, Stl.	.35	.75
☐	454	Doug Griffin, Bos.	.35	.75
☐	455	Don Wilson, Hou.	.35	.75
☐	456	Bob Coluccio, Mil.	.35	.75
☐	**457**	**Mario Mendoza, Pgh., RC**	**.35**	**.75**
☐	458	Ross Grimsley, Bal.	.35	.75
☐	459	A.L.: A's: 3 Games Orioles: 1 Game	.75	1.50
☐	460	N.L.: Dodgers: 3 Games Pirates: 1 Game	.75	1.50
☐	461	WS-Game 1: Oakland 3; Los Angeles 2	2.75	5.50
☐	462	WS-Game 2: Los Angeles 3; Oakland 2	.75	1.50
☐	463	WS-Game 3: Oakland 3; Los Angeles 2	.75	1.50
☐	464	WS-Game 4: Oakland 5; Los Angeles 2	.75	1.50
☐	465	WS-Game 5: Oakland 3; Los Angeles 2	.75	1.50
☐	466	A's Do It Again! Win 3rd Straight World Series!	.75	1.50
☐	**467**	**Ed Halicki, S.F., RC**	**.75**	**1.50**
☐	468	Bobby Mitchell, Mil.	.35	.75
☐	**469**	**Tom Dettore, Chi.-N.L., RC**	**.35**	**.75**
☐	470	AS: Jeff Burroughs, Tex.	.35	.75
☐	471	Bob Stinson, Mtl.	.35	.75
☐	472	Bruce Dal Canton, K.C.	.35	.75
☐	473	Ken McMullen, L.A.	.35	.75
☐	474	Luke Walker, Det.	.35	.75
☐	475	Darrell Evans, Atl.	.75	1.50
☐	**476**	**Ed Figueroa, Cal., RC**	**.35**	**.75**
☐	477	Tom Hutton, Pha.	.35	.75
☐	478	Tom Burgmeier, Min.	.35	.75
☐	479	Ken Boswell, Hou.	.35	.75
☐	480	Carlos May, Chi.-A.L.	.35	.75
☐	**481**	**Will McEnaney, Cin., RC**	**.35**	**.75**
☐	482	Tom McCraw, Cle.	.35	.75
☐	483	Steve Ontiveros, S.F.	.35	.75
☐	484	Glenn Beckert, S.D.	.35	.75
☐	485	Sparky Lyle, NYY.	.35	.75
☐	486	Ray Fosse, Oak.	.35	.75
☐	487	Hou.: Preston Gomez, Mgr.	.35	.75
☐	**488**	**Bill Travers, Mil., RC**	**.35**	**.75**
☐	489	Cecil Cooper, Bos.	.35	.75
☐	490	Reggie Smith, Stl.	.35	.75
☐	491	Doyle Alexander, Bal.	.35	.75
☐	492	Rich Hebner, Pgh.	.35	.75
☐	493	Don Stanhouse, Tex.	.35	.75
☐	**494**	**Pete LaCock, Chi.-N.L., RC**	**.35**	**.75**
☐	495	Nelson Briles, K.C.	.35	.75
☐	496	Pepe Frias, Mtl.	.35	.75
☐	497	Jim Nettles, Det.	.35	.75
☐	498	Al Downing, L.A.	.35	.75
☐	499	Marty Perez, Atl.	.35	.75
☐	500	Nolan Ryan	50.00	100.00
☐	501	Bill Robinson, Pha.	.35	.75
☐	502	Pat Bourque, Oak.	.35	.75
☐	503	Fred Stanley, NYY.	.35	.75
☐	504	Buddy Bradford, Chi.-A.L.	.35	.75
☐	505	Chris Speier, S.F.	.35	.75
☐	506	Leron Lee, Cle.	.35	.75
☐	**507**	**Tom Carroll, Cin., RC**	**.35**	**.75**
☐	**508**	**Bob Hansen, Mil., RC**	**.35**	**.75**
☐	509	Dave Hilton, S.D.	.35	.75
☐	510	Vida Blue, Oak.	.35	.75
☐	511	Tex.: Billy Martin, Mgr.	.75	1.50
☐	**512**	**Larry Milbourne, Hou., RC**	**.35**	**.75**
☐	**513**	**Dick Pole, Bos., RC**	**.35**	**.75**
☐	514	Jose Cruz, Hou.	.35	.75
☐	515	Manny Sanguillen, Pgh.	.35	.75
☐	516	Don Hood, Bal.	.35	.75
☐	517	Checklist 4 (397 - 528)	.75	1.50
☐	518	Leo Cardenas, Tex.	.35	.75
☐	**519**	**Jim Todd, Chi.-N.L., RC**	**.35**	**.75**
☐	520	Amos Otis, K.C.	.35	.75
☐	**521**	**Dennis Blair, Mtl., RC**	**.35**	**.75**
☐	522	Gary Sutherland, Det.	.35	.75
☐	523	Tom Paciorek, L.A.	.35	.75
☐	**524**	**John Doherty, Cal., RC**	**.35**	**.75**
☐	525	Tom House, Atl.	.35	.75
☐	526	Larry Hisle, Min.	.35	.75
☐	527	Mac Scarce, Pha.	.35	.75
☐	528	Eddie Leon, Chi.-A.L.	.35	.75
☐	529	Gary Thomasson, S.F.	.35	.75
☐	530	AS: Gaylord Perry, Cle.	1.25	2.50
☐	531	Cin.: Sparky Anderson, Mgr.	.75	1.50
☐	532	Gorman Thomas, Mil.	.35	.75
☐	533	Rudi Meoli, Cal.	.35	.75
☐	534	Alex Johnson, NYY.	.35	.75
☐	535	Gene Tenace, Oak.	.35	.75
☐	536	Bob Moose, Pgh.	.35	.75
☐	537	Tommy Harper, Bos.	.35	.75
☐	538	Duffy Dyer, Pgh.	.35	.75
☐	539	Jesse Jefferson, Bal.	.35	.75
☐	540	Lou Brock, Stl.	3.50	7.00
☐	541	Roger Metzger, Hou.	.35	.75
☐	542	Pete Broberg, Tex.	.35	.75
☐	543	Larry Biittner, Mtl.	.35	.75
☐	544	Steve Mingori, K.C.	.35	.75
☐	545	Billy Williams, Oak.	1.50	3.00
☐	546	John Knox, Det.	.35	.75
☐	547	Von Joshua, L.A.	.35	.75
☐	548	Charlie Sands, Cal.	.35	.75
☐	549	Bill Butler, Min.	.35	.75
☐	550	Ralph Garr, Atl.	.35	.75
☐	551	Larry Christenson, Pha.	.35	.75
☐	552	Jack Brohamer, Cle.	.35	.75
☐	553	John Boccabella, S.F.	.35	.75
☐	554	Rich Gossage, Chi.-A.L.	.75	1.50
☐	555	Al Oliver, Pgh.	.35	.75
☐	556	Tim Johnson, Mil.	.75	1.50
☐	557	Larry Gura, NYY.	.35	.75
☐	558	Dave Roberts, S.D.	.35	.75
☐	559	Bob Montgomery, Bos.	.35	.75
☐	560	Tony Perez, Cin.	.75	1.50
☐	561	Oak.: Alvin Dark, Mgr.	.35	.75
☐	562	Gary Nolan, Cin.	.35	.75
☐	563	Wilbur Howard, Hou.	.35	.75
☐	564	Tommy Davis, Bal.	.35	.75
☐	565	Joe Torre, NYM.	.35	.75
☐	566	Ray Burris, Chi.-N.L.	.35	.75
☐	**567**	**Jim Sundberg, Tex., RC**	**1.25**	**2.50**
☐	**568**	**Dale Murray, Mtl., RC**	**.35**	**.75**
☐	569	Frank White, K.C.	.35	.75
☐	570	AS: Jim Wynn, L.A.	.35	.75
☐	**571**	**Dave Lemanczyk, Det., RC**	**.35**	**.75**
☐	572	Roger Nelson, Chi.-A.L.	.35	.75
☐	573	Orlando Pena, Cal.	.35	.75
☐	574	Tony Taylor, Pha.	.35	.75
☐	575	Gene Clines, NYM.	.35	.75
☐	576	Phil Roof, Min.	.35	.75
☐	577	John Morris, S.F.	.35	.75
☐	**578**	**Dave Tomlin, S.D., RC**	**.35**	**.75**
☐	579	Skip Pitlock, Chi.-A.L.	.35	.75
☐	580	Frank Robinson, Cle.	3.75	7.50
☐	581	Darrel Chaney, Cin.	.35	.75
☐	582	Eduardo Rodriguez, Mil.	.35	.75
☐	583	Andy Etchebarren, Bal.	.35	.75
☐	**584**	**Mike Garman, Stl., RC**	**.35**	**.75**
☐	585	Chris Chambliss, NYY.	.35	.75

☐ 586	Tim McCarver, Bos.	.35	.75
☐ **587**	**Chris Ward, Chi.-N.L., RC**	**.35**	**.75**
☐ 588	Rick Auerbach, L.A.	.35	.75
☐ 589	Atl.: Clyde King, Mgr.	.35	.75
☐ 590	Cesar Cedeno, Hou.	.35	.75
☐ 591	Glenn Abbott, Oak.	.35	.75
☐ 592	Balor Moore, Mtl.	.35	.75
☐ **593**	**Gene Lamont, Det., RC**	**.35**	**.75**
☐ 594	Jim Fuller, Bal.	.35	.75
☐ 595	Joe Niekro, Atl.	.35	.75
☐ 596	Ollie Brown, Pha.	.35	.75
☐ 597	Winston Llenas, Cal.	.35	.75
☐ 598	Bruce Kison, Pgh.	.35	.75
☐ 599	Nate Colbert, Det.	.35	.75
☐ 600	AS: Rod Carew, Min.	3.75	7.50
☐ 601	Juan Beniquez, Bos.	.35	.75
☐ 602	John Vukovich, Cin.	.35	.75
☐ 603	Lew Krausse, Atl.	.35	.75
☐ **604**	**Oscar Zamora, Chi.-N.L., RC**	**.35**	**.75**
☐ 605	John Ellis, Cle.	.35	.75
☐ **606**	**Bruce Miller, S.F., RC**	**.35**	**.75**
☐ 607	Jim Holt, Oak.	.35	.75
☐ 608	Gene Michael, NYY.	.35	.75
☐ 609	Ellie Hendricks, Bal.	.35	.75
☐ 610	Ron Hunt, Stl.	.35	.75
☐ 611	NYY.: Bill Virdon, Mgr.	.35	.75
☐ 612	Terry Hughes, Bos.	.35	.75
☐ 613	Bill Parsons, Oak.	.35	.75
☐ 614	J. Kucek/ D. Miller/ V. Ruhle/ P. Siebert	.35	.75
☐ 615	P. Darcy/ D. Leonard/ T. Underwood/ H. Webb	.35	.75
☐ 616	D. Augustine/ P. Mangual/ J. Rice/ J. Scott	7.00	14.00
☐ 617	M. Cubbage/ D. DeCinces/ R. Sanders/ M. Trillo	.75	1.50
☐ 618	J. Easterly/ T/ Johnson/ S. McGregor/ R. Rhoden	.75	1.50
☐ 619	B. Ayala/ N. Nyman/ T. Smith/ J. Turner	.35	.75
☐ 620	G. Carter/ M. Hill/ D. Meyer/ L. Roberts	17.50	35.00
☐ 621	J. Denny/ R. Eastwick/ J. Kern/ J. Veintidos	.35	.75
☐ 622	E. Armbrister/ F. Lynn/ T. Poquette/ Terry Whitfield	3.00	6.00
☐ 623	P. Garner/ K. Hernandez/ B. Sheldon/ T. Veryzer	4.00	8.00
☐ 624	D. Konieczny/ G. Lavelle/ J. Otten/ E. Solomon	.35	.75
☐ 625	Boog Powell, Bal.	.35	.75
☐ 626	Larry Haney, Oak.	.35	.75
☐ 627	Tom Walker, Mtl.	.35	.75
☐ **628**	**Ron LeFlore, Det., RC**	**.75**	**1.50**
☐ 629	Joe Hoerner, K.C.	.35	.75
☐ 630	Greg Luzinski, Pha.	.35	.75
☐ 631	Lee Lacy, L.A.	.35	.75
☐ **632**	**Morris Nettles, Cal., RC**	**.35**	**.75**
☐ 633	Paul Casanova, Atl.	.35	.75
☐ 634	Cy Acosta, Chi.-A.L.	.35	.75
☐ 635	Chuck Dobson, Cal.	.35	.75
☐ **636**	**Charlie Moore, Mil., RC**	**.35**	**.75**
☐ 637	Ted Martinez, NYM.	.35	.75
☐ 638	Chi.: Jim Marshall, Mgr.	.35	.75
☐ 639	Steve Kline, Cle.	.35	.75
☐ 640	Harmon Killebrew, Min.	3.25	6.50
☐ 641	Jim Northrup, Bal.	.35	.75
☐ 642	Mike Phillips, S.F.	.35	.75
☐ 643	Brent Strom, S.D.	.35	.75
☐ 644	Bill Fahey, Tex.	.35	.75
☐ 645	Danny Cater, Bos.	.35	.75
☐ 646	Checklist 5 (529-660)	.75	1.50
☐ **647**	**Claudell Washington, Oak., RC**	**.75**	**1.50**
☐ **648**	**Dave Pagan, NYY., RC**	**1.00**	**2.00**
☐ 649	Jack Heidemann	.35	.75
☐ 650	Dave May, Atl.	.35	.75
☐ **651**	**John Morlan, Pgh., RC**	**.35**	**.75**
☐ 652	Lindy McDaniel, K.C.	.35	.75
☐ 653	Lee Richard, Chi.-A.L., Error	.35	.75
☐ 654	Jerry Terrell, Min.	.35	.75
☐ 655	Rico Carty, Cle.	.35	.75
☐ 656	Bill Plummer, Cin.	.35	.75
☐ 657	Bob Oliver, Bal.	.35	.75
☐ 658	Vic Harris, Chi.-N.L.	.35	.75
☐ **659**	**Bob Apodaca, NYM., RC**	**.35**	**.75**
☐ 660	Hank Aaron, Mil.	22.50	45.00

1976 O-PEE-CHEE

Card Size: 2 1/2" x 3 1/2"
Face: Four colour, coloured border; name, position, team
Back: Green and brown on card stock; number, resume, trivia, bilingual
Imprint: O.P.C. PTD. IN CANADA

Complete Set (660 cards):		**240.00**	**475.00**
Common Player:		**.25**	**.50**
No.	**Player**	**EX**	**NRMT**
☐ 1	Hank Aaron, Mil.	11.00	22.00
☐ 2	Bobby Bonds, NYY.	.50	1.00
☐ 3	Mickey Lolich, Det.	.25	.50
☐ 4	Dave Lopes, L.A.	.25	.50
☐ 5	Tom Seaver, NYM.	3.00	6.00
☐ 6	Rennie Stennett, Pgh.	.25	.50
☐ **7**	**Jim Umbarger, Tex., RC**	**.25**	**.50**
☐ 8	Tito Fuentes, S.D.	.25	.50
☐ 9	Paul Lindblad, Oak.	.25	.50
☐ 10	N.L. All-Star: Lou Brock, Stl.	1.50	3.00
☐ **11**	**Jim Hughes, Min., RC**	**.25**	**.50**
☐ 12	Richie Zisk, Pgh.	.25	.50
☐ **13**	**Johnny Wockenfuss, Det., RC**	**.25**	**.50**
☐ 14	Gene Garber, Pha.	.25	.50
☐ 15	George Scott, Mil.	.25	.50
☐ 16	Bob Apodaca, NYM.	.25	.50
☐ 17	NYY.: Billy Martin, Mgr.	.50	1.00
☐ 18	Dale Murray, Mtl.	.25	.50
☐ 19	George Brett, K.C.	42.50	85.00
☐ 20	Bob Watson, Hou.	.25	.50
☐ 21	Dave LaRoche, Cle.	.25	.50
☐ 22	Bill Russell, L.A.	.25	.50
☐ 23	Brian Downing, Chi.-A.L.	.25	.50
☐ 24	Cesar Geronimo, Cin.	.25	.50
☐ 25	Mike Torrez, Bal.	.25	.50
☐ 26	Andy Thornton, Chi.-N.L.	.25	.50
☐ 27	Ed Figueroa, Cal.	.25	.50
☐ 28	Dusty Baker, Atl.	.25	.50
☐ 29	Rick Burleson, Bos.	.25	.50
☐ **30**	**John Montefusco, S.F., RC**	**.25**	**.50**
☐ 31	Lenny Randle, Tex.	.25	.50
☐ 32	Danny Frisella, S.D.	.25	.50
☐ 33	Bill North, Oak.	.25	.50
☐ 34	Mike Garman, Chi.-N.L.	.25	.50
☐ 35	Tony Oliva, Min.	.75	1.50
☐ 36	Frank Taveras, Pgh.	.25	.50
☐ 37	John Hiller, Det.	.75	1.50

	No.	Player		
☐	38	Garry Maddox, Pha.	.25	.50
☐	39	Pete Broberg, Mil.	.25	.50
☐	40	Dave Kingman, NYM.	.25	.50
☐	**41**	**Tippy Martinez, NYY., RC**	**.25**	**.50**
☐	42	Barry Foote, Mtl.	.25	.50
☐	43	Paul Splittorff, K.C.	.25	.50
☐	44	Doug Rader, Hou.	.25	.50
☐	45	Boog Powell, Cle.	.25	.50
☐	46	L.A.: Walter Alston, Mgr.	.50	1.00
☐	47	Jesse Jefferson, Chi.-A.L.	.25	.50
☐	48	AS: Dave Concepcion, Cin.	.25	.50
☐	49	Dave Duncan, Bal.	.25	.50
☐	50	Fred Lynn, Bos.	.75	1.50
☐	51	Ray Burris, Chi.-N.L.	.25	.50
☐	52	Dave Chalk, Cal.	.25	.50
☐	**53**	**Mike Beard, Atl., RC**	**.25**	**.50**
☐	54	Dave Rader, S.F.	.25	.50
☐	55	Gaylord Perry, Tex.	1.25	2.50
☐	56	Bob Tolan, S.D.	.25	.50
☐	57	Phil Garner, Oak.	.25	.50
☐	58	Ron Reed, Stl.	.25	.50
☐	59	Larry Hisle, Min.	.25	.50
☐	60	AS: Jerry Reuss, Pgh.	.25	.50
☐	61	Ron LeFlore, Det.	.25	.50
☐	62	Johnny Oates, Pha.	.25	.50
☐	63	Bobby Darwin, Mil.	.25	.50
☐	64	Jerry Koosman, NYM.	.25	.50
☐	65	Chris Chambliss, NYY.	.25	.50
☐	66	Gus Bell, Cin./ Buddy Bell, Cle.	.50	1.00
☐	67	Ray Boone, Det./ Bob Boone, Pha.	.50	1.00
☐	68	Joe Coleman, Bal./ Joe Coleman Jr., Det.	.50	1.00
☐	69	Jim Hegan, Cle./ Mike Hegan, Mil.	.50	1.00
☐	70	Roy Smalley, Mil./ Roy Smalley, Tex.	.50	1.00
☐	71	Steve Rogers, Mtl.	.25	.50
☐	72	Hal McRae, K.C.	.25	.50
☐	73	Bal.: Earl Weaver, Mgr.	1.00	2.00
☐	74	Oscar Gamble, Cle.	.25	.50
☐	75	Larry Dierker, Hou.	.25	.50
☐	76	Willie Crawford, L.A.	.25	.50
☐	77	Pedro Borbon, Cin.	.25	.50
☐	78	Cecil Cooper, Bos.	.25	.50
☐	79	Jerry Morales, Chi.-N.L.	.25	.50
☐	80	Jim Kaat, Chi.-A.L.	.25	.50
☐	81	Darrell Evans, Atl.	.25	.50
☐	82	Von Joshua, S.F.	.25	.50
☐	83	Jim Spencer, Tex.	.25	.50
☐	84	Brent Strom, S.D.	.25	.50
☐	85	Mickey Rivers, Cal.	.25	.50
☐	86	Mike Tyson, Stl.	.25	.50
☐	87	Tom Burgmeier, Min.	.25	.50
☐	88	Duffy Dyer, Pgh.	.25	.50
☐	89	Vern Ruhle, Det.	.25	.50
☐	90	Sal Bando, Oak.	.25	.50
☐	91	Tom Hutton, Pha.	.25	.50
☐	92	Eduardo Rodriguez, Mil.	.25	.50
☐	93	Mike Phillips, NYM.	.25	.50
☐	94	Jim Dwyer, Mtl.	.25	.50
☐	95	Brooks Robinson, Bal.	3.75	7.50
☐	96	Doug Bird, K.C.	.25	.50
☐	97	Wilbur Howard, Hou.	.25	.50
☐	**98**	**Dennis Eckersley, Cle., RC**	**25.00**	**50.00**
☐	99	Lee Lacy, L.A.	.25	.50
☐	100	Jim Hunter, NYY.	1.25	2.50
☐	101	Pete LaCock, Chi.-N.L.	.25	.50
☐	102	Jim Willoughby, Bos.	.25	.50
☐	103	Biff Pocoroba, Atl.	.25	.50
☐	104	Cin.: Sparky Anderson, Mgr.	2.00	4.00
☐	105	Gary Lavelle, S.D.	.25	.50
☐	106	Tom Grieve, Tex.	.25	.50
☐	107	Dave Roberts, S.D.	.25	.50
☐	**108**	**Don Kirkwood, Cal., RC**	**.25**	**.50**
☐	109	Larry Lintz, Oak.	.25	.50
☐	110	Carlos May, Chi.-A.L.	.25	.50
☐	111	Danny Thompson, Min.	.25	.50
☐	**112**	**Kent Tekulve, Pgh., RC**	**1.25**	**2.50**
☐	113	Gary Sutherland, Det.	.25	.50
☐	114	Jay Johnstone, Pha.	.25	.50
☐	115	Ken Holtzman, Oak.	.25	.50
☐	116	Charlie Moore, Mil.	.25	.50
☐	117	Mike Jorgensen, Mtl.	.25	.50
☐	118	Bos.: Darrell Johnson, Mgr.	.25	.50
☐	119	1976 Checklist 1 (1 - 132)	.50	1.00
☐	120	Rusty Staub, NYM.	1.25	2.50
☐	121	Tony Solaita, K.C.	.25	.50
☐	122	Mike Cosgrove, Hou.	.25	.50
☐	123	Walt Williams, NYY.	.25	.50
☐	124	Doug Rau, L.A.	.25	.50
☐	125	Don Baylor, Bal.	.25	.50
☐	126	Tom Dettore, Chi.-N.L.	.25	.50
☐	127	Larvell Blanks, Atl.	.25	.50
☐	128	Ken Griffey, Cin.	.50	1.00
☐	129	Andy Etchebarren, Cal.	.25	.50
☐	130	Luis Tiant, Bos.	.25	.50
☐	**131**	**Bill Stein, Chi.-A.L., RC**	**.25**	**.50**
☐	132	Don Hood, Cle.	.25	.50
☐	133	Gary Matthews, S.F.	.25	.50
☐	134	Mike Ivie, S.D.	.25	.50
☐	135	Bake McBride, Stl.	.25	.50
☐	136	Dave Goltz, Min.	.25	.50
☐	137	Bill Robinson, Pgh.	.25	.50
☐	138	Lerrin LaGrow, Det.	.25	.50
☐	139	Gorman Thomas, Mil.	.25	.50
☐	140	AS: Vida Blue, Oak.	.25	.50
☐	**141**	**Larry Parrish, Mtl., RC**	**.50**	**1.00**
☐	142	Dick Drago, Bos.	.25	.50
☐	143	Jerry Grote, NYM.	.25	.50
☐	144	Al Fitzmorris, K.C.	.25	.50
☐	145	Larry Bowa, Pha.	.25	.50
☐	146	George Medich, NYY.	.25	.50
☐	147	Hou.: Bill Virdon, Mgr.	.25	.50
☐	**148**	**Stan Thomas, Tex., RC**	**.25**	**.50**
☐	149	Tommy Davis, Bal.	.25	.50
☐	150	AS: Steve Garvey, L.A.	.75	1.50
☐	151	Bill Bonham, Chi.-N.L.	.25	.50
☐	152	Leroy Stanton, Cal.	.25	.50
☐	153	Buzz Capra, Atl.	.25	.50
☐	154	Bucky Dent, Chi.-A.L.	.25	.50
☐	155	Jack Billingham, Cin.	.25	.50
☐	156	Rico Carty, Cle.	.25	.50
☐	157	Mike Caldwell, S.F.	.25	.50
☐	158	Ken Reitz, Stl.	.25	.50
☐	159	Jerry Terrell, Min.	.25	.50
☐	160	Dave Winfield, S.D.	15.00	30.00
☐	161	Bruce Kison, Pgh.	.25	.50
☐	**162**	**Jack Pierce, Det., RC**	**.25**	**.50**
☐	163	Jim Slaton, Mil.	.25	.50
☐	164	Pepe Mangual, Mtl.	.25	.50
☐	165	AS: Gene Tenace, Oak.	.25	.50
☐	166	Skip Lockwood, NYM.	.25	.50
☐	167	Freddie Patek, K.C.	.25	.50
☐	168	Tom Hilgendorf, Pha.	.25	.50
☐	169	AS: Graig Nettles, NYY.	.25	.50
☐	170	Rick Wise, Bos.	.25	.50
☐	171	Greg Gross, Hou.	.25	.50
☐	172	Tex. Frank Lucchesi, Mgr.	.25	.50
☐	173	Steve Swisher, Chi.-N.L.	.25	.50
☐	174	Charlie Hough, L.A.	.25	.50
☐	175	Ken Singleton, Bal.	.25	.50

	No.	Player		
☐	176	Dick Lange, Cal.	.25	.50
☐	177	Marty Perez, Atl.	.25	.50
☐	178	Tom Buskey, Cle.	.25	.50
☐	179	George Foster, Cin.	.25	.50
☐	180	Rich Gossage, Chi.-A.L.	.50	1.00
☐	181	Willie Montanez, S.F.	.25	.50
☐	**182**	**Harry Rasmussen, Stl., RC**	**.25**	**.50**
☐	183	Steve Braun, Min.	.25	.50
☐	184	Bill Greif, S.D.	.25	.50
☐	185	Dave Parker, Pgh.	.50	1.00
☐	186	Tom Walker, Det.	.25	.50
☐	187	Pedro Garcia, Mil.	.25	.50
☐	188	Fred Scherman, Mtl.	.25	.50
☐	189	Claudell Washington, Oak.	.25	.50
☐	190	Jon Matlack, NYM.	.25	.50
☐	191	LL: B. Madlock/ T. Simmons/ M. Sanguillen	.50	1.00
☐	192	LL: R. Carew/ F. Lynn/ T. Munson	.75	1.50
☐	193	LL: D. Kingman/ G. Luzinski/ M. Schmidt	.75	1.50
☐	194	LL: R. Jackson/ G. Scott/ J. Mayberry	.75	1.50
☐	195	LL: G. Luzinski/ J. Bench/ T. Perez	.75	1.50
☐	196	LL: G. Scott/ J. Mayberry/ F. Lynn	.50	1.00
☐	197	LL: D. Lopes/ J. Morgan/ L. Brock	1.00	2.00
☐	198	LL: M. Rivers/ C.I Washington/ A. Otis	.50	1.00
☐	199	LL: T. Seaver/ R. Jones/; A. Messersmith	.75	1.50
☐	200	LL: J. Hunter/ J. Palmer/ V. Blue	1.00	2.00
☐	201	LL: R. Jones/ A. Messersmith/ T. Seaver	.75	1.50
☐	202	LL: J. Palmer/ J. Hunter/ D. Eckersley	1.25	2.50
☐	203	LL: T. Seaver/ J. Montefusco/ A. Messersmith	.75	1.50
☐	204	LL: F. Tanana/ B. Blyleven/ G. Perry	1.00	2.00
☐	205	LL: Al Hrabosky/ Rich Gossage	.50	1.00
☐	206	Manny Trillo, Chi.-N.L.	.25	.50
☐	207	Andy Hassler, Cal.	.25	.50
☐	208	Mike Lum, Atl.	.25	.50
☐	**209**	**Alan Ashby, Cle., RC**	**.25**	**.50**
☐	210	Lee May, Bal.	.25	.50
☐	211	Clay Carroll, Cin.	.25	.50
☐	212	Pat Kelly, Chi.-A.L.	.25	.50
☐	**213**	**Dave Heaverlo, S.F., RC**	**.25**	**.50**
☐	214	Eric Soderholm, Min.	.25	.50
☐	215	Reggie Smith, Stl.	.25	.50
☐	216	Mtl.: Karl Kuehl, Mgr.	.25	.50
☐	217	Dave Freisleben, S.D.	.25	.50
☐	218	John Knox, Det.	.25	.50
☐	219	Tom Murphy, Mil.	.25	.50
☐	220	Manny Sanguillen, Pgh.	.25	.50
☐	221	Jim Todd, Oak.	.25	.50
☐	222	Wayne Garrett, NYM.	.25	.50
☐	223	Ollie Brown, Pha.	.25	.50
☐	224	Jim York, Hou.	.25	.50
☐	225	Roy White, NYY.	.25	.50
☐	226	Jim Sundberg, Tex.	.25	.50
☐	227	Oscar Zamora, Chi.-N.L.	.25	.50
☐	**228**	**John Hale, L.A., RC**	**.25**	**.50**
☐	**229**	**Jerry Remy, Cal., RC**	**.25**	**.50**
☐	230	Carl Yastrzemski, Bos.	3.75	7.50
☐	231	Tom House, Atl.	.25	.50
☐	232	Frank Duffy, Cle.	.25	.50
☐	233	Grant Jackson, Bal.	.25	.50
☐	234	Mike Sadek, S.F.	.25	.50
☐	235	Bert Blyleven, Min.	.50	1.00
☐	236	K.C.: Whitey Herzog, Mgr.	.25	.50
☐	237	Dave Hamilton, Chi.-A.L.	.25	.50
☐	238	Larry Biittner, Mtl.	.25	.50
☐	239	John Curtis, Stl.	.25	.50
☐	240	AS: Pete Rose, Cin.	7.50	15.00
☐	241	Hector Torres, S.D.	.25	.50
☐	**242**	**Dan Meyer, Det., RC**	**.25**	**.50**
☐	243	Jim Rooker, Pgh.	.25	.50
☐	244	Bill Sharp, Mil.	.25	.50
☐	245	Felix Millan, NYM.	.25	.50
☐	246	Cesar Tovar, Oak.	.25	.50
☐	247	Terry Harmon, Pha.	.25	.50
☐	248	Dick Tidrow, NYY.	.25	.50
☐	249	Cliff Johnson, Hou.	.25	.50
☐	250	Fergie Jenkins, Tex.	2.00	4.00
☐	251	Rick Monday, Chi.-N.L.	.25	.50
☐	**252**	**Tim Nordbrook, Bal., RC**	**.25**	**.50**
☐	253	Bill Buckner, L.A.	.25	.50
☐	254	Rudi Meoli, Cal., Error	.25	.50
☐	255	Fritz Peterson, Cle.	.25	.50
☐	256	Rowland Office, Atl.	.25	.50
☐	257	Ross Grimsley, Bal.	.25	.50
☐	258	Nyls Nyman, Chi.-A.L.	.25	.50
☐	259	Darrel Chaney, Cin.	.25	.50
☐	260	Steve Busby, K.C.	.25	.50
☐	261	Gary Thomasson, S.F.	.25	.50
☐	262	1976 Checklist 2 (133 - 264)	.50	1.00
☐	**263**	**Lyman Bostock, Min., RC**	**.75**	**1.50**
☐	264	Steve Renko, Mtl.	.25	.50
☐	265	Willie Davis, S.D.	.25	.50
☐	266	Alan Foster, S.D.	.25	.50
☐	267	Aurelio Rodriguez, Det.	.25	.50
☐	268	Del Unser, NYM.	.25	.50
☐	269	Rick Austin, Mil.	.25	.50
☐	270	Willie Stargell, Pgh.	2.00	4.00
☐	271	Jim Lonborg, Pha.	.25	.50
☐	272	Rick Dempsey, NYY.	.25	.50
☐	273	Joe Niekro, Hou.	.25	.50
☐	274	Tommy Harper, Oak.	.25	.50
☐	**275**	**Rick Manning, Cle., RC**	**.25**	**.50**
☐	276	Mickey Scott, Cal.	.25	.50
☐	277	Chi.: Jim Marshall, Mgr.	.25	.50
☐	278	Bernie Carbo, Bos.	.25	.50
☐	279	Roy Howell, Tex.	.25	.50
☐	280	Burt Hooton, L.A.	.25	.50
☐	281	Dave May, Atl.	.25	.50
☐	**282**	**Dan Osborn, Chi.-A.L., RC**	**.25**	**.50**
☐	283	Merv Rettenmund, Cin.	.25	.50
☐	284	Steve Ontiveros, S.F.	.25	.50
☐	285	Mike Cuellar, Bal.	.25	.50
☐	286	Jim Wohlford, K.C.	.25	.50
☐	**287**	**Pete Mackanin, Mtl., RC**	**.25**	**.50**
☐	288	Bill Campbell, Min.	.25	.50
☐	289	Enzo Hernandez, S.D.	.25	.50
☐	290	Ted Simmons, Stl.	.25	.50
☐	291	Ken Sanders, NYM.	.25	.50
☐	292	Leon Roberts, Det.	.25	.50
☐	**293**	**Bill Castro, Mil., RC**	**.25**	**.50**
☐	294	Ed Kirkpatrick, Pgh.	.25	.50
☐	295	Dave Cash, Pha.	.25	.50
☐	296	Pat Dobson, NYY.	.25	.50
☐	297	Roger Metzger, Hou.	.25	.50
☐	298	Dick Bosman, Oak.	.25	.50
☐	**299**	**Champ Summers, Chi.-N.L., RC**	**.25**	**.50**
☐	300	AS: Johnny Bench, Cin.	5.00	10.00
☐	301	Jackie Brown, Cle.	.25	.50
☐	302	Rick Miller, Bos.	.25	.50
☐	303	Steve Foucault, Tex.	.25	.50
☐	304	Cal.: Dick Williams, Mgr.	.25	.50
☐	305	Andy Messersmith, L.A.	.25	.50
☐	306	Rod Gilbreath, Atl.	.25	.50
☐	307	Al Bumbry, Bal.	.25	.50
☐	308	Jim Barr, S.F.	.25	.50
☐	309	Bill Melton, Chi.-A.L.	.25	.50
☐	310	Randy Jones, S.D.	.25	.50
☐	311	Cookie Rojas, K.C.	.25	.50
☐	312	Don Carrithers, Mtl.	.25	.50
☐	**313**	**Dan Ford, Min., RC**	**.25**	**.50**

	No.	Player		
☐	314	Ed Kranepool, NYM.	.25	.50
☐	315	Al Hrabosky, Stl.	.25	.50
☐	316	Robin Yount, Mil.	20.00	40.00
☐	**317**	**John Candelaria, Pgh., RC**	**1.00**	**2.00**
☐	318	Bob Boone, Pha.	.25	.50
☐	319	Larry Gura, K.C.	.25	.50
☐	320	Willie Horton, Det.	.25	.50
☐	321	Jose Cruz, Hou.	.25	.50
☐	322	Glenn Abbott, Oak.	.25	.50
☐	**323**	**Rob Sperring, Chi.-N.L., RC**	**.25**	**.50**
☐	324	Jim Bibby, Cle.	.25	.50
☐	325	Tony Perez, Cin.	.50	1.00
☐	326	Dick Pole, Bos.	.25	.50
☐	**327**	**Dave Moates, Tex., RC**	**.25**	**.50**
☐	328	Carl Morton, Atl.	.25	.50
☐	329	Joe Ferguson, L.A.	.25	.50
☐	330	Nolan Ryan, Cal.	45.00	90.00
☐	331	S.D.: John McNamara, Mgr.	.25	.500
☐	332	Charlie Williams, S.F.	.25	.50
☐	333	Bob Coluccio, Chi.-A.L.	.25	.50
☐	**334**	**Dennis Leonard, K.C., RC**	**.25**	**.50**
☐	335	Bobby Grich, Bal.	.25	.50
☐	336	Vic Albury, Min.	.25	.50
☐	337	Bud Harrelson, NYM.	.25	.50
☐	338	Bob Bailey, Mtl.	.25	.50
☐	339	John Denny, Stl.	.25	.50
☐	340	Jim Rice, Bos.	2.50	5.00
☐	341	Lou Gehrig	7.50	15.00
☐	342	Rogers Hornsby	2.00	4.00
☐	343	Pie Traynor	1.25	2.50
☐	344	Honus Wagner	3.25	6.50
☐	345	Babe Ruth	10.00	20.00
☐	346	Ty Cobb	1.25	2.50
☐	347	Ted Williams	7.50	15.00
☐	348	Mickey Cochrane	1.00	2.00
☐	349	Walter Johnson	2.25	4.50
☐	350	Lefty Grove	1.00	2.00
☐	351	Randy Hundley, S.D.	.25	.50
☐	352	Dave Giusti, Pgh.	.25	.50
☐	**353**	**Sixto Lezcano, Mil., RC**	**.25**	**.50**
☐	354	Ron Blomberg, NYY.	.25	.50
☐	355	Steve Carlton, Pha.	4.50	9.00
☐	356	Ted Martinez, Oak.	.25	.50
☐	357	Ken Forsch, Hou.	.25	.50
☐	358	Buddy Bell, Cle.	.40	.80
☐	359	Rick Reuschel, Chi.-N.L.	.25	.50
☐	360	Jeff Burroughs, Tex.	.25	.50
☐	361	Det.: Ralph Houk, Mgr.	.25	.50
☐	362	Will McEnaney, Cin.	.25	.50
☐	**363**	**Dave Collins, Cal., RC**	**.25**	**.50**
☐	364	Elias Sosa, Atl.	.25	.50
☐	365	Carlton Fisk, Bos.	4.50	9.00
☐	366	Bobby Valentine, S.D.	.25	.50
☐	367	Bruce Miller, S.F.	.25	.50
☐	368	Wilbur Wood, Chi.-A.L.	.25	.50
☐	369	Frank White, K.C.	.25	.50
☐	370	AS: Ron Cey, L.A.	.25	.50
☐	371	Ellie Hendricks, Bal.	.25	.50
☐	**372**	**Rick Baldwin, NYM., RC**	**.25**	**.50**
☐	373	Johnny Briggs, Min.	.25	.50
☐	**374**	**Dan Warthen, Mtl., RC**	**.25**	**.50**
☐	375	Ron Fairly, Stl.	.25	.50
☐	376	Rich Hebner, Pgh.	.25	.50
☐	377	Mike Hegan, Mil.	.25	.50
☐	378	Steve Stone, Chi.-N.L.	.25	.50
☐	379	Ken Boswell, Hou.	.25	.50
☐	380	AS: Bobby Bonds, Cal.	.25	.50
☐	381	Denny Doyle, Bos.	.25	.50
☐	**382**	**Matt Alexander, Oak., RC**	**.25**	**.50**
☐	383	John Ellis, Cle.	.25	.50
☐	384	Pha.: Danny Ozark, Mgr.	.25	.50
☐	385	Mickey Lolich, Det.	.25	.50
☐	386	Ed Goodson, L.A.	.25	.50
☐	**387**	**Mike Miley, Cal., RC**	**.25**	**.50**
☐	**388**	**Stan Perzanowski, Tex., RC**	**.25**	**.50**
☐	**389**	**Glenn Adams, S.F., RC**	**.25**	**.50**
☐	390	Don Gullett, Cin.	.25	.50
☐	391	Jerry Hairston, Chi.-A.L.	.25	.50
☐	392	1976 Checklist 3 (265 - 396)	.50	1.00
☐	**393**	**Paul Mitchell, Bal., RC**	**.25**	**.50**
☐	394	Fran Healy, K.C.	.25	.50
☐	395	N.L. All-Star: Jim Wynn, Atl	.25	.50
☐	396	Bill Lee, Bos.	.25	.50
☐	397	Tim Foli, Mtl.	.25	.50
☐	398	Dave Tomlin, S.D.	.25	.50
☐	399	Luis Melendez, Stl.	.25	.50
☐	400	AS: Rod Carew, Min.	3.00	6.00
☐	401	Ken Brett, Pgh.	.25	.50
☐	402	Don Money, Mil.	.25	.50
☐	403	Geoff Zahn, Chi.-N.L.	.25	.50
☐	404	Enos Cabell, Hou.	.25	.50
☐	405	Rollie Fingers, Oak.	1.75	3.50
☐	406	Ed Herrmann, NYY.	.25	.50
☐	407	Tom Underwood, Pha.	.25	.50
☐	408	Charlie Spikes, Cle.	.25	.50
☐	409	Dave Lemanczyk, Det.	.25	.50
☐	410	Ralph Garr, Atl.	.25	.50
☐	411	Bill Singer, Cal.	.25	.50
☐	412	Toby Harrah, Tex.	.25	.50
☐	**413**	**Pete Varney, Chi.-A.L., RC**	**.25**	**.50**
☐	414	Wayne Garland, Bal.	.25	.50
☐	415	Vada Pinson, K.C.	.25	.50
☐	416	Tommy John, L.A.	.25	.50
☐	417	Gene Clines, NYM.	.25	.50
☐	**418**	**Jose Morales, Mtl., RC**	**.25**	**.50**
☐	419	Reggie Cleveland, Bos.	.50	1.00
☐	420	AS: Joe Morgan, Cin.	3.00	6.00
☐	421	Oakland A's	.50	1.00
☐	422	Johnny Grubb, S.D.	.25	.50
☐	423	Ed Halicki, S.F.	.25	.50
☐	424	Phil Roof, Min.	.25	.50
☐	425	Rennie Stennett, Pgh.	.25	.50
☐	426	Bob Forsch, Stl.	.25	.50
☐	427	Kurt Bevacqua, Mil.	.25	.50
☐	428	Jim Crawford, Hou.	.25	.50
☐	429	Fred Stanley, NYY.	.25	.50
☐	430	Jose Cardenal, Chi.-N.L.	.25	.50
☐	431	Dick Ruthven, Pha.	.25	.50
☐	**432**	**Tom Veryzer, Det., RC**	**.25**	**.50**
☐	**433**	**Rick Waits, Cle., RC**	**.25**	**.50**
☐	434	Morris Nettles, Cal.	.25	.50
☐	435	Phil Niekro, Atl.	1.00	2.00
☐	436	Bill Fahey, Tex.	.25	.50
☐	437	Terry Forster, Chi.-A.L.	.25	.50
☐	438	Doug DeCinces, Bal.	.25	.50
☐	439	Rick Rhoden, L.A.	.25	.50
☐	440	John Mayberry, K.C.	.25	.50
☐	441	Gary Carter, Mtl.	5.00	10.00
☐	442	Hank Webb, NYM.	.25	.50
☐	443	San Francisco Giants	.50	1.00
☐	444	Gary Nolan, Cin.	.25	.50
☐	445	Rico Petrocelli, Bos.	.25	.50
☐	446	Larry Haney, Oak.	.25	.50
☐	447	Gene Locklear, S.D.	.25	.50
☐	448	Tom Johnson, Min.	.25	.50
☐	449	Bob Robertson, Pgh.	.25	.50
☐	450	Jim Palmer, Bal.	3.00	6.00
☐	451	Buddy Bradford, Stl.	.25	.50

	No.	Card		
☐	**452**	**Tom Hausman, Mil., RC**	**.25**	**.50**
☐	453	Lou Piniella, NYY.	.25	.50
☐	454	Tom Griffin, Hou.	.25	.50
☐	455	Dick Allen, Pha.	.25	.50
☐	456	Joe Coleman, Det.	.25	.50
☐	457	Ed Crosby, Cle.	.25	.50
☐	458	Earl Williams, Atl.	.25	.50
☐	459	Jim Brewer, Cal.	.25	.50
☐	460	Cesar Cedeno, Hou.	.25	.50
☐	461	N.L. & A.L. Championships: Bosox surprise A's; Reds sweep Bucs in 3	.50	1.00
☐	462	1975 World Series: First Time Since 1940 Reds Champs!	.75	1.50
☐	463	Steve Hargan, Tex.	.25	.50
☐	464	Ken Henderson, Chi.-A.L.	.25	.50
☐	465	Mike Marshall, L.A.	.25	.50
☐	466	Bob Stinson, K.C.	.25	.50
☐	467	Woodie Fryman, Mtl.	.25	.50
☐	468	Jesus Alou, NYM.	.25	.50
☐	469	Rawly Eastwick, Cin.	.25	.50
☐	470	Bobby Murcer, S.F.	.25	.50
☐	**471**	**Jim Burton, Bos., RC**	**.25**	**.50**
☐	472	Bob Davis, S.D.	.25	.50
☐	473	Paul Blair, Bal.	.25	.50
☐	474	Ray Corbin, Min.	.25	.50
☐	475	AS: Joe Rudi, Oak.	.25	.50
☐	476	Bob Moose, Pgh.	.25	.50
☐	477	Cle.: Frank Robinson, Mgr.	1.00	2.00
☐	478	Lynn McGlothen, Stl.	.25	.50
☐	479	Bobby Mitchell, Mil.	.25	.50
☐	480	Mike Schmidt, Pha.	15.00	30.00
☐	481	Rudy May, NYY.	.25	.50
☐	**482**	**Tim Hosley, Chi.-N.L., RC**	**.25**	**.50**
☐	483	Mickey Stanley, Det.	.25	.50
☐	**484**	**Eric Raich, Cle., RC**	**.25**	**.50**
☐	485	Mike Hargrove, Tex.	.50	1.00
☐	486	Bruce Dal Canton, Atl.	.25	.50
☐	487	Leron Lee, L.A.	.25	.50
☐	488	Claude Osteen, Chi.-A.L.	.25	.50
☐	489	Skip Jutze, Hou.	.25	.50
☐	490	Frank Tanana, Cal.	.25	.50
☐	491	Terry Crowley, Cin.	.25	.50
☐	492	Marty Pattin, K.C.	.25	.50
☐	493	Derrel Thomas, S.F.	.25	.50
☐	**494**	**Craig Swan, NYM., RC**	**.25**	**.50**
☐	495	Nate Colbert, Mtl.	.25	.50
☐	496	Juan Beniquez, Tex.	.25	.50
☐	**497**	**Joe McIntosh, S.D., RC**	**.25**	**.50**
☐	498	Glenn Borgmann, Min.	.25	.50
☐	499	Mario Guerrero, Stl.	.25	.50
☐	500	AS: Reggie Jackson, Oak.	10.00	20.00
☐	501	Billy Champion, Mil.	.25	.50
☐	502	Tim McCarver, Pha.	.25	.50
☐	503	Elliott Maddox, NYY.	.25	.50
☐	504	Pgh.: Danny Murtaugh, Mgr.	.50	1.00
☐	505	Mark Belanger, Bal.	.25	.50
☐	506	George Mitterwald, Chi.-N.L.	.25	.50
☐	**507**	**Ray Bare, Det., RC**	**.25**	**.50**
☐	**508**	**Duane Kuiper, Cle., RC**	**.50**	**1.00**
☐	509	Bill Hands, Tex.	.25	.50
☐	510	Amos Otis, K.C.	.25	.50
☐	511	Jamie Easterly, Atl.	.25	.50
☐	512	Ellie Rodriguez, Cal.	.25	.50
☐	513	Bart Johnson, Chi.-A.L.	.25	.50
☐	514	Dan Driessen, Cin.	.25	.50
☐	515	Steve Yeager, L.A.	.25	.50
☐	516	Wayne Granger, Hou.	.25	.50
☐	517	John Milner, NYM.	.25	.50
☐	**518**	**Doug Flynn, Cin., RC**	**.25**	**.50**
☐	519	Steve Brye, Min.	.25	.50
☐	520	Willie McCovey, S.D.	2.50	5.00
☐	521	Jim Colborn, Mil.	.25	.50
☐	522	Ted Sizemore, Stl.	.25	.50
☐	523	Bob Montgomery, Bos.	.25	.50
☐	**524**	**Pete Falcone, S.F., RC**	**.25**	**.50**
☐	525	Billy Williams, Oak.	1.25	2.50
☐	526	1976 Checklist 4 (397-528)	.50	1.00
☐	527	Mike Anderson, Pha.	.25	.50
☐	528	Dock Ellis, Pgh.	.25	.50
☐	529	Deron Johnson, Bos.	.50	1.00
☐	530	Don Sutton, L.A.	1.25	2.50
☐	531	NYM.: Joe Frazier, Mgr.	.50	1.00
☐	532	Milt May, Hou.	.25	.50
☐	533	Lee Richard, Chi.-A.L.	.25	.50
☐	534	Stan Bahnsen, Oak.	.25	.50
☐	535	Dave Nelson, K.C.	.25	.50
☐	536	Mike Thompson, Atl.	.25	.50
☐	537	Tony Muser, Bal.	.25	.50
☐	**538**	**Pat Darcy, Cin., RC**	**.25**	**.50**
☐	**539**	**John Balaz, Cal., RC**	**.50**	**1.00**
☐	540	Bill Freehan, Det.	.25	.50
☐	541	Steve Mingori, K.C.	.25	.50
☐	542	Keith Hernandez, Stl.	.50	1.00
☐	543	Wayne Twitchell, Pha.	.25	.50
☐	544	Pepe Frias, Mtl.	.25	.50
☐	545	Sparky Lyle, NYY.	.25	.50
☐	**546**	**Dave Rosello, Chi.-N.L., RC**	**.25**	**.50**
☐	547	Roric Harrison, Cle.	.25	.50
☐	548	Manny Mota, L.A.	.25	.50
☐	**549**	**Randy Tate, NYM., RC**	**.25**	**.50**
☐	550	Hank Aaron, Mil.	15.00	30.00
☐	551	Jerry DaVanon, Hou.	.25	.50
☐	552	Terry Humphrey, Det.	.25	.50
☐	553	Randy Moffitt, S.F.	.25	.50
☐	554	Ray Fosse, Oak.	.25	.50
☐	555	Dyar Miller, Bal.	.25	.50
☐	556	Min.: Gene Mauch, Mgr.	.50	1.00
☐	557	Dan Spillner, S.D.	.25	.50
☐	558	Clarence Gaston, Atl.	.25	.50
☐	559	Clyde Wright, Tex.	.25	.50
☐	560	Jorge Orta, Chi.-A.L.	.25	.50
☐	561	Tom Carroll, Cin.	.25	.50
☐	562	Adrian Garrett, Cal.	.25	.50
☐	563	Larry Demery, Pgh.	.25	.50
☐	564	1975 Joe Garagiola, Bazooka Bubble Gum Blowing Champ: Kurt Bevacqua, Mil.	.50	1.00
☐	565	Tug McGraw, Pha.	.25	.50
☐	566	Ken McMullen, L.A.	.25	.50
☐	567	George Stone, NYM.	.25	.50
☐	**568**	**Rob Andrews, Hou., RC**	**.25**	**.50**
☐	569	Nelson Briles, Tex.	.25	.50
☐	570	George Hendrick, Cle.	.25	.50
☐	571	Don DeMola, Mtl.	.25	.50
☐	572	Rich Coggins, NYY.	.25	.50
☐	573	Bill Travers, Mil.	.25	.50
☐	574	Don Kessinger, Stl.	.25	.50
☐	575	Dwight Evans, Bos.	.25	.50
☐	576	Maximino Leon, Atl.	.25	.50
☐	577	Marc Hill, S.F.	.25	.50
☐	578	Ted Kubiak, S.D.	.25	.50
☐	579	Clay Kirby, Cin.	.25	.50
☐	580	AS: Bert Campaneris, Oak.	.25	.50
☐	581	Stl.: Red Schoendienst, Mgr.	.50	1.00
☐	582	Mike Kekich, Tex.	.25	.50
☐	583	Tommy Helms, Hou.	.25	.50
☐	**584**	**Stan Wall, L.A., RC**	**.25**	**.50**
☐	585	Joe Torre, NYM.	.25	.50
☐	586	Ron Schueler, Pha.	.25	.50

	No.	Player		
☐	587	Leo Cardenas, Tex.	.25	.50
☐	588	Kevin Kobel, Mil.	.25	.50
☐	589	S. Alcala/ M. Flanagan/ J. Pactwa/ P. Torrealba	1.25	2.50
☐	590	H. Cruz/ C. Lemon/ E. Valentine/ T. Whitfield	.75	1.50
☐	591	S. Grilli/ C. Mitchell/ J. Sosa/ G. Throop	.50	1.00
☐	592	W. Randolph/ D. McKay/ J. Royster/ R. Staiger	3.00	6.00
☐	593	L. Anderson/ K. Crosby/ M. Littell/ B. Metzger	.50	1.00
☐	594	A. Merchant/ E. Ott/ R. Stillman/ J. White	.50	1.00
☐	595	A. DeFilippis/ R. Lerch/ S. Monge/ S. Barr	.50	1.00
☐	596	C/ Reynolds/ L. Johnson/ J. LeMaster / J. Manuel	.50	1.00
☐	597	D. Aase/ J. Kucek/ F. LaCorte/ M. Pazik	.50	1.00
☐	598	H. Cruz/ J. Quirk/ J. Turner/ J. Wallis	.50	1.00
☐	599	R. Dressler/ R. Guidry/ B. McClure/ P. Zachry	3.00	6.00
☐	600	Tom Seaver, NYM.	5.00	10.00
☐	601	Ken Rudolph, Stl.	.25	.50
☐	602	Doug Konieczny, Hou.	.25	.50
☐	603	Jim Holt, Oak.	.25	.50
☐	604	Joe Lovitto, Tex.	.25	.50
☐	605	Al Downing, L.A.	.25	.50
☐	606	Mil.: Alex Grammas, Mgr.	.50	1.00
☐	607	Rich Hinton, Chi.-A.L.	.25	.50
☐	608	Vic Correll, Atl.	.25	.50
☐	609	Fred Norman, Cin.	.25	.50
☐	610	Greg Luzinski, Pha.	.25	.50
☐	611	Rich Folkers, S.D.	.25	.50
☐	612	Joe Lahoud, Cal.	.25	.50
☐	613	Tim Johnson, Mil.	.50	1.00
☐	**614**	**Fernando Arroyo, Det., RC**	**.25**	**.50**
☐	615	Mike Cubbage, Tex.	.25	.50
☐	616	Buck Martinez, K.C.	.25	.50
☐	617	Darold Knowles, Chi.-N.L.	.25	.50
☐	618	Jack Brohamer, Cle.	.25	.50
☐	619	Bill Butler, Min.	.25	.50
☐	620	Al Oliver, Pgh.	.25	.50
☐	621	Tom Hall, NYM.	.25	.50
☐	622	Rick Auerbach, L.A.	.25	.50
☐	**623**	**Bob Allietta, Cal., RC**	**.25**	**.50**
☐	624	Tony Taylor, Pha.	.25	.50
☐	625	J.R. Richard, Hou.	.25	.50
☐	626	Bob Sheldon, Mil.	.25	.50
☐	627	Bill Plummer, Cin.	.25	.50
☐	628	John D'Acquisto, S.F.	.25	.50
☐	629	Sandy Alomar, NYY.	.25	.50
☐	630	Chris Speier, S.F.	.25	.50
☐	631	Atl.: Dave Bristol, Mgr.	.50	1.00
☐	632	Rogelio Moret, Bos.	.25	.50
☐	**633**	**John Stearns, NYM., RC**	**.25**	**.50**
☐	634	Larry Christenson, Pha.	.25	.50
☐	635	Jim Fregosi, Tex.	.25	.50
☐	636	Joe Decker, Min.	.25	.50
☐	637	Bruce Bochte, Cal.	.25	.50
☐	638	Doyle Alexander, Bal.	.25	.50
☐	639	Fred Kendall, S.D.	.25	.50
☐	640	Bill Madlock, Chi.-N.L.	.25	.50
☐	641	Tom Paciorek, Atl.	.25	.50
☐	642	Dennis Blair, Mtl.	.25	.50
☐	643	1976 Checklist 5 (529 - 660)	.50	1.00
☐	644	Tom Bradley, S.F.	.25	.50
☐	645	Darrell Porter, Mil.	.25	.50
☐	646	John Lowenstein, Cle.	.25	.50
☐	647	Ramon Hernandez, Pgh.	.25	.50
☐	648	Al Cowens, K.C.	.25	.50
☐	649	Dave Roberts, Hou.	.25	.50
☐	650	AS: Thurman Munson, NYY.	2.50	5.00
☐	651	John Odom, Atl.	.25	.50
☐	652	Ed Armbrister, Cin.	.25	.50
☐	**653**	**Mike Norris, Oak., RC**	**.25**	**.50**
☐	654	Doug Griffin, Bos.	.25	.50
☐	**655**	**Mike Vail, NYM., RC**	**.25**	**.50**
☐	656	Chi.-A.L. Chuck Tanner, Mgr.	.25	.50
☐	**657**	**Roy Smalley, Tex., RC**	**.50**	**1.00**
☐	658	Jerry Johnson, S.D.	.25	.50
☐	659	Ben Oglivie, Det.	.25	.50
☐	660	Dave Lopes, L.A.	.25	.50

1977 - 83 DIMANCHE / DERNIERE HEURE

1977 ISSUES

Stamp Size: 8" x 10"
Face: Four colour, white border, name, jersey number, position, resume, French
Back: Blank
Imprint: DIMANCHE / DERNIERE HEURE

	Player	MINT
☐	Gary Carter	8.00
☐	Dave Cash	3.00
☐	Andre Dawson	8.00
☐	Tim Foli	3.00
☐	Jose Morales	3.00
☐	Steve Rogers	3.00
☐	Don Stanhouse	3.00
☐	Ellis Valentine	3.00
☐	Dick Williams, Mgr.	3.00

1978 ISSUES

Stamp Size: 8" x 10"
Face:Four colour, white border, name, jersey number, position, resume, French
Back: Blank
Imprint: DIMANCHE / DERNIERE HEURE

	Player	MINT
☐	Jim Brewer, Coach	3.00
☐	Woodie Fryman	3.00
☐	Mike Garman	3.00
☐	Ross Grimsley	3.00
☐	Ed Hermann	3.00
☐	Darold Knowles	3.00
☐	Rudy May	3.00
☐	Stan Papi	3.00
☐	Bob Reece	3.00
☐	Dan Schatzeder	3.00
☐	Norm Sherry, Coach	3.00

1979 ISSUES

Stamp Size: 8" x 10"
Face: Four colour, white border, name, jersey number, position, resume, French
Back: Blank
Imprint: DIMANCHE / DERNIERE HEURE

	Player	MINT
☐	Tommy Hutton	3.00
☐	Bill Lee	5.00
☐	Kem Macha	3.00
☐	Jim Mason	3.00
☐	Tony Solaita	3.00
☐	Elias Sosa	3.00

1980 ISSUES

Stamp Size: 8" x 10"
Face: Four colour, white border, name, jersey number, position, resume, French
Back: Blank
Imprint: DIMANCHE / DERNIERE HEURE

	Player	MINT
☐	Bill Almon	3.00

	Player	MINT
☐	Stan Bahnsen	3.00
☐	Tony Bernazard	3.00
☐	Gary Carter	8.00
☐	Warren Cromartie	5.00
☐	André Dawson	8.00
☐	Woodie Fryman	3.00
☐	Tommy Hutton	3.00
☐	Bill Lee	5.00
☐	Ron Leflore	3.00
☐	Ken Macha	3.00
☐	Fred Norman	3.00
☐	David Palmer	3.00
☐	Larry Parrish	5.00
☐	Steve Rogers	5.00
☐	Rodney Scott	3.00
☐	Elias Sosa	3.00
☐	Chris Speier	3.00
☐	John Tamargo	3.00
☐	Ellis Valentine	3.00
☐	Jerry White	3.00
☐	Dick Williams, Mgr.	3.00

1981 ISSUES

Stamp Size: 8" x 10"
Face: Four colour, white border, name, jersey number, position, resume, French
Back: Blank
Imprint: DIMANCHE / DERNIERE HEURE

	Player	MINT
☐	Ray Burris	3.00
☐	Gary Carter	8.00
☐	Bill Gullickson	3.00
☐	Charlie Lea	3.00
☐	Tim Raines	6.00
☐	Tim Wallach	5.00

1982 ISSUES

Stamp Size: 8" x 10"
Face: Four colour, white border, name, jersey number, position, resume, French
Back: Blank
Imprint: DIMANCHE / DERNIERE HEURE

	Player	MINT
☐	Tim Blackwell	3.00
☐	J. Fanning, S. Boros, G. Cisco, B. DeMars, B. Gebhard, V. Rapp, Coaching staff	3.00
☐	Steve Rogers	5.00
☐	Joel Youngblood	3.00

1983 ISSUES

Stamp Size 8" x 10"
Face: Four colour, white border, name, jersey number, position, resume, French
Back: Blank
Imprint: DIMANCHE / DERNIERE HEURE

	Player	MINT
☐	Greg Bargar	3.00
☐	Ray Burris	3.00
☐	Gary Carter	6.00
☐	Terry Crowley	3.00
☐	Bill Gullickson	3.00
☐	Bob James	3.00
☐	Charlie Lea	3.00
☐	G. Mauch, Coach; B. Stoneman, C. Laboy, C. Raymond	3.00
☐	Al Oliver	5.00
☐	Tim Raines	5.00
☐	Steve Rogers	3.00
☐	Angel Salazar	3.00
☐	Dan Schatzeder	3.00
☐	Chris Speier	3.00
☐	Billy Virdon, Manager	3.00
☐	Jim Wohlford	3.00

1977 O-PEE-CHEE

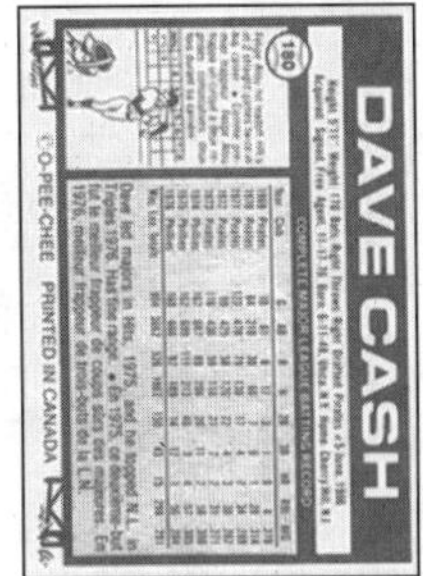

The card numbers on this 264-card set are not the same as those for the corresponding players in the 660-card Topps issue for 1977. This set is often in high demand by collectors of Toronto Blue Jays cards, and the number of Blue Jays cards figures prominently in this set, as this was the Jays' first year in major league baseball.

Card Size: 2 1/2" x 3 1/2"
Face: Four colour, white border; position, facsimile autograph
Back: Green on card stock; number, résumé, bilingual, baseball trivia
Imprint: © O-PEE-CHEE PRINTED IN CANADA

Complete Set (264 cards): 275.00
Common Player: .35

	No.	Player	MINT
☐	1	LL: George Brett/ Bill Madlock	9.00
☐	2	LL: Graig Nettles/ Mike Schmidt	1.00
☐	3	LL: Lee May/ George Foster	.75
☐	4	LL: Bill North/ Dave Lopes	.75
☐	5	LL: Jim Palmer/ Randy Jones	1.00
☐	6	LL: Nolan Ryan/ Tom Seaver	20.00
☐	7	LL: Mark Fidrych/ John Denny	.75
☐	8	LL: Bill Campbell/ Rawly Eastwick	.75
☐	9	Mike Jorgensen, Mtl.	.35
☐	10	Jim Hunter, NYY.	1.50
☐	11	Ken Griffey, Cin.	.35
☐	12	Bill Campbell, Bos.	.35
☐	13	Otto Velez, Tor.	.35
☐	14	Milt May, Det.	.35
☐	15	Dennis Eckersley, Cle.	7.00
☐	16	John Mayberry, K.C.	.35
☐	17	Larry Bowa, Pha.	.35
☐	18	Don Carrithers, Mtl.	.35
☐	19	Ken Singleton, Bal.	.35
☐	20	Bill Stein, Sea.	.35
☐	21	Ken Brett, Chi.-A.L.	.35
☐	**22**	**Gary Woods, Tor., RC, Error**	**.35**
☐	23	Steve Swisher, Chi.-N.L.	.35
☐	24	Don Sutton, L.A.	1.50
☐	25	Willie Stargell, Pgh.	3.50
☐	26	Jerry Koosman, NYM.	.35
☐	27	Del Unser, Mtl.	.35
☐	28	Bob Grich, Cal.	.35
☐	29	Jim Slaton, Mil.	.35
☐	30	Thurman Munson, NYY	4.00
☐	31	Dan Driessen, Cin.	.35
☐	**32**	**Tom Bruno, Tor., RC**	**.35**
☐	33	Larry Hisle, Min.	.35
☐	34	Phil Garner, Pgh.	.35
☐	35	Mike Hargrove, Tex.	.35

	No.	Player	Price
☐	36	Jackie Brown, Mtl.	.35
☐	37	Carl Yastrzemski, Bos.	6.00
☐	38	Dave Roberts, Det.	.35
☐	39	Ray Fosse, Cle.	.35
☐	40	Dave McKay, Tor.	.75
☐	41	Paul Splittorff, K.C.	.35
☐	42	Garry Maddox, Pha.	.35
☐	43	Phil Niekro, Atl.	1.00
☐	44	Roger Metzger, Hou.	.35
☐	45	Gary Carter, Mtl.	6.00
☐	46	Jim Spencer, Chi.-A.L.	.35
☐	47	Ross Grimsley, Bal.	.35
☐	**48**	**Bob Bailor, Tor., RC**	**.75**
☐	49	Chris Chambliss, NYY.	.35
☐	50	Will McEnaney, Mtl.	.35
☐	51	Lou Brock, Stl.	4.50
☐	52	Rollie Fingers, S.D.	3.00
☐	53	Chris Speier, S.F.	.35
☐	**54**	**Bombo Rivera, Mtl., RC**	**.35**
☐	55	Pete Broberg, Sea.	.35
☐	56	Bill Madlock, S.F.	.35
☐	57	Rick Rhoden, L.A.	.35
☐	58	Tor.: Coaches: D. Leppert/ B. Miller/ J. Moore/ H. Warner	.75
☐	59	John Candelaria, Pgh.	.35
☐	60	Ed Kranepool, NYM.	.35
☐	61	Dave LaRoche, Cle.	.35
☐	62	Jim Rice, Bos.	3.25
☐	63	Don Stanhouse, Mtl.	.35
☐	**64**	**Jason Thompson, Det. RC**	**.35**
☐	65	Nolan Ryan, Cal.	60.00
☐	**66**	**Tom Poquette, K.C., RC**	**.35**
☐	**67**	**Leon Hooten, Tor., RC**	**.35**
☐	68	Bob Boone, Pha.	.35
☐	69	Mickey Rivers, NYY.	.35
☐	70	Gary Nolan, Cin.	.35
☐	71	Sixto Lezcano, Mil.	.35
☐	72	Larry Parrish, Mtl.	.35
☐	73	Dave Goltz, Min.	.35
☐	74	Bert Campaneris, Tex.	.35
☐	75	Vida Blue, Oak.	.35
☐	**76**	**Rick Cerone, Tor., RC**	**.35**
☐	77	Ralph Garr, Chi.-A.L.	.35
☐	78	Ken Forsch, Hou.	.35
☐	79	Willie Montanez, Atl.	.35
☐	80	Jim Palmer, Bal.	4.50
☐	81	Jerry White, Mtl.	.35
☐	82	Gene Tenace, S.D.	.35
☐	83	Bobby Murcer, Chi.-N.L.	.35
☐	**84**	**Garry Templeton, Stl., RC**	**1.00**
☐	85	Bill Singer, Tor.	.35
☐	86	Buddy Bell, Cle.	.35
☐	87	Luis Tiant, Bos.	.35
☐	88	Rusty Staub, Det.	1.50
☐	89	Sparky Lyle, NYY.	.35
☐	90	Jose Morales, Mtl.	.35
☐	91	Dennis Leonard, K.C.	.35
☐	**92**	**Tommy Smith, Sea., RC**	**.35**
☐	93	Steve Carlton, Pha.	7.50
☐	94	John Scott, Tor.	.35
☐	95	Bill Bonham, Chi.-N.L.	.35
☐	96	Dave Lopes, L.A.	.35
☐	97	Jerry Reuss, Pgh.	.35
☐	98	Dave Kingman, NYM.	.35
☐	99	Dan Warthen, Mtl.	.35
☐	100	Johnny Bench, Cin.	9.00
☐	101	Bert Blyleven, Tex.	.35
☐	102	Cecil Cooper, Mil.	.35
☐	**103**	**Mike Willis, Tor., RC**	**.35**
☐	104	Dan Ford, Min.	.35
☐	105	Frank Tanana, Cal.	.35
☐	106	Bill North, Oak.	.35
☐	107	Joe Ferguson, Hou.	.35
☐	108	Dick Williams, Mgr., Mtl.	.35
☐	109	John Denny, Stl.	.35
☐	110	Willie Randolph, NYY.	.35
☐	111	Reggie Cleveland, Bos.	.75
☐	**112**	**Doug Howard, Tor., RC**	**.35**
☐	113	Randy Jones, S.D.	.35
☐	114	Rico Carty, Cle.	.35
☐	**115**	**Mark Fidrych, Det., RC**	**7.00**
☐	116	Darrell Porter, K.C.	.35
☐	117	Wayne Garrett, Mtl.	.35
☐	118	Greg Luzinski, Pha.	.35
☐	119	Jim Barr, S.F.	.35
☐	120	George Foster, Cin.	.35
☐	121	Phil Roof, Tor.	.35
☐	122	Bucky Dent (NYY.)	.35
☐	123	Steve Braun, Sea.	.35
☐	124	Checklist 1 (1-132)	1.00
☐	125	Lee May, Bal.	.35
☐	126	Woodie Fryman, Cin.	.35
☐	127	Jose Cardenal, Chi.-N.L.	.35
☐	128	Doug Rau, L.A.	.35
☐	129	Rennie Stennett, Pgh.	.35
☐	**130**	**Pete Vuckovich, Tor., RC**	**.75**
☐	131	Cesar Cedeno, Hou.	.35
☐	132	Jon Matlack, NYM.	.35
☐	133	Don Baylor, Cal.	.35
☐	134	Darrel Chaney, Atl.	.35
☐	135	Tony Perez, Mtl.	.75
☐	136	Aurelio Rodriguez, Det.	.35
☐	137	Carlton Fisk, Bos.	6.50
☐	138	Wayne Garland, Cle.	.35
☐	139	Dave Hilton, Tor.	.35
☐	140	Rawly Eastwick, Cin.	.35
☐	141	Amos Otis, K.C.	.35
☐	142	Tug McGraw, Pha.	.35
☐	143	Rod Carew, Min.	4.50
☐	144	Mike Torrez, Oak.	.35
☐	145	Sal Bando, Mil.	.35
☐	146	Dock Ellis, NYY.	.35
☐	147	Jose Cruz, Hou.	.35
☐	148	Alan Ashby, Tor.	.35
☐	149	Gaylord Perry, Tex.	1.00
☐	150	Keith Hernandez, Stl.	.35
☐	151	Dave Pagan, Sea.	.75
☐	152	Richie Zisk, Chi.-A.L.	.35
☐	153	Steve Rogers, Mtl.	.35
☐	154	Mark Belanger, Bal., Error	.35
☐	155	Andy Messersmith, Atl.	.35
☐	156	Dave Winfield, S.D.	20.00
☐	157	Chuck Hartenstein, Tor.	.35
☐	158	Manny Trillo, Chi.-N.L.	.35
☐	159	Steve Yeager, L.A.	.35
☐	160	Cesar Geronimo, Cin.	.35
☐	161	Jim Rooker, Pgh.	.35
☐	162	Tim Foli, Mtl.	.35
☐	163	Fred Lynn, Bos.	.75
☐	164	Ed Figueroa, NYY.	.35
☐	165	Johnny Grubb, Cle.	.35
☐	166	Pedro Garcia, Tor.	.35
☐	167	Ron LeFlore, Det.	.35
☐	168	Rich Hebner, Pha.	.35
☐	**169**	**Larry Herndon, S.F., RC**	**.35**
☐	170	George Brett, K.C.	50.00
☐	**171**	**Joe Kerrigan, Mtl., RC**	**.35**
☐	172	Bud Harrelson, NYM.	.35
☐	173	Bobby Bonds, Cal.	.35

	No.	Player	MINT
☐	174	Bill Travers, Mil.	.35
☐	175	John Lowenstein, (Cle.)	.35
☐	**176**	**Butch Wynegar, Min., RC**	**.35**
☐	177	Pete Falcone, Stl.	.35
☐	178	Claudell Washington, Oak.	.35
☐	179	Checklist 2 (133 - 264)	1.00
☐	180	Dave Cash, Mtl.	.35
☐	181	Fred Norman, Cin.	.35
☐	182	Roy White, NYY.	.35
☐	183	Marty Perez, NYY.	.35
☐	184	Jesse Jefferson, Tor.	.35
☐	185	Jim Sundberg, Tex.	.35
☐	186	Dan Meyer, Sea.	.35
☐	187	Fergie Jenkins, Bos.	3.25
☐	188	Tom Veryzer, Det.	.35
☐	189	Dennis Blair, Mtl.	.35
☐	190	Rick Manning, Cle.	.35
☐	191	Doug Bird, K.C.	.35
☐	192	Al Bumbry, Bal.	.35
☐	193	Dave Roberts, S.D.	.35
☐	194	Larry Christenson, Pha.	.35
☐	195	Chet Lemon, Chi.-A.L.	.35
☐	196	Ted Simmons, Stl.	.35
☐	197	Ray Burris, Chi.-N.L.	.35
☐	198	Mtl.: Coaches: J. Brewer/ B. Gardner/ M. Vernon/ O. Virgil	.75
☐	199	Ron Cey, L.A.	.35
☐	200	Reggie Jackson, NYY.	15.00
☐	201	Pat Zachry, Cin.	.35
☐	**202**	**Doug Ault, Tor., RC, Error**	**.75**
☐	203	Al Oliver, Pgh.	.75
☐	204	Robin Yount, Mil.	25.00
☐	205	Tom Seaver, NYM.	7.50
☐	206	Joe Rudi, Cal.	.35
☐	207	Barry Foote, Mtl.	.35
☐	208	Toby Harrah, Tex.	.35
☐	209	Jeff Burroughs, Atl.	.35
☐	210	George Scott, Bos.	.35
☐	211	Jim Mason, Tor.	.35
☐	212	Vern Ruhle, Det.	.35
☐	213	Fred Kendall, Cle.	.35
☐	214	Rick Reuschel, Chi.-N.L.	.35
☐	215	Hal McRae, K.C.	.35
☐	**216**	**Chip Lang, Mtl., RC**	**.35**
☐	217	Graig Nettles, NYY.	.35
☐	218	George Hendrick, S.D.	.35
☐	219	Glenn Abbott, Sea.	.35
☐	220	Joe Morgan, Cin.	4.50
☐	**221**	**Sam Ewing, Tor., RC**	**.35**
☐	222	George Medich, Oak.	.35
☐	223	Reggie Smith, L.A.	.35
☐	224	Dave Hamilton, Chi.-A.L.	.35
☐	225	Pepe Frias, Mtl.	.35
☐	226	Jay Johnstone, Pha.	.35
☐	227	J.R. Richard, Hou.	.35
☐	228	Doug DeCinces, Bal.	.35
☐	229	Dave Lemanczyk, Tor.	.35
☐	230	Rick Monday, L.A.	.35
☐	231	Manny Sanguillen, Oak.	.35
☐	232	John Montefusco, S.F.	.35
☐	233	Duane Kuiper, Cle.	.35
☐	234	Ellis Valentine, Mtl.	.35
☐	235	Dick Tidrow, NYY.	.35
☐	236	Ben Oglivie, Det.	.35
☐	237	Rick Burleson, Bos.	.35
☐	238	Roy Hartsfield, Mgr., Tor.	.75
☐	239	Lyman Bostock, Min.	.35
☐	240	Pete Rose, Cin.	12.00
☐	241	Mike Ivie, S.D.	.35
☐	242	Dave Parker, Pgh.	.75
☐	243	Bill Greif, Mtl.	.35
☐	244	Freddie Patek, K.C.	.35
☐	245	Mike Schmidt, Pha.	22.00
☐	246	Brian Downing, Chi.-A.L.	.35
☐	247	Steve Hargan, Tor.	.35
☐	248	Dave Collins, Sea.	.35
☐	249	Felix Millan, NYM.	.35
☐	250	Don Gullett, NYY.	.35
☐	251	Jerry Royster, Atl.	.35
☐	252	Earl Williams, Mtl. (Oak.)	.35
☐	253	Frank Duffy, Cle.	.35
☐	254	Tippy Martinez, Bal.	.35
☐	255	Steve Garvey, L.A.	.75
☐	**256**	**Alvis Woods, Tor., RC**	**.35**
☐	257	John Hiller, Det.	.75
☐	258	Dave Concepcion, Cin.	.35
☐	259	Dwight Evans, Bos.	.35
☐	260	Pete MacKanin, Mtl.	.35
☐	261	George Brett, K.C.;	15.00
☐	262	Minnie Minoso, Chi.-A.L.	.75
☐	263	Jose Morales, Mtl.	.35
☐	264	Nolan Ryan, Cal.	22.00

1978 O-PEE-CHEE

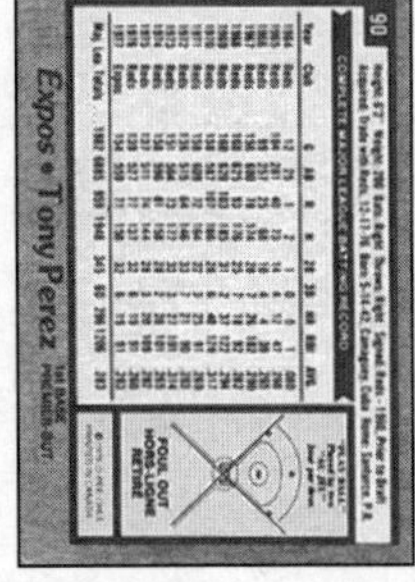

The card numbers on this 242-card set are not the same as those for the corresponding players in the 726-card Topps issue for 1978. The imprint "O-PEE-CHEE PRINTED IN CANADA" appears on the back of the cards, distingushing them from the Topps set.

Card Size: 2 1/2" x 3 1/2"
Face: Four colour; name, position, team
Back: Brown on card stock; number, résumé, "Play Ball", bilingual
Imprint: © 1978 O-PEE-CHEE PRINTED IN CANADA

Complete Set (242 cards): 215.00
Common Player: .35

	No.	Player	MINT
☐	1	LL: Dave Parker, Pgh./ Rod Carew, Min.	1.00
☐	2	LL: Jim Rice, Bos./ George Foster, Cin.	.75
☐	3	LL: George Foster, Cin./ Larry Hisle, Min.	.75
☐	4	LL: Frank Taveras, Pgh./ Freddie Patek, K.C.	.75
☐	5	LL: Steve Carlton, Phi./ Dave Goltz, Min./ Dave Goltz, Min. / Dennis Leonard, K.C./ Jim Palmer, Bal.	1.25
☐	6	LL: Nolan Ryan, Cal./ Phil Niekro, Atl.	6.50
☐	7	LL: John Candelaria, Pgh./ Frank Tanana, Cal.	.75
☐	8	LL: Rollie Fingers, S.D./ Bill Campbell, Bos.	1.00
☐	9	Steve Rogers, Mtl.	.35
☐	10	Graig Nettles, NYY.	.35
☐	**11**	**Doug Capilla, Cin., RC**	**.35**
☐	12	George Scott, Bos.	.35
☐	13	Gary Woods, Tor.	.35
☐	14	Tom Veryzer, (Cle.)	.35
☐	15	Wayne Garland, Cle.	.35
☐	16	Amos Otis, K.C.	.35
☐	17	Larry Christenson, Pha.	.35

☐ 18 Dave Cash, Mtl. .35
☐ 19 Jim Barr, S.F. .35
☐ 20 Ruppert Jones, Sea. .35
☐ 21 Eric Soderholm, Chi.-A.L. .35
☐ 22 Jesse Jefferson, Tor. .35
☐ 23 Jerry Morales, Chi.-N.L. .35
☐ 24 Doug Rau, L.A. .35
☐ 25 Rennie Stennett, Pgh. .35
☐ 26 Lee Mazzilli, NYM. .35
☐ 27 Dick Williams, Mgr., Mtl. .35
☐ 28 Joe Rudi, Cal. .35
☐ 29 Robin Yount, Mil. 15.00
☐ 30 Don Gullett, NYY. .35
☐ 31 Roy Howell, Tor. .35
☐ 32 Cesar Geronimo, Cin. .35
☐ **33 Rick Langford, Oak., RC .35**
☐ 34 Dan Ford, Min. .35
☐ 35 Gene Tenace, S.D. .35
☐ **36 Santo Alcala, Mtl., RC .35**
☐ 37 AS: Rick Burleson, Bos. .35
☐ **38 Dave Rozema, Det., RC .35**
☐ 39 Duane Kuiper, Cle. .35
☐ 40 Ron Fairly, (Cal.) .35
☐ 41 Dennis Leonard, K.C. .35
☐ 42 AS: Greg Luzinski, Pha. .35
☐ 43 Willie Montanez, (NYM.) .35
☐ 44 Enos Cabell, Hou. .35
☐ 45 Ellis Valentine, Mtl. .35
☐ 46 Steve Stone, Chi.-A.L. .35
☐ 47 Lee May, Bal. .35
☐ 48 Roy White, NYY. .35
☐ **49 Jerry Garvin, Tor., RC .75**
☐ 50 AS: Johnny Bench, Cin. 4.50
☐ 51 Garry Templeton, Stl. .35
☐ 52 Doyle Alexander, Tex. .35
☐ **53 Steve Henderson, NYM., RC .35**
☐ 54 Stan Bahnsen, Mtl. .35
☐ 55 Dan Meyer, Sea. .35
☐ 56 Rick Reuschel, Chi.-N.L. .35
☐ 57 Reggie Smith, L.A. .35
☐ 58 Team Checklist: Blue Jays 1.00
☐ 59 John Montefusco, S.F. .35
☐ 60 AS: Dave Parker, Pgh. .35
☐ 61 Jim Bibby, Cle. .35
☐ 62 Fred Lynn, Bos. .75
☐ 63 Jose Morales, Mtl. .35
☐ 64 Aurelio Rodriguez, Det. .35
☐ 65 Frank Tanana, Cal. .35
☐ 66 Darrell Porter, K.C. .35
☐ 67 Otto Velez, Tor. .35
☐ 68 Larry Bowa, Pha. .35
☐ 69 Jim Hunter, NYY. 1.50
☐ 70 AS: George Foster, Cin. .35
☐ 71 Cecil Cooper, Mil. .35
☐ 72 Gary Alexander, S.F. .35
☐ **73 Paul Thormodsgard, Min., RC .35**
☐ 74 Toby Harrah, Tex. .35
☐ **75 Mitchell Page, Oak.; RC .35**
☐ 76 Alan Ashby, Tor. .35
☐ 77 Jorge Orta, Chi.-A.L. .35
☐ 78 Dave Winfield, S.D. 15.00
☐ 79 Andy Messersmith, (NYY.) .35
☐ 80 Ken Singleton, Bal. .35
☐ 81 Will McEnaney, Mtl. .35
☐ 82 Lou Piniella, NYY. .35
☐ 83 Bob Forsch, Stl. .35
☐ 84 Dan Driessen, Cin. .35
☐ 85 Dave Lemanczyk, Tor. .35
☐ **86 Paul Dade, Cle., RC .35**
☐ 87 Bill Campbell, Bos. .35
☐ 88 Ron LeFlore, Det. .35
☐ 89 Bill Madlock, S.F. .35
☐ 90 Tony Perez, Mtl. .75
☐ 91 Freddie Patek, K.C. .35
☐ 92 Glenn Abbott, Sea. .35
☐ 93 Garry Maddox, Pha. .35
☐ **94 Steve Staggs, Tor., RC .35**
☐ 95 Bobby Murcer, Chi.-N.L. .35
☐ 96 AS: Don Sutton, L.A. 1.50
☐ 97 Al Oliver, (Tex.) .75
☐ 98 Jon Matlack, (Tex.) .35
☐ 99 Sam Mejias, Mtl. .35
☐ 100 Pete Rose, Cin. 6.00
☐ 101 Randy Jones, S.D. .35
☐ 102 Sixto Lezcano, Mil. .35
☐ **103 Jim Clancy, Tor., RC .75**
☐ 104 Butch Wynegar, Min. .35
☐ 105 Nolan Ryan, Cal. 55.00
☐ 106 Wayne Gross, Oak. .35
☐ 107 Bob Watson, Hou. .35
☐ 108 Joe Kerrigan, (Bal.) .35
☐ 109 Keith Hernandez, Stl. .35
☐ 110 AS: Reggie Jackson, NYY. 12.00
☐ 111 Denny Doyle, Bos. .35
☐ 112 Sam Ewing, Tor. .35
☐ 113 Bert Blyleven, (Pgh.) .35
☐ 114 Andre Thornton, Cle. .35
☐ 115 Milt May, Det. .35
☐ 116 Jim Colborn, K.C. .35
☐ **117 Warren Cromartie, Mtl., RC .75**
☐ 118 Ted Sizemore, Pha. .35
☐ 119 Checklist 1 (1 - 121) .75
☐ 120 Tom Seaver, Cin. 6.00
☐ 121 Luis Gomez, Tor. .35
☐ 122 Jim Spencer, (NYY.) .35
☐ 123 Leroy Stanton, Sea. .35
☐ 124 Luis Tiant, Bos. .35
☐ 125 Mark Belanger, Bal. .35
☐ 126 Jackie Brown, Mtl. .35
☐ 127 Bill Buckner, Chi.-N.L. .35
☐ 128 Bill Robinson, Pgh. .35
☐ 129 Rick Cerone, Tor. .35
☐ 130 AS: Ron Cey, L.A. .35
☐ 131 Jose Cruz, Hou. .35
☐ 132 Len Randle, NYM. .35
☐ 133 Bob Grich, Cal. .35
☐ 134 Jeff Burroughs, Atl. .35
☐ 135 Gary Carter, Mtl. 3.50
☐ 136 Milt Wilcox, Det. .35
☐ 137 AS: Carl Yastrzemski, Bos. 4.50
☐ 138 Dennis Eckersley, Cle. 4.50
☐ 139 Tim Nordbrook, Tor. .35
☐ 140 Ken Griffey, Cin. .35
☐ 141 Bob Boone, Pha. .35
☐ 142 Dave Goltz, Min. .35
☐ 143 Al Cowens, K.C. .35
☐ **144 Bill Atkinson, Mtl., RC .75**
☐ 145 Chris Chambliss, NYY. .35
☐ 146 Jim Slaton, (Det.) .35
☐ 147 Bill Stein, Sea. .35
☐ 148 Bob Bailor, Tor. .35
☐ 149 J.R. Richard, Hou. .35
☐ 150 Ted Simmons, Stl. .35
☐ 151 Rick Manning, Cle. .35
☐ 152 Lerrin LaGrow, Chi.-A.L. .35
☐ 153 Larry Parrish, Mtl. .35
☐ **154 Eddie Murray, Bal., RC 140.00**
☐ 155 Phil Niekro, Atl. 1.00

☐ 156 Bake McBride, Pha. .35
☐ 157 Pete Vuckovich, Tor. .35
☐ **158 Ivan DeJesus, Chi.-N.L., RC .35**
☐ 159 Rick Rhoden, L.A. .35
☐ 160 AS: Joe Morgan, Cin. 3.50
☐ **161 Ed Ott, Pgh., RC .35**
☐ 162 Don Stanhouse, Mtl. .35
☐ 163 Jim Rice, Bos. .75
☐ 164 Bucky Dent, NYY. .35
☐ **165 Jim Kern, Cle., RC .35**
☐ 166 Doug Rader, Tor. .35
☐ 167 Steve Kemp, Det. .35
☐ 168 John Mayberry, K.C. .35
☐ 169 Tim Foli, (NYM.) .35
☐ 170 Steve Carlton, Pha. 4.50
☐ 171 Pepe Frias, Mtl. .35
☐ 172 Pat Zachry, NYM. .35
☐ 173 Don Baylor, Cal. .35
☐ 174 Sal Bando, Mil. .35
☐ 175 Alvis Woods, Tor. .35
☐ 176 Mike Hargrove, Tex. .35
☐ 177 Vida Blue, Oak. .35
☐ 178 George Hendrick, S.D. .35
☐ 179 AS: Jim Palmer, Bal. 3.50
☐ 180 Andre Dawson, Mtl. 18.00
☐ 181 Paul Moskau, Cin. .35
☐ 182 Mickey Rivers, NYY. .35
☐ 183 Checklist 2 (122 - 242) .75
☐ 184 Jerry Johnson, Tor. .35
☐ 185 Willie McCovey, S.F. 3.50
☐ **186 Enrique Romo, Sea., RC .35**
☐ 187 Butch Hobson, Bos. .35
☐ 188 Rusty Staub, Det. 1.50
☐ 189 Wayne Twitchell, Mtl. .35
☐ 190 AS: Steve Garvey, L.A. 1.00
☐ 191 Rick Waits, Cle. .35
☐ 192 Doug DeCinces, Bal. .35
☐ 193 Tom Murphy, Tor. .35
☐ 194 Rich Hebner, Pha. .35
☐ 195 Ralph Garr, Chi.-A.L. .35
☐ 196 Bruce Sutter, Chi.-N.L. .35
☐ 197 Tom Poquette, K.C. .35
☐ 198 Wayne Garrett, Mtl. .35
☐ 199 Pedro Borbon, Cin. .35
☐ 200 Thurman Munson, NYY. 3.50
☐ 201 Rollie Fingers, S.D. 2.25
☐ 202 Doug Ault, Tor. .35
☐ 203 Phil Garner, Pgh. .35
☐ 204 Lou Brock, Stl. 3.50
☐ 205 Ed Kranepool, NYM. .35
☐ 206 Bobby Bonds, (Chi.-A.L.) .35
☐ 207 Team Checklist: Expos 1.00
☐ 208 Bump Wills, Tex. .35
☐ 209 Gary Matthews, Atl. .35
☐ 210 AS: Carlton Fisk, Bos. 3.50
☐ **211 Jeff Byrd, Tor., RC .35**
☐ 212 Jason Thompson, Det. .35
☐ 213 Larvell Blanks, Cle. .35
☐ 214 Sparky Lyle, NYY. .35
☐ 215 AS: George Brett, K.C. 30.00
☐ 216 Del Unser, Mtl. .35
☐ 217 Manny Trillo, Chi.-N.L. .35
☐ 218 Roy Hartsfield, Mgr., Tor. .75
☐ 219 Carlos Lopez, (Bal.) .35
☐ 220 AS: Dave Concepcion, Cin. .35
☐ 221 John Candelaria, Pgh. .35
☐ 222 Dave Lopes, L.A. .35
☐ **223 Tim Blackwell, (Chi.-N.L.), RC .35**
☐ 224 Chet Lemon, Chi.-A.L. .35
☐ 225 Mike Schmidt, Pha. 15.00
☐ 226 Cesar Cedeno, Hou. .35
☐ 227 Mike Willis, Tor. .35
☐ 228 AS: Willie Randolph, NYY. .35
☐ **229 Doug Bair, Oak., RC .35**
☐ 230 AS: Rod Carew, Min. 3.50
☐ 231 Mike Flanagan, Bal. .75
☐ 232 Chris Speier, Mtl. .35
☐ 233 Don Aase, (Cal.) .35
☐ 234 Buddy Bell, Cle. .35
☐ 235 Mark Fidrych, Det. .75
☐ 236 Lou Brock, Stl. 3.50
☐ 237 Sparky Lyle, NYY. .35
☐ 238 Willie McCovey, S.F. 1.00
☐ 239 Brooks Robinson, Bal. 2.50
☐ 240 Pete Rose, Cin. 4.00
☐ 241 Nolan Ryan, Cal. 18.00
☐ 242 Reggie Jackson, NYY. 5.00

1979 O-PEE-CHEE

The card numbers on this 374-card set are not the same as those for the corresponding players in the 726-card Topps issue for 1979. Cards in the O-Pee-Chee set are identical in design to the Topps set with the exception the the O-Pee-Chee logo appears for the first time on the front of their baseball cards. The imprint reads "© 1979 O-PEE-CHEE PRTN. IN CANADA" on the back of the Canadian cards.

Card Size: 2 1/2" x 3 1/2"
Face: Four colour; name, position, team, O-Pee-Chee logo
Back: Green and black on card stock; number, résumé, trivia, bilingual
Imprint: © 1979 O-PEE-CHEE PRTD. IN CANADA
Complete Set (374 cards): 165.00
Common Player: .30

	No.	Player	MINT
☐	1	Lee May, Bal.	.30
☐	2	Dick Drago, Bos.	.30
☐	3	Paul Dade, Cle.	.30
☐	4	Ross Grimsley, Mtl.	.30
☐	5	AS: Joe Morgan, Cin.	1.25
☐	6	Kevin Kobel, NYM.	.30
☐	7	Terry Forster, L.A.	.30
☐	8	Paul Molitor, Mil.	30.00
☐	9	Steve Carlton, Pha.	3.50
☐	10	Dave Goltz, Min.	.30
☐	11	Dave Winfield, S.D.	10.00
☐	12	Dave Rozema, Det.	.30
☐	13	Ed Figueroa, NYY.	.30
☐	14	Alan Ashby, Hou. (Tor.)	.30
☐	15	Dale Murphy, Atl.	5.00
☐	16	Dennis Eckersley, Bos.	2.25
☐	17	Ron Blomberg, Chi.-A.L.	.30
☐	18	Wayne Twitchell, NYM.	.30
☐	19	Al Hrabosky, K.C.	.30
☐	20	Fred Norman, Cin.	.30

	No.	Player	Price
☐	21	AS: Steve Garvey, L.A.	.75
☐	22	Willie Stargell, Pgh.	1.25
☐	23	John Hale, Sea.	.30
☐	24	Mickey Rivers, NYY.	.30
☐	25	Jack Brohamer, Bos.	.30
☐	26	Tom Underwood, Tor.	.30
☐	27	Mark Belanger, Bal.	.30
☐	28	Elliott Maddox, NYM.	.30
☐	29	John Candelaria, Pgh.	.30
☐	**30**	**Shane Rawley, Sea., RC**	**.30**
☐	31	Steve Yeager, L.A.	.30
☐	32	Warren Cromartie, Mtl.	.30
☐	33	Jason Thompson, Det.	.30
☐	**34**	**Roger Erickson, Min., RC**	**.30**
☐	35	Gary Matthews, Atl.	.30
☐	36	Pete Falcone, NYM.	.30
☐	37	Dick Tidrow, NYY.	.30
☐	38	Bob Boone, Pha.	.30
☐	39	Jim Bibby, Pgh.	.30
☐	40	Len Barker, Cle.	.30
☐	41	Robin Yount, Mil.	10.00
☐	42	Sam Mejias, Chi.-N.L.	.30
☐	43	Ray Burris, Chi.-N.L.	.30
☐	44	Tom Seaver, Cin.	4.00
☐	45	Roy Howell, Tor.	.30
☐	46	Jim Todd, Oak.	.30
☐	47	Frank Duffy, Bos.	.30
☐	48	Joel Youngblood, NYM.	.30
☐	49	AS: Vida Blue, S.F.	.30
☐	50	Cliff Johnson, NYY.	.30
☐	51	Nolan Ryan, Cal.	40.00
☐	**52**	**Ozzie Smith, S.D., RC**	**115.00**
☐	53	Jim Sundberg, Tex.	.30
☐	54	Mike Paxton, Cle.	.30
☐	55	Lou Whitaker, Det.	10.00
☐	56	Dan Schatzeder, Mtl.	.30
☐	57	Rick Burleson, Bos.	.30
☐	58	Doug Bair, Cin.	.30
☐	59	Ted Martinez, L.A.	.30
☐	60	Bob Watson, Hou.	.30
☐	61	Jim Clancy, Tor.	.30
☐	62	Rowland Office, Atl.	.30
☐	63	Bobby Murcer, Chi.-N.L.	.30
☐	64	Don Gullett, NYY.	.30
☐	65	Tom Paciorek, Sea.	.30
☐	66	Rick Rhoden, L.A.	.30
☐	67	Duane Kuiper, Cle.	.30
☐	68	Bruce Boisclair, NYM.	.30
☐	69	Manny Sarmiento, Cin.	.30
☐	70	Wayne Cage, Cle.	.30
☐	71	John Hiller, Det.	.50
☐	72	Rick Cerone, Tor.	.30
☐	73	Dwight Evans, Bos.	.30
☐	74	Buddy Solomon, Atl.	.30
☐	75	Roy White, NYY.	.30
☐	76	Mike Flanagan, Bal.	.30
☐	77	Tom Johnson, Min.	.30
☐	78	Glenn Burke, Oak.	.30
☐	79	Frank Taveras, Pgh.	.30
☐	80	Don Sutton, L.A.	1.25
☐	81	Leon Roberts, Sea.	.30
☐	82	George Hendrick, Stl.	.30
☐	83	Aurelio Rodriguez, Det.	.30
☐	84	Ron Reed, Pha.	.30
☐	85	Alvis Woods, Tor.	.30
☐	**86**	**Jim Beattie, NYY., RC**	**.50**
☐	87	Larry Hisle, Mil.	.30
☐	88	Mike Garman, Mtl.	.30
☐	89	Tim Johnson, Tor.	.75
☐	90	Paul Splittorff, K.C.	.30
☐	91	Darrel Chaney, Atl.	.30
☐	92	Mike Torrez, Bos.	.30
☐	93	Eric Soderholm, Chi.-A.L.	.30
☐	94	Ron Cey, L.A.	.30
☐	95	Randy Jones, S.D.	.30
☐	96	Bill Madlock, S.F.	.30
☐	97	Steve Kemp, Det.	.30
☐	98	Bob Apodaca, NYM.	.30
☐	99	Johnny Grubb, Tex.	.30
☐	100	Larry Milbourne, Sea.	.30
☐	101	AS: Johnny Bench, Cin.	3.00
☐	102	Dave Lemanczyk, Tor.	.30
☐	103	Reggie Cleveland, Tex.	.50
☐	104	AS: Larry Bowa, Pha.	.30
☐	105	Denny Martinez, Bal.	.50
☐	106	Bill Travers, Mil.	.30
☐	107	Willie McCovey, S.F.	3.00
☐	108	Wilbur Wood, Chi.-A.L.	.30
☐	109	Dennis Leonard, K.C.	.30
☐	110	Roy Smalley, Min.	.30
☐	111	Cesar Geronimo, Cin.	.30
☐	112	Jesse Jefferson, Tor.	.30
☐	113	Dave Revering, Oak.	.30
☐	114	Rich Gossage, NYY.	.50
☐	115	Steve Stone, Bal.	.30
☐	116	Doug Flynn, NYM.	.30
☐	117	Bob Forsch, Stl.	.30
☐	118	Paul Mitchell, Sea.	.30
☐	119	Toby Harrah, Cle.	.30
☐	120	Steve Rogers, Mtl.	.50
☐	121	Checklist 1 (1 - 125)	.75
☐	122	Balor Moore, Tor.	.30
☐	123	Rick Reuschel, Chi.-N.L.	.30
☐	124	Jeff Burroughs, Atl.	.30
☐	125	Willie Randolph, NYY.	.30
☐	126	Bob Stinson, Sea.	.30
☐	127	Rick Wise, Cle.	.30
☐	128	Luis Gomez, Tor.	.30
☐	129	Tommy John, NYY.	.30
☐	130	AS: Richie Zisk, Tex.	.30
☐	131	Mario Guerrero, Oak.	.30
☐	132	Oscar Gamble, Tex. (S.D.)	.30
☐	133	AS: Don Money, Mil.	.30
☐	134	Joe Rudi, Cal.	.30
☐	135	Woodie Fryman, Mtl.	.30
☐	136	Butch Hobson, Bos.	.30
☐	137	Jim Colborn, Sea.	.30
☐	138	Tom Grieve, Stl.	.30
☐	139	Andy Messersmith, L.A.	.30
☐	140	Andre Thornton, Cle.	.30
☐	**141**	**Ken Kravec, Chi.-A.L., RC**	**.30**
☐	142	Bobby Bonds, Cle. (Tex.)	.30
☐	143	Jose Cruz, Hou.	.30
☐	144	Dave Lopes, L.A.	.30
☐	145	Jerry Garvin, Tor.	.30
☐	146	Pepe Frias, Mtl.	.30
☐	147	Mitchell Page, Oak.	.30
☐	148	Ted Sizemore, Chi.-N.L.	.30
☐	**149**	**Rich Gale, K.C., RC**	**.30**
☐	150	Steve Ontiveros, Chi.-N.L.	.30
☐	151	AS: Rod Carew, Cal.	3.00
☐	152	Lary Sorensen, Mil.	.30
☐	153	Willie Montanez, NYM.	.30
☐	154	Floyd Bannister, Sea.	.30
☐	155	Bert Blyleven, Pgh.	.30
☐	156	Ralph Garr, Chi.-A.L.	.30
☐	157	Thurman Munson, NYY.	2.50
☐	158	Bob Robertson, K.C.	.30

	No.	Player	Price
☐	159	Jon Matlack, Tex.	.30
☐	160	Carl Yastrzemski, Bos.	3.50
☐	161	Gaylord Perry, S.D.	1.00
☐	162	Mike Tyson, Stl.	.30
☐	163	Cecil Cooper, Mil.	.30
☐	164	Pedro Borbon, Cin.	.30
☐	165	Art Howe, Hou.	.30
☐	166	Joe Coleman, S.F.	.30
☐	167	AS: George Brett, K.C.	25.00
☐	168	Gary Alexander, Cle.	.30
☐	169	Chet Lemon, Chi.-A.L.	.30
☐	170	Craig Swan, NYM.	.30
☐	171	Chris Chambliss, NYY.	.30
☐	172	John Montague, Sea.	.30
☐	173	Ron Jackson, Min.	.30
☐	174	AS: Jim Palmer, Bal.	3.00
☐	**175**	**Willie Upshaw, Tor. RC**	**.75**
☐	176	Tug McGraw, Pha.	.30
☐	177	Bill Buckner, Chi.-N.L.	.30
☐	178	Doug Rau, L.A.	.30
☐	179	Andre Dawson, Mtl.	9.00
☐	**180**	**Jim Wright, Bos., RC**	**.30**
☐	181	Garry Templeton, Stl.	.30
☐	182	Bill Bonham, Cin.	.30
☐	183	Lee Mazzilli, NYM.	.30
☐	184	Alan Trammell, Det.	13.00
☐	185	Amos Otis, K.C.	.30
☐	**186**	**Tom Dixon, Hou., RC**	**.30**
☐	187	Mike Cubbage, Min.	.30
☐	188	Sparky Lyle, Tex.	.30
☐	189	Juan Bernhardt, Sea.	.30
☐	190	Bump Wills, Tex.	.30
☐	191	Dave Kingman, Chi.-N.L.	.30
☐	192	Lamar Johnson, Chi.-A.L.	.30
☐	193	Lance Rautzhan, L.A.	.30
☐	194	Ed Herrmann, Mtl.	.30
☐	195	Bill Campbell, Bos.	.30
☐	196	Gorman Thomas, Mil.	.30
☐	197	Paul Moskau, Cin.	.30
☐	198	Dale Murray, NYM.	.30
☐	199	John Mayberry, Tor.	.30
☐	200	Phil Garner, Pgh.	.30
☐	201	Dan Ford, Cal.	.30
☐	202	Gary Thomasson, L.A.	.30
☐	203	Rollie Fingers, S.D.	1.25
☐	204	Al Oliver, Tex.	.50
☐	205	Doug Ault, Tor.	.30
☐	206	Scott McGregor, Bal.	.30
☐	207	Dave Cash, Mtl.	.30
☐	208	Bill Plummer, Sea.	.30
☐	209	Ivan DeJesus, Chi.-N.L.	.30
☐	210	AS: Jim Rice, Bal.	.75
☐	211	Ray Knight, Cin.	.30
☐	**212**	**Paul Hartzell, Min., RC**	**.30**
☐	213	Tim Foli, NYM.	.30
☐	214	Butch Wynegar, Min.	.30
☐	215	Darrell Evans, S.F.	.30
☐	216	Ken Griffey, Cin.	.30
☐	217	Doug DeCinces, Bal.	.30
☐	218	Ruppert Jones, Sea.	.30
☐	219	Bob Montgomery, Bos.	.30
☐	220	Rick Manning, Cle.	.30
☐	221	Chris Speier, Mtl.	.30
☐	222	Bobby Valentine, NYM.	.30
☐	223	Dave Parker, Pgh.	.30
☐	224	Larry Biittner, Chi.-N.L.	.30
☐	225	Ken Clay, NYY.	.30
☐	226	Gene Tenace, S.D.	.30
☐	227	Frank White, K.C.	.30
☐	228	Rusty Staub, Det.	1.00
☐	229	Lee Lacy, L.A.	.30
☐	230	Doyle Alexander, Tex.	.30
☐	231	Bruce Bochte, Sea.	.30
☐	232	Steve Henderson, NYM.	.30
☐	233	Jim Lonborg, Pha.	.30
☐	234	Dave Concepcion, Cin.	.30
☐	235	Jerry Morales, Det.	.30
☐	236	Len Randle, NYM.	.30
☐	237	Bill Lee, Mtl.	.30
☐	238	Bruce Sutter, Chi.-N.L.	.30
☐	239	Jim Essian, Oak.	.30
☐	240	Graig Nettles, NYY.	.30
☐	241	Otto Velez, Tor.	.30
☐	242	Checklist 2 (126 - 250)	.75
☐	243	Reggie Smith, L.A.	.30
☐	244	Stan Bahnsen, Mtl.	.30
☐	245	Garry Maddox, Pha.	.30
☐	246	Joaquin Andujar, Hou.	.30
☐	247	Dan Driessen, Cin.	.30
☐	248	Bob Grich, Cal.	.30
☐	249	Fred Lynn, Bos.	.75
☐	250	Skip Lockwood, NYM.	.30
☐	251	Craig Reynolds, Hou.	.30
☐	252	Willie Horton, Tor.	.30
☐	253	Rick Waits, Cle.	.30
☐	254	Bucky Dent, NYY.	.30
☐	255	Bob Knepper, S.F.	.30
☐	256	Miguel Dilone, Oak.	.30
☐	257	Bob Owchinko, S.D.	.30
☐	258	Al Cowens, K.C.	.30
☐	259	Bob Bailor, Tor.	.30
☐	260	Larry Christenson, Pha.	.30
☐	261	Tony Perez, Mtl.	.75
☐	262	TC: Blue Jays Roy Hartsfield, Mgr.	.75
☐	263	Glenn Abbott, Sea.	.30
☐	264	Ron Guidry, NYY.	.30
☐	265	Ed Kranepool, NYM.	.30
☐	266	Charlie Hough, L.A.	.30
☐	267	Ted Simmons, Stl.	.30
☐	268	Jack Clark, S.F.	.30
☐	269	Enos Cabell, Hou.	.30
☐	270	Gary Carter, Mtl.	1.00
☐	271	Sam Ewing, Tor.	.30
☐	272	Tom Burgmeier, Bos.	.30
☐	273	Freddie Patek, K.C.	.30
☐	274	Frank Tanana, Cal.	.30
☐	275	Leroy Stanton, Sea.	.30
☐	276	Ken Forsch, Hou.	.30
☐	277	Ellis Valentine, Mtl.	.30
☐	278	AS: Greg Luzinski, Pha.	.30
☐	279	Rick Bosetti, Tor.	.30
☐	280	John Stearns, NYM.	.30
☐	281	Enrique Romo, Pgh.	.30
☐	282	Bob Bailey, Bos.	.30
☐	283	Sal Bando, Mil.	.30
☐	284	Matt Keough, Oak.	.30
☐	285	Biff Pocoroba, Atl.	.30
☐	286	Mike Lum, Atl.	.30
☐	287	Jay Johnstone, NYY.	.30
☐	288	John Montefusco, S.F.	.30
☐	289	Ed Ott, Pgh.	.30
☐	290	Dusty Baker, L.A.	.30
☐	291	Rico Carty, Tor. (Oak.)	.30
☐	292	Nino Espinosa, NYM.	.30
☐	293	Rich Hebner, Pha.	.30
☐	294	Cesar Cedeno, Hou.	.30
☐	295	Darrell Porter, K.C.	.30
☐	296	Rod Gilbreath, Atl.	.30

	No.	Player	MINT
☐	297	Jim Kern, Tex. (Cle.)	.30
☐	298	Claudell Washington, Chi.-A.L.	.30
☐	299	Luis Tiant, NYY.	.30
☐	**300**	**Mike Parrott, Sea., RC**	**.30**
☐	301	Pete Broberg, L.A.	.30
☐	302	Greg Gross, Pha.	.30
☐	303	Darold Knowles, Stl.	.30
☐	304	Paul Blair, NYY.	.30
☐	305	Julio Cruz, Sea.	.30
☐	306	Hal McRae, K.C.	.30
☐	307	Ken Reitz, Stl.	.30
☐	308	Tom Murphy, Tor.	.30
☐	309	Terry Whitfield, S.F.	.30
☐	310	J.R. Richard, Hou.	.30
☐	311	Mike Hargrove, S.D. (Tex.)	.30
☐	312	Rick Dempsey, Bal.	.30
☐	313	Phil Niekro, Atl.	1.00
☐	314	Bob Stanley, Bos.	.30
☐	315	Jim Spencer, NYY.	.30
☐	316	AS: George Foster, Cin.	.30
☐	317	Dave LaRoche, Cal.	.30
☐	318	Rudy May, Mtl.	.30
☐	319	Jeff Newman, Oak.	.30
☐	320	AS: Rick Monday, L.A.	.30
☐	321	Omar Moreno, Pgh.	.30
☐	322	Dave McKay, Tor.	.50
☐	323	Mike Schmidt, Pha.	10.00
☐	324	Ken Singleton, Bal.	.30
☐	325	Jerry Remy, Bos.	.30
☐	326	Bert Campaneris, Tex.	.30
☐	327	Pat Zachry, NYM.	.30
☐	328	Larry Herndon, S.F.	.30
☐	329	Mark Fidrych, Det.	.75
☐	330	Del Unser, Mtl.	.30
☐	331	Gene Garber, Atl.	.30
☐	332	Bake McBride, Pha.	.30
☐	333	Jorge Orta, Chi.-A.L.	.30
☐	334	Don Kirkwood, Tor.	.30
☐	335	Don Baylor, Cal.	.30
☐	336	Bill Robinson, Pgh.	.30
☐	337	Manny Trillo, Pha.	.30
☐	338	Eddie Murray, Bal.	35.00
☐	339	Tom Hausman, NYM.	.30
☐	340	George Scott, Bos.	.30
☐	**341**	**Rick Sweet, S.D., RC**	**.30**
☐	342	Lou Piniella, NYY.	.30
☐	343	AS: Pete Rose, Pha.	6.00
☐	**344**	**Stan Papi, Bos., RC**	**.30**
☐	345	Jerry Koosman, Min.	.30
☐	**346**	**Hosken Powell, Min. RC**	**.30**
☐	347	George Medich, Tex.	.30
☐	348	Ron LeFlore, Det.	.30
☐	349	TC: Expos; Dick Williams, Mgr.	.30
☐	350	Lou Brock, Stl.	3.00
☐	351	Bill North, L.A.	.30
☐	352	Jim Hunter, NYY.	1.25
☐	353	Checklist 3 (251 - 374)	.75
☐	354	Ed Halicki, S.F.	.30
☐	355	Tom Hutton, Mtl.	.30
☐	356	Mike Caldwell, Mil.	.30
☐	357	Larry Parrish, Mtl.	.30
☐	358	Geoff Zahn, Min.	.30
☐	359	Derrel Thomas, L.A.	.30
☐	360	AS: Carlton Fisk, Bos.	3.50
☐	**361**	**John Henry Johnson, Oak., RC**	**.30**
☐	362	Dave Chalk, Cal.	.30
☐	363	Dan Meyer, Sea.	.30
☐	364	Sixto Lezcano, Mil.	.30
☐	365	Rennie Stennett, Pgh.	.30
☐	366	Mike Willis, Tor.	.30
☐	367	Buddy Bell, Tex.	.30
☐	368	Mickey Stanley, Det.	.30
☐	369	Dave Rader, Pha.	.30
☐	370	Burt Hooton, L.A.	.30
☐	371	Keith Hernandez, Stl.	.30
☐	372	Bill Stein, Sea.	.30
☐	**373**	**Hal Dues, Mtl., RC**	**.30**
☐	374	AS: Reggie Jackson, NYY.	5.00

1980 O-PEE-CHEE

The card numbers on this 374-card set are not the same as those for the corresponding players in the 726-card Topps issue for 1980. The Topps set included the Rickey Henderson Rookie card (#482), but the Canadian issue did not.

Card Size: 2 1/2" x 3 1/2"
Face: Four colour; name, position, team, facsimile autograph
Back: Blue and black on card stock; number, position, trivia, bilingual
Imprint: © 1980 O-PEE-CHEE PRINTED IN CANADA

Complete Set (374 cards):			**120.00**
Common Player:			**.30**
	No.	**Player**	**MINT**
☐	1	Craig Swan, NYM.	.30
☐	2	Denny Martinez, Bal.	.50
☐	3	Dave Cash, (S.D.)	.30
☐	4	Bruce Sutter, Chi.-N.L.	.50
☐	5	Ron Jackson, Min.	.30
☐	6	Balor Moore, Tor.	.30
☐	7	Dan Ford, Cal.	.30
☐	8	Pat Putnam, Tex.	.30
☐	9	Derrel Thomas, L.A.	.30
☐	10	Jim Slaton, Mil.	.30
☐	11	Lee Mazzilli, NYM.	.30
☐	12	Del Unser, Pha.	.30
☐	13	Mark Wagner, Det.	.30
☐	14	Vida Blue, S.F.	.30
☐	15	Jay Johnstone, (L.A.)	.30
☐	16	Julio Cruz, Sea.	.30
☐	17	Tony Scott, Stl.	.30
☐	18	Jeff Newman, Oak.	.30
☐	19	Luis Tiant, NYY.	.30
☐	20	Carlton Fisk, Bos.	2.50
☐	**21**	**Dave Palmer, Mtl., RC**	**.30**
☐	22	Bombo Rivera, Min.	.30
☐	23	Bill Fahey, S.D.	.30
☐	24	AS: Frank White, K.C.	.30
☐	25	Rico Carty, Tor.	.30
☐	26	Bill Bonham, Cin.	.30
☐	27	Rick Miller, Cal.	.30
☐	28	J.R. Richard, Hou.	.30
☐	29	Joe Ferguson, L.A.	.30
☐	30	Bill Madlock, Pgh.	.30
☐	31	Pete Vuckovich, Stl.	.30

☐	32	Doug Flynn, NYM.	.30
☐	33	Bucky Dent, NYY.	.30
☐	34	Mike Ivie, S.F.	.30
☐	35	Bob Stanley, Bos.	.30
☐	36	Al Bumbry, Bal.	.30
☐	37	Gary Carter, Mtl.	1.50
☐	38	John Milner, Pgh.	.30
☐	39	Sid Monge, Cle.	.30
☐	40	Bill Russell, L.A.	.30
☐	41	John Stearns, NYM.	.30
☐	**42**	**Dave Stieb, Tor., RC**	**2.00**
☐	43	Ruppert Jones, (NYY.)	.30
☐	44	Bob Owchinko, (Cle.), Error	.30
☐	45	Ron LeFlore, (Mtl.)	.30
☐	46	Ted Sizemore, Bos.	.30
☐	47	AS: Ted Simmons, Stl.	.30
☐	48	Pepe Frias, (Tex.)	.30
☐	49	Ken Landreaux, Min.	.30
☐	50	Manny Trillo, Pha.	.30
☐	51	Rick Dempsey, Bal.	.30
☐	52	Cecil Cooper, Mil.	.30
☐	53	Bill Lee, Mtl.	.30
☐	54	Victor Cruz, Cle.	.30
☐	55	Johnny Bench, Cin.	4.00
☐	56	Rich Dauer, Bal.	.30
☐	57	Frank Tanana, Cal.	.30
☐	58	Francisco Barrios, Chi.-A.L.	.30
☐	59	Bob Horner, Atl.	.50
☐	60	AS: Fred Lynn, Bos.	.50
☐	61	Bob Knepper, S.F.	.30
☐	62	Sparky Lyle, Tex.	.30
☐	63	Larry Cox, Sea.	.30
☐	64	Dock Ellis, (Pgh.)	.30
☐	65	Phil Garner, Pgh.	.30
☐	66	Greg Luzinski, Pha.	.30
☐	67	Checklist 1 (1 - 125)	.50
☐	68	Dave Lemanczyk, Tor.	.30
☐	69	Tony Perez, (Bos.)	.50
☐	70	Gary Thomasson, L.A.	.30
☐	71	Craig Reynolds, Hou.	.30
☐	72	Amos Otis, K.C.	.30
☐	73	Biff Pocoroba, Atl.	.30
☐	74	Matt Keough, Oak.	.30
☐	75	Bill Buckner, Chi.-N.L.	.30
☐	**76**	**John Castino, Min., RC**	**.30**
☐	77	Rich Gossage, NYY.	.50
☐	78	Gary Alexander, Cle.	.30
☐	**79**	**Phil Huffman, Tor., RC**	**.30**
☐	80	Bruce Bochte, Sea.	.30
☐	81	Darrell Evans, S.F.	.30
☐	82	Terry Puhl, Hou.	.75
☐	83	Jason Thompson, Det.	.30
☐	84	Lary Sorenson, Mil.	.30
☐	85	Jerry Remy, Bos.	.30
☐	**86**	**Tony Brizzolara, Atl., RC**	**.30**
☐	87	Willie Wilson, K.C.	.30
☐	88	Eddie Murray, Bal.	18.00
☐	89	Larry Christenson, Pha.	.30
☐	90	Bob Randall, Min.	.30
☐	91	Greg Pryor, Chi.-A.L.	.30
☐	92	Glenn Abbott, Sea.	.30
☐	93	Jack Clark, S.F.	.30
☐	94	Rick Waits, Cle.	.30
☐	95	Luis Gomez, (Atl.)	.30
☐	96	Burt Hooton, L.A.	.30
☐	97	John Henry Johnson, Tex.	.30
☐	98	Ray Knight, Cin.	.30
☐	99	Rick Reuschel, Chi.-N.L.	.30
☐	100	Champ Summers, Det.	.30
☐	101	Ron Davis, NYY.	.30
☐	102	Warren Cromartie, Mtl.	.30
☐	103	Ken Reitz, Stl.	.30
☐	104	Hal McRae, K.C.	.30
☐	105	Alan Ashby, Hou.	.30
☐	106	Kevin Kobel, NYM.	.30
☐	107	Buddy Bell, Tex.	.30
☐	108	Dave Goltz, (L.A.)	.30
☐	109	John Montefusco, S.F.	.30
☐	110	Lance Parrish, Det.	.30
☐	111	Mike LaCoss, Cin.	.30
☐	112	AS: Jim Rice, Bos.	.50
☐	113	AS: Steve Carlton, Pha.	3.00
☐	114	Sixto Lezcano, Mil.	.30
☐	115	Ed Halicki, S.F.	.30
☐	116	Jose Morales, Min.	.30
☐	117	Dave Concepcion, Cin.	.30
☐	**118**	**Joe Cannon, Tor., RC**	**.30**
☐	119	Willie Montanez, (S.D.), Error	.30
☐	120	Lou Piniella, NYY.	.30
☐	121	Bill Stein, Sea.	.30
☐	122	AS: Dave Winfield, S.D.	8.00
☐	123	Alan Trammell, Det.	5.00
☐	124	Andre Dawson, Mtl.	6.00
☐	125	Marc Hill, S.F.	.30
☐	126	Don Aase, Cal.	.30
☐	127	Dave Kingman, Chi.-N.L.	.30
☐	128	Checklist 2 (126 - 250)	.50
☐	129	Dennis Lamp, Chi.-N.L.	.30
☐	130	Phil Niekro, Atl.	1.00
☐	131	Tim Foli, Pgh.	.30
☐	132	Jim Clancy, Tor.	.30
☐	133	Bill Atkinson, (Chi.-A.L.), Error	.50
☐	134	Paul Dade, S.D.	.30
☐	135	Dusty Baker, L.A.	.30
☐	136	Al Oliver, Tex.	.50
☐	137	Dave Chalk, Oak.	.30
☐	138	Bill Robinson, Pgh.	.30
☐	139	Robin Yount, Mil.	8.00
☐	140	Dan Schatzeder, (Det.)	.30
☐	141	AS: Mike Schmidt, Pha.	5.00
☐	142	Ralph Garr, (Cal.)	.30
☐	143	Dale Murphy, Atl.	3.00
☐	144	Jerry Koosman, Min.	.30
☐	145	Tom Veryzer, Cle.	.30
☐	146	Rick Bosetti, Tor.	.30
☐	147	Jim Spencer, NYY.	.30
☐	148	Gaylord Perry, (Tex.) Error	1.00
☐	149	Paul Blair, Cin.	.30
☐	150	Don Baylor, Cal.	.30
☐	151	Dave Rozema, Det.	.30
☐	152	AS: Steve Garvey, L.A.	.50
☐	153	Elias Sosa, Mtl.	.30
☐	154	Larry Gura, K.C.	.30
☐	155	Tim Johnson, Tor.	.75
☐	156	Steve Henderson, NYM.	.30
☐	157	Ron Guidry, NYY.	.50
☐	158	Mike Edwards, Oak.	.30
☐	159	Butch Wynegar, Min.	.30
☐	160	Randy Jones, S.D.	.30
☐	161	Denny Walling, Hou.	.30
☐	162	Mike Hargrove, Cle.	.30
☐	163	AS: Dave Parker, Pgh.	.50
☐	164	Roger Metzger, S.F.	.30
☐	165	Johnny Grubb, Tex.	.30
☐	166	Steve Kemp, Det.	.30
☐	167	Bob Lacey, Oak.	.30
☐	168	Chris Speier, Mtl.	.30
☐	169	Dennis Eckersley, Bos.	.75

	No.	Player	Price
☐	170	Keith Hernandez, Stl.	.30
☐	171	Claudell Washington, Chi.-A.L.	.30
☐	172	Tom Underwood, (NYY.)	.30
☐	173	Dan Driessen, Cin.	.30
☐	174	Al Cowens, (Cal.)	.30
☐	175	Rich Hebner, (Det.)	.30
☐	176	Willie McCovey, S.F.	2.25
☐	177	Carney Lansford, Cal.	.30
☐	178	Ken Singleton, Bal.	.30
☐	179	Jim Essian, Oak.	.30
☐	180	Mike Vail, Chi.-N.L.	.30
☐	181	Randy Lerch, Pha.	.30
☐	182	Larry Parrish, Mtl.	.30
☐	183	Checklist 3 (251-374)	.50
☐	184	George Hendrick, Stl.	.30
☐	185	Bob Davis, Tor.	.30
☐	186	Gary Matthews, Atl.	.30
☐	187	Lou Whitaker, Det.	3.00
☐	188	AS: Darrell Porter, K.C.	.30
☐	189	Wayne Gross, Oak.	.30
☐	190	Bobby Murcer, NYY.	.30
☐	**191**	**Willie Aikens, (K.C.), RC**	**.30**
☐	192	Jim Kern, Tex.	.30
☐	193	Cesar Cedeno, Hou.	.30
☐	194	Joel Youngblood, NYM.	.30
☐	195	Ross Grimsley, Mtl.	.30
☐	196	Jerry Mumphrey, (S.D.), Error	.30
☐	197	Kevin Bell, Chi.-A.L.	.30
☐	198	Garry Maddox, Pha.	.30
☐	199	Dave Freisleben, Tor.	.30
☐	200	Ed Ott, Pgh.	.30
☐	201	Enos Cabell, Hou.	.30
☐	202	Pete LaCock, K.C.	.30
☐	203	Fergie Jenkins, Tex.	2.00
☐	204	Milt Wilcox, Det.	.30
☐	205	Ozzie Smith, S.D.	22.00
☐	206	Ellis Valentine, Mtl.	.30
☐	207	Dan Meyer, Sea.	.30
☐	208	Barry Foote, Chi.-N.L.	.30
☐	209	AS: George Foster, Cin.	.30
☐	210	Dwight Evans, Bos.	.30
☐	211	Paul Molitor, Mil.	18.00
☐	212	Tony Solaita, Tor.	.30
☐	213	Bill North, S.F.	.30
☐	214	Paul Splittorff, K.C.	.30
☐	215	Bobby Bonds, (Stl.)	.50
☐	216	Butch Hobson, Bos.	.30
☐	217	Mark Belanger, Bal.	.30
☐	218	Grant Jackson, Pgh.	.30
☐	219	Tom Hutton, Mtl.	.30
☐	220	Pat Zachry, NYM.	.30
☐	221	Duane Kuiper, Cle.	.30
☐	222	Larry Hisle, Mil.	.30
☐	223	Mike Krukow, Chi.-N.L.	.30
☐	**224**	**Johnnie LeMaster, S.F., RC**	**.30**
☐	225	Billy Almon, (Mtl.)	.30
☐	226	Joe Niekro, Hou.	.30
☐	227	Dave Revering, Oak.	.30
☐	228	Don Sutton, L.A.	1.00
☐	229	John Hiller, Det.	.50
☐	230	Alvis Woods, Tor.	.30
☐	231	Mark Fidrych, Det.	.50
☐	232	Duffy Dyer, Mtl.	.30
☐	233	Nino Espinosa, Pha.	.30
☐	234	Doug Bair, Cin.	.30
☐	235	AS: George Brett, K.C.	18.00
☐	236	Mike Torrez, Bos.	.30
☐	237	Frank Taveras, NYM.	.30
☐	238	Bert Blyleven, Pgh.	.30
☐	239	Willie Randolph, NYY.	.30
☐	240	Mike Sadek, S.F.	.30
☐	241	Jerry Royster, Atl.	.30
☐	242	John Denny, (Cle.)	.30
☐	243	Rick Monday, L.A.	.30
☐	244	Jesse Jefferson, Tor.	.30
☐	245	Aurelio Rodriguez, (S.D.)	.30
☐	246	Bob Boone, Pha.	.30
☐	247	Cesar Geronimo, Cin.	.30
☐	248	Bob Shirley, S.D.	.30
☐	249	TC: Expos; Dick Williams, Mgr.	.50
☐	250	Bob Watson, (NYY.)	.30
☐	251	Mickey Rivers, Tex.	.30
☐	252	Mike Tyson, (Chi.-N.L.)	.30
☐	253	Wayne Nordhagen, Chi.-A.L.	.30
☐	254	Roy Howell, Tor.	.30
☐	255	Lee May, Bal.	.30
☐	256	Jerry Martin, Chi.-N.L.	.30
☐	257	Bake McBride, Pha.	.30
☐	258	Silvio Martinez, Stl.	.30
☐	259	Jim Mason, Mtl.	.30
☐	260	Tom Seaver, Cin.	5.00
☐	**261**	**Rich Wortham, Chi.-A.L., RC**	**.30**
☐	262	Mike Cubbage, Min.	.30
☐	263	Gene Garber, Atl.	.30
☐	264	Bert Campaneris, Cal.	.30
☐	265	Tom Buskey, Tor.	.30
☐	266	Leon Roberts, Sea.	.30
☐	267	Ron Cey, L.A.	.30
☐	268	Steve Ontiveros, Chi.-N.L.	.30
☐	269	Mike Caldwell, Mil.	.30
☐	**270**	**Nelson Norman, Tex., RC**	**.30**
☐	271	Steve Rogers, Mtl.	.50
☐	272	Jim Morrison, Chi.-A.L.	.30
☐	273	Clint Hurdle, K.C.	.30
☐	274	Dale Murray, Mtl.	.30
☐	275	Jim Barr, Cal.	.30
☐	276	Jim Sundberg, Tex.	.30
☐	277	Willie Horton, Sea.	.30
☐	278	Andre Thornton, Cle.	.30
☐	279	Bob Forsch, Stl.	.30
☐	280	Joe Strain, S.F.	.30
☐	281	Rudy May, (NYY.)	.30
☐	282	Pete Rose, Pha.	5.00
☐	283	Jeff Burroughs, Atl.	.30
☐	284	Rick Langford, Oak.	.30
☐	285	Ken Griffey, Cin.	.50
☐	286	Bill Nahorodny, (Atl.)	.30
☐	287	Art Howe, Hou.	.30
☐	288	Ed Figueroa, NYY.	.30
☐	289	Joe Rudi, Cal.	.30
☐	290	Alfredo Griffin, Tor.	.30
☐	291	AS: Dave Lopes, L.A.	.30
☐	292	Rick Manning, Cle.	.30
☐	293	Dennis Leonard, K.C.	.30
☐	294	Bud Harrelson, Pha.	.30
☐	295	Skip Lockwood, (Bos.)	.30
☐	296	AS: Roy Smalley, Min.	.30
☐	297	Kent Tekulve, Pgh.	.30
☐	298	Scot Thompson, Chi.-N.L.	.30
☐	299	Ken Kravec, Chi.-A.L.	.30
☐	300	TC: Blue Jays; Bobby Mattick, Mgr.	.50
☐	301	Scott Sanderson, Mtl.	.30
☐	302	Charlie Moore, Mil.	.30
☐	303	AS: Nolan Ryan, (Hou.)	28.00
☐	304	Bob Bailor, Tor.	.30
☐	305	Bob Stinson, Sea.	.30
☐	306	Al Hrabosky, (Atl.)	.30
☐	307	Mitchell Page, Oak.	.30

☐	308	Garry Templeton, Stl.	.30
☐	309	Chet Lemon, Chi.-A.L.	.30
☐	310	Jim Palmer, Bal.	2.25
☐	311	Rick Cerone, (NYY.)	.30
☐	312	Jon Matlack, Tex.	.30
☐	313	Don Money, Mil.	.30
☐	314	Reggie Jackson, NYY.	5.00
☐	315	Brian Downing, Cal.	.30
☐	316	Woodie Fryman, Mtl.	.30
☐	317	Alan Bannister, Chi.-A.L.	.30
☐	318	Ron Reed, Pha.	.30
☐	319	Willie Stargell, Pgh.	1.00
☐	320	Jerry Garvin, Tor.	.30
☐	321	Cliff Johnson, Cle.	.30
☐	322	Doug DeCinces, Bal.	.30
☐	323	Gene Richards, S.D.	.30
☐	324	Joaquin Andujar, Hou.	.30
☐	325	Richie Zisk, Tex.	.30
☐	326	Bob Grich, Cal.	.30
☐	327	Gorman Thomas, Mil.	.30
☐	328	Chris Chambliss, (Atl.)	.30
☐	329	Blue Jays Future Stars: B. Edge/ Pat Kelly/ Ted Wilborn	.30
☐	330	AS: Larry Bowa, Pha.	.30
☐	331	Barry Bonnell, (Tor.)	.30
☐	332	John Candelaria, Pgh.	.30
☐	333	Toby Harrah, Cle.	.30
☐	334	Larry Biittner, Chi.-N.L.	.30
☐	335	Mike Flanagan, Bal.	.30
☐	336	Ed Kranepool, NYM.	.30
☐	337	Ken Forsch, Hou.	.30
☐	338	John Mayberry, Tor.	.30
☐	339	Rick Burleson, Bos.	.30
☐	340	Milt May, (S.F.)	.30
☐	341	Roy White, NYY.	.30
☐	342	Joe Morgan, (Hou.)	.30
☐	343	Rollie Fingers, S.D.	1.00
☐	344	Mario Mendoza, Sea.	.30
☐	345	Stan Bahnsen, Mtl.	.30
☐	346	Tug McGraw, Pha.	.30
☐	347	Rusty Staub, Mtl.	1.00
☐	348	Tommy John, NYY.	.30
☐	349	Ivan DeJesus, Chi.-N.L.	.30
☐	350	Reggie Smith, L.A.	.30
☐	351	Expos Future Stars: T. Bernazard/ R. Miller/ J. Tamargo	.30
☐	352	Floyd Bannister, Sea.	.30
☐	353	AS: Rod Carew, Cal.	1.00
☐	354	Otto Velez, Tor.	.30
☐	355	Gene Tenace, S.D.	.30
☐	356	Freddie Patek, (Cal.)	.30
☐	357	Elliott Maddox, NYM.	.30
☐	**358**	**Pat Underwood, Det. RC**	**.30**
☐	359	Graig Nettles, NYY.	.30
☐	360	Rodney Scott, Mtl.	.30
☐	361	Terry Whitfield, S.F.	.30
☐	362	Fred Norman, (Mtl.)	.30
☐	363	Sal Bando, Mil.	.30
☐	364	Greg Gross, Pha.	.30
☐	365	AS: Carl Yastrzemski, Bos.	1.00
☐	366	Paul Hartzell, Min.	.30
☐	367	Jose Cruz, Hou.	.30
☐	368	Shane Rawley, Sea.	.30
☐	369	Jerry White, Mtl.	.30
☐	370	Rick Wise, (S.D.)	.30
☐	371	Steve Yeager, L.A.	.30
☐	372	Omar Moreno, Pgh.	.30
☐	373	Bump Wills, Tex.	.30
☐	374	Craig Kusick, (S.D.)	.30

1981 O-PEE-CHEE

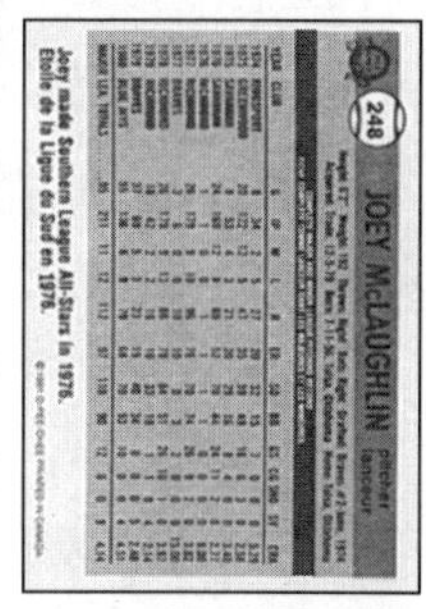

The card numbers on this 374-card set are not the same as those for the corresponding players in the 726-card Topps issue for 1981. The Canadian set was printed on two different card stocks, one grey and the other buff. A complete set all printed on the same stock would command a small premium. Complete sets on the grey stock command a slightly higher premium than a complete set on buff stock. The imprint on the Canadian issue reads "A, B, C or D *" O-PEE-CHEE PRINTED IN CANADA." The letters designate the sheet the cards were printed on.

Card Size: 2 1/2" x 3 1/2"

Face: Four colour, coloured border; name, position, team

Back: Red and black on grey or buff card stock; number, résumé, bilingual

Imprint: A, B, C, or D *© 1981 O-PEE-CHEE PRINTED IN CANADA

Complete Set (374 cards): **45.00**

Common Player: **.20**

	No.	Player	MINT
☐	1	Frank Pastore, Cin.	.20
☐	2	Phil Huffman, Tor.	.20
☐	3	Len Barker, Cle.	.20
☐	4	Robin Yount, Mil.	2.00
☐	5	Dave Stieb, Tor.	.50
☐	6	Gary Carter, Mtl.	.75
☐	7	Butch Hobson, Cal. (Ana.)	.20
☐	8	Lance Parrish, Det.	.20
☐	9	AS: Bruce Sutter, (Stl.)	.35
☐	10	Mike Flanagan, Bal.	.20
☐	**11**	**Paul Mirabeila, Tor., RC**	**.20**
☐	12	Craig Reynolds, Hou.	.20
☐	**13**	**Joe Charboneau, Cle., RC**	**1.00**
☐	14	Dan Driessen, Cin.	.20
☐	15	Larry Parrish, Mtl.	.20
☐	16	Ron Davis, NYY.	.20
☐	17	Cliff Johnson, (Oak.)	.20
☐	18	Bruce Bochte, Sea.	.20
☐	19	Jim Clancy, Tor.	.20
☐	20	ASr: Bill Russell, L.A.	.20
☐	21	Ron Oester, Cin.	.20
☐	22	Danny Darwin, Tex.	.20
☐	23	Willie Aikens, K.C.	.20
☐	24	Don Stanhouse, L.A.	.20
☐	25	Sixto Lezcano, (Stl.)	.20
☐	26	U. L. Washington, K.C.	.20
☐	27	Champ Summers, Det.	.20
☐	28	Enrique Romo, Pgh.	.20
☐	29	Gene Tenace, S.D.	.20
☐	30	Jack Clark, S.F.	.20
☐	31	Checklist 1 (1 - 125)	.35
☐	32	Ken Oberkfell, Stl.	.20
☐	33	Rick Honeycutt, (Tex.)	.20
☐	34	Al Bumbry, Bal.	.20
☐	35	John Tamargo, Mtl.	.20
☐	36	Ed Farmer, Chi.-A.L.	.20

	No.	Player	Price
☐	37	Gary Roenicke, Bal.	.20
☐	38	Tim Foli, Pgh.	.20
☐	39	Eddie Murray, Bal.	6.00
☐	40	Roy Howell, (Mil.)	.20
☐	**41**	**Bill Gullickson, Mtl., RC**	**.50**
☐	42	Jerry White, Mtl.	.20
☐	43	Tim Blackwell, Chi.-N.L.	.20
☐	44	Steve Henderson, NYM.	.20
☐	45	Enos Cabell, (S.F.)	.20
☐	46	Rick Bosetti, Tor.	.20
☐	47	Bill North, S.F.	.20
☐	48	AS: Rich Gossage, NYY.	.35
☐	49	Bob Shirley, (Stl.)	.20
☐	50	AS: Dave Lopes, L.A.	.20
☐	51	Shane Rawley, Sea.	.20
☐	**52**	**Lloyd Moseby, Tor., RC**	**.75**
☐	53	Burt Hooton, L.A.	.20
☐	54	Ivan DeJesus, Chi.-N.L.	.20
☐	55	Mike Norris, Oak.	.20
☐	56	Del Unser, Pha.	.20
☐	57	Dave Revering, Oak.	.20
☐	58	Joel Youngblood, NYM.	.20
☐	59	Steve McCatty, Oak.	.20
☐	60	Willie Randolph, NYY.	.20
☐	61	Butch Wynegar, Min.	.20
☐	62	Gary Lavelle, S.F.	.20
☐	63	Willie Montanez, Mtl.	.20
☐	64	Terry Puhl, Hou.	.50
☐	65	Scott McGregor, Bal.	.20
☐	66	Buddy Bell, Tex.	.20
☐	67	Toby Harrah, Cle.	.20
☐	68	Jim Rice, Bos.	.20
☐	69	Darrell Evans, S.F.	.20
☐	70	Al Oliver, Tex.	.20
☐	71	Hal Dues, Mtl.	.20
☐	**72**	**Barry Evans, S.D., RC**	**.20**
☐	73	Doug Bair, Cin.	.20
☐	74	Mike Hargrove, Cle.	.20
☐	75	AS: Reggie Smith, L.A.	.20
☐	76	Mario Mendoza, (Tex.)	.20
☐	77	Mike Barlow, Tor.	.20
☐	78	Garth Iorg, Tor.	.20
☐	**79**	**Jeff Reardon, NYM., RC**	**2.00**
☐	80	Roger Erickson, Min.	.20
☐	**81**	**Dave Stapleton, Bos., RC**	**.20**
☐	82	Barry Bonnell, Tor.	.20
☐	83	Dave Concepcion, Cin.	.20
☐	84	Johnnie LeMaster, S.F.	.20
☐	85	Mike Caldwell, Mil.	.20
☐	86	Wayne Gross, Oak.	.20
☐	87	Rick Camp, Atl.	.20
☐	**88**	**Joe Lefebvre, NYY., RC**	**.20**
☐	89	Darrell Jackson, Min.	.20
☐	90	Bake McBride, Pha.	.20
☐	91	Tim Stoddard, Bal.	.20
☐	92	Mike Easler, Pgh.	.20
☐	93	AS: Jim Bibby, Pgh.	.20
☐	94	Kent Tekulve, Pgh.	.20
☐	95	Jim Sundberg, Tex.	.20
☐	96	Tommy John, NYY.	.20
☐	97	Chris Speier, Mtl.	.20
☐	98	Clint Hurdle, K.C.	.20
☐	99	Phil Garner, Pgh.	.20
☐	100	AS: Rod Carew, Cal.	1.50
☐	101	AS: Steve Stone, Bal.	.20
☐	102	Joe Niekro, Hou.	.20
☐	103	Jerry Martin, (S.F.)	.20
☐	104	Ron LeFlore, Mtl. (Chi.-A.L.)	.20
☐	105	Jose Cruz, Hou.	.20
☐	106	Don Money, Mil.	.20
☐	107	Bobby Brown, NYY.	.20
☐	108	Larry Herndon, S.F.	.20
☐	109	Dennis Eckersley, Bos.	.35
☐	110	Carl Yastrzemski, Bos.	1.00
☐	111	Greg Minton, S.F.	.20
☐	112	Dan Schatzeder, Det.	.20
☐	113	AS: George Brett, K.C.	6.00
☐	114	Tom Underwood, NYY.	.20
☐	115	Roy Smalley, Min.	.20
☐	116	AS: Carlton Fisk, Bos. (Chi.-A.L.)	1.00
☐	117	Pete Falcone, NYM.	.20
☐	118	Dale Murphy, Atl.	.75
☐	119	Tippy Martinez, Bal.	.20
☐	120	Larry Bowa, Pha.	.20
☐	121	Julio Cruz, Sea.	.20
☐	122	Jim Gantner, Mil.	.20
☐	123	Al Cowens, Det.	.20
☐	124	Jerry Garvin, Tor.	.20
☐	125	Andre Dawson, Mtl.	2.50
☐	**126**	**Charlie Leibrandt, Cin., RC**	**.20**
☐	127	Willie Stargell, Pgh.	1.00
☐	128	Andre Thornton, Cle.	.20
☐	129	Art Howe, Hou.	.20
☐	130	AS: Larry Gura, K.C.	.20
☐	131	Jerry Remy, Bos.	.20
☐	132	Rick Dempsey, Bal.	.20
☐	133	Alan Trammell, Det.	1.00
☐	134	Mike LaCoss, Cin.	.20
☐	135	Gorman Thomas, Mil.	.20
☐	**136**	**Expos Future Stars: T. Raines/ R. Ramos/ B. Pate, RCs**	**6.50**
☐	137	Bill Madlock, Pgh.	.20
☐	**138**	**Rich Dotson, Chi.-A.L., RC**	**.20**
☐	139	Oscar Gamble, NYY.	.20
☐	140	Bob Forsch, Stl.	.20
☐	141	Miguel Dilone, Cle.	.20
☐	142	Jackson Todd, Tor.	.20
☐	143	Dan Meyer, Sea.	.20
☐	144	Garry Templeton, Stl.	.20
☐	145	Mickey Rivers, Tex.	.20
☐	146	Alan Ashby, Hou.	.20
☐	147	Dale Berra, Pgh.	.20
☐	148	Randy Jones, (NYM.)	.20
☐	149	Joe Nolan, Cin.	.20
☐	150	Mark Fidrych, Det.	.35
☐	151	Tony Armas, Oak.	.20
☐	152	Steve Kemp, Det.	.20
☐	153	Jerry Reuss, L.A.	.20
☐	154	Rick Langford, Oak.	.20
☐	155	Chris Chambliss, Atl.	.20
☐	156	Bob McClure, Mil.	.20
☐	157	John Wathan, K.C.	.20
☐	158	John Curtis, S.D.	.20
☐	**159**	**Steve Howe, L.A., RC**	**.50**
☐	160	Garry Maddox, Pha.	.20
☐	161	Dan Graham, Bal.	.20
☐	**162**	**Doug Corbett, Min., RC**	**.20**
☐	163	Rob Dressler, Sea.	.20
☐	164	AS: Bucky Dent, NYY.	.20
☐	165	Alvis Woods, Tor.	.20
☐	166	Floyd Bannister, Sea.	.20
☐	167	Lee Mazzilli, NYM.	.20
☐	168	Don Robinson, Pgh.	.20
☐	169	John Mayberry, Tor.	.20
☐	170	Woodie Fryman, Mtl.	.20
☐	171	Gene Richards, S.D.	.20
☐	172	Rick Burleson, Bos. (Cal.)	.20
☐	173	Bump Wills, Tex.	.20
☐	174	Glenn Abbott, Sea.	.20

- ☐ 175 Dave Collins, Cin. .20
- ☐ 176 Mike Krukow, Chi.-N.L. .20
- ☐ 177 Rick Monday, L.A. .20
- ☐ 178 AS: Dave Parker, Pgh. .20
- ☐ 179 Rudy May, NYY. .20
- ☐ 180 Pete Rose, Pha. 2.50
- ☐ 181 Elias Sosa, Mtl. .20
- ☐ 182 Bob Grich, Cal. .20
- ☐ 183 Fred Norman, Mtl. .20
- ☐ 184 Jim Dwyer, (Bal.) .20
- ☐ 185 Dennis Leonard, K.C. .20
- ☐ 186 Gary Matthews, Atl. .20
- ☐ 187 Ron Hassey, Cle. .20
- ☐ 188 Doug DeCinces, Bal. .20
- ☐ 189 Craig Swan, NYM. .20
- ☐ 190 Cesar Cedeno, Hou. .20
- ☐ 191 Rick Sutcliffe, L.A. .20
- ☐ 192 Kiko Garcia, Bal. .20
- ☐ 193 Pete Vuckovich, (Mil.) .20
- ☐ 194 Tony Bernazard, (Chi.-A.L.) .20
- ☐ 195 Keith Hernandez, Stl. .20
- ☐ 196 Jerry Mumphrey, S.D. .20
- ☐ 197 Jim Kern, Tex. .20
- ☐ **198 Jerry Dybzinski, Cle., RC .20**
- ☐ 199 John Lowenstein, Bal. .20
- ☐ 200 George Foster, Cin. .20
- ☐ 201 Phil Niekro, Atl. .75
- ☐ 202 Bill Buckner, Chi.-N.L. .20
- ☐ 203 AS: Steve Carlton, Pha. 2.00
- ☐ 204 John D'Acquisto, Pha. (Ana.) .20
- ☐ 205 Rick Reuschel, Chi.-N.L. .20
- ☐ 206 Dan Quisenberry, K.C. .20
- ☐ 207 AS: Mike Schmidt, Pha. 2.50
- ☐ 208 Bob Watson, NYY. .20
- ☐ 209 Jim Spencer, NYY. .20
- ☐ 210 Jim Palmer, Bal. 1.50
- ☐ 211 Derrel Thomas, L.A. .20
- ☐ 212 Steve Nicosia, Pgh. .20
- ☐ 213 Omar Moreno, Pgh. .20
- ☐ 214 Richie Zisk, (Sea.) .20
- ☐ 215 Larry Hisle, Mil. .20
- ☐ 216 Mike Torrez, Bos. .20
- ☐ 217 Rich Hebner, Det. .20
- ☐ **218 Britt Burns, Chi.-A.L. RC .20**
- ☐ 219 Ken Landreaux, Min. .20
- ☐ 220 Tom Seaver, Cin. 2.50
- ☐ 221 Bob Davis, (Cal.) .20
- ☐ 222 Jorge Orta, Cle. .20
- ☐ 223 Bobby Bonds, Stl. .20
- ☐ 224 Pat Zachry, NYM. .20
- ☐ 225 Ruppert Jones, NYY. .20
- ☐ 226 Duane Kuiper, Cle. .20
- ☐ 227 Rodney Scott, Mtl. .20
- ☐ 228 Tom Paciorek, Sea. .20
- ☐ 229 Rollie Fingers, S.D. (Mil.) .75
- ☐ 230 George Hendrick, Stl. .20
- ☐ 231 Tony Perez, Bos. .35
- ☐ 232 Grant Jackson, Pgh. .20
- ☐ **233 Damaso Garcia, Tor., RC .20**
- ☐ 234 Lou Whitaker, Det. 1.50
- ☐ 235 Scott Sanderson, Mtl. .20
- ☐ 236 Mike Ivie, S.F. .20
- ☐ 237 Charlie Moore, Mil. .20
- ☐ 238 Blue Jays Future Stars: L. Leal/ B. Milner/ K. Schrom .20
- ☐ 239 Rick Miller, (Bos.) .20
- ☐ 240 Nolan Ryan, Hou. 9.00
- ☐ 241 Checklist 2 (126 - 250) .35
- ☐ 242 Chet Lemon, Chi.-A.L. .20
- ☐ 243 Dave Palmer, Mtl. .20
- ☐ 244 Ellis Valentine, Mtl. .20
- ☐ 245 Carney Lansford, Cal. (Bos.) .20
- ☐ 246 Ed Ott, Pgh. .20
- ☐ 247 Glenn Hubbard, Atl. .20
- ☐ 248 Joey McLaughlin, Tor. .20
- ☐ 249 Jerry Narron, Sea. .20
- ☐ 250 Ron Guidry, NYY. .35
- ☐ 251 AS: Steve Garvey, L.A. .35
- ☐ 252 Victor Cruz, (Pgh.) .20
- ☐ 253 Bobby Murcer, NYY. .20
- ☐ 254 Ozzie Smith, S.D. 6.00
- ☐ 255 John Stearns, NYM. .20
- ☐ 256 Bill Campbell, Bos. .20
- ☐ 257 Rennie Stennett, S.F. .20
- ☐ 258 Rick Waits, Cle. .20
- ☐ **259 Gary Lucas, S.D., RC .20**
- ☐ 260 Ron Cey, L.A. .20
- ☐ 261 Rickey Henderson, Oak. 6.00
- ☐ 262 Sammy Stewart, Bal. .20
- ☐ 263 Brian Downing, Cal. .20
- ☐ **264 Mark Bomback, NYM., RC .20**
- ☐ 265 John Candelaria, Pgh. .20
- ☐ 266 Renie Martin, K.C. .20
- ☐ 267 Stan Bahnsen, Mtl. .20
- ☐ 268 TC: Montreal Expos; Dick Williams, Mgr. .35
- ☐ 269 Ken Forsch, Hou. .20
- ☐ 270 Greg Luzinski, Pha. .20
- ☐ 271 Ron Jackson, Min. .20
- ☐ 272 Wayne Garland, Cle. .20
- ☐ 273 Milt May, S.F. .20
- ☐ 274 Rick Wise, S.D. .20
- ☐ 275 Dwight Evans, Bos. .20
- ☐ 276 Sal Bando, Mil. .20
- ☐ 277 Alfredo Griffin, Tor. .20
- ☐ 278 Rick Sofield, Min. .20
- ☐ 279 Bob Knepper, (Hou.) .20
- ☐ 280 Ken Griffey, Cin. .35
- ☐ 281 Ken Singleton, Bal. .20
- ☐ 282 Ernie Whitt, Tor. .20
- ☐ 283 Billy Sample, Tex. .20
- ☐ 284 Jack Morris, Det. .20
- ☐ 285 Dick Ruthven, Pha. .20
- ☐ 286 AS: Johnny Bench, Cin. 2.00
- ☐ **287 Dave Smith, Hou., RC .50**
- ☐ 288 Amos Otis, K.C. .20
- ☐ 289 Dave Goltz, L.A. .20
- ☐ 290 Bob Boone, Pha. .20
- ☐ 291 Aurelio Lopez, Det. .20
- ☐ 292 Tom Hume, Cin. .20
- ☐ **293 Charlie Lea, Mtl., RC .20**
- ☐ 294 Bert Blyleven, (Cle.) .20
- ☐ 295 Hal McRae, K.C. .20
- ☐ 296 Bob Stanley, Bos. .20
- ☐ 297 Bob Bailor, (NYM.) .20
- ☐ 298 Jerry Koosman, Min. .20
- ☐ 299 Elliott Maddox, (NYY.) .20
- ☐ 300 AS: Paul Molitor, Mil. 2.50
- ☐ 301 Matt Keough, Oak. .20
- ☐ 302 Pat Putnam, Tex. .20
- ☐ 303 Dan Ford, Cal. .20
- ☐ 304 John Castino, Min. .20
- ☐ 305 Barry Foote, Chi.-N.L. .20
- ☐ 306 Lou Pinieila, NYY. .20
- ☐ 307 Gene Garber, Atl. .20
- ☐ 308 Rick Manning, Cle. .20
- ☐ 309 Don Baylor, Cal. .20
- ☐ 310 Vida Blue, S.F. .20
- ☐ 311 Doug Flynn, NYM. .20
- ☐ 312 Rick Rhoden, Pgh. .20

	No.	Player	Price
☐	313	AS: Fred Lynn, (Cal.)	.20
☐	314	Rich Dauer, Bal.	.20
☐	**315**	**Kirk Gibson, Det., RC**	**3.00**
☐	316	Ken Reitz, (Chi.-N.L.)	.20
☐	317	Lonnie Smith, Pha.	.20
☐	318	Steve Yeager, L.A.	.20
☐	319	Rowland Office, Mtl.	.20
☐	320	Tom Burgmeier, Bos.	.20
☐	321	Leon Durham, (Chi.-N.L.)	.20
☐	322	Neil Allen, NYM.	.20
☐	323	Ray Burris, (Mtl.)	.20
☐	324	Mike Willis, Tor.	.20
☐	325	Ray Knight, Cin.	.20
☐	326	Rafael Landestoy, Hou.	.20
☐	327	Moose Haas, Mil.	.20
☐	328	Ross Baumgarten, Chi.-A.L.	.20
☐	329	Joaquin Andujar, Hou.	.20
☐	330	Frank White, K.C.	.20
☐	331	TC: Toronto Blue Jays; Bobby Mattick, Mgr.	.35
☐	332	Dick Drago, Bos.	.20
☐	333	Sid Monge, Cle.	.20
☐	334	Joe Sambito, Hou.	.20
☐	335	Rick Cerone, NYY.	.20
☐	336	Eddie Whitson, S.F.	.20
☐	337	Sparky Lyle, Pha.	.20
☐	338	Checklist 3 (251-374)	.35
☐	339	Jon Matlack, Tex.	.20
☐	340	Ben Oglivie, Mil.	.20
☐	341	Dwayne Murphy, Oak.	.20
☐	342	Terry Crowley, Bal.	.20
☐	343	Frank Taveras, NYM.	.20
☐	344	Steve Rogers, Mtl.	.35
☐	345	Warren Cromartie, Mtl.	.20
☐	346	Bill Caudill, Chi.-N.L.	.20
☐	**347**	**Harold Baines, Chi.-A.L., RC**	**3.50**
☐	348	Frank LaCorte, Hou.	.20
☐	**349**	**Glenn Hoffman, Bos., RC**	**.20**
☐	350	J.R. Richard, Hou.	.20
☐	351	Otto Velez, Tor.	.20
☐	352	Ted Simmons, (Mil.)	.20
☐	353	Terry Kennedy, Stl. (S.D.)	.20
☐	354	Al Hrabosky, Atl.	.20
☐	355	Bob Horner, Atl.	.20
☐	356	Cecil Cooper, Mil.	.20
☐	357	Bob Welch, L.A.	.20
☐	358	Paul Moskau, Cin.	.20
☐	359	Dave Rader, (Cal.)	.20
☐	360	Willie Wilson, K.C.	.20
☐	361	AS: Dave Kingman, Chi.-N.L.	.20
☐	362	Joe Rudi, (Bos.)	.20
☐	363	Rich Gale, K.C.	.20
☐	364	Steve Trout, Chi.-A.L.	.20
☐	365	Graig Nettles, NYY.	.20
☐	366	Lamar Johnson, Chi.-A.L.	.20
☐	367	Denny Martinez, Bal.	.20
☐	368	Manny Trillo, Pha.	.20
☐	369	Frank Tanana, (Bos.)	.20
☐	370	AS: Reggie Jackson, NYY.	2.50
☐	371	Bill Lee, Mtl.	.20
☐	372	Jay Johnstone, L.A.	.20
☐	373	Jason Thompson, Cal.	.20
☐	374	Tom Hutton, Mtl.	.20

POSTER INSERTS

These posters were folded twice and inserted in the regular wax packs.

Poster Size: 4 7/8" x 6 7/8"

Face: Four colour, white border; name, position, team, numbered _ of 24, bilingual

Back: Blank

Imprint: ©1981 O-Pee-Chee Co. Ltd. Printed in Canada - imprimé au Canada

Insert Set (24 posters): 15.00

	No.	Player	MINT
☐	1	Willie Montanez, Mtl.	.75
☐	2	Rodney Scott, Mtl.	.75
☐	3	Chris Speier, Mtl.	.75
☐	4	Larry Parrish, Mtl.	.75
☐	5	Warren Cromartie, Mtl.	.75
☐	6	André Dawson, Mtl.	2.50
☐	7	Ellis Valentine, Mtl.	.75
☐	8	Gary Carter, Mtl.	2.00
☐	9	Steve Rogers, Mtl.	1.00
☐	10	Woodie Fryman, Mtl.	.75
☐	11	Jerry White, Mtl.	.75
☐	12	Scott Sanderson, Mtl.	.75
☐	13	John Mayberry, Tor.	.75
☐	14	Damaso Garcia, Tor., Error (Damasa)	.75
☐	15	Alfredo Griffin, Tor.	.75
☐	16	Garth Iorg, Tor.	.75
☐	17	Alvis Woods, Tor.	.75
☐	18	Rick Bosetti, Tor.	.75
☐	19	Barry Bonnell, Tor.	.75
☐	20	Ernie Whitt, Tor.	.75
☐	21	Jim Clancy, Tor.	.75
☐	22	Dave Stieb, Tor.	1.50
☐	23	Otto Velez, Tor.	.75
☐	24	Lloyd Moseby, Tor.	1.25

1982 FBI FOODS BOX BOTTOMS

This set appeared on the bottom of FBI drink boxes. There were two round disks per box bottom. Each was perforated. A 50-100% premium applies to intact box bottoms. Four of the players remain unkown.

Card Size: 2 7/8" Diameter

Face: Black and white photo; name, position, team, colour FBI logo, bilingual

Back: Blank

Imprint: © 1982 M.L.B.P.A. M.S.A.

Complete Set (32 discs): 1,000.00

	Player	MINT
□	Vida Blue	30.00
□	George Brett, K.C.	75.00
□	Rod Carew, Cal.	60.00
□	Steve Carlton	60.00
□	Gary Carter, Mtl.	50.00
□	Warren Cromartie, Mtl.	30.00
□	Andre Dawson, Mtl.	50.00
□	Rollie Fingers, Mil.	50.00
□	Steve Garvey, L.A.	40.00
□	Rich Gossage, NYY.	40.00
□	Bill Gullickson, Mtl.	30.00
□	Steve Henderson, Chi.-N.L.	30.00
□	Keith Hernandez	30.00
□	John Mayberry, Tor.	30.00
□	Al Oliver	30.00
□	Dave Parker, Pgh.	40.00
□	Tim Raines, Mtl.	40.00
□	Jim Rice, Bos.	40.00
□	Steve Rogers, Mtl.	35.00
□	Pete Rose, Pha.	65.00
□	Nolan Ryan, Hou.	150.00
□	Mike Schmidt, Pha.	75.00
□	Tom Seaver, Cin.	60.00
□	Ken Singleton, Bal.	30.00
□	Dave Stieb, Tor.	40.00
□	Bruce Sutter, Stl.	40.00
□	Ellis Valentine, NYM.	30.00
□	Dave Winfield, NYY.	60.00

1982 O-PEE-CHEE

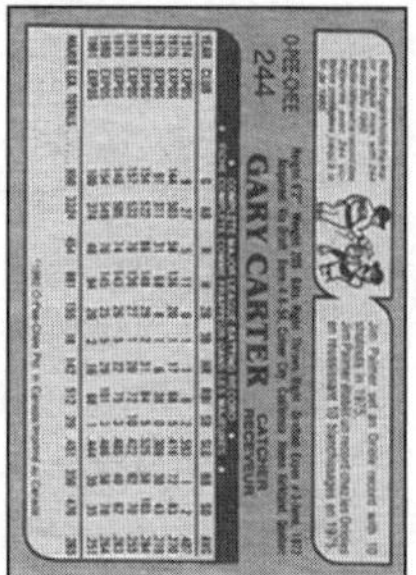

The card numbers on this 396-card set are not the same as those for the corresponding players in the 792-card Topps issue for 1982. Canadian cards bear the imprint "© 1982 O-Pee-Chee Ptd. in Canada/imprimé au Canada."

Card Size: 2 1/2" x 3 1/2"

Face: Four colour, white border; name, position, team, facsimile autograph, O-Pee-Chee logo

Back: Green and blue on card stock; number, position, résumé, trivia bilingual

Imprint: © O-Pee-Chee Ptd. in Canada/imprimé au Canada

Complete Set (396 cards): 60.00

Common Player: .20

	No.	Player	MINT
□	1	Dan Spillner, Cle.	.20
□	2	AS: Ken Singleton, Bal.	.20
□	3	John Candelaria, Pgh.	.20
□	4	Frank Tanana, (Tex.)	.20
□	5	Reggie Smith, L.A.	.20
□	6	Rick Monday, L.A.	.20
□	7	Scott Sanderson, Mtl.	.20
□	8	Rich Dauer, Bal.	.20
□	9	Ron Guidry, NYY.	.20
□	10	In Action: Ron Guidry, NYY.	.20
□	11	Tom Brookens, Det.	.20
□	12	Moose Haas, Mil.	.20
□	13	Chet Lemon, (Det.)	.20
□	14	Steve Howe, L.A.	.20
□	15	Ellis Valentine, NYM.	.20
□	16	Toby Harrah, Cle.	.20
□	17	Darrell Evans, S.F.	.20
□	18	Johnny Bench, Cin.	.75
□	19	Ernie Whitt, Tor.	.20
□	20	Garry Maddox, Pha.	.20
□	21	In Action: Graig Nettles, NYY.	.20
□	22	In Action: Al Oliver, Tex.	.20
□	23	Bob Boone, (Cal.)	.20
□	24	In Action: Pete Rose, Cal.	1.00
□	25	Jerry Remy, Bos.	.20
□	26	Jorge Orta, (L.A.)	.20
□	27	Bobby Bonds, Chi.-N.L.	.20
□	28	Jim Clancy, Tor.	.20
□	29	Dwayne Murphy, Oak.	.20
□	30	Tom Seaver, Cin.	2.00
□	31	In Action: Tom Seaver, Cin.	1.00
□	32	Claudell Washington, Atl.	.20
□	33	Bob Shirley, Stl.	.20
□	34	Bob Forsch, Stl.	.20
□	35	Willie Aikens, K.C.	.20
□	36	AS: Rod Carew, Cal.	.75
□	37	Willie Randolph, NYY.	.20
□	38	Charlie Lea, Mtl.	.20
□	39	Lou Whitaker, Det.	.20
□	40	Dave Parker, Pgh.	.20

	No.	Card	Price
☐	41	In Action: Dave Parker, Pgh.	.20
☐	42	Mark Belanger, (L.A.)	.20
☐	43	Rick Langford, Oak.	.20
☐	44	In Action: Rollie Fingers, Sea.	.35
☐	45	Rick Cerone, NYY.	.20
☐	46	Johnny Wockenfuss, Det.	.20
☐	47	AS: Jack Morris, Det.	.20
☐	48	Cesar Cedeno, (Cin.)	.20
☐	49	Alvis Woods, Tor.	.20
☐	50	Buddy Bell, Tex.	.20
☐	51	In Action: Mickey Rivers, Tex.	.20
☐	52	Steve Rogers, Mtl.	.20
☐	53	TC: John Mayberry/ Dave Stieb	.35
☐	54	Ron Hassey, Cle.	.20
☐	55	Rick Burleson, Cal.	.20
☐	56	Harold Baines, Chi.-A.L.	1.00
☐	57	Craig Reynolds, Hou.	.20
☐	58	AS: Carlton Fisk, Chi.-A.L.	.50
☐	59	Jim Kern, (Cin.)	.20
☐	60	Tony Armas, Oak.	.20
☐	61	Warren Cromartie, Mtl.	.20
☐	62	Graig Nettles, NYY.	.20
☐	63	Jerry Koosman, Chi.-A.L.	.20
☐	64	Pat Zachry, NYM.	.20
☐	65	Terry Kennedy, S.D.	.20
☐	66	Richie Zisk, Sea.	.20
☐	67	Rich Gale, (S.F.)	.20
☐	68	Steve Carlton, Pha.	1.50
☐	69	In Action: Greg Luzinski, Chi.-A.L.	.20
☐	70	Tim Raines, Mtl.	1.50
☐	71	Roy Lee Jackson, Tor.	.20
☐	72	Carl Yastrzemski, Bos.	.75
☐	73	John Castino, Min.	.20
☐	74	Joe Niekro, Hou.	.20
☐	75	Tommy John, NYY.	.20
☐	76	AS: Dave Winfield, NYY.	1.00
☐	77	Miguel Dilone, Cle.	.20
☐	78	Gary Gray, Sea.	.20
☐	79	Tom Hume, Cin.	.20
☐	80	Jim Palmer, Bal.	1.00
☐	81	In Action: Jim Palmer, Bal.	.50
☐	82	In Action: Vida Blue, S.F.	.20
☐	83	Garth Iorg, Tor.	.20
☐	84	Rennie Stennett, S.F.	.20
☐	85	In Action: Dave Lopes, (Oak.)	.20
☐	86	Dave Concepcion, Cin.	.20
☐	87	Matt Keough, Oak.	.20
☐	88	Jim Spencer, Oak.	.20
☐	89	Steve Henderson, Chi.-N.L.	.20
☐	90	Nolan Ryan, Hou.	10.00
☐	91	Carney Lansford, Bos.	.20
☐	92	Bake McBride, Pha.	.20
☐	93	Dave Stapleton, Bos.	.20
☐	94	TC: Warren Cromartie	.35
☐	95	Ozzie Smith, (Stl.)	4.00
☐	96	Rich Hebner, Det.	.20
☐	97	Tim Foli, (Cal.)	.20
☐	98	Darrell Porter, Stl.	.20
☐	99	Barry Bonnell, Tor.	.20
☐	100	Mike Schmidt, Pha.	2.00
☐	101	In Action: Mike Schmidt, Pha.	1.00
☐	102	Dan Briggs, Mtl.	.20
☐	103	Al Cowens, Det.	.20
☐	104	Grant Jackson, (K.C.)	.20
☐	105	Kirk Gibson, Det.	.50
☐	106	Dan Schatzeder, (S.F.)	.20
☐	107	Juan Berenguer, Tor.	.20
☐	108	Jack Morris, Det.	.75
☐	109	Dave Revering, NYY.	.20
☐	110	Carlton Fisk, Chi.-A.L.	1.00
☐	111	In Action: Carlton Fisk, Error	.20
☐	112	Billy Sample, Tex.	.50
☐	113	Steve McCatty, Oak.	.20
☐	114	Ken Landreaux, L.A.	.20
☐	115	Gaylord Perry, Atl.	.50
☐	116	Elias Sosa, Mtl.	.20
☐	117	In Action: Rich Gossage, NYY.	.20
☐	118	Mtl.: Terry Francona/ Brad Mills/ Bryn Smith	.20
☐	119	Billy Almon, Chi.-A.L.	.20
☐	120	Gary Lucas, S.D.	.20
☐	121	Ken Oberkfell, Stl.	.20
☐	122	In Action: Steve Carlton, Pha.	.75
☐	123	Jeff Reardon, Mtl.	.20
☐	124	Bill Buckner, Chi.-N.L.	.20
☐	125	Danny Ainge, Tor.	2.75
☐	126	Paul Splittorff, K.C.	.20
☐	127	Lonnie Smith, (Stl.)	.20
☐	128	Rudy May, NYY.	.20
☐	129	Checklist (1 - 132)	.35
☐	130	Julio Cruz, Sea.	.20
☐	131	Stan Bahnsen, Mtl.	.20
☐	132	Pete Vuckovich, Mil.	.20
☐	133	Luis Salazar, S.D.	.20
☐	134	Dan Ford, (Bal.)	.20
☐	135	Denny Martinez, Bal.	.35
☐	136	Lary Sorensen, (Cle.)	.20
☐	137	Fergie Jenkins, (Chi.-N.L.)	1.00
☐	138	Rick Camp, Atl.	.20
☐	139	Wayne Nordhagen, Chi.-A.L.	.20
☐	140	Ron LeFlore, Chi.-A.L.	.20
☐	141	Rick Sutcliffe, L.A.	.20
☐	142	Rick Waits, Cle.	.20
☐	143	Mookie Wilson, NYM.	.20
☐	144	Greg Minton, S.F.	.20
☐	145	Bob Horner, Atl.	.20
☐	146	In Action: Joe Morgan, S.F.	.35
☐	147	Larry Gura, K.C.	.20
☐	148	Alfredo Griffin, Tor.	.20
☐	149	Pat Putnam, Tex.	.20
☐	150	Ted Simmons, Mil.	.20
☐	151	Gary Matthews, Pha.	.20
☐	152	Greg Luzinski, Chi.-A.L.	.20
☐	153	Mike Flanagan, Bal.	.20
☐	154	Jim Morrison, Chi.-A.L.	.20
☐	155	Otto Velez, Tor.	.20
☐	156	Frank White, K.C.	.20
☐	157	Doug Corbett, Min.	.20
☐	158	Brian Downing, Cal.	.20
☐	159	In Action: Willie Randolph, NYY.	.20
☐	160	Luis Tiant, Pgh.	.20
☐	161	Andre Thornton, Cle.	.20
☐	162	Amos Otis, K.C.	.20
☐	163	Paul Mirabella, Tor.	.20
☐	164	Bert Blyleven, Cle.	.20
☐	165	Rowland Office, Mtl.	.20
☐	166	Gene Tenace, Stl.	.20
☐	167	Cecil Cooper, Mil.	.20
☐	168	Bruce Benedict, Atl.	.20
☐	169	Mark Clear, Bos.	.20
☐	170	Jim Bibby, Pgh.	.20
☐	171	In Action: Ken Griffey, (NYY.)	.20
☐	172	Bill Gullickson, Mtl.	.20
☐	173	Mike Scioscia, L.A.	.20
☐	174	Doug DeCinces, (Cal.)	.20
☐	175	Jerry Mumphrey, NYY.	.20
☐	176	Rollie Fingers, Mil.	.50
☐	177	In Action: George Foster, (NYM.)	.20
☐	178	Mitchell Page, Oak.	.20

☐	179	Steve Garvey, L.A.	.35
☐	180	In Action: Steve Garvey, L.A.	.20
☐	181	Woodie Fryman, Mtl.	.20
☐	182	Larry Herndon, (Det.)	.20
☐	183	In Action: Frank White, K.C.	.20
☐	184	Alan Ashby, Hou.	.20
☐	185	Phil Niekro, Atl.	.50
☐	186	Leon Roberts, Tex.	.20
☐	187	Rod Carew, Cal.	1.25
☐	188	In Action: Willie Stargell, Pgh.	.35
☐	189	Joel Youngblood, NYM.	.20
☐	190	J.R. Richard, Hou.	.20
☐	**191**	**Tim Wallach, Mtl., RC**	**.75**
☐	192	Broderick Perkins, S.D.	.20
☐	193	Johnny Grubb, Tex.	.20
☐	194	Larry Bowa, (Chi.-N.L.)	.20
☐	195	Paul Molitor, Mil.	2.00
☐	196	Willie Upshaw, Tor.	.20
☐	197	Roy Smalley, Min.	.20
☐	198	Chris Speier, Mtl.	.20
☐	199	Don Aase, Cal.	.20
☐	200	George Brett, K.C.	3.50
☐	201	In Action: George Brett, K.C.	2.00
☐	202	Rick Manning, Cle.	.20
☐	**203**	**Tor.: Jesse Barfield/ Brian Milner/ Boomer Wells, RCs**	**.75**
☐	204	Rick Reuschel, NYY.	.20
☐	205	Neil Allen, NYM.	.20
☐	206	Leon Durham, Chi.-N.L.	.20
☐	207	Jim Gantner, Mil.	.20
☐	208	Joe Morgan, S.F.	.75
☐	209	Gary Lavelle, S.F.	.20
☐	210	Keith Hernandez, Stl.	.20
☐	211	Joe Charboneau, Cle.	.20
☐	212	Mario Mendoza, Tex.	.20
☐	213	AS: Willie Randolph, NYY.	.20
☐	214	Lance Parrish, Det.	.20
☐	215	Mike Krukow, (Pha.)	.20
☐	216	Ron Cey, L.A.	.20
☐	217	Ruppert Jones, S.D.	.20
☐	218	Dave Lopes, (Oak.)	.20
☐	219	Steve Yeager, L.A.	.20
☐	220	Manny Trillo, Pha.	.20
☐	221	In Action: Dave Concepcion, Cin.	.20
☐	222	Butch Wynegar, Min.	.20
☐	223	Lloyd Moseby, Tor.	.30
☐	224	Bruce Bochte, Sea.	.20
☐	225	Ed Ott, Cal.	.20
☐	226	Checklist (133 - 264)	.35
☐	227	Ray Burris, Mtl.	.20
☐	228	In Action: Reggie Smith, L.A.	.20
☐	229	Oscar Gamble, NYY.	.20
☐	230	Willie Wilson, K.C.	.20
☐	231	Brian Kingman, Oak.	.20
☐	232	John Stearns, NYM.	.20
☐	233	Duane Kuiper, (S.F.)	.20
☐	234	Don Baylor, Cal.	.20
☐	235	Mike Easler, Pgh.	.20
☐	236	Lou Piniella, NYY.	.20
☐	237	Robin Yount, Mil.	1.25
☐	238	Kevin Saucier, Det.	.20
☐	239	Jon Matlack, Tex.	.20
☐	240	Bucky Dent, NYY.	.20
☐	241	In Action: Bucky Dent, NYY.	.20
☐	242	Milt May, S.F.	.20
☐	243	Lee Mazzilli, NYM.	.20
☐	244	Gary Carter, Mtl.	.75
☐	245	Ken Reitz, Chi.-N.L.	.20
☐	246	AS: Scott McGregor, Bal.	.20
☐	247	Pedro Guerrero, L.A.	.20
☐	248	Art Howe, Hou.	.20
☐	249	Dick Tidrow, Chi.-N.L.	.20
☐	250	Tug McGraw, Pha.	.20
☐	251	Fred Lynn, Cal.	.20
☐	252	In Action: Fred Lynn, Cal.	.20
☐	253	Gene Richards, S.D.	.20
☐	**254**	**Jorge Bell, Tor., RC**	**1.00**
☐	255	Tony Perez, Bos.	.35
☐	256	In Action: Tony Perez, Bos.	.20
☐	257	Rich Dotson, Chi.-A.L.	.20
☐	258	Bo Diaz, (Pha.)	.20
☐	259	Rodney Scott, Mtl.	.20
☐	260	Bruce Sutter, Stl.	.20
☐	261	AS: George Brett, K.C.	2.50
☐	262	Rick Dempsey, Bal.	.20
☐	263	Mike Phillips, Mtl.	.20
☐	264	Jerry Garvin, Tor.	.20
☐	265	Al Bumbry, Bal.	.20
☐	266	Hubie Brooks, NYM.	.20
☐	267	Vida Blue, S.F.	.20
☐	268	Rickey Henderson, Oak.	3.00
☐	269	Rick Peters, Det.	.20
☐	270	Rusty Staub, NYM.	.50
☐	271	Sixto Lezcano, (S.D.)	.20
☐	272	Bump Wills, Tex.	.20
☐	273	Gary Allenson, Bos.	.20
☐	274	Randy Jones, NYM.	.20
☐	275	Bob Watson, NYY.	.20
☐	276	Dave Kingman, NYM.	.20
☐	277	Terry Puhl, Hou.	.35
☐	278	Jerry Reuss, L.A.	.20
☐	279	Sammy Stewart, Bal.	.20
☐	280	Ben Oglivie, Mil.	.20
☐	281	Kent Tekulve, Pgh.	.20
☐	282	Ken Macha, Tor.	.20
☐	283	Ron Davis, NYY.	.20
☐	284	Bob Grich, Cal.	.20
☐	285	Sparky Lyle, Pha.	.20
☐	286	AS: Rich Gossage, NYY.	.20
☐	287	Dennis Eckersley, Bos.	.20
☐	288	Garry Templeton, (S.D.)	.20
☐	289	Bob Stanley, Bos.	.20
☐	290	Ken Singleton, Bal.	.20
☐	291	Mickey Hatcher, Min.	.20
☐	292	Dave Palmer, Mtl.	.20
☐	293	Damaso Garcia, Tor.	.20
☐	294	Don Money, Mil.	.20
☐	295	George Hendrick, Stl.	.20
☐	296	Steve Kemp, (Chi.-A.L.)	.20
☐	297	Dave Smith, Hou.	.20
☐	298	AS: Bucky Dent, NYY.	.20
☐	299	Steve Trout, Chi.-A.L.	.20
☐	300	Reggie Jackson, (Cal.)	2.00
☐	301	In Action: Reggie Jackson, (Cal.)	1.00
☐	302	Doug Flynn, (Tex.)	.20
☐	303	Wayne Gross, Oak.	.20
☐	304	In Action: Johnny Bench, Cin.	.50
☐	305	Don Sutton, Hou.	.50
☐	306	In Action: Don Sutton, Hou.	.35
☐	307	Mark Bomback, Tor.	.20
☐	308	Charlie Moore, Mil.	.20
☐	309	Jeff Burroughs, Sea.	.20
☐	310	Mike Hargrove, Cle.	.20
☐	311	Enos Cabell, S.F.	.20
☐	312	Lenny Randle, Sea.	.20
☐	313	Ivan DeJesus, (Pha.)	.20
☐	314	Buck Martinez, Tor.	.20
☐	315	Burt Hooton, L.A.	.20
☐	316	Scott McGregor, Bal.	.20

	No.	Player	Price
☐	317	Dick Ruthven, Pha.	.20
☐	318	Mike Heath, Oak.	.20
☐	319	Ray Knight, (Hou.)	.20
☐	320	Chris Chambliss, Atl.	.20
☐	321	In Action: Chris Chambliss, Atl.	.20
☐	322	Ross Baumgarten, Chi.-A.L.	.20
☐	323	Bill Lee, Mtl.	.20
☐	324	Gorman Thomas, Mil.	.20
☐	325	Jose Cruz, Hou.	.20
☐	326	Al Oliver, Tex.	.20
☐	327	Jackson Todd, Tor.	.20
☐	328	Ed Farmer, (Pha.)	.20
☐	329	U.L. Washington, K.C.	.20
☐	330	Ken Griffey, (NYY.)	.35
☐	331	John Milner, Mtl.	.20
☐	332	Don Robinson, Pgh.	.20
☐	333	Cliff Johnson, Oak.	.20
☐	334	Fernando Valenzuela, L.A.	.50
☐	335	Jim Sundberg, Tex.	.20
☐	336	George Foster, (NYM.)	.20
☐	337	AS: Pete Rose, Pha.	1.00
☐	338	AS: Dave Lopes, (Oak.)	1.00
☐	339	AS: Mike Schmidt, Pha.	.20
☐	340	AS: Dave Concepcion, Cin.	.20
☐	341	AS: Andre Dawson, Mtl.	1.00
☐	342	AS: George Foster, (NYM.)	.20
☐	343	AS: Dave Parker, Pgh.	.20
☐	344	AS: Gary Carter, Mtl.	.50
☐	345	AS: Fernando Valenzuela, L.A.	.35
☐	346	AS: Tom Seaver, Chi.-N.L.	1.00
☐	347	AS: Bruce Sutter, Stl.	.20
☐	348	In Action: Darrell Porter, Stl.	.20
☐	349	Dave Collins, (NYY.)	.20
☐	350	In Action: Amos Otis, K.C.	.20
☐	351	Frank Taveras, (Mtl.)	.20
☐	352	Dave Winfield, NYY.	1.25
☐	353	Larry Parrish, Mtl.	.20
☐	354	Roberto Ramos, Mtl.	.20
☐	355	Dwight Evans, Bos.	.20
☐	356	Mickey Rivers, Tex.	.20
☐	357	Butch Hobson, Cal.	.20
☐	358	In Action: Carl Yastrzemski, Bos.	.50
☐	359	Ron Jackson, Det.	.20
☐	360	Len Barker, Cle.	.20
☐	361	Pete Rose, Pha.	2.00
☐	**362**	**Kevin Hickey, Chi.-A.L., RC**	**.20**
☐	363	In Action: Rod Carew, Cal.	.75
☐	364	Hector Cruz, Chi.-N.L.	.20
☐	365	Bill Madlock, Pgh.	.20
☐	366	Jim Rice, Bos.	.20
☐	367	In Action: Ron Cey, L.A.	.20
☐	368	Luis Leal, Tor.	.20
☐	369	Dennis Leonard, K.C.	.20
☐	370	Mike Norris, Oak.	.20
☐	371	Tom Paciorek, (Chi.-A.L.)	.20
☐	372	Willie Stargell, Pgh.	.75
☐	373	Dan Driessen, Cin.	.20
☐	374	In Action: Larry Bowa, (Chi.-N.L.)	.20
☐	375	Dusty Baker, L.A.	.20
☐	376	Joey McLaughlin, Tor.	.20
☐	377	AS: Reggie Jackson, (Cal.)	1.00
☐	378	Mike Caldwell, Mil.	.20
☐	379	Andre Dawson, Mtl.	2.00
☐	380	Dave Stieb, Tor.	.20
☐	381	Alan Trammell, Det.	.20
☐	382	John Mayberry, Tor.	.20
☐	383	John Wathan, K.C.	.20
☐	384	Hal McRae, K.C.	.20
☐	385	Ken Forsch, Cal.	.20
☐	386	Jerry White, Mtl.	.20
☐	387	Tom Veryzer, (NYM.)	.20
☐	388	Joe Rudi, (Oak.)	.20
☐	389	Bob Knepper, Hou.	.20
☐	390	Eddie Murray, Bal.	2.50
☐	391	Dale Murphy, Atl.	.50
☐	392	In Action: Bob Boone, (Cal.)	.20
☐	393	Al Hrabosky, Atl.	.20
☐	394	Checklist (265 - 396)	.35
☐	395	Omar Moreno, Pgh.	.20
☐	396	Rich Gossage, NYY.	.20

1982 POSTER INSERTS

These posters were inserted into O-Pee-Chee wax packs in 1982.

Poster Size: 4 7/78" x 6 7/8"

Face: Four colour; name, position, team, numbered _ of 24, bilingual

Back: Blank

Imprint: © 1982 O-Pee-Chee Co. Ltd. Printed in Canada - imprimé au Canada

Complete Set (24 posters): 15.00

	No.	**Player**	**MINT**
☐	1	John Mayberry, Tor.	.75
☐	2	Damaso Garcia, Tor.	.75
☐	3	Ernie Whitt, Tor.	.75
☐	4	Lloyd Moseby, Tor.	.75
☐	5	Alvis Woods, Tor.	.75
☐	6	Dave Stieb, Tor.	.75
☐	7	Roy Lee Jackson, Tor.	.75
☐	8	Joey McLaughlin, Tor.	.75
☐	9	Luis Leal, Tor.	.75
☐	10	Aurelio Rodriguez, Tor.	.75
☐	11	Otto Velez, Tor.	.75
☐	12	Juan Berenguer, Tor., Error	.75
☐	13	Warren Cromartie, Mtl.	.75
☐	14	Rodney Scott, Mtl.	.75
☐	15	Larry Parrish, Mtl.	.75
☐	16	Gary Carter, Mtl.	2.00
☐	17	Tim Raines, Mtl.	1.50
☐	18	Andre Dawson, Mtl.	2.50
☐	19	Terry Francona, Mtl.	.75
☐	20	Steve Rogers, Mtl.	1.00
☐	21	Bill Gullickson, Mtl.	.75
☐	22	Scott Sanderson, Mtl.	.75
☐	23	Jeff Reardon, Mtl.	.75
☐	24	Jerry White, Mtl.	.75

1982 O-PEE-CHEE STICKERS

These stickers were produced in Italy by Panini for O-Pee-Chee.
Sticker Size: 1 15/16" x 2 9/16"
Face: Four colour, coloured border; name
Back: Black print on card stock; name, number, position, bilingual
Imprint: © 1982 O-PEE-CHEE CO., LTD.

Complete Set (260 stickers):		**40.00**
Album Price:		**6.00**
Common Player:		**.20**

	No.	Player	MINT
☐	1	LL: Bill Madlock, Pgh.	.20
☐	2	LL: Carney Lansford, Bos.	.20
☐	3	LL: Mike Schmidt, Pha.	.50
☐	4	LL: A: T. Armas.; B: D. Evans; C: B. Grich; D: E. Murray	.50
☐	5	LL: Mike Schmidt, Pha.	.50
☐	6	LL: Eddie Murray, Bal.	.50
☐	7	LL: Tim Raines, Mtl.	.20
☐	8	LL: Rickey Henderson, Oak.	.50
☐	9	LL: Tom Seaver, Cin.	.20
☐	10	LL: A: D. Martinez; B: S. McCatty; C: J. Morris; D: P. Vuckovich, Mil.	.20
☐	11	LL: Fernando Valenzuela, L.A.	.20
☐	12	LL: Len Barker, Cle.	.20
☐	13	LL: Nolan Ryan, Hou.	2.00
☐	14	LL: Steve McCatty, Oak.	.20
☐	15	LL: Bruce Sutter, Stl.	.20
☐	16	LL: Rollie Fingers, Mil.	.20
☐	17	Chris Chambliss, Atl.	.20
☐	18	Bob Horner, Atl.	.20
☐	19	Dale Murphy, Atl.	.20
☐	20	Phil Niekro, Atl.	.50
☐	21	Bruce Benedict, Atl.	.20
☐	22	Claudell Washington, Atl.	.20
☐	23	Glenn Hubbard, Atl.	.20
☐	24	Rick Camp, Atl.	.20
☐	25	Leon Durham, Chi.	.20
☐	26	Ken Reitz, Chi.	.20
☐	27	Dick Tidrow, Chi.	.20
☐	28	Tim Blackwell, Chi.	.20
☐	29	Bill Buckner, Chi.	.20
☐	30	Steve Henderson, Chi.	.20
☐	31	Mike Krukow, Chi.	.20
☐	32	Ivan DeJesus, Chi.	.20
☐	33	Dave Collins, Cin.	.20
☐	34	Ron Oester, Cin.	.20
☐	35	Johnny Bench, Cin.	.60
☐	36	Tom Seaver, Cin.	.75
☐	37	Dave Concepcion, Cin.	.20
☐	38	Tom Hume, Cin.	.20
☐	39	Ray Knight, Cin.	.20
☐	40	George Foster, Cin.	.20
☐	41	Nolan Ryan, Hou.	4.00
☐	42	Terry Puhl, Hou.	.35
☐	43	Art Howe, Hou.	.20
☐	44	Jose Cruz, Hou.	.20
☐	45	Bob Knepper, Hou.	.20
☐	46	Craig Reynolds, Hou.	.20
☐	47	Cesar Cedeno, Hou.	.20
☐	48	Alan Ashby, Hou.	.20
☐	49	Ken Landreaux, L.A.	.20
☐	50	Fernando Valenzuela, L.A.	.20
☐	51	Ron Cey, L.A.	.20
☐	52	Dusty Baker, L.A.	.20
☐	53	Burt Hooton, L.A.	.20
☐	54	Steve Garvey, L.A.	.35
☐	55	Pedro Guerrero, L.A.	.20
☐	56	Jerry Reuss, L.A.	.20
☐	57	Andre Dawson, Mtl.	.35
☐	58	Chris Speier, Mtl.	.20
☐	59	Steve Rogers, Mtl.	.35
☐	60	Warren Cromartie, Mtl.	.20
☐	61	Gary Carter, Mtl.	.35
☐	62	Tim Raines, Mtl.	.35
☐	63	Scott Sanderson, Mtl.	.20
☐	64	Larry Parrish, Mtl.	.20
☐	65	Joel Youngblood, NYM.	.20
☐	66	Neil Allen, NYM.	.20
☐	67	Lee Mazzilli, NYM.	.20
☐	68	Hubie Brooks, NYM.	.20
☐	69	Ellis Valentine, NYM.	.20
☐	70	Doug Flynn, NYM.	.20
☐	71	Pat Zachry, NYM.	.20
☐	72	Dave Kingman, NYM.	.20
☐	73	Garry Maddox, Pha.	.20
☐	74	Mike Schmidt, Pha.	1.00
☐	75	Steve Carlton, Pha.	.75
☐	76	Manny Trillo, Pha.	.20
☐	77	Bob Boone, Pha.	.20
☐	78	Pete Rose, Pha.	1.00
☐	79	Gary Matthews, Pha.	.20
☐	80	Larry Bowa, Pha.	.20
☐	81	Omar Moreno, Pgh.	.20
☐	82	Rick Rhoden, Pgh.	.20
☐	83	Bill Madlock, Pgh.	.20
☐	84	Mike Easler, Pgh.	.20
☐	85	Willie Stargell, Pgh.	.50
☐	86	Jim Bibby, Pgh.	.20
☐	87	Dave Parker, Pgh.	.20
☐	88	Tim Foli, Pgh.	.20
☐	89	Ken Oberkfell, Stl.	.20
☐	90	Bob Forsch, Stl.	.20
☐	91	George Hendrick, Stl.	.20
☐	92	Keith Hernandez, Stl.	.20
☐	93	Darrell Porter, Stl.	.20
☐	94	Bruce Sutter, Stl.	.20
☐	95	Sixto Lezcano, Stl.	.20
☐	96	Garry Templeton, Stl.	.20
☐	97	Juan Eichelberger, S.D.	.20
☐	98	Broderick Perkins, S.D.	.20
☐	99	Ruppert Jones, S.D.	.20
☐	100	Terry Kennedy, S.D.	.20
☐	101	Luis Salazar, S.D.	.20
☐	102	Gary Lucas, S.D.	.20
☐	103	Gene Richards, S.D.	.20
☐	104	Ozzie Smith, S.D.	1.50
☐	105	Enos Cabell, S.F.	.20
☐	106	Jack Clark, S.F.	.20
☐	107	Greg Minton, S.F.	.20
☐	108	Johnnie LeMaster, S.F.	.20
☐	109	Larry Herndon, S.F.	.20
☐	110	Milt May, S.F.	.20
☐	111	Vida Blue, S.F.	.20

☐ 112 Darrell Evans, S.F. .20
☐ 113 HL: Len Barker, Cle. .20
☐ 114 HL: Julio Cruz, Sea. .20
☐ 115 HL: Billy Martin, Coach, Oak. .20
☐ 116 HL: Tim Raines, Mtl. .20
☐ 117 HL: Pete Rose, Pha. .50
☐ 118 HL: Bill Stein, Tex. .20
☐ 119 HL: Fernando Valenzuela, L.A. .20
☐ 120 HL: Carl Yastrzemski, Bos. .50
☐ 121 AS: Pete Rose, Pha. .50
☐ 122 AS: Manny Trillo, Pha. .20
☐ 123 AS: Mike Schmidt, Pha. .50
☐ 124 AS: Dave Concepcion, Cin. .20
☐ 125 AS: Andre Dawson, Mtl. .20
☐ 126 AS: George Foster, Cin. .20
☐ 127 AS: Dave Parker, Pgh. .20
☐ 128 AS: Gary Carter, Mtl. .20
☐ 129 AS: Steve Carlton, Pha. .50
☐ 130 AS: Bruce Sutter, Stl. .20
☐ 131 AS: Rod Carew, Cal. .35
☐ 132 AS: Jerry Remy, Bos. .20
☐ 133 AS: George Brett, K.C. 1.00
☐ 134 AS: Rick Burleson, Cal. .20
☐ 135 AS: Dwight Evans, Bos. .20
☐ 136 AS: Ken Singleton, Bal. .20
☐ 137 AS: Dave Winfield, NYY. .50
☐ 138 AS: Carlton Fisk, Chi.-A.L. .35
☐ 139 AS: Jack Morris, Det. .20
☐ 140 AS: Rich Gossage, NYY. .20
☐ 141 Al Bumbry, Bal. .20
☐ 142 Doug DeCinces, Bal. .20
☐ 143 Scott McGregor, Bal. .20
☐ 144 Ken Singleton, Bal. .20
☐ 145 Eddie Murray, Bal. 1.25
☐ 146 Jim Palmer, Bal. .50
☐ 147 Rich Dauer, Bal. .20
☐ 148 Mike Flanagan, Bal. .20
☐ 149 Jerry Remy, Bos. .20
☐ 150 Jim Rice, Bos. .20
☐ 151 Mike Torrez, Bos. .20
☐ 152 Tony Perez, Bos. .35
☐ 153 Dwight Evans, Bos. .20
☐ 154 Mark Clear, Bos. .20
☐ 155 Carl Yastrzemski, Bos. .75
☐ 156 Carney Lansford, Bos. .20
☐ 157 Rick Burleson, Cal. .20
☐ 158 Don Baylor, Cal. .20
☐ 159 Ken Forsch, Cal. .20
☐ 160 Rod Carew, Cal. .50
☐ 161 Fred Lynn, Cal. .20
☐ 162 Bob Grich, Cal. .20
☐ 163 Dan Ford, Cal. .20
☐ 164 Butch Hobson, Cal. .20
☐ 165 Greg Luzinski, Chi.-A.L. .20
☐ 166 Rich Dotson, Chi.-A.L. .20
☐ 167 Billy Almon, Chi.-A.L. .20
☐ 168 Chet Lemon, Chi.-A.L. .20
☐ 169 Steve Trout, Chi.-A.L. .20
☐ 170 Carlton Fisk, Chi.-A.L. .60
☐ 171 Tony Bernazard, Chi.-A.L. .20
☐ 172 Ron LeFlore, Chi.-A.L. .20
☐ 173 Bert Blyleven, Cle. .20
☐ 174 Andre Thornton, Cle. .20
☐ 175 Jorge Orta, Cle. .20
☐ 176 Bo Diaz, Cle. .20
☐ 177 Toby Harrah, Cle. .20
☐ 178 Len Barker, Cle. .20
☐ 179 Rick Manning, Cle. .20
☐ 180 Mike Hargrove, Cle. .20
☐ 181 Alan Trammell, Det. .20
☐ 182 Al Cowens, Det. .20
☐ 183 Jack Morris, Det. .20
☐ 184 Kirk Gibson, Det. .20
☐ 185 Steve Kemp, Det. .20
☐ 186 Milt Wilcox, Det. .20
☐ 187 Lou Whitaker, Det. .20
☐ 188 Lance Parrish, Det. .20
☐ 189 Willie Wilson, K.C. .20
☐ 190 George Brett, K.C. 2.00
☐ 191 Dennis Leonard, K.C. .20
☐ 192 John Wathan, K.C. .20
☐ 193 Frank White, K.C. .20
☐ 194 Amos Otis, K.C. .20
☐ 195 Larry Gura, K.C. .20
☐ 196 Willie Aikens, K.C. .20
☐ 197 Ben Oglivie, Mil. .20
☐ 198 Rollie Fingers, Mil. .35
☐ 199 Cecil Cooper, Mil. .20
☐ 200 Paul Molitor, Mil. 1.50
☐ 201 Ted Simmons, Mil. .20
☐ 202 Pete Vuckovich, Mil. .20
☐ 203 Robin Yount, Mil. 1.00
☐ 204 Gorman Thomas, Mil. .20
☐ 205 Rob Wilfong, Min. .20
☐ 206 Hosken Powell, Min. .20
☐ 207 Roy Smalley, Min. .20
☐ 208 Butch Wynegar, Min. .20
☐ 209 John Castino, Min. .20
☐ 210 Doug Corbett, Min. .20
☐ 211 Roger Erickson, Min. .20
☐ 212 Mickey Hatcher, Min. .20
☐ 213 Dave Winfield, NYY. 1.00
☐ 214 Tommy John, NYY. .20
☐ 215 Graig Nettles, NYY. .20
☐ 216 Reggie Jackson, NYY. 1.00
☐ 217 Rich Gossage, NYY. .20
☐ 218 Rick Cerone, NYY. .20
☐ 219 Willie Randolph, NYY. .20
☐ 220 Jerry Mumphrey, NYY. .20
☐ 221 Rickey Henderson, Oak. 1.00
☐ 222 Mike Norris, Oak. .20
☐ 223 Jim Spencer, Oak. .20
☐ 224 Tony Armas, Oak. .20
☐ 225 Matt Keough, Oak. .20
☐ 226 Cliff Johnson, Oak. .20
☐ 227 Dwayne Murphy, Oak. .20
☐ 228 Steve McCatty, Oak. .20
☐ 229 Richie Zisk, Sea. .20
☐ 230 Lenny Randle, Sea. .20
☐ 231 Jeff Burroughs, Sea. .20
☐ 232 Bruce Bochte, Sea. .20
☐ 233 Gary Gray, Sea. .20
☐ 234 Floyd Bannister, Sea. .20
☐ 235 Julio Cruz, Sea. .20
☐ 236 Tom Paciorek, Sea. .20
☐ 237 Danny Darwin, Tex. .20
☐ 238 Buddy Bell, Tex. .20
☐ 239 Al Oliver, Tex. .20
☐ 240 Jim Sundberg, Tex. .20
☐ 241 Pat Putnam, Tex. .20
☐ 242 Steve Comer, Tex. .20
☐ 243 Mickey Rivers, Tex. .20
☐ 244 Bump Wills, Tex. .20
☐ 245 Damaso Garcia, Tor. .20
☐ 246 Lloyd Moseby, Tor. .20
☐ 247 Ernie Whitt, Tor. .20
☐ 248 John Mayberry, Tor. .20
☐ 249 Otto Velez, Tor. .20

	No.	Player	MINT
☐	250	Dave Stieb, Tor.	.20
☐	251	Barry Bonnell, Tor.	.20
☐	252	Alfredo Griffin, Tor.	.20
☐	253	1981 N.L. Championship: Dodgers edge Montreal in 5	.50
☐	254	1981 A.L. Championship: Yankees sweep A's	.50
☐	255	Los Angeles Dodgers	.35
☐	256	Los Angeles Dodgers	.35
☐	257	Game 3	.35
☐	258	Game 4	.35
☐	259	Game 5	.35
☐	260	Game 6	.35

1983 O-PEE-CHEE

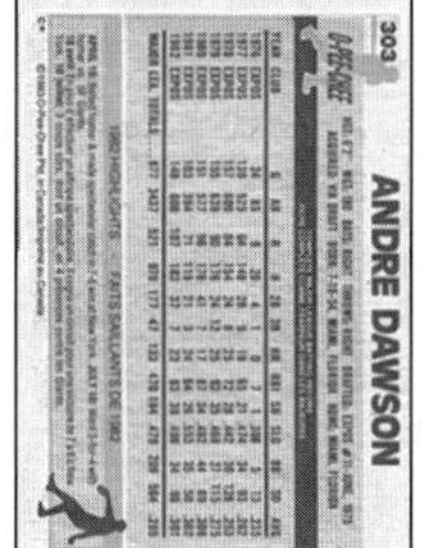

The card numbers in this 396-card set are not the same as those for the corresponding players in the 792-card Topps issue for 1983. This set is one of the more popular O-Pee-Chee baseball card series. It marked the first time dual pictures appeared on the front of O-Pee-Chee cards. The set also contains Rookie cards for Ryne Sandberg (#83) and Tony Gwynn (#143).

Card Size: 2 1/2" x 3 1/2"
Face: Four colour, white border; name, position, team
Back: Orange and black on card stock; name, number, résumé, highlights, bilingual
Imprint: A, B, C, D or E* © 1983 O-Pee-Chee Ptd. in Canada/imprimé au Canada

Complete Set (396 cards): 75.00
Common Player: .20

	No.	Player	MINT
☐	1	Rusty Staub, NYM.	.50
☐	2	Larry Parrish, Tex.	.20
☐	3	George Brett, K.C.	3.00
☐	4	Carl Yastrzemski, Bos.	1.00
☐	5	Super Veteran: Al Oliver, Mtl.	.20
☐	6	Bill Virdon, Manager, Mtl.	.20
☐	7	Gene Richards, S.D.	.20
☐	8	Steve Balboni, NYY.	.20
☐	9	Joey McLaughlin, Tor.	.20
☐	10	Gorman Thomas, Mil.	.20
☐	11	Chris Chambliss, Atl.	.20
☐	12	Ray Burris, Mtl.	.20
☐	13	Larry Herndon, Det.	.20
☐	14	Ozzie Smith, Stl.	3.00
☐	15	Ron Cey, (Chi.-N.L.)	.20
☐	16	Willie Wilson, K.C.	.20
☐	17	Kent Tekulve, Pgh.	.20
☐	18	Super Veteran: Kent Tekulve, Pgh.	.20
☐	19	Oscar Gamble, NYY.	.20
☐	20	Carlton Fisk, Chi.-A.L.	1.00
☐	21	N.L. All Star: Dale Murphy, Atl.	.20
☐	22	Randy Lerch, Mtl.	.20
☐	23	Dale Murphy, Atl.	.20
☐	24	Steve Mura, (Chi.-A.L.)	.20
☐	25	Hal McRae, K.C.	.20
☐	26	Dennis Lamp, Chi.-A.L.	.20
☐	27	Ron Washington, Min.	.20
☐	28	Bruce Bochte, Sea.	.20
☐	29	Randy Jones, (Pgh.)	.20
☐	30	Jim Rice, Bos.	.20
☐	31	Bill Gullickson, Mtl.	.20
☐	32	AS: Dave Concepcion, Cin.	.20
☐	33	Super Veteran: Ted Simmons, Mil.	.20
☐	34	Bobby Cox, Manager, Tor.	.20
☐	35	Rollie Fingers, Mil.	.50
☐	36	Super Veteran: Rollie Fingers, Mil.	.35
☐	37	Mike Hargrove, Cle.	.20
☐	38	Roy Smalley, NYY.	.20
☐	39	Terry Puhl, Hou.	.35
☐	40	Fernando Valenzuela, L.A.	.20
☐	41	Garry Maddox, Pha.	.20
☐	42	Dale Murray, (NYY.)	.20
☐	43	Bob Dernier, Pha.	.20
☐	44	Don Robinson, Pgh.	.20
☐	45	John Mayberry, NYY.	.20
☐	46	Richard Dotson, Chi.-A.L.	.20
☐	47	Wayne Nordhagen, (Chi.-N.L.)	.20
☐	48	Lary Sorensen, Cle.	.20
☐	**49**	**Willie McGee, Stl., RC**	**.75**
☐	50	Bob Horner, Atl.	.20
☐	51	Super Veteran: Rusty Staub, NYM.	.35
☐	52	Tom Seaver, (NYM.)	2.00
☐	53	Chet Lemon, Det.	.20
☐	54	Scott Sanderson, Mtl.	.20
☐	55	Mookie Wilson, NYM.	.20
☐	56	Reggie Jackson, Cal.	2.00
☐	57	Tim Blackwell, Mtl.	.20
☐	58	Keith Moreland, Chi.-N.L.	.20
☐	59	Alvis Woods, (Oak.)	.20
☐	60	Johnny Bench, Cin.	1.50
☐	61	Super Veteran: Johnny Bench, Cin.	.75
☐	**62**	**Jim Gott, Tor., RC**	**.20**
☐	63	Rick Monday, L.A.	.20
☐	64	Gary Matthews, Pha.	.20
☐	65	Jack Morris, Det.	.75
☐	66	Lou Whitaker, Det.	.20
☐	67	U.L. Washinton, K.C.	.20
☐	68	Eric Show, S.D.	.20
☐	69	Lee Lacy, Pgh.	.20
☐	70	Steve Carlton, Pha.	1.50
☐	71	Super Veteran: Steve Carlton, Pgh.	.75
☐	72	Tom Paciorek, Chi.-A.L.	.20
☐	73	Manny Trillo, (Cle.)	.20
☐	74	Super Veteran: Tony Perez, (Pha.)	.20
☐	75	Amos Otis, K.C.	.20
☐	76	Rick Mahler, Atl.	.20
☐	77	Hosken Powell, Tor.	.20
☐	78	Bill Caudill, Sea.	.20
☐	79	Dan Petry, Det.	.20
☐	80	George Foster, NYM.	.20
☐	81	Joe Morgan, (Pha.)	.75
☐	82	Burt Hooton, L.A.	.20
☐	**83**	**Ryne Sandberg, Chi.-N.L., RC**	**25.00**
☐	84	Alan Ashby, Hou.	.20
☐	85	Ken Singleton, Bal.	.20
☐	86	Tom Hume, Cin.	.20
☐	87	Dennis Leonard, K.C.	.20
☐	88	Jim Gantner, Mil.	.20
☐	89	Leon Roberts, (K.C.)	.20
☐	90	Jerry Reuss, L.A.	.20
☐	91	Ben Oglivie, Mil.	.20
☐	92	Super Veteran: Sparky Lyle, Chi.-A.L.	.20
☐	93	John Castino, Min.	.20
☐	94	Phil Niekro, Atl.	.50
☐	95	Alan Trammell, Det.	.20

	No.	Player	Price
☐	96	Gaylord Perry, Sea.	.50
☐	97	Tom Herr, Stl.	.20
☐	98	Vance Law, Chi.-A.L.	.20
☐	99	Dickie Noles, Chi.-N.L.	.20
☐	100	Pete Rose, Pha.	2.00
☐	101	Super Veteran: Pete Rose, Pha.	1.00
☐	102	Dave Concepcion, Cin.	.20
☐	103	Darrell Porter, Stl.	.20
☐	104	Ron Guidry, NYY.	.20
☐	105	Don Baylor, (NYY.)	.20
☐	106	AS: Steve Rogers, Mtl.	.20
☐	107	Greg Minton, S.F.	.20
☐	108	Glenn Hoffman, Bos.	.20
☐	109	Luis Leal, Tor.	.20
☐	110	Ken Griffey, NYY.	.35
☐	111	Mtl.: Al Oliver/ Steve Rogers	.20
☐	112	Luis Pujols, Hou.	.20
☐	113	Julio Cruz, Sea.	.20
☐	114	Jim Slaton, Mil.	.20
☐	115	Chili Davis, S	.20
☐	116	Pedro Guerrero, L.A.	.20
☐	117	Mike Ivie, Det.	.20
☐	118	Chris Welsh, S.D.	.20
☐	119	Frank Pastore, Cin.	.20
☐	120	Len Barker, Cle.	.20
☐	121	Chris Speier, Mtl.	.20
☐	122	Bobby Murcer, NYY.	.20
☐	123	Bill Russell, L.A.	.20
☐	124	Lloyd Moseby, Tor.	.20
☐	125	Leon Durham, Chi.-N.L.	.20
☐	126	Super Veteran: Carl Yastrzemski, Bos.	.50
☐	127	John Candelaria, Pgh.	.20
☐	128	Phil Garner, Hou.	.20
☐	129	Checklist 1 (1 - 132)	.35
☐	130	Dave Stieb, Tor.	.20
☐	131	Geoff Zahn, Cal.	.20
☐	132	Todd Cruz, Sea.	.20
☐	133	Tony Pena, Pgh.	.20
☐	134	Hubie Brooks, NYM.	.20
☐	135	Dwight Evans, Bos.	.20
☐	136	Willie Aikens, K.C.	.20
☐	137	Woodie Fryman, Mtl.	.20
☐	138	Rick Dempsey, Bal.	.20
☐	139	Bruce Berenyi, Cin.	.20
☐	140	Willie Randolph, NYY.	.20
☐	141	Eddie Murray, Bal.	2.00
☐	142	Mike Caldwell, Mil.	.20
☐	**143**	**Tony Gwynn, S.D., RC**	**45.00**
☐	144	Super Veteran: Tommy John, Cal.	.20
☐	145	Don Sutton, Mil.	.50
☐	146	Super Veteran: Don Sutton, Mil.	.35
☐	147	Rick Manning, Cle.	.20
☐	148	George Hendrick, Stl.	.20
☐	149	Johnny Ray, Pgh.	.20
☐	150	Bruce Sutter, Stl.	.20
☐	151	Super Veteran: Bruce Sutter, Stl.	.20
☐	152	Jay Johnstone, Chi.-N.L.	.20
☐	153	Jerry Koosman, Chi.-A.L.	.20
☐	154	Johnnie LeMaster, S.F.	.20
☐	155	Dan Quisenberry, K.C.	.20
☐	156	Luis Salazar, S.D.	.20
☐	157	Steve Bedrosian, Atl.	.20
☐	158	Jim Sundberg, Tex.	.20
☐	159	Super Veteran: Gaylord Perry, Sea.	.35
☐	160	Dave Kingman, NYM.	.20
☐	161	Super Veteran: Dave Kingman, NYM.	.20
☐	162	Mark Clear, Bos.	.20
☐	163	Cal Ripken, Bal.	20.00
☐	164	Dave Palmer, Mtl.	.20
☐	165	Dan Driessen, Cin.	.20
☐	166	Tug McGraw, Pha.	.20
☐	167	Denny Martinez, Bal.	.20
☐	168	Juan Eichelberger, (Cle.)	.20
☐	169	Doug Flynn, Mtl.	.20
☐	170	Steve Howe, L.A.	.20
☐	171	Frank White, K.C.	.20
☐	172	Mike Flanagan, Bal.	.20
☐	173	AS: Andre Dawson, Mtl.	.75
☐	174	AS:: Manny Trillo, (Cle.)	.20
☐	175	Bo Diaz, Pha.	.20
☐	176	Dave Righetti, NYY.	.20
☐	177	Harold Baines, Chi.-A.L.	.20
☐	178	Vida Blue, K.C.	.20
☐	179	Super Veteran: Luis Tiant, Cal.	.20
☐	180	Rickey Henderson, Oak.	1.25
☐	181	Rick Rhoden, Pgh.	.20
☐	182	Fred Lynn, Cal.	.20
☐	**183**	**Ed VandeBerg, Sea., RC**	**.20**
☐	184	Dwayne Murphy, Oak.	.20
☐	185	Tim Lollar, S.D.	.20
☐	186	Dave Tobik, Det.	.20
☐	187	Super Veteran: Tug McGraw, Pha.	.20
☐	188	Rick Miller, Bos.	.20
☐	189	Dan Schatzeder, Mtl.	.20
☐	190	Cecil Cooper, Mil.	.20
☐	191	Jim Beattie, Sea.	.20
☐	192	Rich Dauer, Bal.	.20
☐	193	Al Cowens, Sea.	.20
☐	194	Roy Lee Jackson, Tor.	.20
☐	**195**	**Mike Gates, Mtl., RC**	**.20**
☐	196	Tommy John, Cal.	.20
☐	197	Bob Forsch, Stl.	.20
☐	198	Steve Garvey, (S.D.)	.35
☐	199	Brad Mills, Mtl.	.20
☐	200	Rod Carew, Cal.	1.25
☐	201	Super Veteran: Rod Carew, Cal.	.75
☐	202	Tor.: Damaso Garcia/ Dave Stieb, Error	.20
☐	203	Floyd Bannister, (Chi.-A.L.)	.20
☐	204	Bruce Benedict, Atl.	.20
☐	205	Dave Parker, Pgh.	.20
☐	206	Ken Oberkfell, Stl.	.20
☐	207	Super Veteran: Graig Nettles, NYY.	.20
☐	208	Sparky Lyle, Chi.-A.L.	.20
☐	209	Jason Thompson, Pgh.	.20
☐	210	Jack Clark, S.F.	.20
☐	211	Jim Kaat, Stl.	.20
☐	212	John Stearns, NYM.	.20
☐	213	Tom Burgmeier, Oak.	.20
☐	214	Jerry White, Mtl.	.20
☐	215	Mario Soto, Cin.	.20
☐	216	Scott McGregor, Bal.	.20
☐	217	Tim Stoddard, Bal.	.20
☐	**218**	**Bill Laskey, S.F., RC**	**.20**
☐	219	Super Veteran: Reggie Jackson, Cal.	1.00
☐	220	Dusty Baker, L.A.	.20
☐	221	Joe Niekro, Hou.	.20
☐	222	Damaso Garcia, Tor.	.20
☐	223	John Montefusco, S.D.	.20
☐	224	Mickey Rivers, Tex.	.20
☐	225	Enos Cabell, Det.	.20
☐	226	LaMarr Hoyt, Chi.-A.L.	.20
☐	227	Tim Raines, Mtl.	.20
☐	228	Joaquin Andujar, Stl.	.20
☐	229	Tim Wallach, Mtl.	.20
☐	230	Fergie Jenkins, Chi.-N.L.	1.00
☐	231	Super Veteran: Fergie Jenkins, Chi.-N.L.	.50
☐	232	Tom Brunansky, Min.	.20
☐	233	Ivan DeJesus, Pha.	.20

- ☐ 234 Bryn Smith, Mtl. .20
- ☐ 235 Claudell Washington, Atl. .20
- ☐ 236 Steve Renko, Cal. .20
- ☐ 237 Dan Norman, Mtl. .20
- ☐ 238 Cesar Cedeno, Cin. .20
- ☐ 239 Dave Stapleton, Bos. .20
- ☐ 240 Rich Gossage, NYY. .20
- ☐ 241 Super Veteran: Rich Gossage, NYY. .20
- ☐ 242 Bob Stanley, Bos. .20
- ☐ 243 Rich Gale, (Cin.) .20
- ☐ 244 Sixto Lezcano, S.D. .20
- ☐ 245 Steve Sax, L.A. .20
- ☐ 246 Jerry Mumphrey, NYY. .20
- ☐ 247 Dave Smith, Hou. .20
- ☐ 248 Bake McBride, Cle. .20
- ☐ 249 Checklist 2 (133 - 264) .35
- ☐ 250 Bill Buckner, Chi.-N.L. .20
- ☐ 251 Kent Hrbek, Min. .20
- ☐ 252 Gene Tenace, (Pgh.) .20
- ☐ 253 Charlie Lea, Mtl. .20
- ☐ 254 Rick Cerone, NYY. .20
- ☐ 255 Gene Garber, Atl. .20
- ☐ 256 Super Veteran: Gene Garber, Atl. .20
- ☐ 257 Jesse Barfield, Tor .20
- ☐ 258 Dave Winfield, NYY. 1.00
- ☐ 259 Don Money, Mil. .20
- ☐ 260 Steve Kemp, (NYY.) .20
- ☐ 261 Steve Yeager, L.A. .20
- ☐ 262 Keith Hernandez, Stl. .20
- ☐ 263 Tippy Martinez, Bal. .20
- ☐ 264 Super Veteran: Joe Morgan, (Pha.) .50
- ☐ 265 Joel Youngblood, (S.F.) .20
- ☐ 266 AS: Bruce Sutter, Stl. .20
- ☐ 267 Terry Francona, Mtl. .20
- ☐ 268 Neil Allen, NYM. .20
- ☐ 269 Ron Oester, Cin. .20
- ☐ 270 Dennis Eckersley, Bos. .20
- ☐ 271 Dale Berra, Pgh. .20
- ☐ 272 Al Bumbry, Bal. .20
- ☐ 273 Lonnie Smith, Stl. .20
- ☐ 274 Terry Kennedy, S.D. .20
- ☐ 275 Ray Knight, Hou. .20
- ☐ 276 Mike Norris, Oak. .20
- ☐ 277 Rance Mulliniks, Tor. .20
- ☐ 278 Dan Spillner, Cle. .20
- ☐ 279 Bucky Dent, Tex. .20
- ☐ 280 Bert Blyleven, Cle. .20
- ☐ 281 Barry Bonnell, Tor. .20
- ☐ 282 Reggie Smith, S.F. .20
- ☐ 283 Super Veteran: Reggie Smith, S.F. .20
- ☐ 284 Ted Simmons, Mil. .20
- ☐ 285 Lance Parrish, Det. .20
- ☐ 286 Larry Christenson, Pha. .20
- ☐ 287 Ruppert Jones, S.D. .20
- ☐ 288 Bob Welch, L.A. .20
- ☐ 289 John Wathan, K.C. .20
- ☐ 290 Jeff Reardon, Mtl. .20
- ☐ 291 Dave Revering, Sea. .20
- ☐ 292 Craig Swan, NYM. .20
- ☐ 293 Graig Nettles, NYY. .20
- ☐ 294 Alfredo Griffin, Tor. .20
- ☐ 295 Jerry Remy, Bos. .20
- ☐ 296 Joe Sambito, Hou. .20
- ☐ 297 Ron LeFlore, Chi.-A.L. .20
- ☐ 298 Brian Downing, Cal. .20
- ☐ 299 Jim Palmer, Bal. 1.00
- ☐ 300 Mike Schmidt, Pha. 1.00
- ☐ 301 Super Veteran: Mike Schmidt, Pha. .50
- ☐ 302 Ernie Whitt, Tor. .20
- ☐ 303 Andre Dawson, Mtl. 1.25
- ☐ 304 Super Veteran: Bobby Murcer, NYY. .20
- ☐ 305 Larry Bowa, Chi.-N.L. .20
- ☐ 306 Lee Mazzilli, (Pgh.) .20
- ☐ 307 Lou Piniella, NYY. .20
- ☐ 308 Buck Martinez, Tor. .20
- ☐ 309 Jerry Martin, K.C. .20
- ☐ 310 Greg Luzinski, Chi.-A.L. .20
- ☐ 311 Al Oliver, Mtl. .20
- ☐ 312 Mike Torrez, (NYM.) .20
- ☐ 313 Dick Ruthven, Pha. .20
- ☐ 314 AS: Gary Carter, Mtl. .50
- ☐ 315 Rick Burleson, Cal. .20
- ☐ 316 Super Veteran: Phil Niekro, Atl. .35
- ☐ 317 Moose Haas, Mil. .20
- ☐ 318 Carney Lansford, (Oak.) .20
- ☐ 319 Tim Foli, Cal. .20
- ☐ 320 Steve Rogers, Mtl. .20
- ☐ 321 Kirk Gibson, Det. .20
- ☐ 322 Glenn Hubbard, Atl. .20
- ☐ 323 Luis DeLeon, S.D. .20
- ☐ 324 Mike Marshall, L.A. .20
- ☐ 325 Von Hayes, (Pha.) .20
- ☐ 326 Garth Iorg, Tor. .20
- ☐ 327 Jose Cruz, Hou. .20
- ☐ 328 Super Veteran: Jim Palmer, Bal. .50
- ☐ 329 Darrell Evans, S.F. .20
- ☐ 330 Buddy Bell, Tex. .20
- ☐ 331 Mike Krukow, (S.F.) .20
- ☐ 332 Omar Moreno, (Hou.) .20
- ☐ 333 Dave LaRoche, NYY. .20
- ☐ 334 Super Veteran: Dave LaRoche, NYY. .20
- ☐ 335 Bill Madlock, Pgh. .20
- ☐ 336 Garry Templeton, S.D. .20
- ☐ 337 John Lowenstein, Bal. .20
- ☐ 338 Willie Upshaw, Tor. .20
- ☐ **339 Dave Hostetler, Tex. RC .20**
- ☐ 340 Larry Gura, K.C. .20
- ☐ 341 Doug DeCinces, Cal. .20
- ☐ 342 AS: Mike Schmidt, Pha. 1.00
- ☐ 343 Charlie Hough, Tex. .20
- ☐ 344 Andre Thornton, Cle. .20
- ☐ 345 Jim Clancy, Tor. .20
- ☐ 346 Ken Forsch, Cal. .20
- ☐ 347 Sammy Stewart, Bal. .20
- ☐ 348 Alan Bannister, Cle. .20
- ☐ 349 Checklist 3 (265 - 396) .35
- ☐ 350 Robin Yount, Mil. 1.25
- ☐ 351 Warren Cromartie, Mtl. .20
- ☐ 352 AS: Tim Raines, Mtl. .20
- ☐ 353 Tony Armas, (Bos.) .20
- ☐ 354 Super Veteran: Tom Seaver, (NYM.) 1.00
- ☐ 355 Tony Perez, (Pha.) .35
- ☐ 356 Toby Harrah, Cle. .20
- ☐ 357 Dan Ford, Bal. .20
- ☐ **358 Charlie Puleo, (Cin.), RC .20**
- ☐ 359 Dave Collins, (Tor.) .20
- ☐ 360 Nolan Ryan, Hou. 8.00
- ☐ 361 Super Veteran: Nolan Ryan, Hou. 4.00
- ☐ 362 Bill Almon, (Oak.) .20
- ☐ **363 Eddie Milner, Cin., RC .20**
- ☐ 364 Gary Lucas, S.D. .20
- ☐ 365 Dave Lopes, Oak. .20
- ☐ 366 Bob Boone, Cal. .20
- ☐ 367 Biff Pocoroba, Atl. .20
- ☐ 368 Richie Zisk, Sea. .20
- ☐ 369 Tony Bernazard, Chi.-A.L. .20
- ☐ 370 Gary Carter, Mtl. .75
- ☐ 371 Paul Molitor, Mil. 2.00

	No.	Player	MINT
☐	372	Art Howe, Hou.	.20
☐	373	AS: Pete Rose, Pha.	1.00
☐	374	Glenn Adams, Tor.	.20
☐	375	Pete Vuckovich, Mil.	.20
☐	376	Gary Lavelle, S.F.	.20
☐	377	Lee May, K.C.	.20
☐	378	Super Veteran: Lee May, K.C.	.20
☐	379	Butch Wynegar, NYY.	.20
☐	380	Ron Davis, Min.	.20
☐	381	Bob Grich, Cal.	.20
☐	382	Gary Roenicke, Bal.	.20
☐	383	Super Veteran: Jim Kaat, Stl.	.20
☐	384	AS: Steve Carlton, Pha.	.75
☐	385	Mike Easler, Pgh.	.20
☐	386	AS: Rod Carew, Cal.	.75
☐	387	AS: Bob Grich, Cal.	.20
☐	388	AS: George Brett, K.C.	1.50
☐	389	AS: Robin Yount, Mil.	.75
☐	390	AS: Reggie Jackson, Cal.	1.00
☐	391	AS: Rickey Henderson, Oak.	.75
☐	392	AS: Fred Lynn, Cal.	.20
☐	393	AS: Carlton Fisk, Chi.-A.L.	.50
☐	394	AS: Pete Vuckovich, Mil.	.20
☐	395	AS: Larry Gura, K.C.	.20
☐	396	AS: Dan Quisenberry, K.C.	.20

1983 O-PEE-CHEE STICKERS

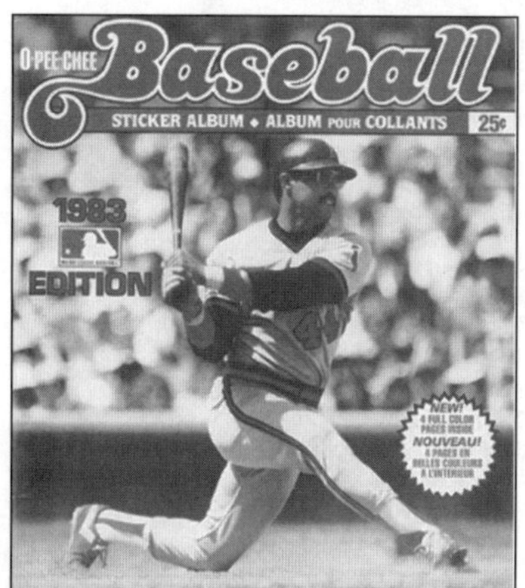

224 SEND HERE AND PEEL BACK / PLIER ICI ET PELER
FERGIE JENKINS
MISSING SOME STICKERS?
- See special offer on inside back cover of album
- Only $1.00 for any 10 stickers of your choice
- Details in O-Pee-Chee Baseball Album

TE MANQUE-T-IL CERTAINS COLLANTS?
- Il y a une offre spéciale sur la couverture arrière intérieure de l'album.
- Tu ne paieras que $1.00 pour 10 collants de ton choix.
- Les détails sont dans l'Album de Baseball O-Pee-Chee.

PRINTED IN ITALY FABRIQUE EN ITALIE

The 1983 sticker set was produced by Panini of Italy for O-Pee-Chee.
Sticker Size: 1 15/16" x 2 9/16"
Face: Four colour, white border; number
Back: Red on card stock; name, number, bilingual
Imprint: © 1983 O-PEE-CHEE CO. LTD. PRINTED IN ITALY FABRIQUE EN ITALIE

Complete Set (330 stickers): 40.00
Album: 6.00
CommonSticker: .20

	No.	Player	MINT
☐	1	Hank Aaron	1.50
☐	2	Babe Ruth	2.50
☐	3	Willie Mays	1.50
☐	4	Frank Robinson	.50
☐	5	Reggie Jackson, Cal.	.75
☐	6	Carl Yastrzemski, Bos.	.50
☐	7	Johnny Bench, Cin.	.35
☐	8	Tony Perez, Pha.	.20
☐	9	Lee May, K.C.	.20
☐	10	Mike Schmidt, Pha.	.75
☐	11	Dave Kingman, NYM.	.20
☐	12	Reggie Smith, S.F.	.20
☐	13	Graig Nettles, NYY.	.20
☐	14	Rusty Staub, NYM.	.20
☐	15	LL: Willie Wilson, K.C.	.20
☐	16	LL: LaMarr Hoyt, Chi.-A.L.	.20
☐	17	LL: Reggie Jackson, Cal./ Gorman Thomas, Mil.	.75
☐	18	LL: Floyd Bannister, Sea.	.20
☐	19	LL: Hal McRae, K.C.	.20
☐	20	LL: Rick Sutcliffe, Cle.	.20
☐	21	LL: Rickey Henderson, Oak.	.20
☐	22	LL: Dan Quisenberry, K.C.	.20
☐	23	Jim Palmer, Bal.	.50
☐	24	John Lowenstein, Bal.	.20
☐	25	Mike Flanagan, Bal.	.20
☐	26	Cal Ripken, Bal.	5.00
☐	27	Rich Dauer, Bal.	.20
☐	28	Ken Singleton, Bal.	.20
☐	29	Eddie Murray, Bal.	1.00
☐	30	Rick Dempsey, Bal.	.20
☐	31	Carl Yastrzemski, Bos.	.75
☐	32	Carney Lansford, Bos.	.20
☐	33	Jerry Remy, Bos.	.20
☐	34	Dennis Eckersley, Bos.	.20
☐	35	Dave Stapleton, Bos.	.20
☐	36	Mark Clear, Bos.	.20
☐	37	Jim Rice, Bos.	.20
☐	38	Dwight Evans, Bos.	.20
☐	39	Rod Carew, Cal.	.50
☐	40	Don Baylor, Cal.	.20
☐	41	Reggie Jackson, Cal.	1.00
☐	42	Geoff Zahn, Cal.	.20
☐	43	Bob Grich, Cal.	.20
☐	44	Fred Lynn, Cal.	.20
☐	45	Bob Boone, Cal.	.20
☐	46	Doug DeCinces, Cal.	.20
☐	47	Tom Paciorek, Chi.-A.L.	.20
☐	48	Britt Burns, Chi.-A.L.	.20
☐	49	Tony Bernazard, Chi.-A.L.	.20
☐	50	Steve Kemp, Chi.-A.L.	.20
☐	51	Greg Luzinski, Chi.-A.L.	.20
☐	52	Harold Baines, Chi.-A.L.	.20
☐	53	LaMarr Hoyt, Chi.-A.L.	.20
☐	54	Carlton Fisk, Chi.-A.L.	.60
☐	55	Andre Thornton, Cle.	.20
☐	56	Mike Hargrove, Cle.	.20
☐	57	Len Barker, Cle.	.20
☐	58	Toby Harrah, Cle.	.20
☐	59	Dan Spillner, Cle.	.20
☐	60	Rick Manning, Cle.	.20
☐	61	Rick Sutcliffe, Cle.	.20
☐	62	Ron Hassey, Cle.	.20
☐	63	Lance Parrish, Det.	.20
☐	64	John Wockenfuss, Det.	.20

☐	65	Lou Whitaker, Det.	.20
☐	66	Alan Trammell, Det.	.20
☐	67	Kirk Gibson, Det.	.20
☐	68	Larry Herndon, Det.	.20
☐	69	Jack Morris, Det.	.20
☐	70	Dan Petry, Det.	.20
☐	71	Frank White, K.C.	.20
☐	72	Amos Otis, K.C.	.20
☐	73	Willie Wilson, K.C.	.20
☐	74	Dan Quisenberry, K.C.	.20
☐	75	Hal McRae, K.C.	.20
☐	76	George Brett, K.C.	2.00
☐	77	Larry Gura, K.C.	.20
☐	78	John Wathan, K.C.	.20
☐	79	Rollie Fingers, Mil.	.35
☐	80	Cecil Cooper, Mil.	.20
☐	81	Robin Yount, Mil.	1.00
☐	82	Ben Oglivie, Mil.	.20
☐	83	Paul Molitor, Mil.	1.00
☐	84	Gorman Thomas, Mil.	.20
☐	85	Ted Simmons, Mil.	.20
☐	86	Pete Vuckovich, Mil.	.20
☐	87	Gary Gaetti, Min.	.20
☐	88	Kent Hrbek, Min.	.20
☐	89	John Castino, Min.	.20
☐	90	Tom Brunansky, Min.	.20
☐	91	Bobby Mitchell, Min.	.20
☐	92	Gary Ward, Min.	.20
☐	93	Tim Laudner, Min.	.20
☐	94	Ron Davis, Min.	.20
☐	95	Willie Randolph, NYY.	.20
☐	96	Roy Smalley, NYY.	.20
☐	97	Jerry Mumphrey, NYY.	.20
☐	98	Ken Griffey, NYY.	.35
☐	99	Dave Winfield, NYY.	1.00
☐	100	Rich Gossage, NYY.	.20
☐	101	Butch Wynegar, NYY.	.20
☐	102	Ron Guidry, NYY.	.20
☐	103	Rickey Henderson, Oak.	1.00
☐	104	Mike Heath, Oak.	.20
☐	105	Dave Lopes, Oak.	.20
☐	106	Rick Langford, Oak.	.20
☐	107	Dwayne Murphy, Oak.	.20
☐	108	Tony Armas, Oak.	.20
☐	109	Matt Keough, Oak.	.20
☐	110	Dan Meyer, Oak.	.20
☐	111	Bruce Bochte, Sea.	.20
☐	112	Julio Cruz, Sea.	.20
☐	113	Floyd Bannister, Sea.	.20
☐	114	Gaylord Perry, Sea.	.35
☐	115	Al Cowens, Sea.	.20
☐	116	Richie Zisk, Sea.	.20
☐	117	Jim Essian, Sea.	.20
☐	118	Bill Caudill, Sea.	.20
☐	119	Buddy Bell, Tex.	.20
☐	120	Larry Parrish, Tex.	.20
☐	121	Danny Darwin, Tex.	.20
☐	122	Bucky Dent, Tex.	.20
☐	123	Johnny Grubb, Tex.	.20
☐	124	George Wright, Tex.	.20
☐	125	Charlie Hough, Tex.	.20
☐	126	Jim Sundberg, Tex.	.20
☐	127	Dave Stieb, Tor.	.20
☐	128	Willie Upshaw, Tor.	.20
☐	129	Alfredo Griffin, Tor.	.20
☐	130	Lloyd Moseby, Tor.	.20
☐	131	Ernie Whitt, Tor.	.20
☐	132	Jim Clancy, Tor.	.20
☐	133	Barry Bonnell, Tor.	.20
☐	134	Damaso Garcia, Tor.	.20
☐	135	Jim Kaat, Stl.	.20
☐	136	Jim Kaat, Stl.	.20
☐	137	Greg Minton, S.F.	.20
☐	138	Greg Minton, S.F.	.20
☐	139	Paul Molitor, Mil.	.50
☐	140	Paul Molitor, Mil.	.50
☐	141	Manny Trillo, Pha.	.20
☐	142	Manny Trillo, Pha.	.20
☐	143	Joel Youngblood, Mtl.	.20
☐	144	Joel Youngblood, Mtl.	.20
☐	145	Robin Yount, Mil.	.50
☐	146	Robin Yount, Mil.	.50
☐	147	Willie McGee, Stl.	.20
☐	148	Darrell Porter, Stl.	.20
☐	149	Darrell Porter, Stl.	.20
☐	150	Robin Yount, Mil.	.50
☐	151	Bruce Benedict, Atl.	.20
☐	152	Bruce Benedict, Atl.	.20
☐	153	George Hendrick, Stl.	.20
☐	154	Bruce Benedict, Atl.	.20
☐	155	Doug DeCinces, Cal.	.20
☐	156	Paul Molitor, Mil.	.50
☐	157	Charlie Moore, Mil.	.20
☐	158	Fred Lynn, Cal.	.20
☐	159	AS: Rickey Henderson, Oak.	.50
☐	160	AS: Dale Murphy, Hou.	.20
☐	161	AS.: Willie Wilson, K.C.	.20
☐	162	AS: Jack Clark, S.F.	.20
☐	163	AS: Reggie Jackson, Cal.	.50
☐	164	AS: Andre Dawson, Mtl.	.20
☐	165	AS: Dan Quisenberry, K.C.	.20
☐	166	AS: Bruce Sutter, Stl.	.20
☐	167	AS: Robin Yount, Mil.	.50
☐	168	AS: Ozzie Smith, Stl.	.75
☐	169	AS: Frank White, K.C.	.20
☐	170	AS: Phil Garner, Hou.	.20
☐	171	AS: Doug DeCinces, Cal.	.20
☐	172	AS: Mike Schmidt, Pha.	.50
☐	173	AS: Cecil Cooper, Mil.	.20
☐	174	AS: Al Oliver, Mtl.	.20
☐	175	AS: Jim Palmer, Bal.	.35
☐	176	AS: Steve Carlton, Pha.	.35
☐	177	AS: Carlton Fisk, Chi.-A.L.	.35
☐	178	AS: Gary Carter, Mtl.	.20
☐	179	HL: Joaquin Andujar, Stl.	.20
☐	180	HL: Ozzie Smith, Stl.	.75
☐	181	HL: Cecil Cooper, Mil.	.20
☐	182	HL: Darrell Porter, Stl.	.20
☐	183	HL: Darrell Porter, Stl.	.20
☐	184	HL: Mike Caldwell, Mil.	.20
☐	185	HL: Mike Caldwell, Mil.	.20
☐	186	HL: Ozzie Smith, Stl.	.75
☐	187	HL: Bruce Sutter, Stl.	.20
☐	188	HL: Keith Hernandez, Stl.	.20
☐	189	HL: Dane Iorg, Stl.	.20
☐	190	HL: Dane Iorg, Stl.	.20
☐	191	Tony Armas, Oak.	.20
☐	192	Tony Armas, Oak.	.20
☐	193	Lance Parrish, Det.	.20
☐	194	Lance Parrish, Det.	.20
☐	195	John Wathan, K.C.	.20
☐	196	John Wathan, K.C.	.20
☐	197	Rickey Henderson, Oak.	.35
☐	198	Rickey Henderson, Oak.	.35
☐	199	Rickey Henderson, Oak.	.35
☐	200	Rickey Henderson, Oak.	.35
☐	201	Rickey Henderson, Oak.	.35
☐	202	Rickey Henderson, Oak.	.35

- ☐ 203 LL: Steve Carlton, Pha. .35
- ☐ 204 LL: Steve Carlton, Pha. .35
- ☐ 205 LL: Al Oliver, Mtl. .20
- ☐ 206 LL: Dale Murphy, Atl.; Al Oliver, Mtl. .20
- ☐ 207 LL: Dave Kingman, NYM. .20
- ☐ 208 LL: Steve Rogers, Mtl. .20
- ☐ 209 LL: Bruce Sutter, Stl. .20
- ☐ 210 LL: Tim Raines, Mtl. .20
- ☐ 211 Dale Murphy, Atl. .35
- ☐ 212 Chris Chambliss, Atl. .20
- ☐ 213 Gene Garber, Atl. .20
- ☐ 214 Bob Horner, Atl. .20
- ☐ 215 Glenn Hubbard, Atl. .20
- ☐ 216 Claudell Washington, Atl. .20
- ☐ 217 Bruce Benedict, Atl. .20
- ☐ 218 Phil Niekro, Atl. .50
- ☐ 219 Leon Durham, Chi.-N.L. .20
- ☐ 220 Jay Johnstone, Chi.-N.L. .20
- ☐ 221 Larry Bowa, Chi.-N.L. .20
- ☐ 222 Keith Moreland, Chi.-N.L. .20
- ☐ 223 Bill Buckner, Chi.-N.L. .20
- ☐ 224 Fergie Jenkins, Chi.-N.L. .50
- ☐ 225 Dick Tidrow, Chi.-N.L. .20
- ☐ 226 Jody Davis, Chi.-N.L. .20
- ☐ 227 Dave Concepcion, Cin. .20
- ☐ 228 Dan Driessen, Cin. .20
- ☐ 229 Johnny Bench, Cin. .50
- ☐ 230 Ron Oester, Cin. .20
- ☐ 231 Cesar Cedeno, Cin. .20
- ☐ 232 Alex Trevino, Cin. .20
- ☐ 233 Tom Seaver, Cin. .60
- ☐ 234 Mario Soto, Cin. .20
- ☐ 235 Nolan Ryan, Hou. 3.50
- ☐ 236 Art Howe, Hou. .20
- ☐ 237 Phil Garner, Hou. .20
- ☐ 238 Ray Knight, Hou. .20
- ☐ 239 Terry Puhl, Hou. .35
- ☐ 240 Joe Niekro, Hou. .20
- ☐ 241 Alan Ashby, Hou. .20
- ☐ 242 Jose Cruz, Hou. .20
- ☐ 243 Steve Garvey, L.A. .35
- ☐ 244 Ron Cey, L.A. .20
- ☐ 245 Dusty Baker, L.A. .20
- ☐ 246 Ken Landreaux, L.A. .20
- ☐ 247 Jerry Reuss, L.A. .20
- ☐ 248 Pedro Guerrero, L.A. .20
- ☐ 249 Bill Russell, L.A. .20
- ☐ 250 Fernando Valenzuela, L.A. .20
- ☐ 251 Al Oliver, Mtl. .20
- ☐ 252 Andre Dawson, Mtl. .35
- ☐ 253 Tim Raines, Mtl. .20
- ☐ 254 Jeff Reardon, Mtl. .20
- ☐ 255 Gary Carter, Mtl. .35
- ☐ 256 Steve Rogers, Mtl. .20
- ☐ 257 Tim Wallach, Mtl. .20
- ☐ 258 Chris Speier, Mtl. .20
- ☐ 259 Dave Kingman, NYM. .20
- ☐ 260 Bob Bailor, NYM. .20
- ☐ 261 Hubie Brooks, NYM. .20
- ☐ 262 Craig Swan, NYM. .20
- ☐ 263 George Foster, NYM. .20
- ☐ 264 John Stearns, NYM. .20
- ☐ 265 Neil Allen, NYM. .20
- ☐ 266 Mookie Wilson, NYM. .20
- ☐ 267 Steve Carlton, Pha. .75
- ☐ 268 Manny Trillo, Pha. .20
- ☐ 269 Gary Matthews, Pha. .20
- ☐ 270 Mike Schmidt, Pha. 1.00
- ☐ 271 Ivan DeJesus, Pha. .20
- ☐ 272 Pete Rose, Pha. 1.00
- ☐ 273 Bo Diaz, Pha. .20
- ☐ 274 Sid Monge, Pha. .20
- ☐ 275 Bill Madlock, Pgh. .20
- ☐ 276 Jason Thompson, Pgh. .20
- ☐ 277 Don Robinson, Pgh. .20
- ☐ 278 Omar Moreno, Pgh. .20
- ☐ 279 Dale Berra, Pgh. .20
- ☐ 280 Dave Parker, Pgh. .20
- ☐ 281 Tony Pena, Pgh. .20
- ☐ 282 John Candelaria, Pgh. .20
- ☐ 283 Lonnie Smith, Stl. .20
- ☐ 284 Bruce Sutter, Stl. .20
- ☐ 285 George Hendrick, Stl. .20
- ☐ 286 Tom Herr, Stl. .20
- ☐ 287 Ken Oberkfell, Stl. .20
- ☐ 288 Ozzie Smith, Stl. 1.50
- ☐ 289 Bob Forsch, Stl. .20
- ☐ 290 Keith Hernandez, Stl. .20
- ☐ 291 Garry Templeton, S.D. .20
- ☐ 292 Broderick Perkins, S.D. .20
- ☐ 293 Terry Kennedy, S.D. .20
- ☐ 294 Gene Richards, S.D. .20
- ☐ 295 Ruppert Jones, S.D. .20
- ☐ 296 Tim Lollar, S.D. .20
- ☐ 297 John Montefusco, S.D. .20
- ☐ 298 Sixto Lezcano, S.D. .20
- ☐ 299 Greg Minton, S.F. .20
- ☐ 300 Jack Clark, S.F. .20
- ☐ 301 Milt May, S.F. .20
- ☐ 302 Reggie Smith, S.F. .20
- ☐ 303 Joe Morgan, S.F. .50
- ☐ 304 Johnnie LeMaster, S.F. .20
- ☐ 305 Darrell Evans, S.F. .20
- ☐ 306 Al Holland, S.F. .20
- ☐ 307 Jesse Barfield, Tor. .20
- ☐ 308 Wade Boggs, Bos. 3.00
- ☐ 309 Tom Brunansky, Min. .20
- ☐ 310 Storm Davis, Bal. .20
- ☐ 311 Von Hayes, Cle. .20
- ☐ 312 Dave Hostetler, Tex. .20
- ☐ 313 Kent Hrbek, Min. .20
- ☐ 314 Tim Laudner, Min. .20
- ☐ 315 Cal Ripken, Bal. 5.00
- ☐ 316 Andre Robertson, NYY. .20
- ☐ 317 Ed VandeBerg, Sea. .20
- ☐ 318 Glenn Wilson, Det. .20
- ☐ 319 Chili Davis, S.F. .20
- ☐ 320 Bob Dernier, Pha. .20
- ☐ 321 Terry Francona, Mtl. .20
- ☐ 322 Brian Giles, NYM. .20
- ☐ 323 David Green, Stl. .20
- ☐ 324 Atlee Hammaker, S.F. .20
- ☐ 325 Bill Laskey, S.F. .20
- ☐ 326 Willie McGee, Stl. .35
- ☐ 327 Johnny Ray, Pgh. .20
- ☐ 328 Ryne Sandberg, Chi.-N.L. 4.00
- ☐ 329 Steve Sax, L.A. .20
- ☐ 330 Eric Show, S.D. .20

1984 O-PEE-CHEE

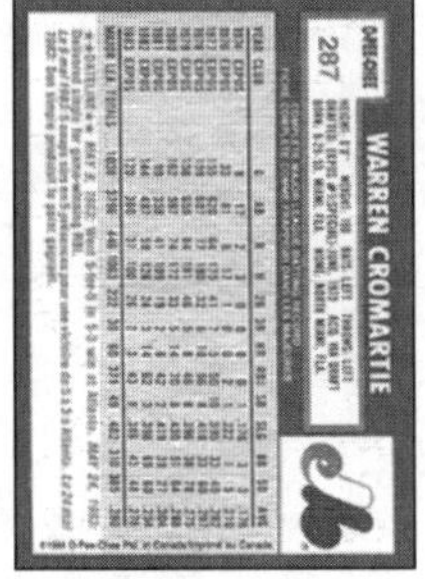

Card Size: 2 1/2" x 3 1/2"
Face: Four colour, white border; name, position, team
Back: Blue and red on card stock; name, number, résumé, team logo, dateline, bilingual
Imprint: © 1984 O-Pee-Chee Ptd. in Canada/imprimé au Canada

Complete Set (396 cards): 40.00
Common Player: .15

	No.	Player	MINT
☐	1	Pascual Perez, Atl.	.15
☐	2	AS: Cal Ripken, Bal.	4.00
☐	3	AS: Lloyd Moseby, Tor.	.15
☐	4	Mel Hall, Chi.-N.L.	.15
☐	5	Willie Wilson, K.C.	.15
☐	6	Mike Morgan, Tor	.15
☐	7	Gary Lucas, (Mtl.)	.15
☐	**8**	**Don Mattingly, NYY., RC**	**10.00**
☐	9	Jim Gott, Tor.	.15
☐	10	Robin Yount, Mil.	.75
☐	11	Joey McLaughlin, Tor.	.15
☐	12	Billy Sample, Tex.	.15
☐	13	Oscar Gamble, NYY.	.15
☐	14	Bill Russell, L.A.	.15
☐	15	Burt Hooton, L.A.	.15
☐	16	Omar Moreno, NYY.	.15
☐	17	Dave Lopes, Oak.	.15
☐	18	Dale Berra, Pgh.	.15
☐	19	Rance Mulliniks, Tor.	.15
☐	20	Greg Luzinski, Chi.-A.L.	.15
☐	**21**	**Doug Sisk, NYM., RC**	**.15**
☐	22	Don Robinson, Pgh.	.15
☐	23	Keith Moreland, Chi.-N.L.	.15
☐	24	Richard Dotson, Chi.-A.L.	.15
☐	25	Glenn Hubbard, Atl.	.15
☐	26	Rod Carew, Cal.	.75
☐	27	Alan Wiggins, S.D.	.15
☐	28	Frank Viola, Min.	.15
☐	29	Phil Niekro, (NYY.)	.50
☐	30	Wade Boggs, Bos.	1.25
☐	31	Dave Parker, (Cin.)	.15
☐	32	Bobby Ramos, Mtl.	.15
☐	33	Tom Burgmeier, Oak.	.15
☐	34	Eddie Milner, Cin.	.15
☐	35	Don Sutton, Mil.	.50
☐	36	Glenn Wilson, Det.	.15
☐	37	Mike Krukow, S.F.	.15
☐	38	Dave Collins, Tor.	.15
☐	39	Garth Iorg, Tor.	.15
☐	40	Dusty Baker, L.A.	.15
☐	41	Tony Bernazard, (Cle.)	.15
☐	42	Claudell Washington, Atl.	.15
☐	43	Cecil Cooper, Mil.	.15
☐	44	Dan Driessen, Cin.	.15
☐	45	Jerry Mumphrey, Hou.	.15
☐	46	Rick Rhoden, Pgh.	.15
☐	47	Rudy Law, Chi.-A.L.	.15
☐	48	Julio Franco, Cle.	.15
☐	49	Mike Norris, Oak.	.15
☐	50	Chris Chambliss, Atl.	.15
☐	51	Pete Falcone, Atl.	.15
☐	52	Mike Marshall, L.A.	.15
☐	53	Amos Otis, (Pgh.)	.15
☐	54	Jesse Orosco, NYM.	.15
☐	55	Dave Concepcion, Cin.	.15
☐	56	Gary Allenson, Bos.	.15
☐	57	Dan Schatzeder, Mtl.	.15
☐	58	Jerry Remy, Bos.	.15
☐	59	Carney Lansford, Oak.	.15
☐	60	Paul Molitor, Mil.	1.25
☐	**61**	**Chris Codiroli, Oak., RC**	**.15**
☐	62	Dave Hostetler, Tex.	.15
☐	63	Ed VandeBerg, Sea.	.15
☐	64	Ryne Sandberg, Chi.-N.L.	2.50
☐	65	Kirk Gibson, Det.	.15
☐	66	Nolan Ryan, Hou.	6.00
☐	67	Gary Ward, (Tex.)	.15
☐	68	Luis Salazar, S.D.	.15
☐	69	AS: Dan Quisenberry, K.C.	.15
☐	70	Gary Matthews, Pha.	.15
☐	**71**	**Pete O'Brien, Tex., RC**	**.15**
☐	72	John Wathan, K.C.	.15
☐	73	Jody Davis, Chi.-N.L.	.15
☐	74	Kent Tekulve, Pgh.	.15
☐	75	Bob Forsch, Stl.	.15
☐	76	Alfredo Griffin, Tor.	.15
☐	77	Bryn Smith, Mtl.	.15
☐	78	Mike Torrez, NYM.	.15
☐	79	Mike Hargrove, Cle.	.15
☐	80	Steve Rogers, Mtl.	.25
☐	81	Bake McBride, Cle.	.15
☐	82	Doug DeCinces, Cal.	.15
☐	83	Richie Zisk, Sea.	.15
☐	**84**	**Randy Bush, Min., RC**	**.15**
☐	85	Atlee Hammaker, S.F.	.15
☐	86	Chet Lemon, Det.	.15
☐	87	Frank Pastore, Cin.	.15
☐	88	Alan Trammell, Det.	.15
☐	89	Terry Francona, Mtl.	.15
☐	90	Pedro Guerrero, L.A.	.15
☐	91	Dan Spillner, Cle.	.15
☐	92	Lloyd Moseby, Tor.	.15
☐	93	Bob Knepper, Hou.	.15
☐	94	AS: Ted Simmons, Mil.	.15
☐	95	Aurelio Lopez, Det.	.15
☐	96	Bill Buckner, Chi.-N.L.	.15
☐	97	LaMarr Hoyt, Chi.-A.L.	.15
☐	98	Tom Brunansky, Min.	.15
☐	99	Ron Oester, Cin.	.15
☐	100	Reggie Jackson, Cal.	1.25
☐	101	Ron Davis, Min.	.15
☐	102	Ken Oberkfell, Stl.	.15
☐	103	Dwayne Murphy, Oak.	.15
☐	104	Jim Slaton, (Cal.)	.15
☐	105	Tony Armas, Bos.	.15
☐	106	Ernie Whitt, Tor.	.15
☐	107	Johnnie LeMaster, S.F.	.15
☐	108	Randy Moffitt, Tor.	.15
☐	109	Terry Forster, Atl.	.15
☐	110	Ron Guidry, NYY.	.15
☐	111	Bill Virdon, Manager, Mtl.	.15
☐	112	Doyle Alexander, Tor.	.15
☐	113	Lonnie Smith, Stl.	.15

	No.	Player	Price
☐	114	Checklist 1 (1 - 132)	.25
☐	115	Andre Thornton, Cle.	.15
☐	116	Jeff Reardon, Mtl.	.15
☐	117	Tom Herr, Stl.	.15
☐	118	Charlie Hough, Tex.	.15
☐	119	Phil Garner, Hou.	.15
☐	120	Keith Hernandez, NYM.	.15
☐	121	Rich Gossage, (S.D.)	.15
☐	122	Ted Simmons, Mil.	.15
☐	123	Butch Wynegar, NYY.	.15
☐	124	Damaso Garcia, Tor.	.15
☐	125	Britt Burns, Chi.-A.L.	.15
☐	126	Bert Blyleven, Cle.	.15
☐	127	Carlton Fisk, Chi.-A.L.	.35
☐	128	Rick Manning, Mil.	.15
☐	129	Bill Laskey, S.F.	.15
☐	130	Ozzie Smith, Stl.	1.50
☐	131	Bo Diaz, Pha.	.15
☐	132	Tom Paciorek, Chi.-A.L.	.15
☐	133	Dave Rozema, Det.	.15
☐	134	Dave Stieb, Tor.	.15
☐	135	Brian Downing, Cal.	.15
☐	136	Rick Camp, Atl.	.15
☐	137	Willie Aikens, (Tor.)	.15
☐	138	Charlie Moore, Mil.	.15
☐	139	George Frazier, (Cle.)	.15
☐	140	Storm Davis, Bal.	.15
☐	141	Glenn Hoffman, Bos.	.15
☐	142	Charlie Lea, Mtl.	.15
☐	143	Mike Vail, Mtl.	.15
☐	144	Steve Sax, L.A.	.15
☐	145	Gary Lavelle, S.F.	.15
☐	146	Gorman Thomas, (Sea.)	.15
☐	147	Dan Petry, Det.	.15
☐	148	Mark Clear, Bos.	.15
☐	149	Dave Beard, (Sea.)	.15
☐	150	Dale Murphy, Atl.	.35
☐	151	Steve Trout, Chi.-N.L.	.15
☐	152	Tony Pena, Pgh.	.15
☐	153	Geoff Zahn, Cal.	.15
☐	154	Dave Henderson, Sea.	.15
☐	155	Frank White, K.C.	.15
☐	156	Dick Ruthven, Chi.-N.L.	.15
☐	157	Gary Gaetti, Min.	.15
☐	158	Lance Parrish, Det.	.15
☐	159	Joe Price, Cin.	.15
☐	160	Mario Soto, Cin.	.15
☐	161	Tug McGraw, Pha.	.15
☐	162	Bob Ojeda, Bos.	.15
☐	163	George Hendrick, Stl.	.15
☐	164	Scott Sanderson, (Chi.-N.L.)	.15
☐	165	Ken Singleton, Bal.	.15
☐	166	Terry Kennedy, S.D.	.15
☐	167	Gene Garber, Atl.	.15
☐	168	Juan Bonilla, S.D.	.15
☐	169	Larry Parrish, Tex.	.15
☐	170	Jerry Reuss, L.A.	.15
☐	171	John Tudor, (Pgh.)	.15
☐	172	Dave Kingman, NYM.	.15
☐	173	Garry Templeton, S.D.	.15
☐	174	Bob Boone, Cal.	.15
☐	175	Graig Nettles, NYY.	.15
☐	176	Lee Smith, Chi.-N.L.	.35
☐	177	AS: LaMarr Hoyt, Chi.-A.L.	.15
☐	**178**	**Bill Krueger, Oak., RC**	**.15**
☐	179	Buck Martinez, Tor.	.15
☐	180	Manny Trillo, (S.F.)	.15
☐	181	AS: Lou Whitaker, Det.	.15
☐	**182**	**Darryl Strawberry, NYM., RC**	**2.25**
☐	183	Neil Allen, Stl.	.15
☐	184	AS: Jim Rice, Bos.	.15
☐	185	Sixto Lezcano, Pha.	.15
☐	186	Tom Hume, Cin.	.15
☐	187	Garry Maddox, Pha.	.15
☐	**188**	**Bryan Little, Mtl., RC**	**.15**
☐	189	Jose Cruz, Hou.	.15
☐	190	Ben Oglivie, Mil.	.15
☐	191	Cesar Cedeno, Cin.	.15
☐	**192**	**Nick Esasky, Cin., RC**	**.15**
☐	193	Ken Forsch, Cal.	.15
☐	194	Jim Palmer, Bal.	.50
☐	195	Jack Morris, Det.	.15
☐	196	Steve Howe, L.A.	.15
☐	197	Harold Baines, Chi.-A.L.	.15
☐	**198**	**Bill Doran, Hou., RC**	**.15**
☐	199	Willie Hernandez, Pha.	.15
☐	200	Andre Dawson, Mtl.	.75
☐	201	Bruce Kison, Cal.	.15
☐	202	Bobby Cox, Manager, Tor.	.15
☐	203	Matt Keough, NYY.	.15
☐	204	AS: Ron Guidry, NYY.	.15
☐	205	Greg Minton, S.F.	.15
☐	206	Al Holland, Pha.	.15
☐	207	Luis Leal, Tor.	.15
☐	**208**	**Jose Oquendo, NYM., RC**	**.15**
☐	209	Leon Durham, Chi.-N.L.	.15
☐	210	Joe Morgan, (Oak.)	.50
☐	211	Lou Whitaker, Det.	.15
☐	212	George Brett, K.C.	1.00
☐	213	Bruce Hurst, Bos.	.15
☐	214	Steve Carlton, Pha.	1.00
☐	215	Tippy Martinez, Bal.	.15
☐	216	Ken Landreaux, L.A.	.15
☐	217	Alan Ashby, Hou.	.15
☐	218	Dennis Eckersley, Bos.	.15
☐	**219**	**Craig McMurtry, Atl., RC**	**.15**
☐	220	Fernando Valenzuela, L.A.	.15
☐	221	Cliff Johnson, Tor.	.15
☐	222	Rick Honeycutt, L.A.	.15
☐	223	AS: George Brett, K.C.	1.75
☐	224	Rusty Staub, NYM.	.50
☐	225	Lee Mazzilli, Pgh.	.15
☐	226	Pat Putnam, Sea.	.15
☐	227	Bob Welch, L.A.	.15
☐	228	Rick Cerone, NYY.	.15
☐	229	Lee Lacy, Pgh.	.15
☐	230	Rickey Henderson, Oak.	.75
☐	**231**	**Gary Redus, Cin., RC**	**.15**
☐	232	Tim Wallach, Mtl.	.15
☐	233	Checklist 2 (33 - 264)	.25
☐	234	Rafael Ramirez, Atl.	.15
☐	**235**	**Matt Young, Sea., RC**	**.15**
☐	236	Ellis Valentine, Cal.	.15
☐	237	John Castino, Min.	.15
☐	238	Eric Show, S.D.	.15
☐	239	Bob Horner, Atl.	.15
☐	240	Eddie Murray, Bal.	1.25
☐	241	Billy Almon, Oak.	.15
☐	242	Greg Brock, L.A.	.15
☐	243	Bruce Sutter, Stl.	.15
☐	244	Dwight Evans, Bos.	.15
☐	245	Rick Sutcliffe, Cle.	.15
☐	246	Terry Crowley, Mtl.	.15
☐	247	Fred Lynn, Cal.	.15
☐	248	Bill Dawley, Hou.	.15
☐	249	Dave Stapleton, Bos.	.15
☐	250	Bill Madlock, Pgh.	.15
☐	251	Jim Sundberg, (Mil.)	.15

- ☐ 252 Steve Yeager, L.A. .15
- ☐ 253 Jim Wohlford, Mtl. .15
- ☐ 254 Shane Rawley, NYY. .15
- ☐ 255 Bruce Benedict, Atl. .15
- ☐ 256 Dave Geisel, (Sea.) .15
- ☐ 257 Julio Cruz, Chi.-A.L. .15
- ☐ 258 Luis Sanchez, Cal. .15
- ☐ 259 Von Hayes, Pha. .15
- ☐ 260 Scott McGregor, Bal. .15
- ☐ 261 Tom Seaver, (Chi.-A.L.) 1.25
- ☐ 262 Doug Flynn, Mtl. .15
- ☐ 263 Wayne Gross, (Bal.) .15
- ☐ 264 Larry Gura, K.C. .15
- ☐ 265 John Montefusco, NYY. .15
- ☐ 266 AS: Dave Winfield, NYY. .50
- ☐ 267 Tim Lollar, S.D. .15
- ☐ 268 Ron Washington, Min. .15
- ☐ 269 Mickey Rivers, Tex. .15
- ☐ 270 Mookie Wilson, NYM. .15
- ☐ 271 Moose Haas, Mil. .15
- ☐ 272 Rick Dempsey, Bal. .15
- ☐ 273 Dan Quisenberry, K.C. .15
- ☐ 274 Steve Henderson, Sea. .15
- ☐ 275 Len Matuszek, Pha. .15
- ☐ 276 Frank Tanana, Tex. .15
- ☐ 277 Dave Righetti, NYY. .15
- ☐ 278 Jorge Bell, Tor. .15
- ☐ 279 Ivan DeJesus, Pha. .15
- ☐ 280 Floyd Bannister, Chi.-A.L. .15
- ☐ 281 Dale Murray, NYY. .15
- ☐ 282 Andre Robertson, NYY. .15
- ☐ 283 Rollie Fingers, Mil. .50
- ☐ 284 Tommy John, Cal. .15
- ☐ 285 Darrell Porter, Stl. .15
- ☐ 286 Lary Sorensen, (Oak.) .15
- ☐ 287 Warren Cromartie, (Mtl.) .15
- ☐ 288 Jim Beattie, Sea. .15
- ☐ 289 Tor.: Lloyd Moseby/ Dave Stieb .15
- ☐ 290 Dave Dravecky, S.D. .15
- ☐ 291 AS: Eddie Murray, Bal. .75
- ☐ **292 Greg Bargar, Mtl., RC .15**
- ☐ 293 Tom Underwood, (Bal.) .15
- ☐ 294 U.L. Washington, K.C. .15
- ☐ 295 Mike Flanagan, Bal. .15
- ☐ 296 Rich Gedman, Bos. .15
- ☐ 297 Bruce Berenyi, Cin. .15
- ☐ 298 Jim Gantner, Mil. .15
- ☐ 299 Bill Caudill, (Oak.) .15
- ☐ 300 Pete Rose, (Mtl.) 1.25
- ☐ 301 Steve Kemp, NYY. .15
- ☐ 302 Barry Bonnell, (Sea.) .15
- ☐ 303 Joel Youngblood, S.F. .15
- ☐ 304 Rick Langford, Oak. .15
- ☐ 305 Roy Smalley, NYY. .15
- ☐ 306 Ken Griffey, NYY. .25
- ☐ 307 Al Oliver, Mtl. .15
- ☐ 308 Ron Hassey, Cle. .15
- ☐ 309 Len Barker, Atl. .15
- ☐ 310 Willie McGee, Stl. .15
- ☐ 311 Jerry Koosman, (Pha.) .15
- ☐ 312 Jorge Orta, (K.C.) .15
- ☐ 313 Pete Vuckovich, Mil. .15
- ☐ 314 George Wright, Tex. .15
- ☐ 315 Bob Grich, Cal. .15
- ☐ 316 Jesse Barfield, Tor. .15
- ☐ 317 Willie Upshaw, Tor. .15
- ☐ 318 Bill Gullickson, Mtl. .15
- ☐ 319 Ray Burris, (Oak.) .15
- ☐ 320 Bob Stanley, Bos. .15
- ☐ 321 Ray Knight, Hou. .15
- ☐ 322 Ken Schrom, Min. .15
- ☐ 323 Johnny Ray, Pgh. .15
- ☐ 324 Brian Giles, NYM. .15
- ☐ 325 Darrell Evans, (Det.) .15
- ☐ 326 Mike Caldwell, Mil. .15
- ☐ 327 Ruppert Jones, S.D. .15
- ☐ 328 Chris Speier, Mtl. .15
- ☐ 329 Bobby Castillo, Min. .15
- ☐ 330 John Candelaria, Pgh. .15
- ☐ 331 Bucky Dent, Tex. .15
- ☐ 332 Mtl.: Al Oliver/ Charlie Lea .15
- ☐ 333 Larry Herndon, Det. .15
- ☐ 334 Chuck Rainey, Chi.-N.L. .15
- ☐ 335 Don Baylor, NYY. .15
- ☐ **336 Bob James, Mtl, RC .15**
- ☐ 337 Jim Clancy, Tor. .15
- ☐ 338 Duane Kuiper, S.F. .15
- ☐ 339 Roy Lee Jackson, Tor. .15
- ☐ 340 Hal McRae, K.C. .15
- ☐ 341 Larry McWilliams, Pgh. .15
- ☐ 342 Tim Foli, (NYY.) .15
- ☐ 343 Fergie Jenkins, Chi.-N.L. .75
- ☐ 344 Dickie Thon, Hou. .15
- ☐ 345 Kent Hrbek, Min. .15
- ☐ 346 Larry Bowa, Chi.-N.L. .15
- ☐ 347 Buddy Bell, Tex. .15
- ☐ 348 Toby Harrah, (NYY.) .15
- ☐ 349 Dan Ford, Bal. .15
- ☐ 350 George Foster, NYM. .15
- ☐ 351 Lou Piniella, NYY. .15
- ☐ 352 Dave Stewart, Tex. .15
- ☐ 353 Mike Easler, (Bos.) .15
- ☐ 354 Jeff Burroughs, Oak. .15
- ☐ 355 Jason Thompson, Pgh. .15
- ☐ 356 Glenn Abbott, Det. .15
- ☐ 357 Ron Cey, Chi.-N.L. .15
- ☐ 358 Bob Dernier, Pha. .15
- ☐ **359 Jim Acker, Tor., RC .15**
- ☐ 360 Willie Randolph, NYY. .15
- ☐ 361 Mike Schmidt, Pha. 1.25
- ☐ 362 David Green, Stl. .15
- ☐ 363 Cal Ripken, Bal. 7.00
- ☐ 364 Jim Rice, Bos. .15
- ☐ 365 Steve Bedrosian, Atl. .15
- ☐ 366 Gary Carter, Mtl. .50
- ☐ 367 Chili Davis, S.F. .15
- ☐ 368 Hubie Brooks, NYM. .15
- ☐ 369 Steve McCatty, Oak. .15
- ☐ 370 Tim Raines, Mtl. .15
- ☐ 371 Joaquin Andujar, Stl. .15
- ☐ 372 Gary Roenicke, Bal. .15
- ☐ 373 Ron Kittle, Chi.-A.L. .15
- ☐ 374 Rich Dauer, Bal. .15
- ☐ 375 Dennis Leonard, K.C. .15
- ☐ 376 Rick Burleson, Cal. .15
- ☐ 377 Eric Rasmussen, K.C. .15
- ☐ 378 Dave Winfield, NYY. .50
- ☐ 379 Checklist 3 (265 - 396) .25
- ☐ 380 Steve Garvey, S.D. .25
- ☐ 381 Jack Clark, S.F. .15
- ☐ 382 Odell Jones, Tex. .15
- ☐ 383 Terry Puhl, Hou. .35
- ☐ 384 Joe Niekro, Hou. .15
- ☐ 385 Tony Perez, (Cin.) .25
- ☐ 386 AS: George Hendrick, Stl. .15
- ☐ 387 AS: Johnny Ray, Pgh. .15
- ☐ 388 AS: Mike Schmidt, Pha. .75
- ☐ 389 AS: Ozzie Smith, Stl. .75

	No.	Player	MINT
☐	390	AS: Tim Raines, Mtl.	.15
☐	391	AS: Dale Murphy, Atl.	.15
☐	392	AS: Andre Dawson, Mtl.	.50
☐	393	AS: Gary Carter, Mtl.	.25
☐	394	AS: Steve Rogers, Mtl.	.15
☐	395	AS: Steve Carlton, Pha.	.50
☐	396	AS: Jesse Orosco, NYM.	.15

1984 O-PEE-CHEE STICKERS

As with the 1983 sticker set, the 1984 stickers were produced by Panini of Italy for O-Pee-Chee.

Sticker Size: 1 15/16" x 2 9/16"
Face: Four colour, white border; number
Back: Red on card stock; name, number, bilingual
Imprint: © 1984 O-PEE-CHEE CO., LTD. PRINTED IN ITALY - IMPRIMÉ EN ITALIE

Complete Set (290 stickers):	**30.00**
Common Sticker:	**.20**
Album:	**6.00**

	No.	Player	MINT
☐	1	HL: Steve Carlton, Pha.	.50
☐	2	HL: Steve Carlton, Pha.	.50
☐	3	HL: Rickey Henderson, Oak.	.50
☐	4	HL: Rickey Henderson, Oak.	.50
☐	5	HL: Fred Lynn, Cal.	.20
☐	6	HL: Fred Lynn, Cal.	.20
☐	7	HL: Greg Luzinski, Chi.-A.L.	.20
☐	8	HL: Greg Luzinski, Chi.-A.L.	.20
☐	9	HL: Dan Quisenberry, K.C.	.20
☐	10	HL: Dan Quisenberry, K.C.	.20
☐	11	LaMarr Hoyt, Chi.-A.L.	.20
☐	12	Mike Flanagan, Bal.	.20
☐	13	Mike Boddicker, Bal.	.20
☐	14	Tito Landrum, Bal.	.20
☐	15	Steve Carlton, Pha.	.50
☐	16	Fernando Valenzuela, L.A.	.20
☐	17	Charles Hudson, Pha.	.20
☐	18	Gary Matthews, Pha.	.20
☐	19	John Denny, Pha.	.20
☐	20	John Lowenstein, Bal.	.20
☐	21	Jim Palmer, Bal.	.50
☐	22	Benny Ayala, Bal.	.20
☐	23	Rick Dempsey, Bal.	.20
☐	24	Rich Dauer, Bal.	.20
☐	25	Sammy Stewart, Bal.	.20
☐	26	Eddie Murray, Bal.	.50
☐	27	Dale Murphy, Atl.	.20
☐	28	Chris Chambliss	.20
☐	29	Glenn Hubbard	.20
☐	30	Bob Horner	.20
☐	31	Phil Niekro	.35
☐	32	Claudell Washington	.20
☐	33	Rafael Ramirez	.20
☐	34	Bruce Benedict	.20
☐	35	Gene Garber	.20
☐	36	Pascual Perez	.20
☐	37	Jerry Royster	.20
☐	38	Steve Bedrosian	.20
☐	39	Keith Moreland, Chi.-N.L.	.20
☐	40	Leon Durham, Chi.-N.L.	.20
☐	41	Ron Cey, Chi.-N.L.	.20
☐	42	Bill Buckner, Chi.-N.L.	.20
☐	43	Jody Davis, Chi.-N.L.	.20
☐	44	Lee Smith, Chi.-N.L.	.20
☐	45	Ryne Sandberg, Chi.-N.L.	2.00
☐	46	Larry Bowa, Chi.-N.L.	.20
☐	47	Chuck Rainey, Chi.-N.L.	.20
☐	48	Fergie Jenkins, Chi.-N.L.	.50
☐	49	Dick Ruthven, Chi.-N.L.	.20
☐	50	Jay Johnstone, Chi.-N.L.	.20
☐	51	Mario Soto, Cin.	.20
☐	52	Gary Redus, Cin.	.20
☐	53	Ron Oester, Cin.	.20
☐	54	Cesar Cedeno, Cin.	.20
☐	55	Dan Driessen, Cin.	.20
☐	56	Dave Concepcion, Cin.	.20
☐	57	Dann Bilardello, Cin.	.20
☐	58	Joe Price, Cin.	.20
☐	59	Tom Hume, Cin.	.20
☐	60	Eddie Milner, Cin.	.20
☐	61	Paul Householder, Cin.	.20
☐	62	Bill Scherrer, Cin.	.20
☐	63	Phil Garner, Hou.	.20
☐	64	Dickie Thon, Hou.	.20
☐	65	Jose Cruz, Hou.	.20
☐	66	Nolan Ryan, Hou.	3.00
☐	67	Terry Puhl, Hou.	.25
☐	68	Ray Knight, Hou.	.20
☐	69	Joe Niekro, Hou.	.20
☐	70	Jerry Mumphrey, Hou.	.20
☐	71	Bill Dawley, Hou.	.20
☐	72	Alan Ashby, Hou.	.20
☐	73	Denny Walling, Hou.	.20
☐	74	Frank DiPino, Hou.	.20
☐	75	Pedro Guerrero, L.A.	.20
☐	76	Ken Landreaux, L.A.	.20
☐	77	Bill Russell, L.A.	.20
☐	78	Steve Sax, L.A.	.20
☐	79	Fernando Valenzuela, L.A.	.20
☐	80	Dusty Baker, L.A.	.20
☐	81	Jerry Reuss, L.A.	.20
☐	82	Alejandro Pena, L.A.	.20
☐	83	Rick Monday, L.A.	.20
☐	84	Rick Honeycutt, L.A.	.20
☐	85	Mike Marshall, L.A.	.20
☐	86	Steve Yeager, L.A.	.20
☐	87	Al Oliver, Mtl.	.20
☐	88	Steve Rogers, Mtl.	.20
☐	89	Jeff Reardon, Mtl.	.20
☐	90	Gary Carter, Mtl.	.35
☐	91	Tim Raines, Mtl.	.20
☐	92	Andre Dawson, Mtl.	.35
☐	93	Manny Trillo, Mtl.	.20
☐	94	Tim Wallach, Mtl.	.20
☐	95	Chris Speier, Mtl.	.20
☐	96	Bill Gullickson, Mtl.	.20
☐	97	Doug Flynn, Mtl.	.20
☐	98	Charlie Lea, Mtl.	.20
☐	99	Bill Madlock, Pgh.	.20
☐	100	Wade Boggs, Bos.	.75
☐	101	Mike Schmidt, Pha.	.50
☐	102A	Jim Rice, Bos.	.20

- ☐ 102B Reggie Jackson, Cal. .35
- ☐ 103 Hubie Brooks, NYM. .20
- ☐ 104 Jesse Orosco, NYM. .20
- ☐ 105 George Foster, NYM. .20
- ☐ 106 Tom Seaver, NYM. .50
- ☐ 107 Keith Hernandez, NYM. .20
- ☐ 108 Mookie Wilson, NYM. .20
- ☐ 109 Bob Bailor, NYM. .20
- ☐ 110 Walt Terrell, NYM. .20
- ☐ 111 Brian Giles, NYM. .20
- ☐ 112 Jose Oquendo, NYM. .20
- ☐ 113 Mike Torrez, NYM. .20
- ☐ 114 Junior Ortiz, NYM. .20
- ☐ 115 Pete Rose, Pha. 1.00
- ☐ 116 Joe Morgan, Pha. .50
- ☐ 117 Mike Schmidt, Pha. 1.00
- ☐ 118 Gary Matthews, Pha. .20
- ☐ 119 Steve Carlton, Pha. 1.00
- ☐ 120 Bo Diaz, Pha. .20
- ☐ 121 Ivan DeJesus, Pha. .20
- ☐ 122 John Denny, Pha. .20
- ☐ 123 Garry Maddox, Pha. .20
- ☐ 124 Von Hayes, Pha. .20
- ☐ 125 Al Holland, Pha. .20
- ☐ 126 Tony Perez, Pha. .35
- ☐ 127 John Candelaria, Pgh. .20
- ☐ 128 Jason Thompson, Pgh. .20
- ☐ 129 Tony Pena, Pgh. .20
- ☐ 130 Dave Parker, Pgh. .20
- ☐ 131 Bill Madlock, Pgh. .20
- ☐ 132 Kent Tekulve, Pgh. .20
- ☐ 133 Larry McWilliams, Pgh. .20
- ☐ 134 Johnny Ray, Pgh. .20
- ☐ 135 Marvell Wynne, Pgh. .20
- ☐ 136 Dale Berra, Pgh. .20
- ☐ 137 Mike Easler, Pgh. .20
- ☐ 138 Lee Lacy, Pgh. .20
- ☐ 139 George Hendrick, Stl. .20
- ☐ 140 Lonnie Smith, Stl. .20
- ☐ 141 Willie McGee, Stl. .20
- ☐ 142 Tom Herr, Stl. .20
- ☐ 143 Darrell Porter, Stl. .20
- ☐ 144 Ozzie Smith, Stl. 1.50
- ☐ 145 Bruce Sutter, Stl. .20
- ☐ 146 Dave LaPoint, Stl. .20
- ☐ 147 Neil Allen, Stl. .20
- ☐ 148 Ken Oberkfell, Stl. .20
- ☐ 149 David Green, Stl. .20
- ☐ 150 Andy Van Slyke, Stl. .20
- ☐ 151 Garry Templeton, S.D. .20
- ☐ 152 Juan Bonilla, S.D. .20
- ☐ 153 Alan Wiggins, S.D. .20
- ☐ 154 Terry Kennedy, S.D. .20
- ☐ 155 Dave Dravecky, S.D. .20
- ☐ 156 Steve Garvey, S.D. .35
- ☐ 157 Bobby Brown, S.D. .20
- ☐ 158 Ruppert Jones, S.D. .20
- ☐ 159 Luis Salazar, S.D. .20
- ☐ 160 Tony Gwynn, S.D. 4.00
- ☐ 161 Gary Lucas, S.D. .20
- ☐ 162 Eric Show, S.D. .20
- ☐ 163 Darrell Evans, S.F. .20
- ☐ 164 Gary Lavelle, S.F. .20
- ☐ 165 Atlee Hammaker, S.F. .20
- ☐ 166 Jeff Leonard, S.F. .20
- ☐ 167 Jack Clark, S.F. .20
- ☐ 168 Johnnie LeMaster, S.F. .20
- ☐ 169 Duane Kuiper, S.F. .20
- ☐ 170 Tom O'Malley, S.F. .20

- ☐ 171 Chili Davis, S.F. .20
- ☐ 172 Bill Laskey, S.F. .20
- ☐ 173 Joel Youngblood, S.F. .20
- ☐ 174 Bob Brenly, S.F. .20
- ☐ 175 Atlee Hammaker, S.F. .20
- ☐ 176 Rick Honeycutt, Tex. .20
- ☐ 177 John Denny, Pha. .20
- ☐ 178 LaMarr Hoyt, Chi.-A.L. .20
- ☐ 179 AS: Tim Raines, Mtl. .20
- ☐ 180 AS: Dale Murphy, Atl. .20
- ☐ 181 AS: Andre Dawson, Mtl. .20
- ☐ 182 AS: Steve Rogers, Mtl. .20
- ☐ 183 AS: Gary Carter, Mtl. .20
- ☐ 184 AS: Steve Carlton, Pha. .50
- ☐ 185 AS: George Hendrick, Stl. .20
- ☐ 186 AS: Johnny Ray, Pgh. .20
- ☐ 187 AS: Ozzie Smith, Stl. .75
- ☐ 188 AS: Mike Schmidt, Pha. .50
- ☐ 189 AS: Jim Rice, Bos. .20
- ☐ 190 AS: Dave Winfield, NYY. .50
- ☐ 191 AS: Lloyd Moseby, Tor. .20
- ☐ 192 AS: LaMarr Hoyt, Chi.-A.L. .20
- ☐ 193 AS: Ted Simmons, Mil. .20
- ☐ 194 AS: Ron Guidry, NYY. .20
- ☐ 195 AS: Eddie Murray, Bal. .50
- ☐ 196 AS: Lou Whitaker, Det. .20
- ☐ 197 AS: Cal Ripken, Bal. 1.50
- ☐ 198 AS: George Brett, K.C. .75
- ☐ 199 Dale Murphy, Atl. .20
- ☐ 200 Cecil Cooper, Mil./ Jim Rice, Bos. .20
- ☐ 201 Tim Raines, Mtl. .20
- ☐ 202 Rickey Henderson, Oak. .50
- ☐ 203 Eddie Murray, Bal. 1.00
- ☐ 204 Cal Ripken, Bal. 3.00
- ☐ 205 Gary Roenicke, Bal. .20
- ☐ 206 Ken Singleton, Bal. .20
- ☐ 207 Scott McGregor, Bal. .20
- ☐ 208 Tippy Martinez, Bal. .20
- ☐ 209 John Lowenstein, Bal. .20
- ☐ 210 Mike Flanagan, Bal. .20
- ☐ 211 Jim Palmer, Bal. .50
- ☐ 212 Dan Ford, Bal. .20
- ☐ 213 Rick Dempsey, Bal. .20
- ☐ 214 Rich Dauer, Bal. .20
- ☐ 215 Jerry Remy, Bos. .20
- ☐ 216 Wade Boggs, Bos. 1.50
- ☐ 217 Jim Rice, Bos. .20
- ☐ 218 Tony Armas, Bos. .20
- ☐ 219 Dwight Evans, Bos. .20
- ☐ 220 Bob Stanley, Bos. .20
- ☐ 221 Dave Stapleton, Bos. .20
- ☐ 222 Rich Gedman, Bos. .20
- ☐ 223 Glenn Hoffman, Bos. .20
- ☐ 224 Dennis Eckersley, Bos. .20
- ☐ 225 John Tudor, Bos. .20
- ☐ 226 Bruce Hurst, Bos. .20
- ☐ 227 Rod Carew, Cal. .50
- ☐ 228 Bobby Grich, Cal. .20
- ☐ 229 Doug DeCinces, Cal. .20
- ☐ 230 Fred Lynn, Cal. .20
- ☐ 231 Reggie Jackson, Cal. 1.00
- ☐ 232 Tommy John, Cal. .20
- ☐ 233 Luis Sanchez, Cal. .20
- ☐ 234 Bob Boone, Cal. .20
- ☐ 235 Bruce Kison, Cal. .20
- ☐ 236 Brian Downing, Cal. .20
- ☐ 237 Ken Forsch, Cal. .20
- ☐ 238 Rick Burleson, Cal. .20
- ☐ 239 Dennis Lamp, Chi.-A.L. .20

☐ 240 LaMarr Hoyt, Chi.-A.L. .20
☐ 241 Richard Dotson, Chi.-A.L. .20
☐ 242 Harold Baines, Chi.-A.L. .20
☐ 243 Carlton Fisk, Chi.-A.L. .50
☐ 244 Greg Luzinski, Chi.-A.L. .20
☐ 245 Rudy Law, Chi.-A.L. .20
☐ 246 Tom Paciorek, Chi.-A.L. .20
☐ 247 Floyd Bannister, Chi.-A.L. .20
☐ 248 Julio Cruz, Chi.-A.L. .20
☐ 249 Vance Law, Chi.-A.L. .20
☐ 250 Scott Fletcher, Chi.-A.L. .20
☐ 251 Toby Harrah, Cle. .20
☐ 252 Pat Tabler, Cle. .20
☐ 253 Gorman Thomas, Cle. .20
☐ 254 Rick Sutcliffe, Cle. .20
☐ 255 Andre Thornton, Cle. .20
☐ 256 Bake McBride, Cle. .20
☐ 257 Alan Bannister, Cle. .20
☐ 258 Jamie Easterly, Cle. .20
☐ 259 Lary Sorensen, Cle. .20
☐ 260 Mike Hargrove, Cle. .20
☐ 261 Bert Blyleven, Cle. .20
☐ 262 Ron Hassey, Cle. .20
☐ 263 Jack Morris, Det. .20
☐ 264 Larry Herndon, Det. .20
☐ 265 Lance Parrish, Det. .20
☐ 266 Alan Trammell, Det. .20
☐ 267 Lou Whitaker, Det. .20
☐ 268 Aurelio Lopez, Det. .20
☐ 269 Dan Petry, Det. .20
☐ 270 Glenn Wilson, Det. .20
☐ 271 Chet Lemon, Det. .20
☐ 272 Kirk Gibson, Det. .20
☐ 273 Enos Cabell, Det. .20
☐ 274 Johnny Wockenfuss., Det. .20
☐ 275 George Brett, K.C. 1.50
☐ 276 Willie Aikens, K.C. .20
☐ 277 Frank White, K.C. .20
☐ 278 Hal McRae, K.C. .20
☐ 279 Dan Quisenberry, K.C. .20
☐ 280 Willie Wilson, K.C. .20
☐ 281 Paul Splittorff, K.C. .20
☐ 282 U.L. Washington, K.C. .20
☐ 283 Bud Black, K.C. .20
☐ 284 John Wathan, K.C. .20
☐ 285 Larry Gura, K.C. .20
☐ 286 Pat Sheridan, K.C. .20
☐ 287 Rusty Staub/ Dave Righetti, NYY. .20
☐ 288 Bob Forsch, Stl./ Mike Warren, Oak. .20
☐ 289 Al Holland .20
☐ 290 Dan Quisenberry .20
☐ 291 Cecil Cooper, Mil. .20
☐ 292 Moose Haas, Mil. .20
☐ 293 Ted Simmons, Mil. .20
☐ 294 Paul Molitor, Mil. 1.00
☐ 295 Robin Yount, Mil. 1.00
☐ 296 Ben Oglivie, Mil. .20
☐ 297 Tom Tellmann, Mil. .20
☐ 298 Jim Gantner, Mil. .20
☐ 299 Rick Manning, Mil. .20
☐ 300 Don Sutton, Mil. .35
☐ 301 Charlie Moore, Mil. .20
☐ 302 Jim Slaton, Mil. .20
☐ 303 Gary Ward, Min. .20
☐ 304 Tom Brunansky, Min. .20
☐ 305 Kent Hrbek, Min. .20
☐ 306 Gary Gaetti, Min. .20
☐ 307 John Castino, Min. .20
☐ 308 Ken Schrom, Min. .20
☐ 309 Ron Davis, Min. .20
☐ 310 Lenny Faedo, Min. .20
☐ 311 Darrell Brown, Min. .20
☐ 312 Frank Viola, Min. .20
☐ 313 Dave Engle, Min. .35
☐ 314 Randy Bush, Min. .20
☐ 315 Dave Righetti, NYY. .20
☐ 316 Rich Gossage, NYY. .20
☐ 317 Ken Griffey, NYY. .20
☐ 318 Ron Guidry, NYY. .20
☐ 319 Dave Winfield, NYY. 1.00
☐ 320 Don Baylor, NYY. .20
☐ 321 Butch Wynegar, NYY. .20
☐ 322 Omar Moreno, NYY. .20
☐ 323 Andre Robertson, NYY. .20
☐ 324 Willie Randolph, NYY. .20
☐ 325 Don Mattingly, NYY. 3.00
☐ 326 Graig Nettles, NYY. .20
☐ 327 Rickey Henderson, Oak. 1.00
☐ 328 Carney Lansford, Oak. .20
☐ 329 Jeff Burroughs, Oak. .20
☐ 330 Chris Codiroli, Oak. .20
☐ 331 Dave Lopes, Oak. .20
☐ 332 Dwayne Murphy, Oak. .20
☐ 333 Wayne Gross, Oak. .20
☐ 334 Bill Almon, Oak. .20
☐ 335 Tom Underwood, Oak. .20
☐ 336 Dave Beard, Oak. .20
☐ 337 Mike Heath, Oak. .20
☐ 338 Mike Davis, Oak. .20
☐ 339 Pat Putnam, Sea. .20
☐ 340 Tony Bernazard, Sea. .20
☐ 341 Steve Henderson, Sea. .20
☐ 342 Richie Zisk, Sea. .20
☐ 343 Dave Henderson, Sea. .20
☐ 344 Al Cowens, Sea. .20
☐ 345 Bill Caudill, Sea. .20
☐ 346 Jim Beattie, Sea. .20
☐ 347 Ricky Nelson, Sea. .20
☐ 348 Roy Thomas, Sea. .20
☐ 349 Spike Owen, Sea. .20
☐ 350 Jamie Allen, Sea. .20
☐ 351 Buddy Bell, Tex. .20
☐ 352 Billy Sample, Tex. .20
☐ 353 George Wright, Tex. .20
☐ 354 Larry Parrish, Tex. .20
☐ 355 Jim Sundberg, Tex. .20
☐ 356 Charlie Hough, Tex. .20
☐ 357 Pete O'Brien, Tex. .20
☐ 358 Wayne Tolleson, Tex. .20
☐ 359 Danny Darwin, Tex. .20
☐ 360 Dave Stewart, Tex. .20
☐ 361 Mickey Rivers, Tex. .20
☐ 362 Bucky Dent, Tex. .20
☐ 363 Willie Upshaw, Tor. .20
☐ 364 Damaso Garcia, Tor. .20
☐ 365 Lloyd Moseby, Tor. .20
☐ 366 Cliff Johnson, Tor. .20
☐ 367 Jim Clancy, Tor. .20
☐ 368 Dave Stieb, Tor. .20
☐ 369 Alfredo Griffin, Tor. .20
☐ 370 Barry Bonnell, Tor. .20
☐ 371 Luis Leal, Tor. .20
☐ 372 Jesse Barfield, Tor. .20
☐ 373 Ernie Whitt, Tor. .20
☐ 374 Rance Mulliniks, Tor. .20
☐ 375 Mike Boddicker, Bal. .20
☐ 376 Greg Brock, L.A. .20
☐ 377 Bill Doran, Hou. .20

	No.	Player	MINT
☐	378	Nick Esasky, Cin.	.20
☐	379	Julio Franco, Cle.	.20
☐	380	Mel Hall, Chi.-N.L.	.20
☐	381	Bob Kearney, Oak.	.20
☐	382	Ron Kittle, Chi.-A.L.	.20
☐	383	Carmelo Martinez, Chi.-N.L.	.20
☐	384	Craig McMurtry, Atl.	.20
☐	385	Darryl Strawberry, NYM.	.50
☐	386	Matt Young, Sea.	.20

1985 GENERAL MILLS

In 1985 General Mills of Canada inserted a panel of two stickers into each box of Cheerios. The four colour player's portrait on each sticker has the team insignia removed. The stickers are unnumbered and are listed alphabetically by the player on the left of the panel. There may have been a second printing of this set.

Sticker Size: 2 3/8" x 3 3/4"
Face: Four colour; name, position, team, General Mills logo, bilingual
Back: Blank
Imprint: None

Complete Set (15 panels):		**30.00**
Common Panel:		**2.00**
	Player	**MINT**
☐	Gary Carter / Tom Brunansky	3.00
☐	Gary Carter / Dave Stieb	3.50
☐	Andre Dawson / Alvin Davis	3.00
☐	Andre Dawson / Dave Stieb	3.50
☐	Steve Garvey / Buddy Bell	2.00
☐	Steve Garvey / Jim Rice	2.00
☐	Jeff Leonard / Eddie Murray	3.50
☐	Dale Murphy / Robin Yount	3.00
☐	Terry Puhl / Reggie Jackson	4.00
☐	Johnny Ray / Lou Whitaker	2.00
☐	Ryne Sandberg / Mike Hargrove	3.00
☐	Mike Schmidt / George Brett	5.00
☐	Ozzie Smith / Dave Winfield	4.00
☐	Mario Soto / Carlton Fisk	3.00
☐	Fernando Valenzuela / Dwayne Murphy	2.00

1985 LEAF

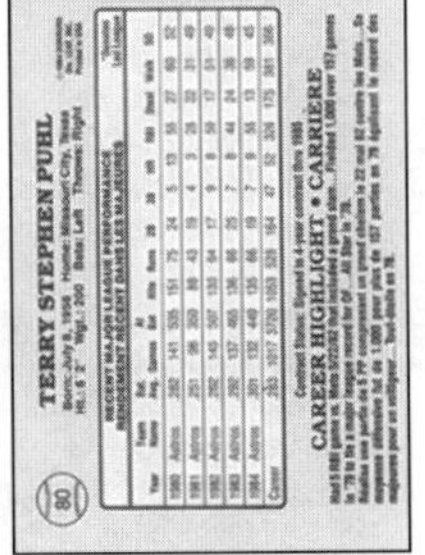

There are a number of differences between this 264-card set and the 660-card Donruss set of the same year. The players on the first 26 cards are the same as those on the corresponding Donruss cards but cards 27 to 258 of the Canadian set have a stylized green leaf in the upper left corner of the face. Also, players on these cards are not the same as those on the corresponding Donruss cards. The Canadian set also features two "Canadian Greats" cards of Dave Stieb and Tim Raines. There is a Lou Gehrig card and a Gehrig puzzle consisting of 21 perforated cards. Each puzzle piece is individually numbered. The Gehrig portrait was painted by the official Hall of Fame artist, Dick Perez. There are Cy Young overprints on the backs of the Rick Sutcliffe, Dwight Gooden and Willie Hernandez cards. The write ups on the backs of the cards are in English and French.

Card Size: 2 1/2" x 3 1/2"
Face: Four colour, black border; position, team logo
Back: Yellow and black on card stock; number, resume, career highlights
Imprint: Cards No. 1-26: © 1985 DONRUSS, MADE & PRINTED IN U.S.A. PEREZ-STEELE GALLERIES Cards No. 27 - 259 © 1984 DONRUSS Div. LEAF, Printed in USA

Complete Set (264 cards):			**100.00**
Common Player:			**.20**
	No.	**Player**	**MINT**
☐	1	Ryne Sandberg, Chi.-N.L.	2.75
☐	2	Doug DeCinces, Cal.	.20
☐	3	Rich Dotson, Chi.-A.L.	.20
☐	4	Bert Blyleven, Chi.-N.L.	.20
☐	5	Lou Whitaker, Det.	.20
☐	6	Dan Quisenberry, K.C.	.20
☐	7	Don Mattingly, NYY.	3.50
☐	8	Carney Lans.f.ord, Oak.	.20
☐	9	Frank Tanana, Tex.	.20
☐	10	Willie Upshaw, Tor.	.20
☐	11	Claudell Washington, Atl.	.20
☐	12	Mike Marshall, L.A.	.20
☐	13	Joaquin Andujar, Stl..	.20
☐	14	Cal Ripken Jr., Bal.	5.50
☐	15	Jim Rice, Bos.	.20
☐	16	Don Sutton, Mil.	.60
☐	17	Frank Viola, Min.	.20
☐	18	Alvin Davis, Sea.	.20
☐	19	Mario Soto, Cin.	.20
☐	20	Jose Cruz, Hou.	.20
☐	21	Charlie Lea, Mtl.	.20
☐	22	Jesse Orosco, NYY.	.20
☐	23	Juan Samuel, Pha.	.20
☐	24	Tony Pena, Pgh.	.20
☐	25	Tony Gwynn, S.D.	4.50
☐	26	Bob Brenly, S.F.	.20
☐	27	Rated Rookie: Steve Keifer, Oak.	.20
☐	28	Joe Morgan, Oak.	.75
☐	29	Luis Leal, Tor.	.20
☐	30	Dan Gladden, S.F.	.20
☐	31	Shane Rawley, Pha.	.20
☐	32	Mark Clear, Bos.	.20
☐	33	Terry Kennedy, S.D.	.20
☐	34	Hal McRae, K.C.	.20
☐	35	Mickey Rivers, Tex.	.20
☐	36	Tom Brunansky, Min.	.20
☐	37	LaMarr Hoyt, Chi.-A.L.	.20
☐	**38**	**Orel Hershiser, L.A., RC**	**1.00**
☐	39	Chris Bando, Cle.	.20
☐	40	Lee Lacy, Pgh.	.20
☐	41	Lance Parrish, Det.	.20
☐	42	George Foster, NYM.	.20
☐	43	Kevin McReynolds, S.D.	.20
☐	44	Robin Yount, Mil.	.75
☐	45	Craig McMurtry, Atl.	.20
☐	46	Mike Witt, Cal.	.20
☐	47	Gary Redus, Cin.	.20
☐	48	Dennis Rasmussen, NYY.	.20
☐	49	Gary Woods, Chi.-N.L.	.20
☐	50	Phil Bradley, Sea.	.20
☐	51	Steve Bedrosian, Atl.	.20
☐	52	Duane Walker, Cin.	.20
☐	53	Geoff Zahn, Cal.	.20
☐	54	Dave Stieb, Tor.	.20
☐	55	Pascual Perez, Atl.	.20
☐	**56**	**Mark Langston, Sea., RC**	**.50**
☐	57	Bob Dernier, Chi.-N.L.	.20
☐	58	Joe Cowley, NYY.	.20

	No.	Player	Price
☐	59	Dan Schatzeder, Mtl.	.20
☐	60	Ozzie Smith, Stl.	2.50
☐	61	Bob Knepper, Hou.	.20
☐	62	Keith Hernandez, NYM.	.20
☐	63	Rick Rhoden, Pgh.	.20
☐	64	Alejandro Pena, L.A.	.20
☐	65	Damaso Garcia, Tor.	.20
☐	66	Chili Davis, S.F.	.20
☐	67	Al Oliver, Pha.	.20
☐	68	Alan Wiggins, S.D.	.20
☐	69	Darryl Motley, K.C.	.20
☐	70	Gary Ward, Tex.	.20
☐	71	John Butcher, Min.	.20
☐	72	Scott McGregor, Bal.	.20
☐	73	Bruce Hurst, Bos.	.20
☐	74	Dwayne Murphy, Oak.	.20
☐	75	Greg Luzinski, Chi.-A.L.	.20
☐	76	Pat Tabler, Cle.	.20
☐	77	Chet Lemon, Det.	.20
☐	78	Jim Sundberg, Mil.	.20
☐	79	Wally Backman, NYM.	.20
☐	80	Terry Puhl, Hou.	.35
☐	81	Storm Davis, Bal.	.20
☐	82	Jim Wohlford, Mtl.	.20
☐	83	Willie Randolph, NYY.	.20
☐	84	Ron Cey, Chi.-N.L.	.20
☐	85	Jim Beattie, Sea.	.20
☐	86	Rafael Ramirez, Atl.	.20
☐	87	Cesar Cedeno, Cin.	.20
☐	88	Bobby Grich, Cal.	.20
☐	89	Jason Thompson, Pgh.	.20
☐	90	Steve Sax, L.A.	.20
☐	91	Tony Fernandez, Tor.	.20
☐	92	Jeff Leonard, S.F.	.20
☐	93	Von Hayes, Pha.	.20
☐	94	Steve Garvey, S.D.	.20
☐	95	Steve Balboni, K.C.	.20
☐	96	Larry Parrish, Tex.	.20
☐	97	Tim Teufel, Min.	.20
☐	98	Sammy Stewart, Bal.	.20
☐	**99**	**Roger Clemens, Bos., RC**	**30.00**
☐	100	Steve Kemp, NYY.	.20
☐	101	Tom Seaver, Chi.-A.L.	.75
☐	102	Andre Thornton, Cle.	.20
☐	103	Kirk Gibson, Det.	.20
☐	104	Ted Simmons, Mil.	.20
☐	105	David Palmer, Mtl.	.20
☐	106	Roy Lee Jackson, Tor.	.20
☐	**107**	**Kirby Puckett, Min., RC**	**20.00**
☐	108	Charlie Hough, Tex.	.20
☐	109	Mike Boddicker, Bal.	.20
☐	110	Willie Wilson, K.C.	.20
☐	111	Tim Lollar, S.D.	.20
☐	112	Tony Armas, Bos.	.20
☐	113	Steve Carlton, Pha.	.75
☐	114	Gary Lavelle, S.F.	.20
☐	115	Cliff Johnson, Tor.	.20
☐	116	Ray Burris, Oak.	.20
☐	117	Rudy Law, Chi.-A.L.	.20
☐	118	Mike Scioscia, L.A.	.20
☐	119	Kent Tekulve, Pgh.	.20
☐	120	George Vukovich, Cle.	.20
☐	121	Barbaro Garbey, Det.	.20
☐	122	Mookie Wilson, NYM.	.20
☐	123	Ben Oglivie, Mil.	.20
☐	124	Jerry Mumphrey, Hou.	.20
☐	125	Willie McGee, Stl.	.20
☐	126	Jeff Reardon, Mtl.	.20
☐	127	Dave Winfield, NYY.	.75
☐	128	Lee Smith, Chi.-N.L.	.20
☐	129	Ken Phelps, Sea.	.20
☐	130	Rick Camp, Atl.	.20
☐	131	Dave Concepcion, Cin.	.20
☐	132	Rod Carew, Cal.	.75
☐	133	AndrÇ Dawson, Mtl.	.75
☐	134	Doyle Alexander, Tor.	.20
☐	135	Miguel Dilone, Mtl.	.20
☐	136	Jim Gott, Tor.	.20
☐	137	Eric Show, S.D.	.20
☐	138	Phil Niekro, NYY.	.75
☐	139	Rick Sutcliffe, Chi.-N.L.	.20
☐	140	Two For The Title: D. Winfield; D. Mattingly, NYY.	3.50
☐	141	Ken Oberkfell, Atl.	.20
☐	142	Jack Morris, Det.	.20
☐	143	Lloyd Moseby, Tor.	.20
☐	144	Pete Rose, Cin.	1.00
☐	145	Gary Gaetti, Min.	.20
☐	146	Don Baylor, NYY.	.20
☐	147	Bobby Meacham, NYY.	.20
☐	148	Frank White, K.C.	.20
☐	149	Mark Thurmond, S.D.	.20
☐	150	Dwight Evans, Bos.	.20
☐	151	Al Holland, Pha.	.20
☐	152	Joel Youngblood, S.F.	.20
☐	153	Rance Mulliniks, Tor.	.20
☐	154	Bill Caudill, Oak.	.20
☐	155	Carlton Fisk, Chi.-A.L.	.50
☐	156	Rick Honeycutt, L.A.	.20
☐	157	John Candelaria, Pgh.	.20
☐	158	Alan Trammell, Det.	.20
☐	159	Darryl Strawberry, NYM.	.75
☐	160	Aurelio Lopez, Det.	.20
☐	161	Enos Cabell, Hou.	.20
☐	162	Dion James, Mil.	.20
☐	163	Bruce Sutter, Stl.	.20
☐	**164**	**Razor Shines, Mtl., RC**	**.20**
☐	165	Butch Wynegar, NYY.	.20
☐	166	Rich Bordi, Chi.-N.L.	.20
☐	167	Spike Owen, Sea.	.20
☐	168	Chris Chambliss, Atl.	.20
☐	169	Dave Parker, Cin.	.20
☐	170	Reggie Jackson, Cal.	.75
☐	171	Bryn Smith, Mtl.	.20
☐	172	Dave Collins, Tor.	.20
☐	173	Dave Engle, Min.	.20
☐	174	Buddy Bell, Tex.	.20
☐	175	Mike Flanagan, Bal.	.20
☐	176	George Brett, K.C.	4.50
☐	177	Graig Nettles, S.D.	.20
☐	178	Jerry Koosman, Pha.	.20
☐	179	Wade Boggs, Bos.	3.00
☐	180	Jody Davis, Chi.-N.L.	.20
☐	181	Ernie Whitt, Tor.	.20
☐	182	Dave Kingman, Oak.	.20
☐	183	Vance Law, Chi.-A.L.	.20
☐	184	Fernando Valenzuela, L.A.	.20
☐	185	Bill Madlock, Pgh.	.20
☐	186	Brett Butler, Cle.	.20
☐	187	Doug Sisk, NYM.	.20
☐	188	Dan Petry, Det.	.20
☐	189	Joe Niekro, Hou.	.20
☐	190	Rollie Fingers, Mil.	.50
☐	191	David Green, Stl.	.20
☐	192	Steve Rogers, Mtl.	.20
☐	193	Ken Griffey, NYY.	.35
☐	194	Scott Sanderson, Chi.-N.L.	.20
☐	195	Barry Bonnell, Sea.	.20
☐	196	Bruce Benedict, Atl.	.20

	No.	Player	MINT
☐	197	Keith Moreland, Chi.-N.L.	.20
☐	198	Fred Lynn, Cal.	.20
☐	199	Tim Wallach, Mtl.	.20
☐	200	Kent Hrbek, Min.	.20
☐	201	Pete O'Brien, Tex.	.20
☐	202	Bud Black, K.C.	.20
☐	203	Eddie Murray, Bal.	2.50
☐	204	Goose Gossage, S.D.	.20
☐	205	Mike Schmidt, Pha.	.75
☐	206	Mike Easler, Bos.	.20
☐	207	Jack Clark, S.F.	.20
☐	208	Rickey Henderson, Oak.	.35
☐	209	Jesse Barfield, Tor.	.20
☐	210	Ron Kittle, Chi.-A.L.	.20
☐	211	Pedro Guerrero, L.A.	.20
☐	212	Johnny Ray, Pgh.	.20
☐	213	Julio Franco, Cle.	.20
☐	214	Hubie Brooks, NYM.	.20
☐	215	Darrell Evans, Det.	.20
☐	216	Nolan Ryan, Hou.	11.00
☐	217	Jim Gantner, Mil.	.20
☐	218	Tim Raines, Mtl.	.20
☐	219	Dave Righetti, NYY.	.20
☐	220	Gary Matthews, Chi.-N.L.	.20
☐	221	Jack Perconte, Sea.	.20
☐	222	Dale Murphy, Atl.	.35
☐	223	Brian Downing, Cal.	.20
☐	224	Mickey Hatcher, Min.	.20
☐	225	Lonnie Smith, Stl.	.20
☐	226	Jorge Orta, K.C.	.20
☐	227	Milt Wilcox, Det.	.20
☐	228	John Denny, Pha.	.20
☐	229	Marty Barrett, Bos.	.20
☐	230	Alfredo Griffin, Tor.	.20
☐	231	Harold Baines, Chi.-A.L.	.20
☐	232	Bill Russell, L.A.	.20
☐	233	Marvell Wynne, Pgh.	.20
☐	**234**	**Dwight Gooden, NYM., RC**	**3.00**
☐	235	Willie Hernandez, Det.	.20
☐	236	Bill Gullickson, Mtl.	.20
☐	237	Ron Guidry, NYY.	.20
☐	238	Leon Durham, Chi.-N.L.	.20
☐	239	Al Cowens, Sea.	.20
☐	240	Bob Horner, Atl.	.20
☐	241	Gary Carter, Mtl.	.75
☐	242	Glenn Hubbard, Atl.	.20
☐	243	Steve Trout, Chi.-N.L.	.20
☐	244	Jay Howell, NYY.	.20
☐	245	Terry Francona, Mtl.	.20
☐	246	Cecil Cooper, Mil.	.20
☐	247	Larry McWilliams, Pgh.	.20
☐	248	George Bell, Tor.	.20
☐	249	Larry Herndon, Det.	.20
☐	250	Ozzie Virgil, Pha.	.20
☐	251	Dave Stieb, Tor.	.20
☐	252	Tim Raines, Mtl.	.20
☐	253	Ricky Horton, Stl.	.20
☐	254	Bill Buckner, Bos.	.20
☐	255	Dan Driessen, Mtl.	.20
☐	256	Ron Darling, NYM.	.20
☐	257	Doug Flynn, Mtl.	.20
☐	258	Darrell Porter, Stl.	.20
☐	259	George Hendrick, Stl.	.20
☐	635	Lou Gehrig	.50
☐	1	Checklist 27-102	.35
☐	2	Checklist 103-178	.35
☐	3	Checklist 179-259	.35

LOU GEHRIG PUZZLE

This 1985 Hall of Fame puzzle features Lou Gehrig, the "Iron Horse" of baseball. The words "Collect all 63 pieces to complete puzzle" appear on the back. All pieces are individually numbered. The puzzle art was painted by Dick Perez, the official Hall of Fame artist.

Card Size: 2 1/2" x 3 1/2"
Face: Four colour, white border
Back: Black on card stock; puzzle piece number
Imprint: © DONRUSS DIAMOND KING PUZZLE
Complete Set No.: 21 (3 pcs. per card)
Complete Set Price: 5.00

1985 O-PEE-CHEE

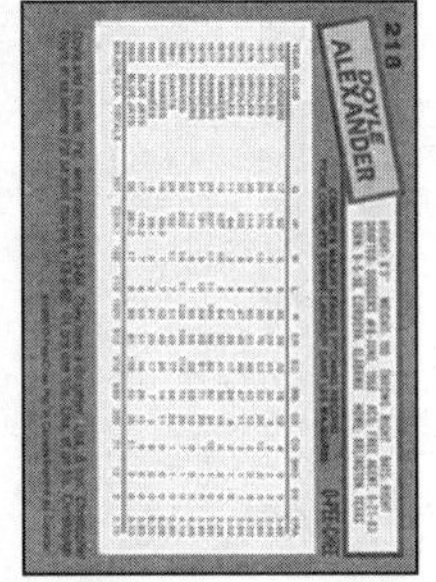

The card numbers on this 396-card set are not the same as those for the corresponding players in the 792-card Topps issue for 1985. It includes Rookie cards for Kirby Puckett (#10), Bret Saberhagen (#23), Dwight Gooden (#41) and Orel Hershiser (#273).

Card Size: 2 1/2" x 3 1/2"
Face: Four colour, white border; name, position, team, team logo
Back: Olive green and burgundy on card stock; name, number résumé, bilingual
Imprint: © 1985 O-Pee-Chee Ptd. In Canada/imprimé au Canada
Complete Set (396 cards): **30.00**
Common Player: **.15**

	No.	Player	MINT
☐	1	Tom Seaver, Chi.-A.L.	1.00
☐	2	Gary Lavelle, (Tor.)	.15
☐	3	Tim Wallach, Mtl.	.15
☐	4	Jim Wohlford, Mtl.	.15
☐	**5**	**Jeff Robinson, S.F., RC**	**.15**
☐	6	Willie Wilson, K.C.	.15
☐	7	Cliff Johnson (Tex.)	.15
☐	8	Willie Randolph, NYY.	.15
☐	9	Larry Herndon, Det.	.15
☐	**10**	**Kirby Puckett, Min., RC**	**8.00**
☐	11	Mookie Wilson, NYM.	.15
☐	12	Dave Lopes, (Chi.-N.L.)	.15
☐	13	Tim Lollar, (Chi.-A.L.)	.15
☐	14	Chris Bando, Cle.	.15
☐	15	Jerry Koosman, Pha.	.15
☐	16	Bobby Meacham, NYY.	.15
☐	17	Mike Scott, Hou.	.15
☐	18	Rich Gedman, Bos.	.15
☐	19	George Frazier, Chi.-N.L.	.15
☐	20	Chet Lemon, Det.	.15
☐	21	Dave Concepcion, Cin.	.15
☐	22	Jason Thompson, Pgh.	.15
☐	**23**	**Bret Saberhagen, K.C., RC**	**.50**
☐	24	Jesse Barfield, Tor.	.15
☐	25	Steve Bedrosian, Atl.	.15
☐	26	Roy Smalley, (Min.)	.15
☐	27	Bruce Berenyi, NYM.	.15

	No.	Player	Price
☐	28	Butch Wynegar, NYY.	.15
☐	29	Alan Ashby, Hou.	.15
☐	30	Cal Ripken, Bal.	4.00
☐	31	Luis Leal, Tor.	.15
☐	32	Dave Dravecky, S.D.	.15
☐	33	Tito Landrum, Stl.	.15
☐	34	Pedro Guerrero, L.A.	.15
☐	35	Graig Nettles, S.D.	.15
☐	36	Fred Breining, Mtl.	.15
☐	37	Roy Lee Jackson, Tor.	.15
☐	38	Steve Henderson, Sea.	.15
☐	39	Gary Pettis, Cal.	.15
☐	40	Phil Niekro, NYY.	.50
☐	**41**	**Dwight Gooden, NYM., RC**	**1.75**
☐	42	Luis Sanchez, Cal.	.15
☐	43	Lee Smith, Chi.-N.L.	.35
☐	44	Dickie Thon, Hou.	.15
☐	45	Greg Minton, S.F.	.15
☐	46	Mike Flanagan, Bal.	.15
☐	47	Bud Black, K.C.	.15
☐	48	Tony Fernandez, Tor.	.35
☐	49	Carlton Fisk, Chi.-A.L.	.50
☐	50	John Candelaria, Pgh.	.15
☐	51	Bob Watson, Atl.	.15
☐	52	Rick Leach, Tor.	.15
☐	53	Rick Rhoden, Pgh.	.15
☐	54	Cesar Cedeno, Cin.	.15
☐	55	Frank Tanana, Tex.	.15
☐	56	Larry Bowa, Chi.-N.L.	.15
☐	57	Willie McGee, Stl.	.15
☐	58	Rich Dauer, Bal.	.15
☐	59	Jorge Bell, Tor.	.15
☐	60	George Hendrick, (Pgh.)	.15
☐	61	Donnie Moore, (Cal.)	.15
☐	62	Mike Ramsey, Mtl.	.15
☐	63	Nolan Ryan, Hou.	4.00
☐	**64**	**Mark Bailey, Hou., RC**	**.15**
☐	65	Bill Buckner, Bos.	.15
☐	66	Jerry Reuss, L.A.	.15
☐	67	Mike Schmidt, Pha.	1.00
☐	68	Von Hayes, Pha.	.15
☐	69	Phil Bradley, Sea.	.15
☐	70	Don Baylor, NYY.	.15
☐	71	Julio Cruz, Chi.-A.L.	.15
☐	72	Rick Sutcliffe, Chi.-N.L.	.15
☐	73	Storm Davis, Bal.	.15
☐	74	Mike Krukow, S.F.	.15
☐	75	Willie Upshaw, Tor.	.15
☐	76	Craig Lefferts, S.D.	.15
☐	77	Lloyd Moseby, Tor.	.15
☐	78	Ron Davis, Min.	.15
☐	79	Rick Mahler, Atl.	.15
☐	80	Keith Hernandez, NYM.	.15
☐	81	Vance Law, (Mtl.)	.15
☐	82	Joe Price, Cin.	.15
☐	83	Dennis Lamp, Tor.	.15
☐	84	Gary Ward, Tex.	.15
☐	85	Mike Marshall, L.A.	.15
☐	86	Marvell Wynne, Pgh.	.15
☐	87	David Green, S.F.	.15
☐	88	Bryn Smith, Mtl.	.15
☐	89	Sixto Lezcano, (Pgh.)	.15
☐	90	Rich Gossage, S.D.	.15
☐	91	Jeff Burroughs, (Tor.)	.15
☐	92	Bobby Brown, S.D.	.15
☐	93	Oscar Gamble, NYY.	.15
☐	94	Rick Dempsey, Bal.	.15
☐	95	Jose Cruz, Hou.	.15
☐	96	Johnny Ray, Pgh.	.15
☐	97	Joel Youngblood, S.F.	.15
☐	98	Eddie Whitson, (NYY.)	.15
☐	99	Milt Wilcox, Det.	.15
☐	100	George Brett, K.C.	1.50
☐	101	Jim Acker, Tor.	.15
☐	102	Jim Sundberg, (K.C.)	.15
☐	103	Ozzie Virgil, Pha.	.15
☐	104	Mike Fitzgerald, (Mtl.)	.15
☐	105	Ron Kittle, Chi.-A.L.	.15
☐	106	Pascual Perez, Atl.	.15
☐	107	Barry Bonnell, Sea.	.15
☐	108	Lou Whitaker, Det.	.15
☐	109	Gary Roenicke, Bal.	.15
☐	110	Alejandro Pena, L.A.	.15
☐	111	Doug DeCinces, Cal.	.15
☐	112	Doug Flynn, Mtl.	.15
☐	113	Tom Herr, Stl.	.15
☐	114	Bob James, (Chi.-A.L.)	.15
☐	115	Rickey Henderson, (NYY.)	.35
☐	116	Pete Rose, Manager, Cin.	1.00
☐	117	Greg Gross, Pha.	.15
☐	118	Eric Show, S.D.	.15
☐	119	Buck Martinez, Tor.	.15
☐	120	Steve Kemp, (Pgh.)	.15
☐	121	Checklist 1 - 132	.25
☐	122	Tom Brunansky, Min.	.15
☐	123	Dave Kingman, Oak.	.15
☐	124	Garry Templeton, S.D.	.15
☐	125	Kent Tekulve, Pgh.	.15
☐	126	Darryl Strawberry, NYM.	.35
☐	**127**	**Mark Gubicza, K.C., RC**	**.15**
☐	128	Ernie Whitt, Tor.	.15
☐	129	Don Robinson, Pgh.	.15
☐	130	Al Oliver, (L.A.)	.15
☐	131	Mario Soto, Cin.	.15
☐	132	Jeff Leonard, S.F.	.15
☐	133	Andre Dawson, Mtl.	.75
☐	134	Bruce Hurst, Bos.	.15
☐	135	Bobby Cox, Manager, Tor.	.15
☐	136	Matt Young, Sea.	.15
☐	137	Bob Forsch, Stl.	.15
☐	138	Ron Darling, NYM.	.15
☐	139	Steve Trout, Chi.-N.L.	.15
☐	140	Geoff Zahn, Cal.	.15
☐	141	Ken Forsch, Cal.	.15
☐	142	Jerry Willard, Cle.	.15
☐	143	Bill Gullickson, Mtl.	.15
☐	**144**	**Mike Mason, Tex., RC**	**.15**
☐	**145**	**Alvin Davis, Sea., RC**	**.15**
☐	146	Gary Redus, Cin.	.15
☐	147	Willie Aikens, Tor.	.15
☐	148	Steve Yeager, L.A.	.15
☐	149	Dickie Noles, Tex.	.15
☐	150	Jim Rice, Bos.	.15
☐	151	Moose Haas, Mil.	.15
☐	152	Steve Balboni, K.C.	.15
☐	153	Frank LaCorte, Cal.	.15
☐	154	Argenis Salazar, (Stl.)	.15
☐	155	Bob Grich, Cal.	.15
☐	156	Craig Reynolds, Hou.	.15
☐	157	Bill Madlock, Pgh.	.15
☐	158	Pat Tabler, Cle.	.15
☐	159	Don Slaught, (Tex.)	.15
☐	160	Lance Parrish, Det.	.15
☐	161	Ken Schrom, Min.	.15
☐	162	Wally Backman, NYM.	.15
☐	163	Dennis Eckersley, Chi.-N.L.	.15
☐	164	Dave Collins, (Oak.)	.15
☐	165	Dusty Baker, S.F.	.15

	#	Player	Price
☐	166	Claudell Washington, Atl.	.15
☐	167	Rick Camp, Atl.	.15
☐	168	Garth Iorg, Tor.	.15
☐	169	Shane Rawley, Pha.	.15
☐	170	George Foster, NYM.	.15
☐	171	Tony Bernazard, Cle.	.15
☐	172	Don Sutton, Oak.	.50
☐	173	Jerry Remy, Bos.	.15
☐	174	Rick Honeycutt, L.A.	.15
☐	175	Dave Parker, Cin.	.15
☐	176	Buddy Bell, Tex.	.15
☐	177	Steve Garvey, S.D.	.35
☐	178	Miguel Dilone, Mtl.	.15
☐	179	Tommy John, Cal.	.15
☐	180	Dave Winfield, NYY.	.50
☐	181	Alan Trammell, Det.	.15
☐	182	Rollie Fingers, Mil.	.50
☐	183	Larry McWilliams, Pgh.	.15
☐	184	Carmen Castillo, Cle.	.15
☐	185	Al Holland, Pha.	.15
☐	186	Jerry Mumphrey, Hou.	.15
☐	187	Chris Chambliss, Atl.	.15
☐	188	Jim Clancy, Tor.	.15
☐	189	Glenn Wilson, Pha.	.15
☐	190	Rusty Staub, NYM.	.25
☐	191	Ozzie Smith, Stl.	1.25
☐	192	Howard Johnson, (NYM.)	.15
☐	**193**	**Jimmy Key, Tor., RC**	**1.00**
☐	194	Terry Kennedy, S.D.	.15
☐	195	Glenn Hubbard, Atl.	.15
☐	196	Pete O'Brien, Tex.	.15
☐	197	Keith Moreland, Chi.-N.L.	.15
☐	198	Eddie Milner, Cin.	.15
☐	199	Dave Engle, Min.	.15
☐	200	Reggie Jackson, Cal.	1.00
☐	201	Burt Hooton, (Tex.)	.15
☐	202	Gorman Thomas, Sea.	.15
☐	203	Larry Parrish, Tex.	.15
☐	204	Bob Stanley, Bos.	.15
☐	205	Steve Rogers, Mtl.	.15
☐	206	Phil Garner, Hou.	.15
☐	207	Ed VandeBerg, Sea.	.15
☐	208	Jack Clark, (Stl.)	.15
☐	209	Bill Campbell, Pha.	.15
☐	210	Gary Matthews, Chi.-N.L.	.15
☐	211	Dave Palmer, Mtl.	.15
☐	212	Tony Perez, Cin.	.35
☐	213	Sammy Stewart, Bal.	.15
☐	214	John Tudor, (Stl.)	.15
☐	215	Bob Brenly, S.F.	.15
☐	216	Jim Gantner, Mil.	.15
☐	217	Bryan Clark, Tor.	.15
☐	218	Doyle Alexander, Tor.	.15
☐	219	Bo Diaz, Pha.	.15
☐	220	Fred Lynn, (Bal.)	.15
☐	221	Eddie Murray, Bal.	1.00
☐	222	Hubie Brooks, (Mtl.)	.15
☐	223	Tom Hume, Cin.	.15
☐	224	Al Cowens, Sea.	.15
☐	225	Mike Boddicker, Bal.	.15
☐	226	Len Matuszek, Pha.	.15
☐	227	Danny Darwin, (Mil.)	.15
☐	228	Scott McGregor, Bal.	.15
☐	229	Dave LaPoint, (S.F.)	.15
☐	230	Gary Carter, (NYM.)	.50
☐	231	Joaquin Andujar, Stl.	.15
☐	232	Rafael Ramirez, Atl.	.15
☐	233	Wayne Gross, Bal.	.15
☐	234	Neil Allen, Stl.	.15
☐	235	Garry Maddox, Pha.	.15
☐	236	Mark Thurmond, S.D.	.15
☐	237	Julio Franco, Cle.	.15
☐	238	Ray Burris, (Mil.)	.15
☐	239	Tim Teufel, Min.	.15
☐	240	Dave Stieb, Tor.	.15
☐	241	Brett Butler, Cle.	.15
☐	242	Greg Brock, L.A.	.15
☐	**243**	**Barbaro Garbey, Det., RC**	**.15**
☐	244	Greg Walker, Chi.-A.L.	.15
☐	245	Chili Davis, S.F.	.15
☐	246	Darrell Porter, Stl.	.15
☐	247	Tippy Martinez, Bal.	.15
☐	248	Terry Forster, Atl.	.15
☐	249	Harold Baines, Chi.-A.L.	.15
☐	250	Jesse Orosco, NYM.	.15
☐	251	Brad Gulden, Cin.	.15
☐	252	Mike Hargrove, Cle.	.15
☐	253	Nick Esasky, Cin.	.15
☐	**254**	**Frank Williams, S.F., RC**	**.15**
☐	255	Lonnie Smith, Stl.	.15
☐	256	Daryl Sconiers, Cal.	.15
☐	257	Brian Little, (Chi.-A.L.), Error	.15
☐	258	Terry Francona, Mtl.	.15
☐	**259**	**Mark Langston, Sea., RC**	**.35**
☐	260	Dave Righetti, NYY.	.15
☐	261	Checklist (133 - 264)	.25
☐	262	Bob Horner, Atl.	.15
☐	263	Mel Hall, Cle.	.15
☐	264	John Shelby, Bal.	.15
☐	265	Juan Samuel, Pha.	.15
☐	266	Frank Viola, Min.	.15
☐	267	Jim Fanning, Manager, Mtl.	.15
☐	268	Dick Ruthven, Chi.-N.L.	.15
☐	269	Bobby Ramos, Mtl.	.15
☐	270	Dan Quisenberry, K.C.	.15
☐	271	Dwight Evans, Bos.	.15
☐	272	Andre Thornton, Cle.	.15
☐	**273**	**Orel Hershiser, L.A., RC**	**.75**
☐	274	Ray Knight, NYM.	.15
☐	275	Bill Caudill, (Tor.)	.15
☐	276	Charlie Hough, Tex.	.15
☐	277	Tim Raines, Mtl.	.15
☐	278	Mike Squires, Chi.-A.L.	.15
☐	279	Alex Trevino, Atl.	.15
☐	**280**	**Ron Romanick, Cal., RC**	**.15**
☐	281	Tom Niedenfuer, L.A.	.15
☐	282	Mike Stenhouse, (Min.)	.15
☐	283	Terry Puhl, Hou.	.35
☐	284	Hal McRae, K.C.	.15
☐	285	Dan Driessen, Mtl.	.15
☐	286	Rudy Law, Chi.-A.L.	.15
☐	287	Walt Terrell, (Det.)	.15
☐	**288**	**Jeff Kunkel, Tex., RC**	**.15**
☐	289	Bob Knepper, Hou.	.15
☐	290	Cecil Cooper, Mil.	.15
☐	291	Bob Welch, L.A.	.15
☐	292	Frank Pastore, Cin.	.15
☐	293	Dan Schatzeder, Mtl.	.15
☐	294	Tom Nieto, Stl.	.15
☐	295	Joe Niekro, Hou.	.15
☐	296	Ryne Sandberg, Chi.-N.L.	1.00
☐	297	Gary Lucas, Mtl.	.15
☐	298	John Castino, Min.	.15
☐	299	Bill Doran, Hou.	.15
☐	300	Rod Carew, Cal.	.50
☐	301	John Montefusco, NYY.	.15
☐	302	Johnnie LeMaster, S.F.	.15
☐	303	Jim Beattie, Sea.	.15

☐ 304 Gary Gaetti, Min. .15
☐ 305 Dale Berra, (NYY.) .15
☐ 306 Rick Reuschel, Chi.-N.L. .15
☐ 307 Ken Oberkfell, Atl. .15
☐ 308 Kent Hrbek, Min. .15
☐ 309 Mike Witt, Cal. .15
☐ 310 Manny Trillo, S.F. .15
☐ 311 Jim Gott, (S.F.) .15
☐ 312 LaMarr Hoyt, (S.D.) .15
☐ 313 Dave Schmidt, Tex. .15
☐ 314 Ron Oester, Cin. .15
☐ 315 Doug Sisk, NYM. .15
☐ 316 John Lowenstein, Bal. .15
☐ 317 Derrel Thomas, (Cal.) .15
☐ 318 Ted Simmons, Mil. .15
☐ 319 Darrell Evans, Det. .15
☐ 320 Dale Murphy, Atl. .15
☐ **321 Ricky Horton, Stl., RC .15**
☐ 322 Ken Phelps, Sea. .15
☐ 323 Lee Mazzilli, Pgh. .15
☐ 324 Don Mattingly, NYY. 3.00
☐ 325 John Denny, Pha. .15
☐ 326 Ken Singleton, Bal. .15
☐ 327 Brook Jacoby, Cle. .15
☐ 328 Greg Luzinski, Chi.-A.L. .15
☐ 329 Bob Ojeda, Bos. .15
☐ 330 Leon Durham, Chi.-N.L. .15
☐ 331 Bill Laskey, S.F. .15
☐ 332 Ben Oglivie, Mil. .15
☐ 333 Willie Hernandez, Det. .15
☐ 334 Bob Dernier, Chi.-N.L. .15
☐ 335 Bruce Benedict, Atl. .15
☐ 336 Rance Mulliniks, Tor. .15
☐ 337 Rick Cerone, (Atl.) .15
☐ 338 Britt Burns, Chi.-A.L. .15
☐ 339 Danny Heep, NYM. .15
☐ 340 Robin Yount, Mil. .50
☐ 341 Andy Van Slyke, Stl. .15
☐ 342 Curt Wilkerson, Tex. .15
☐ 343 Bill Russell, L.A. .15
☐ 344 Dave Henderson, Sea. .15
☐ 345 Charlie Lea, Mtl. .15
☐ **346 Terry Pendleton, Stl., RC .50**
☐ 347 Carney Lansford, Oak. .15
☐ 348 Bob Boone, Cal. .15
☐ 349 Mike Easler, Bos. .15
☐ 350 Wade Boggs, Bos. .75
☐ 351 Atlee Hammaker, S.F. .15
☐ 352 Joe Morgan, Oak. .50
☐ 353 Damaso Garcia, Tor. .15
☐ 354 Floyd Bannister, Chi.-A.L. .15
☐ 355 Bert Blyleven, Cle. .15
☐ 356 John Butcher, Min. .15
☐ 357 Fernando Valenzuela, L.A. .15
☐ 358 Tony Péna, Pgh. .15
☐ 359 Mike Smithson, Min. .15
☐ 360 Steve Carlton, Pha. .50
☐ 361 Alfredo Griffin, (Oak.) .15
☐ 362 Craig McMurtry, Atl. .15
☐ 363 Bill Dawley, Hou. .15
☐ 364 Richard Dotson, Chi.-A.L. .15
☐ 365 Carmelo Martinez, S.D. .15
☐ 366 Ron Cey, Chi.-N.L. .15
☐ 367 Tony Scott, Mtl. .15
☐ 368 Dave Bergman, Det. .15
☐ 369 Steve Sax, L.A. .15
☐ 370 Bruce Sutter, (Atl.) .15
☐ 371 Mickey Rivers, Tex. .15
☐ 372 Kirk Gibson, Det. .15
☐ 373 Scott Sanderson, Chi.-N.L. .15
☐ 374 Brian Downing, Cal. .15
☐ 375 Jeff Reardon, Mtl. .15
☐ 376 Frank DiPino, Hou. .15
☐ 377 Checklist 265 - 396 .25
☐ 378 Alan Wiggins, S.D. .15
☐ 379 Charles Hudson, Pha. .15
☐ 380 Ken Griffey, NYY. .25
☐ 381 Tom Paciorek, Chi.-A.L. .15
☐ 382 Jack Morris, Det. .15
☐ 383 Tony Gwynn, S.D. 3.50
☐ 384 Jody Davis, Chi.-N.L. .15
☐ 385 Jose DeLeon, Pgh. .15
☐ 386 Bob Kearney, Sea. .15
☐ 387 George Wright, Tex. .15
☐ 388 Ron Guidry, NYY. .15
☐ 389 Rick Manning, Mil. .15
☐ 390 Sid Fernandez, NYM. .15
☐ 391 Bruce Bochte, Oak. .15
☐ 392 Dan Petry, Det. .15
☐ 393 Tim Stoddard, (S.D.) .15
☐ 394 Tony Armas, Bos. .15
☐ 395 Paul Molitor, Mil. 1.00
☐ 396 Mike Heath, Oak. .15

1985 POSTER INSERTS

This 24-card poster insert featured players from the Montreal Expos and the Toronto Blue Jays. The posters were inserted in the 1985 regular wax packs. The posters are folded twice.

Poster Size: 4 14/16" x 6 13/16'

Face: Four colour, blue or red border; name, position, team numbered _ of 24, bilingual

Back: Blank

Imprint: © 1985 O-Pee-Chee Co. Ltd. Printed in Canada/imprimé au Canada

Complete Set (24 posters): 15.00

Common Player: .75

	No.	Player	MINT
☐	1	Mike Fitzgerald, Mtl.	.75
☐	2	Dan Driessen, Mtl.	.75
☐	3	Dave Palmer, Mtl.	.75
☐	4	U.L. Washington, Mtl.	.75
☐	5	Hubie Brooks, Mtl.	.75
☐	6	Tim Wallach, Mtl.	.75
☐	7	Tim Raines, Mtl.	1.25
☐	8	Herm Winningham, Mtl.	.75
☐	9	Andre Dawson, Mtl.	2.00
☐	10	Charlie Lea, Mtl.	.75
☐	11	Steve Rogers, Mtl.	.75
☐	12	Jeff Reardon, Mtl.	.75

	No.	Player	MINT
☐	13	Buck Martinez, Tor.	.75
☐	14	Willie Upshaw, Tor.	.75
☐	15	Damaso Garcia, Tor., Error	.75
☐	16	Tony Fernandez, Tor.	.75
☐	17	Rance Mulliniks, Tor.	.75
☐	18	Jorge Bell, Tor.	.75
☐	19	Lloyd Moseby, Tor.	.75
☐	20	Jesse Barfield, Tor.	.75
☐	21	Doyle Alexander, Tor.	.75
☐	22	Dave Stieb, Tor.	.75
☐	23	Bill Caudill, Tor.	.75
☐	24	Gary Lavelle, Tor.	.75

1985 O-PEE-CHEE STICKERS

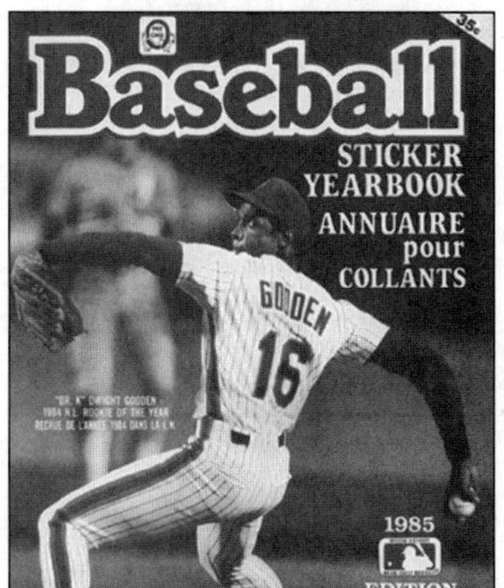

58–NOLAN RYAN

O-PEE-CHEE BASEBALL CARDS
THE REAL ONES
—a baseball tradition
★
Collect the full series 396 cards
★
Complete with all statistics

CARTES DE BASEBALL O-PEE-CHEE
LES VRAIES
—une tradition du baseball
★
Collectionne toute la série de 396 cartes
★
Cartes complètes avec toutes les statistiques

© 1985 O-PEE-CHEE CO. LTD. PRINTED IN ITALY - IMPRIMÉ EN ITALIE

Sticker Size: 2 1/8" x 3"
Face: Four colour, white border; number
Back: Blue on card stock; name, number, bilingual
Imprint: © 1985 O-PEE-CHEE CO., LTD. PRINTED IN ITALY IMPRIMê EN ITALIE

Complete Set (376 stickers):	**30.00**
Album:	**5.00**
Common Sticker:	**.15**

	No.	Player	MINT
☐	1	Steve Garvey, S.D.	.25
☐	2	Steve Garvey, S.D.	.25
☐	3	Dwight Gooden, NYM.	.25
☐	4	Dwight Gooden, NYM.	.25
☐	5	Joe Morgan, Oak.	.35
☐	6	Joe Morgan, Oak.	.35
☐	7	Don Sutton, Mil.	.35
☐	8	Don Sutton, Mil.	.35
☐	9	Jack Morris, Det.	.15
☐	10	Milt Wilcox, Det.	.15
☐	11	Kirk Gibson, Det.	.15
☐	12	Gary Matthews, Chi.-N.L.	.15
☐	13	Steve Garvey, S.D.	.25
☐	14	Steve Garvey, S.D.	.25
☐	15	Jack Morris, S.D.	.15
☐	16	Kurt Bevacqua, S.D.	.15
☐	17	Milt Wilcox, Det.	.15
☐	18	Alan Trammell, Det.	.15
☐	19	Kirk Gibson, Det.	.15
☐	20	Alan Trammell, Det.	.15
☐	21	Tigers Celebrate	.15
☐	22	Dale Murphy, Atl.	.25
☐	23	Steve Bedrosian, Atl.	.15
☐	24	Bob Horner, Atl.	.15
☐	25	Claudell Washington, Atl.	.15
☐	34	Ryne Sandberg, Chi.-N.L.	1.00
☐	35	Rick Sutcliffe, Chi.-N.L.	.15
☐	36	Leon Durham, Chi.-N.L.	.15
☐	37	Jody Davis, Chi.-N.L.	.15
☐	46	Mario Soto, Cin.	.15
☐	47	Dave Parker, Cin.	.15
☐	48	Dave Concepcion, Cin.	.15
☐	49	Gary Redus, Cin.	.15
☐	58	Nolan Ryan, Hou.	3.00
☐	59	Jose Cruz, Hou.	.15
☐	60	Jerry Mumphrey, Hou.	.15
☐	61	Enos Cabell, Hou.	.15
☐	70	Pedro Guerrero, L.A.	.15
☐	71	Fernando Valenzuela, L.A.	.15
☐	72	Mike Marshall, L.A.	.15
☐	73	Alejandro Pena, L.A.	.15
☐	82	Tim Raines, Mtl.	.15
☐	83	Gary Carter, Mtl.	.35
☐	84	Charlie Lea, Mtl.	.15
☐	85	Jeff Reardon, Mtl.	.15
☐	98	Keith Hernandez, NYM.	.15
☐	99	George Foster, NYM.	.15
☐	100	Darryl Strawberry, NYM.	.35
☐	101	Jesse Orosco, NYM.	.15
☐	110	Ozzie Virgil, Pha.	.15
☐	111	Mike Schmidt, Pha.	.50
☐	112	Steve Carlton, Pha.	.75
☐	113	Al Holland, Pha.	.15
☐	122	Bill Madlock, Pgh.	.15
☐	123	John Candelaria, Pgh.	.15
☐	124	Tony Pena, Pgh.	.15
☐	125	Jason Thompson, Pgh.	.15
☐	134	George Hendrick, Stl.	.15
☐	135	Bruce Sutter, Stl.	.15
☐	136	Joaquin Andujar, Stl.	.15
☐	137	Ozzie Smith, Stl.	1.50
☐	146	Tony Gwynn, S.D.	3.00
☐	147	Rich Gossage, S.D.	.15
☐	148	Terry Kennedy, S.D.	.15
☐	149	Steve Garvey, S.D.	.25
☐	158	Bob Brenly, S.F.	.15
☐	159	Gary Lavelle, S.F.	.15
☐	160	Jack Clark, S.F.	.15
☐	161	Jeff Leonard, S.F.	.15
☐	174	Tony Gwynn, S.D.	1.50
☐	175	Ryne Sandberg, ChiC	.50
☐	176	Steve Garvey, S.D.	.25
☐	177	Dale Murphy, Atl.	.25
☐	178	Mike Schmidt, Pha.	.25
☐	179	Darryl Strawberry, NYM.	.15
☐	180	Gary Carter, Mtl.	.25

- ☐ 181 Ozzie Smith, Stl. .75
- ☐ 182 Charlie Lea, Mtl. .15
- ☐ 183 Lou Whitaker, Det. .15
- ☐ 184 Rod Carew, Cal. .25
- ☐ 185 Cal Ripken, Bal. 1.50
- ☐ 186 Dave Winfield, NYY. .25
- ☐ 187 Reggie Jackson, Cal. .50
- ☐ 188 George Brett, K.C. .75
- ☐ 189 Lance Parrish, Det. .15
- ☐ 190 Chet Lemon, Det. .15
- ☐ 191 Dave Stieb, Tor. .15
- ☐ 196 Eddie Murray, Bal. 1.00
- ☐ 197 Cal Ripken, Bal. 3.00
- ☐ 198 Scott McGregor, Bal. .15
- ☐ 199 Rick Dempsey, Bal. .15
- ☐ 208 Jim Rice, Bos. .15
- ☐ 209 Tony Armas, Bos. .15
- ☐ 210 Wade Boggs, Bos. 1.00
- ☐ 211 Bruce Hurst, Bos. .15
- ☐ 220 Reggie Jackson, Cal. 1.00
- ☐ 221 Geoff Zahn, Cal. .15
- ☐ 222 Doug DeCinces, Cal. .15
- ☐ 223 Rod Carew, Cal. .50
- ☐ 232 Ron Kittle, ChiW .15
- ☐ 233 Richard Dotson, Chi.-A.L. .15
- ☐ 234 Harold Baines, Chi.-A.L. .15
- ☐ 235 Tom Seaver, Chi.-A.L. .35
- ☐ 244 Andre Thornton, Cle. .15
- ☐ 245 Julio Franco, Cle. .15
- ☐ 246 Brett Butler, Cle. .15
- ☐ 247 Bert Blyleven, Cle. .15
- ☐ 256 Jack Morris, Det. .15
- ☐ 257 Willie Hernandez, Det. .15
- ☐ 258 Alan Trammell, Det. .15
- ☐ 259 Lance Parrish, Det. .15
- ☐ 268 George Brett, K.C. 1.50
- ☐ 269 Dan Quisenberry, K.C. .15
- ☐ 270 Hal McRae, K.C. .15
- ☐ 271 Steve Balboni, K.C. .15
- ☐ 284 Robin Yount, Mil. .75
- ☐ 285 Rollie Fingers, Mil. .35
- ☐ 286 Jim Sundberg, Mil. .15
- ☐ 287 Cecil Cooper, Mil. .15
- ☐ 296 Kent Hrbek, Min. .15
- ☐ 297 Ron Davis, Min. .15
- ☐ 298 Dave Engle, Min. .15
- ☐ 299 Tom Brunansky, Min. .15
- ☐ 308 Dave Winfield, NYY. .50
- ☐ 309 Phil Niekro, NYY. .50
- ☐ 310 Don Mattingly, NYY. 2.00
- ☐ 311 Don Baylor, NYY. .15
- ☐ 320 Dave Kingman, Oak. .15
- ☐ 321 Rickey Henderson, Oak. .75
- ☐ 322 Bill Caudill, Oak. .15
- ☐ 323 Dwayne Murphy, Oak. .15
- ☐ 332 Alvin Davis, Sea. .15
- ☐ 333 Al Cowens, Sea. .15
- ☐ 334 Jim Beattie, Sea. .15
- ☐ 335 Bob Kearney, Sea. .15
- ☐ 344 Pete O'Brien, Tex. .15
- ☐ 345 Charlie Hough, Tex. .15
- ☐ 346 Larry Parrish, Tex. .15
- ☐ 347 Buddy Bell, Tex. .15
- ☐ 356 Dave Stieb, Tor. .15
- ☐ 357 Damaso Garcia, Tor. .15
- ☐ 358 Willie Upshaw, Tor. .15
- ☐ 359 Lloyd Moseby, Tor. .15
- ☐ 368 Alvin Davis, Sea. .15
- ☐ 369 Juan Samuel, Pha. .15
- ☐ 370 Brook Jacoby, Cle. .15
- ☐ 371 Mark Langston, Sea./Dwight Gooden, NYM. .25
- ☐ 372 Mike Fitzgerald, NYM. .15
- ☐ 373 Jackie Gutierrez, Bos. .15
- ☐ 374 Dan Gladden, S.F. .15
- ☐ 375 Carmelo Martinez, S.D. .15
- ☐ 376 Kirby Puckett, Min. 3.50

MULTIPLE STICKERS

- ☐ 26/212 Rick Mahler, Atl./ Dwight Evans, Bos. .15
- ☐ 27/213 Rafael Ramirez, Atl./ Mike Easler, Bos. .15
- ☐ 28/214 Craig McMurtry, Atl./ Bill Buckner, Bos. .15
- ☐ 29/215 Chris Chambliss, Atl./ Bob Stanley, Bos. .15
- ☐ 30/216 Alex Trevino, Atl./ Jackie Gutierrez, Bos. .15
- ☐ 31/217 Bruce Benedict, Atl./ Rich Gedman, Bos. .15
- ☐ 32/218 Ken Oberkfell, Atl./ Jerry Remy, Bos. .15
- ☐ 33/219 Glenn Hubbard, Atl./ Marty Barrett, Bos. .15
- ☐ 38/224 Bob Dernier, Chi.-N.L./ Brian Downing, Cal. .15
- ☐ 39/225 Keith Moreland, Chi.-N.L./ Fred Lynn, Cal. .15
- ☐ 40/226 Scott Anderson, Chi.-N.L./ Gary Pettis, Cal. .15
- ☐ 41/227 Lee Smith, Chi.-N.L./ Mike Witt, Cal. .25
- ☐ 42/228 Ron Cey, Chi.-N.L./ Bob Boone, Cal. .15
- ☐ 43/229 Steve Trout, Chi.-N.L./ Tommy John, Cal. .15
- ☐ 44/230 Gary Matthews, Chi.-N.L./ Bobby Grich, Cal. .15
- ☐ 45/231 Larry Bowa, Chi.-N.L./ Ron Romanick, Cal. .15
- ☐ 50/236 Ted Power, Cin./ Greg Walker, Chi.-A.L. .15
- ☐ 51/237 Nick Esasky, Cin./ Roy Smalley, Chi.-A.L. .15
- ☐ 52/238 Duane Walker, Cin./ Greg Luzinski, Chi.-A.L. .15
- ☐ 53/239 Eddie Milner, Cin./ Julio Cruz, Chi.-A.L. .15
- ☐ 54/240 Ron Oester, Cin./ Scott Fletcher, Chi.-A.L. .15
- ☐ 55/241 Cesar Cedeno, Cin./ Rudy Law, Chi.-A.L. .15
- ☐ 56/242 Joe Price, Cin./ Vance Law, Chi.-A.L. .15
- ☐ 57/243 Pete Rose, Cin./ Carlton Fisk, Chi.-A.L. 1.00
- ☐ 62/248 Bob Knepper, Hou./ Mike Hargrove, Cle. .15
- ☐ 63/249 Dickie Thon, Hou./ George Vukovich, Cle. .15
- ☐ 64/250 Phil Garner, Hou./ Pat Tabler, Cle. .15
- ☐ 65/251 Craig Reynolds, Hou./ Brook Jacoby, Cle. .15
- ☐ 66/252 Frank DiPino, Hou./ Tony Bernazard, Cle. .15
- ☐ 67/253 Terry Puhl, Hou./ Ernie Camacho, Cle. .25
- ☐ 68/254 Bill Doran, Hou./ Mel Hall, Cle. .15
- ☐ 69/255 Joe Niekro, Hou./ Carmen Castillo, Cle. .15
- ☐ 74/260 Orel Hershiser, L.A./ Chet Lemon, Det. .35
- ☐ 75/261 Ken Landreaux, L.A./ Lou Whitaker, Det. .15
- ☐ 76/262 Bill Russell, L.A./ Howard Johnson, Det. .15
- ☐ 77/263 Steve Sax, L.A./ Barbaro Garbey, Det. .15
- ☐ 78/264 Rick Honeycutt, L.A./ Dan Petry, Det. .15
- ☐ 79/265 Mike Scioscia, L.A./ Aurelio Lopez, Det. .15
- ☐ 80/266 Tom Niedenfuer, L.A./ Larry Herndon, Det. .15
- ☐ 81/267 Candy Maldonado, L.A./ Kirk Gibson, Det. .15
- ☐ 86/272 Andre Dawson, Mtl./ Pat Sheridan, K.C. .35
- ☐ 87/273 Tim Wallach, Mtl./ Jorge Orta, K.C. .15
- ☐ 88/274 Terry Francona, Mtl./ Frank White, K.C. .15
- ☐ 89/275 Steve Rogers, Mtl./ Bud Black, K.C. .15
- ☐ 90/276 Bryn Smith, Mtl./ Darryl Motley, K.C. .15
- ☐ 91/277 Bill Gullickson, Mtl./ Willie Wilson, K.C. .15
- ☐ 92/278 Dan Driessen, Mtl./ Larry Gura, K.C. .15
- ☐ 93/279 Doug Flynn, Mtl./ Don Slaught, K.C. .15
- ☐ 102/288 Mookie Wilson, NYM./ Jaime Cocanower, Mil. .15
- ☐ 103/289 Doug Sisk, NYM./ Mike Caldwell, Mil. .15
- ☐ 104/290 Hubie Brooks, NYM./ Don Sutton, Mil. .35
- ☐ 105/291 Ron Darling, NYM./ Rick Manning, Mil. .15
- ☐ 106/292 Wally Backman, NYM./ Ben Oglivie, Mil. .15
- ☐ 107/293 Dwight Gooden, NYM./ Moose Haas, Mil. .15
- ☐ 108/294 Mike Fitzgerald, NYM./ Ted Simmons, Mil. .15
- ☐ 109/295 Walt Terrell, NYM./ Jim Gantner, Mil. .15
- ☐ 114/300 Juan Samuel, Pha./ Frank Viola, Min. .15
- ☐ 115/301 Von Hayes, Pha./ Mike Smithson, Min. .15
- ☐ 116/302 Jeff Stone, Pha./ Gary Gaetti, Min. .15
- ☐ 117/303 Jerry Koosman, Pha./ Tim Teufel, Min. .15
- ☐ 118/304 Al Oliver, Pha./ Mickey Hatcher, Min. .15

- ☐ 119/305 John Denny, Pha./ John Butcher, Min. .15
- ☐ 120/306 Charles Hudson, Pha./ Darrell Brown, Min. .15
- ☐ 121/307 Garry Maddox, Pha./ Kirby Puckett, Min. 3.00
- ☐ 126/312 Lee Lacy, Pgh./ Willie Randolph, NYY. .15
- ☐ 127/313 Rick Rhoden, Pgh./ Ron Guidry, NYY. .15
- ☐ 128/314 Doug Frobel, Pgh./ Dave Righetti, NYY. .15
- ☐ 129/315 Kent Tekulve, Pgh./ Bobby Meacham, NYY. .15
- ☐ 130/316 Johnny Ray, Pgh./ Butch Wynegar, NYY. .15
- ☐ 131/317 Marvell Wynne, Pgh./ Mike Pagliarulo, Pgh. .15
- ☐ 132/318 Larry McWilliams, Pgh./ Joe Cowley, Pgh. .15
- ☐ 133/319 Dale Berra, Pgh./ John Montefusco, NYY. .15
- ☐ 138/324 Andy Van Slyke, Stl./ Steve McCatty, Oak. .15
- ☐ 139/325 Lonnie Smith, Stl./ Joe Morgan, Oak. .50
- ☐ 140/326 Darrell Porter, Stl. /Mike Heath, Oak. .15
- ☐ 141/327 Willie McGee, Stl./ Chris Codiroli, Oak. .15
- ☐ 142/328 Tom Herr, Stl./ Ray Burris, Oak. .15
- ☐ 143/329 Dave LaPoint, Stl./ Tony Phillips, Oak. .15
- ☐ 144/330 Neil Allen, Stl./ Carney Lansford, Oak. .15
- ☐ 145/331 David Green, Stl./ Bruce Bochte, Oak. .15
- ☐ 150/336 Alan Wiggins, S.D./ Ed VandeBerg, Sea. .15
- ☐ 151/337 Garry Templeton, S.D./ Mark Langston, Sea. .35
- ☐ 152/338 Eddie Whitson, S.D./ Dave Henderson, Sea. .15
- ☐ 153/339 Tim Lollar, S.D./ Spike Owen, Sea. .15
- ☐ 154/340 Dave Dravecky, S.D./ Matt Young, Sea. .15
- ☐ 155/341 Craig Nettles, S.D./ Jack Perconte, Sea. .15
- ☐ 156/342 Eric Show, S.D./ Barry Bonnell, Sea. .15
- ☐ 157/352 Carmelo Martinez, S.D./ Mike Stanton, Sea. .15
- ☐ 162/348 Chili Davis, S.F./ Frank Tanana, Tex. .15
- ☐ 163/349 Mike Krukow, S.F./ Curt Wilkerson, Tex. .15
- ☐ 164/350 Johnnie LeMaster, S.F./ Jeff Kunkel, Tex. .15
- ☐ 165/351 Atlee Hammeker, S.F./ Billy Sample, Tex. .15
- ☐ 166/352 Dan Gladden, S.F./ Danny Darwin, Tex. .15
- ☐ 167/353 Greg Minton, S.F./ Gary Ward, Tex. .15
- ☐ 168/354 Joel Youngblood, S.F./ Mike Mason, Tex. .15
- ☐ 169/355 Frank Williams, S.F./ Mickey Rivers, Tex. .15
- ☐ 200/360 Tippy Martinez, Bal./ George Bell, Tor. .15
- ☐ 201/361 Ken Singleton, Bal./ Luis Leal, Tor. .15
- ☐ 202/362 Mike Boddicker, Bal./ Jesse Barfield, Tor. .15
- ☐ 203/363 Rich Dauer, Bal./ Dave Collins, Tor. .15
- ☐ 204/364 John Shelby, Bal./ Roy Lee Jackson, Tor. .15
- ☐ 205/365 Al Bumbry, Bal./ Doyle Alexander, Tor. .15
- ☐ 206/366 John Lowenstein, Bal./ Alfredo Griffin, Tor. .15
- ☐ 207/367 Mike Flanagan, Bal. Cliff Johnson, Tor. .15
- ☐ 94/95/96/97 M.Schmidt/ T.Armas/ D.Murphy/ R.Sutcliffe .50
- ☐ 170/171/172/173 T.Gwynn/ D.Mattingly/ B.Sutter/ D.Quisenberry .75
- ☐ 192/193/194/195 G.Carter/ M.Schmidt/ T.Armas/ M.Witt .50
- ☐ 280/281/282/283 D.Gooden/ M.Langston/ T.Raines/ R.Henderson .35

1986 GENERAL MILLS

Six booklets were issued by General Mills and appeared in specially marked boxes of Cheerios during 1986. The team logos have been removed from the player's uniforms.

Booklet Size: 15" x 3 3/4"
Face: Four colour; name, number, position, team, resume, bilingual
Back: Four colour; name, number, position, team, resume, bilingual
Imprint: None
Complete Set (6 booklets): 40.00

	No.	Player	MINT
☐	1	A. L. East: W. Boggs; K. Gibson; R. Henderson; D. Mattingly; J. Morris; L. Parrish; J. Rice; D. Righetti; C. Ripken; L. Whitaker	18.00
☐	2	A. L. West: H. Baines; P. Bradley; G. Brett; C. Fisk; O. Guillen; K. Hebek; R. Jackson; D. Quisenberry; B. Saberhagen; F. White	10.00
☐	3	A. L. Players, Toronto: J. Barfield; G. Bell; B. Caudill; T. Fernandez; D. Garcia; L. Moseby; R. Mullikins; D. Steib; E. Whitt	7.50
☐	4	N. L. East: G. Carter; J. Clark; G. Foster; D. Gooden; G. Matthews; W. McGee; R. Sandberg; M. Schmidt; L. Smith; O. Smith	10.00
☐	5	N. L. West: T. Kennedy; D. Concepcion; P. Guerrero; D. Murphy; G. Nettles; D. Parker; T. Perez; S. Sax; B. Sutter; F. Valenzuela	6.50
☐	6	N. L. Players, Montreal: H. Brooks; A. Dawson; Mi. Fitzgerald; V. Law; T. Raines; J. Reardon; B. Smith; J. Thompson; T. Wallach; Mi. Webster	7.50

1986 LEAF

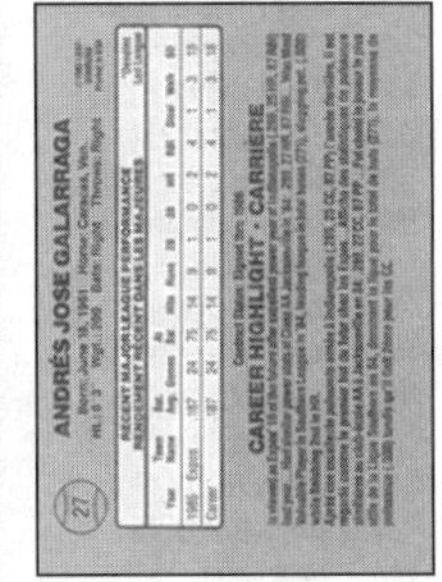

The faces of cards 1 to 26 bear the words "Donruss Diamond Kings." Cards 27 to 258 with the exception of the "Canadian Greats" painted portrait cards of Jeff Reardon and Jesse Barfield bear the words "Leaf '86" on the face. Players do not match those on the corresponding cards of the 660-card Donruss set of 1986, and the backs of the Canadian cards are in English and French. The set includes a Hank Aaron card and a 21-piece Hank Aaron puzzle.

Card Size: 2 1/2" x 3 1/2"
Face: Four colour, blue border; position, team logo
Back: Blue and black on card stock; number, resume, career highlights, bilingual
Imprint: Cards No. 1-26: © 1985 DONRUSS, MADE & PRINTED IN U.S.A. PEREZ-STEELE GALLERIES Card No. 27-258: © 1985 DONRUSS Div. LEAF, INC. Printed in USA
Complete Set (264 cards): 45.00
Common Player: .20

	No.	Player	MINT
☐	1	Kirk Gibson, Det.	.20
☐	2	Goose Gossage, S.D.	.20
☐	3	Willie McGee, Stl..	.20
☐	4	George Bell, Tor.	.20
☐	5	Tony Armas, Bos.	.20
☐	6	Chili Davis, S.F.	.20
☐	7	Cecil Cooper, Mil.	.20
☐	8	Mike Boddicker, Bal.	.20
☐	9	Davey Lopes, Chi.-N.L.	.20
☐	10	Bill Doran, Hou.	.20
☐	11	Bret Saberhagen, K.C.	.20
☐	12	Brett Butler, Chi.-N.L.	.20
☐	13	Harold Baines, Chi.-A.L.	.20
☐	14	Mike Davis, Oak.	.20
☐	15	Tony Perez, Cin.	.35
☐	16	Willie Randolph, NYY.	.20
☐	17	Bob Boone, Cal.	.20
☐	18	Orel Hershiser, L.A.	.20
☐	19	Johnny Ray, Pgh.	.20
☐	20	Gary Ward, Tex.	.20
☐	21	Rick Mahler, Atl.	.20
☐	22	Phil Bradley, Sea.	.20
☐	23	Jerry Koosman, Pha.	.20
☐	24	Tom Brunansky, Min.	.20
☐	25	Andre Dawson, Mtl.	1.00
☐	26	Dwight Gooden, NYY.	.20

	No.	Player	Price
☐	**27**	**Andres Galarraga, Mtl., RC**	**7.50**
☐	**28**	**Fred McGriff, Tor., RC**	**15.00**
☐	**29**	**Dave Shipanoff, Pha., RC**	**.20**
☐	30	Danny Jackson, K.C.	.20
☐	31	Robin Yount, Mil.	.75
☐	32	Mike Fitzgerald, Mtl.	.20
☐	33	Lou Whitaker, Det.	.20
☐	34	Alfredo Griffin, Oak.	.20
☐	35	Oil Can Boyd, Bos.	.20
☐	36	Ron Guidry, NYY.	.20
☐	37	Rickey Henderson, NYY.	.35
☐	38	Jack Morris, Det.	.20
☐	39	Brian Downing,	.20
☐	40	Mike Marshall, L.A.	.20
☐	41	Tony Gwynn, S.D.	2.50
☐	42	George Brett, K.C.	2.50
☐	43	Jim Gantner, Mil.	.20
☐	44	Hubie Brooks, Mtl.	.20
☐	45	Tony Fernandez, Tor.	.20
☐	46	Oddibe McDowell, Tex.	.20
☐	47	Ozzie Smith, Stl..	2.00
☐	48	Ken Griffey, NYY.	.20
☐	49	Jose Cruz, Hou.	.20
☐	50	Mariano Duncan, L.A.	.20
☐	51	Mike Schmidt, Pha.	1.00
☐	52	Pat Tabler, Cle.	.20
☐	53	Pete Rose, Cin.	1.25
☐	54	Frank White, K.C.	.20
☐	55	Carney Lansford, Oak.	.20
☐	56	Steve Garvey, S.D.	.35
☐	57	Vance Law, Mtl.	.20
☐	58	Tony Pena, Pgh.	.20
☐	59	Wayne Tolleson, Tex.	.20
☐	60	Dale Murphy, Atl.	.35
☐	61	LaMarr Hoyt, S.D.	.20
☐	62	Ryne Sandberg, Chi.-N.L.	1.00
☐	63	Gary Carter, NYM.	1.00
☐	64	Lee Smith, Chi.-N.L.	.20
☐	65	Alvin Davis, Sea.	.20
☐	66	Edwin Nunez, Sea.	.20
☐	67	Kent Hrbek, Min.	.20
☐	68	Dave Stieb, Tor.	.20
☐	69	Kirby Puckett, Min.	5.00
☐	70	Paul Molitor, Mil.	1.00
☐	71	Glenn Hubbard, Atl.	.20
☐	72	Lloyd Moseby, Tor.	.20
☐	73	Mike Smithson, Min.	.20
☐	74	Jeff Leonard, S.F.	.20
☐	75	Danny Darwin, Mil.	.20
☐	76	Kevin McReynolds, S.D.	.20
☐	77	Bill Buckner, Bos.	.20
☐	78	Ron Oester, Cin.	.20
☐	79	Tommy Herr, Stl..	.20
☐	80	Mike Pagliarulo, NYY.	.20
☐	81	Ron Romanick, Cal.	.20
☐	82	Brook Jacoby, Cle.	.20
☐	83	Eddie Murray, Bal.	2.00
☐	84	Gary Pettis, Cal.	.20
☐	85	Chet Lemon, Det.	.20
☐	86	Toby Harrah, Tex.	.20
☐	87	Mike Scioscia, L.A.	.20
☐	88	Bert Blyleven, Min.	.20
☐	89	Dave Righetti, NYY.	.20
☐	90	Bob Knepper, Hou.	.20
☐	91	Fernando Valenzuela, L.A.	.20
☐	92	Dave Dravecky, S.D.	.20
☐	93	Julio Franco, Cle.	.20
☐	94	Keith Moreland, Chi.-N.L.	.20
☐	95	Darryl Motley, K.C.	.20
☐	96	Jack Clark, Stl..	.20
☐	97	Tim Wallach, Mtl.	.20
☐	98	Steve Balboni, K.C.	.20
☐	99	Storm Davis, Bal.	.20
☐	100	Jay Howell, Oak.	.20
☐	101	Alan Trammell, Det.	.20
☐	102	Willie Hernandez, Det.	.20
☐	103	Don Mattlingly, NYY.	2.50
☐	104	Lee Lacy, Bal.	.20
☐	105	Pedro Guerrero, L.A.	.20
☐	106	Willie Wilson, K.C.	.20
☐	107	Craig Reynolds, Hou.	.20
☐	108	Tim Raines, Mtl.	.20
☐	109	Shane Rawley, Pha.	.20
☐	110	Larry Parrish, Tex.	.20
☐	111	Eric Show, S.D.	.20
☐	112	Mike Witt, Cal.	.20
☐	113	Dennis Eckersley, Chi.-N.L.	.20
☐	114	Mike Moore, Sea.	.20
☐	**115**	**Vince Coleman, Stl., RC**	**.50**
☐	116	Damaso Garcia, Tor.	.20
☐	117	Steve Carlton, Pha.	.75
☐	118	Floyd Bannister, Chi.-A.L.	.20
☐	119	Mario Soto, Cin.	.20
☐	120	Fred Lynn, Bal.	.20
☐	121	Bob Horner, Atl.	.20
☐	122	Rick Sutcliffe, Chi.-N.L.	.20
☐	123	Walt Terrell, Det.	.20
☐	124	Keith Hernandez, NYM.	.20
☐	125	Dave Winfield, NYY.	.75
☐	126	Frank Viola, Min.	.20
☐	127	Dwight Evans, Bos.	.20
☐	128	Willie Upshaw, Tor.	.20
☐	129	Andre Thornton, Cle.	.20
☐	130	Donnie Moore, Cal.	.20
☐	131	Darryl Strawberry, NYM.	.35
☐	132	Nolan Ryan, Hou.	5.00
☐	133	Garry Templeton, S.D.	.20
☐	134	John Tudor, Stl.	.20
☐	135	Dave Parker, Cin.	.20
☐	136	Larry McWilliams, Pgh.	.20
☐	137	Terry Pendleton, Stl.	.20
☐	138	Terry Puhl, Hou.	.50
☐	139	Bob Dernier, Chi.-N.L.	.20
☐	140	Ozzie Guillen, Chi.-A.L.	.20
☐	141	Jim Clancy, Tor.	.20
☐	142	Cal Ripken Jr., Bal.	5.00
☐	143	Mickey Hatcher, Min.	.20
☐	144	Dan Petry, Det.	.20
☐	145	Rich Gedman, Bos.	.20
☐	146	Jim Rice, Bos.	.20
☐	147	Butch Wynegar, NYY.	.20
☐	148	Donnie Hill, Oak.	.20
☐	149	Jim Sundberg, K.C.	.20
☐	150	Joe Hesketh, Mtl.	.20
☐	151	Chris Codiroli, Oak.	.20
☐	152	Charlie Hough, Tex.	.20
☐	**153**	**Herman Winningham, Mtl., RC**	**.20**
☐	154	Dave Rozema, Tex.	.20
☐	155	Don Slaught, Tex.	.20
☐	156	Juan Beniquez, Cal.	.20
☐	157	Ted Higuera, Mil.	.20
☐	158	Andy Hawkins, S.D.	.20
☐	159	Don Robinson, Pgh.	.20
☐	160	Glenn Wilson, Pha.	.20
☐	**161**	**Ernest Riles, Mil., RC**	**.20**
☐	162	Nick Esasky, Cin.	.20
☐	163	Carlton Fisk, Chi.-A.L.	.50
☐	164	Claudell Washington, Atl.	.20

☐ 165 Scott McGregor, Bal. .20
☐ **166 Nate Snell, Bal., RC .20**
☐ 167 Ted Simmons, Mil. .20
☐ 168 Wade Boggs, Bos. .75
☐ 169 Marty Barrett, Bos. .20
☐ 170 Bud Black, K.C. .20
☐ 171 Charlie Leibrandt, K.C. .20
☐ 172 Charlie Lea, Mtl. .20
☐ 173 Reggie Jackson, Cal. .75
☐ 174 Bryn Smith, Mtl. .20
☐ 175 Glenn Davis, Hou. .20
☐ 176 Von Hayes, Pha. .20
☐ 177 Danny Cox, Stl. .20
☐ 178 Sam Khalifa, Pgh. .20
☐ 179 Tom Browning, Cin. .20
☐ 180 Scott Garrelts, S.F. .20
☐ 181 Shawon Dunston, Chi.-N.L. .20
☐ 182 Doyle Alexander, Tor. .20
☐ 183 Jim Presley, Sea. .20
☐ 184 Al Cowens, Sea. .20
☐ 185 Mark Salas, Min. .20
☐ 186 Tom Niedenfuer, L.A. .20
☐ 187 Dave Henderson, Sea. .20
☐ 188 Lonnie Smith, K.C. .20
☐ 189 Bruce Bochte, Oak. .20
☐ 190 Leon Durham, Chi.-N.L. .20
☐ 191 Terry Francona, Mtl. .20
☐ 192 Bruce Sutter, Atl. .20
☐ 193 Steve Crawford, Bos. .20
☐ 194 Bob Brenly, S.F. .20
☐ 195 Dan Pasqua, NYY. .20
☐ 196 Juan Samuel, Pha. .20
☐ 197 Floyd Rayford, Bal. .20
☐ 198 Tim Burke, Mtl. .20
☐ 199 Ben Oglivie, Sea. .20
☐ 200 Don Carman, Pha. .20
☐ 201 Lance Parrish, Det. .20
☐ 202 Terry Forster, Atl. .20
☐ 203 Neal Heaton, Cle. .20
☐ **204 Ivan Calderon, Sea., RC .20**
☐ 205 Jorge Orta, K.C. .20
☐ 206 Tom Henke, Tor. .20
☐ 207 Rick Reuschel, Pgh. .20
☐ 208 Dan Quisenberry, K.C. .20
☐ 209 Ty-Breaking: Pete Rose Hit #4191; Hit #4192 .50
☐ **210 Floyd Youmans, Mtl., RC .20**
☐ 211 Tom Filer, Tor. .20
☐ 212 R.J. Reynolds, Pgh. .20
☐ 213 Gorman Thomas, Sea. .20
☐ 214 Canadian Greats: Jeff Reardon, Mtl. .20
☐ 215 Chris Brown, S.F. .20
☐ **216 Rick Aguilera, NYM., RC .35**
☐ 217 Ernie Whitt, Tor. .20
☐ **218 Joe Orsulak, Pgh., RC .20**
☐ 219 Jimmy Key, Tor. .35
☐ 220 Atlee Hammaker, S.F. .20
☐ 221 Ron Darling, NYM. .20
☐ 222 Zane Smith, Atl. .20
☐ 223 Bob Welch, L.A. .20
☐ 224 Reid Nichols, Chi.WS .20
☐ 225 Fleet Feet: Willie McGee, Stl./ Vince Coleman, Stl. .20
☐ 226 Mark Gubicza, K.C. .20
☐ 227 Tim Birtsas, Oak. .20
☐ 228 Mike Hargrove, Cle. .20
☐ **229 Randy St. Claire, Mtl., RC .20**
☐ 230 Larry Herndon, Det. .20
☐ 231 Dusty Baker, Oak. .20
☐ 232 Mookie Wilson, NYM. .20
☐ 233 Jeff Lahti, Stl.. .20
☐ 234 Tom Seaver, Chi.-A.L. 1.00
☐ 235 Mike Scott, Hou. .20
☐ 236 Don Sutton, Cal. .75
☐ 237 Roy Smalley, Min. .20
☐ 238 Bill Madlock, L.A. .20
☐ 239 Charles Hudson, Pha. .20
☐ 240 John Franco, Cin. .20
☐ 241 Frank Tanana, Det. .20
☐ 242 Sid Fernandez, NYM. .20
☐ 243 Knuckle Brothers: Joe Niekro, NYY; Phil Niekro, NYY. .35
☐ 244 Dennis Lamp, Tor. .20
☐ 245 Gene Nelson, Chi.WS .20
☐ 246 Terry Harper, Atl. .20
☐ 247 Vida Blue, S.D. .20
☐ 248 Roger McDowell, NYM. .35
☐ 249 Tony Bernazard, Cle. .20
☐ 250 Cliff Johnson, Tor. .20
☐ 251 Hal McRae, K.C. .20
☐ 252 Garth Iorg, Tor. .20
☐ 253 Mitch Webster, Mtl. .20
☐ 254 Canadian Greats: Jesse Barfield, Tor. .20
☐ 255 Dan Driessen, S.F. .20
☐ 256 Mike Brown, Pgh. .20
☐ 257 Ron Kittle, Chi.-A.L. .20
☐ 258 Bo Diaz, Cin. .20
☐ 259 Hank Aaron .50
☐ 260 Pete Rose .50
☐ no # Checklist 1-26 .35
☐ 1 Checklist 27-106 .35
☐ 2 Checklist 107-186 .35
☐ 3 Checklist 187-260 .35

HANK AARON PUZZLE

The words "Collect all 63 pieces to complete puzzle" appear on the backs of the 21 perforated cards. The puzzle art was painted by Dick Perez, the official Hall of Fame artist, and all pieces are numbered.

Card Size: 2 1/2" x 3 1/2"
Face: Four colour, white border
Back: Black on card stock; puzzle piece number
Imprint: © DONRUSS DIAMOND KING PUZZLE
Complete Set (21 cards, 3 pcs. per card): 5.00
Common Puzzle piece: .20

1986 O-PEE-CHEE

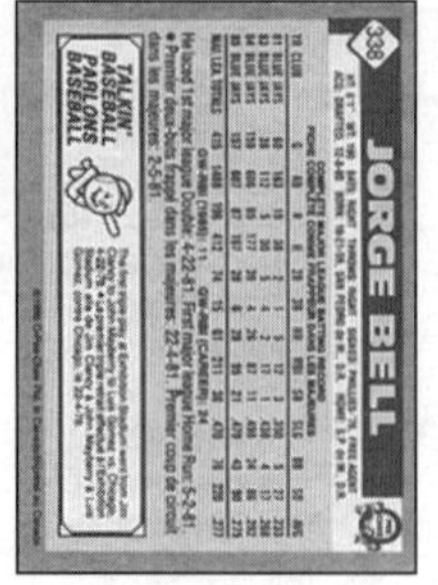

The card numbers on this 396-card set are not the same as those for the corresponding players in the 792-card Topps issue for 1986. This set is difficult to find in high grades. This is because the black border at the top of the cards was often cracked or chipped when originally trimmed at the printer.

Card Size: 2 1/2" x 3 1/2"
Face: Four colour, black and white border; name, position, team
Back: Red and black on card stock; name, number, résumé, bilingual
Imprint: © 1986 O-Pee-Chee Ptd. in Canada/imprimé au Canada

Complete Set (396 cards): 20.00
Common Player: .10

	No.	Player	MINT
☐	1	Pete Rose, Mgr., Cin.	.75
☐	2	Ken Landreaux, L.A.	.10
☐	3	Rob Picciolo, Oak.	.10
☐	4	Steve Garvey, S.D.	.25
☐	5	Andy Hawkins, S.D.	.10
☐	6	Rudy Law, Chi.-A.L.	.10
☐	7	Lonnie Smith, K.C.	.10
☐	8	Dwayne Murphy, Oak.	.10
☐	9	Moose Haas, Mil.	.10
☐	10	Tony Gwynn, S.D.	1.25
☐	11	Bob Ojeda, (NYM.)	.10
☐	**12**	**Jose Uribe, S.F., RC**	**.10**
☐	13	Bob Kearney, Sea.	.10
☐	14	Julio Cruz, Chi.-A.L.	.10
☐	15	Eddie Whitson, NYY.	.10
☐	16	Rick Schu, Pha.	.10
☐	17	Mike Stenhouse, (Bos.)	.10
☐	**18**	**Lou Thornton, Tor., RC**	**.10**
☐	19	Ryne Sandberg, Chi.-N.L.	.50
☐	20	Andre Dawson, (Mtl.)	.50
☐	21	Mark Brouhard, Mil.	.10
☐	22	Gary Lavelle, Tor.	.10
☐	23	Manny Lee, Tor.	.10
☐	24	Don Slaught, Tex.	.10
☐	25	Willie Wilson, K.C.	.10
☐	26	Mike Marshall, L.A.	.10
☐	27	Ray Knight, NYM.	.10
☐	28	Mario Soto, Cin.	.10
☐	29	Dave Anderson, L.A.	.10
☐	30	Eddie Murray, Bal.	.75
☐	31	Dusty Baker, Oak.	.10
☐	32	Steve Yeager, (Sea.)	.10
☐	33	Andy Van Slyke, Stl.	.10
☐	34	Dave Righetti, NYY.	.10
☐	35	Jeff Reardon, Mtl.	.10
☐	36	Burt Hooton, Tex.	.10
☐	37	Johnny Ray, Pgh.	.10
☐	38	Glenn Hoffman, Bos.	.10
☐	39	Rick Mahler, Atl.	.10
☐	40	Ken Griffey, NYY.	.10
☐	41	Brad Wellman, S.F.	.10
☐	42	Joe Hesketh, Mtl.	.10
☐	43	Mark Salas, Min.	.10
☐	44	Jorge Orta, K.C.	.10
☐	45	Damaso Garcia, Tor.	.10
☐	46	Jim Acker, Tor.	.10
☐	47	Bill Madlock, L.A.	.10
☐	48	Bill Almon, Pgh.	.10
☐	49	Rick Manning, Mil.	.10
☐	50	Dan Quisenberry, K.C.	.10
☐	51	Jim Gantner, Mil.	.10
☐	52	Kevin Bass, Hou.	.10
☐	**53**	**Len Dykstra, NYM., RC**	**.50**
☐	54	John Franco, Cin.	.10
☐	55	Fred Lynn, Bal.	.10
☐	56	Jim Morrison, Pgh.	.10
☐	57	Bill Doran, Hou.	.10
☐	58	Leon Durham, Chi.-N.L.	.10
☐	59	Andre Thornton, Cle.	.10
☐	60	Dwight Evans, Bos.	.10
☐	61	Larry Herndon, Det.	.10
☐	62	Bob Boone, Cal.	.10
☐	63	Kent Hrbek, Min.	.10
☐	64	Floyd Bannister, Chi.-A.L.	.10
☐	65	Harold Baines, Chi.-A.L.	.10
☐	66	Pat Tabler, Cle.	.10
☐	67	Carmelo Martinez, S.D.	.10
☐	68	Ed Lynch, NYM.	.10
☐	69	George Foster, NYM.	.10
☐	70	Dave Winfield, NYY.	.50
☐	71	Ken Schrom, (Cle.)	.10
☐	72	Toby Harrah, Tex.	.10
☐	73	Jackie Gutierrez, (Bal.)	.10
☐	74	Rance Mulliniks, Tor.	.10
☐	75	Jose DeLeon, Pgh.	.10
☐	76	Ron Romanick, Cal.	.10
☐	77	Charlie Leibrandt, K.C.	.10
☐	78	Bruce Benedict, Atl.	.10
☐	79	Dave Schmidt, (Chi.-A.L.)	.10
☐	80	Darryl Strawberry, NYM.	.10
☐	81	Wayne Krenchicki, Cin.	.10
☐	82	Tippy Martinez, Bal.	.10
☐	83	Phil Garner, Hou.	.10
☐	84	Darrell Porter, (Tex.)	.10
☐	85	Tony Perez, Cin.	.25
☐	86	Tom Waddell, Cle.	.10
☐	87	Tim Hulett, Chi.-A.L.	.10
☐	88	Barbaro Garbey, (Oak.)	.10
☐	**89**	**Randy St. Claire, Mtl., RC**	**.10**
☐	90	Garry Templeton, S.D.	.10
☐	91	Tim Teufel, (NYM.)	.10
☐	92	Al Cowens, Sea.	.10
☐	93	Scot Thompson, Mtl.	.10
☐	94	Tom Herr, Stl.	.10
☐	95	Ozzie Virgil, (Atl.)	.10
☐	96	Jose Cruz, Hou.	.10
☐	97	Gary Gaetti, Min.	.10
☐	98	Roger Clemens, Bos.	2.50
☐	99	Vance Law, Mtl.	.10
☐	100	Nolan Ryan, Hou.	2.00
☐	101	Mike Smithson, Min.	.10
☐	102	Rafael Santana, NYM.	.10
☐	103	Darrell Evans, Det.	.10
☐	104	Rich Gossage, S.D.	.10
☐	105	Gary Ward, Tex.	.10
☐	106	Jim Gott, S.F.	.10
☐	107	Rafael Ramirez, Atl.	.10
☐	108	Ted Power, Cin.	.10
☐	109	Ron Guidry, NYY.	.10
☐	110	Scott McGregor, Bal.	.10

- ☐ 111 Mike Scioscia, L.A. .10
- ☐ 112 Glenn Hubbard, Atl. .10
- ☐ 113 U.L. Washington, Mtl. .10
- ☐ 114 Al Oliver, Tor. .10
- ☐ 115 Jay Howell, Oak. .10
- ☐ 116 Brook Jacoby, Cle. .10
- ☐ 117 Willie McGee, Stl. .10
- ☐ 118 Jerry Royster, S.D. .10
- ☐ 119 Barry Bonnell, Sea. .10
- ☐ 120 Steve Carlton, Pha. .50
- ☐ 121 Alfredo Griffin, Oak. .10
- ☐ 122 David Green, (Mil.) .10
- ☐ 123 Greg Walker, Chi.-A.L. .10
- ☐ 124 Frank Tanana, Det. .10
- ☐ 125 Dave Lopes, Chi.-N.L. .10
- ☐ 126 Mike Krukow, S.F. .10
- ☐ 127 Jack Howell, Cal. .10
- ☐ 128 Greg Harris, Tex. .10
- ☐ **129 Herm Winningham, Mtl., RC .10**
- ☐ 130 Alan Trammell, Det. .10
- ☐ 131 Checklist 1 - 132 .25
- ☐ 132 Razor Shines, Mtl. .10
- ☐ 133 Bruce Sutter, Atl. .10
- ☐ 134 Carney Lansford, Oak. .10
- ☐ 135 Joe Niekro, NYY. .10
- ☐ 136 Ernie Whitt, Tor. .10
- ☐ 137 Charlie Moore, Mil. .10
- ☐ 138 Mel Hall, Cle. .10
- ☐ **139 Roger McDowell, NYM., RC .25**
- ☐ 140 John Candelaria, Cal. .10
- ☐ 141 Bob Rogers, Mgr., Mtl. .10
- ☐ 142 Manny Trillo, (Chi.-N.L.) .10
- ☐ 143 Dave Palmer, (Atl.) .10
- ☐ 144 Robin Yount, Mil. .50
- ☐ 145 Pedro Guerrero, L.A. .10
- ☐ 146 Von Hayes, Pha. .10
- ☐ 147 Lance Parrish, Det. .10
- ☐ 148 Mike Heath, (Stl.) .10
- ☐ 149 Brett Butler, Cle. .10
- ☐ 150 Joaquin Andujar, (Oak.) .10
- ☐ 151 Graig Nettles, S.D. .10
- ☐ 152 Pete Vuckovich, Mil. .10
- ☐ 153 Jason Thompson, Pgh. .10
- ☐ 154 Bert Roberge, Mtl. .10
- ☐ 155 Bob Grich, Cal. .10
- ☐ 156 Roy Smalley, Min. .10
- ☐ 157 Ron Hassey, NYY. .10
- ☐ 158 Bob Stanley, Bos. .10
- ☐ 159 Orel Hershiser, L.A. .10
- ☐ 160 Chet Lemon, Det. .10
- ☐ 161 Terry Puhl, Hou. .25
- ☐ 162 Dave LaPoint, (Det.) .10
- ☐ 163 Onix Concepcion, K.C. .10
- ☐ 164 Steve Balboni, K.C. .10
- ☐ 165 Mike Davis, Oak. .10
- ☐ 166 Dickie Thon, Hou. .10
- ☐ 167 Zane Smith, Atl. .10
- ☐ 168 Jeff Burroughs, Tor. .10
- ☐ 169 Alex Trevino, (L.A.) .10
- ☐ 170 Gary Carter, NYM. .50
- ☐ 171 Tito Landrum, Stl. .10
- ☐ 172 Sammy Stewart, (Bos.) .10
- ☐ 173 Wayne Gross, Bal. .10
- ☐ 174 Britt Burns, (NYY.) .10
- ☐ 175 Steve Sax, L.A. .10
- ☐ 176 Jody Davis, Chi.-N.L. .10
- ☐ 177 Joel Youngblood, S.F. .10
- ☐ 178 Fernando Valenzuela, L.A. .10
- ☐ 179 Storm Davis, Bal. .10
- ☐ 180 Don Mattingly, NYY. 1.25
- ☐ 181 Steve Bedrosian, (Pha.) .10
- ☐ 182 Jesse Orosco, NYM. .10
- ☐ 183 Gary Roenicke, (NYY.) .10
- ☐ 184 Don Baylor, NYY. .10
- ☐ 185 Rollie Fingers, Mil. .50
- ☐ 186 Ruppert Jones, Cal. .10
- ☐ 187 Scott Fletcher, (Tex.) .10
- ☐ 188 Bob Dernier, Chi.-N.L. .10
- ☐ 189 Mike Mason, Tex. .10
- ☐ 190 George Hendrick, Cal. .10
- ☐ 191 Wally Backman, NYM. .10
- ☐ 192 Oddibe McDowell, Tex. .10
- ☐ 193 Bruce Hurst, Bos. .10
- ☐ 194 Ron Cey, Chi.-N.L. .10
- ☐ 195 Dave Concepcion, Cin. .10
- ☐ 196 Doyle Alexander, Tor. .10
- ☐ 197 Dale Murphy, Atl. .25
- ☐ 198 Mark Langston, Sea. .10
- ☐ 199 Dennis Eckersley, Chi.-N.L. .10
- ☐ 200 Mike Schmidt, Pha. .50
- ☐ 201 Nick Esasky, Cin. .10
- ☐ 202 Ken Dayley, Stl. .10
- ☐ 203 Rick Cerone, Atl. .10
- ☐ 204 Larry McWilliams, Pgh. .10
- ☐ 205 Brian Downing, Cal. .10
- ☐ 206 Danny Darwin, Mil. .10
- ☐ 207 Bill Caudill, Tor. .10
- ☐ 208 Dave Rozema, Tex. .10
- ☐ 209 Eric Show, S.D. .10
- ☐ 210 Brad Komminsk, Atl. .10
- ☐ 211 Chris Bando, Cle. .10
- ☐ 212 Chris Speier, Chi.-N.L. .10
- ☐ 213 Jim Clancy, Tor. .10
- ☐ 214 Randy Bush, Min. .10
- ☐ 215 Frank White, K.C. .10
- ☐ 216 Dan Petry, Det. .10
- ☐ 217 Tim Wallach, Mtl. .10
- ☐ **218 Mitch Webster, Mtl., RC .10**
- ☐ 219 Dennis Lamp, Tor. .10
- ☐ 220 Bob Horner, Atl. .10
- ☐ 221 Dave Henderson, Sea. .10
- ☐ 222 Dave Smith, Hou. .10
- ☐ 223 Willie Upshaw, Tor. .10
- ☐ 224 Cesar Cedeno, Stl. .10
- ☐ 225 Ron Darling, NYM. .10
- ☐ 226 Lee Lacy, Bal. .10
- ☐ 227 John Tudor, Stl. .10
- ☐ 228 Jim Presley, Sea. .10
- ☐ 229 Bill Gullickson, (Cin.) .10
- ☐ 230 Terry Kennedy, S.D. .10
- ☐ 231 Bob Knepper, Hou. .10
- ☐ 232 Rick Rhoden, Pgh. .10
- ☐ 233 Richard Dotson, Chi.-A.L. .10
- ☐ 234 Jesse Barfield, Tor. .10
- ☐ 235 Butch Wynegar, NYY. .10
- ☐ 236 Jerry Reuss, L.A. .10
- ☐ 237 Juan Samuel, Pha. .10
- ☐ 238 Larry Parrish, Tex. .10
- ☐ 239 Bill Buckner, Bos. .10
- ☐ 240 Pat Sheridan, K.C. .10
- ☐ 241 Tony Fernandez, Tor. .10
- ☐ **242 Rich Thompson, (Mil.), RC .10**
- ☐ 243 Rickey Henderson, NYY. .25
- ☐ 244 Craig Lefferts, S.D. .10
- ☐ 245 Jim Sundberg, K.C. .10
- ☐ 246 Phil Niekro, NYY. .50
- ☐ 247 Terry Harper, Atl. .10
- ☐ 248 Spike Owen, Sea. .10

	No.	Player	Price
☐	249	Bret Saberhagen, K.C.	.10
☐	250	Dwight Gooden, NYM.	.10
☐	251	Rich Dauer, Bal.	.10
☐	252	Keith Hernandez, NYM.	.10
☐	253	Bo Diaz, Cin.	.10
☐	**254**	**Ozzie Guillen, Chi.-A.L.., RC**	**.35**
☐	255	Tony Armas, Bos.	.10
☐	256	Andre Dawson, Mtl.	.25
☐	257	Doug DeCinces, Cal.	.10
☐	258	Tim Burke, Mtl.	.10
☐	259	Dennis Boyd, Bos.	.10
☐	260	Tony Péna, Pgh.	.10
☐	261	Sal Butera, (Cin.)	.10
☐	262	Wade Boggs, Bos.	.50
☐	263	Checklist 133 - 264	.25
☐	264	Ron Oester, Cin.	.10
☐	265	Ron Davis, Min.	.10
☐	266	Keith Moreland, Chi.-N.L.	.10
☐	267	Paul Molitor, Mil.	.50
☐	268	John Denny, (Cin.)	.10
☐	269	Frank Viola, Min.	.10
☐	270	Jack Morris, Det.	.10
☐	271	Dave Collins, (Det.)	.10
☐	272	Bert Blyleven, Min.	.10
☐	273	Jerry Willard, Cle.	.10
☐	274	Matt Young, Sea.	.10
☐	275	Charlie Hough, Tex.	.10
☐	276	Dave Dravecky, S.D.	.10
☐	277	Garth Iorg, Tor.	.10
☐	278	Hal McRae, K.C.	.10
☐	279	Curt Wilkerson, Tex.	.10
☐	280	Tim Raines, Mtl.	.10
☐	281	Bill Laskey, (S.F.)	.10
☐	282	Jerry Mumphrey, (Chi.-N.L.)	.10
☐	283	Pat Clements, Pgh.	.10
☐	284	Bob James, Chi.-A.L.	.10
☐	285	Buddy Bell, Cin.	.10
☐	286	Tom Brookens, Det.	.10
☐	287	Dave Parker, Cin.	.10
☐	288	Ron Kittle, Chi.-A.L.	.10
☐	289	Johnnie LeMaster, Pgh.	.10
☐	290	Carlton Fisk, Chi.-A.L.	.10
☐	291	Jimmy Key, Tor.	.10
☐	292	Gary Matthews, Chi.-N.L.	.10
☐	293	Marvell Wynne, Pgh.	.10
☐	294	Danny Cox, Stl.	.10
☐	295	Kirk Gibson, Det.	.10
☐	296	Mariano Duncan, L.A.	.10
☐	297	Ozzie Smith, Stl.	1.00
☐	298	Craig Reynolds, Hou.	.10
☐	299	Bryn Smith, Mtl.	.10
☐	300	George Brett, K.C.	1.25
☐	301	Walt Terrell, Det.	.10
☐	302	Greg Gross, Pha.	.10
☐	303	Claudell Washington, Atl.	.10
☐	304	Howard Johnson, NYM.	.10
☐	305	Phil Bradley, Sea.	.10
☐	306	R.J. Reynolds, Pgh.	.10
☐	307	Bob Brenly, S.F.	.10
☐	308	Hubie Brooks, Mtl.	.10
☐	309	Alvin Davis, Sea.	.10
☐	310	Donnie Hill, Oak.	.10
☐	311	Dick Schofield, Cal.	.10
☐	312	Tom Filer, Tor.	.10
☐	313	Mike Fitzgerald, Mtl.	.10
☐	314	Marty Barrett, Bos.	.10
☐	315	Mookie Wilson, NYM.	.10
☐	316	Alan Knicely, Pha.	.10
☐	317	Ed Romero, (Bos.)	.10
☐	318	Glenn Wilson, Pha.	.10
☐	319	Bud Black, K.C.	.10
☐	320	Jim Rice, Bos.	.10
☐	321	Terry Pendleton, Stl.	.10
☐	322	Dave Kingman, Oak.	.10
☐	323	Gary Pettis, Cal.	.10
☐	324	Dan Schatzeder, Mtl.	.10
☐	325	Juan Beniquez, (Bal.)	.10
☐	326	Kent Tekulve, Pha.	.10
☐	327	Mike Pagliarulo, NYY.	.10
☐	328	Pete O'Brien, Tex.	.10
☐	329	Kirby Puckett, Min.	1.75
☐	330	Rick Sutcliffe, Chi.-N.L.	.10
☐	331	Alan Ashby, Hou.	.10
☐	332	Willie Randolph, NYY.	.10
☐	333	Tom Henke, Tor.	.10
☐	334	Ken Oberkfell, Atl.	.10
☐	335	Don Sutton, Cal.	.35
☐	336	Dan Gladden, S.F.	.10
☐	337	George Vukovich, Cle.	.10
☐	338	George Bell, Tor.	.10
☐	339	Jim Dwyer, Bal.	.10
☐	340	Cal Ripken, Bal.	2.00
☐	341	Willie Hernandez, Det.	.10
☐	342	Gary Redus, (Pha.)	.10
☐	343	Jerry Koosman, Pha.	.10
☐	344	Jim Wohlford, Mtl.	.10
☐	345	Donnie Moore, Cal.	.10
☐	**346**	**Floyd Youmans, Mtl., RC**	**.10**
☐	347	Gorman Thomas, Sea.	.10
☐	348	Cliff Johnson, Tor.	.10
☐	349	Ken Howell, L.A.	.10
☐	350	Jack Clark, Stl.	.10
☐	351	Gary Lucas, (Cal.)	.10
☐	352	Bob Clark, Mil.	.10
☐	353	Dave Stieb, Tor.	.10
☐	354	Tony Bernazard, Cle.	.10
☐	355	Lee Smith, Chi.-N.L.	.10
☐	356	Mickey Hatcher, Min.	.10
☐	357	Ed VandeBerg, (L.A.)	.10
☐	358	Rick Dempsey, Bal.	.10
☐	359	Bobby Cox, Manager, Tor. (Atl.)	.10
☐	360	Lloyd Moseby, Tor.	.10
☐	361	Shane Rawley, Pha.	.10
☐	362	Garry Maddox, Pha.	.10
☐	363	Buck Martinez, Tor.	.10
☐	364	Ed Nunez, Sea.	.10
☐	365	Luis Leal, Tor.	.10
☐	366	Dale Berra, NYY.	.10
☐	367	Mike Boddicker, Bal.	.10
☐	368	Greg Brock, L.A.	.10
☐	369	Al Holland, Cal.	.10
☐	**370**	**Vince Coleman, Stl., RC**	**.25**
☐	371	Rod Carew, Cal.	.50
☐	372	Ben Oglivie, Mil.	.10
☐	373	Lee Mazzilli, Pgh.	.10
☐	374	Terry Francona, Mtl.	.10
☐	375	Rich Gedman, Bos.	.10
☐	376	Charlie Lea, Mtl.	.10
☐	377	Joe Carter, Cle.	1.00
☐	378	Bruce Bochte, Oak.	.10
☐	379	Bobby Meacham, NYY.	.10
☐	380	LaMarr Hoyt, S.D.	.10
☐	381	Jeff Leonard, S.F.	.10
☐	**382**	**Ivan Calderon, Sea., RC**	**.10**
☐	383	Chris Brown, S.F.	.10
☐	384	Steve Trout, Chi.-N.L.	.10
☐	385	Cecil Cooper, Mil.	.10
☐	**386**	**Cecil Fielder, Tor., RC**	**1.75**

	No.	Player	
☐	387	Tim Flannery, S.D.	.10
☐	388	Chris Codiroli, Oak.	.10
☐	389	Glenn Davis, Hou.	.10
☐	390	Tom Seaver, Chi.-A.L.	.50
☐	391	Julio Franco, Cle.	.10
☐	392	Tom Brunansky, Min.	.10
☐	393	Rob Wilfong, Cal.	.10
☐	394	Reggie Jackson, Cal.	.75
☐	395	Scott Garrelts, S.F.	.10
☐	396	Checklist (265 - 396)	.25

1986 BOX BOTTOMS

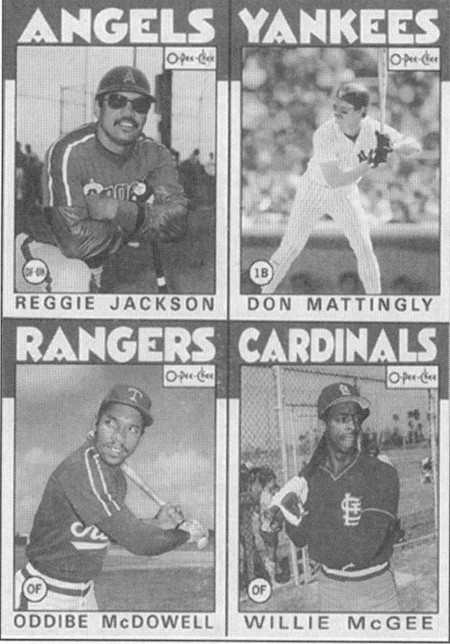

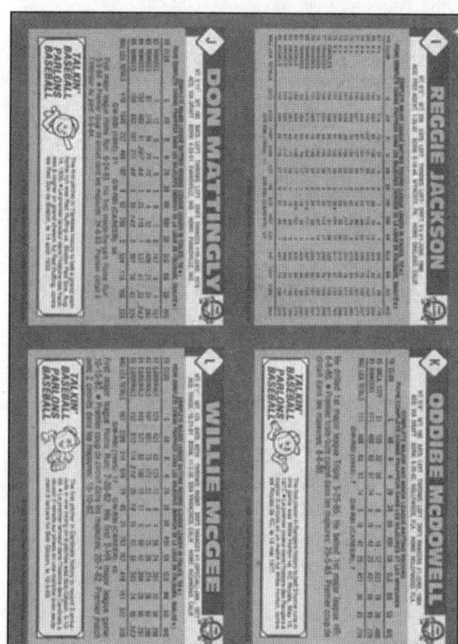

Panel Size: 5" x 7"
Face: Four colour, red and white; name, position, team
Back: Red and black on card stock; name, letter, résumé, "Talkin' Baseball," bilingual
Imprint: © 1986 O-Pee-Chee Ptd. in Canada/imprimé au Canada

Complete Set (16 cards):			**14.00**
Panel A-D:			**8.00**
Panel E-H:			**4.00**
Panel I-L:			**7.00**
Panel M-P:			**6.00**
		Player	**MINT**
☐	A	George Bell, Tor.	.50
☐	B	Wade Boggs, Bos.	1.50
☐	C	George Brett, K.C.	4.00
☐	D	Vince Coleman, Stl.	.50
☐	E	Carlton Fisk, Chi.-A.L.	1.50
☐	F	Dwight Gooden, NYM.	1.00
☐	G	Pedro Guerrero, L.A.	.50
☐	H	Ron Guidry, NYY.	.50
☐	I	Reggie Jackson, Cal.	1.50
☐	J	Don Mattingly, NYY.	3.50
☐	K	Oddibe McDowell, Tex.	.50
☐	L	Willie McGee, Stl.	.50
☐	M	Dale Murphy	1.00
☐	N	Pete Rose	2.50
☐	O	Bret Saberhagen	1.00
☐	P	Fernando Valenzuela	.50

1986 OPC STICKERS

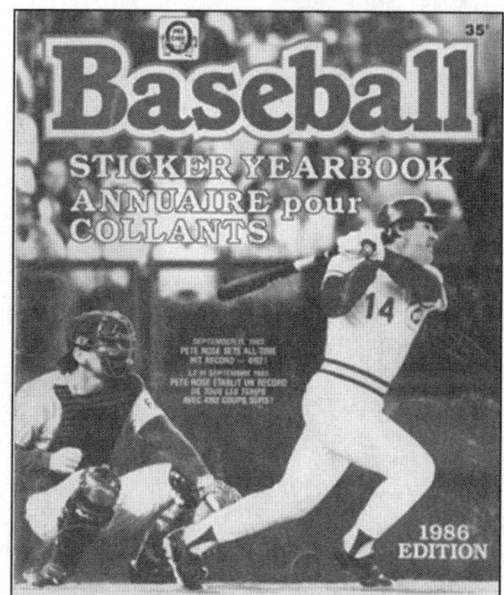

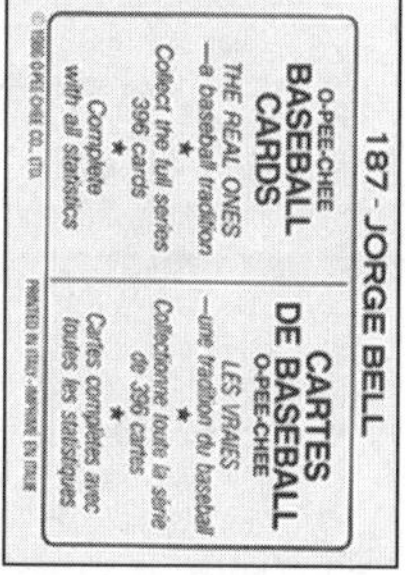

Sticker Size: 2 1/8" x 3"
Face: Four colour, white border; number
Back: Black on card stock; name, number, bilingual
Imprint: © 1986 O-PEE-CHEE LTD., PRINTED IN TIALY IMPRIMÉ EN ITALIE

Complete Set (200 stickers):	**30.00**
Album:	**5.00**
Common Sticker:	**.15**

	No.	Player	MINT
☐	1	Pete Rose, Cin.	.35
☐	2	Pete Rose, Cin.	.35
☐	11	Ozzie Smith, Stl.	.75
☐	12	Bill Madlock, L.A.	.15
☐	13	Cardinals Celebrate	.15
☐	14	Al Oliver, Tor.	.15
☐	15	Jim Sundberg, K.C.	.15
☐	16	George Brett, K.C.	.35
☐	17	Bret Saberhagen, K.C.	.15
☐	18	Dane Iorg, K.C.	.15
☐	19	Tito Landrum, Stl.	.15
☐	20	John Tudor, Stl.	.15
☐	21	Buddy Biancalana, K.C.	.15
☐	22	Darryl Motley, K.C.	.15
☐	23	George Brett, K.C./Frank White, K.C.	.35
☐	24	Nolan Ryan, Hou.	2.50
☐	25	Bill Doran, Hou.	.15
☐	34	Bob Horner, Atl.	.15
☐	35	Dale Murphy, Atl.	.25
☐	44	Joaquin, Andujar, Stl.	.15
☐	45	Willie McGee, Stl.	.15
☐	54	Keith Moreland, Chi.-N.L.	.15
☐	55	Ryne Sandberg, Chi.-N.L.	.75
☐	64	Fernando Valenzuela, L.A.	.15
☐	65	Pedro Guerrero, L.A.	.15
☐	74	Andre Dawson, Mtl.	.35
☐	75	Tim Raines, Mtl.	.15
☐	84	Jeff Leonard, S.F.	.15
☐	85	Chris Brown, S.F.	.15
☐	94	Dwight Gooden, NYM.	.15
☐	95	Darryl Strawberry, NYM.	.25
☐	104	Steve Garvey, S.D.	.25
☐	105	Tony Gwynn, S.D.	1.00
☐	114	Mike Schmidt, Pha.	.50
☐	115	Ozzie Virgil, Pha.	.15
☐	124	Johnny Ray, Pgh.	.15
☐	125	Tony Pena, Pgh.	.15
☐	134	Pete Rose, Cin.	.75
☐	135	Dave Parker, Cin.	.15
☐	146	Tony Gwynn, S.D.	.50
☐	147	Tom Herr, Stl.	.15
☐	148	Steve Garvey, S.D.	.25
☐	149	Dale Murphy, Atl.	.15
☐	150	Darryl Strawberry, NYM.	.25
☐	151	Craig Nettles, S.D.	.15
☐	152	Terry Kennedy, S.D.	.15
☐	153	Ozzie Smith, Stl.	1.50
☐	154	LaMarr Hoyt, S.D.	.15
☐	155	Rickey Henderson, NYY.	.25
☐	156	Lou Whitaker, Det.	.15
☐	157	George Brett, K.C.	.75
☐	158	Eddie Murray, Bal.	.50
☐	159	Cal Ripken, Bal.	1.25
☐	160	Dave Winfield, NYY.	.50
☐	161	Jim Rice, Bos.	.15
☐	162	Carlton Fisk, Chi.-A.L.	.25
☐	163	Jack Morris, Det.	.15
☐	166	Mike Davis, Oak.	.15
☐	167	Dave Kingman, Oak.	.15
☐	176	Rod Carew, Cal.	.50
☐	177	Reggie Jackson, Cal.	.75
☐	186	Dave Stieb, Tor.	.15
☐	187	George Bell, Tor.	.15
☐	196	Cecil Cooper, Mil.	.15
☐	197	Robin Yount, Mil.	.50
☐	206	Brett Butler, Cle.	.15
☐	207	Brook Jacoby, Cle.	.15
☐	216	Gorman Thomas, Sea.	.15
☐	217	Phil Bradley, Sea.	.15
☐	226	Cal Ripken, Bal.	2.50
☐	227	Eddie Murray, Bal.	1.00
☐	236	Pete O'Brien, Tex.	.15
☐	237	Oddibe McDowell, Tex.	.15
☐	246	Jim Rice, Bos.	.15
☐	247	Wade Boggs, Bos.	.75
☐	256	George Brett, K.C.	1.50
☐	257	Dan Quisenberry, K.C.	.15
☐	266	Kirk Gibson, Det.	.15
☐	267	Alan Trammell, Det.	.15
☐	276	Tom Brunansky, Min.	.15
☐	277	Kent Hrbek, Min.	.15
☐	286	Carlton Fisk, Chi.-A.L.	.50
☐	287	Tom Seaver, Chi.-A.L.	.25
☐	296	Don Mattingly, NYY.	1.50
☐	297	Rickey Henderson, NYY.	.50

MULTIPLE STICKERS

	No.	Player	MINT
☐	3/175	George Brett, K.C./ Jay Howell, Oak.	1.00
☐	4/178	Rod Carew, Cal./ Doug DeCinces, Cal.	.35
☐	5/179	Vince Coleman, Stl./ Bob Boone, Cal.	.15
☐	6/180	Dwight Gooden, NYM./ Ron Romanick, Cal.	.15
☐	7/181	Phil Niekro, NYY./ Bob Grich, Cal.	.35
☐	8/182	Tony Perez, Cin./ Donnie Moore, Cal.	.25
☐	9/183	Nolan Ryan, Hou./ Brian Downing, Cal.	2.00
☐	10/184	Tom Seaver, Chi.-A.L./ Ruppert Jones, Cal.	.25
☐	26/185	Jose Cruz, Hou./ Juan Beniquez, Cal.	.15
☐	27/188	Mike Scott, Hou./ Willie Upshaw, Tor.	.15
☐	28/189	Kevin Blass, Hou./ Tom Henke, Tor.	.15
☐	29/190	Glenn Davis, Hou./ Damaso Garcia, Tor.	.15
☐	30/191	Mark Bailey, Hou./ Jimmy Key, Tor.	.25
☐	31/192	Dave Smith, Hou./ Jesse Barfield, Tor.	.15
☐	32/193	Phil Garner, Hou./ Dennis Lamp, Tor.	.15
☐	33/194	Dickie Thon, Hou./ Tony Fernandez, Tor.	.15
☐	36/195	Glenn Hubbard, Atl./ Lloyd Moseby, Tor.	.15
☐	37/198	Bruce Sutter, Atl./ Rollie Fingers, Mil.	.25
☐	38/199	Ken Oberkfell, Atl./ Ted Simmons, Mil.	.15
☐	39/200	Claudell Washington, Atl./ Ben Ogilvie, Mil.	.15
☐	40/201	Steve Bedrosian, Atl./ Moose Haas, Mil.	.15
☐	41/202	Terry Harper, Atl./ Jim Gantner, Mil.	.15
☐	42/203	Rafael Ramirez, Atl./ Paul Molitor, Mil.	.50
☐	43/204	Rick Mahler, Atl./ Charlie Moore, Mil.	.15
☐	46/205	Ozzie Smith, Stl./ Danny Darwin, Mil.	1.25
☐	47/208	Vince Coleman, Stl./ Andre Thornton, Cle.	.15
☐	48/209	Danny Cox, Stl./ Tom Waddell, Cle.	.15
☐	49/210	Tom Herr, Stl./ Tony Bernazard, Cle.	.15
☐	50/211	Jack Clark, Stl./ Julio Franco, Cle.	.15
☐	51/212	Andy Van Slyke, Stl./ Pat Tabler, Cle.	.15
☐	52/213	John Tudor, Stl./ Joe Carter, Cle.	.75
☐	53/214	Terry Pendleton, Stl./ George Vukovich, Cle.	.15
☐	56/215	Lee Smith, Chi.-N.L./ Rich Thompson, Cle.	.25
☐	57/218	Steve Trout, Chi.-N.L./ Alvin Davis, Sea.	.15
☐	58/219	Jody Davis, Chi.-N.L./ Jim Presley, Sea.	.15
☐	59/220	Gary Matthews, Chi.-N.L./ Matt Young, Sea.	.15
☐	60/221	Leon Durham, Chi.-N.L./ Mike Moore, Sea.	.15
☐	61/222	Rick Sutcliffe, Chi.-N.L./ Dave Henderson, Sea.	.15
☐	62/223	Dennis Eckersley, Chi.-N.L./ Ed Nunez, Sea.	.15
☐	63/224	Bob Dernier, Chi.-N.L./ Spike Owen, Sea.	.15
☐	66/225	Jerry Reuss, L.A./ Mark Langston, Sea.	.15
☐	67/228	Greg Brock, L.A./ Fred Lynn, Bal.	.15
☐	68/229	Mike Scioscia, L.A./ Lee Lacy, Bal.	.15
☐	69/230	Ken Howell, L.A./ Scott McGregor, Bal.	.15
☐	70/231	Bill Madlock, L.A./ Storm Davis, Bal.	.15
☐	71/232	Mike Marshall, L.A./ Rick Dempsey, Bal.	.15
☐	72/233	Steve Sax, L.A./ Mike Boddicker, Bal.	.15
☐	73/234	Orel Hershiser, L.A./ Mike Young, Bal.	.15
☐	76/235	Jeff Reardon, Mtl./ Sammy Stewart, Bal.	.15
☐	77/238	Hubie Brooks, Mtl./ Toby Harrah, Tex.	.15
☐	78/239	Bill Gullickson, Mtl./ Gary Ward, Tex.	.15

☐ 79/240 Bryn Smith, Mtl./ Larry Parrish, Tex. .15
☐ 80/241 Terry Francona, Mtl./ Charlie Hough, Tex. .15
☐ 81/242 Vance Law, Mtl./ Burt Hooton, Tex. .15
☐ 82/243 Tim Wallach, Mtl./ Don Slaught, Tex. .15
☐ 83/244 Herm Winningham, Mtl./ Curt Wilkerson, Tex. .15
☐ 86/245 Scott Garrelts, S.F./ Greg Harris, Tex. .15
☐ 87/248 Jose Uribe, S.F./ Rich Gedman, Bos. .15
☐ 88/249 Manny Trillo, S.F./ Dennis Boyd, Bos. .15
☐ 89/250 Dan Driessen, S.F./ Marty Barrett, Bos. .15
☐ 90/251 Dan Gladden, S.F./ Dwight Evans, Bos. .15
☐ 91/252 Mark Davis, S.F./ Bill Buckner, Bos. .15
☐ 92/253 Bob Brenly, S.F./ Bob Stanley, Bos. .15
☐ 93/254 Mike Krukow, S.F./ Tony Armas, Bos. .15
☐ 96/255 Gary Carter, NYM./ Mike Easler, Bos. .35
☐ 97/258 Wally Backman, NYM./ Willie Wilson, K.C. .15
☐ 98/259 Ron Darling, NYM./ Jim Sundberg, K.C. .15
☐ 99/260 Keith Hernandez, NYM./ Bret Saberhagen, K.C. .15
☐ 100/261 George Foster, NYM./ Bud Black, K.C. .15
☐ 101/262 Howard Johnson, NYM./ Charlie Leibrandt, K.C. .15
☐ 102/263 Rafael Santana, NYM./ Frank White, K.C. .15
☐ 103/264 Roger McDowell, NYM./ Lonnie Smith, K.C. .15
☐ 106/265 Craig Nettles, S.D./ Steve Balboni, K.C. .15
☐ 107/268 Rich Gossage, S.D./ Jack Morris, Det. .15
☐ 108/269 Andy Hawkins, S.D./ Darrell Evans, Det. .15
☐ 109/270 Carmelo Martinez, S.D./ Dan Petry, Det. .15
☐ 110/271 Garry Templeton, S.D./ Larry Herndon, Det. .15
☐ 111/272 Terry Kennedy, S.D./ Lou Whitaker, Det. .15
☐ 112/273 Tim Flannery, S.D./ Lance Parrish, Det. .15
☐ 113/274 LaMarr Hoyt, S.D./ Chet Lemon, Det. .15
☐ 116/275 Steve Carlton, Pha./ Willie Hernandez, Det. .35
☐ 117/278 Garry Maddox, Pha./ Mark Salas, Min. .15
☐ 118/279 Glenn Wilson, Pha./ Bert Blyleven, Min. .15
☐ 119/280 Kevin Gross, Pha./ Tim Teufel, Min. .15
☐ 120/281 Von Hayes, Pha/ Ron Davis, Min. .15
☐ 121/282 Juan Samuel, Pha./ Mike Smithson, Min. .15
☐ 122/283 Rick Schu, Pha./ Gary Gaetti, Min. .15
☐ 123/284 Shane Rawley, Pha./ Frank Viola, Min. .15
☐ 126/285 Rick Reuschel, Pgh./ Kirby Puckett, Min. 1.50
☐ 127/288 Sammy Khalifa, Pgh./ Harold Baines, Chi.-A.L. .15
☐ 128/289 Marvell Wynne, Pgh./ Ron Kittle, Chi.-A.L. .15
☐ 129/290 Jason Thompson, Pgh./ Bob James, Chi.-A.L. .15
☐ 130/291 Rick Rhoden, Pgh./ Rudy Law, Chi.-A.L. .15
☐ 131/292 Bill Almon, Pgh./ Britt Burns, Chi.-A.L. .15
☐ 132/293 Joe Orsulak, Pgh./ Greg Walker, Chi.-A.L. .15
☐ 133/293 Jim Morrison, Pgh./ Ozzie Guillen, Chi.-A.L. .15
☐ 136/295 Mario Soto, Cin./ Tim Hulett, Chi.-A.L. .15
☐ 137/298 Dave Concepcion, Cin./ Dave Winfield, NYY. .35
☐ 138/299 Ron Oester, Cin./ Butch Wynegar, NYY. .15
☐ 139/300 Buddy Bell, Cin./ Don Baylor, NYY. .15
☐ 140/301 Ted Power, Cin./ Eddie Whitson, NYY. .15
☐ 141/302 Tom Browning, Cin./ Ron Guidry, NYY. .15
☐ 142/303 John Franco, Cin./ Dave Righetti, NYY. .15
☐ 143/304 Tony Perez, Cin./ Bobby Meacham, NYY. .25
☐ 144/305 Willie McGee, Stl./ Willie Randolph, NYY. .15
☐ 145/306 Dale Murphy, Atl./ Vince Coleman, Stl. .15
☐ 164/307 Wade Boggs, Bos./ Oddibe McDowell, Tex. .25
☐ 165/308 Darrell Evans, Pgh./ Larry Sheets, Bal. .15
☐ 168/309 Alfredo Griffin, Oak./ Ozzie Guillen, Chi.-A.L. .15
☐ 169/310 Carney Lansford, Oak./ Earnie Riles, Mil. .15
☐ 170/311 Bruce Bochte, Oak./ Chris Brown, S.F. .15
☐ 171/312 Dwayne Murphy, Oak./ B.Fisher & R.McDowell .15
☐ 172/313 Dave Collins, Oak./ Tom Browning, Cin. .15
☐ 173/314 Chris Codiroli, Oak./ Glenn Davis, Hou. .15
☐ 174/315 Mike Heath, Oak./ Mark Salas, Min. .15

1986 O-PEE-CHEE TATTOOS

Transfer Size: 3 5/16" x 14 1/8"
Face: Four colour, white border; name, team, numbered _ of 24
Back: Blank
Imprint: © 1966 O-PEE-CHEE PTD. IN CANADA/IMPRIMê AU CANADA
Complete Set (24 sheets; 384 transfers): 30.00
Sheet No. Players MINT

☐ SHEET No. 1: Charlie Leibrandt, K.C.; Dickie Thon, Hou.; Lee Smith, Chi.-N.L.; Dave Winfield, NYY., Julio Franco, Cle.; Keith Hernandez, NYM.; Jack Perconte, Sea.; Rich Gossage, S.D., 2.00
☐ SHEET No. 2: Brian Fisher, Pitcher, NYY.; Dale Murphy, Atl.; Shawon Dunston. Chi.-N.L.; Bret Saberhagen, K.C.; Jesse Barfield, Tor.; Moose Haas, Mil.; Dennis Eckersley, Chi.-N.L.; Mike Moore, Sea. 1.50
☐ SHEET No. 3: Dan Quisenberry, K.C.; Steve Carlton, Phil.; Bob Brenly, S.F.; Bob James, Chi.-A.L.; George Bell, Tor.; Jose DeLeon, Pgh.; Andre Thornton, Cle.; Chicago Cubs Caricature; Bob Horner, Atl. 1.50
☐ SHEET No. 4: Darrell Evans, Det.; Johnny Ray, Pgh.; Leon Durham. Chi.-N.L.; Mike Davis, Oak.; Harold Baines. Chi.-A.L.; Cal Ripken, Bal., Glenn Hubbard, Atl.; Ted Simmons, Mitl. 3.00
☐ SHEET No. 5: Rick Dempsey, Bal.; Jesse Orosco, NYM.; Tony Pena, Pgh.; John Candelaria, Cal.; Brook Jacoby, Cle.; Gary Matthews, Chi.-N.L.; Ozzie Guillen, Chi.-A.L.; Steve Garvey, S.D. 1.00
☐ SHEET No. 6: Pete Rose, Cin.; Ron Kittle, Chi.-A.L.; Bruce Bochte, Oak; Sam Khalifa, Pgh.; Scott McGregor, Bal.; Mookie Wilson, NYM.; George Brett, K.C.; Cecil Cooper, Mil. 2.50
☐ SHEET No. 7: John Franco, Cin.; Larry Sheets, Bal.; Don Mattingly, NYY.; Graig Nettles, S.D.; Carney Lansford, Oak.; Rick Reuschel, Pgh.; Don Sutton, Cal.; Mike Schmidt, Pha. 2.50
☐ SHEET No. 8: Ryne Sandberg, Chi.-N.L.; Phil Niekro, NYY.; Fred Lynn, Bal.; Mike Krukow, S.F.; Willie Hernandez, Det.; Pat Tabler, Cle.; Ed Nunez, Sea.; Cecilio Guante, Pgh. 2.00
☐ SHEET No. 9: Glenn Wilson, Pha.; Chris Codiroli, Oak.; Brett Butler, Cle.; Rick Rhoden, Pgh.; Robin Yount, Mil.; Dave Parker, Cin.; Jim Gantner, Mil.; Charlie Hough, Tex. 1.50
☐ SHEET No. 10: Mike Smithson, Min.; Chet Lemon, Det.; Tom Seaver, Chi.-A.L.; Ron Darling, NYM.; Von Hayes, Pha.; Tom Browning, Cin.; Bruce Sutter, Atl.; Alan Trammell, Det. 1.50
☐ SHEET No. 11: Dave Righetti, NYY.; Rick Mahler, Atl.; Jose Cruz, Hou.; Jay Howell, Oak.; Jack Morris, Det.; Tony Armas, Bos.; Mike Young, Bal.; Rafael Ramirez, Atl. 1.00
☐ SHEET No. 12: Alvin Davis, Sea.; Keith Moreland, Chi.-N.L.; John Tudor, Stl.; Doug DeCinces, Cal.; Jim Presley, Sea.; Andy Hawkins, S.D.; Dennis Lamp, Tor.; Mario Soto, Cin. 1.00
☐ SHEET No. 13: Dwight Evans, Bos.; Charles Hudson, Pha.; Jody Davis, Chi.-N.L.; Kirby Puckett, Min.; Eddie Murray, Bal.; Jose Uribe, S.F.; Ron Hassey, NYY.; Hubie Brooks, Mtl. 2.50
☐ SHEET No. 14: Brian Downing, Cal.; LaMarr Hoyt, S.D.; Dan Driessen, S.F.; Ron Guidry, NYY.; Tony Bernazard, Cle.; Garry Maddox, Pha.; Phil Bradley, Sea.; Bill Buckner, Bos. 1.00
☐ SHEET No. 15: Hal McRae, K.C.; Tito Landrum, Stl.; Jeff Leonard, S.F.; Joe Carter, Cle.; Tony Fernandez, Tor.; Juan Samuel, Pha.; Buddy Bell, Cin.; Willie Randolph, NYY.; 1.50
☐ SHEET No. 16: Dennis Boyd, Bos.; Scott Garrelts, S.F.; Tony Perez,

Cin.; Donnie Moore, Cal.; Vince Coleman, Stl.; Alfredo Griffin, Oak.; Frank White, K.C.; Ozzie Smith, Stl. 2.00

☐ SHEET No. 17: Rich Gedman, Bos.; Clardell Washington, Atl.; Terry Pendleton, Stl.; Reggie Jackson, Cal.; Mark Salas, Min.; Mike Marshall, L.A.; Ken Hrbek, Min.; Tim Raines, Mtl. 2.00

☐ SHEET No. 18: Glenn Davis, Hou.; Ron Davis, Min.; Burt Hooton, Tex.; Chris Brown, S.F.; Darryl Strawberry, NYM.; Tom Brunansky, Min.; Tim Wallach, Mtl.; Frank Viola, Min. 1.00

☐ SHEET No. 19: Toby Harrah, Tex.; Jack Clark, Stl.; Mike Scioscia, L.A.; Larry Parrish, Tex.; Pete O'Brien, Tex.; Bill Dorran, Hou.; Garry Templeton, S.D.; Bill Madlock, L.A. 1.00

☐ SHEET No. 20: Andre Dawson, Mtl.; Dwight Gooden, NYM.; Oddibe McDowell, NYY.; Roger McDowell, NYM.; Gary Carter, NYM.; Orel Hershiser, L.A.; Jim Rice, Bos.; Dwayne Murphy, Oak. 1.50

☐ SHEET No. 21: Rick Sutcliffe, Chi.-N.L.; Steve Balboni, K.C.; Mike Easler, Bos.; Charlie Lea, Mtl.; Steve Sax, L.A.; Gary Ward, Tex.; Lloyd Moseby, Tor.; Willie Wilson, K.C. 1.00

☐ SHEET No. 22: Tom Herr, Stl.; Lance Parrish, Det.; Kirk Gibson, Det.; Bryn Smith, Mtl.; Jeff Reardon, Mtl.; Gorman Thomas, Sea.; Wade Boggs, Bos.; Dave Concepcion, Cin. 1.50

☐ SHEET No. 23: Willie McGee, Stl.; Dave Steib, Tor.; Paul Molitor, Mil.; Bob Grich, Cal.; Pedro Guerrero, L.A.; Carlton Fisk, Chi.-A.L.; Mike Scott, Hou.; Lou Whitaker, Det. 2.00

☐ SHEET No. 24: Rickey Henderson, NYY.; Tony Gwynn, S.D.; Nolan Ryan, Hou.; Damaso Garcia, Tor.; Bret Blyleven, Min.; Fernando Valenzuela, L.A.; Ben Oglivie, Mil.; Phil Garner, Hou. 5.00

1987 GENERAL MILLS

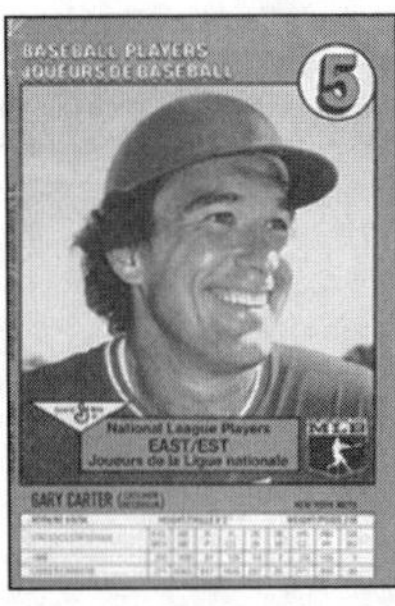

In 1987, General Mills again inserted booklets into specially marked cereal boxes. This booklet set also had the team insignias removed.

Booklet Size: 15" x 3 3/4"
Face: Four colour; name, number, position, team, résumé, bilingual
Back: Four colour; name, number, position, team, résumé, bilingual
Imprint: Mike Schechter Associates, Inc. Printed in Canada
Complete Set (6 booklets): 25.00

	No.	Player	MINT
☐	1	A. L. Players, Toronto: E. Whitt; J. Barfield; G. Bell; T. Fernandez; K. Gruber; T. Henke; J. Key; L. Moseby; D. Steib; W. Upshaw	7.50
☐	2	A. L. East: K. Gibson; W. Boggs; R. Clemens; R. Henderson; D. Mattingly; J. Morris; E. Murray; P. Tabler; D. Winfield; R. Yount	18.00
☐	3	A. L. West: C. Fisk; P. Bradley; G. Brett; J. Canseco; R. Jackson; W. Joyner; K. McCaskill; L. Parrish; K. Puckett; D. Quisenberry	10.00
☐	4	N. L. Players, Montreal: M. Fitzgerald; H. Brooks; A. Galarraga; V. Law; A. McGaffigan; B. Smith; J. Thompson; T. Wallach; M. Webster; F. Youmans	7.50
☐	5	N. L. East: G. Carter; D. Gooden; K. Hernandez; W. McGee; T. Raines; R.J. Reynolds; R. Sandberg; Mi. Schmidt; O. Smith; D. Strawberry	10.00
☐	6	N. L. West: K. Bass; C. Davis; B. Doran; P. Guerrero; T. Gwynn; D. Murphy; D. Parker; S. Sax; M. Scott; F. Valenzuela	6.50

1987 HOSTESS

Issued in bags of Hostess Potato Chips during the summer of 1987, this sticker set contains a good roster of stars for the season. It is believed that some of these small cards were reprinted and that these reprints are scarcer than those produced in the first printing. Collectors with any knowledge of this set are invited to contact the publisher. A small premium applies to stickers still enclosed in the cellophane wrapper.

Card Size: 1 3/8" x 1 3/4"
Face: Four colour; name, number
Back: Black on sticker back; position, hostess and MLB logos, bilingual
Imprint: *TM/M de C
Complete Set (30 cards): 35.00

	No.	Player	MINT
☐	1	Jesse Barfield, Tor.	.50
☐	2	Ernie Whitt, Tor.	.50
☐	3	George Bell, Tor.	.35
☐	4	Hubie Brooks, Mtl.	.35
☐	5	Tim Wallach, Mtl.	.35
☐	6	Floyd Youmans, Mtl.	.35
☐	7	Dale Murphy, Atl.	.75
☐	8	Ryne Sandberg, Chi.-N.L.	2.50
☐	9	Eric Davis, Cin.	.35
☐	10	Mike Scott, Hou.	.35
☐	11	Fernando Valenzuela, L.A.	.35
☐	12	Gary Carter, NYM.	1.00
☐	13	Mike Schmidt, Pha.	3.00
☐	14	Tony Pena, Pgh.	.35
☐	15	Ozzie Smith, Stl.	3.00
☐	16	Tony Gwynn, S.D.	4.00
☐	17	Mike Krukow, S.F.	.35
☐	18	Eddie Murray, Bal.	2.50
☐	19	Wade Boggs, Bos.	2.00
☐	20	Wally Joyner, Cal.	.35
☐	21	Harold Baines, Chi.-A.L.	.35
☐	22	Brook Jacoby, Cle.	.35
☐	23	Lou Whitaker, Det.	.35
☐	24	George Brett, K.C.	3.50
☐	25	Robin Yount, Mil.	2.00
☐	26	Kirby Puckett, Min.	3.50
☐	27	Don Mattingly, NYY.	3.00
☐	28	Jose Canseco, Oak.	2.00
☐	29	Phil Bradley, Sea.	.35
☐	30	Pete O'Brien, Tex.	.35

1987 LEAF

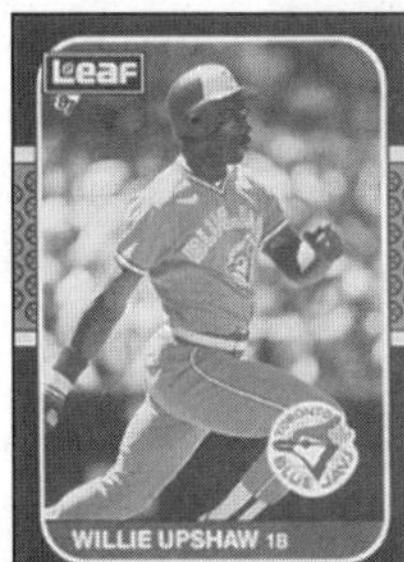

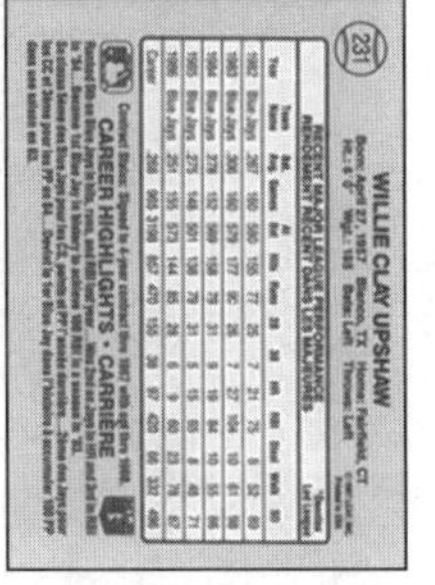

For the third consecutive year Leaf-Donruss issued a 264-card set, which was different from the 660-card Donruss issue. The first 26 cards bear painted portraits of the players. The word Donruss has been replaced on the face of this set by the word Leaf, and the backs are bilingual. The "Canadian Greats" cards of this issue feature Floyd Youmans and Mark Eichhorn. There is also a Roberto Clemente puzzle card and a Clemente puzzle of 21 perforated pieces.

Card Size: 2 1/2" x 3 1/2"
Face: Four colour, black border; position, team logo
Back: Orange and black on card stock; number, résumé, career highlights, bilingual
Imprint: Cards No. 1-26: © 1987 LEAF, INC. MADE & PRINTED IN U.S.A. PEREZ-STEELE GALLERIES Cards No. 27-263: © 1987 LEAF, INC. Printed in U.S.A.

Complete Set (264 cards):			**30.00**
Common Player:			**.15**
	No.	**Player**	**MINT**
☐	1	Wally Joyner, Cal.	.25
☐	2	Roger Clemens, Bos.	.75
☐	3	Dale Murphy, Atl.	.25
☐	4	Darryl Strawberry, NYM.	.25
☐	5	Ozzie Smith, Stl.	.50
☐	6	Jose Canseco, Oak.	.15
☐	7	Charlie Hough, Min.	.15
☐	8	Brook Jacoby, Cle.	.15
☐	9	Fred Lynn, Bal.	.15
☐	10	Rick Rhoden, Pgh.	.15
☐	11	Chris Brown, S.F.	.15
☐	12	Von Hayes, Pha.	.15
☐	13	Jack Morris, Det.	.15
☐	14	Kevin McReynolds, S.D.	.15
☐	15	George Brett, K.C.	.50
☐	16	Ted Higuera, Mil.	.15
☐	17	Hubie Brooks, Mtl.	.15
☐	18	Mike Scott, Hou.	.15
☐	19	Kirby Puckett, Min.	.50
☐	20	Dave Winfield, NYY.	.25
☐	21	Lloyd Moseby, Tor.	.15
☐	22	Eric Davis, Cin.	.15
☐	23	Jim Presley, Sea.	.15
☐	24	Keith Moreland, Chi.-N.L.	.15
☐	25	Greg Walker, Chi.-A.L.	.15
☐	26	Steve Sax, L.A.	.15
☐	27	Checklist 1-27	.15
☐	**28**	**B.J. Surhoff, Mil., RC**	**.50**
☐	**29**	**Randy Myers, NYM., RC**	**.50**
☐	**30**	**Ken Gerhart, Bal., RC**	**.15**
☐	31	Benito Santiago, S.D.	.15
☐	**32**	**Greg Swindell, Cle., RC**	**.15**
☐	**33**	**Mike Birkbeck, Mil., RC**	**.15**
☐	**34**	**Terry Steinbach, Oak., RC**	**.15**
☐	**35**	**Bo Jackson, K.C., RC**	**.75**
☐	**36**	**Greg Maddux, Chi.-N.L., RC**	**12.00**
☐	**37**	**Jim Lindeman, Stl., RC**	**.15**
☐	**38**	**Devon White, Cal., RC**	**.50**
☐	**39**	**Eric Bell, Bal., RC**	**.15**
☐	**40**	**Will Fraser, Cal., RC**	**.15**
☐	**41**	**Jerry Browne, Tex., RC**	**.15**
☐	**42**	**Chris James, Pha., RC**	**.15**
☐	**43**	**Rafael Palmeiro, Chi.-N.L., RC**	**2.00**
☐	**44**	**Pat Dodson, Bos., RC**	**.15**
☐	**45**	**Duane Ward, Tor., RC**	**.15**
☐	46	Mark McGwire, Oak.	5.00
☐	**47**	**Bruce Fields, Det., RC**	**.15**
☐	48	Jody Davis, Chi.-N.L.	.15
☐	49	Roger McDowell, NYM.	.15
☐	50	Jose Guzman, Tex.	.15
☐	51	Oddibe McDowell, Tex.	.15
☐	52	Harold Baines, Chi.-A.L.	.15
☐	53	Dave Righetti, NYY.	.15
☐	54	Moose Haas, Oak.	.15
☐	55	Mark Langston, Sea.	.15
☐	56	Kirby Puckett, Min.	1.00
☐	57	Dwight Evans, Bos.	.15
☐	58	Willie Randolph, NYY.	.15
☐	59	Wally Backman, NYM.	.15
☐	60	Bryn Smith, Mtl.	.15
☐	61	Tim Wallach, Mtl.	.15
☐	62	Joe Hesketh, Mtl.	.15
☐	63	Garry Templeton, S.D.	.15
☐	**64**	**Rob Thompson, S.F., RC**	**.15**
☐	65	Canadian Greats: Floyd Youmans, Mtl.	.15
☐	66	Ernest Riles, Mil.	.15
☐	67	Robin Yount, Mil.	.50
☐	68	Darryl Strawberry, NYM.	.25
☐	69	Ernie Whitt, Tor.	.15
☐	70	Dave Winfield, NYY.	.50
☐	71	Paul Molitor, Mil.	.50
☐	72	Dave Stieb, Tor.	.15
☐	73	Tom Henke, Tor.	.15
☐	74	Frank Viola, Min.	.15
☐	75	Scott Garrelts, S.F.	.15
☐	76	Mike Boddicker, Bal.	.15
☐	77	Keith Moreland, Chi.-N.L.	.15
☐	78	Lou Whitaker, Det.	.15
☐	79	Dave Parker, Cin.	.15
☐	80	Lee Smith, Chi.-N.L.	.15
☐	81	Tom Candiotti, Cle.	.15
☐	82	Greg Harris, Tex.	.15
☐	83	Fred Lynn, Bal.	.15
☐	84	Dwight Gooden, NYM.	.15
☐	85	Ron Darling, NYM.	.15
☐	86	Mike Krukow, S.F.	.15
☐	87	Spike Owen, Bos.	.15
☐	88	Lenny Dykstra, NYM.	.15
☐	89	Rick Aguilera, NYM.	.15
☐	90	Jim Clancy, Tor.	.15
☐	91	Joe Johnson, Tor.	.15
☐	92	Damaso Garcia, Tor.	.15
☐	93	Sid Fernandez, NYM.	.15
☐	94	Bob Ojeda, NYM.	.15
☐	95	Ted Higuera, Mil.	.15
☐	96	George Brett, K.C.	1.00
☐	97	Willie Wilson, K.C.	.15
☐	98	Cal Ripken, Bal.	2.25
☐	99	Kent Hrbek, Min.	.15
☐	100	Bert Blyleven, Min.	.15
☐	101	Ron Guidry, NYY.	.15
☐	**102**	**Andy Allanson, Cle., RC**	**.15**
☐	103	Dave Henderson, Bos.	.15
☐	104	Kirk Gibson, Det.	.15

	No.	Player	Price
☐	105	Lloyd Moseby, Tor.	.15
☐	106	Tony Fernandez, Tor.	.15
☐	107	Lance Parrish, Det.	.15
☐	108	Ozzie Smith, Stl.	.75
☐	109	Gary Carter, NYM.	.35
☐	110	Eddie Murray, Bal.	.75
☐	111	Mike Witt, Cal.	.15
☐	**112**	**Bobby Witt, Tex., RC**	**.15**
☐	113	Willie McGee, Stl.	.15
☐	114	Steve Garvey, S.D.	.25
☐	115	Glenn Davis, Hou.	.15
☐	116	Jose Cruz, Hou.	.15
☐	117	Ozzie Guillen, Chi.-A.L.	.15
☐	118	Alvin Davis, Sea.	.15
☐	119	Jose Rijo, Oak.	.15
☐	120	Bill Madlock, L.A.	.15
☐	121	Tommy Herr, Stl.	.15
☐	122	Mike Schmidt, Pha.	.50
☐	123	Mike Scioscia, L.A.	.15
☐	124	Terry Pendleton, Stl.	.15
☐	125	Leon Durham, Chi.-N.L.	.15
☐	126	Alan Trammell, Det.	.15
☐	127	Jesse Barfield, Tor.	.15
☐	128	Shawon Dunston, Chi.-N.L.	.15
☐	129	Pete Rose, Cin.	.50
☐	130	Von Hayes, Pha.	.15
☐	131	Julio Franco, Cle.	.15
☐	132	Juan Samuel, Pha.	.15
☐	133	Joe Carter, Cle.	.25
☐	134	Brook Jacoby, Cle.	.15
☐	135	Jack Morris, Det.	.15
☐	136	Bob Horner, Atl.	.15
☐	137	Calvin Schiraldi, Bos.	.15
☐	138	Tom Browning, Cin.	.15
☐	139	Shane Rawley, Pha.	.15
☐	140	Mario Soto, Cin.	.15
☐	141	Dale Murphy, Atl.	.25
☐	142	Hubie Brooks, Mtl.	.15
☐	143	Jeff Reardon, Mtl.	.15
☐	**144**	**Will Clark, S.F., RC**	**2.00**
☐	145	Ed Correa, Tex.	.15
☐	146	Glenn Wilson, Pha.	.15
☐	147	Johnny Ray, Pgh.	.15
☐	148	Fernando Valenzuela, L.A.	.15
☐	149	Tim Raines, Mtl.	.15
☐	150	Don Mattingly, NYY.	1.00
☐	151	Jose Canseco, Oak.	.50
☐	152	Gary Pettis, Cal.	.15
☐	153	Don Sutton, Cal.	.35
☐	154	Jim Presley, Sea.	.15
☐	155	Checklist 28-105	.15
☐	**156**	**Dale Sveum, Mil., RC**	**.15**
☐	157	Cory Snyder, Cle.	.15
☐	**158**	**Jeff Sellers, Bos., RC**	**.15**
☐	159	Denny Walling, Hou.	.15
☐	160	Danny Cox, Stl.	.15
☐	161	Bob Forsch, Stl.	.15
☐	162	Joaquin Andujar, Oak.	.15
☐	163	Roberto Clemente, Puzzle Card	.35
☐	**164**	**Paul Assenmacher, Mil., RC**	**.15**
☐	165	Marty Barrett, Bos.	.15
☐	166	Ray Knight, NYM.	.15
☐	167	Rafael Santana, NYM.	.15
☐	**168**	**Bruce Ruffin, Pha., RC**	**.15**
☐	169	Buddy Bell, Cin.	.15
☐	**170**	**Kevin Mitchell, NYM., RC**	**.35**
☐	171	Ken Oberkfell, Atl.	.15
☐	172	Gene Garber, Atl.	.15
☐	173	Canadian Greats: Mark Eichorn, Tor.	.15
☐	174	Don Carman, Pha.	.15
☐	175	Jesse Orosco, NYM.	.15
☐	176	Mookie Wilson, NYM.	.15
☐	177	Gary Ward, Tex.	.15
☐	178	John Franco, Cin.	.15
☐	179	Eric Davis, Cin.	.15
☐	180	Walt Terrell, Det.	.15
☐	181	Phil Niekro, Cle.	.50
☐	182	Pat Tabler, Cle.	.15
☐	183	Brett Butler, Cle.	.15
☐	184	George Bell, Tor.	.15
☐	185	Pete Incaviglia, Tex.	.15
☐	186	Pete O'Brien, Tex.	.15
☐	187	Jimmy Key, Tor.	.15
☐	188	Frank White, K.C.	.15
☐	189	Mike Pagliarulo, NYY.	.15
☐	190	Roger Clemens, Bos.	1.50
☐	191	Rickey Henderson, NYY.	.15
☐	192	Mike Easler, NYY.	.15
☐	193	Wade Boggs, Bos.	.35
☐	194	Vince Coleman, Stl.	.15
☐	195	Charlie Kerfeld, Hou.	.15
☐	196	Dickie Thon, Hou.	.15
☐	197	Bill Doran, Hou.	.15
☐	198	Alfredo Griffin, Oak.	.15
☐	199	Carlton Fisk, Chi.-A.L.	.35
☐	200	Phil Bradley, Sea.	.15
☐	201	Reggie Jackson, Cal.	.50
☐	202	Bob Boone, Cal.	.15
☐	203	Steve Sax, L.A.	.15
☐	204	Tom Niedenfuer, L.A.	.15
☐	205	Tim Burke, Mtl.	.15
☐	206	Floyd Youmans, Mtl.	.15
☐	207	Jay Tibbs, Mtl.	.15
☐	208	Chili Davis, S.F.	.15
☐	209	Larry Parrish, Tex.	.15
☐	210	John Cerutti, Tor.	.15
☐	211	Kevin Bass, Hou.	.15
☐	212	Andre Dawson, Mtl.	.35
☐	**213**	**Bob Sebra, Mtl., RC**	**.15**
☐	214	Kevin McReynolds, S.D.	.15
☐	215	Jim Morrison, Pgh.	.15
☐	216	Candy Maldonado, S.F.	.15
☐	217	John Kruk, S.D.	.15
☐	218	Todd Worrell, Stl.	.15
☐	**219**	**Barry Bonds, Pgh., RC**	**5.00**
☐	220	Andy McGaffigan, Mtl.	.15
☐	221	Andres Galarraga, Mtl.	.50
☐	222	Mike Fitzgerald, Mtl.	.15
☐	**223**	**Kirk McCaskill, Cal., RC**	**.35**
☐	224	Dave Smith, Hou.	.15
☐	**225**	**Ruben Sierra, Tex., RC**	**.35**
☐	226	Scott Fletcher, Tex.	.15
☐	227	Chet Lemon, Det.	.15
☐	228	Dan Petry, Det.	.15
☐	229	Mark Eichhorn, Tor.	.15
☐	230	Cecil Cooper, Mil.	.15
☐	231	Willie Upshaw, Tor.	.15
☐	232	Don Baylor, Bos.	.15
☐	233	Keith Hernandez, NYM.	.15
☐	234	Ryne Sandberg, Chi.-N.L.	.50
☐	235	Tony Gwynn, S.D.	1.00
☐	236	Chris Brown, S.F.	.15
☐	237	Pedro Guerrero, L.A.	.15
☐	238	Mark Gubicza, K.C.	.15
☐	239	Sid Bream, Pgh.	.15
☐	240	Joe Cowley, Chi.-A.L.	.15
☐	241	Bill Buckner, Bos.	.15
☐	242	John Candelaria, Cal.	.15

	No.	Player	Price
☐	243	Scott McGregor, Bal.	.15
☐	244	Tom Brunansky, Min.	.15
☐	245	Gary Gaetti, Min.	.15
☐	246	Orel Hershiser, L.A.	.15
☐	247	Jim Rice, Bos.	.15
☐	248	Oil Can Boyd, Bos.	.15
☐	249	Bob Knepper, Hou.	.15
☐	250	Danny Tartabull, Sea.	.15
☐	251	John Cangelosi, Chi.-A.L.	.15
☐	**252**	**Wally Joyner, Cal., RC**	**.50**
☐	253	Bruce Hurst, Bos.	.15
☐	254	Rich Gedman, Bos.	.15
☐	255	Jim Deshaies, Hou.	.15
☐	256	Tony Pena, Pgh.	.15
☐	257	Nolan Ryan, Hou.	1.75
☐	258	Mike Scott, Hou.	.15
☐	259	Checklist 106-183	.15
☐	260	Dennis Rasmussen, NYY.	.15
☐	261	Bret Saberhagen, K.C.	.15
☐	262	Steve Balboni, K.C.	.15
☐	263	Tom Seaver, Bos.	.25
☐	264	Checklist 184-264	.15

ROBERTO CLEMENTE PUZZLE

This puzzle features Roberto Clemente. The words "Collect all 63 Donruss puzzle pieces and complete puzzle" appear on the backs of the 21 perforated cards. The puzzle art was painted by Dick Perez, the official Hall of Fame artist.

Card Size: 2 1/2" x 3 1/2"
Face: Four colour, white border
Back: Black on card stock; puzzle piece number
Imprint: ©LEAF INC. DIAMOND KING PUZZLE
Complete Set (21 cards): 5.00

1987 O-PEE-CHEE

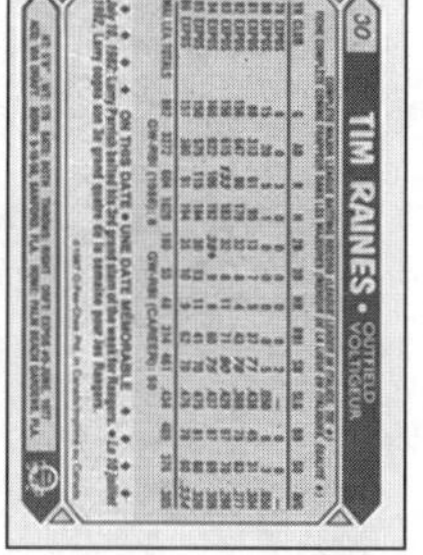

The card numbers on this 396-card set are not the same as those for the corresponding players in the 792-card Topps issue for 1987. **Card Size: 2 1/2" x 3 1/2"**
Face: Four colour, wood-grain border; name, team logo
Back: Yellow and blue on card stock; name, number, position, résumé, bilingual
Imprint: © 1987 O-Pee-Chee Ptd. in Canada/imprimé au Canada
Complete Set (396 cards): 12.00
Common Player: .10

	No.	**Player**	**MINT**
☐	1	Ken Oberkfell, Atl.	.10
☐	2	Jack Howell, Cal.	.10
☐	3	Hubie Brooks, Mtl.	.10
☐	4	Bob Grich, Cal.	.10
☐	5	Rick Leach, Tor.	.10
☐	6	Phil Niekro, Cle.	.35
☐	7	Rickey Henderson, NYY.	.10
☐	8	Terry Pendleton, Stl.	.10
☐	9	Jay Tibbs, Mtl.	.10
☐	10	Cecil Cooper, Mil.	.10
☐	11	Mario Soto, Cin.	.10
☐	12	George Bell, Tor.	.10
☐	13	Nick Esasky, Cin.	.10
☐	14	Larry McWilliams, Pgh.	.10
☐	15	Dan Quisenberry, K.C.	.10
☐	16	Ed Lynch, Chi.-N.L.	.10
☐	17	Pete O'Brien, Tex.	.10
☐	18	Luis Aguayo, Pha.	.10
☐	19	Matt Young, (L.A.)	.10
☐	20	Gary Carter, NYM.	.35
☐	21	Tom Paciorek, Tex.	.10
☐	22	Doug DeCinces, Cal.	.10
☐	23	Lee Smith, Chi.-N.L.	.10
☐	24	Jesse Barfield, Tor.	.10
☐	25	Bert Blyleven, Min.	.10
☐	26	Greg Brock, (Mil.)	.10
☐	27	Dan Petry, Det.	.10
☐	28	Rick Dempsey, Cle.	.10
☐	29	Jimmy Key, Tor.	.10
☐	30	Tim Raines, Mtl.	.10
☐	31	Bruce Hurst, Bos.	.10
☐	32	Manny Trillo, Chi.-N.L.	.10
☐	33	Andy Van Slyke, Stl.	.10
☐	34	Ed VandeBerg, (Cle.)	.10
☐	35	Sid Bream, Pgh.	.10
☐	36	Dave Winfield, NYY.	.35
☐	37	Scott Garrelts, S.F.	.10
☐	38	Dennis Leonard, K.C.	.10
☐	39	Marty Barrett, Bos.	.10
☐	40	Dave Righetti, NYY.	.10
☐	41	Bo Diaz, Cin.	.10
☐	42	Gary Redus, Pha.	.10
☐	43	Tom Niedenfuer, L.A.	.10
☐	44	Greg Harris, Tex.	.10
☐	45	Jim Presley, Sea.	.10
☐	46	Danny Gladden, S.F.	.10
☐	47	Roy Smalley, Min.	.10
☐	48	Wally Backman, NYM.	.10
☐	49	Tom Seaver, Bos.	.35
☐	50	Dave Smith, Hou.	.10
☐	51	Mel Hall, Cle.	.10
☐	52	Tim Flannery, S.D.	.10
☐	53	Julio Cruz, Chi.-A.L.	.10
☐	54	Dick Schofield, Cal.	.10
☐	55	Tim Wallach, Mtl.	.10
☐	56	Glenn Davis, Hou.	.10
☐	57	Darren Daulton, Pha.	.10
☐	**58**	**Chico Walker, Chi.-N.L., RC**	**.10**
☐	59	Garth Iorg, Tor.	.10
☐	60	Tony Pena, Pgh.	.10
☐	61	Ron Hassey, Chi.-A.L.	.10
☐	62	Dave Dravecky, S.D.	.10
☐	63	Jorge Orta, K.C.	.10
☐	64	Al Nipper, Bos.	.10
☐	65	Tom Browning, Cin.	.10
☐	66	Marc Sullivan, Bos.	.10
☐	67	Todd Worrell, Stl.	.10
☐	68	Glenn Hubbard, Atl.	.10
☐	69	Carney Lansford, Oak.	.10
☐	70	Charlie Hough, Tex.	.10
☐	71	Lance McCullers, S.D.	.10
☐	72	Walt Terrell, Det.	.10
☐	73	Bob Kearney, Sea.	.10
☐	74	Dan Pasqua, NYY.	.10
☐	75	Ron Darling, NYM.	.10

	No.	Player	Price
☐	76	Robin Yount, Mil.	.35
☐	77	Pat Tabler, Cle.	.10
☐	78	Tom Foley, Mtl.	.10
☐	79	Juan Nieves, Mil.	.10
☐	80	Wally Joyner, Cal.	.10
☐	81	Wayne Krenchinlki, Mtl.	.10
☐	82	Kirby Puckett, Min.	.75
☐	83	Bob Ojeda, NYM.	.10
☐	84	Mookie Wilson, NYM.	.10
☐	85	Kevin Bass, Hou.	.10
☐	86	Kent Tekulve, Pha.	.10
☐	87	Mark Salas, Min.	.10
☐	88	Brian Downing, Cal.	.10
☐	89	Ozzie Guillen, Chi.-A.L.	.10
☐	90	Dave Stieb, Tor.	.10
☐	91	Rance Mulliniks, Tor.	.10
☐	92	Mike Witt, Cal.	.10
☐	93	Charlie Moore, Mil.	.10
☐	94	Jose Uribe, S.F.	.10
☐	95	Oddibe McDowell, Tex.	.10
☐	**96**	**Ray Soff, Stl., RC**	**.10**
☐	97	Glenn Wilson, Pha.	.10
☐	98	Brook Jacoby, Cle.	.10
☐	99	Darryl Motley, K.C., Error (Atl.)	.10
☐	100	Steve Garvey, S.D.	.25
☐	101	Frank White, Tex.	.10
☐	102	Mike Moore, Sea.	.10
☐	103	Rick Aguilera, NYM.	.10
☐	104	Buddy Bell, Cin.	.10
☐	105	Floyd Youmans, Mtl.	.10
☐	106	Lou Whitaker, Det.	.10
☐	107	Ozzie Smith, Stl.	.35
☐	108	Jim Gantner, Mil.	.10
☐	109	R.J. Reynolds, Pgh.	.10
☐	110	John Tudor, Stl.	.10
☐	111	Alfredo Griffin, Oak.	.10
☐	112	Mike Flanagan, Bal.	.10
☐	113	Neil Allen, Chi.-A.L.	.10
☐	114	Ken Griffey, Atl.	.25
☐	115	Donnie Moore, Cal.	.10
☐	116	Bob Horner, Atl.	.10
☐	**117**	**Ron Shepherd, Tor., RC**	**.10**
☐	118	Cliff Johnson, Tor.	.10
☐	119	Vince Coleman, Stl.	.10
☐	120	Eddie Murray, Bal.	.35
☐	121	Dwayne Murphy, Oak.	.10
☐	122	Jim Clancy, Tor.	.10
☐	123	Ken Landreaux, L.A.	.10
☐	124	Tom Nieto, (Min.)	.10
☐	125	Bob Brenly, S.F.	.10
☐	126	George Brett, K.C.	.50
☐	127	Vance Law, Mtl.	.10
☐	128	Checklist 1 (1 - 132), Error	.10
☐	129	Bob Knepper, Hou.	.10
☐	130	Dwight Gooden, NYM.	.10
☐	131	Juan Bonilla, Bal.	.10
☐	132	Tim Burke, Mtl.	.10
☐	133	Bob McClure, Mtl.	.10
☐	134	Scott Bailes, Cle.	.10
☐	135	Mike Easler, (Pha.)	.10
☐	136	Ron Romanick, (NYY.)	.10
☐	137	Rich Gedman, Bos.	.10
☐	138	Bob Dernier, Chi.-N.L.	.10
☐	139	John Denny, Cin.	.10
☐	140	Bret Saberhagen, K.C.	.10
☐	141	Herm Winningham, Mtl.	.10
☐	142	Rick Sutcliffe, Chi.-N.L.	.10
☐	143	Ryne Sandberg, Chi.-N.L.	.35
☐	144	Mike Scioscia, L.A.	.10
☐	145	Charlie Kerfeld, Hou.	.10
☐	146	Jim Rice, Bos.	.10
☐	147	Steve Trout, Chi.-N.L.	.10
☐	148	Jesse Orosco, NYM.	.10
☐	149	Mike Boddicker, Bal.	.10
☐	150	Wade Boggs, Bos.	.25
☐	151	Dane Iorg, S.D.	.10
☐	152	Rick Burleson, (Bal.)	.10
☐	**153**	**Duane Ward, Tor., RC**	**.10**
☐	154	Rick Reuschel, Pgh.	.10
☐	155	Nolan Ryan, Hou.	1.00
☐	156	Bill Caudill, Tor.	.10
☐	157	Danny Darwin, Hou.	.10
☐	158	Ed Romero, Bos.	.10
☐	159	Bill Almon, Pgh.	.10
☐	160	Julio Franco, Cle.	.10
☐	161	Kent Hrbek, Min.	.10
☐	162	Chili Davis, S.F.	.10
☐	163	Kevin Gross, Pha.	.10
☐	164	Carlton Fisk, Chi.-A.L.	.25
☐	165	Jeff Reardon, (Min.)	.10
☐	166	Bob Boone, Cal.	.10
☐	167	Rick Honeycutt, L.A.	.10
☐	168	Dan Schatzeder, Pha.	.10
☐	169	Jim Wohlford, Mtl.	.10
☐	170	Phil Bradley, Sea.	.10
☐	171	Ken Schrom, Cle.	.10
☐	172	Ron Oester, Cin.	.10
☐	173	Juan Beniquez, (K.C.)	.10
☐	174	Tony Armas, Bos.	.10
☐	175	Bob Stanley, Bos.	.10
☐	176	Steve Buechele, Tex.	.10
☐	177	Keith Moreland, Chi.-N.L.	.10
☐	178	Cecil Fielder, Tor.	.25
☐	179	Gary Gaetti, Min.	.10
☐	180	Chris Brown, S.F.	.10
☐	181	Tom Herr, Stl.	.10
☐	182	Lee Lacy, Bal.	.10
☐	183	Ozzie Virgil, Atl.	.10
☐	184	Paul Molitor, Mil.	.35
☐	185	Roger McDowell, NYM.	.10
☐	186	Mike Marshall, L.A.	.10
☐	187	Ken Howell, L.A.	.10
☐	188	Rob Deer, Mil.	.10
☐	189	Joe Hesketh, Mtl.	.10
☐	190	Jim Sundberg, K.C.	.10
☐	191	Kelly Gruber, Tor.	.10
☐	192	Cory Snyder, Cle.	.10
☐	193	Dave Concepcion, Cin.	.10
☐	194	Kirk McCaskill, Cal.	.25
☐	195	Mike Pagliarulo, NYY.	.10
☐	196	Rick Manning, Mil.	.10
☐	197	Brett Butler, Cle.	.10
☐	198	Tony Gwynn, S.D.	.75
☐	199	Mariano Duncan, L.A.	.10
☐	200	Pete Rose, Cin.	.35
☐	201	John Cangelosi, Chi.-A.L.	.10
☐	202	Danny Cox, Stl.	.10
☐	203	Butch Wynegar, (Cal.)	.10
☐	204	Chris Chambliss, Atl.	.10
☐	205	Graig Nettles, S.D.	.10
☐	206	Chet Lemon, Det.	.10
☐	207	Don Aase, Bal.	.10
☐	208	Mike Mason, Tex.	.10
☐	209	Alan Trammell, Det.	.10
☐	210	Lloyd Moseby, Tor.	.10
☐	211	Richard Dotson, Chi.-A.L.	.10
☐	212	Mike Fitzgerald, Mtl.	.10
☐	213	Darrell Porter, Tex.	.10

☐ 214 Checklist 2 (133 - 264), Error .10
☐ 215 Mark Langston, Sea. .10
☐ 216 Steve Farr, K.C. .10
☐ 217 Dann Bilardello, Mtl. .10
☐ 218 Gary Ward, (NYY.) .10
☐ 219 Cecilio Guante, (NYY.) .10
☐ 220 Joe Carter, Cle. .25
☐ 221 Ernie Whitt, Tor. .10
☐ 222 Denny Walling, Hou. .10
☐ 223 Charlie Leibrandt, K.C. .10
☐ 224 Wayne Tolleson, NYY. .10
☐ 225 Mike Smithson, Min. .10
☐ 226 Zane Smith, Atl. .10
☐ 227 Terry Puhl, Hou. .25
☐ 228 Eric Davis, Cin. .10
☐ 229 Don Mattingly, NYY. .75
☐ 230 Don Baylor, Bos. .10
☐ 231 Frank Tanana, Det. .10
☐ 232 Tom Brookens, Det. .10
☐ 233 Steve Bedrosian, Pha. .10
☐ 234 Wallace Johnson, Mtl. .10
☐ 235 Alvin Davis, Sea. .10
☐ 236 Tommy John, NYY. .10
☐ 237 Jim Morrison, Pgh. .10
☐ 238 Ricky Horton, Stl. .10
☐ 239 Shane Rawley, Pha. .10
☐ 240 Steve Balboni, K.C. .10
☐ 241 Mike Krukow, S.F. .10
☐ 242 Rick Mahler, Atl. .10
☐ 243 Bill Doran, Hou. .10
☐ 244 Mark Clear, Mil. .10
☐ 245 Willie Upshaw, Tor. .10
☐ 246 Hal McRae, K.C. .10
☐ 247 Jose Canseco , Oak. .35
☐ 248 George Hendrick, Cal. .10
☐ 249 Doyle Alexander, Atl. .10
☐ 250 Teddy Higuera, Mil. .10
☐ 251 Tom Hume, Pha. .10
☐ 252 Dennis Martinez, Mtl. .10
☐ 253 Eddie Milner, (S.F.) .10
☐ 254 Steve Sax, L.A. .10
☐ 255 Juan Samuel, Pha. .10
☐ 256 Dave Bergman, Det. .10
☐ 257 Bob Forsch, Stl. .10
☐ 258 Steve Yeager, Sea. .10
☐ 259 Don Sutton, Cal. .25
☐ 260 Vida Blue, (Oak.) .10
☐ 261 Tom Brunansky, Min. .10
☐ 262 Joe Sambito, Bos. .10
☐ 263 Mitch Webster, Mtl. .10
☐ 264 Checklist 3 (265 - 396), Error .10
☐ 265 Darrell Evans, Det. .10
☐ 266 Dave Kingman, Oak. .10
☐ 267 Howard Johnson, NYM. .10
☐ 268 Greg Pryor, K.C. .10
☐ 269 Tippy Martinez, Bal. .10
☐ 270 Jody Davis, Chi.-N.L. .10
☐ 271 Steve Carlton, Chi.-A.L. .35
☐ 272 Andres Galarraga, Mtl. .35
☐ 273 Fernando Valenzuela, L.A. .10
☐ 274 Jeff Hearron, Tor. .10
☐ 275 Ray Knight, (Bal.) .10
☐ 276 Bill Madlock, L.A. .10
☐ 277 Tom Henke, Tor. .10
☐ 278 Gary Pettis, Cal. .10
☐ 279 Jimy Williams, Manager, Tor. .10
☐ 280 Jeffrey Leonard, S.F. .10
☐ 281 Bryn Smith, Mtl. .10
☐ **282 John Cerutti, Tor., RC .10**
☐ 283 Gary Roenicke, Atl. .10
☐ 284 Joaquin Andujar, Oak. .10
☐ 285 Dennis Boyd, Bos. .10
☐ 286 Tim Hulett, Chi.-A.L. .10
☐ 287 Craig Lefferts, S.D. .10
☐ 288 Tito Landrum, Stl. .10
☐ 289 Manny Lee, Tor. .10
☐ 290 Leon Durham, Chi.-N.L. .10
☐ 291 Johnny Ray, Pgh. .10
☐ 292 Franklin Stubbs, L.A. .10
☐ 293 Bob Rodgers, Manager, Mtl. .10
☐ 294 Terry Francona, Chi.-N.L. .10
☐ 295 Len Dykstra, NYM. .10
☐ 296 Tom Candiotti, Cle. .10
☐ 297 Frank DiPino, Chi.-N.L. .10
☐ 298 Craig Reynolds, Hou. .10
☐ 299 Jerry Hairston, Chi.-A.L. .10
☐ 300 Reggie Jackson, (Oak.) .35
☐ **301 Luis Aquino, Tor., RC .10**
☐ 302 Greg Walker, Chi.-A.L. .10
☐ 303 Terry Kennedy, (Bal.) .10
☐ 304 Phil Garner, Hou. .10
☐ 305 John Franco, Cin. .10
☐ 306 Bill Buckner, Bos. .10
☐ **307 Kevin Mitchell, (S.D.), RC .25**
☐ 308 Don Slaught, Tex. .10
☐ 309 Harold Baines, Chi.-A.L. .10
☐ 310 Frank Viola, Min. .10
☐ 311 Dave Lopes, Hou. .10
☐ 312 Cal Ripken, Bal. 1.00
☐ 313 John Candelaria, Cal. .10
☐ **314 Bob Sebra, Mtl., RC .10**
☐ 315 Bud Black, K.C. .10
☐ 316 Brian Fisher, (Pgh.) .10
☐ 317 Clint Hurdle, Stl. .10
☐ 318 Ernie Riles, Mil. .10
☐ 319 Dave LaPoint, (Stl.) .10
☐ **320 Barry Bonds, Pgh., RC 1.50**
☐ 321 Tim Stoddard, NYY. .10
☐ 322 Ron Cey, (Oak.) .10
☐ **323 Al Newman, Mtl., RC .10**
☐ 324 Jerry Royster, (Chi.-A.L.) .10
☐ 325 Garry Templeton, S.D. .10
☐ 326 Mark Gubicza, K.C. .10
☐ 327 Andre Thornton, Cle. .10
☐ 328 Bob Welch, L.A. .10
☐ 329 Tony Fernandez, Tor. .10
☐ 330 Mike Scott, Hou. .10
☐ 331 Jack Clark, Stl. .10
☐ 332 Danny Tartabull, (K.C.) .10
☐ 333 Greg Minton, S.F. .10
☐ 334 Ed Correa, Tex. .10
☐ 335 Candy Maldonado, S.F. .10
☐ 336 Dennis Lamp, (Cle.) .10
☐ 337 Sid Fernandez, NYM. .10
☐ 338 Greg Gross, Pha. .10
☐ 339 Willie Hernandez, Det. .10
☐ 340 Roger Clemens, Bos. 1.00
☐ 341 Mickey Hatcher, Min. .10
☐ 342 Bob James, Chi.-A.L. .10
☐ 343 Jose Cruz, Hou. .10
☐ 344 Bruce Sutter, Atl. .10
☐ 345 Andre Dawson, Mtl. .35
☐ 346 Shawon Dunston, Chi.-N.L. .10
☐ 347 Scott McGregor, Bal. .10
☐ 348 Carmelo Martinez, S.D. .10
☐ 349 Storm Davis, (S.D.) .10
☐ 350 Keith Hernandez, NYM. .10
☐ 351 Andy McGaffigan,Pitcher, Mtl. .10

	No.	Player	Price
☐	352	Dave Parker, Cin.	.10
☐	353	Ernie Camacho, Cle.	.10
☐	354	Eric Show, S.D.	.10
☐	355	Don Carman, Pha.	.10
☐	356	Floyd Bannister, Chi.-A.L.	.10
☐	357	Willie McGee, Stl.	.10
☐	358	Atlee Hammaker, S.F.	.10
☐	359	Dale Murphy, Atl.	.25
☐	360	Pedro Guerrero, L.A.	.10
☐	**361**	**Will Clark, S.F., RC**	**.75**
☐	362	Bill Campbell, Det.	.10
☐	363	Alejandro Pena, L.A.	.10
☐	364	Dennis Rasmussen, NYY.	.10
☐	365	Rick Rhoden, NYY.	.10
☐	366	Randy St. Claire, Mtl.	.10
☐	367	Willie Wilson, K.C.	.10
☐	368	Dwight Evans, Bos.	.10
☐	369	Moose Haas, Oak.	.10
☐	370	Fred Lynn, Bal.	.10
☐	371	Mark Eichhorn, Tor.	.10
☐	372	Dave Schmidt, (Bal.)	.10
☐	373	Jerry Reuss, L.A.	.10
☐	374	Lance Parrish, Det.	.10
☐	375	Ron Guidry, NYY.	.10
☐	376	Jack Morris, Det.	.10
☐	377	Willie Randolph, NYY.	.10
☐	378	Joel Youngblood, S.F.	.10
☐	379	Darryl Strawberry, NYM.	.25
☐	380	Rich Gossage, S.D.	.10
☐	381	Dennis Eckersley, Chi.-N.L.	.10
☐	382	Gary Lucas, Cal.	.10
☐	383	Ron Davis, Chi.-N.L.	.10
☐	**384**	**Pete Incaviglia, Tex., RC**	**.10**
☐	385	Orel Hershiser, L.A.	.10
☐	386	Kirk Gibson, Det.	.10
☐	387	Don Robinson, Pgh.	.10
☐	388	Darnell Coles, Det.	.10
☐	389	Von Hayes, Pha.	.10
☐	390	Gary Matthews, Chi.-N.L.	.10
☐	391	Jay Howell, Oak.	.10
☐	392	Tim Laudner, Min.	.10
☐	393	Rod Scurry, NYY.	.10
☐	394	Tony Bernazard, Cle.	.10
☐	395	Damaso Garcia, (Atl.)	.10
☐	396	Mike Schmidt, Pha.	.35

1987 BOX BOTTOMS

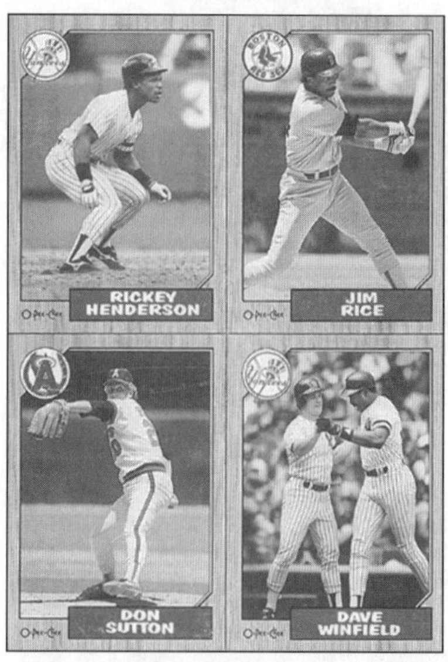

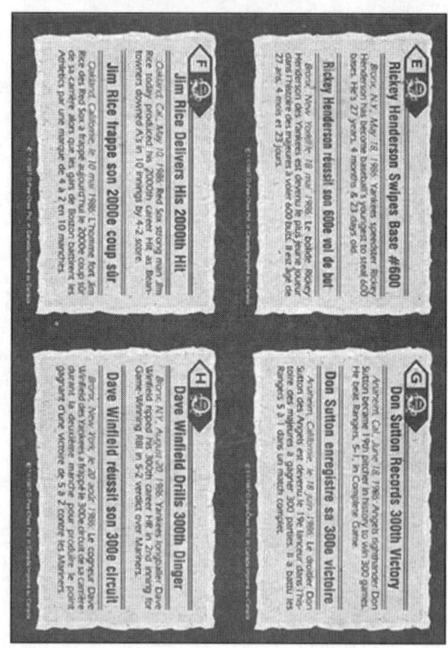

Panel Size: 4 1/4" x 6"
Face: Four colour, woodgrain border; name, team logo
Back: Yellow with blue border on card; name, letter, bilingual
Imprint: 1 or 1987 O-Pee-Chee Ptd. in Canada/imprimé au Canada

Complete Set (8 cards):			**7.00**
Panel A-D:			**4.00**
Panel E-H:			**5.00**
☐	A	Don Baylor, Bos.	.50
☐	B	Steve Carlton, S.F.	1.50
☐	C	Ron Cey, Chi.-N.L.	.50
☐	D	Cecil Cooper, Sea.	.50
☐	E	Rickey Henderson, NYY.	1.00
☐	F	Jim Rice, Bos.	.50
☐	G	Don Sutton, Cal.	1.00
☐	H	Dave Winfield, NYY.	1.50

1987 O-PEE-CHEE STICKERS

101-GARY CARTER

MISSING SOME STICKERS?
• See special offer on inside back cover of yearbook.
• Only $1.00 for any 10 stickers of your choice.
• Details in O-Pee-Chee Baseball Yearbook.

TE MANQUE-T-IL CERTAINS COLLANTS?
• Il y a une offre spéciale sur la couverture arrière intérieure de l'annuaire pour collants.
• Tu ne paieras que $1.00 pour 10 collants de ton choix.
• Les détails sont dans l'annuaire pour collants de Baseball O-Pee-Chee.

Sticker Size: 2 1/8" x 3"
Face: Four colour, white border; number
Back: Red on card stock; name, number, bilingual
Imprint: @ 1987 0-PEE-CHEE CO., LTD. PRINTED IN ITALY – IMPRIMÉ EN ITALIE

Complete Set (198 stickers):		**25.00**
Common Sticker:		**.15**
Album:		**5.00**
No.	**Player**	**MINT**
☐ 13	Lenny Dykstra,NYM.	.15
☐ 14	Gary Carter,NYM.	.25
☐ 15	Mike Scott, Hou.	.15
☐ 16	Gary Pettis, Cal.	.15
☐ 17	Jim Rice, Bos.	.15
☐ 18	Marty Barrett, Bos.	.15
☐ 19	Bruce Hurst, Bos.	.15
☐ 20	Dwight Evans, Bos.	.15
☐ 21	Lenny Dykstra,NYM.	.15
☐ 22	Gary Carter,NYM.	.25
☐ 23	Dave Henderson, Bos.	.15
☐ 24	Ray Knight,NYM.	.15
☐ 25	Gary Carter and Mets Celebrate	.25
☐ 26	Glenn Davis, Hou.	.15
☐ 35	Mike Scott, Hou.	.15
☐ 36	Dale Murphy, Atl.	.15
☐ 41	Bob Horner, Atl.	.15
☐ 46	Ozzie Smith, Stl.	1.00
☐ 55	Todd Worrell, Stl.	.15
☐ 56	Lee Smith, Chi.-N.L.	.15
☐ 61	Ryne Sandberg, Chi.-N.L.	.50
☐ 70	Steve Sax, L.A.	.15
☐ 75	Fernando Valenzuela, L.A.	.15
☐ 76	Hubie Brooks, Mtl.	.15
☐ 85	Tim Raines, Mtl.	.15
☐ 86	Chris Brown, S.F.	.15
☐ 95	Chili Davis, S.F.	.15
☐ 96	Dwight Gooden,NYM.	.15
☐ 101	Gary Carter,NYM.	.35
☐ 106	Tony Gwynn, S.D.	1.00
☐ 115	Steve Garvey, S.D.	.25
☐ 116	Mike Schmidt, Pha.	.75
☐ 121	Von Hayes, Pha.	.15
☐ 130	Rick Rhoden, Pgh.	.15
☐ 135	Johnny Ray, Pgh.	.15
☐ 136	Eric Davis, Cin.	.15
☐ 145	Dave Parker, Cin.	.15
☐ 146	Kirby Puckett, Min.	.75
☐ 147	Rickey Henderson, NYY.	.50
☐ 148	Wade Boggs, Bos.	.50
☐ 149	Lance Parrish, Det.	.15
☐ 150	Wally Joyner, Cal.	.15
☐ 151	Cal Ripken, Bal.	1.50
☐ 152	Dave Winfield, NYY.	.50
☐ 153	Lou Whitaker, Det.	.15
☐ 154	Roger Clemens, Bos.	1.50
☐ 155	Tony Gwynn, S.D.	.60
☐ 156	Ryne Sandberg, Chi.-N.L.	.35
☐ 157	Keith Hernandez, NYM.	.15
☐ 158	Gary Carter, NYM.	.25
☐ 159	Darryl Strawberry, NYM.	.25
☐ 160	Mike Schmidt, Pha.	.50
☐ 161	Dale Murphy, Atl.	.25
☐ 162	Ozzie Smith, Stl.	.60
☐ 163	Dwight Gooden, NYM.	.15
☐ 164	Jose Canseco, Oak.	.35
☐ 173	Dave Kingman, Oak.	.15
☐ 174	Wally Joyner, Cal.	.15
☐ 179	Mike Witt, Cal.	.15
☐ 184	Jesse Barfield, Tor.	.15
☐ 193	George Bell, Tor.	.15
☐ 194	Rob Deer, Mil.	.15
☐ 199	Teddy Higuera, Mil.	.15
☐ 208	Joe Carter, Cle.	.50
☐ 213	Cory Snyder, Cle.	.15
☐ 214	Jim Presley, Sea.	.15
☐ 223	Danny Tartabull, Sea.	.15
☐ 224	Eddie Murray, Bal.	1.00
☐ 233	Cal Ripken, Bal.	2.50
☐ 234	Larry Parrish, Tex.	.15
☐ 239	Pete O'Brien, Tex.	.15
☐ 248	Jim Rice, Bos.	.15
☐ 253	Wade Boggs, Bos.	.75
☐ 254	George Brett, K.C.	1.00
☐ 263	Steve Balboni, K.C.	.15
☐ 264	Darrell Evans, Det.	.15
☐ 273	Kirk Gibson, Det.	.15
☐ 274	Kirk Puckett, Min.	1.50
☐ 279	Gary Gaetti, Min.	.15
☐ 284	Harold Baines, Chi.-A.L.	.15
☐ 293	John Cangelosi, Chi.-A.L.	.15
☐ 294	Don Mattingly, NYY.	1.50
☐ 299	Dave Righetti, NYY.	.15

MULTIPLE STICKERS

☐ 1/172	Jim Deshaies, Hou./ Joaquin Andujar, Oak.	.15
☐ 2/175	Roger Clemens, Bos./ Gary Pettis, Cal.	1.00
☐ 3/176	Roger Clemens, Bos./ Dick Schofield, Cal.	1.00
☐ 4/177	Dwight Evans, Bos./ Donnie Moore, Cal.	.15
☐ 5/178	Dwight Gooden,NYM./ Brian Downing, Cal.	.15
☐ 6/180	Dwight Gooden,NYM./ Bob Boone, Cal.	.15
☐ 7/181	Dave Lopes, Hou./ Kirk McCaskill, Cal.	.25

	No.	Players	Price
☐	8/182	Dave Righetti, NYY./ Doug DeCinces, Cal.	.15
☐	9/183	Dave Righetti, NYY./ Don Sutton, Cal.	.25
☐	10/185	Ruben Sierra, Tex./ Tom Henke, Tor.	.15
☐	11/186	Todd Worrell, Stl./ Willie Upshaw, Tor.	.15
☐	12/187	Todd Worrell, Stl./ Mark Eichhorn, Tor.	.15
☐	27/188	Nolan Ryan, Hou./ Damaso Garcia, Tor.	.35
☐	28/189	Charlie Kerfeld, Hou./ Jim Clancy, Tor.	.15
☐	29/190	Jose Cruz, Hou./ Lloyd Moseby, Tor.	.15
☐	30/191	Phil Garner, Hou./ Tony Fernandez, Tor.	.15
☐	31/192	Bill Doran, Hou./ Jimmy Key, Tor.	.15
☐	32/195	Bob Knepper, Hou./ Mark Clear, Mil.	.15
☐	33/196	Denny Walling, Hou./ Robin Yount, Mil.	.35
☐	34/197	Kevin Bass, Hou./ Jim Gantner, Mil.	.15
☐	37/198	Paul Assenmacher, Atl./ Cecil Cooper, Mil.	.15
☐	38/200	Ken Oberkfell, Atl./ Paul Molitor, Mil.	.35
☐	39/201	Andres Thomas, Atl./ Don Plesac, Mil.	.15
☐	40/202	Gene Garber, Atl./ Billy Jo Robidoux, Mil.	.15
☐	42/203	Rafael Ramirez, Atl./ Earnie Riles, Mil.	.15
☐	43/204	Rick Mahler, Atl./ Ken Schrom, Cle.	.15
☐	44/205	Omar Moreno, Atl./ Pat Tabler, Cle.	.15
☐	45/206	Dave Palmer, Atl./ Mel Hal, Cle.	.15
☐	47/207	Bob Forsch, Stl./ Tony Bernazard, Cle.	.15
☐	48/209	Willie McGee, Stl./ Ernie Camacho, Cle.	.15
☐	49/210	Tom Herr, Stl./ Julio Franco, Cle.	.15
☐	50/211	Vince Coleman, Stl./ Tom Candiotti, Cle.	.15
☐	51/212	Andy Van Slyke, Stl./ Brook Jacoby, Cle.	.15
☐	52/215	Jack Clark, Stl./ Mike Moore, Sea.	.15
☐	53/216	John Tudor, Stl./ Harold Reynolds, Sea.	.15
☐	54/217	Terry Pendleton, Stl./ Scott Bradley, Sea.	.15
☐	57/218	Leon Durham, Chi.-N.L./ Matt Young, Sea.	.15
☐	58/219	Jerry Mumphrey, Chi.-N.L./ Mark Langston, Sea.	.15
☐	59/220	Shawon Dunston, Chi.-N.L./ Alvin Davis, Sea.	.15
☐	60/221	Scott Sanderson, Chi.-N.L./ Phil Bradley, Sea.	.15
☐	62/222	Gary Matthews, Chi.-N.L./ Ken Phelps, Sea.	.15
☐	63/225	Dennis Eckersley, Chi.-N.L./ Rick Dempsey, Bal.	.15
☐	64/226	Jody Davis, Chi.-N.L./ Fred Lynn, Bal.	.15
☐	65/227	Keith Moreland, Chi.-N.L./ Mike Boddicker, Bal.	.15
☐	66/228	Mike Marshall, L.A./ Don Aase, Bal.	.15
☐	67/229	Bill Madlock, L.A./ Larry Sheets, Bal.	.15
☐	68/230	Greg Brock, L.A./ Storm Davis, Bal.	.15
☐	69/231	Pedro Guerrero, L.A./ Lee Lacy, Bal.	.15
☐	71/232	Rick Honeycutt, L.A./ Jim Traber, Bal.	.15
☐	72/235	Franklin Stubbs, L.A./ Gary Ward, Tex.	.15
☐	73/236	Mike Scioscia, L.A./ Pete Incaviglia, Tex.	.15
☐	74/237	Mariano Duncan, L.A./ Scott Fletcher, Tex.	.15
☐	77/238	Andre Dawson, Mtl./ Greg Harris, Tex.	.25
☐	78/240	Tim Burke, Mtl./ Charlie Hough, Tex.	.15
☐	79/241	Floyd Youmans, Mtl./ Don Slaught, Tex.	.15
☐	80/242	Tim Wallach, Mtl./ Steve Buechele, Tex.	.15
☐	81/243	Jeff Reardon, Mtl./ Oddibe McDowell, Tex.	.15
☐	82/244	Mitch Webster, Mtl./ Roger Clemens, Bos.	.50
☐	83/245	Bryn Smith, Mtl./ Bob Stanley, Bos.	.15
☐	84/246	Andres Galarraga, Mtl./ Tom Seaver, Bos.	.35
☐	87/247	Bob Brenly, S.F./ Rich Gedman, Bos.	.15
☐	88/249	Will Clark, S.F./ Dennis Boyd, Bos.	.35
☐	89/250	Scott Garrelts, S.F./ Bill Buckner, Bos.	.15
☐	90/251	Jeffrey Leonard, S.F./ Dwight Evans, Bos.	.15
☐	91/252	Bobby Thompson, S.F./ Don Baylor, Bos.	.15
☐	92/255	Mike Krukow, S.F./ Steve Farr, K.C.	.15
☐	93/256	Danny Gladden, S.F./ Jim Sundberg, K.C.	.15
☐	94/257	Candy Maldonado, S.F./ Dan Quisenberry, K.C.	.15
☐	97//258	Sid Fernandez, NYM./ Charlie Leibrandt, K.C.	.15
☐	98/259	Lenny Dykstra, NYM./ Argenis Salazar, K.C.	.15
☐	99/260	Bob Ojeda, NYM./ Frank White, K.C.	.15
☐	100/261	Wally Backman, NYM./ Willie Wilson, K.C.	.15
☐	102/262	Keith Hernandez, NYM./ Lonnie Smith, K.C.	.15
☐	103/265	Darryl Strawberry, NYM./ Johnny Grubb, Det.	.25
☐	104/266	Roger McDowell, NYM./ Jack Morris, Det.	.15
☐	105/267	Ron Darling, NYM./ Lou Whitaker, Det.	.15
☐	107/268	Dave Dravecky, S.D./ Chet Lemon, Det.	.15
☐	108/269	Terry Kennedy, S.D./ Lance Parrish, Det.	.15
☐	109/270	Rich Gossage, S.D./ Alan Trammell, Det.	.15
☐	110/271	Garry Templeton, S.D./ Darnell Coles, Det.	.15
☐	111/272	Lance McCullers, S.D./ Willie Hernandez, Det.	.15
☐	112/275	Eric Show, S.D./ Mike Smithson, Min.	.15
☐	113/276	John Kruk, S.D./ Mickey Hatcher, Min.	.15
☐	114/277	Tim Flannery, S.D./ Frank Viola, Min.	.15
☐	117/278	Glenn Wilson, Pha./ Bert Blyleven, Min.	.15
☐	118/280	Kent Tekulve, Pha./ Tom Brunansky, Min.	.15
☐	119/281	Gary Redus, Pha./ Kent Hrbek, Min.	.15
☐	120/282	Shane Rawley, Pha./ Roy Smalley, Min.	.15
☐	122/283	Don Carman, Pha./ Greg Gagne, Min.	.15
☐	123/285	Bruce Ruffin, Pha./ Ron Hassey, Chi.-A.L.	.15
☐	124/286	Steve Bedrosian, Pha./ Floyd Bannister, Chi.-A.L.	.15
☐	125/287	Juan Samuel, Pha./ Ozzie Guillen, Chi.-A.L.	.15
☐	126/288	Sid Bream, Pgh./ Carlton Fisk, Chi.-A.L.	.35
☐	127/289	Cecilio Guante, Pgh./ Tim Hulett, Chi.-A.L.	.15
☐	128/290	Rick Reuschel, Pgh./ Joe Cowley, Chi.-A.L.	.15
☐	129/291	Tony Pena, Pgh./ Greg Walker, Chi.-A.L.	.15
☐	131/292	Barry Bonds, Pgh./ Neil Allen, Chi.-A.L.	1.00
☐	132/295	Joe Orsulak, Pgh./ Mike Easler, NYY.	.15
☐	133/296	Jim Morrison, Pgh./ Rickey Henderson, NYY.	.35
☐	134/297	R.J. Reynolds, Pgh./ Dan Pasqua, NYY.	.15
☐	137/298	Tom Browning, Cin./ Dave Winfield, NYY.	.35
☐	138/300	John Franco, Cin./ Mike Pagliarulo, NYY.	.15
☐	139/301	Pete Rose, Cin./ Ron Guidry, NYY.	.50
☐	140/302	Bill Gullickson, Cin./ Willie Randolph, NYY.	.15
☐	141/303	Ron Oester, Cin./ Dennis Ramussen, NYY.	.15
☐	142/304	Bo Diaz, Cin./ Jose Canseco, Oak.	.15
☐	143/305	Buddy Bell, Cin./ Andres Thomas, Atl.	.15
☐	144/306	Eddie Milner, Cin./ Danny Tartabull, Sea.	.15
☐	165/307	Curt Young, Oak./ Robby Thompson, S.F.	.15
☐	166/308	Alfredo Griffin, Oak./ P.Incaviglia & C.Snyder	.15
☐	167/309	Dave Stewart, Oak./ Dale Sveum, Mil.	.15
☐	168/310	Mike Davis, Oak./ Todd Worrell, Stl.	.15
☐	169/311	Bruce Bochte, Oak./ Andy Allanson, Clev.	.15
☐	170/312	Dwayne Murphy, Oak./ Bruce Ruffin, Pha.	.15
☐	171/313	Carney Lansford, Oak./ Wally Joyner, Cal.	.15

1987 STUART BAKERY

Issued in Canada only, this 28-panel set features three players and one offer card per panel. All major league teams are represented, with the Blue Jays and Expos having two panels each. Team logos are airbrushed out of the photos. A complete set comprises 84 player cards and 28 offer cards. Offer cards are not individually priced here.

Card Size: 2 1/2" x 3 1/2"

Face: Four colour, blue and white border; position, perforated, Stuart and M.L.B. logos

Back: Black on card stock; numbered _ of 28, résumé, bilingual

Imprint: © MSA

Complete Panel Set (28 panels; 112 cards) 55.00

No.	Panel	MINT
☐ 1	PANEL - NEW YORK METS Gary Carter Keith Hernandez Darryl Strawberry, Error	3.00
☐ 2	PANEL - ATLANTA BRAVES Dale Murphy Ken Griffey Bruce Benedict	1.50
☐ 3	PANEL - CHIAGO CUBS Andre Dawson Jody Davis Leon Durham	2.50
☐ 4	PANEL CINCINNATI REDS Eric Davis Dave Parker Buddy Bell	1.50
☐ 5	PANEL - HOUSTON ASTROS Glenn Davis Nolan Ryan Mike Scott	6.50
☐ 6	PANEL - LOS ANGELES DODGERS Pedro Guerrero Fernando Valenzuela Mike Marshall	1.50
☐ 7	PANEL - MONTREAL EXPOS Tim Raines Tim Wallach Mitch Webster	2.50
☐ 8	PANEL - MONTREAL EXPOS Floyd Youmans Hubie Brooks Bryn Smith	2.00
☐ 9	PANEL - PHILADELPHIA PHILLIES Mike Schmidt Shane Rawley Juan Samuel	3.50
☐ 10	PANEL -PITTSBURGH PIRATES Johnny Ray R.J. Reynolds Jim Morrison	1.50
☐ 11	PANEL - ST LOUIS CARDINALS Jack Clark Vince Coleman Ozzie Smith	2.75
☐ 12	PANEL - SAN DIEGO PADRES Steve Garvey Tony Gwynn John Kruk	5.00
☐ 13	PANEL - SAN FRANCISCO GIANTS Chili Davis Jeffrey Leonard Robby Thompson	1.50
☐ 14	PANEL - BALTIMORE ORIOLES Cal Ripken Eddie Murray Fred Lynn	8.00
☐ 15	PANEL - BOSTON RED SOCKS Don Baylor Wade Boggs Roger Clemens	5.00
☐ 16	PANEL - CALIFORNIA ANGELS Doug DeCinces Wally Joyner Mike Witt	1.50
☐ 17	PANEL - CHIAGO WHITE SOX Harold Baines Carlton Fisk Ozzie Guillen	2.50
☐ 18	PANEL - CLEVELAND INDIANS Pat Tabler Julio Franco Joe Carter	3.25
☐ 19	PANEL - DETROIT TIGERS Jack Morris Alan Trammell Kirk Gibson	1.50
☐ 20	PANEL - KANSAS CITY ROYALS George Brett Bret Saberhagen Willie Wilson	4.00
☐ 21	PANEL - MILWAUKEE BREWERS Cecil Cooper Robin Yount Paul Molitor	3.50
☐ 22	PANEL - MINNESSOTA TWINS Tom Brunansky Kent Hrbek Kirby Puckett	3.50
☐ 23	PANEL - NEW YORK YANKEES Rickey Henderson Don Mattingly Dave Winfield	5.00
☐ 24	PANEL - OAKLAND ATHLETICS Jose Canseco Carney Lansford Alfredo Griffin	2.50
☐ 25	PANEL - SEATTLE MARINERS Alvin Davis Phil Bradley Mark Langston	1.50
☐ 26	PANEL - TEXAS RANGERS Pete Incaviglia Pete O'Brien Larry Parrish	1.50
☐ 27	PANEL - TORONTO BLUE JAYS Jesse Barfield Tony Fernandez George Bell	2.75
☐ 28	PANEL - TORONTO BOUE JAYS Dave Stieb Lloyd Moseby Ernie Whitt	2.50

1988 FANTASTIC SAM'S

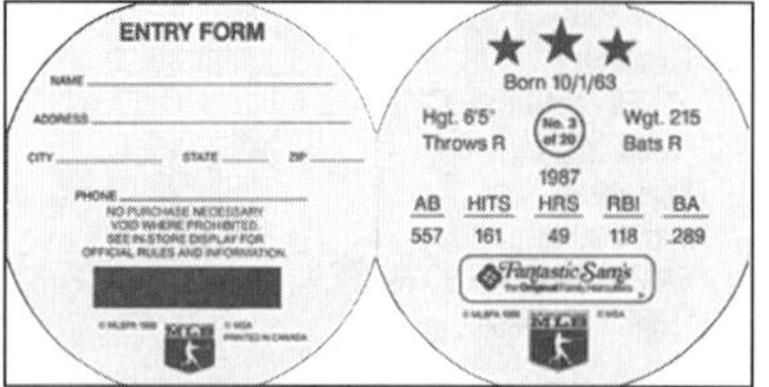

Each of these 20 two-disk perforated cards features a player photo and a grand prize offer, with a metalic scratch-off bar on the front. There is an entry form and player stats on the back.

Disk Size: 2 5/8" Diameter
Face: Four colour, orange border; name, team
Back: Black on card stock; numbered _ of 20, résumé
Imprint: None

		Complete Set (20 cards):	**30.00**
	No.	**Player**	**MINT**
☐	1	Kirby Puckett, Min.	3.00
☐	2	George Brett, K.C.	3.00
☐	3	Mark McGwire, Oak.	4.00
☐	4	Wally Joyner, Cal.	1.50
☐	5	Paul Molitor, Mil.	2.00
☐	6	Alan Trammell, Det.	1.50
☐	7	George Bell, Tor.	1.50
☐	8	Wade Boggs, Bos.	2.00
☐	9	Don Mattingly, NYY.	3.00
☐	10	Julio Franco, Cle.	1.50
☐	11	Ozzie Smith, Stl.	2.50
☐	12	Will Clark, S.F.	1.50
☐	13	Dale Murphy, Atl.	1.50
☐	14	Eric Davis, Cin.	1.50
☐	15	Andre Dawson, Chi.-N.L.	2.00
☐	16	Tim Raines, Mtl.	1.50
☐	17	Darryl Strawberry, NYM.	1.50
☐	18	Tony Gwynn, S.D.	4.00
☐	19	Mike Schmidt, Pha.	2.50
☐	20	Pedro Guerrero, L.A.	1.50

1988 HOSTESS

One panel of this set of 24 cards on 12 perforated panels was inserted in Hostess Potato Chips.

Disc Size: 2 5/8" Diameter
Face: Four colour, name, portrait, Hostess logo
Back: Blue on card stock; position, 1987 stats, numbered _ of 24, bilingual
Imprint: ©MSA ©MLBPA

		Complete Set (12 panels):	**10.00**
	No.	**Player**	**MINT**
☐	1	Mitch Webster, Mtl.	.50
☐	2	Tim Burke, Mtl.	.50
☐	3	Tom Foley, Mtl.	.50
☐	4	Herm Winningham, Mtl.	.50
☐	5	Hubie Brooks, Mtl.	.50
☐	6	Mike Fitzgerald, Mtl.	.50
☐	7	Tim Wallach, Mtl.	.50
☐	8	Andres Galarraga, Mtl.	2.00
☐	9	Floyd Youmans, Mtl.	.50
☐	10	Neal Heaton, Mtl.	.50
☐	11	Tim Raines, Mtl.	1.00
☐	12	Casey Candaele, Mtl.	.50
☐	13	Jim Clancy, Tor.	.50
☐	14	Rance Mulliniks, Tor.	.50
☐	15	Fred McGriff, Tor.	1.00
☐	16	Ernie Whitt, Tor.	.50
☐	17	Dave Stieb, Tor.	.50
☐	18	Mark Eichhorn, Tor.	.50
☐	19	Jesse Barfield, Tor.	.50
☐	20	Lloyd Moseby, Tor.	.50
☐	21	Tony Fernandez, Tor.	.50
☐	22	George Bell, Tor.	.50
☐	23	Tom Henke, Tor.	.50
☐	24	Jimmy Key, Tor.	.50

1988 LEAF

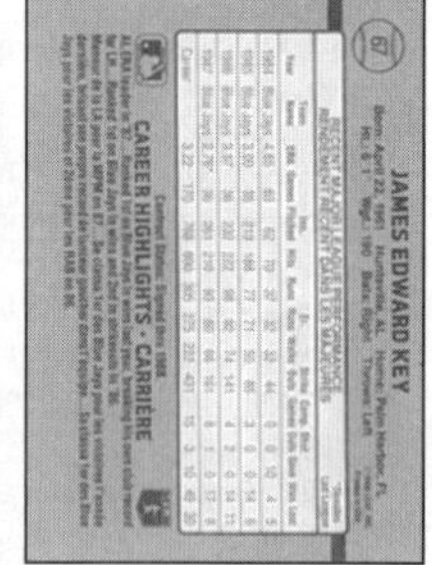

The 264-card Leaf set of this year has different player photos than the 660-card Donruss set of 1988. Again this year, the first 26 Donruss Diamond Kings cards feature painted portraits of the players. The remaining card faces feature player photos and the word Leaf appears in the upper left corner. The "Canadian Greats" cards in this set feature painted portraits of George Bell and Tim Wallach. The set also includes a puzzle card of Stan Musial and a 21-piece Musial puzzle.

Card Size: 2 1/2" x 3 1/2"
Face: Four colour, blue border; position, team logo
Back: Blue and black on card stock; number, résumé, career highlights, bilingual
Imprint: Card No. 1-26: ©1988 LEAF, INC. *MADE & PRINTED IN U.S.A. * PEREZ-STEELE GALLERIES Card No. 27-262: ©1988 LEAD, INC. Printed in U.S.A.

		Complete Set (264 cards):	**10.00**
		Common Player:	**.10**
	No.	**Player**	**MINT**
☐	1	Mark McGwire, Oak.	.35
☐	2	Tim Raines, Mtl.	.10

	No.	Player	Price
☐	3	Benito Santiago, S.D.	.10
☐	4	Alan Trammell, Det.	.10
☐	5	Danny Tartabull, K.C.	.10
☐	6	Ron Darling, NYM.	.10
☐	7	Paul Molitor, Mil.	.25
☐	8	Devon White, Cal.	.10
☐	9	Andre Dawson, Chi.-N.L.	.10
☐	10	Julio Franco, Cle.	.10
☐	11	Scott Fletcher, Tex.	.10
☐	12	Tony Fernandez, Tor.	.10
☐	13	Shane Rawley, Pha.	.10
☐	14	Kal Daniels, Cin.	.10
☐	15	Jack Clark, Stl.	.10
☐	16	Dwight Evans, Bos.	.10
☐	17	Tommy John, NYY.	.10
☐	18	Andy Van Slyke, Pgh.	.10
☐	19	Gary Gaetti, Min.	.10
☐	20	Mark Langston, Sea.	.10
☐	21	Will Clark, S.F.	.10
☐	22	Glenn Hubbard, Atl.	.10
☐	23	Billy Hatcher, Hou.	.10
☐	24	Bob Welch, L.A.	.10
☐	25	Ivan Calderon, Chi.-A.L.	.10
☐	26	Cal Ripken Jr., Bal.	.50
☐	27	Checklist 1-26	.10
☐	**28**	**Mackey Sasser, Pgh., RC**	**.10**
☐	**29**	**Jeff Treadway, Cin., RC**	**.10**
☐	**30**	**Mike Campbell, Sea., RC**	**.10**
☐	**31**	**Lance Johnson, Stl., RC**	**.10**
☐	**32**	**Nelson Liriano, Tor., RC**	**.10**
☐	33	Shawn Abner, S.D.	.10
☐	**34**	**Roberto Alomar, S.D., RC**	**2.25**
☐	**35**	**Shawn Hillegas, L.A., RC**	**.10**
☐	36	Joey Meyer, Sea.	.10
☐	37	Kevin Elster, NYM.	.10
☐	**38**	**Jose Lind, Pgh., RC**	**.10**
☐	**39**	**Kirt Manwaring, S.D., RC**	**.10**
☐	**40**	**Mark Grace, Chi.-N.L., RC**	**.50**
☐	**41**	**Jody Reed, Bos., RC**	**.10**
☐	**42**	**John Farrell, Cle., RC**	**.10**
☐	**43**	**Al Leiter, NYY., RC**	**.25**
☐	**44**	**Gary Thurman, K.C., RC**	**.10**
☐	**45**	**Vicente Palacios, Pgh., RC**	**.10**
☐	**46**	**Eddie Williams, Cle., RC**	**.10**
☐	**47**	**Jack McDowell, Chi.WS, RC**	**.10**
☐	48	Dwight Gooden, NYM.	.10
☐	49	Mike Witt, Cal.	.10
☐	50	Wally Joyner, Cal.	.10
☐	51	Brook Jacoby, Cle.	.10
☐	52	Bert Blyleven, Min.	.10
☐	53	Ted Higuera, Mil.	.10
☐	54	Mike Scott, Hou.	.10
☐	55	Jose Guzman, Tex.	.10
☐	56	Roger Clemens, Bos.	.50
☐	57	Dave Righetti, NYY.	.10
☐	58	Benito Santiago, S.D.	.10
☐	59	Ozzie Guillen, Chi.-A.L.	.10
☐	60	Matt Nokes, Det. RC	.10
☐	61	Fernando Valenzuela, L.A.	.10
☐	62	Orel Hershiser, L.A.	.10
☐	63	Sid Fernandez, NYM.	.10
☐	64	Ozzie Virgil, Atl.	.10
☐	65	Wade Boggs, Bos.	.35
☐	66	Floyd Youmans, Mtl.	.10
☐	67	Jimmy Key, Tor.	.10
☐	68	Bret Saberhagen, K.C.	.10
☐	69	Jody Davis, Chi.-N.L.	.10
☐	70	Shawon Dunston, Chi.-N.L.	.10
☐	71	Julio Franco, Cle.	.10
☐	72	Danny Cox, Stl.	.10
☐	73	Jim Clancy, Tor.	.10
☐	74	Mark Eichhorn, Tor.	.10
☐	75	Scott Bradley, Sea.	.10
☐	76	Charlie Liebrandt, K.C.	.10
☐	77	Nolan Ryan, Hou.	.85
☐	78	Ron Darling, NYM.	.10
☐	79	John Franco, Cin.	.10
☐	80	Dave Stieb, Tor.	.10
☐	81	Mike Fitzgerald, Mtl.	.10
☐	82	Steve Bedrosian, Pha.	.10
☐	83	Dale Murphy, Atl.	.10
☐	84	Tim Burke, Mtl.	.10
☐	85	Jack Morris, Det.	.10
☐	86	Greg Walker, Chi.-A.L.	.10
☐	87	Kevin Mitchell, S.F.	.10
☐	88	Doug Drabek, Pgh.	.10
☐	89	Charlie Hough, Tex.	.10
☐	90	Tony Gwynn, S.D.	.50
☐	91	Rick Sutcliffe, Chi.-N.L.	.10
☐	92	Shane Rawley, Pha.	.10
☐	93	George Brett, K.C.	.50
☐	94	Frank Viola, Min.	.10
☐	95	Tony Pena, Stl.	.10
☐	96	Jim Deshaies, Hou.	.10
☐	97	Mike Scioscia, L.A.	.10
☐	98	Rick Rhoden, NYY.	.10
☐	99	Terry Kennedy, Bal.	.10
☐	100	Cal Ripkin, Bal.	.85
☐	101	Pedro Guerrero, L.A.	.10
☐	102	Andy Van Slyke, Pgh.	.10
☐	103	Willie McGee, Stl.	.10
☐	104	Mike Kingery, Sea.	.10
☐	105	Kevin Seitzer, K.C.	.10
☐	106	Robin Yount, Mil.	.35
☐	107	Tracy Jones, Cin.	.10
☐	108	Dave Magadan, NYM.	.10
☐	109	Mel Hall, Cle.	.10
☐	110	Billy Hatcher, Hou.	.10
☐	111	Todd Benzinger, Bos.	.10
☐	112	Mike LaValliere, Pgh.	.10
☐	113	Barry Bonds, Pgh.	.35
☐	114	Tim Raines, Mtl.	.10
☐	115	Ozzie Smith, Stl.	.35
☐	116	Dave Winfield, NYY.	.25
☐	117	Keith Hernandez, NYM.	.10
☐	118	Jeffrey Leonard, S.F.	.10
☐	119	Larry Parrish, Tex.	.10
☐	120	Rob Thompson, S.F.	.10
☐	121	Andres Galarraga, Mtl.	.25
☐	122	Mickey Hatcher, L.A.	.10
☐	123	Mark Langston, Sea.	.10
☐	124	Mike Schmidt, Pha.	.35
☐	125	Cory Snyder, Cle.	.10
☐	126	Andre Dawson, Chi.-N.L.	.10
☐	127	Devon White, Cal.	.10
☐	128	Vince Coleman, Stl.	.10
☐	129	Bryn Smith, Mtl.	.10
☐	130	Lance Parrish, Pha.	.10
☐	131	Willie Upshaw, Tor.	.10
☐	132	Pete O'Brien, Tex.	.10
☐	133	Tony Fernandez, Tor.	.10
☐	**134**	**Billy Ripken, Stl., RC**	**.10**
☐	135	Len Dykstra, NYM.	.10
☐	136	Kirk Gibson, Det.	.10
☐	137	Kevin Bass, Hou.	.10
☐	138	Jose Canseco, Oak.	.25
☐	139	Kent Hrbek, Min.	.10
☐	140	Lloyd Moseby, Tor.	.10

☐ 141 Marty Barrett, Bos. .10
☐ 142 Carmelo Martinez, S.D. .10
☐ 143 Tom Foley, Mtl. .10
☐ 144 Kirby Puckett, Min. .50
☐ 145 Rickey Henderson, NYY. .25
☐ 146 Juan Samuel, Pha. .10
☐ 147 Pete Incaviglia, Tex. .10
☐ 148 Greg Brock, Mil. .10
☐ 149 Eric Davis, Cin. .10
☐ 150 Kal Daniels, Cin. .10
☐ 151 Bob Boone, Cal. .10
☐ 152 John Cerutti, Tor. .10
☐ 153 Mike Greenwell, Bos. .10
☐ 154 Oddibe McDowell, Tex. .10
☐ 155 Scott Fletcher, Tex. .10
☐ 156 Gary Carter, NYM. .25
☐ 157 Harold Baines, Chi.-A.L. .10
☐ 158 Greg Swindell, Cle. .10
☐ 159 Mark McLemore, Cal. .10
☐ 160 Keith Moreland, Chi.-N.L. .10
☐ 161 Jim Gantner, Mil. .10
☐ 162 Willie Randolph, NYY. .10
☐ 163 Fred Lynn, Bal. .10
☐ 164 B.J. Surhoff, Mil. .10
☐ 165 Ken Griffey, Atl. .10
☐ 166 Chet Lemon, Det. .10
☐ 167 Alan Trammell, Det. .10
☐ 168 Paul Molitor, Mil. .35
☐ 169 Lou Whitaker, Det. .10
☐ 170 Will Clark, S.F. .10
☐ 171 Dwight Evans, Bos. .10
☐ 172 Eddie Murray, Bal. .35
☐ 173 Darrell Evans, Det. .10
☐ **174 Ellis Burks, Bos., RC .35**
☐ 175 Ivan Calderon, Chi.-A.L. .10
☐ 176 John Kruk, S.D. .10
☐ 177 Don Mattingly, NYY. .50
☐ 178 Dick Schofield, Cal. .10
☐ 179 Bruce Hurst, Bos. .10
☐ 180 Ron Guidry, NYY. .10
☐ 181 Jack Clark, Stl. .10
☐ 182 Franklin Stubbs, L.A. .10
☐ 183 Bill Doran, Hou. .10
☐ 184 Joe Carter, Cle. .25
☐ 185 Steve Sax, L.A. .10
☐ 186 Glenn Davis, Hou. .10
☐ 187 Bo Jackson, K.C. .10
☐ 188 Bobby Bonilla, Pgh. .10
☐ 189 Willie Wilson, Pha. .10
☐ 190 Danny Tartabull, K.C. .10
☐ 191 Bo Diaz, Cin. .10
☐ 192 Buddy Bell, Cin. .10
☐ 193 Tim Wallach, Mtl. .10
☐ 194 Mark McGwire, Oak. .60
☐ 195 Carney Lansford, Oak. .10
☐ 196 Alvin Davis, Sea. .10
☐ 197 Von Hayes, Pha. .10
☐ 198 Mitch Webster, Mtl. .10
☐ 199 Casey Candaele, Mtl. .10
☐ 200 Gary Gaetti, Min. .10
☐ 201 Tommy Herr, Stl. .10
☐ 202 Wally Backman, NYM. .10
☐ 203 Brian Downing, Cal. .10
☐ 204 Rance Mulliniks, Tor. .10
☐ 205 Craig Reynolds, Hou. .10
☐ 206 Ruben Sierra, Tex. .10
☐ 207 Ryne Sandberg, Chi.-N.L. .35
☐ 208 Carlton Fisk, Chi.-A.L. .25
☐ 209 Checklist 28-107 .10
☐ **210 Gerald Young, Hou., RC .10**
☐ 211 Donruss MVP: Tim Raines, Mtl. .10
☐ 212 John Tudor, Stl. .10
☐ 213 Canadian Greats: George Bell, Tor. .10
☐ 214 Donruss MVP: George Bell, Tor. .10
☐ 215 Jim Rice, Bos. .10
☐ 216 Gerald Perry, Atl. .10
☐ 217 Dave Stewart, Oak. .10
☐ 218 Jose Uribe, S.F. .10
☐ 219 Rick Reuschel, S.F. .10
☐ 220 Darryl Strawberry, NYM. .25
☐ 221 Chris Brown, S.D. .10
☐ 222 Ted Simmons, Atl. .10
☐ 223 Lee Mazzilli, NYM. .10
☐ 224 Denny Walling, Hou. .10
☐ 225 Jesse Barfield, Tor. .10
☐ 226 Barry Larkin, Cin. .25
☐ 227 Harold Reynolds, Sea. .10
☐ 228 Kevin McReynolds, NYM. .10
☐ 229 Todd Worrell, Stl. .10
☐ 230 Tommy John, NYY. .10
☐ 231 Rick Aguilera, NYM. .10
☐ 232 Bill Madlock, Det. .10
☐ 233 Roy Smalley, Min. .10
☐ 234 Jeff Musselman, Tor. .10
☐ 235 Mike Dunne, Pgh. .10
☐ 236 Jerry Browne, Tex. .10
☐ 237 Sam Horn, Bos. .10
☐ 238 Howard Johnson, NYM. .10
☐ 239 Candy Maldonado, S.F. .10
☐ 240 Nick Esasky, Cin. .10
☐ 241 Geno Petralli, Tex. .10
☐ 242 Herm Winningham, Mtl. .10
☐ 243 Roger McDowell, NYM. .10
☐ 244 Brian Fisher, Pgh. .10
☐ 245 John Marzano, Bos. .10
☐ 246 Terry Pendleton, Stl. .10
☐ 247 Rick Leach, Tor. .10
☐ 248 Pascual Perez, Mtl. .10
☐ 249 Mookie Wilson, NYM. .10
☐ 250 Ernie Whitt, Tor. .10
☐ 251 Ron Kittle, NYY. .10
☐ 252 Oil Can Boyd, Bos. .10
☐ 253 Jim Gott, Pgh. .10
☐ 254 George Bell, Tor. .10
☐ 255 Canadian Greats: Tim Wallach, Mtl. .10
☐ 256 Luis Polonia, Oak. .10
☐ 257 Hubie Brooks, Mtl. .10
☐ 258 Mickey Brantley, Sea. .10
☐ **259 Gregg Jefferies, NYM., RC .25**
☐ 260 Johnny Ray, Cal. .10
☐ 261 Checklist 108-187 .10
☐ 262 Dennis Martinez, Mtl. .10
☐ 263 Stan Musial .25
☐ 264 Checklist 188-264 .10

STAN MUSIAL PUZZLE

These 21 cards feature Stan Musial, with the words "Collect all 63 Donruss puzzle pieces to complete puzzle" on the back. All pieces are individually numbered for easy collecting.

Card Size: 2 1/2" x 3 1/2"
Face: Four colour, white border
Back: Black on card stock; puzzle piece number
Imprint: © LEAF INC. DIAMOND KING PUZZLE
Complete Set (21 cards): 4.00

1988 O-PEE-CHEE

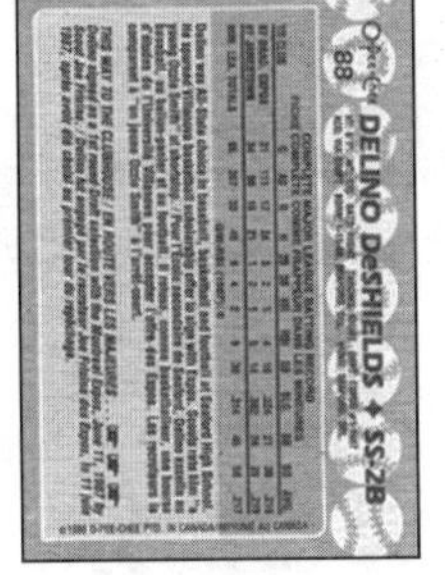

Card Size: 2 1/2" x 3 1/2"
Face: Four colour, white border; name, team
Back: Orange and black on card stock; name, number, résumé, player trivia, bilingual
Imprint: © 1988 O-PEE-CHEE PRD. IN CANADA/IMPRIMê AU CANADA

Complete Set (396 cards): 12.00
Common Player: .10

	No.	Player	MINT
☐	1	Chris James, Pha.	.10
☐	2	Steve Buechele, Tex.	.10
☐	**3**	**Mike Henneman, Det., RC**	**.10**
☐	4	Eddie Murray, Bal.	.35
☐	5	Bret Saberhagen, K.C.	.10
☐	**6**	**Nathan Minchey, Mtl., RC**	**.10**
☐	7	Harold Reynolds, Sea.	.10
☐	8	Bo Jackson, K.C.	.10
☐	9	Mike Easler, NYY.	.10
☐	10	Ryne Sandberg, Chi.-N.L.	.25
☐	11	Mike Young, Bal.	.10
☐	12	Tony Phillips, Oak.	.10
☐	13	Andres Thomas, Atl.	.10
☐	14	Tim Burke, Mtl.	.10
☐	15	Chili Davis, (S.F.)	.10
☐	16	Jim Lindeman, Stl.	.10
☐	17	Ron Oester, Cin.	.10
☐	18	Craig Reynolds, Hou.	.10
☐	19	Juan Samuel, Pha.	.10
☐	20	Kevin Gross, Pha.	.10
☐	21	Cecil Fielder, Tor.	.10
☐	22	Greg Swindell, Cle.	.10
☐	23	Jose DeLeon, Chi.-A.L.	.10
☐	24	Jim Deshaies, Hou.	.10
☐	25	Andres Galarraga, Mtl.	.10
☐	26	Mitch Williams, Tex.	.10
☐	27	R.J. Reynolds, Pgh.	.10
☐	**28**	**Jose Nunez, Tor., RC**	**.10**
☐	29	Angel Salazar, K.C.	.10
☐	30	Sid Fernandez, NYM.	.10
☐	31	Keith Moreland, Chi.-N.L.	.10
☐	32	John Kruk, S.D.	.10
☐	33	Rob Deer, Mil.	.10
☐	34	Ricky Horton, Stl.	.10
☐	35	Harold Baines, Chi.-A.L.	.10
☐	36	Jamie Moyer, Chi.-N.L.	.10
☐	37	Kevin McReynolds, NYM.	.10
☐	38	Ron Darling, NYM.	.10
☐	39	Ozzie Smith, Stl.	.35
☐	40	Orel Hershiser, L.A.	.10
☐	41	Bob Melvin, S.F.	.10
☐	42	Alfredo Griffin, (Oak.)	.10
☐	43	Dick Schofield, Cal.	.10
☐	44	Terry Steinbach, Oak.	.10
☐	45	Kent Hrbek, Min.	.10
☐	46	Darnell Coles, Pgh.	.10
☐	47	Jimmy Key, Tor.	.10
☐	48	Alan Ashby, Hou.	.10
☐	49	Julio Franco, Cle.	.10
☐	50	Hubie Brooks, Mtl.	.10
☐	51	Chris Bando, Cle.	.10
☐	52	Fernando Valenzuela, L.A.	.10
☐	53	Kal Daniels, Cin.	.10
☐	54	Jim Clancy, Tor.	.10
☐	55	Phil Bradley, (Sea.)	.10
☐	56	Andy McGaffigan, Mtl.	.10
☐	57	Mike LaVaillere, Pgh.	.10
☐	58	Dave Magadan, NYM.	.10
☐	59	Danny Cox, Stl.	.10
☐	60	Rickey Henderson, Oak.	.25
☐	61	Jim Rice, Bos.	.10
☐	62	Calvin Schiraldi, (Bos.)	.10
☐	63	Jerry Mumphrey, Chi.-N.L.	.10
☐	**64**	**Ken Caminiti, Hou., RC**	**.75**
☐	65	Leon Durham, Chi.-N.L.	.10
☐	66	Shane Rawley, Pha.	.10
☐	67	Ken Oberkfell, Atl.	.10
☐	68	Keith Hernandez, NYM.	.10
☐	69	Bob Brenly, S.F.	.10
☐	70	Roger Clemens, Bos.	.50
☐	71	Gary Pettis, Cal. (Det)	.10
☐	72	Dennis Eckersley, Oak.	.10
☐	73	Dave Smith, Hou.	.10
☐	74	Cal Ripken, Bal.	.75
☐	75	Joe Carter, Cle.	.10
☐	76	Denny Martinez, Mtl.	.10
☐	77	Juan Beniquez, Tor.	.10
☐	78	Tim Laudner, Min.	.10
☐	79	Ernie Whitt, Tor.	.10
☐	80	Mark Langston, Sea.	.10
☐	81	Dale Sveum, Mil.	.10
☐	82	Dion James, Atl.	.10
☐	83	Dave Valle, Sea.	.10
☐	84	Bill Wegman, Mil.	.10
☐	85	Howard Johnson, NYM.	.10
☐	86	Benny Santiago, S.D.	.10
☐	87	Casey Candaele, Mtl.	.10
☐	**88**	**Delino DeShields, Mtl., RC**	**2.00**
☐	89	Dave Winfield, NYY.	.25
☐	90	Dale Murphy, Atl.	.10
☐	91	Jay Howell, (Oak.)	.10
☐	**92**	**Ken Williams, Chi.-A.L., RC**	**.10**
☐	93	Bob Sebra, Mtl.	.10
☐	94	Tim Wallach, Mtl.	.10
☐	95	Lance Parrish, Pha.	.10
☐	**96**	**Todd Benzinger, Bos., RC**	**.10**
☐	97	Scott Garrelts, S.F.	.10
☐	98	Jose Guzman, Tex.	.10
☐	99	Jeff Reardon, Min.	.10
☐	100	Jack Clark, Stl.	.10
☐	101	Tracy Jones, Cin.	.10
☐	102	Barry Larkin, Cin.	.35
☐	103	Curt Young, Oak.	.10
☐	104	Juan Nieves, Mil.	.10
☐	105	Terry Pendleton, Stl.	.10
☐	**106**	**Rob Ducey, Tor., RC**	**.35**
☐	107	Scott Bailes, Cle.	.10
☐	108	Eric King, Det.	.10
☐	109	Mike Pagliarulo, NYY.	.10
☐	110	Teddy Higuera, Mil.	.10
☐	111	Pedro Guerrero, L.A.	.10
☐	112	Chris Brown, S.D.	.10
☐	113	Kelly Gruber, Tor.	.10

	No.	Player	Price
☐	114	Jack Howell, Cal.	.10
☐	115	Johnny Ray, Cal.	.10
☐	116	Mark Eichhorn, Tor.	.10
☐	117	Tony Pena, Stl.	.10
☐	118	Bob Welch, (L.A.)	.10
☐	119	Mike Kingery, Sea.	.10
☐	120	Kirby Puckett, Min.	.50
☐	121	Charlie Hough, Tex.	.10
☐	122	Tony Bernazard, Oak.	.10
☐	123	Tom Candiotti, Cle.	.10
☐	124	Ray Knight, Bal.	.10
☐	125	Bruce Hurst, Bos.	.10
☐	126	Steve Jeltz, Pha.	.10
☐	127	Ron Guidry, NYY.	.10
☐	128	Duane Ward, Tor.	.10
☐	129	Greg Minton, Cal.	.10
☐	130	Buddy Bell, Cin.	.10
☐	131	Denny Walling, Hou.	.10
☐	132	Donnie Hill, Chi.-A.L.	.10
☐	133	Wayne Tolleson, NYY.	.10
☐	134	Robert (Buck) Rodgers, Mgr, Mtl.	.10
☐	135	Todd Worrell, Stl.	.10
☐	136	Brian Dayett, Chi.-N.L.	.10
☐	137	Chris Bosio, Mil.	.10
☐	138	Mitch Webster, Mtl.	.10
☐	139	Jerry Browne, Tex.	.10
☐	140	Jesse Barfield, Tor.	.10
☐	141	Doug DeCinces, (Cal.)	.10
☐	142	Andy Van Slyke, Pgh.	.10
☐	143	Doug Drabek, Pgh.	.10
☐	**144**	**Jeff Parrett, Mtl., RC**	**.10**
☐	145	Bill Madlock, Det.	.10
☐	146	Larry Herndon, Det.	.10
☐	147	Bill Buckner, Cal.	.10
☐	148	Carmelo Martinez, S.D.	.10
☐	149	Ken Howell, L.A.	.10
☐	150	Eric Davis, Cin.	.10
☐	151	Randy Ready, S.D.	.10
☐	152	Jeffrey Leonard, S.F.	.10
☐	153	Dave Stieb, Tor.	.10
☐	154	Jeff Stone, Pha.	.10
☐	155	Dave Righetti, NYY.	.10
☐	156	Gary Matthews, Sea.	.10
☐	157	Gary Carter, NYM.	.25
☐	158	Bob Boone, Cal.	.10
☐	159	Glenn Davis, Hou.	.10
☐	160	Willie McGee, Stl.	.10
☐	161	Bryn Smith, Mtl.	.10
☐	162	Mark McLemore, Cal.	.10
☐	163	Dale Mohorcic, Tex.	.10
☐	164	Mike Flanagan, Tor.	.10
☐	165	Robin Yount, Mil.	.25
☐	166	Bill Doran, Hou.	.10
☐	167	Rance Mulliniks, Tor.	.10
☐	168	Wally Joyner, Cal.	.10
☐	169	Cory Snyder, Cle.	.10
☐	170	Rich Gossage, S.D.	.10
☐	171	Rick Mahler, Atl.	.10
☐	172	Henry Cotto, NYY.	.10
☐	173	George Bell, Tor.	.10
☐	174	B.J. Surhoff, Mil.	.10
☐	175	Kevin Bass, Hou.	.10
☐	176	Jeff Reed, Mtl.	.10
☐	177	Frank Tanana, Det.	.10
☐	178	Darryl Strawberry, NYM.	.25
☐	179	Lou Whitaker, Det.	.10
☐	180	Terry Kennedy, Bal.	.10
☐	181	Mariano Duncan, L.A.	.10
☐	182	Ken Phelps, Sea.	.10
☐	183	Bob Dernier, (Chi.-N.L.)	.10
☐	184	Ivan Calderon, Chi.-A.L.	.10
☐	185	Rick Rhoden, NYY.	.10
☐	186	Rafael Palmeiro, Chi.-N.L.	.10
☐	187	Kelly Downs, S.F.	.10
☐	188	Spike Owen, Bos.	.10
☐	189	Bobby Bonilla, Pgh.	.10
☐	190	Candy Maldonado, S.F.	.10
☐	191	John Cerutti, Tor.	.10
☐	192	Devon White, Cal.	.10
☐	193	Brian Fisher, Pgh.	.10
☐	**194**	**Alex Sanchez, Tor., RC**	**.10**
☐	195	Dan Quisenberry, K.C.	.10
☐	196	Dave Engle, Mtl.	.10
☐	197	Lance McCullers, S.D.	.10
☐	198	Franklin Stubbs, L.A.	.10
☐	199	Scott Bradley, Sea.	.10
☐	200	Wade Boggs	.35
☐	201	Kirk Gibson, Det.	.10
☐	202	Brett Butler, (Cle.)	.10
☐	203	Dave Anderson, L.A.	.10
☐	204	Donnie Moore, Cal.	.10
☐	**205**	**Nelson Liriano, Tor., RC**	**.10**
☐	206	Dan Gladden, Min.	.10
☐	207	Dan Pasqua, (NYY.)	.10
☐	208	Robby Thompson, S.F.	.10
☐	209	Richard Dotson, (Chi.-A.L.)	.10
☐	210	Willie Randolph, NYY.	.10
☐	211	Danny Tartabull, K.C.	.10
☐	212	Greg Brock, Mil.	.10
☐	213	Albert Hall, Atl.	.10
☐	214	Dave Schmidt, Bal.	.10
☐	215	Von Hayes, Pha.	.10
☐	216	Herm Winningham, Mtl.	.10
☐	217	Mike Davis, Oak. (L.A.)	.10
☐	218	Charlie Leibrandt, K.C.	.10
☐	219	Mike Stanley, Tex.	.10
☐	220	Tom Henke, Tor.	.10
☐	221	Dwight Evans, Bos.	.10
☐	222	Willie Wilson, K.C.	.10
☐	223	Stan Jefferson, S.D.	.10
☐	224	Mike Dunne, Pgh.	.10
☐	225	Mike Scioscia, L.A.	.10
☐	226	Larry Parrish	.10
☐	227	Mike Scott, Hou.	.10
☐	228	Wallace Johnson, Mtl.	.10
☐	229	Jeff Musselman, Tor.	.10
☐	230	Pat Tabler, Cle.	.10
☐	231	Paul Molitor, Mil.	.35
☐	232	Bob James, Chi.-A.L.	.10
☐	233	Joe Niekro, Min.	.10
☐	234	Oddibe McDowell, Tex.	.10
☐	235	Gary Ward, NYY.	.10
☐	236	Ted Power, Cin.	.10
☐	237	Pascual Perez, Mtl.	.10
☐	**238**	**Luis Polonia, Oak., RC**	**.10**
☐	239	Mike Diaz, Pgh.	.10
☐	240	Lee Smith, (Chi.-N.L.)	.10
☐	241	Willie Upshaw, Tor.	.10
☐	242	Tom Niedenfuer, Bal.	.10
☐	243	Tim Raines, Mtl.	.10
☐	244	Jeff Robinson, Pgh.	.10
☐	245	Rich Gedman, Bos.	.10
☐	246	Scott Bankhead, Sea.	.10
☐	247	Andre Dawson, Chi.-N.L.	.25
☐	248	Brook Jacoby, Cle.	.10
☐	249	Mike Marshall, L.A.	.10
☐	250	Nolan Ryan, Hou.	1.50
☐	251	Tom Foley, Mtl.	.10

- ☐ 252 Bob Brower, Tex. .10
- ☐ 253 Checklist (1 - 132) .10
- ☐ 254 Scott McGregor, Bal. .10
- ☐ 255 Ken Griffey, Atl. .10
- ☐ 256 Ken Schrom, Cle. .10
- ☐ 257 Gary Gaetti, Min. .10
- ☐ 258 Ed Nunez, Sea. .10
- ☐ 259 Frank Viola, Min. .10
- ☐ 260 Vince Coleman, Stl. .10
- ☐ 261 Reid Nichols, Mtl. .10
- ☐ 262 Tim Flannery, S.D. .10
- ☐ 263 Glenn Braggs, Mil. .10
- ☐ 264 Garry Templeton, S.D. .10
- ☐ 265 Bo Diaz, Cin. .10
- ☐ **266 Matt Nokes, Det., RC .10**
- ☐ 267 Barry Bonds, Pgh. .35
- ☐ 268 Bruce Ruffin, Pha. .10
- ☐ **269 Ellis Burks, Bos., RC .35**
- ☐ 270 Mike Witt, Cal. .10
- ☐ 271 Ken Gerhart, Bal. .10
- ☐ 272 Lloyd Moseby, Tor. .10
- ☐ 273 Garth Iorg, Tor. .10
- ☐ 274 Mike Greenwell, Bos. .10
- ☐ 275 Kevin Seitzer, K.C. .10
- ☐ 276 Luis Salazar, S.D. .10
- ☐ 277 Shawon Dunston, Chi.-N.L. .10
- ☐ 278 Rick Reuschel, S.F. .10
- ☐ 279 Randy St. Claire, Mtl. .10
- ☐ 280 Pete Incaviglia, Tex. .10
- ☐ 281 Mike Boddicker, Bal. .10
- ☐ 282 Jay Tibbs, Mtl. .10
- ☐ 283 Shane Mack, S.D. .10
- ☐ 284 Walt Terrell, Det. .10
- ☐ 285 Jim Presley, Sea. .10
- ☐ 286 Greg Walker, Chi.-A.L. .10
- ☐ 287 Dwight Gooden, NYM. .10
- ☐ 288 Jim Morrison, Det. .10
- ☐ 289 Gene Garber, K.C. .10
- ☐ 290 Tony Fernandez, Tor. .10
- ☐ 291 Ozzie Virgil, Atl. .10
- ☐ 292 Carney Lansford, Oak. .10
- ☐ 293 Jim Acker, Atl. .10
- ☐ **294 Tommy Hinzo, Cle., RC .10**
- ☐ 295 Bert Blyleven, Min. .10
- ☐ 296 Ozzie Guillen, Chi.-A.L. .10
- ☐ 297 Zane Smith, Atl. .10
- ☐ 298 Milt Thompson, Pha. .10
- ☐ 299 Len Dykstra, NYM. .10
- ☐ 300 Don Mattingly, NYY. .50
- ☐ 301 Bud Black, K.C. .10
- ☐ 302 Jose Uribe, S.F. .10
- ☐ 303 Manny Lee, Tor. .10
- ☐ 304 Sid Bream, Pgh. .10
- ☐ 305 Steve Sax, L.A. .10
- ☐ 306 Billy Hatcher, Hou. .10
- ☐ 307 John Shelby, L.A. .10
- ☐ 308 Lee Mazzilli, NYM. .10
- ☐ **309 Bill Long, Chi.-A.L., RC .10**
- ☐ 310 Tom Herr, Stl. .10
- ☐ **311 Derek Bell, Tor., RC 1.00**
- ☐ 312 George Brett, K.C. .50
- ☐ 313 Bob McClure, Mtl. .10
- ☐ 314 Jimy Williams, Manager, Tor. .10
- ☐ 315 Dave Parker, Cin. (Oak.) .10
- ☐ 316 Doyle Alexander, Det. .10
- ☐ 317 Dan Plesac, Mil. .10
- ☐ 318 Mel Hall, Cle. .10
- ☐ 319 Ruben Sierra, Tex. .10
- ☐ 320 Alan Trammell, Det. .10
- ☐ 321 Mike Schmidt, Pha. .35
- ☐ **322 Wally Ritchie, Pha., RC .10**
- ☐ 323 Rick Leach, Tor. .10
- ☐ 324 Danny Jackson, K.C. (Cin.) .10
- ☐ 325 Glenn Hubbard, Atl. .10
- ☐ 326 Frank White, K.C. .10
- ☐ 327 Larry Sheets, Bal. .10
- ☐ 328 John Cangelosi, Pgh. .10
- ☐ 329 Bill Gullickson, NYY. .10
- ☐ 330 Eddie Whitson .10
- ☐ 331 Brian Downing, Cal. .10
- ☐ 332 Gary Redus, Chi.-A.L. .10
- ☐ 333 Wally Backman, NYM. .10
- ☐ 334 Dwayne Murphy, Oak. .10
- ☐ 335 Claudell Washington, NYY. .10
- ☐ 336 Dave Concepcion, Cin. .10
- ☐ 337 Jim Gantner, Mil. .10
- ☐ 338 Marty Barrett, Bos. .10
- ☐ 339 Mickey Hatcher, L.A. .10
- ☐ 340 Jack Morris, Det. .10
- ☐ 341 John Franco, Cin. .10
- ☐ 342 Ron Robinson, Cin. .10
- ☐ 343 Greg Gagne, Min. .10
- ☐ 344 Steve Bedrosian, Pha. .10
- ☐ 345 Scott Fletcher, Tex. .10
- ☐ 346 Vance Law, Mtl. (Chi.-N.L.) .10
- ☐ 347 Joe Johnson, Tor. (Ana.) .10
- ☐ 348 Jim Eisenreich, K.C. .10
- ☐ 349 Alvin Davis, Sea. .10
- ☐ 350 Will Clark, S.F. .10
- ☐ 351 Mike Aldrete, S.F. .10
- ☐ **352 Billy Ripken, Bal., RC .10**
- ☐ 353 Dave Stewart, Oak. .10
- ☐ 354 Neal Heaton, Mtl. .10
- ☐ 355 Roger McDowell, NYM. .10
- ☐ 356 John Tudor, Stl. .10
- ☐ 357 Floyd Bannister, Chi.-A.L. (K.C.) .10
- ☐ 358 Rey Quinones, Sea. .10
- ☐ 359 Glenn Wilson, Pha. (Sea.) .10
- ☐ 360 Tony Gwynn, S.D. .50
- ☐ 361 Greg Maddux, Chi.-N.L. 1.75
- ☐ 362 Juan Castillo, Mil. .10
- ☐ 363 Willie Fraser, Cal. .10
- ☐ 364 Nick Esasky, Cin. .10
- ☐ 365 Floyd Youmans, Mtl. .10
- ☐ 366 Chet Lemon, Det. .10
- ☐ 367 Matt Young, L.A. (Oak.) .10
- ☐ **368 Gerald Young, Hou., RC .10**
- ☐ 369 Bob Stanley, Bos. .10
- ☐ 370 Jose Canseco, Oak. .25
- ☐ 371 Joe Hesketh, Mtl. .10
- ☐ 372 Rick Sutcliffe, Chi.-N.L. .10
- ☐ 373 Checklist (133 - 264) .10
- ☐ 374 Checklist (265-396) .10
- ☐ 375 Tom Brunansky, Min. .10
- ☐ 376 Jody Davis, Chi.-N.L. .10
- ☐ **377 Sam Horn, Bos., RC .10**
- ☐ 378 Mark Gubicza, K.C. .10
- ☐ 379 Rafael Ramirez, Atl. (Hou.) .10
- ☐ **380 Joe Magrane, Stl., RC .10**
- ☐ 381 Pete O'Brien, Tex. .10
- ☐ 382 Lee Guetterman, Sea. .10
- ☐ 383 Eric Bell, Bal. .10
- ☐ **384 Gene Larkin, Min., RC .10**
- ☐ 385 Carlton Fisk, Chi.-A.L. .25
- ☐ 386 Mike Fitzgerald, Mtl. .10
- ☐ 387 Kevin Mitchell, S.F. .10
- ☐ 388 Jim Winn, Chi.-A.L. .10
- ☐ 389 Mike Smithson, Min. .10

	No.	Player	MINT
☐	390	Darrell Evans, Det.	.10
☐	391	Terry Leach	.10
☐	392	Charlie Kerfeld, Hou.	.10
☐	393	Mike Krukow, S.F.	.10
☐	394	All-Star: Mark McGwire, Oak.	.60
☐	395	Fred McGriff, Tor.	.25
☐	**396**	**DeWayne Buice, Cal., RC**	**.10**

1988 BOX BOTTOMS

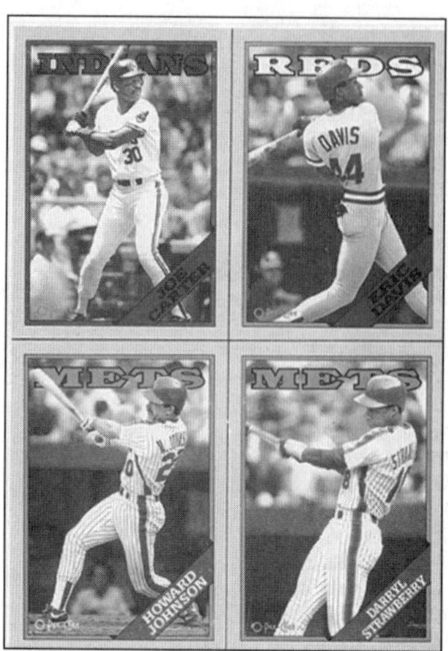

Panel Size: 5 1/4" x 7 1/4"
Face: Four colour, blue border; name, team
Back: Orange and black on card stock; letter, records
Imprint: © 1988 O-PEE-CHEE PTD. IN CANADA/ IMPRIMÉ AU CANADA

Complete Set (16 cards):	**15.00**
Panel A-D:	**2.50**
Panel E-H:	**5.00**
Panel I-L:	**4.00**
Panel M-P:	**9.00**

	No.	Player	MINT
☐	A	Don Baylor, Bos.	.50
☐	B	Steve Bedrosian, Pha.	.50
☐	C	Juan Beniquez, Tor.	.50
☐	D	Bob Boone, Cal.	.50
☐	E	Darrell Evans, Det.	.50
☐	F	Tony Gwynn, S.D.	2.50
☐	G	John Kruk, S.D.	.50
☐	H	Marvell Wynne, S.D.	.50
☐	I	Joe Carter, Cle.	1.00
☐	J	Eric Davis, Cin.	.50
☐	K	Howard Johnson, NYM.	.50
☐	L	Darryl Strawberry, NYM.	1.00
☐	M	Rickey Henderson, NYY.	1.00
☐	N	Nolan Ryan, Hou.	4.00
☐	O	Mike Schmidt, Pha.	2.00
☐	P	Kent Tekulve, Pha.	.50

1988 O-PEE-CHEE STICKERS

Sticker Size: 2 1/2" x 3 1/2"
Face: Four colour, yellow boeder; number
Back: Blank / O-Pee-Chee Super Star
Imprint: © 1988 O-Pee-Chee Ptd. in Canada/imprimé au Canada

Complete Set (198 stickers):	**20.00**
Album:	**5.00**
Common Sticker:	**.15**

	No.	Player	MINT
☐	13	John Tudor, Stl.	.15
☐	14	Jeff Reardon, Min.	.15
☐	15	Tom Brunansky, Min.	.15
☐	16	Jeffrey Leonard, Stl.	.15
☐	17	Gary Gaetti, Min.	.15

☐	18	Cardinals NLCS	.15
☐	19	Danny Gladden, Min.	.15
☐	20	Bert Blyleven, Min.	.15
☐	21	John Tudor, Stl.	.15
☐	22	Tom Lawless, Stl.	.15
☐	23	Curt Ford, Stl.	.15
☐	24	Kent Hrbek, Min.	.15
☐	25	Frank Viola, Min.	.15
☐	30	Mike Scott, Hou.	.15
☐	35	Glenn Davis, Hou.	.15
☐	36	Ozzie Virgil, Atl.	.15
☐	45	Dale Murphy, Atl.	.25
☐	46	Jack Clark, Stl.	.15
☐	55	Willie McGee, Stl.	.15
☐	56	Andre Dawson, Chi.-N.L.	.35
☐	61	Rick Sutcliffe, Chi.-N.L.	.15
☐	70	Fernando Valenzuela, L.A.	.15
☐	75	Pedro Guerrero, L.A.	.15
☐	76	Tim Raines, Mtl.	.15
☐	85	Tim Wallach, Mtl.	.15
☐	86	Jeffrey Leonard, S.F.	.15
☐	95	Candy Maldonado, S.F.	.15
☐	96	Darryl Strawberry, NYM.	.25
☐	101	Dwight Gooden, NYM.	.15
☐	110	John Kruk, S.D.	.15
☐	115	Tony Gwynn, S.D.	1.00
☐	116	Steve Bedrosian, Pha.	.15
☐	125	Mike Schmidt, Pha.	.50
☐	126	Andy Van Slyke, Pgh.	.15
☐	135	Barry Bonds, Pgh.	.75
☐	136	Dave Parker, Cin.	.15
☐	141	Eric Davis, Cin.	.15
☐	146	Eric Davis, Cin.	.15
☐	147	Ryne Sandberg, Chi.-N.L.	.35
☐	148	Andre Dawson, Chi.-N.L.	.25
☐	149	Mike Schmidt, Pha.	.35
☐	150	Jack Clark, Stl.	.15
☐	151	Darryl Strawberry, NYM.	.25
☐	152	Gary Carter, NYM.	.35
☐	153	Ozzie Smith, Stl.	.15
☐	154	Mike Scott, Hou.	.15
☐	155	Rickey Henderson, NYY.	.35
☐	156	Don Mattingly, NYY.	.50
☐	157	Wade Boggs, Bos.	.25
☐	158	George Bell, Tor.	.15
☐	159	Dave Winfield, NYY.	.35
☐	160	Cal Ripken, Bal.	1.50
☐	161	Terry Kennedy, Bal.	.15
☐	162	Willie Randolph, NYY.	.15
☐	163	Bret Saberhagen, K.C.	.15
☐	164	Mark McGwire, Oak.	2.00
☐	173	Jose Canseco, Oak.	.25
☐	174	Mike Witt, Cal.	.15
☐	179	Wally Joyner, Cal.	.15
☐	188	George Bell, Tor.	.15
☐	193	Tony Fernandez, Tor.	.15
☐	194	Paul Molitor, Mil.	.35
☐	203	Dan Plesac, Mil.	.15
☐	204	Pat Tabler, Cle.	.15
☐	213	Joe Carter, Cle.	.35
☐	214	Mark Langston, Sea.	.15
☐	219	Alvin Davis, Sea.	.15
☐	228	Cal Ripken, Bal.	2.50
☐	233	Eddie Murray, Bal.	.75
☐	234	Ruben Sierra, Tex.	.15
☐	243	Larry Parrish, Tex.	.15
☐	244	Wade Boggs, Bos.	.50
☐	253	Bruce Hurst, Bos.	.15
☐	254	Bret Saberhagen, K.C.	.15
☐	259	George Brett, K.C.	1.00
☐	268	Jack Morris, Det.	.15
☐	273	Alan Trammell, Det.	.15
☐	274	Kent Hrbek, Min.	.15
☐	283	Kirby Puckett, Min.	.75
☐	284	Ozzie Guillen, Chi.-A.L.	.15
☐	293	Harold Baines, Chi.-A.L.	.15
☐	294	Willie Randolph, NYY.	.15
☐	299	Don Mattingly, NYY.	.75

MULTIPLE STICKERS

☐	1/263	Mark McGwire, Oak./ Willie Wilson, K.C.	1.00
☐	2/304	Benny Santiago, S.D./ Al Pedrique, Pgh.	.15
☐	3/187	Don Mattingly, Bal./ Ernie Whitt, Tor.	.50
☐	4/223	Vince Coleman, Stl./ Gary Matthews, Sea.	.15
☐	5/272	Bob Boone, Cal./ Jim Morrison, Det.	.15
☐	6/278	Steve Bedrosian, NYY./ Tim Laudner, Min.	.15
☐	7/276	Nolan Ryan, Hou./ Bert Blyleven, Min.	1.00
☐	8/306	Darrell Evans, Det./ Kevin Seitzer, K.C.	.15
☐	9/255	Mike Schmidt, Pha./ Frank White, K.C.	.25
☐	10/256	Don Baylor, Bos./ Dan Quisenberry, K.C.	.15
☐	11/145	Eddie Murray, Bal./ Dennis Rasmussen, Cin.	.50
☐	12/237	Juan Beniquez, Tor./ Oddibe McDowell, Tex.	.15
☐	26/216	Dave Smith, Hou./ Ed Nunez, Sea.	.15
☐	27/240	Jim Deshaies, Hou./ Pete O'Brian, Tex.	.15
☐	28/171	Billy Hatcher, Hou./ Mike Davis, Oak.	.15
☐	29/196	Kevin Bass, Hou./ Teddy Higuera, Mil.	.15
☐	31/224	Denny Walling, Hou./ Eric Bell, Bal.	.15
☐	32/185	Alan Ashby, Hou./ Willie Upshaw, Tor.	.15
☐	33/ 292	Ken Caminiti, Hou./Greg Walker, Chi.-A.L.	.25
☐	34/245	Bill Doran, Hou./ Dwight Evans, Bos.	.15
☐	37/260	Ken Oberkfell, Atl./ Charlie Leibrandt, K.C.	.15
☐	38/183	Ken Griffey, Atl./ Devon White, Cal.	.15
☐	39/287	Albert Hall, Atl./ Ken Williams, Chi.-A.L.	.15
☐	40/310	Zane Smith, Atl./ Ellis Burks, Bos.	.15
☐	41/207	Andres Thomas, Atl./ Julio Franco, Cle.	.15
☐	42/178	Dion James, Atl./ Gary Pettis, Cal.	.15
☐	43/249	Jim Acker, Atl./ Mike Greenwell, Bos.	.15
☐	44/226	Tom Glavine, Atl./ Dave Schmidt, Bal.	.15
☐	47/269	Vince Coleman, Stl./ Matt Nokes, Det.	.15
☐	48/221	Ricky Horton, Stl./ Harold Reynolds, Sea.	.15
☐	49/303	Terry Pendleton, Stl./ Gary Ward, NYY.	.15
☐	50/271	Tom Herr, Stl./ Eric King, Det.	.15
☐	51/265	Joe Magrane, Stl./ Darrell Evans, Det.	.15
☐	52/211	Tony Pena, Stl./ Brook Jacoby, Cle.	.15
☐	53/298	Ozzie Smith, Stl./ Rick Rhodden, NYY.	.75
☐	54/169	Todd Worrell, Stl./ Alfredo Griffin, Oak.	.15
☐	57/255	Ryne Sandberg, Chi.-N.L./ Frank White, K.C.	.35
☐	58/291	Kieth Moreland, Chi.-N.L./ Richard Dotson, Chi.-A.L.	.15
☐	59/198	Greg Maddux, Chi.-N.L./ Rob Deer, Mil.	2.00
☐	60/290	Jody Davis, Chi.-N.L./ Carlton Fisk, Chi.-A.L.	.35
☐	62/295	Jamie Moyer, Chi.-N.L./ Mike Pagliarulo, NYY.	.15
☐	63/172	Leon Durham, Chi.-N.L./ Luis Polonia, Oak.	.15
☐	64/313	Lee Smith, Chi.-N.L./ Devon White, Cal.	.15
☐	65/250	Shawon Dunston, Chi.-N.L./ Ellis Burks, Bos.	.15
☐	66/257	Franklin Stubbs, L.A./ Danny Tartabull, K.C.	.15
☐	67/235	Mike Scioscia, L.A./ Steve Buechele, Tex.	.15
☐	68/177	Orel Hershiser, L.A./ Dick Schofield, Cal.	.15
☐	69/289	Mike Marshall, L.A./ Bob James, Chi.-A.L.	.15
☐	71/281	Mickey Hatcher, L.A./ Danny Gladden, Min.	.15
☐	72/166	Matt Young, L.A./Jay Howell, Oak.	.15
☐	73/236	Bob Welch, L.A./ Charlie Hough, Tex.	.15
☐	74/170	Steve Sax, L.A./ Dennis Eckersley, Oak.	.15
☐	77/252	Casey Candaele, Mtl./ Rich Gedman, Bos.	.15
☐	78/248	Mike Fitzgerald, Mtl./ Marty Barrett, Bos.	.15
☐	79/301	Andres Galarraga, Mtl./ Claudell Washington, NYY.	.25
☐	80/212	Neal Heaton, Mtl./ Brett Butler, Cle.	.15
☐	81/296	Hubie Brooks, Mtl./ Ron Guidry, NYY.	.15
☐	82/258	Floyd Youmans, Mtl./ Bo Jackson, K.C.	.15
☐	83/201	Herm Winningham, Mtl./ Robin Yount, Mil.	.25

☐ 84/307	Denny Martinez, Mtl./ Mike Dunne, Pgh.	.15
☐ 87/251	Will Clark, S.F./ Roger Clemens, Bos.	.50
☐ 88/288	Kevin Mitchell, S.F./ Jim Winn, Chi.-A.L.	.15
☐ 89/267	Mike Aldrete, S.F./ Kirk Gibson, Det.	.15
☐ 90/191	Scott Garrelts, S.F./ Dave Stieb, Tor.	.15
☐ 91/231	Jose Uribe, S.F./ Mike Boddicker, Bal.	.15
☐ 92/246	Bob Brenly, S.F./ Sam Horn, Bos.	.15
☐ 93/189	Robby Thompson, S.F./ Lloyd Moseby, Tor.	.15
☐ 94/217	Don Robinson, S.F./ Jim Presley, Sea.	.15
☐ 97/192	Keith Hernandez, NYM./ Jesse Barfield, Tor	.15
☐ 98/220	Ron Darling, NYM./ Dave Valle, Sea.	.15
☐ 99/218	Howard Johnson, NYM./ Phil Bradley, Sea.	.15
☐ 100/190	Roger McDowell, NYM./ Jimmy Key, Tor.	.15
☐ 102/165	Kevin McReynolds, NYM./ Tony Phillips, Oak.	.15
☐ 103/275	Sid Fernandez, NYM./ Tom Brunansky, Min.	.15
☐ 104/241	Dave Magadan, NYM./ Scott Fletcher, Tex.	.15
☐ 105/167	Gary Carter, NYM./ Carney Lansford, Oak.	.35
☐ 106/302	Carmelo Martinez, S.D./ Dave Winfield, NYY.	.35
☐ 107/205	Eddie Whitson, S.D./ Mel Hall, Cle.	.15
☐ 108/180	Time Flannery, S.D./ DeWayne Buice, Cal.	.15
☐ 109/266	Stan Jeffierson, S.D./ Bill Madlock, Det.	.15
☐ 111/168	Chris Brown, S.D./ Dave Stewart, Oak.	.15
☐ 112/215	Benny Santiago, S.D./ Rey Quinones, Sea.	.15
☐ 113/270	Garry Templeton, S.D./ Lou Whitaker, Det.	.15
☐ 114/186	Lance McCullers, S.D./ Tom Henke, Tor.	.15
☐ 117/247	Von Hayes, Pha./ Jim Rice, Bos.	.15
☐ 118/279	Kevin Gross, Pha./ Gene Larkin, Min.	.15
☐ 119/238	Bruce Ruffin, Pha./ Mike Stanley, Tex.	.15
☐ 120/184	Juan Samuel, Pha./ Jim Clancy, Tor.	.15
☐ 121/182	Shane Rawley, Pha./ Bob Boone, Cal.	.15
☐ 122/222	Chris James, Pha./ Scott Bradley, Sea.	.15
☐ 123/199	Lance Parrish, Pha./ Dave Sveum, Mil.	.15
☐ 124/181	Glenn Wilson, Pha./ Brian Downing, Cal.	.15
☐ 127/297	Jose Lind, Pgh./ Rickey Henderson, NYY.	.35
☐ 128/176	Al Pedrique, Pgh./ Greg Minton, Cal.	.15
☐ 129/277	Bobby Bonilla, Pgh./ Gary Gaetti, Min.	.15
☐ 130/175	Sid Bream, Pgh./ Jack Howell, Cal.	.15
☐ 131/230	Mike LaValliere, Pgh./ Larry Sheets, Bal.	.15
☐ 132/197	Mike Dunne, Pgh./ Glenn Braggs, Mil.	.15
☐ 133/232	Jeff Robinson, Pgh./ Tom Niedenfuer, Bal.	.15
☐ 134/195	Doug Drabek, Pgh./ Jim Gantner, Mil.	.15
☐ 137/208	Nick Esasky, Cin./ Cory Snyder, Cle.	.15
☐ 138/280	Buddy Bell, Cin./ Jeff Reardon, Min.	.15
☐ 139/239	Kal Daniels, Cin./ Pete Incaviglia, Tex	.15
☐ 140/285	Barry Larkin, Cin./ Ivan Calderon, Chi.-A.L.	.50
☐ 142/227	John Franco, Cin./ Billy Ripken, Bal.	.15
☐ 143/229	Bo Diaz, Cin./ Ray Knight, Bal.	.15
☐ 144/261	Ron Oester, Cin./ Kevin Seitzer, K.C.	.15
☐ 200/308	Bill Wegman, Mil./ Jeff Musselman, Tor.	.15
☐ 202/309	Robin Yount, Mil./ Mark McGwire, Oak.	1.50
☐ 206/305	Scott Bailes, Cle./ Casey Candeale, Mtl.	.15
☐ 209/312	Chris Bando, Cle./ Mike Greenwell, Bos.	.15
☐ 210/311	Greg Swindell, Cle./ Matt Nokes, Det.	.15
☐ 242/300	Dale Mohoric, Tex./ Dave Righetti, NYY.	.15
☐ 262/282	Mark Gubicza, K.C./ Frank Viola, Min.	.15
☐ 264/286	Frank Tanana, Det./ Donnie Hill, Chi.-N.L.	.15

1988 SUPER STAR

The 1988 O-Pee-Chee Super Star is a subset of the 1988 Stickers. The cards are on the back of the stickers. After the stickers are removed, you are left with the Super Star subset.

Card Size: 2 1/8" x 3"
Face: Four colour, white border; name, number, résumé, O-Pee-Chee logo
Back: 1988 O-Pee-Chee Stickers
Imprint: © 1988 O-Pee-Chee Ptd. in Canada/imprimé au Canada

Complete Set (67 stickers):	**10.00**
Common Player:	**.10**

	No.	Player	MINT
☐	1	Jack Clark, Stl.	.10
☐	2	Andres Galarraga, Mtl.	.25
☐	3	Keith Hernandez, NYM.	.10
☐	4	Tom Herr, Stl.	.10
☐	5	Juan Samuel, Pha.	.10
☐	6	Ryne Sandberg, Chi.-N.L.	.35
☐	7	Terry Pendleton, Stl.	.10
☐	8	Mike Schmidt, Pha.	.35
☐	9	Tim Wallach, Mtl.	.10
☐	10	Hubie Brooks, Mtl.	.10
☐	11	Shawon Dunston, Chi.-N.L.	.10
☐	12	Ozzie Smith, Stl.	.50
☐	13	Andre Dawson, Chi.-N.L.	.35
☐	14	Eric Davis, Cin.	.10
☐	15	Pedro Guerrero, L.A.	.10
☐	16	Tony Gwynn, S.D.	.50
☐	17	Jeffrey Leonard, S.F.	.10
☐	18	Dale Murphy, Atl.	.25
☐	19	Dave Parker, Cin.	.10
☐	20	Tim Raines, Mtl.	.10
☐	21	Darryl Strawberry, NYM.	.25
☐	22	Gary Carter, NYM.	.25
☐	23	Jody Davis, Chi.-N.L.	.10
☐	24	Ozzie Virgil, Atl.	.10
☐	25	Dwight Gooden, NYM.	.10
☐	26	Mike Scott, Hou.	.10
☐	27	Rick Sutcliffe, Chi.-N.L.	.10
☐	28	Sid Fernandez, NYM.	.10
☐	29	Neal Heaton, Mtl.	.10
☐	30	Fernando Valenzuela, L.A.	.10
☐	31	Steve Bedrosian, Pha.	.10
☐	32	John Franco, Cin.	.10
☐	33	Lee Smith, Chi.-N.L.	.10
☐	34	Wally Joyner, Cal.	.10
☐	35	Don Mattingly, NYY.	.35
☐	36	Mark McGwire, Oak.	.35
☐	37	Willie Randolph, NYY.	.10
☐	38	Lou Whitaker, Det.	.10
☐	39	Frank White, K.C.	.10
☐	40	Wade Boggs, Bos.	.25
☐	41	George Brett, K.C.	.50
☐	42	Paul Molitor, Mil.	.25
☐	43	Tony Fernandez, Tor.	.10
☐	44	Cal Ripken, Bal.	1.50
☐	45	Alan Trammell, Det.	.10
☐	46	Jesse Barfield, Tor.	.10
☐	47	George Bell, Tor.	.10
☐	48	Jose Canseco, Oak.	.25
☐	49	Joe Carter, Cle.	.25
☐	50	Dwight Evans, Bos.	.10
☐	51	Rickey Henderson, NYY.	.25
☐	52	Kirby Puckett, Min.	.35
☐	53	Cory Snyder, Cle.	.10
☐	54	Dave Winfield, NYY.	.25
☐	55	Terry Kennedy, Bal.	.10
☐	56	Matt Nokes, Det.	.10
☐	57	B.J. Surhoff, Mil.	.10
☐	58	Roger Clemens, Bos.	.50
☐	59	Jack Morris, Det.	.10
☐	60	Bret Saberhagen, K.C.	.10
☐	61	Ron Guidry, NYY.	.10
☐	62	Bruce Hurst, Bos.	.10
☐	63	Mark Langston, Sea.	.10
☐	64	Tom Henke, Tor.	.10
☐	65	Dan Plesac, Mil.	.10
☐	66	Dave Righetti, NYY.	.10
☐	67	CL: Superstar Checklist	.10

1988 PANINI STICKERS

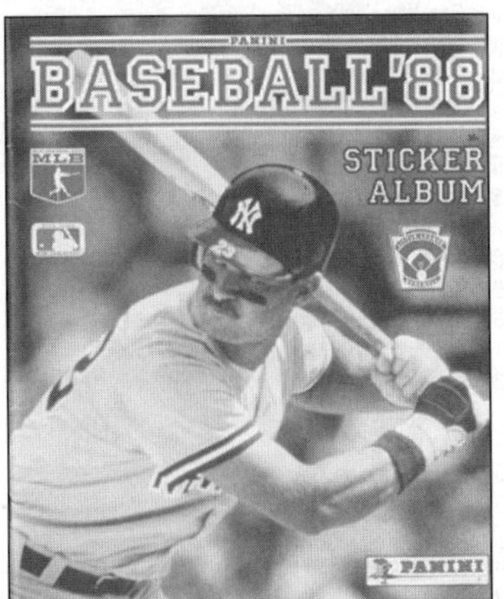

The 64-page Panini "Baseball '88 Sticker Album" for this 480-sticker set was printed in Canada. The stickers were printed by Panini in Italy. There was also a French version of the album.

Sticker Size: 1 3/4" x 2 7/8"
Face: Four colour, white border; name, team, MLB logo
Back: Black and white; number, Panini and MLB logos
Imprint: None

Complete Set (480 stickers):	**25.00**
Common Sticker:	**.20**
Album:	**5.00**

	No.	Player	MINT
☐	1	1987 World Series Trophy	.20
☐	2	Team Emblem, Bal.	.20
☐	3	Team Uniform, Bal.	.20
☐	4	Eric Bell, Bal.	.20
☐	5	Mike Boddicker, Bal.	.20
☐	6	Dave Schmidt, Bal.	.20
☐	7	Terry Kennedy, Bal.	.20
☐	8	Eddie Murray, Bal.	.75
☐	9	Bill Ripken, Bal.	.20
☐	10	Orioles' Action: Tony Armas; Cal Ripken, Jr., Bal.	.35
☐	11	Orioles' Action: Tony Armas; Cal Ripken, Jr., Bal.	.35
☐	12	Ray Knight, Bal.	.20
☐	13	Cal Ripken, Jr., Bal.	2.50
☐	14	Ken Gerhart, Bal.	.20
☐	15	Fred Lynn, Bal.	.20
☐	16	Larry Sheets, Bal.	.20
☐	17	Mike Young, Bal.	.20
☐	18	Team Emblem, Bos.	.20
☐	19	Team Uniform, Bos.	.20
☐	20	"Oil Can" Boyd, Bos.	.20
☐	21	Roger Clemens, Bos.	1.25
☐	22	Bruce Hurst, Bos.	.20
☐	23	Bob Stanley, Bos.	.20
☐	24	Rich Gedman, Bos.	.20
☐	25	Dwight Evans, Bos.	.20
☐	26	Red Sox Action: Marty Barrett; Tim Laudner, Bos.	.20
☐	27	Red Sox Action: Marty Barrett; Tim Laudner, Bos.	.20
☐	28	Marty Barrett, Bos.	.20
☐	29	Wade Boggs, Bos.	.50
☐	30	Spike Owen, Bos.	.20
☐	31	Ellis Burks, Bos.	.35
☐	32	Mike Greenwell, Bos.	.20
☐	33	Jim Rice, Bos.	.20
☐	34	Team Emblem, Cal.	.20
☐	35	Team Uniform, Cal.	.20
☐	36	Kirk McCaskill, Cal.	.25
☐	37	Don Sutton, Cal.	.25
☐	38	Mike Witt, Cal.	.20
☐	39	Bob Boone, Cal.	.20
☐	40	Wally Joyner, Cal.	.20
☐	41	Mark McLemore, Cal.	.20
☐	42	Angels' Action: Juan Bonilla; Devon White, Cal.	.20
☐	43	Angels' Action: Juan Bonilla; Devon White, Cal.	.20
☐	44	Jack Howell, Cal.	.20
☐	45	Dick Schofield, Cal.	.20
☐	46	Brian Downing, Cal.	.20
☐	47	Ruppert Jones, Cal.	.20
☐	48	Gary Pettis, Cal.	.20
☐	49	Devon White, Cal.	.20
☐	50	Team Emblem, Chi.-A.L.	.20
☐	51	Team Uniform, Chi.-A.L.	.20
☐	52	Floyd Bannister, Chi.-A.L.	.20
☐	53	Richard Dotson	.20
☐	54	Bob James, Chi.-A.L.	.20
☐	55	Carlton Fisk, Chi.-A.L.	.25
☐	56	Greg Walker, Chi.-A.L.	.20
☐	57	Fred Manrique, Chi.-A.L.	.20
☐	58	White Sox Action: Ozzie Guillen, Donnie Hill; Pat Sheridan, Chi.-A.L.	.20
☐	59	White Sox Action: Ozzie Guillen Donnie Hill; Pat Sheridan, Chi.-A.L.	
☐	60	Steve Lyons, Chi.-A.L.	.20
☐	61	Ozzie Guillen, Chi.-A.L.	.20
☐	62	Harold Baines, Chi.-A.L.	.20
☐	63	Ivan Calderon, Chi.-A.L.	.20
☐	64	Gary Redus, Chi.-A.L.	.20
☐	65	Ken Williams, Chi.-A.L.	.20
☐	66	Team Emblem, Cle.	.20
☐	67	Team Uniform, Cle.	.20
☐	68	Scott Bailes, Cle.	.20
☐	69	Tom Candiotti, Cle.	.20
☐	70	Greg Swindell, Cle.	.20
☐	71	Chris Bando, Cle.	.20
☐	72	Joe Carter, Cle.	.25
☐	73	Tommy Hinzo, Cle.	.20
☐	74	Indians' Action: Joe Carter; Juan Bonilla, Cle.	.25
☐	75	Indians' Action: Joe Carter; Juan Bonilla, Cle.	.25
☐	76	Brook Jacoby, Cle.	.20
☐	77	Julio Franco, Cle.	.20
☐	78	Brett Butler, Cle.	.20
☐	79	Mel Hall, Cle.	.20
☐	80	Cory Snyder, Cle.	.20
☐	81	Pat Tabler, Cle.	.20
☐	82	Team Emblem, Det.	.20
☐	83	Team Uniform, Det.	.20
☐	84	Willie Hernandez, Det.	.20
☐	85	Jack Morris, Det.	.20
☐	86	Frank Tanana, Det.	.20
☐	87	Walt Terrell, Det.	.20

	No.	Player	Price
☐	88	Matt Nokes, Det.	.20
☐	89	Darrell Evans, Det.	.20
☐	90	Tigers' Action: Darrell Evans; Carlton Fisk, Det.	.25
☐	91	Tigers' Action: Darrell Evans; Carlton Fisk, Det.	.25
☐	92	Lou Whitaker, Det.	.20
☐	93	Tom Brookens, Det.	.20
☐	94	Alan Trammell, Det.	.20
☐	95	Kirk Gibson, Det.	.20
☐	96	Chet Lemon, Det.	.20
☐	97	Pat Sheridan, Det.	.20
☐	98	Team Emblem, K.C.	.20
☐	99	Team Uniform, Det.	.20
☐	100	Charlie Leibrandt, Det.	.20
☐	101	Dan Quisenberry, Det.	.20
☐	102	Bret Saberhagen, Det.	.20
☐	103	Jamie Quirk, Det.	.20
☐	104	George Brett, Det.	1.00
☐	105	Frank White, Det.	.20
☐	106	Royals' Action: Bret Saberhagen, Det.	.20
☐	107	Royals' Action: Bret Saberhagen, Det.	.20
☐	108	Keven Seitzer, Det.	.20
☐	109	Angel Salazar, Det.	.20
☐	110	Bo Jackson, Det.	.20
☐	111	Lonnie Smith, Det.	.20
☐	112	Danny Tartabull, Det.	.20
☐	113	Willie Wilson, Det.	.20
☐	114	Team Emblem, Mil.	.20
☐	115	Team Uniform, Mil.	.20
☐	116	Ted Higuera, Mil.	.20
☐	117	Juan Nieves, Mil.	.20
☐	118	Dan Plesac, Mil.	.20
☐	119	Bill Wegman, Mil.	.20
☐	120	B.J. Surhoff, Mil.	.20
☐	121	Greg Brock, Mil.	.20
☐	122	Brewers' Action: Jim Gantner; Lou Whitaker, Mil.	.20
☐	123	Brewers' Action: Jim Gantner; Lou Whitaker, Mil.	.20
☐	124	Jim Gantner, Mil.	.20
☐	125	Paul Molitor, Mil.	.50
☐	126	Dale Sveum, Mil.	.20
☐	127	Glenn Braggs, Mil.	.20
☐	128	Rob Deer, Mil.	.20
☐	129	Robin Yount, Mil.	.50
☐	130	Team Emblem, Min.	.20
☐	131	Team Uniform, Min.	.20
☐	132	Bert Blyleven, Min.	.20
☐	133	Jeff Reardon, Min.	.20
☐	134	Frank Viola, Min.	.20
☐	135	Tim Laudner, Min.	.20
☐	136	Kent Hrbek	.20
☐	137	Steve Lombardozzi, Min.	.20
☐	138	Twins' Action: Steve Lombardozzi; Frank White, Min.	.20
☐	139	Twins' Action: Steve Lombardozzi; Frank White, Min.	.20
☐	140	Gary Gaetti, Min.	.20
☐	141	Greg Gagne, Min.	.20
☐	142	Tom Brunansky, Min.	.20
☐	143	Dan Gladden, Min.	.20
☐	144	Kirby Puckett, Min.	1.00
☐	145	Gene Larkin, Min.	.20
☐	146	Team Emblem, NYY.	.20
☐	147	Team Uniform, NYY.	.20
☐	148	Tommy John, NYY.	.20
☐	149	Rick Rhoden, NYY.	.20
☐	150	Dave Righetti, NYY.	.20
☐	151	Rick Cerone, NYY.	.20
☐	152	Don Mattingly, NYY.	1.00
☐	153	Willie Randolph, NYY.	.20
☐	154	Yankees' Action: Scott Fletcher; Don Mattingly, NYY.	.20
☐	155	Yankees' Action: Scott Fletcher; Don Mattingly, NYY.	.20
☐	156	Mike Pagliarulo, NYY.	.20
☐	157	Wayne Tolleson, NYY.	.20
☐	158	Rickey Henderson, NYY.	.35
☐	159	Dan Pasqua, NYY.	.20
☐	160	Gary Ward, NYY.	.20
☐	161	Dave Winfield, NYY.	.35
☐	162	Team Emblem, Oak.	.20
☐	163	Team Uniform, Oak.	.20
☐	164	Dave Stewart, Oak.	.20
☐	165	Curt Young, Oak.	.20
☐	166	Terry Steinbach, Oak.	.20
☐	167	Mark McGwire, Oak.	1.50
☐	168	Tony Phillips, Oak.	.20
☐	169	Carney Lansford, Oak.	.20
☐	170	Athletics' Action: Mike Gallego; Tony Phillips, Oak.	.20
☐	171	Athletics' Action: Mike Gallego; Tony Phillips, Oak.	.20
☐	172	Alfredo Griffin, Oak.	.20
☐	173	Jose Canseco, Oak.	.35
☐	174	Mike Davis, Oak.	.20
☐	175	Reggie Jackson, Oak.	.50
☐	176	Dwayne Murphy, Oak.	.20
☐	177	Luis Polonia, Oak.	.20
☐	178	Team Emblem, Sea.	.20
☐	179	Team Uniform, Sea.	.20
☐	180	Scot Bankhead, Sea.	.20
☐	181	Mark Langston, Sea.	.20
☐	182	Edwin Nunez, Sea.	.20
☐	183	Scott Bradley, Sea.	.20
☐	184	Dale Valle, Sea.	.20
☐	185	Alvin Davis, Sea.	.20
☐	186	Mariners' Action: Jack Howell; Rey Quinones, Sea.	.20
☐	187	Mariners' Action: Jack Howell; Rey Quinones, Sea.	.20
☐	188	Harold Reynolds, Sea.	.20
☐	189	Jim Presley, Sea.	.20
☐	190	Rey Quinones, Sea.	.20
☐	191	Phil Bradley, Sea.	.20
☐	192	Mickey Brantley, Sea.	.20
☐	193	Mike Kingery, Sea.	.20
☐	194	Team Emblem, Tex.	.20
☐	195	Team Uniform, Tex.	.20
☐	196	Edwin Correa, Tex.	.20
☐	197	Charlie Hough, Tex.	.20
☐	198	Bobby Witt, Tex.	.20
☐	199	Mike Stanley, Tex.	.20
☐	200	Pete O'Brien, Tex.	.20
☐	201	Jerry Browne, Tex.	.20
☐	202	Rangers' Action: Eddie Murray; Steve Buechele, Tex.	.25
☐	203	Rangers' Action: Eddie Murray; Steve Buechele, Tex.	.25
☐	204	Steve Buechele, Tex.	.20
☐	205	Larry Parrish, Tex.	.20
☐	206	Scott Fletcher, Tex.	.20
☐	207	Pete Incaviglia, Tex.	.20
☐	208	Oddibe McDowell, Tex.	.20
☐	209	Ruben Sierra, Tex.	.20
☐	210	Team Emblem, Tor.	.20
☐	211	Team Uniform, Tor.	.20
☐	212	Mark Eichhorn, Tor.	.20
☐	213	Tom Henke, Tor.	.20
☐	214	Jimmy Key, Tor.	.20
☐	215	Dave Steib, Tor.	.20
☐	216	Ernie Whitt, Tor.	.20
☐	217	Willie Upshaw, Tor.	.20
☐	218	Blue Jays' Action: Harold Reynolds; Willie Upshaw, Tor.	.20
☐	219	Blue Jays' Action: Harold Reynolds; Willie Upshaw, Tor.	.20
☐	220	Garth Iorg, Tor.	.20
☐	221	Kelly Gruber, Tor.	.20
☐	222	Tony Fernandez, Tor.	.20
☐	223	Jesse Barfield, Tor.	.20
☐	224	George Bell, Tor.	.20
☐	225	Lloyd Moseby, Tor.	.20

- ☐ 226A American League Logo .20
- ☐ 226B National League Logo .20
- ☐ 227 Terry Kennedy, Bal.; Don Mattingly, NYY. .50
- ☐ 228 Willie Randolph, NYY.; Wade Boggs, Bos. .35
- ☐ 229 Bret Saberhagen, K.C. .20
- ☐ 230 Cal Ripken, Jr., Bal.; George Bell, Tor. 1.50
- ☐ 231 Rickey Henderson, NYY.; Dave Winfield, NYY. .35
- ☐ 232 Gary Carter, NYM; Jack Clark, Stl. .35
- ☐ 233 Mike Scott, Hou. .20
- ☐ 234 Ryne Sandberg, Chi.C; Mike Schmidt, Pha. .50
- ☐ 235 Ozzie Smith, St.L; Eric Davis, Cin. .50
- ☐ 236 Andre Dawson, Chi.C; Darryl Strawberry, NYM. .35
- ☐ 237 Team Emblem, Atl. .20
- ☐ 238 Team Uniform, Atl. .20
- ☐ 239 Rick Mahler, Atl. .20
- ☐ 240 Zane Smith, Atl. .20
- ☐ 241 Ozzie Virgil, Atl. .20
- ☐ 242 Gerald Perry, Atl. .20
- ☐ 243 Glenn Hubbard, Atl. .20
- ☐ 244 Ken Oberkfell, Atl. .20
- ☐ 245 Braves' Action: Glenn Hubbard; Jeffrey Leonard, Atl. .20
- ☐ 246 Braves' Action: Glenn Hubbard; Jeffrey Leonard, Atl. .20
- ☐ 247 Rafael Ramirez, Atl. .20
- ☐ 248 Ken Griffey, Atl. .20
- ☐ 249 Albert Hall, Atl. .20
- ☐ 250 Dion James, Atl. .20
- ☐ 251 Dale Murphy, Atl. .25
- ☐ 252 Gary Roenicke, Atl. .20
- ☐ 253 Team Emblem, Chi.-N.L. .20
- ☐ 254 Team Uniform, Chi.-N.L. .20
- ☐ 255 Jamie Moyer, Chi.-N.L. .20
- ☐ 256 Lee Smith, Chi.-N.L. .20
- ☐ 257 Rick Sutcliffe, Chi.-N.L. .20
- ☐ 258 Jody Davis, Chi.-N.L. .20
- ☐ 259 Leon Durham, Chi.-N.L. .20
- ☐ 260 Ryne Sandberg, Chi.-N.L. .50
- ☐ 261 Cubs' Action: Jody Davis, Chi.-N.L. .20
- ☐ 262 Cubs' Action: Jody Davis, Chi.-N.L. .20
- ☐ 263 Keith Moreland, Chi.-N.L. .20
- ☐ 264 Shawon Dunston, Chi.-N.L. .20
- ☐ 265 Andre Dawson, Chi.-N.L. .35
- ☐ 266 Dave Martinez, Chi.-N.L. .20
- ☐ 267 Jerry Mumphrey, Chi.-N.L. .20
- ☐ 268 Rafael Palmeiro, Chi.-N.L. .35
- ☐ 269 Team Emblem, Cin. .20
- ☐ 270 Team Uniform, Cin. .20
- ☐ 271 John Franco, Cin. .20
- ☐ 272 Ted Power, Cin. .20
- ☐ 273 Bo Diaz, Cin. .20
- ☐ 274 Nick Esasky, Cin. .20
- ☐ 275 Dave Concepcion, Cin. .20
- ☐ 276 Kurt Stillwell, Cin. .20
- ☐ 277 Reds' Action: Bob Melvin; Dave Parker, Cin. .20
- ☐ 278 Reds' Action: Bob Melvin; Dave Parker, Cin. .20
- ☐ 279 Buddy Bell, Cin. .20
- ☐ 280 Barry Larkin, Cin. .35
- ☐ 281 Kal Daniels, Cin. .20
- ☐ 282 Eric Davis, Cin. .20
- ☐ 283 Tracey Jones, Cin. .20
- ☐ 284 Dave Parker, Cin. .20
- ☐ 285 Team Emblem, Hou. .20
- ☐ 286 Team Uniform, Hou. .20
- ☐ 287 Jim Deshaies, Hou. .20
- ☐ 288 Nolan Ryan, Hou. 2.50
- ☐ 289 Mike Scott, Hou. .20
- ☐ 290 Dave Smith, Hou. .20
- ☐ 291 Alan Ashby, Hou. .20
- ☐ 292 Glenn Davis, Hou. .20
- ☐ 293 Astros' Action: Alan Ashby; Gary Carter, Hou. .20
- ☐ 294 Astros' Action: Alan Ashby; Gary Carter, Hou. .20
- ☐ 295 Bill Doran, Hou. .20
- ☐ 296 Denny Walling, Hou. .20
- ☐ 297 Craig Reynolds, Hou. .20
- ☐ 298 Kevin Bass, Hou. .20
- ☐ 299 Jose Cruz, Hou. .20
- ☐ 300 Billy Hatcher, Hou. .20
- ☐ 301 Team Emblem, L.A. .20
- ☐ 302 Team Uniform, L.A. .20
- ☐ 303 Orel Hershiser, L.A. .20
- ☐ 304 Fernando Valenzuela, L.A. .20
- ☐ 305 Bob Welch, L.A. .20
- ☐ 306 Matt Young, L.A. .20
- ☐ 307 Mike Scioscia, L.A. .20
- ☐ 308 Franklin Stubbs, L.A. .20
- ☐ 309 Dodgers' Action: Mariano Duncan; Junior Ortiz, L.A. .20
- ☐ 310 Dodgers' Action: Mariano Duncan; Junior Ortiz, L.A. .20
- ☐ 311 Steve Sax, L.A. .20
- ☐ 312 Jeff Hamilton, L.A. .20
- ☐ 313 Dave Anderson, L.A. .20
- ☐ 314 Pedro Guerrero, L.A. .20
- ☐ 315 Mike Marshall, L.A. .20
- ☐ 316 John Shelby, L.A. .20
- ☐ 317 Team Emblem, Mtl. .20
- ☐ 318 Team Uniform, Mtl. .20
- ☐ 319 Neal Heaton, Mtl. .20
- ☐ 320 Bryn Smith, Mtl. .20
- ☐ 321 Floyd Youmans, Mtl. .20
- ☐ 322 Mike Fitzgerald, Mtl. .20
- ☐ 323 Andres Galarraga, Mtl. .35
- ☐ 324 Vance Law, Mtl. .20
- ☐ 325 Expos' Action: John Kruk; Tim Raines, Mtl. .20
- ☐ 326 Expos' Action: John Kruk; Tim Raines, Mtl. .20
- ☐ 327 Tim Wallach, Mtl. .20
- ☐ 328 Hubie Brooks, Mtl. .20
- ☐ 329 Casey Candaele, Mtl. .20
- ☐ 330 Tim Raines, Mtl. .20
- ☐ 331 Mitch Webster, Mtl. .20
- ☐ 332 Herm Winningham , Mtl. .20
- ☐ 333 Team Emblem, NYM. .20
- ☐ 334 Team Uniform, NYM. .20
- ☐ 335 Ron Darling, NYM. .20
- ☐ 336 Sid Fernandez, NYM. .20
- ☐ 337 Dwight Gooden, NYM. .20
- ☐ 338 Gary Carter, NYM. .35
- ☐ 339 Keith Hernandez, NYM. .20
- ☐ 340 Wally Backman, NYM. .20
- ☐ 341 Mets' Action: Mike Diaz; Darryl Strawberry; Tim Teufel; Mookie Wilson, NYM. .20
- ☐ 342 Mets' Action: Mike Diaz; Darryl Strawberry; Tim Teufel; Mookie Wilson, NYM. .20
- ☐ 343 Howard Johnson, NYM. .20
- ☐ 344 Rafael Santana, NYM. .20
- ☐ 345 Lenny Dykstra, NYM. .20
- ☐ 346 Kevin McReynolds, NYM. .20
- ☐ 347 Darryl Strawberry, NYM. .25
- ☐ 348 Mookie Wilson, NYM. .20
- ☐ 349 Team Emblem, Pha. .20
- ☐ 350 Team Uniform, Pha. .20
- ☐ 351 Steve Bedrosian, Pha. .20
- ☐ 352 Shane Rawley, Pha. .20
- ☐ 353 Bruce Ruffin, Pha. .20
- ☐ 354 Kent Tekulve, Pha. .20
- ☐ 355 Lance Parrish, Pha. .20
- ☐ 356 Von Hayes, Pha. .20
- ☐ 357 Phillies' Action: Tony Pena; Glenn Wilson, Pha. .20
- ☐ 358 Phillies' Action: Tony Pena; Glenn Wilson, Pha. .20
- ☐ 359 Juan Samuel, Pha. .20
- ☐ 360 Mike Schmidt, Pha.

- ☐ 361 Steve Jeltz, Pha. .20
- ☐ 362 Chris James, Pha. .20
- ☐ 363 Milt Thompson, Pha. .20
- ☐ 364 Glenn Wilson, Pha. .20
- ☐ 365 Team Emblem, Pgh. .20
- ☐ 366 Team Uniform, Pgh. .20
- ☐ 367 Mike Dunne, Pgh. .20
- ☐ 368 Brian Fisher, Pgh. .20
- ☐ 369 Mike LaValliere, Pgh. .20
- ☐ 370 Sid Bream, Pgh. .20
- ☐ 371 Jose Lind, Pgh. .20
- ☐ 372 Bobby Bonilla, Pgh. .20
- ☐ 373 Pirates' Action: Bobby Bonilla, Pgh. .20
- ☐ 374 Pirates' Action: Bobby Bonilla, Pgh. .20
- ☐ 375 Al Pedrique, Pgh. .20
- ☐ 376 Barry Bonds, Pgh. .50
- ☐ 377 John Cangelosi, Pgh. .20
- ☐ 378 Mike Diaz, Pgh. .20
- ☐ 379 R.J. Reynolds, Pgh. .20
- ☐ 380 Andy Van Slyke, Pgh. .20
- ☐ 381 Team Emblem, Stl. .20
- ☐ 382 Team Uniform, Stl. .20
- ☐ 383 Danny Cox, Stl. .20
- ☐ 384 Bob Forsch, Stl. .20
- ☐ 385 Joe Magrane, Stl. .20
- ☐ 386 Todd Worrell, Stl. .20
- ☐ 387 Tony Pena, Stl. .20
- ☐ 388 Jack Clark, Stl. .20
- ☐ 389 Cardinals' Action: Jody Davis; Tom Herr, Stl. .20
- ☐ 390 Cardinals' Action: Jody Davis; Tom Herr, Stl. .20
- ☐ 391 Tom Herr, Stl. .20
- ☐ 392 Terry Pendleton, Stl. .20
- ☐ 393 Ozzie Smith, Stl. .75
- ☐ 394 Vince Coleman, Stl. .20
- ☐ 395 Curt Ford, Stl. .20
- ☐ 396 Willie McGee, Stl. .20
- ☐ 397 Team Emblem, S.D. .20
- ☐ 398 Team Uniform, S.D. .20
- ☐ 399 Lance McCullers, S.D. .20
- ☐ 400 Eric Show, S.D. .20
- ☐ 401 Ed Whitson, S.D. .20
- ☐ 402 Benito Santiago, S.D. .20
- ☐ 403 John Kruk, S.D. .20
- ☐ 404 Tim Flannery, S.D. .20
- ☐ 405 Padres' Action: Randy Ready; Benito Santiago, S.D. .20
- ☐ 406 Padres' Action: Randy Ready; Benito Santiago, S.D. .20
- ☐ 407 Randy Ready, S.D. .20
- ☐ 408 Chris Brown, S.D. .20
- ☐ 409 Garry Templeton, S.D. .20
- ☐ 410 Tony Gwynn, S.D. 1.00
- ☐ 411 Stan Jefferson, S.D. .20
- ☐ 412 Carmelo Martinez, S.D. .20
- ☐ 413 Team Emblem, S.F. .20
- ☐ 414 Team Uniform, S.F. .20
- ☐ 415 Kelly Downs, S.F. .20
- ☐ 416 Scott Garrelts, S.F. .20
- ☐ 417 Mike Krukow, S.F. .20
- ☐ 418 Mike LaCoss, S.F. .20
- ☐ 419 Bob Brenly, S.F. .20
- ☐ 420 Will Clark, S.F. .35
- ☐ 421 Giants' Action: Will Clark; Mike Fitzgerald, S.F. .25
- ☐ 422 Giants' Action: Will Clark; Mike Fitzgerald, S.F. .25
- ☐ 423 Robby Thompson, S.F. .20
- ☐ 424 Kevin Mitchell, S.F. .20
- ☐ 425 Jose Uribe, S.F. .20
- ☐ 426 Mike Aldrete, S.F. .20
- ☐ 427 Jeffrey Leonard, S.F. .20
- ☐ 428 Candy Maldonado, S.F. .20
- ☐ 429 MIke Schmidt, Pha. .50
- ☐ 430 Don Mattingly, NYY. .50
- ☐ 431 Juan Nieves, Mil. .20
- ☐ 432 Paul Molitor, Mil. .35
- ☐ 433 Benito Santiago, S.D. .20
- ☐ 434 Rickey Henderson, NYY. .35
- ☐ 435 Nolan Ryan, Hou. 1.50
- ☐ 436 Kevin Seitzer, K.C. .20
- ☐ 437 Tony Gwynn, S.D. .60
- ☐ 438 Mark MGwire, Oak. 1.00
- ☐ 439 Howard Johnson, NYM. .20
- ☐ 440 Steve Bedrosian, Pha. .20
- ☐ 441 Darrell Evans, Det. .20
- ☐ 442 Eddie Murray, Bal. .50
- ☐ 443 Kirby Puckett, Min. .50
- ☐ 444 Kirby Puckett, Min. .50
- ☐ 445 Gary Gaetti, Min. .20
- ☐ 446 Jeffrey Leonard, S.F. .20
- ☐ 447 Tony Pena .20
- ☐ 448 Tony Pena .20
- ☐ 449 WS: Randy Bush .20
- ☐ 450 WS: Tony Pena .20
- ☐ 451 World Series Celebration .20
- ☐ 452 World Series Celebration .20
- ☐ 453 World Series Celebration .20
- ☐ 454 World Series Celebration .20

AMERICAN LEAGUE

- ☐ A1 Orioles Logo/Pennant .20
- ☐ B1 Red Sox/Pennant .20
- ☐ C-1 Angels Logo/Pennant .20
- ☐ D-1 WhiteSox Logo/Pennant .20
- ☐ E-1 Indians Logo/Pennant .20
- ☐ F-1 Tigers Logo/Pennant .20
- ☐ G-1 Royals Logo/Pennant .20
- ☐ H-1 Brewers Logo/Pennant .20
- ☐ I-1 Twins Logo/Pennant .20
- ☐ J-1 Yankees Logo/Pennant .20
- ☐ K-1 Athletics Logo/Pennant .20
- ☐ L-1 Mariners Logo/Pennant .20
- ☐ M-1 Rangers Logo/Pennant .20
- ☐ N-1 Blue Jays Logo/Pennant .20

NATIONAL LEAGUE

- ☐ O-1 Braves Logo/Pennant .20
- ☐ P-1 Cubs Logo/Pennant .20
- ☐ Q-1 Reds Logo/Pennant .20
- ☐ R-1 Astros Logo/Pennant .20
- ☐ S-1 Dodgers Logo/Pennant .20
- ☐ T-1 Expos Logo/Pennant .20
- ☐ U-1 Mets Logo/Pennant .20
- ☐ V-1 Phillies Logo/Pennant .20
- ☐ W-1 Pirates Logo/Pennant .20
- ☐ X-1 Cardinals Logo/Pennant .20
- ☐ Y-1 Padres Logo/Pennant .20
- ☐ Z-1 Giants Logo/Pennant .20

1989 BEN'S / HOLSUMS DISKS

Ben's Limited, of Halifax, N.S., issued Holsum promotional disks as premiums in their packages of hot dog and hamburger buns and in other products. The disks were designed by Michael Schechter and Associates (MSA) and distributed under their licence. The team logos on all players' uniforms were removed by airbrushing.

The 1989 20-disk set has the Holsum and Schafer logos. The disks are unnumbered and are listed here alphabetically.

Disk Size: 2 3/4" Diameter

Face: Four colour, white border; name, position, team Holsum's and Schafer's logos

Back: Blue on card stock; name, resume, numbered _ of 20

Imprint: "MLBPA 1989" MSA

Complete Set (20 disks): 40.00

	No.	Player	MINT
☐	1	Wade Boggs, Bos.	2.00
☐	2	Bobby Bonilla, Pgh.	1.25
☐	3	Jose Canseco, Atl.	2.00
☐	4	Roger Clemens, Bos.	6.00
☐	5	David Cone, NYM.	1.25
☐	6	Eric Davis, Cin.	1.25
☐	7	Kirk Gibson, L.A.	1.25
☐	8	Mark Grace, Chi.-N.L.	1.25
☐	9	Tony Gwynn, S.D.	6.00
☐	10	Orel Hershiser, L.A.	1.25
☐	11	Gregg Jefferies, NYM.	1.25
☐	12	Wayne Joyner, Cal.	1.25
☐	13	Don Mattingly, NYY.	5.00
☐	14	Mark McGwire, Oak.	6.00
☐	15	Matt Nokes, Det.	1.25
☐	16	Kirby Puckett, Min.	5.00
☐	18	Ozzie Smith, Stl.	3.00
☐	19	Darryl Strawberry, NYM.	2.00
☐	20	Frank Viola, Min.	1.25

1989 O-PEE-CHEE

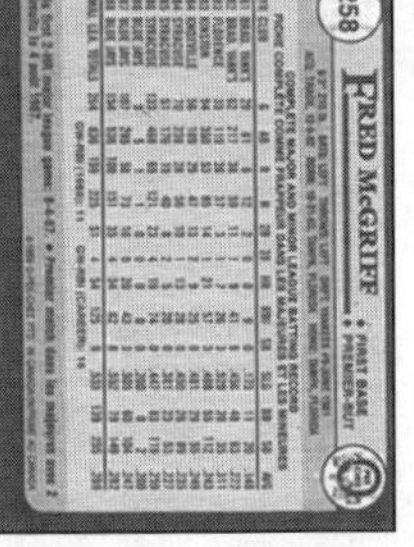

The card numbers on this 396-card set are not the same as those for the corresponding players in the 792-card Topps issue for 1989. The O-Pee-Chee set also has the Canadian imprint on the back of the cards.

Card Size: 2 1/2" x 3 1/2"

Face: Four colour, white border; name, team

Back: Pink and black on card stock; name, number, position, résumé, bilingual

Imprint: © 1989 O-PEE-CHEE PTD. IN CANADA IMPRIMê AU CANADA

Complete Set (396 cards): 10.00

Common Player: .10

	No.	Player	MINT
☐	1	Brook Jacoby, Cle.	.10
☐	2	Atlee Hammaker, S.F.	.10
☐	3	Jack Clark, NYY. (S.D.)	.10
☐	4	Dave Stieb, Tor.	.10
☐	5	Bud Black, Cle.	.10
☐	6	Damon Berryhill, Chi.-N.L.	.10
☐	7	Mike Scioscia, L.A.	.10
☐	8	Jose Uribe, S.F.	.10
☐	9	Mike Aldrete, S.F. (Mtl.)	.10
☐	10	Andre Dawson, Chi.-N.L.	.25
☐	11	Bruce Sutter, Atl.	.10
☐	12	Dale Sveum, Mil.	.10
☐	13	Dan Quisenberry, Stl.	.10
☐	14	Tom Niedenfuér, Bal. (Sea.)	.10
☐	15	Robby Thompson, S.F.	.10
☐	16	Ron Robinson, Cin.	.10
☐	17	Brian Downing, Cal.	.10
☐	18	Rick Rhoden, NYY.	.10
☐	19	Greg Gagne, Min.	.10
☐	20	Allan Anderson, Min.	.10
☐	21	Eddie Whitson, S.D.	.10
☐	22	Billy Ripken, Bal.	.10
☐	23	Mike Fitzgerald, Mtl.	.10
☐	24	Shane Rawley, Pha. (Min.)	.10
☐	25	Frank White, K.C.	.10
☐	26	Don Mattingly, NYY.	.75
☐	27	Fred Lynn, Det.	.10
☐	28	Mike Moore, Sea.	.10
☐	29	Kelly Gruber, Tor.	.10
☐	30	Doc Gooden, NYM.	.10
☐	31	Dan Pasqua, Chi.-A.L.	.10
☐	32	Dennis Rasmussen, S.D.	.10
☐	33	B.J. Surhoff, Mil.	.10
☐	34	Sid Fernandez, NYM.	.10
☐	35	John Tudor, L.A.	.10
☐	36	Mitch Webster, Chi.-N.L.	.10
☐	37	Doug Drabek, Pgh.	.10
☐	38	Bobby Witt, Tex.	.10
☐	39	Mike Maddux, Pha.	.10
☐	40	Steve Sax, L.A. (NYY.)	.10
☐	41	Orel Hershiser, L.A.	.10
☐	42	Pete Incaviglia, Tex.	.10
☐	43	Guillermo Hernandez, Det.	.10
☐	44	Kevin Coffman, Atl. (Chi.-N.L.)	.10
☐	45	Kal Daniels, Cin.	.10
☐	46	Carlton Fisk, Chi.-A.L.	.25
☐	47	Carney Lansford, Oak.	.10
☐	48	Tim Burke, Mtl.	.10
☐	49	Alan Trammell, Det.	.10
☐	50	George Bell, Tor.	.10
☐	51	Tony Gwynn, S.D.	.75
☐	52	Bob Brenly, S.F.	.10
☐	53	Ruben Sierra, Tex.	.10
☐	54	Otis Nixon, Mtl.	.10
☐	55	Julio Franco, Cle. (Tex.)	.10
☐	56	Pat Tabler, K.C.	.10
☐	57	Alvin Davis, Sea.	.10
☐	58	Kevin Seitzer, K.C.	.10
☐	59	Mark Davis, S.D.	.10
☐	60	Tom Brunansky, Stl.	.10
☐	61	Jeff Treadway, Cin.	.10
☐	62	Alfredo Griffin, L.A.	.10

	No.	Player	Price
☐	63	Keith Hernandez, NYM.	.10
☐	64	Alex Trevino, Hou.	.10
☐	65	Rick Reuschel, S.F.	.10
☐	66	Bob Walk, Pgh.	.10
☐	67	Dave Palmer, Pha.	.10
☐	68	Pedro Guerrero, Stl.	.10
☐	69	Jose Oquendo, Stl.	.10
☐	70	Mark McGwire, Oak.	1.00
☐	71	Mike Boddicker, Bos.	.10
☐	72	Wally Backman, NYM. (Min.)	.10
☐	73	Pascual Perez, Mtl.	.10
☐	74	Joe Hesketh, Mtl.	.10
☐	75	Tom Henke, Tor.	.10
☐	76	Nelson Liriano, Tor.	.10
☐	77	Doyle Alexander, Det.	.10
☐	78	Tim Wallach, Mtl.	.10
☐	79	Scott Bankhead, Sea.	.10
☐	80	Cory Snyder, Cle.	.10
☐	81	Dave Magadan, NYM.	.10
☐	82	Randy Ready, S.D.	.10
☐	83	Steve Buechele, Tex.	.10
☐	84	Bo Jackson, K.C.	.10
☐	85	Kevin McReynolds, NYM.	.10
☐	86	Jeff Reardon, Min.	.10
☐	87	Rock Raines, Mtl.	.10
☐	88	Melido Perez, Chi.-A.L.	.10
☐	89	Dave LaPoint, Pgh. (NYY.)	.10
☐	90	Vince Coleman, Stl.	.10
☐	91	Floyd Youmans, Mtl. (Pha.)	.10
☐	92	Buddy Bell, Hou.	.10
☐	93	Andres Galarraga, Mtl.	.25
☐	94	Tony Péna, Stl.	.10
☐	95	Gerald Young, Hou.	.10
☐	96	Rick Cerone, Bos.	.10
☐	97	Ken Oberkfell, Pgh.	.10
☐	98	Larry Sheets, Bal.	.10
☐	99	Chuck Crim, Mil.	.10
☐	100	Mike Schmidt, Pha.	.35
☐	101	Ivan Calderon, Chi.-A.L.	.10
☐	102	Kevin Bass, Hou.	.10
☐	103	Chili Davis, Cal.	.10
☐	104	Randy Myers, NYM.	.10
☐	105	Ron Darling, NYM.	.10
☐	106	Willie Upshaw, Cle.	.10
☐	107	Jose DeLeon, Stl.	.10
☐	108	Fred Manrique, Chi.-A.L.	.10
☐	109	Johnny Ray, Cal.	.10
☐	110	Paul Molitor, Mil.	.25
☐	111	Rance Mulliniks, Tor.	.10
☐	112	Jim Presley, Sea.	.10
☐	113	Lloyd Moseby, Tor.	.10
☐	114	Lance Parrish, Pha. (Ana.)	.10
☐	115	Jody Davis, Chi.-N.L. (Atl.)	.10
☐	116	Matt Nokes, Det.	.10
☐	117	Dave Anderson, L.A.	.10
☐	118	Checklist (133 - 264)	.10
☐	119	Rafael Belliard, Pgh.	.10
☐	120	Frank Viola, Min.	.10
☐	121	Roger Clemens, Bos.	.75
☐	122	Luis Salazar, Det.	.10
☐	123	Mike Stanley, Tex.	.10
☐	124	Jim Traber, Bal.	.10
☐	125	Mike Krukow, S.F.	.10
☐	126	Sid Bream, Pgh.	.10
☐	127	Joel Skinner, NYY.	.10
☐	128	Milt Thompson, Pha.	.10
☐	**129**	**Terry Clark, Cal., RC**	**.10**
☐	130	Gerald Perry, Atl.	.10
☐	131	Bryn Smith, Mtl.	.10
☐	132	Kirby Puckett, Min.	.75
☐	133	Bill Long, Chi.-A.L.	.10
☐	134	Jim Gantner, Mil.	.10
☐	135	Jose Rijo, Cin.	.10
☐	136	Joey Meyer, Mil.	.10
☐	137	Geno Petralli, Tex.	.10
☐	138	Wallace Johnson, Mtl.	.10
☐	139	Mike Flanagan, Tor.	.10
☐	140	Shawon Dunston, Chi.-N.L.	.10
☐	141	Eric Plunk, Oak.	.10
☐	142	Bobby Bonilla, Pgh.	.10
☐	143	Jack McDowell, Chi.-A.L.	.10
☐	144	Mookie Wilson, NYM.	.10
☐	145	Dave Stewart, Oak.	.10
☐	146	Gary Pettis, Det.	.10
☐	147	Eric Show, S.D.	.10
☐	148	Eddie Murray, Bal. (L.A.)	.35
☐	149	Lee Smith, Bos.	.10
☐	150	Fernando Valenzuela, L.A.	.10
☐	151	Bob Welch, Oak.	.10
☐	152	Harold Baines, Chi.-A.L.	.10
☐	153	Albert Hall, Atl.	.10
☐	154	Don Carman, Pha.	.10
☐	155	Marty Barrett, Bos.	.10
☐	**156**	**Chris Sabo, Cin. RC**	**.10**
☐	157	Bret Saberhagen, K.C.	.10
☐	158	Danny Cox, Stl.	.10
☐	159	Tom Foley, Mtl.	.10
☐	160	Jeffrey Leonard, Mil. (Sea.)	.10
☐	**161**	**Brady Anderson, Bal., RC**	**.50**
☐	162	Rich Gossage, Chi.-N.L.	.10
☐	163	Greg Brock, Mil.	.10
☐	164	Joe Carter, Cle.	.25
☐	165	Mike Dunne, Pgh.	.10
☐	166	Jeff Russell, Tex.	.10
☐	167	Dan Plesac, Mil.	.10
☐	168	Willie Wilson, K.C.	.10
☐	169	Mike Jackson, Sea.	.10
☐	170	Tony Fernandez, Tor.	.10
☐	171	Jamie Moyer, Chi.-N.L. (Tex.)	.10
☐	172	Jim Gott, Pgh.	.10
☐	173	Mel Hall, Cle.	.10
☐	174	Mark McGwire, Oak.; 1988 Dodgers vs. Athletics	1.00
☐	175	John Shelby, L.A.	.10
☐	176	Jeff Parrett, Mtl. (Pha.)	.10
☐	177	Tim Belcher, L.A.; 1988 Dodgers vs. Athletics	.10
☐	178	Rich Gedman, Bos.	.10
☐	179	Ozzie Virgil, Atl.	.10
☐	180	Mike Scott, Hou.	.10
☐	181	Dickie Thon, S.D.	.10
☐	182	Rob Murphy, Cin.	.10
☐	183	Oddibe McDowell, Tex.	.10
☐	184	Wade Boggs, Bos.	.25
☐	185	Claudell Washington, NYY.	.10
☐	**186**	**Randy Johnson, Mtl., RC**	**1.50**
☐	187	Paul O'Neill, Bos.	.10
☐	188	Todd Benzinger, Cin. (Cin.)	.10
☐	189	Kevin Mitchell, S.F.	.10
☐	190	Mike Witt, Cal.	.10
☐	**191**	**Sil Campusano, Tor., RC**	**.10**
☐	192	Ken Gerhart, Bal.	.10
☐	193	Bob Rodgers, Manager, Mtl.	.10
☐	194	Floyd Bannister, K.C.	.10
☐	195	Ozzie Guillen, Chi.-A.L.	.10
☐	196	Ron Gant, Atl.	.10
☐	197	Neal Heaton, Mtl.	.10
☐	198	Bill Swift, Sea.	.10
☐	199	Dave Parker, Oak.	.10
☐	200	George Brett, K.C.	.50

	No.	Player	Price
☐	201	Bo Diaz, Cin.	.10
☐	**202**	**Brad Moore, Pha., RC**	**.10**
☐	203	Rob Ducey, Tor.	.25
☐	204	Bert Blyleven, Cal. (Ana.)	.10
☐	205	Dwight Evans, Bos.	.10
☐	206	Roberto Alomar, S.D.	.35
☐	207	Henry Cotto, Sea.	.10
☐	208	Harold Reynolds, Sea.	.10
☐	209	Jose Guzman, Tex.	.10
☐	210	Dale Murphy, Atl.	.25
☐	211	Mike Pagliarulo, NYY.	.10
☐	212	Jay Howell, L.A.	.10
☐	213	Rene Gonzales, Bal.	.10
☐	214	Scott Garrelts, S.F.	.10
☐	215	Kevin Gross, Pha. (Mtl.)	.10
☐	216	Jack Howell, Cal.	.10
☐	217	Kurt Stillwell, K.C.	.10
☐	218	Mike LaValliere, Pgh.	.10
☐	219	Jim Clancy, Tor. (Hou.)	.10
☐	220	Gary Gaetti, Min.	.10
☐	221	Hubie Brooks, Mtl.	.10
☐	222	Bruce Ruffin, Pha.	.10
☐	223	Jay Buhner, Sea.	.25
☐	224	Cecil Fielder, Tor.	.25
☐	225	Willie McGee, Stl.	.10
☐	226	Bill Doran, Hou.	.10
☐	227	John Farrell, Cle.	.10
☐	**228**	**Nelson Santovenia, Mtl., RC**	**.10**
☐	229	Jimmy Key, Tor.	.10
☐	230	Ozzie Smith, Stl.	.35
☐	231	Dave Schmidt, Bal.	.10
☐	232	Jody Reed, Bos.	.10
☐	233	Gregg Jefferies, NYM.	.10
☐	234	Tom Browning, Cin.	.10
☐	235	John Kruk, S.D.	.10
☐	236	Charles Hudson, NYY.	.10
☐	237	Todd Stottlemyre, Tor.	.10
☐	238	Don Slaught, NYY.	.10
☐	239	Tim Laudner, Min.	.10
☐	240	Greg Maddux, Chi.-N.L.	1.00
☐	241	Brett Butler, S.F.	.10
☐	242	Checklist (1-132)	.10
☐	243	Bob Boone, Cal. (K.C.)	.10
☐	244	Willie Randolph, NYY. (L.A.)	.10
☐	245	Jim Rice, Bos.	.10
☐	246	Rey Quinones, Sea.	.10
☐	247	Checklist 3 (265 - 396)	.10
☐	248	Stan Javier, Oak.	.10
☐	249	Tim Leary, L.A.	.10
☐	250	Cal Ripken, Bal.	1.00
☐	**251**	**John Dopson, Mtl., RC (Bos.)**	**.10**
☐	252	Billy Hatcher, Hou.	.10
☐	253	Robin Yount, Mil.	.25
☐	254	Mickey Hatcher, L.A.; Dodgers vs. Athletics	.10
☐	255	Bob Horner, Stl. 1988	.10
☐	256	Benny Santiago, S.D.	.10
☐	257	Luis Rivera, Mtl., (Bos.)	.10
☐	258	Fred McGriff, Tor.	.25
☐	259	David Wells, Tor.	.10
☐	260	Dave Winfield, NYY.	.35
☐	261	Rafael Ramirez, Hou.	.10
☐	262	Nick Esasky, (Cin.)	.10
☐	263	Barry Bonds, Pgh.	.35
☐	264	Joe Magrane, Stl.	.10
☐	265	Kent Hrbek, Min.	.10
☐	266	Jack Morris, Det.	.10
☐	267	Jeff Robinson, Det.	.10
☐	268	Ron Kittle, Cle. (Chi.-A.L.)	.10
☐	269	Candy Maldonado, S.F.	.10
☐	270	Wally Joyner, Cal.	.10
☐	271	Glenn Braggs, Mil.	.10
☐	272	Ron Hassey, Oak.	.10
☐	273	Jose Lind, Pgh.	.10
☐	274	Mark Eichhorn, Tor.	.10
☐	275	Danny Tartabull, K.C.	.10
☐	276	Paul Kilgus, Tex., (Chi.-N.L.)	.10
☐	277	Mike Davis, L.A.	.10
☐	278	Andy McGaffigan, Mtl.	.10
☐	279	Scott Bradley, Sea.	.10
☐	280	Bob Knepper, Hou.	.10
☐	281	Gary Redus, Pgh.	.10
☐	282	Rickey Henderson, NYY.	.25
☐	283	Andy Allanson, Cle.	.10
☐	284	Rick Leach, Tor.	.10
☐	285	John Candelaria, NYY.	.10
☐	286	Dick Schofield, Cal.	.10
☐	**287**	**Bryan Harvey, Cal., RC**	**.10**
☐	288	Randy Bush, Min.	.10
☐	289	Ernie Whitt, Tor.	.10
☐	290	John Franco, Cin.	.10
☐	291	Todd Worrell, Stl.	.10
☐	292	Teddy Higuera, Mil.	.10
☐	293	Keith Moreland, S.D. (Det.)	.10
☐	294	Juan Berenguer, Min.	.10
☐	295	Scott Fletcher, Tex.	.10
☐	296	Roger McDowell, NYM. (Cle.)	.10
☐	297	Mark Grace, Chi.-N.L.	.10
☐	298	Chris James, Pha.	.10
☐	299	Frank Tanana, Det.	.10
☐	300	Darryl Strawberry, NYM.	.25
☐	301	Charlie Leibrandt, K.C.	.10
☐	302	Gary Ward, NYY.	.10
☐	303	Brian Fisher, Pgh.	.10
☐	304	Terry Steinbach, Oak.	.10
☐	305	Dave Smith, Hou.	.10
☐	306	Greg Minton, Cal.	.10
☐	307	Lance McCullers, S.D. (NYY.)	.10
☐	308	Phil Bradley, Pha. (Bal.)	.10
☐	309	Terry Kennedy, Bal.	.10
☐	310	Rafael Palmeiro, Chi.-N.L. (Tex.)	.10
☐	311	Ellis Burks, Bos.	.10
☐	312	Doug Jones, Cle.	.10
☐	313	Denny Martinez, Mtl.	.10
☐	314	Pete O'Brien, Tex. (Cle.)	.10
☐	315	Greg Swindell, Cle.	.10
☐	316	Walt Weiss, Oak.	.10
☐	317	Pete Stanicek, Bal.	.10
☐	318	Gene Larkin, Min.	.10
☐	319	Danny Jackson, Cin.	.10
☐	320	Lou Whitaker, Det.	.10
☐	321	Will Clark, S.F.	.10
☐	322	John Smiley, Pgh.	.10
☐	323	Mike Marshall, L.A.	.10
☐	324	Gary Carter, NYM.	.25
☐	325	Jesse Barfield, Tor.	.10
☐	326	Dennis Boyd, Bos.	.10
☐	327	Dave Henderson, Oak.	.10
☐	328	Chet Lemon, Det.	.10
☐	329	Bob Melvin, S.F.	.10
☐	330	Eric Davis, Cin.	.10
☐	331	Ted Power, Det.	.10
☐	332	Carmelo Martinez, S.D.	.10
☐	333	Bob Ojeda, NYM.	.10
☐	334	Steve Lyons, Chi.-A.L.	.10
☐	335	Dave Righetti, NYY.	.10
☐	336	Steve Balboni, Sea.	.10
☐	337	Calvin Schiraldi, Chi.-N.L.	.10
☐	338	Vance Law, Chi.-N.L.	.10

	No.	Player	MINT
☐	339	Zane Smith, Atl.	.10
☐	340	Kirk Gibson, L.A.	.10
☐	341	Jim Deshaies, Hou.	.10
☐	342	Tom Brookens, Det.	.10
☐	**343**	**Pat Borders, Tor., RC**	**.10**
☐	344	Devon White, Cal.	.10
☐	345	Charlie Hough, Tex.	.10
☐	346	Rex Hudler, Mtl.	.10
☐	347	John Cerutti, Tor.	.10
☐	348	Kirk McCaskill, Cal.	.25
☐	349	Len Dykstra, NYM.	.10
☐	350	Andy Van Slyke, Pgh.	.10
☐	351	Jeff Robinson, Pgh.	.10
☐	352	Rick Schu, Bal.	.10
☐	353	Bruce Benedict, Atl.	.10
☐	354	Bill Wegman, Mil.	.10
☐	355	Mark Langston, Sea.	.10
☐	356	Steve Farr, K.C.	.10
☐	357	Richard Dotson, NYY.	.10
☐	358	Andres Thomas, Atl.	.10
☐	359	Alan Ashby, Hou.	.10
☐	360	Ryne Sandberg, Chi.-N.L.	.25
☐	361	Kelly Downs, S.F.	.10
☐	362	Jeff Musselman, Tor.	.10
☐	363	Barry Larkin, Cin.	.25
☐	364	Rob Deer, Mil.	.10
☐	365	Mike Henneman, Det.	.10
☐	366	Nolan Ryan, Hou. (Tex.)	1.00
☐	**367**	**Johnny Paredes, Mtl., RC**	**.10**
☐	368	Bobby Thigpen, Chi.-A.L.	.10
☐	369	Mickey Brantley, Sea.	.10
☐	370	Dennis Eckersley, Oak.	.10
☐	371	Manny Lee, Tor.	.10
☐	372	Juan Samuel, Pha.	.10
☐	373	Tracy Jones, Mtl. (NYG.)	.10
☐	374	Mike Greenwell, Bos.	.10
☐	375	Terry Pendleton, Stl.	.10
☐	376	Steve Lombardozzi, Min.	.10
☐	377	Mitch Williams, Tex. (Chi.-N.L.)	.10
☐	378	Glenn Davis, Hou.	.10
☐	379	Mark Gubicza, K.C.	.10
☐	380	Orel Hershiser, L.A. 1988 Dodgers vs. Athletics	.10
☐	381	Jimy Williams, Manager, Tor.	.10
☐	382	Kirk Gibson, L.A.; 1988 Dodgers vs. Athletics	.25
☐	383	Howard Johnson, NYM.	.10
☐	384	Dave Cone, NYM.	.10
☐	385	Von Hayes, Pha.	.10
☐	386	Luis Polonia, Oak.	.10
☐	387	Danny Gladden, Min.	.10
☐	388	Pete Smith, Atl.	.10
☐	389	Jose Canseco, Oak.	.25
☐	390	Mickey Hatcher, L.A.	.10
☐	391	Wil Tejada, Mtl., (NYG.)	.10
☐	392	Duane Ward, Tor.	.10
☐	393	Rick Mahler, Atl. (Cin.)	.10
☐	394	Rick Sutcliffe, Chi.-N.L.	.10
☐	395	Dave Martinez, Mtl.	.10
☐	396	Ken Dayley, Stl.	.10

1989 BOX BOTTOMS

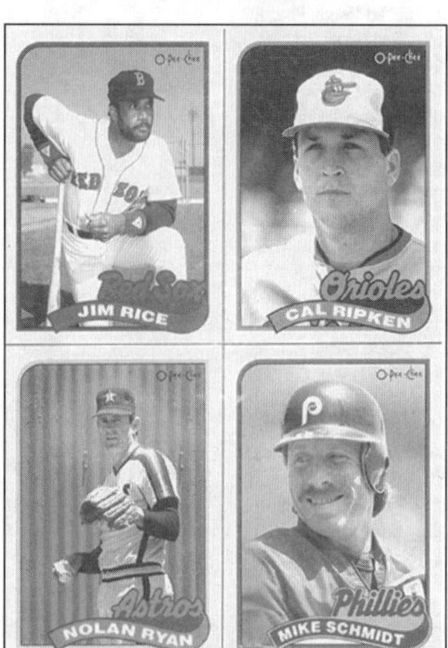

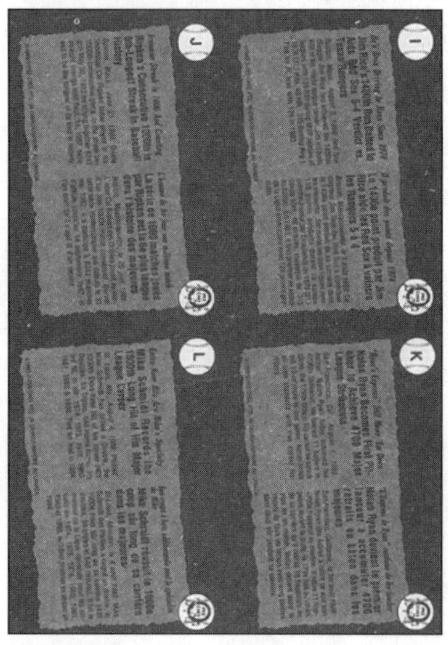

Panel Size: 5" x 7"
Face: Four colour, light blue border; name, team
Back: Pink and black on card stock; letter, headline
Imprint: © 1989 O-PEE-CHEE PTD. IN CANADA/IMPRIMê AU CANADA

Complete Set (16 cards):		**10.00**
Panel A-D:		**3.00**
Panel E-H:		**2.00**
Panel I-L:		**8.00**
Panel M-P:		**2.00**

	No.	Player	MINT
☐	A	George Brett, K.C.	1.50
☐	B	Bill Buckner, K.C.	.25
☐	C	Darrell Evans, Det.	.25
☐	D	Rich Gossage, Chi.-N.L.	.25
☐	E	Greg Gross, Pha.	.25
☐	F	Rickey Henderson, NYY.	.50

☐	G	Keith Hernandez, NYM.	.25
☐	H	Tom Lasorda, Manager, L.A.	.50
☐	I	Jim Rice, Bos.	.25
☐	J	Cal Ripken, Bal.	2.00
☐	K	Nolan Ryan, Hou.	2.50
☐	L	Mike Schmidt, Pha.	1.25
☐	M	Bruce Sutter, Atl.	.25
☐	N	Don Sutton, L.A.	.50
☐	O	Kent Tekulve, Pha.	.25
☐	P	Dave Winfield, NYY.	.50

1989 O-PEE-CHEE STICKERS

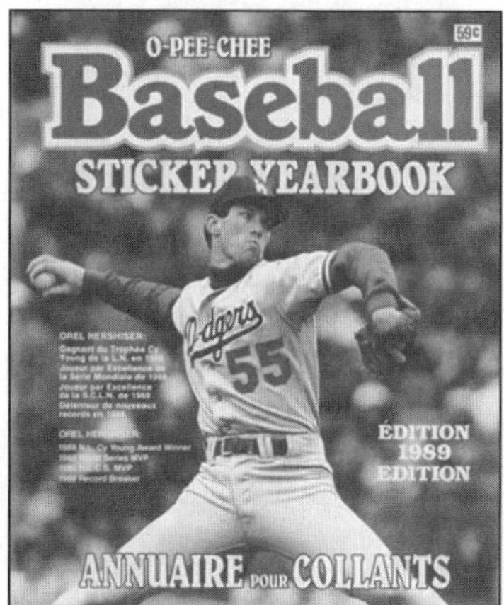

Sticker Size: 1 7/16" x 2 1/8"
Face: Four colour, white border; number
Back: 1989 O-Pee-Chee Super Stars
Imprint: © 1989 O-PEE-CHEE PTD. IN CANADA/IMPRIMê AU CANADA
Complete Set (198 stickers): 20.00
Album: 4.00
CommonSticker: .15

	No.	Player	MINT
☐	21	Glenn Davis, Hou.	.15
☐	22	Bob Knepper, Hou.	.15
☐	32	Dale Murphy, Atl.	.25
☐	33	Gerald Perry, Atl.	.35
☐	43	Vince Coleman, Stl.	.15
☐	44	Ozzie Smith, Stl.	.65
☐	54	Andre Dawson, Chi.-N.L.	.25
☐	55	Ryne Sandberg, Chi.-N.L.	.35
☐	65	Orel Hershiser, L.A.	.15
☐	66	Kirk Gibson, L.A.	.15
☐	76	Andres Galarraga, Mtl.	.35
☐	77	Tim Raines, Mtl.	.15
☐	87	Robby Thompson, S.F.	.15
☐	88	Will Clark, S.F.	.25
☐	98	Darryl Strawberry, NYM.	.25
☐	99	Doc Godden, NYM.	.15
☐	109	Tony Gwynn, S.D.	.75
☐	110	Mark Davis, S.D.	.15
☐	120	Mike Schmidt, Pha.	.35
☐	121	Don Carman, Pha.	.15
☐	131	Bobby Bonilla, Pgh.	.15
☐	132	Andy Van Slyke, Pgh.	.15
☐	142	Chris Sabo, Cin.	.15
☐	143	Danny Jackson, Cin.	.15
☐	145	Rickey Henderson, NYY	.25
☐	146	Paul Molitor, Mil.	.25
☐	147	Wade Boggs, Bos.	.25
☐	148	Jose Canseco, Oak.	.25
☐	149	Dave Winfield, NYY	.25
☐	150	Cal Ripken, Bal.	1.00
☐	151	Mark McGwire, Oak.	.75
☐	152	Terry Steinbach, Oak.	.15
☐	153	Frank Viola, Min.	.15
☐	154	Vince Coleman, Stl.	.15
☐	155	Ryne Sandberg, Chi.-N.L.	.25
☐	156	Andre Dawson, Chi.-N.L.	.25
☐	157	Darryl Strawberry, NYM.	.25
☐	158	Bobby Bonilla, Pgh.	.15
☐	159	Will Clark, S.F.	.15
☐	160	Gary Carter, NYM.	.25
☐	161	Ozzie Smith, Stl.	.35
☐	162	Doc Gooden, NYM.	.15
☐	171	Jose Canseco, Oak.	.25
☐	172	Mark McGwire, Oak.	1.25
☐	182	Johnny Ray, Cal.	.15
☐	183	Wally Joyner, Cal.	.15
☐	193	George Bell, Tor.	.15
☐	194	Dave Stieb, Tor.	.15
☐	204	Paul Molitor, Mil.	.35
☐	205	Robin Yount, Mil.	.35
☐	215	Doug Jones, Cle.	.15
☐	216	Joe Carter, Cle.	.35
☐	226	Harold Reynolds, Sea.	.15
☐	227	Alvin Davis, Sea.	.15
☐	237	Cal Ripken, Bal.	2.00
☐	238	Eddie Murray, Bal.	.50
☐	248	Pete O'Brien, Tex.	.15
☐	249	Pete Incaviglia, Tex.	.15
☐	259	Roger Clemens, Bos.	1.00
☐	260	Wade Boggs, Bos.	.35
☐	270	George Brett, K.C.	.75
☐	271	Mark Gubicza, K.C.	.15
☐	281	Alan Trammell, Det.	.15
☐	282	Lou Whitaker, Det.	.15
☐	292	Frank Viola, Min.	.15
☐	293	Kirby Puckett, Min.	.75
☐	303	Ozzie Guillen, Chi.-A.L.	.15
☐	304	Harold Baines, Chi.-A.L.	.15
☐	314	Don Mattingly, NYY	.75
☐	315	Dave Winfield, NYY	.35

MULTIPLE STICKERS

☐	1/230	George Bell, Tor./ Jeff Ballard, Bal.	.15
☐	2/272	Gary Carter, NYM./ Steve Farr, K.C.	.25
☐	3/324	Doug Jones, Cle./ Mark Grace, Chi.-N.L.	.15
☐	4/320	John Franco, Cin./ Cecil Espy, Tex.	.15
☐	5/322	Andre Dawson, Chi.-N.L./ Ron Gant, Atl.	.25
☐	6/326	Pat Tabler, Cle./ Walt Weiss, Oak.	.15
☐	7/317	Tom Browning, Cin./ Tim Belcher, L.A.	.15
☐	8/239	Jeff Reardon, Min./ Larry Sheets, Bal.	.15
☐	9/325	Wade Boggs, Bos./ Chris Sabo, Cin.	.25
☐	10/319	Kevin McReynolds, NYM./ Jay Buhner, Sea.	.25
☐	11/323	Jose Canseco, Oak./ Paul Gibson, Det.	.25
☐	12/318	Orel Hershiser, L.A./ Damon Berryhill, Chi.-N.L.	.15
☐	13/231	Dave Smith, Hou./ Mickey Tettleton, Bal.	.15
☐	14/302	Kevin Bass, Hou./ Jack McDowell, Chi.-A.L.	.15
☐	15/232	Mike Scott, Hou./ Pete Stanicek, Bal.	.15
☐	16/256	Bill Doran, Hou./ Jim Rice, Bos.	.15
☐	17/207	Rafael Ramirez, Hou./ Andy Allanson, Cle.	.15
☐	18/181	Buddy Bell, Hou./ Jack Howell, Cal.	.15
☐	19/214	Billy Hatcher, Hou./ John Farrell, Cle.	.15
☐	20/275	Nolan Ryan, Hou./ Frank Tanana, Det.	1.50
☐	23/211	Gerald Young, Hou./ Tom Candiotti	.15
☐	24/208	Dion James, Atl./ Julio Franco, Cle.	.15
☐	25/243	Bruce Sutter, Atl./ Jeff Russell, Tex.	.15
☐	26/310	Andres Thomas, Atl./ Tommy John, NYY	.15
☐	27/200	Zane Smith, Atl./ B.J. Surhoff, Mil.	.15

☐ 28/198	Ozzie Virgil, Atl./ Teddy Higuera, Mil.	.15
☐ 29/269	Rick Mahler, Atl./ Floyd Bannister, K.C.	.15
☐ 30/219	Albert Hall, Atl./ Mickey Brantley, Sea.	.15
☐ 31/203	Pete Smith, Atl./ Jim Gantner, Mil.	.15
☐ 34/177	Ron Gant, Atl./ Chili Davis, Cal.	.15
☐ 35/244	Bob Horner, Stl./ Mike Stanley, Tex.	.15
☐ 36/313	Willie McGee, Stl./ Rafael Santana, NYY	.15
☐ 37/288	Luis Alicea, Stl./ Greg Gagne, Min.	.15
☐ 38/279	Tony Pena, Stl./ Gary Pettis, Det.	.15
☐ 39/184	Todd Worrell, Stl./ Kirk McCaskill, Cal.	.25
☐ 40/228	Pedro Guerrero, Stl./ Bill Swift, Sea.	.15
☐ 41/174	Tom Brunansky, Stl./ Dick Shofield, Cal.	.15
☐ 42/262	Terry Pendleton, Stl./ Frank White, K.C.	.15
☐ 45/240	Jose Oquendo, Stl./ Cecil Espy, Tex	.15
☐ 46/191	Vance Law, Chi.-N.L./ Pat Borders, Tor.	.15
☐ 47/258	Rafael Palmeiro, Chi.-N.L./ Bob Stanley, Bos.	.35
☐ 48/213	Greg Maddux, Chi.-N.L./ Greg Swindell, Cle.	1.50
☐ 49/229	Shawon Dunston, Chi.-N.L./ Jose Bautista, Bal.	.15
☐ 50/210	Mark Grace, Chi.-N.L./ Cory Snyder, Cle.	.25
☐ 51/187	Damon Berryhill, Chi.-N.L./ Kelly Gruber, Tor.	.15
☐ 52/192	Rick Sutcliffe, Chi.-N.L./ Rance Mulliniks, Tor.	.15
☐ 53/291	Jamie Moyer, Chi.-N.L./ Juan Berenguer, Min.	.15
☐ 56/284	Calvin Schiraldi, Chi.-N.L./ Jeff Reardon, Min.	.15
☐ 57/308	Steve Sax, L.A./ Jack Clark, NYY	.15
☐ 58/263	Mike Scioscia, L.A./ Bret Saberhagen, K.C.	.15
☐ 59/298	Alfredo Griffin, L.A./ Steve Lyons, Chi.-A.L.	.15
☐ 60/202	Fernando Valenzuela, L.A./ Rob Deer, Mil.	.15
☐ 61/286	Jay Howell, L.A./ Danny Gladden, Min.	.15
☐ 62/305	Tim Leary, L.A./ Bobby Thigpen, Chi.-A.L.	.15
☐ 63/212	John Shelby, L.A./ Brook Jacoby, Cle.	.15
☐ 64/306	John Tudor, L.A./ John Candelaria, NYY	.15
☐ 67/223	Mike Marshall, L.A./ Jim Presley, Sea.	.15
☐ 68/206	Luis Rivera, Mtl./ Dale Sveum, Mil.	.15
☐ 69/311	Tim Burke, Mtl./ Mike Pagliarulo, NYY	.15
☐ 70/253	Tim Wallach, Mtl./ Rich Gedman, Bos.	.15
☐ 71/265	Pascual Perez, Mtl./ Bo Jackson, K.C.	.15
☐ 72/185	Hubie Brooks, Mtl./ Fred McGriff, Tor.	.25
☐ 73/250	Jeff Parrett, Mtl./ Steve Buechele, Tex.	.15
☐ 74/316	Denny Martinez, Mtl./ Richard Dotson, NYY	.15
☐ 75/285	Andy McGaffigan, Mtl./ Bert Blyleven, Min.	.15
☐ 78/287	Nelson Santovenia, Mtl./ Kent Hrbek, Min.	.15
☐ 79/261	Rick Reushel, S.F./ Mike Boddicker, Bos.	.15
☐ 80/276	Mike Aldrete, S.F./ Luis Salazar, Det.	.15
☐ 81/247	Kelly Downs, S.F./ Mitch Williams, Tex.	.15
☐ 82/283	Jose Uribe, S.F./ Chet Lemon, Det.	.15
☐ 83/190	Mike Krukow, S.F./ Mike Flanagan, Tor.	.15
☐ 84/179	Kevin Mitchell, S.F./ Devon White, Cal.	.25
☐ 85/195	Brett Butler, S.F./ Tom Heinke, Tor.	.15
☐ 86/252	Don Robinson, S.F./ Dwight Evans, Bos.	.15
☐ 89/188	Candy Maldonado, S.F./ Lloyd Moseby, Tor.	.15
☐ 90/180	Lenny Dykstra, NYM./ Bryan Harvey, Cal.	.15
☐ 91/234	Howard Johnson, NYM./ Rene Gonzales, Bal.	.15
☐ 92/266	Roger McDowell, NYM./ Kurt Stillwell, K.C.	.15
☐ 93/222	Keith Hernandez, NYM./ Steve Balboni, Sea.	.15
☐ 94/178	Gary Carter, NYM./ Brian Downing, Cal.	.25
☐ 95/277	Kevin McReynolds, NYM./ Jack Morris, Det.	.15
☐ 96/307	Dave Cone, NYM./ Dave Righetti, NYY	.15
☐ 97/175	Randy Myers, NYM./ Bob Boone, Cal.	.15
☐ 100/257	Ron Darling, NYM./ Marty Barrett, Bos.	.15
☐ 101/201	Benny Santiago, S.D./ Greg Brock, Mil.	.15
☐ 102/273	John Kruk, S.D./ Mike Henneman, Det.	.15
☐ 103/242	Chris Brown, S.D./ Ruben Sierra, Tex.	.15
☐ 104/255	Roberto Alomar, S.D./ Mike Greenwell, Bos.	.50
☐ 105/290	Keith Moreland, S.D./ Tim Laudner, Min.	.15
☐ 106/217	Randy Ready, S.D./ Scott Bailes, Cle.	.15
☐ 107/267	Marvell Wynne, S.D./ Danny Tartabull, K.C.	.15
☐ 108/176	Lance McCullers, S.D./ Mike Witt, Cal.	.15
☐ 111/236	Andy Hawkins, S.D./ Terry Kennedy, Bal.	.15
☐ 112/233	Steve Bedrosian, Pha./ Jim Traber, Bal.	.15
☐ 113/196	Phil Bradley, Pha./ Glenn Braggs, Mil.	.15
☐ 114/189	Steve Jeltz, Pha./ Tony Fernandez, Tor.	.15
☐ 115/209	Von Hayes, Pha./ Julio Franco, Cle.	.15
☐ 116/245	Kevin Gross, Pha./ Charlie Hough, Tex.	.15
☐ 117/218	Juan Samuel, Pha./ Henry Cotto, Sea.	.15
☐ 118/274	Shane Rawley, Pha./ Doyle Alexander, Det.	.15
☐ 119/186	Chris James, Pha./ Lloyd Moseby, Tor.	.15
☐ 122/280	Bruce Ruffin, Pha./ Matt Nokes, Det.	.15
☐ 123/246	Bob Walk, Pgh./ Scott Fletcher, Tex.	.15
☐ 124/278	John Smiley, Pgh./ Tom Brookens, Det.	.15
☐ 125/301	Sid Bream, Pgh./ Dan Pasqua, Chi.-A.L.	.15
☐ 126/251	Jose Lind, Pgh./ Lee Smith, Bos.	.15
☐ 127/309	Barry Bonds, Pgh./ Willie Randolph, NYY.	.35
☐ 128/294	Mike LaValliere, Pgh./ Gene Larkin, Min.	.15
☐ 129/225	Jeff D. Robinson, Pgh./ Scott Bradley, Sea.	.15
☐ 130/295	Mike Dunne, Pgh./ Dave Gallagher, Chi.-A.L.	.15
☐ 133/241	Rafael Belliard, Pgh./ Jose Guzman, Tex.	.15
☐ 134/197	Nick Esasky, Cin./ Dan Plesac, Mil.	.15
☐ 135/300	Bo Diaz, Cin./ Fred Manrique, Chi.-A.L.	.15
☐ 136/221	John Franco, Cin./ Mark Langston, Sea.	.15
☐ 137/312	Barry Larkin, Cin./ Rickey Henderson, NYY.	.25
☐ 138/173	Eric Davis, Cin./ Ron Hassey, Oak.	.15
☐ 139/299	Jeff Treadway, Cin./ Carlton Fisk, Chi.-A.L.	.25
☐ 140/254	Jose Rijo, Cin./ Ellis Burks, Bos.	.15
☐ 141/220	Tom Browning, Cin./ Mike Moore, Sea.	.15
☐ 144/199	Kal Daniels, Cin./ Jeffrey Leonard, Mil.	.15
☐ 163/268	Dave Stewart, Oak./ Willie Wilson, K.C.	.15
☐ 164/297	Dave Henderson, Oak./ Ivan Calderon, Chi.-A.L.	.15
☐ 165/321	Terry Steinbach, Oak./ Dave Gallagher, Chi.-A.L.	.15
☐ 166/264	Bob Welch, Oak./ Kevin Seitzer, K.C.	.15
☐ 167/224	Dennis Eckersley, Oak./ Rey Quinones, Sea.	.15
☐ 168/235	Walt Weiss, Oak./ Terry Kennedy, Bal.	.15
☐ 169/296	Dave Parker, Oak./ Melido Perez, Chi.-A.L.	.15
☐ 170/289	Carney Lansford, Oak./ Gary Gaetti, Min.	.15

1989 SUPER STAR

The 1989 O-Pee-Chee Super Star is a subset of the 1989 Stickers. The cards are on the back of the stickers. After the stickers are removed, you are left with the Super Star subset.

Card Size: 2 1/8" x 3"
Face: Four colour, white border; number, résumé, O-Pee-Chee logo
Back: 1989 O-Pee-Chee sticker
Imprint: © 1989 O-PEE-CHEE LTD. PTD. IN CANADA/IMPRIMê AU CANADA

Complete Set (67 stickers):		**10.00**
Common Player:		**.10**

	No.	Player	MINT
☐	1	George Brett, K.C.	.50
☐	2	Don Mattingly, NYM.	.50
☐	3	Mark McGwire, Oak.	.50
☐	4	Julio Franco, Cle.	.10
☐	5	Harold Reynolds, Sea.	.10
☐	6	Lou Whitaker, Det.	.10
☐	7	Wade Boggs, Bos.	.25
☐	8	Gary Gaetti, Min.	.10
☐	9	Paul Molitor, Mil.	.25
☐	10	Tony Fernandez, Tor.	.10
☐	11	Cal Ripken, Bal.	2.00
☐	12	Alan Trammell, Det.	.10
☐	13	Jose Canseco, Oak.	.25
☐	14	Joe Carter, Cle.	.25
☐	15	Dwight Evans, Bos.	.10
☐	16	Mike Greenwell, Bos.	.10
☐	17	Dave Henderson, Oak.	.10
☐	18	Rickey Henderson, NYY.	.25
☐	19	Kirby Puckett, Min.	.50
☐	20	Dave Winfield, NYY.	.25
☐	21	Robin Yount, Mil.	.25
☐	22	Bob Boone, Cal.	.10

	No.	Player	
□	23	Carlton Fisk, Chi.-N.L.	.25
□	24	Geno Petralli, Tex.	.10
□	25	Roger Clemens, Bos.	.75
□	26	Mark Gubicza, K.C.	.10
□	27	Dave Stewart, Oak.	.10
□	28	Teddy Higuera, Mil.	.10
□	29	Bruce Hurst, Bos.	.10
□	30	Frank Viola, Min.	.10
□	31	Dennis Eckersley, Oak.	.10
□	32	Doug Jones, Cle.	.10
□	33	Jeff Reardon, Min.	.10
□	34	Will Clark, S.F.	.25
□	35	Glenn Davis, Hou.	.10
□	36	Andres Galarraga, Mtl.	.25
□	37	Juan Samuel, Pha.	.10
□	38	Ryne Sandberg, Chi.-N.L.	.25
□	39	Steve Sax, L.A.	.10
□	40	Bobby Bonilla, Pgh.	.10
□	41	Howard Johnson, NYM.	.10
□	42	Vance Law, Chi.-N.L.	.10
□	43	Shawon Dunston, Chi.-N.L.	.10
□	44	Barry Larkin, Cin.	.25
□	45	Ozzie Smith, Stl.	.35
□	46	Barry Bonds, Pgh.	.35
□	47	Eric Davis, Cin.	.10
□	48	Andre Dawson, Chi.-N.L.	.25
□	49	Kirk Gibson, L.A.	.10
□	50	Tony Gwynn, S.D.	.50
□	51	Kevin McReynolds, NYM.	.10
□	52	Rafael Palmeiro, Chi.-N.L.	.10
□	53	Darryl Strawberry, NYM.	.25
□	54	Andy Van Slyke, Pgh.	.10
□	55	Gary Carter, NYM.	.25
□	56	Mike LaValliere, Pgh.	.10
□	57	Benny Santiago, S.D.	.10
□	58	Dave Cone, NYM.	.10
□	59	Doc Gooden, NYM.	.10
□	60	Orel Hershiser, L.A.	.10
□	61	Tom Browning, Cin.	.10
□	62	Danny Jackson, Cin.	.10
□	63	Bob Knepper, Hou.	.10
□	64	Mark Davis, S.D.	.10
□	65	John Franco, Cin.	.10
□	66	Randy Myers, NYM.	.10
□	67	CL: Superstar Checklist	.10

1989 PANINI STICKERS

Panini made a 64-page, colour "Baseball '89 Sticker Album" to hold this 480-sticker set. It was written in French and English and was printed in the United States. Panini made the stickers in Italy.

Sticker Size: 2 15/16" x 2 3/4"

Face: Four colour, white border; name, team, MLB logo

Back: Black and white; number, Panini and MLB logos

Imprint: None

Complete Set (480 stickers): 20.00

Common Sticker: .15

Album: 4.00

	No.	Player	MINT
□	1	1988 World Series Trophy	.15
□	2	1988 World Series Trophy	.15
□	3	HL: Mike Schmidt, Pha.	.35
□	4	HL: Tom Browning, Cin.	.15
□	5	HL: Doug Jones, Cle.	.15
□	6	HL: Wrigley Field	.15
□	7	HL: Wade Boggs, Bos.	.25
□	8	HL: Jose Canseco, Oak.	.25
□	9	HL: Orel Hershiser, L.A.	.15
□	10	Oakland Athletics	.15
□	11	Oakland Athletics	.15
□	12	1988 ALCS - MVP: Dennis Eckersley, Oak.	.15
□	13	1988 NLCS - MVP: Orel Hershiser, L.A.	.15
□	14	Dodgers Beat Mets	.15
□	15	Dodgers Beat Mets	.15
□	16	WS: Kirk Gibson, L.A.	.15
□	17	WS: Kirk Gibson, L.A.	.15
□	18	WS: Orel Hershiser, L.A.	.15
□	19	WS: Orel Hershiser, L.A.	.15
□	20	WS: Mark McGwire, Oak.	1.00
□	21	WS: Tim Belcher. LA	.15
□	22	WS: Jay Howell, L.A..	.15
□	23	WS: Mickey Hatcher, L.A.	.15
□	24	WS: Mike Davis, L.A.	.15
□	25	1988 World Series MVP: Orel Hershiser, L.A.	.15
□	26	World Series Celebration	.15
□	27	World Series Celebration	.15
□	28	World Series Celebration	.15
□	29	World Series Celebration	.15
□	30	Team Logo, Atl.	.15
□	31	Jose Alvarez, Atl.	.15
□	32	Tommy Gregg, Atl.	.15
□	33	Paul Assenmacher, Atl.	.15
□	34	Tom Glavine, Atl.	.35
□	35	Rick Mahler, Atl.	.15
□	36	Pete Smith, Atl.	.15
□	37	Atlanta-Fulton County Stadium, Atl.	.15
□	38	Team Lettering, Atl.	.15
□	39	Bruce Sutter, Atl.	.15
□	40	Gerald Perry, Atl.	.15
□	41	Jeff Blauser, Atl.	.15
□	42	Ron Gant, Atl.	.15
□	43	Andres Thomas, Atl.	.15
□	44	Dion James, Atl.	.15
□	45	Dale Murphy, Atl.	.25
□	46	Team Logo, Chi.-N.L.	.15
□	47	Doug Dascenzo, Chi.-N.L.	.15
□	48	Mike Harkey, Chi.-N.L.	.15
□	49	Greg Maddux, Chi.-N.L.	1.50
□	50	Jeff Pico, Chi.-N.L.	.15
□	51	Rick Sutcliffe, Chi.-N.L.	.15
□	52	Damon Berryhill, Chi.-N.L.	.15
□	53	Wrigley Field, Chi.-N.L.	.15
□	54	Team Lettering, Chi.-N.L.	.15
□	55	Mark Grace, Chi.-N.L.	.35
□	56	Ryne Sandberg, Chi.-N.L.	.50
□	57	Vance Law, Chi.-N.L.	.15
□	58	Shawon Dunston, Chi.-N.L.	.15
□	59	Andre Dawson, Chi.-N.L.	.35
□	60	Rafael Palmeiro, Chi.-N.L.	.35
□	61	Mitch Webster, Chi.-N.L.	.15
□	62	Team Logo, Cin.	.15
□	63	Jack Armstrong, Cin.	.15
□	64	Chris Sabo, Cin.	.15

	No.	Player	Price
☐	65	Tom Browning, Cin.	.15
☐	66	John Franco, Cin.	.15
☐	67	Danny Jackson, Cin.	.15
☐	68	Jose Rijo, Cin.	.15
☐	69	Riverfront Stadium, Cin.	.15
☐	70	Team Lettering, Cin.	.15
☐	71	Bo Diaz, Cin.	.15
☐	72	Nick Esasky, Cin.	.15
☐	73	Jeff Treadway, Cin.	.15
☐	74	Barry Larkin, Cin.	.25
☐	75	Kal Daniels, Cin.	.15
☐	76	Eric Davis, Cin.	.15
☐	77	Paul O'Neill, Cin.	.15
☐	78	Team Logo, Hou.	.15
☐	79	Craig Biggio, Hou.	.25
☐	80	John Fishel, Hou.	.15
☐	81	Juan Agosto, Hou.	.15
☐	82	Bob Knepper, Hou.	.15
☐	83	Nolan Ryan, Hou.	2.50
☐	84	Mike Scott, Hou.	.15
☐	85	The Astrodome, Hou.	.15
☐	86	Team Lettering, Hou.	.15
☐	87	Dave Smith, Hou.	.15
☐	88	Glenn Davis, Hou.	.15
☐	89	Bill Doran, Hou.	.15
☐	90	Rafael Ramirez, Hou.	.15
☐	91	Kevin Bass, Hou.	.15
☐	92	Billy Hatcher, Hou.	.15
☐	93	Gerald Young, Hou.	.15
☐	94	Team Logo, L.A.	.15
☐	95	Tim Belcher, L.A.	.15
☐	96	Tim Crews, L.A.	.15
☐	97	Orel Hershiser, L.A.	.15
☐	98	Jay Howell, L.A.	.15
☐	99	Tim Leary, L.A.	.15
☐	100	John Tudor, L.A.	.15
☐	101	Dodger Stadium, L.A.	.15
☐	102	Team Lettering, L.A.	.15
☐	103	Fernando Valenzuela, L.A.	.15
☐	104	Mike Scioscia, L.A.	.15
☐	105	Mickey Hatcher, L.A.	.15
☐	106	Steve Sax, L.A.	.15
☐	107	Kirk Gibson, L.A.	.15
☐	108	Mike Marshall, L.A.	.15
☐	109	John Shelby, L.A.	.15
☐	110	Team Logo, Mtl.	.15
☐	111	Randy Johnson, Mtl.	.50
☐	112	Nelson Santovenia, Mtl.	.15
☐	113	Tim Burke, Mtl.	.15
☐	114	Dennis Martinez, Mtl.	.15
☐	115	Pascual Perez, Mtl.	.15
☐	116	Bryn Smith, Mtl.	.15
☐	117	Olympic Stadium, Mtl.	.15
☐	118	Team Lettering, Mtl.	.15
☐	119	Andres Galarraga, Mtl.	.35
☐	120	Wallace Johnson, Mtl.	.15
☐	121	Tom Foley, Mtl.	.15
☐	122	Tim Wallach, Mtl.	.15
☐	123	Hubie Brooks, Mtl.	.15
☐	124	Tracey Jones, Mtl.	.15
☐	125	Tim Raines, Mtl.	.15
☐	126	Team Logo, NYM.	.15
☐	127	Kevin Elster, NYM.	.15
☐	128	Gregg Jefferies, NYM.	.15
☐	129	David Cone, NYM.	.35
☐	130	Ron Darling, NYM.	.15
☐	131	Dwight Gooden, NYM.	.15
☐	132	Roger McDowell, NYM.	.15
☐	133	Shea Stadium, NYM.	.15
☐	134	Team Lettering, NYM.	.15
☐	135	Randy Myers, NYM.	.15
☐	136	Gary Carter, NYM.	.35
☐	137	Keith Hernandez, NYM.	.15
☐	138	Lenny Dykstra, NYM.	.15
☐	139	Kevin McReynolds, NYM.	.15
☐	140	Darryl Strawberry, NYM.	.25
☐	141	Mookie Wilson, NYM.	.15
☐	142	Team Logo, Pha.	.15
☐	143	Ron Jones, Pha.	.15
☐	144	Rickey Jordan, Pha.	.15
☐	145	Steve Bedrosian, Pha.	.15
☐	146	Don Carman, Pha.	.15
☐	147	Kevin Gross, Pha.	.15
☐	148	Bruce Ruffin, Pha.	.15
☐	149	Veterans Stadium, Pha.	.15
☐	150	Team Lettering, Pha.	.15
☐	151	Von Hayes, Pha.	.15
☐	152	Juan Samuel, Pha.	.15
☐	153	Mike Schmidt, Pha.	.50
☐	154	Phil Bradley, Pha.	.15
☐	155	Bob Dernier, Pha.	.15
☐	156	Chris James, Pha.	.15
☐	157	Milt Thompson, Pha.	.15
☐	158	Team Logo, Pgh.	.15
☐	159	Randy Kramer, Pgh.	.15
☐	160	Scott Medvin, Pgh.	.15
☐	161	Doug Drabek, Pgh.	.15
☐	162	Mike Dunne, Pgh.	.15
☐	163	Jim Gott, Pgh.	.15
☐	164	Jeff Robinson, Pgh.	.15
☐	165	Three Rivers Stadium, Pgh.	.15
☐	166	Team Lettering, Pgh.	.15
☐	167	John Smiley, Pgh.	.15
☐	168	Mike LaValliere, Pgh.	.15
☐	169	Sid Bream, Pgh.	.15
☐	170	Jose Lind, Pgh.	.15
☐	171	Bobby Bonilla, Pgh.	.15
☐	172	Barry Bonds, Pgh.	.50
☐	173	Andy Van Slyke, Pgh.	.15
☐	174	Team Logo, Stl.	.15
☐	175	Luis Alicea, Stl.	.15
☐	176	John Costello, Stl.	.15
☐	177	Jose DeLeon, Stl.	.15
☐	178	Joe Magrane, Stl.	.15
☐	179	Todd Worrell, Stl.	.15
☐	180	Tony Pena, Stl.	.15
☐	181	Busch Stadium, Stl.	.15
☐	182	Team Lettering, Stl.	.15
☐	183	Pedro Guerrero, Stl.	.15
☐	184	Jose Oquendo, Stl.	.15
☐	185	Terry Pendleton, Stl.	.15
☐	186	Ozzie Smith, Stl.	.75
☐	187	Tom Brunansky, Stl.	.15
☐	188	Vince Coleman, Stl.	.15
☐	189	Willie McGee, Stl.	.15
☐	190	Team Logo, S.D.	.15
☐	191	Roberto Alomar, S.D.	.50
☐	192	Sandy Alomar, Jr., S.D.	.35
☐	193	Mark Davis, S.D.	.15
☐	194	Andy Hawkins, S.D.	.15
☐	195	Dennis Rasmussen, S.D.	.15
☐	196	Eric Show, S.D.	.15
☐	197	San Diego Murphy Stadium, S.D.	.15
☐	198	Team Lettering, S.D.	.15
☐	199	Benito Santiago, S.D.	.15
☐	200	John Kruk, S.D.	.15
☐	201	Randy Ready, S.D.	.15
☐	202	Garry Templeton, S.D.	.15

	No.	Sticker	Value
☐	203	Tony Gwynn, S.D.	1.00
☐	204	Carmelo Martinez, S.D.	.15
☐	205	Marvell Wynne, S.D.	.15
☐	206	Team Logo, S.F.	.15
☐	207	Dennis Cook, S.F.	.15
☐	208	Kirt Manwaring, S.F.	.15
☐	209	Kelly Downs, S.F.	.15
☐	210	Rick Reuschel, S.F.	.15
☐	211	Don Robinson, S.F.	.15
☐	212	Will Clark, S.F.	.25
☐	213	Candlestick Park, S.F.	.15
☐	214	Team Lettering, S.F.	.15
☐	215	Robby Thompson, S.F.	.15
☐	216	Kevin Mitchell, S.F.	.15
☐	217	Jose Uribe, S.F.	.15
☐	218	Matt Williams, S.F.	.35
☐	219	Mike Aldrete, S.F.	.15
☐	220	Brett Butler, S.F.	.15
☐	221	Candy Maldonado, S.F.	.15
☐	222	1988 Statistics	.15
☐	223	1988 Statistics	.15
☐	224	1988 Statistics	.15
☐	225	1988 Statistics	.15
☐	226	1988 Statistics	.15
☐	227	AS: Dwight Gooden, NYM.	.15
☐	228	AS: Gary Carter, NYM.	.25
☐	229	AS: Vince Coleman, Stl.	.15
☐	230	AS: Andre Dawson, Chi.-N.L.	.25
☐	231	AS: Darryl Strawberry, NYM.	.25
☐	232	AS: Will Clark, S.F.	.25
☐	233	AS: Ryne Sandberg, Chi.-N.L.	.25
☐	234	AS: Bobby Bonilla, Pgh.	.15
☐	235	AS: Ozzie Smith, Stl.	.50
☐	236	AS: Terry Steinbach, Oak.	.15
☐	237	AS: Frank Viola, Min.	.15
☐	238	AS: Jose Canseco, Oak.	.25
☐	239	AS: Rickey Henderson, Oak.	.25
☐	240	AS: Dave Winfield, NYY.	.25
☐	241	AS: Cal Ripken. Jr., Bal.	1.50
☐	242	AS: Wade Boggs, Bos.	.50
☐	243	AS: Paul Molitor, Mil.	.25
☐	244	AS: Mark McGwire, Oak.	1.00
☐	245	1988 Statistics	.15
☐	246	1988 Statistics	.15
☐	247	1988 Statistics	.15
☐	248	1988 Statistics	.15
☐	249	1988 Statistics	.15
☐	250	Team Logo, Bal.	.15
☐	251	Bob Milacki, Bal.	.15
☐	252	Craig Worthington, Bal.	.15
☐	253	Jeff Ballard, Bal.	.15
☐	254	Tom Niedenfuer, Bal.	.15
☐	255	Dave Schmidt, Bal.	.15
☐	256	Terry Kennedy, Bal.	.15
☐	257	Memorial Stadium, Bal.	.15
☐	258	Team Lettering, Bal.	.15
☐	259	Mickey Tettleton, Bal.	.15
☐	260	Eddie Murray, Bal.	.75
☐	261	Bill Ripken, Bal.	.15
☐	262	Cal Ripken, Jr., Bal.	2.50
☐	263	Joe Orsulak, Bal.	.15
☐	264	Larry Sheets, Bal.	.15
☐	265	Pete Stanicek, Bal.	.15
☐	266	Team Logo, Bos.	.15
☐	267	Steve Curry, Bos.	.15
☐	268	Jody Reed, Bos.	.15
☐	269	"Oil Can" Boyd, Bos.	.15
☐	270	Roger Clemens, Bos.	1.25
☐	271	Bruce Hurst, Bos.	.15
☐	272	Lee Smith, Bos.	.15
☐	273	Fenway Park, Bos.	.15
☐	274	Team Lettering, Bos.	.15
☐	275	Todd Benzinger, Bos.	.15
☐	276	Marty Barrett, Bos.	.15
☐	277	Wade Boggs, Bos.	.75
☐	278	Ellis Burks, Bos.	.15
☐	278	Dwight Evans, Bos.	.25
☐	280	Mike Greenwell, Bos.	.15
☐	281	Jim Rice, Bos.	.15
☐	282	Team Logo, Cal.	.15
☐	283	Dante Bichette, Cal.	.15
☐	284	Bryan Harvey, Cal.	.15
☐	285	Kirk McCaskill, Cal.	.25
☐	286	Mike Witt, Cal.	.15
☐	287	Bob Boone, Cal.	.15
☐	288	Brian Downing, Cal.	.15
☐	289	Anaheim Stadium, Cal.	.15
☐	290	Team Lettering, Cal.	.15
☐	291	Wally Joyner, Cal.	.15
☐	292	Johnny Ray, Cal.	.15
☐	293	Jack Howell, Cal.	.15
☐	294	Dick Schofield, Cal.	.15
☐	295	Tony Armas, Cal.	.15
☐	296	Chili Davis, Cal.	.15
☐	297	Devon White, Cal.	.15
☐	298	Team Logo, Chi.-A.L.	.15
☐	299	Dave Gallagher, Chi.-A.L.	.15
☐	300	Melido Perez, Chi.-A.L.	.15
☐	301	Shawn Hillegas, Chi.-A.L.	.15
☐	302	Jack McDowell, Chi.-A.L.	.15
☐	303	Bobby Thigpen, Chi.-A.L.	.15
☐	304	Carlton Fisk, Chi.-A.L.	.35
☐	305	Comiskey Park, Chi.-A.L.	.15
☐	306	Team Lettering, Chi.-A.L.	.15
☐	307	Greg Walker, Chi.-A.L.	.15
☐	308	Steve Lyons, Chi.-A.L.	.15
☐	309	Ozzie Guillen, Chi.-A.L.	.15
☐	310	Harold Baines, Chi.-A.L.	.15
☐	311	Daryl Boston, Chi.-A.L.	.15
☐	312	Lance Johnson, Chi.-A.L.	.15
☐	313	Dan Pasqua, Chi.-A.L.	.15
☐	314	Team Logo, Cle.	.15
☐	315	Luis Medina	.15
☐	316	Ron Tingley, Cle.	.15
☐	317	Tom Candiotti, Cle.	.15
☐	318	John Farrell, Cle.	.15
☐	319	Doug Jones, Cle.	.15
☐	320	Greg Swindell, Cle.	.15
☐	321	Cleveland Stadium, Cle.	.15
☐	322	Team Lettering, Cle.	.15
☐	323	Andy Allanson, Cle.	.15
☐	324	Willie Upshaw, Cle.	.15
☐	325	Julio Franco, Cle.	.15
☐	326	Brook Jacoby, Cle.	.15
☐	327	Joe Carter, Cle.	.25
☐	328	Mel Hall, Cle.	.15
☐	329	Cory Snyder, Cle.	.15
☐	330	Team Logo, Det.	.15
☐	331	Paul Gibson, Det.	.15
☐	332	Torey Lovullo, Det.	.15
☐	333	Mike Henneman, Det.	.15
☐	334	Jack Morris, Det.	.15
☐	335	Jeff Robinson, Det.	.15
☐	336	Frank Tanana, Det.	.15
☐	337	Tiger Stadium, Det.	.15
☐	338	Team Lettering, Det.	.15
☐	339	Matt Nokes, Det.	.15
☐	340	Tom Brookens, Det.	.15

	No.	Card	Price
☐	341	Lou Whitaker, Det.	.15
☐	342	Luis Salazar, Det.	.15
☐	343	Alan Trammell, Det.	.15
☐	344	Chet Lemon, Det.	.15
☐	345	Gary Pettis, Det.	.15
☐	346	Team Logo, K.S.	.15
☐	347	Luis de los Santos, K.S.	.15
☐	348	Gary Thurman, K.S.	.15
☐	349	Steve Farr, K.S.	.15
☐	350	Mark Gubicza, K.S.	.15
☐	351	Charlie Leibrandt, K.S.	.15
☐	352	Bret Saberhagen, K.S.	.15
☐	353	Royals Stadium, K.S.	.15
☐	354	Team Lettering, K.S.	.15
☐	355	George Brett, K.S.	1.00
☐	356	Frank White, K.S.	.15
☐	357	Kevin Seitzer, K.S.	.15
☐	358	Bo Jackson, K.S.	.15
☐	359	Pat Tabler, K.S.	.15
☐	360	Danny Tartabull, K.S.	.15
☐	361	Willie Wilson, K.S.	.15
☐	362	Team Logo, Mil.	.15
☐	363	Joey Meyer, Mil.	.15
☐	364	Gary Sheffield, Mil.	.35
☐	365	Don August, Mil.	.15
☐	366	Ted Higuera, Mil.	.15
☐	367	Dan Plesac, Mil.	.15
☐	368	B.J. Surhoff, Mil.	.15
☐	369	Milwaukee County Stadium, Mil.	.15
☐	370	Team Lettering, Mil.	.15
☐	371	Greg Brock, Mil.	.15
☐	372	Jim Gantner, Mil.	.15
☐	373	Paul Molitor, Mil.	.50
☐	374	Dale Sveum, Mil.	.15
☐	375	Glenn Braggs, Mil.	.15
☐	376	Rob Deer, Mil.	.15
☐	377	Robin Yount, Mil.	.50
☐	378	Team Logo, Min.	.15
☐	379	German Gonzalez, Min.	.15
☐	380	Kelvin Torve, Min.	.15
☐	381	Allan Anderson, Min.	.15
☐	382	Jeff Reardon, Min.	.15
☐	383	Frank Viola, Min.	.15
☐	384	Tim Laudner, Min.	.15
☐	385	Hubert H. Humphrey Metrodome, Min.	.15
☐	386	Team Lettering, Min.	.15
☐	387	Kent Hrbek, Min.	.15
☐	388	Gene Larkin, Min.	.15
☐	389	Gary Gaetti, Min.	.15
☐	390	Greg Gagne, Min.	.15
☐	391	Randy Bush, Min.	.15
☐	392	Dan Gladden, Min.	.15
☐	393	Kirby Puckett, Min.	1.00
☐	394	Team Logo, NYY.	.15
☐	395	Roberto Kelly, NYY.	.15
☐	396	Al Leiter, NYY.	.15
☐	397	John Candelaria, NYY.	.15
☐	398	Rich Dotson, NYY.	.15
☐	399	Rick Rhoden, NYY.	.15
☐	400	Dave Righetti, NYY.	.15
☐	401	Yankee Stadium, NYY.	.15
☐	402	Team Lettering, NYY.	.15
☐	403	Don Slaught, NYY.	.15
☐	404	Don Mattingly, NYY.	1.00
☐	405	Willie Randolph, NYY.	.15
☐	406	Mike Pagliarulo, NYY.	.15
☐	407	Rafael Santana, NYY.	.15
☐	408	Rickey Henderson, NYY.	.35
☐	409	Dave Winfield, NYY.	.35
☐	410	Team Logo, Oak.	.15
☐	411	Todd Burns, Oak.	.15
☐	412	Walt Weiss, Oak.	.15
☐	413	Storm Davis, Oak.	.15
☐	414	Dennis Eckersley, Oak.	.15
☐	415	Dave Stewart, Oak.	.15
☐	416	Bob Welch, Oak.	.15
☐	417	Oakland Alameda County Coliseum, Oak.	.15
☐	418	Team Lettering, Oak.	.15
☐	419	Terry Steinbach, Oak.	.15
☐	420	Mark McGwire, Oak.	1.50
☐	421	Carney Lansford, Oak.	.15
☐	422	Jose Canseco, Oak.	.25
☐	423	Dave Henderson, Oak.	.15
☐	424	Dave Parker, Oak.	.15
☐	425	Luis Polonia, Oak.	.15
☐	426	Team Logo, Sea.	.15
☐	427	Mario Diaz, Sea.	.15
☐	428	Edgar Martinez, Sea.	.15
☐	429	Scott Bankhead, Sea.	.15
☐	430	Mark Langston, Sea.	.15
☐	431	Mike Moore, Sea.	.15
☐	432	Scott Bradley, Sea.	.15
☐	433	The Kingdome, Sea.	.15
☐	434	Team Lettering, Sea.	.15
☐	435	Alvin Davis, Sea.	.15
☐	436	Harold Reynolds, Sea.	.15
☐	437	Jim Presley, Sea.	.15
☐	438	Rey Quinones, Sea.	.15
☐	439	Mickey Brantley, Sea.	.15
☐	440	Jay Buhner, Sea.	.25
☐	441	Henry Cotto, Sea.	.15
☐	442	Team Logo, Tex.	.15
☐	443	Cecil Espy, Tex.	.15
☐	444	Chad Kreuter, Tex.	.15
☐	445	Jose Guzman, Tex.	.15
☐	446	Charlie Hough, Tex.	.15
☐	447	Jeff Russell, Tex.	.15
☐	448	Bobby Witt, Tex.	.15
☐	449	Arlington Stadium, Tex.	.15
☐	450	Team Lettering, Tex.	.15
☐	451	Geno Petralli, Tex.	.15
☐	452	Pete O'Brien, Tex.	.15
☐	453	Steve Buechele, Tex.	.15
☐	454	Scott Fletcher, Tex.	.15
☐	455	Pete Incaviglia, Tex.	.15
☐	456	Oddibe McDowell, Tex.	.15
☐	457	Ruben Sierra, Tex.	.15
☐	458	Team Logo, Tor.	.15
☐	459	Rob Ducey, Tor.	.25
☐	460	Todd Stottlemyre, Tor.	.15
☐	461	Tom Henke, Tor.	.15
☐	462	Jimmy Key, Tor.	.15
☐	463	Dave Steib, Tor.	.15
☐	464	Pat Borders, Tor.	.15
☐	465	Exhibition Stadium, Tor.	.15
☐	466	Team Lettering, Tor.	.15
☐	467	Fred McGriff, Tor.	.35
☐	468	Manny Lee, Tor.	.15
☐	469	Kelly Gruber, Tor.	.15
☐	470	Tony Fernandez, Tor.	.15
☐	471	Jesse Barfield, Tor.	.15
☐	472	George Bell, Tor.	.15
☐	473	Lloyd Moseby, Tor.	.15
☐	474	N.L. Cy Young Award: Orel Hershiser	.15
☐	475	A.L. Cy Young Award: Frank Viola	.15
☐	476	N.L. Rookie of the Year: Chris Sabo	.15
☐	477	Associated Press Player of the Year: Jose Canseco	.25
☐	478	A.L. Rookie of the Year: Walt Weiss	.15
☐	479	N.L. Most Valuable Player: Kirk Gibson	.15
☐	480	A.L. Most Valuable Player: Jose Canseco	.25

1990 BEN'S / HOLSUMS DISKS

These 20 disks carry only the Holsum logo; Schafer's has been removed.

Disk Size: 2 3/4" Diameter

Face: Four colour, orange border; name, position, team, Holsum's logo

Back: Black on card stock; name, résumé, numbered _ of 20

Imprint: "MLBPA 1990" MSA Printed in U.S.A.

	No.	Player	MINT
		Complete Set (20 disks):	**35.00**
☐	1	George Bell, Tor.	1.25
☐	2	Tim Raines, Mtl.	1.25
☐	3	Tom Henke, Tor.	1.25
☐	4	Andres Galarraga, Mtl.	2.50
☐	5	Bret Saberhagen, K.C.	1.25
☐	6	Mark Davis, K.C.	1.25
☐	7	Robin Yount, Mil.	2.00
☐	8	Rickey Henderson, Oak.	2.00
☐	9	Kevin Mitchell, S.F.	1.25
☐	10	Howard Johnson, NYM.	1.25
☐	11	Will Clark, S.F.	1.75
☐	12	Orel Hershiser, L.A.	1.25
☐	13	Fred McGriff, Tor.	1.75
☐	14	Dave Stewart, Oak.	1.25
☐	15	Vince Coleman, Stl.	1.25
☐	16	Steve Sax, NYY.	1.25
☐	17	Kirby Puckett, Min.	5.00
☐	18	Tony Gwynn, S.D.	5.00
☐	19	Jerome Walton, Chi.-N.L.	1.25
☐	20	Gregg Olson, Bal.	1.25

1990 FLEER CANADIAN ISSUE

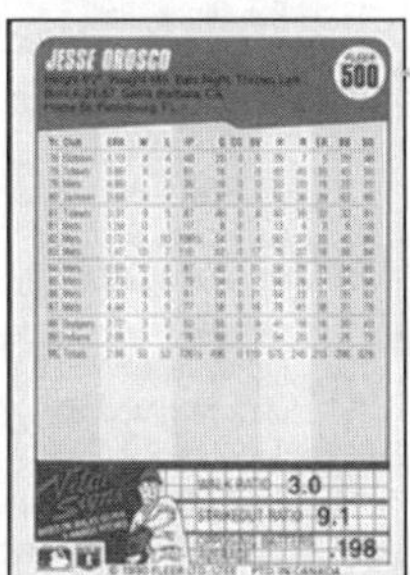

In 1990 Fleer contacted a Canadian printer to produce its set in Canada for the Canadian market. This set carries a "Printed in Canada" imprint. Also during 1990, three U.S. chain stores (Ben Franklin, Toys R Us and Walgreens) sold Fleer sets that were printed in Canada, although they were distributed in the United States.

Card Size: 2 1/2"x 3 1/2"

Face: Four colour, coloured border; name, position, team logo

Back: Red and blue on card stock; name, number, résumé,

Imprint: ©1990 FLEER LTD./LTEE PTD. IN CANADA

	No.	Player	MINT
		Complete Set (660 cards):	**85.00**
		Common Player:	**.25**
☐	1	Lance Blankenship, Oak.	.25
☐	2	Todd Burns, Oak.	.25
☐	3	Jose Canseco, Oak.	.75
☐	4	Jim Corsi, Oak.	.25
☐	5	Storm Davis, Oak.	.25
☐	6	Dennis Eckersley, Oak.	.25
☐	7	Mike Gallego, Oak.	.25
☐	8	Ron Hassey, Oak.	.25
☐	9	Dave Henderson, Oak.	.25
☐	10	Rickey Henderson, Oak.	.50
☐	11	Rick Honeycutt, Oak.	.25
☐	12	Stan Javier, Oak.	.25
☐	13	Felix Jose, Oak.	.25
☐	14	Carney Lansford, Oak.	.25
☐	15	Mark McGwire, Oak.	4.00
☐	16	Mike Moore, Oak.	.25
☐	17	Gene Nelson, Oak.	.25
☐	18	Dave Parker, Oak.	.25
☐	19	Tony Phillips, Oak.	.25
☐	20	Terry Steinbach, Oak.	.25
☐	21	Dave Stewart, Oak.	.25
☐	22	Walt Weiss, Oak.	.25
☐	23	Bob Welch, Oak.	.25
☐	24	Curt Young, Oak.	.25
☐	25	Paul Assenmacher, Chi.-N.L.	.25
☐	26	Damon Berryhill, Chi.-N.L.	.25
☐	27	Mike Bielecki, Chi.-N.L.	.25
☐	28	Kevin Blankenship, Chi.-N.L.	.25
☐	29	Andre Dawson, Chi.-N.L.	.75
☐	30	Shawon Dunston, Chi.-N.L.	.25
☐	31	Joe Girardi, Chi.-N.L.	.25
☐	32	Mark Grace, Chi.-N.L.	.25
☐	33	Mike Harkey, Chi.-N.L.	.25
☐	34	Paul Kilgus, Chi.-N.L.	.25
☐	35	Les Lancaster, Chi.-N.L.	.25
☐	36	Vance Law, Chi.-N.L.	.25
☐	37	Greg Maddux, Chi.-N.L.	5.00
☐	38	Lloyd McClendon, Chi.-N.L.	.25
☐	39	Jeff Pico, Chi.-N.L.	.25
☐	40	Ryne Sandberg, Chi.-N.L.	2.00
☐	41	Scott Sanderson, Chi.-N.L.	.25
☐	42	Dwight Smith, Chi.-N.L.	.25
☐	43	Rick Sutcliffe, Chi.-N.L.	.25
☐	44	Jerome Walton, Chi.-N.L.	.25
☐	45	Mitch Webster, Chi.-N.L.	.25
☐	46	Curt Wilkerson, Chi.-N.L.	.25
☐	47	Dean Wilkins, Chi.-N.L.	.25
☐	48	Mitch Williams, Chi.-N.L.	.25
☐	49	Steve Wilson, Chi.-N.L.	.50
☐	50	Steve Bedrosian, S.F.	.25
☐	51	Mike Benjamin, S.F.	.25
☐	**52**	**Jeff Brantley, S.F., RC**	**.25**
☐	53	Brett Butler, S.F.	.25
☐	54	Will Clark, S.F.	.75
☐	55	Kelly Downs, S.F.	.25
☐	56	Scott Garrelts, S.F.	.25
☐	57	Atlee Hammaker, S.F.	.25
☐	58	Terry Kennedy, S.F.	.25
☐	59	Mike LaCoss, S.F.	.25
☐	60	Craig Lefferts, S.F.	.25
☐	61	Greg Litton, S.F.	.25
☐	62	Candy Maldonado, S.F.	.25
☐	63	Kirt Manwaring, S.F.	.25
☐	64	Randy McCament, S.F.	.25
☐	65	Kevin Mitchell, S.F.	.25
☐	66	Donell Nixon, S.F.	.25
☐	67	Ken Oberkfell, S.F.	.25
☐	68	Rick Reuschel, S.F.	.25
☐	69	Ernest Riles, S.F.	.25
☐	70	Don Robinson, S.F.	.25
☐	71	Pat Sheridan, S.F.	.25
☐	72	Chris Speier, S.F.	.25
☐	73	Robby Thompson, S.F.	.25
☐	74	Jose Uribe, S.F.	.25
☐	75	Matt Willaims, S.F.	.75
☐	76	George Bell, Tor.	.25
☐	77	Pat Borders, Tor.	.25
☐	78	John Cerutti, Tor.	.25

	No.	Player	Price
☐	79	Junior Felix, Tor.	.25
☐	80	Tony Fernandez, Tor.	.25
☐	81	Mike Flanagan, Tor.	.25
☐	**82**	**Mauro Gozzo, Tor., RC**	**.25**
☐	83	Kelly Gruber, Tor.	.25
☐	84	Tom Henke, Tor.	.25
☐	85	Jimmy Key, Tor.	.25
☐	86	Manny Lee, Tor.	.25
☐	87	Nelson Liriano, Tor.	.25
☐	88	Lee Mazzilli, Tor.	.25
☐	89	Fred McGriff, Tor.	.50
☐	90	Lloyd Moseby, Tor.	.25
☐	91	Rance Mulliniks, Tor.	.25
☐	92	Alex Sanchez, Tor.	.25
☐	93	Dave Stieb, Tor.	.25
☐	94	Todd Stottlemyre, Tor.	.25
☐	95	Duane Ward, Tor.	.25
☐	96	David Wells, Tor.	.25
☐	97	Ernie Whitt, Tor.	.25
☐	98	Frank Wills, Tor.	.25
☐	99	Mookie Wilson, Tor.	.25
☐	**100**	**Kevin Appier, K.C., RC**	**.75**
☐	101	Luis Aquino, K.C.	.25
☐	102	Bob Boone, K.C.	.25
☐	103	George Brett, K.C.	3.50
☐	104	Jose DeJesus, K.C.	.25
☐	105	Luis de los Santos, K.C.	.25
☐	106	Jim Eisenreich, K.C.	.25
☐	107	Steve Farr, K.C.	.25
☐	108	Tom Gordon, K.C.	.25
☐	109	Mark Gubicza, K.C.	.25
☐	110	Bo Jackson, K.C.	.50
☐	111	Terry Leach, K.C.	.25
☐	112	Charlie Leibrandt, K.C.	.25
☐	113	Rick Luecken, K.C.	.25
☐	114	Mike Macfarlane, K.C.	.25
☐	115	Jeff Montgomery, K.C.	.25
☐	116	Bret Saberhagen, K.C.	.25
☐	117	Kevin Seitzer, K.C.	.25
☐	118	Kurt Stillwell, K.C.	.25
☐	119	Pat Tabler, K.C.	.25
☐	120	Danny Tartabull, K.C.	.25
☐	121	Gary Thurman, K.C.	.25
☐	122	Frank White, K.C.	.25
☐	123	Willie Wilson, K.C.	.25
☐	124	Matt Winters, K.C.	.25
☐	125	Jim Abbott, Cal.	.25
☐	126	Tony Armas, Cal.	.25
☐	127	Dante Bichette, Cal.	.25
☐	128	Bert Blyleven, Cal.	.25
☐	129	Chili Davis, Cal.	.25
☐	130	Brian Downing, Cal.	.25
☐	131	Mike Fetters, Cal.	.25
☐	132	Chuck Finley, Cal.	.25
☐	133	Willie Fraser, Cal.	.25
☐	134	Bryan Harvey, Cal.	.25
☐	135	Jack Howell, Cal.	.25
☐	136	Wally Joyner, Cal.	.25
☐	**137**	**Jeff Manto, Cal., RC**	**.25**
☐	138	Kirk McCaskill, Cal.	.75
☐	139	Bob McClure, Cal.	.25
☐	140	Greg Minton, Cal.	.25
☐	141	Lance Parrish, Cal.	.25
☐	142	Dan Petry, Cal.	.25
☐	143	Johnny Ray, Cal.	.25
☐	144	Dick Schofield, Cal.	.25
☐	**145**	**Lee Stevens, Cal., RC**	**.50**
☐	146	Claudell Washington, Cal.	.25
☐	147	Devon White, Cal.	.25
☐	148	Mike Witt, Cal.	.25
☐	149	Roberto Alomar, S.D.	1.50
☐	150	Sandy Alomar, Jr., S.D.	.25
☐	151	Andy Benes, S.D.	.25
☐	152	Jack Clark, S.D.	.25
☐	153	Pat Clements, S.D.	.25
☐	154	Joey Cora, S.D.	.25
☐	155	Mark Davis, S.D.	.25
☐	156	Mark Grant, S.D.	.25
☐	157	Tony Gwynn, S.D.	3.50
☐	158	Greg Harris, S.D.	.25
☐	159	Bruce Hurst, S.D.	.25
☐	160	Darrin Jackson, S.D.	.25
☐	161	Chris James, S.D.	.25
☐	162	Carmelo Martinez, S.D.	.25
☐	163	Mike Pagliarulo, S.D.	.25
☐	164	Mark Parent, S.D.	.25
☐	165	Dennis Rasmussen, S.D.	.25
☐	166	Bip Roberts, S.D.	.25
☐	167	Benito Santiago, S.D.	.25
☐	168	Calvin Schiraldi, S.D.	.25
☐	169	Eric Show, S.D.	.25
☐	170	Garry Templeton, S.D.	.25
☐	171	Ed Whitson, S.D.	.25
☐	172	Brady Anderson, Bal.	.25
☐	173	Jeff Ballard, Bal.	.25
☐	174	Phil Bradley, Bal.	.25
☐	175	Mike Devereaux, Bal.	.25
☐	176	Steve Finley, Bal.	.25
☐	177	Pete Harnisch, Bal.	.25
☐	178	Kevin Hickey, Bal.	.25
☐	179	Brian Holton, Bal.	.25
☐	**180**	**Ben McDonald, Bal., RC**	**.25**
☐	181	Bob Melvin, Bal.	.25
☐	182	Bob Milacki, Bal.	.25
☐	183	Randy Milligan, Bal.	.25
☐	**184**	**Gregg Olson, Bal., RC**	**.50**
☐	185	Joe Orsulak, Bal.	.25
☐	186	Bill Ripken, Bal.	.25
☐	187	Cal Ripken, Jr., Bal.	6.50
☐	188	Dave Schmidt, Bal.	.25
☐	189	Larry Sheets, Bal.	.25
☐	190	Mickey Tettleton, Bal.	.25
☐	191	Mark Thurmond, Bal.	.25
☐	192	Jay Tibbs, Bal.	.25
☐	193	Jim Traber, Bal.	.25
☐	194	Mark Williamson, Bal.	.25
☐	195	Craig Worthington, Bal.	.25
☐	196	Dan Aase, NYM.	.25
☐	197	Blaine Beatty, NYM.	.25
☐	198	Mark Carreon, NYM.	.25
☐	199	Gary Carter, NYM.	1.00
☐	200	David Cone, NYM.	.25
☐	201	Ron Darling, NYM.	.25
☐	202	Kevin Elster, NYM.	.25
☐	203	Sid Fernandez, NYM.	.25
☐	204	Dwight Gooden, NYM.	.25
☐	205	Keith Hernandez, NYM.	.25
☐	**206**	**Jeff Innis, NYM., RC**	**.25**
☐	207	Gregg Jefferies, NYM.	.25
☐	208	Howard Johnson, NYM.	.25
☐	209	Barry Lyons, NYM.	.25
☐	210	Dave Magadan, NYM.	.25
☐	211	Kevin McReynolds, NYM.	.25
☐	212	Jeff Musselman, NYM.	.25
☐	213	Randy Myers, NYM.	.25
☐	214	Bob Ojeda, NYM.	.25
☐	215	Juan Samuel, NYM.	.25
☐	216	Mackey Sasser, NYM.	.25

	No.	Player	Price
☐	217	Darryl Strawberry, NYM.	.75
☐	218	Tim Teufel, NYM.	.25
☐	219	Frank Viola, NYM.	.25
☐	220	Juan Agosto, Hou.	.25
☐	221	Larry Andersen, Hou.	.25
☐	**222**	**Eric Anthony, Hou., RC**	**.25**
☐	223	Kevin Bass, Hou.	.25
☐	224	Craig Biggio, Hou.	.25
☐	225	Ken Caminiti, Hou.	.75
☐	226	Jim Clancy, Hou.	.25
☐	227	Danny Darwin, Hou.	.25
☐	228	Glenn Davis, Hou.	.25
☐	229	Jim Deshaies, Hou.	.25
☐	230	Bill Doran, Hou.	.25
☐	231	Bob Forsch, Hou.	.25
☐	232	Brian Meyer, Hou.	.25
☐	233	Terry Puhl, Hou.	.50
☐	234	Rafael Ramirez, Hou.	.25
☐	235	Rick Rhoden, Hou.	.25
☐	236	Dan Schatzeder, Hou.	.25
☐	237	Mike Scott, Hou.	.25
☐	238	Dave Smith, Hou.	.25
☐	239	Alex Trevino, Hou.	.25
☐	240	Glenn Wilson, Hou.	.25
☐	241	Gerald Young, Hou.	.25
☐	242	Tom Brunansky, Stl.	.25
☐	243	Chris Carpenter, Stl.	.25
☐	**244**	**Alex Cole, Stl., RC**	**.25**
☐	245	Vince Coleman, Stl.	.25
☐	246	John Costello, Stl.	.25
☐	247	Ken Dayley, Stl.	.25
☐	248	Jose DeLeon, Stl.	.25
☐	249	Frank DiPino, Stl.	.25
☐	250	Pedro Guerrero, Stl.	.25
☐	251	Ken Hill, Stl.	.25
☐	252	Joe Magrane, Stl.	.25
☐	253	Willie McGee, Stl.	.25
☐	254	John Morris, Stl.	.25
☐	255	Jose Oquendo, Stl.	.25
☐	256	Tony Pena, Stl.	.25
☐	257	Terry Pendleton, Stl.	.25
☐	258	Ted Power, Stl.	.25
☐	259	Dan Quisenberry, Stl.	.25
☐	260	Ozzie Smith, Stl.	2.00
☐	261	Scott Terry, Stl.	.25
☐	262	Milt Thompson, Stl.	.25
☐	263	Denny Walling, Stl.	.25
☐	264	Todd Worrell, Stl.	.25
☐	265	Todd Zeile, Stl.	.25
☐	266	Marty Barrett, Bos.	.25
☐	267	Mike Boddicker, Bos.	.25
☐	268	Wade Boggs, Bos.	.75
☐	269	Ellis Burks, Bos.	.50
☐	270	Rick Cerone, Bos.	.25
☐	271	Roger Clemens, Bos.	4.00
☐	272	John Dopson, Bos.	.25
☐	273	Nick Esasky, Bos.	.25
☐	274	Dwight Evans, Bos.	.25
☐	275	Wes Gardner, Bos.	.25
☐	276	Rich Gedman, Bos.	.25
☐	277	Mike Greenwell, Bos.	.25
☐	278	Danny Heep, Bos.	.25
☐	279	Eric Hetzel, Bos.	.25
☐	280	Dennis Lamp, Bos.	.25
☐	281	Rob Murphy, Bos.	.25
☐	282	Joe Price, Bos.	.25
☐	283	Carlos Quintana, Bos.	.25
☐	284	Jody Reed, Bos.	.25
☐	285	Luis Rivera, Bos.	.25
☐	286	Kevin Romine, Bos.	.25
☐	287	Lee Smith, Bos.	.25
☐	288	Mike Smithson, Bos.	.25
☐	289	Bob Stanley, Bos.	.25
☐	290	Harold Baines, Tex.	.25
☐	291	Kevin Brown, Tex.	.25
☐	292	Steve Buechele, Tex.	.25
☐	**293**	**Scott Coolbaugh, Tex., RC**	**.25**
☐	294	Jack Daugherty, Tex.	.25
☐	295	Cecil Espy, Tex.	.25
☐	296	Julio Franco, Tex.	.25
☐	**297**	**Juan Gonzalez, Tex., RC**	**5.00**
☐	298	Cecilio Guante, Tex.	.25
☐	299	Drew Hall, Tex.	.25
☐	300	Charlie Hough, Tex.	.25
☐	301	Pete Incaviglia, Tex.	.25
☐	302	Mike Jeffcoat, Tex.	.25
☐	303	Chad Kreuter, Tex.	.25
☐	304	Jeff Kunkel, Tex.	.25
☐	305	Rick Leach, Tex.	.25
☐	306	Fred Manrique, Tex.	.25
☐	307	Jamie Moyer, Tex.	.25
☐	308	Rafael Palmeiro, Tex.	.50
☐	309	Geno Petralli, Tex.	.25
☐	310	Kevin Reimer, Tex.	.50
☐	**311**	**Kenny Rogers, Tex., RC**	**.25**
☐	312	Jeff Russell, Tex.	.25
☐	313	Nolan Ryan, Tex.	6.50
☐	314	Ruben Sierra, Tex.	.25
☐	315	Bobby Witt, Tex.	.25
☐	316	Chris Bosio, Mil.	.25
☐	317	Glenn Braggs, Mil.	.25
☐	318	Greg Brock, Mil.	.25
☐	319	Chuck Crim, Mil.	.25
☐	320	Rob Deer, Mil.	.25
☐	321	Mike Felder, Mil.	.25
☐	322	Tom Filer, Mil.	.25
☐	323	Tony Fossas, Mil.	.25
☐	324	Jim Gantner, Mil.	.25
☐	325	Darryl Hamilton, Mil.	.25
☐	326	Ted Higuera, Mil.	.25
☐	327	Mark Knudson, Mil.	.25
☐	328	Bill Krueger, Mil.	.25
☐	329	Tim McIntosh, Mil.	.25
☐	330	Paul Molitor, Mil.	.75
☐	331	Jaime Navarro, Mil.	.25
☐	332	Charlie O'Brien, Mil.	.25
☐	333	Jeff Peterek, Mil.	.25
☐	334	Dan Plesac, Mil.	.25
☐	335	Jerry Reuss, Mil.	.25
☐	336	Gary Sheffield, Mil.	.50
☐	337	Bill Spiers, Mil.	.25
☐	338	B.J. Surhoff, Mil.	.25
☐	**339**	**Greg Vaughn, Mil., RC**	**1.00**
☐	340	Robin Yount, Mil.	.75
☐	341	Hubie Brooks, Mtl.	.25
☐	342	Tim Burke, Mtl.	.25
☐	343	Mike Fitzgerald, Mtl.	.25
☐	344	Tom Foley, Mtl.	.25
☐	345	Andres Galarraga, Mtl.	1.50
☐	346	Damaso Garcia, Mtl.	.25
☐	**347**	**Marquis Grissom, Mtl., RC**	**1.50**
☐	348	Kevin Gross, Mtl.	.25
☐	349	Joe Hesketh, Mtl.	.25
☐	350	Jeff Huson, Mtl.	.25
☐	351	Wallace Johnson, Mtl.	.25
☐	352	Mark Langston, Mtl.	.25
☐	353	Dave Martinez, Mtl.	.25
☐	354	Dennis Martinez, Mtl.	.25

	No.	Player	Price
☐	355	Andy McGaffigan, Mtl.	.25
☐	356	Otis Nixon, Mtl.	.25
☐	357	Spike Owen, Mtl.	.25
☐	358	Pascual Perez, Mtl.	.25
☐	359	Tim Raines, Mtl.	.25
☐	360	Nelson Santovenia, Mtl.	.25
☐	361	Bryn Smith, Mtl.	.25
☐	362	Zane Smith, Mtl.	.25
☐	**363**	**Larry Walker, Mtl., RC**	**3.50**
☐	364	Tim Wallach, Mtl.	.25
☐	365	Rick Aguilera, Min.	.25
☐	366	Allan Anderson, Min.	.25
☐	367	Wally Backman, Min.	.25
☐	368	Doug Baker, Min.	.25
☐	369	Juan Berenguer, Min.	.25
☐	370	Randy Bush, Min.	.25
☐	371	Carmen Castillo, Min.	.25
☐	372	Mike Dyer, Min.	.25
☐	373	Gary Gaetti, Min.	.25
☐	374	Greg Gagne, Min.	.25
☐	375	Dan Gladden, Min.	.25
☐	376	German Gonzalez, Min.	.25
☐	377	Brian Harper, Min.	.25
☐	378	Kent Hrbek, Min.	.25
☐	379	Gene Larkin, Min.	.25
☐	380	Tim Laudner, Min.	.25
☐	381	John Moses, Min.	.25
☐	382	Al Newman, Min.	.25
☐	383	Kirby Puckett, Min.	3.50
☐	384	Shane Rawley, Min.	.25
☐	385	Jeff Reardon, Min.	.25
☐	386	Roy Smith, Min.	.25
☐	387	Gary Wayne, Min.	.25
☐	388	Dave West, Min.	.25
☐	389	Tim Belcher, L.A.	.25
☐	390	Tim Crews, L.A.	.25
☐	391	Mike Davis, L.A.	.25
☐	392	Rick Dempsey, L.A.	.25
☐	393	Kirk Gibson, L.A.	.25
☐	394	Jose Gonzalez, L.A.	.25
☐	395	Alfredo Griffin, L.A.	.25
☐	396	Jeff Hamilton, L.A.	.25
☐	397	Lenny Harris, L.A.	.25
☐	398	Mickey Hatcher, L.A.	.25
☐	399	Orel Hershiser, L.A.	.25
☐	400	Jay Howell, L.A.	.25
☐	401	Mike Marshall, L.A.	.25
☐	402	Ramon Martinez, L.A.	.25
☐	403	Mike Morgan, L.A.	.25
☐	404	Eddie Murray, L.A.	.75
☐	405	Alejandro Pena, L.A.	.25
☐	406	Willie Randolph, L.A.	.25
☐	407	Mike Scioscia, L.A.	.25
☐	408	Ray Searage, L.A.	.25
☐	409	Fernando Valenzuela, L.A.	.25
☐	410	Jose Vizcaino, L.A.	.25
☐	**411**	**John Wetteland, L.A., RC**	**1.00**
☐	412	Jack Armstrong, Cin.	.25
☐	413	Todd Benzinger, Cin.	.25
☐	414	Tim Birtsas, Cin.	.25
☐	415	Tom Browning, Cin.	.25
☐	416	Norm Charlton, Cin.	.25
☐	417	Eric Davis, Cin.	.25
☐	418	Rob Dibble, Cin.	.25
☐	419	John Franco, Cin.	.25
☐	420	Ken Griffey, Cin.	.25
☐	**421**	**Chris Hammond, Cin., RC**	**.25**
☐	422	Danny Jackson, Cin.	.25
☐	423	Barry Larkin, Cin.	.50
☐	424	Tim Leary, Cin.	.25
☐	425	Rick Mahler, Cin.	.25
☐	426	Joe Oliver, Cin.	.25
☐	427	Paul O'Neill, Cin.	.25
☐	428	Luis Quinones, Cin.	.25
☐	429	Jeff Reed, Cin.	.25
☐	430	Jose Rijo, Cin.	.25
☐	431	Ron Robinson, Cin.	3.00
☐	432	Rolando Roomes, Cin.	.25
☐	433	Chris Sabo, Cin.	.25
☐	434	Scott Scudder, Cin.	.25
☐	435	Herm Winningham, Cin.	.25
☐	436	Steve Balboni, NYY.	.25
☐	437	Jesse Barfield, NYY.	.25
☐	438	Mike Blowers, NYY.	.25
☐	439	Tom Brookens, NYY.	.25
☐	440	Greg Cadaret, NYY.	.25
☐	441	Alvaro Espinoza, NYY.	.25
☐	442	Bob Geren, NYY.	.25
☐	443	Lee Guetterman, NYY.	.25
☐	444	Mel Hall, NYY.	.25
☐	445	Andy Hawkins, NYY.	.25
☐	446	Roberto Kelly, NYY.	.25
☐	447	Don Mattingly, NYY.	3.50
☐	448	Lance McCullers, NYY.	.25
☐	449	Hensley Meulens, NYY.	.25
☐	450	Dale Mohorcic, NYY.	.25
☐	451	Clay Parker, NYY.	.25
☐	452	Eric Plunk, NYY.	.25
☐	453	Dave Righetti, NYY.	.25
☐	**454**	**Deion Sanders, NYY., RC**	**1.00**
☐	455	Steve Sax, NYY.	.25
☐	456	Don Slaught, NYY.	.25
☐	457	Walt Terrell, NYY.	.25
☐	458	Dave Winfield, NYY.	1.00
☐	459	Jay Bell, Pgh.	.25
☐	460	Rafael Belliard, Pgh.	.25
☐	461	Barry Bonds, Pgh.	3.00
☐	462	Bobby Bonilla, Pgh.	.25
☐	463	Sid Bream, Pgh.	.25
☐	464	Benny Distefano, Pgh.	.25
☐	465	Doug Drabek, Pgh.	.25
☐	466	Jim Gott, Pgh.	.25
☐	467	Billy Hatcher, Pgh.	.25
☐	468	Neal Heaton, Pgh.	.25
☐	469	Jeff King, Pgh.	.25
☐	470	Bob Kipper, Pgh.	.25
☐	471	Randy Kramer, Pgh.	.25
☐	472	Bill Landrum, Pgh.	.25
☐	473	Mike Lavalliere, Pgh.	.25
☐	474	Jose Lind, Pgh.	.25
☐	475	Junior Ortiz, Pgh.	.25
☐	476	Gary Redus, Pgh.	.25
☐	477	Rick Reed, Pgh.	.25
☐	478	R.J. Reynolds, Pgh.	.25
☐	479	Jeff Robinson, Pgh.	.25
☐	480	John Smiley, Pgh.	.25
☐	481	Andy Van Slyke, Pgh.	.25
☐	482	Bob Walk, Pgh.	.25
☐	483	Andy Allanson, Cle.	.25
☐	484	Scott Bailes, Cle.	.25
☐	**485**	**Albert Belle, Cle., RC**	**2.00**
☐	486	Bud Black, Cle.	.25
☐	487	Jerry Browne, Cle.	.25
☐	488	Tom Candiotti, Cle.	.25
☐	489	Joe Carter, Cle.	.75
☐	490	Dave Clark, Cle.	.25
☐	491	John Farrell, Cle.	.25
☐	492	Felix Fermin, Cle.	.25

- ☐ 493 Brook Jacoby, Cle. .25
- ☐ 494 Dion James, Cle. .25
- ☐ 495 Doug Jones, Cle. .25
- ☐ 497 Rod Nichols, Cle. .25
- ☐ 498 Pete O'Brien, Cle. .25
- ☐ **499 Steve Olin, Cle., RC .25**
- ☐ 500 Jesse Orosco, Cle. .25
- ☐ 501 Joel Skinner, Cle. .25
- ☐ 502 Cory Snyder, Cle. .25
- ☐ 503 Greg Swindell, Cle. .25
- ☐ 504 Rich Yett, Cle. .25
- ☐ 505 Scott Bankhead, Sea. .25
- ☐ 506 Scott Bradley, Sea. .25
- ☐ 507 Greg Briley, Sea. .25
- ☐ 508 Jay Buhner, Sea. .25
- ☐ 509 Darnell Coles, Sea. .25
- ☐ 510 Keith Comstock, Sea. .25
- ☐ 511 Henry Cotto, Sea. .25
- ☐ 512 Alvin Davis, Sea. .25
- ☐ 513 Ken Griffey, Jr., Sea. 10.00
- ☐ 514 Erik Hanson, Sea. .25
- ☐ 515 Gene Harris, Sea. .25
- ☐ 516 Brian Holman, Sea. .25
- ☐ 517 Mike Jackson, Sea. .25
- ☐ 518 Randy Johnson, Sea. .75
- ☐ 519 Jeffrey Leonard, Sea. .25
- ☐ 520 Edgar Martinez, Sea. .25
- ☐ 521 Dennis Powell, Sea. .25
- ☐ 522 Jim Presley, Sea. .25
- ☐ 523 Jerry Reed, Sea. .25
- ☐ 524 Harold Reynolds, Sea. .25
- ☐ 525 Mike Schooler, Sea. .25
- ☐ 526 Bill Swift, Sea. .25
- ☐ 527 David Valle, Sea. .25
- ☐ 528 Omar Vizquel, Sea. .25
- ☐ 529 Ivan Calderon, Chi.-A.L. .25
- ☐ 530 Carlton Fisk, Chi.-A.L. .75
- ☐ 531 Scott Fletcher, Chi.-A.L. .25
- ☐ 532 Dave Gallagher, Chi.-A.L. .25
- ☐ 533 Ozzie Guillen, Chi.-A.L. .25
- ☐ 534 Greg Hibbard, Chi.-A.L. .25
- ☐ 535 Shawn Hillegas, Chi.-A.L. .25
- ☐ 536 Lance Johnson, Chi.-A.L. .25
- ☐ 537 Eric King, Chi.-A.L. .25
- ☐ 538 Ron Kittle, Chi.-A.L. .25
- ☐ 539 Steve Lyons, Chi.-A.L. .25
- ☐ **540 Carlos Martinez, Chi.-A.L., RC .25**
- ☐ 541 Tom McCarthy, Chi.-A.L. .25
- ☐ 542 Matt Merullo, Chi.-A.L. .25
- ☐ 543 Donn Pall, Chi.-A.L. .25
- ☐ 544 Dan Pasqua, Chi.-A.L. .25
- ☐ 545 Ken Patterson, Chi.-A.L. .25
- ☐ 546 Melido Perez, Chi.-A.L. .25
- ☐ 547 Steve Rosenberg, Chi.-A.L. .25
- ☐ 548 Sammy Sosa, Chi.-A.L. 3.50
- ☐ 549 Bobby Thigpen, Chi.-A.L. .25
- ☐ 550 Robin Ventura, Chi.-A.L. .50
- ☐ 551 Greg Walker, Chi.-A.L. .25
- ☐ 552 Don Carman, Pha. .25
- ☐ 553 Pat Combs, Pha. .25
- ☐ 554 Dennis Cook, Pha. .25
- ☐ 555 Darren Daulton, Pha. .25
- ☐ 556 Lenny Dykstra, Pha. .25
- ☐ 557 Curt Ford, Pha. .25
- ☐ 558 Charlie Hayes, Pha. .25
- ☐ 559 Von Hayes, Pha. .25
- ☐ 560 Tom Herr, Pha. .25
- ☐ 561 Ken Howell, Pha. .25
- ☐ 562 Steve Jeltz, Pha. .25
- ☐ 563 Ron Jones, Pha. .25
- ☐ 564 Ricky Jordan, Pha. .25
- ☐ 565 John Kruk, Pha. .25
- ☐ 566 Steve Lake, Pha. .25
- ☐ 567 Roger McDowell, Pha. .25
- ☐ 568 Terry Mulholland, Pha. .25
- ☐ 569 Dwayne Murphy, Pha. .25
- ☐ 570 Jeff Parrett, Pha. .25
- ☐ 571 Randy Ready, Pha. .25
- ☐ 572 Bruce Ruffin, Pha. .25
- ☐ 573 Dickie Thon, Pha. .25
- ☐ 574 Jose Alvarez, Atl. .25
- ☐ 575 Geronimo Berroa, Atl. .25
- ☐ 576 Jeff Blauser, Atl. .25
- ☐ 577 Joe Boever, Atl. .25
- ☐ 578 Martin Clary, Atl. .25
- ☐ 579 Jody Davis, Atl. .25
- ☐ 580 Mark Eichhorn, Atl. .25
- ☐ 581 Darrell Evans, Atl. .25
- ☐ 582 Ron Gant, Atl. .25
- ☐ 583 Tom Glavine, Atl. .75
- ☐ **584 Tommy Greene, Atl., RC .25**
- ☐ 585 Tommy Gregg, Atl. .25
- ☐ **586 David Justice, Atl., RC 2.00**
- ☐ 587 Mark Lemke, Atl. .25
- ☐ 588 Derek Lilliquist, Atl. .25
- ☐ 589 Oddibe McDowell, Atl. .25
- ☐ **590 Kent Mercker, Atl., RC .25**
- ☐ 591 Dale Murphy, Atl. .75
- ☐ 592 Gerald Perry, Atl. .25
- ☐ 593 Lonnie Smith, Atl. .25
- ☐ 594 Pete Smith, Atl. .25
- ☐ 595 John Smoltz, Atl. .25
- ☐ 596 Mike Stanton, Atl. .25
- ☐ 597 Andres Thomas, Atl. .25
- ☐ 598 Jeff Treadway, Atl. .25
- ☐ 599 Doyle Alexander, Det. .25
- ☐ 600 Dave Bergman, Det. .25
- ☐ 601 Brian Dubois, Det. .25
- ☐ 602 Paul Gibson, Det. .25
- ☐ 603 Mike Heath, Det. .25
- ☐ 604 Mike Henneman, Det. .25
- ☐ 605 Guillermo Hernandez, Det. .25
- ☐ 606 Shawn Holman, Det. .25
- ☐ 607 Tracy Jones, Det. .25
- ☐ 608 Chet Lemon, Det. .25
- ☐ 609 Fred Lynn, Det. .25
- ☐ 610 Jack Morris, Det. .25
- ☐ 611 Matt Nokes, Det. .25
- ☐ 612 Gary Pettis, Det. .25
- ☐ 613 Kevin Ritz, Det. .25
- ☐ 614 Jeff Robinson, Det. .25
- ☐ 615 Steve Searcy, Det. .25
- ☐ 616 Frank Tanana, Det. .25
- ☐ 617 Alan Trammell, Det. .25
- ☐ 618 Gary Ward, Det. .25
- ☐ 619 Lou Whitaker, Det. .25
- ☐ 620 Frank Williams, Det. .25
- ☐ 621 George Brett, K.C. 2.00
- ☐ 622 Fernando Valenzuela, L.A. .25
- ☐ 623 Dale Murphy, Atl. .50
- ☐ 624 Cal Ripken, Jr., Bal. 3.50
- ☐ 625 Ryne Sandberg, Chi.-N.L. 1.00
- ☐ 626 Don Mattingly, NYY. 2.00
- ☐ 627 Roger Clemens, Bos. 2.00
- ☐ 628 George Bell, Tor. .25
- ☐ 629 Jose Canseco, Oak. .50
- ☐ 630 Will Clark, S.F. .50
- ☐ 631 Mark Davis, S.F./ Mitch Williams, Chi.-N.L. .25

	No.	Player	Price
☐	632	Wade Boggs, Bos./ Mike Greenwell, Bos.	.50
☐	633	Mark Gubicza, K.C./ Jeff Russell, Tex.	.25
☐	634	Tony Fernandez, Tor./ Cal Ripken, Jr., Bal.	3.50
☐	635	Kirby Puckett, Min./ Bo Jackson, K.C.	2.00
☐	636	Nolan Ryan, Tex./ Mike Scott, Hou.	3.50
☐	637	Will Clark, S.F./ Kevin Mitchell, S.F.	.50
☐	638	Don Mattingly, NYY./ Mark McGwire, Oak.	2.50
☐	639	Howard Johnson, NYM./ Ryne Sandberg, Chi.-N.L.	1.00
☐	**640**	**Rudy Seanez, Cle., RC/ Colin Charland, Cal., RC**	**.25**
☐	**641**	**George Canale, Mil., RC/ Kevin Maas, NYY., RC**	**.25**
☐	**642**	**Kelly Mann, Atl., RC/ Dave Hansen, L.A., RC**	**.25**
☐	**643**	**Greg Smith, Chi.-N.L., RC/ Stu Tate, S.F., RC**	**.25**
☐	**644**	**Tom Drees, Chi.-A.L. RC/ Dann Howitt, Oak., RC**	**.25**
☐	**645**	**Mike Roesler, Cin, RC/ Derrick May, Chi.-N.L., RC**	**.25**
☐	**646**	**Scott Hemond, Oak. RC/ Mark Gardner, Mtl., RC**	**.25**
☐	**647**	**John Orton, Cal., RC/ Scott Leius, Min., RC**	**.25**
☐	**648**	**Rich Monteleone, Cal., RC/ Dana Williams, Bos., RC**	**.25**
☐	**649**	**Mike Huff, L.A., RC/ Steve Frey, Mtl., RC**	**.25**
☐	**650**	**Chuck McElroy, Pha., RC/ Moises Alou, Pgh., RC**	**1.50**
☐	**651**	**Bobby Rose, Cal., RC/ Mike Hartley, L.A., RC**	**.25**
☐	**652**	**Matt Kinzer, Stl.., RC/ Wayne Edwards, Chi.-A.L., RC**	**.25**
☐	**653**	**Delino Deshields, Mtl./ Jason Grimsley, Pha., RC**	**.25**
☐	654	Checklist 1 (1-99)	.25
☐	655	Checklist 2 (100-195)	.25
☐	656	Checklist 3 (196-289)	.25
☐	657	Checklist 4 (290-388)	.25
☐	658	Checklist 5 (389-482)	.25
☐	659	Checklist 6 (483-573)	.25
☐	660	Checklist 7 (574-660)	.25

1990 O-PEE-CHEE

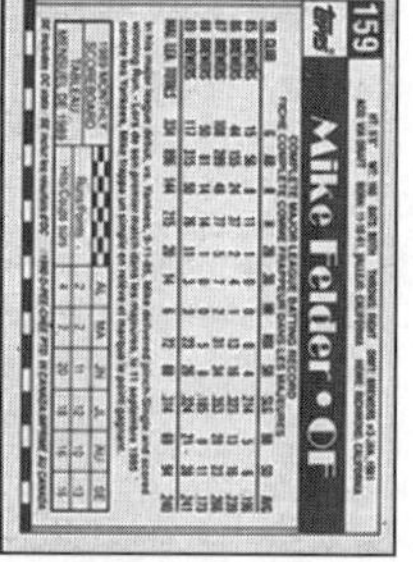

Card Size: 2 1/2" x 3 1/2"
Face: Four colour, white border; name, team, Topps logo
Back: Yellow and black on card stock; name, number, position, résumé, bilingual
Imprint: © 1990 O-PEE-CHEE
Complete Set (792 cards): **20.00**
Common Player: **.15**

	No.	Player	MINT
☐	1	Nolan Ryan, Tex.	1.25
☐	2	Nolan Ryan, NYM.	.50
☐	3	Nolan Ryan, Cal.	.50
☐	4	Nolan Ryan, Hou.	.50
☐	5	Nolan Ryan, Tex.	.50
☐	6	Vince Coleman, Stl.	.15
☐	7	Rickey Henderson, Cle.	.25
☐	8	Cal Ripken, Bal.	.75
☐	9	Eric Plunk, NYY.	.15
☐	10	Barry Larkin, Cin.	.25
☐	11	Paul Gibson, Det.	.15
☐	12	Joe Girardi, Chi.-N.L.	.15
☐	13	Mark Williamson, Bal.	.15
☐	14	Mike Fetters, Cal.	.15
☐	15	Teddy Higuera, Mil.	.15
☐	**16**	**Kent Anderson, Cal., RC**	**.15**
☐	17	Kelly Downs, S.F.	.15
☐	18	Carlos Quintana, Bos.	.15
☐	19	Al Newman, Min.	.15
☐	20	Mark Gubicza, K.C.	.15
☐	21	Jeff Torborg, Mgr., Chi.-A.L.	.15
☐	22	Bruce Ruffin, Pha.	.15
☐	23	Randy Velarde, NYY.	.15
☐	24	Joe Hesketh, Mtl.	.15
☐	25	Willie Randolph, L.A.	.15
☐	26	Don Slaught, NYY. (Pgh.)	.15
☐	27	Rick Leach, Tex.	.15
☐	28	Duane Ward, Tor.	.15
☐	29	John Cangelosi, Pgh.	.15
☐	30	David Cone, NYM.	.15
☐	31	Henry Cotto, Sea.	.15
☐	32	John Farrell, Cle.	.15
☐	33	Greg Walker, Chi.-A.L.	.15
☐	34	Tony Fossas, Mil.	.15
☐	35	Benny Santiago, S.D.	.15
☐	36	John Costello, Stl.	.15
☐	37	Domingo Ramos, Chi.-N.L.	.15
☐	38	Wes Gardner, Bos.	.15
☐	39	Curt Ford, Pha.	.15
☐	40	Jay Howell, L.A.	.15
☐	41	Matt Williams, S.F.	.25
☐	42	Jeff Robinson, Det.	.15
☐	43	Dante Bichette, Cal.	.15
☐	**44**	**Roger Salkeld, Sea., RC**	**.15**
☐	45	Dave Parker, Oak	.15
☐	46	Rob Dibble, Cin.	.15
☐	47	Brian Harper, Min.	.15
☐	48	Zane Smith, Mtl.	.15
☐	49	Tom Lawless, Tor.	.15
☐	50	Glenn Davis, Hou.	.15
☐	51	Doug Rader, Mgr., Cal.	.15
☐	52	Jack Daugherty, Tex.	.15
☐	53	Mike LaCoss, S.F.	.15
☐	54	Joel Skinner, Cle.	.15
☐	55	Darrell Evans, Atl.	.15
☐	56	Franklin Stubbs, L.A.	.15
☐	**57**	**Greg Vaughn, Mil., RC**	**.35**
☐	58	Keith Miller, NYM.	.15
☐	59	Ted Power, Stl. (Pgh.)	.15
☐	60	George Brett, K.C.	.50
☐	**61**	**Deion Sanders, NYY., RC**	**.35**
☐	62	Ramon Martinez, L.A.	.15
☐	63	Mike Pagliarulo, S.D.	.15
☐	64	Danny Darwin, Hou.	.15
☐	65	Devon White, Cal.	.15
☐	**66**	**Greg Litton, S.F., RC**	**.15**
☐	67	Scott Sanderson, Chi.-N.L. (Oak.)	.15
☐	68	Dave Henderson, Oak.	.15
☐	69	Todd Frohwirth, Pha.	.15
☐	70	Mike Greenwell, Bos.	.15
☐	71	Allan Anderson, Min.	.15
☐	72	Jeff Huson, Mtl.	.15
☐	73	Bob Milacki, Bal.	.15
☐	74	#1 Draft Pick: Jeff Jackson, Pha.	.15
☐	75	Doug Jones, Cle.	.15
☐	76	Dave Valle, Sea.	.15
☐	77	Dave Bergman, Det.	.15
☐	78	Mike Flanagan, Tor.	.15
☐	79	Ron Kittle, Chi.-A.L.	.15
☐	80	Jeff Russell, Tex.	.15
☐	81	Bob Rodgers, Mgr., Mtl.	.15
☐	82	Scott Terry, Stl.	.15
☐	83	Hensley Meulens, NYY.	.15

	No.	Player	Price
☐	84	Ray Searage, L.A.	.15
☐	85	Juan Samuel, NYM. (L.A.)	.15
☐	86	Paul Kilgus, Chi.-N.L. (Tor.)	.15
☐	**87**	**Rick Luecken, K.C., (Atl.), RC**	**.15**
☐	88	Glenn Braggs, Mil.	.15
☐	**89**	**Clint Zavaras, Sea., RC**	**.15**
☐	90	Jack Clark, S.D.	.15
☐	91	Steve Frey, Mtl.	.15
☐	92	Mike Stanley, Tex.	.15
☐	93	Shawn Hillegas, Chi.-A.L.	.15
☐	94	Herm Winningham, Cin.	.15
☐	95	Todd Worrell, Stl.	.15
☐	96	Jody Reed, Bos.	.15
☐	97	Curt Schilling, Bal.	.15
☐	**98**	**Jose Gonzalez, L.A., RC**	**.15**
☐	**99**	**Rich Monteleone, Cal., RC**	**.15**
☐	100	Will Clark, S.F.	.25
☐	101	Shane Rawley, Min. (Bos.)	.15
☐	102	Stan Javier, Oak.	.15
☐	103	Marvin Freeman, Pha.	.15
☐	104	Bob Knepper, S.F.	.15
☐	105	Randy Myers, NYM. (Cin.)	.15
☐	106	Charlie O'Brien, Mil.	.15
☐	107	Fred Lynn, Det., (S.D.)	.15
☐	108	Rod Nichols, Cle.	.15
☐	109	Roberto Kelly, NYY.	.15
☐	110	Tommy Helms, Mgr., Cin.	.15
☐	**111**	**Ed Whited, Atl., RC**	**.15**
☐	112	Glenn Wilson, Hou.	.15
☐	113	Manny Lee, Tor.	.15
☐	114	Mike Bielecki, Chi.-N.L.	.15
☐	115	Tony Pena, Stl., (Bos.)	.15
☐	116	Floyd Bannister, K.C.	.15
☐	117	Mike Sharperson, L.A.	.15
☐	118	Erik Hanson, Sea.	.15
☐	119	Billy Hatcher, Pgh.	.15
☐	120	John Franco, Cin. (NYM.)	.15
☐	121	Robin Ventura, Chi.-A.L.	.25
☐	122	Shawn Abner, S.D.	.15
☐	123	Rich Gedman, Bos.	.15
☐	124	Dave Dravecky, S.F.	.15
☐	125	Kent Hrbek, Min.	.15
☐	126	Randy Kramer, Pgh.	.15
☐	127	Mike Devereaux, Bal.	.15
☐	128	Checklist 1 of 6	.15
☐	129	Ron Jones, Pha.	.15
☐	130	Bert Blyleven, Cal.	.15
☐	131	Matt Nokes, Det.	.15
☐	132	Lance Blankenship, Oak.	.15
☐	133	Ricky Horton, Stl.	.15
☐	**134**	**DP: Earl Cunningham, Chi.-N.L., RC**	**.15**
☐	135	Dave Magadan, NYM.	.15
☐	136	Kevin Brown, Tex.	.15
☐	**137**	**Marty Pevey, Mtl., RC**	**.15**
☐	138	Al Leiter, Tor.	.15
☐	139	Greg Brock, Mil.	.15
☐	140	Andre Dawson, Chi.-N.L.	.25
☐	141	John Hart, Mgr., Cle.	.15
☐	**142**	**Jeff Wetherby, Atl., RC**	**.15**
☐	143	Rafael Belliard, Pgh.	.15
☐	144	Bud Black, Cle.	.15
☐	145	Terry Steinbach, Oak.	.15
☐	**146**	**Rob Richie, Det., RC**	**.15**
☐	147	Chuck Finley, Cal.	.15
☐	148	Edgar Martinez, Sea.	.15
☐	149	Steve Farr, K.C.	.15
☐	150	Kirk Gibson, L.A.	.15
☐	151	Rick Mahler, Cin.	.15
☐	152	Lonnie Smith, Atl.	.15
☐	153	Randy Milligan, Bal.	.15
☐	154	Mike Maddux, Pha. (L.A.)	.15
☐	155	Ellis Burks, Bos.	.25
☐	156	Ken Patterson, Chi.-A.L.	.15
☐	157	Craig Biggio, Hou.	.25
☐	158	Craig Lefferts, S.F. (S.D.)	.15
☐	159	Mike Fedler, Mil.	.15
☐	160	Dave Righetti, NYY.	.15
☐	161	Harold Reynolds, Sea.	.15
☐	162	Todd Zeile, Stl.	.15
☐	163	Phil Bradley, Bal.	.15
☐	**164**	**Jeff Juden, Hou., RC**	**.15**
☐	165	Walt Weiss, Oak.	.15
☐	166	Bobby Witt, Tex.	.15
☐	**167**	**Kevin Appier, K.C., RC**	**.25**
☐	168	Jose Lind, Pgh.	.15
☐	169	Richard Dotson, Chi.-A.L. (K.C.)	.15
☐	170	George Bell, Tor.	.15
☐	171	Russ Nixon, Mgr., Atl.	.15
☐	172	Tom Lampkin, Cle.	.15
☐	173	Tim Belcher, L.A.	.15
☐	174	Jeff Kunkel, Tex.	.15
☐	175	Mike Moore, Oak.	.15
☐	176	Luis Quinones, Cin.	.15
☐	177	Mike Henneman, Det.	.15
☐	178	Chris James, S.D. (Cle.)	.15
☐	179	Brian Holton, Bal.	.15
☐	180	Rock (Tim) Raines, Mtl.	.15
☐	181	Juan Agosto, Hou.	.15
☐	182	Mookie Wilson, Tor.	.15
☐	183	Steve Lake, Pha.	.15
☐	184	Danny Cox, Stl.	.15
☐	185	Ruben Sierra, Tex.	.15
☐	186	Dave LaPoint, NYY.	.15
☐	**187**	**Rick Wrona, Chi.-N.L., RC**	**.15**
☐	188	Mike Smithson, Bos. (Ana.)	.15
☐	189	Dick Schofield, Cal.	.15
☐	190	Rick Reuschel, S.F.	.15
☐	191	Pat Borders, Tor.	.15
☐	192	Don August, Mil.	.15
☐	193	Andy Benes, S.D.	.15
☐	194	Glenallen Hill, Tor.	.15
☐	195	Tim Burke, Mtl.	.15
☐	196	Gerald Young, Hou.	.15
☐	197	Doug Drabek, Pgh.	.15
☐	198	Mike Marshall, L.A. (NYM.)	.15
☐	**199**	**Sergio Valdez, Atl., RC**	**.15**
☐	200	Don Mattingly, NYY.	.75
☐	201	Cito Gaston, Mgr., Tor.	.15
☐	202	Mike MacFarlane, K.C.	.15
☐	**203**	**Mike Roesler, Cin., RC**	**.15**
☐	204	Bob Dernier, Pha.	.15
☐	205	Mark Davis, S.D. (K.C.)	.15
☐	206	Nick Esasky, Bos. (Atl.)	.15
☐	207	Bob Ojeda, NYM.	.15
☐	208	Brook Jacoby, Cle.	.15
☐	209	Greg Mathews, Stl.	.15
☐	210	Ryne Sandberg, Chi.-N.L.	.25
☐	211	John Cerutti, Tor.	.15
☐	212	Joe Orsulak, Bal.	.15
☐	213	Scott Bankhead, Sea.	.15
☐	214	Terry Francona, Mil.	.15
☐	215	Kirk McCaskill, Cal.	.25
☐	216	Ricky Jordan, Pha.	.15
☐	217	Don Robinson, S.F.	.15
☐	218	Wally Backman, Min.	.15
☐	219	Donn Pall, Chi.-A.L.	.15
☐	220	Barry Bonds, Pgh.	.35
☐	**221**	**Gary Mielke, Tex., RC**	**.15**

☐ 222 Kurt Stillwell, K.C. .15
☐ 223 Tommy Gregg, Atl. .15
☐ 224 Delino DeShields, Mtl. .15
☐ 225 Jim Deshaies, Hou. .15
☐ 226 Mickey Hatcher, L.A. .15
☐ **227 Kevin Tapani, Min., RC .15**
☐ 228 Dave Martinez, Mtl. .15
☐ 229 David Wells, Tor. .15
☐ 230 Keith Hernandez, NYM. (Cle.) .15
☐ 231 Jack McKeon, Mgr., S.D. .15
☐ 232 Darnell Coles, Sea. .15
☐ 233 Ken Hill, Stl. .15
☐ 234 Mariano Duncan, Cin. .15
☐ 235 Jeff Reardon, Min. (Bos.) .15
☐ 236 Hal Morris, NYY., (Cin.) .15
☐ **237 Kevin Ritz, Det., RC .15**
☐ 238 Felix Jose, Oak. .15
☐ 239 Eric Show, S.D. .15
☐ 240 Mark Grace, Chi.-N.L. .15
☐ 241 Mike Krukow, S.F. .15
☐ 242 Fred Manrique, Tex. .15
☐ 243 Barry Jones, Chi.-A.L. .15
☐ 244 Bill Schroeder, Cal. .15
☐ 245 Roger Clemens, Bos. .75
☐ 246 Jim Eisenreich, K.C. .15
☐ 247 Jerry Reed, Sea. .15
☐ 248 Dave Anderson, L.A. .15
☐ **249 Mike Smith, Bal., RC .15**
☐ 250 Jose Canseco, Oak. .25
☐ 251 Jeff Blauser, Atl. .15
☐ 252 Otis Nixon, Mtl. .15
☐ 253 Mark Portugal, Hou. .15
☐ 254 Francisco Cabrera, Atl. .15
☐ 255 Bobby Thigpen, Chi.-A.L. .15
☐ 256 Marvell Wynne, Chi.-N.L. .15
☐ 257 Jose DeLeon, Stl. .15
☐ 258 Barry Lyons, NYM. .15
☐ 259 Lance McCullers, NYY. .15
☐ 260 Eric Davis, Cin. .15
☐ 261 Whitey Herzog, Mgr., Stl. .15
☐ 262 Checklist 2 of 6 .15
☐ 263 Mel Stottlemyre Jr., K.C. .15
☐ 264 Bryan Clutterbuck, Mil. .15
☐ 265 Pete O'Brien, Sea. .15
☐ 266 German Gonzalez, Min. .15
☐ 267 Mark Davidson, Hou. .15
☐ 268 Rob Murphy, Bos. .15
☐ 269 Dickie Thon, Pha. .15
☐ 270 Dave Stewart, Oak. .15
☐ 271 Chet Lemon, Det. .15
☐ 272 Bryan Harvey, Cal. .15
☐ 273 Bobby Bonilla, Pgh. .15
☐ 274 Goose Gozzo, Cle. .15
☐ 275 Mickey Tettleton, Bal. .15
☐ 276 Gary Thurman, K.C. .15
☐ 277 Lenny Harris, L.A. .15
☐ 278 Pascual Perez, NYY. .15
☐ 279 Steve Buechele, Tex. .15
☐ 280 Lou Whitaker, Det. .15
☐ 281 Kevin Bass, S.F. .15
☐ 282 Derek Lilliquist, Atl. .15
☐ **283 Albert Belle, Cle., RC .50**
☐ **284 Mark Gardner, Mtl., RC .15**
☐ 285 Willie McGee, Stl. .15
☐ 286 Lee Guetterman, NYY. .15
☐ 287 Vance Law, Chi.-N.L. .15
☐ 288 Greg Briley, Sea. .15
☐ 289 Norm Charlton, Cin. .15
☐ 290 Robin Yount, Mil. .25
☐ 291 Dave Johnson, Bal. .15
☐ 292 Jim Gott, L.A. .15
☐ 293 Mike Gallego, Oak. .15
☐ 294 Craig McMurtry, Tex. .15
☐ 295 Fred McGriff, Tor. .25
☐ 296 Jeff Ballard, Bal. .15
☐ 297 Tom Herr, NYM. .15
☐ 298 Danny Gladden, Min. .15
☐ 299 Adam Peterson, Chi.-A.L. .15
☐ 300 Bo Jackson, K.C. .15
☐ 301 Don Aase, NYM. .15
☐ 302 Marcus Lawton, NYY. .15
☐ 303 Rick Cerone, Bos. (NYY.) .15
☐ 304 Marty Clary, Atl. .15
☐ 305 Eddie Murray, L.A. .25
☐ 306 Tom Niedenfuer, Sea. .15
☐ 307 Bip Roberts, S.D. .15
☐ 308 Jose Guzman, Tex. .15
☐ **309 Eric Yelding, Hou., RC .15**
☐ 310 Steve Bedrosian, S.F. .15
☐ 311 Dwight Smith, Chi.-N.L. .15
☐ 312 Dan Quisenberry, Stl. .15
☐ 313 Gus Polidor, Mil. .15
☐ **314 DP: Donald Harris, Tex., RC .15**
☐ 315 Bruce Hurst, S.D. .15
☐ 316 Carney Lansford, Oak. .15
☐ 317 Mark Guthrie, Min. .15
☐ 318 Wallace Johnson, Mtl. .15
☐ 319 Dion James, Cle. .15
☐ 320 Dave Stieb, Tor. .15
☐ 321 Joe Morgan, Mgr., Bos. .15
☐ 322 Junior Ortiz, Pgh. .15
☐ 323 Willie Wilson, K.C. .15
☐ 324 Pete Harnisch, Bal. .15
☐ 325 Robby Thompson, S.F. .15
☐ **326 Tom McCarthy, Chi.-A.L., RC .15**
☐ 327 Ken Williams, Det. .15
☐ 328 Curt Young, Oak. .15
☐ 329 Oddibe McDowell, Atl. .15
☐ 330 Ron Darling, NYM. .15
☐ **331 Juan Gonzalez, Tex., RC 3.00**
☐ 332 Paul O'Neill, Cin. .15
☐ 333 Bill Wegman, Mil. .15
☐ 334 Johnny Ray, Cal. .15
☐ 335 Andy Hawkins, NYY. .15
☐ 336 Ken Griffey Jr., Sea. 2.50
☐ 337 Lloyd McClendon, Chi.-N.L. .15
☐ 338 Dennis Lamp, Bos. .15
☐ 339 Dave Clark, Cle. (Chi.-N.L.) .15
☐ 340 Fernando Valenzuela, L.A. .15
☐ 341 Tom Foley, Mtl. .15
☐ 342 Alex Trevino, Hou. .15
☐ 343 Frank Tanana, Det. .15
☐ 344 George Canale, Mil. .15
☐ 345 Harold Baines, Tex. .15
☐ 346 Jim Presley, Sea. .15
☐ 347 Junior Felix, Tor. .15
☐ **348 Gary Wayne, Min., RC .15**
☐ 349 Steve Finley, Bal. .15
☐ 350 Bret Saberhagen, K.C. .15
☐ 351 Roger Craig, Mgr., S.F. .15
☐ 352 Bryn Smith, Mtl. (Stl.) .15
☐ 353 Sandy Alomar, S.D., (Cle.) .25
☐ 354 Stan Belinda, Pgh. .15
☐ 355 Marty Barrett, Bos. .15
☐ 356 Randy Ready, Pha. .15
☐ 357 Dave West, Min. .15
☐ 358 Andres Thomas, Atl. .15
☐ 359 Jimmy Jones, NYY. .15

	No.	Card	Value
☐	360	Paul Molitor, Mil.	.25
☐	**361**	**Randy McCament, S.F., RC**	**.15**
☐	362	Damon Berryhill, Chi.-N.L.	.15
☐	363	Dan Petry, Cal.	.15
☐	364	Rolando Roomes, Cin.	.15
☐	365	Ozzie Guillen, Chi.-A.L.	.15
☐	366	Mike Heath, Det.	.15
☐	367	Mike Morgan, L.A.	.15
☐	368	Bill Doran, Hou.	.15
☐	369	Todd Burns, Oak.	.15
☐	370	Tim Wallach, Mtl.	.15
☐	371	Jimmy Key, Tor.	.15
☐	372	Terry Kennedy, S.F.	.15
☐	373	Alvin Davis, Sea.	.15
☐	374	Steve Cummings, Tor.	.15
☐	375	Dwight Evans, Bos.	.15
☐	376	Checklist 3 of 6	.15
☐	**377**	**Mickey Weston, Bal., RC**	**.15**
☐	378	Luis Salazar, Chi.-N.L.	.15
☐	379	Steve Rosenberg, Chi.-A.L.	.15
☐	380	Dave Winfield, NYY.	.25
☐	381	Frank Robinson, Mgr., Bal.	.25
☐	382	Jeff Musselman, NYM.	.15
☐	383	John Morris, Stl.	.15
☐	384	Pat Combs, Pha.	.15
☐	385	Fred McGriff, Tor.	.25
☐	386	Julio Franco, Tex.	.15
☐	387	Wade Boggs, Bos.	.25
☐	388	Cal Ripken, Bal.	.75
☐	389	Robin Yount, Mil.	.25
☐	390	Ruben Sierra, Tex.	.15
☐	391	Kirby Puckett, Min.	.50
☐	392	Carlton Fisk, Chi.-A.L.	.25
☐	393	Bret Saberhagen, K.C.	.15
☐	394	Jeff Ballard, Bal.	.15
☐	395	Jeff Russell, Tex.	.15
☐	396	A. Bartlett Giamatti, President	.15
☐	397	Will Clark, S.F.	.25
☐	398	Ryne Sandberg, Chi.-N.L.	.25
☐	399	Howard Johnson, NYM.	.15
☐	400	Ozzie Smith, Stl.	.35
☐	401	Kevin Mitchell, S.F.	.15
☐	402	Eric Davis, Cin.	.15
☐	403	Tony Gwynn, S.D.	.50
☐	404	Craig Biggio, Hou.	.15
☐	405	Mike Scott, Hou.	.15
☐	406	Joe Magrane, Cin.	.15
☐	407	Mark Davis, S.D. (K.C.)	.15
☐	408	Trevor Wilson, S.F.	.15
☐	409	Tom Brunansky, Stl.	.15
☐	410	Joe Boever, Atl.	.15
☐	411	Ken Phelps, Oak.	.15
☐	412	Jamie Moyer, Tex.	.15
☐	413	Brian Dubois, Det.	.15
☐	**414**	**DP: Frank Thomas, Chi.-A.L., RC**	**6.00**
☐	415	Shawon Dunston, Chi.-N.L.	.15
☐	416	Dave Johnson, Bal.	.15
☐	417	Jim Gantner, Mil.	.15
☐	418	Tom Browning, Cin.	.15
☐	**419**	**Beau Allred, Cle., RC**	**.15**
☐	420	Carlton Fisk, Chi.-A.L.	.25
☐	421	Greg Minton, Cal.	.15
☐	422	Pat Sheridan, S.F.	.15
☐	423	Fred Toliver, S.D., (NYY.)	.15
☐	424	Jerry Reuss, Mil.	.15
☐	425	Bill Landrum, Pgh.	.15
☐	426	Jeff Hamilton, L.A.	.15
☐	427	Carmelo Castillo, Min.	.15
☐	428	Steve Davis, Cle. (L.A.)	.15
☐	429	Tom Kelly, Mgr., Min.	.15
☐	430	Pete Incaviglia, Tex.	.15
☐	431	Randy Johnson, Sea.	.50
☐	432	Damaso Garcia, Mtl. (NYY.)	.15
☐	**433**	**Steve Olin, Cle., RC**	**.15**
☐	434	Mark Carreon, NYM.	.15
☐	435	Kevin Seitzer, K.C.	.15
☐	436	Mel Hall, NYY.	.15
☐	437	Les Lancaster, Chi.-N.L.	.15
☐	438	Greg Myers, Tor.	.15
☐	439	Jeff Parrett, Pha.	.15
☐	440	Alan Trammell, Det.	.15
☐	441	Bob Kipper, Pgh.	.15
☐	442	Jerry Browne, Cle.	.15
☐	443	Cris Carpenter, Stl.	.15
☐	**444**	**Kyle Abbott, Cal., RC**	**.15**
☐	445	Danny Jackson, Cin.	.15
☐	446	Dan Pasqua, Chi.-A.L.	.15
☐	447	Atlee Hammaker, S.F.	.15
☐	448	Greg Gagne, Min.	.15
☐	449	Dennis Rasmussen, S.D.	.15
☐	450	Rickey Henderson, Oak.	.25
☐	451	Mark Lemke, Atl.	.15
☐	452	Luis De Los Santos, K.C.	.15
☐	453	Jody Davis, Atl.	.15
☐	454	Jeff King, Pgh.	.15
☐	455	Jeffrey Leonard, Sea.	.15
☐	456	Chris Gwynn, L.A.	.15
☐	457	Gregg Jefferies, NYM.	.15
☐	458	Bob McClure, Cal.	.15
☐	459	Jim Lefebvre, Mgr., Sea.	.15
☐	460	Mike Scott, Hou.	.15
☐	**461**	**Carlos Martinez, Chi.-A.L., RC**	**.15**
☐	462	Denny Walling, Stl.	.15
☐	463	Drew Hall, Tex.	.15
☐	464	Jerome Walton, Chi.-N.L.	.15
☐	465	Kevin Gross, Mtl.	.15
☐	466	Rance Mulliniks, Tor.	.15
☐	467	Juan Nieves, Mil.	.15
☐	468	Billy Ripken, Bal.	.15
☐	469	John Kruk, Pha.	.15
☐	470	Frank Viola, NYM.	.15
☐	471	Mike Brumley, Det. (Bal.)	.15
☐	472	Jose Uribe, S.F.	.15
☐	473	Joe Price, Bos.	.15
☐	474	Rich Thompson, Mtl.	.15
☐	475	Bob Welch, Oak.	.15
☐	476	Brad Komminsk, Cle.	.15
☐	477	Willie Fraser, Cal.	.15
☐	478	Mike LaValliere, Pgh.	.15
☐	479	Frank White, K.C.	.15
☐	480	Sid Fernandez, NYM.	.15
☐	481	Garry Templeton, S.D.	.15
☐	482	Steve Carter, Pgh.	.15
☐	483	Alejandro Pena, L.A. (NYM.)	.15
☐	484	Mike Fitzgerald, Mtl.	.15
☐	485	John Candelaria, Mtl.	.15
☐	486	Jeff Treadway, Atl.	.15
☐	487	Steve Searcy, Det.	.15
☐	488	Ken Oberkfell, S.F. (Hou.)	.15
☐	489	Nick Leyva, Mgr., Pha.	.15
☐	490	Dan Plesac, Mil.	.15
☐	491	Dave Cochrane, Sea.	.15
☐	492	Ron Oester, Cin.	.15
☐	493	Jason Grimsley, Pha.	.15
☐	494	Terry Puhl, Hou.	.25
☐	495	Lee Smith, Bos.	.15
☐	496	Cecil Espy, Tex.	.15
☐	497	Dave Schmidt, Bal. (Mtl.)	.15

	No.	Player	Price
☐	498	Rick Schu, Det.	.15
☐	499	Bill Long, Chi.-A.L.	.15
☐	500	Kevin Mitchell, S.F.	.15
☐	501	Matt Young, Oak. (Sea.)	.15
☐	502	Mitch Webster, Chi.-N.L. (Cle.)	.15
☐	503	Randy St. Claire, Min.	.15
☐	504	Tom O'Malley, NYM.	.15
☐	505	Kelly Gruber, Tor.	.15
☐	506	Tom Glavine, Atl.	.25
☐	507	Gary Redus, Pgh.	.15
☐	508	Terry Leach, K.C.	.15
☐	509	Tom Pagnozzi, Stl.	.15
☐	510	Doc Gooden, NYM.	.15
☐	511	Clay Parker, NYY.	.15
☐	512	Gary Pettis, Det. (Tex.)	.15
☐	513	Mark Eichhorn, Atl. (Ana.)	.15
☐	514	Andy Allanson, Cle.	.15
☐	515	Len Dykstra, Pha.	.15
☐	516	Tim Leary, Cin. (NYY.)	.15
☐	517	Roberto Alomar, S.D.	.35
☐	518	Bill Krueger, Mil.	.15
☐	519	Bucky Dent, Mgr., NYY.	.15
☐	520	Mitch Williams, Chi.-N.L.	.15
☐	521	Craig Worthington, Bal.	.15
☐	522	Mike Dunne, Sea. (S.D.)	.15
☐	523	Jay Bell, Pgh.	.15
☐	524	Daryl Boston, Chi.-A.L.	.15
☐	525	Wally Joyner, Cal.	.15
☐	526	Checklist 4 of 6	.15
☐	527	Ron Hassey, Oak.	.15
☐	528	Kevin Wickander, Cle.	.15
☐	529	Greg Harris, Bos.	.15
☐	530	Mark Langston, Mtl. (Ana.)	.15
☐	531	Ken Caminiti, Hou.	.25
☐	532	Cecilio Guante, Tex. (Cle.)	.15
☐	533	Tim Jones, Stl.	.15
☐	534	Louie Meadows, Hou.	.15
☐	535	John Smoltz, Atl.	.15
☐	536	Bob Geren, NYY.	.15
☐	537	Mark Grant, S.D.	.15
☐	538	Billy Spiers, Mil.	.15
☐	539	Neal Heaton, Pgh.	.15
☐	540	Danny Tartabull, K.C.	.15
☐	541	Pat Perry, Chi.-N.L.	.15
☐	542	Darren Daulton, Phi	.15
☐	543	Nelson Liriano, Tor	.15
☐	544	Dennis Boyd, Bos. (Mtl.)	.15
☐	545	Kevin McReynolds, NYM.	.15
☐	546	Kevin Hickey, Bal.	.15
☐	547	Jack Howell, Cal.	.15
☐	548	Pat Clements, S.D.	.15
☐	549	Don Zimmer, Mgr., Chi.-N.L.	.15
☐	550	Julio Franco, Tex.	.15
☐	551	Tim Crews, L.A.	.15
☐	**552**	**Mike Smith, Pgh., RC**	**.15**
☐	**553**	**Scott Scudder, Cin., RC**	**.15**
☐	554	Jay Buhner, Sea.	.25
☐	555	Jack Morris, Det.	.15
☐	556	Gene Larkin, Min.	.15
☐	557	Jeff Innis, NYM.	.15
☐	558	Rafael Ramirez, Hou.	.15
☐	559	Andy McGaffigan, Mtl.	.15
☐	560	Steve Sax, NYY.	.15
☐	561	Ken Dayley, Stl.	.15
☐	562	Chad Kreuter, Tex.	.15
☐	563	Alex Sanchez, Tor.	.15
☐	564	Tyler Houston, Atl.	.15
☐	565	Scott Fletcher, Chi.-A.L.	.15
☐	566	Mark Knudson, Mil.	.15
☐	567	Ron Gant, Atl.	.15
☐	568	John Smiley, Pgh.	.15
☐	569	Ivan Calderon, Chi.-A.L.	.15
☐	570	Cal Ripken, Bal.	1.25
☐	571	Brett Butler, S.F.	.15
☐	572	Greg Harris, S.D.	.15
☐	573	Danny Heep, Bos.	.15
☐	574	Bill Swift, Sea.	.15
☐	575	Lance Parrish, Cal.	.15
☐	576	Mike Dyer, Min.	.15
☐	577	Charlie Hayes, Pha.	.15
☐	578	Joe Magrane, Stl.	.15
☐	579	Art Howe, Mgr., Hou.	.15
☐	580	Joe Carter, Cle. (S.D.)	.25
☐	581	Ken Griffey, Cin.	.15
☐	582	Rick Honeycutt, Oak.	.15
☐	583	Bruce Benedict, Atl.	.15
☐	**584**	**Phil Stephenson, S.D., RC**	**.15**
☐	585	Kal Daniels, L.A.	.15
☐	586	Ed Nunez, Det.	.15
☐	587	Lance Johnson, Chi.-A.L.	.15
☐	588	Rick Rhoden, Hou.	.15
☐	589	Mike Aldrete, Mtl.	.15
☐	590	Ozzie Smith, Stl.	.35
☐	591	Todd Stottlemyre, Tor.	.15
☐	592	R.J. Reynolds, Pgh.	.15
☐	593	Scott Bradley, Sea.	.15
☐	**594**	**Luis Sojo, Tor., RC**	**.15**
☐	595	Greg Swindell, Cle.	.15
☐	596	Jose DeJesus, K.C.	.15
☐	597	Chris Bosio, Mil.	.15
☐	598	Brady Anderson, Bal.	.15
☐	599	Frank Williams, Det.	.15
☐	600	Darryl Strawberry, NYM.	.25
☐	601	Luis Rivera, Bos.	.15
☐	602	Scott Garrelts, S.F.	.15
☐	603	Tony Armas, Cal.	.15
☐	604	Ron Robinson, Cin.	.15
☐	605	Mike Scioscia, L.A.	.15
☐	606	Storm Davis, Oak. (K.C.)	.15
☐	607	Steve Jeltz, Pha.	.15
☐	**608**	**Eric Anthony, Hou., RC**	**.15**
☐	609	Sparky Anderson, Mgr., Det.	.15
☐	610	Pedro Guerrero, Stl.	.15
☐	611	Walt Terrell, NYY. (Pgh.)	.15
☐	612	Dave Gallagher, Chi.-A.L.	.15
☐	**613**	**Jeff Pico, Chi.-N.L., RC**	**.15**
☐	614	Nelson Santovenia, Mtl.	.15
☐	615	Rob Deer, Mil.	.15
☐	616	Brian Holman, Sea.	.15
☐	617	Geronimo Berroa, Alt.	.15
☐	618	Eddie Whitson, S.D.	.15
☐	619	Rob Ducey, Tor.	.25
☐	620	Tony Castillo, Atl.	.15
☐	621	Melido Perez, Chi.-A.L.	.15
☐	622	Sid Bream, Pgh.	.15
☐	623	Jim Corsi, Oak.	.15
☐	624	Darrin Jackson, S.D.	.15
☐	625	Roger McDowell, Pha.	.15
☐	626	Bob Melvin, Bal.	.15
☐	627	Jose Rijo, Cin.	.15
☐	628	Candy Maldonado, S.F. (Cle.)	.15
☐	629	Eric Hetzel, Bos.	.15
☐	630	Gary Gaetti, Min.	.15
☐	**631**	**John Wetteland, L.A., RC**	**.35**
☐	632	Scott Lusader, Det.	.15
☐	633	Dennis Cook, Pha.	.15
☐	634	Luis Polonia, NYY.	.15
☐	635	Brian Downing, Cal.	.15

☐ 636 Jesse Orosco, Cle. .15
☐ 637 Craig Reynolds, Hou. .15
☐ 638 Jeff Montgomery, K.C. .15
☐ 639 Tony LaRussa, Mgr., Oak. .15
☐ 640 Rick Sutcliffe, Chi.-N.L. .15
☐ **641 Doug Strange, Det., RC .15**
☐ 642 Jack Armstrong, Cin. .15
☐ 643 Alfredo Griffin, L.A. .15
☐ 644 Paul Assenmacher, Chi.-N.L. .15
☐ 645 Jose Oquendo, Stl. .15
☐ 646 Checklist 5 of 6 .15
☐ 647 Rex Hudler, Mtl. .15
☐ 648 Jim Clancy, Hou. .15
☐ 649 Dan Murphy, S.D. .15
☐ 650 Mike Witt, Cal. .15
☐ 651 Rafael Santana, NYY. (Cle.) .15
☐ 652 Mike Boddicker, Bos. .15
☐ 653 John Moses, Min. .15
☐ 655 Paul Coleman, Stl. .15
☐ 655 Gregg Olson, Bal. .15
☐ 656 Mackey Sasser, NYM. .15
☐ 657 Terry Mulholland, Pha. .15
☐ 658 Donell Nixon, S.F. .15
☐ 659 Greg Cadaret, NYY. .15
☐ 660 Vince Coleman, Stl. .15
☐ 661 1985: Dick Howser, Mgr., K.C. .15
☐ 662 1980: Mike Schmidt, Pha. .35
☐ 663 1975: Fred Lynn, Bos. .15
☐ 664 1970: Johnny Bench, Cin. .35
☐ 665 1965: Sandy Koufax, L.A. .35
☐ 666 Brian Fisher, Pgh. .15
☐ 667 Curt Wilkerson, Chi.-N.L. .15
☐ **668 Joe Oliver, Cin., RC .15**
☐ 669 Tom Lasorda, Mgr., L.A. .35
☐ 670 Dennis Eckersley, Oak. .15
☐ 671 Bob Boone, K.C. .15
☐ 672 Roy Smith, Min. .15
☐ 673 Joey Meyer, Mil. .15
☐ 674 Spike Owen, Mtl. .15
☐ 675 Jim Abbott, Cal. .15
☐ 676 Randy Kutcher, Bos. .15
☐ 677 Jay Tibbs, Bal. .15
☐ 678 Kirt Manwaring, S.F. .15
☐ 679 Gary Ward, Det. .15
☐ 680 Howard Johnson, NYM. .15
☐ 681 Mike Schooler, Sea. .15
☐ 682 Dann Bilardello, Pgh. .15
☐ **683 Kenny Rogers, Tex., RC .15**
☐ **684 Julio Machado, NYM., RC .15**
☐ 685 Tony Fernandez, Tor. .15
☐ 686 Carmelo Martinez, S.D. (Pha.) .15
☐ 687 Tim Birtsas, Cin. .15
☐ 688 Milt Thompson, Stl. .15
☐ 689 Rich Yett, Cle., (Min.) .15
☐ 690 Mark McGwire, Oak. .75
☐ 691 Chuck Cary, NYY. .15
☐ **692 Sammy Sosa, Chi.-A.L., RC 2.00**
☐ 693 Calvin Schiraldi, S.D. .15
☐ 694 Mike Stanton, Atl. .15
☐ 695 Tom Henke, Tor. .15
☐ 696 B.J. Surhoff, Mil. .15
☐ 697 Mike Davis, L.A. .15
☐ 698 Omar Vizquel, Sea. .15
☐ 699 Jim Leyland, Mgr., Pgh. .15
☐ 700 Kirby Puckett, Min. .75
☐ **701 Bernie Williams, RC .75**
☐ 702 Tony Phillips, Oak. (Det.) .15
☐ 703 Jeff Brantley, S.F. .15
☐ 704 Chip Hale, Min. .15
☐ 705 Claudell Washington, Cal. .15
☐ 706 Geno Petralli, Tex. .15
☐ 707 Luis Aquino, K.C. .15
☐ 708 Larry Sheets, Bal. (Det.) .15
☐ 709 Juan Berenguer, Min. .15
☐ 710 Von Hayes, Pha. .15
☐ 711 Rick Aguilera, Min. .15
☐ 712 Todd Benzinger, Cin. .15
☐ 713 Tim Drummond, Min. .15
☐ **714 Marquis Grissom, Mtl., RC .75**
☐ 715 Greg Maddux, Chi.-N.L. 1.00
☐ 716 Steve Balboni, NYY. .15
☐ 717 Ron Karkovice, Chi.-A.L. .15
☐ 718 Gary Sheffield, Mil. .25
☐ 719 Wally Whitehurst, NYM. .15
☐ 720 Andres Galarraga, Mtl. .25
☐ 721 Lee Mazzilli, Tor. .15
☐ 722 Felix Fermin, Cle. .15
☐ 723 Jeff Robinson, Pgh. .15
☐ 724 Juan Bell, Bal. .15
☐ 725 Terry Pendleton, Stl. .15
☐ 726 Gene Nelson, Oak. .15
☐ 727 Pat Tabler, K.C. .15
☐ 728 Jim Acker, Tor. .15
☐ 729 Bobby Valentine, Mgr., Tex. .15
☐ 730 Tony Gwynn, S.D. .75
☐ 731 Don Carman, Pha. .15
☐ 732 Ernie Riles, S.F. .15
☐ 733 John Dopson, Bos. .15
☐ 734 Kevin Elster, NYM. .15
☐ 735 Charlie Hough, Tex. .15
☐ 736 Rick Dempsey, L.A. .15
☐ 737 Chris Sabo, Cin. .15
☐ 738 Gene Harris, Sea. .15
☐ 739 Dale Sveum, Mil. .15
☐ 740 Jesse Barfield, NYY. .15
☐ 741 Steve Wilson, Chi.-N.L. .25
☐ 742 Ernie Whitt, Tor. (Atl.) .15
☐ 743 Tom Candiotti, Cle. .15
☐ **744 Kelly Mann, Alt., RC .15**
☐ 745 Hubie Brooks, Mtl. (L.A.) .15
☐ 746 Dave Smith, Hou. .15
☐ 747 Randy Bush, Min. .15
☐ 748 Doyle Alexander, Det. .15
☐ 749 Mark Parent, S.D. .15
☐ 750 Dale Murphy, Atl. .25
☐ 751 Steve Lyons, Chi.-A.L. .15
☐ 752 Tom Gordon, K.C. .15
☐ 753 Chris Speier, S.F. .15
☐ 754 Bob Walk, Pgh. .15
☐ 755 Rafael Palmeiro, Tex. .25
☐ 756 Ken Howell, Pha. .15
☐ **757 Larry Walker, Mtl., RC 2.00**
☐ 758 Mark Thurmond, Bal. .15
☐ 759 Tom Trebelhorn, Mgr., Mil. .15
☐ 760 Wade Boggs, Bos. .25
☐ 761 Mike Jackson, Sea. .15
☐ 762 Doug Dascenzo, Chi.-N.L. .15
☐ 763 Denny Martinez, Mtl. .15
☐ 764 Tim Teufel, NYM. .15
☐ 765 Chili Davis, Cal. .15
☐ 766 Brian Meyer, Hou. .15
☐ 767 Tracy Jones, Det. .15
☐ 768 Chuck Crim, Mil. .15
☐ 769 Greg Hibbard, Chi.-A.L. .15
☐ 770 Cory Snyder, Cle. .15
☐ 771 Pete Smith, Atl. .15
☐ 772 Jeff Reed, Cin. .15
☐ 773 Dave Leiper, S.D. .15

	No.	Player	Price
☐	**774**	**Ben McDonald, Bal., RC**	**.15**
☐	775	Andy Van Slyke, Pgh.	.15
☐	776	Charlie Leibrandt, K.C. (Atl.)	.15
☐	777	Tim Laudner, Min.	.15
☐	778	Mike Jeffcoat, Tex.	.15
☐	779	Lloyd Moseby, Tor. (Det.)	.15
☐	780	Orel Hershiser, L.A.	.15
☐	781	Mario Diaz, Sea.	.15
☐	782	Jose Alvarez, Atl., (NYG.)	.15
☐	783	Checklist 6 of 6	.15
☐	784	Scott Bailes, Cle. (Ana.)	.15
☐	785	Jim Rice, Bos.	.15
☐	786	Eric King, Chi.-A.L.	.15
☐	787	Rene Gonzales, Bal.	.15
☐	788	Frank DiPino, Stl.	.15
☐	789	John Wathan, Mgr., K.C.	.15
☐	790	Gary Carter, NYM.	.25
☐	791	Alvaro Espinoza, NYY.	.15
☐	792	Gerald Perry, Atl. (K.C.)	.15

1990 BOX BOTTOMS

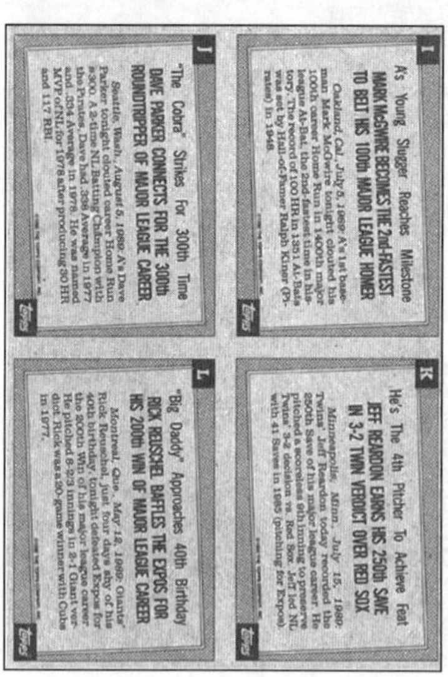

Panel Size: 5" x 7"

Complete Set (4 panels; 16 cards):			**13.00**
Panel A-D:			**4.00**
Panel E-H:			**2.00**
Panel I-L:			**4.00**
Panel M-P:			**10.00**
	No.	**Player**	**MINT**
☐	A	Wade Boggs	.75
☐	B	George Brett	1.50
☐	C	Andre Dawson	.50
☐	D	Darrell Evans	.25
☐	E	Doc Gooden	.25
☐	F	Rickey Henderson	.50
☐	G	Tom Lasorda	.50
☐	H	Fred Lynn	.25
☐	I	Mark McGwire	2.50
☐	J	Dave Parker	.25
☐	K	Jeff Reardon	.25
☐	L	Rick Reuschel	.25
☐	M	Jim Rice	.25
☐	N	Cal Ripken	3.50
☐	O	Nolan Ryan	4.00
☐	P	Ryne Sandberg	1.25

1990 PANINI STICKERS

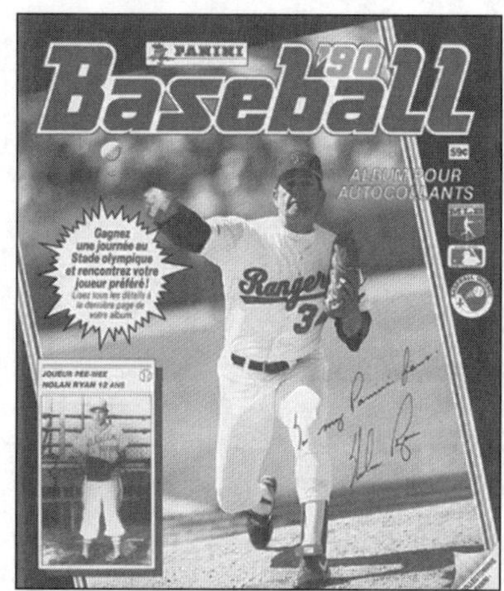

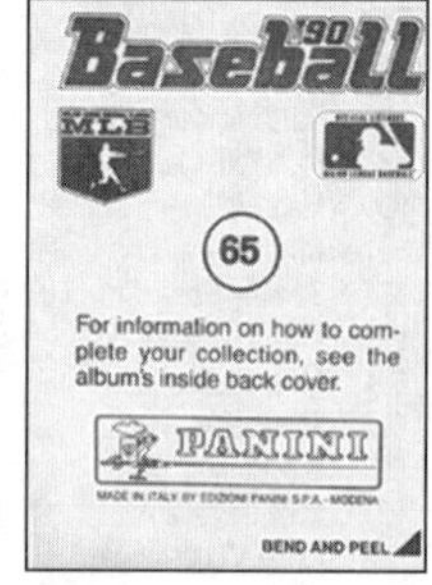

There was a 68-page colour album issued to house this sticker set. It was available in both English and French and was printed in the United States. The stickers were made in Italy by Panini.

Sticker Size: 2 1/8" x 3"

Face: Four colour, white border; name, team

Back: Black and white; number, Panini and MLB logos

Imprint: MLB '90
Complete Set (388 stickers): 20.00
Common Player: .15
Album: 3.50

	No.	Player	MINT
☐	1	Randy Milligan, Bal.	.15
☐	2	Gregg Olson, Bal.	.15
☐	3	Bill Ripken, Bal.	.15
☐	4	Phil Bradley, Bal.	.15
☐	5	Joe Orsulak, Bal.	.15
☐	6	Bob Milacki, Bal.	.15
☐	7	AS: Cal Ripken, Bal.	2.00
☐	8	AS: Mickey Tettleton, Bal.	.15
☐	9	Team Logo, Bal.	.15
☐	10	Team Helmet, Bal.	.15
☐	11	Craig Worthington, Bal.	.15
☐	12	Mike Devereaux, Bal.	.15
☐	13	Jeff Ballard, Bal.	.15
☐	14	Lee Smith, Bos.	.15
☐	15	Marty Barrett, Bos.	.15
☐	16	AS: Mike Greenwell, Bos.	.15
☐	17	Dwight Evans, Bos.	.15
☐	18	John Dopson, Bos.	.15
☐	19	AS: Wade Boggs, Bos.	.35
☐	20	Mike Boddicker, Bos.	.15
☐	21	Ellis Burks, Bos.	.25
☐	22	Team Logo, Bos.	.15
☐	23	Team Helmet, Bos.	.15
☐	24	Roger Clemens, Bos.	1.00
☐	25	Jody Reed, Bos.	.15
☐	26	Nick Esasky, Bos.	.15
☐	27	Brian Downing, Cal.	.15
☐	28	Bert Blyleven, Cal.	.15
☐	29	AS: Devon White, Cal.	.15
☐	30	Claudell Washington, Cal.	.15
☐	31	Wally Joyner, Cal.	.15
☐	32	AS: Chuck Finley, Cal.	.15
☐	33	Johnny Ray, Cal.	.15
☐	34	Jim Abbott, Cal.	.15
☐	35	Team Logo, Cal.	.15
☐	36	Team Helmet, Cal.	.15
☐	37	Kirk McCaskill, Cal.	.25
☐	38	Lance Parrish, Cal.	.15
☐	39	Chili Davis, Cal.	.15
☐	40	Steve Lyons, Chi.-A.L.	.15
☐	41	Ozzie Guillen, Chi.-A.L.	.15
☐	42	Melido Perez, Chi.-A.L.	.15
☐	43	Scott Fletcher, Chi.-A.L.	.15
☐	44	Carlton Fisk, Chi.-A.L.	.35
☐	45	Greg Walker, Chi.-A.L.	.15
☐	46	Dave Gallagher, Chi.-A.L.	.15
☐	47	Ivan Calderon, Chi.-A.L.	.15
☐	48	Team Logo, Chi.-A.L.	.15
☐	49	Team Helmet, Chi.-A.L.	.15
☐	50	Bobby Thigpen, Chi.-A.L.	.15
☐	51	Ron Kittle, Chi.-A.L.	.15
☐	52	Daryl Boston, Chi.-A.L.	.15
☐	53	John Farrell, Cle.	.15
☐	54	Jerry Browne, Cle.	.15
☐	55	Pete O'Brien, Cle.	.15
☐	56	Cory Snyder, Cle.	.15
☐	57	Tom Candiotti, Cle.	.15
☐	58	Brook Jacoby, Cle.	.15
☐	59	AS: Greg Swindell, Cle.	.15
☐	60	Felix Fermin, Cle.	.15
☐	61	Team Logo, Cle.	.15
☐	62	Team Helmet, Cle.	.15
☐	63	AS: Doug Jones, Cle.	.15
☐	64	Dion James, Cle.	.15
☐	65	Joe Carter, Cle.	.25
☐	66	Mike Heath, Det.	.15
☐	67	Dave Bergman, Det.	.15
☐	68	Gary Ward, Det.	.15
☐	69	AS: Mike Henneman, Det.	.15
☐	70	Alan Trammell, Det.	.15
☐	71	Lou Whitaker, Det.	.15
☐	72	Frank Tanana, Det.	.15
☐	73	Fred Lynn, Det.	.15
☐	74	Team Logo, Det.	.15
☐	75	Team Helmet, Det.	.15
☐	76	Jack Morris, Det.	.15
☐	77	Chet Lemon, Det.	.15
☐	78	Gary Pettis, Det.	.15
☐	79	Kurt Stillwell, K.C.	.15
☐	80	Jim Eisenreich, K.C.	.15
☐	81	Bret Saberhagen, K.C.	.15
☐	82	AS: Mark Gubicza, K.C.	.15
☐	83	Frank White, K.C.	.15
☐	84	AS: Bo Jackson, K.C.	.15
☐	85	Jeff Montgomery, K.C.	.15
☐	86	Kevin Seitzer, K.C.	.15
☐	87	Team Logo, K.C.	.15
☐	88	Team Helmet, K.C.	.15
☐	89	Tom Gordon, K.C.	.15
☐	90	Danny Tartabull, K.C.	.15
☐	91	George Brett, K.C.	.75
☐	92	Robin Yount, Mil.	.35
☐	93	B.J. Surhoff, Mil.	.15
☐	94	Jim Gantner, Mil.	.15
☐	95	AS: Dan Plesac, Mil.	.15
☐	96	Ted Higuera, Mil.	.15
☐	97	Glenn Braggs, Mil.	.15
☐	98	Paul Molitor, Mil.	.35
☐	99	Chris Bosio, Mil.	.15
☐	100	Team Logo, Mil.	.15
☐	101	Team Helmet, Mil.	.15
☐	102	Rob Deer, Mil.	.15
☐	103	Chuck Crim, Mil.	.15
☐	104	Greg Brock, Mil.	.15
☐	105	AS: Kirby Puckett, Min.	.75
☐	106	AS: Gary Gaetti, Min.	.15
☐	107	Roy Smith, Min.	.15
☐	108	Jeff Reardon, Min.	.15
☐	109	Randy Bush, Min.	.15
☐	110	Al Newman, Min.	.15
☐	111	Dan Gladden, Min.	.15
☐	112	Kent Hrbek, Min.	.15
☐	113	Team Logo, Min.	.15
☐	114	Team Helmet, Min.	.15
☐	115	Greg Gagne, Min.	.15
☐	116	Brian Harper, Min.	.15
☐	117	Allan Anderson, Min.	.15
☐	118	Lee Guetterman, NYY.	.15
☐	119	Roberto Kelly, NYY.	.15
☐	120	Jesse Barfield, NYY.	.15
☐	121	Alvaro Espinoza, NYY.	.15
☐	122	Mel Hall, NYY.	.15
☐	123	Chuck Cary, NYY.	.15
☐	124	Dave Righetti, NYY.	.15
☐	125	AS: Don Mattingly, NYY.	.75
☐	126	Team Logo, NYY.	.15
☐	127	Team Helmet, NYY.	.15
☐	128	Bob Geren, NYY.	.15
☐	129	AS: Steve Sax, NYY.	.15
☐	130	Andy Hawkins, NYY.	.15
☐	131	Bob Welch, Oak.	.15
☐	132	AS: Mark McGwire, Oak.	1.25
☐	133	Dave Henderson, Oak.	.15

	No.	Player	Price
☐	134	Carney Lansford, Oak.	.15
☐	135	Walt Weiss, Oak.	.15
☐	136	AS: Mike Moore, Oak.	.15
☐	137	Dennis Eckersley, Oak.	.15
☐	138	Rickey Henderson, Oak.	.25
☐	139	Team Logo, Oak.	.15
☐	140	Team Helmet, Oak.	.15
☐	141	AS: Dave Stewart, Oak.	.15
☐	142	Jose Canseco, Oak.	.25
☐	143	AS: Terry Steinbach, Oak.	.15
☐	144	Harold Reynolds, Sea.	.15
☐	145	Darnell Coles, Sea.	.15
☐	146	Brian Holman, Sea.	.15
☐	147	Scott Bankhead, Sea.	.15
☐	148	Greg Briley, Sea.	.15
☐	149	Alvin Davis, Sea.	.15
☐	150	AS: Jeffrey Leonard, Sea.	.15
☐	151	Mike Schooler, Sea.	.15
☐	152	Team Logo, Sea.	.15
☐	153	Team Helmet, Sea.	.15
☐	154	Randy Johnson, Sea.	.35
☐	155	Ken Griffey, Jr., Sea.	4.00
☐	156	Dave Valle, Sea.	.15
☐	157	Pete Incaviglia, Tex.	.15
☐	158	Fred Manrique, Tex.	.15
☐	159	AS: Jeff Russell, Tex.	.15
☐	160	AS: Nolan Ryan, Tex.	2.00
☐	161	Geno Petralli, Tex.	.15
☐	162	AS: Ruben Sierra, Tex.	.15
☐	163	AS: Julio Franco, Tex.	.15
☐	164	Rafael Palmeiro, Tex.	.15
☐	165	Team Logo, Tex.	.15
☐	166	Team Helmet, Tex.	.15
☐	167	AS: Harold Baines, Tex.	.15
☐	168	Kevin Brown, Tex.	.15
☐	169	Steve Buechele, Tex.	.15
☐	170	Fred McGriff, Tor.	.15
☐	171	AS: Kelly Gruber, Tor.	.15
☐	172	Todd Stottlemyre, Tor.	.15
☐	173	Dave Steib, Tor.	.15
☐	174	Mookie Wilson, Tor.	.15
☐	175	Pat Borders, Tor.	.15
☐	176	AS: Tony Fernandez, Tor.	.15
☐	177	John Cerutti, Tor.	.15
☐	178	Team Logo, Tor.	.15
☐	179	Team Helmet, Tor.	.15
☐	180	George Bell, Tor.	.15
☐	181	Jimmy Key, Tor.	.15
☐	182	Nelson Liriano, Tor.	.15
☐	183	1989 Statistics	.15
☐	184	1989 Statistics	.15
☐	185	1989 Statistics	.15
☐	186	American League	.15
☐	187	National League	.15
☐	188	Giants vs Athletics	.15
☐	189	Athletics vs Dodgers	.15
☐	190	Cardinals vs Twins	.15
☐	191	Red Sox vs Mets	.15
☐	192	Cardinals vs Royals	.15
☐	193	Tigers vs Padres	.15
☐	194	Phillies vs Orioles	.15
☐	195	Brewers vs Cardinals	.15
☐	196	Dodgers vs Yankees	.15
☐	197	Royals vs Phillies	.15
☐	198	Dave Stewart, Oak.; Bo Jackson, K.C.	.15
☐	199	Wade Boggs, Bos.; Kirby Puckett, Min.	.35
☐	200	Harold Baines, Chi.WS	.15
☐	201	Julio Franco, Tex.	.15
☐	202	Cal Ripken, Jr., Bal.	1.00
☐	203	Ruben Sierra, Tex	.15
☐	204	Mark McGwire, Oak.	.75
☐	205	Terry Steinbach, Oak.	.15
☐	206	Rick Reuschel, S.F.; Ozzie Smith, Stl.	.25
☐	207	Tony Gwynn, S.D.; Will Clark, S.F.	.25
☐	208	Kevin Mitchell, S.F.	.15
☐	209	Eric Davis, Cin.	.15
☐	210	Howard Johnson, NYM.	.15
☐	211	Pedro Guerrero, Stl.	.15
☐	212	Ryne Sandberg, Chi.-N.L.	.25
☐	213	Benito Santiago, S.D.	.15
☐	214	1989 Statistics	.15
☐	215	1989 Statistics	.15
☐	216	1989 Statistics	.15
☐	217	Jeff Blauser, Atl.	.15
☐	218	Jeff Treadway, Atl.	.15
☐	219	Tom Glavine, Atl.	.25
☐	220	Joe Boever, Atl.	.15
☐	221	Oddibe McDowell, Atl.	.15
☐	222	Dale Murphy, Atl.	.25
☐	223	Derek Lilliquist, Atl.	.15
☐	224	Tommy Gregg, Atl.	.15
☐	225	Team Logo, Atl.	.15
☐	226	Team Helmet, Atl.	.15
☐	227	Lonnie Smith, Atl.	.15
☐	228	AS: John Smoltz, Atl.	.25
☐	229	Andres Thomas, Atl.	.15
☐	230	Jerome Walton, Chi.-N.L.	.15
☐	231	AS: Ryne Sandberg, Chi.-N.L.	.35
☐	232	AS: Mitch Williams, Chi.-N.L.	.15
☐	233	Rick Sutcliffe, Chi.-N.L.	.15
☐	234	Damon Berryhill, Chi.-N.L.	.15
☐	235	Dwight Smith, Chi.-N.L.	.15
☐	236	Shawon Dunston, Chi.-N.L.	.15
☐	237	Greg Maddux, Chi.-N.L.	2.00
☐	238	Team Logo, Chi.-N.L.	.15
☐	239	Team Helmet, Chi.-N.L.	.15
☐	240	Andre Dawson, Chi.-N.L.	.35
☐	241	Mark Grace, Chi.-N.L.	.15
☐	242	Mike Bielecki, Chi.-N.L.	.15
☐	243	Jose Rijo, Cin.	.15
☐	244	AS: John Franco, Cin.	.15
☐	245	Paul O'Neill, Cin.	.15
☐	246	AS: Eric Davis, Cin.	.15
☐	247	Tom Browning, Cin.	.15
☐	248	Chris Sabo, Cin.	.15
☐	249	Rob Dibble, Cin.	.15
☐	250	Todd Benzinger, Cin.	.15
☐	251	Team Logo, Cin.	.15
☐	252	Team Helmet, Cin.	.15
☐	253	AS: Barry Larkin, Cin.	.25
☐	254	Rolando Roomes, Cin.	.15
☐	255	Danny Jackson, Cin.	.15
☐	256	Terry Puhl, Hou.	.25
☐	257	Dave Smith, Hou.	.15
☐	258	AS: Glenn Davis, Hou.	.15
☐	259	Craig Biggio, Hou.	.15
☐	260	Ken Caminiti, Hou.	.15
☐	261	Kevin Bass, Hou.	.15
☐	262	AS: Mike Scott, Hou.	.15
☐	263	Gerald Young, Hou.	.15
☐	264	Team Logo, Hou.	.15
☐	265	Team Helmet, Hou.	.15
☐	266	Rafael Ramirez, Hou.	.15
☐	267	Jim Deshaies, Hou.	.15
☐	268	Bill Doran, Hou.	.15
☐	269	Fernando Valenzuela, L.A.	.15
☐	270	Alfredo Griffin, L.A.	.15
☐	271	Kirk Gibson, L.A.	.15

- ☐ 272 Mike Marshall, L.A. .15
- ☐ 273 Eddie Murray, L.A. .50
- ☐ 274 AS: Jay Howell, L.A. .15
- ☐ 275 AS: Orel Hershiser, L.A. .15
- ☐ 276 AS: Mike Scioscia, L.A. .15
- ☐ 277 Team Logo, L.A. .15
- ☐ 278 Team Helmet, L.A. .15
- ☐ 279 AS: Willie Randolph, L.A. .15
- ☐ 280 Kal Daniels, L.A. .15
- ☐ 281 Tim Belcher, L.A. .15
- ☐ 282 Pascual Perez, Mtl. .15
- ☐ 283 Tim Raines, Mtl. .15
- ☐ 284 Andres Galarraga, Mtl. .25
- ☐ 285 Spike Owen, Mtl. .15
- ☐ 286 AS: Tim Wallach, Mtl. .15
- ☐ 287 Mark Langston, Mtl. .15
- ☐ 288 Dennis Martinez, Mtl. .15
- ☐ 289 Nelson Santovenia, Mtl. .15
- ☐ 290 Team Logo, Mtl. .15
- ☐ 291 Team Helmet, Mtl. .15
- ☐ 292 Tom Foley, Mtl. .15
- ☐ 293 Dave Martinez, Mtl. .15
- ☐ 294 AS: Tim Burke, Mtl. .15
- ☐ 295 Ron Darling, NYM. .15
- ☐ 296 Kevin Elster, NYM. .15
- ☐ 297 Dwight Gooden, NYM. .15
- ☐ 298 Gregg Jeffries, NYM. .15
- ☐ 299 Sid Fernandez, NYM. .15
- ☐ 300 Dave Magadan, NYM. .15
- ☐ 301 David Cone, NYM. .15
- ☐ 302 AS: Darryl Strawberry, NYM. .25
- ☐ 303 Team Logo, NYM. .15
- ☐ 304 Team Helmet, NYM. .15
- ☐ 305 Kevin McReynolds, NYM. .15
- ☐ 306 AS: Howard Johnson, NYM. .15
- ☐ 307 Randy Myers, NYM. .15
- ☐ 308 Roger McDowell, Pha. .15
- ☐ 309 Tom Herr, Pha. .15
- ☐ 310 John Kruk, Pha. .15
- ☐ 311 Randy Ready, Pha. .15
- ☐ 312 Jeff Parrett, Pha. .15
- ☐ 313 Lenny Dykstra, Pha. .15
- ☐ 314 Ken Howell, Pha. .15
- ☐ 315 Ricky Jordan, Pha. .15
- ☐ 316 Team Logo .15
- ☐ 317 Team Helmet, Pha. .15
- ☐ 318 Dickie Thon, Pha. .15
- ☐ 319 AS: Von Hayes, Pha. .15
- ☐ 320 Dennis Cook, Pha. .15
- ☐ 321 Jay Bell, Pgh. .15
- ☐ 322 Barry Bonds, Pgh. .35
- ☐ 323 John Smiley, Pgh. .15
- ☐ 324 Andy Van Slyke, Pgh. .15
- ☐ 325 AS: Bobby Bonilla, Pgh. .15
- ☐ 326 Bill Landrum, Pgh. .15
- ☐ 327 Randy Kramer, Pgh. .15
- ☐ 328 Jose Lind, Pgh. .15
- ☐ 329 Team Logo, Pgh. .15
- ☐ 330 Team Helmet, Pgh. .15
- ☐ 331 Gary Redus, Pgh. .15
- ☐ 332 Doug Drabek, Pgh. .15
- ☐ 333 Mike LaValliere, Pgh. .15
- ☐ 334 Jose DeLeon, Stl. .15
- ☐ 335 AS: Pedro Guerrero, Stl. .15
- ☐ 336 AS: Vince Coleman, Stl. .15
- ☐ 337 Terry Pendleton, Stl. .15
- ☐ 338 AS: Ozzie Smith, Stl. .50
- ☐ 339 Wille McGee, Stl. .15
- ☐ 340 Todd Worrell, Stl. .15
- ☐ 341 Jose Oquendo, Stl. .15
- ☐ 342 Team Logo, Stl. .15
- ☐ 343 Team Helmet, Stl. .15
- ☐ 344 Tom Brunansky, Stl. .15
- ☐ 345 Milt Thompson, Stl. .15
- ☐ 346 Joe Magrane, Stl. .15
- ☐ 347 Ed Whitson, S.D. .15
- ☐ 348 Jack Clark, S.D. .15
- ☐ 349 Roberto Alomar, S.D. .50
- ☐ 350 Chris James, S.D. .15
- ☐ 351 AS: Tony Gwynn, S.D. .75
- ☐ 352 AS: Mark Davis, S.D. .15
- ☐ 353 Greg Harris, S.D. .15
- ☐ 354 Garry Templeton, S.D. .15
- ☐ 355 Team Logo, S.D. .15
- ☐ 356 Team Helmet, S.D. .15
- ☐ 357 Bruce Hurst, S.D. .15
- ☐ 358 AS: Benito Santiago, S.D. .15
- ☐ 359 Bip Roberts, S.D. .15
- ☐ 360 Dave Dravecky, S.F. .15
- ☐ 361 AS: Kevin Mitchell, S.F. .15
- ☐ 362 Craig Lefferts, S.F. .15
- ☐ 363 AS: Will Clark, S.F. .15
- ☐ 364 Steve Bedrosian, S.F. .15
- ☐ 365 Brett Butler, S.F. .15
- ☐ 366 Matt Williams, S.F. .25
- ☐ 367 Scott Garrelts, S.F. .15
- ☐ 368 Team Logo, S.F. .15
- ☐ 369 Team Helmet, S.F. .15
- ☐ 370 AS: Rick Reuschel, S.F. .15
- ☐ 371 Robby Thompson, S.F. .15
- ☐ 372 Jose Uribe, S.F. .15
- ☐ 373 Pitcher .15
- ☐ 374 First Base .15
- ☐ 375 Pitcher .15
- ☐ 376 Outfield .15
- ☐ 377 Outfield .15
- ☐ 378 Catcher .15
- ☐ 379 Outfield .15
- ☐ 380 Pitcher .15
- ☐ 381 Catcher .15
- ☐ 382 Pitcher .15
- ☐ 383 HL: Vince Coleman .15
- ☐ 384 HL: Bo Jackson .15
- ☐ 385 HL: Howard Johnson .15
- ☐ 386 HL: Dave Dravecky .15
- ☐ 387 HL: Nolan Ryan 1.00
- ☐ 388 HL: Cal Ripken, Jr. 1.00

1991 BEN'S / HOLSUMS DISKS

This is the first year the Holsum disks were printed in Canada, and they were produced solely for distribution by Ben's in their bread products.

Disk Size: 2 3/4" Diameter

Face: Four colour, white border; name, position, team, Holsum's logo

Back: Black on card stock; name, résumé, numbered _ of 20

Imprint: "MLBPA 1991" MSA MADE IN CANADA

Complete Set (20 disks): 75.00

	No.	Player	MINT
☐	1	Darryl Strawberry, L.A.	3.00
☐	2	Eric Davis, Cin.	2.00
☐	3	Tim Wallach, Mtl.	2.00
☐	4	Kevin Mitchell, S.F.	2.00
☐	5	Tony Gwynn, S.D.	6.50
☐	6	Ryne Sandberg, Chi.-N.L.	3.50
☐	7	Doug Drabek, Pgh.	2.00
☐	8	Randy Myers, Cin.	2.00
☐	9	Ken Griffey, Jr., Sea.	25.00

	No.	Player	MINT
□	10	AlanTrammell, Det.	2.00
□	11	Ken Griffey, Sr., Sea.	2.00
□	12	Rickey Henderson, Oak.	3.00
□	13	Roger Clemens, Bos.	8.00
□	14	Bob Welch, Oak.	2.00
□	15	Kelly Gruber, Tor.	2.00
□	16	Mark McGwire, Oak.	8.00
□	17	Cecil Fielder, Det.	2.00
□	18	Dave Stieb, Tor.	2.00
□	19	Nolan Ryan, Tex.	18.00
□	20	Cal Ripken, Jr., Bal.	18.00

1991 O-PEE-CHEE

Card Size: 2 1/2" x 3 1/2"
Face: Four colour, white border; name, position, team, Topps logo
Back: Orange and blue on card stock; name, number, position, résumé, bilingual
Imprint: © 1991 O-PEE-CHEE

Complete Set (792 cards):			**20.00**
Common Player:			**.15**

	No.	Player	MINT
□	1	Nolan Ryan, Tex.	1.25
□	2	George Brett, K.C.	.35
□	3	Carlton Fisk, Chi.-A.L.	.25
□	4	Kevin Maas, NYY.	.15
□	5	Cal Ripken, Bal.	.75
□	6	Nolan Ryan, Tex.	.75
□	7	Ryne Sandberg, Chi.-N.L.	.25
□	8	Bobby Thigpen, Chi.-A.L.	.15
□	9	Darrin Fletcher, Pha.	.15
□	10	Gregg Olson, Bal.	.15
□	11	Roberto Kelly, NYY.	.15
□	12	Paul Assenmacher, Chi.-N.L.	.15
□	13	Mariano Duncan, Cin.	.15
□	14	Dennis Lamp, Bos.	.15
□	15	Von Hayes, Pha.	.15
□	16	Mike Heath, Det.	.15
□	17	Jeff Brantley, S.F.	.15
□	18	Nelson Liriano, Min.	.15
□	19	Jeff Robinson, NYY.	.15
□	20	Pedro Guerrero, Stl.	.15
□	21	Joe Morgan, Mgr., Bos.	.15
□	22	Storm Davis, K.C.	.15
□	23	Jim Gantner, Mil.	.15
□	24	Dave Martinez, Mtl.	.15
□	25	Tim Belcher, L.A.	.15
□	26	Luis Sojo, Tor., (Ana.)	.15
□	27	Bobby Witt, Tex.	.15
□	28	Alvaro Espinoza, NYY.	.15
□	29	Bob Walk, Pgh.	.15
□	30	Gregg Jefferies, NYM.	.15
□	**31**	**Colby Ward, Cle., RC**	**.15**
□	32	Mike Simms, Hou.	.15
□	33	Barry Jones, Chi.-A.L.	.15
□	34	Atlee Hammaker, S.D.	.15
□	35	Greg Maddux, Chi.-N.L.	1.00
□	36	Donnie Hill, Cal.	.15
□	37	Tom Bolton, Bos.	.15
□	38	Scott Bradley, Sea.	.15
□	**39**	**Jim Neidlinger, L.A., RC**	**.15**
□	40	Kevin Mitchell, S.F.	.15
□	41	Ken Dayley, Stl. (Tor.)	.15
□	42	Chris Hoiles, Bal.	.15
□	43	Roger McDowell, Pha.	.15
□	44	Mike Felder, Mil.	.15
□	45	Chris Sabo, Cin.	.15
□	46	Tim Drummond, Min.	.15
□	47	Brook Jacoby, Cle.	.15
□	48	Dennis Boyd, Mtl.	.15
□	49	Pat Borders, Tor.	.15
□	50	Bob Welch, Oak.	.15
□	51	Art Howe, Mgr., Hou.	.15
□	52	Francisco Oliveras, S.F.	.15
□	53	Mike Sharperson, L.A.	.15
□	54	Gary Mielke, Tex.	.15
□	55	Jeffrey Leonard, Sea.	.15
□	56	Jeff Parrett, Atl.	.15
□	57	Jack Howell, Cal.	.15
□	58	Mel Stottlemyre, K.C.	.15
□	59	Eric Yelding, Hou.	.15
□	60	Frank Viola, NYM.	.15
□	61	Stan Javier, L.A.	.15
□	62	Lee Guetterman, NYY.	.15
□	63	Milt Thompson, Stl.	.15
□	64	Tom Herr, NYM.	.15
□	65	Bruce Hurst, S.D.	.15
□	66	Terry Kennedy, S.F.	.15
□	67	Rick Honeycutt, Oak.	.15
□	68	Gary Sheffield, Mil.	.15
□	69	Steve Wilson, Chi.-N.L.	.25
□	70	Ellis Burks, Bos.	.25
□	71	Jim Acker, Tor.	.15
□	72	Junior Ortiz, Min.	.15
□	73	Craig Worthington, Bal.	.15
□	**74**	**Shane Andrews, Mtl., RC**	**.25**
□	75	Jack Morris, Det.	.15
□	76	Jerry Browne, Cle.	.15
□	77	Drew Hall, Mtl.	.15
□	78	Geno Petralli, Tex.	.15
□	79	Frank Thomas, Chi.-A.L.	2.00
□	80	Fernando Valenzuela, L.A.	.15
□	81	Cito Gaston, Mgr., Tor.	.15
□	82	Tom Glavine, Atl.	.15
□	83	Daryl Boston, NYM.	.15
□	84	Bob McClure, Cal.	.15
□	85	Jesse Barfield, NYY.	.15
□	86	Les Lancaster, Chi.-N.L.	.15
□	87	Tracy Jones, Sea.	.15
□	88	Bob Tewksbury, Stl.	.15
□	89	Darren Daulton, Pha.	.15
□	90	Danny Tartabull, K.C.	.15
□	**91**	**Greg Colbrunn, Mtl., RC**	**.15**
□	92	Danny Jackson, Cin. (Chi.-N.L.)	.15
□	93	Ivan Calderon, Chi.-A.L. (Mtl.)	.15
□	94	John Dopson, Bos.	.15
□	95	Paul Molitor, Mil.	.25
□	96	Trevor Wilson, S.F.	.15
□	97	Brady Anderson, Bal.	.15
□	98	Sergio Valdez, Cle.	.15
□	99	Chris Gwynn, L.A.	.15
□	100	Don Mattingly, NYY.	.75
□	101	Rob Ducey, Tor.	.25

- ☐ 102 Gene Larkin, Min. .15
- ☐ 103 Tim Costo, Cle. .15
- ☐ 104 Don Robinson, S.F. .15
- ☐ 105 Kevin McReynolds, NYM. .15
- ☐ 106 Ed Nunez, Det. (Atl.) .15
- ☐ 107 Luis Polonia, Cal. .15
- ☐ 108 Matt Young, Sea. (Bos.) .15
- ☐ 109 Greg Riddoch, Mgr., S.D. .15
- ☐ 110 Tom Henke, Tor. .15
- ☐ 111 Andres Thomas, Atl. .15
- ☐ 112 Frank DiPino, Stl. .15
- ☐ **113 Carl Everett, NYY., RC .15**
- ☐ **114 Lance Dickson, Chi.-N.L., RC .15**
- ☐ 115 Hubie Brooks, L.A. (NYM.) .15
- ☐ 116 Mark Davis, K.C. .15
- ☐ 117 Dion James, Cle. .15
- ☐ **118 Tom Edens, Mil., RC .15**
- ☐ 119 Carl Nichols, Hou. .15
- ☐ 120 Joe Carter, S.D. (Tor,) .15
- ☐ 121 Eric King, Chi.-A.L. (Cle.) .15
- ☐ 122 Paul O'Neill, Cin. .15
- ☐ 123 Greg Harris, Bos. .15
- ☐ 124 Randy Bush, Min. .15
- ☐ 125 Steve Bedrosian, S.F. (Min.) .15
- ☐ 126 Bernard Gilkey, Stl. .15
- ☐ 127 Joe Price, Bal. .15
- ☐ 128 Travis Fryman, Det. .25
- ☐ 129 Mark Eichhorn, Cal. .15
- ☐ 130 Ozzie Smith, Stl. .25
- ☐ 131 1991 Checklist No. 1 of 6 .15
- ☐ 132 Jamie Quirk, Oak. .15
- ☐ 133 Greg Briley, Sea. .15
- ☐ 134 Kevin Elster, NYM. .15
- ☐ 135 Jerome Walton, Chi.-N.L. .15
- ☐ 136 Dave Schmidt, Mtl. .15
- ☐ 137 Randy Ready, Pha. .15
- ☐ 138 Jamie Moyer, Tex. (Stl.) .15
- ☐ 139 Jeff Treadway, Atl. .15
- ☐ 140 Fred McGriff, Tor. (S.D.) .25
- ☐ 141 Nick Leyva, Mgr., Pha. .15
- ☐ 142 Curt Wilkerson, Chi.-N.L. (Pgh.) .15
- ☐ 143 John Smiley, Pgh. .15
- ☐ 144 Dave Henderson, Oak. .15
- ☐ 145 Lou Whitaker, Det. .15
- ☐ 146 Dan Plesac, Mil. .15
- ☐ 147 Carlos Baerga, Cle. .15
- ☐ 148 Rey Palacios, K.C. .15
- ☐ **149 Al Osuna, Hou., RC .15**
- ☐ 150 Cal Ripken, Bal. 1.25
- ☐ 151 Tom Browning, Cin. .15
- ☐ 152 Mickey Hatcher, L.A. .15
- ☐ 153 Bryan Harvey, Cal. .15
- ☐ 154 Jay Buhner, Sea. .15
- ☐ 155 Dwight Evans, Bos. (Bal.) .15
- ☐ 156 Carlos Martinez, Chi.-A.L. .15
- ☐ 157 John Smoltz, Atl. .15
- ☐ 158 Jose Uribe, S.F. .15
- ☐ 159 Joe Boever, Pha. .15
- ☐ 160 Vince Coleman, Stl. (NYM.) .15
- ☐ 161 Tim Leary, NYY. .15
- ☐ 162 Ozzie Canseco, Oak. .15
- ☐ 163 Dave Johnson, Bal. .15
- ☐ 164 Edgar Diaz, Mil. .15
- ☐ 165 Sandy Alomar, Cle. .15
- ☐ 166 Harold Baines, Oak .15
- ☐ **167 Randy Tomlin, Pgh., RC .15**
- ☐ 168 John Olerud, Tor. .25
- ☐ 169 Luis Aquino, K.C. .15
- ☐ 170 Carlton Fisk, Chi.-A.L. .25
- ☐ 171 Tony LaRussa, Mgr., Oak. .15
- ☐ 172 Pete Incaviglia, Tex. .15
- ☐ 173 Jason Grimsley, Pha. .15
- ☐ 174 Ken Caminiti, Hou. .25
- ☐ 175 Jack Armstrong, Cin. .15
- ☐ 176 John Orton, Cal. .15
- ☐ 177 Reggie Harris, Oak. .15
- ☐ 178 Dave Valle, Sea. .15
- ☐ 179 Pete Harnisch, Bal. (Hou.) .15
- ☐ 180 Tony Gwynn, S.D. .50
- ☐ 181 Duane Ward, Tor. .15
- ☐ 182 Junior Noboa, Mtl. .15
- ☐ 183 Clay Parker, Det. .15
- ☐ 184 Gary Green, Tex. .15
- ☐ 185 Joe Magrane, Stl. .15
- ☐ 186 Rod Booker, Phi. .15
- ☐ 187 Greg Cadaret, NYY. .15
- ☐ 188 Damon Berryhill, Chi.-N.L. .15
- ☐ **189 Daryl Irvine, Bos., RC .15**
- ☐ 190 Matt Williams, S.F. .15
- ☐ 191 Willie Blair, Tor., (Cle.) .15
- ☐ 192 Rob Deer, Mil. (Det.) .15
- ☐ 193 Felix Fermin, Cle. .15
- ☐ 194 Xavier Hernandez, Hou. .15
- ☐ 195 Wally Joyner, Cal. .15
- ☐ **196 Jim Vatcher, Atl., RC .15**
- ☐ **197 Chris Nabholz, Mtl., RC .15**
- ☐ 198 R.J. Reynolds, Pgh. .15
- ☐ 199 Mike Hartley, L.A. .15
- ☐ 200 Darryl Strawberry, NYM. (L.A.) .25
- ☐ 201 Tom Kelly, Mgr., Min. .15
- ☐ 202 Jim Leyritz, NYY. .15
- ☐ 203 Gene Harris, Sea. 15.
- ☐ 204 Herm Winningham, Cin. .15
- ☐ **205 Mike Perez, Stl., RC .15**
- ☐ 206 Carlos Quintana, Bos. .15
- ☐ 207 Gary Wayne, Min. .15
- ☐ 208 Willie Wilson, K.C. (Oak.) .15
- ☐ 209 Ken Howell, Pha. .15
- ☐ 210 Lance Parrish, Cal. .15
- ☐ **211 Brian Barnes, Mtl., RC .15**
- ☐ 212 Steve Finley, Bal. (Hou.) .15
- ☐ 213 Frank Wills, Tor. .15
- ☐ 214 Joe Girardi, Chi.-N.L. .15
- ☐ 215 Dave Smith, Hou. (Chi.-N.L.) .15
- ☐ 216 Greg Gagne, Min. .15
- ☐ 217 Chris Bosio, Mil. .15
- ☐ 218 Rick Parker, S.F. .15
- ☐ 219 Jack McDowell, Chi.-A.L. .15
- ☐ 220 Tim Wallach, Mtl. .15
- ☐ 221 Don Slaught, Pgh. .15
- ☐ **222 Brian McRae, K.C., RC .25**
- ☐ 223 Allan Anderson, Min. .15
- ☐ 224 Juan Gonzalez, Tex. .75
- ☐ 225 Randy Johnson, Sea. .25
- ☐ 226 Alfredo Griffin, L.A. .15
- ☐ 227 Steve Avery, Atl. .15
- ☐ 228 Rex Hudler, Stl. .15
- ☐ 229 Rance Mulliniks, Tor. .15
- ☐ 230 Sid Fernandez, NYM. .15
- ☐ 231 Doug Rader, Mgr., Cal. .15
- ☐ 232 Jose DeJesus, Pha. .15
- ☐ 233 Al Leiter, Tor. .15
- ☐ **234 Scott Erickson, Min., RC .25**
- ☐ 235 Dave Parker, Mil. .15
- ☐ 236 Frank Tanana, Det. .15
- ☐ 237 Rick Cerone, NYY. .15
- ☐ 238 Mike Dunne, S.D. .15
- ☐ 239 Darren Lewis, Oak., (NYG.) .15

☐ 240 Mike Scott, Hou. .15
☐ 241 Dave Clark, Chi.-N.L. .15
☐ 242 Mike LaCoss, S.F. .15
☐ 243 Lance Johnson, Chi.-A.L. .15
☐ 244 Mike Jeffcoat, Tex. .15
☐ 245 Kal Daniels, L.A. .15
☐ 246 Kevin Wickander, Cle. .15
☐ 247 Jody Reed, Bos. .15
☐ 248 Tom Gordon, K.C. .15
☐ 249 Bob Melvin, Bal. .15
☐ 250 Dennis Eckersley, Oak. .15
☐ 251 Mark Lemke, Atl. .15
☐ 252 Mel Rojas, Mtl. .15
☐ 253 Garry Templeton, S.D. .15
☐ 254 Shawn Boskie, Chi.-N.L. .15
☐ 255 Brian Downing, Cal. .15
☐ 256 Greg Hibbard, Chi.-A.L. .15
☐ 257 Tom O'Malley, NYM. .15
☐ 258 Chris Hammond, Cin. .15
☐ 259 Hensley Meulens, NYY. .15
☐ 260 Harold Reynolds, Sea. .15
☐ 261 Bud Harrelson, Mgr., NYM. .15
☐ 262 Tim Jones, Stl. .15
☐ 263 1991 Checklist No. 2 of 6 .15
☐ 264 Dave Hollins, Phi. .15
☐ 265 Mark Gubicza, K.C. .15
☐ 266 Carmelo Castillo, Min. .15
☐ 267 Mark Knudson, Mil. .15
☐ 268 Tom Brookens, Cle. .15
☐ 269 Joe Hesketh, Bos. .15
☐ 270 Mark McGwire, Oak. .75
☐ **271 Omar Olivares, Stl., RC .15**
☐ 272 Jeff King, Pgh. .15
☐ 273 Johnny Ray, Cal. .15
☐ 274 Ken Williams, Tor. .15
☐ 275 Alan Trammell, Det. .15
☐ 276 Bill Swift, Sea. .15
☐ 277 Scott Coolbaugh, Tex., (S.D.) .15
☐ 278 Alex Fernandez, Chi.-A.L. .15
☐ 279 Jose Gonzalez, L.A. .15
☐ 280 Bret Saberhagen, K.C. .15
☐ 281 Larry Sheets, Det. .15
☐ 282 Don Carman, Pha. .15
☐ 283 Marquis Grissom, Mtl. .15
☐ 284 Billy Spiers, Mil. .15
☐ 285 Jim Abbott, Cal. .15
☐ 286 Ken Oberkfell, Hou. .15
☐ 287 Mark Grant, Atl. .15
☐ 288 Derrick May, Chi.-N.L. .15
☐ 289 Tim Birtsas, Cin. .15
☐ 290 Steve Sax, NYY. .15
☐ 291 John Wathan, Mgr., K.C. .15
☐ 292 Bud Black, Tor. (NYG.) .15
☐ 293 Jay Bell, Pgh. .15
☐ 294 Mike Moore, Oak. .15
☐ 295 Rafael Palmeiro, Tex. .15
☐ 296 Mark Williamson, Bal. .15
☐ 297 Manny Lee, Tor. .15
☐ 298 Omar Vizquel, Sea. .15
☐ 299 Scott Radinsky, Chi.-A.L. .15
☐ 300 Kirby Puckett, Min. .75
☐ 301 Steve Farr, K.C. (NYY.) .15
☐ 302 Tim Teufel, NYM. .15
☐ 303 Mike Boddicker, Bos. (K.C.) .15
☐ 304 Kevin Reimer, Tex. .25
☐ 305 Mike Scioscia, L.A. .15
☐ 306 Lonnie Smith, Atl. .15
☐ 307 Andy Benes, S.D. .15
☐ 308 Tom Pagnozzi, Stl. .15
☐ 309 Norm Charlton, Cin. .15
☐ 310 Gary Carter, S.F. .25
☐ 311 Jeff Pico, Chi.-N.L. .15
☐ 312 Charlie Hayes, Pha. .15
☐ 313 Ron Robinson, Mil. .15
☐ 314 Gary Pettis, Tex. .15
☐ 315 Roberto Alomar, S.D. (Tor.) .35
☐ 316 Gene Nelson, Oak. .15
☐ 317 Mike Fitzgerald, Mtl. .15
☐ 318 Rick Aguilera, Min. .15
☐ 319 Jeff McKnight, Bal. .15
☐ 320 Tony Fernandez, Tor. (S.D.) .15
☐ 321 Bob Rodgers, Mgr., Mtl. .15
☐ 322 Terry Shumpert, K.C. .15
☐ 323 Cory Snyder, Cle. (Bos.) .15
☐ 324 Ron Kittle, Bal. .15
☐ 325 Brett Butler, S.F. (L.A.) .15
☐ 326 Ken Patterson, Chi.-A.L. .15
☐ 327 Ron Hassey, Oak. .15
☐ 328 Walt Terrell, Det. .15
☐ 329 David Justice, Atl. .25
☐ 330 Doc Gooden, NYM. .15
☐ 331 Eric Anthony, Hou. .15
☐ 332 Kenny Rogers, Tex. .15
☐ **333 Chipper Jones, Atl., RC 4.00**
☐ 334 Todd Benzinger, Cin. .15
☐ 335 Mitch Williams, Chi.-N.L. .15
☐ 336 Matt Nokes, NYY. .15
☐ 337 Keith Comstock, Sea. .15
☐ 338 Luis Rivera, Bos. .15
☐ 339 Larry Walker, Mtl. 1.00
☐ 340 Ramon Martinez, L.A. .15
☐ 341 John Moses, Min. .15
☐ 342 Mickey Morandini, Pha. .15
☐ 343 Jose Oquendo, Stl. .15
☐ 344 Jeff Russell, Tex. .15
☐ 345 Len Dykstra, Pha. .15
☐ 346 Jesse Orosco, Cle. .15
☐ 347 Greg Vaughn, Mil. .15
☐ 348 Todd Stottlemyre, Tor. .15
☐ 349 Dave Gallagher, Bal. (Ana.) .15
☐ 350 Glenn Davis, Hou. (Bal.) .15
☐ 351 Joe Torre, Mgr., Stl. .15
☐ 352 Frank White, K.C. .15
☐ 353 Tony Castillo, Atl. .15
☐ 354 Sid Bream, Pgh. (Atl.) .15
☐ 355 Chili Davis, Cal. .15
☐ 356 Mike Marshall, .15
☐ 357 Jack Savage, Min. .15
☐ 358 Mark Parent, S.D. (Tex.) .15
☐ 359 Chuck Cary, NYY. .15
☐ 360 Tim Raines, Mtl. (Chi.-A.L.) .15
☐ 361 Scott Garrelts, S.F. .15
☐ 362 Hector Villanueva, Chi.-N.L. .15
☐ 363 Rick Mahler, Cin. .15
☐ 364 Dan Pasqua, Chi.-A.L. .15
☐ 365 Mike Schooler, Sea. .15
☐ 366 1991 Checklist No. 3 of 6 .15
☐ 367 Dave Walsh .15
☐ 368 Felix Jose, Stl. .15
☐ 369 Steve Searcy, Det. .15
☐ 370 Kelly Gruber, Tor. .15
☐ 371 Jeff Montgomery, K.C. .15
☐ 372 Spike Owen, Mtl. .15
☐ 373 Darrin Jackson, S.D. .15
☐ **374 Larry Casian, Min., RC .15**
☐ 375 Tony Pena, Bos. .15
☐ 376 Mike Harkey, Chi.-N.L. .15
☐ 377 Rene Gonzales, Bal. .15

- ☐ 378 Wilson Alvarez, Chi.-A.L. .15
- ☐ 379 Randy Velarde, NYY. .15
- ☐ 380 Willie McGee, Oak. .15
- ☐ 381 Jim Leyland, Mgr., Pgh. .15
- ☐ 382 Mackey Sasser, NYM. .15
- ☐ 383 Pete Smith, Atl. .15
- ☐ 384 Gerald Perry, K.C. (Stl.) .15
- ☐ 385 Mickey Tettleton, Bal. (Det.) .15
- ☐ 386 AS: Cecil Fielder, Det. .15
- ☐ 387 AS: Julio Franco, Tex. .15
- ☐ 388 AS: Kelly Gruber, Tor. .15
- ☐ 389 AS: Alan Trammell, Det. .15
- ☐ 390 AS: Jose Canseco, Oak. .25
- ☐ 391 AS: Rickey Henderson, Oak. .15
- ☐ 392 AS: Ken Griffey Jr., Sea. .15
- ☐ 393 AS: Carlton Fisk, Chi.-N.L. .25
- ☐ 394 AS: Bob Welch, Oak. .15
- ☐ 395 AS: Chuck Finley, Cal. .15
- ☐ 396 AS: Bobby Thigpen, Chi.-N.L. .15
- ☐ 397 AS: Eddie Murray, L.A. .25
- ☐ 398 AS: Ryne Sandberg, Chi.-N.L. .25
- ☐ 399 AS: Matt Williams, S.F. .15
- ☐ 400 AS: Barry Larkin .15
- ☐ 401 AS: Barry Bonds, Pgh. .25
- ☐ 402 AS: Darryl Strawberry, NYM. .25
- ☐ 403 AS: Bobby Bonilla, Pgh. .15
- ☐ 404 AS: Mike Scioscia, L.A. .15
- ☐ 405 AS: Doug Drabek, Pgh. .15
- ☐ 406 AS: Frank Viola, NYM. .15
- ☐ 407 AS: John Franco, NYM. .15
- ☐ 408 Ernie Riles, S.F. (Oak.) .15
- ☐ 409 Mike Stanley, Tex. .15
- ☐ 410 Dave Righetti, NYY. .15
- ☐ 411 Lance Blankenship, Oak. .15
- ☐ 412 Dave Bergman, Det. .15
- ☐ 413 Terry Mulholland, Pha. .15
- ☐ 414 Sammy Sosa, Chi.-A.L. .25
- ☐ 415 Rick Sutcliffe, Chi.-N.L. .15
- ☐ 416 Randy Milligan, Bal. .15
- ☐ 417 Bill Krueger, Mil. (Sea.) .15
- ☐ 418 Nick Esasky, Atl. .15
- ☐ 419 Jeff Reed, Cin. .15
- ☐ 420 Bobby Thigpen, Chi.-A.L. .15
- ☐ 421 Alex Cole, Cle. .15
- ☐ 422 Rick Reuschel, S.F. .15
- ☐ 423 Rafael Ramirez, Hou. .15
- ☐ 424 Calvin Schiraldi, S.D. .15
- ☐ 425 Andy Van Slyke, Pgh. .15
- ☐ **426 Joe Grahe, Cal., RC .15**
- ☐ 427 Rick Dempsey, L.A. .15
- ☐ **428 John Barfield, Tex., RC .15**
- ☐ 429 Stump Merrill, Mgr., NYY. .15
- ☐ 430 Gary Gaetti, Min. .15
- ☐ 431 Paul Gibson, Det. .15
- ☐ 432 Delino DeShields, Mtl. .15
- ☐ 433 Pat Tabler, NYM. (Tor.) .15
- ☐ 434 Julio Machado, Mil. .15
- ☐ 435 Kevin Maas, NYY. .15
- ☐ 436 Scott Bankhead, Sea. .15
- ☐ 437 Doug Dascenzo, Chi.-N.L. .15
- ☐ 438 Vincente Palacios, Pgh. .15
- ☐ 439 Dickie Thon, Pha. .15
- ☐ 440 George Bell, Tor. (Chi.-N.L.) .15
- ☐ 441 Zane Smith, Pgh. .15
- ☐ 442 Charlie O'Brien, NYM. .15
- ☐ 443 Jeff Innis, NYM. .15
- ☐ 444 Glenn Braggs, Cin. .15
- ☐ 445 Greg Swindell, Cle. .15
- ☐ 446 Craig Grebeck, Chi.-A.L. .15
- ☐ 447 John Burkett, S.F. .15
- ☐ 448 Craig Lefferts, S.D. .15
- ☐ 449 Juan Berenguer, Min. .15
- ☐ 450 Wade Boggs, Bos. .35
- ☐ 451 Neal Heaton, Pgh. .15
- ☐ 452 Bill Schroeder, Cal. .15
- ☐ 453 Lenny Harris, L.A. .15
- ☐ 454 Kevin Appier, K.C. .15
- ☐ 455 Walt Weiss, Oak. .15
- ☐ 456 Charlie Leibrandt, Atl. .15
- ☐ 457 Todd Hundley, NYM. .15
- ☐ 458 Brian Holman, Sea. .15
- ☐ 459 Tom Trebelhorn, Mgr., Mil. .15
- ☐ 460 Dave Stieb, Tor. .15
- ☐ 461 Robin Ventura, Chi.-A.L. .15
- ☐ 462 Steve Frey, Mtl. .15
- ☐ 463 Dwight Smith, Chi.-N.L. .15
- ☐ 464 Steve Buechele, Tex. .15
- ☐ 465 Ken Griffey, Sea. .15
- ☐ 466 Charles Nagy, Cle. .15
- ☐ 467 Dennis Cook, L.A. .15
- ☐ 468 Tim Hulett, Bal. .15
- ☐ 469 Chet Lemon, Det. .15
- ☐ 470 Howard Johnson, NYM. .15
- ☐ 471 Mike Lieberthal, Pha. .15
- ☐ 472 Kirt Manwaring, S.F. .15
- ☐ 473 Curt Young, Oak. .15
- ☐ **474 Phil Plantier, Bos., RC .15**
- ☐ 475 Teddy Higuera, Mil. .15
- ☐ 476 Glenn Wilson, Hou. .15
- ☐ 477 Mike Fetters, Cal. .15
- ☐ 478 Kurt Stillwell, K.C. .15
- ☐ 479 Bob Patterson, Pgh. .15
- ☐ 480 Dave Magadan, NYM. .15
- ☐ 481 Eddie Whitson, S.D. .15
- ☐ 482 Tino Martinez, Sea. .15
- ☐ 483 Mike Aldrete, Mtl. .15
- ☐ 484 Dave LaPoint, NYY. .15
- ☐ 485 Terry Pendleton, Stl. (Atl.) .15
- ☐ 486 Tommy Greene, Pha. .15
- ☐ 487 Rafael Belliard, Pgh. (Atl.) .15
- ☐ 488 Jeff Manto, Cle. .15
- ☐ 489 Bobby Valentine, Mgr., Tex. .15
- ☐ 490 Kirk Gibson, L.A. (K.C.) .15
- ☐ 491 Kurt Miller, Pgh. .15
- ☐ 492 Ernie Whitt, Atl. .15
- ☐ 493 Jose Rijo, Cin. .15
- ☐ 494 Chris James, Cle. .15
- ☐ 495 Charlie Hough, Tex. (Chi.-A.L.) .15
- ☐ 496 Marty Barrett, Bos. (S.D.) .15
- ☐ 497 Ben McDonald, Bal. .15
- ☐ 498 Mark Salas, Det. .15
- ☐ 499 Melido Perez, Chi.-A.L. .15
- ☐ 500 Will Clark, S.F. .25
- ☐ 501 Mike Bielecki, Chi.-N.L. .15
- ☐ 502 Carney Lansford, Oak. .15
- ☐ 503 Roy Smith, Min. .15
- ☐ 504 Julio Valera, NYM. .15
- ☐ 505 Chuck Finley, Cal. .15
- ☐ 506 Darnell Coles, Det. .15
- ☐ 507 Steve Jeltz, K.C. .15
- ☐ **508 Mike York, Pgh., RC .15**
- ☐ 509 Glenallen Hill, Tor. .15
- ☐ 510 John Franco, NYM. .15
- ☐ 511 Steve Balboni, NYY. .15
- ☐ 512 Jose Mesa, Bal. .15
- ☐ 513 Jerald Clark, S.D. .15
- ☐ 514 Mike Stanton, Atl. .15
- ☐ 515 Alvin Davis, Sea. .15

	No.	Player	Price
☐	516	Karl Rhodes, Hou.	.15
☐	517	Joe Oliver, Cin.	.15
☐	518	Cris Carpenter, Stl.	.15
☐	519	Sparky Anderson, Mgr., Det.	.15
☐	520	Mark Grace, Chi.-N.L.	.15
☐	521	Joe Orsulak, Bal.	.15
☐	522	Stan Belinda, Pgh.	.15
☐	**523**	**Rodney McCray, Chi.-A.L., RC**	**.15**
☐	524	Darrel Akerfelds, Pha.	.15
☐	525	Willie Randolph, Oak.	.15
☐	526	Moises Alou, Mtl.	.50
☐	527	1991 Checklist No. 4 of 6	.15
☐	528	Denny Martinez, Mtl.	.15
☐	529	Marc Newfield, Sea.	.15
☐	530	Roger Clemens, Bos.	.75
☐	531	Dave Rohde, Hou.	.15
☐	532	Kirk McCaskill, Cal.	.25
☐	533	Oddibe McDowell, Atl.	.15
☐	534	Mike Jackson, Sea.	.15
☐	535	Ruben Sierra, Tex.	.15
☐	536	Mike Witt, NYY.	.15
☐	537	Jose Lind, Pgh.	.15
☐	538	Bip Roberts, S.D.	.15
☐	539	Scott Terry, Stl.	.15
☐	540	George Brett, K.C.	.50
☐	541	Domingo Ramos, Chi.-N.L.	.15
☐	542	Rob Murphy, Bos.	.15
☐	543	Junior Felix, Tor. (Ana.)	.15
☐	544	Alejandro Pena, NYM.	.15
☐	545	Dale Murphy, Pha.	.25
☐	546	Jeff Ballard, Bal.	.15
☐	547	Mike Pagliarulo, S.D.	.15
☐	548	Jamie Navarro, Mil.	.15
☐	549	John McNamara, Mgr., Cle.	.15
☐	550	Eric Davis, Cin.	.15
☐	551	Bob Kipper, Pgh.	.15
☐	552	Jeff Hamilton, L.A.	.15
☐	553	Joe Klink, Oak.	.15
☐	554	Brian Harper, Min.	.15
☐	**555**	**Turner Ward, Cle., RC**	**.15**
☐	556	Gary Ward, Det.	.15
☐	557	Wally Whitehurst, NYM.	.15
☐	558	Otis Nixon, Mtl.	.15
☐	559	Adam Peterson, Chi.-A.L.	.15
☐	560	Greg Smith, Chi.-N.L. (L.A.)	.15
☐	561	Future Star: Tim McIntosh, Mil.	.15
☐	562	Jeff Kunkel, Tex.	.15
☐	**563**	**Brent Knackert, Sea., RC**	**.15**
☐	564	Dante Bichette, Cal.	.15
☐	565	Craig Biggio, Hou.	.15
☐	**566**	**Craig Wilson, Stl., RC**	**.15**
☐	567	Dwayne Henry, Atl.	.15
☐	568	Ron Karkovice, Chi.-A.L.	.15
☐	569	Curt Schilling, Bal. (Hou.)	.15
☐	570	Barry Bonds, Pgh.	.35
☐	571	Pat Combs, Pha.	.15
☐	572	Dave Anderson, S.F.	.15
☐	**573**	**Rich Rodriguez, S.D., RC**	**.15**
☐	574	John Marzano, Bos.	.15
☐	575	Robin Yount, Mil.	.25
☐	576	Jeff Kaiser, Cle.	.15
☐	577	Bill Doran, Cin.	.15
☐	578	Dave West, Min.	.15
☐	579	Roger Craig, Mgr., S.F.	.15
☐	580	Dave Stewart, Oak.	.15
☐	581	Luis Quinones, Cin.	.15
☐	582	Marty Clary, Atl.	.15
☐	583	Tony Phillips, Det.	.15
☐	584	Kevin Brown, Tex.	.15
☐	585	Pete O'Brien, Sea.	.15
☐	586	Fred Lynn, S.D.	.15
☐	587	Jose Offerman, L.A.	.15
☐	588	Mark Whiten, Tor.	.15
☐	589	Scott Ruskin, Mtl.	.15
☐	590	Eddie Murray, L.A.	.25
☐	591	Ken Hill, Stl.	.15
☐	592	B.J. Surhoff, Mil.	.15
☐	593	Mike Walker, Cle.	.15
☐	**594**	**Rich Garces, Min., RC**	**.15**
☐	595	Bill Landrum, Pgh.	.15
☐	596	Ronnie Walden, L.A.	.15
☐	597	Jerry Don Gleaton, Det.	.15
☐	598	Sam Horn, Bal.	.15
☐	599	Greg Myers, Tor.	.15
☐	600	Bo Jackson, K.C.	.15
☐	601	Bob Ojeda, NYM. (L.A.)	.15
☐	602	Casey Candaele, Hou.	.15
☐	**603**	**Wes Chamberlain, Pha., RC**	**.15**
☐	604	Billy Hatcher, Cin.	.15
☐	605	Jeff Reardon, Bos.	.15
☐	606	Jim Gott, L.A.	.15
☐	607	Edgar Martinez, Sea.	.15
☐	608	Todd Burns, Oak.	.15
☐	609	Jeff Torborg, Mgr., Chi.-A.L.	.15
☐	610	Andres Galarraga, Mtl.	.25
☐	611	Dave Eiland, NYY.	.15
☐	612	Steve Lyons, Chi.-A.L.	.15
☐	613	Eric Show, S.D. (Oak.)	.15
☐	614	Luis Salazar, Chi.-N.L.	.15
☐	615	Bert Blyleven, Cal.	.15
☐	616	Todd Zeile, Stl.	.15
☐	617	Bill Wegman, Mil.	.15
☐	618	Sil Campusano, Pha.	.15
☐	619	David Wells, Tor.	.15
☐	620	Ozzie Guillen, Chi.-A.L.	.15
☐	621	Ted Power, Pgh. (Cin.)	.15
☐	622	Jack Daugherty, Tex.	.15
☐	623	Jeff Blauser, Atl.	.15
☐	624	Tom Candiotti, Cle.	.15
☐	625	Terry Steinbach, Oak.	.15
☐	626	Gerald Young, Hou.	.15
☐	627	Tim Layana, Cin.	.15
☐	628	Greg Litton, S.F.	.15
☐	629	Wes Gardner, Bos. (S.D.)	.15
☐	630	Dave Winfield, Cal.	.25
☐	631	Mike Morgan, L.A.	.15
☐	632	Lloyd Moseby, Det.	.15
☐	633	Kevin Tapini, Min.	.15
☐	634	Henry Cotto, Sea.	.15
☐	635	Andy Hawkins, NYY.	.15
☐	**636**	**Geronimo Pena, Stl., RC**	**.15**
☐	637	Bruce Ruffin, Pha.	.15
☐	638	Mike Macfarlane, K.C.	.15
☐	639	Frank Robinson, Mgr., Bal.	.25
☐	640	Andre Dawson, Chi.-N.L.	.25
☐	641	Mike Henneman, Det.	.15
☐	642	Hal Morris, Cin.	.15
☐	643	Jim Presley, Atl.	.15
☐	644	Chuck Crim, Mil.	.15
☐	645	Juan Samuel, L.A.	.15
☐	646	Andujar Cedeno, Hou.	.15
☐	647	Mark Portugal, Hou.	.15
☐	648	Lee Stevens, Cal.	.15
☐	649	Bill Sampen, Mtl.	.15
☐	650	Jack Clark, S.D., (Bos.)	.15
☐	651	Alan Mills, NYY.	15
☐	652	Kevin Romine, Bos.	.15
☐	**653**	**Anthony Telford, Bal., RC**	**.15**

- ☐ 654 Paul Sorrento, Min. .15
- ☐ 655 Erik Hanson, Sea. .15
- ☐ 656 1991 Checklist No. 5 .15of 6 .15
- ☐ 657 Mike Kingery, S.F. .15
- ☐ 658 Scott Aldred, Det. .15
- ☐ **659 Oscar Azocar, NYY., (S.D.), RC .15**
- ☐ 660 Lee Smith, Stl. .15
- ☐ 661 Steve Lake, Pha. .15
- ☐ 662 Rob Dibble, Cin. .15
- ☐ 663 Greg Brock, Mil. .15
- ☐ 664 John Farrell, Cle. .15
- ☐ 665 Mike LaValliere, Pgh. .15
- ☐ 666 Danny Darwin, Hou. (Bos.) .15
- ☐ 667 Kent Anderson, Cal. .15
- ☐ 668 Bill Long, Chi.-N.L. .15
- ☐ 669 Lou Piniella, Mgr., Cin. .15
- ☐ 670 Rickey Henderson, Oak. .25
- ☐ 671 Andy McGaffigan, K.C. .15
- ☐ 672 Shane Mack, Min. .15
- ☐ 673 Greg Olson, Atl. .15
- ☐ 674 Kevin Gross, Mtl. (L.A.) .15
- ☐ 675 Tom Brunansky, Bos. .15
- ☐ **676 Scott Chiamparino, Tex., RC .15**
- ☐ 677 Billy Ripken, Bal. .15
- ☐ 678 Mark Davidson, Hou. .15
- ☐ 679 Bill Bathe, S.F. .15
- ☐ 680 David Cone, NYM. .15
- ☐ **681 Jeff Schaefer, Sea., RC .15**
- ☐ 682 Ray Lankford, Stl. .15
- ☐ 683 Derek Lilliquist, S.D. .15
- ☐ 684 Milt Cuyler, Det. .15
- ☐ 685 Doug Drabek, Pgh. .15
- ☐ 686 Mike Gallego, Oak. .15
- ☐ 687 John Cerutti, Tor. .15
- ☐ **688 Rosario Rodriguez, Cin., (Pgh.), RC .15**
- ☐ 689 John Kruk, Pha. .15
- ☐ 690 Orel Hershiser, L.A. .15
- ☐ 691 Mike Blowers, NYY. .15
- ☐ **692 Efrain Valdez, Cle., RC .15**
- ☐ 693 Francisco Cabrera, Atl. .15
- ☐ 694 Randy Veres, Mil. .15
- ☐ 695 Kevin Seitzer, K.C. .15
- ☐ 696 Steve Olin, Cle. .15
- ☐ 697 Shawn Abner, S.D. .15
- ☐ 698 Mark Guthrie, Min. .15
- ☐ 699 Jim Lefebvre, Mgr., Sea. .15
- ☐ 700 Jose Canseco, Oak. .25
- ☐ 701 Pascual Perez, NYY. .15
- ☐ **702 Tim Naehring, Bos., RC .15**
- ☐ 703 Juan Agosto, Hou. (Stl.) .15
- ☐ 704 Devon White, Cal. (Tor.) .15
- ☐ 705 Robby Thompson, S.F. .15
- ☐ 706 Brad Arnsberg, Tex. .15
- ☐ 707 Jim Eisenreich, K.C. .15
- ☐ 708 John Mitchell, Bal. .15
- ☐ 709 Matt Sinatro, Sea. .15
- ☐ 710 Kent Hrbek, Min. .15
- ☐ 711 Jose DeLeon, Stl. .15
- ☐ 712 Ricky Jordan, Pha. .15
- ☐ 713 Scott Scudder, Cin. .15
- ☐ 714 Marvell Wynne, Chi.-N.L. .15
- ☐ 715 Tim Burke, Mtl. .15
- ☐ 716 Bob Geren, NYY. .15
- ☐ 717 Phil Bradley, Chi.-A.L. .15
- ☐ 718 Steve Crawford, K.C. .15
- ☐ 719 Keith Miller, NYM. .15
- ☐ 720 Cecil Fielder, Det. .15
- ☐ 721 Mark Lee, Mil. .15
- ☐ 722 Wally Backman, Pgh. (Pha.) .15
- ☐ 723 Candy Maldonado, Cle. .15
- ☐ 724 David Segui, Bal. .15
- ☐ 725 Ron Gant, Atl. .15
- ☐ 726 Phil Stephenson, S.D. .15
- ☐ 727 Mookie Wilson, Tor. .15
- ☐ 728 Scott Sanderson, Oak. (NYY.) .15
- ☐ 729 Don Zimmer, Mgr., Chi.-N.L. .15
- ☐ 730 Barry Larkin, Cin. .25
- ☐ **731 Jeff Gray, Bos., RC .15**
- ☐ 732 Franklin Stubbs, Hou. .15
- ☐ 733 Kelly Downs, S.F. .15
- ☐ 734 John Russell, Tex. .15
- ☐ 735 Ron Darling, NYM. .15
- ☐ 736 Dick Schofield, Cal. .15
- ☐ 737 Tim Crews, L.A. .15
- ☐ 738 Mel Hall, NYY. .15
- ☐ 739 Russ Swan, Sea. .15
- ☐ 740 Ryne Sandberg, Chi.-N.L. .25
- ☐ 741 Jimmy Key, Tor. .15
- ☐ 742 Tommy Gregg, Atl. .15
- ☐ 743 Bryn Smith, Stl. .15
- ☐ 744 Nelson Santovenia, Mtl. .15
- ☐ 745 Doug Jones, Cle. .15
- ☐ 746 John Shelby, Det. .15
- ☐ 747 Tony Fossas, Mil. .15
- ☐ 748 Al Newman, Min. .15
- ☐ 749 Greg Harris, S.D. .15
- ☐ 750 Bobby Bonilla, Pgh., .15
- ☐ 751 Wayne Edwards, Chi.-A.L. .15
- ☐ 752 Kevin Bass, S.F. .15
- ☐ **753 Paul Marak, Atl., RC .15**
- ☐ 754 Bill Pecota, K.C. .15
- ☐ 755 Mark Langston, Cal. .15
- ☐ 756 Topps All-Star Rookie: Jeff Huson, Tex. .15
- ☐ 757 Mark Gardner, Mtl. .15
- ☐ 758 Mike Devereaux, Bal. .15
- ☐ 759 Bobby Cox, Mgr., Atl. .15
- ☐ 760 Benny Santiago, S.D. .15
- ☐ 761 Larry Andersen, Bos. (S.D.) .15
- ☐ 762 Mitch Webster, Cle. .15
- ☐ 763 Dana Kiecker, Bos. .15
- ☐ 764 Mark Carreon, NYM. .15
- ☐ 765 Shawon Dunston, Chi.-N.L. .15
- ☐ 766 Jeff Robinson, Det. (Bal.) .15
- ☐ **767 DP: Dan Wilson, Cin., RC .15**
- ☐ 768 Donn Pall, Chi.-A.L. .15
- ☐ **769 Tim Sherrill, Stl, RC .15**
- ☐ 770 Jay Howell, L.A. .15
- ☐ 771 Gary Redus, Pgh. .15
- ☐ 772 Kent Mercker, Atl. .15
- ☐ 773 Tom Foley, Mtl. .15
- ☐ 774 Dennis Rasmussen, S.D. .15
- ☐ 775 Julio Franco, Tex. .15
- ☐ 776 Brent Mayne, K.C. .15
- ☐ 777 John Candelaria, Tor. .15
- ☐ 778 Danny Gladden, Min. .15
- ☐ 779 Carmelo Martinez, Pgh. .15
- ☐ 780 Randy Myers, Cin. .15
- ☐ 781 Darryl Hamilton, Mil. .15
- ☐ 782 Jim Deshaies, Hou. .15
- ☐ 783 Joel Skinner, Cle. .15
- ☐ 784 Willie Fraser, Cal. (Tor.) .15
- ☐ 785 Scott Fletcher, Chi.-A.L. .15
- ☐ 786 Eric Plunk, NYY. .15
- ☐ 787 1991 Checklist No. 6 of 6 .15
- ☐ 788 Bob Milacki, Bal. .15
- ☐ 789 Tom Lasorda, Mgr., L.A. .15
- ☐ 790 Ken Griffey Jr., Sea. 2.00
- ☐ 791 Mike Benjamin, S.F. .15
- ☐ 792 Mike Greenwell, Bos. .15

1991 BOX BOTTOMS

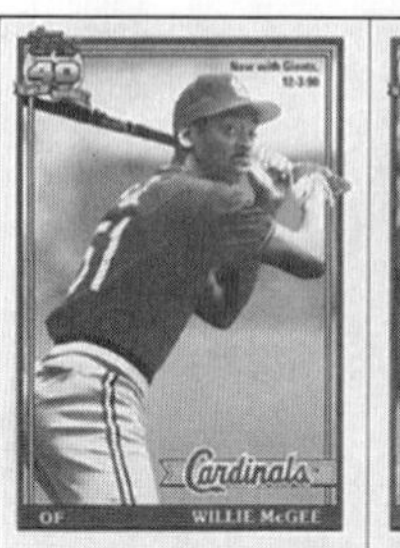

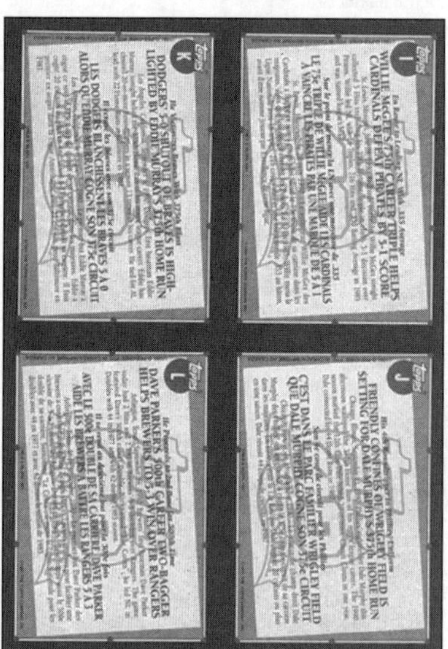

Panel Size: 5" x 7"

Complete Set (16 cards):		**7.00**
Panel A-D:		**3.00**
Panel E-H:		**2.00**
Panel I-L:		**2.50**
Panel M-P:		**5.00**
No.	**Player**	**MINT**
☐ A	Bert Blyleven, Cal.	.25
☐ B	George Brett, K.C.	1.50
☐ C	Brett Butler, L.A.	.25
☐ D	Andre Dawson, Chi.-N.L.	.50
☐ E	Dwight Evans, Bal.	.25
☐ E	Carlton Fisk, Chi.-A.L.	.50
☐ G	Alfredo Griffin, L.A.	.25
☐ H	Rickey Henderson, Oak.	.50
☐ I	Willie McGee, St.L (N.Y.)	.25
☐ J	Dale Murphy, Pha.	.50
☐ K	Eddie Murray, L.A.	1.00
☐ L	Dave Parker, Mil.	.25
☐ M	Jeff Reardon, Bos.	.25
☐ N	Nolan Ryan, Tex.	3.50
☐ O	Juan Samuel, L.A.	.25
☐ P	Robin Yount, Mil.	.50

1991 O-PEE-CHEE PREMIER

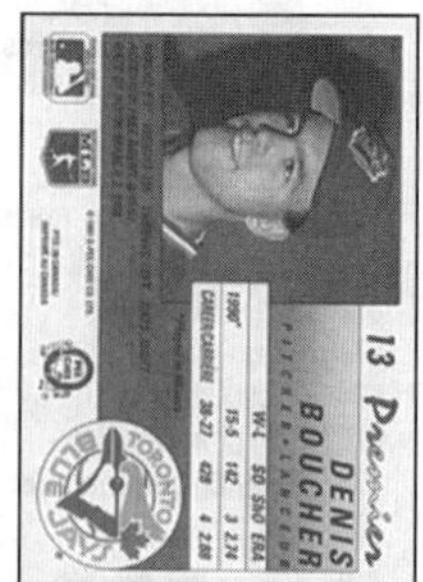

These 132 cards comprise the first O-Pee-Chee Premier set. This set was manufactured to meet the increasing demand by collectors for higher quality in design and production, as well as the desire to see more star players represented on cards.

Card Size: 2 1/2" x 3 1/2"
Face: Four colour, white border; name, position, team
Back: Four colour; name, number, position, résumé, team logo, bilingual
Imprint: © 1991 O-PEE-CHEE CO. LTD.

Complete Set (132 cards):		**10.00**
Common Player:		**.10**
No.	**Player**	**MINT**
☐ 1	Roberto Alomar, Tor.	.35
☐ 2	Sandy Alomar, Cle.	.10
☐ 3	Moises Alou, Mtl.	.50
☐ 4	Brian Barnes, Mtl.	.10
☐ 5	Steve Bedrosian, Min.	.10
☐ 6	George Bell, Chi.-N.L.	.10
☐ 7	Juan Bell, Bal.	.10
☐ 8	Albert Belle, Cle.	.75
☐ 9	Bud Black, S.F.	.10
☐ 10	Mike Boddicker, K.C.	.35
☐ 11	Wade Boggs, Bos.	.50
☐ 12	Barry Bonds, Pgh.	.10
☐ **13**	**Denis Boucher, Tor., RC**	**.25**
☐ 14	George Brett, K.C.	.50
☐ 15	Hubie Brooks, NYM.	.10
☐ 16	Brett Butler, L.A.	.10
☐ 17	Ivan Calderon, Mtl.	.10
☐ 18	Jose Canseco, Oak.	.35
☐ 19	Gary Carter, L.A.	.25
☐ 20	Joe Carter, Tor.	.25
☐ 21	Jack Clark, Bos.	.10
☐ 22	Will Clark, S.F.	.25
☐ 23	Roger Clemens, Bos.	.50
☐ 24	Alex Cole, Cle.	.10
☐ 25	Vince Coleman, NYM.	.10
☐ **26**	**Jeff Conine, K.C., RC**	**.10**
☐ 27	Milt Cuyler, Det.	.10
☐ 28	Danny Darwin, Bos.	.10
☐ 29	Eric Davis, Cin.	.10
☐ 30	Glenn Davis, Bal.	.10
☐ 31	Andre Dawson, Chi.-N.L.	.25
☐ 32	Ken Dayley, Tor.	.10

☐ **33 Steve Decker, S.F., RC .10**
☐ 34 Delino DeShields, Mtl. .10
☐ **35 Lance Dickson, Chi.-N.L., RC .10**
☐ **36 Kirk Dressendorfer, Oak., RC .10**
☐ 37 Shawon Dunston, Chi.-N.L. .10
☐ 38 Dennis Eckersley, Oak. .10
☐ 39 Dwight Evans, Bal. .10
☐ 40 Howard Farmer, Mtl. .10
☐ 41 Junior Felix, Cal. .10
☐ **42 Alex Fernandez, Chi.-A.L., RC .10**
☐ 43 Tony Fernandez, S.D. .10
☐ 44 Cecil Fielder, Det. .10
☐ 45 Carleton Fisk, Chi.-A.L. .25
☐ 46 Willie Fraser, Tor. .10
☐ 47 Gary Gaetti, Cal. .10
☐ 48 Andres Galarraga, Mtl. .35
☐ 49 Ron Gant, Atl. .10
☐ 50 Kirk Gibson, K.C. .10
☐ 51 Bernard Gilkey, Stl. .10
☐ 52 Leo Gomez, Bal. .10
☐ 53 Rene Gonzales, Tor. .10
☐ 54 Juan Gonzalez, Tex. 1.00
☐ 55 Doc Gooden, NYM. .10
☐ 56 Ken Griffey Jr., Sea. 2.00
☐ 57 Kelly Gruber, Tor. .10
☐ 58 Pedro Guerrero, Stl. .10
☐ 59 Tony Gwynn, S.D. .50
☐ 60 Chris Hammond, Cin. .10
☐ 61 Ron Hassey, Mtl. .10
☐ 62 HL: Rickey Henderson, Oak. .25
☐ 63 Tom Henke, Tor. .10
☐ 64 Orel Hershiser, L.A. .10
☐ 65 Chris Hoiles, Bal. .10
☐ 66 Todd Hundley, NYM. .10
☐ 67 Pete Incaviglia, Det. .10
☐ 68 Danny Jackson, Chi.-N.L. .10
☐ 69 Barry Jones, Mtl. .10
☐ 70 David Justice, Atl. .25
☐ 71 Jimmy Key, Tor. .10
☐ 72 Ray Lankford, Stl. .10
☐ 73 Darren Lewis, S.F. .10
☐ 74 Kevin Maas, NYY. .10
☐ 75 Denny Martinez, Mtl. .10
☐ 76 Tino Martinez, Sea. .25
☐ 77 Don Mattingly, NYY. .50
☐ 78 Willie McGee, S.F. .10
☐ 79 Fred McGriff, S.D. .35
☐ 80 Hensley Meulens, NYY. .10
☐ 81 Kevin Mitchell, S.F. .10
☐ 82 Paul Molitor, Mil. .25
☐ 83 Mickey Morandini, Pha. .10
☐ 84 Jack Morris, Min. .10
☐ 85 Dale Murphy, Pha. .25
☐ 86 Eddie Murray, L.A. .25
☐ **87 Chris Nabholz, Mtl., RC .10**
☐ **88 Tim Naehring, Bos., RC .10**
☐ 89 Otis Nixon, Atl. .10
☐ 90 Jose Offerman .10
☐ 91 Bob Ojeda, L.A. .10
☐ 92 John Olerud, Tor. .25
☐ 93 Gregg Olson, Bal. .10
☐ 94 Dave Parker, Cal. .10
☐ 95 Terry Pendleton, Atl. .10
☐ 96 Kirby Puckett, Min. .50
☐ 97 Rock Raines, Chi.-A.L. .10
☐ 98 Jeff Reardon, Bos. .10
☐ 99 Dave Righetti, S.F. .10
☐ 100 Cal Ripken, Bal. 1.00
☐ 101 Mel Rojas, Mtl. .10
☐ 102 HL: Nolan Ryan, Tex. 1.00
☐ 103 Ryne Sandberg, Chi.-N.L. .25
☐ 104 Scott Sanderson, NYY. .10
☐ 105 Benny Santiago, S.D. .10
☐ **106 Pete Schourek, NYM., RC .10**
☐ **107 Gary Scott, Chi.-N.L., RC .10**
☐ 108 Terry Shumpert, K.C. .10
☐ 109 Ruben Sierra, Tex. .10
☐ **110 Doug Simons, NYM., RC .10**
☐ 111 Dave Smith, Chi.-N.L. .10
☐ 112 Ozzie Smith, Stl. .25
☐ 113 Cory Snyder, Chi.-A.L. .10
☐ 114 Luis Sojo, Cal. .10
☐ 115 Dave Stewart, Oak. .10
☐ 116 Dave Stieb, Tor. .10
☐ 117 Darryl Strawberry, L.A. .25
☐ 118 Pat Tabler, Tor. .10
☐ **119 Wade Taylor, NYY., RC .10**
☐ 120 Bobby Thigpen, Chi.-A.L. .10
☐ 121 Frank Thomas, Chi.-A.L. 2.00
☐ **122 Mike Timlin, Tor., RC .10**
☐ 123 Alan Trammell, Det. .10
☐ 124 Mo Vaughn, Bos. .50
☐ 125 Tim Wallach, Mtl. .10
☐ 126 Devon White, Tor. .10
☐ 127 Mark Whiten, Tor. .10
☐ 128 Bernie Williams, NYY. .25
☐ 129 Willie Wilson, Oak. .10
☐ 130 Dave Winfield, Cal. .25
☐ 131 Robin Yount, Mil. .25
☐ 132 Checklist (1-132) .10

1991 PANINI STICKERS

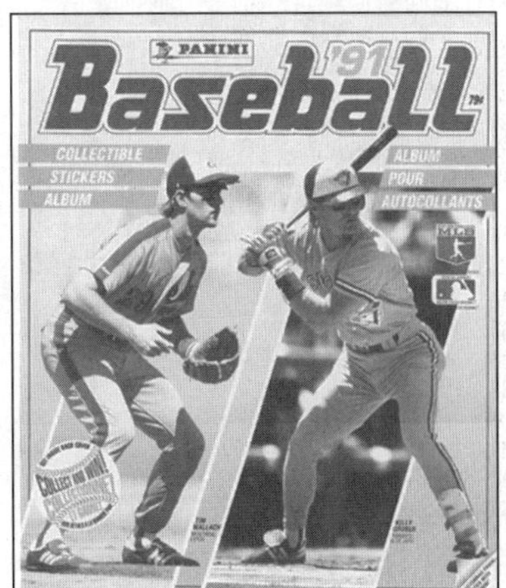

This 360-sticker set was printed in Italy by Panini and appears in both English and French. The 65-page album to house the stickers is also bilingual. It was printed in Canada.

Sticker Size: 2 1/8" x 3"
Face: Four colour, white border; name, Team
Back: Black and white; number, Panini and MLB logo, bilingual
Imprint: Printed in Italy by Panini S.r.l. - Modena

Complete Set (360 stickers):		**20.00**
Common Player:		**.15**
Album:		**3.50**

	No.	Player	MINT
☐	1	MLB Logo	.15
☐	2	MLBPA Logo	.15
☐	3	Panini Baseball 91 Logo	.15
☐	4	Team Pennant, Hou.	.15
☐	5	Team Logo, Hou.	.15
☐	6	Craig Biggio, Hou.	.15
☐	7	Glenn Davis, Hou.	.15
☐	8	Casey Candaele, Hou.	.15
☐	9	Ken Caminiti, Hou.	.25
☐	10	Rafael Ramirez, Hou.	.15
☐	11	Glenn Wilson, Hou.	.15
☐	12	Eric Yelding, Hou.	.15
☐	13	Franklin Stubbs, Hou.	.15
☐	14	Mike Scott, Hou.	.15
☐	15	Danny Darwin, Hou.	.15
☐	16	Team Pennant, Atl.	.15
☐	17	Team Logo, Atl.	.15
☐	18	AS: Greg Olson, Atl.	.15
☐	19	Tommy Gregg, Atl.	.15
☐	20	Jeff Treadway, Atl.	.15
☐	21	Jim Presley, Atl.	.15
☐	22	Jeff Blauser, Atl.	.15
☐	23	Ron Gant, Atl.	.15
☐	24	Lonnie Smith, Atl.	.15
☐	25	Dave Justice, Atl.	.25
☐	26	John Smoltz, Atl.	.25
☐	27	Charlie Leibrandt, Atl.	.15
☐	28	Team Pennant, Stl.	.15
☐	29	Team Logo, Stl.	.15
☐	30	Tom Pagnozzi, Stl.	.15
☐	31	Pedro Guerrero, Stl.	.15
☐	32	Jose Oquendo, Stl.	.15
☐	33	Todd Zeile, Stl.	.15
☐	34	AS: Ozzie Smith, Stl.	.75
☐	35	Vince Coleman, Stl.	.15
☐	36	Milt Thompson, Stl.	.15
☐	37	Rex Hudler, Stl.	.15
☐	38	Joe Magrane, Stl.	.15
☐	39	Lee Smith, Stl.	.15
☐	40	Team Pennant, Chi.-N.L.	.15
☐	41	Team Logo, Chi.-N.L.	.15
☐	42	Joe Girardi, Chi.-N.L.	.15
☐	43	Mark Grace, Chi.-N.L.	.15
☐	44	AS: Ryne Sandberg, Chi.-N.L.	.50
☐	45	Luis Salazar, Chi.-N.L.	.15
☐	46	AS: Shawon Dunston, Chi.-N.L.	.15
☐	47	Dwight Smith, Chi.-N.L.	.15
☐	48	Jerome Walton, Chi.-N.L.	.15
☐	49	AS: Andre Dawson, Chi.-N.L.	.25
☐	50	Greg Maddux, Chi.-N.L.	2.00
☐	51	Mike Harkey, Chi.-N.L.	.15
☐	52	Team Pennant, L.A.	.15
☐	53	Team Logo, L.A.	.15
☐	54	AS: Mike Scioscia, L.A.	.15
☐	55	Eddie Murray, L.A.	.50
☐	56	Juan Samuel, L.A.	.15
☐	57	Lenny Harris, L.A.	.15
☐	58	Alfredo Griffin, L.A.	.15
☐	59	Hubie Brooks, L.A.	.15
☐	60	Kal Daniels, L.A.	.15
☐	61	Stan Javier, L.A.	.15
☐	62	AS: Ramon Martinez, L.A.	.25
☐	63	Mike Morgan, L.A.	.15
☐	64	Team Pennant, S.F.	.15
☐	65	Team Logo, S.F.	.15
☐	66	Terry Kennedy, S.F.	.15
☐	67	AS: Will Clark, S.F.	.25
☐	68	Robby Thompson, S.F.	.15
☐	69	AS: Matt Williams, S.F.	.15
☐	70	Jose Uribe, S.F.	.15
☐	71	AS: Kevin Mitchell, S.F.	.15
☐	72	Brett Butler, S.F.	.15
☐	73	Don Robinson, S.F.	.15
☐	74	John Burkett, S.F.	.15
☐	75	AS: Jeff Brantley, S.F.	.15
☐	76	Team Pennant, NYM.	.15
☐	77	Team Logo, NYM.	.15
☐	78	Mackey Sasser, NYM.	.15
☐	79	Dave Magadan, NYM.	.15
☐	80	Gregg Jefferies, NYM.	.15
☐	81	Howard Johnson, NYM.	.15
☐	82	Kevin Elster, NYM.	.15
☐	83	Kevin McReynolds, NYM.	.15
☐	84	Daryl Boston, NYM.	.15
☐	85	AS: Darryl Strawberry, NYM.	.25
☐	86	Dwight Gooden, NYM.	.15
☐	87	AS: Frank Viola, NYM.	.15
☐	88	Team Pennant, S.D.	.15
☐	89	Team Logo, S.D.	.15
☐	90	AS: Benito Santiago, S.D.	.15
☐	91	Jack Clark, S.D.	.15
☐	92	AS: Roberto Alomar, S.D.	.35
☐	93	Mike Pagliarulo, S.D.	.15
☐	94	Garry Templeton, S.D.	.15
☐	95	Joe Carter, S.D.	.35
☐	96	Bip Roberts, S.D.	.15
☐	97	AS: Tony Gwynn, S.D.	1.00
☐	98	Ed Whitson, S.D.	.15
☐	99	Andy Benes, S.D.	.15
☐	100	Team Pennant, Pha.	.15
☐	101	Team Logo, Pha.	.15
☐	102	Darren Daulton, Pha.	.15
☐	103	Ricky Jordan, Pha.	.15
☐	104	Randy Ready, Pha.	.15
☐	105	Charlie Hayes, Pha.	.15
☐	106	Dickie Thon, Pha.	.15
☐	107	Von Hayes, Pha.	.15
☐	108	AS: Lenny Dykstra, Pha.	.15
☐	109	Dale Murphy, Pha.	.25
☐	110	Ken Howell, Pha.	.15
☐	111	Roger McDowell, Pha.	.15
☐	112	Team Pennant, Pgh.	.15
☐	113	Team Logo, Pgh.	.15
☐	114	Mike LaValliere, Pgh.	.15
☐	115	Sid Bream, Pgh.	.15
☐	116	Jose Lind, Pgh.	.15
☐	117	Jeff King, Pgh.	.15
☐	118	Jay Bell, Pgh.	.15
☐	119	AS: Barry Bonds, Pgh.	.50
☐	120	AS: Bobby Bonilla, Pgh.	.15
☐	121	Andy Van Slyke, Pgh.	.15
☐	122	Doug Drabek, Pgh.	.15
☐	123	AS: Neal Heaton, Pgh.	.15
☐	124	Team Pennant, Cin.	.15
☐	125	Team Logo, Cin.	.15
☐	126	Joe Oliver, Cin.	.15
☐	127	Todd Benzinger, Cin.	.15

	No.	Name	Value
☐	128	Mariano Duncan, Cin.	.15
☐	129	AS: Chris Sabo, Cin.	.15
☐	130	AS: Barry Larkin, Cin.	.25
☐	131	Eric Davis, Cin.	.15
☐	132	Billy Hatcher, Cin.	.15
☐	133	Paul O'Neill, Cin.	.15
☐	134	Jose Rijo, Cin.	.15
☐	135	AS: Randy Myers, Cin.	.15
☐	136	Team Pennant, Mtl.	.15
☐	137	Team Logo, Mtl.	.15
☐	138	Mike Fitzgerald, Mtl.	.15
☐	139	Andres Galarraga, Mtl.	.25
☐	140	Delino DeShields, Mtl.	.15
☐	141	AS: Tim Wallach, Mtl.	.15
☐	142	Spike Owen, Mtl.	.15
☐	143	Tim Raines, Mtl.	.15
☐	144	Dave Martinez, Mtl.	.15
☐	145	Larry Walker, Mtl.	1.00
☐	146	Team Helmet, Mtl.	.15
☐	147	Dennis Boyd, Mtl.	.15
☐	148	Tim Burke, Mtl.	.15
☐	149	Bill Sampen, Mtl.	.15
☐	150	AS: Dennis Martinez, Mtl.	.15
☐	151	Marquis Grissom, Mtl.	.35
☐	152	Otis Nixon, Mtl.	.15
☐	153	Jerry Goff, Mtl.	.15
☐	154	Steve Frey, Mtl.	.15
☐	155	National League Emblem	.15
☐	156	American League Emblem	.15
☐	157	AS: Benito Santiago, S.D.	.15
☐	158	AS: Will Clark, S.F.	.25
☐	159	AS: Ryne Sandberg, Chi.-N.L.	.25
☐	160	AS: Chris Sabo, Cin.	.15
☐	161	AS: Ozzie Smith, Stl.	.25
☐	162	AS: Kevin Mitchell, S.F.	.15
☐	163	AS: Lenny Dykstra, Pha.	.15
☐	164	AS: Darryl Strawberry, NYM.	.25
☐	165	AS: Jack Armstrong, Cin.	.15
☐	166	AS: Sandy Alomar Jr., Cle.	.15
☐	167	AS: Mark McGwire, Oak.	1.00
☐	168	AS: Steve Sax, NYY.	.15
☐	169	AS: Wade Boggs, Bos.	.25
☐	170	AS: Cal Ripken, Bal.	1.00
☐	171	AS: Rickey Henderson, Oak.	.25
☐	172	AS: Ken Griffey Jr., Sea.	2.00
☐	173	AS: Jose Canseco, Oak.	.25
☐	174	AS: Bob Welch, Oak.	.15
☐	175	AS: Wrigley Field Stadium	.15
☐	176	World Series Trophy	.15
☐	177	Team Pennant, Cal.	.15
☐	178	Team Logo, Cal.	.15
☐	179	AS: Lance Parrish, Cal.	.15
☐	180	Wally Joyner, Cal.	.15
☐	181	Johnny Ray, Cal.	.15
☐	182	Jack Howell, Cal.	.15
☐	183	Dick Schofield, Cal.	.15
☐	184	Dave Winfield, Cal.	.35
☐	185	Devon White, Cal.	.15
☐	186	Dante Bichette, Cal.	.15
☐	187	AS: Chuck Finley, Cal.	.15
☐	188	Jim Abbott, Cal.	.15
☐	189	Team Pennant, Oak.	.15
☐	190	Team Logo, Oak.	.15
☐	191	Terry Steinbach, Oak.	.15
☐	192	Mark McGwire, Oak.	1.50
☐	193	Willie Randolph, Oak.	.15
☐	194	Carney Lansford, Oak.	.15
☐	195	Walt Weiss, Oak.	.15
☐	196	AS: Rickey Henderson, Oak.	.25
☐	197	Dave Henderson, Oak.	.15
☐	198	AS: Jose Canseco, Oak.	.25
☐	199	Dave Stewart, Oak.	.15
☐	200	AS: Dennis Eckersley, Oak.	.15
☐	201	Team Pennant, Mil.	.15
☐	202	Team Logo, Mil.	.15
☐	203	B.J. Surhoff, Mil.	.15
☐	204	Greg Brock, Mil.	.15
☐	205	Paul Molitor, Mil.	.35
☐	206	Gary Sheffield, Mil.	.35
☐	207	Bill Spiers, Mil.	.15
☐	208	Robin Yount, Mil.	.35
☐	209	Rob Deer, Mil.	.15
☐	210	AS: Dave Parker, Mil.	.15
☐	211	Mark Knudson, Mil.	.15
☐	212	Dan Plesac, Mil.	.15
☐	213	Team Pennant, Cle.	.15
☐	214	Team Logo, Cle.	.15
☐	215	AS: Sandy Alomar, Jr., Cle.	.15
☐	216	AS: Brook Jacoby, Cle.	.15
☐	217	Jerry Browne, Cle.	.15
☐	218	Carlos Baerga, Cle.	.15
☐	219	Felix Fermin, Cle.	.15
☐	220	Candy Maldonado, Cle.	.15
☐	221	Cory Snyder, Cle.	.15
☐	222	Alex Cole Jr., Cle.	.15
☐	223	Tom Candiotti, Cle.	.15
☐	224	AS: Doug Jones, Cle.	.15
☐	225	Team Pennant, Sea.	.15
☐	226	Team Logo, Sea.	.15
☐	227	Dave Valle, Sea.	.15
☐	228	Pete O'Brien, Sea.	.15
☐	229	Harold Reynolds, Sea.	.15
☐	230	Edgar Martinez, Sea.	.15
☐	231	Omar Vizquel, Sea.	.15
☐	232	Henry Cotto, Sea.	.15
☐	233	AS: Ken Griffey, Jr., Sea.	3.00
☐	234	Jay Buhner, Sea.	.15
☐	235	Erik Hanson, Sea.	.15
☐	236	Mike Schooler, Sea.	.15
☐	237	Team Pennant, Bal.	.15
☐	238	Team Logo, Bal.	.15
☐	239	Mickey Tettleton, Bal.	.15
☐	240	Randy Milligan, Bal.	.15
☐	241	Bill Ripken, Bal.	.15
☐	242	Craig Worthington, Bal.	.15
☐	243	AS: Cal Ripken, Bal.	2.00
☐	244	Steve Finley, Bal.	.15
☐	245	Mike Devereaux, Bal.	.15
☐	246	Joe Orsulak, Bal.	.15
☐	247	Ben McDonald, Bal.	.15
☐	248	AS: Gregg Olson, Bal.	.15
☐	249	Team Pennant, Tex.	.15
☐	250	Team Logo, Tex.	.15
☐	251	Geno Petralli, Tex.	.15
☐	252	Rafael Palmeiro, Tex.	.35
☐	253	AS: Julio Franco, Tex.	.15
☐	254	Steve Buechele, Tex.	.15
☐	255	Jeff Huson, Tex.	.15
☐	256	Gary Pettis, Tex.	.15
☐	257	Ruben Sierra, Tex.	.15
☐	258	Pete Incaviglia, Tex.	.15
☐	259	Nolan Ryan, Tex.	2.00
☐	260	Bobby Witt, Tex.	.15
☐	261	Team Pennant, Bos.	.15
☐	262	Team Logo, Bos.	.15
☐	263	Tony Pena, Bos.	.15
☐	264	Carlos Quintana, Bos.	.15
☐	265	Jody Reed, Bos.	.15

	No.	Player	Price
☐	266	AS: Wade Boggs, Bos.	.35
☐	267	Luis Rivera, Bos.	.15
☐	268	Mike Greenwell, Bos.	.15
☐	269	Ellis Burks, Bos.	.15
☐	270	Tom Brunansky, Bos.	.15
☐	271	AS: Roger Clemens, Bos.	1.25
☐	272	Jeff Reardon, Bos.	.15
☐	273	Team Pennant, K.C.	.15
☐	274	Team Logo, K.C.	.15
☐	275	Mike MacFarlane, K.C.	.15
☐	276	George Brett, K.C.	1.00
☐	277	Bill Pecota, K.C.	.15
☐	278	Kevin Seitzer, K.C.	.15
☐	279	Kurt Stillwell, K.C.	.15
☐	280	Jim Eisenreich, K.C.	.15
☐	281	Bo Jackson, K.C.	.15
☐	282	Danny Tartabull, K.C.	.15
☐	283	AS: Bret Saberhagen, K.C.	.15
☐	284	Tom Gordon, K.C.	.15
☐	285	Team Pennant, Det.	.15
☐	286	Team Logo, Det.	.15
☐	287	Mike Heath, Det.	.15
☐	288	AS: Cecil Fielder, Det.	.15
☐	289	Lou Whitaker, Det.	.15
☐	290	Tony Phillips, Det.	.15
☐	291	AS: Alan Trammell, Det.	.15
☐	292	Chet Lemon, Det.	.15
☐	293	Lloyd Moseby, Det.	.15
☐	294	Gary Ward, Det.	.15
☐	295	Dan Petry, Det.	.15
☐	296	Jack Morris, Det.	.15
☐	297	Team Pennant, Min.	.15
☐	298	Team Logo, Min.	.15
☐	299	Brian Harper, Min.	.15
☐	300	Kent Hrbek, Min.	.15
☐	301	Al Newman, Min.	.15
☐	302	Gary Gaetti, Min.	.15
☐	303	Greg Gagne, Min.	.15
☐	304	Dan Gladden, Min.	.15
☐	305	AS: Kirby Puckett, Min.	1.00
☐	306	Gene Larkin, Min.	.15
☐	307	Kevin Tapani, Min.	.15
☐	308	Rick Aguilera, Min.	.15
☐	309	Team Pennant, Chi.-A.L.	.15
☐	310	Team Logo, Chi.-A.L.	.15
☐	311	Carlton Fisk, Chi.-A.L.	.35
☐	312	Carlos Martinez, Chi.-A.L.	.15
☐	313	Scott Fletcher, Chi.-A.L.	.15
☐	314	Robin Ventura, Chi.-A.L.	.15
☐	315	AS: Ozzie Guillen, Chi.-A.L.	.15
☐	316	Sammy Sosa, Chi.-A.L.	.25
☐	317	Lance Johnson, Chi.-A.L.	.15
☐	318	Ivan Calderon, Chi.-A.L.	.15
☐	319	Greg Hibbard, Chi.-A.L.	.15
☐	320	AS: Bobby Thigpen, Chi.-A.L.	.15
☐	321	Team Pennant, NYY.	.15
☐	322	Team Logo, NYY.	.15
☐	323	Bob Geren, NYY.	.15
☐	324	Don Mattingly, NYY.	1.00
☐	325	AS: Steve Sax, NYY.	.15
☐	326	Jim Leyritz, NYY.	.15
☐	327	Alvaro Espinoza, NYY.	.15
☐	328	Roberto Kelly, NYY.	.15
☐	329	AS: Oscar Azocar, NYY.	.15
☐	330	Jesse Barfield, NYY.	.15
☐	331	Chuck Cary, NYY.	.15
☐	332	Dave Righetti, NYY.	.15
☐	333	Team Pennant, Tor.	.15
☐	334	Team Logo, Tor.	.15
☐	335	Pat Borders, Tor.	.15
☐	336	Fred McGriff, Tor.	.25
☐	337	Manny Lee, Tor.	.15
☐	338	AS: Kelly Gruber, Tor.	.15
☐	339	Tony Fernandez, Tor.	.15
☐	340	AS: George Bell, Tor.	.15
☐	341	Mookie Wilson, Tor.	.15
☐	342	Junior Felix, Tor.	.15
☐	343	Team Helmet, Tor.	.15
☐	344	AS: Dave Stieb, Tor.	.15
☐	345	Tom Henke, Tor.	.15
☐	346	Greg Myers, Tor.	.15
☐	347	Glenallen Hill, Tor.	.15
☐	348	John Olerud, Tor.	.15
☐	349	Todd Stottlemyre, Tor.	.15
☐	350	David Wells, Tor.	.15
☐	351	Jimmy Key, Tor.	.15
☐	352	Mark Langston, Cal.	.15
☐	353	Randy Johnson, Sea.	.25
☐	354	Nolan Ryan, Tex.	1.00
☐	355	Dave Stewart, Oak.	.15
☐	356	Fernando Valenzuela, L.A.	.15
☐	357	Andy Hawkins, NYY.	.15
☐	358	Melido Perez, Chi.-A.L.	.15
☐	359	Terry Mulholland, Pha.	.15
☐	360	Dave Stieb, Tor.	.15

1991 PANINI TOP 15 STICKERS

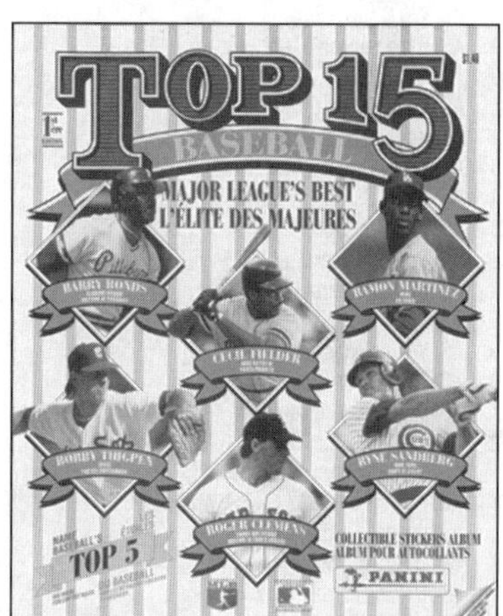

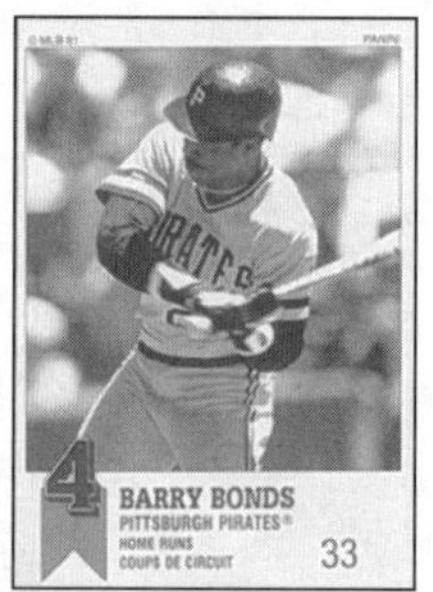

The 36-page album is an integral part of the set. It is bilingual and is printed in Canada.

Sticker Size: 2 1/2" x 3 1/2"

Face: Four colour, white border; name, position, team, bilingual
Back: Black and white; number, Panini and MLB logos, bilingual
Imprint: Printed in Italy/imprimé en Italie

Complete Set (136 stickers):			**35.00**
Common Player:			**.10**
Album:			**5.00**
	No.	**Player**	**MINT**
BATTING AVERAGE			
☐	1	Willie McGee, Stl.	.10
☐	2	Eddie Murray, L.A.	1.00
☐	3	Dave Magadan, NYM.	.10
☐	4	Lenny Dykstra, Pha.	.10
☐	5	George Brett, K.C.	1.50
☐	6	Rickey Henderson, Oak.	.25
☐	7	Rafael Palmeiro, Tex.	.25
☐	8	Alan Trammell, Det.	.15
HOME RUNS			
☐	9	Ryne Sandberg, Chi.-N.L.	1.00
☐	10	Darryl Strawberry, NYM.	.25
☐	11	Kevin Mitchell, S.F.	.10
☐	12	Barry Bonds, Pgh.	1.50
☐	13	Cecil Fielder, Det.	.10
☐	14	Mark McGwire, Oak.	2.50
☐	15	Jose Canseco, Oak.	.50
☐	16	Fred McGriff, Tor.	.25
RUNS BATTED IN			
☐	17	Mitch Williams, S.F.	.10
☐	18	Bobby Bonilla, Pgh.	.10
☐	19	Joe Carter, S.D.	.25
☐	20	Barry Bonds, Pgh.	1.50
☐	21	Cecil Fielder, Det.	.10
☐	22	Kelly Gruber, Tor.	.10
☐	23	Mark McGwire, Oak.	2.50
☐	24	Jose Canseco, Oak.	.50
HITS			
☐	25	Brett Butler, S.F.	.10
☐	26	Lenny Dykstra, Pha.	.10
☐	27	Ryne Sandberg, Chi.	1.00
☐	28	Barry Larkin, Cin.	.75
☐	29	Rafael Palmeiro, Tex.	.25
☐	30	Wade Boggs, Bos.	1.00
☐	31	Roberto Kelly, NYY.	.10
☐	32	Mike Greenwell, Bos.	.10
SLUGGING AVERAGE			
☐	33	Barry Bonds, Pgh.	1.50
☐	34	Ryne Sandberg, Chi.	1.00
☐	35	Kevin Mitchell, S.F.	.10
☐	36	Ron Gant, Atl.	.10
☐	37	Cecil Fielder, Det.	.10
☐	38	Rickey Henderson, Oak.	.25
☐	39	Jose Canseco, Oak.	.50
☐	40	Fred McGriff, Tor.	.25
STOLEN BASES			
☐	41	Vince Coleman, Stl.	.10
☐	42	Eric Yelding, Hou.	.10
☐	43	Barry Bonds, Pgh.	1.50
☐	44	Brett Butler, S.F.	.10
☐	45	Rickey Henderson, Oak.	.25
☐	46	Steve Sax, NYY.	.10
☐	47	Roberto Kelly, NYY.	.10
☐	48	Alex Cole, Jr., Cle.	.10
RUNS			
☐	49	Ryne Sandberg, Chi.	1.00
☐	50	Bobby Bonilla, Pgh.	.10
☐	51	Brett Butler, S.F.	.10
☐	52	Ron Gant, Atl.	.10
☐	53	Rickey Henderson, Oak.	.25
☐	54	Cecil Fielder, Det.	.10
☐	55	Harold Reynolds, Sea.	.10
☐	56	Robin Yount, Mil.	.50
WINS			
☐	57	Doug Drabek, Pgh.	.10
☐	58	Ramon Martinez, L.A.	.10
☐	59	Frank Viola, NYM.	.10
☐	60	Dwight Gooden, NYM.	.10
☐	61	Bob Welch, Oak.	.10
☐	62	Dave Stewart, Oak.	.10
☐	63	Roger Clemens, Bos.	1.50
☐	64	Dave Stieb, Tor.	.10
EARNED RUN AVERAGE			
☐	65	Danny Darwin, Hou.	.10
☐	66	Zane Smith, Pgh.	.10
☐	67	Eddie Whitson, S.D.	.10
☐	68	Frank Viola, NYM.	.10
☐	69	Roger Clemens, Bos.	1.50
☐	70	Chuck Finley, Cal.	.10
☐	71	Dave Stewart, Oak.	.10
☐	72	Kevin Appier, K.C.	.10
STRIKEOUTS			
☐	73	David Cone, NYM.	.10
☐	74	Dwight Gooden, NYM.	.10
☐	75	Ramon Martinez, L.A.	.10
☐	76	Frank Viola, NYM.	.10
☐	77	Nolan Ryan, Tex.	4.00
☐	78	Bobby Witt, Tex.	.10
☐	79	Erik Hanson, Sea.	.10
☐	80	Roger Clemens, Bos.	1.50
SAVES			
☐	81	John Franco, NYM.	.10
☐	82	Randy Myers, Cin.	.10
☐	83	Lee Smith, Stl.	.10
☐	84	Craig Lefferts, S.D.	.10
☐	85	Bobby Thigpen, Chi.WS	.10
☐	86	Dennis Eckersley, Oak.	.10
☐	87	Dennis Jones, Cle.	.10
☐	88	Gregg Olson, Bal.	.10
SHUTOUTS			
☐	89	Mike Morgan, L.A.	.10
☐	90	Bruce Hurst, S.D.	.10
☐	91	Mike Gardner, Mon.	.10
☐	92	Doug Drabek, Pgh.	.10
☐	93	Dave Stewart, Oak.	.10
☐	94	Roger Clemens, Bos.	1.50
☐	95	Kevin Appier, K.C.	.10
☐	96	Melido Perez, Chi.-A.L.	.10
THE GOLD GLOVES NATIONAL LEAGUE			
☐	97	National League Emblem	.10
☐	98	Greg Maddux, Chi.-N.L.	2.50
☐	99	Benito Santiago, S.D.	.10
☐	100	Andres Galarraga, Mtl.	.50
☐	101	Ryne Sandberg, Chi.-N.L.	1.00
☐	102	Tim Wallach, Mtl.	.10
☐	103	Ozzie Smith, Stl.	1.00
☐	104	Tony Gwynn, S.D.	2.00
☐	105	Barry Bonds, Pgh.	1.50
☐	106	Andy Van Slyke, Pgh.	.10
AMERICAN LEAGUE			
☐	107	American League Emblem	.10
☐	108	Mike Boddicker, K.C.	.10
☐	109	Sandy Alomar, Jr., Cle.	.10
☐	110	Mark McGwire, Oak.	2.50
☐	111	Harold Reynolds, Sea.	.10
☐	112	Kelly Gruber, Tor.	.10
☐	113	Ozzie Guillen, Chi.-A.L.	.10
☐	114	Ellis Burks, Bos.	.50
☐	115	Gary Pettis, Tex.	.10

☐	116	Ken Griffey, Jr., Sea.	6.50

THE BEST OFFENSIVE TEAMS

☐	117	Cincinnati Reds:	.10

HIGHEST BATTING AVERAGE

☐	118	New York Mets: Most Home Runs	.10
☐	119	New York Mets: Most Runs Scored	.10
☐	120	Chicago Cubs: Most Hits	.10
☐	121	Montreal Expos: Most Stolen Bases	.10
☐	122	Boston Red Sox:	.10

HIGHEST BATTING AVERAGE

☐	123	Detroit Tigers: Most Home Runs	.10
☐	124	Toronto Blue Jays:	.10

MOST RUNS SCORED

☐	125	Boston Red Sox: Most Hits	.10
☐	126	Milwaukee Brewers:	.10

THE BEST DEFENSIVE TEAMS

☐	127	Philadelphia Phillies:	.10

MOST DOUBLE PLAYS

☐	128	Cincinnati Reds: Fewest Errors	.10
☐	129	Montreal Expos:	.10

BEST EARNED RUN AVERAGE

☐	130	New York Mets: Most Shutouts	.10
☐	131	Cincinnati Reds: Most Saves	.10
☐	132	California Angels:	.10

MOST DOUBLE PLAYS

☐	133	Toronto Blue Jays:	.10

FEWEST ERRORS

☐	134	Oakland Athletics:	.10

BEST EARNED RUN AVERAGE

☐	135	Oakland Athletics: Most Shutouts	.10
☐	136	Chicago White Sox: Most Saves	.10

1991 PETRO-CANADA ALL-STAR

This set was issued by Petro-Canada for the All Star Game Fanfest, which was held in Toronto during the first week in July, 1991. It is die cut, the players stand up when the cards are opened.

Card Size: 2 7/8" x 3 13/16"
Face: Four colour; number
Back: Four colour on card stock; highlights, quiz
Imprint: Promotions International Ltd.

Complete Set (26 cards):			**25.00**
Common Player:			**.50**
	No.	**Player**	**MINT**
☐	1	Cal Ripken, Jr., Bal.	4.00
☐	2	Greg Olson, Atl.	.50
☐	3	Roger Clemens, Bos.	1.50
☐	4	Ryne Sandberg, Chi.-N.L.	1.00
☐	5	Dave Winfield, Cal.	1.00
☐	6	Eric Davis, Cin.	.50
☐	7	Carlton Fisk, Chi.-A.L.	1.00
☐	8	Mike Scott, Hou.	.50
☐	9	Sandy Alomar, Jr., Cle.	.50
☐	10	Tim Wallach, Mtl.	.50
☐	11	Cecil Fielder, Det.	.50
☐	12	Dwight Gooden, NYM.	.50
☐	13	George Brett, K.C.	1.75
☐	14	Dale Murphy, Pha.	1.00
☐	15	Paul Molitor, Mil.	1.00
☐	16	Barry Bonds, Pgh.	1.00
☐	17	Kirby Puckett, Min.	1.75
☐	18	Ozzie Smith, Stl.	1.25
☐	19	Don Mattingly, NYY.	1.75
☐	20	Will Clark, S.F.	1.00
☐	21	Rickey Henderson, Oak.	1.00
☐	22	Orel Hershiser, L.A.	.50
☐	23	Ken Griffey, Jr., Sea.	5.50
☐	24	Tony Gwynn, S.D.	1.75
☐	25	Nolan Ryan, Tex.	4.00
☐	26	Kelly Gruber, Tor.	.50

1991 POST

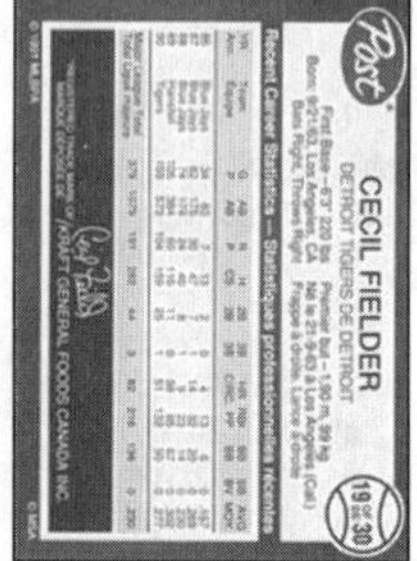

This 30-card set features stars from both the National and American leagues.

Card Size: 2 1/2" x 3 1/2"
Face: Four colour, red or blue border; name, team, Post logo
Back: Black and red on card stock; name, team, résumé, facsimile autograph, numbered _ of 30, bilingual
Imprint: ©1991 MLBPA © MSA

Complete Set (30 cards):			**15.00**
	No.	**Player**	**MINT**
☐	1	Delino DeShields, Mtl.	.35
☐	2	Tim Wallach, Mtl.	.35
☐	3	Andres Galarraga, Mtl.	.75
☐	4	Dave Magadan, NYM.	.35
☐	5	Barry Bonds, Pgh.	1.00
☐	6	Len Dykstra, Pha.	.35
☐	7	André Dawson, Chi.-N.L.	.50
☐	8	Ozzie Smith, Stl.	.75
☐	9	Will Clark, S.F.	.50
☐	10	Chris Sabo, Cin.	.35
☐	11	Eddie Murray, L.A.	.75
☐	12	David Justice, Atl.	.50
☐	13	Benito Santiago, S.D.	.35
☐	14	Glenn Davis, Hou.	.35
☐	15	Kelly Gruber, Tor.	.35
☐	16	Dave Stieb, Tor.	.35
☐	17	John Olerud, Tor.	.35
☐	18	Roger Clemens, Bos.	1.50
☐	19	Cecil Fielder, Det.	.35
☐	20	Kevin Maas, NNY.	.35
☐	21	Robin Yount, Mil.	.75
☐	22	Cal Ripken, Jr., Bal.	2.00
☐	23	Sandy Alomar, Jr., Cle.	.35
☐	24	Rickey Henderson, Oak.	.50
☐	25	Bobby Thigpen, Chi.-A.L.	.35
☐	26	Ken Griffey, Jr., Sea.	3.00

	No.	Player	MINT
☐	27	Nolan Ryan, Tex.	2.00
☐	28	Dave Winfield, Cal.	.75
☐	29	George Brett, K.C.	1.00
☐	30	Kirby Puckett, Min.	1.25

1991 SCORE ALL-STAR

This 11-card set features players from the 1991 All Star Game held in Toronto's SkyDome in July 1991.

Card Size: 2 1/2" x 3 1/2"

Face: Four colour, green border; name, team

Back: Four colour, red, yellow and green on card stock; name, position, team logo, numbered _ of 10

Imprint: © 1991 SCORE PRINTED IN U.S.A.

Complete Set (10 cards):

	No.	Player	MINT
☐		Title Card: Score The Intelligent Choice	8.00
☐	1	Ray Lankford, Stl.	1.25
☐	2	Steve Decker, S.F.	.75
☐	3	Gary Scott, Chi.-N.L.	.75
☐	4	Hensley Meulens, NYY.	.75
☐	5	Tim Naehring, Bos.	.75
☐	6	Mark Whiten, Tor.	.75
☐	7	Ed Sprague, Tor.	.75
☐	8	Charles Nagy, Cle.	.75
☐	9	Terry Shumpert, K.C.	.75
☐	10	Chuck Knoblauch, Min.	1.75

1992 BEN'S / HOLSUMS DISKS

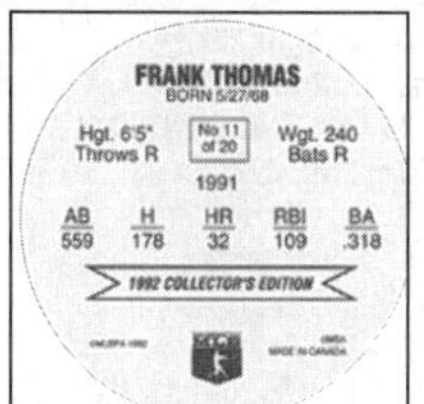

The Ben's Limited logo replaced the Holsum logo on their disks in 1992.

Disk Size: 2 3/4" Diameter

Face: Four colour, white border; name, position, team, Ben's logo

Back: Black on card stock; name, résumé, numbered _ of 20

Imprint: "MLBPA 1992" MSA MADE IN CANADA

Complete Set (20 disks): 45.00

	No.	Player	MINT
☐	1	Cecil Fielder, Det.	1.25
☐	2	Joe Carter, Tor.	2.00
☐	3	Roberto Alomar, Tor.	2.50
☐	4	Devon White, Tor.	1.25
☐	5	Kelly Gruber, Tor.	1.25
☐	6	Cal Ripken, Bal.	8.00
☐	7	Kirby Puckett, Min.	5.00
☐	8	Paul Molitor, Mil.	2.50
☐	9	Julio Franco, Tex.	1.25
☐	10	Ken Griffey, Jr., Sea.	12.00
☐	11	Frank Thomas, Chi.-A.L.	10.00
☐	12	Jose Canseco, Oak.	2.00
☐	13	Danny Tartabull, NYY.	1.25
☐	14	Terry Pendleton, Atl.	1.25
☐	15	Tony Gwynn, S.D.	5.00
☐	16	Howard Johnson, NYM.	1.25
☐	17	Will Clark, S.F.	2.00
☐	18	Barry Bonds, Pgh.	2.50
☐	19	Ryne Sandberg, Chi.-N.L.	2.00
☐	20	Bobby Bonilla, NYM.	1.25

1992 CSC PREMIUM SHEET

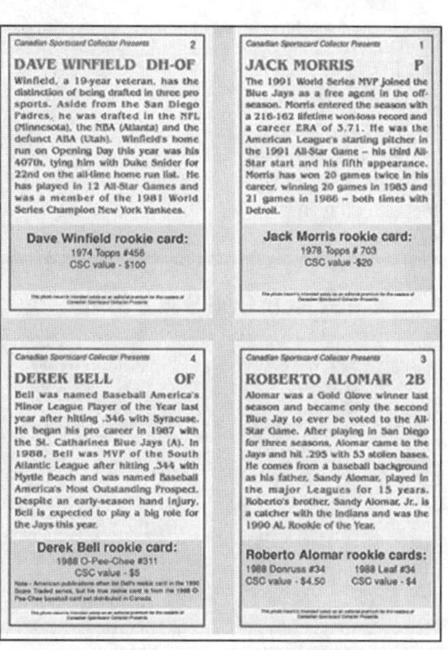

The four cards on this sheet cut out to the standadrd 2 1/2" x 3 1/2" size. The sheet was a premium in the CSC Presents Baseball Card Preview.

Sheet Size: 8 5/8" x 10 9/16"

	No.	Player	MINT
☐	1	Jack Morris, Tor.	4.00
	2	Dave Winfield, Tor.	
	3	Roberto Alomar, Tor.	
	4	Derek Bell, Tor.	

1992 HOMERS CLASSIC HALL OF FAME

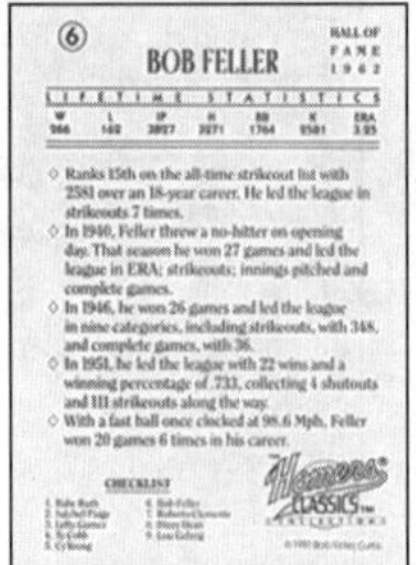

Distributed in Canada by B.L. Marks Sales Co. Ltd. of Toronto, this 9-card set was a premium offering in Homers Vanilla Cookies. While the cards are not bilingual, the package was.

Card Size: 2 1/2" x 3 1/2"
Face: Sepia, white border; name
Back: Black on card stock; name, number, résumé, checklist, Homers Classic logo
Imprint: © 1991 Curtis
Complete Set (9 cards): 11.00

	No.	Player	MINT
☐	1	Babe Ruth, Bos.	3.00
☐	2	Satchel Page, Stl.	2.25
☐	3	Lefty Gomez, NYY.	1.00
☐	4	Ty Cobb, Det.	2.25
☐	5	Cy Young, Cle.	2.00
☐	6	Bob Feller, Cle.	2.00
☐	7	Roberto Clemente, Pgh.	2.50
☐	8	Dizzy Dean, Chi.-N.L.	1.75
☐	9	Lou Gehrig, NYY.	2.50

1992 KELLOGG'S ALL-STAR

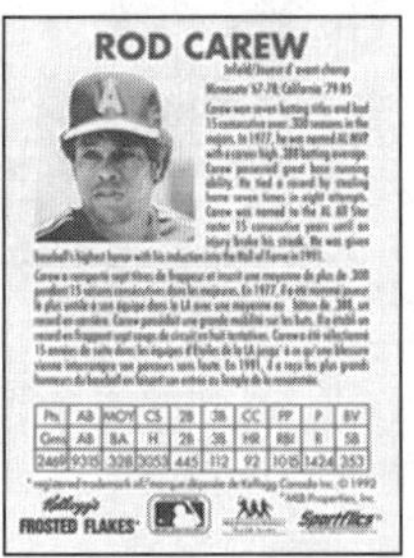

These 10 cards feature some of baseball's greatest players. In addition to the colour photo on the face which appears to move when the card is moved, there is a black and white photo on the back. The set was made available by Kellogg on the back of boxes of Frosted Flakes. There is also a special display board to hold the set. The cards are unnumbered and are listed here alphabetically.

Card Size: 2 1/2" x 3 1/4"
Face: Four colour, white border; name, team, Kellogg logo
Back: Black and red on laminated plastic card; name, position, résumé, stats, bilingual
Imprint: *registered trademark of/marque deposee de Kellogg Canada Inc. © 1992
Complete Set (10 cards) 12.00
Display Board: 5.00

	No.	Player	MINT
☐		Rod Carew, Cal.	2.50
☐		Bill Madlock, L.A.	1.00
☐		Phil Niekro, Atl.	2.00
☐		Jim Palmer, Bal.	2.50
☐		Tony Perez, Cin.	1.50
☐		Dan Quisenbery, K.C.	1.00
☐		Jim Rice, Bos.	1.00
☐		Mike Schmidt, Pha.	3.00
☐		Tom Seaver, NYM.	3.00
☐		Willie Stargell, Pgh.	2.00

1992 MCDONALD'S MVP SERIES

Card Size: 2 1/2" x 3 1/2"
Face: Four colour, white border; name, position, team
Back: Four colour, red, blue and black on card stock; name, résumé, numbered _ of 26
Imprint: © 1992 MCDONALD'S RESTAURANTS OF CANADA LIMITED © 1992 LEAF, INC. PRINTED IN U.S.A.
Complete Set (27 cards): 10.00

	No.	Player	MINT
☐		Title Card / Checklist	1.00
☐	1	Cal Ripken, Jr., Bal.	1.00
☐	2	Frank Thomas, Chi.-A.L.	1.75
☐	3	George Brett, K.C.	.50
☐	4	Roberto Kelly, NYY.	.25
☐	5	Nolan Ryan, Tex.	1.00
☐	6	Ryne Sandberg, Chi.-N.L.	.50
☐	7	Darryl Strawberry, L.A.	.35
☐	8	Lenny Dykstra, Pha.	.25
☐	9	Fred McGriff, S.D.	.35
☐	10	Roger Clemens, Bos.	.75
☐	11	Sandy Alomar, Jr., Cle.	.25
☐	12	Robin Yount, Mil.	.50
☐	13	Jose Canseco, Oak.	.35
☐	14	Jimmy Key, Tor.	.25
☐	15	Barry Larkin, Cin.	.35
☐	16	Dennis Martinez, Mtl.	.25
☐	17	Andy Van Slyke, Pgh.	.25
☐	18	Will Clark, S.F.	.35
☐	19	Mark Langston, Cal.	.25
☐	20	Cecil Fielder, Det.	.25
☐	21	Kirby Puckett, Min.	.50
☐	22	Ken Griffey, Jr., Sea.	2.00
☐	23	David Justice, Atl.	.35
☐	24	Jeff Bagwell, Hou.	.50
☐	25	Howard Johnson, NYM.	.25
☐	26	Ozzie Smith, Stl.	.50

1992 GOLD SERIES

A prize card was randomly inserted into foil packs. This card entitled the holder to redeem it for a card autographed by Roberto Alomar.

The face of the Roberto Alomar autographed card has the words "Authorized

Autograph" printed near the bottom. Above these words is Alomar's signature in dark blue ink. On the back of the card, near the top, is the limited-edition number, in blue ink, out of a total of 1,000 produced.

Card Size: 2 1/2" x 3 1/2"
Face: Four colour, gold striped border; name
Back: Red, blue and black on card stock; name, résumé, numbered _ of 6
Imprint: © 1992 MCDONALD'S RESTAURANTS OF CANADA LIMITED © 1992 LEAF, INC. PRINTED IN U.S.A.
Complete Set (6 cards): 2.00
Roberto Alomar Autographed 100.00

	No.	Player	MINT
☐	1	Roberto Alomar	.75
☐	2	Joe Carter	.50
☐	3	Kelly Gruber	.25
☐	4	Jack Morris	.25
☐	5	Tom Henke	.25
☐	6	Devon White	.25

1992 NABISCO TRADITION

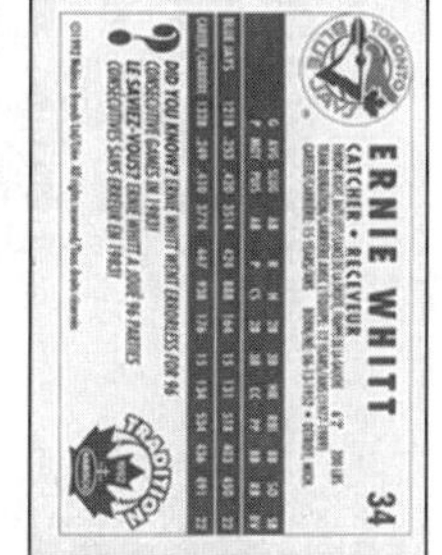

This 36-card set was issued by Nabisco during 1992 as a premium in its cereal. This set features the Toronto Blue Jays and the Montreal Expos. A blue 9 1/4" x 12" album was made to hold the set.

Card Size: 2 1/2" x 3 1/2"
Face: Four colour, white border; name, bilingual
Back: Blue, red and black on card stock; number, position, résumé,
Imprint: © 1992 Nabisco Brands Ltd/Ltee
Complete Set (36 cards): 15.00
Album: 3.00

	No.	Player	MINT
☐	1	Bill Lee, Mtl.	1.00
☐	2	Cliff Johnson, Tor.	.50
☐	3	Ken Singleton, Mtl.	.50
☐	4	Al Woods, Tor.	.50
☐	5	Ron Hunt, Mtl.	.50
☐	6	Barry Bonnell, Tor.	.50
☐	7	Tony Perez, Mtl.	1.00
☐	8	Willie Upshaw, Tor.	.50
☐	9	Coco Laboy, Mtl.	.50
☐	10	Famous Moments: Toronto Blue Jays (October 5, 1985)	.50
☐	11	Bob Bailey, Mtl.	.50
☐	12	Dave McKay, Tor.	.50
☐	13	Rodney Scott, Mtl.	.50
☐	14	Jerry Garvin, Tor.	.50
☐	15	Famous Moments: Montreal Expos (October 11, 1981)	.50
☐	16	Rick Bosetti, Tor.	.50
☐	17	Larry Parrish, Mtl.	.50
☐	18	Bill Singer, Tor.	.50
☐	19	Ron Fairly, Mtl.	.50
☐	20	Damaso Garcia, Tor.	.50
☐	21	Al Oliver, Mtl.	.50
☐	22	Famous Moments: Toronto Blue Jays (September 30, 1989)	.50
☐	23	Claude Raymond, Mtl.	.50
☐	24	Buck Martinez, Tor.	.50
☐	25	Rusty Staub, Mtl.	1.50
☐	26	Otto Velez, Tor.	.50
☐	27	Mack Jones, Mtl.	.50
☐	28	Garth Iorg, Tor.	.50
☐	29	Bill Stoneman, Mtl.	.50
☐	30	Doug Ault, Tor.	.50
☐	31	Famous Moments: Montreal Expos (July 6, 1982)	.50
☐	32	Jesse Jefferson, Tor.	.50
☐	33	Steve Rogers, Mtl.	.50
☐	34	Ernie Whitt, Tor.	.50
☐	35	John Boccabella, Mtl.	.50
☐	36	Bob Bailor, Tor.	.50

1992 O-PEE-CHEE

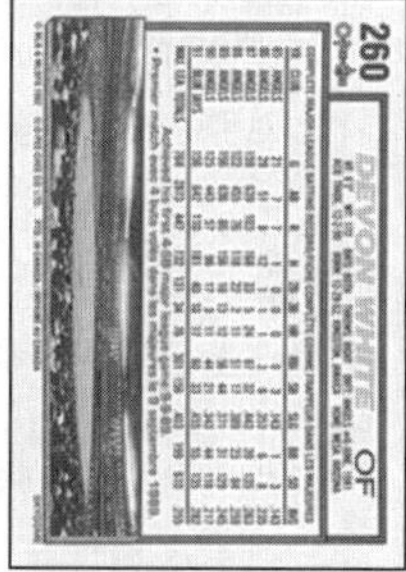

Card Size: 2 1/2" x 3 1/2"
Face: Four colour, white border; name, team
Back: Four colour, white border; name, number, position, résumé, Stadium
Imprint: @ O-PEE-CHEE CO. LTD.
Complete Set (792 cards): 20.00
Common Player: .15

	No.	Player	MINT
☐	1	Nolan Ryan, Tex.	.25
☐	2	Rickey Henderson, Oak.	.15
☐	3	Jeff Reardon, Bos.	.15
☐	4	Nolan Ryan, Tex.	.75
☐	5	Dave Winfield, Cal.	.25
☐	**6**	**Brien Taylor, NYY., RC**	**.15**
☐	**7**	**Jim Olander, Mil., RC**	**.15**
☐	**8**	**Bryan Hickerson, S.F., RC**	**.15**
☐	**9**	**Jon Farrell, RC**	**.15**
☐	10	Wade Boggs, Bos.	.25
☐	11	Jack McDowell, Chi.-A.L.	.15
☐	12	All-Star Rookie: Luis Gonzalez, Hou.	.15
☐	13	Mike Scioscia, L.A.	.15
☐	14	Wes Chamberlain, Pha.	.15
☐	15	Denny Martinez, Mtl.	.15
☐	16	Jeff Montgomery, K.C.	.15
☐	17	Randy Milligan, Bal.	.15
☐	18	Greg Cadaret, NYY.	.15
☐	19	Jamie Quirk, Oak.	.15
☐	20	Bip Roberts, S.D., (Bos.)	.15
☐	21	Buck Rodgers, Mgr., Cal.	.15
☐	22	Bill Wegman, Mil.	.15
☐	23	All-Star Rookie: Chuck Knoblauch, Min.	.25
☐	24	Randy Myers, Cin.	.15
☐	25	Ron Gant, Atl.	.15
☐	26	Mike Bielecki, Atl.	.15
☐	27	Juan Gonzalez, Tex.	.75
☐	28	Mike Schooler, Sea.	.15
☐	29	Micke Tettleton, Det.	.15
☐	30	John Kruk, Pha.	.15

	No.	Player	Price
☐	31	Bryn Smith, Stl.	.15
☐	32	Chris Nabholz, Mtl.	.15
☐	33	Carlos Baerga, Cle.	.15
☐	34	Jeff Juden, Hou.	.15
☐	35	Dave Righetti, S.F.	.15
☐	36	Major League Draft Pick: Scott Ruffcorn	.15
☐	37	Luis Polonia, Cal.	.15
☐	38	Tom Candiotti, Tor. (L.A.).	.15
☐	39	Greg Olson, Atl.	.15
☐	40	Cal Ripken, Bal.	3.00
☐	41	Craig Lefferts, S.D.	.15
☐	42	Mike Macfarlane, K.C.	.15
☐	43	Jose Lind, Pgh.	.15
☐	44	Rick Aguilera, Min.	.15
☐	45	Gary Carter, Mtl.	.25
☐	46	Steve Farr, NYY.	.15
☐	47	Rex Hudler, Stl.	.15
☐	48	Scott Scudder, Cin. (Cle.)	.15
☐	49	Damon Berryhill, Atl.	.15
☐	50	Ken Griffey Jr., Sea.	2.00
☐	51	Tom Runnells, Mgr., Mtl.	.15
☐	52	Juan Bell, Bal.	.15
☐	53	Tommy Gregg, Atl.	.15
☐	54	David Wells, Tor.	.15
☐	55	Rafael Palmeiro, Tex.	.25
☐	56	Charlie O'Brien, NYM.	.15
☐	57	Donn Pall, Chi WS	.15
☐	**58**	**Brad Ausmus, RC/ Jim Campanis, RC/ Dave Nilsson, RC/ Doug Robbins, RC**	**.15**
☐	59	Mo Vaughn, Bos.	.35
☐	60	Tony Fernandez, S.D.	.15
☐	61	Paul O'Neill, Cin.	.15
☐	62	Gene Nelson, Oak.	.15
☐	63	Randy Ready, Pha.	.15
☐	64	Bob Kipper, Pgh. (Min.)	.15
☐	65	Willie McGee, S.F.	.15
☐	66	Major League Draft Pick: Scott Stahoviak	.15
☐	67	Luis Salazar, Chi C	.15
☐	68	Marvin Freeman, Atl.	.15
☐	69	Kenny Lofton, Hou. (Cle.)	.75
☐	70	Gary Gaetti, Cal.	.15
☐	71	Erik Hanson, Sea.	.15
☐	72	Eddie Zosky, Tor.	.15
☐	73	Brian Barnes, Mtl.	.15
☐	74	Scott Leius, Min.	.15
☐	75	Bret Saberhagen, K.C. (NYM.)	.15
☐	76	Mike Gallego, Oak.	.15
☐	77	Jack Armstrong, Cin. (Cle.)	.15
☐	78	All-Star Rookie: Ivan Rodriguez, Tex.	.50
☐	79	Jesse Orosco, Cle. (Mil.)	.15
☐	80	David Justice, Atl.	.25
☐	81	Ced Landrum, Chi.-N.L.	.15
☐	82	Doug Simons, NYM.	.15
☐	83	Tommy Greene, Pha.	.15
☐	84	All-Star Rookie: Leo Gomez, Bal.	.15
☐	85	Jose DeLeon, St.L	.15
☐	86	Steve Finley, Hou.	.15
☐	87	Bob MacDonald, Tor.	.15
☐	88	Darrin Jackson, S.D.	.15
☐	89	Neal Heaton, Pgh.	.15
☐	90	Robin Yount, Mil.	.25
☐	91	Jeff Reed, Cin.	.15
☐	92	Lenny Harris, L.A.	.15
☐	93	Reggie Jefferson, Cle.	.15
☐	94	Sammy Sosa, Chi.-A.L.	.25
☐	95	Scott Bailes, Cal.	.15
☐	**96**	**Major League Draft Pick: Tom McKinnon, RC**	**.15**
☐	97	Luis Rivera, Bos.	.15
☐	98	Mike Harkey, Chi.-N.L.	.15
☐	99	Jeff Treadway, Atl.	.15
☐	100	Jose Canseco, Oak.	.25
☐	101	Omar Vizquel, Sea.	.15
☐	102	Scott Kamieniecki, NYY.	.15
☐	103	Ricky Jordan, Pha.	.15
☐	104	Jeff Ballard, Bal.	.15
☐	105	Felix Jose, Stl.	.15
☐	106	Mike Boddicker, K.C.	.15
☐	107	Dan Pasqua, Chi.-A.L.	.15
☐	108	Mike Timlin, Tor.	.15
☐	109	Roger Craig, Mgr., S.F.	.15
☐	110	Ryne Sandberg, Chi.-N.L.	.25
☐	111	Mark Carreon, NYM.	.15
☐	112	Oscar Azocar, S.D.	.15
☐	113	Mike Greenwell, Bos.	.15
☐	114	Mark Portugal, Hou.	.15
☐	115	Terry Pendleton, Atl.	.15
☐	116	Willie Randolph, Mil. (NYM.)	.15
☐	117	Scott Terry, Stl.	.15
☐	118	Chili Davis, Min.	.15
☐	119	Mark Gardner, Mtl.	.15
☐	120	Alan Trammell, Det.	.15
☐	121	Derek Bell, Tor.	.15
☐	122	Gary Varsho, Pgh.	.15
☐	123	Bob Ojeda, L.A.	.15
☐	**124**	**Major League Draft Pick: Shawn Livsey, RC**	**.15**
☐	125	Chris Hoiles, Bal.	.15
☐	126	Rico Brogna/ **John Jaha, RC/** Ryan Klesko/ Dave Staton	.25
☐	127	Carlos Quintana, Bos.	.15
☐	128	Kurt Stillwell, K.C.	.15
☐	129	Melido Perez, Chi.-A.L.	.15
☐	130	Alvin Davis, Sea.	.15
☐	131	1992 Checklist No. 1 of 6	.15
☐	132	Eric Show, Oak.	.15
☐	133	Rance Mulliniks, Tor.	.15
☐	134	Darryl Kile, Hou.	.15
☐	135	Von Hayes, Pha. (Ana.)	.15
☐	136	Bill Doran, Cin.	.15
☐	137	Jeff Robinson, Cal.	.15
☐	138	Monty Fariss, Tex.	.15
☐	139	Jeff Innis, NYM.	.15
☐	140	Mark Grace, Chi.-N.L.	.15
☐	141	Jim Leyland, Pgh.	.15
☐	142	Todd Van Poppel, Oak.	.15
☐	143	Paul Gibson, Det.	.15
☐	144	Bill Swift, Sea.	.15
☐	145	Danny Tartabull, K.C. (NYY.)	.15
☐	146	Al Newman, Min.	.15
☐	147	Cris Carpenter, Stl.	.15
☐	148	Anthony Young, NYM.	.15
☐	149	Brian Bohanon, Tex.	.15
☐	150	Roger Clemens, Bos.	.75
☐	151	Jeff Hamilton, L.A.	.15
☐	152	Charlie Leibrandt, Atl.	.15
☐	153	Ron Karkovice, Chi.-A.L.	.15
☐	154	Hensley Meulens, NYY.	.15
☐	155	Scott Bankhead, Sea.	.15
☐	**156**	**Major League Draft Pick: Manny Ramirez, RC**	**1.50**
☐	157	Keith Miller, NYM. (K.C.)	.15
☐	158	Todd Frohwirth, Bal.	.15
☐	159	Darrin Fletcher, Pha. (Mtl.)	.15
☐	160	Bobby Bonilla, Pgh. (NYM.)	.15
☐	161	Casey Candaele, Hou.	.15
☐	162	Paul Faries, S.D.	.15
☐	163	Dana Kiecker, Bos.	.15
☐	164	Shane Mack, Min.	.15
☐	165	Mark Langston, Cal.	.15
☐	166	Geronimo Pena, Stl.	.15

- ☐ 167 Andy Allanson, Det. .15
- ☐ 168 Dwight Smith, Chi.-N.L. .15
- ☐ 169 Chuck Crim, Mil. (Cal.) .15
- ☐ 170 Alex Cole, Cle. .15
- ☐ 171 Bill Plummer, Mgr., Sea. .15
- ☐ 172 Juan Berenguer, Atl. .15
- ☐ 173 Brian Downing, Tex. .15
- ☐ 174 Steve Frey, Mtl. .15
- ☐ 175 Orel Hershiser, L.A. .15
- ☐ **176 Ramon Garcia, Chi.-A.L., RC .15**
- ☐ 177 Danny Gladden, Min. (Det.) .15
- ☐ 178 Jim Acker, Tor. .15
- ☐ **179** C. Bernhardt/ **B. De Jardin, RC/ A. Moreno, RC/ A. Stankiewicz, RC .15**
- ☐ 180 Kevin Mitchell, S.F. (Sea.) .15
- ☐ 181 Hector Villanueva, Chi.-N.L. .15
- ☐ 182 Jeff Reardon, Bos. .15
- ☐ 183 Brent Mayne, K.C. .15
- ☐ 184 Jimmy Jones, Hou. .15
- ☐ 185 Benny Santiago, S.D. .15
- ☐ **186 Cliff Floyd, Mtl., RC .35**
- ☐ 187 Ernie Riles, Oak. .15
- ☐ 188 Jose Guzman, Tex. .15
- ☐ 189 Junior Felix, Cal. .15
- ☐ 190 Glenn Davis, Bal. .15
- ☐ 191 Charlie Hough, Chi.-A.L. .15
- ☐ 192 Dave Fleming, Sea. .15
- ☐ 193 Omar Olivares, StL, .15
- ☐ 194 Eric Karros, L.A. .15
- ☐ 195 David Cone, NYM. .15
- ☐ **196 Frank Castillo, Chi.-N.L., RC .15**
- ☐ 197 Glenn Braggs, Cin. .15
- ☐ 198 Scott Aldred, Det. .15
- ☐ 199 Jeff Blauser, Atl. .15
- ☐ 200 Lenny Dykstra, Pha. .15
- ☐ 201 Buck Showalter, Mgr., NYY. .15
- ☐ 202 Rick Honeycutt, Oak. .15
- ☐ 203 Greg Myers, Tor. .15
- ☐ 204 Trevor Wilson, S.F. .15
- ☐ 205 Jay Howell, L.A. .15
- ☐ 206 Luis Sojo, Cal. .15
- ☐ 207 Jack Clark, Bos. .15
- ☐ 208 Julio Machado, Mil. .15
- ☐ 209 Lloyd McClendon, Pgh. .15
- ☐ 210 Ozzie Guillen, Chi.-A.L. .15
- ☐ **211 Jeremy Hernandez, S.D., RC .15**
- ☐ 212 Randy Velarde, NYY. .15
- ☐ 213 Les Lancaster, Chi.-N.L. .15
- ☐ **214 Andy Mota, Hou., RC .15**
- ☐ 215 Rich Gossage, Tex. .15
- ☐ **216 Major League Draft Pick: Brent Gates, RC .15**
- ☐ 217 Brian Harper, Min. .15
- ☐ 218 Mike Flanagan, Bal. .15
- ☐ 219 Jerry Browne, Cle. .15
- ☐ 220 Jose Rijo, Cin. .15
- ☐ 221 Skeeter Barnes, Det. .15
- ☐ 222 Jaime Navarro, Mil. .15
- ☐ 223 Mel Hall, NYY. .15
- ☐ **224 Bret Barberie, Mtl., RC .15**
- ☐ 225 Roberto Alomar, Tor. .25
- ☐ 226 Pete Smith, Atl. .15
- ☐ 227 Daryl Boston, NYM. .15
- ☐ 228 Eddie Whitson, S.D. .15
- ☐ 229 Shawn Boskie, Chi.-N.L. .15
- ☐ 230 Dick Schofield, Cal. .15
- ☐ 231 Brian Drahman, Chi.-A.L. .15
- ☐ 232 John Smiley, Pgh. .15
- ☐ 233 Mitch Webster, L.A. .15
- ☐ 234 Terry Steinbach, Oak. .15
- ☐ 235 Jack Morris, Min. (Tor.) .15
- ☐ 236 Bill Pecota, K.C. .15
- ☐ **237 Jose Hernandez, Tex., RC .15**
- ☐ 238 Greg Litton, S.F. .15
- ☐ 239 Brian Holman, Sea. .15
- ☐ 240 Andres Galarraga, Mtl. (Stl.) .25
- ☐ 241 Gerald Young, Hou. .15
- ☐ 242 Mike Mussina, Bal. .35
- ☐ 243 Alvaro Espinoza, NYY. .15
- ☐ 244 Darren Daulton, Pha. .15
- ☐ 245 John Smoltz, Atl. .15
- ☐ **246 Major League Draft Pick: Jason Pruitt, RC .15**
- ☐ 247 Chuck Finley, Cal. .15
- ☐ 248 Jim Gantner, Mil. .15
- ☐ 249 Tony Fossas, Bos. .15
- ☐ 250 Ken Griffey, Sea. .15
- ☐ 251 Kevin Elster, NYM. .15
- ☐ 252 Dennis Rasmussen, S.D. .15
- ☐ 253 Terry Kennedy, S.F. .15
- ☐ 254 Ryan Bowen, Hou. .15
- ☐ 255 Robin Ventura, Chi.-A.L. .15
- ☐ 256 Mike Aldrete, Cle. .15
- ☐ 257 Jeff Russell, Tex. .15
- ☐ 258 Jim Lindeman, Pha. .15
- ☐ 259 Ron Darling, Oak. .15
- ☐ 260 Devon White, Tor. .15
- ☐ 261 Tom Lasorda, Mgr., L.A. .25
- ☐ 262 Terry Lee, Cin. .15
- ☐ 263 Bob Patterson, Pgh. .15
- ☐ 264 1992 Checklist No. 2 of 6 .15
- ☐ 265 Teddy Higuera, Mil. .15
- ☐ 266 Roberto Kelly, NYY. .15
- ☐ 267 Steve Bedrosian, Min. .15
- ☐ 268 Brady Anderson, Bal. .15
- ☐ 269 Ruben Amaro, Cal. (Pha.) .15
- ☐ 270 Tony Gwynn, S.D. .75
- ☐ 271 Tracy Jones, Sea. .15
- ☐ 272 Jerry Don Gleaton, Det. .15
- ☐ 273 Craig Grebeck, Chi.-A.L. .15
- ☐ 274 Bob Scanlan, Chi.-N.L. .15
- ☐ 275 Todd Zeile, Stl .15
- ☐ **276 Major League Draft Pick: Shawn Green, RC .35**
- ☐ 277 Scott Chiamparino, Tex. .15
- ☐ 278 Darryl Hamilton, Mil. .15
- ☐ 279 Jim Clancy, Atl. .15
- ☐ 280 Carlos Martinez, Cle. .15
- ☐ 281 Kevin Appier, K.C. .15
- ☐ **282 John Wehner, Pgh., RC .15**
- ☐ 283 Reggie Sanders, Cin. .15
- ☐ 284 Gene Larkin, Min. .15
- ☐ 285 Bob Welch, Oak. .15
- ☐ 286 Gilberto Reyes, Mtl. .15
- ☐ 287 Pete Schourek, NYM. .15
- ☐ 288 All-Star Rookie: Andujar Cedeno, Hou. .15
- ☐ 289 Mike Morgan, LA (Chi.-N.L.) .15
- ☐ 290 Bo Jackson, Chi.-A.L. .15
- ☐ 291 Phil Garner, Mgr., Mil. .15
- ☐ 292 All-Star Rookie: Ray Lankford, Stl. .15
- ☐ 293 Mike Henneman, Det. .15
- ☐ 294 Dave Valle, Sea. .15
- ☐ 295 Alonzo Powell, Sea. .15
- ☐ 296 Tom Brunansky, Bos. .15
- ☐ 297 Kevin Brown, Tex. .15
- ☐ 298 Kelly Gruber, Tor. .15
- ☐ 299 Charles Nagy, Cle. .15
- ☐ 300 Don Mattingly, NYY. .75
- ☐ 301 Kirk McCaskill, Cal. .25
- ☐ 302 Joey Cora, Chi.-A.L. .15
- ☐ 303 Dan Plesac, Mil. .15

- ☐ 304 Joe Oliver, Cin. .15
- ☐ 305 Tom Glavine, Atl. .15
- ☐ **306 Major League Draft Pick: Al Shirley, RC .15**
- ☐ 307 Bruce Ruffin, Pha. (Mil.) .15
- ☐ 308 Craig Shipley, S.D. .15
- ☐ 309 Dave Martinez, Mtl. (Bos.) .15
- ☐ 310 Jose Mesa, Bal. .15
- ☐ 311 Henry Cotto, Sea. .15
- ☐ 312 Mike LaValliere, Pgh. .15
- ☐ 313 Kevin Tapani, Min. .15
- ☐ 314 Jeff Huson, Tex. .15
- ☐ 315 Juan Samuel, L.A. .15
- ☐ 316 Curt Schilling, Hou. .15
- ☐ 317 Mike Bordick, Oak. .15
- ☐ 318 Steve Howe, NYY. .15
- ☐ 319 Tony Phillips, Det. .15
- ☐ 320 George Bell, Chi.-N.L. .15
- ☐ 321 Lou Piniella, Mgr., Cin. .15
- ☐ 322 Tim Burke, NYM. .15
- ☐ 323 Milt Thompson, Stl. .15
- ☐ 324 Danny Darwin, Bos. .15
- ☐ 325 Joe Orsulak, Bal. .15
- ☐ 326 Eric King, Cle. .15
- ☐ 327 Jay Buhner, Sea. .15
- ☐ 328 Joel Johnston, K.C. .15
- ☐ 329 Franklin Stubbs, Mil. .15
- ☐ 330 Will Clark, S.F. .25
- ☐ 331 Steve Lake, Pha. .15
- ☐ 332 Chris Jones, Cin. (Hou.) .15
- ☐ 333 Pat Tabler, Tor. .15
- ☐ 334 Kevin Gross, L.A. .15
- ☐ 335 Dave Henderson, Oak. .15
- ☐ **336 Major League Draft Pick: Greg Anthony, RC .15**
- ☐ 337 Alejandro Pena, Atl. .15
- ☐ 338 Shawn Abner, Cal. .15
- ☐ 339 Tom Browning, Cin. .15
- ☐ 340 Otis Nixon, Atl. .15
- ☐ 341 Bob Geren, NYY. (Bos.) .15
- ☐ 342 Tim Spehr, K.C. .15
- ☐ **343 John Vander Wal, Mtl., RC .15**
- ☐ 344 Jack Daugherty, Tex. .15
- ☐ 345 Zane Smith, Pgh. .15
- ☐ 346 Rheal Cormier, Stl. .25
- ☐ 347 Kent Hrbek, Min. .15
- ☐ 348 Rick Wilkins, Chi.-N.L. .15
- ☐ 349 Steve Lyons, Bos. .15
- ☐ 350 Gregg Olson, Bal. .75
- ☐ 351 Greg Riddoch, Mgr., S.D. .15
- ☐ 352 Ed Nunez, Mil. .15
- ☐ **353 Braulio Castillo, Pha., RC .15**
- ☐ 354 Dave Bergman, Det. .15
- ☐ **355 Warren Newson, Chi.-A.L., RC .15**
- ☐ 356 Luis Quinones, Cin. (Min.) .15
- ☐ 357 Mike Witt, NYY. .15
- ☐ 358 Ted Wood, S.F. .15
- ☐ 359 Mike Moore, Oak. .15
- ☐ 360 Lance Parrish, Cal. .15
- ☐ 361 Barry Jones, Mtl. .15
- ☐ 362 Javier Ortiz, Hou. .15
- ☐ 363 John Candelaria, L.A. .15
- ☐ 364 Glenallen Hill, Cle. .15
- ☐ 365 Duane Ward, Tor. .15
- ☐ 366 1992 Checklist No. 3 of 6 .15
- ☐ 367 Rafael Belliard, Atl. .15
- ☐ 368 Bill Krueger, Sea. .15
- ☐ 369 Major League Draft Pick: Steve Whitaker .15
- ☐ 370 Shawon Dunston, Chi.-N.L. .15
- ☐ 371 Dante Bichette, Mil. .15
- ☐ **372 Kip Gross, Cin. (L.A.), RC .15**
- ☐ 373 Don Robinson, S.F. (Cal.) .15
- ☐ 374 Bernie Williams, NYY. .25
- ☐ 375 Bert Blyleven, Cal. .15
- ☐ 376 Chris Donnells, NYM., Error .15
- ☐ **377 Bob Zupcic, Bos., RC .15**
- ☐ 378 Joel Skinner, Cle. .15
- ☐ 379 Steve Chitren, Oak. .15
- ☐ 380 Barry Bonds, Pgh. .50
- ☐ 381 Sparky Anderson, Mgr., Det. .15
- ☐ 382 Sid Fernandez, NYM. .15
- ☐ 383 Dave Hollins, Pha. .15
- ☐ 384 Mark Lee, Mil. .15
- ☐ 385 Tim Wallach, Mtl. .15
- ☐ 386 Lance Blankenship, Oak. .15
- ☐ 387 Tribute: Gary Carter, Mtl. .25
- ☐ 388 Ron Tingley, Cal. .15
- ☐ 389 Tribute: Gary Carter, NYM. .25
- ☐ 390 Gene Harris, Sea. .15
- ☐ 391 Jeff Schaefer, Sea. .15
- ☐ 392 Mark Grant, Atl. .15
- ☐ 393 Carl Willis, Min. .15
- ☐ 394 Al Leiter, Tor. .15
- ☐ 395 Ron Robinson, Mil. .15
- ☐ 396 Tim Hulett, Bal. .15
- ☐ 397 Craig Worthington, Bal. .15
- ☐ 398 John Orton, Cal. .15
- ☐ 399 Tribute: Gary Carter, L.A. .25
- ☐ 400 John Dopson, Bos. .15
- ☐ 401 Moises Alou, Mtl. .25
- ☐ 402 Tribute: Gary Carter, S.F. .25
- ☐ 403 Matt Young, Bos. .15
- ☐ 404 Wayne Edwards, Chi.-A.L. .15
- ☐ 405 Nick Esasky, Atl. .15
- ☐ 406 Dave Eiland, NYY. .15
- ☐ 407 Mike Brumley, Bos. .15
- ☐ 408 Bob Milacki, Bal. .15
- ☐ 409 Geno Petralli, Tex. .15
- ☐ 410 Dave Stewart, Oak. .15
- ☐ 411 Mike Jackson, Sea. (NYG.) .15
- ☐ 412 Luis Aquino, K.C. .15
- ☐ 413 Tim Teufel, S.D. .15
- ☐ **414 Major League Draft Pick: Jeff Ware, RC .15**
- ☐ 415 Jim Deshaies, Hou. .15
- ☐ 416 Ellis Burks, Bos. .25
- ☐ 417 Allan Anderson, Min. .15
- ☐ 418 Alfredo Griffin, L.A. .15
- ☐ 419 Wally Whitehurst, NYM. .15
- ☐ 420 Sandy Alomar, Cle. .15
- ☐ 421 Juan Agosto, Stl. .15
- ☐ 422 Sam Horn, Bal. .15
- ☐ **423 Jeff Fassero, Mtl., RC .25**
- ☐ 424 Paul McClellan, S.F. .15
- ☐ 425 Cecil Fielder, Det. .15
- ☐ 426 Tim Raines, Chi.-A.L. .15
- ☐ **427 Eddie Taubensee, Cle. (Hou.), RC .25**
- ☐ 428 Dennis Boyd, Tex. .15
- ☐ 429 Tony LaRussa, Mgr., Oak. .15
- ☐ 430 Steve Sax, NYY. .15
- ☐ 431 Tom Gordon, K.C. .15
- ☐ 432 Billy Hatcher, Cin. .15
- ☐ 433 Cal Eldred, Mil. .15
- ☐ 434 Wally Backman, Pha. .15
- ☐ 435 Mark Eichhorn, Cal. .15
- ☐ 436 Mookie Wilson, Tor. .15
- ☐ 437 Scott Servais, Hou. .15
- ☐ 438 Mike Maddux, S.D. .15
- ☐ 439 Chico Walker, Chi.-N.L. .15
- ☐ 440 Doug Drabek, Pgh. .15
- ☐ 441 Rob Deer, Det. .15

- ☐ 442 Dave West, Min. .15
- ☐ 443 Spike Owen, Mtl. .15
- ☐ **444 Major League Draft Pick: Tyrone Hill, RC .15**
- ☐ 445 Matt Williams, S.F. .15
- ☐ 446 Mark Lewis, Cle. .15
- ☐ 447 David Segui, Bal. .15
- ☐ 448 Tom Pagnozzi, Stl. .15
- ☐ 449 Jeff Johnson, NYY. .15
- ☐ 450 Mark McGwire, Oak. .75
- ☐ 451 Tom Henke, Tor. .15
- ☐ 452 Wilson Alvarez, Chi.-A.L. .15
- ☐ 453 Gary Redus, Pgh. .15
- ☐ 454 Dareen Holmes, Mil. .15
- ☐ 455 Pete O'Brien, Sea. .15
- ☐ 456 Pat Combs, Pha. .15
- ☐ 457 Hubie Brooks, NYM. (Ana.) .15
- ☐ 458 Frank Tanana, Det. .15
- ☐ 459 Tom Kelly, Mgr., Min. .15
- ☐ 460 Andre Dawson, Chi.-N.L. .25
- ☐ 461 Doug Jones, Cle. .15
- ☐ 462 Rich Rodriguez, S.D. .15
- ☐ 463 Mike Simms, Hou. .15
- ☐ 464 Mike Jeffcoat, Tex. .15
- ☐ 465 Barry Larkin, Cin. .25
- ☐ 466 Stan Belinda, Pgh. .15
- ☐ 467 Lonnie Smith, Atl. .15
- ☐ 468 Greg Harris, Bos. .15
- ☐ 469 Jim Eisenreich, K.C. .15
- ☐ 470 Pedro Guerrero, Stl. .15
- ☐ 471 Jose DeJesus, Pha. .15
- ☐ 472 Rich Rowland, Det. .15
- ☐ 473 F. Bolick/ C. Paquette/ **T. Redington, RC**/ P. Russo .15
- ☐ **474 Major League Draft Pick: Mike Rossiter, RC .15**
- ☐ 475 Robby Thompson, S.F. .15
- ☐ 476 Randy Bush, Min. .15
- ☐ 477 Greg Hibbard, Chi.-A.L. .15
- ☐ 478 Dale Sveum, Mil. (Pgh.) .15
- ☐ **479 Chito Martinez, Bal., RC .15**
- ☐ 480 Scott Sanderson, NYY. .15
- ☐ 481 Tino Martinez, Sea. .25
- ☐ 482 Jimmy Key, Tor. .15
- ☐ 483 Terry Shumpert, K.C. .15
- ☐ 484 Mike Hartley, Pha. .15
- ☐ 485 Chris Sabo, Cin. .15
- ☐ 486 Bob Walk, Pgh. .15
- ☐ 487 John Cerutti, Det. .15
- ☐ 488 Scott Cooper, Bos. .15
- ☐ 489 Bobby Cox, Mgr., Atl. .15
- ☐ 490 Julio Franco, Tex. .15
- ☐ 491 Jeff Brantley, S.F. .15
- ☐ 492 Mike Devereaux, Bal. .15
- ☐ 493 Jose Offerman, L.A. .15
- ☐ 494 Gary Thurman, K.C. .15
- ☐ 495 Carney Lans.f.ord, Oak. .15
- ☐ 496 Joe Grahe, Cal. .15
- ☐ 497 Andy Ashby, Pha. .15
- ☐ 498 Gerald Perry, Stl. .15
- ☐ 499 Dave Otto, Cle. .15
- ☐ 500 Vince Coleman, NYM. .15
- ☐ 501 Rob Mallicoat, Hou. .15
- ☐ 502 Greg Briley, Sea. .15
- ☐ 503 Pasqual Perez, NYY. .15
- ☐ **504 Major League Draft Pick: Aaron Sele, RC .25**
- ☐ 505 Bobby Thigpen, Chi.-A.L. .15
- ☐ 506 Todd Benzinger, K.C. (L.A.) .15
- ☐ 507 Candy Maldonado, Tor. .15
- ☐ 508 Bill Gullickson, Det. .15
- ☐ 509 Doug Dascenzo, Chi.-N.L. .15
- ☐ 510 Frank Viola, NYM. (Bosl) .15
- ☐ 511 Kenny Rogers, Tex. .15
- ☐ 512 Mike Heath, Atl. .15
- ☐ 513 Kevin Bass, S.F. .15
- ☐ 514 Kim Batiste, Pha. .15
- ☐ 515 Delino DeShields, Mtl. .15
- ☐ 516 Ed Sprague, Tor. .15
- ☐ 517 Jim Gott, L.A. .15
- ☐ 518 Jose Melendez, S.D. .15
- ☐ 519 Hal McRae, Mgr., K.C. .15
- ☐ 520 All-Star Rookie: Jeff Bagwell, Hou. .75
- ☐ 521 Joe Hesketh, Bos. .15
- ☐ 522 All-Star Rookie: Milt Cuyler, Det. .15
- ☐ 523 Shawn Hillegas, Cle. .15
- ☐ 524 Don Slaught, Pgh. .15
- ☐ 525 Randy Johnson, Sea. .25
- ☐ **526 Doug Piatt, Mtl., RC .15**
- ☐ 527 1992 Checklist No. 4 of 6 .15
- ☐ **528 Steve Foster, Cin., RC .15**
- ☐ 529 Joe Girardi, Chi.-N.L. .15
- ☐ 530 Jim Abbott, Cal. .15
- ☐ 531 Larry Walker, Mtl. 1.00
- ☐ 532 Mike Huff, Chi.-A.L. .15
- ☐ 533 Mackey Sasser, NYM. .15
- ☐ **534 Major League Draft Pick: Benji Gil, RC .15**
- ☐ 535 Dave Stieb, Tor. .15
- ☐ 536 Willie Wilson, Oak. .15
- ☐ 537 All-Star Rookie: Mark Leiter, Det. .15
- ☐ 538 Jose Uribe, S.F. .15
- ☐ 539 Thomas Howard, S.D. .15
- ☐ 540 Ben McDonald, Bal. .15
- ☐ 541 Jose Tolentino, Hou. .15
- ☐ 542 Keith Mitchell, Atl. .15
- ☐ 543 Jerome Walton, Chi.-N.L. .15
- ☐ 544 Cliff Brantley, S.F. .15
- ☐ 545 Andy Van Slyke, Pgh. .15
- ☐ 546 Paul Sorrento, Min. .15
- ☐ 547 Herm Winningham, Cin. .15
- ☐ 548 Mark Guthrie, Min. .15
- ☐ 549 Joe Torre, Mgr., Stl. .15
- ☐ 550 Darryl Strawberry, L.A. .25
- ☐ 551 **Manny Alexander,RC/ Alex Arias, RC/** Wil Cordero/ Chipper Jones 2.00
- ☐ 552 Dave Gallagher, Cal. (NYM.) .15
- ☐ 553 Edgar Martinez, Sea. .15
- ☐ 554 Donald Harris, Tex. .15
- ☐ 555 Frank Thomas, Chi.-A.L. 1.50
- ☐ 556 Storm Davis, K.C. (Bal.) .15
- ☐ 557 Dickie Thon, Pha., (Tex.) .15
- ☐ 558 Scott Garrelts, S.F. .15
- ☐ 559 Steve Olin, Cle. .15
- ☐ 560 Rickey Henderson, Oak. .25
- ☐ 561 Jose Vizcaino, Chi.-N.L. .15
- ☐ 562 Wade Taylor, NYY. .15
- ☐ 563 Pat Borders, Tor. .15
- ☐ **564 ML Draft Pick: Jimmy Gonzalez, RC .15**
- ☐ 565 Lee Smith, Stl. .15
- ☐ 566 Bill Sampen, Mtl. .15
- ☐ 567 Dean Palmer, Tex. .15
- ☐ 568 Bryan Harvey, Cal. .15
- ☐ 569 Tony Pena, Bos. .15
- ☐ 570 Lou Whitaker, Det. .15
- ☐ 571 Randy Tomlin, Pgh. .15
- ☐ 572 Greg Vaughn, Mil. .15
- ☐ 573 Kelly Downs, S.F. .15
- ☐ 574 Steve Avery, Atl. .15
- ☐ 575 Kirby Puckett, Min. .75
- ☐ 576 Heathcliff Slocumb, Chi.-N.L. .15
- ☐ 577 Kevin Seitzer, K.C. .15

☐ 578 Lee Guetterman, NYY. .15
☐ 579 Johnny Oates, Mgr., Bal. .15
☐ 580 Greg Maddux, Chi.-N.L. 1.00
☐ 581 Stan Javier, L.A. .15
☐ 582 Vincente Palacios, Pgh. .15
☐ 583 Mel Rojas, Mtl. .15
☐ **584 Wayne Rosenthal, Tex., RC .15**
☐ 585 Lenny Webster, Min. .15
☐ 586 Rod Nichols, Cle. .15
☐ 587 Mickey Morandini, Pha. .15
☐ 588 Russ Swan, Sea. .15
☐ 589 Mariano Duncan, Cin. (Pha.) .15
☐ 590 Howard Johnson, NYM. .15
☐ 591 **J Brumfield, RC**/ **J. Burnitz**/
A. Cockrell, RC/ D.J. Dozier .15
☐ 592 Denny Neagle, Min. .15
☐ 593 Steve Decker, S.F. .15
☐ **594 Major League Draft Pick: Brian Barber, RC .15**
☐ 595 Bruce Hurst, S.D. .15
☐ 596 Kent Mercker, Atl. .15
☐ **597 Mike Magnante, K.C., RC .15**
☐ 598 Jody Reed, Bos. .15
☐ 599 Steve Searcy, Pha. .15
☐ 600 Paul Molitor, Mil. .25
☐ 601 Dave Smith, Chi.-N.L. .15
☐ 602 Mike Fetters, Cal. (Mil.) .15
☐ 603 Luis Mercedes, Bal. .15
☐ 604 Chris Gwynn, L.A. (K.C.) .15
☐ 605 Scott Erickson, Min. .15
☐ 606 Brook Jacoby, Oak. .15
☐ 607 Todd Stottlemyre, Tor. .15
☐ 608 Scott Bradley, Sea. .15
☐ 609 Mike Hargrove, Mgr., Cle. .15
☐ 610 Eric Davis, Cin. (L.A.) .15
☐ **611 Brian Hunter, Atl., RC .15**
☐ 612 Pat Kelly, NYY. .15
☐ 613 Pedro Munoz, Min. .15
☐ 614 Al Osuna, Hou. .15
☐ 615 Matt Merullo, Chi.-A.L. .15
☐ 616 Larry Andersen, S.D. .15
☐ 617 Junior Ortiz, Min., (Cle.) .15
☐ 618 C. Hernandez/ S. Hosey/ D. Peltier/ J. McNeely .15
☐ 619 Danny Jackson, Chi.-N.L. .15
☐ 620 George Brett, K.C. .50
☐ 621 Dan Gakeler, Det. .15
☐ 622 Steve Buechele, Pgh. .15
☐ 623 Bob Tewksbury, Stl. .15
☐ **624 Major League Draft Pick: Shawn Estes, RC .25**
☐ 625 Kevin McReynolds, NYM. (K.C.) .15
☐ 626 Chris Haney, Mtl. .15
☐ 627 Mike Sharperson, L.A. .15
☐ 628 Mark Williamson, Bal. .15
☐ 629 Wally Joyner, Cal. (K.C.) .15
☐ 630 Carlton Fisk, Chi.-A.L. .25
☐ **631 Armando Reynoso, Atl., RC .15**
☐ 632 Felix Fermin, Cle. .15
☐ 633 Mitch Williams, Pha. .15
☐ 634 Manuel Lee, Tor. .15
☐ 635 Harold Baines, Oak. .15
☐ 636 Greg Harris, S.D. .15
☐ 637 Orlando Merced, Pgh., Error .15
☐ 638 Chris Bosio, Mil. .15
☐ **639 Wayne Housie, Bos., RC .15**
☐ 640 Xavier Hernandez, Hou. .15
☐ 641 David Howard, K.C. .15
☐ 642 Tim Crews, L.A. .15
☐ 643 Rick Cerone, NYM. .15
☐ 644 Terry Leach, Min. .15
☐ 645 Deion Sanders, Atl. .15
☐ 646 Craig Wilson, Stl. .15
☐ 647 Marquis Grissom, Mtl. .15
☐ 648 Scott Fletcher, Chi.-A.L. .15
☐ 649 Norm Charlton, Cin. .15
☐ 650 Jesse Barfield, NYY. .15
☐ 651 Joe Slusarski, Oak. .15
☐ 652 Bobby Rose, Cal. .15
☐ 653 Dennis Lamp, Bos. .15
☐ **654 Major League Draft Pick: Allen Watson, RC .15**
☐ 655 Brett Butler, L.A. .15
☐ 656 **Rudy Pemberton, RC**/ Henry Rodriguez/
Lee Tinsley, RC/ Gerald Williams .15
☐ 657 Dave Johnson, Bal. .15
☐ 658 1992 Checklist No. 5 of 6 .15
☐ 659 Brian McRae, K.C. .15
☐ 660 Fred McGriff, S.D. .25
☐ 661 Bill Landrum, Pgh. .15
☐ **662 Juan Guzman, Tor., RC .35**
☐ 663 Greg Gagne, Min. .15
☐ 664 Ken Hill, St.L .15
☐ 665 Dave Haas, Det. .15
☐ 666 Tom Foley, Mtl. .15
☐ 667 Roberto Hernandez, Chi.-A.L. .15
☐ 668 Dwayne Henry, Hou. (Cin.) .15
☐ 669 Jim Fregosi, Mgr., Pha. .15
☐ 670 Harold Reynolds, Sea. .15
☐ 671 Mark Whiten, Cle. .15
☐ 672 Eric Plunk, NYY. (Tor.) .15
☐ 673 Todd Hundley, NYM. .15
☐ **674 Mo Sanford, Cin., RC .15**
☐ 675 Bobby Witt, Tex. .15
☐ **676 Pat Mahomes, RC**/ Sam Militello/
Roger Salkeld/ **Turk Wendell, RC .15**
☐ 677 John Marzano, Bos. .15
☐ 678 Joe Klink, Oak. .15
☐ 679 Pete Incaviglia, Det. .15
☐ 680 Dale Murphy, Pha. .25
☐ 681 Rene Gonzales, Tor. .15
☐ 682 Andy Benes, S.D. .15
☐ 683 Jim Poole, Bal. .15
☐ **684 Major League Draft Pick: Trever Miller, RC .15**
☐ 685 Scott Livingstone, Det. .15
☐ 686 Rich DeLucia, Sea. .15
☐ 687 Harvey Pulliam, K.C. .15
☐ 688 Tim Belcher, L.A. (Cin.) .15
☐ 689 Mark Lemke, Atl. .15
☐ 690 John Franco, NYM. .15
☐ 691 Walt Weiss, Oak. .15
☐ 692 Scott Ruskin, Mtl. (Cin.) .15
☐ 693 Jeff King, Pgh. .15
☐ 694 Mike Gardiner, Bos. .25
☐ 695 Gary Sheffield, Mil. .25
☐ 696 Joe Boever, Pha. .15
☐ 697 Mike Felder, S.F. .15
☐ 698 John Habyan, NYY. .15
☐ 699 Cito Gaston, Mgr., Tor. .15
☐ 700 Ruben Sierra, Tex. .15
☐ 701 Scott Radinsky, Chi.-A.L. .15
☐ 702 Lee Stevens, Cal. .15
☐ 703 Mark Wohlers, Atl. .15
☐ 704 Curt Young, Oak. .15
☐ 705 Dwight Evans, Bal. .15
☐ 706 Rob Murphy, Sea. .15
☐ 707 Gregg Jefferies, NYM. (K.C.) .15
☐ 708 Tom Bolton, Bos. .15
☐ 709 Chris James, Cle. .15
☐ 710 Kevin Maas, NYY. .15
☐ 711 Ricky Bones, S.D. .15
☐ 712 Curt Wilkerson, Pgh. .15

	No.	Player	Price
☐	713	Roger McDowell, L.A.	.15
☐	**714**	**Major League Draft Pick: Calvin Reese, RC**	**.15**
☐	715	Craig Biggio, Hou.	.25
☐	716	Kirk Dressendorfer, Oak.	.15
☐	717	Ken Dayley, Tor.	.15
☐	718	B.J. Surhoff, Mil.	.15
☐	719	Terry Mulholland, Pha.	.15
☐	720	Kirk Gibson, K.C.	.15
☐	721	Mike Pagliarulo, Min.	.15
☐	722	Walt Terrell, Det.	.15
☐	723	Jose Oquendo, Stl.	.15
☐	724	Kevin Morton, Bos.	.15
☐	725	Doc Gooden, NYM.	.15
☐	726	Kirt Manwaring, S.F.	.15
☐	727	Chuck McElroy, Chi.-N.L.	.15
☐	**728**	**Dave Burba, Sea. (NYG.)**	**.15**
☐	729	Art Howe, Mgr., Hou.	.15
☐	730	Ramon Martinez, L.A.	.15
☐	731	Donnie Hill, Cal.	.15
☐	732	Nelson Santovenia, Mtl.	.15
☐	733	Bob Melvin, Bal. (K.C.)	.15
☐	**734**	**ML Draft Pick: Scott Hatteberg, RC**	**.15**
☐	735	Greg Swindell, Cle. (Cin.)	.15
☐	736	Lance Johnson, Chi.-A.L.	.15
☐	737	Kevin Reimer, Tex.	.25
☐	738	Dennis Eckersley, Oak.	.15
☐	739	Rob Ducey, Tor.	.25
☐	740	Ken Caminiti, Hou.	.25
☐	741	Mark Gubicza, K.C.	.15
☐	742	Billy Spiers, Mil.	.15
☐	743	Darren Lewis, S.F.	.15
☐	744	Chris Hammond, Cin.	.15
☐	745	Dave Magadan, NYM.	.15
☐	746	Bernard Gilkey, St.L	.15
☐	747	Willie Banks, Min.	.15
☐	748	Matt Nokes, NYY.	.15
☐	749	Jerald Clark, S.D.	.15
☐	750	Travis Fryman, Det.	.15
☐	751	Steve Wilson, L.A.	.25
☐	752	Billy Ripken, Bal.	.15
☐	753	Paul Assenmacher, Chi.-N.L.	.15
☐	754	Charlie Hayes, Pha.	.15
☐	755	Alex Fernandez, Chi.-A.L.	.15
☐	756	Gary Pettis, Tex.	.15
☐	757	Rob Dibble, Cin.	.15
☐	758	Tim Naehring, Bos.	.15
☐	759	Jeff Torborg, Mgr., NYM.	.15
☐	760	Ozzie Smith, Stl.	.25
☐	761	Mike Fitzgerald, Mtl.	.15
☐	762	John Burkett, S.F.	.15
☐	763	Kyle Abbott, Cal.	.15
☐	764	Tyler Green, Pha.	.15
☐	765	Pete Harnisch, Hou.	.15
☐	766	Mark Davis, K.C.	.15
☐	767	Kal Daniels, L.A.	.15
☐	768	Jim Thome, Cle.	.75
☐	769	Jack Howell, S.D.	.15
☐	770	Sid Bream, Atl.	.15
☐	771	Authur Rhodes, Bal.	.15
☐	772	Garry Templeton, NYM.	.15
☐	773	Hal Morris, Cin.	.15
☐	774	Bud Black, S.F.	.15
☐	775	Ivan Calderon, Mtl.	.15
☐	**776**	**Doug Henry, Mil., RC**	**.15**
☐	777	John Olerud, Tor.	.15
☐	778	Tim Leary, NYY.	.15
☐	779	Jay Bell, Pgh.	.15
☐	780	Eddie Murray, L.A. (NYM.)	.25
☐	781	Paul Abbott, Min.	.15
☐	782	Phil Plantier, Bos.	.15
☐	783	Joe Magrane, Stl.	.15
☐	784	Ken Patterson, Chi.-A.L.	.15
☐	785	Albert Belle, Cle.	.35
☐	786	Royce Clayton,	.15
☐	787	1992 Checklist No. 6 of 6	.15
☐	788	Mike Stanton, Atl.	.15
☐	789	Bobby Valentine, Mgr., Tex.	.15
☐	790	Joe Carter, Tor.	.25
☐	791	Danny Cox, Pha.	.15
☐	792	Dave Winfield, Cal. (Tor.)	.25

1992 BOX BOTTOMS

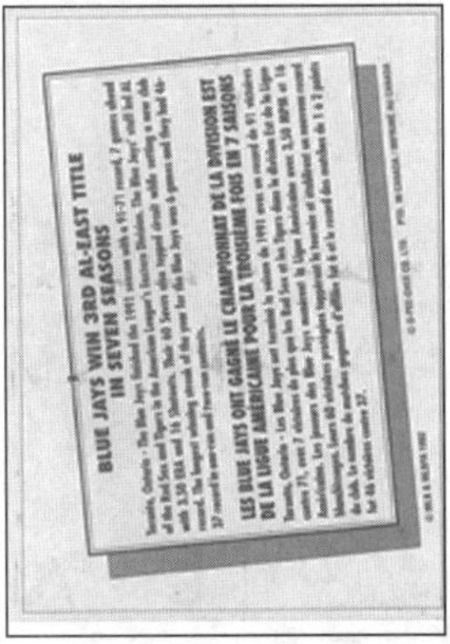

The bottom panels of the 1992 boxes are devoted to four different group pictures of the 1991 Championships, instead of the usual four cards, as in the previous years. The cards are not numbered.

Panel Size: 5"x 7"

Complete Set (4 cards): 6.00

	Player	MINT
☐	1991 A.L. - Eastern Division: Blue Jays Claim Crown	3.00
☐	1991 N.L. - Eastern Division: Pirates Prevail	1.00
☐	1991 N. L. Champions: Braves Beat Bucs	1.00
☐	1991 World Series: Twins Tally In Tenth	3.00

1992 O-PEE-CHEE PREMIER

The 1991 concept of a high-quality card set was continued in 1992, with O-Pee-Chee producing another 198-card set of similar quality. The backs of the cards bear the company logo, as well as two logos of major league baseball.

Card Size: 2 1/2"x 3 1/2"
Face: Four colour, white border; name, position, team
Back: Four colour, gold, green and black on card stock; name, number, position, résumé, team logo
Imprint: © 1992 O-PEE-CHEE CO. LTD.

Complete Set (198 cards): 12.00
Common Player: .10

	No.	Player	MINT
□	1	Wade Boggs, Bos.	.25
□	2	John Smiley, Min.	.10
□	3	Checklist 1	.10
□	4	Ron Gant, Atl.	.10
□	5	Mike Bordick, Oak.	.10
□	6	Charlie Hayes, NYY.	.10
□	7	Kevin Morton, Bos.	.10
□	8	Checklist 2	.10
□	9	Chris Gwynn, K.C.	.10
□	10	Melido Perez, NYY.	.10
□	11	Danny Gladden, Min.	.10
□	12	Brian McRae, K.C.	.10
□	13	Denny Martinez, Mtl.	.10
□	14	Bob Scanlan, Chi.-N.L.	.10
□	15	Julio Franco, Tex.	.10
□	16	Ruben Amaro, Pha.	.10
□	17	Mo Sanford, Cin.	.10
□	18	Scott Bankhead, Cin.	.10
□	19	Dickie Thon, Pha.	.10
□	20	Chris James, S.F.	.10
□	21	Mike Huff, Chi.-A.L.	.10
□	22	Orlando Merced, Pgh.	.10
□	23	Chris Sabo, Cin.	.10
□	24	Jose Canseco, Oak.	.25
□	25	Reggie Sanders, Cin.	.10
□	26	Chris Nabholz, Mtl.	.10
□	27	Kevin Seitzer, Mil.	.10
□	28	Ryan Bowen, Hou.	.10
□	29	Gary Carter,	.25
□	**30**	**Wayne Rosenthal, Tex., RC**	**.10**
□	31	Alan Trammell, Det.	.10
□	32	Doug Drabek, Pgh.	.10
□	33	Craig Shipley, S.D.	.10
□	34	Ryne Sandberg, Chi.-N.L.	.25
□	35	Chuck Knoblauch, Min.	.25
□	36	Bret Barberie, Mtl.	.10
□	37	Tim Naehring, Bos.	.10
□	38	Omar Olivares, Stl.	.10
□	39	Royce Clayton, S.F.	.10
□	40	Brent Mayne, K.C.	.10
□	41	Darrin Fletcher, Mtl.	.10
□	42	Howard Johnson, NYM.	.10
□	43	Steve Sax, Chi.-A.L.	.10
□	44	Greg Swindell, Cin.	.10
□	45	Andre Dawson, Chi.-N.L.	.25
□	46	Kent Hrbek, Min.	.10
□	47	Doc Gooden, NYM.	.10
□	48	Mark Leiter, Det.	.10
□	49	Tom Glavine, Atl.	.10
□	50	Mo Vaughn, Bos.	.35
□	51	Doug Jones, Cle.	.10
□	52	Brian Barnes, Mtl.	.10
□	53	Rob Dibble, Cin.	.10
□	54	Kevin McReynolds, NYM.	.10
□	55	Ivan Rodriguez, Tex.	.50
□	56	Scott Livingstone, Det.	.10
□	**57**	**Mike Magnante, K.C., RC**	**.10**
□	58	Pete Schourek, NYM.	.10
□	59	Frank Thomas, Chi.-A.L.	2.00
□	60	Kirk McCaskill, Chi.-A.L.	.20
□	61	Wally Joyner, K.C.	.10
□	62	Rick Aguilera, Min.	.10
□	63	Eric Karros, L.A.	.10
□	64	Tino Martinez, Sea.	.25
□	65	Bryan Hickerson, S.F.	.10
□	66	Ruben Sierra, Tex.	.10
□	67	Willie Randolph, NYM.	.10
□	68	Bill Landrum, Mtl.	.10
□	69	Bip Roberts, Cin.	.10
□	70	Cecil Fielder, Det.	.10
□	71	Pat Kelly, NYY.	.10
□	72	Kenny Lofton, Cle.	1.50
□	73	John Franco, NYM.	.10
□	74	Phil Plantier, Bos.	.10
□	75	Dave Martinez, Cin.	.10
□	76	Warren Newson, Chi.-A.L.	.10
□	**77**	**Chito Martinez, Bal., RC**	**.10**
□	78	Brian Hunter, Atl.	.10
□	79	Jack Morris, Tor.	.10
□	80	Eric King, Det.	.10
□	81	Nolan Ryan, Tex.	1.25
□	82	Bret Saberhagen, NYM.	.10
□	83	Roberto Kelly, NYY.	.10
□	84	Ozzie Smith, Stl.	.25
□	85	Chuck McElroy, Chi.-N.L.	.10
□	86	Carlton Fisk, Chi.-A.L.	.25
□	87	Mike Mussina, Bal.	.35
□	88	Mark Carreon, Det.	.10
□	89	Ken Hill, Stl.	.10
□	90	Rick Cerone, Mtl.	.10
□	91	Deion Sanders, Atl.	.10
□	92	Don Mattingly, NYY.	.50
□	93	Danny Tartabull, NYY.	.10
□	94	Keith Miller, K.C.	.10
□	95	Gregg Jefferies, K.C.	.10
□	96	Barry Larkin, Cin.	.10
□	97	Kevin Mitchell, Sea.	.10
□	98	Rick Sutcliffe, Bal.	.10
□	99	Mark McGwire, Oak.	.75
□	100	Albert Belle, Cle.	.35
□	101	Gregg Olson, Bal.	.10
□	102	Kirby Puckett, Min.	.50
□	103	Luis Gonzalez, Hou., Error	.10
□	104	Randy Myers, S.D.	.10
□	105	Roger Clemens, Bos.	.75
□	106	Tony Gwynn, S.D.	.50
□	107	Jeff Bagwell, Hou.	.50
□	108	John Wetteland, L.A.	.10
□	109	Bernie Williams, NYY.	.25
□	110	Scott Kamieniecki, NYY.	.10

	No.	Player	
☐	111	Robin Yount, Mil.	.25
☐	112	Dean Palmer, Tex.	.10
☐	113	Tim Belcher, Cin.	.10
☐	114	George Brett, K.C.	.50
☐	115	Frank Viola, Bos.	.10
☐	116	Kelly Gruber, Tor.	.10
☐	117	David Justice, Atl.	.25
☐	118	Scott Leius, Min.	.10
☐	**119**	**Jeff Fassero, Mtl., RC**	**.25**
☐	120	Sammy Sosa, Chi.-N.L.	.10
☐	121	Al Osuna, Hou.	.10
☐	122	Wilson Alvarez, Chi.-A.L.	.10
☐	123	Jose Offerman, L.A.	.10
☐	124	Mel Rojas, Mtl.	.10
☐	125	Shawon Dunston, Chi.-N.L.	.10
☐	126	Pete Incaviglia, Det.	.10
☐	127	Von Hayes, Cal.	.10
☐	128	Dave Gallagher, Cal.	.10
☐	129	Eric Davis, L.A.	.10
☐	130	Roberto Alomar, Tor.	.25
☐	131	Mike Gallego, Oak.	.10
☐	132	Robin Ventura, Chi.-A.L.	.10
☐	133	Bill Swift, S.F.	.10
☐	134	John Kruk, Pha.	.10
☐	135	Craig Biggio, Hou.	.25
☐	**136**	**Eddie Taubensee, Hou., RC**	**.25**
☐	137	Cal Ripken, Bal.	1.50
☐	138	Charles Nagy, Cle.	.10
☐	139	Jose Melendez, S.D.	.10
☐	140	Jim Abbott, Cal.	.10
☐	141	Paul Molitor, Mil.	.25
☐	142	Tom Candiotti, Cle.	.10
☐	143	Bobby Bonilla, NYM.	.10
☐	144	Matt Williams, S.F.	.10
☐	145	Brett Butler, L.A.	.10
☐	146	Will Clark, S.F.	.25
☐	147	Rickey Henderson, Oak.	.25
☐	148	Ray Lankford, Stl.	.10
☐	149	Bill Pecota, K.C.	.10
☐	150	Dave Winfield, Cal.	.25
☐	151	Darren Lewis, S.F.	.10
☐	152	Bob MacDonald, Tor.	.10
☐	153	David Segui, Bal.	.10
☐	154	Benny Santiago, S.D.	.10
☐	155	Chuck Finley, Cal.	.10
☐	156	Andujar Cedeno, Hou.	.10
☐	157	Barry Bonds, Pgh.	.50
☐	158	Joe Grahe, Cal.	.10
☐	159	Frank Castillo, Chi.-N.L.	.10
☐	**160**	**Dave Burba, Sea., RC**	**.10**
☐	161	Leo Gomez, Bal.	.10
☐	162	Orel Hershiser, L.A.	.10
☐	163	Delino DeShields, Mtl.	.10
☐	164	Sandy Alomar, Cle.	.10
☐	165	Denny Neagle, Pgh.	.10
☐	166	Fred McGriff, S.D.	.25
☐	167	Ken Griffey Jr., Sea.	2.25
☐	168	Juan Guzman, Tor.	.35
☐	169	Bobby Rose, Cal.	.10
☐	170	Steve Avery, Atl.	.10
☐	**171**	**Rich DeLucia, Sea., RC**	**.10**
☐	172	Mike Timlin, Tor.	.10
☐	173	Randy Johnson, Sea.	.25
☐	174	Paul Gibson, NYM.	.10
☐	175	David Cone, NYM.	.10
☐	176	Marquis Grissom, Mtl.	.10
☐	177	Kurt Stillwell, S.D.	.10
☐	178	Mark Whiten, Cle.	.10
☐	179	Darryl Strawberry, L.A.	.25
☐	180	Mike Morgan, Chi.-N.L.	.10
☐	181	Scott Scudder, Cle.	.10
☐	182	George Bell, Chi.-A.L.	.10
☐	183	Alvin Davis, Cal.	.10
☐	184	Len Dykstra, Pha.	.10
☐	185	Kyle Abbott, Pha.	.10
☐	186	Chris Haney, Mtl.	.10
☐	187	Junior Noboa,	.10
☐	188	Dennis Eckersley, Oak.	.10
☐	189	Derek Bell, Tor.	.10
☐	190	Lee Smith, Stl.	.10
☐	191	Andres Galarraga, Stl.	.25
☐	192	Jack Armstrong, Cle.	.10
☐	193	Eddie Murray, NYM.	.25
☐	194	Joe Carter, Tor.	.25
☐	195	Terry Pendleton, Atl.	.10
☐	196	Darryl Kile, Hou.	.10
☐	197	Rod Beck, S.F.	.10
☐	198	Hubie Brooks, NYM.	.10

1992 PANINI STICKERS

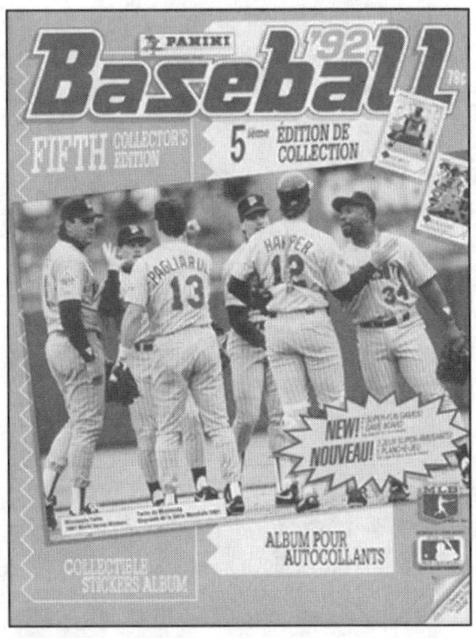

This sticker set has a colour album with 60 bilingual pages. The album was printed in Canada, but the stickers were printed in Italy by Panini.

Sticker Size: 2 1/8" x 2 15/16"
Face: Four colour, white border; name, position, bilingual
Back: Four colour on card stock; baseball trivia, Panini and MLB logos, bilingual
Imprint: PRINTED IN ITALY / IMPRIMê EN ITALIE

Complete Set (288 stickers):			**20.00**
Common Player:			**.15**
Album:			**3.00**
	No.	**Player**	**MINT**
☐	1	Panini Baseball '92 Logo	.15
☐	2	MLB Logo	.15
☐	3	MLBPA Logo	.15
☐	4	Lance Parrish, Cal.	.15
☐	5	Wally Joyner, Cal.	.15
☐	6	Luis Sojo, Cal.	.15
☐	7	Gary Gaetti, Cal.	.15
☐	8	Dick Schofield, Cal.	.15
☐	9	Junior Felix, Cal.	.15
☐	10	Luis Polonia, Cal.	.15
☐	11	Mark Langston, Cal.	.15
☐	12	Jim Abbott, Cal.	.15
☐	13	California Angels Logo, Cal.	.15

	No.	Player	Price
☐	14	Terry Steinbach, Oak.	.15
☐	15	Mark McGwire, Oak.	1.50
☐	16	Mike Gallego, Oak.	.15
☐	17	Carney Lansford, Oak.	.15
☐	18	Walt Weiss, Oak.	.15
☐	19	Jose Canseco, Oak.	.25
☐	20	Dave Henderson, Oak.	.15
☐	21	Rickey Henderson, Oak.	.25
☐	22	Dennis Eckersley, Oak.	.15
☐	23	Oakland Athletics Logo, Oak.	.15
☐	24	Pat Borders, Tor.	.15
☐	25	John Olerud, Tor.	.15
☐	26	Roberto Alomar, Tor.	.35
☐	27	Kelly Gruber, Tor.	.15
☐	28	Manuel Lee, Tor.	.15
☐	29	Joe Carter, Tor.	.35
☐	30	Devon White, Tor.	.15
☐	31	Candy Maldonado, Tor.	.15
☐	32	Dave Steib, Tor.	.15
☐	33	Toronto Blue Jays Logo, Tor.	.15
☐	34	B.J. Surhoff, Mil.	.15
☐	35	Franklin Stubbs, Mil.	.15
☐	36	Willie Randolph, Mil.	.15
☐	37	Jim Gantner, Mil.	.15
☐	38	Bill Spiers, Mil.	.15
☐	39	Dante Bichette, Mil.	.15
☐	40	Robin Yount, Mil.	.35
☐	41	Greg Vaughn, Mil.	.15
☐	42	Chris Bosio, Mil.	.15
☐	43	Milwaukee Brewers Logo, Mil.	.15
☐	44	Sandy Alomar, Cle.	.15
☐	45	Mike Aldrete, Cle.	.15
☐	46	Mark Lewis, Cle.	.15
☐	47	Carlos Baerga, Cle.	.15
☐	48	Felix Fermin, Cle.	.15
☐	49	Mark Whiten, Cle.	.15
☐	50	Alex Cole, Cle.	.15
☐	51	Albert Belle, Cle.	.35
☐	52	Greg Swindell, Cle.	.15
☐	53	Cleveland Indians Logo, Cle.	.15
☐	54	Dave Valle, Sea.	.15
☐	55	Pete O'Brien, Sea.	.15
☐	56	Harold Reynolds, Sea.	.15
☐	57	Edgar Martinez, Sea.	.15
☐	58	Omar Vizquel, Sea.	.15
☐	59	Jay Buhner, Sea.	.15
☐	60	Ken Griffey, Jr., Sea.	3.00
☐	61	Greg Briley, Sea.	.15
☐	62	Randy Johnson, Sea.	.35
☐	63	Seattle Mariners Logo, Sea.	.15
☐	64	Chris Hoiles, Bal.	.15
☐	65	Randy Milligan, Bal.	.15
☐	66	Billy Ripken, Bal.	.15
☐	67	Leo Gomez, Bal.	.15
☐	68	Cal Ripken, Bal.	2.00
☐	69	Dwight Evans, Bal.	.15
☐	70	Mike Devereaux, Bal.	.15
☐	71	Joe Orsulak, Bal.	.15
☐	72	Gregg Olson, Bal.	.15
☐	73	Baltimore Orioles Logo, Bal.	.15
☐	74	Ivan Rodriguez, Tex.	.25
☐	75	Rafael Palmeiro, Tex.	.25
☐	76	Julio Franco, Tex.	.15
☐	77	Dean Palmer, Tex.	.15
☐	78	Jeff Huson, Tex.	.15
☐	79	Ruben Sierra, Tex.	.15
☐	80	Gary Pettis, Tex.	.15
☐	81	Juan Gonzalez, Tex.	.35
☐	82	Nolan Ryan, Tex.	2.00
☐	83	Texas Rangers Logo, Tex.	.15
☐	84	Tony Pena, Bos.	.15
☐	85	Carlos Quintana, Bos.	.15
☐	86	Jody Reed, Bos.	.15
☐	87	Wade Boggs, Bos.	.35
☐	88	Luis Rivera, Bos.	.15
☐	89	Tom Brunansky, Bos.	.15
☐	90	Ellis Burks, Bos.	.25
☐	91	Mike Greenwell, Bos.	.15
☐	92	Roger Clemens, Bos.	1.25
☐	93	Boston Red Sox Logo, Bos.	.15
☐	94	Todd Benzinger, K.C.	.15
☐	95	Terry Shumpert, K.C.	.15
☐	96	Bill Pecota, K.C.	.15
☐	97	Kurt Stillwell, K.C.	.15
☐	98	Danny Tartabull, K.C.	.15
☐	99	Brian McRae, K.C.	.15
☐	100	Kirk Gibson, K.C.	.15
☐	101	Bret Saberhagen, K.C.	.15
☐	102	George Brett, K.C.	.35
☐	103	Kansas City Royals Logo, K.C.	.15
☐	104	Mickey Tettleton, Tex.	.15
☐	105	Cecil Fielder, Tex.	.15
☐	106	Lou Whitaker, Tex.	.15
☐	107	Travis Fryman, Tex.	.15
☐	108	Alan Trammell, Tex.	.15
☐	109	Rob Deer, Tex.	.15
☐	110	Milt Cuyler, Tex.	.15
☐	111	Lloyd Moseby, Tex.	.15
☐	112	Bill Gullickson, Tex.	.15
☐	113	Detriot Tigers Logo, Tex.	.15
☐	114	Brian Harper, Min.	.15
☐	115	Kent Hrbek, Min.	.15
☐	116	Chuck Knoblauch, Min.	.25
☐	117	Mike Pagliarulo, Min.	.15
☐	118	Greg Gagne, Min.	.15
☐	119	Shane Mack, Min.	.15
☐	120	Kirby Puckett, Min.	1.00
☐	121	Dan Gladden, Min.	.15
☐	122	Jack Morris, Min.	.15
☐	123	Minnesota Twins Logo, Min.	.15
☐	124	Carlton Fisk, Chi.-A.L.	.25
☐	125	Frank Thomas, Chi.-A.L.	3.00
☐	126	Joey Cora, Chi.-A.L.	.15
☐	127	Robin Ventura, Chi.-A.L.	.15
☐	128	Ozzie Guillen, Chi.-A.L.	.15
☐	129	Sammy Sosa, Chi.-A.L.	.35
☐	130	Lance Johnson, Chi.-A.L.	.15
☐	131	Tim Raines, Chi.-A.L.	.15
☐	132	Bobby Thigpen, Chi.-A.L.	.15
☐	133	Chicago White Sox Logo, Chi.-A.L.	.15
☐	134	Matt Nokes, NYY.	.15
☐	135	Don Mattingly, NYY	1.00
☐	136	Steve Sax, NYY	.15
☐	137	Pat Kelly, NYY	.15
☐	138	Alvaro Espinoza, NYY	.15
☐	139	Jesse Barfield, NYY	.15
☐	140	Roberto Kelly, NYY	.15
☐	141	Mel Hall, NYY	.15
☐	142	Scott Sanderson, NYY	.15
☐	143	New York Yankees Logo, NYY	.15
☐	144	Cecil Fielder, Det.; Jose Canseco, Oak.	.25
☐	145	Julio Franco, Tex.	.15
☐	146	Roger Clemens, Bos.	.75
☐	147	Howard Johnson, NYM.	.15
☐	148	Terry Pendleton, Atl.	.15
☐	149	Dennis Martinez, Mon.	.15
☐	150	Houston Astros Logo, Hou.	.15
☐	151	Craig Biggio, Hou.	.25

☐ 152 Jeff Bagwell, Hou. 1.00
☐ 153 Casey Candaele, Hou. .15
☐ 154 Ken Caminiti, Hou. .25
☐ 155 Adujar Cedeno, Hou. .15
☐ 156 Mike Simms, Hou. .15
☐ 157 Steve Finley, Hou. .15
☐ 158 Luis Gonzalez, Hou. .15
☐ 159 Pete Harnisch, Hou. .15
☐ 160 Atlanta Braves Logo, Atl. .15
☐ 161 Greg Olson, Atl. .15
☐ 162 Sid Bream, Atl. .15
☐ 163 Mark Lemke, Atl. .15
☐ 164 Terry Pendleton, Atl. .15
☐ 165 Rafael Belliard, Atl. .15
☐ 166 David Justice, Atl. .25
☐ 167 Ron Gant, Atl. .15
☐ 168 Lonnie Smith, Atl. .15
☐ 169 Steve Avery, Atl. .15
☐ 170 St. Louis Cardinals Logo, Stl. .15
☐ 171 Tom Pagnozzi, Stl. .15
☐ 172 Pedro Guerrero, Stl. .15
☐ 173 Jose Oquendo, Stl. .15
☐ 174 Todd Zeile, Stl. .15
☐ 175 Ozzie Smith, Stl. .85
☐ 176 Felix Jose, Stl. .15
☐ 177 Ray Lankford, Stl. .15
☐ 178 Jose DeLeon, Stl. .15
☐ 179 Lee Smith, Stl. .15
☐ 180 Chicago Cubs Logo, Chi.-N.L. .15
☐ 181 Hector Villanueva, Chi.-N.L. .15
☐ 182 Mark Grace, Chi.-N.L. .15
☐ 183 Ryne Sandberg, Chi.-N.L. .35
☐ 184 Luis Salazar, Chi.-N.L. .15
☐ 185 Shawon Dunston, Chi.-N.L. .15
☐ 186 Andre Dawson, Chi.-N.L. .25
☐ 187 Jerome Walton, Chi.-N.L. .15
☐ 188 George Bell, Chi.-N.L. .15
☐ 189 Greg Maddux, Chi.-N.L. 2.00
☐ 190 Los Angeles Dodgers Logo, L.A. .15
☐ 191 Mike Scioscia, L.A. .15
☐ 192 Eddie Murray, L.A. .50
☐ 193 Juan Samuel, L.A. .15
☐ 194 Lenny Harris, L.A. .15
☐ 195 Alfredo Griffin, L.A. .15
☐ 196 Darryl Strawberry, L.A. .25
☐ 197 Brett Butler, L.A. .15
☐ 198 Kal Daniels, L.A. .15
☐ 199 Orel Hershieser, L.A. .15
☐ 200 Montréal Expos Logo, Mtl. .15
☐ 201 Gilberto Reyes, Mtl. .15
☐ 202 Andres Galarraga, Mtl. .25
☐ 203 Delino DeShields, Mtl. .15
☐ 204 Tim Wallach, Mtl. .15
☐ 205 Spike Owen, Mtl. .15
☐ 206 Larry Walker, Mtl. 1.00
☐ 207 Marquis Grissom, Mtl. .15
☐ 208 Ivan Calderon, Mtl. .15
☐ 209 Dennis Martinez, Mtl. .15
☐ 210 San Francisco Giants Logo, S.F. .15
☐ 211 Steve Decker, S.F. .15
☐ 212 Will Clark, S.F. .25
☐ 213 Robby Thompson, S.F. .15
☐ 214 Matt Williams, S.F. .15
☐ 215 Jose Uribe, S.F. .15
☐ 216 Kevin Bass, S.F. .15
☐ 217 Willie McGee, S.F. .15
☐ 218 Kevin Mitchell, S.F. .15
☐ 219 Dave Righetti, S.F. .15
☐ 220 New York Mets Logo, NYM. .15
☐ 221 Rick Cerone, NYM. .15
☐ 222 Dave Magadan, NYM. .15
☐ 223 Gregg Jefferies, NYM. .15
☐ 224 Howard Johnson, NYM. .15
☐ 225 Kevin Elster, NYM. .15
☐ 226 Hubie Brooks, NYM. .15
☐ 227 Vince Coleman, NYM. .15
☐ 228 Kevin McReynolds, NYM. .15
☐ 229 Frank Viola, NYM. .15
☐ 230 San Diego Padres Logo, S.D. .15
☐ 231 Benito Santiago, S.D. .15
☐ 232 Fred McGriff, S.D. .25
☐ 233 Bip Roberts, S.D. .15
☐ 234 Jack Howell, S.D. .15
☐ 235 Tony Fernandez, S.D. .15
☐ 236 Tony Gwynn, S.D. 1.00
☐ 237 Darrin Jackson, S.D. .15
☐ 238 Bruce Hurst, S.D. .15
☐ 239 Craig Lefferts, S.D. .15
☐ 240 Philadelphia Phillies Logo, Pha. .15
☐ 241 Darren Daulton, Pha. .15
☐ 242 John Kruk, Pha. .15
☐ 243 Mickey Morandini, Pha. .15
☐ 244 Charlie Hayes, Pha. .15
☐ 245 Dickie Thon, Pha. .15
☐ 246 Dale Murphy, Pha. .15
☐ 247 Lenny Dykstra, Pha. .15
☐ 248 Von Hayes, Pha. .15
☐ 249 Terry Mulholland, Pha. .15
☐ 250 Pittsburgh Pirates Logo, Pgh. .15
☐ 251 Mike LaValliere, Pgh. .15
☐ 252 Orlando Merced, Pgh. .15
☐ 253 Jose Lind, Pgh. .15
☐ 254 Steve Buechele, Pgh. .15
☐ 255 Jay Bell, Pgh. .15
☐ 256 Bobby Bonilla, Pgh. .15
☐ 257 Andy Van Slyke, Pgh. .15
☐ 258 Barry Bonds, Pgh. .35
☐ 259 Doug Drabek, Pgh. .15
☐ 260 Cincinnati Reds Logo, Cin. .15
☐ 261 Joe Oliver, Cin. .15
☐ 262 Hal Morris, Cin. .15
☐ 263 Bill Doran, Cin. .15
☐ 264 Chris Sabo, Cin. .15
☐ 265 Barry Larkin, Cin. .25
☐ 266 Paul O'Neill, Cin. .15
☐ 267 Eric Davis, Cin. .15
☐ 268 Glenn Braggs, Cin. .15
☐ 269 Jose Rijo, Cin. .15
☐ 270 AS: Toronto SkyDome .15
☐ 271 AS: Sandy Alomar Jr. .15
☐ 272 AS: Cecil Fielder .15
☐ 273 AS: Roberto Alomar .25
☐ 274 AS: Wade Boggs .25
☐ 275 AS: Cal Ripken 1.00
☐ 276 AS: Dave Henderson .15
☐ 277 AS: Ken Griffey, Jr. 1.50
☐ 278 AS: Rickey Henderson .25
☐ 279 AS: Jack Morris .15
☐ 280 AS: Benito Santiago .15
☐ 281 AS: Will Clark .25
☐ 282 AS: Ryne Sandberg .25
☐ 283 AS: Chris Sabo .15
☐ 284 AS: Ozzie Smith .50
☐ 285 AS: Andre Dawson .25
☐ 286 AS: Tony Gwynn .60
☐ 287 AS: Ivan Calderon .15
☐ 288 AS: Tom Glavine .15

1992 PIZZA HUT / DIET PEPSI

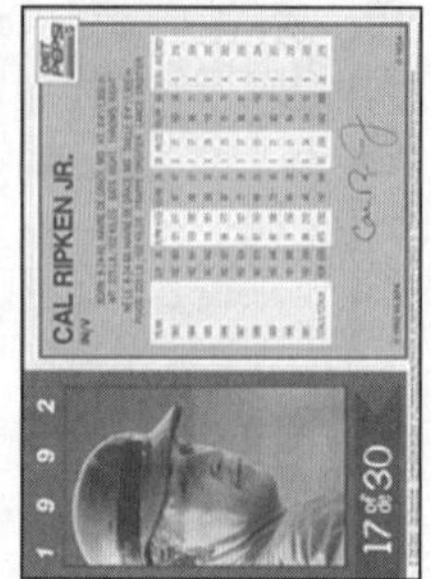

This 30-card set was available through Shoppers Drug Mart, Pharma Plus and Pizza Pizza. The Pizza Pizza offer was specially packaged by Pepsi. The signature series was marketed on specially designed cans of Diet Pepsi. The logos on the players' jerseys and hats have been airbrushed out.

Card Size: 2 1/2" x 3 1/2"
Face: Four colour, blue and red border; name, Diet Pepsi logo
Back: Four colour, blue and black on card stock; name, position, résumé, autograph, numbered _ of 30, bilingual
Imprint: "1992 MLBPA" MSA

	No.	Player	MINT
Complete Set (20 cards):			**20.00**
☐	1	Roger Clemens, Bos.	2.00
☐	2	Dwight Gooden, NYM.	.50
☐	3	Tom Henke, Tor.	.50
☐	4	Dennis Martinez, Mtl.	.50
☐	5	Tom Glavine, Bal.	.50
☐	6	Jack Morris, Tor.	.50
☐	7	Dennis Eckersley, Oak.	.50
☐	8	Jeff Reardon, Bos.	.50
☐	9	Bryan Harvey, Cal.	.50
☐	10	Sandy Alomar, Jr., Cle.	.50
☐	11	Carlton Fisk, Chi.-A.L.	1.00
☐	12	Gary Carter, Mtl.	1.00
☐	13	Cecil Fielder, Det.	.50
☐	14	Will Clark, S.F.	1.00
☐	15	Roberto Alomar, Tor.	1.50
☐	16	Ryne Sandberg, Chi.-N.L.	1.00
☐	17	Cal Ripken, Bal.	2.50
☐	18	Barry Larkin, Cin.	1.00
☐	19	Ozzie Smith, Stl.	1.50
☐	20	Kelly Gruber, Tor.	.50
☐	21	Wade Boggs, Bos.	1.00
☐	22	Tim Wallach, Mtl.	.50
☐	23	Howard Johnson, NYM.	.50
☐	24	Jose Canseco, Oak.	1.00
☐	25	Joe Carter, Tor.	1.00
☐	26	Ken Griffey, Jr., Sea.	4.50
☐	27	Kirby Puckett, Min.	1.50
☐	28	Rickey Henderson, Oak.	1.00
☐	29	Barry Bonds, Pgh.	2.00
☐	30	Dave Winfield, Tor.	1.00

1992 POST

Card Size: 2 1/2" x 3 1/2"
Face: Four colour, white border; name, team, Post logo
Back: Four colour, red or blue band within white border; name, number, position, team, bilingual
Imprint: None

	No.	Player	MINT
Complete Set (18 cards):			**10.00**
☐	1	Dennis Martinez, Mtl.	.35
☐	2	Benito Santiago, S.D.	.35
☐	3	Will Clark, S.F.	.60
☐	4	Ryne Sandberg, Chi.-N.L.	.60
☐	5	Tim Wallach, Mtl.	.35
☐	6	Ozzie Smith, Stl.	.75
☐	7	Darryl Strawberry, L.A.	.50
☐	8	Brett Butler, L.A.	.35
☐	9	Barry Bonds, Pgh.	1.00
☐	10	Roger Clemens, Bos.	1.50
☐	11	Sandy Alomar, Jr., Cle.	.35
☐	12	Cecil Fielder, Det.	.35
☐	13	Roberto Alomar, Tor.	.60
☐	14	Kelly Gruber, Tor.	.35
☐	15	Cal. Ripken, Jr., Bal.	2.00
☐	16	Jose Canseco, Oak.	.60
☐	17	Kirby Puckett, Min.	1.00
☐	18	Rickey Henderson, Oak.	.50

1993 BEN'S / HOLSUMS DISKS

This 20-disk set was distributed exclusively through Ben's Limited

Disk Size: 2 3/4" Diameter
Face: Four colour, white border; name, position, team, Ben's logo
Back: Black on card stock; name, résumé, numbered _ of 20
Imprint: "1993 MLBPA" MSA MADE IN CANADA

	No.	Player	MINT
Complete Set (20 disks):			**20.00**
☐	1	Dennis Eckersley, Oak.	1.25
☐	2	Chris Bosio, Sea.	1.25
☐	3	Jack Morris, Tor.	1.25
☐	4	Greg Maddux, Alt.	6.00
☐	5	Dennis Martinez, Mtl.	1.25
☐	6	Tom Glavine, Alt.	1.25
☐	7	Doug Drabek. Hou.	1.25
☐	8	John Smoltz, Atl.	1.25
☐	9	Randy Myers, Chi.-N.L.	1.25
☐	10	Jack McDowell, Chi.-A.L.	1.25
☐	11	John Wetteland, Mtl.	1.25
☐	12	Roger Clemens, Bos.	5.00
☐	13	Mike Mussina, Bal.	2.00
☐	14	Juan Guzman, Tor.	1.75
☐	15	Jose Rijo, Cin.	1.25
☐	16	Tom Henke, Tex.	1.25
☐	17	Gregg Olson, Bal.	1.25
☐	18	Jim Abbott, NYY.	1.25
☐	19	Jimmy Key, NYY.	1.25
☐	20	Rheal Cormier, Stl.	1.75

1993 HIT THE BOOKS

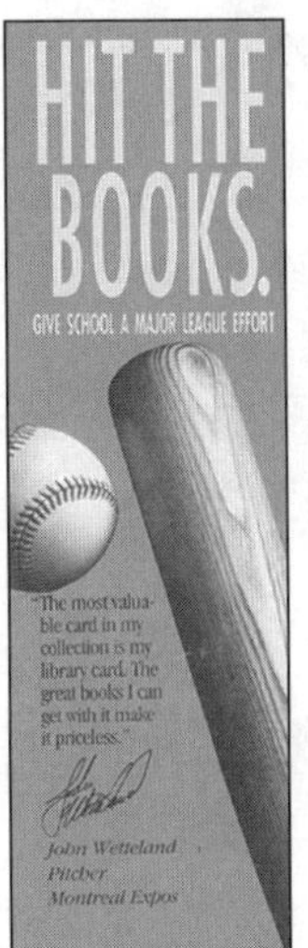

These bookmarks do not feature player photos like later issues do. Other Blue Jays' bookmarks may exist. The "Hit the Books" poster features head shots of Ken Hill and Larry Walker.

Card Size: 2" x 6 3/8"

Sponsors: Canadian Teachers' Association, National Literacy Secreteriat

Poster (Hill/ Walker; 17" x 22"):		**5.00**
	Player	**MINT**
□	Wil Cordero, Mtl.	.75
□	Delino DeShields, Mtl.	.75
□	Ken Hill, Mtl.	.75
□	Mike Lansing, Mtl.	1.00
□	Chris Nabholz, Mtl.	.75
□	Larry Walker, Mtl.	3.00
□	John Wetteland, Mtl.	1.00

1993 HUMPTY DUMPTY

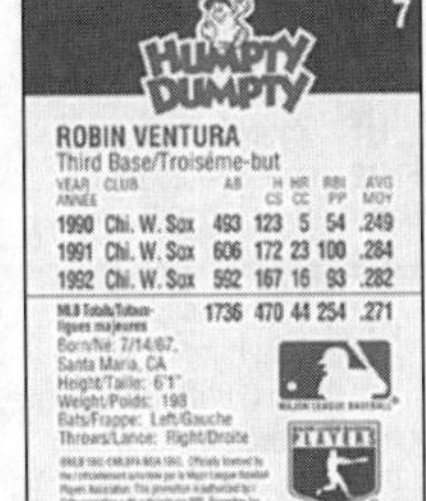

Sticker Size: 1 7/16" x 1 15/16"

Face: Four colour, borderless; team logo

Back: Four colour on card stock; name, position, résumé

Imprint: none

Complete Set (51 cards):			**35.00**
Checklist (no #)			**2.50**
	No.	**Player**	**MINT**
□	1	Cal Ripken, Jr., Bal.	3.50
□	2	Mike Mussina, Bal.	1.00
□	3	Roger Clemens, Bos.	2.00
□	4	Chuck Finley, Cal.	.50
□	5	Sandy Alomar, Jr., Cle.	.50
□	6	Frank Thomas, Chi.-A.L.	4.00
□	7	Robin Ventura, Chi.-A.L.	.50
□	8	Cecil Fielder, Det.	.50
□	9	George Brett, K.C.	1.25
□	10	Cal. Eldred, Mil.	.50
□	11	Kirby Puckett, Minn.	1.50
□	12	Dave Winfield, Minn.	1.00
□	13	Jim Abbott, NYY.	.50
□	14	Rickey Henderson, Oak.	1.00
□	15	Ken Griffey, Jr., Sea.	5.00
□	16	Nolan Ryan, Tex.	3.50
□	17	Ivan Rodriguez, Tex.	1.00
□	18	Paul Molitor, Tor.	1.00
□	19	John Olerud, Tor.	.50
□	20	Joe Carter, Tor.	1.00
□	21	Jack Morris, Tor.	.50
□	22	Roberto Alomar, Tor.	1.00
□	23	Pat Borders, Tor.	.50
□	24	Devon White, Tor.	.50
□	25	Juan Guzman, Tor.	.75
□	26	Steve Avery, Atl.	.50
□	27	John Smoltz, Atl.	.50
□	28	Mark Grace, Chi.-N.L.	.50
□	29	Jose Rijo, Cin.	.50
□	30	David Nied, Col.	.50
□	31	Benito Santiago, Fl.	.50
□	32	Jeff Bagwell, Hus.	1.50
□	33	Tim Wallach, L.A.	.50
□	34	Erik Karros, L.A.	.50
□	35	Delino DeShields, Mtl.	.50
□	36	Will Cordero, Mtl.	.50
□	37	Marquis Grissom, Mtl.	.50
□	38	Ken Hill, Mtl.	.50
□	39	Moises Alou, Mon	1.00
□	40	Chris Nabholz, Mtl.	.50
□	41	Dennis Martinez, Mtl.	.50
□	42	Larry Walker, Mtl.	1.50
□	43	Bobby Bonilla, NYM.	.50
□	44	Lenny Dykstra, Pha.	.50
□	45	Tim Wakefield, Pgh.	.50
□	46	Andy Van Slyke, Pgh.	.50
□	47	Tony Gwynn, S.D.	1.50
□	48	Fred McGriff, S.D.	.75
□	49	Barry Bonds, S.F.	1.00
□	50	Ozzie Smith, Stl.	1.00

1993 O-PEE-CHEE

This 396-card set was advertised by O-Pee-Chee as being a series "totally independent of the Topps 1993 Series." The set features a special 18-card insert set commemorating the 1992 World Series Champion Toronto Blue

Jays, as well as an additional 4-card random insert series featuring the Blue Jays.

Card Size: 2 1/2" x 3 1/2"
Face: Four colour, white border; name, position, team
Back: Four colour, name, number, résumé, bilingual
Imprint: © 1993 O-PEE-CHEE CO. LTD.

Complete Set No (396 cards): 40.00
Common Player: .15

	No.	Player	MINT
☐	1	Jim Abbott, Cal. (NYY.)	.15
☐	2	Eric Anthony, Hou.	.15
☐	3	Harold Baines, Oak.	.15
☐	4	Roberto Alomar, Tor.	.25
☐	5	Steve Avery, Atl.	.15
☐	6	James Austin, Atl.	.15
☐	7	Mark Wohlers, Atl.	.15
☐	8	Steve Buechele, Chi.-N.L.	.15
☐	9	Pedro Astacio, L.A.	.15
☐	10	Moises Alou, Mtl.	.25
☐	11	Rod Beck, S.F.	.15
☐	12	Sandy Alomar, Cle.	.15
☐	13	Bret Boone, Sea.	.15
☐	14	Bryan Harvey, Fla.	.15
☐	15	Bobby Bonilla, NYM.	.15
☐	16	Brady Anderson, Bal.	.15
☐	17	Andy Benes, S.D.	.15
☐	18	Ruben Amaro, Pha.	.15
☐	19	Jay Bell, Pgh.	.15
☐	20	Kevin Brown, Tex.	.15
☐	21	Scott Bankhead, Cin. (Bos.)	.15
☐	22	Denis Boucher, Col.	.25
☐	23	Kevin Appier, K.C.	.15
☐	24	Pat Kelly, NYY.	.15
☐	25	Rick Agullera, Min.	.15
☐	26	George Bell, Chi.-A.L.	.15
☐	27	Steve Farr, NYY.	.15
☐	28	Chad Curtis, Cal.	.15
☐	29	Jeff Bagwell, Hou.	.75
☐	30	Lance Blankenship, Oak.	.15
☐	31	Derek Bell, Tor.	.15
☐	32	Damon Berryhill, Atl.	.15
☐	33	Ricky Bones, Mil.	.15
☐	34	Rheal Cormier, Cin.	.25
☐	35	Andre Dawson, Chi.-N.L. (Bos.)	.25
☐	36	Brett Butler, L.A.	.15
☐	37	Sean Berry, Mtl.	.15
☐	38	Bud Black, S.F.	.15
☐	39	Carlos Baerga, Cle.	.15
☐	40	Jay Buhner, Sea.	.15
☐	41	Charlie Hough, Fla.	.15
☐	42	Sid Fernandez, NYM.	.15
☐	43	Luis Mercedes, Bal.	.15
☐	44	Jerald Clark, S.D. (Col.)	.15
☐	45	Wes Chamberlain, Pha.	.15
☐	46	Barry Bonds, S.F.	.35
☐	47	Jose Canseco, Tex.	.25
☐	48	Tim Belcher, Cin.	.15
☐	49	David Nied, Col.	.15
☐	50	George Brett, K.C.	.35
☐	51	Cecil Fielder, Det.	.15
☐	52	Chilli Davis, Cal. (Ana.)	.15
☐	53	Alex Fernandez, Chi.-A.L.	.15
☐	54	Charlie Hayes, NYY. (Col.)	.15
☐	55	Rob Ducey, Cal.	.25
☐	56	Craig Biggio, Hou.	.25
☐	57	Mike Bordick, Oak.	.15
☐	58	Pat Borders, Tor.	.15
☐	59	Jeff Blauser, Atl.	.15
☐	60	Chris Bosio, Fla. (Sea.)	.15
☐	61	Bernard Gilkey, Stl.	.15
☐	62	Shawon Dunston, Chi.-N.L.	.15
☐	63	Tom Candiotti, L.A.	.15
☐	64	Darrin Fletcher, Mtl.	.15
☐	65	Jeff Brantley, S.F.	.15
☐	66	Albert Belle, Cle.	.25
☐	67	Dave Fleming, Sea.	.15
☐	68	John Franco, NYM.	.15
☐	69	Glenn Davis, Bal.	.15
☐	70	Tony Fernandez, S.D. (NYM.)	.15
☐	71	Darren Daulton, Pha.	.15
☐	72	Doug Drabek, Pgh. (Hou.)	.15
☐	73	Julio Franco, Tex.	.15
☐	74	Tom Browning, Cin.	.15
☐	75	Tom Gordon, K.C.	.15
☐	76	Travis Fryman, Det.	.15
☐	77	Scott Erickson, Min.	.15
☐	78	Carlton Fisk, Chi.-A.L.	.25
☐	79	Roberto Kelly, NYY. (Cin.)	.15
☐	80	Gary DiSarcina, Cal.	.15
☐	81	Ken Caminiti, Hou.	.25
☐	82	Ron Darling, Oak.	.15
☐	83	Joe Carter, Tor.	.25
☐	84	Sid Bream, Mil.	.15
☐	85	Cal Eldred, Mil.	.15
☐	86	Mark Grace, Chi.-N.L.	.15
☐	87	Eric Davis, L.A.	.15
☐	88	Ivan Calderon, Mtl. (Bos.)	.15
☐	89	John Burkett, S.F.	.15
☐	90	Felix Fermin, Cle.	.15
☐	91	Ken Griffey Jr., Sea.	3.50
☐	92	Doc Gooden, NYM.	.15
☐	93	Mike Devereaux, Bal.	.15
☐	94	Tony Gwynn, S.D.	.75
☐	95	Mariano Duncan, Pha.	.15
☐	96	Jeff King, Pgh.	.15
☐	97	Juan Gonzalez, Tex.	.50
☐	98	Norm Charlton, (Sea.)	.15
☐	99	Mark Gubicza, K.C.	.15
☐	100	Danny Gladden, Det.	.15
☐	101	Greg Gagne, Min. (K.C.)	.15
☐	102	Ozzie Guillen, Chi.-A.L.	.15
☐	103	Don Mattingly, NYY.	.75
☐	104	Damion Easley, Cal.	.15
☐	105	Casey Candaele, Hou.	.15
☐	106	Dennis Eckersley, Oak.	.15
☐	107	David Cone, K.C. (K.C.)	.15
☐	108	Ron Gant, Atl.	.15
☐	109	Mike Fetters, Mil.	.15
☐	110	Mike Harkey, Chi.-N.L.	.15
☐	111	Kevin Gross, L.A.	.15
☐	112	Archi Cianfrocco, Mtl.	.15
☐	113	Will Clark, S.F.	.15
☐	114	Glenallen Hill, Cle.	.15
☐	115	Erik Hanson, Sea.	.15
☐	116	Todd Hundley, NYM.	.15
☐	117	Leo Gomez, Bal.	.15
☐	118	Bruce Hurst, S.D.	.15
☐	119	Len Dykstra, Pha.	.15
☐	120	Jose Lind, K.C. (K.C.)	.15
☐	121	Jose Guzman, (Chi.-N.L.)	.15
☐	122	Rob Dibble, Cin.	.15
☐	123	Gregg Jefferies, K.C.	.15
☐	124	Bill Gullickson, Det.	.15
☐	125	Brian Harper, Min.	.15
☐	126	Roberto Hernandez, Chi.-A.L.	.15
☐	127	Sam Militello, NYY.	.15
☐	128	Junior Felix, Cal. (Fla.)	.15
☐	129	Andujar Cedeno, Hou.	.15

- ☐ 130 Rickey Henderson, Oak. .15
- ☐ 131 Bob MacDonald, Tor. .15
- ☐ 132 Tom Glavine, Atl. .15
- ☐ 133 Scott Fletcher, Mil. (Bos.) .15
- ☐ 134 Brian Jordan, Stl. .15
- ☐ 135 Greg Maddux, Chi.-N.L. (Atl.) 2.50
- ☐ 136 Orel Hershiser, L.A. .15
- ☐ 137 Greg Colbrunn, Mtl. .15
- ☐ 138 Royce Clayton, S.F. .15
- ☐ 139 Thomas Howard, Cle. .15
- ☐ 140 Randy Johnson, Sea. .25
- ☐ 141 Jeff Innis NYM. .15
- ☐ 142 Chris Hoiles, Bal. .15
- ☐ 143 Darrin Jackson, S.D. .15
- ☐ 144 Tommy Greene, Pha. .15
- ☐ 145 Mike LaValliere, Pgh. .15
- ☐ **146 David Hulse, Tex., RC .15**
- ☐ 147 Barry Larkin, Cin. .25
- ☐ 148 Wally Joyner, K.C. .15
- ☐ 149 Mike Henneman, Det. .15
- ☐ 150 Kent Hrbek, Min. .15
- ☐ 151 Bo Jackson, Chi.-A.L. .15
- ☐ 152 Rich Monteleone, NYY. .15
- ☐ 153 Chuck Finley, Cal. .15
- ☐ 154 Steve Finley, Hou. .15
- ☐ 155 Dave Henderson, Oak. .15
- ☐ 156 Kelly Gruber, L.A. (Ana.) .15
- ☐ 157 Brian Hunter, Atl. .15
- ☐ 158 Darryl Hamilton, Mil. .15
- ☐ 159 Derrick May, Chi.-N.L. .15
- ☐ 160 Jay Howell, L.A. .15
- ☐ 161 Will Cordero, Mtl. .15
- ☐ 162 Bryan Hickerson, S.F. .15
- ☐ 163 Reggie Jefferson, Cle. .15
- ☐ 164 Edgar Martinez, Sea. .15
- ☐ 165 Nigel Wilson, Fla. .25
- ☐ 166 Howard Johnson, NYM. .15
- ☐ 167 Tim Hulett, Bal. .15
- ☐ 168 Mike Maddux, (NYM) .15
- ☐ 169 Dave Hollins, Pha. .15
- ☐ 170 Zane Smith, Pgh. .15
- ☐ 171 Rafael Palmeiro, Tex. .15
- ☐ 172 Dave Martinez, Cin. (S.F.) .15
- ☐ 173 Rusty Meacham, K.C. .15
- ☐ 174 Mark Leiter, Det. .15
- ☐ 175 Chuck Knoblauch, Min. .25
- ☐ 176 Lance Johnson, Chi.-A.L. .15
- ☐ 177 Matt Nokes, NYY. .15
- ☐ 178 Luis Gonzales, Hou. .15
- ☐ 179 Jack Morris, Tor. .15
- ☐ 180 David Justice, Atl. .25
- ☐ 181 Doug Henry, Mil. .15
- ☐ 182 Felix Jose, St.L .15
- ☐ 183 Delino DeShields, Mtl. .15
- ☐ 184 Rene Gonzales, Cal. .15
- ☐ 185 Pete Harnisch, Hou. .15
- ☐ 186 Mike Moore, Oak. (Det.) .15
- ☐ 187 Juan Guzman, Tor. .15
- ☐ 188 John Olerud, Tor. .15
- ☐ 189 Ryan Klesko, Atl. .15
- ☐ 190 John Jaha, Mil. .15
- ☐ 191 Ray Lankford, St.L .15
- ☐ 192 Jeff Fassero, Mtl. .15
- ☐ 193 Darren Lewis, S.F. .15
- ☐ 194 Mark Lewis, Cle. .15
- ☐ 195 Alan Mills, Bal. .15
- ☐ 196 Wade Boggs, (NYY.) .25
- ☐ 197 Hal Morris, Cin. .15
- ☐ 198 Ron Karkovice, Chi.-A.L. .15
- ☐ 199 Joe Grahe, Cal. .15
- ☐ 200 Butch Henry, Hou. (Col.) .15
- ☐ 201 Mark McGwire, Oak. 1.50
- ☐ 202 Tom Henke, Tor. (Tex.) .15
- ☐ 203 Ed Sprague, Tor. .15
- ☐ 204 Charlie Leibrandt, Atl. (Tex.) .15
- ☐ 205 Pat Listach, Mil. .15
- ☐ 206 Omar Olivares, Stl. .15
- ☐ 207 Mike Morgan, Chi.-N.L. .15
- ☐ 208 Erik Karros, L.A. .15
- ☐ 209 Marquis Grissom, Mtl. .15
- ☐ 210 Willie McGee, S.F. .15
- ☐ 211 Derek Lilliquest, Cle. .15
- ☐ 212 Tino Martinez, Sea. .15
- ☐ 213 Jeff Kent, NYM. .15
- ☐ 214 Mike Mussina, Bal. .25
- ☐ 215 Randy Myers, (Chi.-N.L.) .15
- ☐ 216 John Kruk, Pha. .15
- ☐ 217 Tom Brunansky, Bos .15
- ☐ 218 Paul O'Neill, Cin. (NYY.) .15
- ☐ 219 Scott Livingstone, Det. .15
- ☐ 220 John Valentin, Bos. .15
- ☐ 221 Eddie Zosky, Tor. .15
- ☐ 222 Pete Smith, Atl. .15
- ☐ 223 Bill Wegman, Mil. .15
- ☐ 224 Todd Zeile, St.L .15
- ☐ 225 Tim Wallach, Mtl (L.A.) .15
- ☐ 226 Mitch Williams, Pha. .15
- ☐ 227 Tim Wakefield, Pgh. .15
- ☐ 228 Frank Viola, Bos. .15
- ☐ 229 Nolan Ryan, Tex. 2.50
- ☐ 230 Kirk McCaskill, Chi.-A.L. .25
- ☐ 231 Melido Perez, NYY. .15
- ☐ 232 Mark Langston, Cal. .15
- ☐ 233 Xavier Hernandez, Hou. .15
- ☐ 234 Jerry Browne, Oak. .15
- ☐ 235 Dave Stieb, Tor. (Chi.-A.L.) .15
- ☐ 236 Mark Lemke, Atl. .15
- ☐ 237 Paul Molitor, (Tor.) .25
- ☐ 238 Geronimo Pena, Stl. .15
- ☐ 239 Ken Hill, Mtl. .15
- ☐ 240 Jack Clark, Bos. .15
- ☐ 241 Greg Myers, Cal. .15
- ☐ 242 Pete Incaviglia, (Pha.) .15
- ☐ 243 Ruben Sierra, Oak. .15
- ☐ 244 Todd Stottlemyre, Tor. .15
- ☐ 245 Pat Hentgen, Tor., .15
- ☐ 246 Melvin Nieves, Atl. .15
- ☐ 247 Jaime Navarro, Mil. .15
- ☐ 248 Donovan Osborne, Stl. .15
- ☐ 249 Brian Barnes, Mtl. .15
- ☐ 250 Cory Snyder, S.F. (L.A.) .15
- ☐ 251 Kenny Lofton, Cle. .75
- ☐ 252 Kevin Mitchell, (Cin.) .15
- ☐ 253 Dave Magadan, NYM. (Fla.) .15
- ☐ 254 Ben McDonald, Bal. .15
- ☐ 255 Fred McGriff, S.D. .25
- ☐ 256 Mickey Morandini, Pha. .15
- ☐ 257 Randy Tomlin, Pgh. .15
- ☐ 258 Dean Palmer, Tex. .15
- ☐ 259 Roger Clemens, Bos. 1.25
- ☐ 260 Joe Oliver, Cin. .15
- ☐ 261 Jeff Montgomery, K.C. .15
- ☐ 262 Tony Phillips, Det. .15
- ☐ 263 Shane Mack, Min. .15
- ☐ 264 Jack McDowell, Chi.-A.L. .15
- ☐ 265 Mike Macfarlane, K.C. .15
- ☐ 266 Luis Polonia, Cal. .15
- ☐ 267 Doug Jones, Hou. .15

	No.	Player	Price
☐	268	Terry Steinbach, Oak.	.15
☐	269	Jimmy Key, Tor. (NYY.)	.15
☐	270	Pat Tabler, Tor.	.15
☐	271	Otis Nixon, Atl.	.15
☐	272	Dave Nilsson, Mil.	.15
☐	273	Tom Pagnozzi, Stl.	.15
☐	274	Ryne Sandberg, Chi.-N.L.	.25
☐	275	Ramon Martinez, L.A.	.15
☐	**276**	**Tim Laker, Mtl., RC**	**.15**
☐	277	Bill Swift, S.F.	.15
☐	278	Charles Nagy, Cle.	.15
☐	279	Harold Reynolds, Sea. (Bal.)	.15
☐	280	Eddie Murray, NYM.	.25
☐	281	Gregg Olson, Bal.	.15
☐	282	Frank Seminara, S.D.	.15
☐	283	Terry Mulholland, Pha.	.15
☐	284	Kevin Reimer, (Mil.)	.25
☐	285	Mike Greenwell, Bos.	.15
☐	286	Jose Rijo, Cin.	.15
☐	287	Brian McRae, K.C.	.15
☐	288	Frank Tanana, (NYM.)	.15
☐	289	Pedro Munoz, Min.	.15
☐	290	Tim Raines, Chi.-A.L.	.15
☐	291	Andy Stankiewicz, NYY.	.15
☐	292	Tim Salmon, Cal.	.15
☐	293	Jimmy Jones, Hou.	.15
☐	294	Dave Stewart, Oak. (Tor.)	.15
☐	295	Mike Timlin, Tor.	.15
☐	296	Greg Olson, Atl.	.15
☐	297	Dan Plesac, Mil. (Chi.-N.L.)	.15
☐	298	Mike Perez, Stl.	.15
☐	299	Jose Offerman, L.A.	.15
☐	300	Denny Martinez, Mtl.	.15
☐	301	Robby Thompson, S.F.	.15
☐	302	Bret Saberhagen, NYM.	.15
☐	303	Joe Orsulak, Bal. (NYM.)	.15
☐	304	Tim Naehring, Bos.	.15
☐	305	Bip Roberts, Cin.	.15
☐	306	Kirby Puckett, Min.	.75
☐	307	Steve Sax, Chi.-A.L.	.15
☐	308	Danny Tartabull, NYY.	.15
☐	309	Jeff Juden, Hou.	.15
☐	310	Duane Ward, Tor.	.15
☐	311	Alejandro Pena, Atl. (Pgh.)	.15
☐	312	Kevin Seitzer, Mil.	.15
☐	313	Ozzie Smith, Stl.	.25
☐	314	Mike Piazza, L.A.	3.25
☐	315	Chris Nabholz, Mtl.	.15
☐	316	Tony Pena, Bos.	.15
☐	317	Gary Sheffield, S.D.	.15
☐	318	Mark Portugal, Hou.	.15
☐	319	Walt Weiss, (Fla.)	.15
☐	320	Manuel Lee, Tor. (Tex.)	.15
☐	321	David Wells, Tor.	.15
☐	322	Terry Pendleton, Atl.	.15
☐	323	Billy Spiers, Mil.	.15
☐	324	Lee Smith, Stl.	.15
☐	325	Bob Scanlan, Chi.-N.L.	.15
☐	326	Mike Scioscia, L.A.	.15
☐	327	Spike Owen, (NYY.)	.15
☐	328	Mackey Sasser, NYM. (Sea.)	.15
☐	329	Arthur Rhodes, Bal.	.15
☐	330	Ben Rivera, Pha.	.15
☐	331	Ivan Rodriguez, Tex.	.25
☐	332	Phil Plantier, (S.D.)	.15
☐	333	Chris Sabo, Cin.	.15
☐	334	Mickey Tettleton, Det.	.15
☐	335	John Smiley, (Cin.)	.15
☐	336	Bobby Thigpen, Chi.-A.L.	.15
☐	337	Randy Velarde, NYY.	.15
☐	338	Luis Sojo, Cal. (Tor.)	.15
☐	339	Scott Servais, Hou.	.15
☐	340	Tom Welch, Oak.	.15
☐	341	Devon White,Tor.	.15
☐	342	Jeff Reardon, Atl.	.15
☐	343	B.J. Surhoff, Mil.	.15
☐	344	Bob Tewksbury, Stl.	.15
☐	345	Jose Vizcaino, Chi.-N.L.	.15
☐	346	Mike Sharperson, L.A.	.15
☐	347	Mel Rojas, Mtl.	.15
☐	348	Matt Williams, S.F.	.15
☐	349	Steve Olln, Cle.	.15
☐	350	Mike Schooler, Sea.	.15
☐	351	Ryan Thompson, NYM.	.15
☐	352	Cal Ripken, Bal.	2.75
☐	353	Benny Santiago, S.D. (Fla.)	.15
☐	354	Curt Schilling, Pha.	.15
☐	355	Andy Van Slyke, Pgh.	.15
☐	356	Kenny Rogers, Tex.	.15
☐	357	Jody Reed, (L.A.)	.15
☐	358	Reggie Sanders, Cin.	.15
☐	359	Kevin McReynolds, K.C.	.15
☐	360	Alan Trammell, Det.	.15
☐	361	Kevin Tapani, Min.	.15
☐	362	Frank Thomas, Chi.-A.L.	3.25
☐	363	Bernie Williams, NYY.	.25
☐	364	John Smoltz, Atl.	.15
☐	365	Robin Yount, Mil.	.25
☐	366	John Wetteland, Mtl.	.15
☐	367	Bob Zupcic, Bos.	.15
☐	368	Julio Valera, Cal.	.15
☐	369	Brian Williams, Hou.	.15
☐	370	Willie Wilson, (Chi.-N.L.)	.15
☐	371	Dave Winfield, Tor. (Min.)	.25
☐	372	Deion Sanders, Atl.	.15
☐	373	Greg Vaughn, Mil.	.15
☐	374	Todd Worrell, (L.A.)	.15
☐	375	Darryl Strawberry, L.A.	.25
☐	376	John Vander Wal, Mtl.	.15
☐	377	Mike Benjamin, S.F.	.15
☐	378	Mark Whiten, Cle.	.15
☐	379	Omar Vizquel, Sea.	.15
☐	380	Anthony Young, NYM.	.15
☐	381	Rick Sutcliffe, Bal.	.15
☐	382	Candy Maldonado, Tor. (Chi.-N.L.)	.15
☐	383	Francisco Cabrera, Atl.	.15
☐	384	Larry Walker, Mtl.	.50
☐	385	Scott Cooper, Bos.	.15
☐	386	Gerald Williams, NYY.	.15
☐	387	Robin Ventura, Chi.-A.L.	.15
☐	388	Carl Willis, Min.	.15
☐	389	Lou Whitaker, Det.	.15
☐	390	Hipolito Pichardo, K.C.	.15
☐	391	Rudy Seanez, Col.	.15
☐	392	Greg Swindell, (Hou.)	.15
☐	393	Mo Vaughn, Bos.	.25
☐	394	Checklist 1 of 3	.15
☐	395	Checklist 2 of 3	.15
☐	396	Checklist 3 of 3	.15

WORLD SERIES CHAMPIONS

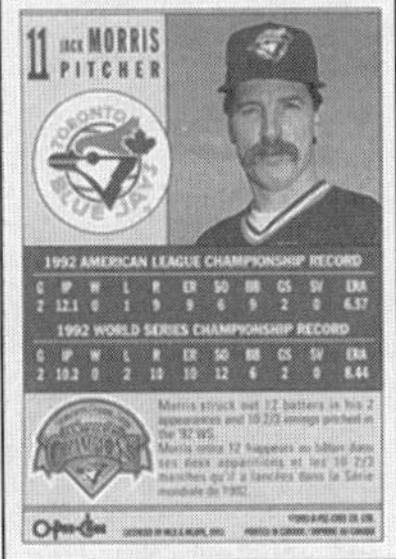

This 18-card set was independent of the Topps 1993 Series. It commemorates "the 1992 World Series Champions, the Toronto Blue Jays," and was inserted into the 1993 regular issue foil packs.

Insert Set (18 cards): 5.00

	No.	Player	MINT
☐	1	Roberto Alomar	1.00
☐	2	Pat Borders	.25
☐	3	Joe Carter	.50
☐	4	David Cone	.25
☐	5	Kelly Gruber	.25
☐	6	Juan Guzman	.25
☐	7	Tom Henke	.25
☐	8	Jimmy Key	.25
☐	9	Manuel Lee	.25
☐	10	Candy Maldonado	.25
☐	11	Jack Morris	.25
☐	12	John Olerud	.25
☐	13	Ed Sprague	.25
☐	14	Todd Stottlemyre	.25
☐	15	Duane Ward	.25
☐	16	Devon White	.25
☐	17	Dave Winfield	.75
☐	18	Cito Gaston, Mgr.	.25

WORLD SERIES HEROES

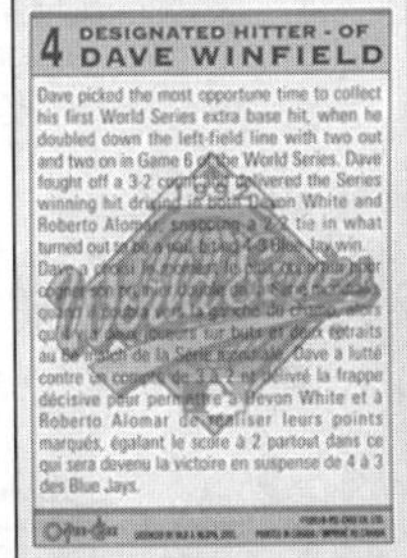

This 4-card set features "the 1992 World Series Heroes" the Toronto Blue Jays, and was randomly inserted into the 1993 regular issue packages.

Insert Set (4 cards): 2.00

	No.	Player	MINT
☐	1	Pat Borders, Tor.	.50
☐	2	Jimmy Key, Tor.	.50
☐	3	Ed Sprague, Tor.	.50
☐	4	Dave Winfield, Tor.	1.50

1993 O-PEE-CHEE PREMIER

Card Size: 2 1/2"x 3 1/2"
Face: Four colour, white border; name, position
Back: Four colour, name, position, team, card number, résumé
Imprint: © 1993 O-PEE-CHEE CO. LTD.
Complete Set (132 cards): 10.00
Common Card: .10

	No.	Player	MINT
☐	1	Barry Bonds, S.F.	.50
☐	2	Chad Curtis, Cal.	.10
☐	3	Chris Bosio, Sea.	.10
☐	4	Cal Eldred, Mil.	.10
☐	5	Dan Walters, S.D.	.10
☐	**6**	**Rene Arocha, Stl., RC**	**.10**
☐	7	Delino DeShields, Mtl.	.10
☐	8	Spike Owen, NYY.	.10
☐	9	Jeff Russell, Bos.	.10
☐	10	Phil Plantier, S.D.	.10
☐	11	Mike Christopher, Cle.	.10
☐	12	Darren Daulton, Pha.	.10
☐	13	Scott Cooper, Bos.	.10
☐	14	Paul O'Neill, NYY.	.10
☐	15	Jimmy Key, NYY.	.10
☐	16	Dickie Thon, Mil	.10
☐	17	Greg Gohr, Det.	.10
☐	18	Andre Dawson, Bos.	.25
☐	19	Steve Cooke, Pgh.	.10
☐	20	Tony Fernandez, NYM.	.10
☐	21	Mark Gardner, K.C.	.10
☐	22	Dave Martinez, S.D.	.10
☐	23	Jose Guzman, Chi.-N.L.	.10
☐	24	Chili Davis, Cal.	.10
☐	25	Randy Knorr, Tor.	.10
☐	26	Mike Piazza. L.A.	2.50
☐	27	Benji Gil, Tex.	.10
☐	28	Dave Winfield, Min.	.25
☐	29	Wil Cordero, Mtl.	.10
☐	30	Butch Henry, Col.	.10
☐	31	Eric Young, Col.	.10
☐	32	Orestes Destrade, Fla.	.10
☐	33	Randy Myers, Chi.-N.L.	.10
☐	34	Tom Brunansky, Mil.	.10
☐	35	Dan Wilson, Cin.	.10
☐	36	Juan Guzman, Tor.	.10
☐	37	Tim Salmon, Cal.	.10
☐	38	Bill Krueger, Det.	.10
☐	39	Larry Walker, Mtl.	.50
☐	40	David Hulse, Tex.	.10
☐	**41**	**Ken Ryan, Bos., RC**	**.10**
☐	42	Jose Lind, K.C.	.10
☐	43	Benito Santiago, Fla.	.10
☐	44	Ray Lankford, Stl.	.10
☐	45	Dave Stewart, Tor.	.10

	No.	Player	Price
☐	46	Don Mattingly, NYY.	1.00
☐	47	Fernando Valenzuela, Bal.	.10
☐	48	Scott Fletcher, Bos.	.25
☐	49	Wade Boggs, NYY.	.10
☐	50	Norn Charlton, Sea.	.10
☐	51	Carlos Baerga, Cle.	.10
☐	52	John Olerud, Tor.	.10
☐	53	Willie Wilson, Chi.-N.L.	.10
☐	**54**	**Dennis Moeller, Pgh., RC**	**.10**
☐	55	Joe Orsulak, NYM.	.10
☐	56	John Smiley, Cin.	.10
☐	57	Al Martin, Pgh.	.10
☐	58	Andres Galarraga, Col.	.25
☐	59	Billy Ripken, Tex.	.10
☐	60	Dave Stieb, Chi.-A.L.	.10
☐	61	Dave Magadan, Fla.	.10
☐	62	Todd Worrell, L.A.	.10
☐	**63**	**Sherman Obando, Bal., RC**	**.10**
☐	64	Kent Bottenfield, Mtl.	.10
☐	65	Vinny Castilla, Col.	.10
☐	66	Charlie Hayes, Col.	.10
☐	67	Mike Hartley, Min.	.10
☐	67	Harold Baines, Bal.	.10
☐	69	John Cummings, Sea.	.10
☐	**70**	**J.T. Snow, Cal., RC**	**.10**
☐	**71**	**Graeme Lloyd, Mil., RC**	**.10**
☐	72	Frank Bolick, Mtl.	.10
☐	73	Doug Drabek, Hou.	.10
☐	74	Milt Thompson, Pha.	.10
☐	**75**	**Tim Pugh, Cin., RC**	**.10**
☐	76	John Kruk, Pha.	.10
☐	77	Tom Henke, Tex.	.10
☐	78	Kevin Young, Pit	.10
☐	**79**	**Ryan Thompson, NYM., RC**	**.10**
☐	80	Mike Hampton, Sea.	.25
☐	81	Jose Canseco, Tex.	.50
☐	**82**	**Mike Lansing, Mtl., RC**	**.10**
☐	83	Candy Maldonado, Chi.-N.L.	.10
☐	84	Alex Arias. Fla.	.10
☐	85	Troy Neel, Oak.	.10
☐	86	Greg Swindell, Hou.	.10
☐	87	Tim Wallach, L.A.	.10
☐	88	Andy Van Slyke, Pgh.	.10
☐	89	Harold Reynolds, Bal.	.10
☐	90	Bryan Harvey, Fla.	.10
☐	91	Jerald Clark, Col.	.10
☐	92	David Cone, K.C.	.10
☐	93	Ellis Burks, Chi.-A.L.	.25
☐	94	Scott Bankhead, Bos.	.10
☐	95	Peter Incaviglia, Pha.	.10
☐	96	Cecil Fielder, Det.	.10
☐	97	Sean Berry, Mtl.	.10
☐	98	Gregg Jefferies, Stl.	.10
☐	**99**	**Billy Brewer, K.C., RC**	**.10**
☐	100	Scott Sanderson, Cal.	.10
☐	101	Walt Weiss, Fla.	.10
☐	102	Travis Fryman, Det.	.10
☐	103	Barry Larkin, Cin.	.25
☐	104	Darren Holmes, Col.	.10
☐	105	Ivan Calderon, Bos.	.10
☐	106	Terry Jorgensen, Min.	.10
☐	107	David Nied, Col.	.10
☐	**108**	**Tim Bogar, NYM., RC**	**.10**
☐	109	Roberto Kelly, Cin.	.10
☐	110	Mike Moore, Det.	.10
☐	111	Carlos Garcia, Pgh.	.10
☐	112	Mike Bielecki, Cle.	.10
☐	113	Trevor Hoffman, Fla.	.10
☐	114	Rich Amaral, Sea.	.10
☐	115	Jody Reed, L.A.	.10
☐	116	Charlie Leibrandt, Tex.	.10
☐	117	Grege Gagne, K.C.	.10
☐	**118**	**Darrell Sherman, S.D., RC**	**.10**
☐	119	Jeff Conine, Fla.	.10
☐	**120**	**Tim Laker, Mtl., RC**	**.10**
☐	121	Kevin Seitzer, Oak.	.10
☐	122	Jeff Mutis, Cle.	.10
☐	123	Rico Rossy, K.C.	.10
☐	124	Paul Molitor, Tor.	25
☐	125	Cal. Ripken, Bal.	1.75
☐	126	Greg Maddux, Atl.	1.50
☐	**127**	**Greg McMichael, Atl., RC**	**.10**
☐	128	Felix Jose, K.C.	.10
☐	129	Dick Schofield, Tor.	.10
☐	130	Jim Abbott, NYY.	.10
☐	131	Kevin Reimer, Mil.	.25
☐	132	Checklist	.10

DRAFT CHOICES

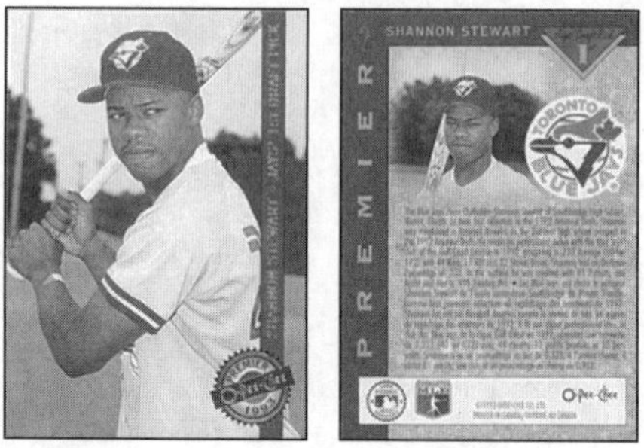

	No.	Player	MINT
Insert Set (4 cards):			**6.00**
☐	1	B.J. Wallace, Expos' 1st draft pick	1.50
☐	2	Shannon Stewart, Jays' 1st draft pick	3.00
☐	3	Rod Henderson, Expos' 2nd draft pick	1.50
☐	4	Todd Steverson, Jays' 2nd draft pick	1.50

STAR PERFORMERS

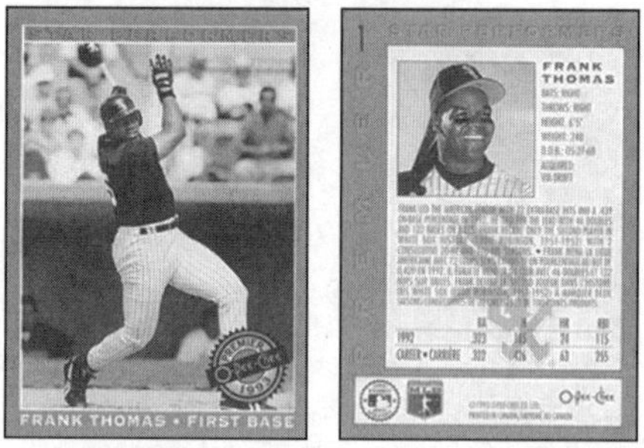

	No.	Player	Foil	Reg.
Insert Set (22 cards):			**40.00**	**8.00**
☐ ☐	1	Frank Thomas, Chi.-A.L.	15.00	2.50
☐ ☐	2	Fred McGriff, S.D.	2.50	.50
☐ ☐	3	Roberto Alomar, Tor.	2.50	.50
☐ ☐	4	Ryne Sandberg, Chi.-N.L.	2.50	.50
☐ ☐	5	Edgar Martinez, Sea.	1.50	.25
☐ ☐	6	Gary Sheffield, S.D.	1.50	.25
☐ ☐	7	Juan Gonzalez, Tex.	3.50	.75
☐ ☐	8	Eric Karros, L.A.	1.50	.25
☐ ☐	9	Ken Griffey Jr., Sea.	18.00	3.00
☐ ☐	10	Deion Sanders, Atl.	1.50	.25

	No.	Player		
□ □	11	Kirby Puckett, Min.	3.50	.75
□ □	12	Will Clark, S.F.	1.50	.25
□ □	13	Joe Carter, Tor.	2.50	.50
□ □	14	Barry Bonds, S.F.	2.50	.50
□ □	15	Pat Listach, Mil.	1.50	.25
□ □	16	Mark McGwire, Oak.	8.00	1.25
□ □	17	Kenny Lofton, Cle.	2.50	.50
□ □	18	Roger Clemens, Bos.	6.00	1.00
□ □	19	Greg Maddux, Atl.	9.00	1.50
□ □	20	Nolan Ryan, Tex.	12.00	2.00
□ □	21	Tom Glavine, Atl.	1.50	.25
□ □	22	Dennis Eckersley, Oak.	1.50	.25

1993 PANINI STICKERS

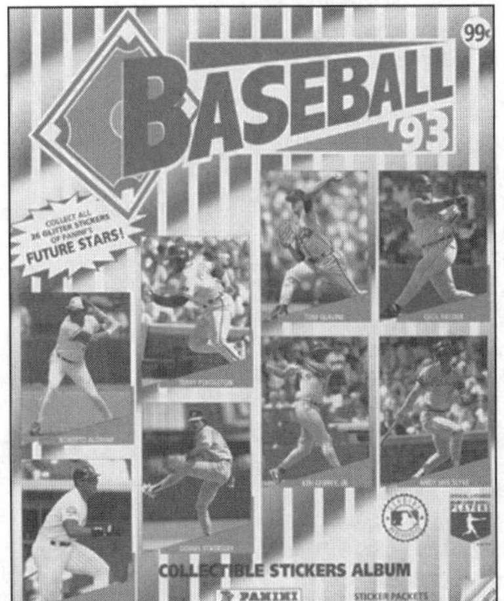

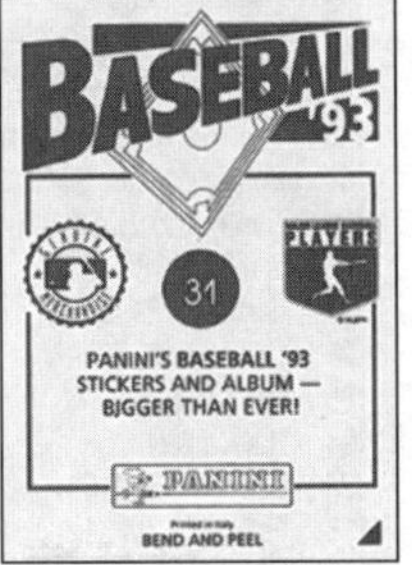

Sticker Size: 2 6/16" x 3 6/16"
Face: Four colour, white border; name, team, team logo
Back: Green on card stock; card number, Panini and MLB logos
Imprint: "MLB 93 " MLBPA Printed in Italy

Complete Set (300 stickers):	**15.00**
Common Player:	**.15**
Album:	**3.00**

	No.	Player	MINT
□	1	California Angels Logo, Cal.	.15
□	2	Mark Langston, Cal.	.15
□	3	Ron Tingley, Cal.	.15
□	4	Gary Gaetti, Cal.	.15
□	5	Kelly Gruber, Cal.	.15
□	6	Gary DiSarcina, Cal.	.15
□	7	Damion Easley (Glitter), Cal.	.15
□	8	Luis Polonia, Cal.	.15
□	9	Lee Stevens, Cal.	.15
□	10	Chad Curtis, Cal.	.15
□	11	Rene Gonzalez, Cal.	.15
□	12	Oakland Athletics Logo, Oak.	.15
□	13	Dennis Eckersley, Oak.	.15
□	14	Terry Steinbach, Oak.	.15
□	15	Mark McGwire, Oak.	1.25
□	16	Mike Bordick (Glitter), Oak.	.15
□	17	Carney Lansford, Oak.	.15
□	18	Jerry Browne, Oak.	.15
□	19	Rickey Henderson, Oak.	.25
□	20	Dave Henderson, Oak.	.15
□	21	Ruben Sierra, Oak.	.15
□	22	Ron Darling, Oak.	.15
□	23	Toronto Blue Jays Logo, Tor.	.15
□	24	Jack Morris, Tor.	.15
□	25	Pat Borders, Tor.	.15
□	26	John Olerud, Tor.	.15
□	27	Roberto Alomar, Tor.	.35
□	28	Luis Sojo, Tor.	.15
□	29	Dave Stewart, Tor.	.15
□	30	Devon White, Tor.	.15
□	31	Joe Carter, Tor.	.25
□	32	Derek Bell, Tor.	.15
□	33	Juan Guzman (Glitter), Tor.	.15
□	34	Milwaukee Brewers Logo, Mil.	.15
□	35	Jaime Navarro, Mil.	.15
□	36	B.J. Surhoff, Mil.	.15
□	37	Franklin Stubbs, Mil.	.15
□	38	Bill Spiers, Mil.	.15
□	39	Pat Listach (Glitter), Mil.	.15
□	40	Kevin Seitzer, Mil.	.15
□	41	Darryl Hamilton, Mil.	.15
□	42	Robin Yount, Mil.	.35
□	43	Kevin Reimer, Mil.	.25
□	44	Greg Vaughn, Mil.	.15
□	45	Cleveland Indians Logo, Cle.	.15
□	46	Charles Nagy, Cle.	.15
□	47	Sandy Alomar, Jr., Cle.	.15
□	48	Reggie Jefferson, Cle.	.15
□	49	Mark Lewis, Cle.	.15
□	50	Felix Fermin, Cle.	.15
□	51	Carlos Baerga, Cle.	.15
□	52	Albert Belle, Cle.	.35
□	53	Kenny Lofton (Glitter), Cle.	.15
□	54	Mark Whiten, Cle.	.15
□	55	Paul Sorrento, Cle.	.15
□	56	Seattle Mariners Logo, Sea.	.15
□	57	Dave Fleming, Sea.	.15
□	58	Dave Valle, Sea.	.15
□	59	Pete O'Brien, Sea.	.15
□	60	Randy Johnson, Sea.	.35
□	61	Omar Vizquel, Sea.	.15
□	62	Edgar Martinez, Sea.	.15
□	63	Ken Griffey, Jr. (Glitter), Sea.	3.50
□	64	Henry Cotto, Sea.	.15
□	65	Jay Buhner, Sea.	.15
□	66	Tino Martinez, Sea.	.15
□	67	Baltimore Orioles Logo, Bal.	.15
□	68	Ben McDonald, Bal.	.15
□	69	Mike Mussina (Glitter), Bal.	.25
□	70	Chris Hoiles, Bal.	.15
□	71	Randy Milligan, Bal.	.15
□	72	Billy Ripken, Bal.	.15
□	73	Cal. Ripken, Jr., Bal.	2.00
□	74	Leo Gomez, Bal.	.15
□	75	Mike Devereaux, Bal.	.15
□	76	Brady Anderson, Bal.	.15
□	77	Joe Orsulak, Bal.	.15

☐ 78 Texas Rangers Logo, Tex. .15
☐ 79 Kevin Brown, Tex. .15
☐ 80 Ivan Rodriguez (Glitter), Tex. .25
☐ 81 Rafael Palmeiro, Tex. .15
☐ 82 Julio Franco, Tex. .15
☐ 83 Jeff Huson, Tex. .15
☐ 84 Dean Palmer, Tex. .15
☐ 85 Jose Canseco, Tex. .25
☐ 86 Juan Gonzalez, Tex. .35
☐ 87 Nolan Ryan, Tex. 2.00
☐ 88 Brian Downing, Tex. .15
☐ 89 Boston Red Sox Logo, Bos. .15
☐ 90 Roger Clemens, Bos. 1.00
☐ 91 Tony Pena, Bos. .15
☐ 92 Mo Vaughn, Bos. .25
☐ 93 Scott Cooper, Bos. .15
☐ 94 Luis Rivera, Bos. .15
☐ 95 Ellis Burks, Bos. .15
☐ 96 Mike Greenwell, Bos. .15
☐ 97 Andre Dawson, Bos. .25
☐ 98 Ivan Calderon, Bos. .15
☐ 99 Phil Plantier (Glitter), Bos. .15
☐ 100 Kansas City Royals Logo, K.C. .15
☐ 101 Kevin Appier, K.C. .15
☐ 102 Mike MacFarlane, K.C. .15
☐ 103 Wally Joyner, K.C. .15
☐ 104 Jim Eisenreich, K.C. .15
☐ 105 Greg Gagne, K.C. .15
☐ 106 Greg Jefferies, K.C. .15
☐ 107 Kevin McReynolds, K.C. .15
☐ 108 Brian McRae (Glitter), K.C. .15
☐ 109 Keith Miller, K.C. .15
☐ 110 George Brett, K.C. .75
☐ 111 Detroit Tigers Logo, Det. .15
☐ 112 Bill Gullickson, Det. .15
☐ 113 Mickey Tettleton, Det. .15
☐ 114 Cecil Fielder, Det. .15
☐ 115 Tony Phillips, Det. .15
☐ 116 Scott Livingstone, Det. .15
☐ 117 Travis Fryman (Glitter), Det. .15
☐ 118 Dan Gladden, Det. .15
☐ 119 Rob Deer, Det. .15
☐ 120 Frank Tanana, Det. .15
☐ 121 Skeeter Barnes, Det. .15
☐ 122 Minnesota Twins Logo, Min. .15
☐ 123 Scott Erickson, Min. .15
☐ 124 Brian Harper, Min. .15
☐ 125 Kent Hrbek, Min. .15
☐ 126 Chuck Knoblauch (Glitter), Min. .25
☐ 127 Willie Banks, Min. .15
☐ 128 Scott Leius, Min. .15
☐ 129 Shane Mack, Min. .15
☐ 130 Kirby Puckett, Min. .75
☐ 131 Chili Davis, Min. .15
☐ 132 Pedro Munoz, Min. .15
☐ 133 Chicago White Sox Logo, Chi.-A.L. .15
☐ 134 Jack McDowell, Chi.-A.L. .15
☐ 135 Carlton Fisk, Chi.-A.L. .25
☐ 136 Frank Thomas (Glitter), Chi.-A.L. 3.00
☐ 137 Steve Sax, Chi.-A.L. .15
☐ 138 Ozzie Guillen, Chi.-A.L. .15
☐ 139 Robin Ventura, Chi.-A.L. .15
☐ 140 Tim Raines, Chi.-A.L. .15
☐ 141 Lance Johnson, Chi.-A.L. .15
☐ 142 Ron Karkovice, Chi.-A.L. .15
☐ 143 George Bell, Chi.-A.L. .15
☐ 144 New York Yankees Logo, NYY. .15
☐ 145 Scott Sanderson, NYY. .15
☐ 146 Matt Nokes, NYY. .15
☐ 147 Kevin Maas (Glitter), NYY. .15
☐ 148 Randy Velarde, NYY. .15
☐ 149 Andy Stankiewicz, NYY. .15
☐ 150 Pat Kelly, NYY. .15
☐ 151 Paul O'Neill, NYY. .15
☐ 152 Wade Boggs, NYY. .25
☐ 153 Danny Tartabull, NYY. 15
☐ 154 Don Mattingly, NYY. .75
☐ 155 Edgar Martinez, Sea. .15
☐ 156 Kevin Brown, Tex. .15
☐ 157 Dennis Eckersley, Oak. .15
☐ 158 Gary Sheffield, S.D. .15
☐ 159 Tom Glavine, Atl.; Greg Maddux, Chi.-N.L. .15
☐ 160 Lee Smith, Stl. .15
☐ 161 Dennis Eckersley, Oak. .15
☐ 162 Dennis Eckersley, Oak. .15
☐ 163 Pat Listach, Mil. .15
☐ 164 Greg Maddux, Chi.-N.L. .35
☐ 165 Barry Bonds, Pgh. .35
☐ 166 Erik Karros, L.A. .15
☐ 167 Houston Astros Logo, Hou. .15
☐ 168 Pete Harnish, Hou. .15
☐ 169 Eddie Taubensee, Hou. .15
☐ 170 Jeff Bagwell (Glitter), Hou. .35
☐ 171 Craig Biggio, Hou. .25
☐ 172 Andujar Cedeno, Hou. .15
☐ 173 Ken Caminiti, Hou. .25
☐ 174 Steve Finley, Hou. .15
☐ 175 Luis Gonzalez, Hou. .15
☐ 176 Eric Anthony, Hou. .15
☐ 177 Casey Candalele, Hou. .15
☐ 178 Atlanta Braves Logo, Atl. .15
☐ 179 Tom Glavine, Atl. .15
☐ 180 Gregg Olson, Atl. .15
☐ 181 Sid Bream, Atl. .15
☐ 182 Mark Lemke, Atl. .15
☐ 183 Jeff Blauser, Atl. .15
☐ 184 Terry Pendleton, Atl. .15
☐ 185 Ron Gant, Atl. .15
☐ 186 Otis Nixon, Atl. .15
☐ 187 David Justice, Atl. .25
☐ 188 Deion Sanders (Glitter), Atl. .15
☐ 189 St. Louis Cardinals Logo, Stl. .15
☐ 190 Bob Tewksbury, Stl. .15
☐ 191 Tom Pagnozzi, Stl. .15
☐ 192 Lee Smith, Stl. .15
☐ 193 Geronimo Pena, Stl. .15
☐ 194 Ozzie Smith, Stl. .50
☐ 195 Todd Zeile, Stl. .15
☐ 196 Ray Lankford, Stl. .15
☐ 197 Bernard Gilkey, Stl. .15
☐ 198 Felix Jose, Stl. .15
☐ 199 Donovan Osborne (Glitter), Stl. .15
☐ 200 Chicago Cubs Logo, Chi.-N.L. .15
☐ 201 Mike Morgan, Chi.-N.L. .15
☐ 202 Rick Wilkins, Chi.-N.L. .15
☐ 203 Mark Grace (Glitter), Chi.-N.L. .15
☐ 204 Ryne Sandberg, Chi.-N.L. .35
☐ 205 Shawon Dunston, Chi.-N.L. .15
☐ 206 Steve Buechele, Chi.-N.L. .15
☐ 207 Kal Daniels, Chi.-N.L. .25
☐ 207 Sammy Sosa .15
☐ 209 Derrick May, Chi.-N.L. .15
☐ 210 Doug Dascenzo, Chi.-N.L. .15
☐ 211 Los Angeles Dodgers Logo, L.A. .15
☐ 212 Ramon Martinez, L.A. .15
☐ 213 Mike Scioscia, L.A. .15
☐ 214 Erik Karros (Glitter), L.A. .15
☐ 215 Tim Wallach, L.A. .15

	No.	Player	Price
☐	216	Jose Offerman, L.A.	.15
☐	217	Mike Sharperson, L.A.	.15
☐	218	Brett Butler, L.A.	.15
☐	219	Darryl Strawberry, L.A.	.25
☐	220	Lenny Harris, L.A.	.15
☐	221	Eric Davis, L.A.	.15
☐	222	Montreal Expos Logo, Mtl.	.15
☐	223	Ken Hill, Mtl.	.15
☐	224	Darrin Fletcher, Mtl.	.15
☐	225	Greg Colbrunn (Glitter), Mtl.	.15
☐	226	Delino DeShields, Mtl.	.15
☐	227	Wilfredo Cordero, Mtl.	.15
☐	228	Dennis Martinez, Mtl.	.15
☐	229	John Vanderwal, Mtl.	.15
☐	230	Marquis Grissom, Mtl.	.15
☐	231	Larry Walker, Mtl.	1.00
☐	232	Moises Alou, Mtl.	.25
☐	233	San Francisco Giants, S.F.	.15
☐	234	Bill Swift, S.F.	.15
☐	235	Kirt Manwaring, S.F.	.15
☐	236	Will Clark, S.F.	.15
☐	237	Robby Thompson, S.F.	.15
☐	238	Royce Clayton (Glitter), S.F.	.15
☐	239	Matt Williams, S.F.	.15
☐	240	Willie McGee, S.F.	.15
☐	241	Mark Leonard, S.F.	.15
☐	242	Cory Snyder, S.F.	.15
☐	243	Barry Bonds, S.F.	.35
☐	244	New York Mets Logo, NYM.	.15
☐	245	Dwight Gooden, NYM.	.15
☐	246	Todd Hundley (Glitter), NYM.	.15
☐	247	Eddie Murray, NYM.	.50
☐	248	Sid Fernandez, NYM.	.15
☐	249	Tony Fernandez, NYM.	.15
☐	250	Dave Magadan, NYM.	.15
☐	251	Howard Johnson, NYM.	.15
☐	252	Vince Coleman, NYM.	.15
☐	253	Bobby Bonilla, NYM.	.15
☐	254	Daryl Boston, NYM.	.15
☐	255	San Diego Padres Logo, S.D.	.15
☐	256	Bruce Hurst, S.D.	.15
☐	257	Dan Walters, S.D.	.15
☐	258	Fred McGriff, S.D.	.25
☐	259	Kurt Stillwell, S.D.	.15
☐	260	Craig Shipley, S.D.	.15
☐	261	Gary Sheffield (Glitter), S.D.	.15
☐	262	Tony Gwynn, S.D.	.75
☐	263	Oscar Azocar, S.D.	.15
☐	264	Darrin Jackson, S.D.	.15
☐	265	Andy Benes, S.D.	.15
☐	266	Philadelphia Phillies Logo, Pha.	.15
☐	267	Terry Mulholland, Pha.	.15
☐	268	Curt Schilling, Pha.	.15
☐	269	Darren Daulton, Pha.	.15
☐	270	John Kruk, Pha.	.15
☐	271	Mickey Morandini (Glitter), Pha.	.15
☐	272	Mariano Duncan, Pha.	.15
☐	273	Dave Hollins, Pha.	.15
☐	274	Lenny Dykstra, Pha.	.15
☐	275	Wes Chamberlain, Pha.	.15
☐	276	Stan Javier, Pha.	.15
☐	277	Pittsburgh Pirates Logo, Pgh.	.15
☐	278	Zane Smith, Pgh.	.15
☐	279	Tim Wakefield (Glitter), Pgh.	.15
☐	280	Mike LaValliere, Pgh.	.15
☐	281	Orlando Merced, Pgh.	.15
☐	282	Stan Belinda, Pgh.	.15
☐	283	Jay Bell, Pgh.	.15
☐	284	Jeff King, Pgh.	.15
☐	285	Andy Van Slyke, Pgh.	.15
☐	286	Bob Walk, Pgh.	.15
☐	287	Gary Varsho, Pgh.	.15
☐	288	Cincinnatti Reds Logo, Cin.	.15
☐	289	Jose Rijo, Cin.	.15
☐	290	Joe Oliver, Cin.	.15
☐	291	Hal Morris, Cin.	.15
☐	292	Bip Roberts, Cin.	.15
☐	293	Barry Larkin, Cin.	.25
☐	294	Chris Sabo, Cin.	.15
☐	295	Roberto Kelly, Cin.	.15
☐	296	Kevin Mitchell, Cin.	.15
☐	297	Rob Dibble, Cin.	.15
☐	298	Reggie Sanders (Glitter), Cin.	.15
☐	299	Florida Marlins Logo, Fla.	.15
☐	300	Colorado Rockies Logo, Col.	.15

1993 POST

This 18-card set was inserted in Post "Sugar Crisp" boxes during 1993. Additional cards (5) were available by mail for $2.99 and 5 UPC's. An album was also available by mail.

Card Size: 2-1/2" x 3-1/2"

Face:

Back:

Imprint:

Complete Set (18 cards): **25.00**

Album: **5.00**

	No.	Player	MINT
☐	1	Pat Borders, Tor.	.50
☐	2	Juan Guzman, Tor.	.50
☐	3	Roger Clemens, Bos.	3.00
☐	4	Joe Carter, Tor.	.75
☐	5	Roberto Alomar, Tor.	1.50
☐	6	Robin Yount, Mil.	1.00
☐	7	Cal Ripken, Bal.	4.00
☐	8	Kirby Puckett, Min.	2.00
☐	9	Ken Griffey, Jr., Sea.	6.00
☐	10	Darren Daulton, Pha.	.50
☐	11	Andy Van Slyke	.50
☐	12	Bobby Bonilla	.50
☐	13	Larry Walker, Mtl.	3.00
☐	14	Ryne Sandberg, Chi.-N.L.	1.50
☐	15	Barry Larkin	1.00
☐	16	Gary Sheffield	.75
☐	17	Ozzy Smith	1.50
☐	18	Terry Pendleton, Atl.	.50

1994 GARCIA PHOTO SERIE SELECTIVA

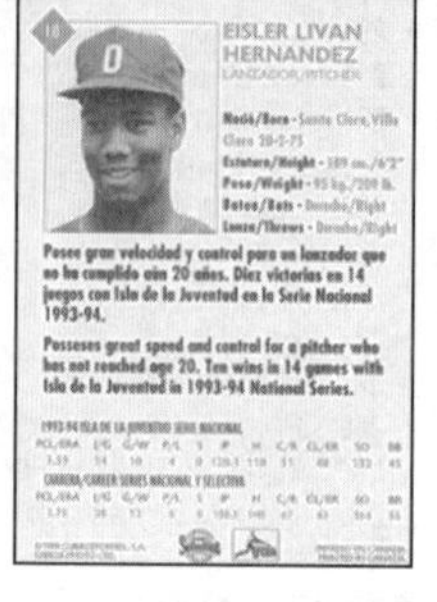

Card Size: 2 1/2" x 3 1/2"
Imprint: © 1994 CUBADEPORTES, S.A. GARCIA PHOTO LTD.
Complete Set (132 cards): 60.00
Common Player: .10

	No.	Player	MINT
☐	1	Juan Manrique, Occidentales	.10
☐	2	Lazaro Arturo Castro, Occidentales	.10
☐	3	Pedro Luis Duenas, Occidentales	.10
☐	4	Julio German Fernandez, Occidentales	.10
☐	5	Alberto Peraza, Occidentales	.10
☐	6	Yobal Dueñas, Occidentales	.10
☐	7	Alexander Ramos, Occidentales	.10
☐	8	Omar Linares, Occidentales	1.50
☐	9	Eduardo Cardenas, Occidentales	.10
☐	10	Reniel Capote, Occidentales	.10
☐	11	Alberto Diaz, Occidentales	.10
☐	12	Lazaro Junco, Occidentales	.10
☐	13	Jose Antonio Estrada, Occidentales	.10
☐	14	Daniel Lazo, Occidentales	.10
☐	15	Juan Carlos Linares, Occidentales	.50
☐	16	Lazaro Madera, Occidentales	.10
☐	17	Felix Isasi, Occidentales	.10
☐	18	Livan Hernandez, Occidentales	35.00
☐	19	Pedro Luis Lazo, Occidentales	.50
☐	20	Faustino Corrales, Occidentales	.10
☐	21	Omar Ajete, Occidentales	.10
☐	22	Jorge Luis Valdes, Occidentales	.10
☐	23	Carlos Yanes, Occidentales	.10
☐	24	Lazaro Garro, Occidentales	.10
☐	25	Jesus Bosmenier, Occidentales	.10
☐	26	Carlos de la Torre, Occidentales	.10
☐	27	Jorge Antonio Martinez, Occidentales	.10
☐	28	Jorge Fuentes, Mgr., Occidentales	.10
☐	29	Pablo Pascual Abreu, Asst., Occidentales	.10
☐	30	Nestor Perez, Asst., Occidentales	.10
☐	31	Roman Suarez, Trainer, Occidentales	.10
☐	32	Armando Johnson, Trainer, Occidentales	.10
☐	33	TC: Occidentales	.10
☐	34	Pedro Luis Rodriguez, Habana	.10
☐	35	Francisco Santiesteban, Habana	.10
☐	36	Ricardo Miranda, Habana	.10
☐	37	Roberto Colina, Habana	.10
☐	38	Juan Carlos Millan, Habana	.10
☐	39	Juan Padilla, Habana	.10
☐	40	Oscar Macias, Habana	.10
☐	41	Andy Morales, Habana	.10
☐	42	Enrique Diaz, Habana	.10
☐	43	German Mesa, Habana	.50
☐	44	Juan Carlos Moreno, Habana	.10
☐	45	Javier Mendez, Habana	.10
☐	46	Gerardo Miranda, Habana	.10
☐	47	Romelio Martinez, Habana	.10
☐	48	Luis Enrique Piloto, Habana	.10
☐	49	Carlos Tabares, Habana	.10
☐	50	Orbe Luis Rodriguez, Habana	.10
☐	51	Orlando Hernandez, Habana	10.00
☐	52	Lazaro Valle, Habana	.50
☐	53	Ariel Prieto, Habana	5.00
☐	54	Jorge Fumero, Habana	.10
☐	55	Jose Ibar, Habana	.10
☐	56	Vladimir Nuñez, Habana	2.50
☐	57	Heriberto Collazo, Habana	.10
☐	58	Jorge Garcia, Habana	.10
☐	59	Euclides Rojas, Habana	.10
☐	60	Osnel Blas Bocourt, Habana	.10
☐	61	Jorge Trigoura, Mgr., Habana	.10
☐	62	Rene Bello, Asst., Habana	.10
☐	63	Jorge Hernandez, Asst., Habana	.10
☐	64	Antonio Jiminez, Trainer, Habana	.10
☐	65	Rene Rojas, Trainer, Habana	.10
☐	66	TC: Habana	.10
☐	67	Angel Lopez, Centrales	.10
☐	68	Jose Raul Delgado, Centrales	.10
☐	69	Ariel Pestano, Centrales	.10
☐	70	Lourdes Gourriel, Centrales	.10
☐	71	Jorge Luis Toca, Centrales	.50
☐	72	Jorge Diaz, Centrales	.10
☐	73	Lazaro Lopez, Centrales	.10
☐	74	Miguel Caldes, Centrales	.10
☐	75	Eduardo Paret, Centrales	.10
☐	76	Luis Ulacia, Centrales	.10
☐	77	Eusebio Miguel Rojas, Centrales	.10
☐	78	Victor Mesa, Centrales	.10
☐	79	Oscar Machado, Centrales	.10
☐	80	Eddy Rojas, Centrales	.10
☐	81	Pablo Primelles, Centrales	.10
☐	82	Rey Issac, Centrales	.10
☐	83	Edel Pacheco, Centrales	.10
☐	84	Luis Rolando Arrojo, Centrales	7.50
☐	85	Jose Ramon Riscart, Centrales	.10
☐	86	Teofilo Perez, Centrales	.10
☐	87	Adiel Palma, Centrales	.10
☐	88	Miguel Arnay Hernandez, Centrales	.10
☐	89	Omar Luis, Centrales	.10
☐	90	Felipe Fernandez, Centrales	.10
☐	91	Ramon Gardon, Centrales	.10
☐	92	Elicer Montes de Oca, Centrales	.10
☐	93	Yovani Aragon, Centrales	.10
☐	94	Pedro Jova, Mgr., Centrales	.10
☐	95	Luis Enrique Gonzalez, Asst., Centrales	.10
☐	96	Roberto Montero, Asst., Centrales	.10
☐	97	Pedro Perez, Trainer, Centrales	.10
☐	98	Antonio Munoz, Trainer, Centrales	.10
☐	99	TC: Centrales	.10
☐	100	Alberto Hernandez, Orientales	.10
☐	101	Luis Enrique Padro, Orientales	.10
☐	102	Carlos Barrabi, Orientales	.10
☐	103	Orestes Kindelan, Orientales	.10
☐	104	Pablo Bejerano, Orientales	.10
☐	105	Antonio Pacheco, Orientales	.50
☐	106	Gabriel Pierre, Orientales	.10
☐	107	Evenecer Godinez, Orientales	.10
☐	108	Manuel Benavides, Orientales	.10
☐	109	Marino Moreno, Orientales	.10
☐	110	Felix Benavides, Orientales	.10
☐	111	Ermidelio Urrutia, Orientales	.10
☐	112	Fausto Alvarez, Orientales	.10
☐	113	Luis Rodriguez, Orientales	.10
☐	114	Jorge Ochoa, Orientales	.10
☐	115	Juan Carlos Bruzon, Orientales	.10
☐	116	Leonel Bueno, Orientales	.10

	No.	Player	
☐	117	Osvaldo Fernandez, Orientales	5.00
☐	118	Ernesto Leonel Guevara, Orientales	.10
☐	119	Jose Luis Aleman, Orientales	.10
☐	120	Osmani Tamayo, Orientales	.10
☐	121	Adolfo Canet, Orientales	.10
☐	122	Jose Miguel Baez, Orientales	.10
☐	123	Alfredo Fonseca, Orientales	.10
☐	124	Miguel Perez, Orientales	.10
☐	125	Ruben Rodriguez, Orientales	.10
☐	126	Misael Lopez, Orientales	.10
☐	127	Frangel Reynaldo, Mgr., Orientales	.10
☐	128	Antonio Sanchez, Asst., Orientales	.10
☐	129	Miguel Giro, Asst., Orientales	.10
☐	130	Rafael Ramos, Trainer, Orientales	.10
☐	131	Jesus Santiago Guerra, Trainer, Orientales	.10
☐	132	TC: Orientales	.10

1994 KELLOGG'S JERSEYS

Kellogg's major breakfast cereals included a premium of one baseball shirt. The display was available through a mail-in offer only. The cost was $7.98 plus 2 upc codes from the boxes of cereal. The shirts are to be inserted into the display in the order of position based on the teams standings and changed when the team changes position. No players were used, just the team logos.

Shirt Size: 2 3/8" x 3 1/8"
Face: Four colour, team logo on cloth
Back: Blank
Imprint: © Major League Baseball 1994 All Rights Reserved
***Registered trademark of Kellogg Canada Inc. © 1994**

Complete Set (28 shirts):	**25.00**
Display Price:	**5.00**
Common Shirt:	**1.00**

	Player		Player
☐	Baltimore Orioles	☐	Boston Red Soxs
☐	California Angels	☐	Chicago White Sox
☐	Cleveland Indians	☐	Detroit Tigers
☐	Kansas City Royals	☐	Milwaukee Brewers
☐	Minnesota Twins	☐	New York Yankees
☐	Oakland Athletics	☐	Seattle Mariners
☐	Texas Rangers	☐	Toronto Blue Jays
☐	Atlanta Braves	☐	Chicago Cubs
☐	Cincinnati Reds	☐	Colorado Rockies
☐	Florida Marlins	☐	Huston Astros
☐	Los Angeles Dodgers	☐	Montreal Expos
☐	New York Mets	☐	Philadelphia Phillies
☐	Pittsburgh Pirates	☐	St. Louis Cardinals
☐	San Diego Padres	☐	San Francisco Giants

1994 O-PEE-CHEE

Card Size: 2 1/2"X 3 1/2"
Face: Four colour, borderless; name, team name, position
Back: Four colour, name, team name, résumé
Imprint: ©1994. O-PEE-CHEE CO. LTD.

Complete Set (270 cards):	**20.00**
Common Player:	**.15**

	No.	Player	MINT
☐	1	Paul Molitor, Tor.	.25
☐	2	Kirt Manwaring, S.F.	.15
☐	3	Brady Anderson, Bal.	.15
☐	4	Scott Cooper, Bos.	.15
☐	5	Kevin Stocker, Pha.	.15
☐	6	Alex Fernandez, Chi.-A.L.	.15
☐	7	Jeff Montgomery, K.C.	.15
☐	8	Danny Tartabull, NYY.	.15
☐	9	Damion Easley, Cal.	.15
☐	10	Andujar Cedeno, Hou.	.15
☐	11	Steve Karsay, Oak.	.15
☐	12	Dave Stewart, Tor.	.15
☐	13	Fred McGriff, Atl.	.15
☐	14	Jaime Navarro, Mil.	.15
☐	15	Allen Watson, Stl.	.15
☐	16	Ryne Sandberg, Chi.-N.L.	.25
☐	17	Arthur Rhodes, Bal.	.15
☐	18	Marquis Grissom, Mtl.	.15
☐	19	John Burkett, S.F.	.15
☐	20	Robby Thompson, S.F.	.15
☐	21	Denny Martinez, Cle.	.15
☐	22	Ken Griffey, Jr., Sea.	3.00
☐	23	Orestes Destrade, Fla.	.15
☐	24	Doc Gooden, NYM.	.15
☐	25	Rafael Palmeiro, Bal.	.15
☐	**26**	**Pedro Martinez, S.D., RC**	**.50**
☐	27	Wes Chamberlain, Pha.	.15
☐	28	Juan Gonzalez, Tex.	.75
☐	29	Kevin Mitchell, Cin.	.15
☐	30	Dante Bichette, Col.	.15
☐	31	Howard Johnson, Col.	.15
☐	32	Mickey Tettleton, Det.	.15
☐	33	Robin Ventura, Chi.-A.L.	.15
☐	34	Terry Mulholland, NYY.	.15
☐	35	Bernie Williams, NYY.	.25
☐	36	Eduardo Perez, Cal.	.15
☐	37	Rickey Henderson, Oak.	.25
☐	38	Terry Pendleton, Atl.	.15
☐	39	John Smoltz, Atl.	.15
☐	40	Derrick May, Chi.-N.L.	.15
☐	41	Pedro Martinez, Mtl.	.15
☐	42	Mark Portugal, S.F.	.15
☐	43	Albert Belle, Cle.	.25
☐	44	Edgar Martinez, Sea.	.15
☐	45	Gary Sheffield, Fla.	.15
☐	46	Bret Saberhagen, NYM.	.15
☐	47	Ricky Gutierrez, S.D.	.15
☐	48	Orlando Merced, Pgh.	.15
☐	49	Mike Greenwell, Bos.	.15
☐	50	Jose Rijo, Cin.	.15
☐	**51**	**Jeff Granger, K.C., RC**	**.15**
☐	52	Mike Henneman, Det.	.15
☐	53	Dave Winfield, Min.	.25
☐	54	Don Mattingly, NYY.	.75
☐	55	J.T. Snow, Cal.	.15
☐	56	Todd Van Poppel, Oak.	.15
☐	57	Chipper Jones, Atl.	1.50
☐	58	Darryl Hamilton, Mil.	.15
☐	59	Delino DeShields, L.A.	.15
☐	60	Rondell White, Mtl.	.15
☐	61	Eric Anthony, Sea.	.15
☐	62	Charlie Hough, Fla.	.15
☐	63	Sid Fernandez, Bal.	.15
☐	64	Derek Bell, S.D.	.15
☐	65	Phil Plantier, S.D.	.15

	No.	Player	Price
☐	66	Curt Schilling, Pha.	.15
☐	67	Roger Clemens, Bos.	1.00
☐	68	Jose Lind, K.C.	.15
☐	69	Andres Galarraga, Col.	.25
☐	70	Tim Belcher, Det.	.15
☐	71	Ron Karkovice, Chi.-A.L.	.15
☐	72	Alan Trammell, Det.	.15
☐	73	Pete Hanisch, Hus.	.15
☐	74	Mark McGwire, Oak.	1.25
☐	75	Ryan Klesko, Atl.	.25
☐	76	Ramon Martinez, L.A.	.15
☐	77	Gregg Jefferies, Cin.	.15
☐	78	Steve Buechele, Chi.-N.L.	.15
☐	79	Bill Swift, S.F.	.15
☐	80	Matt Williams, S.F.	.15
☐	81	Randy Johnson, Sea.	.25
☐	82	Mike Mussina, Bal.	.25
☐	83	Andy Benes, S.D.	.15
☐	84	Dave Staton, S.D.	.15
☐	85	Steve Cooke, Pgh.	.15
☐	86	Andy Van Slyke, Pgh.	.15
☐	87	Ivan Rodriguez, Tex.	.25
☐	88	Frank Viola, Bos.	.15
☐	89	Aaron Sele, Bos.	.15
☐	90	Ellis Burks, Col.	.15
☐	91	Wally Joyner, K.C.	.15
☐	92	Rick Aguilera, Min.	.15
☐	93	Kirby Puckett, Min.	.75
☐	94	Roberto Hernandez, Chi.-A.L.	.15
☐	95	Mike Stanley, NYY.	.15
☐	96	Roberto Alomar, Tor.	.25
☐	97	James Mouton, Hus.	.15
☐	98	Chad Curtis, Cal.	.15
☐	99	Mitch Williams, Pha.	.15
☐	100	Carlos Delgado, Tor.	.25
☐	101	Greg Maddux, Atl.	1.50
☐	102	Brian Harper, Mil.	.15
☐	103	Tom Pagnozzi, Stl.	.15
☐	104	Jose Offerman, L.A.	.15
☐	105	John Wetteland, Mtl.	.15
☐	106	Carlos Baerga, Cle.	.15
☐	107	Dave Magadan, Fla.	.15
☐	108	Bobby Jones, NYM.	.15
☐	109	Tony Gwynn, S.D.	.75
☐	110	Jeromy Burnitz, NYM.	.15
☐	111	Bip Roberts, S.D.	.15
☐	112	Carlos Garcia, Pgh.	.15
☐	113	Jeff Russell, Bos.	.15
☐	114	Armando Reynoso, Col.	.15
☐	115	Ozzie Guillen, Chi.-A.L.	.15
☐	116	Bo Jackson, Cal.	.15
☐	117	Terry Steinbach, Oak.	.15
☐	118	Deion Sanders, Atl.	.15
☐	119	Randy Myers, NYM.	.15
☐	120	Mark Whiten, Stl.	.15
☐	121	Manny Ramirez, Cle.	.25
☐	122	Ben McDonald, Bal.	.15
☐	123	Darren Daulton, Pha.	.15
☐	124	Kevin Young, Pgh.	.15
☐	125	Barry Larkin, Cin.	.25
☐	126	Cecil Fielder, Det.	.15
☐	127	Frank Thomas, Chi.-A.L.	2.50
☐	128	Luis Polonia, NYY.	.15
☐	129	Steve Finley, Hou.	.15
☐	130	John Olerud, Tor.	.15
☐	131	John Jaha, Mil.	.15
☐	132	Darren Lewis, S.F.	.15
☐	133	Orel Hershiser, L.A.	.15
☐	134	Chris Bosio, Sea.	.15
☐	135	Ryan Thompson, NYM.	.15
☐	136	Chris Sabo, Bal.	.15
☐	137	Tommy Greene, Pha.	.15
☐	138	Andre Dawson, Bos.	.15
☐	139	Roberto Kelly, Cin.	.15
☐	140	Ken Hill, Mtl.	.15
☐	141	Greg Gagne, K.C.	.15
☐	142	Julio Franco, Chi.-A.L.	.15
☐	143	Chili Davis, Cal.	.15
☐	144	Dennis Eckersley, Oak.	.15
☐	145	Joe Carter, Tor.	.15
☐	146	Mark Grace, Chi.-N.L.	.15
☐	147	Mike Piazza, L.A.	1.50
☐	148	J.R. Phillips, S.F.	.15
☐	149	Rich Amaral, Sea.	.15
☐	150	Benny Santiago, Fla.	.15
☐	151	Jeff King, Pgh.	.15
☐	152	Dean Palmer, Tex.	.15
☐	153	Hal Morris, Cin.	.15
☐	154	Mike MacFarlane, K.C.	.15
☐	155	Chuck Knoblauch, Min.	.25
☐	156	Pat Kelly, NYY.	.15
☐	157	Greg Swindell, Hou.	.15
☐	158	Chuck Finley, Cal.	.15
☐	159	Devon White, Tor.	.15
☐	160	Duane Ward, Tor.	.15
☐	161	Sammy Sosa, Chi.-N.L.	.25
☐	162	Javy Lopez, Atl.	.15
☐	163	Eric Karros, L.A.	.15
☐	164	Royce Clayton, S.F.	.15
☐	165	Salomon Torres, S.F.	.15
☐	166	Jeff Kent, NYM.	.15
☐	167	Chris Hoiles, Bal.	.15
☐	168	Len Dykstra, Pha.	.15
☐	169	Jose Canseco, Tex.	.25
☐	170	Bret Boone, Cin.	.15
☐	171	Charlie Hayes, Col.	.15
☐	172	Lou Whitaker, Det.	.15
☐	173	Jack McDowell, Chi.-A.L.	.15
☐	174	Jimmy Key, NYY.	.15
☐	175	Mark Langston Cal.	.15
☐	176	Darryl Kile, Hou.	.15
☐	177	Juan Guzman, Tor.	.15
☐	178	Pat Borders, Tor.	.15
☐	179	Cal Eldred, Mil.	.15
☐	180	Jose Guzman, Chi.-N.L.	.15
☐	181	Ozzie Smith, Stl.	.25
☐	182	Rod Beck, S.F.	.15
☐	183	Dave Fleming, Sea.	.15
☐	184	Eddie Murray, Cle.	.25
☐	185	Cal.Ripken, Bal.	2.00
☐	186	Dave Hollins, Pha.	.15
☐	187	Will Clark, Tex.	.15
☐	188	Otis Nixon, Bos.	.15
☐	189	Joe Oliver, Cin.	.15
☐	190	Roberto Mejia, Col.	.15
☐	191	Felix Jose, K.C.	.15
☐	192	Tony Phillips, Det.	.15
☐	193	Wade Boggs, NYY.	.25
☐	194	Tim Salmon, Cal.	.15
☐	195	Ruben Sierra, Oak.	.15
☐	196	Steve Avery, Atl.	.15
☐	197	B.J. Surhoff, Mil.	.15
☐	198	Todd Zeile, Stl.	.15
☐	199	Raul Mondesi, L.A.	.15
☐	200	Barry Bonds, S.F.	.35
☐	201	Sandy Alomar, Cle.	.15
☐	202	Bobby Bonilla, NYM.	.15
☐	203	Mike Devereaux, Bal.	.15

	No.	Player	Price
☐	**204**	**Ricky Bottalico, Pha., RC**	**.15**
☐	205	Kevin Brown, Tex.	.15
☐	206	Jason Bere, Chi.-A.L.	.15
☐	207	Reggie Sanders, Cin.	.15
☐	208	David Nied, Col.	15
☐	209	Travis Fryman, Det.	.15
☐	210	James Baldwin, Chi.-A.L.	.15
☐	211	Jim Abbott, NYY.	.15
☐	212	Jeff Bagwell, Hou.	.75
☐	213	Bob Welch, Oak.	.15
☐	214	Jeff Blauser, Atl.	.15
☐	215	Brett Butler, L.A.	.15
☐	216	Pat Listach, Mil.	.15
☐	217	Bob Tewksbury, Stl.	.15
☐	218	Mike Lansing, Mtl.	.15
☐	219	Wayne Kirby, Cle.	.15
☐	220	Chuck Carr, Fla.	.15
☐	221	Harold Baines, Bal.	.15
☐	222	Jay Bell, Pgh.	.15
☐	223	Cliff Floyd, Mtl.	.15
☐	224	Rob Dibble, Cin.	.15
☐	225	Kevin Appier, K.C.	.15
☐	226	Eric Davis, Det.	.15
☐	227	Matt Walbeck, Min.	.15
☐	228	Tim Raines. Chi.-A.L.	.15
☐	229	Paul O'Neill, NYY.	.15
☐	230	Craig Biggio, Hou.	.15
☐	231	Brent Gates, Oak.	.15
☐	232	Rob Butler, Tor.	.25
☐	233	David Justice, Atl.	.15
☐	234	Rene Arocha, Stl.	.15
☐	235	Mike Morgan, Chi.-N.L.	.15
☐	236	Denis Boucher, Mtl.	.25
☐	237	Kenny Lofton, Cle.	.50
☐	238	Jeff Conine, Fla.	.15
☐	239	Bryan Harvey, Fla.	.15
☐	240	Danny Jackson, Pha.	.15
☐	241	Al Martin, Pgh.	.15
☐	242	Tom Henke, Tex.	.15
☐	243	Erik Hanson, Cin.	.15
☐	244	Walt Weiss, Col.	.15
☐	245	Brian McRae, K.C.	.15
☐	246	Kevin Tapani, Min.	.15
☐	247	David McCarty, Min.	.15
☐	248	Doug Drabek, Hou.	.15
☐	249	Troy Neel, Oak.	.15
☐	250	Tom Glavine, Atl.	.15
☐	251	Ray Lankford, Stl.	.15
☐	252	Wil Cordero, Mtl.	.15
☐	253	Larry Walker, Mtl.	.75
☐	254	Charles Nagy, Cle.	.15
☐	255	Kirk Rueter, Mtl.	.15
☐	256	John Franco, NYM.	.15
☐	257	John Kruk, Pha.	.15
☐	258	Alex Gonzalez, Tor.	.15
☐	259	Mo Vaughn, Bos.	.25
☐	260	David Cone, K.C.	.15
☐	261	Kent Hrbek, Min.	.15
☐	262	Lance Johnson, Chi.-A.L.	.15
☐	263	Luis Gonzalez, Hou.	.15
☐	264	Mike Bordick, Oak.	.15
☐	265	Ed Sprague, Tor.	.15
☐	266	Moises Alou, Mtl.	.15
☐	267	Omar Vizquel, Cle.	.15
☐	268	Jay Buhner, Sea.	.15
☐	269	Checklist	.15
☐	270	Checklist	.15

ALL STARS

Box Insert Size: 5" x 7"
Reg. Card Size: 2-1/2" x 3-1/2"

	No.	Player	5 x 7	Reg.
Insert Set (25 cards):			**20.00**	**12.00**
☐ ☐	1	Frank Thomas, Chi.-A.L.	5.00	3.00
☐ ☐	2	Paul Molitor, Tor.	1.50	.75
☐ ☐	3	Barry Bonds, S.F.	1.50	.75
☐ ☐	4	Juan Gonzalez, Tex.	2.00	1.00
☐ ☐	5	Jeff Bagwell, Hou.	2.00	1.00
☐ ☐	6	Carlos Baerga, Cle.	.50	.25
☐ ☐	7	Ryne Sandberg, Chi.-N.L.	1.50	.75
☐ ☐	8	Ken Griffey Jr. Sea.	6.00	3.50
☐ ☐	9	Mike Piazza, L.A.	4.00	2.00
☐ ☐	10	Tim Salmon, Cal.	.50	.25
☐ ☐	11	Marquis Grissom, Mtl.	.50	.25
☐ ☐	12	Albert Belle, Cle.	1.50	.75
☐ ☐	13	Fred McGriff, Atl.	1.00	.50
☐ ☐	14	Jack McDowell, Chi.-A.L.	.50	.25
☐ ☐	15	Cal. Ripken, Bal.	4.50	2.50
☐ ☐	16	John Olerud, Tor.	1.00	.50
☐ ☐	17	Kirby Puckett, Min.	2.00	1.00
☐ ☐	18	Roger Clemens, Bos.	3.00	1.50
☐ ☐	19	Larry Walker, Mtl.	2.00	1.00
☐ ☐	20	Cecil Fielder, Det.	.50	.25
☐ ☐	21	Roberto Alomar, Tor.	1.50	.75
☐ ☐	22	Greg Maddux, Atl.	4.00	2.00
☐ ☐	23	Joe Carter, Tor.	1.00	.50
☐ ☐	24	David Justice, Atl.	1.00	.50
☐ ☐	25	Kenny Lofton, Cle.	1.50	.75

HOT PROSPECTS

	No.	Player	MINT
Insert Set (9 cards):			**10.00**
☐	1	Cliff Floyd, Mtl.	1.00
☐	2	James Mouton, Hou.	1.00
☐	3	Salomon Torres, S.F.	1.00
☐	4	Raul Mondesi, L.A.	2.00
☐	5	Carlos Delgado, Tor.	1.50
☐	6	Manny Ramirez, Cle.	2.50
☐	7	Javy Lopez, Atl.	1.00
☐	8	Alex Gonzalez, Tor.	1.00
☐	9	Ryan Klesko, Atl.	2.00

DIAMOND DYNAMOS

Insert Set (18 cards):		20.00
No.	Player	MINT
☐ 1	Mike Piazza, L.A.	10.00
☐ 2	Roberto Mejia, Col.	1.00
☐ 3	Wayne Kirby, Cle.	1.00
☐ 4	Kevin Stocker, Pha.	1.00
☐ 5	Chris Gomez, Det.	1.00
☐ 6	Bobby Jones, NYM.	1.00
☐ 7	David McCarty, Min.	1.00
☐ 8	Kirk Rueter, Mtl.	1.00
☐ 9	J.T. Snow, Cal.	1.00
☐ 10	Wil Cordero, Mtl.	1.00
☐ 11	Tim Salmon, Cal.	1.00
☐ 12	Jeff Conine, Fla.	1.00
☐ 13	Jason Bere, Chi.-A.L.	1.00
☐ 14	Greg McMichael, Atl.	1.00
☐ 15	Brent Gates. Oak.	1.00
☐ 16	Allen Watson, Stl.	1.00
☐ 17	Aaron Sele, Bos.	2.00
☐ 18	Carlos Garcia, Pgh.	1.00

TORONTO BLUE JAYS

Insert Set (9 cards):		8.00
No.	Player	MINT
☐ 1	Rickey Henderson	1.00
☐ 2	Devon White	1.00
☐ 3	Paul Molitor	1.00
☐ 4	Joe Carter	1.00
☐ 5	John Olerud	1.00
☐ 6	Roberto Alomar	1.00
☐ 7	Ed Sprague	1.00
☐ 8	Pat Borders	1.00
☐ 9	Tony Fernandez	1.00

1994 PANINI STICKERS

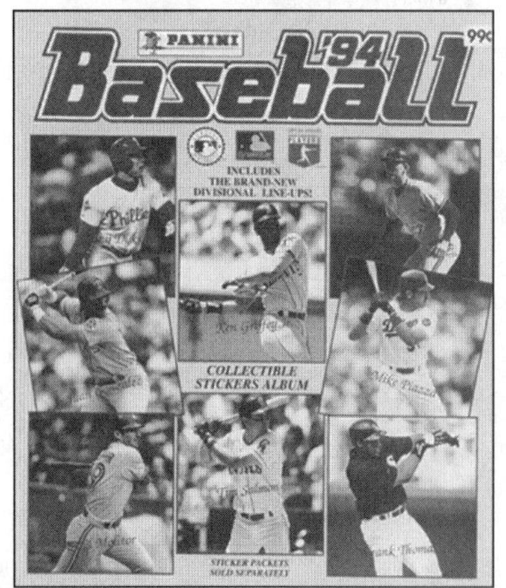

Sticker Size: 2 6/16" x 3 6/16"
Face: Four colour, green border; name, team logo
Back: Black on card stock; card number, Panini and MLB logos
Imprint: " MLB 94" 1994 MLBPA. Printed in Italy by Panini S. r. l.-Modena

Complete Set (268 stickers):		15.00
Common Player:		.15
Album:		3.00
No.	Player	MINT
☐ 1	LL: Rickey Henderson, Tor.	.25
☐ 2	LL: Dave Hollins, Pha.	.15
☐ 3	LL: John Kruk, Pha.	.15
☐ 4	LL: Paul Molitor, Tor.	.25
☐ 5	LL: John Olerud, Tor.	.15
☐ 6	LL: Juan Gonzalez, Tex.	.35
☐ 7	LL: Albert Belle, Cle.	.25
☐ 8	LL: Jack McDowell, Chi.WS	.15
☐ 9	LL: Randy Johnson, Sea.	.25
☐ 10	LL: Jeff Montgomery, KC./ Duane Ward, Tor.	.15
☐ 11	LL: Andres Galarraga, Col.	.25
☐ 12	LL: Barry Bonds, S.F.	.35
☐ 13	LL: Barry Bonds, S.F.	.35
☐ 14	LL: Tom Glavine, Atl./ John Burkett, Pircher, S.F.	.15
☐ 15	LL: Jose Rijo, Cin.	.15
☐ 16	LL: Randy Myers, Chi.-N.L.	.15
☐ 17	Brady Anderson, Bal.	.15
☐ 18	Harold Baines, Bal.	.15
☐ 19	Mike Devereaux, Bal.	.15
☐ 20	Chris Hoiles, Bal.	.15
☐ 21	Mike Mussina, Bal.	.25
☐ 22	Harold Reynolds, Bal.	.15
☐ 23	Cal Ripken Jr., Bal.	2.00
☐ 24	David Segui, Bal.	.15
☐ 25	Fernando Valenzuela, Bal.	.15
☐ 26	Roger Clemens, Bos.	1.00
☐ 27	Scott Cooper, Bos.	.15
☐ 28	Andre Dawson, Bos.	.15
☐ 29	Scott Fletcher, Bos.	.15
☐ 30	Mike Greenwell, Bos.	.15
☐ 31	Billy Hatcher, Bos.	.15
☐ 32	Tony Pena, Bos.	.15
☐ 33	John Valentin, Bos.	.15
☐ 34	Mo Vaughn, Bos.	.25
☐ 35	Chad Curtis, Cal.	.15
☐ 36	Gary DiSarcina, Cal.	.15
☐ 37	Damion Easley, Cal.	.15
☐ 38	Mark Langston, Cal.	.15
☐ 39	Torey Lovullo, Cal.	.15
☐ 40	Greg Myers, Cal.	.15
☐ 41	Luis Polonia, Cal.	.15
☐ 42	Tim Salmon, Cal.	.15
☐ 43	J. T. Snow, Cal.	.15
☐ 44	George Bell, Chi.-A.L.	.15
☐ 45	Ellis Burks, Chi.-A.L.	.25
☐ 46	Joey Cora, Chi.-A.L.	.15

	No.	Sticker	Price
☐	47	Ozzie Guillen, Chi.-A.L.	.15
☐	48	Roberto Hernandez, Chi.-A.L.	.15
☐	49	Bo Jackson, Chi.-A.L.	.15
☐	50	Jack McDowell, Chi.-A.L.	.15
☐	51	Frank Thomas, Chi.-A.L.	3.00
☐	52	Robin Ventura, Chi.-A.L.	.15
☐	53	Sandy Alomar, Jr., Cle.	.15
☐	54	Carlos Baerga, Cle.	.15
☐	55	Albert Belle, Cle.	.35
☐	56	Felix Fermin, Cle.	.15
☐	57	Wayne Kirby, Cle.	.15
☐	58	Kenny Lofton, Cle.	.25
☐	59	Charles Nagy, Cle.	.15
☐	60	Paul Sorrento, Cle.	.15
☐	61	Jeff Treadway, Cle.	.15
☐	62	Eric Davis, Det.	.15
☐	63	Cecil Fielder, Det.	.15
☐	64	Travis Fryman, Det.	.15
☐	65	Bill Gullickson, Det.	.15
☐	66	Mike Moore, Det.	.15
☐	67	Tony Phillips, Det.	.15
☐	68	Mickey Tettleton, Det.	.15
☐	69	Alan Trammell, Det.	.15
☐	70	Lou Whitaker, Det.	.15
☐	71	Kevin Appier, K.C.	.15
☐	72	Greg Gagne, K.C.	.15
☐	73	Tom Gordon, K.C.	.15
☐	74	Felix Jose, K.C.	.15
☐	75	Wally Joyner, K.C.	.15
☐	76	Jose Lind, K.C.	.15
☐	77	Mike Macfarlane, K.C.	.15
☐	78	Brian McRae, K.C.	.15
☐	79	Kevin McReynolds, K.C.	.15
☐	80	Darryl Hamilton, Mil.	.15
☐	81	Teddy Higuera, Mil.	.15
☐	82	John Jaha, Mil.	.15
☐	83	Pat Listach, Mil.	.15
☐	84	Dave Nilsson, Mil.	.15
☐	85	Kevin Reimer, Mil.	.25
☐	86	Kevin Seitzer, Mil.	.15
☐	87	B.J. Surhoff, Mil.	.15
☐	88	Greg Vaughn, Mil.	.15
☐	89	Willie Banks, Min.	.15
☐	90	Brian Harper, Mil.	.15
☐	91	Kent Hrbek, Mil.	.15
☐	92	Chuck Knoblauch, Mil.	.25
☐	93	Shane Mack, Mil.	.15
☐	94	Pat Meares, Mil.	.15
☐	95	Pedro Munoz, Mil.	.15
☐	96	Kirby Puckett, Mil.	.75
☐	97	Dave Winfield, Mil.	.25
☐	98	Jim Abbott, NYY.	.15
☐	99	Wade Boggs, NYY.	.25
☐	100	Mike Gallego, NYY.	.15
☐	101	Pat Kelly, NYY.	.15
☐	102	Don Mattingly, NYY.	.75
☐	103	Paul O'Neill, NYY.	.15
☐	104	Mike Stanley, NYY.	.15
☐	105	Danny Tartabull, NYY.	.15
☐	106	Bernie Williams, NYY.	.15
☐	107	Mike Bordick, Oak.	.15
☐	108	Dennis Eckersley, Oak.	.15
☐	109	Dave Henderson, Oak.	.15
☐	110	Mark McGwire, Oak.	1.25
☐	111	Troy Neel, Oak.	.15
☐	112	Ruben Sierra, Oak.	.15
☐	113	Terry Steinbach, Oak.	.15
☐	114	Todd Van Poppel, Oak.	.15
☐	115	Bob Welch, Oak.	.15
☐	116	Bret Boone, Sea.	.15
☐	117	Jay Buhner, Sea.	.15
☐	118	Ken Griffey, Jr., Sea.	3.50
☐	119	Randy Johnson, Sea.	.35
☐	120	Rich Amaral, Sea.	.15
☐	121	Edgar Martinez, Sea.	.15
☐	122	Tino Martinez, Sea.	.15
☐	123	Dave Valle, Sea.	.15
☐	124	Omar Vizquel, Sea.	.15
☐	125	Jose Canseco, Tex.	.25
☐	126	Julio Franco, Tex.	.15
☐	127	Juan Gonzalez, Tex.	.35
☐	128	Tom Henke, Tex.	.15
☐	129	Manuel Lee, Tex.	.15
☐	130	Rafael Palmeiro, Tex.	.15
☐	131	Dean Palmer, Tex.	.15
☐	132	Ivan Rodriguez, Tex.	.25
☐	133	Doug Strange, Tex.	.15
☐	134	Roberto Alomar, Tor.	.35
☐	135	Pat Borders, Tor.	.15
☐	136	Joe Carter, Tor.	.25
☐	137	Tony Fernandez, Tor.	.15
☐	138	Juan Guzman, Tor.	.15
☐	139	Rickey Henderson, Tor.	.25
☐	140	Paul Molitor, Tor.	.25
☐	141	John Olerud, Tor.	.15
☐	142	Devon White, Tor.	.15
☐	143	Jeff Blauser, Atl.	.15
☐	144	Ron Gant, Atl.	.15
☐	145	Tom Glavine, Atl.	.15
☐	146	David Justice, Atl.	.15
☐	147	Greg Maddux, Atl.	2.00
☐	148	Fred McGriff, Atl.	.15
☐	149	Terry Pendleton, Atl.	.15
☐	150	Deion Sanders, Atl.	.15
☐	151	John Smoltz, Atl.	.15
☐	152	Shawon Dunston, Chi.-N.L.	.15
☐	153	Mark Grace, Chi.-N.L.	.15
☐	154	Derrick May, Chi.-N.L.	.15
☐	155	Randy Myers, Chi.-N.L.	.15
☐	156	Ryne Sandberg, Chi.-N.L.	.35
☐	157	Dwight Smith, Chi.-N.L.	.15
☐	158	Sammy Sosa, Chi.-N.L.	.25
☐	159	Jose Vizcaino, Chi.-N.L.	.15
☐	160	Rick Wilkins, Chi.-N.L.	.15
☐	161	Tom Browning, Cin.	.15
☐	162	Roberto Kelly, Cin.	.15
☐	163	Barry Larkin, Cin.	.25
☐	164	Kevin Mitchell, Cin.	.15
☐	165	Hal Morris, Cin.	.15
☐	166	Joe Oliver, Cin.	.15
☐	167	Jose Rijo, Cin.	.15
☐	168	Chris Sabo, Cin.	.15
☐	169	Reggie Sanders, Cin.	.15
☐	170	Freddie Benavides, Col.	.15
☐	171	Dante Bichette, Col.	.15
☐	172	Vinny Castilla, Col.	.15
☐	173	Jerald Clark, Col.	.15
☐	174	Anres Galarraga, Col.	.35
☐	175	Charlie Hayes, Col.	.15
☐	176	Chris Jones, Col.	.15
☐	177	Roberto Mejia, Col.	.15
☐	178	Eric Young, Col.	.15
☐	179	Bret Barberie, Fla.	.15
☐	180	Chuck Carr, Fla.	.15
☐	181	Jeff Conine, Fla.	.15
☐	182	Orestes Destrade, Fla.	.15
☐	183	Bryan Harvey, Fla.	.15
☐	184	Rich Renteria, Fla.	.15

	No.	Player	MINT
☐	185	Benito Santiago, Fla.	.15
☐	186	Gary Sheffield, Fla.	.15
☐	187	Walt Weiss, Fla.	.15
☐	188	Eric Anthony, Hou.	.15
☐	189	Jeff Bagwell, Hou.	.35
☐	190	Craig Biggio, Hou.	.15
☐	191	Ken Caminiti, Hou.	.25
☐	192	Andujar Cedeno, Hou.	.15
☐	193	Doug Drabek, Hou.	.15
☐	194	Steve Finley, Hou.	.15
☐	195	Doug Jones, Hou.	.15
☐	196	Darryl Kile, Hou.	.15
☐	197	Brett Butler, L.A.	.15
☐	198	Tom Candiotti, Hou.	.15
☐	199	Dave Hansen, Hou.	.15
☐	200	Orel Hershiser, Hou.	.15
☐	201	Eric Karros, Hou.	.15
☐	202	Jose Offerman, Hou.	.15
☐	203	Mike Piazza, Hou.	1.75
☐	204	Cory Snyder, Hou.	.15
☐	205	Darryl Strawberry, Hou.	.25
☐	206	Moises Alou, Mtl.	.15
☐	207	Sean Berry, Mtl.	.15
☐	208	Wil Cordero, Mtl.	.15
☐	209	Delino DeShields, Mtl.	.15
☐	210	Marquis Grissom, Mtl.	.15
☐	211	Ken Hill, Mtl.	.15
☐	212	Mike Lansing, Mtl.	.15
☐	213	Larry Walker, Mtl.	.50
☐	214	John Wetteland, Mtl.	.15
☐	215	Bobby Bonilla, NYM.	.15
☐	216	Jeromy Burnitz, NYM.	.15
☐	217	Dwight Gooden, NYM.	.15
☐	218	Todd Hundley, NYM.	.15
☐	219	Howard Johnson, NYM.	.15
☐	220	Jeff Kent, NYM.	.15
☐	221	Eddie Murray, NYM.	.50
☐	222	Bret Saberhagen, NYM.	.15
☐	223	Ryan Thompson, NYM.	.15
☐	224	Darren Daulton, Pha.	.15
☐	225	Mariano Duncan, Pha.	.15
☐	226	Lenny Dykstra, Pha.	.15
☐	227	Jim Eisenreich, Pha.	.15
☐	228	Dave Hollins, Pha.	.15
☐	229	John Kruk, Pha.	.15
☐	230	Curt Schilling, Pha.	.15
☐	231	Kevin Stocker, Pha.	.15
☐	232	Mitch Williams, Pha.	.15
☐	233	Jay Bell, Pgh.	.15
☐	234	Steve Cooke, Pgh.	.15
☐	235	Carlos Garcia, Pgh.	.15
☐	236	Jeff King, Pgh.	.15
☐	237	Orlando Merced, Pgh.	.15
☐	238	Don Slaught, Pgh.	.15
☐	239	Zame Smith, Pgh.	.15
☐	240	Andy Van Slyke, Pgh.	.15
☐	241	Kevin Young, Pgh.	.15
☐	242	Bernard Gilkey, Stl.	.15
☐	243	Gregg Jefferies, Stl.	.15
☐	244	Brian Jordan, Stl.	.15
☐	245	Ray Lankford, Stl.	.15
☐	246	Tom Pagnozzi, Stl.	.15
☐	247	Geronimo Pena, Stl.	.15
☐	248	Ozzie Smith, Stl.	.50
☐	249	Bob Tewksbury, Stl.	.15
☐	250	Mark Whiten, Stl.	.15
☐	251	Brad Ausmus, S.D.	.15
☐	252	Derek Bell, S.D.	.15
☐	253	Andy Benes, S.D.	.15
☐	254	Phil Clark, S.D.	.15
☐	255	Jeff Gardner, S.D.	.15
☐	256	Tony Gwynn, S.D.	.75
☐	257	Trevor Hoffman, S.D.	.15
☐	258	Phil Plantier, S.D.	.15
☐	259	Craig Shipley, S.D.	.15
☐	260	Rod Beck, S.F.	.15
☐	261	Barry Bonds, S.F.	.35
☐	262	John Burkett, S.F.	.15
☐	263	Will Clark, S.F.	.15
☐	264	Royce Clayton, S.F.	.15
☐	265	Willie McGee, S.F.	.15
☐	266	Bill Swift, S.F.	.15
☐	267	Robby Thompson, S.F.	.15
☐	268	Matt Williams, S.F.	.15

1994 POST

Card Size: 2 1/2" x 3 1/2"
Face: Four colour, borderless; name, position, team, bilingual
Back: Four colour, name, position, team, résumé. numbered _ of 18, bilingual
Imprint:
Complete Set (18 cards): 30.00

	No.	Player	MINT
☐	1	Joe Carter, Tor.	1.25
☐	2	Paul Molitor, Tor.	.75
☐	3	Roberto Alomar, Tor.	1.50
☐	4	John Olerud, Tor.	.75
☐	5	Dave Stewart, Tor.	.75
☐	6	Juan Guzman, Tor.	.75
☐	7	Pat Borders, Tor.	.75
☐	8	Larry Walker, Mtl.	3.00
☐	9	Moises Alou, Mtl.	1.50
☐	10	Ken Griffey Jr. Sea.	6.00
☐	11	Barry Bonds, S.F.	1.50
☐	12	Frank Thomas, Chi.-A.L.	5.00
☐	13	Cal. Ripken Jr., Bal.	4.00
☐	14	Mike Piazza, L.A.	3.50
☐	15	Juan Gonzalez, K.C.	1.50
☐	16	Lenny Dykstra, Pha.	.75
☐	17	David Justice, Atl.	1.25
☐	18	Kirby Puckett, Min.	2.00

1995 POST

Card Size: 2 1/2" x 3 1/2"
Imprint:
Complete Set (18 cards): 50.00

	No.	Player	MINT
☐	1	Ken Griffey, Jr., Sea.	12.00
☐	2	Roberto Alomar, Tor.	3.00
☐	3	Paul Molitor, Tor.	3.00
☐	4	Devon White, Tor.	1.50
☐	5	Moises Alou, Mtl.	3.00
☐	6	Ken Hill, Mtl.	1.50
☐	7	Paul O'Neill, NYY.	1.50
☐	8	Joe Carter, Tor.	2.00
☐	9	Kirby Puckett, Min.	4.00
☐	10	Jimmy Key, NYY.	1.50
☐	11	Frank Thomas, Chi.-A.L.	8.00
☐	12	David Cone, NYY.	1.50
☐	13	Tony Gwynn, S.D.	5.00
☐	14	Matt Williams, S.F.	2.50
☐	15	Jeff Bagwell, Hou.	4.00
☐	16	Greg Maddux, Atl.	6.00
☐	17	Barry Bonds, S.F.	3.00
☐	18	Cal Ripken, Bal.	7.00

1996 HIT THE BOOKS

Other bookmarks may exist.

Card Size: 2 1/2" x 6 1/4"

Sponsors: Canadian Teachers' Association, National Literacy Secreteriat

	Player	MINT
□	Shane Andrews, Mtl.	.50
□	Mark Grudzielanek, Mtl.	.75
□	Tim Scott, Mtl.	.50
□	David Segui, Mtl.	.50
□	Dave Veres, Mtl.	.50
□	Felipe Alou, Mgr., Mtl.	1.00
□	Joe Carter, Tor.	.75
□	Pat Hentgen, Tor.	.75
□	Otis Nixon, Tor.	.50
□	John Olerud, Tor.	.50
□	Ed Sprague, Tor.	.50
□	Woody Williams, Tor.	.50

1997 HIT THE BOOKS

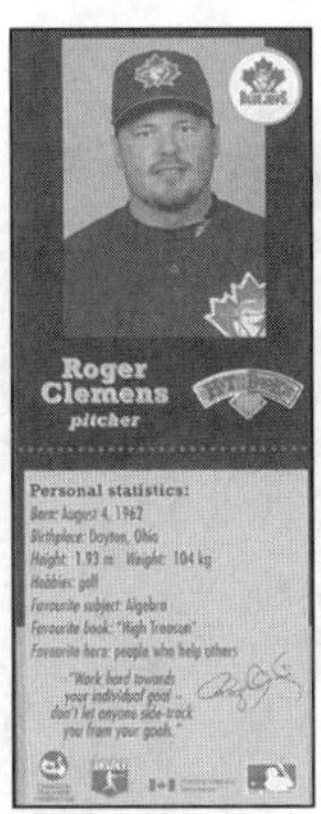

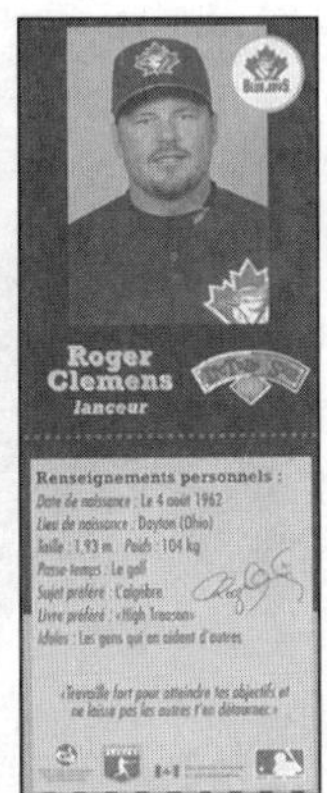

Other Expos' bookmarks exist.

Card Size: 2 1/2" x 6 1/4"

Sponsors: Canadian Teachers' Association, National Literacy Secreteriat

	Player	MINT
□	Joe Carter, Tor.	.75
□	Roger Clemens, Tor.	3.00
□	Tim Crabtree, Tor.	.50
□	Alex Gonzalez, Tor.	.50
□	Shawn Green, Tor.	.50
□	Juan Guzman, Tor.	.50
□	Pat Hentgen, Tor.	.75
□	Otis Nixon, Tor.	.50
□	Charlie O'Brien, Tor.	.50
□	Benito Santiago, Tor.	.50
□	Mike Timlin, Tor.	.50
□	Cito Gaston, Mgr., Tor.	.50

1997 ONTARIO SPECIAL OLYMPICS CLEMENS CARD

Card Size: 3 1/2" x 5"

Sponsors: Ontario Special Olympics, A & P, Super Fresh, Dominion, Ultra food & drug and The Fan 590

	Player	MINT
□	Roger Clemens, Tor.	5.00

1998 HIT THE BOOKS

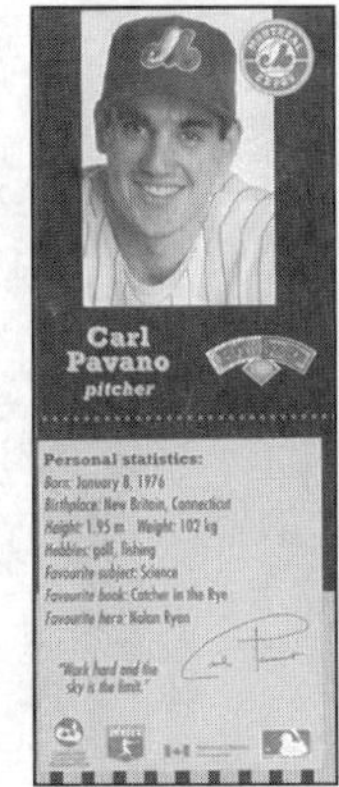

Other bookmarks exist.

Card Size: 2 1/2" x 6 1/4"

Sponsors: Canadian Teachers' Association, National Literacy Secreteriat

	Player	MINT
□	Carl Pavano, Mtl.	.75
□	Randy Myers, Tor.	.50
□	Ed Sprague, Tor.	.50

CHAPTER THREE

MAJOR LEAGUE TEAM ISSUES

MONTREAL EXPOS

(NATIONAL LEAGUE)

1971 EXPOS LA PIZZA ROYALE

These blank-back photos have a blue border.

Card Size: 2 7/16" x 5"

Sponsor: La Pizza Royale

Imprint: None

Complete Set (14 cards):		**40.00**
	Player	**MINT**
☐	Bob Bailey	2.50
☐	John Boccabella	2.50
☐	Ron Fairly	2.50
☐	Jim Gosger	2.50
☐	Coco Laboy	2.50
☐	Rich Nye	2.50
☐	John O'Donoghue	2.50
☐	Adolfo Phillips	2.50
☐	Howie Reed	2.50
☐	Marv Staehle	2.50
☐	Rusty Staub	8.00
☐	Gary Sutherland	2.50
☐	Bobby Wine	2.50
☐	Gene Mauch, Mgr.	2.50

1971 EXPOS PRO STARS

These black-back colour photos are similar in design to the 1971 ProStars regular issue.

Card Size: 3 1/2" x 5 1/2"

Imprint: © PRO STARS PUBLICATIONS 1971

Complete Set (28 cards):		**60.00**
	Player	**MINT**
☐	Bob Bailey	2.50
☐	John Bateman	2.50
☐	John Boccabella	2.50
☐	Ron Brand	2.50
☐	Boots Day	2.50
☐	Jim Fairey	2.50
☐	Ron Fairly	2.50
☐	Jim Gosger	2.50
☐	Don Hahn	2.50
☐	Ron Hunt	2.50
☐	Mack Jones	2.50
☐	Coco Laboy	2.50
☐	Mike Marshall	2.50
☐	Clyde Mashore	2.50
☐	Dan McGinn	2.50
☐	Carl Morton	2.50
☐	John O'Donoghue	2.50
☐	Adolfo Phillips	2.50
☐	Claude Raymond	2.50
☐	Howie Reed	2.50
☐	Steve Renko	2.50
☐	Rusty Staub	8.00
☐	Bill Stoneman	2.50
☐	John Strohmayer	2.50
☐	Gary Sutherland	2.50
☐	Mike Wegener	2.50
☐	Bobby Wine	2.50
☐	Gene Mauch, Mgr.	2.50

1974 EXPOS WESTON

This 10-card set was issued in specially marked packages of Weston B.B.

Bats and features players on the Montreal Expos. The team logo has been airbrushed from the photos.

Card Size: 3 1/2" x 5 1/2"

Sponsor: George Weston, Ltd.

Imprint: COPYRIGHT PRO STAR PROMOTIONS INC.

Complete Set (10 cards): 12.00

	Player	MINT
☐	Bob Bailey	1.50
☐	John Boccabella	1.50
☐	Boots Day	1.50
☐	Tim Foli	1.50
☐	Ron Hunt	1.50
☐	Mike Jorgensen	1.50
☐	Ernie McAnally	1.50
☐	Steve Renko	1.50
☐	Ken Singleton	3.00
☐	Bill Stoneman	1.50

1977 EXPOS

This series was released continuously over several seasons. Other singles exist.

Card Size: 3 1/2" x 5 1/2"

Imprint: None

	Player	MINT
☐	Santo Alcala	1.00
☐	Bill Atkinson	1.00
☐	Stan Bahnsen	1.00
☐	Tim Blackwell	1.00
☐	Gary Carter	5.00
☐	Dave Cash	1.00
☐	Warren Cromartie	1.00
☐	Andre Dawson	5.00
☐	Barry Foote	1.00
☐	Pepe Frias	1.00
☐	Bill Gardner	1.00
☐	Wayne Garrett	1.00
☐	Gerald Hannahs	1.00
☐	Mike Jorgensen	1.00
☐	Joe Kerrigan	1.00
☐	Pete MacKanin	1.00
☐	Will McEnaney	1.00
☐	Sam Mejias	1.00
☐	Jose Morales	1.00
☐	Larry Parrish	1.00
☐	Tony Perez	1.00
☐	Steve Rogers	2.00
☐	Dan Schatzeder	1.00
☐	Chris Speier	1.00
☐	Don Stanhouse	1.00
☐	Jeff Terpko	1.00
☐	Wayne Twitchell	1.00
☐	Del Unser	1.00
☐	Ellis Valentine	1.00
☐	Mickey Vernon	1.00
☐	Tom Walker	1.00
☐	Dan Warthen	1.00
☐	Jerry White	1.00
☐	Dick Williams, Mgr.	1.00
☐	Ossie Virgil, Coach	1.00
☐	Jim Brewer, Coach	1.00
☐	Jackie Brown, Coach	1.00

1977 EXPOS REDPATH SUGAR

Other singles exist.

Card Size: 3 1/4" x 10"

Sponsor: Redpath Sugar

	Player	MINT
☐	Bill Atkinson	1.00
☐	Gary Carter	5.00
☐	David Cash	1.00
☐	Warren Cromartie	1.00
☐	Andre Dawson	5.00
☐	Barry Foote	1.00
☐	Pepe Frias	1.00
☐	Bill Gardner	1.00
☐	Wayne Garrett	1.00
☐	Gerald Hannahs	1.00
☐	Mike Jorgensen	1.00
☐	Joe Kerrigan	1.00
☐	Pete MacKanin	1.00
☐	Sam Mejias	1.00
☐	Will McEnaney	1.00
☐	Jose Morales	1.00
☐	Larry Parrish	1.00
☐	Tony Perez	1.00
☐	Steve Rogers	2.00
☐	Chris Speier	1.00
☐	Don Stanhouse	1.00
☐	Jeff Terpko	1.00
☐	Del Unser	1.00
☐	Ellis Valentine	1.00
☐	Mickey Vernon	1.00
☐	Dan Warthen	1.00
☐	Dick Williams, Mgr.	1.00
☐	Jim Brewer, Coach	1.00
☐	Jackie Brown, Coach	1.00
☐	Ossie Virgil, Coach	1.00

1982 EXPOS HYGRADE

Collectionnez les vingt-quatre cartes de la série Expos-Hygrade pendant tout l'été 1982. Vous en trouverez une dans chaque paquet de saucisses fumées Hygrade spécialement identifié.

Et pour conserver votre collection, procurez-vous un album pratique et attrayant spécialement conçu pour cette promotion. Pour l'obtenir, faites simplement parvenir un chèque ou un mandat: $1.99 + taxe provinciale + frais postaux pour un total de $2.92 à:

Album collection Expos-Hygrade
B.P. 343, Lachine, Québec
H8S 4C2

Photographie par Denis Brodeur

The 24 cards in this set were issued individually with Hygrade Luncheon Meat and were available in Quebec only. They are printed on heavy paper and have rounded corners. The backs of the cards are in French only.

Card Size: 2" x 3"

Imprint: Photographie par Denis Brodeur

Complete Set (24 cards): 60.00

Album: 10.00

	Player	MINT
☐	Tim Blackwell	2.00
☐	Ray Burris	2.00
☐	Gary Carter	10.00
☐	Warren Cromartie	2.00
☐	Andre Dawson	10.00
☐	Terry Francona	2.00
☐	Woodie Fryman	2.00
☐	Bill Gullickson	2.00
☐	Bob James	2.00
☐	Charlie Lea	2.00
☐	Brad Mills	2.00
☐	John Milner	2.00
☐	Dan Norman	2.00
☐	Al Oliver	3.00
☐	Tim Raines	8.00
☐	Jeff Reardon	4.00
☐	Steve Rogers	3.00
☐	Scott Sanderson	2.00
☐	Bryn Smith	2.00
☐	Chris Speier	2.00
☐	Frank Taveras	2.00
☐	Tim Wallach	4.00
☐	Jerry White	2.00
☐	Jim Fanning, Mgr.	2.00

1982 EXPOS ZELLERS

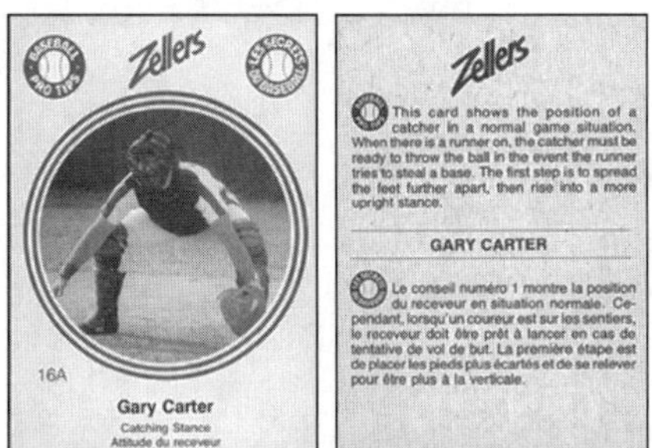

This 60-card standard size set was issued in 20 panels. A 60-card cut-out set sells for $15.

Panel Size: 7 1/2" x 3 1/2"
Sponsor: Zellers
Complete Set (20 panels): 20.00

	No.	Player	MINT
☐	1	Gary Carter, Catching	3.00
☐	2	Steve Rogers, Pitching	1.25
☐	3	Tim Raines, Sliding	2.00
☐	4	Andre Dawson, Batting	3.00
☐	5	Terry Francona, Hitting	1.00
☐	6	Gary Carter, Fielding	3.00
☐	7	Warren Cromartie, Fielding	1.00
☐	8	Chris Speier, Fielding	1.00
☐	9	Billy DeMars, Signals	1.00
☐	10	Andre Dawson, Batting	3.00
☐	11	Terry Francona, Outfield	1.00
☐	12	Woodie Fryman, Holding the Runner	1.00
☐	13	Gary Carter, Fielding	3.00
☐	14	Andre Dawson, Centerfield	3.00
☐	15	Bill Gullickson, Slurve	1.00
☐	16	Gary Carter, Catching	3.00
☐	17	Scott Sanderson, Fielding	1.00
☐	18	Warren Cromartie, Handling Bad Throws	1.00
☐	19	Gary Carter, Hitting	3.00
☐	20	Ray Burris, Holding the Runner	1.00

1983 EXPOS

These blank-back postcards likely follow the same series as those from the late seventies. Other singles exist.

Card Size: 3 1/2" x 5 1/2"
Imprint: None

	Player	MINT
☐	Tim Blackwell	1.00
☐	Ray Burris	1.00
☐	Gary Carter	5.00
☐	Warren Cromartie	1.00
☐	Andre Dawson	5.00
☐	Doug Flynn	1.00
☐	Terry Francona	1.00
☐	Woodie Fryman	1.00
☐	Bill Gullickson	1.00
☐	Charlie Lea	1.00
☐	Bryan Little	1.00
☐	Al Oliver	1.50
☐	David Palmer	1.00
☐	Tim Raines	3.50
☐	Jeff Reardon	2.00
☐	Steve Rogers	1.50
☐	Scott Sanderson	1.00
☐	Dan Schatzeder	1.00
☐	Chris Speier	1.00
☐	Tim Wallach	2.00
☐	Jim Fanning, Mgr.	1.00
☐	Billy DeMars, Coach	1.00

1983 EXPOS STUART BAKERY

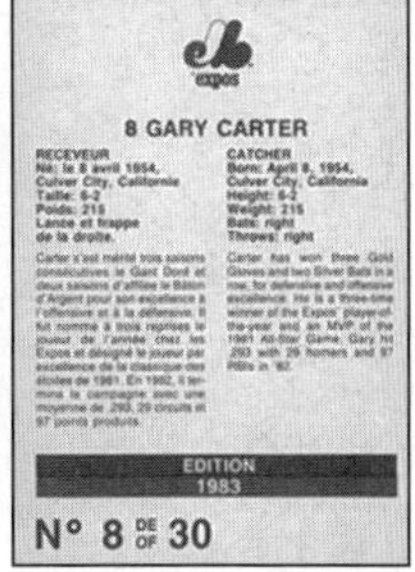

Card Size: 2 1/2" x 3 1/2"
Sponsor: Stuart Bakery
Imprint: Promo Marketing
Complete Set (30 cards): 12.00

	No.	Player	MINT
☐	1	Bill Virdon, Field Mgr.	.50
☐	2	Woodie Fryman	.50
☐	3	Vern Rapp, Coach	.50
☐	4	Andre Dawson	2.50
☐	5	Jeff Reardon	.75
☐	6	Al Oliver	.50
☐	7	Doug Flynn	.50
☐	8	Gary Carter	2.50
☐	9	Tim Raines	1.50
☐	10	Steve Rogers	.50
☐	11	Billy DeMars, Coach	.50
☐	12	Tim Wallach	.75
☐	13	Galen Cisco, Coach	.50
☐	14	Terry Francona	.50
☐	15	Bill Gullickson	.50
☐	16	Ray Burris	.50
☐	17	Scott Sanderson	.50
☐	18	Warren Cromartie	.50
☐	19	Jerry White	.50
☐	20	Bobby Ramos	.50

	No.	Player	MINT
☐	21	Jim Wohlford	.50
☐	22	Dan Schatzeder	.50
☐	23	Charlie Lea	.50
☐	24	Bryan Little, Error (Brian)	.50
☐	25	Mel Wright, Coach	.50
☐	26	Tim Blackwell	.50
☐	27	Chris Speier	.50
☐	28	Randy Lerch	.50
☐	29	Bryn Smith	.50
☐	30	Brad Mills	.50

1984 EXPOS

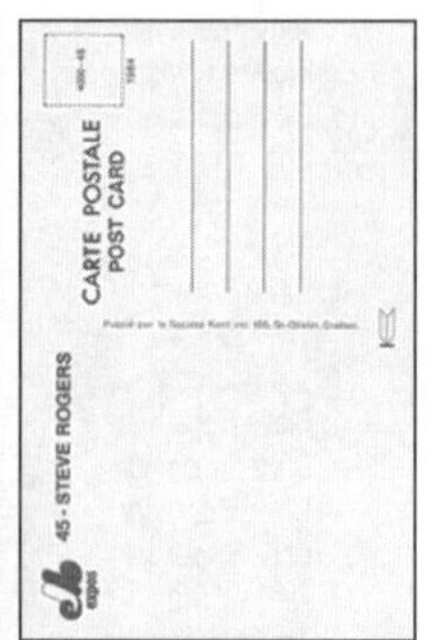

Postcard Size: 3 1/2" x 5 1/2"
Imprint: Publié par la Société Kent Inc.
Complete Set (36 cards): 35.00

	Player	MINT
☐	Fred Breining	1.00
☐	Gary Carter	5.00
☐	Andre Dawson	5.00
☐	Miguel Dilone	1.00
☐	Doug Flynn	1.00
☐	Terry Francona	1.00
☐	Mike Fuentes	1.00
☐	Bill Gullickson	1.00
☐	Greg A. Harris	1.00
☐	Bob James	1.00
☐	Roy Johnson	1.00
☐	Charlie Lea	1.00
☐	Bryan Little	1.00
☐	Gary Lucas	1.00
☐	Andy McGaffigan	1.00
☐	David Palmer	1.00
☐	Tim Raines	3.00
☐	Bobby Ramos	1.00
☐	Jeff Reardon	2.00
☐	Steve Rogers	1.50
☐	Pete Rose	8.00
☐	Argenis Salazar	1.00
☐	Dan Schatzeder	1.00
☐	Bryn Smith	1.00
☐	Chris Speier	1.00
☐	Mike Stenhouse	1.00
☐	Derrel Thomas	1.00
☐	Mike Vail	1.00
☐	Tim Wallach	2.00
☐	Jim Wohlford	1.00
☐	Bill Virdon, Mgr.	1.00
☐	Russ Nixon, Coach	1.00
☐	Joe Kerrigan, Coach	1.00
☐	Billy DeMars, Coach	1.00
☐	Galen Cisco, Coach	1.00
☐	Felipe Alou, Coach	3.00

1984 EXPOS STUART BAKERY

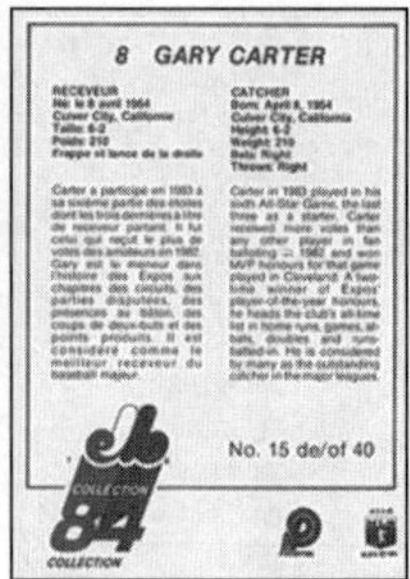

Card Size: 2 1/2"x 3 1/2"
Sponsor: Stuart Bakery
Complete Set (40 cards): 35.00
Album: 5.00

	No.	Player	MINT
☐	1	Youppi Mascot	.50
☐	2	Bill Virdon, Mgr.	.50
☐	3	Billy DeMars, Coach	.50
☐	4	Galen Cisco, Coach	.50
☐	5	Russ Nixon, Coach	.50
☐	6	Felipe Alou, Coach	1.50
☐	7	Dan Schatzeder	.50
☐	8	Charlie Lea	.50
☐	9	Bobby Ramos	.50
☐	10	Bob James	.50
☐	11	Andre Dawson	2.50
☐	12	Gary Lucas	.50
☐	13	Jeff Reardon	.75
☐	14	Tim Wallach	.75
☐	15	Gary Carter	2.50
☐	16	Bill Gullickson	.50
☐	17	Pete Rose	4.00
☐	18	Terry Francona	.50
☐	19	Steve Rogers	.50
☐	20	Tim Raines	1.50
☐	21	Bryn Smith	1.00
☐	22	Greg Harris	1.00
☐	23	David Palmer	1.00
☐	24	Jim Wohlford	1.00
☐	25	Miguel Dilone	1.00
☐	26	Mike Stenhouse	1.00
☐	27	Chris Speier	1.00
☐	28	Derrel Thomas	1.00
☐	29	Doug Flynn	1.00
☐	30	Bryan Little	1.00
☐	31	Argenis Salazar	1.00
☐	32	Mike Fuentes	1.00
☐	33	Joe Kerrigan, Coach	1.00
☐	34	Andy McGaffigan	1.00
☐	35	Fred Breining	1.00
☐	36	Gary Carter; Andre Dawson; Tim Raines; Steve Rogers	2.50
☐	37	Andre Dawson; Tim Raines	2.50
☐	38	B. Virdon; R. Nixon; F. Alou; J. Kerrigan; B. DeMars; G. Cisco	1.50
☐	39	Team Photo	1.00
☐	40	Checklist	1.00

1986 EXPOS PROVIGO FOODS

Each panel features 2 21/2" x 3 3/8" cards plus an advertisement card. A 28-card cut out set sells for $10.

Panel Size: 7 1/2" x 3 3/8"

Sponsors: Proviago Foods, Promo Marketing

Complete Set (14 panels):			**15.00**
Album:			**5.00**
	No.	**Player**	**MINT**
☐	1/2	Hubie Brooks; Dann Bilardello	1.00
☐	3/4	Buck Rodgers, Mgr.; Andy McGaffigan	1.00
☐	5/6	Mitch Webster; Jim Wohlford	1.00
☐	7/8	Tim Raines; Jay Tibbs	3.00
☐	9/10	Andre Dawson; Andres Galarraga	6.00
☐	11/12	Tim Wallach; Dan Schatzeder	1.50
☐	13/14	Jeff Reardon; Joe Kerrigan; Bobby Winkles; L. Bearnarth	1.50
☐	15/16	Jason Thompson; Bert Roberge	1.00
☐	17/18	Tim Burke; Al Newman	1.00
☐	19/20	Bryn Smith; Wayne Krenchicki	1.00
☐	21/22	Joe Hesketh; Herman Winningham	1.00
☐	23/24	Vance Law; Floyd Youmans	1.00
☐	25/26	Jeff Parrett; Mike Fitzgerald	1.00
☐	27/28	Mascot Youppi; Rick Renick; Ron Hansen; Ken Macha	1.00

1986 EXPOS PROVIGO POSTERS

Poster Size: 9" x 14 3/4"

Sponsor: Provigo Foods

Complete Set (12 posters):			**25.00**
	No.	**Player**	**MINT**
☐	1	Tim Raines	4.00
☐	2	Bryn Smith	2.00
☐	3	Hubie Brooks	2.00
☐	4	Buck Rogers, Mgr.	2.00
☐	5	Mitch Webster	2.00
☐	6	Joe Hesketh	2.00
☐	7	Mike Fitzgerald	2.00
☐	8	Andy McGaffigan	2.00
☐	9	Andre Dawson	8.00
☐	10	Tim Wallach	3.00
☐	11	Jeff Reardon	3.00
☐	12	Vance Law	2.00

1992 EXPOS DURIVAGE

This 21-card set was made by Donruss-Leaf and made available through Durivage in Québec. Four players and the manager were replaced in this set.

Card Size: 2 1/2" x 3 1/2"

Imprint: © 1992 LEAF, INC.

Complete Set (27 cards):			**50.00**
Album:			**5.00**
	No.	**Player**	**MINT**
☐		Checklist 1 - 20	1.00
☐	1	Bret Barberie	1.00
☐	2	Chris Haney	1.00
☐	2	Brian Barnes (*)	3.00
☐	3	Bill Sampen	1.00
☐	3	Phil Bradley (*)	3.00
☐	4	Ivan Calderon	1.00
☐	5	Gary Carter	5.00
☐	6	Delino DeShields	1.00
☐	7	Jeff Fassero	1.00
☐	8	Darrin Fletcher	1.00
☐	9	Mark Gardner	1.00
☐	10	Marquis Grissom	5.00
☐	11	Ken Hill	1.00
☐	12	Dennis Martinez	1.00
☐	13	Chris Nabholz	1.00
☐	14	Spike Owen	1.00
☐	15	Tom Runnells, Mgr.	1.00
☐	15	Felipe Alou, Mgr. (*)	6.00
☐	16	John Vander Wal	1.00
☐	16	Matt Stairs (*)	6.00
☐	17	Bill Landrum	1.00
☐	17	Dave Wainhouse (*)	4.00
☐	18	Larry Walker	10.00
☐	19	Tim Wallach	2.00
☐	20	John Wetteland	1.00

1993 EXPOS MCDONALD'S

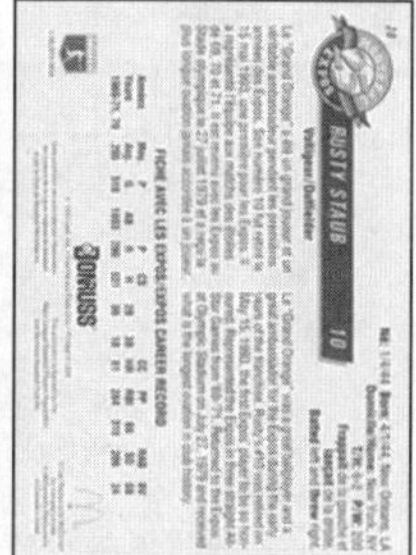

Card Size: 2 1/2" x 3 1/2"

Imprint: © 1993 Leaf, Inc.

Complete Set (33 cards):	**12.00**
Felipe Alou Autograph:	**100.00**

	No.	Player	MINT
☐	1	Moises Alou	1.00
☐	2	Andre Dawson	2.00
☐	3	Delino DeShields	.35
☐	4	Andres Galarraga	1.00
☐	5	Marquis Grissom	.75
☐	6	Tim Raines	1.00
☐	7	Larry Walker	3.00
☐	8	Tim Wallach	.50
☐	9	Ken Hill	.35
☐	10	Dennis Martinez	.35
☐	11	Jeff Reardon	.50
☐	12	Gary Carter	2.00
☐	13	Dave Cash	.35
☐	14	Warren Cromartie	.35
☐	15	Mack Jones	.35
☐	16	Al Oliver	.50
☐	17	Larry Parrish	.35
☐	18	Rodney Scott	.35
☐	19	Ken Singleton	.50
☐	20	Rusty Staub	1.50
☐	21	Ellis Valentine	.35
☐	22	Woodie Fryman	.35
☐	23	Charlie Lea	.35
☐	24	Bill Lee	.35
☐	25	Mike Marshall	.35
☐	26	Claude Raymond	.35
☐	27	Steve Renko	.35
☐	28	Steve Rogers	.50
☐	29	Bill Stoneman	.35
☐	30	Gene Mauch, Mgr.	.35
☐	31	Felipe Alou, Mgr.	1.00
☐	32	Buck Rodgers, Mgr.	.35
☐	33	Checklist	.35

1996 EXPOS DISKS

Photos are credited to Bernard Préfontaine and John Mahoney. This 24-disk set was issued as four 6 3/8" diameter plates with six player disks on each plate. A 4-plate set sells for $12.

Disk Diameter: 1 5/8"

Complete Set (24 disks): 10.00

	Player	MINT
☐	Moises Alou (Batting)	1.00
☐	Moises Alou (Sliding)	1.00
☐	Shane Andrews	.50
☐	Derek Aucoin	.50
☐	Rhéal Cormier	.50
☐	Jeff Fassero	.50
☐	Darrin Fletcher	.50
☐	Mark Grudzielanek (Batting)	.75
☐	Mark Grudzielanek (Fielding)	.75
☐	Mike Lansing	.50
☐	Pedro Martinez (In stance)	2.00
☐	Pedro Martinez (In motion)	2.00
☐	Carlos Perez	.50
☐	Henry Rodriguez	.50
☐	Mel Rojas	.50
☐	Tim Scott	.50
☐	David Segui (Ready to catch)	.50
☐	David Segui (Catching ball)	.50
☐	Tim Spehr	.50
☐	Dave Veres	.50
☐	Rondell White (Batting)	1.00
☐	Rondell White (Running)	1.00
☐	Felipe Alou, Mgr.	1.00
☐	Mascot Youppi	.50

TORONTO BLUE JAYS

(AMERICAN LEAGUE)

1978 BLUE JAYS

These blank-back cards feature black and white photos. This series was apparently issued from 1977 through 1981. Photos were taken by Edwin Brodeur. Other singles exist.

Card Size: 3 1/4" x 5 1/8"

Sponsor: None

	Player	MINT
☐	Doug Ault	1.50
☐	Rico Carty	1.50
☐	Jim Clancy	1.50
☐	Sam Ewing	1.50
☐	Jerry Garvin	1.50
☐	Luis Gomez	1.50
☐	Roy Howell	1.50
☐	Jesse Jefferson	1.50
☐	Tim Johnson	3.00
☐	Don Kirkwood	1.50
☐	Dave Lemanczyk	1.50
☐	Don Leppert	1.50
☐	John Mayberry	1.50
☐	Bob Miller	1.50
☐	Brian Milner	1.50
☐	Balor Moore	1.50
☐	Tom Murphy	1.50
☐	Tom Underwood	1.50
☐	Willie Upshaw	1.50
☐	Otto Velez	1.50

	Player	MINT
☐	Harry Warner	1.50
☐	Mike Willis	1.50
☐	Alvis Woods	1.50
☐	Roy Hartsfield, Mgr.	1.50

1979 BLUE JAYS BUBBLE YUM

This set was issued at two Blue Jays autograph sessions. These cards feature black and white photos.

Card Size: 5 1/2" x 8 1/2"

Sponsor: Bubble Yum

Complete Set (20 cards): 30.00

	Player	MINT
☐	Bob Bailor	1.50
☐	Rick Bosetti	1.50
☐	Tom Buskey	1.50
☐	Rico Carty	1.50
☐	Rick Cerone	1.50
☐	Jim Clancy	1.50
☐	Dave Freisleben	1.50
☐	Luis Gomez	1.50
☐	Alfredo Griffin	1.50
☐	Roy Howell	1.50
☐	Phil Huffman	1.50
☐	Jesse Jefferson	1.50
☐	Dave Lemanczyk	1.50
☐	John Mayberry	1.50
☐	Balor Moore	1.50
☐	Tom Underwood	1.50
☐	Otto Velez	1.50
☐	Avis Woods	1.50
☐	Roy Hartsfield, Mgr.	1.5.0
☐	Bobby Doerr, Coach	1.50

1984 BLUE JAYS FIRE SAFETY

Card Size: 2 1/2" x 3 1/2"

Sponsors: Toronto Sun, Ontario Association of Fire Chiefs

Complete Set (35 cards): 20.00

	Player	MINT
☐	Jim Acker	.75
☐	Willie Aikens	.75
☐	Doyle Alexander	.75
☐	Jesse Barfield	1.00
☐	George Bell	1.00
☐	Jim Clancy	.75
☐	Bryan Clark	.75
☐	Stan Clarke	.75
☐	Dave Collins	.75
☐	Tony Fernandez	1.50
☐	Damaso Garcia	.75
☐	Jim Gott	.75
☐	Alfredo Griffin	.75
☐	Kelly Gruber	.75
☐	Garth Iorg	.75
☐	Roy Lee Jackson	.75
☐	Cliff Johnson	.75
☐	Jimmy Key	3.00
☐	Dennis Lamp	.75
☐	Rick Leach	.75
☐	Luis Leal	.75
☐	Buck Martinez	.75
☐	Lloyd Moseby	.75
☐	Rance Mulliniks	.75
☐	Dave Stieb	1.00
☐	Willie Upshaw	.75
☐	Mitch Webster	.75
☐	Ernie Whitt	.75
☐	Bobby Cox, Mgr.	1.00
☐	Cito Gaston, Coach	1.00
☐	Al Widmar, Coach	.75
☐	Jimy Williams, Coach	.75
☐	Billy Smith, Coach	.75
☐	John Sullivan, Coach	.75
☐	Checklist	.75

1985 BLUE JAYS FIRE SAFETY

Card Size: 2 1/2" x 3 1/2"

Sponsors: Ontario Association of Fire Chiefs, the Ministry of the Solicitor General, The Toronto Star, Midas Muffler, and Brakeshops

Complete Set (36 cards): 15.00

	Player	MINT
☐	Jim Acker	.50
☐	Willie Aikens	.50
☐	Doyle Alexander	.50
☐	Jesse Barfield	.75
☐	George Bell	.75
☐	Jeff Burroughs	.50
☐	Bill Caudill	.50
☐	Jim Clancy	.50
☐	Tony Fernandez	1.00
☐	Damaso Garcia	.50
☐	Kelly Gruber	.50
☐	Tom Henke	.50
☐	Garth Iorg	.50
☐	Jimmy Key	2.00
☐	Dennis Lamp	.50
☐	Gary Lavelle	.50
☐	Luis Leal	.50
☐	Manny Lee	.50
☐	Buck Martinez	.50
☐	Len Matuszek	.50
☐	Lloyd Moseby	.50
☐	Rance Mulliniks	.50
☐	Ron Musselman	.50
☐	Dave Stieb	.75
☐	Lou Thornton	.50
☐	Willie Upshaw	.50
☐	Mitch Webster	.50
☐	Ernie Whitt	.50
☐	Team Photo/Home Schedule	.50
☐	Bobby Cox, Mgr.	.75
☐	Cito Gaston, Coach	.75
☐	Billy Smith, Coach	.50
☐	John Sullivan, Coach	.50
☐	Al Widmar, Coach	.50
☐	Jimy Williams, Coach	.50
☐	Title Card: Checklist	.50

1986 BLUE JAYS AULT FOODS

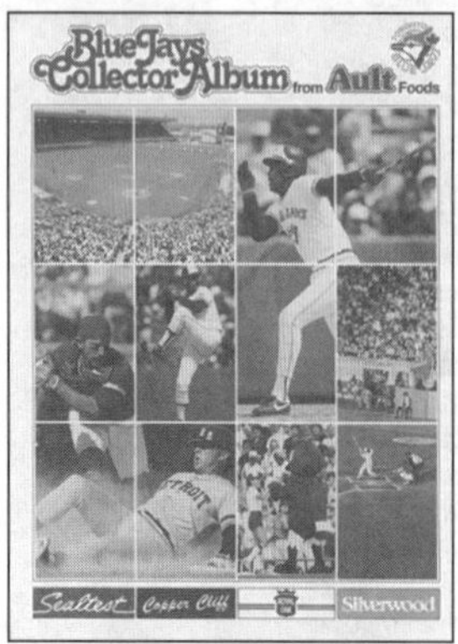

Sticker Size: 2" x 3"
Sponsor: Ault Foods

Complete Set (24 stickers):		**20.00**
Album:		**5.00**
	Player	**MINT**
☐	Jim Acker	.75
☐	Doyle Alexander	.75
☐	Jesse Barfield	1.00
☐	George Bell	1.00
☐	Bill Caudill	.75
☐	Jim Clancy	.75
☐	Steve Davis	.75
☐	Tony Fernandez	1.50
☐	Cecil Fielder	5.00
☐	Damaso Garcia	.75
☐	Don Gordon	.75
☐	Kelly Gruber	.75
☐	Tom Henke	.75
☐	Garth Iorg	.75
☐	Cliff Johnson	.75
☐	Jimmy Key	3.00
☐	Dennis Lamp	.75
☐	Gary Lavelle	.75
☐	Buck Martinez	.75
☐	Lloyd Moseby	.75
☐	Rance Mulliniks	.75
☐	Dave Stieb	1.00
☐	Willie Upshaw	.75
☐	Ernie Whitt	.75

1986 BLUE JAYS FIRE SAFETY

Card Size: 2 1/2" x 3 1/2"
Sponsors: Ontario Association of Fire Chiefs, the Ministry of the Solicitor General, The Toronto Star and Bubble Yum

Complete Set (36 cards):		**15.00**
	Player	**MINT**
☐	Title Card: 10th Anniversary '86	.50
☐	Jim Acker	.50
☐	Doyle Alexander	.50
☐	Jesse Barfield	.75
☐	George Bell	.75
☐	Bill Caudill	.50
☐	Jim Clancy	.50
☐	Steve Davis	.50
☐	Mark Eichhorn	.50
☐	Tony Fernandez	.75
☐	Cecil Fielder	3.00
☐	Tom Filer	.50
☐	Damaso Garcia	.50
☐	Don Gordon	.50
☐	Kelly Gruber	.50
☐	Jeff Hearron	.50
☐	Tom Henke	.50
☐	Garth Iorg	.50
☐	Cliff Johnson	.50
☐	Jimmy Key	2.00
☐	Dennis Lamp	.50
☐	Gary Lavelle	.50
☐	Rick Leach	.50
☐	Buck Martinez	.50
☐	Lloyd Moseby	.50
☐	Rance Mulliniks	.50
☐	Dave Stieb	.75
☐	Willie Upshaw	.50
☐	Ernie Whitt	.50
☐	Jimy Williams, Mgr.	.50
☐	Cito Gaston, Coach	.75
☐	John McLaren, Coach	.50
☐	Billy Smith, Coach	.50
☐	John Sullivan, Coach	.50
☐	Al Widmar, Coach	.50
☐	CL: Team Photo	.50

1987 BLUE JAYS FIRE SAFETY

Card Size: 2 1/2" x 3 1/2"
Sponsors: Ontario Association of Fire Chiefs, the Ministry of the Solicitor General, The Toronto Star and Bubble Yum

Complete Set (36 cards):		**12.00**
	Player	**MINT**
☐	Title Card: Team Logo	.35
☐	Jesse Barfield	.50
☐	George Bell	.50
☐	John Cerutti	.35
☐	Jim Clancy	.35
☐	Rob Ducey	.50
☐	Mark Eichhorn	.35
☐	Tony Fernandez	.50
☐	Cecil Fielder	2.00
☐	Kelly Gruber	.35
☐	Jeff Hearron	.35
☐	Tom Henke	.35
☐	Garth Iorg	.35
☐	Joe Johnson	.35
☐	Jimmy Key	1.50
☐	Gary Lavelle	.35
☐	Rick Leach	.35
☐	Fred McGriff	3.00
☐	Craig McMurtry	.35
☐	Lloyd Moseby	.35

☐	Rance Mulliniks	.35
☐	Jeff Musselman	.35
☐	Jose Nunez	.35
☐	Mike Sharperson	.35
☐	Matt Stark	.35
☐	Dave Stieb	.50
☐	Willie Upshaw	.35
☐	Duane Ward	.35
☐	Ernie Whitt	.35
☐	Al Widmar, Coach	.35
☐	Jimy Williams, Mgr.	.35
☐	Cito Gaston, Coach	.50
☐	John McLaren, Coach	.35
☐	Billy Smith, Coach	.35
☐	John Sullivan, Coach	.35
☐	CL: Team Photo	.35

1988 BLUE JAYS

This 14-postcard set was issued as a promotional package for season ticket sales.

Card Size: 5" x 7"

Imprint: None

Complete Set (14 cards): 8.00

	Player	MINT
☐	Jesse Barfield	1.00
☐	George Bell	1.00
☐	Jim Clancy	.75
☐	Mark Eichhorn	.75
☐	Tony Fernandez	1.00
☐	Tom Henke	.75
☐	Jimmy Key	3.00
☐	Nelson Liriano	.75
☐	Lloyd Moseby	.75
☐	Dave Stieb	1.00
☐	Willie Upshaw	.75
☐	Ernie Whitt	.75
☐	Jimy Williams, Mgr.	.75
☐	Toronto Blue Jays 1988 Schedule	.75

1988 BLUE JAYS FIRE SAFETY

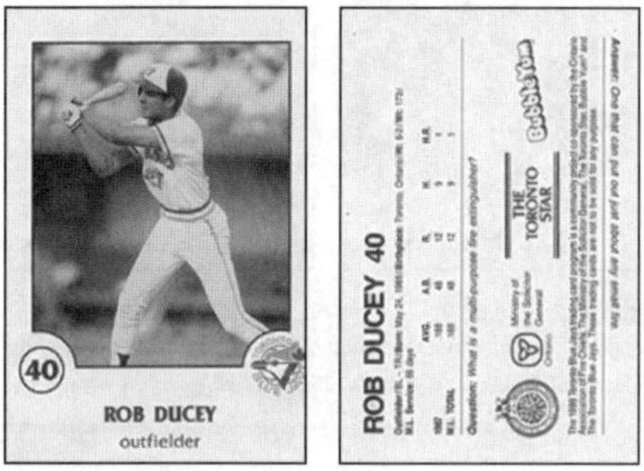

Card Size: 3 1/2" x 5"

Sponsors: Ontario Association of Fire Chiefs, the Ministry of the Solicitor General, TheToronto Star and Bubble Yum

Complete Set (36 cards): 12.00

	Player	MINT
☐	Title Card: Team Logo	.35
☐	Jesse Barfield	.50
☐	George Bell	.50
☐	Juan Beniquez	.35
☐	Pat Borders	.50
☐	Silvestre Campusano	.35
☐	John Cerutti	.35
☐	Jim Clancy	.35
☐	Rob Ducey	.50
☐	Mark Eichhorn	.35
☐	Tony Fernandez	.50
☐	Cecil Fielder	2.00
☐	Mike Flanagan	.35
☐	Kelly Gruber	.35
☐	Tom Henke	.35
☐	Jimmy Key	1.50
☐	Rick Leach	.35
☐	Manny Lee	.35
☐	Nelson Liriano	.35
☐	Lloyd Moseby	.35
☐	Rance Mulliniks	.35
☐	Jeff Musselman	.35
☐	Fred McGriff	3.00
☐	Dave Stieb	.50
☐	Todd Stottlemyre	.35
☐	Duane Ward	.35
☐	David Wells	1.00
☐	Ernie Whitt	.35
☐	Jimy Williams, Mgr.	.35
☐	Cito Gaston, Coach	.50
☐	Winston Llenas, Coach	.35
☐	John McLaren, Coach	.35
☐	Billy Smith, Coach	.35
☐	John Sullivan, Coach	.35
☐	Al Widmar, Coach	.35
☐	CL: Team Photo	.35

1989 BLUE JAYS FIRE SAFETY

Card Size: 2 1/2" x 3 1/2"

Sponsors: Ontario Association of Fire Chiefs, the Ministry of the Solicitor General, A & P-Dominion and Oh Henry

Complete Set (36 cards): 12.00

	Player	MINT
☐	Title Card: On The Move	.35
☐	Jesse Barfield	.50
☐	George Bell	.50
☐	Pat Borders	.50
☐	Bob Brenly	.35
☐	Sal Butera	.35
☐	Silvestre Campusano	.35
☐	John Cerutti	.35
☐	Rob Ducey	.50
☐	Tony Fernandez	.50
☐	Mike Flanagan	.35
☐	Kelly Gruber	.35
☐	Tom Henke	.35
☐	Jimmy Key	1.00
☐	Tom Lawless	.35
☐	Manny Lee	.35
☐	Nelson Liriano	.35
☐	Fred McGriff	2.00
☐	Lloyd Moseby	.35
☐	Rance Mulliniks	.35
☐	Jeff Musselman	.35
☐	Greg Myers	.35
☐	Jose Nunez	.35
☐	Dave Stieb	.50
☐	Todd Stottlemyre	.35
☐	Duane Ward	.35
☐	David Wells	1.00
☐	Ernie Whitt	.35
☐	Frank Wills	.35
☐	Jimy Williams, Mgr.	.35
☐	Cito Gaston, Coach	.50
☐	John McLaren, Coach	.35
☐	Mike Squires, Coach	.35
☐	John Sullivan, Coach	.35
☐	Al Widmar, Coach	.35
☐	CL: Team Photo	.35

1990 BLUE JAYS FIRE SAFETY

Card Size: 2 1/2" x 3 1/2"
Sponsors: The Ontario Association of Fire Chiefs, The Ministry of the Solicitor General, A & P-Dominion and Oh Henry

	Complete Set (36 cards):	12.00
	Player	**MINT**
☐	Title Card: Blue Jays 1990 Fan Club	.35
☐	Jim Acker	.35
☐	George Bell	.50
☐	Willie Blair	.35
☐	Pat Borders	.50
☐	John Cerutti	.35
☐	Junior Felix	.35
☐	Tony Fernandez	.50
☐	Kelly Gruber	.35
☐	Tom Henke	.35
☐	Glenallen Hill	.35
☐	Jimmy Key	1.00
☐	Paul Kilgus	.35
☐	Tom Lawless	.35
☐	Manny Lee	.35
☐	Al Leiter	.35
☐	Nelson Liriano	.35
☐	Fred McGriff	2.00
☐	Rance Mulliniks	.35
☐	Greg Myers	.35
☐	John Olerud	2.50
☐	Alex Sanchez	.35
☐	Dave Stieb	.50
☐	Todd Stottlemyre	.35
☐	Ozzie Virgil	.35
☐	Duane Ward	.35
☐	David Wells	1.00
☐	Frank Wills	.35
☐	Mookie Wilson	.35
☐	Cito Gaston, Mgr.	.50
☐	Galen Cisco, Coach	.35
☐	John McLaren, Coach	.35
☐	Mike Squires, Coach	.35
☐	John Sullivan, Coach	.35
☐	Gene Tenace, Coach	.35
☐	CL: The Sky Dome	.35

1990 BLUE JAYS HOSTESS PANELS

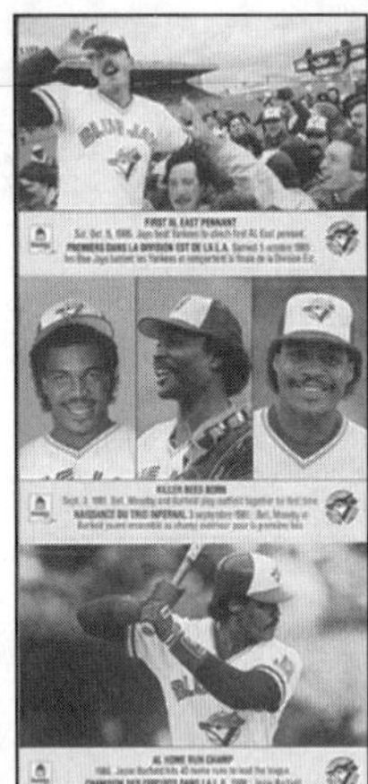

These stickers were issued in packages of Hostess Ding Dongs and Cupcakes.
Panel Size: 7" x 3 5/8"
Sponsor: Hostess

	Complete Set (6 panels):	15.00
	Player	**MINT**
☐	Doyle Alexander/ Bell, Moseby, Barfield/ Jesse Barfield	3.00
☐	Junior Felix/ Dave Stieb/ SkyDome	3.00
☐	Dave Collins/ T. Fernandez; J. Barfield/ Exhibition Goodbye	3.00
☐	Jim Clancy/ Ernie Whitt/ 89 AL East Champs	3.00
☐	Fred McGriff/ Tom Henke/ Jimmy Key	3.00
☐	Damaso Garcia/ George Bell/ Kelly Gruber	3.00

1990 BLUE JAYS VICTORY PRODUCTIONS

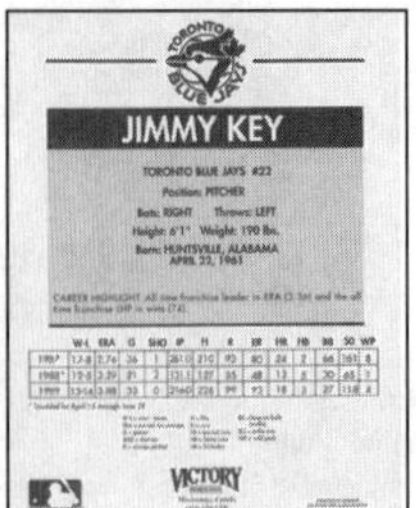

These 8" x 10" poster cards were issued in 1990 as a promotional piece for Victory Productions. We have no pricing information on this set. Other singles may exist.
Card Size: 8" x 10"
Imprint: PRINTED IN CANADA BY ADAM ONE & ASSOCIATES

	Player
☐	George Bell
☐	Jimmy Key
☐	Fred McGriff

1991 BLUE JAYS FIRE SAFETY

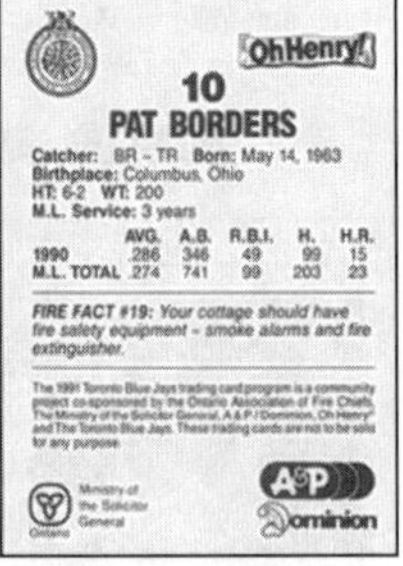

Card Size: 2 1/2" x 3 1/2"
Sponsors: The Ontario Association of Fire Chiefs, the Ministry of the Solicitor General, A & P-Dominion and Oh Henry

	Complete Set (36 cards):	12.00
	Player	**MINT**
☐	Jim Acker	.35
☐	Roberto Alomar	1.00
☐	Pat Borders	.35
☐	Denis Boucher	.50
☐	Joe Carter	1.00
☐	Ken Dayley	.35
☐	Rob Ducey	.50
☐	Rene Gonzales	.35
☐	Kelly Gruber	.35
☐	Tom Henke	.35
☐	Glenallen Hill	.35
☐	Jimmy Key	.75
☐	Manuel Lee	.35
☐	Al Leiter	.35
☐	Rance Mulliniks	.35

	Player	MINT
☐	Greg Myers	.35
☐	John Olerud	1.50
☐	Dave Stieb	.50
☐	Todd Stottlemyre	.35
☐	Pat Tabler	.35
☐	Duane Ward	.35
☐	David Wells	.75
☐	Devon White	.35
☐	Mark Whiten	.35
☐	Kenny Williams	.35
☐	Frank Wills	.35
☐	Mookie Wilson	.35
☐	Cito Gaston, Mgr.	.50
☐	Galen Cisco, Coach	.35
☐	Rich Hacker, Coach	.35
☐	Mike Squires, Coach	.35
☐	John Sullivan, Coach	.35
☐	Gene Tenace, Coach	.35
☐	Hector Torres, Coach	.35
☐	Mascot B.J. Birdy	.35
☐	CL: The All Star Season	.35

1991 BLUE JAYS SCORE

This 40-card set was issued by Score and features members of the Toronto Blue Jays.

Card Size: 2 1/2" x 3 1/2"

Imprint: © 1991 SCORE, PRINTED IN U.S.A.

Complete Set (40 cards): 12.00

	No.	Player	MINT
☐	1	Joe Carter	1.00
☐	2	Tom Henke	.25
☐	3	Jimmy Key	.75
☐	4	Al Leiter	.25
☐	5	Dave Stieb	.50
☐	6	Todd Stottlemyre	.25
☐	7	Mike Timlin	.25
☐	8	Duane Ward	.25
☐	9	David Wells	.75
☐	10	Frank Wills	.25
☐	11	Pat Borders	.25
☐	12	Greg Myers	.25
☐	13	Roberto Alomar	1.00
☐	14	Rene Gonzales	.25
☐	15	Kelly Gruber	.25
☐	16	Manny Lee	.25
☐	17	Rance Mulliniks	.25
☐	18	John Olerud	1.50
☐	19	Pat Tabler	.25
☐	20	Derek Bell	.25
☐	21	Jim Acker	.25
☐	22	Rob Ducey	.50
☐	23	Devon White	.25
☐	24	Mookie Wilson	.25
☐	25	Juan Guzman	.25
☐	26	Ed Sprague	.25
☐	27	Ken Dayley	.25
☐	28	Tom Candiotti	.25
☐	29	Candy Maldonado	.25
☐	30	Eddie Zosky	.25
☐	31	Steve Karsay	.25
☐	32	Bob MacDonald	.25
☐	33	Ray Giannelli	.25
☐	34	Jerry Schunk	.25
☐	35	Dave Weathers	.25
☐	36	Cito Gaston, Mgr.	.50
☐	37	AS: Joe Carter	.75
☐	38	AS: Jimmy Key	.50
☐	39	AS: Roberto Alomar	.75
☐	40	AS: 1991 All-Star Game	.25

1992 BLUE JAYS FIRE SAFETY

Card Size: 2 1/2" x 3 1/2"

Sponsors: The Ontario Association of Fire Chiefs, the Ministry of the Solicitor General, Mac's Milk & Mike's Mart and Oh Henry

Complete Set (36 cards): 12.00

	Player	MINT
☐	Roberto Alomar	1.00
☐	Derek Bell	.35
☐	Pat Borders	.35
☐	Joe Carter	1.00
☐	Ken Dayley	.35
☐	Rob Ducey	.50
☐	Alfredo Griffin	.35
☐	Kelly Gruber	.35
☐	Juan Guzman	.35
☐	Tom Henke	.35
☐	Jimmy Key	.75
☐	Manuel Lee	.35
☐	Bob MacDonald	.35
☐	Candy Maldonado	.35
☐	Jack Morris	.50
☐	Rance Mulliniks	.35
☐	Greg Myers	.35
☐	John Olerud	1.00
☐	Dave Stieb	.50
☐	Todd Stottlemyre	.35
☐	Pat Tabler	.35
☐	Mike Timlin	.35
☐	Duane Ward	.35
☐	Turner Ward	.35
☐	David Wells	.75
☐	Devon White	.35
☐	Dave Winfield	.75
☐	Eddie Zosky	.35
☐	Cito Gaston, Mgr.	.50
☐	Galen Cisco, Coach	.35
☐	Bob Bailor, Coach	.35
☐	Rich Hacker, Coach	.35
☐	Larry Hisle, Coach	.35
☐	John Sullivan, Coach	.35
☐	Gene Tenace, Coach	.35
☐	Checklist	

1993 BLUE JAYS

Card Size: 3 1/2" x 5"
Imprint: © Photography 1993 Barry Colla

Complete Set (15 cards):		10.00
	Player	**MINT**
□	Roberto Alomar	1.50
□	Pat Borders	.75
□	Joe Carter	1.50
□	Juan Guzman	.75
□	Paul Molitor	1.50
□	Dave Stewart	.75
□	Devon White	.75
□	WS: Roberto Alomar	1.50
□	WS: Pat Borders	.75
□	WS: Joe Carter	1.50
□	WS: Juan Guzman	.75
□	WS: Jack Morris	1.00
□	WS: John Olerud	1.00
□	WS: Todd Stottlemyre	.75
□	WS: Devon White	.75

1993 BLUE JAYS DEMPSTER'S

Card Size: 2 1/2" x 3 1/2"
Imprint: © Toronto Blue Jays Baseball Club 1993.

Complete Set (25 cards):			15.00
	No.	**Player**	**MINT**
□	1	Juan Guzman	.50
□	2	Roberto Alomar	1.50
□	3	Danny Cox	.50
□	4	Paul Molitor	1.50
□	5	Todd Stottlemyre	.50
□	6	Joe Carter	1.50
□	7	Jack Morris	.75
□	8	Ed Sprague	.50
□	9	Turner Ward	.50
□	10	John Olerud	1.00
□	11	Duane Ward	.50
□	12	Alfredo Griffin	.50
□	13	Cito Gaston, Mgr.	.75
□	14	Dave Stewart	.50
□	15	Mark Eichhorn	.50
□	16	Darnell Coles	.50
□	17	Randy Knorr	.50
□	18	Al Leiter	.50
□	19	Pat Hentgen	1.50
□	20	Devon White	.50
□	21	Pat Borders	.50
□	22	Darrin Jackson	.50
□	23	Dick Schofield	.50
□	24	Luis Sojo	.50
□	25	Mike Timlin	.50

1993 BLUE JAYS DONRUSS COMMEMORATIVE

Card Size: 2 1/2" x 3 1/2"
Imprint: © 1993 LEAF, INC.

Complete Set (45 cards):			12.00
	No.	**Player**	**MINT**
□	1	Title Card: Checklist	.35
□	2	Roberto Alomar	1.00
□	3	Derek Bell	.35
□	4	Pat Borders	.35
□	5	Joe Carter	1.00
□	6	Alfredo Griffin	.35
□	7	Kelly Gruber	.35
□	8	Manuel Lee	.35
□	9	Candy Maldonado	.35
□	10	John Olerud	.75
□	11	Ed Sprague	.35
□	12	Pat Tabler	.35
□	13	Devon White	.35
□	14	Dave Winfield	.75
□	15	David Cone	.35
□	16	Mark Eichhorn	.35
□	17	Juan Guzman	.35
□	18	Tom Henke	.35
□	19	Jimmy Key	.75
□	20	Jack Morris	.50
□	21	Todd Stottlemyre	.35
□	22	Mike Timlin	.35
□	23	Duane Ward	.35
□	24	David Wells	.75
□	25	Randy Knorr	.35
□	26	Rance Mulliniks	.35
□	27	Tom Quinlin	.35
□	28	Cito Gaston, Mgr.	.50
□	29	Dave Stieb	.50
□	30	Ken Dayley	.35
□	31	Turner Ward	.35
□	32	Eddie Zosky	.35
□	33	Pat Hentgen	1.00
□	34	Al Leiter	.35
□	35	Doug Linton	.35
□	36	Bob MacDonald	.35
□	37	Rick Trlicek	.35

	No.	Player	MINT
☐	38	Domingo Martinez	.35
☐	39	Mike Maksudian	.35
☐	40	Rob Ducey	.50
☐	41	Jeff Kent	.35
☐	42	Greg Myers	.35
☐	43	Dave Weathers	.35
☐	44	SkyDome	.35
☐	45	Trophy Presentation	.35
☐	WS1	HL: Opening of Series	.35
☐	WS2	HL: Game One (Joe Carter)	.50
☐	WS3	HL: Game Two (Derek Bell)	.35
☐	WS4	HL: Game Three (Candy Maldonado)	.35
☐	WS5	HL: Game Four (Jimmy Key)	.50
☐	WS6	HL: Game Five (John Olerud)	.50
☐	WS7	HL: Game Six (Dave Winfield)	.50
☐	WS8	HL: Series MVP (Pat Borders)	.35
☐	WS9	HL: Celebration	.35

1993 BLUE JAYS FIRE SAFETY

Card Size: 2 1/2" x 3 1/2"
Sponsors; The Ontario Association of Fire Chiefs, the Ministry of the Solicitor General of Ontario, Becker's and Oh Henry
Complete Set (35 cards): 12.00

	Player	MINT
☐	Roberto Alomar	1.00
☐	Pat Borders	.35
☐	Joe Carter	1.00
☐	Danny Cox	.35
☐	Darnell Coles	.35
☐	Ken Daley	.35
☐	Alfredo Griffin	.35
☐	Juan Guzman	.35
☐	Pat Hentgen	1.00
☐	Mark Eichhorn	.35
☐	Darren Jackson	.35
☐	Randy Knorr	.35
☐	Al Leiter	.35
☐	Domingo Martinez	.35
☐	Paul Molitor	1.00
☐	John Olerud	.75
☐	Jack Morris	.50
☐	Tom Quinlan	.35
☐	Luis Sojo	.35
☐	Dick Schofield	.35
☐	Todd Stottlemyre	.35
☐	Dave Stewart	.35
☐	Mike Timlin	.35
☐	Ed Sprague	.35
☐	Turner Ward	.35
☐	Devon White	.35
☐	Duane Ward	.35
☐	Eddie Zosky	.35
☐	Cito Gaston, Mgr.	.50
☐	Bob Bailor, Coach	.35
☐	Galen Cisco, Coach	.35
☐	Rich Hacker, Coach	.35
☐	Larry Hisle, Coach	.35
☐	John Sullivan, Coach	.35
☐	Gene Tenace, Coach	.35
☐	Checklist	.35

1993 BLUE JAYS MCDONALD'S

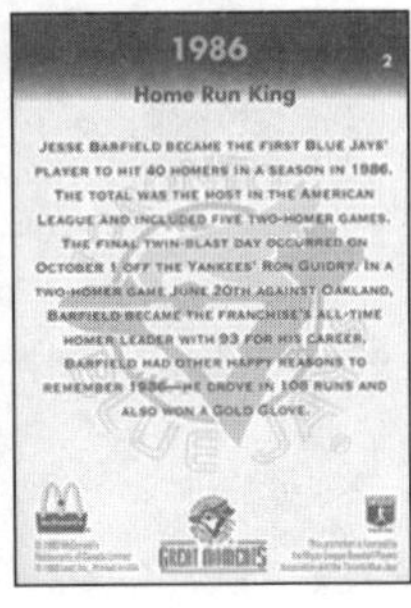

This set features one of two different designs.
Card Size: 2 1/2" x 3 1/2"
Imprint: © 1993 McDonald's Restaurants of Canada Limited, © 1993 Leaf, Inc.
Complete Set (36 cards): 12.00

	No.	Player	MINT
☐	1	1985 First Title	.35
☐	2	1986 Home Run King	.35
☐	3	1987 Major League Home Run Record	.35
☐	4	1988 Opening Bell	.35
☐	5	1989 First Cycle	.35
☐	6	1989 Unbelievable Comeback	.35
☐	7	1989 Winners Again	.35
☐	8	1990 First No-Hitter	.35
☐	9	1992 First 20-Gamer	.35
☐	10	1992 FANtastic	.35
☐	11	1992 Sudden Impact	.35
☐	12	1992 The Turning Point	.35
☐	13	1992 On To Atlanta	.35
☐	14	Ed Sprague - Instant Hero	.35
☐	15	Cito Gaston; Bobby Cox - Old Friends	.35
☐	16	Devon White - The Catch	.35
☐	17	Kelly Gruber - Near Triple Play	.35
☐	18	Roberto Alomar	.35
☐	19	Kelly Gruber - Winning Slide	.35
☐	20	Jimmy Key - Final Farewell	.35
☐	21	Alomar Scores Winning RBI	.35
☐	22	Timlin to Carter - Clincher	.35
☐	23	Blue Jays - World Champions	.35
☐	24	Cito Gaston - Trophy Presentation	.50
☐	25	MVP: Pat Border	.35
☐	26	Parade - Heroes' Welcome	.35
☐	27	John Olerud	.75
☐	28	Roberto Alomar	1.00
☐	29	Ed Sprague	.35
☐	30	Dick Schofield	.35
☐	31	Devon White	.35
☐	32	Joe Carter	1.00
☐	33	Darrin Jackson	.35
☐	34	Pat Borders	.35
☐	35	Paul Molitor	1.00
☐	36	Checklist (1-36)	.35

1994 BLUE JAYS

Four players (*) were available originally only as singles and not part of the set.

Postcard Size: 4" x 6"
Imprint: System 4 Limited
Complete Set (16 cards): 12.00

	Player	MINT
☐	Title card	.50
☐	Roberto Alomar	1.00
☐	Pat Borders	.50
☐	Joe Carter	1.00
☐	Carlos Delgado	2.00
☐	Juan Guzman	.50
☐	Paul Molitor	1.00
☐	John Olerud	.75
☐	Ed Sprague	.50
☐	Devon White	.50
☐	World Series Rings	.50
☐	The 1992 & 1993 World Series Trophies	.50
☐	Pat Hentgen (*)	2.00
☐	Al Leiter (*)	1.00
☐	Dave Stewart (*)	1.00
☐	Duane Ward (*)	1.00

1995 BLUE JAYS OH HENRY

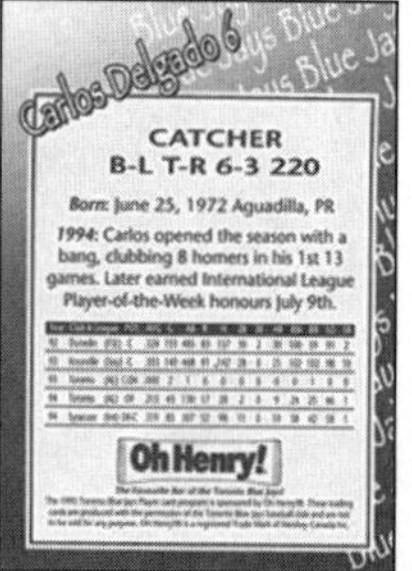

Card Size: 2 1/2" x 3 1/2"
Sponsor: Oh Henry
Complete Set (36 cards): 12.00

	Player	MINT
☐	Roberto Alomar	1.00
☐	Howard Battle	.35
☐	Joe Carter	1.00
☐	Tony Castillo	.35
☐	Domingo Cedeno	.35
☐	David Cone	.35
☐	Brad Cornett	.35
☐	Danny Cox	.35
☐	Tim Crabtree	.35
☐	Carlos Delgado	1.50
☐	Alex Gonzalez	.75
☐	Shawn Green	.75
☐	Juan Guzman	.35
☐	Darren Hall	.35
☐	Pat Hentgen	1.00
☐	Mike Huff	.35
☐	Randy Knorr	.35
☐	Al Leiter	.35
☐	Angel Martinez	.35
☐	Paul Molitor	1.00
☐	John Olerud	.50
☐	Tomas Perez	.35
☐	Aaron Small	.35
☐	Paul Spoljaric	.50
☐	Ed Sprague	.35
☐	Mike Timlin	.35
☐	Duane Ward	.35
☐	Devon White	.35
☐	Woody Williams	.35
☐	Cito Gaston, Mgr.	.50
☐	Bob Bailor, Coach	.35
☐	Galen Cisco, Coach	.35
☐	Larry Hisle, Coach	.35
☐	Dennis Holmberg, Coach	.35
☐	Nick Leyva, Coach	.35
☐	Gene Tenace, Coach	.35

1996 BLUE JAYS OH HENRY

Card Size: 2 1/2" x 3 1/2"
Sponsor: Oh Henry
Complete Set (36 cards): 15.00

	Player	MINT
☐	George Bell	.50
☐	Brian Bohanon	.35
☐	Joe Carter	.75
☐	Tony Castillo	.35
☐	Domingo Cedeno	.35
☐	Tim Crabtree	.35
☐	Felipe Crespo	.35
☐	Carlos Delgado	1.50
☐	Alex Gonzalez	.75
☐	Shawn Green	.75
☐	Kelly Gruber	.35
☐	Juan Guzman	.35
☐	Erik Hanson	.35
☐	Pat Hentgen	.75
☐	Marty Janzen	.35
☐	Sandy Martinez	.35
☐	Lloyd Moseby	.35
☐	Otis Nixon	.35
☐	Charlie O'Brien	.35
☐	John Olerud	.35
☐	Robert Perez	.35
☐	Paul Quantrill	.50
☐	Bill Risley	.35
☐	Juan Samuel	.35
☐	Ed Sprague	.35
☐	Dave Stieb	.35
☐	Mike Timlin	.35
☐	Jeff Ware	.35
☐	Ernie Whitt	.35
☐	Woody Williams	.35
☐	Cito Gaston, Mgr.	.50
☐	Alfredo Griffin, Coach	.35
☐	Nick Leyva, Coach	.35
☐	Mel Queen, Coach	.35
☐	Gene Tenace, Coach	.35
☐	Willie Upshaw, Coach	.35

1997 BLUE JAYS SIZZLER

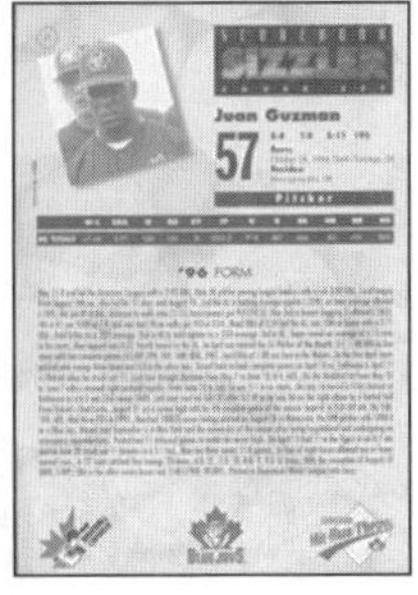

Postcard Size: 4 3/4" x 6 3/4"
Sponsor: Honda

	No.	Player	MINT
Complete Set (60 cards):			**30.00**
Album:			**20.00**
☐	1	Alex Gonzalez	.50
☐	2	Pat Hentgen	.50
☐	3	Joe Carter	1.00
☐	4	Ed Sprague	.50
☐	5	Benito Santiago	.50
☐	6	Roger Clemens	4.00
☐	7	Carlos Garcia	.50
☐	8	Juan Guzman	.50
☐	9	Dan Plesac	.50
☐	10	Carlos Delgado	1.50
☐	11	Orlando Merced	.50
☐	12	Woody Williams	.50
☐	13	Shawn Green	.75
☐	14	Erik Hanson	.50
☐	15	Charlie O'Brien	.50
☐	16	Otis Nixon	.50
☐	17	Paul Spoljaric	.75
☐	18	Jacob Brumfield	.50
☐	19	Mike Timlin	.50
☐	20	Tilson Brito	.50
☐	21	Paul Quantrill	.75
☐	22	Tim Crabtree	.50
☐	23	Jim Lett	.50
☐	24	Cito Gaston, Mgr.	.75
☐	25	Alfredo Griffin, Coach	.50
☐	26	Nick Leyva, Coach	.50
☐	27	Mel Queen, Coach	.50
☐	28	Gene Tenace, Coach	.50
☐	29	Willie Upshaw, Coach	.50
☐	30	Pat Hentgen	1.00
☐	31	Roger Clemens	4.00
☐	32	First Pitcher '77	.50
☐	33	Dave Stieb's No Hitter	.75
☐	34	Moseby/Barfield/Bell	.75
☐	35	'92 World Series	.50
☐	36	'85 Pennant Win	.50
☐	37	MVP: Paul Molitor	1.50
☐	38	Tom Henke & Duane Ward	.50
☐	39	Ernie Whitt	.50
☐	40	WS: Joe Carter	1.00
☐	41	Jack Morris	1.00
☐	42	MVP: Pat Borders	.50
☐	43	Dave Winfield	1.50
☐	44	Damaso Garcia	.50
☐	45	Tony Fernandez	.50
☐	46	Roberto Alomar	.50
☐	47	Dave Stewart	.50
☐	48	Olerud/Molitor/Alomar	1.00
☐	49	Fred McGriff	1.00
☐	50	Kelly Gruber	.50
☐	51	Alex Gonzalez	.75
☐	52	Huck Flener	.50
☐	53	Marty Janzen	.50
☐	54	Sandy Martinez	.50
☐	55	Felipe Crespo	.50
☐	56	Tomas Perez	.50
☐	57	Shannon Stewart	.50
☐	58	Billy Koch	.50
☐	59	Roy Halladay	.50
☐	60	Cris Carpenter	.50

CHAPTER FOUR

MINOR LEAGUE TEAM ISSUES

CALGARY CANNONS

(PACIFIC COAST LEAGUE, AAA)

1985 CANNONS CRAMER

Danny Tartabull is the most expensive single at $2-3. Singles start at 50¢.
Card Size: 2 1/2" x 3 1/2"
Imprint: © 1985 Cramer Sports Promotions
Complete Set (25 cards): 15.00

No.	Player	No.	Player
☐ 76	Karl Best	☐ 77	Jim Lewis
☐ 78	Bobby Floyd, Mgr.	☐ 79	Paul Serna
☐ 80	Al Chambers	☐ 81	Don Scott
☐ 82	Roy Thomas	☐ 83	John Moses
☐ 84	Bobby Cuellar, Coach	☐ 85	Frank Wills
☐ 86	Pat Casey	☐ 87	Dave Tobik
☐ 88	Mickey Brantley	☐ 89	Paul Mirabella
☐ 90	Bob Stoddard	☐ 91	Ricky Nelson
☐ 92	Brian Snyder	☐ 93	Bill Crone
☐ 94	Danny Tartabull	☐ 95	Bob Long
☐ 96	Darnell Coles	☐ 97	Ron Tingley
☐ 98	Rick Luecken	☐ 99	Joe Whitmer
☐ 100	Clay Hill		

1986 CANNONS PROCARDS

Singles start at 35¢.
Card Size: 2 1/2" x 3 1/2"
Imprint: © 1986 ProCards, Inc.
Complete Set (26 cards): 6.00

Player	Player
☐ Greg Bartley	☐ Mickey Brantley
☐ Randy Baun	☐ Pat Casey
☐ Bill Crone	☐ Mario Diaz
☐ Jerry Dybzinski	☐ Steve Fireovid
☐ Dan Firova	☐ Dave Hengel
☐ Clay Hill	☐ Vic Martin
☐ Rich Monteleone	☐ John Moses
☐ Jed Murray	☐ Ricky Nelson
☐ Randy Newman	☐ Jack O'Conner
☐ Jerry Reed	☐ Harold Reynolds
☐ Dave Valle	☐ Bill Wilkinson
☐ Joe Whitmer	☐ Bill Plummer, Mgr.
☐ Ross Grimsley, Coach	☐ Doug Merrifield, Trainer

1987 CANNONS PROCARDS

Edgar Martinez is the most expensive single at $2-3. Singles start at 35¢.
Card Size: 2 1/2" x 3 1/2"
Imprint: 1987 ProCards, Inc.
Complete Set (24 cards): 12.00

No.	Player	No.	Player
☐ 2309	Edgar Martinez	☐ 2310	Mike Watters
☐ 2311	Jim Weaver	☐ 2312	Bill Plummer, Mgr.
☐ 2313	Ross Grimsley, Coach	☐ 2314	Dennis Powell
☐ 2315	Mike Brown	☐ 2316	Paul Schneider
☐ 2317	Dave Hengel	☐ 2318	Karl Best
☐ 2319	Mario Diaz	☐ 2320	Brick Smith
☐ 2321	Roy Thomas	☐ 2322	Mike Campbell
☐ 2323	Randy Braun	☐ 2324	Mike Wishnevski
☐ 2325	Terry Taylor	☐ 2326	Stan Clarke
☐ 2327	Donell Nixon	☐ 2328	Tony Ferreira
☐ 2329	Jerry Narron	☐ 2330	Dave Gallagher
☐ 2331	Doug Gwosdz	☐ 2332	Rich Monteleone

1988 CANNONS CMC

Edgar Martinez is the most expensive single at $1-2. Singles start at 35¢.
Card Size: 2 1/2" x 3 1/2"
Imprint:
Complete Set (25 cards): 6.00

No.	Player	No.	Player
☐ 1	Darren Burroughs	☐ 2	Paul Schneider
☐ 3	Rich Monteleone	☐ 4	Dennis Powell
☐ 5	Jay Baller	☐ 6	Mike Christ
☐ 7	Jim Walker	☐ 8	Matt West
☐ 9	Mike Schooler	☐ 10	Rod Scurry
☐ 11	Donnell Nixon	☐ 12	Phil Ouellette
☐ 13	Greg Briley	☐ 14	Dave Cochrane
☐ 15	Brian Giles	☐ 16	Edgar Martinez
☐ 17	John Christensen	☐ 18	Dave Hengel
☐ 19	Nelson Simmons	☐ 20	Mike Wishnevski
☐ 21	Roger Hansen	☐ 22	Doug Merrifield, Trainer
☐ 23	Mike Watters	☐ 24	Bill Plummer, Mgr.
☐ 25	Dan Warthen, Coach		

1988 CANNONS PROCARDS

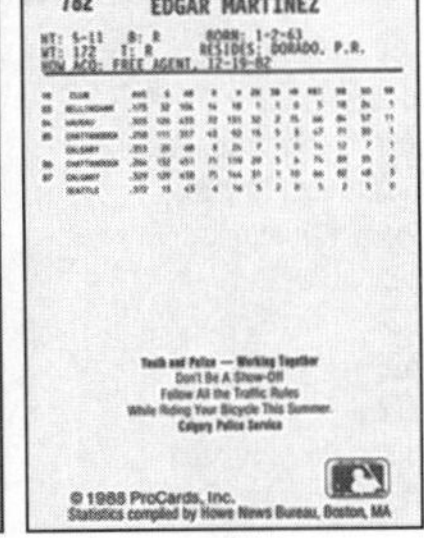

Edgar Martinez is the most expensive single at $1-2. Singles start at 35¢.
Card Size: 2 1/2" x 3 1/2"
Imprint: © 1988 ProCards, Inc.
Complete Set (28 cards): 8.00

No.	Player	No.	Player
☐ no#	Checklist	☐ 779	Rod Scurry
☐ 780	Darren Burroughs	☐ 781	Terry Taylor
☐ 782	Edgar Martinez	☐ 783	Mike Wishnevski
☐ 784	Brian Giles	☐ 785	Dave Cochrane
☐ 786	Erik Hanson	☐ 787	Doug Merrifield, Trainer
☐ 788	Matt West	☐ 789	Dan Warthen, Coach
☐ 790	Roger Hansen	☐ 791	Jim Walker
☐ 792	Jay Baller	☐ 793	Paul Schneider
☐ 794	John Christensen	☐ 795	Mike Schooler
☐ 796	Dennis Powell	☐ 797	Rich Monteleone
☐ 798	Mike Watters	☐ 799	Greg Briley
☐ 800	Bill Plummer	☐ 801	Phil Ouellette
☐ 802	Nelson Simmons	☐ 803	Brick Smith
☐ 804	Mario Diaz	☐ 1550	Dave Hengel

1989 CANNONS CMC

Jay Buhner is the most expensive single at $2-3. Singles start at 35¢.
Card Size: 2 1/2" x 3 1/2"
Imprint:
Complete Set (25 cards): 8.00

No.	Player	No.	Player
☐ 1	Luis DeLeon	☐ 2	Chuck Hensley

	No.	Player		No.	Player
☐	3	Colin McLaughlin	☐	4	Steve Oliverio
☐	5	Reggie Dobie	☐	6	Bill Wilkinson
☐	7	Rich Doyle	☐	8	Jeff Hull
☐	9	Bryan Price	☐	10	Glenn Spagnola
☐	11	Clint Zavaras	☐	12	Dan Boever
☐	13	Jay Buhner, Error (© 1988)	☐	14	Dave Cochrane
☐	15	Roger Hansen	☐	16	Paul Noce
☐	17	Jim Bowie	☐	18	Joe Dunlap
☐	19	Bruce Fields	☐	20	Mike Kingery
☐	21	Bill McGuire	☐	22	Jim Wilson
☐	23	Omar Vizquel			
☐	24	Rich Morales, Mgr., Error (© 1988)			
☐	25	Dan Warthen, Coach, Error (© 1988)			

1989 CANNONS PROCARDS

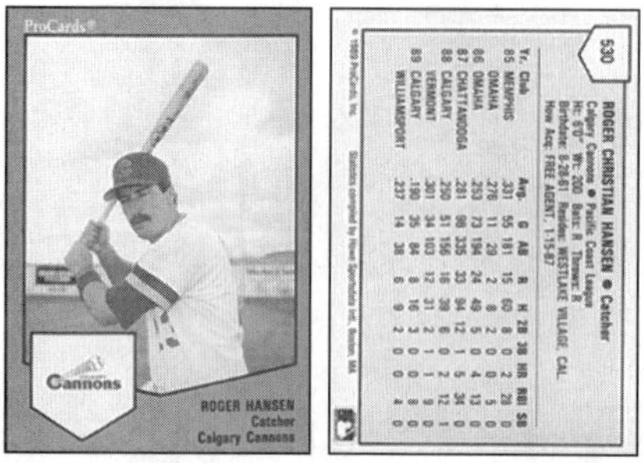

Jay Buhner is the most expensive single at $2-3. Singles start at 35¢.

Card Size: 2 1/2" x 3 1/2"

Imprint: © 1989 ProCards, Inc.

Complete Set (24 cards): 8.00

	No.	Player		No.	Player
☐	522	Checklist	☐	523	Dan Warthen, Coach
☐	524	Greg Fulton	☐	525	Jim Bowie
☐	526	Jeff Hull	☐	527	Glenn Spagnola
☐	528	Reggie Dobie	☐	529	Joe Dunlap
☐	530	Roger Hansen	☐	531	Chuck Hensley
☐	532	Colin McLaughlin	☐	533	Bill McGuire
☐	534	Bruce Fields	☐	535	Dan Boever
☐	536	Jim Wilson	☐	537	Omar Vizquel
☐	538	Rich Morales, Mgr.	☐	539	Paul Noce
☐	540	Bryan Price	☐	541	Rich Doyle
☐	542	Dave Cochrane	☐	543	Steve Oliverio
☐	544	Jay Buhner	☐	545	Mike Kingery

1990 CANNONS CMC

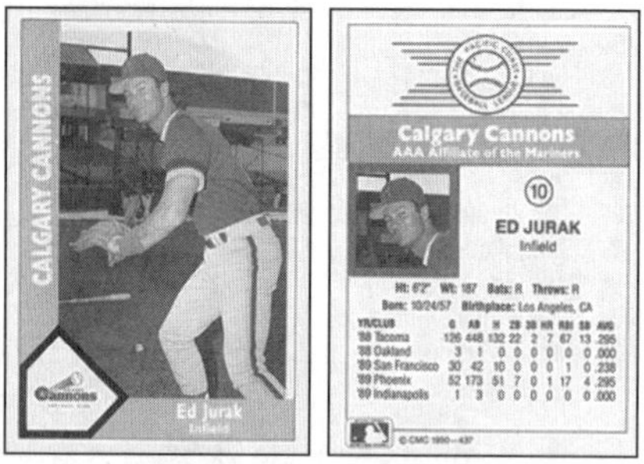

Tino Martinez is the most expensive single at $3-4. Singles start at 35¢.

Card Size: 2 1/2" x 3 1/2"

Imprint: © CMC 1990

Complete Set (25 cards): 10.00

	No.	Player		No.	Player
☐	1	Pat Pacillo	☐	2	Tony Blasucci
☐	3	Mike Walker	☐	4	Pat Rice
☐	5	Terry Taylor	☐	6	Dave Burba
☐	7	Vance Lovelace	☐	8	Ed Vande Berg
☐	9	Greg Fulton	☐	10	Ed Jurak
☐	11	Dave Cochrane	☐	12	Tino Martinez
☐	13	Matt Sinatro	☐	14	Bill McGuire
☐	15	Mickey Brantley	☐	16	Tom Dodd
☐	17	Jim Weaver	☐	18	Todd Haney
☐	19	Casey Close	☐	20	Theo Shaw
☐	21	Keith Helton	☐	22	Jose Melendez
☐	23	Tom Jones, Mgr.	☐	24	Dan Warthen, Coach
☐	25	Randy Roetter, Trainer			

1990 CANNONS PROCARDS

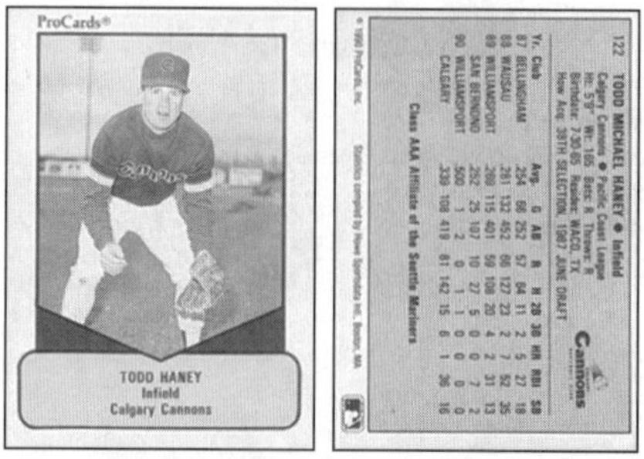

Tino Martinez is the most expensive single at $2-3. Singles start at 35¢.

Card Size: 2 1/2" x 3 1/2"

Imprint: © 1990 ProCards, Inc.

Complete Set (23 cards): 8.00

	No.	Player		No.	Player
☐	643	Checklist	☐	644	Tony Blasucci
☐	645	Dave Burba	☐	646	Keith Helton
☐	647	Vance Lovelace	☐	648	Jose Melendez
☐	649	Pat Pacillo	☐	650	Pat Rice
☐	651	Terry Taylor	☐	652	Mike Walker
☐	653	Bill McGuire	☐	654	Matt Sinatro
☐	655	Mario Diaz	☐	656	Greg Fulton
☐	657	Todd Haney	☐	658	Ed Jurak
☐	659	Tino Martinez	☐	660	Jeff Schaefer
☐	661	Casey Close	☐	662	Tom Dodd
☐	663	Jim Weaver	☐	664	Tommy Jones, Mgr.
☐	665	Dan Warthen, Coach			

1991 CANNONS LINE DRIVE

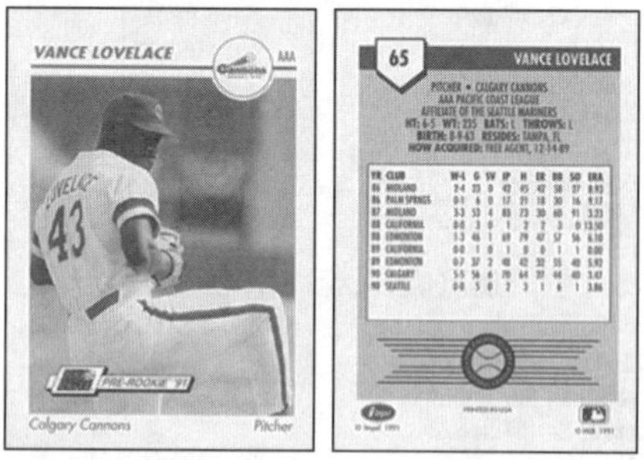

Tino Martinez is the most expensive single at $0.50-1.00. Singles start at 20¢.

Card Size: 2 1/2" x 3 1/2"

Imprint: © Impel 1991

Complete Set (26 cards): 5.00

	No.	Player		No.	Player
☐	no#	Calgary Cannons	☐	51	Rich Amaral
☐	52	Rick Balabon	☐	53	Dave Brundage

☐	54	Dave Burba	☐	55	Dave Cochrane
☐	56	Alan Cockrell	☐	57	Mike Cook
☐	58	Keith Helton	☐	59	Dennis Hood
☐	60	Chris Howard	☐	61	Chuck Jackson
☐	62	Calvin Jones	☐	63	Pat Lennon
☐	64	Shane Letterio	☐	65	Vance Lovelace
☐	66	Tino Martinez	☐	67	John Mitchell
☐	68	Dennis Powell	☐	69	Alonzo Powell
☐	70	Pat Rice	☐	71	Ricky Rojas
☐	72	Steve Springer	☐	73	Ed Vande Berg
☐	74	Keith Bodie, Mgr.	☐	75	Ross Grimsley, Coach

1991 CANNONS PROCARDS

Tino Martinez is the most expensive single at $0.75-1.50. Singles start at 25¢.
Card Size: 2 1/2" x 3 1/2"
Imprint: © 1991 ProCards, Inc.
Complete Set (25 cards): 5.00

	No.	Player		No.	Player
☐	508	Rick Balabon	☐	509	Dave Burba
☐	510	Keith Helton	☐	511	Calvin Jones
☐	512	Vance Lovelace	☐	513	John Mitchell
☐	514	Dennis Powell	☐	515	Pat Rice
☐	516	Ricky Rojas	☐	517	Ed Vande Berg
☐	518	Dave Cochrane	☐	519	Chris Howard
☐	520	Rich Amaral	☐	521	Chuck Jackson
☐	522	Shane Letterio	☐	523	Tino Martinez
☐	524	Steve Springer	☐	525	Dave Brundage
☐	526	Alan Cockrell	☐	527	Dennis Hood
☐	528	Pat Lennon	☐	529	Alonzo Powell
☐	531	Ross Grimsley, Coach	☐	532	Checklist
☐	2649	Keith Bodie, Mgr.			

1992 CANNONS FLEER/PROCARDS

Singles start at 35¢.
Card Size: 2 1/2" x 3 1/2"
Imprint: none
Complete Set (22 cards): 5.00

	No.	Player		No.	Player
☐	3726	Kevin Brown	☐	3727	Mark Grant
☐	3728	Jim Newlin	☐	3729	Mike Remlinger
☐	3730	Pat Rice	☐	3731	Ed Vande Berg
☐	3732	Mike Walker	☐	3733	Kerry Woodson
☐	3734	Bill Haselman	☐	3735	Chris Howard
☐	3736	Greg Pirkl	☐	3737	Rich Amaral
☐	3738	Kent Anderson	☐	3739	Mike Blowers
☐	3740	Bret Boone	☐	3741	Shane Turner
☐	3742	Dave Brundage	☐	3743	John Moses
☐	3744	Jeff Wetherby	☐	3745	Keith Bodie, Mgr.
☐	3746	Ross Grimsley, Coach	☐	3747	Checklist

1992 CANNONS SKYBOX

Singles start at 25¢.
Card Size: 2 1/2" x 3 1/2"
Imprint: © 1992 SKYBOX
Complete Set (26 cards): 5.00

	No.	Player		No.	Player
☐	no#	Checklist	☐	51	Roger Salkeld
☐	52	Kevin Brown	☐	53	Shawn Barton
☐	54	Mike Blowers	☐	55	Bret Boone
☐	56	Jim Bowie	☐	57	Dave Brundage
☐	58	Mario Diaz	☐	59	Andy Hawkins
☐	60	Bret Hefferman	☐	61	Chris Howard
☐	62	Randy Kramer	☐	63	John Moses
☐	64	Pat Lennon	☐	65	Jose Nunez
☐	66	Alonzo Powell	☐	67	Clay Parker
☐	68	Mike Remlinger	☐	69	Pat Rice
☐	70	Dave Schmidt	☐	71	Shane Turner
☐	72	Jim Newlin	☐	73	Clint Zavaras
☐	74	Keith Bodie, Mgr.	☐	75	Ross Grimsley, Coach

1993 CANNONS FLEER PROCARDS

Singles start at 25¢.
Card Size: 2 1/2" x 3 1/2"
Imprint: © 1993 FLEER CORP.
Complete Set (23 cards): 5.00

	No.	Player		No.	Player
☐	1156	Shawn Barton	☐	1157	Kevin Coffman
☐	1158	Jim Converse	☐	1159	Mark Czarkowski
☐	1160	Eric Gunderson	☐	1161	Brad Holman
☐	1162	Troy Kent	☐	1163	Lance McCullers
☐	1164	Rob Parkins	☐	1165	Dennis Powell
☐	1166	Mike Remlinger	☐	1167	Mike Walker
☐	1168	Brian Deak	☐	1169	Bert Hefferman
☐	1170	Chris Howard	☐	1171	Greg Litton
☐	1172	Anthony Manahan	☐	1173	Greg Pirkl
☐	1174	Jack Smith	☐	1175	Brian Turang
☐	1176	Shane Turner	☐	1177	Dann Howitt
☐	1178	Carmelo Martinez	☐	1179	Tow Maynard
☐	1180	Aubrey Waggoner	☐	1181	Keith Bodie, Mgr.
☐	1182	Dave Brundage, Coach	☐	1183	Ross Grimsley, Coach
☐	1184	Checklist			

1994 CANNONS FLEER PROCARDS

Singles start at 25¢.
Card Size: 2 1/2" x 3 1/2"
Imprint:
Complete Set (27 cards): 5.00

	No.	Player		No.	Player
☐	781	Todd Burns	☐	782	Jim Converse
☐	783	Jeff Darwin	☐	784	Brad Holman
☐	785	Bob MacDonald	☐	786	Tony Phillips
☐	787	Bill Risley	☐	788	Roger Salkeld
☐	789	Alex Sanchez	☐	790	Weston Weber
☐	791	Jeff Williams	☐	792	Clint Zavaras
☐	793	Chris Howard	☐	794	Jerry Willard
☐	795	Tommy Hinzo	☐	796	Tommy LeVasseur
☐	797	Anthony Manahan	☐	798	Luis Quinones
☐	799	Luis Sojo	☐	800	Dale Sveum
☐	801	Quinn Mack	☐	802	Marc Newfield
☐	803	John Tejcek	☐	804	Steve Smith, Mgr.
☐	805	Dave Brundage, Coach	☐	806	Bobby Cueller, Coach
☐	807	Checklist			

1997 CANNONS BEST

Ron Wright is the most expensive single at $20. Singles start at 50¢.
Card Size: 2 1/2" x 3 1/2"
Imprint:
Complete Set (30 cards): 30.00

	No.	Player		No.	Player
☐	1	Trent Jewett, Mgr.	☐	2	Ben Oglivie, Coach
☐	3	Dave Rajsich, Coach	☐	4	Sandy Krum, Trainer
☐	5	Jimmy Anderson	☐	6	Tony Beasley
☐	7	Blaine Beatty	☐	8	Joe Boever
☐	9	John Carter	☐	10	Lou Collier
☐	11	Tim Edge	☐	12	Frank Gonzales
☐	13	Jeff Granger	☐	14	Barry Johnson
☐	15	Sean Lawrence	☐	16	Billy Lott
☐	17	Manny Martinez	☐	18	Tim Marx
☐	19	Ramon Morel	☐	20	Kevin Polcovich
☐	21	Chance Sanford	☐	22	Reed Secrist
☐	23	Curtis Shaw	☐	24	Jose Silva
☐	25	T.J. Staton	☐	26	Scott Taylor
☐	27	Jose Tolentino	☐	28	Turner Ward
☐	29	Gary Wilson	☐	30	Ron Wright

EDMONTON TRAPPPERS

(PACIFIC COAST LEAGUE, AAA)

1981 TRAPPERS RED ROOSTER

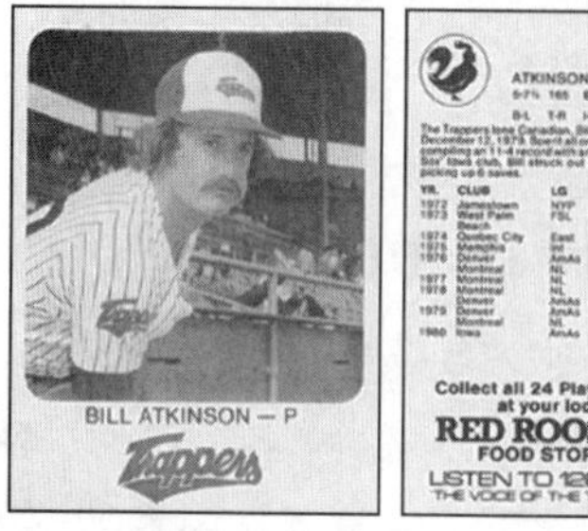

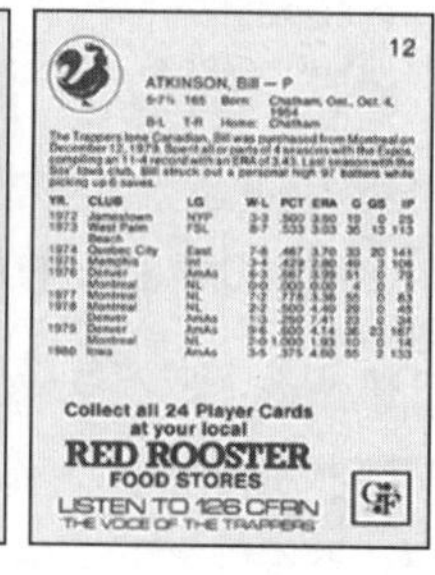

Bill Atkinson is the most expensive single at $1-2. Singles start at 50¢.

Card Size: 2 3/4" x 3 5/8"

Sponsors: Red Rooster, 126 CFRN

Complete Set (24 cards): 12.00

	No.	Player		No.	Player
☐	1	Gary Holle	☐	2	John Poff
☐	3	Dan Williams	☐	4	Nardi Contreras
☐	5	Juan Agosto	☐	6	Guy Hoffman
☐	7	Chris Nyman	☐	8	Gord Lund, Mgr.
☐	9	Vern Thomas	☐	10	Rich Barnes
☐	11	John Flannery	☐	12	Bill Atkinson
☐	13	Hector Eduardo	☐	14	Leo Sutherland
☐	15	Ray Murillo	☐	16	Joe Gates
☐	17	Julio Perez	☐	18	Marv Foley
☐	19	Mike Colbern	☐	20	Fran Mullins
☐	21	Rod Allen	☐	22	Reggie Patterson
☐	23	Jay Loviglio		24	Mark Teutsch

1982 TRAPPERS TCMA

Singles start at 75¢.

Card Size: 2 1/2" x 3 1/2"

Imprint:

Complete Set (25 cards): 18.00

	No.	Player		No.	Player
☐	1	Carlos Ibarra	☐	2	Jose Castro
☐	3	Jim Slwy	☐	4	Steve Dillard
☐	5	Chris Nyman	☐	6	Guy Hoffman
☐	7	Keith Disjalais	☐	8	Jay Loviglio
☐	9	Fran Mullins	☐	10	Lorenzo Gray
☐	11	Leo Sutherland	☐	12	Woody Agosto
☐	13	Ron Kittle	☐	14	Nardi Contreras, Coach
☐	15	Reggie Patterson	☐	16	David Hogg
☐	17	Len Bradley	☐	18	Dom Fucci
☐	19	Rich Barnes	☐	20	Rusty Kuntz
☐	21	Rick Seilheimer	☐	22	Gordy Lund, Mgr.
☐	23	Geoff Combe	☐	24	Dave Grossman, Trainer
☐	25	Jeff Schattinger			

1984 TRAPPERS CRAMER

Singles start at 50¢.

Card Size: 2 1/2" x 3 1/2"

Imprint:

Complete Set (26 cards): 10.00

	No.	Player		No.	Player
☐	97	Moose Stubing, Mgr.	☐	98	Tim Krauss
☐	99	Angel Moreno	☐	100	Marty Kain
☐	101	Sap Randall	☐	102	Rick Steirer
☐	103	Dave Wayne Smith	☐	104	Rick Adams
☐	105	Craig Gerber	☐	106	Steven Finch
☐	107	Steve Liddle	☐	108	Chris Clark
☐	109	Darrell Miller	☐	110	Bill Mooneyham
☐	111	Doug Corbett	☐	112	Steve Lubratich
☐	113	Stewart Cliburn	☐	114	Mike Browning
☐	115	Joe Simpson	☐	116	Reggie West
☐	117	Mike Brown	☐	118	Pat Keedy
☐	119	Jay Kibble	☐	120	Ed Ott, Coach
☐	242	Frank Reberger, Coach	☐	249	Steve Lubratich

1985 TRAPPERS CRAMER

The most expensive singles are Wally Joyner at $4-5 and Kirk McCaskill at $2-3. Singles start at 50¢.

Card Size: 2 1/2" x 3 1/2"

Imprint: © 1985 Cramer Sports Promotions

Complete Set (25 cards): 18.00

	No.	Player		No.	Player
☐	1	Pat Keedy	☐	2	Wally Joyner
☐	3	Mike Madril	☐	4	Bob Grich
☐	5	Scott Oliver	☐	6	TonyLynn Mack
☐	7	Kirk McCaskill	☐	8	Reggie West
☐	9	Rafael Lugo	☐	10	James Randall
☐	11	Marty Kain	☐	12	Gus Polidor
☐	13	Steve Liddle	☐	14	Winston Llenas, Mgr.
☐	15	Bob Ramos	☐	16	Dave Smith
☐	17	Tim Krauss	☐	18	Chris Clark
☐	19	Stewart Cliburn	☐	20	Curt Kaufman
☐	21	Bob Bastian	☐	22	Norman Carrasco
☐	23	Frank Reberger, Coach	☐	24	Jack Howell
☐	25	Al Romero			

1986 TRAPPERS PROCARDS

Devon White is the most expensive single at $2-3. Singles start at 35¢.

Card Size: 2 1/2" x 3 1/2"

Imprint: © 1986 ProCards, Inc.

Complete Set (27 cards): 10.00

	Player		Player
☐	Bob Bastian	☐	Norman Carrasco
☐	Ray Chadwick	☐	Bob Clark
☐	Stan Cliburn	☐	Stewart Cliburn
☐	Steven Finch	☐	Todd Fischer
☐	Tony Fossas	☐	Alan Fowlkes
☐	Craig Gerber	☐	Chris Green
☐	Jack Howell	☐	Pat Keedy
☐	Steven Liddle	☐	Rufino Linares
☐	Tony Lynn Mack	☐	Reggie Montgomery
☐	Gus Polidor	☐	Al Romero
☐	Mark Ryal	☐	Dave Wayne Smith
☐	Devon White	☐	Stan Cliburn/ Stewart Cliburn0
☐	Winston Llenas, Mgr.	☐	Frank Reberger, Coach
☐	Leonard Garcia, Trainer		

1987 TRAPPERS PROCARDS

Singles start at 35¢.

Card Size: 2 1/2" x 3 1/2"

Imprint: © 1987 ProCards, Inc.

Complete Set (23 cards): 6.00

No.	Player	No.	Player
☐ 2061	Jim Eppard	☐ 2062	Jack Lazorko
☐ 2063	David Heath	☐ 2064	Bob Miscik
☐ 2065	Dave Shipanoff, Error (Shippanof)	☐ 2066	Mike Ramsey, Coach
☐ 2067	Doug Banning	☐ 2068	Kevin King
☐ 2069	Allen Morelock	☐ 2070	Tack Wilson
☐ 2071	Ed Amelung	☐ 2072	Tom Kotchman, Mgr.
☐ 2073	Pete Coachman	☐ 2074	Bill Merrifield
☐ 2075	Richard Zaleski, Trainer	☐ 2076	James Randall
☐ 2077	Frank Reberger, Coach	☐ 2078	Sherman Corbett
☐ 2079	Norman Carrasco	☐ 2080	Tony Fossas
☐ 2081	T.R. Bryden	☐ 2082	Terry Clark
☐ 2083	Jack Fimple		

1988 TRAPPERS CMC

Dante Bichette is the most expensive single at $2-3. Singles start at 35¢.

Card Size: 2 1/2" x 3 1/2"

Imprint:

Complete Set (25 cards): 10.00

No.	Player	No.	Player
☐ 1	Terry Clark	☐ 2	Mike Cook
☐ 3	Jack Lazorko	☐ 4	Vance Lovelace
☐ 5	Bryan Harvey	☐ 6	Urbano Lugo
☐ 7	Joe Johnson	☐ 8	Philipo Venturino
☐ 9	Marty Reed	☐ 10	Barry Dacus
☐ 11	Miguel Alicea	☐ 12	Darrell Miller
☐ 13	Pete Coachman	☐ 14	Stan Holmes
☐ 15	Bob Miscik	☐ 16	Brian Brady
☐ 17	Kent Anderson	☐ 18	Doug Davis
☐ 19	Edwin Marquez	☐ 20	Joe Redfield
☐ 21	Jim Eppard	☐ 22	Tom Kotchman, Mgr.
☐ 23	Dante Bichette	☐ 24	Mark Doran
☐ 25	Kevin King		

1988 TRAPPERS PROCARDS

Dante Bichette is the most expensive single at $4-5. Singles start at 35¢.

Card Size: 2 1/2" x 3 1/2"

Imprint: © 1988 ProCards, Inc.

Complete Set (31 cards): 15.00

No.	Player	No.	Player
☐ no#	Checklist	☐ 555	Joe Redfield
☐ 556	Jack Lazorko	☐ 557	Vance Lovelace
☐ 558	Jim Eppard	☐ 559	Doug Davis
☐ 560	Joe Johnson	☐ 561	Chico Walker
☐ 562	Marty Reed	☐ 563	Chuck Hernandez
☐ 564	Junior Noboa	☐ 565	Frank Dimechele
☐ 566	Philipo Venturino	☐ 567	Mike Cook
☐ 568	Barry Dacus	☐ 569	Terry Clark
☐ 570	Mark Doran	☐ 571	Stan Holmes
☐ 572	Brian Brady	☐ 573	Kevin King
☐ 574	Kent Anderson	☐ 575	Edwin Marquez
☐ 576	Dante Bichette	☐ 577	Bob Miscik
☐ 578	Pete Coachman	☐ 579	Darrell Miller
☐ 580	Tom Kotchman, Mgr.	☐ 581	Urbano Lugo
☐ 582	Miguel Alicea	☐ 583	Craig Gerber
☐ 584	Al Olson, Trainer		

1989 TRAPPERS CMC

Singles start at 35¢.

Card Size: 2 1/2" x 3 1/2"

Imprint:

Complete Set (25 cards): 6.00

No.	Player	No.	Player
☐ 1	Jack Lazorko	☐ 2	Rich Monteleone
☐ 3	Carl Willis	☐ 4	Cliff Young
☐ 5	Tim Burcham	☐ 6	Colin Charland
☐ 7	Stewart Cliburn	☐ 8	Sherman Corbett
☐ 9	Mike Fetters	☐ 10	Colby Ward
☐ 11	Stan Holmes	☐ 12	Pete Coachman
☐ 13	Edwin Marquez	☐ 14	Jim Eppard
☐ 15	Doug Davis	☐ 16	Mike Ramsey, Coach
☐ 17	Kent Anderson	☐ 18	Mike Brown
☐ 19	Jamie Nelson	☐ 20	Jeff Manto
☐ 21	Lee Stevens	☐ 22	Jim Thomas
☐ 23	Max Venable	☐ 24	Chuck Hernandez, Coach
☐ 25	Tom Kotchman, Mgr.		

1989 TRAPPERS PROCARDS

Singles start at 35¢.

Card Size: 2 1/2" x 3 1/2"

Imprint: © 1989 ProCards, Inc.

Complete Set (25 cards): 6.00

No.	Player	No.	Player
☐ 546	Checklist	☐ 547	Sherman Corbett
☐ 548	Jim Eppard	☐ 549	Tom Kotchman
☐ 550	Jim Thomas	☐ 551	Doug Davis
☐ 552	Edwin Marquez	☐ 553	Tim Burcham
☐ 554	Lee Stevens	☐ 555	Stan Holmes
☐ 556	Max Venable	☐ 557	Cliff Young
☐ 558	Mike Brown	☐ 559	Vance Lovelace
☐ 560	Don McGann, Trainer	☐ 561	Mike Ramsey, Coach
☐ 562	Chuck Hernandez, Coach	☐ 563	Pete Coachman
☐ 564	Rich Monteleone	☐ 565	Colin Charland
☐ 566	Stewart Cliburn	☐ 567	Carl Willis
☐ 568	Colby Ward	☐ 569	Jamie Nelson
☐ 570	Jeff Manto		

1990 TRAPPERS CMC

Singles start at 35¢.

Card Size: 2 1/2" x 3 1/2"

Imprint: © CMC 1990

Complete Set (24 cards): 6.00

No.	Player	No.	Player
☐ 1	Cliff Young	☐ 2	Max Oliveras, Mgr.
☐ 3	Gary Buckels	☐ 4	Chris Beasley
☐ 4	Tim Burcham	☐ 5	Sherman Corbett
☐ 6	Mike Erb	☐ 7	Mike Fetters
☐ 8	Chuck Hernandez, Coach	☐ 9	Jeff Heathcock
☐ 10	Scott Lewis	☐ 11	Rafael Montalvo
☐ 12	John Skurla	☐ 13	Lee Stevens
☐ 14	Nelson Rood	☐ 15	Bobby Rose

No.	Player	No.	Player
☐ 16	Dan Grunhard	☐ 17	Reed Peters
☐ 18	Doug Davis	☐ 19	Gary DiSarcina
☐ 20	Pete Coachman	☐ 21	Chris Cron
☐ 22	Karl Allaire	☐ 23	Ron Tingley

1990 TRAPPERS PROCARDS

Singles start at 35¢.
Card Size: 2 1/2" x 3 1/2"
Imprint: © 1990 ProCards, Inc.
Complete Set (25 cards): 5.00

No.	Player	No.	Player
☐ 508	Checklist	☐ 509	Chris Beasley
☐ 510	Gary Buckels	☐ 511	Tim Burchman
☐ 512	Sherman Corbett	☐ 513	Mike Erb
☐ 514	Mike Fetters	☐ 515	Jeff Heatchock
☐ 516	Scott Lewis	☐ 517	Rafael Montalvo
☐ 518	Cliff Young	☐ 519	Doug Davis
☐ 520	Ron Tingley	☐ 521	Karl Allaire
☐ 522	Pete Coachman	☐ 523	Chris Cron
☐ 524	Gary DiSarcina	☐ 525	Nelson Rood
☐ 526	Bobby Rose	☐ 527	Lee Stevens
☐ 528	Dan Grunhard	☐ 529	Reed Peters
☐ 530	John Skurla	☐ 531	Max Oliveras, Mgr.
☐ 532	Chuck Hernandez, Coach		

1991 TRAPPERS LINE DRIVE

Singles start at 20¢.
Card Size: 2 1/2" x 3 1/2"
Imprint: © Impel 1991
Complete Set (26 cards): 4.00

No.	Player	No.	Player
☐ no#	Edmonton Trappers	☐ 151	Kyle Abbott
☐ 152	Ruben Amaro	☐ 153	Kent Anderson
☐ 154	Mike Erb	☐ 155	Randy Bockus
☐ 156	Gary Buckels	☐ 157	Tim Burcham
☐ 158	Chris Cron	☐ 159	Chad Curtis
☐ 160	Doug Davis	☐ 161	Mark Davis
☐ 162	Gary DiSarcina	☐ 163	Mike Fetters
☐ 164	Joe Grahe	☐ 165	Dan Grunhard
☐ 166	Dave Leiper	☐ 167	Rafael Montalvo
☐ 168	Reed Peters	☐ 169	Bobby Rose
☐ 170	Lee Stevens	☐ 171	Ron Tingley
☐ 172	Ed Vosberg	☐ 173	Mark Wasinger
☐ 174	Max Oliveras, Mgr.	☐ 175	Coaches: L. Sakata/ G. Ruby

1991 TRAPPERS PROCARDS

Singles start at 25¢.
Card Size: 2 1/2" x 3 1/2"
Imprint: © 1991 ProCards, Inc.
Complete Set (28 cards): 5.00

No.	Player	No.	Player
☐ 1507	Kyle Abbott	☐ 1508	Chris Beasley
☐ 1509	Gary Buckels	☐ 1510	Tim Burchman
☐ 1511	Mike Erb	☐ 1512	Mike Fetters
☐ 1513	Joe Grahe	☐ 1514	Dave Leiper
☐ 1515	Rafael Montalvo	☐ 1516	Ed Vosberg
☐ 1517	Cliff Young	☐ 1518	Doug Davis
☐ 1519	Ron Tingley	☐ 1520	Kent Anderson
☐ 1521	Chris Cron	☐ 1522	Chad Curtis
☐ 1523	Gary DiSarcina	☐ 1524	Bobby Rose
☐ 1525	Mark Wasinger	☐ 1526	Ruben Amaro
☐ 1527	Mark Davis	☐ 1528	Dan Grunhard
☐ 1529	Reed Peters	☐ 1530	Lee Stevens
☐ 1531	Max Oliveras, Mgr.	☐ 1532	Gary Ruby, Coach
☐ 1533	Lenn Sakata, Coach	☐ 1534	Checklist

1992 TRAPPERS FLEER PROCARDS

Tim Salmon is the most expensive single at $1-2. Singles start at 35¢.
Card Size: 2 1/2" x 3 1/2"
Imprint: none
Complete Set (24 cards): 8.00

No.	Player	No.	Player
☐ 3533	Chris Beasley	☐ 3534	Mike Butcher
☐ 3535	Tim Fortugno	☐ 3536	Willie Fraser
☐ 3537	Scott Lewis	☐ 3538	John Pawlowski
☐ 3539	Ray Searage	☐ 3540	Don Vidmar
☐ 3541	Mick Billmeyer	☐ 3542	Larry Gonzalez
☐ 3543	Don Barbara	☐ 3544	Damion Easley
☐ 3545	Kevin Flora	☐ 3546	Ramon Martinez
☐ 3547	Ken Oberkfell	☐ 3548	Ty Van Burkleo
☐ 3549	Mark Wasinger	☐ 3550	Phil Bradley
☐ 3551	Tim Salmon	☐ 3552	Reggie Williams
☐ 3553	Max Oliveras, Mgr.	☐ 3554	Gary Ruby, Coach
☐ 3555	Lenn Sakata, Coach	☐ 3556	Checklist

1992 TRAPPERS SKYBOX

Tim Salmon is the most expensive single at $1-2. Singles start at 25¢.
Card Size: 2 1/2" x 3 1/2"
Imprint: © 1992 SKYBOX
Complete Set (26 cards): 8.00

No.	Player	No.	Player
☐ no#	Checklist	☐ 151	Don Barbara
☐ 152	Chris Beasley	☐ 153	Mike Butcher
☐ 154	Damion Easley	☐ 155	John Orton
☐ 156	Kevin Flora	☐ 157	Tim Fortugno
☐ 158	Willie Fraser	☐ 159	Larry Gonzalez
☐ 160	Jose Gonzalez	☐ 161	Todd James
☐ 162	Dave Johnson	☐ 163	Oddibe McDowell
☐ 164	John Pawlowski	☐ 165	Tim Salmon
☐ 166	Ray Soff	☐ 167	Luis Sojo
☐ 168	Mick Billmeyer	☐ 169	Ty Van Burkleo
☐ 170	Tom Vidmar	☐ 171	Mark Wasinger
☐ 172	Reggie Williams	☐ 173	Cliff Young
☐ 174	Max Oliveras, Mgr.	☐ 175	Coaches: G. Ruby/ L. Sakata

1993 TRAPPERS FLEER PROCARDS

Singles start at 25¢.
Card Size: 2 1/2" x 3 1/2"
Imprint: © 1993 FLEER CORP.
Complete Set (27 cards): 5.00

No.	Player	No.	Player
☐ 1129	Scott Anderson	☐ 1130	Jerry Don Gleaton
☐ 1131	John Johnstone	☐ 1132	Randy Kramer
☐ 1133	Jose Martinez	☐ 1134	Pat Rapp
☐ 1135	Rich Scheid	☐ 1136	Matt Turner
☐ 1137	Gene Walter	☐ 1138	Dave Weathers
☐ 1139	Mitch Lyden	☐ 1140	Terry McGriff
☐ 1141	Bob Natal	☐ 1142	Luis de los Santos
☐ 1143	Chuck Jackson	☐ 1144	Al Pedrique
☐ 1145	Gus Polidor	☐ 1146	Jeff Small
☐ 1147	Geronimo Berroa	☐ 1148	Nick Capra
☐ 1149	Mark Ryal	☐ 1150	Darrell Whitmore
☐ 1151	Nigel Wilson	☐ 1152	Sal Rende, Mgr.
☐ 1153	Fernando Arroyo, Coach	☐ 1154	Adrian Garrett, Coach
☐ 1155	Checklist		

1994 TRAPPERS FLEER PROCARDS

Singles start at 25¢.
Card Size: 2 1/2" x 3 1/2"
Imprint:
Complete Set (27 cards): 5.00

No.	Player	No.	Player
☐ 2867	Darrin Chapin	☐ 2868	Bill Drahman
☐ 2869	Willie Fraser	☐ 2870	Mike Jeffcoat
☐ 2871	John Johnstone	☐ 2872	Steve Long
☐ 2873	Terry Mathews	☐ 2874	Kurt Miller
☐ 2875	Dana Ridenour	☐ 2876	Rich Scheid
☐ 2877	Mitch Lyden	☐ 2878	Bob Natal
☐ 2879	Joe Millette	☐ 2880	Russ Norman
☐ 2881	Al Pedrique	☐ 2882	Vic Rodriguez
☐ 2883	Jim Walewander	☐ 2884	Nick Capra
☐ 2885	Carl Everett	☐ 2886	Monty Fariss
☐ 2887	John Massarelli	☐ 2888	Darrell Whitmore
☐ 2889	Nigel Wilson	☐ 2990	Sal Rende, Mgr.
☐ 2991	Rich Dubee, Coach	☐ 2992	Adrian Garrett, Coach
☐ 2993	Checklist		

1995 TRAPPERS MACRI PHOTOGRAPHIC DESIGN

Jason Giambi is the most expensive single at $1-2. Singles start at 35¢.
Card Size: 2 1/2" x 3 1/2"
Imprint:
Complete Set (27 cards): 10.00

No.	Player	No.	Player
☐ no#	Checklist	☐ no#	Scott Baker
☐ no#	Jim Bowie	☐ no#	Russ Brock
☐ no#	Scott Bryant	☐ no#	Fausto Cruz
☐ no#	Paul Faries	☐ no#	Jason Giambi
☐ no#	Heath Haynes	☐ no#	Walt Horn
☐ no#	Miguel Jimenez	☐ no#	Doug Jones
☐ no#	Scott Lydy	☐ no#	Mike Maksudian
☐ no#	Damon Mashore	☐ no#	Mike Mohler
☐ no#	Steve Phoenix	☐ no#	Todd Revenig
☐ no#	Curtis Shaw	☐ no#	Scott Sheldon
☐ no#	Russ Swan	☐ no#	John Wasdin
☐ no#	Don Wengert	☐ no#	George Williams
☐ no#	Steve Wojciechowski	☐ no#	Jason Wood
☐ no#	Ernie Young	☐ no#	Gary Jones, Mgr.
☐ no#	Orv Franchuk, Coach	☐ no#	Pete Richert, Coach

HAMILTON REDBIRDS

(NEW YORK-PENN LEAGUE, A)

1988 REDBIRDS PROCARDS

Singles start at 35¢.
Card Size: 2 1/2" x 3 1/2"
Imprint: © 1988 ProCards, Inc.
Complete Set (28 cards): 6.00

No.	Player	No.	Player
☐ no#	Checklist	☐ 1719	Chris Houser
☐ 1720	Scott Halama	☐ 1721	John Cebuhar
☐ 1722	Brad DuVall	☐ 1723	Anton Grier
☐ 1724	Rick Christian	☐ 1725	Mark Battell
☐ 1726	Lee Piemel	☐ 1727	Mike Ross
☐ 1728	Dale Kisten	☐ 1729	Tim Redman
☐ 1730	Kevin Robinson	☐ 1731	Cory Saterfield
☐ 1732	Dan Radison	☐ 1733	Luis Melendez
☐ 1734	Mike Evans	☐ 1735	Randy Butts
☐ 1736	Mark Clark	☐ 1737	John Lepley
☐ 1738	Joe Federico	☐ 1739	Steve Fanning
☐ 1740	Rodney Brooks	☐ 1741	Tom Malchesky
☐ 1742	Ed Lampe	☐ 1743	JeanP. Gentleman
☐ 1744	Dean Weese	☐ 1745	Steve Graham
☐ 1746	Frank Moran	☐ 1747	Joe Hall

1989 REDBIRDS STAR

Singles start at 25¢.
Card Size: 2 1/2" x 3 1/2"
Imprint: © 1989 THE STAR CO.
Complete Set (29 cards): 5.00

No.	Player	No.	Player
☐ 1	Scott Banton	☐ 2	Mark Battell
☐ 3	Allan Biggers	☐ 4	Mark Bowlan
☐ 5	David Boss	☐ 6	Cliff Brannon
☐ 7	Mike Campas	☐ 8	John Cebuhar
☐ 9	David Cassidy	☐ 10	Tripp Cromer
☐ 11	Jose Fernandez	☐ 12	Randy Berlin
☐ 13	Steve Graham	☐ 14	Larry Gryskevich
☐ 15	Chris Gorton	☐ 16	Brian Golden
☐ 17	Sean Grubb	☐ 18	Don Green
☐ 19	Tom Infante	☐ 20	Tim Lata
☐ 21	Mike Milchin	☐ 22	Tim Redman
☐ 23	Dan Shannon	☐ 24	Jose Trujillo
☐ 25	Stan Tukes	☐ 26	Mark Wilson
☐ 27	Joseph Pettini, Mgr.	☐ 28	Joseph Cunningham, Coach
☐ 29	Mike Evans, Trainer		

1990 REDBIRDS BEST

Singles start at 25¢.
Card Size: 2 1/2" x 3 1/2"
Imprint:
Complete Set (28 cards): 5.00

No.	Player	No.	Player
☐ 1	Donovan Osborne, Error (Donavan)	☐ 2	Roy Bailey
☐ 3	Marcos Betances	☐ 4	Chris Maloney
☐ 5	Tom Fusco	☐ 6	Kevin McLeod
☐ 7	Mark Smith	☐ 8	David Boss
☐ 9	George Sells	☐ 10	Troy Savior
☐ 11	Mike Newby	☐ 12	Rich Rupkey
☐ 13	Paul Ellis	☐ 14	Marc Ronan
☐ 15	Joe Turvey	☐ 16	Wander Pimentel
☐ 17	Ahmed Rodriguez	☐ 18	Ozzie Perez
☐ 19	Gary Cooper	☐ 20	Rodney Eldridge
☐ 21	Mark MacArthur	☐ 22	Chris Alesio
☐ 23	Terry Bradshaw	☐ 24	John Thomas
☐ 25	Jeff Payne	☐ 26	Juan Belru
☐ 27	Luis Melendez, Mgr.	☐ 28	Checklist

1990 REDBIRDS STAR

Singles start at 25¢.
Card Size: 2 1/2" x 3 1/2"
Imprint:
Complete Set (28 cards): 5.00

No.	Player	No.	Player
☐ 1	Chris Alesio	☐ 2	Jose Arias
☐ 3	Roy Bailey	☐ 4	Andy Beasly
☐ 5	Juan Belru	☐ 6	Marcos Betances
☐ 7	David Boss	☐ 8	Alan Botkin
☐ 9	Gary Cooper	☐ 10	Rodney Eldridge
☐ 11	Paul Ellis	☐ 12	Jeff Fayne
☐ 13	Tom Fusco	☐ 14	Chris Lowe
☐ 15	Mark MacArthur	☐ 16	Kevin McLeod
☐ 17	Mike Newby	☐ 18	Ozzie Perez
☐ 19	Wander Pimentel	☐ 20	Ahmed Rodriguez
☐ 21	Rich Rupkey	☐ 22	Troy Savior
☐ 23	George Sells	☐ 24	Mark Smith
☐ 25	John Thomas	☐ 26	Luis Melendez, Mgr.
☐ 27	Chris Maloney, Coach	☐ 28	Robert Harrison, Trainer

1991 REDBIRDS CLASSIC-BEST

Singles start at 25¢.
Card Size: 2 1/2" x 3 1/2"
Imprint:
Complete Set (30 cards): 6.00

No.	Player	No.	Player
☐ 1	Joe Castaldo	☐ 2	Tim DeGrasse
☐ 3	John Frascatore	☐ 4	Kevin Lucero
☐ 5	Mike Badorek	☐ 6	Rigo Beltran
☐ 7	Al Watson	☐ 8	Jeff Pasquale
☐ 9	Scott Longaker	☐ 10	Duff Brumley
☐ 11	Jason Hisey	☐ 12	Jeff Tanderys
☐ 13	Antonio Boone	☐ 14	Gary Taylor
☐ 15	Mike DiFelice	☐ 16	Garret Blanton
☐ 17	John Mabry	☐ 18	John O'Brien
☐ 19	Mike Cantu	☐ 20	Joe Turvey
☐ 21	Ron Warner	☐ 22	Brent Bohrofen
☐ 23	Keith Black	☐ 24	Jim Davenport
☐ 25	Ben Ellsworth	☐ 26	Rick Mediavilla
☐ 27	Ronnie French	☐ 28	Larry Meza
☐ 29	Rick Colbert, Mgr.	☐ 30	CL: Steve Turco, Coach

1991 REDBIRDS PROCARDS

Singles start at 25¢.
Card Size: 2 1/2" x 3 1/2"
Imprint: © 1991 ProCards, Inc.
Complete Set (33 cards): 6.00

No.	Player	No.	Player
☐ 4026	Mike Badorek	☐ 4027	Rigo Beltran
☐ 4028	Antonio Boone	☐ 4029	Duff Brumley
☐ 4030	Joe Castaldo	☐ 4031	Doug Creek
☐ 4032	Tim DeGrasse	☐ 4033	John Frascatore
☐ 4034	Jason Hisey	☐ 4035	Scott Longaker
☐ 4036	Kevin Lucero	☐ 4037	Jeff Pasquale
☐ 4038	Scott Simmons	☐ 4039	Jeff Tanderys
☐ 4040	Allen Watson	☐ 4041	Mike DiFelice
☐ 4042	Joe Turvey	☐ 4043	Keith Black
☐ 4044	Mike Cantu	☐ 4045	Ben Ellsworth
☐ 4046	Larry Meza	☐ 4047	John O'Brien
☐ 4048	Ron Warner	☐ 4049	Garret Blanton
☐ 4050	Brent Bohrofen	☐ 4051	Jim Davenport
☐ 4052	Ronnie French	☐ 4053	John Mabry
☐ 4054	Rick Mediavilla	☐ 4055	Gary Taylor
☐ 4056	Rick Colbert, Mgr.	☐ 4057	Steve Turco, Coach
☐ 4048	Checklist		

1992 REDBIRDS CLASSIC-BEST

Singles start at 20¢.
Card Size: 2 1/2" x 3 1/2"
Imprint:
Complete Set (30 cards): 5.00

No.	Player	No.	Player
☐ 1	Jeff Tanderys	☐ 2	Kirk Bullinger
☐ 3	Chad Smith	☐ 4	Blaine Milne
☐ 5	Jamie Cochran	☐ 6	Donnie Bellum
☐ 7	Ronnie French	☐ 8	Duff Brumley
☐ 9	Antonio Boone	☐ 10	Steve Jones
☐ 11	Andrew Martin	☐ 12	Keith Johns
☐ 13	Dennis Milius	☐ 14	Al Beavers
☐ 15	Tim DeGrasse	☐ 16	Ken Britt
☐ 17	Trey Ritz	☐ 18	Larry Gilligan
☐ 19	Tim Mathews	☐ 20	Tim Jordan
☐ 21	Alan Robinson	☐ 22	Darren Doucette
☐ 23	Mike DiFelice	☐ 24	Keith Black
☐ 25	Jeff Murphy	☐ 26	Mike Gulan
☐ 27	Todd Henderson	☐ 28	Brad Owens
☐ 29	DeLynn Corry	☐ 30	CL: S. Melvin/ C. Maloney

LETHBRIDGE BLACK DIAMONDS

(PIONEER LEAGUE, ROOKIE)

1997 BLACK DIAMONDS BEST

Singles start at 50¢.
Card Size: 2 1/2" x 3 1/2"
Imprint:
Complete Set (30 cards): 12.00

No.	Player	No.	Player
☐ 1	Tommy Jones	☐ 2	Mike Parrott
☐ 3	Ty Van Burkleo	☐ 4	Gord Watt
☐ 5	Mascot Miner	☐ 6	Steve Doherty
☐ 7	Brian Fox	☐ 8	Keith Jones
☐ 9	Jared Martin	☐ 10	Jeremy Quire
☐ 11	Wyley Steelmon	☐ 12	Jose Taveras
☐ 13	Ron Calloway	☐ 14	Bert Hudson
☐ 15	Wil Madera	☐ 16	Jhensy Sandoval
☐ 17	Jamie Sykes	☐ 18	Dallas Anderson
☐ 19	Chris Bloomer	☐ 20	John Fleming
☐ 21	Reuben Fontanes	☐ 22	David Harper
☐ 23	Jason Jensen	☐ 24	Eric Knott
☐ 25	Jason Martines	☐ 26	Ben Norris
☐ 27	Jamie Puorto	☐ 28	Mike Rooney
☐ 29	Jeff Santa	☐ 30	Jeff Wilson

LONDON TIGERS

(EASTERN LEAGUE, AA)

1989 TIGERS PROCARDS

Travis Fryman is the most expensive single at $5-6. Singles start at 35¢.
Card Size: 2 1/2" x 3 1/2"
Imprint: © 1989 ProCards, Inc.
Complete Set (32 cards): 16.00

No.	Player	No.	Player
☐ 1356	Checklist	☐ 1357	Steve Howe
☐ 1358	Bob Gibson, G.M.	☐ 1359	Bob Eamon, Dir.
☐ 1360	Bill Wilkinson, Asst. G.M.	☐ 1361	Dan Ross, Pres.
☐ 1362	Dave Cooper	☐ 1363	Donnie Rowland
☐ 1364	Bernie Anderson	☐ 1365	John Toale
☐ 1366	Travis Fryman	☐ 1367	Mike Delao, Trainer
☐ 1368	Scott Aldred	☐ 1369	Ron Rightnowar
☐ 1370	Darren Hursey	☐ 1371	Arnie Beyeler
☐ 1372	Dean Decillis	☐ 1373	Tim Leiper

No.	Player	No.	Player
☐ 1374	Don Vesling	☐ 1375	Mike Schwabe
☐ 1376	Mike Hansen	☐ 1377	Randy Nosek
☐ 1378	Chris Chambliss, Mgr.	☐ 1379	Rob Thomson, Coach
☐ 1380	Greg Everson	☐ 1381	Scott Livingstone
☐ 1382	Wayne Housei	☐ 1383	Phil Clark
☐ 1384	Doyle Balthazar	☐ 1385	Manny Jose
☐ 1386	Tom Aldrich	☐ 1387	Jose Ramos

1990 TIGERS PROCARDS

Singles start at 35¢.
Card Size: 2 1/2" x 3 1/2"
Imprint: © 1990 ProCards, Inc.
Complete Set (22 cards): 6.00

No.	Player	No.	Player
☐ 1262	Checklist	☐ 1263	David Haas
☐ 1264	John Kiely	☐ 1265	Mike Lumley
☐ 1266	Rusty Meacham	☐ 1267	Dave Richards
☐ 1268	Ron Rightnowar	☐ 1269	Mike Wilkins
☐ 1270	Ken Williams	☐ 1271	Rich Rowland
☐ 1272	Tom Aldrich	☐ 1273	Chris Alvarez
☐ 1274	Arnie Beyeler	☐ 1275	Rico Brogna
☐ 1276	Lou Frazier	☐ 1277	Luis Galindo
☐ 1278	Basilio Cabrera	☐ 1279	Steve Green
☐ 1280	Riccardo Ingram	☐ 1281	Tim Leiper
☐ 1282	Steve Pegues	☐ 1283	John Toale

1991 TIGERS LINE DRIVE

Singles start at 20¢.
Card Size: 2 1/2" x 3 1/2"
Imprint: © Impel 1991
Complete Set (26 cards): 4.00

No.	Player	No.	Player
☐ no#	Checklist	☐ 376	Doyle Balthazar
☐ 377	Basilio Cabrera	☐ 378	Ron Cook
☐ 379	Ivan Cruz	☐ 380	Dean Decillis
☐ 381	John DeSilva	☐ 382	John Doherty
☐ 383	Lou Frazier	☐ 384	Luis Galindo
☐ 385	Greg Gohr	☐ 386	Bud Groom
☐ 387	Darren Hursey	☐ 388	Riccardo Ingram
☐ 389	Keith Kimberlin	☐ 390	Todd Krumm
☐ 391	Randy Marshall	☐ 392	Domingo Michel
☐ 393	Steve Pegues	☐ 394	Jose Ramos
☐ 395	Bob Reimink	☐ 396	Ruben Rodriguez
☐ 397	Eric Stone	☐ 398	Marty Willis
☐ 399	Gene Roff, Mgr.	☐ 400	Coaches: J. Jones/ D. Raley

1991 TIGERS PROCARDS

Singles start at 25¢.
Card Size: 2 1/2" x 3 1/2"
Imprint: © 1991 ProCards, Inc.
Complete Set (27 cards): 5.00

No.	Player	No.	Player
☐ 1869	John DeSilva	☐ 1870	John Doherty
☐ 1871	Greg Gohr	☐ 1872	Bud Groom
☐ 1873	Darren Hursey	☐ 1875	Todd Krumm
☐ 1876	Randy Marshall	☐ 1877	Jose Ramos
☐ 1878	Eric Stone	☐ 1879	Marty Willis
☐ 1880	Doyle Balthazar	☐ 1881	Ruben Rodriguez
☐ 1882	Ivan Cruz	☐ 1883	Dean Decillis
☐ 1884	Luis Galindo	☐ 1885	Keith Kimberlin
☐ 1886	Domingo Michel	☐ 1887	Bob Reimink
☐ 1888	Basilio Cabrera	☐ 1889	Lou Frazier
☐ 1890	Riccardo Ingram	☐ 1891	Steve Pegues
☐ 1892	Gene Roof, Mgr.	☐ 1893	Jeff Jones, Coach
☐ 1894	Dan Raley, Coach	☐ 2232	Kurt Knudsen
☐ 2232	Checklist		

1992 TIGERS FLEER PROCARDS

Singles start at 35¢.
Card Size: 2 1/2" x 3 1/2"
Imprint: none
Complete Set (29 cards): 5.00

No.	Player	No.	Player
☐ 623	Don August	☐ 624	Jeff Braley
☐ 625	Sherman Corbett	☐ 626	Dan Freed
☐ 627	Mike Garcia	☐ 628	Frank Gonzales
☐ 629	Jimmy Henry	☐ 630	Mike Lumley
☐ 631	Rick Rojas	☐ 632	Don Vesling
☐ 633	Brian Warren	☐ 634	Marty Willis
☐ 635	Steve Wolf	☐ 636	Mike Gillette
☐ 637	Rick Sellers	☐ 638	Ivan Cruz
☐ 639	Mike DeButch	☐ 640	Kirk Mendenhall
☐ 641	Bob Reimink	☐ 642	Rod Robertson
☐ 643	Basilio Cabrera	☐ 644	Brian Cornelius
☐ 645	Lou Frazier	☐ 646	Tyrone Kingwood
☐ 647	Greg Sparks	☐ 648	Mark DeJohn, Mgr.
☐ 649	Bruce Fields, Coach	☐ 650	Jeff Jones, Coach
☐ 651	Checklist		

1992 TIGERS SKYBOX

Singles start at 25¢.
Card Size: 2 1/2" x 3 1/2"
Imprint: © 1992 SKYBOX
Complete Set (26 cards): 5.00

No.	Player	No.	Player
☐ no#	Checklist	☐ 401	Jeff Braley
☐ 402	Basilio Cabrera	☐ 403	Brian Cornelius
☐ 404	Ivan Cruz	☐ 405	Mike DeButch
☐ 406	Lou Frazier	☐ 407	Dan Freed
☐ 408	Mike Garcia	☐ 409	Mike Gillette
☐ 410	Frank Gonzales	☐ 411	Tyrone Kingwood
☐ 412	Mike Lumley	☐ 413	Kirk Mendenhall
☐ 414	Jose Ramos	☐ 415	Robert Reimink
☐ 416	Rod Robertson	☐ 417	Rick Rojas
☐ 418	Rick Sellers	☐ 419	Greg Sparks
☐ 420	Leo Torres	☐ 421	Don Vesling
☐ 422	Brian Warren	☐ 423	Marty Willis
☐ 424	Mark DeJohn, Mgr.	☐ 425	Bruce Fields, Coach

MONTRÉAL ROYALS

(INTERNATIONAL LEAGUE)

1943 - 47 ROYALS PARADE SPORTIVE

These cards have black and white photos and blank backs. Other singles may exist.

Card Size: 5" x 8 5/8"

Imprint: None

Complete Set (14 cards):

	Player	NRMT
☐	Jack Banta	8.00
☐	Stan Breard	8.00
☐	Al Campanis	12.00
☐	Red Durrett	8.00
☐	Herman Franks	8.00
☐	John Gabbard	8.00
☐	Ronald Gladu	8.00
☐	Ray Hathaway	8.00
☐	John Jorgenson	8.00
☐	Paul Pepper Martn	8.00
☐	Marvin Rackley	8.00
☐	Jackie Robinson	8.00
☐	Jean-Pierre Roy	8.00
☐	Le Club Montreal (les Royaux) 1944	20.00
☐	Le Club Montreal (les Royaux) 1945	20.00

OTTAWA LYNX

(INTERNATIONAL LEAGUE, AAA)

1993 LYNX FLEER PROCARDS

The most expensive singles are Matt Stairs at $1-2 and F.P. Santangelo at 75¢-$1.50. Singles start at 25¢.

Card Size: 2 1/2" x 3 1/2"

Imprint: © 1993 FLEER CORP.

Complete Set (23 cards): 7.00

No.	Player	No.	Player
☐ 2428	Tavo Alvarez	☐ 2429	Tim Fortugno
☐ 2430	Gil Heredia	☐ 2431	Jonathan Hurst
☐ 2432	Mike Mathile	☐ 2433	Len Picota
☐ 2434	Bill Risley	☐ 2435	Doug Simons
☐ 2436	Sergio Valdez	☐ 2437	Pete Young
☐ 2438	Gary Hymel	☐ 2439	Joe Siddall
☐ 2440	Tim Barker	☐ 2441	Vince Castaldo
☐ 2442	Todd Haney	☐ 2443	Charlie Montoyo
☐ 2444	Hector Vargas	☐ 2445	Terrel Hansen
☐ 2446	Rick Hirtensteiner	☐ 2447	F.P. Santangelo
☐ 2448	Matt Stairs	☐ 2449	Mike Quade, Mgr.
☐ 2450	Checklist		

1994 LYNX FLEER PROCARDS

Rondell White is the most expensive single at $1-2. Singles start at 25¢.

Card Size: 2 1/2" x 3 1/2"

Imprint:

Complete Set (19 cards): 7.00

No.	Player	No.	Player
☐ 2894	Rick Cornelius	☐ 2895	Ralph Diaz
☐ 2896	Joey Eischen	☐ 2897	Heath Haynes
☐ 2898	Shawn Holman	☐ 2899	Benny Puig
☐ 2900	Darrin Winston	☐ 2901	Joe Siddall
☐ 2902	Shane Andrews	☐ 2903	Ben Figueroa
☐ 2904	Oreste Marrero	☐ 2905	Chris Martin
☐ 2906	F.P. Santangelo	☐ 2907	Derrick White
☐ 2908	Derek Lee	☐ 2909	Rondell White
☐ 2910	Ted Wood	☐ 2911	Tyrone Woods
☐ 2912	Checklist		

ST. CATHARINES BLUE JAYS

(NEW YORK-PENN LEAGUE, A)

1988 BLUE JAYS PROCARDS

Singles start at 35¢.

Card Size: 2 1/2" x 3 1/2"

Imprint: © 1988 ProCards, Inc.

Complete Set (35 cards): 6.00

No.	Player	No.	Player
☐ no#	Checklist	☐ 2005	Armando Pagliari, Trainer
☐ 2006	Luis Salazar	☐ 2007	Timothy Brown
☐ 2008	Jose Villa	☐ 2009	Benigno Placeres
☐ 2010	Brad Evaschuk	☐ 2011	Jose Guarache
☐ 2012	Pablo Castro	☐ 2013	Donn Wolfe
☐ 2014	Eddie Dennis, Mgr.	☐ 2015	Mike McAlpin, Coach
☐ 2016	Timothy Hodge	☐ 2017	Nigel Wilson
☐ 2018	Daniel Dodd	☐ 2019	Greg Williams
☐ 2020	Greg McCutcheon	☐ 2021	Robert Montalvo
☐ 2022	Curtis Johnson	☐ 2023	David Weathers
☐ 2024	Jose Martinez	☐ 2025	Edgar Marquez
☐ 2026	Rafael Martinez	☐ 2027	Jason Townley
☐ 2028	Marcos Taveras	☐ 2029	Greg Harding
☐ 2030	Bryan Dixon	☐ 2031	Mike Jockish
☐ 2032	Mike Taylor	☐ 2033	Rick Vaughan
☐ 2034	Anthony Ward	☐ 2035	Ryan Thompson
☐ 2036	Darrin Wade	☐ 2037	Armando Serra
☐ 2038	Patrick Guerrero, Batboy		

1989 BLUE JAYS PROCARDS

Carlos Delgado is the most expensive single at $15-20. Singles start at 35¢.

Card Size: 2 1/2" x 3 1/2"

Imprint: © 1989 ProCards, Inc.

Complete Set (28 cards): 30.00

No.	Player	No.	Player
☐ 2069	Checklist	☐ 2070	Gregg Martin
☐ 2071	Bill Abara III	☐ 2072	Ryan Thompson

☐ 2073 Daren Brown
☐ 2074 Scott Hutson
☐ 2075 Oscar Garcia
☐ 2076 Darewn Kizziah
☐ 2077 Carlos Delgado
☐ 2078 Mike Jockish
☐ 2079 Greg O'Halloran
☐ 2080 Hector Mercedes
☐ 2081 Nigel Wilson
☐ 2082 Billy Parese
☐ 2083 Gonzalo Vargas
☐ 2084 Anton Mobley
☐ 2085 Chris Beacom
☐ 2086 John Wanish
☐ 2087 Ernsto Santana
☐ 2088 Rob Blumberg
☐ 2089 Sterling Stock
☐ 2090 Greg Bicknell
☐ 2091 Jeff Kent
☐ 2092 Armando Pagliari, Trainer
☐ 2093 Mike McAlpin, Coach
☐ 2094 Greg McCutcheon
☐ 2095 Bob Shirley, Mgr.
☐ 2096 Rick Holifield

1990 BLUE JAYS PROCARDS

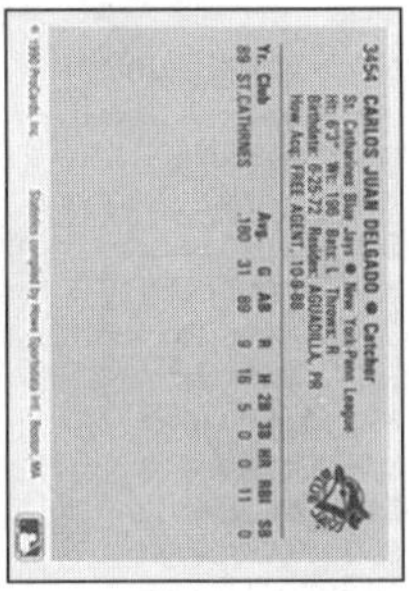

Carlos Delgado is the most expensive single at $5-6. Singles start at 35¢.
Card Size: 2 1/2" x 3 1/2"
Imprint: © 1990 ProCards, Inc.
Complete Set (34 cards): 16.00

No. Player
☐ 3451 Checklist
☐ 3452 Matt Hudik
☐ 3453 Juan Querecuto
☐ 3454 Carlos Delgado
☐ 3455 Edgar Marquez
☐ 3456 Robert Perez
☐ 3457 Tom Singer
☐ 3458 Scott Brow
☐ 3459 Sam Mandia
☐ 3460 Matt Watson
☐ 3461 Joe Ganote
☐ 3462 Frank Kowar
☐ 3463 Dave Marcon
☐ 3464 Paul Menhart
☐ 3465 Bobby Aylmer
☐ 3466 Rob Matalvo
☐ 3467 Ciro Ambrosio
☐ 3468 Rusty Filter
☐ 3469 Allen Rhea
☐ 3470 Huck Flener
☐ 3471 David Tollison
☐ 3472 Steve Karsay
☐ 3473 Rick Steed
☐ 3474 Mike Taylor
☐ 3475 Jeff Irish
☐ 3476 Andy Carlton
☐ 3477 Wally Heckel
☐ 3478 Wilberto Rojas
☐ 3479 Anton Mobley
☐ 3480 Shawn Scott
☐ 3481 Jacinto Yorro
☐ 3482 Doug Ault, Mgr.
☐ 3483 Mike McAlpin, Coach
☐ 3484 Darren Balsley, Coach

1991 BLUE JAYS CLASSIC-BEST

Singles start at 25¢.
Card Size: 2 1/2" x 3 1/2"
Imprint:
Complete Set (30 cards): 6.00

No. Player
☐ no# St.Catharines
☐ no# Toronto
☐ no# M.L.B.
☐ 1 Mike Morland
☐ 2 Keiver Campbell
☐ 3 Lou Benbow, Jr.
☐ 4 Kris Harmes
☐ 5 Sharnol Adriana
☐ 6 Chris Weinke
☐ 7 Mike Coolbaugh
☐ 8 Robert Butler
☐ 9 Joe Lis, Jr.
☐ 10 Craig Quinlan
☐ 11 Kurt Heble
☐ 12 Keith Hines
☐ 13 Giovanni Carrara
☐ 14 James O'Connor
☐ 15 Gary Miller
☐ 16 Dennis Gray, Jr.
☐ 17 Chris Kotes
☐ 18 Paul Barton
☐ 19 Ben Weber
☐ 20 Paul Spoljaric
☐ 21 Tim Lindsay
☐ 22 Darin Nolan
☐ 23 Angel Lugo
☐ 24 Scott Shannon, Trainer
☐ 25 Julio Division, Coach
☐ 26 Doug Ault, Mgr.
☐ 27 Checklist

1991 BLUE JAYS PROCARDS

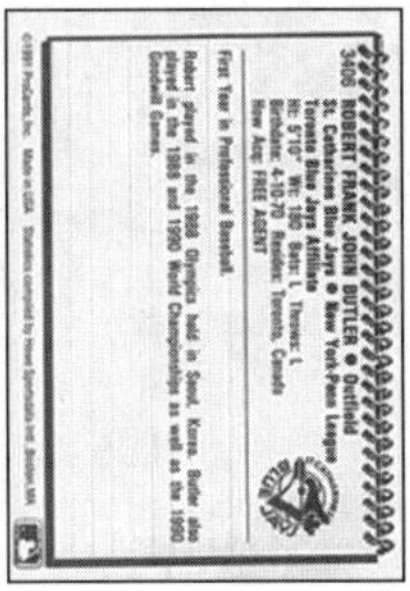

Singles start at 25¢.
Card Size: 2 1/2" x 3 1/2"
Imprint: © 1991 ProCards, Inc.
Complete Set (28 cards): 5.00

No. Player
☐ 3386 Paul Barton
☐ 3387 Giovanni Carrara
☐ 3388 Dennis Gray, Jr.
☐ 3389 Chris Kotes
☐ 3390 Tim Lindsay
☐ 3391 Angel Lugo
☐ 3392 Gary Miller
☐ 3394 Darin Nolan
☐ 3395 Paul Spoljaric
☐ 3396 Ben Weber
☐ 3397 Kris Harmes
☐ 3398 Mike Morland
☐ 3399 Craig Quinlan
☐ 3400 Sharnol Adriana
☐ 3401 Lou Benbow, Jr.
☐ 3402 Mike Coolbaugh
☐ 3403 Kurt Heble
☐ 3404 Joe Lis, Jr.
☐ 3405 Chris Weinke
☐ 3406 Robert Butler
☐ 3407 Keiver Campbell
☐ 3408 Keith Hines
☐ 3409 Felix Septimo
☐ 3410 Jacinto Yorro
☐ 3411 Doug Ault, Mgr.
☐ 3412 Julio Division, Coach
☐ 3413 Checklist

1992 BLUE JAYS CLASSIC-BEST

Singles start at 20¢.
Card Size: 2 1/2" x 3 1/2"
Imprint:
Complete Set (30 cards): 5.00

No. Player
☐ 1 Todd Steverson
☐ 2 Keith Hines
☐ 3 Mike Coolbaugh
☐ 4 Juan Querecuto
☐ 5 Adam Meinershagen
☐ 6 Trevor Mallory
☐ 7 Roger Doman
☐ 8 Ned Darley
☐ 9 Lee Daniels
☐ 10 Santiago Henry
☐ 11 D.J. Boston
☐ 12 Lou Benbow, Jr.
☐ 13 Mark Choate
☐ 14 Keiver Campbell
☐ 15 Rob Adkins
☐ 16 Kris Harmes
☐ 17 Lonell Roberts
☐ 18 Jeff Ladd
☐ 19 Gary Miller
☐ 20 Scot McCloughan
☐ 21 Chris Chandler
☐ 22 Brad Cornett
☐ 23 Timothy Crabtree
☐ 24 Derek Brandow
☐ 25 Levon Largusa
☐ 26 Aaron Jersild
☐ 27 J.J. Cannon, Mgr.
☐ 28 Reggie Cleveland, Coach
☐ 29 Scott Shannon, Trainer
☐ 30 CL: Rolando Pino, Coach

1992 BLUE JAYS FLEER PROCARDS

Singles start at 35¢.
Card Size: 2 1/2" x 3 1/2"
Imprint: none
Complete Set (29 cards): 5.00

No. Player
☐ 2813 Checklist
☐ 3376 Rob Adkins

No.	Player	No.	Player
☐ 3377	Derek Brandow	☐ 3378	Brad Cornett
☐ 3379	Tim Crabtree	☐ 3380	Lee Daniels
☐ 3381	Ned Darley	☐ 3382	Roger Doman
☐ 3383	Aaron Jersild	☐ 3384	Levon Largusa
☐ 3385	Trevor Mallory	☐ 3386	Adam Meinershagen
☐ 3387	Gary Miller	☐ 3388	Kris Harmes
☐ 3389	Jeff Ladd	☐ 3390	Juan Querecuto
☐ 3391	Lou Benbow, Jr.	☐ 3392	D.J. Boston
☐ 3393	Chris Chandler	☐ 3394	Mark Choate
☐ 3395	Mike Coolbaugh	☐ 3396	Santiago Henry
☐ 3397	Keiver Campbell	☐ 3398	Scot McCloughan
☐ 3399	Lonell Roberts	☐ 3400	Todd Steverson
☐ 3401	J.J. Cannon, Mgr.	☐ 3402	Rolando Pino, Coach
☐ 3403	Team Photo		

1993 BLUE JAYS CLASSIC-BEST

Shannon Stewart is the most expensive single at $1-2. Singles start at 20¢.
Card Size: 2 1/2" x 3 1/2"
Imprint:
Complete Set (30 cards): 6.00

No.	Player	No.	Player
☐ 1	Shannon Stewart	☐ 2	Tim Adkins
☐ 3	Alonso Beltran	☐ 4	Chad Brown
☐ 5	Jeff Cheek	☐ 6	Brandon Cromer
☐ 7	Rafael Debrand	☐ 8	Joe Druso
☐ 9	Emmanuel Hayes	☐ 10	Sean Hearn
☐ 11	Edwin Hurtado	☐ 12	Jay Maldonado
☐ 13	Doug Meiners	☐ 14	Adam Meinershagen
☐ 15	Adam Melhuse	☐ 16	Patrick Moultrie
☐ 17	Harry Muir	☐ 18	Rob Mummau
☐ 19	David Pearlman	☐ 20	Juan Querecuto
☐ 21	Kip Roggendorf	☐ 22	Rob Steinert
☐ 23	Dilson Torres	☐ 24	Craig Vaught
☐ 25	J.J. Cannon, Mgr.	☐ 26	Rolando Pino, Coach
☐ 27	Scott Breeden, Coach	☐ 28	Reggie Cleveland, Coach
☐ 29	Scott Shannon, Trainer	☐ 30	CL: Team Photo

1993 BLUE JAYS FLEER PROCARDS

Shannon Stewart is the most expensive single at $1-2. Singles start at 25¢.
Card Size: 2 1/2" x 3 1/2"
Imprint: © 1993 FLEER CORP.
Complete Set (27 cards): 6.00

No.	Player	No.	Player
☐ 3965	Tim Adkins	☐ 3966	Alonso Beltran
☐ 3967	Chad Brown	☐ 3968	Jeff Cheek
☐ 3969	Edwin Hurtado	☐ 3970	Jay Maldonado
☐ 3971	Doug Meiners	☐ 3972	Adam Meinershagen
☐ 3973	Harry Muir	☐ 3974	David Pearlman
☐ 3975	Rob Steinert	☐ 3976	Dilson Torres
☐ 3977	Joe Durso	☐ 3978	Juan Querecuto
☐ 3979	Brandon Cromer	☐ 3980	Emmanuel Hayes
☐ 3981	Adam Melhuse	☐ 3982	Rob Mummau
☐ 3983	Kip Roggendorf	☐ 3984	Craig Vaught
☐ 3985	Rafael Debrand	☐ 3986	Sean Hearn
☐ 3987	Patrick Moultrie	☐ 3988	Shannon Stewart
☐ 3989	J.J. Cannon, Mgr.	☐ 3990	Rolando Pino, Coach
☐ 3991	Checklist		

1994 BLUE JAYS CLASSIC

Singles start at 35¢.
Card Size: 2 1/2" x 3 1/2"
Imprint:
Complete Set (30 cards): 8.00

No.	Player	No.	Player
☐ 1	Chris McBride	☐ 2	Alfredo Arias
☐ 3	Brent Bearden	☐ 4	Ed Budz
☐ 5	Carlos Cabrera	☐ 6	Ben Candelaria
☐ 7	John Crowther	☐ 8	Willy Daunic
☐ 9	Freddy Garcia	☐ 10	Brian Grant
☐ 11	Michael Halperin	☐ 12	Battle Holley
☐ 13	Wayne Hoy	☐ 14	Jeff Ladd
☐ 15	Jeremy Lee	☐ 16	Jeff Leystra
☐ 17	John Reilly	☐ 18	Omat Sanchez
☐ 19	Anthony Sanders	☐ 20	Jeff Schneider
☐ 21	Mark Sievert	☐ 22	Keilan Smith
☐ 23	Randy Smith	☐ 24	Fausto Solano
☐ 25	Shayne Timmons	☐ 26	Eddy Vasquez
☐ 27	J.J. Cannon, Mgr.	☐ 28	Kip Roggendorf
☐ 29	Rolando Pino, Coach	☐ 30	CL: Al Widmar, Coach

1994 BLUE JAYS FLEER PROCARDS

Singles start at 25¢.
Card Size: 2 1/2" x 3 1/2"
Imprint:
Complete Set (30 cards): 6.00

No.	Player	No.	Player
☐ 3631	Alfredo Arias	☐ 3632	Brent Bearden
☐ 3633	Ed Budz	☐ 3634	Jeff Cheek
☐ 3635	John Crowther	☐ 3636	Brian Grant
☐ 3637	Michael Halperin	☐ 3638	Wayne Hoy
☐ 3639	Jeremy Lee	☐ 3640	Jeff Leystra
☐ 3641	Chris McBride	☐ 3642	Jeff Schneider
☐ 3643	Mark Sievert	☐ 3644	Keilan Smith
☐ 3645	Randy Smith	☐ 3646	Jeff Ladd
☐ 3647	John Reilly	☐ 3648	Shayne Timmons
☐ 3649	Carlos Cabrera	☐ 3650	Willy Daunic
☐ 3651	Freddy Garcia	☐ 3652	Battle Holley
☐ 3653	Kip Roggendorf	☐ 3654	Fausto Solano
☐ 3655	Eddy Vasquez	☐ 3656	Ben Candelaria
☐ 3657	Omar Sanchez	☐ 3658	Anthony Sanders
☐ 3659	J.J. Cannon, Mgr.	☐ 3660	Checklist

ST. CATHARINES STOMPERS

(NEW YORK-PENN LEAGUE, A)

1995 STOMPERS TIM HORTONS

Singles start at 50¢.
Card Size: 2 1/2" x 3 1/2"
Sponsors: Tim Horton's, Jaycees
Imprint: none

Complete Set (36 cards): **12.00**

	No.	Player		No.	Player
☐	1	Tom Davey	☐	2	Joe Young
☐	3	Tyson Hartshorn	☐	4	Benny Lowe
☐	5	John Crowther	☐	6	Rusty Volkert
☐	7	Wayne Hoy	☐	8	Randy Smith
☐	9	Eric Horton	☐	10	Narcisco Delacruz
☐	11	Jose Peguero	☐	12	Scott Fitterer
☐	13	Ernie Peterman	☐	14	Luis Rodriguez
☐	15	John Reilly	☐	16	Bryan Williams
☐	17	Ryan Freel	☐	18	Battle Holley
☐	19	Chris Hayes	☐	20	Mark Landers
☐	21	Fausto Solano	☐	22	Damon Johnson
☐	23	Felix Rosario	☐	24	Tim Bourne
☐	25	Omar Sanchez	☐	26	J.J. Cannon, Mgr.
☐	27	Al Widmar, Coach	☐	28	CL-Bat Boys: J. Brown & M. Hogan
☐	29	Mark Spridzans, Club House	☐	30	John Belford, G.M.
☐	31	Ernie Whitt, Owner	☐	32	Paul Pettipiece, Sales&Promotions
☐	33	Chris Marotta, Group Sales	☐	34	St. Catharines Jaycees
☐	35	Timbit Safety Licence	☐	36	CL: Stompers Logo

1996 STOMPERS BEST

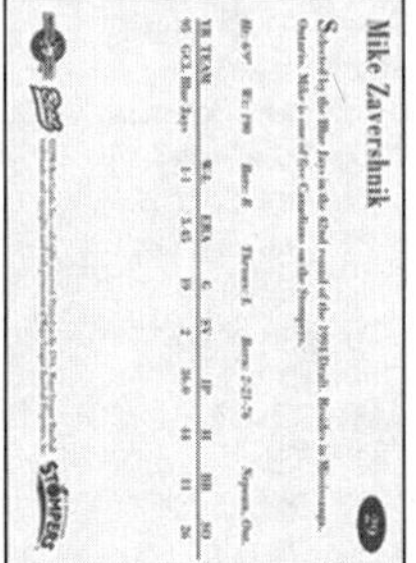

Singles start at 50¢.
Card Size: 2 1/2" x 3 1/2"
Imprint:
Complete Set (30 cards): **12.00**

	No.	Player		No.	Player
☐	1	Rocket Wheeler, Mgr.	☐	2	Neil Allen, Coach
☐	3	Mike Frostad, Trainer	☐	4	John Bale
☐	5	Josh Bradford	☐	6	Steve Charles
☐	7	Joe Davenport	☐	8	Blaine Fortin
☐	9	Derek Gaskill	☐	10	Beiker Graterol
☐	11	Robbie Hampton	☐	12	Alejandro Hueda
☐	13	Damon Johnson	☐	14	Jason Koehler
☐	15	Yan LaChapelle	☐	16	Clint Lawrence
☐	17	Luis Lopez	☐	18	Jim Mann
☐	19	Chris McBride	☐	20	Ryan Meyers
☐	21	Chad Needle	☐	22	Abraham Nunez
☐	23	Mike Rodriguez	☐	24	Victor Rodriguez
☐	25	Andy Shatley	☐	26	Will Skett
☐	27	Allen Snelling	☐	28	Paxton Stewart
☐	29	Mike Zavershnik	☐	30	Checklist

1997 STOMPERS BEST

Vernon Wells is the most expensive single at $4-5. Singles start at 50¢.
Card Size: 2 1/2" x 3 1/2"
Imprint:
Complete Set (30 cards): **15.00**

	No.	Player		No.	Player
☐	1	Lloyd Moseby, Coach	☐	2	Rocket Wheeter, Mgr.
☐	3	Bill Monbouquette, Coach	☐	4	Mike Brady, Trainer
☐	5	Randy Albaral	☐	6	Lorenzo Bagley
☐	7	Brian Barnett	☐	8	Stanley Baston
☐	9	Brian Bowles	☐	10	Kyle Burchart
☐	11	Joseph Casey	☐	12	Paul Chiaffredo
☐	13	Pascual Coco	☐	14	Ken Folkers
☐	15	Woody Heath	☐	16	Tim Huff
☐	17	David Huggins	☐	18	Cesar Izturis
☐	19	Tim Lacefield	☐	20	Selwyn Langaigne
☐	21	Diegomar Markwell	☐	22	Robert Medina
☐	23	Brad Moon	☐	24	Juan Nieves
☐	25	Jaron Seabury	☐	26	Pablo Sencion
☐	27	Matthew Weimer	☐	28	Vernon Wells
☐	29	Orlando Woodards	☐	30	Michael Young

TORONTO MAPLE LEAFS

(INTERNATIONAL LEAGUE)

1961 MAPLE LEAFS BEEHIVES

These cards feature black and white photos. An album was also available.
Card Size: 2 1/2" X 3 1/2"
Imprint: BEE HIVE PLAYER PHOTO
Complete Set (24 cards): **1,000.00**

	Player	NRMT
☐	Sparky Anderson	250.00
☐	Fritzie Brickell	45.00
☐	Willis Burton	30.00
☐	Bob Chakales	30.00
☐	Rip Coleman	45.00
☐	Steve Demeter	45.00
☐	Joe Hannah	30.00
☐	Earl Hersh	30.00
☐	Lou Jackson	30.00
☐	Ken Johnson	70.00
☐	Lou Johnson	40.00
☐	John Lipon	45.00
☐	Carl Mathias	30.00
☐	Bill Moran	45.00
☐	Ron Negray	30.00
☐	Herb Plews	30.00
☐	Dave Pope	30.00
☐	Steve Ridzik	45.00
☐	Paul Sanchez	30.00
☐	Pat Scantlebury	30.00
☐	Bill Smith	30.00
☐	Bob Smith	30.00
☐	Chuck Tanner	100.00
☐	Tim Thompson	30.00

TROIS-RIVIÈRES AIGLES

(EASTERN LEAGUE, AA)

1973 AIGLES CLICK-CLICK

This set features black and white photos and have blank backs. Other singles may exist.

Card Size: 7" x 8 3/4"

Sponsor: Click-Click

Complete Set (18 cards):

	Player		Player
☐	Santo Alcala	☐	Joaquin Andujar (Jack Anduyar)
☐	Marc Bombard	☐	Eric Boyd
☐	Kent Burdick	☐	Art Cover
☐	Arturo DeFreitas	☐	Darrell Devitt
☐	Doug Flynn, Error (Flinn)	☐	Ken Hansen
☐	Mike Heintz	☐	Tom Hume
☐	Ray Knight	☐	Gary Polczynski
☐	Greg Sinatro	☐	Tom Spencer
☐	Don Werner	☐	Pat Zachary, Error (Zachry)

VANCOUVER CANADIANS

(PACIFIC COAST LEAGUE, AAA)

1979 CANADIANS TCMA

Singles start at 75¢.

Card Size: 2 1/2" x 3 1/2"

Imprint: © TCMA 1979

Complete Set (25 cards): 12.00

	No.	Player		No.	Player
☐	1	Skip James	☐	2	Vic Harris
☐	3	Ron Jacobs	☐	4	Marshall Edwards
☐	5	Craig Ryan	☐	6	Tim Nordbrook
☐	7	Mark Bomback	☐	8	Andy Replogle
☐	9	Danny Boitano	☐	10	Rickey Keeton
☐	11	Gus Quiros	☐	12	Juan Lopez
☐	13	Ned Yost	☐	14	Clay Carroll
☐	15	Kuni Ogawa	☐	16	Randy Stein
☐	17	Ed Romero	☐	18	Jeff Yurak
☐	19	Sam Hinds	☐	20	John Felske, Mgr.
☐	21	Billy Severns	☐	22	Kent Biggerstaff, Trainer
☐	22	Lenn Sakata	☐	23	Willie Mueller
☐	23	Creighton Tevlin			

1980 CANADIANS TCMA

Singles start at 75¢.

Card Size: 2 1/2" x 3 1/2"

Imprint:

Complete Set (22 cards): 18.00

	No.	Player		No.	Player
☐	1	Lawrence Rush	☐	2	Willie Mueller
☐	3	Ned Yost	☐	4	Gus Quiros
☐	5	Bobby Glen Smith	☐	6	Terry Bevington
☐	7	Dave LaPoint	☐	8	Bill Severns
☐	9	Lance Rautzhan	☐	10	Tim Nordbrook
☐	11	Bob Didier, Mgr.	☐	12	Kent Biggerstaff, Trainer
☐	13	Ed Romero	☐	14	Dan Boitano
☐	15	Craig Ryan	☐	16	Rene Quinones
☐	17	Mike Henderson	☐	18	Fred Holdsworth
☐	19	Marshall Edwards	☐	20	Bob Galasso
☐	21	Vic Harris	☐	22	Rick Olsen

1981 CANADIANS TCMA

Kevin Bass is the most expensive single at $2-3. Singles start at 75¢.

Card Size: 2 1/2" x 3 1/2"

Imprint:

Complete Set (25 cards): 16.00

	No.	Player		No.	Player
☐	1	Jamie Cocanower	☐	2	Chuck Porter
☐	3	Doug Wanz	☐	4	Dwight Bernard
☐	5	Mark Schuster	☐	6	Frank Thomas
☐	7	Brian Thorson, Trainer	☐	8	Ivan Rodriguez
☐	9	Gil Kubski	☐	10	Baylor Moore
☐	11	Gus Quiros	☐	12	Lawrence Rush
☐	13	Rich Olsen	☐	14	Terry Lee
☐	15	Willie Mueller	☐	16	Andy Replogie
☐	17	Frank DiPino	☐	18	Rene Quinones
☐	19	Bobby Smith	☐	20	Lee Stigman
☐	21	John Flinn	☐	22	Gerry Ako
☐	23	Tom Soto	☐	24	Kevin Bass
☐	25	Steve Lake			

1982 CANADIANS TCMA

Kevin Bass is the most expensive single at $2-3. Singles start at 75¢.

Card Size: 2 1/2" x 3 1/2"

Imprint:

Complete Set (24 cards): 16.00

	No.	Player		No.	Player
☐	1	Bob Skube	☐	2	Frank Thomas
☐	3	Bill Schroeder	☐	4	Kevin Bass
☐	5	Willie Lozada	☐	6	John Skorochocki
☐	7	Lawrence Rush	☐	8	Ed Irvine
☐	9	Stan Davis	☐	10	Doug Loman
☐	11	Steve Herz	☐	12	Tim Cook
☐	13	Doug Jones	☐	14	Mike Madden
☐	15	Rich Olsen	☐	16	Frank DiPino
☐	17	Pete Ladd	☐	18	Chuck Valley
☐	19	Rick Kranitz	☐	20	Jamie Cocanower
☐	21	Chuck Porter	☐	22	Mike Anderson
☐	23	Eli Grba, Coach	☐	24	Brian Thorson, Trainer

1984 CANADIANS CRAMER

Tom Candiotti is the most expensive single at $2-3. Singles start at 50¢.

Card Size: 2 1/2" x 3 1/2"

Imprint: © 1985 Cramer Sports Promotions

Complete Set (25 cards): 15.00

	No.	Player		No.	Player
☐	25	Ron Koenigsfeld	☐	26	Andy Beene
☐	27	Tony Muser, Mgr.	☐	28	Doug Loman
☐	29	Dan Davidsmeier	☐	30	Ray Searage
☐	31	Kelvin Moore	☐	32	Tom Candiotti
☐	33	Frank Thomas	☐	34	Carlos Ponce

☐ 35	Ernie Riles	☐ 36	Dan Boone
☐ 37	Dan Huppert	☐ 38	Hosken Powell
☐ 39	Doug Jones	☐ 40	Bob Gibson
☐ 41	Eric Peyton	☐ 42	Scott Roberts
☐ 43	Jamie Nelson	☐ 44	Ed Irvine
☐ 45	Jim Koontz	☐ 46	Mike Anderson
☐ 47	Marshall Edwards	☐ 48	Jack Lazorko
☐ 243	Don Rowe, Coach		

1985 CANADIANS CRAMER

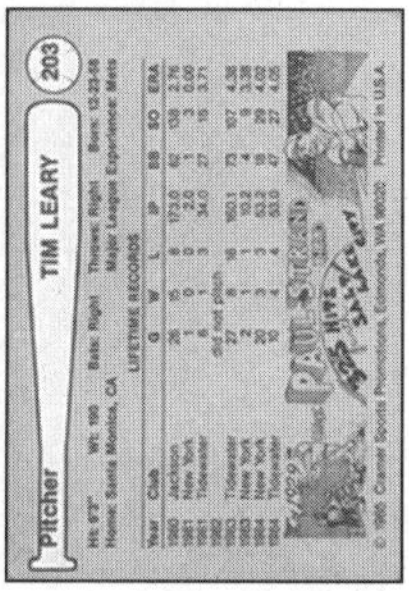

Singles start at 50¢.

Card Size: 2 1/2" x 3 1/2"

Imprint: © 1985 Cramer Sports Promotions

Complete Set (25 cards): 10.00

No.	Player	No.	Player
☐ 201	David Davidsmeier	☐ 202	Brad Lesley
☐ 203	Tim Leary	☐ 204	Bobby Clark
☐ 205	Juan Castillo	☐ 206	Jim Adduci
☐ 207	Ernie Riles	☐ 208	Mike Paul, Coach
☐ 209	Dale Sveum	☐ 210	Jamie Cocanower
☐ 211	Mike Felder	☐ 212	Brian Duquette
☐ 213	Jim Paciorek	☐ 214	Bob Skube
☐ 215	Tom Treblehorn	☐ 216	Bill Wegman
☐ 217	Mike Martin	☐ 218	Scott Roberts
☐ 219	Rick Waits	☐ 220	Chuck Crim
☐ 221	Jamie Nelson	☐ 222	Bryan Clutterbuck
☐ 223	Garrett Nago	☐ 224	Carlos Ponce
☐ 225	Al Price, Trainer		

1986 CANADIANS PROCARDS

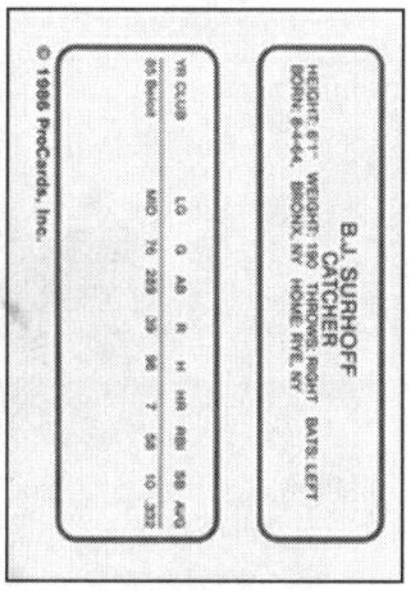

B.J. Surhoff is the most expensive single at $1-2. Singles start at 35¢.

Card Size: 2 1/2" x 3 1/2"

Imprint: © 1986 ProCards, Inc.

Complete Set (27 cards): 10.00

Player	Player
☐ Jim Adduci	☐ Terry Bevington, Mgr.
☐ Mike Birbeck	☐ Chris Bosio
☐ Glenn Braggs	☐ Mark Ciardi
☐ Bryan Clutterbuck	☐ Chuck Crim
☐ Dan Davidsmeier	☐ Ed Diaz
☐ Brian Duquette	☐ Bob Gibson
☐ Dion James	☐ John Johnson
☐ Steve Kiefer	☐ Dave Klipstein
☐ Joe Meyer	☐ Ed Myers
☐ Charlie O'Brien	☐ Jim Paciorek
☐ Mike Paul, Coach	☐ Chuck Porter
☐ Ray Searage	☐ B.J. Surhoff
☐ Rich Thompson	☐ Rick Watts

1987 CANADIANS PROCARDS

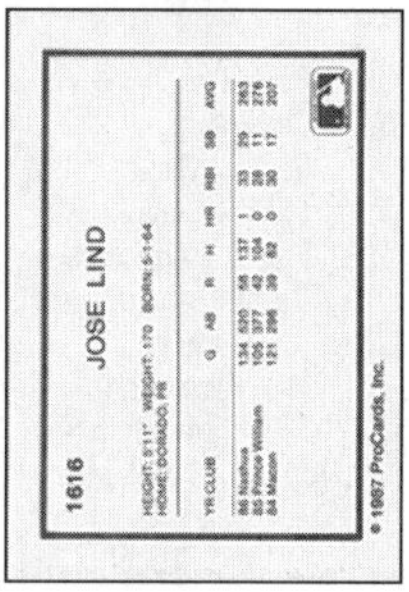

Singles start at 35¢.

Card Size: 2 1/2" x 3 1/2"

Imprint: © 1987 ProCards, Inc.

Complete Set (27 cards): 6.00

No.	Player	No.	Player
☐ 1598	Mike Bielicki	☐ 1599	Jackie Brown
☐ 1600	Jeff Cox	☐ 1601	Carlos Ledezma, Trainer
☐ 1602	Mark Ross	☐ 1603	Tommy Dunbar
☐ 1604	Stan Fransler	☐ 1605	Rocky Bridges, Mgr.
☐ 1606	Dave Johnson	☐ 1607	Sammy Haro
☐ 1608	Sammy Khalifa	☐ 1609	Houston Jimenez
☐ 1610	Tim Drummond	☐ 1611	Dave Leeper
☐ 1612	Mike Dunne	☐ 1613	Randy Kramer
☐ 1614	Butch Davis	☐ 1615	Hipolito Pena
☐ 1616	Jose Lind	☐ 1617	Larry Ray
☐ 1618	Danny Bilardello	☐ 1619	Vincente Palacios
☐ 1620	Ruben Rodriquez	☐ 1621	Dorn Taylor
☐ 1622	U.L. Washington		

1987 CANADIANS BLACK & WHITE PHOTOS

Singles start at 75¢. Other singles exist.

Card Size: 5" x 7"

Imprint: none

Player	Player
☐ Glenn Braggs	☐ Sammy Haro

1988 CANADIANS CMC

Singles start at 35¢.

Card Size: 2 1/2" x 3 1/2"

Imprint:

Complete Set (25 cards): 5.00

No.	Player	No.	Player
☐ 1	Jeff Bittiger	☐ 2	Joel Davis
☐ 3	Steve Rosenberg	☐ 4	Carl Willis
☐ 5	Edward Wojna	☐ 6	Ken Patterson
☐ 7	Adam Peterson	☐ 8	Grady Hall
☐ 9	Donn Pall	☐ 10	Jack Hardy
☐ 11	Greg Hibbard	☐ 12	Kelly Paris
☐ 13	Santiago Garcia	☐ 14	Mike Woodard
☐ 15	Ron Karkovice	☐ 16	Bill Lindsey
☐ 17	Russ Morman	☐ 18	Troy Thomas
☐ 19	Mike Yastrzemski	☐ 20	James Randall
☐ 21	Jeff Schaefer	☐ 22	Daryl Sconiers
☐ 23	Jorge Alcazar	☐ 24	Dave Gallagher
☐ 25	Marlin McPhail		

1988 CANADIANS PROCARDS

Singles start at 35¢.
Card Size: 2 1/2" x 3 1/2"
Imprint: © 1988 ProCards, Inc.
Complete Set (27 cards): 6.00

No.	Player	No.	Player
☐ no#	Checklist	☐ 753	Jeff Schaefer
☐ 754	Steve Rosenberg	☐ 755	Jack Hardy
☐ 756	Edward Wojna	☐ 757	Ken Patterson
☐ 758	Bill Lindsey	☐ 759	Donn Pall
☐ 760	Russ Morman	☐ 761	Grady Hall
☐ 762	Carl Willis	☐ 763	Joel Davis
☐ 764	Santiago Garcia	☐ 765	James Randall
☐ 766	Daryl Sconiers	☐ 767	Mike Woodard
☐ 768	Ron Jackson, Coach	☐ 769	Eli Grba, Coach
☐ 770	Greg Hibbard	☐ 771	Dave Gallagher
☐ 772	Jorge Alcazar	☐ 773	Ron Karkovice
☐ 774	Mike Yastrzemski	☐ 775	Troy Thomas
☐ 776	Adam Peterson	☐ 777	Marlin McPhail
☐ 778	Terry Bevington, Mgr.		

1989 CANADIANS CMC

Lance Johnson is the most expensive single at $1-2.Singles start at 35¢.
Card Size: 2 1/2" x 3 1/2"
Imprint:
Complete Set (25 cards): 10.00

No.	Player	No.	Player
☐ 1	Jeff Bittiger	☐ 2	Adam Peterson
☐ 3	Greg Hibbard	☐ 4	Tom McCarthy
☐ 5	Jack Hardy	☐ 6	Jose Segura
☐ 7	John Pawlowski	☐ 8	Rick Rodriguez
☐ 9	John Davis	☐ 10	Tom Drees
☐ 11	Kelly Paris	☐ 12	Steve Springer
☐ 13	Keith Smith	☐ 14	Jim Weaver
☐ 15	Marlin McPhail	☐ 16	Russ Morman
☐ 17	Carlos Martinez	☐ 18	Lance Johnson
☐ 19	Jerry Willard	☐ 20	Tom Fornester
☐ 21	Cal Emery, Coach	☐ 22	Mark Davis
☐ 23	Marv Foley, Mgr.	☐ 24	Jeff Schaefer
☐ 25	Moe Drabowsky, Coach		

1989 CANADIANS PROCARDS

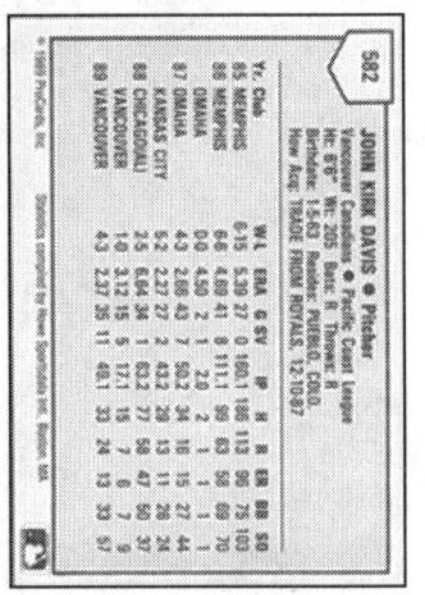

Lance Johnson is the most expensive single at 75¢-$1.50. Singles start at 35¢.
Card Size: 2 1/2" x 3 1/2"
Imprint: © 1989 ProCards, Inc.
Complete Set (31 cards): 8.00

No.	Player	No.	Player
☐ 571	Checklist	☐ 572	Cal Emery, Coach
☐ 573	Marv Foley, Mgr.	☐ 574	Greg Latta, Trainer
☐ 575	Doug Masolino, Coach	☐ 576	Lance Johnson
☐ 577	Jack McDowell	☐ 578	Keith Smith
☐ 579	Carlos Martinez	☐ 580	Rick Rodriquez
☐ 581	Moe Drabowsky, Coach	☐ 582	John Davis
☐ 583	Jim Weaver	☐ 584	Greg Hibbard
☐ 585	Mark Davis	☐ 586	Jack Hardy
☐ 587	Jerry Willard	☐ 588	Tom Drees
☐ 589	Adam Peterson	☐ 590	Russ Morman
☐ 591	Jose Segura	☐ 592	Steve Springer
☐ 593	Tom McCarthy	☐ 594	Kelly Paris
☐ 595	John Pawlowski	☐ 596	Marlin McPhail
☐ 597	Tom Forrester		

1990 CANADIANS CMC

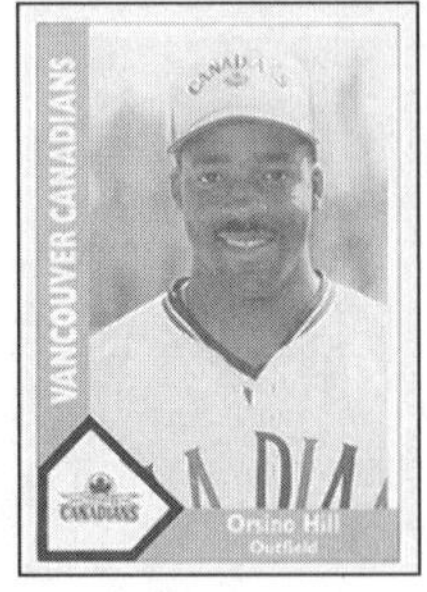

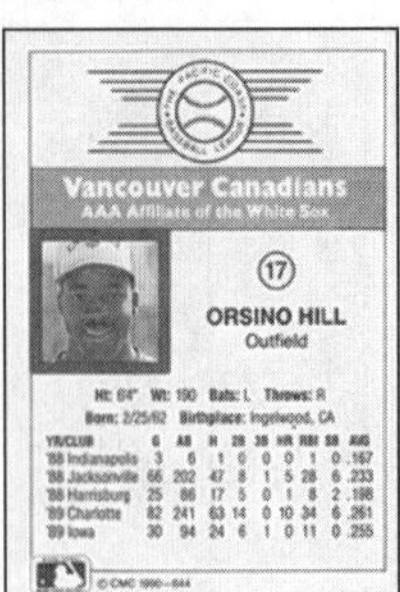

Singles start at 35¢.
Card Size: 2 1/2" x 3 1/2"
Imprint: © CMC 1990
Complete Set (27 cards): 6.00

No.	Player	No.	Player
☐ 1	Wilson Alvarez	☐ 2	Adam Peterson
☐ 3	Tom Drees	☐ 4	Ravelo Manzanillo
☐ 5	Marv Foley, Mgr.	☐ 6	Grady Hall
☐ 7	Mike Campbell	☐ 7	Shawn Hillegas
☐ 9	C.L. Penigar	☐ 10	John Pawlowski
☐ 11	Steve Rosenberg	☐ 12	Jose Segura
☐ 13	Rich Amaral	☐ 14	Pete Dalena
☐ 15	Ramon Sambo	☐ 16	Marcus Lawton
☐ 17	Orsino Hill	☐ 18	Marlin McPhail
☐ 19	Keith Smith	☐ 20	Todd Trafton
☐ 21	Norberto Martin	☐ 22	Don Wakamatsu
☐ 23	Jerry Willard	☐ 24	Dana Williams
☐ 25	Tracy Woodson	☐ 26	Moe Drabowsky, Coach
☐ 27	Roger LaFrancois, Coach		

1990 CANADIANS PROCARDS

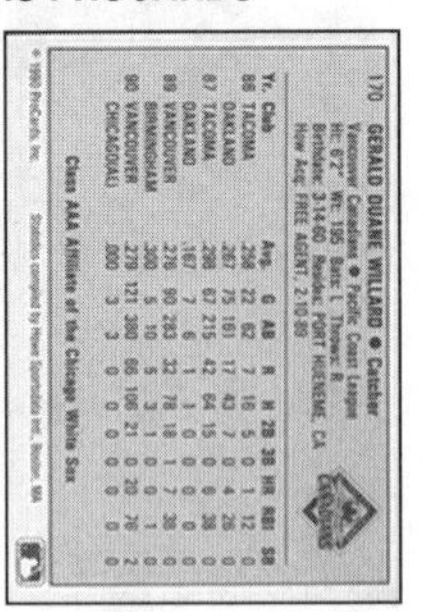

Singles start at 35¢.
Card Size: 2 1/2" x 3 1/2"
Imprint: © 1989 ProCards, Inc.
Complete Set (28 cards): 7.00

No.	Player	No.	Player
☐ 480	Checklist	☐ 481	Wilson Alvarez
☐ 482	Mike Campbell	☐ 483	Tom Drees
☐ 484	Grady Hall	☐ 485	Shawn Hillegas
☐ 486	Ravelo Manzanillo	☐ 487	John Pawlowski

☐ 488	Adam Peterson	☐ 489	Steve Rosenberg
☐ 490	Jose Segura	☐ 491	Don Wakamatsu
☐ 492	Jerry Willard	☐ 493	Rich Amaral
☐ 494	Pete Dalena	☐ 495	Norberto Martin
☐ 496	Keith Smith	☐ 497	Todd Trafton
☐ 498	Tracy Woodson	☐ 499	Orsino Hill
☐ 500	Marcus Lawton	☐ 501	Marlin McPhail
☐ 502	C.L. Penigar	☐ 503	Ramon Sambo
☐ 504	Dana Williams	☐ 505	Marv Foley, Mgr.
☐ 506	Moe Drabowsky, Coach	☐ 507	Roger LaFrancois, Coach

1991 CANADIANS LINE DRIVE

Singles start at 20¢.
Card Size: 2 1/2" x 3 1/2"
Imprint: © Impel 1991
Complete Set (26 cards): 4.00

No.	Player	No.	Player
☐ no#	Vancouver Canadians	☐ 626	Cesar Bernhardt
☐ 627	Mario Brito	☐ 628	Kurt Brown
☐ 629	John Cangelosi	☐ 630	Jeff Carter
☐ 631	Tom Drees	☐ 632	Grady Hall
☐ 633	Joe Hall	☐ 634	Curt Hasler
☐ 635	Danny Heep	☐ 636	Dan Henley
☐ 637	Roberto Hernandez	☐ 638	Orsino Hill
☐ 639	Jerry Kutzler	☐ 640	Norberto Martin
☐ 641	Rod McCray	☐ 642	Rob Nelson
☐ 643	Warren Newson	☐ 644	Greg Perschke
☐ 645	Rich Scheid	☐ 646	Matt Stark
☐ 647	Ron Stephens	☐ 648	Don Wakamatsu
☐ 649	Marv Foley, Mgr.		
☐ 650	Coaches: Roger LaFrancois/ Moe Drabowsky		

1991 CANADIANS PROCARDS

Singles start at 25¢.
Card Size: 2 1/2" x 3 1/2"
Imprint: © 1991 ProCards, Inc.
Complete Set (27 cards): 5.00

No.	Player	No.	Player
☐ 1586	Mario Brito	☐ 1587	Jeff Carter
☐ 1588	Tom Drees	☐ 1589	Grady Hall
☐ 1590	Curt Hasler	☐ 1591	Roberto Hernandez
☐ 1592	Jerry Kutzler	☐ 1593	Gre Perschke
☐ 1594	Rich Scheid	☐ 1595	Ron Stephens
☐ 1596	Kurt Brown	☐ 1597	Matt Stark
☐ 1598	Don Wakamatsu	☐ 1599	Ceasr Bernhardt
☐ 1600	Joe Hall	☐ 1601	Danny Heep
☐ 1602	Dan Henley	☐ 1603	Norberto Martin
☐ 1604	Rob Nelson	☐ 1605	John Cangelosi
☐ 1606	Orsino Hill	☐ 1607	Rod McCray
☐ 1608	Warren Newson	☐ 1609	Marv Foley, Mgr.
☐ 1610	Moe Drabowsky, Coach	☐ 1611	Roger LaFrancois, Coach
☐ 1612	Checklist		

1992 CANADIANS FLEER PROCARDS

Singles start at 35¢.
Card Size: 2 1/2" x 3 1/2"
Imprint: none
Complete Set (24 cards): 5.00

No.	Player	No.	Player
☐ 2713	Rodney Bolton	☐ 2714	Jeff Carter
☐ 2715	Mike Dunne	☐ 2716	Ramon Garcia
☐ 2717	Chris Howard	☐ 2718	John Hudek
☐ 2719	Bo Kennedy	☐ 2720	Greg Perschke
☐ 2721	Rich Scheid	☐ 2722	Jeff Shcwarz
☐ 2723	Ron Stephens	☐ 2724	Steve Wapnick
☐ 2725	Matt Merullo	☐ 2726	Nelson Santovenia
☐ 2727	Ron Coomer	☐ 2728	Chris Cron
☐ 2729	Drew Denson	☐ 2730	Joe Hall
☐ 2731	Ever Magallanes	☐ 2732	Norberto Martin
☐ 2733	Derek Lee	☐ 2734	Rick Renick, Mgr.
☐ 2735	Roger LaFrancois, Coach	☐ 2736	Checklist

1992 CANADIANS SKYBOX

Singles start at 25¢.
Card Size: 2 1/2" x 3 1/2"
Imprint: © 1992 SKYBOX
Complete Set (26 cards): 5.00

No.	Player	No.	Player
☐ no#	Checklist	☐ 626	Shawn Abner
☐ 627	Steve Wapnick	☐ 628	Rod Bolton
☐ 629	Brian Guinn	☐ 630	Jeff Carter
☐ 631	Ron Coomer	☐ 632	Chris Cron
☐ 633	Brian Drahman	☐ 634	Mike Dunne
☐ 635	Ramon Garcia	☐ 636	Joe Hall
☐ 637	Drew Denson	☐ 638	Chris Howard
☐ 639	Shawn Jeter	☐ 640	Roberto Hernandez
☐ 641	John Judek	☐ 624	Derek Lee
☐ 643	Ever Magallanes	☐ 644	Norberto Martin
☐ 645	Greg Perschke	☐ 646	Nelson Santovenia
☐ 647	Rich Scheid	☐ 648	Ron Stephens
☐ 649	Rick Renick, Mgr.	☐ 650	Roger LaFrancois, Coach

1993 CANADIANS FLEER PROCARDS

Garret Anderson and Jim Edmonds are the most expensive singles at 75¢-$1.50. Singles start at 25¢.
Card Size: 2 1/2" x 3 1/2"
Imprint: © 1993 FLEER CORP.
Complete Set (28 cards): 8.00

No.	Player	No.	Player
☐ 2589	Otis Green	☐ 2590	Hilly Hathaway
☐ 2591	Mark Holzemer	☐ 2592	Phil Leftwich
☐ 2593	Jerry Nielsen	☐ 2594	Steve Peck
☐ 2595	Troy Percival	☐ 2596	Darryl Scott
☐ 2597	Russ Springer	☐ 2598	Paul Swingle
☐ 2599	Julain Vasquez	☐ 2600	Mark Zappelli
☐ 2601	Larry Gonzales	☐ 2602	Chris Turner
☐ 2603	Rod Correia	☐ 2604	Ramon Martinez
☐ 2605	Eduardo Perez	☐ 2606	Ty Van Burkleo
☐ 2607	Jim Walewander	☐ 2608	Garret Anderson
☐ 2609	Jim Edmonds	☐ 2610	Jeff Kipila
☐ 2611	Jerome Walton	☐ 2612	Reggie Williams
☐ 2613	Max Oliveras, Mgr.	☐ 2614	Gary Ruby, Coach
☐ 2615	Lenn Sakata, Coach	☐ 2616	Checklist

1994 CANADIANS FLEER PROCARDS

Garret Anderson and J.T. Snow are the most expensive singles at 75¢-$1.50. Singles start at 25¢.
Card Size: 2 1/2" x 3 1/2"
Imprint:
Complete Set (26 cards): 8.00

No.	Player	No.	Player
☐ 1856	Erik Bennett	☐ 1857	Ken Edenfield
☐ 1858	John Farrell	☐ 1859	John Fritz
☐ 1860	David Holdridge	☐ 1861	Mark Holzemer
☐ 1862	Mike James	☐ 1863	Andrew Lorraine
☐ 1864	Troy Percival	☐ 1865	Russ Springer
☐ 1866	Mark Dalesandro	☐ 1867	Jorge Fabreas
☐ 1868	Rod Correia	☐ 1869	P.J. Forbes
☐ 1870	Orlando Munoz	☐ 1871	Ernie Riles
☐ 1872	J.T. Snow	☐ 1873	Garret Anderson
☐ 1874	Steve Hosey	☐ 1875	John Jackson
☐ 1876	Orlando Palmeiro	☐ 1877	Mike Sweeney
☐ 1878	Don Long, Mgr.	☐ 1879	Gary Ruby, Coach
☐ 1880	Lenn Sakata, Coach	☐ 1881	Checklist

1996 CANADIANS BEST

The most expensive singles are Darin Erstad at $8-10 and Jason Dickson at $4-6. Singles start at 50¢. 1000 sets were produced.
Card Size: 2 1/2" x 3 1/2"
Imprint:
Complete Set (30 cards): 20.00

No.	Player	No.	Player
☐ 1	Don Long, Mgr.	☐ 2	Frank Reberger, Coach
☐ 3	John Morris, Coach	☐ 4	Jim Abbott
☐ 5	George Arias	☐ 6	Jamie Burke
☐ 7	Vince Coleman	☐ 8	Alfredo Diaz
☐ 9	Jason Dickson	☐ 10	Geoff Edsell
☐ 11	Robert Ellis	☐ 12	Darin Erstad
☐ 13	P.J. Forbes	☐ 14	Brian Grebeck
☐ 15	Todd Greene	☐ 16	Ryan Hancock
☐ 17	Pep Harris	☐ 18	Pete Janicki
☐ 19	Aaron Ledsma	☐ 20	Orlando Palmeiro
☐ 21	Brad Pennington	☐ 22	Will Pennyfeather
☐ 23	Chris Pritchett	☐ 24	Joe Roselli
☐ 25	Jeff Schmidt	☐ 26	Paul Swingle
☐ 27	Fausto Tejero	☐ 28	Chris Turner
☐ 29	Shad Williams	☐ 30	Michael Wolff

1997 CANADIANS BEST

Todd Greene is the most expensive single at $4-5.Singles start at 50¢.

Card Size: 2 1/2" x 3 1/2"

Imprint:

Complete Set (30 cards): 15.00

No.	Player	No.	Player
☐ 1	Bruce Hines, Mgr.	☐ 2	Leon Durham, Coach
☐ 3	Howie Gershberg, Coach	☐ 4	Don McGann, Trainer
☐ 5	Geroge Arias	☐ 6	William Bene
☐ 7	Frnk Bolick	☐ 8	Travis Buckley
☐ 9	Edgar Caceres	☐ 10	Jovino Caravajal
☐ 11	Fausto Cruz	☐ 12	Geoff Edsell
☐ 13	Robert Eenhorn	☐ 14	Robert Ellis
☐ 15	Steve Frey	☐ 16	Todd Greene
☐ 17	Ryan Hancock	☐ 18	Pete Janicki
☐ 19	Fausto Macey	☐ 20	Darrell May
☐ 21	Ben Molina	☐ 22	Jose Monzon
☐ 23	Chris Pritchett	☐ 24	Marquis Riley
☐ 25	Jeff Schmidt	☐ 26	Duane Singleton
☐ 27	Jerrey Thurston	☐ 28	Derrick White
☐ 29	Shad Williams	☐ 30	Michael Wolff

WELLAND PIRATES

(NEW YORK-PENN LEAGUE, A)

1989 PIRATES PUCKO

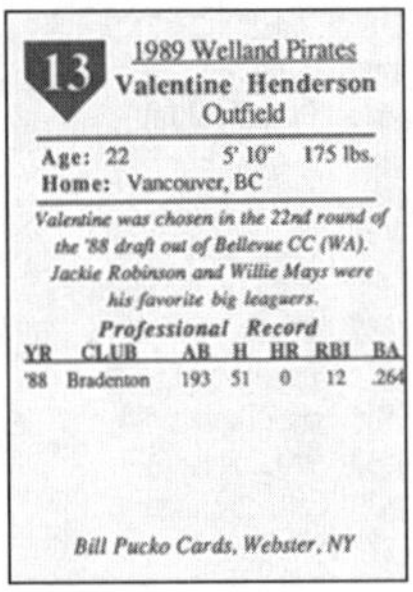

Singles start at 25¢.

Card Size: 2 1/2" x 3 1/2"

Imprint: Bill Pucko Cards

Complete Set (35 cards): 6.00

No.	Player	No.	Player
☐ 1	William Pennyfeather	☐ 2	Scott Arvesen
☐ 3	Robert Bailey, Jr.	☐ 4	Angel Beltran
☐ 5	David Bird	☐ 6	Mike Brewington
☐ 7	Kim Broome	☐ 8	Rod Byerly
☐ 9	Nelson Caraballo	☐ 10	Tom Deller
☐ 11	Raymond Doss	☐ 12	Mike Fortuna
☐ 13	Valentine Henderson	☐ 14	Deron Johnson
☐ 15	Paul Keefer	☐ 16	Jeff Kuder
☐ 17	John Latham	☐ 18	Javier Magria
☐ 19	Erik Nelson	☐ 20	Rob Peterson
☐ 21	Winston Seymour	☐ 22	Garland Slaughter
☐ 23	Mark Thomas	☐ 24	Ken Trusky
☐ 25	Tom Tuholski	☐ 26	Paul Wagner
☐ 27	Tim Wakefield	☐ 28	Ron Way
☐ 29	Flavio Williams	☐ 30	U.L. Washington, Mgr.
☐ 31	Larry Smith, Coach	☐ 32	Paul Allen, Trainer
☐ 33	Bill Kuehn, G.M.	☐ 34	Bob Burgess, Asst. G.M.
☐ 35	John Belford & Norma Chaney		

1990 PIRATES PUCKO

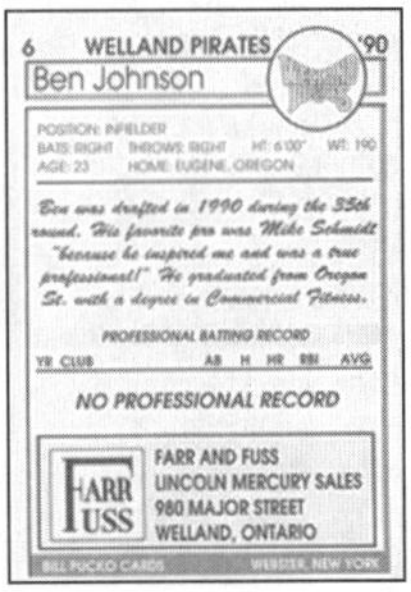

Singles start at 25¢.

Card Size: 2 1/2" x 3 1/2"

Sponsor: Farr & Fuss Mercury Sales

Imprint: Bill Pucko Cards

Complete Set (35 cards): 6.00

No.	Player	No.	Player
☐ 1	Kurt Miller	☐ 2	Michael Brown
☐ 3	Genaro Campusano	☐ 4	Jon Martin
☐ 5	Janiero Feliz	☐ 6	Ben Johnson
☐ 7	Steve Polewski	☐ 8	Kevin Young
☐ 9	John Schulte	☐ 10	Anthony Brown
☐ 11	Scott Bullett, Error (Bullet)	☐ 12	John Curtis
☐ 13	Thomas Green	☐ 14	Joe Ronca
☐ 15	Wes Grisham	☐ 16	Tim Edge
☐ 17	Marcus Hamel	☐ 18	Rob Peterson
☐ 19	Lynn Carlson	☐ 20	Steve Cooke
☐ 21	Mark Futrell	☐ 22	Jeff Lyle
☐ 23	Troy Mooney	☐ 24	Alex Pacheco
☐ 25	Andre Redmond	☐ 26	Richard Robertson
☐ 27	Steve Roeder	☐ 28	Brian Shouse
☐ 29	Shelton Simpson	☐ 30	David Tellers
☐ 31	Michael Zimmerman	☐ 32	Jim Mallon, Mgr.
☐ 33	Coaches: Jerry Nyman/ Rocky Bridges		
☐ 34	Bob Burgess, G.M.	☐ 35	Farr & Fuss
☐ 36	CL: Welland Sports Complex		

1991 PIRATES CLASSIC-BEST

Singles start at 25¢.

Card Size: 2 1/2" x 3 1/2"

Imprint:

Complete Set (30 cards): 5.00

No.	Player	No.	Player
☐ 1	Jon Farrell	☐ 2	Tony Womack
☐ 3	Todd Schroeder	☐ 4	Don Garvey
☐ 5	Tony Mitchell	☐ 6	James Cardona
☐ 7	Mitch House	☐ 8	James Krevokuch
☐ 9	Dean Hinson III	☐ 10	Angelo Encarnacion
☐ 11	Chuck Tooch	☐ 12	Gregg Leavell
☐ 13	Joe McLin, Jr.	☐ 14	Trace Ragland
☐ 15	Craig Shotton	☐ 16	Marty Neff
☐ 17	Jeff Leatherman	☐ 18	Deon Danner

☐ 19	Steve Roeder	☐ 20	Matt Ruebel
☐ 21	John Douris	☐ 22	Mike Maguire
☐ 23	David Bradley	☐ 24	Roberto Ramirez
☐ 25	Glenn Coombs	☐ 26	John Hope
☐ 27	Mike Teich	☐ 28	Jason Bullard
☐ 29	Dan Jones	☐ 30	Checklist

1991 PIRATES PROCARDS

Singles start at 25¢.
Card Size: 2 1/2" x 3 1/2"
Imprint: © 1991 ProCards, Inc.
Complete Set (31 cards): 5.00

No.	Player	No.	Player
☐ 3563	Jason Bullard	☐ 3564	Glenn Coombs
☐ 3565	Deon Danner	☐ 3566	John Douris
☐ 3567	John Hoper	☐ 3568	Dan Jones
☐ 3569	Mike Maguire	☐ 3570	Marc Pisciotta
☐ 3571	Roberto Ramirez	☐ 3572	Matt Ruebel
☐ 3573	Mike Teich	☐ 3574	Angelo Encarnacion
☐ 3575	Jon Farrell	☐ 3576	Dean Hinson III
☐ 3577	Don Garvey	☐ 3578	Mitch House
☐ 3579	James Krevokuch	☐ 3580	Jeff Leatherman
☐ 3581	Joe McLin, Jr.	☐ 3582	Todd Schroeder
☐ 3583	Chuck Tooch	☐ 3584	Tony Womack
☐ 3585	James Cardona	☐ 3586	Gregg Leavell
☐ 3587	Tony Mitchell	☐ 3588	Marty Neff
☐ 3589	Trace Ragland	☐ 3590	Craig Shotton
☐ 3591	Lee Driggers, Mgr.	☐ 3592	Jerry Nyman, Coach
☐ 3593	Checklist		

1992 PIRATES CLASSIC-BEST

Singles start at 20¢.
Card Size: 2 1/2" x 3 1/2"
Imprint:
Complete Set (30 cards): 5.00

No.	Player	No.	Player
☐ 1	Jacob Austin	☐ 2	Miguel Bonilla
☐ 3	Aaron Cannaday	☐ 4	John Carter
☐ 5	John Cranford	☐ 6	Angel Colon
☐ 7	Ramon Espinosa	☐ 8	Frank Garcia-Luna
☐ 9	Rico Gholston	☐ 10	Riegal Hunt, Error (Riegel)
☐ 11	Matt Jones	☐ 12	Erskine Kelly
☐ 13	Dennis Konuszewski	☐ 14	Ted Klamm
☐ 15	Michel LaPlante, Error (Michael)	☐ 16	Sean Lawrence
☐ 17	Pat Lussier	☐ 18	Dave Maize
☐ 19	Gil Perez	☐ 20	Chance Sanford
☐ 21	Craig Shotton	☐ 22	Larry Stahlhoefer
☐ 23	Chuck Tooch	☐ 24	Richard Townsend
☐ 25	Marc Wilkins	☐ 26	Gary Wilson
☐ 27	Stanley Wiltz	☐ 28	Trent Jewett, Mgr.
☐ 29	Julio Garcia, Coach	☐ 30	CL: Tom Barnard, Coach

1993 PIRATES CLASSIC-BEST

Singles start at 25¢.
Card Size: 2 1/2" x 3 1/2"
Imprint:
Complete Set (30 cards): 5.00

No.	Player	No.	Player
☐ 1	Mitch House	☐ 2	Brian Beck
☐ 3	Aaron Cannaday	☐ 4	Lou Collier
☐ 5	Kenny Fairfax	☐ 6	G.G. Harris
☐ 7	Riegal Hunt	☐ 8	Jeff Isom
☐ 9	Tom Johnston	☐ 10	Erskine Kelly
☐ 11	Richard Luna	☐ 12	Jeff Lutt
☐ 13	Sergio Mendez	☐ 14	Johnny Mitchell
☐ 15	Ramon Morel	☐ 16	Jamison Nuttle
☐ 17	Paul Paez	☐ 18	Brian Pelka
☐ 19	Gil Perez	☐ 20	Chris Peters
☐ 21	Jason Phillips	☐ 22	Jeff Pickish
☐ 23	Alan Purdy	☐ 24	Pat Reed
☐ 25	Maximo Rivera	☐ 26	Joe Serna
☐ 27	Stanley Wiltz	☐ 28	John Yselonia
☐ 29	Larry Smith, Mgr.	☐ 30	CL: Julio Garcia, Coach

1993 PIRATES FLEER PROCARDS

Singles start at 25¢.
Card Size: 2 1/2" x 3 1/2"
Imprint: © 1993 FLEER CORP.
Complete Set (31 cards): 5.00

No.	Player	No.	Player
☐ 3346	Jason Abramvicius	☐ 3347	Brian Beck
☐ 3348	Matt Chamberlain	☐ 3349	Kenny Fairfax
☐ 3350	Jeff Isom	☐ 3351	Jeff Lutt
☐ 3352	Ramon Morel	☐ 3353	Jamison Nuttle
☐ 3354	Brian Pelka	☐ 3355	Gil Perez
☐ 3356	Chris Peters	☐ 3357	Jason Phillips
☐ 3358	Jeff Pickish	☐ 3359	Aaron Cannaday
☐ 3360	Sergio Mendez	☐ 3361	Joel Williamson
☐ 3362	Lou Collier	☐ 3363	Pat Gosselin
☐ 3364	G.G. Harris	☐ 3365	Mitch House
☐ 3366	Tom Johnston	☐ 3367	Rich Luna
☐ 3368	Paul Perez	☐ 3369	Maximo Rivera
☐ 3370	Stanley Wiltz	☐ 3371	Jermaine Allensworth
☐ 3372	Riegal Hunt	☐ 3373	Erskine Kelly
☐ 3374	Johnny Mitchell	☐ 3375	Pat Reed
☐ 3376	Checklist		

1994 PIRATES CLASSIC

Singles start at 35¢.
Card Size: 2 1/2" x 3 1/2"
Imprint:
Complete Set (30 cards): 7.00

No.	Player	No.	Player
☐ 1	Mark Farris	☐ 2	Matt Amman
☐ 3	Mike Asche	☐ 4	Richie Blackwell
☐ 5	Keith Brietenstein	☐ 6	Greg Chew
☐ 7	Kane Davis	☐ 8	Elcilio deLeon
☐ 9	Aaron France	☐ 10	Ramon Garcia
☐ 11	Jonnie Gendron	☐ 12	Tim Leger
☐ 13	Joe Mashkivish, Jr.	☐ 14	Tonka Maynor
☐ 15	Rick Paugh	☐ 16	Brian Pelka
☐ 17	Gil Perez	☐ 18	Kevin Pickford
☐ 19	Felipe Polanco	☐ 20	Shannon Puttmann
☐ 21	Miguel Ojeda	☐ 22	Trevor Skjerpen
☐ 23	Matthew Spade	☐ 24	Tarrence Staton
☐ 25	Derek Swafford	☐ 26	Jonathan Sweet
☐ 27	Steven Thobe	☐ 28	Rich Venezia
☐ 29	Jeff Banister, Mgr.	☐ 30	CL: Larry Smith, Coach

1994 PIRATES FLEER PROCARDS

Singles start at 25¢.
Card Size: 2 1/2" x 3 1/2"
Imprint:
Complete Set (31 cards): 5.00

No.	Player	No.	Player
☐ 3483	Richie Blackwell	☐ 3484	Keith Brietenstein
☐ 3485	Greg Chew	☐ 3486	Kane Davis
☐ 3487	Elcilio DeLeon	☐ 3488	Aaron France
☐ 3489	Ramon Garcia	☐ 3490	Jon Gendron
☐ 3491	Joe Mashkivish, Jr.	☐ 3492	Rick Paugh
☐ 3493	Brian Pelka	☐ 3494	Gil Perez
☐ 3495	Kevin Pickford	☐ 3496	Shannon Puttmann
☐ 3497	Trevor Skjerpen	☐ 3498	Matthew Spade
☐ 3499	Miguel Ojeda	☐ 3500	Jonathan Sweet
☐ 3501	Mike Asche	☐ 3502	Mark Farris
☐ 3503	Felipe Polanco	☐ 3504	Steven Thobe
☐ 3505	Derek Swafford	☐ 3506	Rich Venezia
☐ 3507	Matt Amman	☐ 3508	Tim Leger
☐ 3509	Tonka Maynor	☐ 3510	Tarrence Staton
☐ 3511	Jeff Banister, Mgr.	☐ 3512	Larry Smith, Coach
☐ 3513	Checklist		

CHAPTER FIVE

ALPHABETICAL INDEX

This alphabetical index cross-references player cards in chapters one through four. Chapter One (Vintage) and chapter two (Post WWII) sets are listed first in alphabetical order by brand, then Chapter Three sets (Expos and Blue Jays teams issue) and at last Chapter Four sets (Minor League team issues). The index does not include cards listed in Chapter Six (Canadian-born players checklist and price guide).

A

ALLEN, NEIL
81 O-Pee-Chee 322
82 O-Pee-Chee 205
83 O-Pee-Chee 268
84 O-Pee-Chee 183
85 O-Pee-Chee 234
87 O-Pee-Chee 113
82 opcSticker 66
83 opcSticker 265
84 opcSticker 147
85 opcSticker 144
87 opcSticker 292
96 StCatharines/Best 2

ALLEN, PAUL
89 Welland/Pucko 32

ALLEN, RICHIE
66 O-Pee-Chee 80
69 O-Pee-Chee 6, -Deckle 1
70 O-Pee-Chee 40
71 O-Pee-Chee 650
72 O-Pee-Chee 240
75 O-Pee-Chee 210

ALLEN, ROD
81 Edmonton/RedRooster 21

ALLENSON, GARY
82 O-Pee-Chee 273
84 O-Pee-Chee 56

ALLENSWORTH, JERMAINE
93 Welland/ProCards 3371

ALLEY, GENE
65 O-Pee-Chee 121
68 O-Pee-Chee 53
71 O-Pee-Chee 416
72 O-Pee-Chee 286
73 O-Pee-Chee 635

ALLIETTA, BOB
76 O-Pee-Chee 623

ALLISON, BOB
65 O-Pee-Chee 180
67 O-Pee-Chee 194
69 O-Pee-Chee 30
60 opcTattoo 2
62 PostCereal 83
62 ShirriffCoin 22

ALLRED, BEAU
90 O-Pee-Chee 419

ALMON, BILL
80 Dimanche/DernièreHeure
80 O-Pee-Chee 225
82 O-Pee-Chee 119
83 O-Pee-Chee 362
84 O-Pee-Chee 241
86 O-Pee-Chee 48
87 O-Pee-Chee 159
82 opcSticker 167
84 opcSticker 334
86 opcSticker 131

ALOMAR, ROBERTO
92 Ben'sDisk 3
92 CSCSheet
90 FleerCdn. 149
93 HumptyDumpty 22
88 Leaf 34
92 McDonald's 1
89 O-Pee-Chee 206
90 O-Pee-Chee 517
91 O-Pee-Chee 315
92 O-Pee-Chee 225
93 O-Pee-Chee 4, -WSC 1
94 OPC 96, -AS 21, -TOR 6
91 opcPremier 1
92 opcPremier 130
93 opcPremier-StarPerf. 3
89 opcSticker 104
89 PaniniSticker 191
90 PaniniSticker 349
91 PaniniSticker 92
92 PaniniSticker 26, 273
93 PaniniSticker 27
94 PaniniSticker 134
92 PizzaHut/DietPepsi 15
92 PostCdn. 13
93 PostCdn. 5
94 PostCdn. 3
95 PostCdn. 2
91 TOR/FireSafety
91 TOR/Score 13, 39
92 TOR/FireSafety
93 TOR (x2)
93 TOR/Dempster's 2
93 TOR/FireSafety
93 TOR/McDonald's 18, 21, 28
94 TOR
95 TOR/OhHenry
97 TOR/Sizzler 46, 48

ALOMAR, SANDY (SR.)
65 O-Pee-Chee 82
70 O-Pee-Chee 29
71 O-Pee-Chee 745
72 O-Pee-Chee 253
73 O-Pee-Chee 123
74 O-Pee-Chee 347
75 O-Pee-Chee 266
76 O-Pee-Chee 629

ALOMAR, SANDY (JR.)
90 FleerCdn. 150
93 HumptyDumpty 5
92 McDonald's 11
90 O-Pee-Chee 353
91 O-Pee-Chee 165
92 O-Pee-Chee 420
93 O-Pee-Chee 12
94 O-Pee-Chee 201
91 opcPremier 2
92 opcPremier 164
89 PaniniSticker 192
91 PaniniSticker 166, 215
93 PaniniSticker 47
94 PaniniSticker 53
91 PaniniTopFifteen 109
91 PetroCanada 9
92 PizzaHut/DietPepsi 10
91 PostCdn. 23

ALOU, FELIPE
96 HitTheBooks
66 O-Pee-Chee 96
68 O-Pee-Chee 55, -Poster 3
69 O-Pee-Chee 2
70 O-Pee-Chee 434
71 O-Pee-Chee 495
72 O-Pee-Chee 263
73 O-Pee-Chee 65-
74 O-Pee-Chee 485
62 PostCereal 133
62 ShirriffCoins 130
84 MTL
84 MTL/StuartBakery 6,38
92 MTL/Durivage 15
93 MTL/McDonald's 31
96 MTL/Disk

ALOU, JESUS
69 O-Pee-Chee 22
70 O-Pee-Chee 248
71 O-Pee-Chee 253
76 O-Pee-Chee 468

ALOU, MATTY
66 O-Pee-Chee 94
67 O-Pee-Chee 10
68 O-Pee-Chee 1, -Poster 4
69 O-Pee-Chee 2
70 O-Pee-Chee 30, 460
71 O-Pee-Chee 720
72 O-Pee-Chee 395
73 O-Pee-Chee 132
74 O-Pee-Chee 430

ALOU, MOISES
90 FleerCdn. 650
93 HumptyDumpty 39
91 O-Pee-Chee 526
92 O-Pee-Chee 401
93 O-Pee-Chee 10
94 O-Pee-Chee 266
91 opcPremier 3
93 PaniniSticker 232
94 PaniniSticker 206
94 PostCdn. 9
94 PostCdn. 5
93 MTL/McDonald's 1
96 MTL/Disk (x2)

ALPERMAN, WHITEY
1912 ImperialTobacco(C46) 7

ALSTON, WALTER EMMONS
53 Exhibits 61
65 O-Pee-Chee 217
66 O-Pee-Chee 116
69 O-Pee-Chee 24
70 O-Pee-Chee 242
71 O-Pee-Chee 567
73 O-Pee-Chee 569
74 O-Pee-Chee 144
75 O-Pee-Chee 361
76 O-Pee-Chee 46
52 Parkhurst 66

ALTMAN, GEORGE
66 O-Pee-Chee 146
67 O-Pee-Chee 87
62 PostCereal 187
62 ShirriffCoin 128

ALVARADO, LUIS
70 O-Pee-Chee 317
71 O-Pee-Chee 489
73 O-Pee-Chee 627
74 O-Pee-Chee 462

ALVAREZ, CHRIS
90 London/ProCards 1273

ALVAREZ, FAUSTO
94 GarciaPhoto 112

ALVAREZ, JOSE
90 FleerCdn. 574
90 O-Pee-Chee 782
89 PaniniSticker 31

ALVAREZ, TAVO
93 Ottawa/ProCards 2428

ALVAREZ, WILSON
91 O-Pee-Chee 378
92 O-Pee-Chee 452
92 opcPremier 122
90 Vancouver/CMC 1
90 Vancouver/ProCards 481

ALVIS, MAX
65 O-Pee-Chee 185
69 O-Pee-Chee 145
70 O-Pee-Chee 85

ALYEA, BRANT
66 O-Pee-Chee 11
69 O-Pee-Chee 48
70 O-Pee-Chee 303
71 O-Pee-Chee 449
72 O-Pee-Chee 383

AMALFITANO, JOE
73 O-Pee-Chee 252
74 O-Pee-Chee 78
62 PostCereal 144
62 ShirriffCoin 193

AMARAL, RICH
94 O-Pee-Chee 149
93 opcPremier 114
94 PaniniSticker 120
91 Calgary/LineDrive 51
91 Calgary/ProCards 520
92 Calgary/ProCards 3737
90 Vancouver/CMC 13
90 Vancouver/ProCards 493

AMARO, RUBEN
66 O-Pee-Chee 186
68 O-Pee-Chee 138
62 PostCereal 194
62 ShirriffCoin 163
91 Edmonton/LineDrive 152
91 Edmonton/ProCards 1526

AMARO, RUBEN
92 O-Pee-Chee 269
93 O-Pee-Chee 18
92 opcPremier 16

AMBROSIA, CIRO
90 StCatharines/ProCards 346

AMELUNG, ED
87 Edmonton/ProCards 2071

AMMAN, MATT
94 Welland/Classic 2
94 Welland/ProCards 3507

AMOROS, EDMUNDO
53 Exhibits 43

ANDERSEN, LARRY
90 FleerCdn. 221
91 O-Pee-Chee 761
92 O-Pee-Chee 616

ANDERSON, ALLAN
90 FleerCdn. 366
89 O-Pee-Chee 20
90 O-Pee-Chee 71
91 O-Pee-Chee 223
92 O-Pee-Chee 417
89 PaniniSticker 381
90 PaniniSticker 117

ANDERSON, BERNIE
89 London/ProCards 1364

ANDERSON, BRADY
90 FleerCdn. 172
89 O-Pee-Chee 161
90 O-Pee-Chee 598
91 O-Pee-Chee 97
92 O-Pee-Chee 268
93 O-Pee-Chee 16
94 O-Pee-Chee 3
93 PaniniSticker 76
94 PaniniSticker 17

ANDERSON, DALLAS
97 Lethbridge/ Best 18

ANDERSON, DAVE
86 O-Pee-Chee 29
88 O-Pee-Chee 203
89 O-Pee-Chee 117
90 O-Pee-Chee 248
91 O-Pee-Chee 572
88 PaniniSticker 313

ANDERSON, DWAIN
72 O-Pee-Chee 268
73 O-Pee-Chee 241

ANDERSON, FERRELL (ANDY)
52 Parkhurst 17

ANDERSON, GARRETT
93 Vancouver/ProCards 2608
94 Vancouver/ProCards 1873

ANDERSON, GEORGE LEE (SPARKY)
70 O-Pee-Chee 181
71 O-Pee-Chee 688
72 O-Pee-Chee 358
73 O-Pee-Chee 296
74 O-Pee-Chee 326
75 O-Pee-Chee 531
76 O-Pee-Chee 104
90 O-Pee-Chee 609
91 O-Pee-Chee 519
92 O-Pee-Chee 381
43-47 Toronto/BeeHive

ANDERSON, JIMMY
97 Calgary/Best 5

ANDERSON, KENT
90 O-Pee-Chee 16
91 O-Pee-Chee 667
92 Calgary/ProCards 3738
88 Edmonton/CMC 17
88 Edmonton/ProCards 574
89 Edmonton/CMC 17
91 Edmonton/LineDrive 153
91 Edmonton/ProCards 1520

ANDERSON, LARRY
76 O-Pee-Chee 593

ANDERSON, MIKE
72 O-Pee-Chee 14
73 O-Pee-Chee 147
74 O-Pee-Chee 619
75 O-Pee-Chee 118
76 O-Pee-Chee 527
82 Vancouver/TCMA 22
84 Vancouver/Cramer 46

ANDERSON, SCOTT
84 O-Pee-Chee 164
93 Edmonton/ProCards 1129

ANDREWS, MIKE
69 O-Pee-Chee 52
70 O-Pee-Chee 406
71 O-Pee-Chee 191
72 O-Pee-Chee 361
73 O-Pee-Chee 42

ANDREWS, ROB
76 O-Pee-Chee 568

ANDREWS, SHANE
96 HitTheBooks
91 O-Pee-Chee 74
96 MTL/Disk
94 Ottawa/ProCards 2902

ANDUJAR, JOAQUIN
85 Leaf 13
87 Leaf 162
79 O-Pee-Chee 246
80 O-Pee-Chee 324
81 O-Pee-Chee 329
83 O-Pee-Chee 228
84 O-Pee-Chee 371
85 O-Pee-Chee 231
86 O-Pee-Chee 150
87 O-Pee-Chee 284
83 opcSticker 179
85 opcSticker 136
86 opcSticker 44
87 opcSticker 172

ANDUX, ORLANDO
52 Laval Dairy 107

ANGELINI, NORM
73 O-Pee-Chee 616

ANTHONY, ERIC
90 FleerCdn. 222
90 O-Pee-Chee 608
91 O-Pee-Chee 331
93 O-Pee-Chee 2
94 O-Pee-Chee 61
93 PaniniSticker 176
94 PaniniSticker 188

ANTHONY, GREG
92 O-Pee-Chee 336

ANTONELLI, JOHN
60 opcTattoo 3

APARICIO, LIUS
69 O-Pee-Chee 90, -Deckle 2
67 O-Pee-Chee 60
69 O-Pee-Chee 75
70 O-Pee-Chee 315
71 O-Pee-Chee 740
72 O-Pee-Chee 313, 314
73 O-Pee-Chee 165
74 O-Pee-Chee 61
62 PostCereal 49
62 ShirriffCoin 71

APODACA, BOB
74 O-Pee-Chee 608
75 O-Pee-Chee 659
76 O-Pee-Chee 16
79 O-Pee-Chee 98

APPIER, KEVIN
90 FleerCdn. 100
90 O-Pee-Chee 167
91 O-Pee-Chee 454
92 O-Pee-Chee 281
93 O-Pee-Chee 23
94 O-Pee-Chee 225
93 PaniniSticker 101
94 PaniniSticker 71
91 PaniniTopFifteen 72, 95

APPLING, LUKE
37 O-Pee-Chee(V300)
34 WWGum(V354) 84
36 WWGum(V355) 113

AQUINO, LUIS
90 FleerCdn. 101
87 O-Pee-Chee 301
90 O-Pee-Chee 707
91 O-Pee-Chee 169
92 O-Pee-Chee 412

ARAGON, YOVANI
94 GarciaPhoto 93

ARCHER, JIM
62 PostCereal 98
62 ShirriffCoin 75

ARCIA, JOSE
71 O-Pee-Chee 134
73 O-Pee-Chee 466

ARDUNIN, SALVATORE (SOL)
52 LavalDairy 84

ARIAS, ALEX
92 O-Pee-Chee 551
93 opcPremier 84

ARIAS, ALFREDO
94 StCatharines/Classic 2
94 StCatharines/ProCards 3631

ARIAS, GEORGE
96 Vancouver/Best 5
97 Vancouver/Best 5

ARIAS, JOSE
90 Hamilton/Star 2

ARLIN, STEVE
72 O-Pee-Chee 78
73 O-Pee-Chee 294
74 O-Pee-Chee 406
75 O-Pee-Chee 159

ARMAS, TONY
90 FleerCdn. 126
85 Leaf 112
86 Leaf 5
81 O-Pee-Chee 151
82 O-Pee-Chee 60
83 O-Pee-Chee 353
84 O-Pee-Chee 105
85 O-Pee-Chee 394
86 O-Pee-Chee 255
87 O-Pee-Chee 174
90 O-Pee-Chee 603
82 opcSticker 4, 224
83 opcSticker 108, 191, 192
84 opcSticker 218
85 opcSticker 95, 194, 209
86 opcSticker 254
86 opcTattoo 11
88 PaniniSticker 10, 11
89 PaniniSticker 295

ARMBRISTER, ED
72 O-Pee-Chee 524
74 O-Pee-Chee 601
75 O-Pee-Chee 622
76 O-Pee-Chee 652

ARMSTRONG, JACK
90 FleerCdn. 412
90 O-Pee-Chee 642
91 O-Pee-Chee 175
92 O-Pee-Chee 77
92 opcPremier 192
89 PaniniSticker 63
91 PaniniSticker 165

ARNOLD, CHRIS
72 O-Pee-Chee 232
73 O-Pee-Chee 584
74 O-Pee-Chee 43

ARNSBERG, BRAD
91 O-Pee-Chee 706

ARNOVICH, MORRIS
39 WWGum(V351A)

AROCHA, RENE
94 O-Pee-Chee 234
93 opcPremier 6

ARRIGO, JERRY
65 O-Pee-Chee 39
69 O-Pee-Chee 213
70 O-Pee-Chee 274

ARROJO, LUIS ROLANDO
94 GarciaPhoto 84

ARROYO, FERNANDO
76 O-Pee-Chee 614
93 Edmonton/ProCards 1153

ARROYO, LUIS
62 PostCereal 12

ARVESEN, SCOTT
89 Welland/Pucko 2

ASHBURN, RICHIE
60 opcTattoo 4, 72
50 PalmDairies
62 PostCereal 186
62 ShirriffCoin171

ASHBY, ALAN
76 O-Pee-Chee 209
77 O-Pee-Chee 148
78 O-Pee-Chee 76
79 O-Pee-Chee 14
80 O-Pee-Chee 105
81 O-Pee-Chee 146
82 O-Pee-Chee 184
83 O-Pee-Chee 84
84 O-Pee-Chee 217
85 O-Pee-Chee 29
86 O-Pee-Chee 331
88 O-Pee-Chee 48
89 O-Pee-Chee 359
82 opcSticker 48
83 opcSticker 241
84 opcSticker 72
88 opcSticker 32
88 PaniniSticker 291, 293, 294
78 TOR

ASHBY, ANDY
92 O-Pee-Chee 497

ASHE, MIKE
94 Welland/Classic 3
94 Welland/ProCards 3501

ASPROMONTE, BOB
65 O-Pee-Chee 175
68 O-Pee-Chee 95
70 O-Pee-Chee 529
71 O-Pee-Chee 469

ASPROMONTE, KEN
73 O-Pee-Chee 449
74 O-Pee-Chee 521
62 ShirriffCoin 7

ASSENMACHER, PAUL
90 FleerCdn. 25
87 Leaf 164
90 O-Pee-Chee 644
91 O-Pee-Chee 12
92 O-Pee-Chee 753
87 opcSticker 37
89 PaniniSticker 33

ASTACIO, PEDRO
93 O-Pee-Chee 9

ATKINSON, BILL
78 O-Pee-Chee 144
80 O-Pee-Chee 133
77 MTL
77 MTL/RedpathSugar
81 Edmonton/RedRooster 12

ATWELL, TOBY
50 WWGum(V362) 34

AUBIN, YVES
52 Laval Dairy 101

AUCOIN, DEREK
96 MTL/Disk

AUERBACH, RICK
72 O-Pee-Chee 153
73 O-Pee-Chee 427
74 O-Pee-Chee 289
75 O-Pee-Chee 588
76 O-Pee-Chee 622

AUGUST, DON
90 O-Pee-Chee 192
89 PaniniSticker 365
92 London/ProCards 623

AUGUSTINE, DAVE
74 O-Pee-Chee 598
75 O-Pee-Chee 616

AULT, DOUG
92 Nabisco 30
77 O-Pee-Chee 202
78 O-Pee-Chee 202
79 O-Pee-Chee 205
78 TOR
90 StCatharines/ProCards 3482
91 StCatharines/ClassicBest 26
91 StCatharines/ProCards 3411

AUSMUS, BRAD
92 O-Pee-Chee 58
94 PaniniSticker 251

AUST, DENNIS
66 O-Pee-Chee 179

AUSTIN, JACOB
92 Welland/ClassicBest 1

AUSTIN, JAMES
93 O-Pee-Chee 6

AUSTIN, JAMES P.
23 WillardsChocolate(V100) 3

AUSTIN, RICK
71 O-Pee-Chee 41
76 O-Pee-Chee 269

AVERILL, EARL
37 O-Pee-Chee(V300) 103
62 PostCereal 80
62 ShirriffCoin 24
39 WWGum(V351B)

AVERY, STEVE
93 Humpty Dumpty 26
91 O-Pee-Chee 227
92 O-Pee-Chee 574
93 O-Pee-Chee 5
94 O-Pee-Chee 196
92 opcPremier 170
92 PaniniSticker 169

AYALA, BENNY
75 O-Pee-Chee 619
84 opcSticker 22

AYLMER, BOBBY
90 StCatharines/ProCards 3465

AZCUE, JOE
69 O-Pee-Chee 176
70 O-Pee-Chee 294
71 O-Pee-Chee 657

AZOCAR, OSCAR
91 O-Pee-Chee 659
92 O-Pee-Chee 112
93 O-Pee-Chee 263
91 PaniniSticker 329

B

BABIK, BILL
52 LavalDairy 72

BACKMAN, WALLY
90 FleerCdn. 367
85 Leaf 79
87 Leaf 59
88 Leaf 202
85 O-Pee-Chee 162
86 O-Pee-Chee 191
87 O-Pee-Chee 48
88 O-Pee-Chee 333
89 O-Pee-Chee 72
90 O-Pee-Chee 218
91 O-Pee-Chee 722
92 O-Pee-Chee 434
85 opcSticker 106
86 opcSticker 97
87 opcSticker 100
88 PaniniSticker 340

BADDREK, MIKE
91 Hamilton/ClassicBest 5
91 Hamilton/ProCards 4026

BAERGA, CARLOS
91 O-Pee-Chee 147
92 O-Pee-Chee 33
93 O-Pee-Chee 39
94 O-Pee-Chee 106, -AS 6
93 opcPremier 51
91 PaniniSticker 218
92 PaniniSticker 47
93 PaniniSticker 51
94 PaniniSticker 54

BAEZ, JOSE MIGUEL
94 GarciaPhoto 122

BAGBY, JAMES C.
23 WillardsChocolate(V100) 4

BAGLEY, LORENZO
97 St.Catharines/Best 6

BAGWELL, JEFF
93 HumptyDumpty 32
92 McDonald's 24
92 O-Pee-Chee 520
93 O-Pee-Chee 29
94 O-Pee-Chee 212, -AS 5
92 PaniniSticker 152
93 PaniniSticker 170
94 PaniniSticker 189
95 PostCdn. 15

BAHNSEN, STAN
80 Dimanche/DernièreHeure
67 O-Pee-Chee 93
71 O-Pee-Chee 184
73 O-Pee-Chee 20
74 O-Pee-Chee 254
75 O-Pee-Chee 161
76 O-Pee-Chee 534
78 O-Pee-Chee 54
79 O-Pee-Chee 244
80 O-Pee-Chee 345
81 O-Pee-Chee 267
82 O-Pee-Chee 131
77 MTL

BAILES, SCOTT
90 FleerCdn. 484
87 O-Pee-Chee 134
88 O-Pee-Chee 107
90 O-Pee-Chee 784
92 O-Pee-Chee 95
88 opcSticker 206
89 opcSticker 217
88 PaniniSticker 68

BAILEY, BOB
72 Dimanche/DernièreHeure
92 Nabisco 11
67 O-Pee-Chee 32
70 O-Pee-Chee 293
71 O-Pee-Chee 157
72 O-Pee-Chee 493
73 O-Pee-Chee 505
74 O-Pee-Chee 97
75 O-Pee-Chee 365
76 O-Pee-Chee 338
79 O-Pee-Chee 282
71 ProStarPostcard
71 MTL/LaPizzaRoyale
71 MTL/ProStar
74 MTL/GeorgeWeston

BAILEY, ED
62 PostCereal 137
62 ShirriffCoin 113

BAILEY, MARK
85 O-Pee-Chee 64
86 opcSticker 30

BAILEY, ROBERT JR.
89 Welland/Pucko 3

BAILEY, ROY
90 Hamilton/Best 2
90 Hamilton/Star 3

BAILOR, BOB
92 Nabisco 36
77 O-Pee-Chee 48
78 O-Pee-Chee 148
79 O-Pee-Chee 259
80 O-Pee-Chee 304
81 O-Pee-Chee 297
83 opcSticker 260
84 opcSticker 109
79 TOR/BubbleYum
92 TOR/FireSafety
93 TOR/FireSafety
95 TOR/OhHenry

BAINES, HAROLD
90 FleerCdn. 290
85 Leaf 231
86 Leaf 13
87 Leaf 52
88 Leaf 157
86 GeneralMills 2
87 HostessSticker 21
81 O-Pee-Chee 347
82 O-Pee-Chee 56
83 O-Pee-Chee 177
84 O-Pee-Chee 197
85 O-Pee-Chee 249
86 O-Pee-Chee 65
87 O-Pee-Chee 309
88 O-Pee-Chee 35
89 O-Pee-Chee 152
90 O-Pee-Chee 345
91 O-Pee-Chee 166
92 O-Pee-Chee 635
93 O-Pee-Chee 3
94 O-Pee-Chee 221
93 opcPremier 67
83 opcSticker 52
84 opcSticker 242
85 opcSticker 234
86 opcSticker 288
87 opcSticker 284
88 opcSticker 293
89 opcSticker 304
86 opcTattoo 4
88 PaniniSticker 62
89 PaniniSticker 310
90 PaniniSticker 167, 200
94 PaniniSticker 18
87 StuartBakery 17

BAIR, DOUG
78 O-Pee-Chee 229
79 O-Pee-Chee 58
80 O-Pee-Chee 234
81 O-Pee-Chee 73

BAKER, DEL
36 WWGum(V355) 31

BAKER, DOUG
90 FleerCdn. 368

BAKER, DUSTY
86 Leaf 231
71 O-Pee-Chee 709
73 O-Pee-Chee 215
74 O-Pee-Chee 320
75 O-Pee-Chee 33
76 O-Pee-Chee 28
79 O-Pee-Chee 290
80 O-Pee-Chee 135
82 O-Pee-Chee 375
83 O-Pee-Chee 220
84 O-Pee-Chee 40
85 O-Pee-Chee 165
86 O-Pee-Chee 31
82 opcSticker 52
83 opcSticker 245
84 opcSticker 80

BAKER, FRANK
71 O-Pee-Chee 213, 689
72 O-Pee-Chee 409
74 O-Pee-Chee 411

BAKER, J. FRANKLIN
23 WillardsChocolate(V100) 5

BAKER, SCOTT
95 Edmonton/Macri

BALABON, RICK
91 Calgary/LineDrive 52
91 Calgary/ProCards 508

BALAZ, JOHN
76 O-Pee-Chee 539

BALBONI, STEVE
90 FleerCdn. 436
85 Leaf 95
86 Leaf 98
87 Leaf 262
83 O-Pee-Chee 8
85 O-Pee-Chee 152
86 O-Pee-Chee 164
87 O-Pee-Chee 240
89 O-Pee-Chee 336
90 O-Pee-Chee 716
91 O-Pee-Chee 511
85 opcSticker 271
86 opcSticker 265
87 opcSticker 263
89 opcSticker 222
86 opcTattoo 21

BALCENA, ROBERT L.
52 Parkhurst 20

BALDSCHUN, JACK
70 O-Pee-Chee 284

BALDWIN, DAVE
69 O-Pee-Chee 132
71 O-Pee-Chee 48

BALDWIN, JAMES
94 O-Pee-Chee 210

BALDWIN, RICK
76 O-Pee-Chee 372

BALE, JOHN
96 StCatharines/Best 4

BALES, WESLEY (LEE)
67 O-Pee-Chee 51

BALLARD, JEFF
90 FleerCdn. 173
90 O-Pee-Chee 296, 394
91 O-Pee-Chee 546
92 O-Pee-Chee 104
89 opcSticker 230
89 PaniniSticker 253
90 PaniniSticker 13

BALLER, JAY
88 Calgary/CMC 5
88 Calgary/ProCards 792

BALSCHUN, JACK
67 O-Pee-Chee 114

BALSLEY, DARREN
90 StCatharines/ProCards 3484

BALTHAZAR, DOYLE
89 London/ProCards 1384
91 London/LineDrive 376
91 London/ProCards 1880

BAMBERGER, GEORGE
73 O-Pee-Chee 136
74 O-Pee-Chee 306

BANCROFT, DAVID J.
23 WillardsChocolate(V100) 6
22 WilliamPaterson(V89) 38

BANDO, CHRIS
85 Leaf 39
85 O-Pee-Chee 14
86 O-Pee-Chee 211
88 O-Pee-Chee 51
88 opcSticker 209
88 PaniniSticker 71

BANDO, SAL
67 O-Pee-Chee 33
68 O-Pee-Chee 146
70 O-Pee-Chee 120
71 O-Pee-Chee 285
72 O-Pee-Chee 348
73 O-Pee-Chee 155
74 O-Pee-Chee 103
75 O-Pee-Chee 380
76 O-Pee-Chee 90
77 O-Pee-Chee 145
78 O-Pee-Chee 174
79 O-Pee-Chee 283
80 O-Pee-Chee 363
81 O-Pee-Chee 276

BANE, ED
74 O-Pee-Chee 592

BANEY, DICK
70 O-Pee-Chee 88
74 O-Pee-Chee 608

BANISTER, JEFF
94 Welland/Classic 29
94 Welland/ProCards 3511

BANKHEAD, DAN
52 Parkhurst 64

BANKHEAD, SCOTT
90 FleerCdn. 505
88 O-Pee-Chee 246
89 O-Pee-Chee 79
90 O-Pee-Chee 213
91 O-Pee-Chee 436
92 O-Pee-Chee 155
93 O-Pee-Chee 21
92 opcPremier 18
94 opcPremier 94
88 PaniniSticker 180
89 PaniniSticker 429
90 PaniniSticker 147

BANKS, ERNIE
66 O-Pee-Chee 110
69 O-Pee-Chee 6, 20
70 O-Pee-Chee 14
71 O-Pee-Chee 525
73 O-Pee-Chee 81
75 O-Pee-Chee 196, 197
60 opcTattoo 5
62 PostCereal 188
62 ShirriffCoin 177

BANKS, WILLIE
92 O-Pee-Chee 747
93 PaniniSticker 127
94 PaniniSticker 89

BANNING, DOUG
87 Edmonton/ProCards 2067

BANNISTER, ALAN
80 O-Pee-Chee 317
83 O-Pee-Chee 348
84 opcSticker 257

BANNISTER, FLOYD
86 Leaf 118
79 O-Pee-Chee 154
80 O-Pee-Chee 352
81 O-Pee-Chee 166
83 O-Pee-Chee 203
84 O-Pee-Chee 280
85 O-Pee-Chee 354
86 O-Pee-Chee 64
87 O-Pee-Chee 356
88 O-Pee-Chee 357
89 O-Pee-Chee 194
90 O-Pee-Chee 116
82 opcSticker 234
83 opcSticker 18, 113
84 opcSticker 247
86 opcSticker 286
88 PaniniSticker 52

BANTA, JACK
43-47 Montréal/ParadeSportive

BANTON, SCOTT
89 Hamilton/Star 1

BARBARA, DON
92 Edmonton/ProCards 3543
92 Edmonton/SkyBox 151

BARBARE, WALT
21 Neilson's(V61) 73

BARBER, BRIAN
92 O-Pee-Chee 594

BARBER, STEVE
65 O-Pee-Chee 113
67 O-Pee-Chee 82
70 O-Pee-Chee 224
72 O-Pee-Chee 333
73 O-Pee-Chee 36
74 O-Pee-Chee 631
62 Shirriff Coin 11

BARBER, TURNER
23 WillardsChocolate(V100) 7

BARBERICH, FRANK
1912 ImperialTobacco(C46) 16

BARBERIE, BRET
92 O-Pee-Chee 224
92 opcPremier 36
94 PaniniSticker 179
91 MTL/Durivage 1

BARBIERI, JIM
67 Durivage 76

BARE, RAY
76 O-Pee-Chee 507

BARFIELD, JESSE
90 FleerCdn. 437
86 GeneralMills 3
87 GeneralMills 1
87 HostessSticker 1
88 HostessDisk 19
85 Leaf 209
86 Leaf 254
87 Leaf 127
88 Leaf 225
82 O-Pee-Chee 203
83 O-Pee-Chee 257
84 O-Pee-Chee 316
85 O-Pee-Chee 24, -Poster 20
86 O-Pee-Chee 234
87 O-Pee-Chee 24
88 O-Pee-Chee 140
89 O-Pee-Chee 325
90 O-Pee-Chee 740
91 O-Pee-Chee 85
92 O-Pee-Chee 650
83 opcSticker 307
84 opcSticker 372
85 opcSticker 362
86 opcSticker 192
87 opcSticker 184
88 opcSticker 192,-SStar 46
86 opcTattoo 2
88 PaniniSticker 223
89 PaniniSticker 471
90 PaniniSticker 120
91 PaniniSticker 330
92 PaniniSticker 139
87 StuartBakery 27
84 TOR/FireSafety
85 TOR/FireSafety
86 TOR/AultFoods
86 TOR/FireSafety
87 TOR/FireSafety
88 TOR
88 TOR/FireSafety
89 TOR/FireSafety
90 TOR/Hostess (x3)
97 TOR/Sizzler 34

BARFIELD, JOHN
91 O-Pee-Chee 428

BARGAR, GREG
83 Dimanche/DernièreHeure
84 O-Pee-Chee 292

BARILLARI, AL
52 LavalDairy 50

BARNETT, BRIAN
97 St.Catharines/Best 7

BARKER, LEN
79 O-Pee-Chee 40
81 O-Pee-Chee 3
82 O-Pee-Chee 360
83 O-Pee-Chee 120
84 O-Pee-Chee 309
82 opcSticker 12, 113, 178
83 opcSticker 57

BARKER, TIM
93 Ottawa/ProCards 2440

BARLOW, MIKE
81 O-Pee-Chee 77

BARNARD, TOM
92 Welland/ClassicBest 30

BARNES, BRIAN
91 O-Pee-Chee 211
92 O-Pee-Chee 73
93 O-Pee-Chee 249
91 opcPremier 4
92 opcPremier 52
92 MTL/Durivage 2

BARNES, JESSE L.
20 MapleCrispette(V117) 1
23 WillardsChocolate(V100) 8

BARNES, RICH
81 Edmonton/RedRooster 10
82 Edmonton/TCMA 19

BARNES, SKEETER
92 O-Pee-Chee 221
93 PaniniSticker 121

BARNES, TOM
52 LavalDairy 90

BARNHART, CLYDE
21 Neilson's(V61) 108

BARR, JIM
72 O-Pee-Chee 232
73 O-Pee-Chee 387
74 O-Pee-Chee 233
75 O-Pee-Chee 107
76 O-Pee-Chee 308
77 O-Pee-Chee 119
78 O-Pee-Chee 19
80 O-Pee-Chee 275

BARR, STEVE
76 O-Pee-Chee 595

BARRABI, CARLOS
94 GarciaPhoto 102

BARRETT, C.H. (RED)
52 Parkhurst 14

BARRETT, MARTY
90 FleerCdn. 266
85 Leaf 229
86 Leaf 169
87 Leaf 165
88 Leaf 141
86 O-Pee-Chee 314
87 O-Pee-Chee 39
88 O-Pee-Chee 338
89 O-Pee-Chee 155
90 O-Pee-Chee 355
91 O-Pee-Chee 496
85 opcSticker 219
86 opcSticker 250
87 opcSticker 18
88 opcSticker 248
89 opcSticker 257
88 PaniniSticker 26, 27, 28
89 PaniniSticker 276
90 PaniniSticker 15

96 TOR/OhHenry
97 TOR/Sizzler 34

BELL, GUS
76 O-Pee-Chee 66
62 PostCereal 120
62 ShirriffCoin 158

BELL, JAY
90 FleerCdn. 459
90 O-Pee-Chee 523
91 O-Pee-Chee 293
92 O-Pee-Chee 779
93 O-Pee-Chee 19
94 O-Pee-Chee 222
90 PaniniSticker 321
91 PaniniSticker 118
92 PaniniSticker 255
93 PaniniSticker 283
94 PaniniSticker 233

BELL, JERRY
72 O-Pee-Chee 162
73 O-Pee-Chee 92
74 O-Pee-Chee 261

BELL, JUAN
90 O-Pee-Chee 724
92 O-Pee-Chee 52
91 opcPremier 7

BELL, KEVIN
80 O-Pee-Chee 197

BELL, SAM
39 WWGum(V351A)

BELLE, ALBERT (JOEY)
90 FleerCdn. 485
90 O-Pee-Chee 283
92 O-Pee-Chee 785
93 O-Pee-Chee 66
94 O-Pee-Chee 43, -AS 12
91 opcPremier 8
92 opcPremier 100
92 PaniniSticker 51
93 PaniniSticker 52
94 PaniniSticker 67, 55
88 TOR/FireSafety

BELLIARD, RAFAEL
90 FleerCdn. 460
89 O-Pee-Chee 119
90 O-Pee-Chee 143
91 O-Pee-Chee 487
92 O-Pee-Chee 367
89 opcSticker 133
92 PaniniSticker 165

BELLO, RENE
94 GarciaPhoto 62

BELLUM, DONNIE
92 Hamilton/ClassicBest 6

BELRU, JUAN
90 Hamilton/Best 26
90 Hamilton/Star 5

BELTRAN, ALONSO
93 StCatharines/ClassicBest 3
93 StCatharines/ProCards 3966

BELTRAN, ANGEL
89 Welland/Pucko 4

BELTRAN, RIGO
91 Hamilton/ClassicBest 6
91 Hamilton/ProCards 4027

BENAVIDES, FELIX
94 GarciaPhoto 110

BENAVIDES, FREDDIE
94 PaniniSticker 170

BENAVIDES, MANUEL
94 GarciaPhoto 108

BENBOW, LOU JR.
91 StCatharines/ClassicBest 3
91 StCatharines/ProCards 3401
92 StCatharines/ClassicBest 12
92 StCatharines/ProCards 3391

BENCH, JOHNNY
69 O-Pee-Chee 95
70 O-Pee-Chee 464
71 O-Pee-Chee 64, 66, 250
72 O-Pee-Chee 433, 434
73 O-Pee-Chee 62, 63, 380
74 O-Pee-Chee 10, 331
75 OPC 208, 210, 260, 308
76 O-Pee-Chee 195, 300
77 O-Pee-Chee 100
78 O-Pee-Chee 50
79 O-Pee-Chee 101
80 O-Pee-Chee 55
81 O-Pee-Chee 286
82 O-Pee-Chee 18, 304
83 O-Pee-Chee 60, 61
90 O-Pee-Chee 664
82 opcSticker 35
83 opcSticker 7, 229
71 ProStarPostcard

BENE, WILLIAM
97 Vancouver/Best 6

BENEDICT, BRUCE
85 Leaf 196
82 O-Pee-Chee 168
83 O-Pee-Chee 204
84 O-Pee-Chee 255
85 O-Pee-Chee 335
86 O-Pee-Chee 78
89 O-Pee-Chee 353
90 O-Pee-Chee 583
82 opcSticker 21
83 opcSticker 154, 217
84 opcSticker 34
85 opcSticker 31
87 StuartBakery 2

BENES, ANDY
90 FleerCdn. 151
90 O-Pee-Chee 193
91 O-Pee-Chee 307
92 O-Pee-Chee 682
93 O-Pee-Chee 17
94 O-Pee-Chee 83
91 PaniniSticker 99
93 PaniniSticker 265
94 PaniniSticker 253

BENGE, RAY
34 WWGum(V354) 13, 49

BENGOUGH, BENNY
33 WWGum(V353) 1

BENIQUEZ, JUAN
86 Leaf 156
74 O-Pee-Chee 647
75 O-Pee-Chee 601
76 O-Pee-Chee 496
86 O-Pee-Chee 185, 325
87 O-Pee-Chee 173
88 O-Pee-Chee 77, C
88 opcSticker 12

BENJAMIN, MIKE
90 FleerCdn. 51
91 O-Pee-Chee 791
93 O-Pee-Chee 377

BENNETT, DENNIS
65 O-Pee-Chee 147

BENNETT, ERIK
94 Vancouver/ProCards 1856

BENSON, VERN
73 O-Pee-Chee 497
74 O-Pee-Chee 236

BENTLEY, JACK
22 WilliamPaterson(V89) 26

BENTON, LARRY
33 WWGum(V353) 45

BENZINGER, TODD
90 FleerCdn. 413
88 Leaf 111
88 O-Pee-Chee 96
89 O-Pee-Chee 188
90 O-Pee-Chee 712
91 O-Pee-Chee 334
92 O-Pee-Chee 506
89 PaniniSticker 275
90 PaniniSticker 250
91 PaniniSticker 127
92 PaniniSticker 94

BERE, JASON
94 O-Pee-Chee 206, -DD 13

BERENGUER, JUAN
90 FleerCdn. 369
82 O-Pee-Chee 12, 107
89 O-Pee-Chee 294
90 O-Pee-Chee 709
91 O-Pee-Chee 449
92 O-Pee-Chee 172
89 opcSticker 291

BERENYI, BRUCE
83 O-Pee-Chee 139
84 O-Pee-Chee 297
85 O-Pee-Chee 27

BERG, MOE
33 WWGum(V353) 84

BERGER, WALLY
36 WWGum(V355) 35

BERGMAN, DAVE
90 FleerCdn. 600
85 O-Pee-Chee 368
87 O-Pee-Chee 256
90 O-Pee-Chee 77
91 O-Pee-Chee 412
92 O-Pee-Chee 354
90 PaniniSticker 67

BERGMEIER, TOM
73 O-Pee-Chee 306

BERINGER, CARROLL
73 O-Pee-Chee 486
74 O-Pee-Chee 119

BERLIN, RANDY
89 Hamilton/Star 12

BERLY, JOHN
36 WWGum(V355) 118

BERNARD, DWIGHT
81 Vancouver/TCMA 4

BERNAZARD, TONY
80 Dimanche/DernièreHeure
86 Leaf 249
80 O-Pee-Chee 351
81 O-Pee-Chee 194
83 O-Pee-Chee 369
84 O-Pee-Chee 41
85 O-Pee-Chee 171
86 O-Pee-Chee 354
87 O-Pee-Chee 394
88 O-Pee-Chee 122
82 opcSticker 171
83 opcSticker 49
84 opcSticker 340
85 opcSticker 252
86 opcSticker 210
87 opcSticker 207
86 opcTattoo 14

BERNHARDT, CESAR
92 O-Pee-Chee 179
91 Vancouver/ProCards 1599
91 Vancouver/LineDrive 626

BERNHARDT, JUAN
79 O-Pee-Chee 189

BERRA, DALE
81 O-Pee-Chee 147
83 O-Pee-Chee 271
84 O-Pee-Chee 18
85 O-Pee-Chee 305
86 O-Pee-Chee 366
83 opcSticker 279
84 opcSticker 136
85 opcSticker 133

BERRA, LARRY (YOGI)
73 O-Pee-Chee 257
74 O-Pee-Chee 179
75 OPC 189, 192, 193, 421
60 opcTattoo 6
62 PostCereal 7
62 ShirriffCoin 33

BERROA, GERONIMO
90 FleerCdn. 575
90 O-Pee-Chee 617
93 Edmonton/ProCards 1147

BERRY, KEN
66 O-Pee-Chee 127
67 O-Pee-Chee 67
70 O-Pee-Chee 239
71 O-Pee-Chee 466
72 O-Pee-Chee 379
73 O-Pee-Chee 445
74 O-Pee-Chee 163
75 O-Pee-Chee 432

BERRY, SEAN
93 O-Pee-Chee 37
93 opcPremier 97
94 PaniniSticker 207

BERRYHILL, DAMON
90 FleerCdn. 26
89 O-Pee-Chee 6
90 O-Pee-Chee 362
91 O-Pee-Chee 188
92 O-Pee-Chee 49
93 O-Pee-Chee 32
89 opcSticker 51, 318
89 PaniniSticker 52
90 PaniniSticker 234

BERTAINA, FRANK
68 O-Pee-Chee 131
71 O-Pee-Chee 422

BERTELL, DICK
65 O-Pee-Chee 27

BEST, KARL
85 Calgary/Cramer 76
87 Calgary/ProCards 2318

BETANCES, MARCOS
90 Hamilton/Best 3
90 Hamilton/Star 6

BETTS, HUCK
34 WWGum(V354) 83

BETZ, ROBERT J. (BOB)
52 Parkhurst 80

BEVACQUA, KURT
72 O-Pee-Chee 193
74 O-Pee-Chee 454
76 O-Pee-Chee 427, 564
85 opcSticker 16

BEVINGTON, TERRY
80 Vancouver/TCMA 6
86 Vancouver/ProCards
88 Vancouver/ProCards 778

BEYELER, ARNIE
89 London/ProCards 1371
90 London/ProCards 1274

BIANCALANA, BUDDY
86 opcSticker 21

BIASETTI, HANK
50 WWGum(V362) 44

BIBBY, JIM
72 O-Pee-Chee 316
74 O-Pee-Chee 11
75 O-Pee-Chee 155
76 O-Pee-Chee 324
78 O-Pee-Chee 61
79 O-Pee-Chee 39
81 O-Pee-Chee 93
82 O-Pee-Chee 170
82 opcSticker 86

BICHETTE, DANTE
90 FleerCdn. 127
90 O-Pee-Chee 43
91 O-Pee-Chee 564
92 O-Pee-Chee 371
94 O-Pee-Chee 30
89 PaniniSticker 283
91 PaniniSticker 186
92 PaniniSticker 39
94 PaniniSticker 171
88 Edmonton/CMC 23
88 Edmonton/ProCards 576

BICKNELL, GREG
89 StCatharines/ProCards 2090

BIELECKI, MIKE
90 FleerCdn. 27
90 O-Pee-Chee 114
91 O-Pee-Chee 501
92 O-Pee-Chee 26
93 opcPremier 112
90 PaniniSticker 242
87 Vancouver/ProCards 1598

BIGBEE, CARSON
21 Neilson's(V61) 54

BIGGERS, ALLAN
89 Hamilton/Star 3

BIGGERSTAFF, KENT
79 Vancouver/TCMA 22
80 Vancouver/TCMA 12

BIGGIO, CRAIG
90 FleerCdn. 224
90 O-Pee-Chee 157, 404
91 O-Pee-Chee 565
92 O-Pee-Chee 715
93 O-Pee-Chee 56
94 O-Pee-Chee 230
92 opcPremier 135
89 PaniniSticker 79
90 PaniniSticker 259
91 PaniniSticker 6
92 PaniniSticker 151
93 PaniniSticker 171
94 PaniniSticker 190

BIITTNER, LARRY
72 O-Pee-Chee 122
73 O-Pee-Chee 249
75 O-Pee-Chee 543
76 O-Pee-Chee 238
79 O-Pee-Chee 224
80 O-Pee-Chee 334

BILARDELLO, DANNY
87 O-Pee-Chee 217
90 O-Pee-Chee 682
84 opcSticker 57
86 MTL/ProvigoFoods 2
87 Vancouver/ProCards 1618

BILKO, STEVE
62 PostCereal 74
62 ShirriffCoin 17

BILLINGHAM, JACK
69 O-Pee-Chee 92
71 O-Pee-Chee 162
73 O-Pee-Chee 89
74 O-Pee-Chee 158
75 O-Pee-Chee 235
76 O-Pee-Chee 155

BILLINGS, DICK
71 O-Pee-Chee 729
72 O-Pee-Chee 148
73 O-Pee-Chee 94
74 O-Pee-Chee 466

BILLMEYER, MICK
92 Edmonton/SkyBox 168
92 Edmonton/ProCards 3541

BINKS, GEORGE
50 WWGum(V362) 21

BIRD, DAVID
89 Welland/Pucko 5

BIRD, DOUG
74 O-Pee-Chee 17
75 O-Pee-Chee 364
76 O-Pee-Chee 96
77 O-Pee-Chee 191

BIRKBECK, MIKE
87 Leaf 33
86 Vancouver/ProCards

BIRTSAS, TIM
90 FleerCdn. 414
86 Leaf 227
90 O-Pee-Chee 687
91 O-Pee-Chee 289

BISHOP, CHARLES
52 Parkhurst 98

BISHOP, MAX
33 WWGum(V353) 61

BITTIGER, JEFF
88 Vancouver/CMC 1
89 Vancouver/CMC 1

BLACK, BUD
90 FleerCdn. 486
85 Leaf 202
86 Leaf 170
85 O-Pee-Chee 47
86 O-Pee-Chee 319
87 O-Pee-Chee 315
88 O-Pee-Chee 301
89 O-Pee-Chee 5
90 O-Pee-Chee 144
91 O-Pee-Chee 292
92 O-Pee-Chee 774
93 O-Pee-Chee 38
91 opcPremier 9
84 opcSticker 283
85 opcSticker 275
86 opcSticker 261
89 opcSticker 209

BLACK, KEITH
91 Hamilton/ClassicBest 23
91 Hamilton/ProCards 4043
92 Hamilton/ClassicBest 24

BLACKWELL, RICHIE
94 Welland/Classic 4
94 Welland/ProCards 3483

BLACKWELL,TIM
82 Dimanche/DernièreHeure
78 O-Pee-Chee 223
81 O-Pee-Chee 43
83 O-Pee-Chee 57
82 opcSticker 28
77 MTL
82 MTL/Hygrade
83 MTL
83 MTL/StuartBakery 26

BLADT, RICH
74 O-Pee-Chee 601

BLAEHOLDER, GEORGE
33 WWGum(V353) 16

BLAIR, DENNIS
75 O-Pee-Chee 521
76 O-Pee-Chee 642
77 O-Pee-Chee 189

BLAIR, PAUL
66 O-Pee-Chee 48
68 O-Pee-Chee 135
70 O-Pee-Chee 285
71 O-Pee-Chee 53
73 O-Pee-Chee 528
74 O-Pee-Chee 92
75 O-Pee-Chee 275
76 O-Pee-Chee 473
79 O-Pee-Chee 304
80 O-Pee-Chee 149

BLAIR, WILLIE
91 O-Pee-Chee 191
90 TOR/FireSafety

BLAIS, JEAN-MARC
52 LavalDairy 111

BLANCHARD, JOHN
62 PostCereal 11

BLANKENSHIP, KEVIN
90 FleerCdn. 28

BLANKENSHIP, LANCE
90 FleerCdn. 1
90 O-Pee-Chee 132
91 O-Pee-Chee 411
92 O-Pee-Chee 386
93 O-Pee-Chee 30

BLANKS, LARVELL
73 O-Pee-Chee 609
75 O-Pee-Chee 394
76 O-Pee-Chee 127
78 O-Pee-Chee 213

BLANTON, CY
36 WWGum(V355) 3

BLANTON, GARRET
91 Hamilton/ClassicBest 16
91 Hamilton/ProCards 4049

BLASINGAME, DON
65 O-Pee-Chee 21
62 PostCereal 117
62 ShirriffCoin 103

BLASINGAME, WADE
65 O-Pee-Chee 44
67 O-Pee-Chee 119
71 O-Pee-Chee 79

BLASS, STEVE
65 O-Pee-Chee 232
69 O-Pee-Chee 104
70 O-Pee-Chee 396
71 O-Pee-Chee 143
72 O-Pee-Chee 320
73 O-Pee-Chee 95
74 O-Pee-Chee 595

BLASUCCI, TONY
90 Calgary/CMC 2
90 Calgary/ProCards 644

BLATERIC, STEVE
73 O-Pee-Chee 616

BLAUSER, JEFF
90 FleerCdn. 576
90 O-Pee-Chee 251
91 O-Pee-Chee 623
92 O-Pee-Chee 199
93 O-Pee-Chee 59
94 O-Pee-Chee 214
89 PaniniSticker 41
90 PaniniSticker 217
91 PaniniSticker 22
93 PaniniSticker 183
94 PaniniSticker 143

BLEFARY, CURT
65 O-Pee-Chee 49
67 O-Pee-Chee 180
70 O-Pee-Chee 297
71 O-Pee-Chee 131

BLOCK, SEYMOUR
50 WWGum(V362) 9

BLOMBERG, RON
72 O-Pee-Chee 203
73 O-Pee-Chee 462
74 O-Pee-Chee 117
75 O-Pee-Chee 68
76 O-Pee-Chee 354
79 O-Pee-Chee 17

BLOOMER, CHRIS
97 Lethbridge/Best 19

BLOWERS, MIKE
90 FleerCdn. 438
91 O-Pee-Chee 691
92 Calgary/ProCards 3739
92 Calgary/SkyBox 54

BLUE, LUZERNE A. (LU)
21 Neilson's(V61) 5
23 WillardsChocolate(V100) 10

BLUE, VIDA
82 FBI BoxBottom
86 Leaf 247
70 O-Pee-Chee 21
71 O-Pee-Chee 544
72 OPC 92, 94, 96, 169, 170
73 O-Pee-Chee 430
74 O-Pee-Chee 290
75 O-Pee-Chee 209, 510
76 O-Pee-Chee 140, 200
77 O-Pee-Chee 75
78 O-Pee-Chee 177
79 O-Pee-Chee 49
80 O-Pee-Chee 14
81 O-Pee-Chee 310
82 O-Pee-Chee 82, 267
83 O-Pee-Chee 178
87 O-Pee-Chee 260
82 opcSticker 111
71 ProStarPostcard
71 ProStarPoster

BLUEGE, OSWALD (OSSIE)
33 WWGum(V353) 83

BLUMBERG, ROB
89 StCatharines/ProCards 2088

BLYLEVEN, BERT
90 FleerCdn. 128
85 Leaf 4
86 Leaf 88
87 Leaf 100
88 Leaf 52
71 O-Pee-Chee 26
72 O-Pee-Chee 515
73 O-Pee-Chee 199
74 O-Pee-Chee 98
75 O-Pee-Chee 30
76 O-Pee-Chee 204, 235
77 O-Pee-Chee 101
78 O-Pee-Chee 113
79 O-Pee-Chee 155
80 O-Pee-Chee 238
81 O-Pee-Chee 294
82 O-Pee-Chee 164
83 O-Pee-Chee 280
84 O-Pee-Chee 126
85 O-Pee-Chee 355
86 O-Pee-Chee 272
87 O-Pee-Chee 25
88 O-Pee-Chee 295
89 O-Pee-Chee 204
90 O-Pee-Chee 130
91 O-Pee-Chee 615, A
92 O-Pee-Chee 375
82 opcSticker 172
84 opcSticker 251
85 opcSticker 247
86 opcSticker 279
87 opcSticker 278
88 opcSticker 20
89 opcSticker 285
86 opcTattoo 24
88 PaniniSticker 132
90 PaniniSticker 28

BOBB, RANDY
70 O-Pee-Chee 429
71 O-Pee-Chee 83

BOCCABELLA, JOHN
72 Dimanche/DernièreHeure
92 Nabisco 35
70 O-Pee-Chee 19
71 O-Pee-Chee 452
72 O-Pee-Chee 159
73 O-Pee-Chee 592
74 O-Pee-Chee 253
75 O-Pee-Chee 553
71 ProStarPostcard
71 MTL/ProStar
71 MTL/LaPizzaRoyale
74 MTL/GeorgeWeston

BOCHTE, BRUCE
86 Leaf 189
75 O-Pee-Chee 392
76 O-Pee-Chee 637
79 O-Pee-Chee 231
80 O-Pee-Chee 80
81 O-Pee-Chee 18
82 O-Pee-Chee 224
83 O-Pee-Chee 28
85 O-Pee-Chee 391
86 O-Pee-Chee 378
82 opcSticker 232
85 opcSticker 331
86 opcSticker 170
87 opcSticker 169
86 opcTattoo 6

BOCKUS, RANDY
91 Edmonton/LineDrive 155

BOCOURT, OSNEL BLAS
94 GarciaPhoto 60

BODDICKER, MIKE
90 FleerCdn. 267
85 Leaf 109
86 Leaf 8
87 Leaf 76
85 O-Pee-Chee 225
86 O-Pee-Chee 367
87 O-Pee-Chee 149
88 O-Pee-Chee 281
89 O-Pee-Chee 71
90 O-Pee-Chee 652
91 O-Pee-Chee 303
92 O-Pee-Chee 106
91 opcPremier 10
84 opcSticker 13, 375
85 opcSticker 202
86 opcSticker 233
87 opcSticker 227
88 opcSticker 231
89 opcSticker 261
88 PaniniSticker 5
90 PaniniSticker 20
91 PaniniTopFifteen 108

BODELL, HOWARD J.
52 LavalDairy 81

BODIE, KEITH
91 Calgary/LineDrive 74
91 Calgary/ProCards 2649
92 Calgary/ProCards 3745
93 Calgary/ProCards 3745

BOECKEL, NORMAN D.
21 Neilson's(V61) 80
23 WillardsChocolate(V100) 11

BOEVER, DAN
89 Calgary/CMC 12
89 Calgary/ProCards 535

BOEVER, JOE
90 FleerCdn. 577
90 O-Pee-Chee 410
91 O-Pee-Chee 159
92 O-Pee-Chee 696
90 PaniniSticker 220
97 Calgary/Best 8

BOGGS, WADE
88 FantasticSam's 8
90 FleerCdn. 268, 632
85 Leaf 179
86 Leaf 168
87 Leaf 193
88 Leaf 65
86 GeneralMills 1
87 GeneralMills 2
87 HostessSticker 19
84 O-Pee-Chee 30
85 O-Pee-Chee 350
86 O-Pee-Chee 262, B
87 O-Pee-Chee 150
88 O-Pee-Chee 200
89 O-Pee-Chee 184
90 O-Pee-Chee 387, 760, A
91 O-Pee-Chee 450
92 O-Pee-Chee 10
93 O-Pee-Chee 196
94 O-Pee-Chee 193
91 opcPremier 11
92 opcPremier 1
93 opcPremier 49
83 opcSticker 308
84 opcSticker 100, 216
85 opcSticker 210
86 opcSticker 164, 247
87 opcSticker 148, 157
88 opcSticker 244,-SStar 40
89 opcStick. 9, 147, 260, -SS 7
86 opcTattoo 22
88 PaniniSticker 29, 228
89 PaniniSticker 7, 242, 277
90 PaniniSticker 19, 199
91 PaniniSticker 169, 266
92 PaniniSticker 87, 274
93 PaniniSticker 152
94 PaniniSticker 99
91 PaniniTopFifteen 30
92 PizzaHut/DietPepsi 21
87 StuartBakery 15

BOGAR, TIM
93 opcPremier 108

BOHANON, BRIAN
92 O-Pee-Chee 149
96 TOR/OhHenry

BOHNE, SAMMY
20 MapleCrispette(V117) 20
21 Neilson's(V61) 67

BOHROFEN, BRENT
91 Hamilton/ClassicBest
91 Hamilton/ProCards 4050

BOISCLAIR, BRUCE
79 O-Pee-Chee 68

BOITANO, DANNY
79 Vancouver/TCMA 9
80 Vancouver/TCMA 14

BOLICK, FRANK
92 O-Pee-Chee 473
93 opcPremier 72
97 Vancouver/Best 7

BOLIN, BOB
66 O-Pee-Chee 61
68 O-Pee-Chee 169
69 O-Pee-Chee 8
71 O-Pee-Chee 446
72 O-Pee-Chee 266
73 O-Pee-Chee 541
74 O-Pee-Chee 427

BOLLING, FRANK
65 O-Pee-Chee 269
62 PostCereal 146
62 ShirriffCoin 140

BOLTON, CLIFF
36 WWGum(V355) 133

BOLTON, RODNEY
92 Vancouver/ProCards 2713
92 Vancouver/SkyBox 628

BOLTON, TOM
91 O-Pee-Chee 37
92 O-Pee-Chee 708

BOMBACK, MARK
81 O-Pee-Chee 264
82 O-Pee-Chee 307
79 Vancouver/TCMA 7

BOND, WALT
65 O-Pee-Chee 109
62 ShirriffCoin 208

BONDS, BARRY
92 Ben'sDisk 18
90 FleerCdn. 461
87 Leaf 219
88 Leaf 113
93 HumptyDumpty 49
87 O-Pee-Chee 320
88 O-Pee-Chee 267
89 O-Pee-Chee 263
90 O-Pee-Chee 220
91 O-Pee-Chee 401, 570
92 O-Pee-Chee 380
93 O-Pee-Chee 46
94 O-Pee-Chee 200, -AS 2
91 opcPremier 12
92 opcPremier 157
93 opcPremier 1, -StarPerf. 14
87 opcSticker 131
88 opcSticker 135
89 opcSticker 127,-SStar 46
88 PaniniSticker 376
89 PaniniSticker 172
90 PaniniSticker 322
91 PaniniSticker 119
92 PaniniSticker 258
93 PaniniSticker 165, 243
94 PaniniSticker 12, 13, 261
91 PaniniTop 12,20,33,43,105
92 PizzaHut/DietPepsi 29
94 PostCdn. 11
95 PostCdn. 17
91 PetroCanada 16
91 PostCdn. 5
92 PostCdn. 9

BONDS, BOBBY
70 O-Pee-Chee 425
71 O-Pee-Chee 295
73 O-Pee-Chee 145
74 O-Pee-Chee 30
75 O-Pee-Chee 55
76 O-Pee-Chee 2
76 O-Pee-Chee 380
77 O-Pee-Chee 173
78 O-Pee-Chee 206
79 O-Pee-Chee 142
80 O-Pee-Chee 215
81 O-Pee-Chee 223
82 O-Pee-Chee 27

BONES, RICKY
92 O-Pee-Chee 711
93 O-Pee-Chee 33

BONHAM, BILL
72 O-Pee-Chee 29
73 O-Pee-Chee 328
74 O-Pee-Chee 528
75 O-Pee-Chee 85
76 O-Pee-Chee 151
77 O-Pee-Chee 95
79 O-Pee-Chee 182
80 O-Pee-Chee 26

BONILLA, BOBBY
92 Ben'sDisk 20
90 FleerCdn. 462
93 HumptyDumpty 43
88 Leaf 188
88 O-Pee-Chee 189
89 O-Pee-Chee 142
90 O-Pee-Chee 273
91 O-Pee-Chee 403, 750
92 O-Pee-Chee 160
93 O-Pee-Chee 15
94 O-Pee-Chee 202
92 opcPremier 143
88 opcSticker 129, 131
89 opcSticker 158,-SStar 40
88 PaniniSticker 372, 373, 374
89 PaniniSticker 171, 234
90 PaniniSticker 325
91 PaniniSticker 120
92 PaniniSticker 256
93 PaniniSticker 253
94 PaniniSticker 215
91 PaniniTopFifteen 18, 50
93 PostCdn. 12

BONILLA, JUAN
84 O-Pee-Chee 168
87 O-Pee-Chee 131
84 opcSticker 152
88 PaniniSticker 42, 43, 74, 75

BONILLA, MIGUEL
92 Welland/ClassicBest 2

BONNELL, BARRY
92 Nabisco 6
85 Leaf 195
80 O-Pee-Chee 331
81 O-Pee-Chee 82, -Poster 19
82 O-Pee-Chee 99
83 O-Pee-Chee 281
84 O-Pee-Chee 302
85 O-Pee-Chee 107
86 O-Pee-Chee 119
82 opcSticker 25
83 opcSticker 133
84 opcSticker 370
85 opcSticker 342

BONURA, ZEKE
37 O-Pee-Chee(V300) 116
36 WWGum(V355) 112
39 WWGum(V351A)
39 WWGum(V351B)

BOOKER, ROD
91 O-Pee-Chee 186

BOONE, ANTONIO
91 Hamilton/ClassicBest 13
91 Hamilton/ProCards 4028
92 Hamilton/ClassicBest 9

BOONE, BOB
90 FleerCdn. 102
86 Leaf 17
87 Leaf 202
88 Leaf 151
73 O-Pee-Chee 613
74 O-Pee-Chee 131
75 O-Pee-Chee 351
76 O-Pee-Chee 67, 318
77 O-Pee-Chee 68
78 O-Pee-Chee 141
79 O-Pee-Chee 38
80 O-Pee-Chee 246
81 O-Pee-Chee 290
82 O-Pee-Chee 23, 392
83 O-Pee-Chee 366
84 O-Pee-Chee 174
85 O-Pee-Chee 348
86 O-Pee-Chee 179
87 O-Pee-Chee 166
88 O-Pee-Chee 158, D
89 O-Pee-Chee 243
90 O-Pee-Chee 671
82 opcSticker 77
83 opcSticker 45
84 opcSticker 234
85 opcSticker 228
86 opcSticker 179
87 opcSticker 180
88 opcSticker 5, 182
89 opcSticker 175,-SStar 22
88 PaniniSticker 39
89 PaniniSticker 287

BOONE, BRET
93 O-Pee-Chee 13
94 O-Pee-Chee 170
94 PaniniSticker 116
92 Calgary/ProCards 3740
92 Calgary/SkyBox 55

BOONE, DAN
84 Vancouver/Cramer 36

BOONE, RAY
76 O-Pee-Chee 67

BOOZER, JOHN
65 O-Pee-Chee 184
68 O-Pee-Chee 173

BORBON, PEDRO
70 O-Pee-Chee 358
71 O-Pee-Chee 613
73 O-Pee-Chee 492
74 O-Pee-Chee 410
75 O-Pee-Chee 157
76 O-Pee-Chee 77
78 O-Pee-Chee 199
79 O-Pee-Chee 164

BORDERS, PAT
90 FleerCdn. 77
93 HumptyDumpty 23
89 O-Pee-Chee 343
90 O-Pee-Chee 191
91 O-Pee-Chee 49
92 O-Pee-Chee 563
93 OPC 58, -WSChamp 2
93 OPC-WSHero 1
94 O-Pee-Chee 178, -TOR 8
89 opcSticker 191
89 PaniniSticker 464
90 PaniniSticker 175
91 PaniniSticker 335
92 PaniniSticker 24
93 PaniniSticker 25
94 PaniniSticker 135
93 PostCdn. 1
94 PostCdn. 7
88 TOR/FireSafety
89 TOR/FireSafety
90 TOR/FireSafety
91 TOR/FireSafety
91 TOR/Score 11
92 TOR/FireSafety
93 TOR (x2)
93 TOR/Dempster's 21
93 TOR/Donruss 4, WS8
93 TOR/FireSafety
93 TOR/McDonald's 25, 34
94 TOR
97 TOR/Sizzler 42

BORDI, RICH
85 Leaf 166

BORDICK, MIKE
92 O-Pee-Chee 317
93 O-Pee-Chee 57
94 O-Pee-Chee 264
93 PaniniSticker 16
94 PaniniSticker 107

BORGMANN, GLENN
73 O-Pee-Chee 284
74 O-Pee-Chee 547
75 O-Pee-Chee 127
76 O-Pee-Chee 498

BORK, FRANK
66 O-Pee-Chee 123

BOROS, STEVE
82 Dimanche/DernièreHeure
65 O-Pee-Chee 102
62 PostCereal 16
62 ShirriffCoin 50

BOSCH, DON
70 O-Pee-Chee 527

BOSETTI, RICK
92 Nabisco 16
79 O-Pee-Chee 279
80 O-Pee-Chee 146
81 O-Pee-Chee 46, -Poster 18
79 TOR/BubbleYum

BOSIO, CHRIS
93 Ben'sDisk 2
90 FleerCdn. 316
88 O-Pee-Chee 137
90 O-Pee-Chee 597
91 O-Pee-Chee 217
92 O-Pee-Chee 638
93 O-Pee-Chee 60
94 O-Pee-Chee 134
93 opcPremier 3
90 PaniniSticker 99
92 PaniniSticker 42
86 Vancouver/ProCards

BOSKIE, SHAWN
91 O-Pee-Chee 254
92 O-Pee-Chee 229

BOSMAN, DICK
70 O-Pee-Chee 68, 175
70 O-Pee-Chee 68
71 O-Pee-Chee 60
72 O-Pee-Chee 365
73 O-Pee-Chee 640
74 O-Pee-Chee 465
75 O-Pee-Chee 7, 354
76 O-Pee-Chee 298

BOSMENIER, JESUS
94 GarciaPhoto 25

BOSS, DAVID
89 Hamilton/Star 5
90 Hamilton/Best 8
90 Hamilton/Star 7

BOSTOCK, LYMAN
76 O-Pee-Chee 264
77 O-Pee-Chee 239

BOSTON, DARYL
90 O-Pee-Chee 524
91 O-Pee-Chee 83
92 O-Pee-Chee 227
89 PaniniSticker 311
90 PaniniSticker 52
91 PaniniSticker 84
93 PaniniSticker 254

BOSTON, D.J.
92 StCatharines/ClassicBest 11
92 StCatharines/ProCards 3392

BOSWELL, DAVE
70 O-Pee-Chee 70, 325
71 O-Pee-Chee 675

BOSWELL, KEN
70 O-Pee-Chee 214
71 O-Pee-Chee 492
72 O-Pee-Chee 305, 306
73 O-Pee-Chee 87
74 O-Pee-Chee 645
75 O-Pee-Chee 479
76 O-Pee-Chee 379

BOTKIN, ALAN
90 Hamilton/Star 8

BOTTALICO, RICKY
94 O-Pee-Chee 204

BOTTOMLEY, JIM
20 MapleCrispette(V117) 19
33 WWGum(V353) 44
36 WWGum(V355) 85

BOTTENFIELD, KENT
93 opcPremier 64

BOUCHEE, ED
62 PostCereal 182
62 ShirriffCoin 116

BOUCHER, DENIS
93 O-Pee-Chee 22
94 O-Pee-Chee 236
91 opcPremier 13
91 TOR/FireSafety

BOURNE, TIM
95 StCatharines/TimHortons 24

BOURQUE, PAT
73 O-Pee-Chee 605
74 O-Pee-Chee 141
75 O-Pee-Chee 502

BOUTON, JIM
65 O-Pee-Chee 30

BOWA, LARRY
70 O-Pee-Chee 539
71 O-Pee-Chee 233
72 O-Pee-Chee 520
73 O-Pee-Chee 119
74 O-Pee-Chee 255
75 O-Pee-Chee 420
76 O-Pee-Chee 145
77 O-Pee-Chee 17
78 O-Pee-Chee 68
79 O-Pee-Chee 104
80 O-Pee-Chee 330
81 O-Pee-Chee 120
82 O-Pee-Chee 194, 374
83 O-Pee-Chee 305

84 O-Pee-Chee 346
85 O-Pee-Chee 56
82 opcSticker 80
83 opcSticker 221
84 opcSticker 46
85 opcSticker 45

BOWEN, RYAN
92 O-Pee-Chee 254
92 opcPremier 28

BOWENS, SAM
65 O-Pee-Chee 188
68 O-Pee-Chee 82

BOWERS, GROVER B.
52 Parkhurst 6

BOWIE, JIM
89 Calgary/CMC 17
89 Calgary/ProCards 525
92 Calgary/SkyBox 56
95 Edmonton/Macri

BOWLAN, MARK
89 Hamilton/Star 4

BOWLES, BRIAN
97 St.Catharines/Best 9

BOYD, DENNIS (OIL CAN)
86 Leaf 35
87 Leaf 248
88 Leaf 252
86 O-Pee-Chee 259
87 O-Pee-Chee 285
89 O-Pee-Chee 326
90 O-Pee-Chee 544
91 O-Pee-Chee 48
92 O-Pee-Chee 428
86 opcSticker 249
87 opcSticker 249
86 opcTattoo 16
88 PaniniSticker 20
89 PaniniSticker 269
91 PaniniSticker 147

BOYD, GARY
70 O-Pee-Chee 7

BOYER, CLETE
66 O-Pee-Chee 9
70 O-Pee-Chee 206
71 O-Pee-Chee 374
62 PostCereal 3
62 ShirriffCoin 80

BOYER, KEN
65 O-Pee-Chee 6, 100
67 O-Pee-Chee 105
75 O-Pee-Chee 202
62 PostCereal 159
62 ShirriffCoin 167

BRABENDER, GENE
67 O-Pee-Chee 22
68 O-Pee-Chee 163
70 O-Pee-Chee 289
71 O-Pee-Chee 666

BRACH, JOSE CARREO
52 Parkhurst 24

BRADFORD, BUDDY
68 O-Pee-Chee 142
69 O-Pee-Chee 97
70 O-Pee-Chee 299
71 O-Pee-Chee 552
74 O-Pee-Chee 357
75 O-Pee-Chee 504
76 O-Pee-Chee 451

BRADFORD, JOSH
96 StCatharines/Best 5

BRADLEY, DAVID
91 Welland/Best 23

BRADLEY, LEN
82 Edmonton/TCMA 17

BRADLEY, PHIL
90 FleerCdn. 174
85 Leaf 50
86 Leaf 22
87 Leaf 200
86 GeneralMills 2
87 GeneralMills 3
87 HostessSticker 29
85 O-Pee-Chee 69
86 O-Pee-Chee 305
87 O-Pee-Chee 170
88 O-Pee-Chee 55
89 O-Pee-Chee 308
90 O-Pee-Chee 163
91 O-Pee-Chee 717
86 opcSticker 217
87 opcSticker 221
88 opcSticker 218
89 opcSticker 113
86 opcTattoo 14
88 PaniniSticker 191
89 PaniniSticker 154
90 PaniniSticker 4
87 StuartBakery 25
92 MTL/Durivage 3
92 Edmonton/ProCards 3550

BRADLEY, SCOTT
90 FleerCdn. 506
88 Leaf 75
88 O-Pee-Chee 199
89 O-Pee-Chee 279
90 O-Pee-Chee 593
91 O-Pee-Chee 38
92 O-Pee-Chee 608
87 opcSticker 217
88 opcSticker 222
89 opcSticker 225
88 PaniniSticker 183
89 PaniniSticker 432

BRADLEY, TOM
71 O-Pee-Chee 588
72 O-Pee-Chee 248
73 O-Pee-Chee 336
74 O-Pee-Chee 455
75 O-Pee-Chee 179
76 O-Pee-Chee 644

BRADSHAW, TERRY
90 Hamilton/Best 23

BRADY, BRIAN
88 Edmonton/CMC 16
88 Edmonton/ProCards 572

BRADY, MIKE
97 St.Catharines/Best 4

BRAGGS, GLENN
90 FleerCdn. 317
88 O-Pee-Chee 263
89 O-Pee-Chee 271
90 O-Pee-Chee 88
91 O-Pee-Chee 444
92 O-Pee-Chee 197
88 opcSticker 197
89 opcSticker 196
88 PaniniSticker 127
89 PaniniSticker 375
90 PaniniSticker 97
92 PaniniSticker 268
86 Vancouver/ProCards
87 Vancouver/5x7

BRALEY, JEFF
92 London/ProCards 624
92 London/SkyBox 401

BRANCA, RALPH
53 Exhibits 8

BRAND, RON
65 O-Pee-Chee 212
70 O-Pee-Chee 221
71 O-Pee-Chee 304
71 MTL/ProStar

BRANDON, DARRELL
67 O-Pee-Chee 117
68 O-Pee-Chee 26
72 O-Pee-Chee 283
73 O-Pee-Chee 326

BRANDOW, DEREK
92 StCatharines/ClassicBest 24
92 StCatharines/ProCards 3377

BRANNON, CLIFF
89 Hamilton/Star 6

BRANDT, ED
33 WWGum(V353) 50
34 WWGum(V354) 62

BRANDT, JACKIE
65 O-Pee-Chee 33
67 O-Pee-Chee 142
62 PostCereal 31
62 ShirriffCoin 53

BRANLEY, MICKEY
89 PaniniSticker 439

BRANTLEY, CLIFF
92 O-Pee-Chee 544

BRANTLEY, JEFF
90 FleerCdn. 52
90 O-Pee-Chee 703
91 O-Pee-Chee 17
92 O-Pee-Chee 491
93 O-Pee-Chee 65
91 PaniniSticker 75

BRANTLEY, MICKEY
88 Leaf 258
89 O-Pee-Chee 369
89 opcSticker 219
89 PaniniSticker 192
88 PaniniSticker 192
85 Calgary/Cramer 88
86 Calgary/ProCards
90 Calgary/CMC 15

BRATHWAITE, ALONSO
52 Laval Dairy 58

BRAUN, JOHN
65 O-Pee-Chee 82

BRAUN, STEVE
72 O-Pee-Chee 244
73 O-Pee-Chee 16
74 O-Pee-Chee 321
75 O-Pee-Chee 273
76 O-Pee-Chee 183
77 O-Pee-Chee 123

BRAVO, ANGEL
70 O-Pee-Chee 283
71 O-Pee-Chee 538

BRAZILL, FRANK L.
23 WillardsChocolate(V100) 12

BREAM, SID
90 FleerCdn. 463
87 Leaf 239
87 O-Pee-Chee 35
88 O-Pee-Chee 304
89 O-Pee-Chee 126
90 O-Pee-Chee 622
91 O-Pee-Chee 354
92 O-Pee-Chee 770
93 O-Pee-Chee 84
87 opcSticker 126
88 opcSticker 130
89 opcSticker 125
88 PaniniSticker 370
89 PaniniSticker 169
91 PaniniSticker 115
92 PaniniSticker 162
93 PaniniSticker 181

BREARD, STAN
43-47 Montréal/ParadeSportive

BREAZEALE, JIM
73 O-Pee-Chee 33

BRECHEEN, HARRY
53 Exhibits 14

BREEDEN, DANNY
70 O-Pee-Chee 36

BREEDEN, HAL
73 O-Pee-Chee 173
74 O-Pee-Chee 297
75 O-Pee-Chee 341

BREEDEN, SCOTT
93 StCatharines/ClassicBest 27

BREEDING, MARV
62 PostCereal 28
62 ShirriffCoin 65

BREEN, DICK
12 ImperialTobacco(C46) 88

BREINING, FRED
85 O-Pee-Chee 36
84 MTL
84 MTL/StuartBakery 35

BRENLY, BOB
85 Leaf 26
86 Leaf 194
85 O-Pee-Chee 215
86 O-Pee-Chee 307
87 O-Pee-Chee 125
88 O-Pee-Chee 69
89 O-Pee-Chee 52
84 opcSticker 174
85 opcSticker 158
86 opcSticker 92
87 opcSticker 87
88 opcSticker 92
86 opcTattoo 3
88 PaniniSticker 419
89 TOR/FireSafety

BRESSOUD, ED
67 O-Pee-Chee 12
62 ShirriffCoin 182

BRETT, GEORGE
88 Fant. Sam's 2
90 FleerCdn. 103, 621
85 General Mills 24
86 General Mills 2
87 General Mills 3
87 HostessSticker 24
93 Humpty Dumpty 9
85 Leaf 176
86 Leaf 42
87 Leaf 15, 96
88 Leaf 93
92 McDonald's 3
75 O-Pee-Chee 228
76 O-Pee-Chee 19
77 O-Pee-Chee 1, 170, 261
78 O-Pee-Chee 215
79 O-Pee-Chee 167
80 O-Pee-Chee 235
81 O-Pee-Chee 113
82 O-Pee-Chee 200, 201, 261
83 O-Pee-Chee 3, 388
84 O-Pee-Chee 212, 223
85 O-Pee-Chee 100
86 O-Pee-Chee 300, C
87 O-Pee-Chee 126
88 O-Pee-Chee 312
89 O-Pee-Chee 200, A
90 O-Pee-Chee 60, B
91 O-Pee-Chee 2, 540, B
92 O-Pee-Chee 620
93 O-Pee-Chee 50
91 opcPremier 14
92 opcPremier 114
82 opcSticker 133, 190
83 opcSticker 76
84 opcSticker 198, 275
85 opcSticker 188, 268
86 opcSticker 3,16,23,157, 256
87 opcSticker 254
88 opcSticker 259,-SStar 41
89 opcSticker 270
86 opcTattoo 6
88 PaniniSticker 104
89 PaniniSticker 355
90 PaniniSticker 91
91 PaniniSticker 276
91 PaniniTopFifteen 5
92 PaniniSticker 102
93 PaniniSticker 110
91 PetroCanada 13
91 PostCdn. 29
87 Stuart Bakery 20SS

BRETT, KEN
71 O-Pee-Chee 89
72 O-Pee-Chee 517
73 O-Pee-Chee 444
74 O-Pee-Chee 237
75 O-Pee-Chee 250
76 O-Pee-Chee 401
77 O-Pee-Chee 21

BREWER, BILLY
93 opcPremier 99

BREWER, JIM
78 Dimanch/DernièreHeure
66 O-Pee-Chee 158
67 O-Pee-Chee 31
71 O-Pee-Chee 549
72 O-Pee-Chee 151
73 O-Pee-Chee 126
74 O-Pee-Chee 189
75 O-Pee-Chee 163
76 O-Pee-Chee 459
77 O-Pee-Chee 198
77 MTL
77 MTL/Redpath Sugar

BREWER, TOM
62 ShirriffCoin 4

BREWINGTON, MIKE
89 Welland/Pucko 6

BRICKELL, FRED
33 WWGum(V353) 38

BRICKELL, FRITZIE
61 Toronto/BeeHive

BRIDGES, ROCKY
62 PostCereal 75
50 WWGum(V362) 1

BRIDGES, ROCKY
87 Vancouver/ProCards 1605
90 Welland/Pucko 33

BRIDGES, TOMMY
37 O-Pee-Chee 133
34 WWGum(V354) 87
36 WWGum(V355) 33

BRIETENSTEIN, KEITH
94 Welland/Classic 5
94 Welland/ProCards 3484

BRIGGS, DAN
82 O-Pee-Chee 102

BRIGGS, JOHNNY
65 O-Pee-Chee 163
69 O-Pee-Chee 73
71 O-Pee-Chee 297
72 O-Pee-Chee 197
73 O-Pee-Chee 71
74 O-Pee-Chee 218
75 O-Pee-Chee 123
76 O-Pee-Chee 373

BRILES, NELSON
69 O-Pee-Chee 69
70 O-Pee-Chee 435
71 O-Pee-Chee 257
73 O-Pee-Chee 303
74 O-Pee-Chee 123
75 O-Pee-Chee 495
76 O-Pee-Chee 569

BRILEY, GREG
90 FleerCdn. 507
90 O-Pee-Chee 288
91 O-Pee-Chee 133
92 O-Pee-Chee 502
90 PaniniSticker 148
92 PaniniSticker 61
88 Calgary/CMC 13
88 Calgary/ProCards 799

BRINKMAN, CHUCK
71 O-Pee-Chee 13
73 O-Pee-Chee 404
74 O-Pee-Chee 641

BRINKMAN, ED
68 O-Pee-Chee 49
69 O-Pee-Chee 153
71 O-Pee-Chee 389
73 O-Pee-Chee 5
74 O-Pee-Chee 138
75 O-Pee-Chee 439

BRISTOL, DAVE
67 O-Pee-Chee 21
68 O-Pee-Chee 148
71 O-Pee-Chee 637
73 O-Pee-Chee 377
74 O-Pee-Chee 531
76 O-Pee-Chee 631

BRITO, MARIO
91 Vancouver/LineDrive 627
91 Vancouver/ProCards 1586

BRITO, TILSON
97 TOR/Sizzler 20

BRITT, KEN
92 Hamilton/ClassicBest 16

BRITTON, JIM
68 O-Pee-Chee 76
69 O-Pee-Chee 154
71 O-Pee-Chee 699
72 O-Pee-Chee 351

BRIZZOLARA, TONY
80 O-Pee-Chee 86

BROBERG, PETE
72 O-Pee-Chee 64
73 O-Pee-Chee 162
74 O-Pee-Chee 425
75 O-Pee-Chee 542
76 O-Pee-Chee 39
77 O-Pee-Chee 55
79 O-Pee-Chee 301

BROCK, GREG
90 FleerCdn. 318
88 Leaf 148
84 O-Pee-Chee 242
85 O-Pee-Chee 242
86 O-Pee-Chee 368
87 O-Pee-Chee 26
88 O-Pee-Chee 212
89 O-Pee-Chee 163
90 O-Pee-Chee 139
91 O-Pee-Chee 663
84 opcSticker 376
86 opcSticker 67
87 opcSticker 68
89 opcSticker 201
88 PaniniSticker 121
89 PaniniSticker 371
90 PaniniSticker 104
91 PaniniSticker 204

BROCK, LOU
66 O-Pee-Chee 125
67 O-Pee-Chee 63
69 O-Pee-Chee 85
70 O-Pee-Chee 330
71 O-Pee-Chee 625
72 O-Pee-Chee 200
73 O-Pee-Chee 64, 320
74 O-Pee-Chee 60, 204
75 O-Pee-Chee 2, 309, 540
76 O-Pee-Chee 10, 197
77 O-Pee-Chee 51
78 O-Pee-Chee 204, 236
79 O-Pee-Chee 350

BROCK, RUSS
95 Edmonton/Macri

BROCKETT, LEWIS
1912 ImperialTobacco(C46) 55

BROGLIO, ERNIE
62 PostCereal 164
62 ShirriffCoin 132

BROGNA, RICO
92 O-Pee-Chee 126
90 London/ProCards 1275

BROHAMER, JACK
73 O-Pee-Chee 181
74 O-Pee-Chee 586
75 O-Pee-Chee 552
76 O-Pee-Chee 618
79 O-Pee-Chee 25

BROOKENS, TOM
90 FleerCdn. 439
82 O-Pee-Chee 11
86 O-Pee-Chee 286
87 O-Pee-Chee 232
89 O-Pee-Chee 342
91 O-Pee-Chee 268
89 opcSticker 278
88 PaniniSticker 93
89 PaniniSticker 340

BROOKS, BOBBY
70 O-Pee-Chee 381
71 O-Pee-Chee 633

BROOKS, HUBIE
90 FleerCdn. 341
86 General Mills 6
87 General Mills 4
87 HostessSticker 4
88 HostessDisk 5
85 Leaf 214
86 Leaf 44
87 Leaf 17, 142
88 Leaf 257
82 O-Pee-Chee 266
83 O-Pee-Chee 134
84 O-Pee-Chee 368
85 O-Pee-Chee 222, -Poster 5
86 O-Pee-Chee 308
87 O-Pee-Chee 3
88 O-Pee-Chee 50
89 O-Pee-Chee 221
90 O-Pee-Chee 745
91 O-Pee-Chee 115
92 O-Pee-Chee 457
91 opcPremier 15
92 opcPremier 198
82 opcSticker 68
83 opcSticker 261
84 opcSticker 103
85 opcSticker 104
86 opcSticker 77
87 opcSticker 76
88 opcSticker 81,-SuperStar 10
89 opcSticker 72
86 opcTattoo 13
88 PaniniSticker 328
89 PaniniSticker 123
91 PaniniSticker 59
92 PaniniSticker 226
87 Stuart Bakery 8
86 MTL/Provigo Foods 1
86 MTL/ProvigoFoods-Poster

BROOKS, RODNEY
88 Hamilton/ProCards 1740

BROOME, KIM
89 Welland/Pucko 7

BROSNAN, JIM
62 PostCereal 125

BROUHARD, MARK
86 O-Pee-Chee 21

BROUSSEAU, FERNAND
52 LavalDairy 95

BROW, SCOTT
90 StCatharines/ProCards 3458

BROWER, BOB
88 O-Pee-Chee 252

BROWN, ANTHONY
90 Welland/Pucko 10

BROWN, BOBBY
81 O-Pee-Chee 107
85 O-Pee-Chee 92
84 opcSticker 157

BROWN, CHAD
93 StCatharines/ClassicBest 4
93 StCatharines/ProCards 3967

BROWN, CHRIS
86 Leaf 215
87 Leaf 11, 236
88 Leaf 221
86 O-Pee-Chee 383
87 O-Pee-Chee 180
88 O-Pee-Chee 112
89 O-Pee-Chee 103
86 opcSticker 85, 311
87 opcSticker 86
88 opcSticker 111
86 opcTattoo 18
88 PaniniSticker 408

BROWN, DAREN
89 StCatharines/ProCards 2073

BROWN, DARRELL
84 opcSticker 311
85 opcSticker 306

BROWN, DICK
62 PostCereal 21
62 ShirriffCoin 37

BROWN, GATES
65 O-Pee-Chee 19
67 O-Pee-Chee 134
70 O-Pee-Chee 98
71 O-Pee-Chee 503
72 O-Pee-Chee 187
73 O-Pee-Chee 508
74 O-Pee-Chee 389
75 O-Pee-Chee 371

BROWN, IKE
70 O-Pee-Chee 152
71 O-Pee-Chee 669
72 O-Pee-Chee 284
73 O-Pee-Chee 633
74 O-Pee-Chee 409

BROWN, JACKIE
71 O-Pee-Chee 591
74 O-Pee-Chee 89
75 O-Pee-Chee 316
76 O-Pee-Chee 301
77 O-Pee-Chee 36
78 O-Pee-Chee 126
77 MTL
77 MTL/Redpath Sugar
87 Vancouver/ProCards 1599

BROWN, KEVIN
90 FleerCdn. 291
90 O-Pee-Chee 136
91 O-Pee-Chee 584
92 O-Pee-Chee 297
93 O-Pee-Chee 20
94 O-Pee-Chee 205
90 PaniniSticker 168
93 PaniniSticker 79, 156
92 Calgary/ProCards 3726
92 Calgary/SkyBox 52

BROWN, KURT
91 Vancouver/LineDrive 628
91 Vancouver/ProCards 1596

BROWN, LARRY
66 O-Pee-Chee 16
67 O-Pee-Chee 145
70 O-Pee-Chee 391
71 O-Pee-Chee 539
72 O-Pee-Chee 279

BROWN, MACE
39 WWGum(V351A)

BROWN, MICHAEL
90 Welland/Pucko 2

BROWN, MIKE
86 Leaf 256
87 Calgary/ProCards 2315
84 Edmonton/Cramer 117
89 Edmonton/CMC 18
89 Edmonton/ProCards 558

BROWN, OLLIE
67 O-Pee-Chee 83
69 O-Pee-Chee 149
70 O-Pee-Chee 130
71 O-Pee-Chee 505
73 O-Pee-Chee 526
74 O-Pee-Chee 625
75 O-Pee-Chee 596
76 O-Pee-Chee 223

BROWN, OSCAR
71 O-Pee-Chee 52
72 O-Pee-Chee 516
73 O-Pee-Chee 312

BROWN, TIMOTHY
88 StCatharines/ProCards 2007

BROWNE, BYRON
66 O-Pee-Chee 139
70 O-Pee-Chee 388
71 O-Pee-Chee 659

BROWNE, JERRY
87 Leaf 41
88 Leaf 236
90 FleerCdn. 487
88 O-Pee-Chee 139
90 O-Pee-Chee 442
91 O-Pee-Chee 76
92 O-Pee-Chee 219
93 O-Pee-Chee 234
88 PaniniSticker 201
90 PaniniSticker 54
91 PaniniSticker 217
93 PaniniSticker 18

BROWNING, MIKE
84 Edmonton/Cramer 114

BROWNING, TOM
90 FleerCdn. 415
86 Leaf 179
87 Leaf 138
87 O-Pee-Chee 65
89 O-Pee-Chee 234
90 O-Pee-Chee 418
91 O-Pee-Chee 151
92 O-Pee-Chee 339
93 O-Pee-Chee 74
86 opcSticker 141, 313
87 opcSticker 137
89 opcSticker 7, 141, -SStar 61
86 opcTattoo 10
89 PaniniSticker 4, 65
90 PaniniSticker 247
94 PaniniSticker 161

BRUCE, BOB
65 O-Pee-Chee 240
66 O-Pee-Chee 64

BRUMFIELD, JACOB
92 O-Pee-Chee 591
97 TOR/Sizzler 18

BRUMLEY, DUFF
91 Hamilton/ClassicBest 10
91 Hamilton/ProCards 4029
92 Hamilton/ClassicBest 8

BRUMLEY, MIKE
66 O-Pee-Chee 29
90 O-Pee-Chee 471
92 O-Pee-Chee 407

BRUNANSKY, TOM
90 FleerCdn. 242
85 GeneralMills 2
85 Leaf 36
86 Leaf 24
87 Leaf 244
83 O-Pee-Chee 232
84 O-Pee-Chee 98
85 O-Pee-Chee 122
86 O-Pee-Chee 392
87 O-Pee-Chee 261
88 O-Pee-Chee 375
89 O-Pee-Chee 60
90 O-Pee-Chee 409
91 O-Pee-Chee 675
92 O-Pee-Chee 296
93 O-Pee-Chee 217
93 opcPremier 34
83 opcSticker 90, 309
84 opcSticker 304
85 opcSticker 299
86 opcSticker 276
87 opcSticker 280
88 opcSticker 15, 275
89 opcSticker 41
86 opcTattoo 18
88 PaniniSticker 142, 449, 450
89 PaniniSticker 187
90 PaniniSticker 344
91 PaniniSticker 270
92 PaniniSticker 89
87 Stuart Bakery 22

BRUNDAGE, DAVE
91 Calgary/LineDrive 53
91 Calgary/ProCards 525
92 Calgary/ProCards 3742
92 Calgary/SkyBox 57
93 Calgary/ProCards 1182
94 Calgary/ProCards 805

BRUNET, GEORGE
65 O-Pee-Chee 242
67 O-Pee-Chee 122
70 O-Pee-Chee 328
71 O-Pee-Chee 73

89 O-Pee-Chee 288
90 O-Pee-Chee 747
91 O-Pee-Chee 124
92 O-Pee-Chee 476
84 opcSticker 314
89 PaniniSticker 391
90 PaniniSticker 109

BUSKEY, TOM
75 O-Pee-Chee 403
76 O-Pee-Chee 178
80 O-Pee-Chee 265
79 TOR/BubbleYum

BUSSE, RAY
72 O-Pee-Chee 101
73 O-Pee-Chee 607

BUTCHER, JOHN
85 Leaf 71
85 O-Pee-Chee 356
85 opcSticker 305

BUTCHER, MIKE
92 Edmonton/ProCards 3534
92 Edmonton/SkyBox 153

BUTERA, SAL
86 O-Pee-Chee 261
89 TOR/FireSafety

BUTLER, BILL
70 O-Pee-Chee 377
71 O-Pee-Chee 681
75 O-Pee-Chee 549
76 O-Pee-Chee 619

BUTLER, BRETT
90 FleerCdn. 53
85 Leaf 186
86 Leaf 12
87 Leaf 183
85 O-Pee-Chee 241
86 O-Pee-Chee 149
87 O-Pee-Chee 197
88 O-Pee-Chee 202
89 O-Pee-Chee 241
90 O-Pee-Chee 571
91 O-Pee-Chee 325, C
92 O-Pee-Chee 565
93 O-Pee-Chee 36
94 O-Pee-Chee 215
91 opcPremier 16
92 opcPremier 145
85 opcSticker 246
86 opcSticker 206
88 opcSticker 212
89 opcSticker 85
86 opcTatoo 9
88 PaniniSticker 78
89 PaniniSticker 220
90 PaniniSticker 365
91 PaniniSticker 72
92 PaniniSticker 197
93 PaniniSticker 218
94 PaniniSticker 197
91 PaniniTopFifteen 25, 44, 51
92 PostCdn. 8

BUTLER, JOHN
1912 ImperialTobacco(C46) 46

BUTLER, ROBERT
94 O-Pee-Chee 232
91 StCatharines/ClassicBest 8
91 StCatharines/ProCards 3406

BUTTERS, TOM
65 O-Pee-Chee 246

BUTTS, RANDY
88 Hamilton/ProCards 1735

BUZHARDT, JOHN
67 O-Pee-Chee 178
62 PostCereal 200
62 ShirriffCoin 129

BYARN, GEORGE
50 WWGum(V362) 47

BYERLY, ROD
89 Welland/Pucko 8

BYERS, WILLIAM
1912 ImperialTobacco(C46) 74

BYRD, JEFF
78 O-Pee-Chee 211

BYRD, SAMMY
33 WWGum(V353) 86

C

CABANA, GERRY
52 LavalDairy 37

CABELL, ENOS
85 Leaf 161
73 O-Pee-Chee 605
75 O-Pee-Chee 247
76 O-Pee-Chee 404
78 O-Pee-Chee 44
79 O-Pee-Chee 269
80 O-Pee-Chee 201
81 O-Pee-Chee 45
82 O-Pee-Chee 311
83 O-Pee-Chee 225
82 opcSticker 105
84 opcSticker 273
85 opcSticker 61

CABRERA, BASILIO
90 London/ProCards 1278
91 London/LineDrive 377
91 London/ProCards 1888
92 London/ProCards 643
92 London/SkyBox 402

CABRERA, CARLOS
94 StCatharines/Classic 5
94 StCatharines/ProCards 3649

CABRERA, FRANCISCO
90 O-Pee-Chee 254
91 O-Pee-Chee 693
93 O-Pee-Chee 383

CACERES, EDGAR
97 Vancouver/Best 9

CADARET, GREG
90 FleerCdn. 440
90 O-Pee-Chee 659
91 O-Pee-Chee 187
92 O-Pee-Chee 18

CADORE, LEON
21 Neilson's(V61) 97
23 Neilson's 5
23 WillardsChocolate(V100) 15

CAGE, WAYNE
79 O-Pee-Chee 70

CAIN, LES
71 O-Pee-Chee 101

CALDERON, IVAN
90 FleerCdn. 529
86 Leaf 204
88 Leaf 25, 175
86 O-Pee-Chee 382
88 O-Pee-Chee 184
89 O-Pee-Chee 101
90 O-Pee-Chee 569
91 O-Pee-Chee 93
92 O-Pee-Chee 775
93 O-Pee-Chee 88
91 opcPremier 17
93 opcPremier 105
88 opcSticker 285
89 opcSticker 297
88 PaniniSticker 63
90 PaniniSticker 47
91 PaniniSticker 318
92 PaniniSticker 208, 287
93 PaniniSticker 98
92 MTL/Durivage 4

CALDES, MIGUEL
94 GarciaPhoto 74

CALDWELL, EARL
39 WWGum(V351A)

CALDWELL, MIKE
73 O-Pee-Chee 182
74 O-Pee-Chee 344
75 O-Pee-Chee 347
76 O-Pee-Chee 157
79 O-Pee-Chee 356
79 O-Pee-Chee 356
80 O-Pee-Chee 269
81 O-Pee-Chee 85
82 O-Pee-Chee 378
83 O-Pee-Chee 142
84 O-Pee-Chee 326
83 opcSticker 184, 185
85 opcSticker 289

CALLAGHAN, MARTY
21 Neilson's(V61) 66

CALLISON, JOHN
65 O-Pee-Chee 4, 52
67 O-Pee-Chee 85
68 OPC-Poster 5
69 O-Pee-Chee 133
70 O-Pee-Chee 375
71 O-Pee-Chee 12
72 O-Pee-Chee 364
73 O-Pee-Chee 535
62 ShirriffCoin 204

CALLOWAY, RON
97 Lethbridge/Best 13

CAMACHO, ERNIE
87 O-Pee-Chee 353
85 opcSticker 253
87 opcSticker 209

CAMBRIA, FRED
71 O-Pee-Chee 27
72 O-Pee-Chee 392

CAMILLI, DOUG
65 O-Pee-Chee 77
73 O-Pee-Chee 131

CAMILLI, LOU
71 O-Pee-Chee 612

CAMINITI, KEN
90 FleerCdn. 225
88 O-Pee-Chee 64
90 O-Pee-Chee 531
91 O-Pee-Chee 174
92 O-Pee-Chee 740
93 O-Pee-Chee 81
88 opcSticker 33
90 PaniniSticker 260
91 PaniniSticker 9
92 PaniniSticker 154
93 PaniniSticker 173
94 PaniniSticker 191

CAMP, RICK
85 Leaf 130
81 O-Pee-Chee 87
82 O-Pee-Chee 138
84 O-Pee-Chee 136
85 O-Pee-Chee 167
82 opcSticker 24

CAMPANELLA, ROY
53 Exhibits 20
75 O-Pee-Chee 189, 191, 193

CAMPANERIS, BERT
65 O-Pee-Chee 266
66 O-Pee-Chee 175
68 O-Pee-Chee 109, -Poster 6
70 O-Pee-Chee 205
71 O-Pee-Chee 440
72 O-Pee-Chee 75
73 O-Pee-Chee 64, 295
74 O-Pee-Chee 155, 335
75 O-Pee-Chee 170
76 O-Pee-Chee 580
77 O-Pee-Chee 74
79 O-Pee-Chee 326
80 O-Pee-Chee 264

CAMPANIS, AL
43-47 Montréal/ParadeSportive

CAMPANIS, JIM
67 O-Pee-Chee 12
74 O-Pee-Chee 513
92 O-Pee-Chee 58

CAMPAS, MIKE
89 Hamilton/Star 7

CAMPBELL, BILL
74 O-Pee-Chee 26
75 O-Pee-Chee 226
76 O-Pee-Chee 288
77 O-Pee-Chee 8, 12
78 O-Pee-Chee 8, 87
79 O-Pee-Chee 195
81 O-Pee-Chee 256
85 O-Pee-Chee 209
87 O-Pee-Chee 362

CAMPBELL, DAVE
71 O-Pee-Chee 46
72 O-Pee-Chee 384
73 O-Pee-Chee 488
74 O-Pee-Chee 556

CAMPBELL, KEIVER
91 StCatharines/ClassicBest 2
91 StCatharines/ProCards 3407
92 StCatharines/ClassicBest 14
92 StCatharines/ProCards 2397

CAMPBELL, MIKE
88 Leaf 30
87 Calgary/ProCards 2322
90 Vancouver/CMC 7
90 Vancouver/ProCards 482

CAMPISIS, SAL
71 O-Pee-Chee 568

CAMPOS, TONY
52 LavalDairy 103

CAMPUSANO, GENARO
90 Welland/Pucko 3

CAMPUSANO, SILVESTRE
89 O-Pee-Chee 191
91 O-Pee-Chee 618
88 TOR/FireSafety
89 TOR/FireSafety

CANAELE, CASEY
92 O-Pee-Chee 161

CANALE, GEORGE
90 FleerCdn. 641
90 O-Pee-Chee 344

CANDAELE, CASEY
88 Leaf 199
88 HostessDisk
88 O-Pee-Chee 87
91 O-Pee-Chee 602
93 O-Pee-Chee 105
88 opcSticker 77, 305
88 PaniniSticker 329
91 PaniniSticker 8
92 PaniniSticker 153
93 PaniniSticker 177

CANDELARIA, BEN
94 StCatharines/Classic 6
94 StCatharines/ProCards 3656

CANDELARIA, JOHN
85 Leaf 157
87 Leaf 242
76 O-Pee-Chee 317
77 O-Pee-Chee 59
78 O-Pee-Chee 7, 221
79 O-Pee-Chee 29
80 O-Pee-Chee 332
81 O-Pee-Chee 265
82 O-Pee-Chee 3
83 O-Pee-Chee 127
84 O-Pee-Chee 330
85 O-Pee-Chee 50
86 O-Pee-Chee 140
87 O-Pee-Chee 313
89 O-Pee-Chee 285
90 O-Pee-Chee 485
91 O-Pee-Chee 777
92 O-Pee-Chee 363
83 opcSticker 282
84 opcSticker 127
85 opcSticker 123
89 opcSticker 306
86 opcTattoo 5
89 PaniniSticker 397

CANDIOTTI, TOM
90 FleerCdn. 488
87 Leaf 81
87 O-Pee-Chee 296
88 O-Pee-Chee 123
90 O-Pee-Chee 743
91 O-Pee-Chee 624
92 O-Pee-Chee 38
93 O-Pee-Chee 63
92 opcPremier 142
87 opcSticker 211
89 opcSticker 211
88 PaniniSticker 69
89 PaniniSticker 317
90 PaniniSticker 57
91 PaniniSticker 223
94 PaniniSticker 198
91 TOR/Score 28
84 Vancouver/Cramer 32

CANEPA, VINCENT
52 Laval Dairy 52

CANET, ADOLFO
94 GarciaPhoto 121

CANGELOSI, JOHN
87 Leaf 251
87 O-Pee-Chee 201
88 O-Pee-Chee 328
90 O-Pee-Chee 29
87 opcSticker 293
88 PaniniSticker 377
91 Vancouver/LineDrive 629
91 Vancouver/ProCards 1605

CANIGLIA, PETE
52 LavalDairy 45

CANNADAY, AARON
92 Welland/ClassicBest 3
93 Welland/ClassicBest 3
93 Welland/ProCards 3359

CANNIZZARO, CHRIS
65 O-Pee-Chee 61
69 O-Pee-Chee 131
70 O-Pee-Chee 329
71 O-Pee-Chee 426
75 O-Pee-Chee 355

CANNON, JOE
80 O-Pee-Chee 118

CASANOVA, PAUL
67 O-Pee-Chee 115
70 O-Pee-Chee 84
71 O-Pee-Chee 139
73 O-Pee-Chee 452
74 O-Pee-Chee 272
75 O-Pee-Chee 633

CASE, GEORGE
39 WWGum(V351B)

CASEY, JOSEPH
97 St.Catharines/Best 11

CASEY, PAT
85 Calgary/Cramer 86
86 Calgary/ProCards

CASH, DAVID
77 Dimanche/DernièreHeure
70 O-Pee-Chee 141
71 O-Pee-Chee 582
72 O-Pee-Chee 125
73 O-Pee-Chee 397
74 O-Pee-Chee 198
75 O-Pee-Chee 22
76 O-Pee-Chee 295
77 O-Pee-Chee 180
78 O-Pee-Chee 18
79 O-Pee-Chee 207
80 O-Pee-Chee 3
77 MTL
77 MTL/RedpathSugar
93 MTL/McDonald's 13

CASH, NORM
65 O-Pee-Chee 153
69 O-Pee-Chee 80
71 O-Pee-Chee 599
72 O-Pee-Chee 90, 150
73 O-Pee-Chee 485
74 O-Pee-Chee 367
62 PostCereal 14
62 ShirriffCoin 72

CASH, RON
74 O-Pee-Chee 600

CASIAN, LARRY
91 O-Pee-Chee 374

CASSIDY, DAVID
89 Hamilton/Star 9

CASTALDO, JOE
91 Hamilton/ClassicBest 1
91 Hamilton/ProCards 4030

CASTALDO, VINCE
93 Ottawa/ProCards 2441

CASTILLA, VINNY
93 opcPremier 65
94 PaniniSticker 172

CASTILLO, BOBBY
84 O-Pee-Chee 329

CASTILLO, BRAULIO
92 O-Pee-Chee 353

CASTILLO, CARMELO
90 O-Pee-Chee 427
91 O-Pee-Chee 266

CASTILLO, CARMEN
90 FleerCdn. 371
85 O-Pee-Chee 184
85 opcSticker 255

CASTILLO, FRANK
92 O-Pee-Chee 196
92 opcPremier 159

CASTILLO, JUAN
88 O-Pee-Chee 362
85 Vancouver/Cramer 205

CASTILLO, TONY
90 O-Pee-Chee 620
91 O-Pee-Chee 353
95 TOR/OhHenry
96 TOR/OhHenry

CASTINO, JOHN
80 O-Pee-Chee 76
81 O-Pee-Chee 304
82 O-Pee-Chee 73
83 O-Pee-Chee 93
84 O-Pee-Chee 237
85 O-Pee-Chee 298
82 opcSticker 209
83 opcSticker 89
84 opcSticker 307

CASTLEMAN, SLICK
36 WWGum(V355) 36

CASTRO, BILL
76 O-Pee-Chee 293

CASTRO, JOSE
82 Edmonton/TCMA 2

CASTRO, LAZARO ARTURO
94 GarciaPhoto 2

CASTRO, PABLO
88 StCatharines/ProCards 2012

CATER, DANNY
65 O-Pee-Chee 253
67 O-Pee-Chee 157
69 O-Pee-Chee 1, 44
70 O-Pee-Chee 437
71 O-Pee-Chee 358
73 O-Pee-Chee 317
74 O-Pee-Chee 543
75 O-Pee-Chee 645

CAUDILL, BILL
86 GeneralMills
85 Leaf 154
81 O-Pee-Chee 346
83 O-Pee-Chee 78
84 O-Pee-Chee 299
85 O-Pee-Chee 275, -Poster 23
86 O-Pee-Chee 207
87 O-Pee-Chee 156
83 opcSticker 118
84 opcSticker 345
85 opcSticker 322
85 TOR/FireSafety
86 TOR/AultFoods
86 TOR/FireSafety

CAUSEY, WAYNE
69 O-Pee-Chee 33
62 ShirriffCoin 100

CAVARRETTA, PHIL
36 WWGum(V355) 54

CAVENEY, JAMES
21 Neilson's(V61) 116

CEBUHAR, JOHN
88 Hamilton/ProCards 1721
89 Hamilton/Star 8

CEDENO, ANDUJAR
91 O-Pee-Chee 646
92 O-Pee-Chee 288
93 O-Pee-Chee 129
94 O-Pee-Chee 10
92 opcPremier 156
92 PaniniSticker 155
93 PaniniSticker 172
94 PaniniSticker 192

CEDENO, CESAR
85 Leaf 87
71 O-Pee-Chee 237
72 O-Pee-Chee 65
73 O-Pee-Chee 290
74 O-Pee-Chee 200, 337
75 O-Pee-Chee 590
76 O-Pee-Chee 460
77 O-Pee-Chee 131
78 O-Pee-Chee 226
79 O-Pee-Chee 294
80 O-Pee-Chee 193
81 O-Pee-Chee 190
82 O-Pee-Chee 48
83 O-Pee-Chee 238
84 O-Pee-Chee 191
85 O-Pee-Chee 54
86 O-Pee-Chee 224
82 opcSticker 47
83 opcSticker 231
84 opcSticker 54
85 opcSticker 55

CEDENO, DOMINGO
95 TOR/OhHenry
96 TOR/OhHenry

CEPEDA, ORLANDO
65 O-Pee-Chee 13
66 O-Pee-Chee 132
67 O-Pee-Chee 20
68 O-Pee-Chee 3, -Poster 8
70 OPC-Booklet 13
71 O-Pee-Chee 605
72 O-Pee-Chee 195
73 O-Pee-Chee 545
74 O-Pee-Chee 83
75 O-Pee-Chee 205
60 opcTattoo 8
62 PostCereal 136
62 ShirriffCoin 175

CERONE, RICK
90 FleerCdn. 270
77 O-Pee-Chee 76
78 O-Pee-Chee 129
79 O-Pee-Chee 72
80 O-Pee-Chee 311
81 O-Pee-Chee 335
82 O-Pee-Chee 45
83 O-Pee-Chee 254
84 O-Pee-Chee 228
85 O-Pee-Chee 337
86 O-Pee-Chee 203
89 O-Pee-Chee 96
90 O-Pee-Chee 303
91 O-Pee-Chee 237
92 O-Pee-Chee 643
92 opcPremier 90
82 opcSticker 218
88 PaniniSticker 151
92 PaniniSticker 221
79 TOR/BubbleYum

CERUTTI, JOHN
90 FleerCdn. 78
87 Leaf 210
88 Leaf 152
87 O-Pee-Chee 282
88 O-Pee-Chee 191
89 O-Pee-Chee 347
90 O-Pee-Chee 211
91 O-Pee-Chee 687
92 O-Pee-Chee 487
90 PaniniSticker 177
87 TOR/FireSafety
88 TOR/FireSafety
89 TOR/FireSafety
90 TOR/FireSafety

CEY, RON
85 Leaf 84
73 O-Pee-Chee 615
74 O-Pee-Chee 315
75 O-Pee-Chee 390
76 O-Pee-Chee 370
77 O-Pee-Chee 199
78 O-Pee-Chee 130
79 O-Pee-Chee 94
80 O-Pee-Chee 267
81 O-Pee-Chee 260
82 O-Pee-Chee 216, 367
83 O-Pee-Chee 15
84 O-Pee-Chee 357
85 O-Pee-Chee 366
86 O-Pee-Chee 194
87 O-Pee-Chee 322, C
82 opcSticker 51
83 opcSticker 244
84 opcSticker 41
85 opcSticker 42

CHADWICK, RAY
86 Edmonton/ProCards

CHAKALES, BOB
61 Toronto/BeeHive

CHALK, DAVE
74 O-Pee-Chee 597
75 O-Pee-Chee 64
76 O-Pee-Chee 52
79 O-Pee-Chee 362
80 O-Pee-Chee 137'

CHAMBERLAIN, MATT
93 Welland/ProCards 3348

CHAMBERLAIN, WES
91 O-Pee-Chee 603
92 O-Pee-Chee 14
93 O-Pee-Chee 45
94 O-Pee-Chee 27
93 PaniniSticker 275

CHAMBERS, AL
85 Calgary/Cramer 80

CHAMBLISS, CHRIS
85 Leaf 168
72 O-Pee-Chee 142
73 O-Pee-Chee 11
74 O-Pee-Chee 384
75 O-Pee-Chee 585
76 O-Pee-Chee 65
77 O-Pee-Chee 49
78 O-Pee-Chee 145
79 O-Pee-Chee 171
80 O-Pee-Chee 328
81 O-Pee-Chee 155
82 O-Pee-Chee 320, 321
83 O-Pee-Chee 11
84 O-Pee-Chee 50
85 O-Pee-Chee 187
87 O-Pee-Chee 204
82 opcSticker 17
83 opcSticker 212
84 opcSticker 28
85 opcSticker 29
89 London/ProCards 1378

CHAMPION, BILLY
70 O-Pee-Chee 149
71 O-Pee-Chee 323
73 O-Pee-Chee 74
74 O-Pee-Chee 391
75 O-Pee-Chee 256
76 O-Pee-Chee 501

CHANCE, BOB
65 O-Pee-Chee 224

CHANCE, DEAN
65 O-Pee-Chee 7, 9, 11, 140
68 O-Pee-Chee 10, 12
71 O-Pee-Chee 36

CHANDLER, CHRIS
92 StCatharines/ClassicBest 21
92 StCatharines/ProCards 3393

CHANEY, DARREL
70 O-Pee-Chee 3
71 O-Pee-Chee 632
72 O-Pee-Chee 136
73 O-Pee-Chee 507
74 O-Pee-Chee 559
75 O-Pee-Chee 581
76 O-Pee-Chee 259
77 O-Pee-Chee 134
79 O-Pee-Chee 91

CHANEY, NORMA
89 Welland/Pucko 35

CHAPIN, DARRIN
94 Edmonton/ProCards 2867

CHAPMAN, BEN
37 O-Pee-Chee(V300) 130
34 WWGum(V354) 51
36 WWGum(V355) 90
39 WWGum(V351B)

CHARBONEAU, JOE
81 O-Pee-Chee 13
82 O-Pee-Chee 211

CHARLAND, COLIN
90 FleerCdn. 640
89 Edmonton/CMC 6
89 Edmonton/ProCards 565

CHARLES, ED
65 O-Pee-Chee 35
67 O-Pee-Chee 182

CHARLES, STEVE
96 StCatharines/Best 6

CHARLTON, NORM
90 FleerCdn. 416
90 O-Pee-Chee 289
91 O-Pee-Chee 309
92 O-Pee-Chee 649
93 O-Pee-Chee 98
93 opcPremier 50

CHEEK, JEFF
93 StCatharines/ClassicBest 5
93 StCatharines/ProCards 3968
94 StCatharines/ProCards 3634

CHEEVES, VIRGIL
21 Neilson's(V61) 84
23 Neilson's 6

CHEW, GREG
94 Welland/Classic 6
94 Welland/ProCards 3485

CHIAFFREDO, PAUL
97 St.Catharines/Best 12

CHIAMPARINO, SCOTT
91 O-Pee-Chee 676
92 O-Pee-Chee 277

CHILES, RICH
72 O-Pee-Chee 56
73 O-Pee-Chee 617

CHITREN, STEVE
92 O-Pee-Chee 379

CHLUPSA, BOB
71 O-Pee-Chee 594

CHOATE, MARK
92 StCatharines/ClassicBest 13
92 StCatharines/ProCards 3394

CHRIST, MIKE
88 Calgary/CMC 6

CHRISTENBURY, LLOYD R.
23 WillardsChocolate(V100) 18

CHRISTENSEN, JOHN
88 Calgary/CMC 17
88 Calgary/ProCards 794

COCHRANE, DAVE
90 O-Pee-Chee 491
88 Calgary/CMC 14
88 Calgary/ProCards 785
89 Calgary/CMC 14
89 Calgary/ProCards 542
90 Calgary/CMC 11
91 Calgary/LineDrive 55
91 Calgary/ProCards 518

COCHRANE, GORDON (MICKEY)
33 WWGum(V353) 69
34 WWGum(V354) 59
36 WWGum(V355) 45
76 O-Pee-Chee 348

COCKRELL, ALAN
92 O-Pee-Chee 591
91 Calgary/LineDrive 56
91 Calgary/ProCards 526

COCO, PASCUAL
97 St.Catharines/Best 13

CODIROLI, CHRIS
86 Leaf 151
84 O-Pee-Chee 61
86 O-Pee-Chee 388
84 opcSticker 330
85 opcSticker 327
86 opcSticker 173
86 opcTattoo 9

COFFMAN, KEVIN
89 O-Pee-Chee 44
93 Calgary/ProCards 1157

COFFMAN, RICHARD
34 WWGum(V354) 23

COGGINS, FRANK
68 O-Pee-Chee 96

COGGINS, RICH
73 O-Pee-Chee 611
74 O-Pee-Chee 353
75 O-Pee-Chee 167
76 O-Pee-Chee 572

COHEN, ANDY
33 WWGum(V353) 52

COKER, JIM
65 O-Pee-Chee 192
67 O-Pee-Chee 158

COLAVITO, ROCKY
66 O-Pee-Chee 150
67 O-Pee-Chee 109
68 O-Pee-Chee 99
73 O-Pee-Chee 449
60 opcTattoo 9, 73
62 PostCereal 19
62 ShirriffCoin 28

COLBERN, MIKE
81 Edmonton/RedRooster 19

COLBERT, NATE
70 O-Pee-Chee 11
71 O-Pee-Chee 235
73 O-Pee-Chee 340
74 O-Pee-Chee 125
75 O-Pee-Chee 599
76 O-Pee-Chee 495

COLBERT, RICK
91 Hamilton/ClassicBest 29
91 Hamilton/ProCards 4056

COLBERT, VINCE
71 O-Pee-Chee 231
72 O-Pee-Chee 84

COLBORN, JIM
71 O-Pee-Chee 38
72 O-Pee-Chee 386
73 O-Pee-Chee 408
74 O-Pee-Chee 75
75 O-Pee-Chee 305
76 O-Pee-Chee 521
78 O-Pee-Chee 116
79 O-Pee-Chee 137

COLBRUNN, GREG
91 O-Pee-Chee 91
93 O-Pee-Chee 137
93 PaniniSticker 225

COLE, ALBERT
23 Willards Chocolate 21

COLE, ALEX
90 FleerCdn. 244
91 O-Pee-Chee 421
92 O-Pee-Chee 170
91 opcPremier 24
92 PaniniSticker 50

COLE JR., ALEX
91 PaniniSticker 222
91 PaniniTopFifteen 48

COLE, BERT
21 Neilson's(V61) 28

COLEMAN, ED
34 WWGum(V354) 76

COLEMAN, GORDY
67 O-Pee-Chee 61
62 PostCereal 116
62 ShirriffCoin 110

COLEMAN, GUY
52 LavalDairy 46

COLEMAN, HAMPTON
53 Exhibits 52

COLEMAN, JOE
67 O-Pee-Chee 167
70 O-Pee-Chee 127
71 O-Pee-Chee 403
72 O-Pee-Chee 96
73 O-Pee-Chee 120
74 O-Pee-Chee 240
75 O-Pee-Chee 42
76 O-Pee-Chee 68, 456
79 O-Pee-Chee 166

COLEMAN, JOE JR.
76 O-Pee-Chee 68

COLEMAN, PAUL
90 O-Pee-Chee 655

COLEMAN, RIP
61 Toronto/BeeHive

COLEMAN, SOLOMON HAMPTON
52 Parkhurst 65

COLEMAN, VINCE
90 Ben's/HolsumDisk 15
90 FleerCdn. 245
86 Leaf 115, 225
87 Leaf 194
88 Leaf 128
86 O-Pee-Chee 370, D
87 O-Pee-Chee 119
88 O-Pee-Chee 260
89 O-Pee-Chee 90
90 O-Pee-Chee 6, 660
91 O-Pee-Chee 160
92 O-Pee-Chee 500
91 opcPremier 25
86 opcSticker 5, 47, 306
87 opcSticker 50
88 opcSticker 4, 47
89 opcSticker 43, 154
86 opcTattoo 16
88 PaniniSticker 294
89 PaniniSticker 188, 299
90 PaniniSticker 336, 282
91 PaniniSticker 35
92 PaniniSticker 227
93 PaniniSticker 252
91 PaniniTopFifteen 41
87 Stuart Bakery 11
96 Vancouver/Best 7

COLES, DARNELL
90 FleerCdn. 509
87 O-Pee-Chee 388
88 O-Pee-Chee 46
90 O-Pee-Chee 232
91 O-Pee-Chee 506
87 opcSticker 271
90 PaniniSticker 145
93 TOR
93 TOR/Dempster's 16
93 TOR/FireSafety
85 Calgary/Cramer 96

COLINA, ROBERTO
94 GarciaPhoto 37

COLLAZO, HERIBERTO
94 GarciaPhoto 57

COLLIER, LOU
93 Welland/ClassicBest 4
93 Welland/ProCards 3362
97 Calgary/Best 10

COLLINS, DAVE
85 Leaf 172
76 O-Pee-Chee 363
77 O-Pee-Chee 248
81 O-Pee-Chee 175
82 O-Pee-Chee 349
83 O-Pee-Chee 359
84 O-Pee-Chee 38
85 O-Pee-Chee 164
86 O-Pee-Chee 271
82 opcSticker 33
85 opcSticker 363
86 opcSticker 172
84 TOR/FireSafety
90 TOR/Hostess

COLLINS, EDDIE
20 MapleCrispette(V117) 4
21 Neilson's(V61) 29
22 WilliamPaterson(V89) 35
33 WWGum(V353) 42

COLLINS, JOHN F.
23 WillardsChoc.(V100) 22

COLLINS, KEVIN
69 O-Pee-Chee 127
71 O-Pee-Chee 553

COLLINS, PAT
21 Neilson's(V61) 35

COLLINS, PHIL
33 WWGum(V353) 21

COLLINS, RIPPER
36 WWGum(V355) 18

COLLINS, WILLIAM
1912 ImperialTobacco(C46) 34

COLLUM, JACK
50 WWGum(V362) 30

COLMAN, FRANK
52 Parkhurst 9

COLON, ANGEL
92 Welland/ClassicBest 6

COLPAERT, DICK
73 O-Pee-Chee 608

COLSON, LOYD
71 O-Pee-Chee 111

COLUCCIO, BOB
74 O-Pee-Chee 124
75 O-Pee-Chee 456
76 O-Pee-Chee 333

COMBE, GEOFF
82 Edmonton/TCMA 23

COMBS, EARLE
34 WWGum(V354) 21

COMBS, PAT
90 FleerCdn. 553
90 O-Pee-Chee 384
91 O-Pee-Chee 571
92 O-Pee-Chee 456

COMER, STEVE
82 opcSticker 242

COMER, WAYNE
70 O-Pee-Chee 323

COMOROSKY, ADAM
33 WWGum(V353) 70

COMPTON, MIKE
71 O-Pee-Chee 77

COMSTOCK, KEITH
90 FleerCdn. 510
91 O-Pee-Chee 337

CONCEPCION, DAVE
86 GeneralMills
85 Leaf 131
71 O-Pee-Chee 14
72 O-Pee-Chee 267
73 O-Pee-Chee 554
74 O-Pee-Chee 435
75 O-Pee-Chee 17
76 O-Pee-Chee 48
77 O-Pee-Chee 258
78 O-Pee-Chee 220
79 O-Pee-Chee 234
80 O-Pee-Chee 117
81 O-Pee-Chee 83
82 O-Pee-Chee 86, 221, 340
83 O-Pee-Chee 32, 102
84 O-Pee-Chee 55
85 O-Pee-Chee 21
86 O-Pee-Chee 195
87 O-Pee-Chee 193
88 O-Pee-Chee 336
82 opcSticker 37, 124
83 opcSticker 227
84 opcSticker 56
85 opcSticker 48
86 opcSticker 137
86 opcTattoo 22
88 PaniniSticker 275

CONCEPCION, ONIX
86 O-Pee-Chee 163

CONE, DAVID
90 FleerCdn. 200
89 O-Pee-Chee 384
90 O-Pee-Chee 30
91 O-Pee-Chee 680
92 O-Pee-Chee 195
93 O-Pee-Chee 107, -WSC 4
94 O-Pee-Chee 260
92 opcPremier 175
93 opcPremier 92
89 opcSticker 96, -S.Star 58
89 PaniniSticker 129
90 PaniniSticker 301
91 PaniniTopFifteen 73
95 PostCdn. 12
93 TOR/Donruss 15
95 TOR/OhHenry

CONIGLIARO, BILLY
70 O-Pee-Chee 317
71 O-Pee-Chee 114
72 O-Pee-Chee 481
74 O-Pee-Chee 545

CONIGLIARO, TONY
65 O-Pee-Chee 55
68 O-Pee-Chee 140
70 O-Pee-Chee 340
71 O-Pee-Chee 63, 105

CONINE, JEFF
94 O-Pee-Chee 238, -DD 12
91 opcPremier 26
93 opcPremier 119
94 PaniniSticker 181

CONNALLY, GEORGE
33 WWGum(V353) 27

CONNORS, CHUCK
50 WWGum(V362) 2

CONTRERAS, NARDI
81 Edmonton/RedRooster 4
82 Edmonton/TCMA 14

CONVERSE, JIM
93 Calgary/ProCards 1158
94 Calgary/ProCards 782

CONWAY, JOHN CLEMENTS
52 Parkhurst 96

COOK, DENNIS
90 FleerCdn. 554
90 O-Pee-Chee 633
91 O-Pee-Chee 467
89 PaniniSticker 207
90 PaniniSticker 320

COOK, MIKE
91 Calgary/LineDrive 57
88 Edmonton/CMC 2
88 Edmonton/ProCards 567

COOK, RON
71 O-Pee-Chee 583
72 O-Pee-Chee 339
91 London/LineDrive 378

COOK, TIM
82 Vancouver/TCMA 12

COOKE, STEVE
94 O-Pee-Chee 85
93 opcPremier 19
94 PaniniSticker 234
90 Welland/Pucko 20

COOLBAUGH, MIKE
91 StCatharines/ClassicBest 7
91 StCatharines/ProCards 3402
92 StCatharines/ClassicBest 3
92 StCatharines/ProCards 3395

COOLBAUGH, SCOTT
90 FleerCdn. 293
91 O-Pee-Chee 277

COOMBS, DANNY
71 O-Pee-Chee 126

COOMBS, GLENN
91 Welland/Best 25
91 Welland/ProCards 3564

COOMER, RON
92 Vancouver/ProCards 2727
92 Vancouver/SkyBox 631

COOPER, CECIL
85 Leaf 246
86 Leaf 7
87 Leaf 230
72 O-Pee-Chee 79
74 O-Pee-Chee 523
75 O-Pee-Chee 489
76 O-Pee-Chee 78
77 O-Pee-Chee 102
78 O-Pee-Chee 71
79 O-Pee-Chee 163

80 O-Pee-Chee 52
81 O-Pee-Chee 356
82 O-Pee-Chee 167
83 O-Pee-Chee 190
84 O-Pee-Chee 43, -AS
85 O-Pee-Chee 290
86 O-Pee-Chee 385
87 O-Pee-Chee 10, D
82 opcSticker 199
83 opcSticker 80
84 opcSticker 291
85 opcSticker 287
86 opcSticker 196
87 opcSticker 198
86 opcTattoo 6
87 Stuart Bakery 21

COOPER, DAVE
89 London/ProCards 1362

COOPER, GARY
90 Hamilton/Best 19
90 Hamilton/Star 9

COOPER, SCOTT
92 O-Pee-Chee 488
93 O-Pee-Chee 385
94 O-Pee-Chee 4
93 opcPremier 13
93 PaniniSticker 93
94 PaniniSticker 27

COOPER, WALKER
53 Exhibits 58

COOPER, WILBUR
21 Neilson's(V61) 57

CORA, JOEY
90 FleerCdn. 154
92 O-Pee-Chee 302
92 PaniniSticker 126
94 PaniniSticker 46

CORBETT, DOUG
81 O-Pee-Chee 162
82 O-Pee-Chee 157
82 opcSticker 210
84 Edmonton/Cramer 111

CORBETT, SHERMAN
87 Edmonton/ProCards 2978
89 Edmonton/CMC 8
89 Edmonton/ProCards 546
90 Edmonton/CMC 5
90 Edmonton/ProCards 512
92 London/ProCards 625

CORBIN, RAY
72 O-Pee-Chee 66
73 O-Pee-Chee 411
74 O-Pee-Chee 296
75 O-Pee-Chee 78
76 O-Pee-Chee 474

CORCORAN, MICHAEL
1912 ImperialTobacco(C46) 49

CORDERO, WILL
93 HitTheBooks
93 HumptyDumpty 36
92 O-Pee-Chee 551
93 O-Pee-Chee 161
94 O-Pee-Chee 252, -DD 10
93 opcPremier 29
93 PaniniSticker 226
94 PaniniSticker 208

CORKINS, MIKE
71 O-Pee-Chee 179
73 O-Pee-Chee 461
74 O-Pee-Chee 546

CORMIER, RHÉAL
93 Ben'sDisk 20
92 O-Pee-Chee 346
93 O-Pee-Chee 34
96 MTL/Disk

CORNELIUS, BRIAN
92 London/ProCards 644
92 London/SkyBox 403

CORNELIUS, RICK
94 Ottawa/ProCards 2894

CORNETT, BRAD
95 TOR/OhHenry
92 StCatharines/ClassicBest 22
92 StCatharines/ProCards 3378

CORRALES, FAUSTINO
94 GarciaPhoto 20

CORRALES, PAT
65 O-Pee-Chee 107
66 O-Pee-Chee 137
67 O-Pee-Chee 78
70 O-Pee-Chee 507
71 O-Pee-Chee 293
73 O-Pee-Chee 542
74 O-Pee-Chee 498

CORREA, EDWIN
87 Leaf 145
87 O-Pee-Chee 334
88 PaniniSticker 196

CORREIA, ROD
93 Vancouver/ProCards 2603
94 Vancouver/ProCards 1868

CORRELL, VIC
75 O-Pee-Chee 177
76 O-Pee-Chee 608

CORRIDON, FRANK
1912 ImperialTobacco(C46) 17

CORRY, DELYNN
92 Hamilton/ClassicBest 29

CORSI, JIM
90 FleerCdn. 4
90 O-Pee-Chee 623

COSENZA, VINCENT
52 LavalDairy 40

COSGROVE, MIKE
75 O-Pee-Chee 96
76 O-Pee-Chee 122

COSMAN, JIM
70 O-Pee-Chee 429

COSTELLO, JOHN
90 FleerCdn. 246
90 O-Pee-Chee 36
89 PaniniSticker 176

COSTO, TIM
91 O-Pee-Chee 103

COTTIER, CHUCK
62 PostCereal 66
62 ShirriffCoin 20

COTTO, HENRY
90 FleerCdn. 511
88 O-Pee-Chee 172
89 O-Pee-Chee 207
90 O-Pee-Chee 31
91 O-Pee-Chee 634
92 O-Pee-Chee 311
89 opcSticker 218
89 PaniniSticker 441
91 PaniniSticker 232
93 PaniniSticker 64

COVELESKI, STANLEY
23 WillardsChocolate(V100) 23

COVINGTON, WES
66 O-Pee-Chee 52
62 ShirriffCoin 105

COWAN, BILLY
65 O-Pee-Chee 186
71 O-Pee-Chee 614
72 O-Pee-Chee 19

COWENS, AL
85 Leaf 239
86 Leaf 184
75 O-Pee-Chee 437
76 O-Pee-Chee 648
78 O-Pee-Chee 143
79 O-Pee-Chee 258
80 O-Pee-Chee 174
81 O-Pee-Chee 123
82 O-Pee-Chee 103
83 O-Pee-Chee 193
85 O-Pee-Chee 224
86 O-Pee-Chee 92
82 opcSticker 182
83 opcSticker 115
84 opcSticker 344
85 opcSticker 333

COWLE, JOE
85 Leaf 58
87 Leaf 240
85 opcSticker 318
87 opcSticker 290

COX, BOBBY
83 O-Pee-Chee 34
84 O-Pee-Chee 202
85 O-Pee-Chee 135
86 O-Pee-Chee 359
91 O-Pee-Chee 759
92 O-Pee-Chee 489
84 TOR/FireSafety
85 TOR/FireSafety
93 TOR/McDonald's 15

COX, CASEY
68 O-Pee-Chee 66
70 O-Pee-Chee 281
71 O-Pee-Chee 82
72 O-Pee-Chee 231
73 O-Pee-Chee 419

COX, DANNY
86 Leaf 177
87 Leaf 160
88 Leaf 72
86 O-Pee-Chee 294
87 O-Pee-Chee 202
88 O-Pee-Chee 59
89 O-Pee-Chee 158
90 O-Pee-Chee 184
92 O-Pee-Chee 791
88 PaniniSticker 383
93 TOR/Dempster's 3
93 TOR/FireSafety
95 TOR/OhHenry

COX, JEFF
87 Vancouver/ProCards 1600

COX, JIM
74 O-Pee-Chee 600

COX, LARRY
80 O-Pee-Chee 63

COX, TERRY
71 O-Pee-Chee 559

COZZI, DANTE
52 LavalDairy 73

CRABTREE, ESTEL
36 WWGum(V355) 134

CRABTREE, TIM
97 HitTheBooks
95 TOR/OhHenry
96 TOR/Sizzler 22
92 StCatharines/ClassicBest 23
92 StCatharines/ProCards 3379

CRAIG, PETE
66 O-Pee-Chee 11

CRAIG, ROGER
74 O-Pee-Chee 31
90 O-Pee-Chee 351
91 O-Pee-Chee 579
92 O-Pee-Chee 109
62 ShirriffCoin 189

CRANFORD, JOHN
92 Welland/ClassicBest 5

CRAM, JERRY
71 O-Pee-Chee 247

CRAMER, ROGER
34 WWGum(V354) 74

CRANDALL, DEL
65 O-Pee-Chee 68
73 O-Pee-Chee 646
75 O-Pee-Chee 384

CRAWFORD, JIM
74 O-Pee-Chee 279
76 O-Pee-Chee 428

CRAWFORD, STEVE
86 Leaf 193
91 O-Pee-Chee 718

CRAWFORD, WILLIE
70 O-Pee-Chee 34
71 O-Pee-Chee 519
73 O-Pee-Chee 639
74 O-Pee-Chee 480
75 O-Pee-Chee 186
76 O-Pee-Chee 76

CREEK, DOUG
91 Hamilton/ProCards 4031

CRESPO, FELIPE
96 TOR/OhHenry
97 TOR/Sizzler 55

CREWS, TIM
90 FleerCdn. 390
90 O-Pee-Chee 551
91 O-Pee-Chee 737
92 O-Pee-Chee 642
89 PaniniSticker 96

CRIDER, JERRY
71 O-Pee-Chee 113

CRIM, CHUCK
90 FleerCdn. 319
89 O-Pee-Chee 99
90 O-Pee-Chee 768
91 O-Pee-Chee 644
92 O-Pee-Chee 169
90 PaniniSticker 103
85 Vancouver/Cramer 220
86 Vancouver/ProCards

CRITZ, HUGH
33 WWGum(V353) 3
34 WWGum(V354) 72

CROMARTIE, WARREN
80 Dimanche/DernièreHeure
82 FBI BoxBottoms
78 O-Pee-Chee 117
79 O-Pee-Chee 32
80 O-Pee-Chee 102
81 O-Pee-Chee 345, -Poster 5
82 OPC 61, 94, -Poster 13
83 O-Pee-Chee 351
84 O-Pee-Chee 287
82 opcSticker 60
77 MTL
77 MTL/RedpathSugar
82 MTL/Hygrade
82 MTL/Zellers (x2)
83 MTL
83 MTL/StuartBakery
93 MTL/McDonald's 14

CROMER, BRANDON
93 StCatharines/ClassicBest 6
93 StCatharines/ProCards 3979

CROMER, TRIPP
89 Hamilton/Star 10

CROMPTON, HERBERT B.
52 LavalDairy 80

CRON, CHRIS
90 Edmonton/CMC 21
90 Edmonton/ProCards 523
91 Edmonton/LineDrive 158
91 Edmonton/ProCards 1521
92 Vancouver/ProCards 2728
92 Vancouver/SkyBox 632

CRONE, BILL
85 Calgary/Cramer 93
86 Calgary/ProCards

CRONIN, JOE
37 O-Pee-Chee(V300) 124
33 WWGum(V353) 63
36 WWGum(V355) 46
39 WWGum(V351B)

CROSBY, ED
71 O-Pee-Chee 672
73 O-Pee-Chee 599
76 O-Pee-Chee 457

CROSBY, KEN
76 O-Pee-Chee 593

CROSETTI, FRANK
36 WWGum(V355) 91
39 WWGum (V351A)

CROWDER, ALVIN
33 WWGum(V353) 71
34 WWGum(V354) 65

CROWLEY, TERRY
83 Dimanche/DernièreHeure
70 O-Pee-Chee 121
71 O-Pee-Chee 453
73 O-Pee-Chee 302
74 O-Pee-Chee 648
75 O-Pee-Chee 447
76 O-Pee-Chee 491
81 O-Pee-Chee 342
84 O-Pee-Chee 246

CROWTHER, JOHN
94 StCatharines/Classic 7
94 StCatharines/ProCards 3635
95 StCatharines/TimHortons 5

CRUISE, WALTON E.
23 Willards Chocolate 24

CRUZ, FAUSTO
95 Edmonton/Macri
97 Vancouver/Best 11

CRUZ, HECTOR
76 O-Pee-Chee 598
82 O-Pee-Chee 364

CRUZ, HENRY
76 O-Pee-Chee 590

CRUZ, IVAN
91 London/LineDrive 379
91 London/ProCards 1882
92 London/ProCards 638
92 London/SkyBox 404

CRUZ, JOSE (SR.)
85 Leaf 20
86 Leaf 49
87 Leaf 116
72 O-Pee-Chee 107
73 O-Pee-Chee 292
74 O-Pee-Chee 464
75 O-Pee-Chee 514
76 O-Pee-Chee 321

77 O-Pee-Chee 147
78 O-Pee-Chee 131
79 O-Pee-Chee 143
80 O-Pee-Chee 367
81 O-Pee-Chee 105
82 O-Pee-Chee 325
83 O-Pee-Chee 327
84 O-Pee-Chee 189
85 O-Pee-Chee 95
86 O-Pee-Chee 96
87 O-Pee-Chee 343
82 opcSticker 44
83 opcSticker 242
84 opcSticker 54
85 opcSticker 59
86 opcSticker 26
87 opcSticker 29
86 opcTattoo 11
88 PaniniSticker 299

CRUZ, JULIO
79 O-Pee-Chee 305
80 O-Pee-Chee 16
81 O-Pee-Chee 121
82 O-Pee-Chee 130
83 O-Pee-Chee 113
84 O-Pee-Chee 257
85 O-Pee-Chee 71
86 O-Pee-Chee 14
87 O-Pee-Chee 53
82 opcSticker 114, 235
83 opcSticker 112
84 opcSticker 248
85 opcSticker 239

CRUZ, TODD
83 O-Pee-Chee 132

CRUZ, VICTOR
80 O-Pee-Chee 54
81 O-Pee-Chee 252

CUBBAGE, MIKE
75 O-Pee-Chee 617
76 O-Pee-Chee 615
79 O-Pee-Chee 187
80 O-Pee-Chee 262

CUELLAR, BOBBY
85 Calgary/Cramer 84
94 Calgary/ProCards 806

CUELLAR, MIKE
67 O-Pee-Chee 97
70 OPC 68, 70, -Booklet 1
71 O-Pee-Chee 69, 170
72 O-Pee-Chee 70
73 O-Pee-Chee 470
74 O-Pee-Chee 560
75 O-Pee-Chee 410
76 O-Pee-Chee 285

CULLEN, JACK
66 O-Pee-Chee 31

CULLEN, TIM
67 O-Pee-Chee 167
70 O-Pee-Chee 49
71 O-Pee-Chee 566
72 O-Pee-Chee 461

CULP, RAY
66 O-Pee-Chee 4
67 O-Pee-Chee 168
70 O-Pee-Chee 144
71 O-Pee-Chee 660
72 O-Pee-Chee 2

CULVER, GEORGE
65 O-Pee-Chee 166
70 O-Pee-Chee 92
71 O-Pee-Chee 291
73 O-Pee-Chee 242
74 O-Pee-Chee 632

CUMBERLAND, JOHN
69 O-Pee-Chee 114
71 O-Pee-Chee 108
72 O-Pee-Chee 403

CUMMINGS, STEVE
90 O-Pee-Chee 374
93 opcPremier 69

CUNNINGHAM, BILL
21 Neilson's(V61) 112

CUNNINGHAM, EARL
90 O-Pee-Chee 134

CUNNINGHAM, JOE
60 opcTattoo 10
62 PostCereal 160
62 ShirriffCoin 173

CUNNIGHAM, JOSEPH
89 Hamilton/Star 28

CURRY, STEVE
89 PaniniSticker 267

CURTIS, CHAD
93 O-Pee-Chee 28
94 O-Pee-Chee 98
93 opcPremier 2
93 PaniniSticker 10
94 PaniniSticker 35
91 Edmonton/LineDrive 159
91 Edmonton/ProCards 1522

CURTIS, ED
1912 ImperialTobacco(C46) 90

CURTIS, JOHN
73 O-Pee-Chee 143
74 O-Pee-Chee 373
75 O-Pee-Chee 381
76 O-Pee-Chee 239
81 O-Pee-Chee 158

CURTIS, JOHN
90 Welland/Pucko 12

CUTSHAW, GEORGE W.
23 WillardsChocolate(V100) 25

CUYLER, KIKI
33 WWGum(V353) 23
36 WWGum(V355) 55

CUYLER, MILT
91 O-Pee-Chee 684
92 O-Pee-Chee 522
92 opcPremier 27
92 PaniniSticker 110

CZARKOWSKI, MARK
93 Calgary/ProCards 1159

D

DACUS, BARRY
88 Edmonton/CMC 10
88 Edmonton/ProCards 568

D'ACQUISTO, JOHN
74 O-Pee-Chee 608
75 O-Pee-Chee 372
76 O-Pee-Chee 628
81 O-Pee-Chee 204

DAVANON, JERRY
76 O-Pee-Chee 551

DADE, PAUL
78 O-Pee-Chee 86
79 O-Pee-Chee 3
80 O-Pee-Chee 134

DAL CANTON, BRUCE
70 O-Pee-Chee 52
71 O-Pee-Chee 168
73 O-Pee-Chee 487
74 O-Pee-Chee 308
75 O-Pee-Chee 472
76 O-Pee-Chee 486

DALENA, PETE
90 Vancouver/CMC 14
90 Vancouver/ProCards 494

DALESANDRO, MARK
94 Vancouver/ProCards 1866

DALEY, BUD
65 O-Pee-Chee 262
60 opcTattoo 11
62 ShirriffCoin 203

DALRYMPLE, CLAYTON
67 O-Pee-Chee 53
69 O-Pee-Chee 151
70 O-Pee-Chee 319
71 O-Pee-Chee 617
62 PostCereal 197
62 ShirriffCoin 141

DANFORTH, DAVE
21 Neilson's(V61) 26
23 Neilson's 7

DANIELS, BENNIE
65 O-Pee-Chee 129
62 ShirriffCoin 42

DANIELS, KAL
88 Leaf 14,150
88 O-Pee-Chee 53
89 O-Pee-Chee 45
90 O-Pee-Chee 585
91 O-Pee-Chee 245
92 O-Pee-Chee 767
88 opcSticker 139
89 opcSticker 144
88 PaniniSticker 281
89 PaniniSticker 75
90 PaniniSticker 280
91 PaniniSticker 60
92 PaniniSticker 198
93 PaniniSticker 207

DANIELS, LEE
92 StCatharines/ClassicBest 9
92 StCatharines/ProCards 3380

DANNER, DEON
91 Welland/Best 18
91 Welland/ProCards 3565

DANNING, HARRY
36 WWGum(V355) 22
39 WWGum(V351A)

DARCY, PAT
75 O-Pee-Chee 615
76 O-Pee-Chee 538

DARK, ALVIN
69 O-Pee-Chee 91
70 O-Pee-Chee 524
71 O-Pee-Chee 397
75 O-Pee-Chee 561

DARLEY, NED
92 StCatharines/ClassicBest 8
92 StCatharines/ProCards 3381

DARLING, RON
90 FleerCdn. 201
85 Leaf 256
86 Leaf 221
87 Leaf 85
88 Leaf 6,78
85 O-Pee-Chee 138
86 O-Pee-Chee 225
87 O-Pee-Chee 75
88 O-Pee-Chee 38
89 O-Pee-Chee 105
90 O-Pee-Chee 330
91 O-Pee-Chee 735
92 O-Pee-Chee 259
93 O-Pee-Chee 82
85 opcSticker 105
86 opcSticker 98
87 opcSticker 105
88 opcSticker 98
89 opcSticker 100
86 opcTattoo 10
88 PaniniSticker 335
89 PaniniSticker 130
90 PaniniSticker 295
93 PaniniSticker 22

DARON, BILL
86 O-Pee-Chee 19

DARWIN, BOBBY
73 O-Pee-Chee 228
74 O-Pee-Chee 527
75 O-Pee-Chee 346
76 O-Pee-Chee 63

DARWIN, DANNY
90 FleerCdn. 227
86 Leaf 75
81 O-Pee-Chee 22
85 O-Pee-Chee 227
86 O-Pee-Chee 206
87 O-Pee-Chee 157
90 O-Pee-Chee 64
91 O-Pee-Chee 666
92 O-Pee-Chee 324
82 opcSticker 237
83 opcSticker 121
84 opcSticker 359
85 opcSticker 352
86 opcSticker 206
91 opcPremier 28
91 PaniniSticker 15
91 PaniniTopFifteen 65

DARWIN, JEFF
94 Calgary/ProCards 783

DASCENZO, DOUG
90 O-Pee-Chee 762
91 O-Pee-Chee 437
92 O-Pee-Chee 509
89 PaniniSticker 47
93 PaniniSticker 210

DAUBERT, JACOB E.
23 Neilson's 8
23 WillardsChocolate(V100) 26

DAUBERT, JAKE
21 Neilson's(V61) 99
22 WilliamPaterson(V89) 48

DAUER, RICH
80 O-Pee-Chee 56
81 O-Pee-Chee 314
82 O-Pee-Chee 8
83 O-Pee-Chee 192
84 O-Pee-Chee 374
85 O-Pee-Chee 58
86 O-Pee-Chee 251
82 opcSticker 147
83 opcSticker 27
84 opcSticker 24, 214
85 opcSticker 203

DAUGHERTY, JOCK
90 FleerCdn. 294
90 O-Pee-Chee 52
91 O-Pee-Chee 622
92 O-Pee-Chee 344

DAULTON, DARREN
90 FlerCdn. 555
87 O-Pee-Chee 57
90 O-Pee-Chee 542
91 O-Pee-Chee 89
92 O-Pee-Chee 244
93 O-Pee-Chee 71
94 O-Pee-Chee 123
93 opcPremier 12
91 PaniniSticker 102
92 PaniniSticker 241
93 PaniniSticker 269
94 PaniniSticker 224
93 PostCdn. 10

DAUNIC, WILLY
94 StCatharines/Classic 8
94 StCatharines/ProCards 3650

DAUSS, GEORGE
20 MapleCrispette(V117) 11
21 Neilson's(V61) 18
23 WillardsChocolate(V100) 27

DAVALILLO, VIC
65 O-Pee-Chee 128
67 O-Pee-Chee 69
70 O-Pee-Chee 256
71 O-Pee-Chee 4
73 O-Pee-Chee 163
74 O-Pee-Chee 444

DAVENPORT, JIM
65 O-Pee-Chee 213
66 O-Pee-Chee 176
69 O-Pee-Chee 102
70 O-Pee-Chee 378
62 PostCereal 134
62 ShirriffCoin 169
91 Hamilton/ClassicBest 24
91 Hamilton/ProCards 4051

DAVENPORT, JOE
96 StCatharines/Best 7

DAVEY, TOM
95 StCatharines/TimHortons 1

DAVIDSMEIER, DAN
84 Vancouver/Cramer 29
86 Vancouver/ProCards

DAVIDSMEIER, DAVID
85 Vancouver/Cramer 201

DAVIDSON, MARK
90 O-Pee-Chee 267
91 O-Pee-Chee 678

DAVIDSON, TED
65 O-Pee-Chee 243
66 O-Pee-Chee 89
68 O-Pee-Chee 48

DAVIS, ALVIN
90 FleerCdn. 512
85 GeneralMills
85 Leaf 18
86 Leaf 65
87 Leaf 118
88 Leaf 196
85 O-Pee-Chee 145
86 O-Pee-Chee 309
87 O-Pee-Chee 235
88 O-Pee-Chee 349
89 O-Pee-Chee 57
90 O-Pee-Chee 373
91 O-Pee-Chee 515
92 O-Pee-Chee 130
92 opcPremier 183
85 opcSticker 332, 368
86 opcSticker 218
87 opcSticker 220
88 opcSticker 219
89 opcSticker 227
86 opcTattoo 12
88 PaniniSticker 185
89 PaniniSticker 435
90 PaniniSticker 149
87 StuartBakery 25

DAVIS, BILL
66 O-Pee-Chee 44

DAVIS, BOB
76 O-Pee-Chee 472
80 O-Pee-Chee 185
91 O-Pee-Chee 221

DAVIS, BROCK
71 O-Pee-Chee 576
72 O-Pee-Chee 161
73 O-Pee-Chee 366

DAVIS, BUTCH
87 Vancouver/ProCards 1614

DAVIS, CHILI
90 FleerCdn. 129
87 GeneralMills
85 Leaf 66
86 Leaf 6
87 Leaf 208
83 O-Pee-Chee 115
84 O-Pee-Chee 367
85 O-Pee-Chee 245
87 O-Pee-Chee 162
88 O-Pee-Chee 15
89 O-Pee-Chee 103
90 O-Pee-Chee 765
91 O-Pee-Chee 355
92 O-Pee-Chee 118
93 O-Pee-Chee 52
94 O-Pee-Chee 143
93 opcPremier 24
83 opcSticker 319
84 opcSticker 171
85 opcSticker 162
87 opcSticker 95
89 opcSticker 177
89 PaniniSticker 296
90 PaniniSticker 39
93 PaniniSticker 131
87 StuartBakery 13

DAVIS, DOUG
88 Edmonton/CMC 18
88 Edmonton/ProCards 559
89 Edmonton/CMC 15
89 Edmonton/ProCards 551
90 Edmonton/CMC 18
90 Edmonton/ProCards 519
91 Edmonton/LineDrive 160
91 Edmonton/ProCards 1518

DAVIS, ERIC
91 Ben's/HolsumDisk 2
88 FantasticSam's 14
90 FleerCdn. 417
87 HostessSticker
87 Leaf 22,179
88 Leaf 149
87 O-Pee-Chee 228
88 O-Pee-Chee 150, J
89 O-Pee-Chee 330
90 O-Pee-Chee 260, 402
91 O-Pee-Chee 550
92 O-Pee-Chee 610
93 O-Pee-Chee 87
94 O-Pee-Chee 226
91 opcPremier 29
92 opcPremier 129
87 opcSticker 136
88 opcStick. 141,146,-SStar 14
89 opcSticker 138,-SStar 47
88 PaniniSticker 282
89 PaniniSticker 76
90 PaniniSticker 209,246
91 PaniniSticker 131
92 PaniniSticker 267
93 PaniniSticker 221
94 PaniniSticker 62
91 PetroCanada 6
87 StuartBakery 4

DAVIS, FRANK T.
21 Neilson's(V61) 36
23 WillardsChocolate(V100) 28

DAVIS, GEORGE
36 WWGum(V355) 17

DAVIS, GLENN
90 FleerCdn. 228
86 Leaf 175
87 Leaf 115
88 Leaf 186
86 O-Pee-Chee 389
87 O-Pee-Chee 56
88 O-Pee-Chee 159
89 O-Pee-Chee 378
90 O-Pee-Chee 50
91 O-Pee-Chee 350
92 O-Pee-Chee 190
93 O-Pee-Chee 69
91 opcPremier 30
86 opcSticker 29, 314
87 opcSticker 26
88 opcSticker 35
89 opcSticker 21, -SStar 35
86 opcTattoo 18
88 PaniniSticker 292
89 PaniniSticker 88
90 PaniniSticker 258
91 PaniniSticker 7
91 PostCdn. 14
87 StuartBakery 5

DAVIS, JODY
90 FleerCdn. 579
85 Leaf 180
87 Leaf 48
88 Leaf 69
84 O-Pee-Chee 73
85 O-Pee-Chee 384
86 O-Pee-Chee 176
87 O-Pee-Chee 270
88 O-Pee-Chee 376
89 O-Pee-Chee 115
90 O-Pee-Chee 453
83 opcSticker 226
84 opcSticker 43
85 opcSticker 37
86 opcSticker 58
87 opcSticker 64
88 opcSticker 60, -SStar 23
86 opcTattoo 13
88 PaniniSticker 258,261-62
88 PaniniSticker 389-90
87 StuartBakery 3

DAVIS, JOEL
88 Vancouver/CMC 2
88 Vancouver/ProCards 763

DAVIS, JOHN
89 Vancouver/CMC 9
89 Vancouver/ProCards 582

DAVIS, KANE
94 Welland/Classic 7
94 Welland/ProCards 3486

DAVIS, MARK
90 Ben's/HolsumDisk 6
90 FleerCdn. 155, 631
89 O-Pee-Chee 59
90 O-Pee-Chee 205, 407
91 O-Pee-Chee 116
92 O-Pee-Chee 766
86 opcSticker 91
89 opcSticker 110,-SStar 64
89 PaniniSticker 193
90 PaniniSticker 352
91 Edmonton/LineDrive 161
91 Edmonton/ProCards 1527
89 Vancouver/CMC 22
89 Vancouver/ProCards 585

DAVIS, MIKE
90 FleerCdn. 391
86 Leaf 14
86 O-Pee-Chee 165
88 O-Pee-Chee 217
89 O-Pee-Chee 277
90 O-Pee-Chee 697
84 opcSticker 338
86 opcSticker 166
87 opcSticker 168
88 opcSticker 171
86 opcTattoo 4
88 PaniniSticker 174
89 PaniniSticker 24

DAVIS, RON
68 O-Pee-Chee 21
80 O-Pee-Chee 101
81 O-Pee-Chee 16
82 O-Pee-Chee 283
83 O-Pee-Chee 380
84 O-Pee-Chee 101
85 O-Pee-Chee 78
86 O-Pee-Chee 265
87 O-Pee-Chee 383
83 opcSticker 94
84 opcSticker 309
85 opcSticker 297
86 opcSticker 281
86 opcTattoo 18

DAVIS, SPUD
36 WWGum(V355) 12

DAVIS, STAN
82 Vancouver/TCMA 9

DAVIS, STEVE
90 O-Pee-Chee 428
86 TOR/AultFoods
86 TOR/FireSafety

DAVIS, STORM
90 FleerCdn. 5
85 Leaf 81
86 Leaf 99
84 O-Pee-Chee 140
85 O-Pee-Chee 73
86 O-Pee-Chee 179
87 O-Pee-Chee 349
90 O-Pee-Chee 606
91 O-Pee-Chee 22
92 O-Pee-Chee 556
83 opcSticker 310
86 opcSticker 231
87 opcSticker 230
89 PaniniSticker 413

DAVIS, TOMMY
66 O-Pee-Chee 75
69 O-Pee-Chee 135
71 O-Pee-Chee 151
72 O-Pee-Chee 41,42
74 O-Pee-Chee 396
75 O-Pee-Chee 564
76 O-Pee-Chee 149
62 PostCereak 105
62 ShirriffCoin 154

DAVIS, WILLIE
67 O-Pee-Chee 160
69 O-Pee-Chee 65
70 O-Pee-Chee 390
71 O-Pee-Chee 585
72 O-Pee-Chee 390
73 O-Pee-Chee 35
74 O-Pee-Chee 165
75 O-Pee-Chee 10
76 O-Pee-Chee 265
62 PostCereal 106
62 ShirriffCoin 161

DAVISON, MIKE
71 O-Pee-Chee 276

DAWLEY, BILL
84 O-Pee-Chee 248
85 O-Pee-Chee 363

DAWSON, ANDRE (ANDRÉ)
77 Dimanche/DernièreHeure
80 Dimanche/DernièreHeure
88 FantasticSam's
82 FBI BoxBottoms
90 FleerCdn. 29
85 GeneralMills
86 GeneralMills
85 Leaf 133
86 Leaf 25
87 Leaf 212
88 Leaf 9,126
78 O-Pee-Chee 180
79 O-Pee-Chee 179
80 O-Pee-Chee 124
81 O-Pee-Chee 125, -Poster 6
82 OPC 341, 379, -Poster 18
83 O-Pee-Chee 173, 303
84 O-Pee-Chee 200, 392
85 O-Pee-Chee 133, -Poster 9
86 O-Pee-Chee 256
87 O-Pee-Chee 345, 773
88 O-Pee-Chee 247
89 O-Pee-Chee 10
90 O-Pee-Chee 140, C
91 O-Pee-Chee 640, D
92 O-Pee-Chee 460
93 O-Pee-Chee 35
94 O-Pee-Chee 138
91 opcPremier 31
92 opcPremier 45
93 opcPremier 18
82 opcSticker 57,125
83 opcSticker 164, 252
84 opcSticker 92, 181
85 opcSticker 86
86 opcSticker 74
88 opcSticker 56,148-SStar 13
89 opcSticker 5,54,156,-Star 48
86 opcTattoo 20
88 PaniniSticker 236,265
89 PaniniSticker 59,230
90 PaniniSticker 240
91 PaniniSticker 49
92 PaniniSticker 186,285
93 PaniniSticker 97
94 PaniniSticker 28
91 PostCereal 7
87 StuartBakery 3
77 MTL
77 MTL/RedpathSugar
82 MTL/Hygrade
82 MTL/Zellers (x3)
83 MTL
83 MTL/StuartBakery
84 MTL
84 MTL/StuartBakery (x2)
86 MTL/ProvigoFoods, -Poster
93 MTL/McDonald's 2

DAY, BOOTS
72 Dimanche/DernièreHeure
71 O-Pee-Chee 42
72 O-Pee-Chee 254
73 O-Pee-Chee 307
74 O-Pee-Chee 589
71 ProStarPostcard
71 MTL/ProStar
74 MTL/GeorgeWeston

DAYETT, BRIAN
88 O-Pee-Chee 136

DAYLEY, KEN
90 FleerCdn. 247
86 O-Pee-Chee 202
89 O-Pee-Chee 396
90 O-Pee-Chee 561
91 O-Pee-Chee 41
92 O-Pee-Chee 717
91 opcPremier 32
91 TOR/FireSafety
91 TOR/Score 27
92 TOR/FireSafety
93 TOR/Donruss 30

DEAK, BRIAN
93 Calgary/ProCards 1168

DEAL, CHARLES A.
23 WillardsChocolate(V100) 29

DEAN, JAY (DIZZY)
92 HomersClassic 8
34 WWGum(V354) 55
39 WWGum(V351A)

DEAN, TOMMY
70 O-Pee-Chee 234
71 O-Pee-Chee 364

DEBERRY, HANK
21 Neilson's(V61) 101

DEBRAND, RAFAEL
93 StCatharines/ClassicBest 7
93 StCatharines/ProCards 3985

DEBUTCH, MIKE
92 London/ProCards 639
92 London/SkyBox 405

DECILLIS, DEAN
89 London/ProCards 1372
91 London/LineDrive 380
91 London/ProCards 1883

DECINCES, DOUG
85 Leaf 2
75 O-Pee-Chee 617
76 O-Pee-Chee 438
77 O-Pee-Chee 228
78 O-Pee-Chee 192
79 O-Pee-Chee 217
80 O-Pee-Chee 322
81 O-Pee-Chee 188
82 O-Pee-Chee 174
83 O-Pee-Chee 341
84 O-Pee-Chee 82
85 O-Pee-Chee 111
86 O-Pee-Chee 257
87 O-Pee-Chee 22
88 O-Pee-Chee 141
82 opcSticker 142
83 opcSticker 46, 155, 171
84 opcSticker 229
85 opcSticker 222
86 opcSticker 178
87 opcSticker 182
86 opcTattoo 12
87 StuartBakery 16

DECKER, JOE
71 O-Pee-Chee 98
73 O-Pee-Chee 311
74 O-Pee-Chee 469
75 O-Pee-Chee 102
76 O-Pee-Chee 636

DECKER, STEVE
91 O-Pee-Chee 33
92 O-Pee-Chee 593
91 opcPremier 33
92 PaniniSticker 211
91 ScoreAllStarFanfest 2

DEER, ROB
90 FleerCdn. 320
87 O-Pee-Chee 188
88 O-Pee-Chee 33
89 O-Pee-Chee 364
90 O-Pee-Chee 615
91 O-Pee-Chee 192

92 O-Pee-Chee 441
87 opcSticker 194
88 opcSticker 198
89 opcSticker 202
88 PaniniSticker 128
89 PaniniSticker 376
90 PaniniSticker 102
91 PaniniSticker 209
92 PaniniSticker 109
93 PaniniSticker 119

DEFILIPPIS, ART
76 O-Pee-Chee 595

DEGRASSE, TIM
91 Hamilton/ClassicBest 2
91 Hamilton/ProCards 4032
92 Hamilton/ClassicBest 15

DE JARDIN, BOBBY
92 O-Pee-Chee 179

DEJESUS, IVAN
78 O-Pee-Chee 158
79 O-Pee-Chee 209
80 O-Pee-Chee 349
81 O-Pee-Chee 54
82 O-Pee-Chee 313
83 O-Pee-Chee 233
84 O-Pee-Chee 279
82 opcSticker 32
83 opcSticker 271
84 opcSticker 121

DEJESUS, JOSE
90 FleerCdn. 104
90 O-Pee-Chee 596
91 O-Pee-Chee 232
92 O-Pee-Chee 471

DEJOHN, MARK
92 London/ProCards 648
92 London/SkyBox 424

DE JONGHE, EMILE
39 WWGum(V351A)

DELACRUZ, NARCISCO
95 StCatharines/TimHortons 10

DE LA HOZ, MIKE
65 O-Pee-Chee 182

DELANCEY, BILL
36 WWGum(V355) 15

DELAO, MIKE
89 London/ProCards 1367

DELAHANTY, JOSEPH
1912 ImperialTobacco(C46) 67

DE LA TORRE, CARLOS
94 GarciaPhoto 26

DELBIANCO, RONNIE
52 Laval Dairy 29

DELEON, ELCILIO
94 Welland/Classic 8
94 Welland/ProCards 3487

DELEON, JOSE
90 FleerCdn. 248
85 O-Pee-Chee 385
86 O-Pee-Chee 75
88 O-Pee-Chee 23
89 O-Pee-Chee 107
90 O-Pee-Chee 257
91 O-Pee-Chee 711
92 O-Pee-Chee 85
86 opcTattoo 3
89 PaniniSticker 177
90 PaniniSticker 334
92 PaniniSticker 178

DELEON, LUIS
83 O-Pee-Chee 323
89 Calgary/CMC 1

DELGADO, CARLOS
94 O-Pee-Chee 100, -Hot 5
94 TOR
95 TOR/OhHenry
96 TOR/Oh Henry
97 TOR/Sizzler 10
89 StCatharines/ProCards 2077
90 StCatharines/ProCards 3454

DELGADO, JOSE RAUL
94 GarciaPhoto 68

DEL GRECO, BOBBY
62 ShirriffCoin 16

DELLER, TOM
89 Welland/Pucko 10

DE LOS SANTOS, LUIS
90 FleerCdn. 105
90 O-Pee-Chee 452
89 PaniniSticker 347

DELUCIA, RICH
92 O-Pee-Chee 686
92 opcPremier 171

DEMARS, BILLY
82 Dimanche/DernièreHeure
73 O-Pee-Chee 486
74 O-Pee-Chee 119
52 Parkhusrt 8
82 MTL/Zellers
83 MTL
83 MTL/StuartBakery 11
84 MTL
84 MTL/StuartBakery 3

DEMERIT, JOHN
62 ShirriffCoin 192

DEMERY, LARRY
75 O-Pee-Chee 433
76 O-Pee-Chee 563

DEMETER, DON
66 O-Pee-Chee 98
62 PostCereal 195
62 ShirriffCoin 170

DEMETER, STEVE
61 Toronto/BeeHive

DEMMITT, RAY
1912 ImperialTobacco(C46) 11

DEMOLA, DON
75 O-Pee-Chee 391
76 O-Pee-Chee 571

DEMPSEY, RICK
90 FleerCdn. 392
74 O-Pee-Chee 569
75 O-Pee-Chee 451
76 O-Pee-Chee 272
79 O-Pee-Chee 312
80 O-Pee-Chee 51
81 O-Pee-Chee 132
82 O-Pee-Chee 262
83 O-Pee-Chee 138
84 O-Pee-Chee 272
85 O-Pee-Chee 94
86 O-Pee-Chee 358
87 O-Pee-Chee 28
90 O-Pee-Chee 736
91 O-Pee-Chee 427
83 opcSticker 30
84 opcSticker 23, 213
85 opcSticker 199
86 opcSticker 232
87 opcSticker 225
86 opcTattoo 5

DENNIS, DON
66 O-Pee-Chee 142

DENNIS, EDDIE
88 StCatharines/ProCards 2014

DENNY, JOHN
85 Leaf 228
75 O-Pee-Chee 621
76 O-Pee-Chee 339
77 O-Pee-Chee 7, 109
80 O-Pee-Chee 242
85 O-Pee-Chee 325
86 O-Pee-Chee 268
87 O-Pee-Chee 139
84 opcSticker 19, 122, 177
85 opcSticker 119

DENSON, DREW
92 Vancouver/ProCards 2729
92 Vancouver/SkyBox 637

DENT, BUCKY
74 O-Pee-Chee 582
75 O-Pee-Chee 299
76 O-Pee-Chee 154
77 O-Pee-Chee 122
78 O-Pee-Chee 164
79 O-Pee-Chee 254
80 O-Pee-Chee 33
81 O-Pee-Chee 164
82 O-Pee-Chee 240, 241, 298
83 O-Pee-Chee 279
84 O-Pee-Chee 331
90 O-Pee-Chee 519
83 opcSticker 122
84 opcSticker 362

DE OCA, ELCIER MONTES
94 GarciaPhoto 92

DERNIER, BOB
85 Leaf 57
86 Leaf 139
83 O-Pee-Chee 43
83 O-Pee-Chee 43
84 O-Pee-Chee 358
85 O-Pee-Chee 334
86 O-Pee-Chee 188
87 O-Pee-Chee 138
88 O-Pee-Chee 183
90 O-Pee-Chee 204
83 opcSticker 320
85 opcSticker 38
86 opcSticker 63
89 PaniniSticker 155

DERRINGER, PAUL
36 WWGum(V355) 66
39 WWGum(V351A)

DESERT, HARRY C.
52 Parkhurst 92

DESHAIES, JIM
90 FleerCdn. 229
87 Leaf 255
88 Leaf 96
88 O-Pee-Chee 24
89 O-Pee-Chee 341
90 O-Pee-Chee 225
91 O-Pee-Chee 782
92 O-Pee-Chee 415
87 opcSticker 1
88 opcSticker 27
88 PaniniSticker 287
90 PaniniSticker 267

DESHIELDS, DELINO
90 FleerCdn. 653
93 HitTheBooks
93 HumptyDumpty 35
88 O-Pee-Chee 88
90 O-Pee-Chee 224
91 O-Pee-Chee 432
92 O-Pee-Chee 515
93 O-Pee-Chee 183
94 O-Pee-Chee 59
92 opcPremier 163
93 opcPremier 7

91 PaniniSticker 140
92 PaniniSticker 203
93 PaniniSticker 226
94 PaniniSticker 209
91 PostCdn. 1
92 MTL/Durivage 6
93 MTL/McDonald's 3

DESILVA, JOHN
91 London/LineDrive 381
91 London/ProCards 1869

DESSAU, RUBE
1912 ImperialTobacco(C46) 61

DESTRADE, ORESTES
94 O-Pee-Chee 23
93 opcPremier 32
94 PaniniSticker 182

DETTORE, TOM
75 O-Pee-Chee 469
76 O-Pee-Chee 126

DEVANON, JERRY
71 O-Pee-Chee 32

DEVEREAUX, MIKE
90 FleerCdn. 175
90 O-Pee-Chee 127
91 O-Pee-Chee 758
92 O-Pee-Chee 492
93 O-Pee-Chee 93
94 O-Pee-Chee 203
90 PaniniSticker 12
91 PaniniSticker 245
92 PaniniSticker 70
93 PaniniSticker 75
94 PaniniSticker 19

DEVINE, ADRIAN
74 O-Pee-Chee 614

DEVORMER, LOU
23 Neilson's 9

DIAZ, ALBERTO
94 GarciaPhoto 11

DIAZ, ALFREDO
96 Vancouver/Best 8

DIAZ, ARMANDO
52 LavalDairy 76

DIAZ, BO
86 Leaf 191, 258
82 O-Pee-Chee 258
83 O-Pee-Chee 175
84 O-Pee-Chee 131
85 O-Pee-Chee 219
86 O-Pee-Chee 253
87 O-Pee-Chee 4
88 O-Pee-Chee 265
89 O-Pee-Chee 201
82 opcSticker 176
83 opcSticker 273
84 opcSticker 120
87 opcSticker 142
88 opcSticker 143
89 opcSticker 135
88 PaniniSticker 273
89 PaniniSticker 71

DIAZ, EDGAR
91 O-Pee-Chee 164
86 Vancouver/ProCards

DIAZ, ENRIQUE
94 GarciaPhoto 42

DIAZ, JORGE
94 GarciaPhoto 72

DIAZ, MARIO
90 O-Pee-Chee 781
89 PaniniSticker 427
86 Calgary/ProCards

87 Calgary/ProCards 2319
88 Calgary/ProCards 804
90 Calgary/ProCards 655
92 Calgary/SkyBox 58

DIAZ, MIKE
88 O-Pee-Chee 239
88 PaniniSticker 341, 342, 378

DIAZ, RALPH
94 Ottawa/ProCards 2895

DIBBLE, ROB
90 FleerCdn. 418
90 O-Pee-Chee 46
91 O-Pee-Chee 662
92 O-Pee-Chee 757
93 O-Pee-Chee 122
94 O-Pee-Chee 224
92 opcPremier 53
90 PaniniSticker 249
93 PaniniSticker 297

DICKEY, BILL
37 O-Pee-Chee(V300) 119
33 WWGum(V353) 19
36 WWGum(V355) 34
39 WWGum(V351B)

DICKSON, JASON
96 Vancouver/Best 9

DICKSON, LANCE
91 O-Pee-Chee 114
91 opcPremier 35

DIDIER, BOB
70 O-Pee-Chee 232
71 O-Pee-Chee 432
73 O-Pee-Chee 574
74 O-Pee-Chee 482
80 Vancouver/TCMA 11

DIERKER, LARRY
70 O-Pee-Chee 15
71 O-Pee-Chee 540
72 O-Pee-Chee 155
73 O-Pee-Chee 375
74 O-Pee-Chee 660
75 O-Pee-Chee 49
76 O-Pee-Chee 75

DIETZ, DICK
68 O-Pee-Chee 104
70 O-Pee-Chee 135
71 O-Pee-Chee 545
72 O-Pee-Chee 295, 296
73 O-Pee-Chee 44

DIFELICE, MIKE
91 Hamilton/ClassicBest 15
91 Hamilton/ProCards 4041
92 Hamilton/ClassicBest 23

DIGRACE, JACK
52 LavalDairy 87

DILAURO, JACK
70 O-Pee-Chee 382
71 O-Pee-Chee 677

DILLARD, STEVE
82 Edmonton/TCMA 4

DILLMAN, BILL
69 O-Pee-Chee 141
70 O-Pee-Chee 386

DILONE, MIGUEL
85 Leaf 135
79 O-Pee-Chee 256
81 O-Pee-Chee 141
82 O-Pee-Chee 77
85 O-Pee-Chee 178
84 MTL
84 MTL/StuartBakery 2

DUENAS, PEDRO LUIS
94 GarciaPhoto 3

DUEÑAS, YOBAL
94 GarciaPhoto 6

DUES, HAL
79 O-Pee-Chee 373
81 O-Pee-Chee 71

DUFFALO, JIM
65 O-Pee-Chee 159

DUFFY, FRANK
71 O-Pee-Chee 164
73 O-Pee-Chee 376
74 O-Pee-Chee 81
75 O-Pee-Chee 448
76 O-Pee-Chee 232
77 O-Pee-Chee 253
79 O-Pee-Chee 47

DUFFY, HUGH
23 WillardsChocolate(V100) 32

DUGAN, JAMES A.
23 WillardsChocolate(V100) 33

DUKE, MARVIN
36 WWGum(V355) 116

DUKES, JAN
70 O-Pee-Chee 154

DUKES, TOM
68 O-Pee-Chee 128
71 O-Pee-Chee 106

DULIBA, BOB
66 O-Pee-Chee 53

DUNBAR, TOMMY
87 Vancouver/ProCards 1603

DUNCAN, DAVE
69 O-Pee-Chee 68
71 O-Pee-Chee 178
72 O-Pee-Chee 17
73 O-Pee-Chee 337
74 O-Pee-Chee 284
75 O-Pee-Chee 238
76 O-Pee-Chee 49

DUNCAN, LOUIS (PAT)
21 Neilson's(V61) 109

DUNCAN, LOUIS B.
23 WillardsChocolate(V100) 34

DUNCAN, MARIANO
86 Leaf 50
86 O-Pee-Chee 296
87 O-Pee-Chee 199
88 O-Pee-Chee 181
90 O-Pee-Chee 234
91 O-Pee-Chee 13
92 O-Pee-Chee 589
93 O-Pee-Chee 95
87 opcSticker 74
88 PaniniSticker 309,310
91 PaniniSticker 128
93 PaniniSticker 272
94 PaniniSticker 225

DUNEGAN, JIM
71 O-Pee-Chee 121

DUNLAP, JOE
89 Calgary/CMC 18
89 Calgary/ProCards 529

DUNLAP, PAUL
36 WWGum(V355) 125

DUNLOP, HARRY
73 O-Pee-Chee 593

DUNN, JACK
1912 ImperialTobacco(C46) 19

DUNNE, MIKE
88 Leaf 235
88 O-Pee-Chee 224
89 O-Pee-Chee 165
90 O-Pee-Chee 522
91 O-Pee-Chee 238
88 opcSticker 132, 307
89 opcSticker 130
88 PaniniSticker 367
89 PaniniSticker 162
87 Vancouver/ProCards 1612
92 Vancouver/ProCards 2715
92 Vancouver/SkyBox 634

DUNNING, STEVE
71 O-Pee-Chee 294
73 O-Pee-Chee 53

DUNSTON, SHAWON
90 FleerCdn. 30
86 Leaf 181
87 Leaf 128
88 Leaf 70
87 O-Pee-Chee 346
88 O-Pee-Chee 277
89 O-Pee-Chee 140
90 O-Pee-Chee 415
91 O-Pee-Chee 765
92 O-Pee-Chee 370
93 O-Pee-Chee 62
87 opcSticker 59
91 opcPremier 37
92 opcPremier 125
88 opcSticker 65, -SuperStar 11
89 opcSticker 49, -SStar 43
86 opcTattoo 2
88 PaniniSticker 264
89 PaniniSticker 58
90 PaniniSticker 236
91 PaniniSticker 46
92 PaniniSticker 185
93 PaniniSticker 205
94 PaniniSticker 152

DUQUETTE, BRIAN
85 Vancouver/Cramer 212
86 Vancouver/ProCards

DUREN, RYNE
60 opcTattoo 13
62 PostCereal 81
62 ShirriffCoin 46

DURHAM, DON
73 O-Pee-Chee 548

DURHAM, LEON
85 Leaf 238
86 Leaf 190
87 Leaf 125
81 O-Pee-Chee 321
82 O-Pee-Chee 206
83 O-Pee-Chee 125
84 O-Pee-Chee 209
85 O-Pee-Chee 330
86 O-Pee-Chee 58
87 O-Pee-Chee 290
88 O-Pee-Chee 65
82 opcSticker 25
83 opcSticker 219
84 opcSticker 40
85 opcSticker 36
86 opcSticker 60
87 opcSticker 57
88 opcSticker 63
86 opcTattoo 4
88 PaniniSticker 259
87 StuartBakery 3
97 Vancouver/Best 2

DUROCHER, LEO (SPEEDY)
69 O-Pee-Chee 147
70 O-Pee-Chee 291
71 O-Pee-Chee 609
73 O-Pee-Chee 624
33 WWGum(V353) 74
34 WWGum(V354) 69
36 WWGum(V355) 25

DURRETT, RED
43-47 MontréalParadeSportive

DUVALL, BRAD
88 Hamilton/ProCards 1722

DWORAK, JOHN
52 LavalDairy 61

DWYER, JIM
75 O-Pee-Chee 429
76 O-Pee-Chee 94
81 O-Pee-Chee 184
86 O-Pee-Chee 339

DYBZINSKI, JERRY
81 O-Pee-Chee 198
86 Calgary/ProCards

DYER, DUFFY
71 O-Pee-Chee 136
72 O-Pee-Chee 127
73 O-Pee-Chee 493
74 O-Pee-Chee 536
75 O-Pee-Chee 538
76 O-Pee-Chee 88
80 O-Pee-Chee 232

DYER, MIKE
90 FleerCdn. 372
90 O-Pee-Chee 576

DYGERT, JAMES
1912 ImperialTobacco(C46) 45

DYKES, JAMES
23 Neilson's 10
23 WillardsChocolate(V100) 35
33 WWGum(V353) 6
36 WWGum(V355) 1

DYKSTRA, LENNY
90 FleerCdn. 556
93 HumptyDumpty 44
87 Leaf 88
88 Leaf 135
92 McDonald's 8
86 O-Pee-Chee 53
87 O-Pee-Chee 295
88 O-Pee-Chee 299
89 O-Pee-Chee 349
90 O-Pee-Chee 515
91 O-Pee-Chee 345
92 O-Pee-Chee 200
93 O-Pee-Chee 119
94 O-Pee-Chee 168
92 opcPremier 184
87 opcSticker 13, 21, 98
89 opcSticker 90
88 PaniniSticker 345
89 PaniniSticker 138
90 PaniniSticker 313
91 PaniniSticker 108,163
92 PaniniSticker 247
93 PaniniSticker 274
94 PaniniSticker 226
91 PaniniTopFifteen 4,26
91 PostCdn. 6
94 PostCdn. 16

E

EAMON, BOB
89 London/ProCards 1359

EARNSHAW, GEORGE
34 WWGum(V354) 93

EASLER, MIKE
85 Leaf 206
87 Leaf 192
81 O-Pee-Chee 92
82 O-Pee-Chee 235
83 O-Pee-Chee 385
84 O-Pee-Chee 353
85 O-Pee-Chee 349
87 O-Pee-Chee 135
88 O-Pee-Chee 9
82 opcSticker 84
84 opcSticker 137
85 opcSticker 213
86 opcSticker 255
87 opcSticker 295
86 opcTattoo 21

EASLEY, DAMION
93 O-Pee-Chee 104
94 O-Pee-Chee 9
93 PaniniSticker 7
94 PaniniSticker 37
92 Edmonton/ProCards 3544
92 Edmonton/SkyBox 154

EASTER, LUKE
53 Exhibits 2

EASTERLY, JAMIE
75 O-Pee-Chee 618
76 O-Pee-Chee 511
84 opcSticker 258

EASTWICK, RAWLY
75 O-Pee-Chee 621
76 O-Pee-Chee 469
77 O-Pee-Chee 8, 140

ECKERSLEY, DENNIS
93 Ben'sDisk 1
90 FleerCdn. 6
86 Leaf 113
76 O-Pee-Chee 98, 202
77 O-Pee-Chee 15
78 O-Pee-Chee 138
79 O-Pee-Chee 16
80 O-Pee-Chee 169
81 O-Pee-Chee 109
82 O-Pee-Chee 287
83 O-Pee-Chee 270
84 O-Pee-Chee 218
85 O-Pee-Chee 163
86 O-Pee-Chee 199
87 O-Pee-Chee 381
88 O-Pee-Chee 72
89 O-Pee-Chee 370
90 O-Pee-Chee 670
91 O-Pee-Chee 250
92 O-Pee-Chee 738
93 O-Pee-Chee 106
94 O-Pee-Chee 144
83 opcSticker 34
84 opcSticker 224
86 opcSticker 62
87 opcSticker 63
88 opcSticker 170,-SStar 31
89 opcSticker 167,-SStar 31
86 opcTattoo 2
89 PaniniSticker 12,414
90 PaniniSticker 137
91 PaniniSticker 200
92 PaniniSticker 22
93 PaniniSticker 13,157,161-62
94 PaniniSticker 108
92 PizzaHut/DietPepsi 7

EDDY, DON
72 O-Pee-Chee 413

EDENFIELD, KEN
94 Vancouver/ProCards 1857

EDENS, TOM
91 O-Pee-Chee 118

EDGE, BUTCH
80 O-Pee-Chee 329

EDGE, TIM
90 Welland/Pucko 16
97 Calgary/Best 11

EDMONDS, JIM
93 Vancouver/ProCards 2609

EDMONDSON, PAUL
70 O-Pee-Chee 414

EDSELL, GEOFF
96 Vancouver/Best 10
97 Vancouver/Best 12

EDUARDO, HECTOR
81 Edmonton/RedRooster 13

EDWARDS, DOC
65 O-Pee-Chee 239

EDWARDS, JOHNNY
69 O-Pee-Chee 186
70 O-Pee-Chee 339
71 O-Pee-Chee 44
72 O-Pee-Chee 416
73 O-Pee-Chee 519
64 O-Pee-Chee 635
62 ShirriffCoin 191

EDWARDS, MARSHALL
79 Vancouver/TCMA 4
80 Vancouver/TCMA 19
84 Vancouver/Cramer 47

EDWARDS, MIKE
80 O-Pee-Chee 158

EDWARDS, WAYNE
90 FleerCdn. 652
91 O-Pee-Chee 751
92 O-Pee-Chee 404

EENHORN, ROBERT
97 Vancouver/Best 13

EGAN, TOM
67 O-Pee-Chee 147
70 O-Pee-Chee 4
71 O-Pee-Chee 537
72 O-Pee-Chee 207
73 O-Pee-Chee 648
75 O-Pee-Chee 88

EHMKE, HOWARD J.
23 WillardsChocolate(V100) 36

EICHELBERGER, JUAN
83 O-Pee-Chee 168
82 opcSticker 97

EICHHORN, MARK
90 FleerCdn. 580
88 HostessDisk
87 Leaf 173,229
88 Leaf 74
87 O-Pee-Chee 371
88 O-Pee-Chee 116
89 O-Pee-Chee 274
90 O-Pee-Chee 513
91 O-Pee-Chee 129
92 O-Pee-Chee 435
87 opcSticker 187
88 PaniniSticker 212
86 TOR/FireSafety
87 TOR/FireSafety
88 TOR
88 TOR/FireSafety
93 TOR/Dempster's 15
93 TOR/Donruss 16
93 TOR/FireSafety

EILAND, DAVE
91 O-Pee-Chee 611
92 O-Pee-Chee 406

EISCHEN, JOEY
94 Ottawa/ProCards 2896

EISENREICH, JIM
90 FleerCdn. 106
88 O-Pee-Chee 348
90 O-Pee-Chee 246
91 O-Pee-Chee 707
92 O-Pee-Chee 469
90 PaniniSticker 80
91 PaniniSticker 280
93 PaniniSticker 104
94 PaniniSticker 227

ELDRED, CAL
93 HumptyDumpty 10
92 O-Pee-Chee 433
93 O-Pee-Chee 85
94 O-Pee-Chee 179
93 opcPremier 4

ELDRIDGE, RODNEY
90 Hamilton/Best 20
90 Hamilton/Star 10

ELLERBE, FRANK
21 Neilson's(V61) 51
23 WillardsChocolate(V100) 37

ELLINGSEN, BRUCE
75 O-Pee-Chee 288

ELLIOT, LARRY
67 O-Pee-Chee 23

ELLIOTT, BOB
53 Exhibits 26

ELLIOTT, JAMES
34 WWGum(V354) 6

ELLIS, DOCK
71 O-Pee-Chee 2
72 O-Pee-Chee 179, 180
73 O-Pee-Chee 575
74 O-Pee-Chee 145
75 O-Pee-Chee 385
76 O-Pee-Chee 528
77 O-Pee-Chee 146
80 O-Pee-Chee 64

ELLIS, JOHN
70 O-Pee-Chee 516
71 O-Pee-Chee 263
72 O-Pee-Chee 47, 48
73 O-Pee-Chee 656
74 O-Pee-Chee 128
75 O-Pee-Chee 605
76 O-Pee-Chee 383

ELLIS, PAUL
90 Hamilton/Best 13
90 Hamilton/Star 11

ELLIS, ROBERT
96 Vancouver/Best 11
97 Vancouver/Best 14

ELLIS, SAMMY
67 O-Pee-Chee 176
69 O-Pee-Chee 32

ELLSWORTH, BEN
91 Hamilton/ClassicBest 25
91 Hamilton/ProCards 4050

ELLSWORTH, DICK
65 O-Pee-Chee 165
70 O-Pee-Chee 59
71 O-Pee-Chee 309

ELSTER, KEVIN
90 FleerCdn. 202
88 Leaf 37
90 O-Pee-Chee 734
91 O-Pee-Chee 134
92 O-Pee-Chee 251
89 PaniniSticker 127
90 PaniniSticker 296
91 PaniniSticker 82
92 PaniniSticker 225

ELSTON, CURT
1912 ImperialTobacco(C46) 23

ELSTON, DON
62 PostCereal 190
62 ShirriffCoin 101

EMERY, CAL
89 Vancouver/CMC 21
89 Vancouver/ProCards 572

ENCAMACION, ANGELO
91 Welland/Best 10
91 Welland/ProCards 3574

ENGLE, DAVE
85 Leaf 173
85 O-Pee-Chee 199
88 O-Pee-Chee 196
84 opcSticker 313
85 opcSticker 298

ENGLISH, WOODY (ELWOOD)
34 WWGum(V354) 11,50

ENNIS, DEL
53 Exhibits 60

EPPARD, JIM
87 Edmonton/ProCards 2061
88 Edmonton/CMC 21
88 Edmonton/ProCards 558
89 Edmonton/CMC 14
89 Edmonton/ProCards 548

EPSTEIN, MIKE
70 O-Pee-Cee 235, -Booklet 12
71 O-Pee-Chee 655
73 O-Pee-Chee 38
74 O-Pee-Chee 650

ERB, MIKE
90 Edmonton/CMC 6
90 Edmonton/ProCards 513
91 Edmonton/LineDrive 154
91 Edmonton/ProCards 1511

ERICKSON, ERIC G.
23 WillardsChocolate(V100) 38

ERICKSON, ROGER
79 O-Pee-Chee 34
81 O-Pee-Chee 80
82 opcSticker 211

ERICKSON, SCOTT
91 O-Pee-Chee 234
92 O-Pee-Chee 605
93 O-Pee-Chee 77
93 PaniniSticer 123

ERSTAD, DARIN
96 Vancouver/Best 12

ESASKY, NICK
90 FleerCdn. 273
86 Leaf 162
88 Leaf 240
84 O-Pee-Chee 192
85 O-Pee-Chee 253
86 O-Pee-Chee 201
87 O-Pee-Chee 13
88 O-Pee-Chee364
89 O-Pee-Chee 262
90 O-Pee-Chee 206
91 O-Pee-Chee 418
92 O-Pee-Chee 405
84 opcSticker 378
85 opcSticker 51
88 opcSticker 137
89 opcSticker 134
88 PaniniSticker 274
89 PaniniSticker 72
90 PaniniSticker 26

ESPINOSA, NINO
79 O-Pee-Chee 292
80 O-Pee-Chee 233

ESPINOSA, RAMON
92 Welland/ClassicBest 7

ESPINOZA, ALVARO
90 FleerCdn. 441
90 O-Pee-Chee 791
91 O-Pee-Chee 28
92 O-Pee-Chee 243
90 PaniniSticker 121
91 PaniniSticker 327
92 PaniniSticker 138

ESPY, CECIL
90 FleerCdn. 295
90 O-Pee-Chee 496
89 opcSticker 240, 320
89 PaniniSticker 443

ESSEGIAN, CHUCK
62 PostCereal 45

ESSIAN, JIM
79 O-Pee-Chee 239
80 O-Pee-Chee 179
83 opcSticker 117

ESTELLE, DICK
65 O-Pee-Chee 282

ESTES, SHAWN
92 O-Pee-Chee 624

ESTRADA, CHUCK
73 O-Pee-Chee 549
62 PostCereal 36
62 ShirriffCoin 212

ESTRADA, JOSE ANTONIO
94 GarciaPhoto 13

ETCHEBARREN, ANDY
66 O-Pee-Chee 27
70 O-Pee-Chee 213
71 O-Pee-Chee 501
72 O-Pee-Chee 26
73 O-Pee-Chee 618
74 O-Pee-Chee 488
75 O-Pee-Chee 583
76 O-Pee-Chee 129

ETHERIDGE, BOB
68 O-Pee-Chee 126
70 O-Pee-Chee 107

EVANS, BARRY
81 O-Pee-Chee 72

EVANS, DARRELL
90 FleerCdn. 581
85 Leaf 215
88 Leaf 173
72 O-Pee-Chee 171, 172
73 O-Pee-Chee 374
74 O-Pee-Chee 140
75 O-Pee-Chee 475
76 O-Pee-Chee 81
79 O-Pee-Chee 215
80 O-Pee-Chee 81
81 O-Pee-Chee 69
82 O-Pee-Chee 17
83 O-Pee-Chee 329
84 O-Pee-Chee 325
85 O-Pee-Chee 319
86 O-Pee-Chee 103
87 O-Pee-Chee 265
88 O-Pee-Chee 390, E
89 O-Pee-Chee C
90 O-Pee-Chee 55, D
82 opcSticker 112
83 opcSticker 305
84 opcSticker 163
86 opcSticker 165, 269
87 opcSticker 264
88 opcSticker 8, 265
86 opcTattoo 4
88 PaniniSticker 89,90,91,441

EVANS, DWIGHT
90 FleerCdn. 274
85 Leaf 150
86 Leaf 127
87 Leaf 57
88 Leaf 16,171
73 O-Pee-Chee 614
74 O-Pee-Chee 351
75 O-Pee-Chee 255
76 O-Pee-Chee 575
77 O-Pee-Chee 259
79 O-Pee-Chee 73
80 O-Pee-Chee 210
81 O-Pee-Chee 275
82 O-Pee-Chee 355
83 O-Pee-Chee 135
84 O-Pee-Chee 244
85 O-Pee-Chee 271
86 O-Pee-Chee 60
87 O-Pee-Chee 368
88 O-Pee-Chee 221
89 O-Pee-Chee 205
90 O-Pee-Chee 375
91 O-Pee-Chee 155, E
92 O-Pee-Chee 705
91 opcPremier 39
82 opcSticker 4, 135, 153
83 opcSticker 38
84 opcSticker 219
85 opcSticker 212
86 opcSticker 251
87 opcSticker 4, 20, 251
88 opcSticker 245,-SStar 50
89 opcSticker 252,-SStar 15
86 opcTattoo 13
88 PaniniSticker 25
89 PaniniSticker 279
90 PaniniSticker 17
92 PaniniSticker 69

EVANS, MIKE
88 Hamilton/ProCards 1734
89 Hamilton/Star 29

EVASCHUK, BRAD
88 StCatharines/ProCards 2010

EVERETT, CARL
91 O-Pee-Chee 113
94 Edmonton/ProCards 2885

EVERS, JOHN J.
23 WillardsChocolate(V100) 39

EVERSON, GREG
89 London/ProCards 1380

EWING, SAM
77 O-Pee-Chee 221
78 O-Pee-Chee 112
79 O-Pee-Chee 271
78 TOR

F

FABBRO, ARTHUR
53 Exhibits 45
52 Parkhurst 55

FABER, RED (CHARLES)
21 Neilson's(V61) 14
23 WillardsChocolate(V100) 40
33 WWGum(V353) 54

FABREAS, JORGE
94 Vancouver/ProCards 1867

FACE, ELROY
67 O-Pee-Chee 49
69 O-Pee-Chee 207
60 opcTattoo 14, 74
62 PostCereal 177
62 ShirriffCoin 174

FAEDO, LENNY
84 opcSticker 310

FAHEY, BILL
72 O-Pee-Chee 334
73 O-Pee-Chee 186
74 O-Pee-Chee 558
75 O-Pee-Chee 644
76 O-Pee-Chee 436
80 O-Pee-Chee 23

FAHR, GERALD
52 Parkhurst 23

FAIREY, JIM
69 O-Pee-Chee 117
71 O-Pee-Chee 474
73 O-Pee-Chee 429
71 ProStarPostcard
71 MTL/ProStar

FAIRFAX, KENNY
93 Welland/ClassicBest 5
93 Welland/ProCards 3349

FAIRLY, RON
72 Dimanche/DernièreHeure
92 Nabisco 19
65 O-Pee-Chee 196
67 O-Pee-Chee 94
69 O-Pee-Chee 122
71 O-Pee-Chee 315
72 O-Pee-Chee 405
73 O-Pee-Chee 125
74 O-Pee-Chee 146
75 O-Pee-Chee 270
76 O-Pee-Chee 375
78 O-Pee-Chee 40
71 MTL
71 MTL/LaPizzaRoyale
71 MTL/ProStar

FALCONE, PETE
76 O-Pee-Chee 524
77 O-Pee-Chee 177
79 O-Pee-Chee 36
81 O-Pee-Chee 117
84 O-Pee-Chee 51

FALK, BIBB
21 Neilson's(V61) 15
23 Neilson's 11
23 WillardsChocolate 41

FANNING, JIM
82 Dimanche/DernièreHeure
65 O-Pee-Chee 267
82 MTL/Hygrade
83 MTL

FANNING, STEVE
88 Hamilton/ProCards 1739

FANOVICH, FRANK JOSEPH
52 Parkhurst 84

FANZONE, CARMEN
73 O-Pee-Chee 139
74 O-Pee-Chee 484
75 O-Pee-Chee 363

FARIES, PAUL
92 O-Pee-Chee 162
95 Edmonton/Macri

FARISS, MONTY
92 O-Pee-Chee 138
94 Edmonton/ProCards 2886

FARMER, BILLY
70 O-Pee-Chee 444

FARMER, ED
72 O-Pee-Chee 116
73 O-Pee-Chee 272
74 O-Pee-Chee 506
81 O-Pee-Chee 36
82 O-Pee-Chee 328

FARMER, HOWARD
91 opcPremier 40

FARR, ,STEVE
90 FleerCdn. 107
87 O-Pee-Chee 216
89 O-Pee-Chee 356
90 O-Pee-Chee 149
91 O-Pee-Chee 301
92 O-Pee-Chee 46
93 O-Pee-Chee 27
87 opcSticker 255
89 opcSticker 272
89 PaniniSticker 349

FARRELL, DICK
62 ShirriffCoin 184

FARRELL, EDWARD (DOC)
33 WWGum(V353) 73

FARRELL, JOHN
88 Leaf 42
90 FleerCdn. 491
89 O-Pee-Chee 227
90 O-Pee-Chee 32
91 O-Pee-Chee 664
89 PaniniSticker 318
90 PaniniSticker 53
94 Vancouver/ProCards 1858

FARRELL, JON
92 O-Pee-Chee 9
91 Welland/Best 1
91 Welland/ProCards 3575

FARRELL, TURK
65 O-Pee-Chee 80
67 O-Pee-Chee 190

FARRIS, MARK
94 Welland/Classic 1
94 Welland/ProCards 3502

FASSERO, JEFF
92 O-Pee-Chee 423
93 O-Pee-Chee 192
92 opcPremier 119
92 MTL/Durivage 7
96 MTL/Disk

FAST, DARCY
72 O-Pee-Chee 457

FAYNE, JEFF
90 Hamilton/Star 12

FEDERICO, JOE
88 Hamilton/ProCards 1738

FELDER, MIKE
90 FleerCdn. 321
90 O-Pee-Chee 159
91 O-Pee-Chee 44
92 O-Pee-Chee 697

FELIX, JUNIOR
90 FleerCdn. 79
90 O-Pee-Chee 347
91 O-Pee-Chee 543
92 O-Pee-Chee 189
93 O-Pee-Chee 128
91 opcPremier 41
91 PaniniSticker 342
92 PaniniSticker 9
90 TOR/FireSafety
90 TOR/Hostess

FELIZ, JANIERO
90 Welland/Pucko 5

FELLER, BOB
53 Exhibits 17
92 HomersClassic
37 O-Pee-Chee(V300) 120

FELSKE, JOHN
73 O-Pee-Chee 332
79 Vancouver/TCMA 20

FENWICK, BOB
73 O-Pee-Chee 567

FERGUSON, JOE
73 O-Pee-Chee 621
74 O-Pee-Chee 86
75 O-Pee-Chee 115
76 O-Pee-Chee 329
77 O-Pee-Chee 107
80 O-Pee-Chee 29

FERMIN, FELIX
90 FleerCdn. 492
90 O-Pee-Chee 722
91 O-Pee-Chee 193
92 O-Pee-Chee 632
93 O-Pee-Chee 90
90 PaniniSticker 60
91 PaniniSticker 219
92 PaniniSticker 48
93 PaniniSticker 50
94 PaniniSticker 56

FERNANDEZ, ALEX
91 O-Pee-Chee 278
92 O-Pee-Chee 755
93 O-Pee-Chee 53
94 O-Pee-Chee 6
91 opcPremier 42

FERNANDEZ, CHICO
62 PostCereal 17
62 ShirriffCoin 3

FERNANDEZ, FELIPE
94 GarciaPhoto 90

FERNANDEZ, FRANK
70 O-Pee-Chee 82
71 O-Pee-Chee 466

FERNANDEZ, JOSE
89 Hamilton/Star 11

FERNANDEZ, JULIO GERMAN
94 GarciaPhoto 4

FERNANDEZ, OSVALDO
94 GarciaPhoto 117

FERNANDEZ, SID
90FleerCdn. 203
86 Leaf 242
87 Leaf 93
88 Leaf 63
85 O-Pee-Chee 390
87 O-Pee-Chee 337
88 O-Pee-Chee 30
89 O-Pee-Chee 34
90 O-Pee-Chee 480
91 O-Pee-Chee 230
92 O-Pee-Chee 382
87 opcSticker 97
88 opcSticker 103,-SStar 28
88 PaniniSticker 336
90 PaniniSticker 299
93 PaniniSticker 248

FERNANDEZ, TONY
90 FleerCdn. 80,634
86 GeneralMills
87 GeneralMills
88 HostessDisk
85 Leaf 91
86 Leaf 45
87 Leaf 106
88 Leaf 12,133
85 O-Pee-Chee 48, -Poster 16
86 O-Pee-Chee 241
87 O-Pee-Chee 329
88 O-Pee-Chee 290
89 O-Pee-Chee 170
90 O-Pee-Chee 685
91 O-Pee-Chee 320
92 O-Pee-Chee 60
93 O-Pee-Chee 70
94 O-Pee-Chee-TOR 9
91 opcPremier 43
93 opcPremier 20
86 opcSticker 194
87 opcSticker 194
88 opcSticker 193,-SStar 43
89 opcSticker 189,-SStar 10
86 opcTattoo 15
88 PaniniSticker 222
89 PaniniSticker 470
90 PaniniSticker 176
91 PaniniSticker 339
92 PaniniSticker 235
93 PaniniSticker 249
94 PaniniSticker 137
87 StuartBakery 27
84 TOR/FireSafety
85 TOR/FireSafety
86 TOR/AultFoods
86 TOR/FireSafety
87 TOR/FireSafety
88 TOR
88 TOR/FireSafety
89 TOR/FireSafety
90 TOR/FireSafety
90 TOR/Hostess
97 TOR/Sizzler 45

FERRARA, AL
68 O-Pee-Chee 34
70 OPC 345,-Booklet 23
71 O-Pee-Chee 214

FERRARO, MIKE
69 O-Pee-Chee 83

FERREIRA, TONY
87 Calgary/ProCards 2328

FERRELL, RICK
37 O-Pee-Chee(V300) 132

FERRELL, WES
37 O-Pee-Chee(V300) 138
36 WWGum(V355) 40

FETTERS, MIKE
90 FleerCdn. 131
90 O-Pee-Chee 14
91 O-Pee-Chee 477
92 O-Pee-Chee 602
93 O-Pee-Chee 109
89 Edmonton/CMC 9
90 Edmonton/CMC 7
90 Edmonton/ProCards 514
91 Edmonton/LineDrive 163
91 Edmonton/ProCards 1512

FEWSTER, CHICK
22 WilliamPaterson(V89) 29

FIALA, WALTER
53 Exhibits 48
52 Parkhurst 67

FIDRYCH, MARK
77 O-Pee-Chee 7,115
7 O-Pee-Chee 235
79 O-Pee-Chee 329
80 O-Pee-Chee 231
81 O-Pee-Chee 150

FIELDER, CECIL
91 Ben's/HolsumDisk 17
92 Ben'sDisk 1
93 HumptyDumpty 8
92 McDonald's 20
86 O-Pee-Chee 386
87 O-Pee-Chee 178
88 O-Pee-Chee 21
89 O-Pee-Chee 224
91 O-Pee-Chee 386, 720
92 O-Pee-Chee 425
93 O-Pee-Chee 51
94 O-Pee-Chee 126, -AS 20
91 opcPremier 44
92 opcPremier 70
93 opcPremier 96
91 PaniniSticker 288
92 PaniniSticker 105,144,272
93 PaniniSticker 114
94 PaniniSticker 63
91 PaniniTopFifteen 13,21,37,54
91 PetroCanada 11
92 PizzaHut/DietPepsi 13
91 PostCdn. 19
92 PostCdn. 12
86 TOR/AultFoods
86 TOR/FireSafety
87 TOR/FireSafety
88 TOR/FireSafety

FIELDS, BRUCE
87 Leaf 47
89 Calgary/CMC 19
89 Calgary/ProCards 534
92 London/ProCards 649
92 London/SkyBox 425

FIELDS, WILMER
52 Parkhurst 21

FIFE, DAN
74 O-Pee-Chee 421

FIGUEROA, BEN
94 Ottawa/ProCards 2903

FIGUEROA, ED
75 O-Pee-Chee 476
76 O-Pee-Chee 27
77 O-Pee-Chee 164
79 O-Pee-Chee 13
80 O-Pee-Chee 288

FILER, TOM
90 FleerCdn. 322
86 Leaf 211
86 O-Pee-Chee 312
86 TOR/FireSafety

FILTER, RUSTY
90 StCatharines/ProCards 3468

FIMPLE, JACK
87 Edmonton/ProCards 2083

FINCH, STEVEN
84 Edmonton/Cramer 106
86 Edmonton/ProCards

FINGERS, ROLLIE
85 Leaf 190
70 O-Pee-Chee 502
71 O-Pee-Chee 384
72 O-Pee-Chee 241
73 O-Pee-Chee 84
74 O-Pee-Chee 212
75 O-Pee-Chee 21
76 O-Pee-Chee 405
77 O-Pee-Chee 52
78 O-Pee-Chee 8, 201
79 O-Pee-Chee 203
80 O-Pee-Chee 343
81 O-Pee-Chee 229
82 O-Pee-Chee 44, 176
83 O-Pee-Chee 35, 36
84 O-Pee-Chee 283
85 O-Pee-Chee 182
86 O-Pee-Chee 185
82 opcSticker 16, 198
83 opcSticker 79
85 opcSticker 285
86 opcSticker 198

FINLEY, CHUCK
90 FleerCdn. 132
93 HumptyDumpty 4
90 O-Pee-Chee 147
91 O-Pee-Chee 395, 505
92 O-Pee-Chee 247
93 O-Pee-Chee 153
94 O-Pee-Chee 158
92 opcPremier 155
90 PaniniSticker 32
91 PaniniSticker 187
91 PaniniTopFifteen 70

FINLEY, STEVE
90 FleerCdn. 176
90 O-Pee-Chee 349
91 O-Pee-Chee 212
92 O-Pee-Chee 86
93 O-Pee-Chee 154
94 O-Pee-Chee 129
91 PaniniSticker 244
92 PaniniSticker 157
93 PaniniSticker 174
94 PaniniSticker 194

FINN, JOHN
81 Vancouver/TCMA 21

FINNEY, LOU
36 WWGum(V355) 64

FIORE, MIKE
71 O-Pee-Chee 287
72 O-Pee-Chee 199

FIREOVID, STEVE
86 Calgary/ProCards

FIROVA, DAN
86 Calgary/ProCards

FISHEL, JOHN
89 PaniniSticker 80

FISHER, BRIAN
88 Leaf 244
87 O-Pee-Chee 316
88 O-Pee-Chee 193
89 O-Pee-Chee 303
90 O-Pee-Chee 666
86 opcTattoo 2
86 opcSticker 312
88 PaniniSticker 368

FISHER, EDDIE
66 O-Pee-Chee 85
70 O-Pee-Chee 156
71 O-Pee-Chee 631
73 O-Pee-Chee 439

FISHER, JACK
65 O-Pee-Chee 93

FISHER, ROBERT
1912 ImperialTobacco(C46) 43

FISCHER, TODD
86 Edmonton/ProCards

FISK, CARLTON
90 FleerCdn. 530
85 GeneralMills
86 GeneralMills
87 GeneralMills
85 Leaf 155
86 Leaf 163
87 Leaf 199
88 Leaf 208

72 O-Pee-Chee 79
73 O-Pee-Chee 193
74 O-Pee-Chee 105, 331
75 O-Pee-Chee 80
76 O-Pee-Chee 365
77 O-Pee-Chee 137
78 O-Pee-Chee 210
79 O-Pee-Chee 360
80 O-Pee-Chee 20
81 O-Pee-Chee 116
82 O-Pee-Chee 58, 110, 111
83 O-Pee-Chee 20, 393
84 O-Pee-Chee 127
85 O-Pee-Chee 49
86 O-Pee-Chee 290, E
87 O-Pee-Chee 164
88 O-Pee-Chee 385
89 O-Pee-Chee 46
90 O-Pee-Chee 392, 420
91 O-Pee-Chee 3, 170, 393, F
92 O-Pee-Chee 630
93 O-Pee-Chee 78
91 opcPremier 45
92 opcPremier 86
82 opcSticker 138, 170
83 opcSticker 54, 243
84 opcSticker 243
85 opcSticker 243
86 opcSticker 162, 286
87 opcSticker 288
88 opcSticker 290
89 opcSticker 299,-SuperStar
86 opcTattoo 23
88 PaniniSticker 55,90,91
89 PaniniSticker 304
90 PaniniSticker 44
91 PaniniSticker 311
92 PaniniSticker 124
93 PaniniSticker 135
91 PetroCanada 7
92 PizzaHut/DietPepsi 11
87 StuartBakery 17

FITTERE, SCOTT
95 StCatharines/TimHortons 12

FITZGERALD, MIKE
90 FleerCdn. 343
86 GeneralMills
87 GeneralMills
88 HostessDisk
86 Leaf 32
87 Leaf 222
88 Leaf 81
85 O-Pee-Chee 104, -Poster 1
86 O-Pee-Chee 313
87 O-Pee-Chee 212
88 O-Pee-Chee 386
89 O-Pee-Chee 23
90 O-Pee-Chee 484
91 O-Pee-Chee 317
92 O-Pee-Chee 761
85 opcSticker 108, 372
88 PaniniSticker 322,421,422
91 PaniniSticker 138
86 MTL/ProvigoFoods26
86 MTL/ProvigoFoods-Poster

FITZGERALD, RICHARD
52 Laval Dairy 100

FITZMORRIS, AL
70 O-Pee-Chee 241
71 O-Pee-Chee 564
72 O-Pee-Chee 349
73 O-Pee-Chee 643
74 O-Pee-Chee 191
75 O-Pee-Chee 24
76 O-Pee-Chee 144

FITZPATRICK, EDWARD
1912 ImperialTobacco(C46) 70

FITZSIMMONS, FREDDIE
34 WWGum(V354) 20
36 WWGum(V355) 14

FLACK, MAX
23 WillardsChocolate(V100) 42

FLANAGAN, MIKE
90 FleerCdn. 81
85 Leaf 175
76 O-Pee-Chee 589
78 O-Pee-Chee 231
79 O-Pee-Chee 76
80 O-Pee-Chee 335
81 O-Pee-Chee 10
82 O-Pee-Chee 153
83 O-Pee-Chee 172
84 O-Pee-Chee 295
85 O-Pee-Chee 46
87 O-Pee-Chee 112
88 O-Pee-Chee 164
89 O-Pee-Chee 139
90 O-Pee-Chee 78
92 O-Pee-Chee 218
82 opcSticker 148
83 opcSticker 5
84 opcSticker 12, 210
85 opcSticker 207
89 opcSticker 190
88 TOR/FireSafety
89 TOR/FireSafety

FLANNERY, JOHN
81 Edmonton/RedRooster 11

FLANNERY, TIM
86 O-Pee-Chee 387
87 O-Pee-Chee 52
88 O-Pee-Chee 262
86 opcSticker 112
87 opcSticker 114
88 opcSticker 108
88 PaniniSticker 404

FLEISCHER, HERB
52 LavalDairy 47

FLEMING, DAVE
92 O-Pee-Chee 192
93 O-Pee-Chee 67
94 O-Pee-Chee 183
93 PaniniSticker 57

FLEMING, JOHN
97 Lethbridge/Best 20

FLENER, HUCK
97 TOR/Sizzler 52
90 StCatharines/ProCards 3470

FLETCHER, ART
21 Neilson's(V61) 107

FLETCHER, DARRIN
91 O-Pee-Chee 9
92 O-Pee-Chee 159
93 O-Pee-Chee 64
92 opcPremier 41
93 PaniniSticker 224
92 MTL/Durivage 8
96 MTL/Disk

FLETCHER, SCOTT
90 FleerCdn. 531
87 Leaf 226
88 Leaf 11
88 Leaf 155
84 O-Pee-Chee 250
86 O-Pee-Chee 187
88 O-Pee-Chee 345
89 O-Pee-Chee 295
90 O-Pee-Chee 565
91 O-Pee-Chee 785
92 O-Pee-Chee 648
93 O-Pee-Chee 133
92 opcPremier 48
88 opcSticker 241
89 opcSticker 246
88 PaniniSticker 154-55,206,454
90 PaniniSticker 43
91 PaniniSticker 313
94 PaniniSticker 29

FLOETHE, CHRIS
72 O-Pee-Chee 268

FLOOD, CURT
66 O-Pee-Chee 60
67 O-Pee-Chee 63
68 O-Pee-Chee 180
69 OPC-DeckleEdge 5
70 O-Pee-Chee 360
71 O-Pee-Chee 535
62 PostCereal 166
62 ShirriffCoin 139

FLORA, KEVIN
92 Edmonton/ProCards 3545
92 Edmonton/SkyBox 156

FLORENCE, PAUL
36 WWGum(V355) 117

FLOWERS, JAKE
33 WWGum(V353) 81

FLOYD, BOBBY
70 O-Pee-Chee 101
71 O-Pee-Chee 646
72 O-Pee-Chee 273
74 O-Pee-Chee 41
85 Calgary/Cramer 78

FLOYD, CLIFF
92 O-Pee-Chee 186
94 OPC 223,-HotProsp 1

FLYNN, DOUG
85 Leaf 257
76 O-Pee-Chee 518
79 O-Pee-Chee 116
80 O-Pee-Chee 32
81 O-Pee-Chee 311
82 O-Pee-Chee 302
83 O-Pee-Chee 169
84 O-Pee-Chee 262
85 O-Pee-Chee 112
82 opcSticker 70
84 opcSticker 97
85 opcSticker 93
83 MTL
83 MTL/StuartBakery 7
84 MTL
84 MTL/StuartBakery 29

FOHL, LEE
20 MapleCrispette(V117) 5
23 WillardsChocolate(V100) 43

FOILES, HANK
52 Parkhurst 85

FOLEY, MARV
81 Edmonton/RedRooster
89 Vancouver/CMC 23
89 Vancouver/ProCards 573
90 Vancouver/CMC 5
90 Vancouver/ProCards 505
91 Vancouver/LineDrive 649
91 Vancouver/ProCards 1609

FOLEY, TOM
90 FleerCdn. 344
88 HostessDisk
88 Leaf 143
87 O-Pee-Chee 78
88 O-Pee-Chee 251
89 O-Pee-Chee 159
90 O-Pee-Chee 341
91 O-Pee-Chee 773
92 O-Pee-Chee 666
89 PaniniSticker 121
90 PaniniSticker 292

FOLI, TIM
72 Dimanche/DernièreHeure
73 Dimanche/DernièreHeure
71 O-Pee-Chee 83
73 O-Pee-Chee 19
74 O-Pee-Chee 217
75 O-Pee-Chee 149
76 O-Pee-Chee 397
77 O-Pee-Chee 162
78 O-Pee-Chee 169
79 O-Pee-Chee 213
80 O-Pee-Chee 131
81 O-Pee-Chee 38
82 O-Pee-Chee 97
83 O-Pee-Chee 319
84 O-Pee-Chee 342
82 opcSticker 88
71 ProStarPostcard
74 MTL/GeorgeWeston

FOLKERS, KEN
97 St.Catharines/Best 14

FOLKERS, RICH
71 O-Pee-Chee 648
73 O-Pee-Chee 649
74 O-Pee-Chee 417
75 O-Pee-Chee 98
76 O-Pee-Chee 611

FONSECA, ALFREDO
94 GarciaPhoto 123

FONSECA, LEW
33 WWGum(V353) 43

FONTANES, REUBEN
97 Lethbridge/Best 21

FOOR, JIM
72 O-Pee-Chee 257

FOOTE, BARRY
72 Dimanche/DernièreHeure
74 O-Pee-Chee 603
75 O-Pee-Chee 229
76 O-Pee-Chee 42
77 O-Pee-Chee 207
80 O-Pee-Chee 208
81 O-Pee-Chee 305
77 MTL
77 MTL/RedpathSugar

FORBES, P.J.
94 Vancouver/ProCards 1869
96 Vancouver/Best 13

FORD, CURT
90 FleerCdn. 557
90 O-Pee-Chee 39
88 opcSticker 23
88 PaniniSticker 395

FORD, DAN
76 O-Pee-Chee 313
77 O-Pee-Chee 104
78 O-Pee-Chee 34
79 O-Pee-Chee 201
80 O-Pee-Chee 7
81 O-Pee-Chee 303
82 O-Pee-Chee 134
83 O-Pee-Chee 357
84 O-Pee-Chee 349
82 opcSticker 163
84 opcSticker 212

FORD, HORACE
21 Neilson's(V61) 111
33 WWGum(V353) 24

FORD, TED
71 O-Pee-Chee 612
72 O-Pee-Chee 24
73 O-Pee-Chee 299
74 O-Pee-Chee 617

FORD, WHITEY
66 O-Pee-Chee 160
67 O-Pee-Chee 5
60 opcTattoo 15
62 PostCereal 9
62 ShirriffCoin 8

FORRESTER, TOM
89 Vancouver/CMC 20
89 Vancouver/ProCards 597

FORSCH, BOB
90 FleerCdn. 231
87 Leaf 161
75 O-Pee-Chee 51
76 O-Pee-Chee 426
78 O-Pee-Chee 83
79 O-Pee-Chee 117
80 O-Pee-Chee 279
81 O-Pee-Chee 140
82 O-Pee-Chee 34
83 O-Pee-Chee 197
84 O-Pee-Chee 75
85 O-Pee-Chee 137
87 O-Pee-Chee 257
82 opcSticker 90
83 opcSticker 289
84 opcSticker 288
87 opcSticker 47
88 PaniniSticker 384

FORSCH, KEN
71 O-Pee-Chee 102
72 O-Pee-Chee 394
73 O-Pee-Chee 589
74 O-Pee-Chee 91
75 O-Pee-Chee 357
76 O-Pee-Chee 357
77 O-Pee-Chee 78
79 O-Pee-Chee 276
80 O-Pee-Chee 337
81 O-Pee-Chee 269
82 O-Pee-Chee 385
83 O-Pee-Chee 346
84 O-Pee-Chee 193
85 O-Pee-Chee 141
82 opcSticker 159
84 opcSticker 237

FORSTER, TERRY
86 Leaf 202
73 O-Pee-Chee 129
74 O-Pee-Chee 310
75 O-Pee-Chee 137, 313
76 O-Pee-Chee 437
79 O-Pee-Chee 7
84 O-Pee-Chee 109
85 O-Pee-Chee 248

FORTIN, BLAINE
96 StCatharines/Best 8

FORTUGNO, TIM
92 Edmonton/ProCards 3535
92 Edmonton/SkyBox 157
93 Ottawa/ProCards 2429

FORTUNA, MIKE
89 Welland/Pucko 12

FOSSAS, TONY
90 FleerCdn. 323
90 O-Pee-Chee 34
91 O-Pee-Chee 747
92 O-Pee-Chee 249
86 Edmonton/ProCards
87 Edmonton/ProCards 2080

FOSSE, RAY
70 O-Pee-Chee 184
71 O-Pee-Chee 125
72 O-Pee-Chee 470

73 O-Pee-Chee 226
74 O-Pee-Chee 420
75 O-Pee-Chee 486
76 O-Pee-Chee 554
77 O-Pee-Chee 39

FOSTER, ALAN
70 O-Pee-Chee 369
71 O-Pee-Chee 207
72 O-Pee-Chee 521
73 O-Pee-Chee 543
74 O-Pee-Chee 442
75 O-Pee-Chee 266

FOSTER, GEORGE
86 GeneralMills
85 Leaf 42
71 O-Pee-Chee 276
72 O-Pee-Chee 256
73 O-Pee-Chee 399
74 O-Pee-Chee 646
75 O-Pee-Chee 87
76 O-Pee-Chee 179
77 O-Pee-Chee 3, 120
78 O-Pee-Chee 2,3,70
79 O-Pee-Chee 316
80 O-Pee-Chee 209
81 O-Pee-Chee 200
82 O-Pee-Chee 177, 336, 342
83 O-Pee-Chee 80
84 O-Pee-Chee 350
85 O-Pee-Chee 170
86 O-Pee-Chee 69
82 opcSticker 40, 126
83 opcSticker 263
84 opcSticker 105
85 opcSticker 99
86 opcSticker 100

FOSTER, LEO
74 O-Pee-Chee 607
75 O-Pee-Chee 418

FOSTER, ROY
71 O-Pee-Chee 107
72 O-Pee-Chee 329

FOSTER, STEVE
92 O-Pee-Chee 528

FOUCAULT, STEVE
74 O-Pee-Chee 294
75 O-Pee-Chee 283
76 O-Pee-Chee 303

FOULK, LEON RAY
52 Parkhurst 15

FOURNIER, JACQUES F.
23 WillardsChocolate(V100) 44

FOWLER, ART
73 O-Pee-Chee 323
74 O-Pee-Chee 379

FOWLKES, ALAN
86 Edmonton/ProCards

FOX, BRIAN
97 Lethbridge/Best 7

FOX, CHARLIE
71 O-Pee-Chee 517
72 O-Pee-Chee 129
73 O-Pee-Chee 252
74 O-Pee-Chee 78

FOX, NELLIE
75 O-Pee-Chee 197
60 opcTattoo 16
62 PostCereal 47
62 ShirriffCoin 12

FOX, TERRY
67 O-Pee-Chee 181

FOXX, JIMMIE
37 O-Pee-Chee(V300) 106
33 WWGum(V353) 29,85
34 WWGum(V354) 58
39 WWGum(V351B)

FOY, JOE
69 O-Pee-Chee 93
70 O-Pee-Chee 138
71 O-Pee-Chee 706

FRAILING, KEN
74 O-Pee-Chee 605
75 O-Pee-Chee 436

FRANCE, AARON
94 Welland/Classic 9
94 Welland/ProCards 3488

FRANCHUK, ORV
95 Edmonton/Macri

FRANCO, JOHN
90 FleerCdn. 419
86 Leaf 240
87 Leaf 178
88 Leaf 79
86 O-Pee-Chee 54
87 O-Pee-Chee 305
88 O-Pee-Chee 341
89 O-Pee-Chee 290
90 O-Pee-Chee 120
91 O-Pee-Chee 407, 510
92 O-Pee-Chee 690
93 O-Pee-Chee 68
94 O-Pee-Chee 256
92 opcPremier 73
86 opcSticker 142
87 opcSticker 138
88 opcSticker 142,-SStar 32
89 opcSticker 4,136,-SStar 65
86 opcTattoo 7
88 PaniniSticker 271
89 PaniniSticker 66
90 PaniniSticker 244

FRANCO, JULIO
92 Ben'sDisk 9
88 FantasticSam's 10
90 FleerCdn. 296
85 Leaf 213
86 Leaf 93
87 Leaf 131
88 Leaf 10,71
84 O-Pee-Chee 48
85 O-Pee-Chee 237
86 O-Pee-Chee 391
87 O-Pee-Chee 160
88 O-Pee-Chee 49
89 O-Pee-Chee 55
90 O-Pee-Chee 386
91 O-Pee-Chee 387,775
92 O-Pee-Chee 490
93 O-Pee-Chee 73
94 O-Pee-Chee 142
92 opcPremier 15
84 opcSticker 379
85 opcSticker 245
86 opcSticker 211
87 opcSticker 210
88 opcSticker 207
89 opcSticker 208,-SuperStar 4
86 opcTattoo 1
88 PaniniSticker 77
89 PaniniSticker 325
90 PaniniSticker 163,201
91 PaniniSticker 253
92 PaniniSticker 76,145
93 PaniniSticker 82
94 PaniniSticker 126
91 PaniniTopFifteen 81
87 StuartBakery 18

FRANCONA, TERRY
85 Leaf 245
86 Leaf 191
82 O-Pee-Chee 118, -Poster 19
83 O-Pee-Chee 267
84 O-Pee-Chee 89
85 O-Pee-Chee 258
86 O-Pee-Chee 374
87 O-Pee-Chee 294
90 O-Pee-Chee 214
83 opcSticker 321
85 opcSticker 88
86 opcSticker 80
82 MTL/Hygrade
82 MTL/Zellers 11
83 MTL
83 MTL/StuartBakery
84 MTL
84 MTL/StuartBakery 18

FRANCONA, TITO
65 O-Pee-Chee 256
66 O-Pee-Chee 163
60 opcTattoo 17
62 PostCereal 40
62 ShirriffCoin 15

FRANKHOUSE, FRED
34 WWGum(V354) 19

FRANKS, HERMAN
65 O-Pee-Chee 32
67 O-Pee-Chee 116
43-47 Montréal/ParadeSportive

FRANSLER, STAN
87 Vancouver/ProCards 1604

FRASCATORE, JOHN
91 Hamilton/ClassicBest 3
91 Hamilton/ProCards 4033

FRASER, WILLIE
90 FleerCdn. 133
87 Leaf 40
88 O-Pee-Chee 363
90 O-Pee-Chee 477
91 O-Pee-Chee 784
91 opcPremier 46
92 Edmonton/ProCards 3536
92 Edmonton/SkyBox 158
94 Edmonton/ProCards 2869

FRAZIER, GEORGE
84 O-Pee-Chee 139
85 O-Pee-Chee 19

FRAZIER, JOE
76 O-Pee-Chee 531

FRAZIER, LOU
90 London/ProCards 1276
91 London/LineDrive 383
91 London/ProCards 1889
92 London/ProCards 645
92 London/SkyBox 406

FREDERICK, JOHN
34 WWGum(V354) 85

FREED, DAN
92 London/ProCards 626
92 London/SkyBox 407

FREED, ROGER
70 O-Pee-Chee 477
71 O-Pee-Chee 362
72 O-Pee-Chee 69

FREEHAN, BILL
66 O-Pee-Chee 145
67 O-Pee-Chee 48
69 O-Pee-Chee-Deckle 6
70 OPC 335, 465, -Booklet 6
71 O-Pee-Chee 575
72 O-Pee-Chee 120
73 O-Pee-Chee 460
74 O-Pee-Chee 162
75 O-Pee-Chee 397
76 O-Pee-Chee 540

FREEL, RYAN
95 StCatharines/TimHortons 17

FREEMAN, JIMMY
73 O-Pee-Chee 610

FREEMAN, MARVIN
90 O-Pee-Chee 103
92 O-Pee-Chee 68

FREESE, GENE
60 opcTattoo 18
62 PostCereal 118
62 ShirriffCoin 137

FREGOSI, JIM
65 O-Pee-Chee 210
66 O-Pee-Chee 5
68 O-Pee-Chee 170
71 O-Pee-Chee 360
72 O-Pee-Chee 115, 346
73 O-Pee-Chee 525
75 O-Pee-Chee 339
76 O-Pee-Chee 635
92 O-Pee-Chee 669

FREISLEBEN, DAVE
74 O-Pee-Chee 599
75 O-Pee-Chee 37
76 O-Pee-Chee 217
80 O-Pee-Chee 199
79 TOR/BubbleYum 13

FRENCH, CHARLIE
1912 ImperialTobacco(C46) 25

FRENCH, JIM
69 O-Pee-Chee 199
71 O-Pee-Chee 399

FRENCH, LARRY
34 WWGum(V354) 79

FRENCH, RONNIE
91 Hamilton/ClassicBest 27
91 Hamilton/ProCards 4052
92 Hamilton/ClassicBest 7

FREY, JIM
73 O-Pee-Chee 136
74 O-Pee-Chee 306

FREY, STEVE
90 FleerCdn. 649
90 O-Pee-Chee 91
91 O-Pee-Chee 462
92 O-Pee-Chee 174
91 PaniniSticker 154
97 Vancouver/Best 15

FRIAS, JESUS (ANDUJAR)
77 MTL/RedpathSugar

FRIAS, PEPE
73 O-Pee-Chee 607
74 O-Pee-Chee 468
75 O-Pee-Chee 496
76 O-Pee-Chee 544
77 O-Pee-Chee 225
78 O-Pee-Chee 171
79 O-Pee-Chee 146
80 O-Pee-Chee 48
77 MTL
77 MTL/RedpathSugar

FRIBERG, BARNEY
34 WWGum(V354) 10

FRIEND, BOB
62 PostCereal 178
62 ShirriffCoin 157

FRISCH, FRANK
21 Neilson's(V61) 62
23 Neilson's 12
23 WillardsChocolate(V100) 45
22 WilliamPaterson(V89) 24
33 WWGum(V353) 49
34 WWGum(V354) 64
36 WWGum(V355) 107

FRISELLA, DANNY
68 O-Pee-Chee 191
71 O-Pee-Chee 104
72 O-Pee-Chee 293, 294
73 O-Pee-Chee 432
74 O-Pee-Chee 71
75 O-Pee-Chee 343
76 O-Pee-Chee 32

FRITZ, JOHN
94 Vancouver/ProCards 1859

FROBEL, DOUG
85 opcSticker 128

FROCK, SAMUEL
1912 ImperialTobacco(C46) 13

FROHWIRTH, TODD
90 O-Pee-Chee 69
92 O-Pee-Chee 158

FROSTAD, MIKE
96 StCatharines/Best 3

FRYMAN, TRAVIS
91 O-Pee-Chee 128
92 O-Pee-Chee 750
93 O-Pee-Chee 76
94 O-Pee-Chee 209
93 opcPremier 102
92 PaniniSticker 107
93 PaniniSticker 117
94 PaniniSticker 64
89 London/ProCards 1366

FRYMAN, WOODIE
78 Dimanche/DernièreHeure
80 Dimanche/DernièreHeure
68 O-Pee-Chee 112
69 O-Pee-Chee 51
71 O-Pee-Chee 414
72 O-Pee-Chee 357
73 O-Pee-Chee 146
74 O-Pee-Chee 555
75 O-Pee-Chee 166
76 O-Pee-Chee 467
77 O-Pee-Chee 126
79 O-Pee-Chee 135
80 O-Pee-Chee 316
81 O-Pee-Chee 170, -Poster 10
82 O-Pee-Chee 181
83 O-Pee-Chee 137
82 MTL/Hygrade
82 MTL/Zellers
83 MTL
83 MTL/Stuart Bakery 2
93 MTL/McDonald's 22

FUCCI, DOM
82 Edmonton/TCMA 18

FUENTES, JORGE
94 GarciaPhoto 28

FUENTES, MICKEY
70 O-Pee-Chee 88
84 MTL
84 MTL/StuartBakery 32

FUENTES, TITO
67 O-Pee-Chee 177
70 O-Pee-Chee 42
71 O-Pee-Chee 378
72 O-Pee-Chee 427, 428
73 O-Pee-Chee 236
74 O-Pee-Chee 305
75 O-Pee-Chee 425
76 O-Pee-Chee 8

FULLER, JIM
74 O-Pee-Chee 606
75 O-Pee-Chee 594

FULLER, ERN
68 O-Pee-Chee 71

FULTON, GREG
89 Calgary/ProCards 524
90 Calgary/CMC 9
90 Calgary/ProCards 656

FUMERO, JORGE
94 GarciaPhoto 28

FUSCO, TOM
90 Hamilton/Best 5
90 Hamilton/Star 13

FUTRELL, MARK
90 Welland/Pucko 21

GABBARD, JOHN
43-47 Montréal/ParadeSportive

GABRIELSON, LEN
65 O-Pee-Chee 14
70 O-Pee-Chee 204

GAETA, FRANK
52 LavalDairy 25

GAETTI, GARY
90 FleerCdn. 373
85 Leaf 145
87 Leaf 245
88 Leaf 19,200
84 O-Pee-Chee 157
85 O-Pee-Chee 304
86 O-Pee-Chee 97
87 O-Pee-Chee 179
88 O-Pee-Chee 257
89 O-Pee-Chee 220
90 O-Pee-Chee 630
91 O-Pee-Chee 430
92 O-Pee-Chee 70
91 opcPremier 47
83 opcSticker 87
84 opcSticker 306
85 opcSticker 302
86 opcSticker 283
87 opcSticker 279
88 opcSticker 17, 277
89 opcSticker 289, -SStar 8
88 PaniniSticker 140
89 PaniniSticker 389
90 PaniniSticker 106
91 PaniniSticker 302
92 PaniniSticker 7
93 PaniniSticker 4

GAGLIANO, PHIL
70 O-Pee-Chee 143
71 O-Pee-Chee 302
72 O-Pee-Chee 472
73 O-Pee-Chee 69
74 O-Pee-Chee 622

GAGNE, GREG
90 FleerCdn. 374
88 O-Pee-Chee 343
89 O-Pee-Chee 19
90 O-Pee-Chee 448
91 O-Pee-Chee 216
92 O-Pee-Chee 663
93 O-Pee-Chee 101
94 O-Pee-Chee 141
93 opcPremier 117
87 opcSticker 283
89 opcSticker 288
88 PaniniSticker 141
89 PaniniSticker 390
90 PaniniSticker 115
91 PaniniSticker 303
92 PaniniSticker 118
93 PaniniSticker 105
94 PaniniSticker 72

GAINER, DEL
22 WilliamPaterson(V89) 3

GAINES, JOE
66 O-Pee-Chee 122

GAKELER, DAN
92 O-Pee-Chee 621

GALAN, AUGUST
36 WWGum(V355) 106

GALARRAGA, ANDRES
90 Ben's/HolsumDisks 4
90 FleerCdn. 345
87 GeneralMills
88 HostessDisk 8
86 Leaf 27
87 Leaf 221
88 Leaf 121
87 O-Pee-Chee 272
88 O-Pee-Chee 25
89 O-Pee-Chee 93
90 O-Pee-Chee 720
91 O-Pee-Chee 610
92 O-Pee-Chee 240
94 O-Pee-Chee 69
91 opcPremier 48
93 opcPremier 58
87 opcSticker 84
88 opcSticker 79, -SuperStar 2
89 opcSticker 76, -SStar 36
88 PaniniSticker 323
89 PaniniSticker 119
90 PaniniSticker 284
91 PaniniSticker 139
92 PaniniSticker 202
94 PaniniSticker 174
91 PaniniTopFifteen 100
91 PostCdn. 3
86 MTL/ProvigoFoods 10
93 MTL/McDonald's 4

GALASSO, BOB
80 Vancouver/TCMA 20

GALE, RICH
79 O-Pee-Chee 149
81 O-Pee-Chee 363
82 O-Pee-Chee 67
83 O-Pee-Chee 243

GALINDO, LUIS
90 London/ProCards 1277
91 London/LineDrive 384
91 London/ProCards 1884

GALLAGHER, ALAN
71 O-Pee-Chee 224

GALLAGHER, BOB
74 O-Pee-Chee 21
75 O-Pee-Chee 406

GALLAGHER, DAVE
90 FleerCdn. 532
90 O-Pee-Chee 612
91 O-Pee-Chee 349
92 O-Pee-Chee 552
92 opcPremier 128
89 opcSticker 295, 321
89 PaniniSticker 299
90 PaniniSticker 46
87 Calgary/ProCards 2330
88 Vancouver/CMC 24
88 Vancouver/ProCards 771

GALLEGO, MIKE
90 FleerCdn. 7
90 O-Pee-Chee 293
91 O-Pee-Chee 686
92 O-Pee-Chee 76
92 opcPremier 131
88 PaniniSticker 170,171
92 PaniniSticker 16
94 PaniniSticker 100

GALLOWAY, CLARENCE E.
23 WillardsChocolate(V100) 46

GAMBLE, JOHN
74 O-Pee-Chee 597

GAMBLE, OSCAR
71 O-Pee-Chee 23
72 O-Pee-Chee 423
73 O-Pee-Chee 372
74 O-Pee-Chee 152
75 O-Pee-Chee 213
76 O-Pee-Chee 74
79 O-Pee-Chee 132
81 O-Pee-Chee 139
82 O-Pee-Chee 229
83 O-Pee-Chee 19
84 O-Pee-Chee 13
85 O-Pee-Chee 93

GANDIL, CHICK
1912 ImperialTobacco(C46) 65

GANOTE, JOE
90 StCatharines/ProCards 3461

GANT, RON
90 FleerCdn. 582
89 O-Pee-Chee 196
90 O-Pee-Chee 567
91 O-Pee-Chee 725
92 O-Pee-Chee 25
93 O-Pee-Chee 108
91 opcPremier 49
92 opcPremier 4
89 opcSticker 34, 322
89 PaniniSticker 42
91 PaniniSticker 23
92 PaniniSticker 167
93 PaniniSticker 185
94 PaniniSticker 144
91 PaniniTopFifteen 36,52

GANTNER, JIM
90 FleerCdn. 324
85 Leaf 217
86 Leaf 43
88 Leaf 161
81 O-Pee-Chee 122
82 O-Pee-Chee 207
83 O-Pee-Chee 88
85 O-Pee-Chee 216
86 O-Pee-Chee 51
87 O-Pee-Chee 108
88 O-Pee-Chee 337
89 O-Pee-Chee 134
90 O-Pee-Chee 417
91 O-Pee-Chee 23
92 O-Pee-Chee 248
84 opcSticker 298
85 opcSticker 295
86 opcSticker 202
87 opcSticker 197
88 opcSticker 195
89 opcSticker 203
86 opcTattoo 9
88 PaniniSticker 122-24
89 PaniniSticker 372
90 PaniniSticker 94
92 PaniniSticker 37

GANZALEZ, GERMAN
89 PaniniSticker 379

GANZEL, JOHN
1912 ImperialTobacco(C46) 26

GARBER, GENE
87 Leaf 172
74 O-Pee-Chee 431
75 O-Pee-Chee 444
76 O-Pee-Chee 14
79 O-Pee-Chee 331
80 O-Pee-Chee 263
81 O-Pee-Chee 307
83 O-Pee-Chee 255, 256
84 O-Pee-Chee 167
88 O-Pee-Chee 289
83 opcSticker 213
84 opcSticker 35
87 opcSticker 40

GARBEY, BARBARO
85 Leaf 121
85 O-Pee-Chee 243
86 O-Pee-Chee 88
85 opcSticker 263

GARCES, RICH
91 O-Pee-Chee 594

GARCIA, CARLOS
94 OPC 112, -DD 18
93 opcPremier 111
94 PaniniSticker 235
97 TOR/Sizzler 7

GARCIA, DAMASO
90 FleerCdn. 346
86 GeneralMills
85 Leaf 65
86 Leaf 116
87 Leaf 92
92 Nabisco 20
81 O-Pee-Chee 233, -Poster 14
82 O-Pee-Chee 293, -Poster 2
83 O-Pee-Chee 202, 222
84 O-Pee-Chee 124
85 O-Pee-Chee 353, -Poster 15
86 O-Pee-Chee 45
87 O-Pee-Chee 395
90 O-Pee-Chee 432
82 opcSticker 245
83 opcSticker 134
84 opcSticker 364
85 opcSticker 357
86 opcSticker 190
87 opcSticker 188
86 opcTattoo 24
84 TOR/FireSafety
85 TOR/FireSafety
86 TOR/AultFoods
86 TOR/FireSafety
90 TOR/Hostess
97 TOR/Sizzler

GARCIA, DAVE
73 O-Pee-Chee 12

GARCIA, FREDDY
94 StCatharines/Classic 9
94 StCatharines/ProCards 3651

GARCIA, JORGE
94 GarciaPhoto 58

GARCIA, JULIO
92 Welland/ClassicBest 29
93 Welland/ClassicBest 30

GARCIA, KIKO
81 O-Pee-Chee 192

GARCIA, LEONARD
86 Edmonton/ProCards

GARCIA, MIKE
92 London/ProCards 627
92 London/SkyBox 408

GARCIA, OSCAR
89 StCatharines/ProCards 2075

GARCIA, PEDRO
73 O-Pee-Chee 609
74 O-Pee-Chee 142
75 O-Pee-Chee 147
76 O-Pee-Chee 187
77 O-Pee-Chee 166

GARCIA, RALPH
73 O-Pee-Chee 602

GARCIA, RAMON
92 O-Pee-Chee 176
92 Vancouver/ProCards 2716
92 Vancouver/SkyBox 635
94 Welland/Classic 10
94 Welland/ProCards 3489

GARCIA, SANTIAGO
88 Vancouver/CMC 13
88 Vancouver/ProCards 764

GARCIA-LUNA, FRANK
92 Welland/ClassicBest 8

GARDINER, MIKE
92 O-Pee-Chee 694
91 PaniniTopFifteen 91

GARDNER, BILL
77 O-Pee-Chee 198
62 ShirriffCoin 211
77 MTL
77 MTL/RedpathSugar

GARDNER, JEFF
94 PaniniSticker 255

GARDNER, MARK
90 FleerCdn. 646
90 O-Pee-Chee 284
91 O-Pee-Chee 757
92 O-Pee-Chee 119
93 opcPremier 21
92 MTL/Durivage 9

GARDNER, BOB CLAYTON
52 Parkhurst 88

GARDNER, ROB
71 O-Pee-Chee 734
72 O-Pee-Chee 22
73 O-Pee-Chee 222

GARDNER, WES
90 FleerCdn. 275
90 O-Pee-Chee 38
91 O-Pee-Chee 629

GARDNER, WILLIAM L.
23 WillardsChoc.(V100) 47

GARDON, RAMON
94 GarciaPhoto 91

GARIBALDI, BOB
71 O-Pee-Chee 701

GARLAND, WAYNE
74 O-Pee-Chee 596
76 O-Pee-Chee 414
77 O-Pee-Chee 138
78 O-Pee-Chee 15
81 O-Pee-Chee 272

GARMAN, MIKE
78 Dimanche/DernièreHeure
71 O-Pee-Chee 512
72 O-Pee-Chee 79
73 O-Pee-Chee 616
75 O-Pee-Chee 584
76 O-Pee-Chee 34
79 O-Pee-Chee 88

GARNER, PHIL
75 O-Pee-Chee 623
76 O-Pee-Chee 57
77 O-Pee-Chee 34
78 O-Pee-Chee 203
79 O-Pee-Chee 200
80 O-Pee-Chee 65
81 O-Pee-Chee 99
83 O-Pee-Chee 128
84 O-Pee-Chee 119
85 O-Pee-Chee 206
86 O-Pee-Chee 83

87 O-Pee-Chee 304
92 O-Pee-Chee 291
83 opcSticker 170, 237
84 opcSticker 63
85 opcSticker 64
86 opcSticker 32
87 opcSticker 30
86 opcTattoo 24

GARR, RALPH
70 O-Pee-Chee 172
71 O-Pee-Chee 494
72 O-Pee-Chee 85, 260
73 O-Pee-Chee 15
74 O-Pee-Chee 570
75 O-Pee-Chee 306, 550
76 O-Pee-Chee 410
77 O-Pee-Chee 77
78 O-Pee-Chee 195
79 O-Pee-Chee 156
80 O-Pee-Chee 142

GARRELTS, SCOTT
90 FleerCdn. 56
86 Leaf 180
87 Leaf 75
86 O-Pee-Chee 395
87 O-Pee-Chee 37
88 O-Pee-Chee 97
89 O-Pee-Chee 214
90 O-Pee-Chee 602
91 O-Pee-Chee 361
92 O-Pee-Chee 558
86 opcSticker 86
87 opcSticker 89
88 opcSticker 90
86 opcTansfer 16
88 PaniniSticker 416
90 PaniniSticker 367

GARRETT, ADRIAN
71 O-Pee-Chee 576
74 O-Pee-Chee 656
76 O-Pee-Chee 562
93 Edmonton/ProCards 1154
94 Edmonton/ProCards 2992

GARRETT, GREG
71 O-Pee-Chee 377

GARRETT, RONALD
77 MTL/RedpathSugar

GARRETT, WAYNE
71 O-Pee-Chee 228
72 O-Pee-Chee 518
73 O-Pee-Chee 562
74 O-Pee-Chee 510
75 O-Pee-Chee 111
76 O-Pee-Chee 222
77 O-Pee-Chee 117
78 O-Pee-Chee 198
77 MTL
77 MTL/RedpathSugar

GARRIDO, GIL
70 O-Pee-Chee 48
71 O-Pee-Chee 173

GARRO, LAZARO
94 GarciaPhoto 24

GARVEY, DON
91 Welland/Best 4
91 Welland/ProCards 3577

GARVEY, STEVE
82 FBI BoxBottoms
85 GeneralMills
85 Leaf 94
86 Leaf 56
87 Leaf 114
71 O-Pee-Chee 341
73 O-Pee-Chee 213
74 O-Pee-Chee 575
75 O-Pee-Chee 140, 212
76 O-Pee-Chee 150
77 O-Pee-Chee 255
78 O-Pee-Chee 190
79 O-Pee-Chee 21
80 O-Pee-Chee 152
81 O-Pee-Chee 251
82 O-Pee-Chee 179,180
83 O-Pee-Chee 198
84 O-Pee-Chee 380
85 O-Pee-Chee 177
86 O-Pee-Chee 4
87 O-Pee-Chee 100
82 opcSticker 54
83 opcSticker 243
84 opcSticker 156
85 opcStick. 1,2,13,14,149,176
86 opcSticker 104,148
87 opcSticker 115
86 opcTattoo 5
87 StuartBakery 12

GARVIN, JERRY
92 Nabisco 14
78 O-Pee-Chee 49
79 O-Pee-Chee 145
80 O-Pee-Chee 320
81 O-Pee-Chee 124
82 O-Pee-Chee 264
78 TOR

GASKILL, DEREK
96 StCatharines/Best 9

GASPAR, ROD
70 O-Pee-Chee 371
71 O-Pee-Chee 383

GASTON, CLARENCE (CITO)
97 HitTheBooks
71 O-Pee-Chee 25
72 O-Pee-Chee 431,432
73 O-Pee-Chee 159
74 O-Pee-Chee 364
75 O-Pee-Chee 427
76 O-Pee-Chee 558
90 O-Pee-Chee 201
91 O-Pee-Chee 81
92 O-Pee-Chee 699
93 O-Pee-Chee-WSChamps 18
84 TOR/FireSafety
85 TOR/FireSafety
86 TOR/FireSafety
87 TOR/FireSafety
88 TOR/FireSafety
89 TOR/FireSafety
90 TOR/FireSafety
91 TOR/FireSafety
91 TOR/Score 36
92 TOR/FireSafety
93 TOR/Dempster's 13
93 TOR/Donruss 28
93 TOR/FireSafety
93 TOR/McDonalds 15,24
95 TOR/OhHenry
96 TOR/OhHenry
97 TOR/Sizzler

GASTON, MILT
33 WWGum(V353) 65

GATES, BRENT
92 O-Pee-Chee 216
94 O-Pee-Chee 231, -DD 15

GATES, JOE
81 Edmonton/RedRooster 16

GATES, MIKE
83 O-Pee-Chee 195

GATEWOOD, AUBREY
66 O-Pee-Chee 42

GAUNT,
1912 ImperialTobacco(C46) 69

GEBHARD, BOB
82 Dimanche/DernièreHeure
72 O-Pee-Chee 28

GEDDES, JIM
73 O-Pee-Chee 561

GEDMAN, RICH
90 FleerCdn. 276
86 Leaf 145
87 Leaf 254
84 O-Pee-Chee 296
85 O-Pee-Chee 18
86 O-Pee-Chee 375
87 O-Pee-Chee 137
88 O-Pee-Chee 245
89 O-Pee-Chee 178
90 O-Pee-Chee 123
84 opcSticker 222
85 opcSticker 217
86 opcSticker 248
87 opcSticker 247
88 opcSticker 252
89 opcSticker 253
86 opcTattoo 17
88 PaniniSticker 24

GEHRIG, LOU
92 HomersClassic 9
85 Leaf 635
73 O-Pee-Chee 472
76 O-Pee-Chee 341
33 WWGum(V353) 55
34 WWGum(V354) 92
36 WWGum(V355) 96

GEHRINGER, CHARLIE
37 O-Pee-Chee(V300) 112
34 WWGum(V354) 57
36 WWGum(V355) 42
39 WWGum(V351A)
39 WWGum(V351B)

GEIGER, GARY
62 PostCereal 60
62 ShirriffCoin 38

GEISEL, DAVE
84 O-Pee-Chee 256

GELBERT, CHARLEY
36 WWGum(V355) 49

GELNAR, JOHN
65 O-Pee-Chee 143
70 O-Pee-Chee 393
71 O-Pee-Chee 604

GENDRON, JON
94 Welland/Classic 11
94 Welland/ProCards 3490

GENTILE, JIM
66 O-Pee-Chee 45
62 PostCereal 27
62 ShirriffCoin 1

GENTLEMAN, JEAN P.
88 Hamilton/ProCards 1743

GENTRY, GARY
69 O-Pee-Chee 31
70 O-Pee-Chee 153
71 O-Pee-Chee 725
72 O-Pee-Chee 105
73 O-Pee-Chee 288
74 O-Pee-Chee 415
75 O-Pee-Chee 393

GERARD, ALFONZO (CHICO)
52 LavalDairy 88

GERBER, CRAIG
84 Edmonton/Cramer 105
86 Edmonton/ProCards
88 Edmonton/ProCards 583

GERBER, WALTER
21 Neilson's(V61) 49

GEREN, BOB
90 FleerCdn. 442
90 O-Pee-Chee 536
91 O-Pee-Chee 716
92 O-Pee-Chee 341
90 PaniniSticker 128
91 PaniniSticker 323

GERHART, KEN
87 Leaf 30
88 O-Pee-Chee 271
89 O-Pee-Chee 192
88 PaniniSticker 14

GERONIMO, CESAR
71 O-Pee-Chee 447
73 O-Pee-Chee 156
74 O-Pee-Chee 181
75 O-Pee-Chee 41
76 O-Pee-Chee 24
77 O-Pee-Chee 160
78 O-Pee-Chee 32
79 O-Pee-Chee 111
80 O-Pee-Chee 247

GERSHBERG, HOWIE
97 Vancouver/Best 3

GETTMAN, JAKE
1912 ImperialTobacco(C46) 40

GHARRITY, EDWARD P.
21 Neilson' 50
23 WillardsChoc.(V100) 48

GHOLSTON, RICO
92 Welland/ClassicBest 9

GIAMATTI, A. BARTLETT
90 O-Pee-Chee 396

GIAMBI, JASON
95 Edmonton/Macri

GIANNELLI, RAY
91 TOR/Score 33

GIBBON, JOE
65 O-Pee-Chee 54
68 O-Pee-Chee 32
69 O-Pee-Chee 158
70 O-Pee-Chee 517
72 O-Pee-Chee 382

GIBBS, JAKE
65 O-Pee-Chee 226
66 O-Pee-Chee 117
68 O-Pee-Chee 89
71 O-Pee-Chee 382

GIBSON, BOB
65 O-Pee-Chee 12
68 O-Pee-Chee 100
69 OPC 8,10,12,107,200
69 OPC-DeckleEgde 7
70 OPC 67,71,530, -Booklet 22
71 O-Pee-Chee 72,450
72 O-Pee-Chee 130
73 O-Pee-Chee 190
74 O-Pee-Chee 350
75 O-Pee-Chee 3,150,206
89 London/ProCards 1358
84 Vancouver/Cramer 40
86 Vancouver/ProCards

GIBSON, GEORGE
23 WillardsChoc.(V100) 49

GIBSON, HAL
68 O-Pee-Chee 162
69 O-Pee-Chee 156

GIBSON, KIRK
90 FleerCdn. 393
86 GeneralMills
87 GeneralMills
85 Leaf 103
86 Leaf 1
87 Leaf 104
88 Leaf 136
81 O-Pee-Chee 315
82 O-Pee-Chee 105
83 O-Pee-Chee 321
84 O-Pee-Chee 65
85 O-Pee-Chee 372
86 O-Pee-Chee 295
87 O-Pee-Chee 386
88 O-Pee-Chee 201
89 O-Pee-Chee 340,382
90 O-Pee-Chee 150
91 O-Pee-Chee 490
92 O-Pee-Chee 720
91 opcPremier 50
82 opcSticker 184
83 opcSticker 67
84 opcSticker 272
85 opcSticker 19,267
86 opcSticker 266
87 opcSticker 273
88 opcSticker 267
89 opcSticker 66,-SuperStar 49
86 opcTattoo 22
88 PaniniSticker 95
89 PaniniSticker 16,17,107,479
90 PaniniSticker 271
92 PaniniSticker 100
87 StuartBakery 19

GIBSON, PAUL
90 FleerCdn. 602
90 O-Pee-Chee 11
91 O-Pee-Chee 431
92 O-Pee-Chee 143
92 opcPremier 174
89 opcSticker 323
89 PaniniSticker 331

GIBSON, RUSS
69 O-Pee-Chee 89
70 O-Pee-Chee 237
71 O-Pee-Chee 738

GIL, BENJI
92 O-Pee-Chee 534
93 opcPremier 27

GILBERT, ANDY
73 O-Pee-Chee 252
74 O-Pee-Chee 78

GILBREATH, ROD
74 O-Pee-Chee 93
75 O-Pee-Chee 431
76 O-Pee-Chee 306
79 O-Pee-Chee 296

GILES, BRIAN
84 O-Pee-Chee 234
83 opcSticker 322
84 opcSticker 111
88 Calgary/CMC 15
88 Calgary/ProCards 784

GILKEY, BERNARD
91 O-Pee-Chee 126
92 O-Pee-Chee 746
93 O-Pee-Chee 61
91 opcPremier 51
93 PaniniSticker 197
94 PaniniSticker 242

GILLENWATER, CARDEN
50 WWGum(V362) 32

GILLETTE, MIKE
92 London/ProCards 636
92 London/SkyBox 409

GILLIAM, JIM
52 Parkhurst 68
73 O-Pee-Chee 569
74 O-Pee-Chee 144
60 opcTattoo 19
62 PostCereal 112
62 ShirriffCoin 201

GILLIGAN, LARRY
92 Hamilton/ClassicBest 18

GIONFRIDDO, AL
50 WWGum(V362) 24

GIRARDI, JOE
90 FleerCdn. 31
90 O-Pee-Chee 12
91 O-Pee-Chee 214
92 O-Pee-Chee 529
91 PaniniSticker 42

GIRO, MIGUEL
94 GarciaPhoto 129

GIUSTI, DAVE
68 O-Pee-Chee 182
69 O-Pee-Chee 98
70 O-Pee-Chee 372
71 O-Pee-Chee 562
72 O-Pee-Chee 190
73 O-Pee-Chee 465
74 O-Pee-Chee 82
75 O-Pee-Chee 53
76 O-Pee-Chee 352

GLADDEN, DANNY
90 FleerCdn. 375
85 Leaf 30
86 O-Pee-Chee 336
87 O-Pee-Chee 46
88 O-Pee-Chee 206
89 O-Pee-Chee 387
90 O-Pee-Chee 298
91 O-Pee-Chee 778
92 O-Pee-Chee 177
93 O-Pee-Chee 100
92 opcPremier 11
85 opcSticker 166,374
86 opcSticker 90
87 opcSticker 93
88 opcSticker 19,281
89 opcSticker 286
88 PaniniSticker 143
89 PaniniSticker 392
90 PaniniSticker 111
91 PaniniSticker 304
92 PaniniSticker 121
93 PaniniSticker 118

GLADDING, FRED
65 O-Pee-Chee 37
67 O-Pee-Chee 192
69 O-Pee-Chee 58
70 O-Pee-Chee 208
71 O-Pee-Chee 381
72 O-Pee-Chee 507
73 O-Pee-Chee 17

GLADU, RONALD
43-47 Montréal/ParadeSportive

GLANE, WILLIAM CHARLES
52 Parkhurst 50

GLAVINE, TOM
93 Ben'sDIsk 6
90 FleerCdn. 583
90 O-Pee-Chee 506
91 O-Pee-Chee 82
92 O-Pee-Chee 305
93 O-Pee-Chee 132
94 O-Pee-Chee 250
92 opcPremier 49
93 opcPremier -StarPerf 21
88 opcSticker 44
89 PaniniSticker 34
90 PaniniSticker 219
92 PaniniSticker 288
93 PaniniSticker 159,179
94 PaniniSticker 14,145
92 PizzaHut/DietPepsi 5

GLEASON, WILLIAM J.
23 WillardsChoc.(V100) 50

GLEASON, WILLIAM P.
23 WillardsChoc.(V100) 51

GLEATON, JERRY DON
91 O-Pee-Chee 597
92 O-Pee-Chee 272
93 Edmonton/ProCards 1130

GLYNN, BILL
50 WWGum(V362) 42

GODINEZ, EVENECER
94 GarciaPhoto 107

GOFF, JERRY
91 PaniniSticker 153

GOGGIN, CHUCK
74 O-Pee-Chee 457

GOGOLEWSKI, BILL
71 O-Pee-Chee 559
72 O-Pee-Chee 424
73 O-Pee-Chee 27
74 O-Pee-Chee 242

GOHL, VINCENT LEO (LEFTY)
52 Parkhurst 78

GOHR, GREG
93 opcPremier 17
91 London/LineDrive 385
91 London/ProCards 1871

GOLDEN, BRIAN
89 Hamilton/Star 16

GOLTZ, DAVE
73 O-Pee-Chee 148
74 O-Pee-Chee 636
75 O-Pee-Chee 419
76 O-Pee-Chee 136
77 O-Pee-Chee 73
78 O-Pee-Chee 5,142
79 O-Pee-Chee 10
80 O-Pee-Chee 108
81 O-Pee-Chee 289

GOMEZ, CHRIS
94 O-Pee-Chee-DD 5

GOMEZ, LEFTY
92 Homers 3
36 WWGum(V355) 56

GOMEZ, LEO
92 O-Pee-Chee 84
93 O-Pee-Chee 117
91 opcPremier 52
92 opcPremier 161
92 PaniniSticker 67
93 PaniniSticker 74

GOMEZ, LUIS
78 O-Pee-Chee 121
79 O-Pee-Chee 128
80 O-Pee-Chee 95
78 TOR
79 TOR/BubbleYum

GOMEZ, PRESTON
69 O-Pee-Chee 74
70 O-Pee-Chee 513
71 O-Pee-Chee 737
73 O-Pee-Chee 624
74 O-Pee-Chee 31
75 O-Pee-Chee 487

GONZALES, FRANK
97 Calgary/Best 12

GONZALES, LARRY
93 Vancouver/ProCards 2601

GONZALES, LUIS
93 O-Pee-Chee 178

GONZALES, RENE
89 O-Pee-Chee 213
90 O-Pee-Chee 787
91 O-Pee-Chee 377
92 O-Pee-Chee 681
91 opcPremier 53
89 opcSticker 234
91 TOR/FireSafety
91 TOR/Score 14

GONZALES, TONY
68 O-Pee-Chee 1

GONZALEZ, ALEX
97 HitTheBooks
94 OPC 258, -HotProspect 8
95 TOR/OhHenry
96 TOR/OhHenry
97 TOR/Sizzler 1, 51

GONZALEZ, FERNANDO
74 O-Pee-Chee 649

GONZALEZ, FRANK
92 London/ProCards 628
92 London/SkyBox 410

GONZALEZ, GERMAN
90 FleerCdn. 376
90 O-Pee-Chee 266

GONZALEZ, JIMMY
92 O-Pee-Chee 564

GONZALEZ, JOSE
90 FleerCdn. 394
90 O-Pee-Chee 98
91 O-Pee-Chee 279
92 Edmonton/SkyBox 160

GONZALEZ, JUAN
90 FleerCdn. 297
90 O-Pee-Chee 331
91 O-Pee-Chee 224
92 O-Pee-Chee 27
93 O-Pee-Chee 97
94 O-Pee-Chee 28, -AS 4
91 opcPremier 54
93 opcPremier-StarPerf. 7
92 PaniniSticker 81
93 PaniniSticker 86
94 PaniniSticker 6,127
94 PostCdn. 15

GONZALEZ, LARRY
92 Edmonton/ProCards 3542
92 Edmonton/SkyBox 159

GONZALEZ, LUIS
92 O-Pee-Chee 12
94 O-Pee-Chee 263
92 opcPremier 103
92 PaniniSticker 158
93 PaniniSticker 175

GONZALEZ, LUIS ENRIQUE
94 GarciaPhoto 95

GONZALEZ, PEDRO
65 O-Pee-Chee 97

GONZALEZ, RENE
93 PaniniSticker 11

GONZALEZ, TONY
65 O-Pee-Chee 72
70 O-Pee-Chee 105
71 O-Pee-Chee 256

GOODEN, DWIGHT (DOC.)
90 FleerCdn. 204
86 GeneralMills
87 GeneralMills
85 Leaf 234
86 Leaf 26
87 Leaf 84
88 Leaf 48
85 O-Pee-Chee 41
86 O-Pee-Chee 250, F
87 O-Pee-Chee 130
88 O-Pee-Chee 287
89 O-Pee-Chee 30
90 O-Pee-Chee 510
91 O-Pee-Chee 330
92 O-Pee-Chee 725
93 O-Pee-Chee 92
94 O-Pee-Chee 24
91 opcPremier 55
92 opcPremier 47
85 opcSticker 3,4,107,280,371
86 opcSticker 6,94
87 opcSticker 5,6,96,163
88 opcSticker 101,-SStar 25
89 opcSticker 99,162
89 opcSticker-SuperStar 59
86 opcTattoo 20
88 PaniniSticker 337
89 PaniniSticker 131,227
90 PaniniSticker 297
91 PaniniSticker 86
93 PaniniSticker 245
94 PaniniSticker 217
91 PaniniTopFifteen 60,74
91 PetroCanada 12
92 PizzaHut/DietPepsi 2

GOODMAN, BILLY
53 Exhibits 63

GOODSON, ED
73 O-Pee-Chee 197
74 O-Pee-Chee 494
75 O-Pee-Chee 322
76 O-Pee-Chee 386

GOOSSEN, GREG
70 O-Pee-Chee 271

GORDAN, RICKEY
89 PaniniSticker 144

GORDON, DON
86 TOR/Ault Foods
86 TOR/FireSafety

GORDAN, SIDNEY
50 PalmDairies

GORDON, TOM
90 FleerCdn. 108
90 O-Pee-Chee 752
91 O-Pee-Chee 248
92 O-Pee-Chee 431
93 O-Pee-Chee 75
90 PaniniSticker 89
91 PaniniSticker 284
94 PaniniSticker 73

GORTON, CHRIS
89 Hamilton/Star 15

GOSGER, JIM
66 O-Pee-Chee 114
67 O-Pee-Chee 17
71 O-Pee-Chee 284
71 MTL/ProStar
71 MTL/LaPizzaRoyale

GOSLIN, GOOSE
37 O-Pee-Chee(V300) 111
36 WWGum(V355) 43

GOSLIN, LEON
21 Neilson's(V61) 8

GOSSAGE, RICH (GOOSE)
82 FBI BoxBottoms
85 Leaf 204
86 Leaf 2
73 O-Pee-Chee 174
74 O-Pee-Chee 542
75 O-Pee-Chee 554
76 O-Pee-Chee 180
76 O-Pee-Chee 205
79 O-Pee-Chee 114
80 O-Pee-Chee 77
81 O-Pee-Chee 48
82 O-Pee-Chee 117,286,396
83 O-Pee-Chee 240,241
84 O-Pee-Chee 121
85 O-Pee-Chee 90
86 O-Pee-Chee 104,380
88 O-Pee-Chee 170
89 O-Pee-Chee 162,D
92 O-Pee-Chee 215
82 opcSticker 140,217
83 opcSticker 100
84 opcSticker 316
85 opcSticker 147
86 opcSticker 107
87 opcSticker 109
86 opcTattoo 1

GOSSELIN, PAT
93 Welland/ProCards 3363

GOTAY, JULIO
68 O-Pee-Chee 41

GOTT, JIM
90 FleerCdn. 466
85 Leaf 136
88 Leaf 253
83 O-Pee-Chee 62
84 O-Pee-Chee 9
85 O-Pee-Chee 311
86 O-Pee-Chee 106
89 O-Pee-Chee 172
90 O-Pee-Chee 292
91 O-Pee-Chee 606
92 O-Pee-Chee 517
89 PaniniSticker 162
84 TOR/FireSafety

GOURRIEL, LOURDES
94 GarciaPhoto 70

GOWDY, HENRY M.
23 Neilson's 13
23 WillardsChoc.(V100) 52

GOZZO, MAURO (GOOSE)
90 FleerCdn. 82
90 O-Pee-Chee 274

GRABARKEWITZ, BILLY
70 O-Pee-Chee 446
71 O-Pee-Chee 85
73 O-Pee-Chee 301
74 O-Pee-Chee 214
75 O-Pee-Chee 233

GRACE, EARL
36 WWGum(V355) 103

GRACE, MARK
90 FleerCdn. 32
93 HumptyDumpty 28
88 Leaf 40
89 O-Pee-Chee 297
90 O-Pee-Chee 240
91 O-Pee-Chee 520
92 O-Pee-Chee 140
93 O-Pee-Chee 86
94 O-Pee-Chee 146
89 opcSticker 50, 324
89 PaniniSticker 55
90 PaniniSticker 241
91 PaniniSticker 43
92 PaniniSticker 182
93 PaniniSticker 203
94 PaniniSticker 153

GRAHAM
1912 ImperialTobacco(C46) 63

GRAHAM, DAN
81 O-Pee-Chee 161

GRAHAM, STEVE
88 Hamilton/ProCards 1745
89 Hamilton/Star 13

GRAHE, JOE
91 O-Pee-Chee 426
92 O-Pee-Chee 496
93 O-Pee-Chee 199
92 opcPremier 158
91 Edmonton/LineDrive 164
91 Edmonton/ProCards 1513

GRAMMAS, ALEX
73 O-Pee-Chee 296
74 O-Pee-Chee 326
76 O-Pee-Chee 606
62 PostCereal 168
62 ShirriffCoin 197

GRANGER, JEFF
94 O-Pee-Chee 51
97 Calgary/Best 13

GRANGER, WAYNE
70 O-Pee-Chee 73
71 O-Pee-Chee 379
73 O-Pee-Chee 523
74 O-Pee-Chee 644
76 O-Pee-Chee 516

GRANT, BRIAN
94 StCatharines/Classic 10
94 StCatharines/ProCards 3636

GRANT, CHARLES
52 Parkhurst 10

GRANT, JAMES
62 ShirriffCoin 26

GRANT, JIM
66 O-Pee-Chee 40
71 O-Pee-Chee 509
72 O-Pee-Chee 111

GRANT, MARK
90 FleerCdn. 156
90 O-Pee-Chee 537
91 O-Pee-Chee 287
92 O-Pee-Chee 392
92 Calgary/ProCards 3727

GRANTHAM, GEORGE
33 WWGum(V353) 66

GRATEROL, BEIKER
96 StCatharines/Best 10

GRAY, DENNIS JR.
91 StCatharines/ClassicBest 16
91 StCatharines/ProCards 3388

GRAY, GARY
82 O-Pee-Chee 78
82 opcSticker 233

GRAY, JEFF
91 O-Pee-Chee 731

GRAY, LORENZO
82 Edmonton/TCMA 10

GRBA, ELI
82 Vancouver/TCMA 23
88 Vancouver/ProCards 769

GREBECK, BRIAN
96 Vancouver/Best 14

GREBECK, CRAIG
91 O-Pee-Chee 446
92 O-Pee-Chee 273

GREEN, DALLAS
65 O-Pee-Chee 203
62 ShirriffCoin 219

GREEN, DAVID
85 Leaf 191
84 O-Pee-Chee 362
85 O-Pee-Chee 87
86 O-Pee-Chee 122
83 opcSticker 323
84 opcSticker 149
85 opcSticker 145

GREEN, CHRIS
86 Edmonton/ProCards

GREEN, DICK
65 O-Pee-Chee 168
67 O-Pee-Chee 54
70 O-Pee-Chee 311
71 O-Pee-Chee 258
73 O-Pee-Chee 456
74 O-Pee-Chee 392
75 O-Pee-Chee 91

GREEN, DON
89 Hamilton//Star 18

GREEN, GARY
91 O-Pee-Chee 184

GREEN, GENE
62 PostCereal 72
62 ShirriffCoin 70

GREEN, LENNY
62 PostCereal 87
62 ShirriffCoin 69

GREEN, OTIS
93 Vancouver/ProCards 2589

GREEN, PUMPSIE (ELIJAH)
62 ShirriffCoin 187

GREEN, SHAWN
97 HitTheBooks
92 O-Pee-Chee 276
95 TOR/OhHenry
96 OhHenry
97 TOR/Sizzler 13

GREEN, STEVE
90 London/ProCards 1279

GREEN THOMAS
90 Welland/Pucko 13

GREEN, TYLER
92 O-Pee-Chee 764

GREENBERG, HANK
37 O-Pee-Chee(V300) 107
36 WWGum(V355) 41

GREENE, TODD
96 Vancouver/Best 15
97 Vancouver/Best 16

GREENE, TOMMY
90 FleerCdn. 584
91 O-Pee-Chee 486
92 O-Pee-Chee 83
93 O-Pee-Chee 144
94 O-Pee-Chee 137

GREENWELL, MIKE
90 FleerCdn. 277,632
88 Leaf 153
88 O-Pee-Chee 274
89 O-Pee-Chee 374
90 O-Pee-Chee 70
91 O-Pee-Chee 792
92 O-Pee-Chee 113
93 O-Pee-Chee 285
94 O-Pee-Chee 49
88 opcSticker 249,312
89 opcSticker 255,-SStar 16
88 PaniniSticker 32
89 PaniniSticker 280
90 PaniniSticker 16
91 PaniniSticker 268
92 PaniniSticker 91
93 PaniniSticker 96
94 PaniniSticker 30
91 PaniniTopFifteen 32

GREGG, TOMMY
90 FleerCdn. 585
90 O-Pee-Chee 223
91 O-Pee-Chee 742
92 O-Pee-Chee 53
89 PaniniSticker 32
90 PaniniSticker 224
91 PaniniSticker 19

GREIF, BILL
72 O-Pee-Chee 101
73 O-Pee-Chee 583
74 O-Pee-Chee 102
75 O-Pee-Chee 168
76 O-Pee-Chee 184
77 O-Pee-Chee 243

GREIR, ANTON
88 Hamilton/ProCards 1723

GRICH, BOB
85 Leaf 88
71 O-Pee-Chee 193
72 O-Pee-Chee 338
73 O-Pee-Chee 418
74 O-Pee-Chee 109
75 O-Pee-Chee 225
76 O-Pee-Chee 335
77 O-Pee-Chee 28
78 O-Pee-Chee 133
79 O-Pee-Chee 248
80 O-Pee-Chee 326
81 O-Pee-Chee 182
82 O-Pee-Chee 284
83 O-Pee-Chee 381,387
84 O-Pee-Chee 315
85 O-Pee-Chee 155
86 O-Pee-Chee 155
87 O-Pee-Chee 4
82 opcSticker 4,162
83 opcSticker 43
84 opcSticker 228
85 opcSticker 230
86 opcSticker 181
86 opcTattoo 23
85 Edmonton/Cramer 4

GRIEVE, TOM
71 O-Pee-Chee 167
73 O-Pee-Chee 579
74 O-Pee-Chee 268
75 O-Pee-Chee 234
76 O-Pee-Chee 106
79 O-Pee-Chee 138

GRIFFEY, KEN (SR.)
90 Ben's/HolsumDisks 11
90 FleerCdn. 420
85 Leaf 193
86 Leaf 48
88 Leaf 165
74 O-Pee-Chee 598
75 O-Pee-Chee 284
76 O-Pee-Chee 128
77 O-Pee-Chee 11
78 O-Pee-Chee 140
79 O-Pee-Chee 216
80 O-Pee-Chee 285
81 O-Pee-Chee 280
82 O-Pee-Chee 171,330
83 O-Pee-Chee 110
84 O-Pee-Chee 306
85 O-Pee-Chee 380
86 O-Pee-Chee 40
87 O-Pee-Chee 114
88 O-Pee-Chee 255
90 O-Pee-Chee 581
91 O-Pee-Chee 465
92 O-Pee-Chee 250
83 opcSticker 98
84 opcSticker 317
88 opcSticker 38
88 PaniniSticker 248
87 StuartBakery 2

GRIFFEY, KEN (JR.)
91 Ben's/HolsumDisks 9
92 Ben'sDisk 10
90 FleerCdn. 513
93 HumptyDumpty 14
92 McDonald's 22
90 O-Pee-Chee 336
91 O-Pee-Chee 392,790
92 O-Pee-Chee 50
93 O-Pee-Chee 91
94 O-Pee-Chee 22, -AS 8
91 opcPremier 56
92 opcPremier 167
93 opcPremier-StarPerf. 9
90 PaniniSticker 155
91 PaniniSticker 172,233
92 PaniniSticker 60,277
93 PaniniSticker 63
94 PaniniSticker 118
91 PaniniTopFifteen 116
91 PetroCanada 23
92 PizzaHut/DietPepsi 26
91 PostCdn. 26
93 PostCdn. 9
94 PostCdn. 10
95 PostCdn. 1

GRIFFIN, ALFREDO
90 FleerCdn. 395
85 Leaf 230
86 Leaf 34
87 Leaf 198
80 O-Pee-Chee 290
81 O-Pee-Chee 277, -Poster 15
82 O-Pee-Chee 148
83 O-Pee-Chee 294
84 O-Pee-Chee 76
85 O-Pee-Chee 361
86 O-Pee-Chee 121
87 O-Pee-Chee 111
88 O-Pee-Chee 42
89 O-Pee-Chee 62
90 O-Pee-Chee 643
91 O-Pee-Chee 226, G
82 opcSticker 252
83 opcSticker 129
84 opcSticker 369
85 opcSticker 366
86 opcSticker 168
87 opcSticker 166
88 opcSticker 169
89 opcSticker 59
86 opcTattoo 16
88 PaniniSticker 172
90 PaniniSticker 270
91 PaniniSticker 58
92 PaniniSticker 195
87 StuartBakery 24
79 TOR/BubbleYum
84 TOR/FireSafety
92 TOR/FireSafety
93 TOR/Dempster 12
93 TOR/Donruss 6
93 TOR/FireSafety
96 TOR/OhHenry
97 TOR/Sizzler 25

GRIFFIN, DOUG
71 O-Pee-Chee 176
73 O-Pee-Chee 96
74 O-Pee-Chee 219
75 O-Pee-Chee 454
76 O-Pee-Chee 654

GRIFFIN, IVY M.
23 WillardsChoc.(V100) 53

GRIFFIN, TOM
71 O-Pee-Chee 471
73 O-Pee-Chee 468
74 O-Pee-Chee 256
75 O-Pee-Chee 188
76 O-Pee-Chee 454

GRIFFITH, DERRELL
65 O-Pee-Chee 112

GRIFFITH, TOMMY
21 Neilson's(V61) 58
23 WillardsChoc.(V100) 54

GRILLI, STEVE
76 O-Pee-Chee 591

GRIMES, BURLEIGH A.
21 Neilson's(V61) 89
22 WilliamPaterson(V89) 31
23 WillardsChoc.(V100) 55
33 WWGum(V353) 64

GRIMES, OSCAR RAY
21 Neilson's(V61) 105

GRIMM, CHARLIE
23 WillardsChoc.(V100) 56
22 WilliamPaterson(V89) 43
33 WWGum(V353) 51
34 WWGum(V354) 61
36 WWGum(V355) 89

GRIMSLEY, JASON
90 FleerCdn. 653
90 O-Pee-Chee 493
91 O-Pee-Chee 173

GRIMSLEY, ROSS
78 Dimanche/DernièreHeure
72 O-Pee-Chee 99
73 O-Pee-Chee 357
74 O-Pee-Chee 59
75 O-Pee-Chee 458
76 O-Pee-Chee 257
77 O-Pee-Chee 47
79 O-Pee-Chee 4
80 O-Pee-Chee 195
86 Calgary/ProCards
87 Calgary/ProCards 2313
91 Calgary/LineDrive 75
91 Calgary/ProCards 531
92 Calgary/ProCards 3746
92 Calgary/SkyBox 75
93 Calgary/ProCards 1183

GRISHAM, WES
90 Welland/Pucko 15

GRISSOM, MARQUIS
90 FleerCdn. 347
93 HumptyDumpty 37
90 O-Pee-Chee 714
91 O-Pee-Chee 283
92 O-Pee-Chee 647
93 O-Pee-Chee 209
94 O-Pee-Chee 18, -AS 11
92 opcPremier 176
91 PaniniSticker 151
92 PaniniSticker 207
93 PaniniSticker 230
94 PaniniSticker 210
92 MTL/Durivage 10
93 MTL/McDonald's 5

GROAT, DICK
65 O-Pee-Chee 275
66 O-Pee-Chee 103
75 O-Pee-Chee 198
60 opcTattoo 20
62 PostCereal 172
62 ShirriffCoin 138

GROH, HEINIE
21 Neilson's(V61) 88
22 WilliamPaterson(V89) 23

GROOM, BUD
91 London/LineDrive 366
91 London/ProCards 1872

GROSS, GREG
75 O-Pee-Chee 334
76 O-Pee-Chee 171
79 O-Pee-Chee 302
80 O-Pee-Chee 364
85 O-Pee-Chee 117
86 O-Pee-Chee 302
87 O-Pee-Chee 338
89 O-Pee-Chee E

GROSS, KEVIN
90 FleerCdn. 348
87 O-Pee-Chee 163
88 O-Pee-Chee 20
89 O-Pee-Chee 215
90 O-Pee-Chee 465
91 O-Pee-Chee 674
92 O-Pee-Chee 334
93 O-Pee-Chee 111
86 opcSticker 119
88 opcSticker 118
89 opcSticker 116
89 PaniniSticker 147

GROSS, KIP
92 O-Pee-Chee 372

GROSS, WAYNE
78 O-Pee-Chee 106
80 O-Pee-Chee 189
81 O-Pee-Chee 86
82 O-Pee-Chee 303
84 O-Pee-Chee 263
85 O-Pee-Chee 233
86 O-Pee-Chee 173
84 opcSticker 333

GROSSMAN, DAVE
82 Edmonton/TCMA 24

GROTE, JERRY
69 O-Pee-Chee 55
70 O-Pee-Chee 183
71 O-Pee-Chee 278
73 O-Pee-Chee 113
74 O-Pee-Chee 311
75 O-Pee-Chee 158
76 O-Pee-Chee 143

GROVE, LEFTY
37 O-Pee-Chee(V300) 137
76 O-Pee-Chee 350
34 WWGum(V354) 54
36 WWGum(V355) 88

GRUBB, JOHNNY
74 O-Pee-Chee 32
75 O-Pee-Chee 298
76 O-Pee-Chee 422
77 O-Pee-Chee 165
79 O-Pee-Chee 99
80 O-Pee-Chee 165
82 O-Pee-Chee 193
83 opcSticker 123
87 opcSticker 265

GRUBB, SEAN
89 Hamilton/Star 17

GRUBER, KELLY
91 Ben's/HolsumDisks 15
92 Ben'sDisk 5
90 FleerCdn. 83
87 GeneralMills
92 McDonald's 3
87 O-Pee-Chee 191
88 O-Pee-Chee 113
89 O-Pee-Chee 29
90 O-Pee-Chee 505
91 O-Pee-Chee 370
92 O-Pee-Chee 298
93 OPC 156, -WSChamps 5
91 opcPremier 57
92 opcPremier 116
89 opcSticker 187
88 PaniniSticker 221
89 PaniniSticker 469
90 PaniniSticker 171
91 PaniniSticker 338
92 PaniniSticker 27
93 PaniniSticker 5
91 PaniniTopFifteen 22,112
91 PetroCanada 26
92 PizzaHut/DietPepsi 20
91 PostCdn. 15
92 PostCdn. 14
84 TOR/FireSafety
85 TOR/FireSafety
86 TOR/AultFoods
86 TOR/FireSafety
87 TOR/FireSafety
88 TOR/FireSafety
89 TOR/FireSafety
90 TOR/FireSafety
90 TOR/Hostess
91 TOR/FireSafety
91 TOR/Score 15
92 TOR/FireSafety
93 TOR/Donruss 7
93 TOR/McDonalds 17,19
96 TOR/OhHenry
97 TOR/Sizzler

GRUDZIELANEK MARK
96 HitTheBooks
96 MTL/Disk (x2)

GRUNHARD, DAN
90 Edmonton/CMC 16
90 Edmonton/ProCards 528
91 Edmonton/LineDrive 165
91 Edmonton/ProCards 1528

GRYSKEVICH, LARRY
89 Hamilton/Star 14

GRZENDA, JOE
69 O-Pee-Chee 121
71 O-Pee-Chee 518
72 O-Pee-Chee 13

GUANTE, CECILIO
90 FleerCdn. 298
87 O-Pee-Chee 219
90 O-Pee-Chee 532
87 opcSticker 127
86 opcTattoo 8

GUARACHE, JOSE
88 StCatharines/ProCards 2011

GUBICZA, MARK
90 FleerCdn. 633
86 Leaf 226
87 Leaf 238
85 O-Pee-Chee 127
87 O-Pee-Chee 326
88 O-Pee-Chee 378
89 O-Pee-Chee 379
90 O-Pee-Chee 20
91 O-Pee-Chee 265
92 O-Pee-Chee 741
93 O-Pee-Chee 99
88 opcSticker 262
89 opcSticker 271,-SStar 26
89 PaniniSticker 350
90 PaniniSticker 82

GUERRA, JESUS SANTIAGO
94 GarciaPhoto 131

GUERRERO, MARIO
73 O-Pee-Chee 607
74 O-Pee-Chee 192
75 O-Pee-Chee 152
76 O-Pee-Chee 499
79 O-Pee-Chee 131

GUERRERO, PATRICK
88 StCatharines/ProCards 2038

GUERRERO, PEDRO
88 FantasticSam's 20
90 FleerCdn. 250
86 GeneralMills
87 GeneralMills
85 Leaf 211
86 Leaf 105
87 Leaf 237
88 Leaf 101
82 O-Pee-Chee 247
83 O-Pee-Chee 116
84 O-Pee-Chee 90
85 O-Pee-Chee 34
86 O-Pee-Chee 145, G
87 O-Pee-Chee 360
88 O-Pee-Chee 111
89 O-Pee-Chee 68
90 O-Pee-Chee 610
91 O-Pee-Chee 20
92 O-Pee-Chee 470
91 opcPremier 58
82 opcSticker 55
83 opcSticker 248
84 opcSticker 75
85 opcSticker 70
86 opcSticker 65
87 opcSticker 69
88 opcSticker 75,-SuperStar 15
89 opcSticker 40
86 opcTattoo 23
88 PaniniSticker 314
89 PaniniSticker 183
90 PaniniSticker 211,335
91 PaniniSticker 31
92 PaniniSticker 172
87 StuartBakery 6

GUETTERMAN, LEE
90 FleerCdn. 443
88 O-Pee-Chee 382
90 O-Pee-Chee 286
91 O-Pee-Chee 62
92 O-Pee-Chee 578
90 PaniniSticker 118

GUEVARA, ERNESTO LEONEL
94 GarciaPhoto 118

GUIDRY, RON
85 Leaf 237
86 Leaf 36
87 Leaf 101
88 Leaf 180
76 O-Pee-Chee 599
79 O-Pee-Chee 264
80 O-Pee-Chee 157
81 O-Pee-Chee 250
82 O-Pee-Chee 9,10
83 O-Pee-Chee 104
84 O-Pee-Chee 110,204
85 O-Pee-Chee 388
86 O-Pee-Chee 109,H
87 O-Pee-Chee 375
88 O-Pee-Chee 127
83 opcSticker 102
84 opcSticker 194,318
85 opcSticker 313
86 opcSticker 302
87 opcSticker 301
88 opcSticker 296,-SStar 61
86 opcTattoo 14

GUILLEN, OZZIE
90 FleerCdn. 533
86 GeneralMills
86 Leaf 140
87 Leaf 117
88 Leaf 59
86 O-Pee-Chee 254
87 O-Pee-Chee 89
88 O-Pee-Chee 296
89 O-Pee-Chee 195
90 O-Pee-Chee 365
91 O-Pee-Chee 620
92 O-Pee-Chee 210
93 O-Pee-Chee 102
94 O-Pee-Chee 115
86 opcSticker 294,309
87 opcSticker 287
88 opcSticker 284
89 opcSticker 303
86 opcTattoo 5
88 PaniniSticker 58,59,61
89 PaniniSticker 309
90 PaniniSticker 41
91 PaniniSticker 315
92 PaniniSticker 128
93 PaniniSticker 138
94 PaniniSticker 47
87 StuartBakery 17

GUINN, BRIAN
92 Vancouver/SkyBox 629

GUINN, SKIP
70 O-Pee-Chee 316
71 O-Pee-Chee 741

GULAN, MIKE
92 Hamilton/ClassicBest 26

GULDEN, BRAD
85 O-Pee-Chee 251

GULLETT, DON
71 O-Pee-Chee 124
72 O-Pee-Chee 157
73 O-Pee-Chee 595
74 O-Pee-Chee 385
75 O-Pee-Chee 65
76 O-Pee-Chee 390
77 O-Pee-Chee 250
78 O-Pee-Chee 30
79 O-Pee-Chee 64

GULLICKSON, BILL
81 Dimanche/DernièreHeure
83 Dimanche/DernièreHeure
82 FBI BoxBottoms
85 Leaf 236
81 O-Pee-Chee 41
82 OPC 94,172, -Poster 21
83 O-Pee-Chee 31
84 O-Pee-Chee 318
85 O-Pee-Chee 143
86 O-Pee-Chee 229
88 O-Pee-Chee 329
92 O-Pee-Chee 508
93 O-Pee-Chee 124
84 opcSticker 96
85 opcSticker 91
86 opcSticker 78
87 opcSticker 140
92 PaniniSticker 112
93 PaniniSticker 112
94 PaniniSticker 65
82 MTL/Hygrade
82 MTL/Zellers
83 MTL
83 MTL/StuartBakery 15
84 MTL
84 MTL/StuartBakery 16

GUNDERSON, ERIC
93 Calgary/ProCards 1160

GURA, LARRY
71 O-Pee-Chee 203
73 O-Pee-Chee 501
74 O-Pee-Chee 616
75 O-Pee-Chee 557
76 O-Pee-Chee 319
80 O-Pee-Chee 154
81 O-Pee-Chee 130
82 O-Pee-Chee 147
83 O-Pee-Chee 340
84 O-Pee-Chee 264
82 opcSticker 195
83 opcSticker 395
84 opcSticker 285
85 opcSticker 278

GUTHRIE, MARK
90 O-Pee-Chee 317
91 O-Pee-Chee 698
92 O-Pee-Chee 548

GUTIERREZ, CESAR
69 O-Pee-Chee 16
70 O-Pee-Chee 269
71 O-Pee-Chee 154

GUTIERREZ, JACKIE
86 O-Pee-Chee 73
85 opcSticker 216,373

GUTIERREZ, RICKEY
94 O-Pee-Chee 47

GUTTERIDGE, DON
70 O-Pee-Chee 123

GUZMAN, JOSE
87 Leaf
88 Leaf 55
88 O-Pee-Chee 98
89 O-Pee-Chee 209
90 O-Pee-Chee 308
92 O-Pee-Chee 188
93 O-Pee-Chee 121
94 O-Pee-Chee 180
93 opcPremier 23
89 opcSticker 241
89 PaniniSticker 445

GUZMAN, JUAN
93 Ben'sDisk 14
97 HitTheBooks
93 HumptyDumpty 25
92 O-Pee-Chee 662
93 OPC 187, -WSChamp 6
94 O-Pee-Chee 177
92 opcPremier 168
93 opcPremier 36
93 PaniniSticker 33
94 PaniniSticker 138
93 PostCdn. 2
94 PostCdn. 6
91 TOR/Score 25
92 TOR/FireSafety
93 TOR/Dempster's 1
93 TOR/Donruss 17
93 TOR/FIreSafety (x2)
94 TOR
95 TOR/OhHenry
96 TOR/OhHenry
97 TOR/Sizzler 8

GUZMAN, SANTIAGO
72 O-Pee-Chee 316

GWOSDZ, DOUG
87 Calgary/ProCards 2331

GWYNN, CHRIS
90 O-Pee-Chee 456
91 O-Pee-Chee 99
92 O-Pee-Chee 604
92 opcPremier 9

GWYNN, TONY
90 Ben's/HolsumDisks 18
91 Ben's/HolsumDisks 5
88 FantasticSam's 18
90 FleerCdn. 157
87 HostessSticker
93 HumptyDumpty 47
85 Leaf 25
86 Leaf 41
87 Leaf 235
88 Leaf 90
83 O-Pee-Chee 143
85 O-Pee-Chee 383
86 O-Pee-Chee 10
87 O-Pee-Chee 198
88 O-Pee-Chee 360,F
89 O-Pee-Chee 51
90 O-Pee-Chee 403
91 O-Pee-Chee 180
92 O-Pee-Chee 270
93 O-Pee-Chee 94
94 O-Pee-Chee 109
91 opcPremier 59
92 opcPremier 106
84 opcSticker 160
85 opcSticker 146,170,174
86 opcSticker 105,146
87 opcSticker 106,155
88 opcSticker 115,-SStar 16
89 opcSticker 109,-SStar 50
86 opcTattoo 24
88 PaniniSticker 410,437
89 PaniniSticker 203
90 PaniniSticker 207,351
91 PaniniSticker 97
92 PaniniSticker 236,286
93 PaniniSticker 262
94 PaniniSticker 256
91 PaniniTopFifteen 104
91 PetroCanada 24
95 PostCdn. 13
87 StuartBakery 12

H

HAAS, DAVE
92 O-Pee-Chee 665

HAAS, MIKE
89 London/ProCards 1376

HAAS, MOOSE
87 Leaf 54
81 O-Pee-Chee 327
82 O-Pee-Chee 12
83 O-Pee-Chee 317
84 O-Pee-Chee 271
85 O-Pee-Chee 151
86 O-Pee-Chee 9
87 O-Pee-Chee 369
84 opcSticker 292
85 opcSticker 293
86 opcSticker 201
86 opcTattoo 2

HAAS, MULE
36 WWGum(V355) 68

HABYAN, JOHN
92 O-Pee-Chee 698

HACK, STAN
36 WWGum(V355) 105

HACKER, RICH
91 TOR/FireSafety
92 TOR/FireSafety
93 TOR/FireSafety

HADDIX, HARVEY
65 O-Pee-Chee 67
62 PostCereal 180

HADLEY, BUMP
34 WWGum(V354) 15

HAFEY, CHICK
34 WWGum(V354) 78
36 WWGum(V355) 94

HAGUE, JOE
70 O-Pee-Chee 362
71 O-Pee-Chee 96
73 O-Pee-Chee 447

HAHN, DON
71 O-Pee-Chee 94
72 O-Pee-Chee 269
74 O-Pee-Chee 291
75 O-Pee-Chee 182
71 MTL/ProStar

HAINES, JESSE
21 Neilson's(V61) 103
23 WillardsChoc.(V100) 57
34 WWGum(V354) 44
36 WWGum(V355) 93

HAIRSTON, JERRY
74 O-Pee-Chee 96
75 O-Pee-Chee 327
76 O-Pee-Chee 391
78 O-Pee-Chee 299

HALAMAN, SCOTT
88 Hamilton/ProCards 1720

HALE, CHIP
90 O-Pee-Chee 704

HALE, JOHN
76 O-Pee-Chee 228
79 O-Pee-Chee 23

HALE, ODELL
37 O-Pee-Chee(V300) 128

HALICKI, ED
75 O-Pee-Chee 467
76 O-Pee-Chee 423
79 O-Pee-Chee 354
80 O-Pee-Chee 115

HALL, ALBERT
88 O-Pee-Chee 213
89 O-Pee-Chee 153
88 opcSticker 39
89 opcSticker 30
88 PaniniSticker 249

HALL, DARREN
95 TOR/OhHenry

HALL, DICK
68 O-Pee-Chee 17
70 O-Pee-Chee 182
71 O-Pee-Chee 417

HALL, DREW
90 FleerCdn. 299
90 O-Pee-Chee 463
91 O-Pee-Chee 77

HALL, GRADY
88 Vancouver/CMC 8
88 Vancouver/ProCards 761
90 Vancouver/CMC 6
90 Vancouver/ProCards 484
91 Vancouver/LineDrive 632
91 Vancouver/ProCards 1589

HALL, JIMMIE
66 O-Pee-Chee 190
68 O-Pee-Chee 121
69 O-Pee-Chee 61

HALL, JOE
88 Hamilton/ProCards 1747
91 Vancouver/LineDrive 633
91 Vancouver/ProCards 1600
92 Vancouver/ProCards 2730
92 Vancouver/SkyBox 636

HALL, MEL
90 FleerCdn. 444
88 Leaf 109
84 O-Pee-Chee 4
85 O-Pee-Chee 263
86 O-Pee-Chee 138
87 O-Pee-Chee 51
88 O-Pee-Chee 318
89 O-Pee-Chee 173
90 O-Pee-Chee 436
91 O-Pee-Chee 738
92 O-Pee-Chee 223
84 opcSticker 380
85 opcSticker 254
87 opcSticker 206
88 opcSticker 205
88 PaniniSticker 79
89 PaniniSticker 328
90 PaniniSticker 122
92 PaniniSticker 141

HALL, TOM
70 O-Pee-Chee 169
71 O-Pee-Chee 313
72 O-Pee-Chee 417
73 O-Pee-Chee 8
74 O-Pee-Chee 248
75 O-Pee-Chee 108
76 O-Pee-Chee 621

HALLADAY, ROY
97 TOR/Sizzler 59

HALLAHAN, WILD BILL
36 WWGum(V355) 70

HALLER, TOM
67 O-Pee-Chee 65
68 O-Pee-Chee 185
69 OPC-Deckle 8
71 O-Pee-Chee 639
72 O-Pee-Chee 175,176
73 O-Pee-Chee 454

HALPERIN, MICHAEL
94 StCatharines/Classic 11
94 StCatharines/ProCards 3637

HAMBRIGHT, ROGER
72 O-Pee-Chee 124

HAMEL, MARCUS
90 Welland/Pucko 17

HAMILTON, BILL
52 LavalDairy 55

HAMILTON, DARRYL
90 FleerCdn. 325
91 O-Pee-Chee 781
92 O-Pee-Chee 278
93 O-Pee-Chee 158
94 O-Pee-Chee 58
93 PaniniSticker 41
94 PaniniSticker 80

HAMILTON, DAVE
73 O-Pee-Chee 214
74 O-Pee-Chee 633
75 O-Pee-Chee 428
76 O-Pee-Chee 237
77 O-Pee-Chee 224

HAMILTON, EARL
21 Neilson's(V61) 68

HAMILTON, JACK
67 O-Pee-Chee 2
68 O-Pee-Chee 193

HAMILTON, JEFF
90 FleerCdn. 396
90 O-Pee-Chee 426
91 O-Pee-Chee 552
92 O-Pee-Chee 151
88 PaniniSticker 312

HAMILTON, STEVE
69 O-Pee-Chee 69
70 O-Pee-Chee 349
71 O-Pee-Chee 627

HAMLIN, KEN
66 O-Pee-Chee 69
62 ShirriffCoin 34

HAMM, PETE
71 O-Pee-Chee 74
72 O-Pee-Chee 501

HAMMAKER, ATLEE
90 FleerCdn. 57
86 Leaf 220
84 O-Pee-Chee 85
85 O-Pee-Chee 351
87 O-Pee-Chee 358
89 O-Pee-Chee 2
90 O-Pee-Chee 447
91 O-Pee-Chee 34
83 opcSticker 324
84 opcSticker 165,175
85 opcSticker 165

HAMMOND, CHRIS
90 FleerCdn. 421
91 O-Pee-Chee 258
92 O-Pee-Chee 744
91 opcPremier 60

HAMPTON, ROBBIE
96 StCatharines/Best 11

HAMPTON, MIKE
93 opcPremier 80

HANCOCK, RYAN
96 Vancouver/Best 16
97 Vancouver/Best 17

HAND, RICH
71 O-Pee-Chee 24
72 O-Pee-Chee 317
73 O-Pee-Chee 398
74 O-Pee-Chee 571

HANDS, BILL
67 O-Pee-Chee 16
69 O-Pee-Chee 115
70 O-Pee-Chee 405
71 O-Pee-Chee 670
72 O-Pee-Chee 335
73 O-Pee-Chee 555
74 O-Pee-Chee 271
75 O-Pee-Chee 412
76 O-Pee-Chee 509

HANEY, CHRIS
92 O-Pee-Chee 626
92 opcPremier 186
92 MTL/Durivage 2

HANEY, LARRY
68 O-Pee-Chee 42
69 O-Pee-Chee 209
73 O-Pee-Chee 563
75 O-Pee-Chee 626
76 O-Pee-Chee 446

HANEY, TODD
90 Calgary/CMC 18
90 Calgary/ProCards 657
93 Ottawa/ProCards 2442

HANFORD, CHARLES
1912 ImperialTobacco(C46) 21

HANNAH, JOE
61 Toronto/BeeHive

HANNAHS, GERALD
77 MTL
77 MTL/RedpathSugar

HANNAN, JIM
69 O-Pee-Chee 106
71 O-Pee-Chee 229

HANSEN, BOB
75 O-Pee-Chee 508

HANSEN, DAVE
90 FleerCdn. 642
94 PaniniSticker 199

HANSEN, MIKE
89 London/ProCards 1376

HANSEN, ROGER
88 Calgary/CMC 21
88 Calgary/ProCards 790
89 Calgary/CMC 15
89 Calgary/ProCards 530

HANSEN, RON
65 O-Pee-Chee 146
67 O-Pee-Chee 9
70 O-Pee-Chee 217
71 O-Pee-Chee 410
62 PostCereal 30
62 ShirriffCoin 89
86 MTL/ProvigoFoods 27

HANSEN, TERREL
93 Ottawa/ProCards 2445

HANSON, ERIK
90 FleerCdn. 514
90 O-Pee-Chee 118
91 O-Pee-Chee 655
92 O-Pee-Chee 71
93 O-Pee-Chee 115
94 O-Pee-Chee 243
91 PaniniSticker 235
91 PaniniTopFifteen 79
96 TOR/OhHenry
97 TOR/Sizzler 14
88 Calgary/ProCards 786

HARDIN, JIM
71 O-Pee-Chee 491
72 O-Pee-Chee 287
73 O-Pee-Chee 124

HARDING, GREG
88 StCatharines/ProCards 2029

HARDY, ALEX
1912 ImperialTobacco(C46) 78

HARDY, CARROLL
62 ShirriffCoin 220

HARDY, JACK
88 Vancouver/CMC 10
88 Vancouver/ProCards 755
89 Vancouver/CMC 5
89 Vancouver/ProCards 586

HARDY, LARRY
75 O-Pee-Chee 112

HARGAN, STEVE
68 O-Pee-Chee 35
70 O-Pee-Chee 136
71 O-Pee-Chee 375
75 O-Pee-Chee 362
76 O-Pee-Chee 463
77 O-Pee-Chee 247

HARGRAVE, EUGENE (BUBBLES)
21 Neilson's(V61) 60

HARGROVE, MIKE
85 GeneralMills
86 Leaf 228
75 O-Pee-Chee 106
76 O-Pee-Chee 485
77 O-Pee-Chee 35
78 O-Pee-Chee 176
79 O-Pee-Chee 311
80 O-Pee-Chee 162
81 O-Pee-Chee 74
82 O-Pee-Chee 310
83 O-Pee-Chee 37

84 O-Pee-Chee 79
85 O-Pee-Chee 252
92 O-Pee-Chee 609
82 opcSticker 180
83 opcSticker 56
84 opcSticker 260
85 opcSticker 248

HARKEY, MIKE
90 FleerCdn. 33
91 O-Pee-Chee 376
92 O-Pee-Chee 98
93 O-Pee-Chee 110
89 PaniniSticker 48
91 PaniniSticker 51

HARMES, KRIS
91 StCatharines/ClassicBest 4
91 StCatharines/ProCards 3397
92 StCatharines/ClassicBest 16
92 StCatharines/ProCards 3388

HARMON, TERRY
70 O-Pee-Chee 486
71 O-Pee-Chee 682
72 O-Pee-Chee 377
73 O-Pee-Chee 166
74 O-Pee-Chee 7642
75 O-Pee-Chee 399
76 O-Pee-Chee 247

HARNISCH, PETE
90 FleerCdn. 177
90 O-Pee-Chee 324
91 O-Pee-Chee 179
92 O-Pee-Chee 765
93 O-Pee-Chee 185
94 O-Pee-Chee 73
92 PaniniSticker 159
93 PaniniSticker 168

HARO, SAMMY
87 Vancouver/5x7
87 Vancouver/ProCards 1607

HARPER, BRIAN
90 FleerCdn. 377
90 O-Pee-Chee 47
91 O-Pee-Chee 554
92 O-Pee-Chee 217
93 O-Pee-Chee 125
94 O-Pee-Chee 102
90 PaniniSticker 116
91 PaniniSticker 299
92 PaniniSticker 114
93 PaniniSticker 124
94 PaniniSticker 90

HARPER, DAVID
97 Lethbridge/Best 22

HARPER, TERRY
86 Leaf 246
86 O-Pee-Chee 247
86 opcSticker 41

HARPER, TOMMY
65 O-Pee-Chee 47
69 O-Pee-Chee 42
70 OPC 370, -Booklet 11
71 O-Pee-Chee 260
72 O-Pee-Chee 455
73 O-Pee-Chee 620
74 O-Pee-Chee 204, 325
75 O-Pee-Chee 537
76 O-Pee-Chee 274

HARRAH, TOBY
86 Leaf 86
72 O-Pee-Chee 104
73 O-Pee-Chee 216
74 O-Pee-Chee 511
75 O-Pee-Chee 131
76 O-Pee-Chee 412
77 O-Pee-Chee 208
78 O-Pee-Chee 74
79 O-Pee-Chee 119
80 O-Pee-Chee 333
81 O-Pee-Chee 67
82 O-Pee-Chee 16
83 O-Pee-Chee 356
84 O-Pee-Chee 348
86 O-Pee-Chee 72
82 opcSticker 177
83 opcSticker 58
84 opcSticker 251
86 opcSticker 238
86 opcTattoo 19

HARRELL, JOHN
70 O-Pee-Chee 401

HARRELSON, BUD
68 O-Pee-Chee 132
71 O-Pee-Chee 355
72 O-Pee-Chee 53,54,496
73 O-Pee-Chee 223
74 O-Pee-Chee 380
75 O-Pee-Chee 395
76 O-Pee-Chee 337
77 O-Pee-Chee 172
80 O-Pee-Chee 294
91 O-Pee-Chee 261

HARRELSON, KEN
66 O-Pee-Chee 55
67 O-Pee-Chee 188
69 O-Pee-Chee 3,5,-Deckle 9
70 O-Pee-Chee 545
71 O-Pee-Chee 510

HARRIS, ALONZO
68 O-Pee-Chee 128

HARRIS, BILLY
70 O-Pee-Chee 512

HARRIS, BRYAN
21 Neilson's(V61) 38

HARRIS, BUCKY
20 MapleCrispettes(V117) 21
36 WWGum(V355) 130

HARRIS, BUDDY
71 O-Pee-Chee 404

HARRIS, DAVE
33 WWGum(V353) 9

HARRIS, DONALD
90 O-Pee-Chee 314
92 O-Pee-Chee 554

HARRIS, G.G.
93 Welland/ClassicBest 6
93 Welland/ProCards 3364

HARRIS, GENE
90 FleerCdn. 515
90 O-Pee-Chee 738
91 O-Pee-Chee 203
92 O-Pee-Chee 390

HARRIS, GREG
90 FleerCdn. 158
87 Leaf 82
86 O-Pee-Chee 128
87 O-Pee-Chee 44
90 O-Pee-Chee 529,572
91 O-Pee-Chee 123,749
92 O-Pee-Chee 468,636
86 opcSticker 245
87 opcSticker 238
90 PaniniSticker 353
84 MTL
84 MTL/StuartBakery 22

HARRIS, LENNY
90 FleerCdn. 397
90 O-Pee-Chee 277
91 O-Pee-Chee 453
92 O-Pee-Chee 92
91 PaniniSticker 57
92 PaniniSticker 194
93 PaniniSticker 220

HARRIS, LUM
65 O-Pee-Chee 274
66 O-Pee-Chee 147
69 O-Pee-Chee 196
70 O-Pee-Chee 86
71 O-Pee-Chee 346
72 O-Pee-Chee 484

HARRIS, PEP
96 Vancouver/Best 17

HARRIS, REGGIE
91 O-Pee-Chee 177

HARRIS, STANLEY R.
23 Neilson's 14
23 WillardsChoc.(V100) 58

HARRIS, VIC
73 O-Pee-Chee 594
74 O-Pee-Chee 157
75 O-Pee-Chee 658
79 Vancouver/TCMA 2
79 Vancouver/TCMA 21

HARRIS, WILLIAM M.
23 WillardsChoc.(V100) 59

HARRISON, CHUCK
67 O-Pee-Chee 8
69 O-Pee-Chee 116

HARRISON, ROBERT
90 Hamilton/Star 28

HARRISON, RORIC
72 O-Pee-Chee 474
73 O-Pee-Chee 229
74 O-Pee-Chee 298
75 O-Pee-Chee 287
76 O-Pee-Chee 547

HART, J. RAY
65 O-Pee-Chee 4

HART, JIM
68 O-Pee-Chee 73
70 O-Pee-Chee 176
71 O-Pee-Chee 461
73 O-Pee-Chee 538
74 O-Pee-Chee 159

HART, JOHN
90 O-Pee-Chee 141

HARTENSTEIN, CHUCK
68 O-Pee-Chee 13
70 O-Pee-Chee 216
77 O-Pee-Chee 157

HARTLEY, MIKE
90 FleerCdn. 651
91 O-Pee-Chee 199
92 O-Pee-Chee 484
93 opcPremier 67

HARTNETT, GABBY
36 WWGum(V355) 57

HARTSFIELD, ROY
73 O-Pee-Chee 237
77 O-Pee-Chee 238
78 O-Pee-Chee 218
79 O-Pee-Chee 262
78 TOR
79 TOR/BubbleYum

HARTSHORN, TYSON
95 StCatharines/TimHortons 3

HARTZELL, PAUL
79 O-Pee-Chee 212
80 O-Pee-Chee 366

HARVEY, BRYAN
90 FleerCdn. 134
89 O-Pee-Chee 287
90 O-Pee-Chee 272
91 O-Pee-Chee 153
92 O-Pee-Chee 568
93 O-Pee-Chee 14
94 O-Pee-Chee 239
93 opcPremier 90
89 opcSticker 180
89 PaniniSticker 284
94 PaniniSticker 183
92 PizzaHut/DietPepsi 9

HASELMAN, BILL
92 Calgary/ProCards 3734

HASLER, CURT
91 Vancouver/LineDrive 634
91 Vancouver/ProCards 1590

HASSEY, RON
90 FleerCdn. 8
81 O-Pee-Chee 187
82 O-Pee-Chee 54
84 O-Pee-Chee 308
86 O-Pee-Chee 157
87 O-Pee-Chee 61
89 O-Pee-Chee 272
90 O-Pee-Chee 527
91 O-Pee-Chee 327
91 opcPremier 61
83 opcSticker 62
84 opcSticker 262
87 opcSticker 285
89 opcSticker 173
86 opcTattoo 13

HASSLER, ANDY
75 O-Pee-Chee 261
76 O-Pee-Chee 207

HASSON, GENE
39 WWGum(V351A)

HASTY, ROBERT K.
23 WillardsChocolates(V100)60

HATCHER, BILLY
90 FleerCdn. 467
88 Leaf 23,110
88 O-Pee-Chee 306
89 O-Pee-Chee 252
90 O-Pee-Chee 119
91 O-Pee-Chee 604
92 O-Pee-Chee 432
88 opcSticker 28
89 opcSticker 19
88 PaniniSticker 300
89 PaniniSticker 92
91 PaniniSticker 132
94 PaniniSticker 31

HATCHER, MICKEY
90 FleerCdn. 398
85 Leaf 223
86 Leaf 143
88 Leaf 122
82 O-Pee-Chee 291
86 O-Pee-Chee 356
87 O-Pee-Chee 341
88 O-Pee-Chee 339
89 O-Pee-Chee 254,390
90 O-Pee-Chee 226
91 O-Pee-Chee 152
82 opcSticker 212
85 opcSticker 304
87 opcSticker 276
88 opcSticker 71
89 PaniniSticker 23,105

HATHAWAY, HILLY
93 Vancouver/ProCards 2590

HATHAWAY, RAY
43-47 Montréal/ParadeSportive

HATTEBERG, SCOTT
92 O-Pee-Chee 734

HATTON, GRADY
73 O-Pee-Chee 624
74 O-Pee-Chee 31

HAUSER, JOE
21 Neilson's(V61) 53
23 Neilson's 15

HAUSMAN, TOM
76 O-Pee-Chee 452
79 O-Pee-Chee 339

HAUSMANN, CLEM
50 WWGum(V362) 13

HAWKINS, ANDY
90 FleerCdn. 445
86 Leaf 158
86 O-Pee-Chee 5
90 O-Pee-Chee 335
91 O-Pee-Chee 635
86 opcSticker 108
89 opcSticker 111
86 opcTattoo 12
89 PaniniSticker 194
90 PaniniSticker 130
91 PaniniSticker 357
92 Calgary/SkyBox 59

HAYDEL, HAL
71 O-Pee-Chee 692
72 O-Pee-Chee 28

HAYES, CHARLIE
90 FleerCdn. 558
90 O-Pee-Chee 577
91 O-Pee-Chee 312
92 O-Pee-Chee 754
93 O-Pee-Chee 54
94 O-Pee-Chee 171
92 opcPremier 6
93 opcPremier 66
91 PaniniSticker 105
92 PaniniSticker 244
93 PaniniSticker 175

HAYES, CHRIS
95 StCatharines/TimHortons 19

HAYES, EMMANUEL
93 StCatharines/ClassicBest 9
93 StCatharines/ProCards 3980

HAYES, JACKIE
37 O-Pee-Chee(V300) 102

HAYES, VON
90 FleerCdn. 559
85 Leaf 93
86 Leaf 176
87 Leaf 12,130
88 Leaf 197
83 O-Pee-Chee 325
84 O-Pee-Chee 259
85 O-Pee-Chee 68
86 O-Pee-Chee 146
87 O-Pee-Chee 389
88 O-Pee-Chee 215
89 O-Pee-Chee 385
90 O-Pee-Chee 710
91 O-Pee-Chee 15
92 O-Pee-Chee 135
92 opcPremier 127
83 opcSticker 311
84 opcSticker 124
85 opcSticker 115
86 opcSticker 120
87 opcSticker 121
88 opcSticker 117
89 opcSticker 115

86 opcTattoo 10
88 PaniniSticker 356
89 PaniniSticker 151
90 PaniniSticker 319
91 PaniniSticker 107
92 PaniniSticker 248

HAYNES, HEATH
95 Edmonton/Macri
94 Ottawa/ProCards 2897

HAYWORTH, RAY
36 WWGum(V355) 50

HEALY, FRAN
73 O-Pee-Chee 361
74 O-Pee-Chee 238
75 O-Pee-Chee 251
76 O-Pee-Chee 394

HEAP, JAMES
52 Laval Dairy 79

HEARH, MIKE
82 O-Pee-Chee 318

HEARN, SEAN
93 StCatharines/ClassicBest 10
93 StCatharines/ProCards 3986

HEARRON, JEFF
87 O-Pee-Chee 274
86 TOR/FireSafety
87 TOR/FireSafety

HEATH, BILL
67 O-Pee-Chee 172
70 O-Pee-Chee 541

HEATH, DAVID
87 Edmonton/CMC 9

HEATH, MIKE
90 FleerCdn. 603
85 O-Pee-Chee 396
86 O-Pee-Chee 148
90 O-Pee-Chee 366
91 O-Pee-Chee 16
92 O-Pee-Chee 512
83 opcSticker 104
84 opcSticker 337
85 opcSticker 326
86 opcSticker 174
90 PaniniSticker 66
91 PaniniSticker 287

HEATH, WOODY
97 St.Catharines/Best 15

HEATHCOCK, JEFF
90 Edmonton/CMC 9
90 Edmonton/ProCards 515

HEATHCOTE, CLIFTON
34 WWGum(V354) 9

HEATON, NEAL
90 FleerCdn. 468
88 HostessDisk 10
86 Leaf 203
88 O-Pee-Chee 354
90 O-Pee-Chee 197
90 O-Pee-Chee 539
91 O-Pee-Chee 451
92 O-Pee-Chee 89
88 opcSticker 80,-SuperStar 29
88 PaniniSticker 319
91 PaniniSticker 123

HEAVERLO, DAVE
76 O-Pee-Chee 213

HEBLE, KURT
91 StCatharines/ClassicBest 11
91 StCatharines/ProCards 3403

HEBNER, RICH
69 O-Pee-Chee 82
70 O-Pee-Chee 264
71 O-Pee-Chee 212
73 O-Pee-Chee 2
74 O-Pee-Chee 450
75 O-Pee-Chee 492
76 O-Pee-Chee 376
77 O-Pee-Chee 168
78 O-Pee-Chee 194
79 O-Pee-Chee 293
80 O-Pee-Chee 175
81 O-Pee-Chee 217
82 O-Pee-Chee 96

HECKLE, WALLY
90 StCatharines/ProCards 3477

HEDLUND, MIKE
70 O-Pee-Chee 187
71 O-Pee-Chee 662
72 O-Pee-Chee 81
73 O-Pee-Chee 591

HEEP, DANNY
90 FleerCdn. 278
85 O-Pee-Chee 339
90 O-Pee-Chee 573
91 Vancouver/LineDrive 635
91 Vancouver/ProCards 1601

HEFFERMAN, BRET
92 Calgary/SkyBox 60
93 Calgary/ProCards 1169

HEFFNER, BOB
65 O-Pee-Chee 199

HEGAN ,JIM
73 O-Pee-Chee 116
76 O-Pee-Chee 69

HEGAN, MIKE
70 O-Pee-Chee 111
71 O-Pee-Chee 415
73 O-Pee-Chee 382
74 O-Pee-Chee 517
75 O-Pee-Chee 99
76 O-Pee-Chee 377
76 O-Pee-Chee 69

HEIDEMANN, JACK
71 O-Pee-Chee 87
72 O-Pee-Chee 374
73 O-Pee-Chee 644
75 O-Pee-Chee 649

HEILMANN, HARRY
21 Neilson's(V61) 27
23 Neilson's 16
23 WillardsChoc.(V100) 61
22 WilliamPaterson(V89) 22

HEINTZELMAN, TOM
74 O-Pee-Chee 607

HEISE, BOBBY
70 O-Pee-Chee 478
71 O-Pee-Chee 691
72 O-Pee-Chee 402
73 O-Pee-Chee 547
74 O-Pee-Chee 51
75 O-Pee-Chee 441

HEIST, AL
62 ShirriffCoin 195

HELD, WOODIE
66 O-Pee-Chee 136
62 PostCereal 44
62 ShirriffCoin 5

HELMS, TOMMY
65 O-Pee-Chee 243
69 O-Pee-Chee 70,-Deckle 10
70 O-Pee-Chee 159
71 O-Pee-Chee 272
72 O-Pee-Chee 204
73 O-Pee-Chee 495
74 O-Pee-Chee 67
75 O-Pee-Chee 119
76 O-Pee-Chee 583
90 O-Pee-Chee 110

HELTON, KEITH
90 Calgary/CMC 21
90 Calgary/ProCards 646
91 Calgary/LineDrive 58
91 Calgary/ProCards 510

HEMOND, SCOTT
90 FleerCdn. 646

HENDERSON, DAVE
90 FleerCdn. 9
86 Leaf 187
87 Leaf 103
84 O-Pee-Chee 154
85 O-Pee-Chee 344
86 O-Pee-Chee 221
89 O-Pee-Chee 327
90 O-Pee-Chee 68
91 O-Pee-Chee 144
92 O-Pee-Chee 335
93 O-Pee-Chee 155
84 opcSticker 343
85 opcSticker 338
86 opcSticker 222
87 opcSticker 23
89 opcSticker 164,-SStar 17
89 PaniniSticker 423
90 PaniniSticker 133
91 PaniniSticker 197
92 PaniniSticker 20,276
93 PaniniSticker 20
94 PaniniSticker 109

HENDERSON, KEN
66 O-Pee-Chee 39
70 O-Pee-Chee 298
71 O-Pee-Chee 155
72 O-Pee-Chee 443,444
73 O-Pee-Chee 101
74 O-Pee-Chee 394
75 O-Pee-Chee 59
76 O-Pee-Chee 464

HENDERSON, MIKE
80 Vancouver/TCMA 17

HENDERSON, RICKEY
90 Ben's/HolsumDisks 8
91 Ben's/HolsumDisks 12
90 FleerCdn. 10
86 GeneralMills
87 GeneralMills
93 HumptyDumpty 14
85 Leaf 208
86 Leaf 37
87 Leaf 191
88 Leaf 145
81 O-Pee-Chee 261
82 O-Pee-Chee 268
83 O-Pee-Chee 180,391
84 O-Pee-Chee 230
85 O-Pee-Chee 115
86 O-Pee-Chee 243
87 O-Pee-Chee 7,E
88 O-Pee-Chee 60,M
89 O-Pee-Chee 282,F
90 O-Pee-Chee 7,450
91 O-Pee-Chee 391,670,H
92 O-Pee-Chee 2,560
93 O-Pee-Chee 130
94 O-Pee-Chee 37, -TOR 1
91 opcPremier 62
92 opcPremier 147
82 opcSticker 8,221
83 opcSticker 21,103,159
83 opcSticker 197-202
84 opcSticker 3-4,202,327
85 opcSticker 283,321
86 opcSticker 155,297
87 opcSticker 147,296
88 opcStick. 155,297,-SStar 51
89 opcSticker 145,312-SStar 18
86 opcTattoo 24
88 PaniniSticker 158,231,434
89 PaniniSticker 239,408
90 PaniniSticker 138
91 PaniniSticker 171,196
92 PaniniSticker 21
93 PaniniSticker 19
94 PaniniSticker 1,139
91 PaniniTopFifteen 38,45,53
91 PetroCanada 21
92 PizzaHut/DietPepsi 28
91 PostCdn. 24
92 PostCdn. 18
87 StuartBakery 23

HENDERSON, ROD
93 O-Pee-Chee-DraftPick 3
93 opcPremier-DraftPick 3

HENDERSON, STEVE
78 O-Pee-Chee 53
79 O-Pee-Chee 232
80 O-Pee-Chee 156
81 O-Pee-Chee 44
82 O-Pee-Chee 89
84 O-Pee-Chee 274
85 O-Pee-Chee 38
82 opcSticker 30
84 opcSticker 341

HENDERSON, TODD
92 Hamilton/ClassicBest 27

HENDERSON, VALENTINE
89 Welland/Pucko 13

HENDLEY, BOB
66 O-Pee-Chee 82
69 O-Pee-Chee 144

HENDRICK, GEORGE
85 Leaf 259
72 O-Pee-Chee 406
73 O-Pee-Chee 13
74 O-Pee-Chee 303
75 O-Pee-Chee 109
76 O-Pee-Chee 570
77 O-Pee-Chee 218
78 O-Pee-Chee 178
79 O-Pee-Chee 82
80 O-Pee-Chee 184
81 O-Pee-Chee 230
82 O-Pee-Chee 295
83 O-Pee-Chee 148
84 O-Pee-Chee 163,386
85 O-Pee-Chee 60
86 O-Pee-Chee 190
87 O-Pee-Chee 248
82 opcSticker 91
83 opcSticker 153,285
84 opcSticker 139,185
85 opcSticker 134

HENDRICKS, ELROD (ELLIE)
70 O-Pee-Chee 528
71 O-Pee-Chee 219
72 O-Pee-Chee 508
75 O-Pee-Chee 609
76 O-Pee-Chee 371

HENGEL, DAVE
86 Calgary/ProCards
87 Calgary/ProCards 2317
88 Calgary/CMC 18
88 Calgary/ProCards 1550

HENKE, TOM
90 Ben's/HolsumDisks 3
93 Ben'sDisk 16
90 FleerCdn. 84
87 GeneralMills
88 HostessDisk 23
86 Leaf 206
87 Leaf 73
92 McDonald's 5
86 O-Pee-Chee 333
87 O-Pee-Chee 277
88 O-Pee-Chee 220
89 O-Pee-Chee 75
90 O-Pee-Chee 695
91 O-Pee-Chee 110
92 O-Pee-Chee 451
93 OPC 202, -WSChamp 7
94 O-Pee-Chee 242
91 opcPremier 63
93 opcPremier 77
86 opcSticker 189
87 opcSticker 185
88 opcSticker 186,-SStar 64
89 opcSticker 195
88 PaniniSticker 213
89 PaniniSticker 461
91 PaniniSticker 345
94 PaniniSticker 128
92 PizzaHut/DietPepsi 3
85 TOR/FireSafety
86 TOR/AultFoods
86 TOR/FireSafety
87 TOR/FireSafety
88 TOR/FireSafety
89 TOR/FireSafety
90 TOR/FireSafety
90 TOR/Hostess
91 TOR/FireSafety
91 TOR/Score 2
92 TOR/FireSafety
93 TOR/Donruss 18
97 TOR/Sizzler 38

HENLEY, DAN
91 Vancouver/LineDrive 636
91 Vancouver/ProCards 1602

HENLINE, NOAH
1912 ImperialTobacco(C46) 64

HENLINE, WALTER J.
23 Neilson's 17
23 WillardsChoc.(V100) 62

HENNEMAN, MIKE
90 FleerCdn. 604
88 O-Pee-Chee 3
89 O-Pee-Chee 365
90 O-Pee-Chee 177
91 O-Pee-Chee 641
92 O-Pee-Chee 293
93 O-Pee-Chee 149
94 O-Pee-Chee 52
89 opcSticker 273
89 PaniniSticker 333
90 PaniniSticker 69

HENNIGAN, PHIL
71 O-Pee-Chee 211
73 O-Pee-Chee 107

HENNINGER, RICK
74 O-Pee-Chee 602

HENRICH, TOMMY
53 Exhibits 27
39 WWGum(V351A)

HENRY, BUTCH
93 O-Pee-Chee 200
93 opcPremier 30

HENRY, DOUG
92 O-Pee-Chee 776
93 O-Pee-Chee 181

HENRY, DWAYNE
91 O-Pee-Chee 567
92 O-Pee-Chee 668

HENRY, JIMMY
92 London/ProCards 629

HENRY, SANTIAGO
92 StCatharines/ClassicBest 10
92 StCatharines/ProCards 3396

HENSIEK, PHIL
36 WWGum(V355) 123

HENSLEY, CHUCK
89 Calgary/CMC 2
89 Calgary/ProCards 531

HENTGEN, PAT
96 HitTheBooks
97 HitTheBooks
93 O-Pee-Chee 245
93 TOR/FireSafety
93 TOR/Dempster's 19
93 TOR/Donruss 33
94 TOR
95 TOR/OhHenry
96 TOR/OhHenry
97 TOR/Sizzler 2, 30

HEPLER, BILL
67 O-Pee-Chee 144

HERBEL, RON
65 O-Pee-Chee 84
67 O-Pee-Chee 156
70 O-Pee-Chee 526
71 O-Pee-Chee 387
72 O-Pee-Chee 469

HERBERT, RAY
66 O-Pee-Chee 121
60 opcTattoo 21
62 ShirriffCoin 6

HERBERT, ROGER
52 Laval Dairy 65

HEREDIA, GIL
93 Ottawa/ProCards 2430

HERMAN, BABE
33 WWGum(V353) 5

HERMAN, BILLY
65 O-Pee-Chee 251
66 O-Pee-Chee 37
39 WWGum(V351B)

HERMANN, ED
78 Dimanche/DernièreHeure

HERMOSO, ANGEL
70 O-Pee-Chee 147

HERNANDEZ, ALBERTO
94 GarciaPhoto 100

HERNANDEZ, CESAR
92 O-Pee-Chee 618

HERNANDEZ, CHUCK
88 Edmonton/ProCards 563
89 Edmonton/CMC 24
89 Edmonton/ProCards 562
90 Edmonton/CMC 8
90 Edmonton/ProCards 562

HERNANDEZ, ENZO
71 O-Pee-Chee 529
72 O-Pee-Chee 7
73 O-Pee-Chee 438
74 O-Pee-Chee 572
75 O-Pee-Chee 84
76 O-Pee-Chee 289

HERNANDEZ, GUILLERMO
90 FleerCdn. 605
89 O-Pee-Chee 43

HERNANDEZ, JACKIE
71 O-Pee-Chee 144
72 O-Pee-Chee 502
73 O-Pee-Chee 363
74 O-Pee-Chee 566

HERNANDEZ, JEREMY
92 O-Pee-Chee 211

HERNANDEZ, JORGE
94 GarciaPhoto 63

HERNANDEZ, JOSE
92 O-Pee-Chee 237

HERNANDEZ, KEITH
90 FleerCdn. 205
87 GeneralMills 5
85 Leaf 62
86 Leaf 124
87 Leaf 233
88 Leaf 117
75 O-Pee-Chee 623
76 O-Pee-Chee 542
77 O-Pee-Chee 150
78 O-Pee-Chee 109
79 O-Pee-Chee 371
80 O-Pee-Chee 170
81 O-Pee-Chee 195
82 O-Pee-Chee 210
83 O-Pee-Chee 262
84 O-Pee-Chee 120
85 O-Pee-Chee 80
86 O-Pee-Chee 252
87 O-Pee-Chee 350
88 O-Pee-Chee 68
89 O-Pee-Chee 63,G
90 O-Pee-Chee 230
82 opcSticker 92
83 opcSticker 188, 290
84 opcSticker 107
85 opcSticker 98
86 opcSticker 99
87 opcSticker 102,157
88 opcSticker 97,-SuperStar 3
89 opcSticker 93
86 opcTattoo 1
88 PaniniSticker 339
89 PaniniSticker 137
87 StuartBakery 1

HERNANDEX, LIVAN
94 GarciaPhoto 18

HERNANDEZ, MIGUEL ARNAY
94 GarciaPhoto 88

HERNANDEZ, ORLANDO
94 GarciaPhoto 51

HERNANDEZ, RAMON
73 O-Pee-Chee 117
74 O-Pee-Chee 222
75 O-Pee-Chee 224
76 O-Pee-Chee 647

HERNANDEZ, ROBERTO
92 O-Pee-Chee 667
93 O-Pee-Chee 126
94 O-Pee-Chee 94
94 PaniniSticker 48
91 Vancouver/LineDrive 637
91 Vancouver/ProCards 1591
92 Vancouver/SkyBox 640

HERNANDEZ, WILLIE
85 Leaf 235
86 Leaf 102
84 O-Pee-Chee 199
85 O-Pee-Chee 333
86 O-Pee-Chee 341
87 O-Pee-Chee 339
85 opcSticker 257
86 opcSticker 275
87 opcSticker 272
86 opcTattoo 8
88 PaniniSticker 84

HERNANDEZ, XAVIER
91 O-Pee-Chee 194
92 O-Pee-Chee 640
93 O-Pee-Chee 233

HERNDON, LARRY
85 Leaf 249
86 Leaf 230
77 O-Pee-Chee 169
79 O-Pee-Chee 328
81 O-Pee-Chee 108
82 O-Pee-Chee 182
83 O-Pee-Chee 13
84 O-Pee-Chee 333
85 O-Pee-Chee 9
86 O-Pee-Chee 61
88 O-Pee-Chee 146
82 opcSticker 109
83 opcSticker 68
84 opcSticker 264
85 opcSticker 266
86 opcSticker 271

HERR, TOMMY
90 FleerCdn. 560
86 Leaf 79
87 Leaf 121
88 Leaf 201
83 O-Pee-Chee 97
84 O-Pee-Chee 117
85 O-Pee-Chee 113
86 O-Pee-Chee 94
87 O-Pee-Chee 181
88 O-Pee-Chee 310
90 O-Pee-Chee 297
91 O-Pee-Chee 64
83 opcSticker 286
84 opcSticker 142
85 opcSticker 142
86 opcSticker 49,147
87 opcSticker 49
88 opcSticker 50, -SuperStar 4
86 opcTattoo 22
88 PaniniSticker 389-91
90 PaniniSticker 309

HERRERA, PANCHO
62 PostCereal 192
62 ShirriffCoin 122

HERRMANN, ED
70 O-Pee-Chee 368
71 O-Pee-Chee 169
72 O-Pee-Chee 452
73 O-Pee-Chee 73
74 O-Pee-Chee 438
75 O-Pee-Chee 219
76 O-Pee-Chee 406
79 O-Pee-Chee 194

HERSH, EARL
61 Toronto/BeeHive

HERSHBERGER, MIKE
65 O-Pee-Chee 89
68 O-Pee-Chee 18
71 O-Pee-Chee 149

HERSHISER, OREL
90 Ben's/HolsumDisks 12
90 FleerCdn. 399
85 Leaf 38
86 Leaf 18
87 Leaf 246
88 Leaf 62
85 O-Pee-Chee 273
86 O-Pee-Chee 159
87 O-Pee-Chee 385
88 O-Pee-Chee 40
89 O-Pee-Chee 41,380
90 O-Pee-Chee 780
91 O-Pee-Chee 690
92 O-Pee-Chee 175
93 O-Pee-Chee 136
94 O-Pee-Chee 133
91 opcPremier 64
92 opcPremier 162
85 opcSticker 74
86 opcSticker 73
88 opcSticker 68
89 opcSticker 12,65,-SStar 60
86 opcTattoo 20
88 PaniniSticker 303
89 PaniniSticker 9,13,18-19,
89 PaniniSticker 25,97,474
90 PaniniSticker 275
92 PaniniSticker 199
94 PaniniSticker 200
91 PetroCanada 22

HERZ, STEVE
82 Vancouver/TCMA 11

HERZOG, WHITEY
73 O-Pee-Chee 549
76 O-Pee-Chee 236
90 O-Pee-Chee 261

HESKETH, JOE
90 FleerCdn. 349
86 Leaf 150
87 Leaf 62
86 O-Pee-Chee 42
87 O-Pee-Chee 189
88 O-Pee-Chee 371
89 O-Pee-Chee 74
90 O-Pee-Chee 24
91 O-Pee-Chee 269
92 O-Pee-Chee 521
86 MTL/ProvigoFoods21
86 MTL/ProvigoFoods-Poster

HESLET, HARRY
50 WWGum(V362) 27

HETZEL, ERIC
90 FleerCdn. 279
90 O-Pee-Chee 629

HIATT, JACK
69 O-Pee-Chee 204
70 O-Pee-Chee 13
71 O-Pee-Chee 371
73 O-Pee-Chee 402

HIBBARD, GREG
90 FleerCdn. 534
90 O-Pee-Chee 769
91 O-Pee-Chee 256
92 O-Pee-Chee 477
91 PaniniSticker 319
88 Vancouver/CMC 11
88 Vancouver/ProCards 770
89 Vancouver/CMC 3
89 Vancouver/ProCards 584

HICKERSON, BRYAN
92 O-Pee-Chee 8
93 O-Pee-Chee 162
92 opcPremier 65

HICKEY, KEVIN
90 FleerCdn. 178
82 O-Pee-Chee 362
90 O-Pee-Chee 546

HICKMAN, JIM
65 O-Pee-Chee 114
69 O-Pee-Chee 63
71 O-Pee-Chee 175
73 O-Pee-Chee 565

HICKS, JIM
70 O-Pee-Chee 173

HIGGINS, DENNIS
67 O-Pee-Chee 52
70 O-Pee-Chee 257
71 O-Pee-Chee 479
72 O-Pee-Chee 278

HIGGINS, FRANK
39 WWGum(V351B)

HIGUERA, TEDDY
90 FleerCdn. 326
86 Leaf 157
87 Leaf 16,95
88 Leaf 53
87 O-Pee-Chee 250
88 O-Pee-Chee 110
89 O-Pee-Chee 292
90 O-Pee-Chee 15
91 O-Pee-Chee 475
87 opcSticker 199
88 opcSticker 196
89 opcSticker 198,-SStar 28
88 PaniniSticker 116
89 PaniniSticker 366
90 PaniniSticker 96
94 PaniniSticker 81

HILDEBRAND, ORAL
34 WWGum(V354) 95

HILGENDORF, TOM
70 O-Pee-Chee 482
74 O-Pee-Chee 13
75 O-Pee-Chee 377
76 O-Pee-Chee 168

HILL, CLAY
85 Calgary/Cramer 100
86 Calgary/ProCards

HILL, DONNIE
86 Leaf 148
86 O-Pee-Chee 310
88 O-Pee-Chee 132
91 O-Pee-Chee 36
92 O-Pee-Chee 731
88 opcSticker 286
88 PaniniSticker 58, 59

HILL, GARRY
70 O-Pee-Chee 172

HILL, GLENALLEN
90 O-Pee-Chee 194
91 O-Pee-Chee 509
92 O-Pee-Chee 364
93 O-Pee-Chee 114
91 PaniniSticker 347
90 TOR/FireSafety
91 TOR/FireSafety

HILL, HERMAN
70 O-Pee-Chee 267

HILL, KEN
90 FleerCdn. 251
93 HitTheBooks, -Poster
93 HumptyDumpty 38
90 O-Pee-Chee 233
91 O-Pee-Chee 591
92 O-Pee-Chee 664
93 O-Pee-Chee 239
94 O-Pee-Chee 140
92 opcPremier 89
93 PaniniSticker 223
94 PaniniSticker 211
95 PostCdn. 6
92 MTL/Durivage 11
93 MTL/McDonald's 9

HILL, MARC
75 O-Pee-Chee 620
76 O-Pee-Chee 577
80 O-Pee-Chee 125

HILL, ORSINO
90 Vancouver/CMC 17
90 Vancouver/ProCards 499
91 Vancouver/LineDrive 638
91 Vancouver/ProCards 1606

HILL, TYRONE
92 O-Pee-Chee 444

HILLEGAS, SHAWN
90 FleerCdn. 535
88 Leaf 35
90 O-Pee-Chee 93
92 O-Pee-Chee 523
89 PaniniSticker 301
90 Vancouver/CMC 7
90 Vancouver/ProCards 485

HILLER, CHUCK
66 O-Pee-Chee 154
73 O-Pee-Chee 549
62 ShirriffCoin 106

HILLER, JOHN
70 O-Pee-Chee 12
71 O-Pee-Chee 629
73 O-Pee-Chee 448
74 O-Pee-Chee 24,208
75 O-Pee-Chee 415
76 O-Pee-Chee 37
77 O-Pee-Chee 257
79 O-Pee-Chee 71
80 O-Pee-Chee 229

HILTON, DAVE
74 O-Pee-Chee 148
75 O-Pee-Chee 509
77 O-Pee-Chee 139

HILTON, JOHN
73 O-Pee-Chee 615

HINDS, SAM
79 Vancouver/TCMA 19

HINES, BRUCE
97 Vancouver/Best 1

HINES, KEITH
91 StCatharines/ClassicBest 12
91 StCatharines/ProCards 3408
92 StCatharines/ClassicBest 2

HINSON, DEAN (III)
91 Welland/Best 9
91 Welland/ProCards 3576

HINTON, CHUCK
65 O-Pee-Chee 235
67 O-Pee-Chee 189
70 O-Pee-Chee 27
71 O-Pee-Chee 429

HINTON, RICH
73 O-Pee-Chee 321
76 O-Pee-Chee 607

HINZO, TOMMY
88 O-Pee-Chee 294
88 PaniniSticker 73
94 Calgary/ProCards 795

HIRTENSTEINER, RICK
93 Ottawa/ProCards 2446

HISER, GENE
72 O-Pee-Chee 61
74 O-Pee-Chee 452

HISEY, JASON
91 Hamilton/ClassicBest 11
91 Hamilton/ProCards 4034

HISLE, LARRY
69 O-Pee-Chee 206
70 O-Pee-Chee 288
71 O-Pee-Chee 616
72 O-Pee-Chee 398
73 O-Pee-Chee 622
74 O-Pee-Chee 366
75 O-Pee-Chee 526
76 O-Pee-Chee 59
77 O-Pee-Chee 33
78 O-Pee-Chee 3
79 O-Pee-Chee 87
80 O-Pee-Chee 222
81 O-Pee-Chee 215
92 TOR/FireSafety
93 TOR/FireSafety
95 TOR/OhHenry

HOAK, DON
53 Exhibits 33
52 Parkhurst 57
62 PostCereal 171
62 ShirriffCoin 107

HOBBIE, GLEN
60 opcTattoo 22
62 ShirriffCoin 145

HOBSON, BUTCH
78 O-Pee-Chee 187
79 O-Pee-Chee 136
80 O-Pee-Chee 216
81 O-Pee-Chee 7
82 O-Pee-Chee 357
82 opcSticker 164

HOCKENBURY, BILL
52 Parkhurst 81

HODGE, CLARENCE (SHOVEL)
21 Neilson's(V61) 59

HODGE, TIMOTHY
88 StCatharines/ProCards 2016

HODGES, GIL
53 Exhibits 13
65 O-Pee-Chee 99
68 O-Pee-Chee 27
70 O-Pee-Chee 394
71 O-Pee-Chee 183
72 O-Pee-Chee 465
62 PostCereal 101
62 ShirriffCoin 146

HODGES, RON
74 O-Pee-Chee 448
75 O-Pee-Chee 134

HOEFT, WILLIAM (BILLY)
50 PalmDairies

HOERNER, JOE
67 O-Pee-Chee 41
70 O-Pee-Chee 511
71 O-Pee-Chee 166
72 O-Pee-Chee 482
73 O-Pee-Chee 653
74 O-Pee-Chee 493
75 O-Pee-Chee 629

HOFFMAN, GLENN
81 O-Pee-Chee 349
83 O-Pee-Chee 108
84 O-Pee-Chee 141
86 O-Pee-Chee 38
84 opcSticker 223

HOFFMAN, GUY
81 Edmonton/RedRooster 6
82 Edmonton/TCMA 6

HOFFMAN, TREVOR
93 opcPremier 113
94 PaniniSticker 257

HOGAN, FRANK
33 WWGum(V353) 30
34 WWGum(V354) 66

HOGG, DAVID
82 Edmonton/TCMA 16

HOILES, CHRIS
91 O-Pee-Chee 42
92 O-Pee-Chee 125,142
94 O-Pee-Chee 167
91 opcPremier 65
92 PaniniSticker 64
93 PaniniSticker 70
94 PaniniSticker 20

HOLDSWORTH, FRED
74 O-Pee-Chee 596
75 O-Pee-Chee 323
80 Vancouver/TCMA 18

HOLDRIDGE, DAVID
94 Vancouver/ProCards 1860

HOLIFIELD, RICK
89 StCatharines/ProCards 2096

HOLKE, WALTER M.
23 WillardsChoc.(V100) 63

HOLLAND, AL
85 Leaf 151
84 O-Pee-Chee 206
85 O-Pee-Chee 185
86 O-Pee-Chee 369
83 opcSticker 306
84 opcSticker 125,289
85 opcSticker 113

HOLLEY, BATTLE
94 StCatharines/Classic 12
94 StCatharines/ProCards 3652
95 StCatharines/TimHortons 18

HOLLE, GARY
81 Edmonton/RedRooster 1

HOLLINS, DAVE
91 O-Pee-Chee 264
92 O-Pee-Chee 383
93 O-Pee-Chee 169
94 O-Pee-Chee 186
93 PaniniSticker 273
94 PaniniSticker 3,228

HOLLOCHER, CHARLES J.
21 Neilson's(V61) 110
23 Neilson's 18
23 WillardsChoc.(V100) 64

HOLMAN, BRAD
93 Calgary/ProCards 1161
94 Calgary/ProCards 784

HOLMAN, BRIAN
90 FleerCdn. 516
90 O-Pee-Chee 616
91 O-Pee-Chee 458
92 O-Pee-Chee 239
90 PaniniSticker 146

HOLMAN, SHAWN
90 FleerCdn. 606
94 Ottawa/ProCards 2898

HOLMBERG, DENNIS
95 TOR/OhHenry

HOLMES, BOB
1912 ImperialTobacco(C46) 79

HOLMES, DAREN
92 O-Pee-Chee 454
93 opcPremier 104

HOLMES, DUCKY
1912 ImperialTobacco(C46) 60

HOLMES, STAN
88 Edmonton/CMC 14
88 Edmonton/ProCards 571
89 Edmonton/CMC 11
89 Edmonton/ProCards 555

HOLMES, TOMMY
53 Exhibits 18

HOLT, JIM
71 O-Pee-Chee 7
73 O-Pee-Chee 259
74 O-Pee-Chee 122
75 O-Pee-Chee 607
76 O-Pee-Chee 603

HOLTON, BRIAN
90 FleerCdn. 179
90 O-Pee-Chee 179

HOLTZMAN, KEN
67 O-Pee-Chee 185
68 O-Pee-Chee 60
70 O-Pee-Chee 505
71 O-Pee-Chee 410
73 O-Pee-Chee 60
74 O-Pee-Chee 180
75 O-Pee-Chee 145
76 O-Pee-Chee 115

HOLZEMER, MARK
93 Vancouver/ProCards 2591
94 Vancouver/ProCards 1861

HONEYCUTT, RICK
90 FleerCdn. 11
85 Leaf 156
81 O-Pee-Chee 33
84 O-Pee-Chee 222
85 O-Pee-Chee 174
87 O-Pee-Chee 167
90 O-Pee-Chee 582
91 O-Pee-Chee 67
92 O-Pee-Chee 202
84 opcSticker 84,176
85 opcSticker 78
87 opcSticker 72

HOOD, DENNIS
91 Calgary/LineDrive 59
91 Calgary/ProCards 527

HOOD, DON
74 O-Pee-Chee 436
75 O-Pee-Chee 516
76 O-Pee-Chee 132

HOOPER, HARRY B.
21 Neilson's(V61) 13
23 WillardsChoc.(V100) 65

HOOTEN, LEON
67 O-Pee-Chee 67

HOOTON, BURT
72 O-Pee-Chee 61
73 O-Pee-Chee 367
74 O-Pee-Chee 378
75 O-Pee-Chee 176
76 O-Pee-Chee 280
79 O-Pee-Chee 370
80 O-Pee-Chee 96
81 O-Pee-Chee 53
82 O-Pee-Chee 315
83 O-Pee-Chee 82
84 O-Pee-Chee 15
85 O-Pee-Chee 201
86 O-Pee-Chee 36
82 opcSticker 53
86 opcSticker 242
86 opcTattoo 18

HOPER, JOHN
91 Welland/Best 26
91 Welland/ProCards 3567

HOPKINS, GAIL
70 O-Pee-Chee 483
71 O-Pee-Chee 269
73 O-Pee-Chee 44
74 O-Pee-Chee 652

HORLEN, JOE (JOEL)
65 O-Pee-Chee 7
67 O-Pee-Chee 107
68 O-Pee-Chee 8,125
70 O-Pee-Chee 35
71 O-Pee-Chee 345

HORN, SAM
88 Leaf 237
88 O-Pee-Chee 377
91 O-Pee-Chee 598
92 O-Pee-Chee 422
88 opcSticker 246

HORN, WALT
95 Edmonton/Macri

HORNER, BOB
85 Leaf 240
86 Leaf 121
87 Leaf 136
80 O-Pee-Chee 59
81 O-Pee-Chee 355
82 O-Pee-Chee 145
83 O-Pee-Chee 50
84 O-Pee-Chee 239
85 O-Pee-Chee 262
86 O-Pee-Chee 220
87 O-Pee-Chee 116
89 O-Pee-Chee 255
82 opcSticker 18
83 opcSticker 214
84 opcSticker 30
85 opcSticker 24
86 opcSticker 34
87 opcSticker 41
89 opcSticker 35
86 opcTattoo 3

HORNSBY, ROGERS
21 Neilson's(V61) 81
37 O-Pee-Chee(V300) 140
76 O-Pee-Chee 342
23 WillardsChoc.(V100) 66
22 WilliamPaterson(V89) 21
34 WWGum(V354) 1

HORTON, ERIC
95 StCatharines/TimHortons 9

HORTON, RICKY
85 Leaf 253
85 O-Pee-Chee 321
87 O-Pee-Chee 238
88 O-Pee-Chee 34
90 O-Pee-Chee 1233

HORTON, WILLIE
65 O-Pee-Chee 206
66 O-Pee-Chee 20
69 OPC 5,180-Deckle 11
70 O-Pee-Chee 520
71 O-Pee-Chee 120
72 O-Pee-Chee 494
73 O-Pee-Chee 433
74 O-Pee-Chee 115
75 O-Pee-Chee 66
76 O-Pee-Chee 320
79 O-Pee-Chee 252
80 O-Pee-Chee 277

HOSCHEIT, VERN
73 O-Pee-Chee 179

HOSEY, STEVE
92 O-Pee-Chee 618
94 Vancouver/ProCards 1874

HOSLEY, TIM
72 O-Pee-Chee 257
76 O-Pee-Chee 482

HOSTETLER, DAVE
83 O-Pee-Chee 339
84 O-Pee-Chee 62
83 opcSticker 312

HOUGH, CHARLIE
90 FleerCdn. 300
85 Leaf 108
86 Leaf 152
87 Leaf 7
88 Leaf 89
72 O-Pee-Chee 198
73 O-Pee-Chee 610

74 O-Pee-Chee 408
75 O-Pee-Chee 71
76 O-Pee-Chee 174
79 O-Pee-Chee 266
83 O-Pee-Chee 343
84 O-Pee-Chee 118
85 O-Pee-Chee 276
86 O-Pee-Chee 275
87 O-Pee-Chee 70
88 O-Pee-Chee 121
89 O-Pee-Chee 345
90 O-Pee-Chee 735
91 O-Pee-Chee 495
92 O-Pee-Chee 191
93 O-Pee-Chee 41
94 O-Pee-Chee 62
83 opcSticker 125
84 opcSticker 356
85 opcSticker 345
86 opcSticker 241
87 opcSticker 240
88 opcSticker 236
89 opcSticker 245
86 opcTattoo 9
88 PaniniSticker 197
89 PaniniSticker 446

HOUK, RALPH
68 O-Pee-Chee 47
70 O-Pee-Chee 273
71 O-Pee-Chee 146
73 O-Pee-Chee 116
74 O-Pee-Chee 578
75 O-Pee-Chee 18
76 O-Pee-Chee 361

HOUSE, MITCH
91 Welland/Best 7
91 Welland/ProCards 3578
93 Welland/ClassicBest 1
93 Welland/ProCards 3365

HOUSE, TOM
72 O-Pee-Chee 351
74 O-Pee-Chee 164
75 O-Pee-Chee 525
76 O-Pee-Chee 231

HOUSEHOLDER, PAUL
84 opcSticker 61

HOUSER, CHRIS
88 Hamilton/ProCards 1719

HOUSIE, WAYNE
92 O-Pee-Chee 639
89 London/ProCards 1382

HOUSTON, TYLER
90 O-Pee-Chee 564

HOVLEY, STEVE
70 O-Pee-Chee 514
71 O-Pee-Chee 109
73 O-Pee-Chee 282

HOWARD, BRUCE
65 O-Pee-Chee 41
67 O-Pee-Chee 159

HOWARD, CHRIS
91 Calgary/LineDrive 60
91 Calgary/ProCards 519
92 Calgary/ProCards 3735
92 Calgary/SkyBox 61
93 Calgary/ProCards 1170
94 Calgary/ProCards 793
92 Vancouver/ProCards 2717
92 Vancouver/SkyBox 638

HOWARD, DAVID
92 O-Pee-Chee 641

HOWARD, DOUG
77 O-Pee-Chee 112

HOWARD, ELSTON
65 O-Pee-Chee 1
67 O-Pee-Chee 25
68 O-Pee-Chee 167
73 O-Pee-Chee 116
75 O-Pee-Chee 201
62 PostCereal 8
62 ShirriffCoin 95

HOWARD, FRANK
65 O-Pee-Chee 40
68 O-Pee-Chee 6,-Poster 11
69 OPC 3,5,170, -Deckle 12
70 O-Pee-Chee 66
71 O-Pee-Chee 63,65,620
72 O-Pee-Chee 350
73 O-Pee-Chee 560

HOWARD, LARRY
71 O-Pee-Chee 102

HOWARD, THOMAS
92 O-Pee-Chee 539
93 O-Pee-Chee 139

HOWARD, WILBUR
74 O-Pee-Chee 606
75 O-Pee-Chee 563
76 O-Pee-Chee 97

HOWARTH, JIMMY
73 O-Pee-Chee 459
74 O-Pee-Chee 404

HOWE, ART
79 O-Pee-Chee 165
80 O-Pee-Chee 287
81 O-Pee-Chee 129
82 O-Pee-Chee 248
83 O-Pee-Chee 372
90 O-Pee-Chee 579
91 O-Pee-Chee 51
92 O-Pee-Chee 729
82 opcSticker 43
83 opcSticker 236

HOWE, STEVE
81 O-Pee-Chee 159
82 O-Pee-Chee 14
83 O-Pee-Chee 170
84 O-Pee-Chee 196
92 O-Pee-Chee 318
89 London/ProCards 1357

HOWELL, JACK
90 FleerCdn. 135
86 O-Pee-Chee 127
87 O-Pee-Chee 2
88 O-Pee-Chee 114
89 O-Pee-Chee 216
90 O-Pee-Chee 547
91 O-Pee-Chee 57
92 O-Pee-Chee 769
88 opcSticker 175
89 opcSticker 181
88 PaniniSticker 44,186-87
89 PaniniSticker 293
91 PaniniSticker 182
92 PaniniSticker 234
85 Edmonton/Cramer 24
86 Edmonton/ProCards

HOWELL, JAY
90 FleerCdn. 400
85 Leaf 244
86 Leaf 100
86 O-Pee-Chee 115
87 O-Pee-Chee 391
88 O-Pee-Chee 91
89 O-Pee-Chee 212
90 O-Pee-Chee 40
91 O-Pee-Chee 770
92 O-Pee-Chee 205
93 O-Pee-Chee 160
86 opcSticker 175
88 opcSticker 166
89 opcSticker 61
86 opcTattoo 11
89 PaniniSticker 22,98
90 PaniniSticker 274

HOWELL, KEN
90 FleerCdn. 561
86 O-Pee-Chee 349
87 O-Pee-Chee 187
88 O-Pee-Chee 149
90 O-Pee-Chee 756
91 O-Pee-Chee 209
86 opcSticker 69
90 PaniniSticker 314
91 PaniniSticker 110

HOWELL, ROY
76 O-Pee-Chee 279
78 O-Pee-Chee 31
79 O-Pee-Chee 45
80 O-Pee-Chee 254
81 O-Pee-Chee 40
78 TOR
79 TOR/BubbleYum

HOWITT, DANN
90 FleerCdn. 644
93 Calgary/ProCards 1177

HOWSER, DICK
65 O-Pee-Chee 92
73 O-Pee-Chee 116
90 O-Pee-Chee 661
62 PostCereal 94
62 ShirriffCoin 31

HOY, WAYNE
94 StCatharines/Classic 13
94 StCatharines/ProCards 3638
95 StCatharines/TimHortons 7

HOYT, LAMARR
85 Leaf 37
86 Leaf 61
83 O-Pee-Chee 226
84 O-Pee-Chee 97,177
85 O-Pee-Chee 312
86 O-Pee-Chee 14,380
83 opcSticker 16,53
84 opcSticker 11,178,192,240
86 opcSticker 113,154
86 opcTattoo 14

HOYT, WAITE
20 MapleCrispettes(V117) 7
21 Neilson's(V61) 44
23 Neilson's 67
23 WillardsChoc.(V100) 67
22 WilliamPaterson(V89) 32
33 WWGum(V353) 60
36 WWGum(V355) 39

HRABCSAK, EDWARD
52 Parkhurst 87

HRABOSKY, AL
71 O-Pee-Chee 594
73 O-Pee-Chee 153
74 O-Pee-Chee 108
75 O-Pee-Chee 122
76 O-Pee-Chee 205,315
79 O-Pee-Chee 19
80 O-Pee-Chee 306
81 O-Pee-Chee 354
82 O-Pee-Chee 393

HRBEK, KENT
90 FleerCdn. 378
86 GeneralMills 2
85 Leaf 200
86 Leaf 67
87 Leaf 99
88 Leaf 139
83 O-Pee-Chee 251
84 O-Pee-Chee 345
85 O-Pee-Chee 308
86 O-Pee-Chee 63
87 O-Pee-Chee 161
88 O-Pee-Chee 45
89 O-Pee-Chee 265
90 O-Pee-Chee 125
91 O-Pee-Chee 710
92 O-Pee-Chee 347
93 O-Pee-Chee 150
94 O-Pee-Chee 261
92 opcPremier 46
83 opcSticker 88
84 opcSticker 305
85 opcSticker 296
86 opcSticker 277
87 opcSticker 281
88 opcSticker 24,274
89 opcSticker 287
86 opcTattoo 17
88 PaniniSticker 136
89 PaniniSticker 387
90 PaniniSticker 112
91 PaniniSticker 300
92 PaniniSticker 115
93 PaniniSticker 125
94 PaniniSticker 91
878 StuartBakery 22

HRINIAK, WALT
90 O-Pee-Chee 392

HUBBARD, GLENN
85 Leaf 242
86 Leaf 71
88 Leaf 22
81 O-Pee-Chee 247
83 O-Pee-Chee 322
84 O-Pee-Chee 25
85 O-Pee-Chee 195
86 O-Pee-Chee 112
87 O-Pee-Chee 68
88 O-Pee-Chee 325
82 opcSticker 23
83 opcSticker 215
84 opcSticker 29
85 opcSticker 33
86 opcSticker 36
86 opcTattoo 4
88 PaniniSticker 243,245-46

HUBBELL, CARL
34 WWGum(V354) 71

HUBBELL, WILBERT (BILL)
21 Neilson's(V61) 96

HUDEK, JOHN
92 Vancouver/ProCards 2718

HUDIK, MATT
90 StCatharines/ProCards 3452

HUDLER, REX
89 O-Pee-Chee 346
90 O-Pee-Chee 647
91 O-Pee-Chee 228
92 O-Pee-Chee 47
91 PaniniSticker 37

HUDLIN, WILLIS
33 WWGum(V353) 72

HUDSON, BERT
97 Lethbridge/Best 14

HUDSON, CHARLES
86 Leaf 239
85 O-Pee-Chee 379
89 O-Pee-Chee 236
84 opcSticker 17
85 opcSticker 120
86 opcTattoo 13

HUDSON, JESSE
70 O-Pee-Chee 348

HUEDA, ALEJANDRO
96 StCatharines/Best 12

HUFF, MIKE
90 FleerCdn. 649
92 O-Pee-Chee 532
92 opcPremier 21
95 TOR/OhHenry

HUFF, TIM
97 St.Catharines/Best 16

HUFFMAN, PHIL
80 O-Pee-Chee 79
81 O-Pee-Chee 2
79 TOR/BubbleYum

HUGGINS, DAVID
97 St.Catharines/Best 17

HUGGINS, MILLER
23 WillardsChoc.(V100) 68
22 WilliamPaterson(V89) 10

HUGHES, DICK
69 O-Pee-Chee 39

HUGHES, JAMES ROBERT
52 Parkhurst 56

HUGHES, JIM
76 O-Pee-Chee 11

HUGHES, TERRY
73 O-Pee-Chee 603
74 O-Pee-Chee 604
75 O-Pee-Chee 612

HUGHES, TOM
1912 ImperialTobacco(C46) 66

HULETT, TIM
86 O-Pee-Chee 87
87 O-Pee-Chee 286
91 O-Pee-Chee 468
92 O-Pee-Chee 396
93 O-Pee-Chee 167
86 opcSticker 295
87 opcSticker 289

HULL, JEFF
89 Calgary/CMC 8
89 Calgary/ProCards 526

HULSE, DAVID
93 O-Pee-Chee 146
93 opcPremier 40

HUME, TOM
81 O-Pee-Chee 292
82 O-Pee-Chee 79
83 O-Pee-Chee 86
84 O-Pee-Chee 186
85 O-Pee-Chee 223
87 O-Pee-Chee 251
82 opcSticker 38
84 opcSticker 59

HUMPHREY, TERRY
72 Dimanche/DernièreHeure
72 O-Pee-Chee 489
73 O-Pee-Chee 106
76 O-Pee-Chee 552

HUMPHREYS, BOB
65 O-Pee-Chee 154
69 O-Pee-Chee 84
70 O-Pee-Chee 538
71 O-Pee-Chee 236

HUNDLEY, RANDY
67 O-Pee-Chee 106
68 O-Pee-Chee 136
70 O-Pee-Chee 265
71 O-Pee-Chee 592
72 O-Pee-Chee 258
73 O-Pee-Chee 21

74 O-Pee-Chee 319
76 O-Pee-Chee 21

HUNDLEY, TODD
91 O-Pee-Chee 457
92 O-Pee-Chee 673
93 O-Pee-Chee 116
91 opcPremier 66
93 PaniniSticker 246
94 PaniniSticker 218

HUNT, KEN
62 PostCereal 79,129
62 ShirriffCoin 76

HUNT, RIEGAL
92 Welland/ClassicBest 10
93 Welland/ClassicBest 7
93 Welland/ProCards 3372

HUNT, RON
72 Dimanche/DernièreHeure
92 Nabisco 5
68 O-Pee-Chee 15, -Poster 12
70 O-Pee-Chee 276
71 O-Pee-Chee 161
72 O-Pee-Chee 110
73 O-Pee-Chee 149
74 O-Pee-Chee 275
75 O-Pee-Chee 610
71 ProStarPostcard
71 ProStarPoster
71 MTL/ProStar
74 MTL/GeorgeWeston

HUNTER, BILLY
73 O-Pee-Chee 136
74 O-Pee-Chee 306

HUNTER, BRIAN
92 O-Pee-Chee 611
93 O-Pee-Chee 157
92 opcPremier 78

HUNTER, JIM
66 O-Pee-Chee 36
71 O-Pee-Chee 45
72 O-Pee-Chee 330
73 O-Pee-Chee 235,344
74 O-Pee-Chee 196,339
75 O-Pee-Chee 230,310,311
76 O-Pee-Chee 100,200,202
77 O-Pee-Chee 10
78 O-Pee-Chee 69
79 O-Pee-Chee 352

HUNTZ, STEVE
69 O-Pee-Chee 136
70 O-Pee-Chee 282
71 O-Pee-Chee 486
72 O-Pee-Chee 73

HUPPERT, DAN
84 Vancouver/Cramer 37

HURDLE, CLINT
80 O-Pee-Chee 273
81 O-Pee-Chee 98
87 O-Pee-Chee 317

HURSEY, DARREN
89 London/ProCards 1370
91 London/LineDrive 387
91 London/ProCards 1873

HURST, BRUCE
90 FleerCdn. 159
85 Leaf 73
87 Leaf 253
88 Leaf 179
84 O-Pee-Chee 213
85 O-Pee-Chee 134
86 O-Pee-Chee 193
87 O-Pee-Chee 31
88 O-Pee-Chee 125
90 O-Pee-Chee 315
91 O-Pee-Chee 65
92 O-Pee-Chee 238
93 O-Pee-Chee 256
84 opcSticker 226
85 opcSticker 211
87 opcSticker 19
88 opcSticker 253,-SStar 29
88 PaniniSticker 22
89 PaniniSticker 271
90 PaniniSticker 357
91 PaniniSticker 238
93 PaniniSticker 256
91 PaniniTopFifteen 90

HURST, DON
34 WWGum(V354) 80

HURTADO, EDWIN
93 StCatharines/ClassicBest 11
93 StCatharines/ProCards 3969

HUSON, JEFF
90 FleerCdn. 350
90 O-Pee-Chee 72
91 O-Pee-Chee 756
92 O-Pee-Chee 314
91 PaniniSticker 255
92 PaniniSticker 78
93 PaniniSticker 83

HURST, JONATHAN
93 Ottawa/ProCards 2431

HUTCHINSON, FRED
39 WWGum(V351A)
39 WWGum(V351B)

HUTSON, SCOTT
89 StCatharines/ProCards 2074

HUTTON, TOM
79 Dimanche/DernièreHeure
80 Dimanche/DernièreHeure
73 O-Pee-Chee 271
74 O-Pee-Chee 443
75 O-Pee-Chee 477
76 O-Pee-Chee 91
79 O-Pee-Chee 355
80 O-Pee-Chee 219
81 O-Pee-Chee 374

HYMEL, GARY
93 Ottawa/ProCards 2438

I

IBAR, JOSE
94 GarciaPhoto 55

IBARRA, CARLOS
82 Edmonton/TCMA 1

INCAVIGLIA, PETE
87 Leaf 185
88 Leaf 147
90 FleerCdn. 301
87 O-Pee-Chee 384
88 O-Pee-Chee 280
89 O-Pee-Chee 42
90 O-Pee-Chee 430
91 O-Pee-Chee 172
92 O-Pee-Chee 679
93 O-Pee-Chee 242
91 opcPremier 67
92 opcPremier 126
93 opcPremier 95
87 opcSticker 236, 308
88 opcSticker 239
89 opcSticker 249
88 PaniniSticker 207
89 PaniniSticker 455
90 PaniniSticker 157
91 PaniniSticker 258
87 STuartBakery 26

INFANTE, TOM
89 Hamilton/Star 19

INGRAM, RICCARDO
90 London/ProCards 1280
91 London/LineDrive 388
91 London/ProCards 1890

INNIS, JEFF
90 FleerCdn. 206
90 O-Pee-Chee 557
91 O-Pee-Chee 443
92 O-Pee-Chee 139
93 O-Pee-Chee 141

IORG, DANE
87 O-Pee-Chee 151
83 opcSticker 189,190
86 opcSticker 18

IORG, GARTH
86 Leaf 252
92 Nabisco 28
81 O-Pee-Chee 78,-Poster 16
82 O-Pee-Chee 83
83 O-Pee-Chee 326
84 O-Pee-Chee 39
85 O-Pee-Chee 168
86 O-Pee-Chee 277
87 O-Pee-Chee 59
88 O-Pee-Chee 273
88 PaniniSticker 220
84 TOR/FireSafety
85 TOR/FireSafety
86 TOR/AultFoods
86 TOR/FireSafety
87 TOR/FireSafety

IRISH, JEFF
90 StCatharines/ProCards 3475

IRVIN, MONTY
53 Exhibits 6

IRVINE, DARYL
91 O-Pee-Chee 189

IRVINE, ED
82 Vancouver/TCMA 8
84 Vancouver/Cramer 44

ISASI, FELIX
94 GarciaPhoto 17

ISOM, JEFF
93 Welland/ClassicBest 8
93 Welland/ProCards 3350

ISSAC, REY
94 GarciaPhoto 82

IVIE, MIKE
72 O-Pee-Chee 457
73 O-Pee-Chee 613
76 O-Pee-Chee 134
77 O-Pee-Chee 241
80 O-Pee-Chee 34
81 O-Pee-Chee 236
83 O-Pee-Chee 117

IZTURIS, CESAR
97 St.Catharines/Best 18

J

JABLONOWSKI, PETE
34 WWGum(V354) 34

JACKLITSCH, FRED
1912 ImperialTobacco(C46) 62

JACKSON, AL
67 O-Pee-Chee 195
70 O-Pee-Chee 443

JACKSON, BO
90 FleerCdn. 110,635
87 Leaf 35
88 Leaf 187
88 O-Pee-Chee 8
89 O-Pee-Chee 84
90 O-Pee-Chee 300
91 O-Pee-Chee 600
92 O-Pee-Chee 290
93 O-Pee-Chee 15
94 O-Pee-Chee 116
88 opcSticker 258
89 opcSticker 265
88 PaniniSticker 110
89 PaniniSticker 358
90 PaniniSticker 84,198,384
91 PaniniSticker 281
94 PaniniSticker 49

JACKSON CHUCK
91 Calgary/LineDrive 61
91 Calgary/ProCards 521
93 Edmonton/ProCards 1143

JACKSON, DANNY
90 FleerCdn. 422
86 Leaf 30
88 O-Pee-Chee 324
89 O-Pee-Chee 319
90 O-Pee-Chee 445
91 O-Pee-Chee 92,619
94 O-Pee-Chee 240
91 opcPremier 68
89 opcSticker 143,-SStar 62
89 PaniniSticker 67
90 PaniniSticker 255

JACKSON, DARRELL
81 O-Pee-Chee 89

JACKSON, DARRIN
90 FleerCdn. 160
90 O-Pee-Chee 624
91 O-Pee-Chee 373
92 O-Pee-Chee 88
93 O-Pee-Chee 143
92 PaniniSticker 237
93 PaniniSticker 264
93 TOR/Dempster's 22
93 TOR/FireSafety
93 TOR/McDonalds 33

JACKSON, GRANT
69 O-Pee-Chee 174
70 O-Pee-Chee 6
71 O-Pee-Chee 392
72 O-Pee-Chee 212
73 O-Pee-Chee 396
74 O-Pee-Chee 68
75 O-Pee-Chee 303
76 O-Pee-Chee 233
80 O-Pee-Chee 218
81 O-Pee-Chee 232
82 O-Pee-Chee 104

JACKSON, JEFF
90 O-Pee-Chee 74

JACKSON, JOHN
94 Vancouver/ProCards 1875

JACKSON, LARRY
65 O-Pee-Chee 10
68 O-Pee-Chee 81
62 PostCereal 165

JACKSON, LOY
61 Toronto/BeeHive

JACKSON, MIKE
90 FleerCdn. 517
89 O-Pee-Chee 169
90 O-Pee-Chee 761
91 O-Pee-Chee 534
92 O-Pee-Chee 411

JACKSON, REGGIE
85 GeneralMills
86 GeneralMills
87 GeneralMills
85 Leaf 170
86 Leaf 173
87 Leaf 201
70 OPC 64,66,140,459
70 OPC-Booklet 10
71 O-Pee-Chee 20
72 O-Pee-Chee 90,435-36
73 O-Pee-Chee 255
74 OPC 130,202-03,338
75 O-Pee-Chee 211,300
76 O-Pee-Chee 194,500
77 O-Pee-Chee 200
78 O-Pee-Chee 110,242
79 O-Pee-Chee 374
80 O-Pee-Chee 314
81 O-Pee-Chee 370
82 O-Pee-Chee 300,301,377
83 O-Pee-Chee 56,219,390
84 O-Pee-Chee 100
85 O-Pee-Chee 200
86 O-Pee-Chee 394,I
87 O-Pee-Chee 300
82 opcSticker 216
83 opcSticker 5,17,41,163
84 opcSticker 231,342
85 O-Pee-Chee 187,220
86 O-Pee-Chee 177
86 opcTattoo 17
88 PaniniSticker 175
71 ProStarPostcard

JACKSON, RON
79 O-Pee-Chee 173
80 O-Pee-Chee 5
81 O-Pee-Chee 271
82 O-Pee-Chee 359
88 Vancouver/ProCards 768

JACKSON, ROY LEE
85 Leaf 106
82 O-Pee-Chee 71
83 O-Pee-Chee 194
84 O-Pee-Chee 339
85 O-Pee-Chee 37
85 opcSticker 364
84 TOR/FireSafety

JACKSON, SONNY
65 O-Pee-Chee 16
68 O-Pee-Chee 187
69 O-Pee-Chee 53
70 O-Pee-Chee 413
71 O-Pee-Chee 587
72 O-Pee-Chee 318
73 O-Pee-Chee 403
74 O-Pee-Chee 591

JACKSON, TRAVIS
22 WilliamPaterson(V89) 36
34 WWGum(V354) 24

JACKSON, WILLIAM
52 Laval Dairy 34

JACOBS, FORREST V.
53 Exhibits 46
52 Parkhurst 54

JACOBS, RON
79 Vancouver/TCMA 3

JACOBSON, BILL
20 MapleCrispettes(V117) 18
23 WillardsChoc.(V100) 69

JACOBY, BROOK
90 FleerCdn. 493
86 Leaf 82
87 Leaf 8,134

88 Leaf 51
87 HostessSticker
85 O-Pee-Chee 327
86 O-Pee-Chee 116
87 O-Pee-Chee 98
88 O-Pee-Chee 248
89 O-Pee-Chee 1
90 O-Pee-Chee 208
91 O-Pee-Chee 47
92 O-Pee-Chee 606
85 opcSticker 251,370
86 opcSticker 207
87 opcSticker 212
88 opcSticker 211
89 opcSticker 212
86 opcTattoo 5
88 PaniniSticker 76
89 PaniniSticker 326
90 PaniniSticker 58
91 PaniniSticker 216

JAHA, JOHN
92 O-Pee-Chee 126
93 O-Pee-Chee 190
94 O-Pee-Chee 131
94 PaniniSticker 82

JAMES, BOB
82 Dimanche/DernièreHeure
84 O-Pee-Chee 336
85 O-Pee-Chee 114
86 O-Pee-Chee 284
87 O-Pee-Chee 342
88 O-Pee-Chee 232
86 opcSticker 290
88 opcSticker 289
86 opcTattoo 3
88 PaniniSticker 54
82 MTL/Hygrade
84 MTL
84 MTL/StuartBakery 10

JAMES, CHARLIE
65 O-Pee-Chee 141

JAMES, CHRIS
90 FleerCdn. 161
87 Leaf 42
88 O-Pee-Chee 1
89 O-Pee-Chee 298
90 O-Pee-Chee 178
91 O-Pee-Chee 494
92 O-Pee-Chee 709
88 opcSticker 119,122
88 PaniniSticker 362
89 PaniniSticker 156
90 PaniniSticker 350

JAMES, CLEO
72 O-Pee-Chee 117

JAMES, DION
90 FleerCdn. 494
85 Leaf 162
88 O-Pee-Chee 82
90 O-Pee-Chee 319
91 O-Pee-Chee 117
88 opcSticker 42
89 opcSticker 24
88 PaniniSticker 250
89 PaniniSticker 44
90 PaniniSticker 64
86 Vancouver/ProCards

JAMES, JEFF
70 O-Pee-Chee 302

JAMES, MIKE
94 Vancouver/ProCards 1862

JAMES, SKIP
79 Vancouver/TCMA 1

JAMES, TODD
92 Edmonton/SkyBox 161

JAMIESON, CHARLES D.
23 WillardsChoc.(V100) 70

JANESKI, GERRY
71 O-Pee-Chee 673

JANICKI, PETE
96 Vancouver/Best 18
97 Vancouver/Best 18

JANSEN, LARRY
73 O-Pee-Chee 81

JANZEN, MARTY
96 TOR/OhHenry
97 TOR/Sizzler 53

JARVIS, PAT
67 O-Pee-Chee 57
68 O-Pee-Chee 134
70 O-Pee-Chee 438
71 O-Pee-Chee 623
73 O-Pee-Chee 192

JARVIS, RAY
70 O-Pee-Chee 361
71 O-Pee-Chee 526

JASTER, LARRY
68 O-Pee-Chee 117
70 O-Pee-Chee 124

JATA, PAUL
72 O-Pee-Chee 257

JAVIER, JULIAN
68 O-Pee-Chee 25
70 O-Pee-Chee 415
71 O-Pee-Chee 185

JAVIER, STAN
90 FleerCdn. 12
89 O-Pee-Chee 248
90 O-Pee-Chee 102
91 O-Pee-Chee 61
92 O-Pee-Chee 581
91 PaniniSticker 61
93 PaniniSticker 276

JAY, JOEY
65 O-Pee-Chee 174
62 PostCereal 124
62 ShirriffCoin 126

JEFFCOAT, MIKE
90 FleerCdn. 302
90 O-Pee-Chee 778
91 O-Pee-Chee 244
92 O-Pee-Chee 464
94 Edmonton/ProCards 2870

JEFFERIES, GREGG
90 FleerCdn. 207
88 Leaf 259
89 O-Pee-Chee 233
90 O-Pee-Chee 457
91 O-Pee-Chee 30
92 O-Pee-Chee 707
94 O-Pee-Chee 77
93 O-Pee-Chee 123
92 opcPremier 95
93 opcPremier 98
89 PaniniSticker 128
90 PaniniSticker 298
91 PaniniSticker 80
92 PaniniSticker 223
93 PaniniSticker 106
94 PaniniSticker 243

JEFFERSON, JESSE
92 Nabisco 32
73 O-Pee-Chee 604
74 O-Pee-Chee 509
75 O-Pee-Chee 539
76 O-Pee-Chee 47
77 O-Pee-Chee 184
78 O-Pee-Chee 22
79 O-Pee-Chee 112
80 O-Pee-Chee 244
78 TOR
79 TOR/BubbleYum

JEFFERSON, REGGIE
92 O-Pee-Chee 93
93 O-Pee-Chee 163
93 PaniniSticker 48

JEFFERSON, STAN
88 O-Pee-Chee 223
88 opcSticker 109
88 PaniniSticker 411

JELTZ,STEVE
90 FleerCdn. 562
88 O-Pee-Chee 126
90 O-Pee-Chee 607
91 O-Pee-Chee 507
89 opcSticker 114
88 PaniniSticker 361

JENKINS FERGUSON (FERGIE)
92 CanadianSpiritMedallion
68 O-Pee-Chee 9,11
69 O-Pee-Chee 10,12
70 O-Pee-Chee 69,71,240
71 O-Pee-Chee 70,72,280
72 O-Pee-Chee 93,95,410
73 O-Pee-Chee 180
74 O-Pee-Chee 87
75 O-Pee-Chee 60,310
76 O-Pee-Chee 250
77 O-Pee-Chee 187
80 O-Pee-Chee 203
82 O-Pee-Chee 137
83 O-Pee-Chee 230,231
84 O-Pee-Chee 343
83 opcSticker 224
84 opcSticker 48
71 ProStarPostcard
71 ProStarPoster

JENKINS, JACK
70 O-Pee-Chee 286

JENNINGS, WILLIAM
52 Parkhurst 5

JENSEN, JACKIE
75 O-Pee-Chee 196
60 opcTattoo 23,75
50 PalmDairies
62 PostCereal 62
62 ShirriffCoin 73

JERSLID, AARON
92 StCatharines/ClassicBest 26
92 StCatharines/ProCards 3383

JESTADT, GARRY
70 O-Pee-Chee 109
71 O-Pee-Chee 576
72 O-Pee-Chee 143

JETER, JOHNNY
70 O-Pee-Chee 141
71 O-Pee-Chee 47
72 O-Pee-Chee 288
73 O-Pee-Chee 423
74 O-Pee-Chee 615

JETER, SHAWN
92 Vancouver/SkyBox

JETHROE, SAM
53 Exhibits 10

JEWETT, TRENT
92 Welland/ClassicBest 28
97 Calgary/Best 1

JIMENEZ, ANTONIO
94 GarciaPhoto 64

JIMENEZ, ELVIO
65 O-Pee-Chee 226

JIMENEZ, HOUSTON
87 Vancouver/ProCards 1609

JIMENEZ, MIGUEL
95 Edmonton/Macri

JOCKISH, MIKE
88 StCatharines/ProCards 2031
89 StCatharines/ProCards 2078

JOHN, TOMMY
88 Leaf 17, 230
65 O-Pee-Chee 208
68 O-Pee-Chee 72
70 O-Pee-Chee 180
71 O-Pee-Chee 520
72 O-Pee-Chee 264
73 O-Pee-Chee 258
74 O-Pee-Chee 451
75 O-Pee-Chee 47
76 O-Pee-Chee 416
79 O-Pee-Chee 129
80 O-Pee-Chee 348
81 O-Pee-Chee 96
82 O-Pee-Chee 75
83 O-Pee-Chee 144,196
84 O-Pee-Chee 284
85 O-Pee-Chee 179
87 O-Pee-Chee 236
82 opcSticker 214
84 opcSticker 232
85 opcSticker 229
89 opcSticker 310
88 PaniniSticker 148

JOHNS, KEITH
92 Hamilton/ClassicBest 12

JOHNSON, ALEX
66 O-Pee-Chee 104
67 O-Pee-Chee 108
70 O-Pee-Chee 115
71 O-Pee-Chee 61
72 O-Pee-Chee 215
73 O-Pee-Chee 425
74 O-Pee-Chee 107
75 O-Pee-Chee 534

JOHNSON, ARMANDO
94 GarciaPhoto 32

JOHNSON, BARRY
97 Calgary/Best 14

JOHNSON, BART
71 O-Pee-Chee 156
72 O-Pee-Chee 126
73 O-Pee-Chee 506
74 O-Pee-Chee 147
75 O-Pee-Chee 446
76 O-Pee-Chee 513

JOHNSON, BEN
90 Welland/Pucko 6

JOHNSON, BOB
37 O-Pee-Chee 123
66 O-Pee-Chee 148
67 O-Pee-Chee 38
71 O-Pee-Chee 71,365
72 O-Pee-Chee 27
73 O-Pee-Chee 657
74 O-Pee-Chee 269

JOHNSON, CLIFF
85 Leaf 115
86 Leaf 250
92 Nabisco 2
75 O-Pee-Chee 143
76 O-Pee-Chee 249
79 O-Pee-Chee 50
80 O-Pee-Chee 321
81 O-Pee-Chee 17
82 O-Pee-Chee 333
84 O-Pee-Chee 221
85 O-Pee-Chee 7
86 O-Pee-Chee 348
87 O-Pee-Chee 118
82 opcSticker 226
84 opcSticker 366
85 opcSticker 367
84 TOR/FireSafety
86 TOR/AultFoods
86 TOR/FireSafety

JOHNSON, CURTIS
88 StCatharines/ProCards 2022

JOHNSON, DAMON
95 StCatharines/TimHortons 22
96 StCatharines/Best 13

JOHNSON, DARRELL
74 O-Pee-Chee 403
75 O-Pee-Chee 172
76 O-Pee-Chee 118

JOHNSON, DAVE
69 O-Pee-Chee 203
70 O-Pee-Chee 45
71 O-Pee-Chee 595
73 O-Pee-Chee 550
74 O-Pee-Chee 45
75 O-Pee-Chee 57
90 O-Pee-Chee 291, 416
91 O-Pee-Chee 163
92 O-Pee-Chee 657
92 Edmonton/SkyBox 162
87 Vancouver/ProCards 1606

JOHNSON, DERON
65 O-Pee-Chee 75
67 O-Pee-Chee 135
70 OPC 125,-Booklet 20
71 O-Pee-Chee 490
72 O-Pee-Chee 167,168
73 O-Pee-Chee 590
74 O-Pee-Chee 312
76 O-Pee-Chee 529

JOHNSON, DERON
89 Welland/Pucko 14

JOHNSON, ERNEST
23 WillardsChoc.(V100) 71

JOHNSON, FRANK
71 O-Pee-Chee 128

JOHNSON, HENRY
33 WWGum(V353) 14

JOHNSON, HOWARD
90 Ben's/HolsumDisks 10
90 FleerCdn. 208,639
92 Ben'sDisk 16
88 Leaf 238
92 McDonald's 25
85 O-Pee-Chee 192
86 O-Pee-Chee 304
87 O-Pee-Chee 267
88 O-Pee-Chee 85, K
89 O-Pee-Chee 383
90 O-Pee-Chee 399,680
91 O-Pee-Chee 470
92 O-Pee-Chee 590
93 O-Pee-Chee 166
94 O-Pee-Chee 31
92 opcPremier 42
85 opcSticker 262
86 opcSticker 101
88 opcSticker 99
89 opcSticker 91,-SuperStar 41
88 PaniniSticker 343,439
90 PaniniSticker 210,306,385
91 PaniniSticker 81
92 PaniniSticker 147,224
93 PaniniSticker 251
94 PaniniSticker 219
92 PizzaHut/DietPepsi 23

JOHNSON, JEFF
92 O-Pee-Chee 449

JOHNSON, JERRY
70 O-Pee-Chee 162
71 O-Pee-Chee 412
72 O-Pee-Chee 35,36
73 O-Pee-Chee 248
75 O-Pee-Chee 218
76 O-Pee-Chee 658
78 O-Pee-Chee 184

JOHNSON, JOE
87 Leaf 91
88 O-Pee-Chee 347
87 TOR/FireSafety
88 Edmonton/CMC 7
88 Edmonton/ProCards 560

JOHNSON, JOHN HENRY
79 O-Pee-Chee 361
80 O-Pee-Chee 97
86 Vancouver/ProCards

JOHNSON, KEN
67 O-Pee-Chee 101
61 Toronto/BeeHive

JOHNSON, LAMAR
76 O-Pee-Chee 596
79 O-Pee-Chee 192
81 O-Pee-Chee 366

JOHNSON, LANCE
90 FleerCdn. 536
88 Leaf 31
90 O-Pee-Chee 587
91 O-Pee-Chee 243
92 O-Pee-Chee 736
93 O-Pee-Chee 176
94 O-Pee-Chee 262
89 PaniniSticker 312
91 PaniniSticker 317
92 PaniniSticker 130
93 PaniniSticker 141
89 Vancouver/CMC 18
89 Vancouver/ProCards 576

JOHNSON, LOU
66 O-Pee-Chee 13
68 O-Pee-Chee 184
61 Toronto/BeeHive

JOHNSON, RANDY
90 FleerCdn. 518
89 O-Pee-Chee 186
90 O-Pee-Chee 431
91 O-Pee-Chee 225
92 O-Pee-Chee 525
93 O-Pee-Chee 140
94 O-Pee-Chee 81
92 opcPremier 173
89 PaniniSticker 111
90 PaniniSticker 154
91 PaniniSticker 353
92 PaniniSticker 62
93 PaniniSticker 60
94 PaniniSticker 9,119

JOHNSON, ROY
33 WWGum(V353) 8

JOHNSON, ROY
84 MTL

JOHNSON, SYLVESTER
20 MapleCrispettes(V117) 13
21 Neilson's(V61) 24

JOHNSON, TIM
74 O-Pee-Chee 554
75 O-Pee-Chee 556
76 O-Pee-Chee 613
79 O-Pee-Chee 89
80 O-Pee-Chee 155
78 TOR

JOHNSON, TOM
75 O-Pee-Chee 618
76 O-Pee-Chee 448
79 O-Pee-Chee 77

JOHNSON, TOM
93 Welland/ClassicBest 9
93 Welland/ProCards 3366

JOHNSON, WALLACE
90 FleerCdn. 351
87 O-Pee-Chee 234
88 O-Pee-Chee 228
89 O-Pee-Chee 138
90 O-Pee-Chee 318
89 PaniniSticker 120

JOHNSON, WALTER
20 MapleCrispettes(V117) 30
21 Neilson's(V61) 47
23 Neilson's 20
73 O-Pee-Chee 476,478
76 O-Pee-Chee 349
23 WillardsChoc.(V100) 72
22 WilliamPaterson(V89) 47

JOHNSTON, JAMES H.
23 WillardsChoc.(V100) 73

JOHNSTON, JOEL
92 O-Pee-Chee 328

JOHNSTONE, JAY
69 O-Pee-Chee 59
70 O-Pee-Chee 485-Booklet 3
71 O-Pee-Chee 292
72 O-Pee-Chee 233
75 O-Pee-Chee 242
76 O-Pee-Chee 114
77 O-Pee-Chee 226
79 O-Pee-Chee 2877
80 O-Pee-Chee 15
81 O-Pee-Chee 372
83 O-Pee-Chee 152
83 opcSticker 220
84 opcSticker 50

JOHNSTONE, JOHN
93 Edmonton/ProCards 1131
94 Edmonton/ProCards 2871

JOK, STANLEY (STAN) EDWARD
52 Parkhurst 93

JOLLEY, SMEAD
36 WWGum(V355) 98

JONES, BARRY
90 O-Pee-Chee 243
91 O-Pee-Chee 33
92 O-Pee-Chee 361
91 opcPremier 69

JONES, BOBBY
94 O-Pee-Chee 108, -DD 6

JONES, CALVIN
91 Calgary/LineDrive 62
91 Calgary/ProCards 511

JONES, CHIPPER
91 O-Pee-Chee 333
92 O-Pee-Chee 551
94 O-Pee-Chee 57

JONES, CHRIS
92 O-Pee-Chee 332
94 PaniniSticker 176

JONES, CLEON
66 O-Pee-Chee 67
67 O-Pee-Chee 165
68 O-Pee-Chee-Poster 13
70 OPC 19,61,-Booklet 19
71 O-Pee-Chee 527
72 O-Pee-Chee 31,32
73 O-Pee-Chee 540
74 O-Pee-Chee 245
75 O-Pee-Chee 43

JONES, DALTON
65 O-Pee-Chee 178
67 O-Pee-Chee 139
68 O-Pee-Chee 106
71 O-Pee-Chee 367
72 O-Pee-Chee 83
73 O-Pee-Chee 512

JONES, DAN
91 Welland/Best 29
91 Welland/ProCards 3568

JONES, DEACON
21 Neilson's(V61) 43

JONES, DENNIS
91 PaniniTopFifteen 87

JONES, DOUG
90 FleerCdn. 495
89 O-Pee-Chee 312
90 O-Pee-Chee 75
91 O-Pee-Chee 745
92 O-Pee-Chee 461
93 O-Pee-Chee 267
89 opcSticker 3,215,-SStar 32
89 PaniniSticker 5, 319
90 PaniniSticker 63
91 PaniniSticker 224
94 PaniniSticker 195
95 Edmonton/Macri
84 Vancouver/Cramer39
82 Vancouver/TCMA 13

JONES, ELIJAH
1912 ImperialTobacco(C46) 52

JONES, FELIX
92 PaniniSticker 176

JONES, GARY
71 O-Pee-Chee 559
95 Edmonton/Macri

JONES, JEFF
91 London/LineDrive 400
91 London/ProCards 1893
92 London/ProCards 650

JONES, JIMMY
90 O-Pee-Chee 359
92 O-Pee-Chee 184
93 O-Pee-Chee 293

JONES, KEITH
97 Lethbridge/Best 8

JONES, MACK
92 Nabisco 27
65 O-Pee-Chee 241
70 O-Pee-Chee 38
71 O-Pee-Chee 142
71 MTL/ProStar
93 MTL/McDonald's 15

JONES, MATT
92 Welland/ClassicBest 11

JONES, ODELL
84 O-Pee-Chee 382

JONES, RANDY
74 O-Pee-Chee 173
75 O-Pee-Chee 248
76 O-Pee-Chee 199,201,310
77 O-Pee-Chee 5,113
78 O-Pee-Chee 101
79 O-Pee-Chee 95
80 O-Pee-Chee 160
81 O-Pee-Chee 148
82 O-Pee-Chee 274
83 O-Pee-Chee 29

JONES, ROBERT W.
23 WillardsChoc.(V100) 74

JONES, RON
90 FleerCdn. 563
90 O-Pee-Chee 129
89 PaniniSticker 143

JONES, RUPPERT
78 O-Pee-Chee 20
79 O-Pee-Chee 218
80 O-Pee-Chee 43
81 O-Pee-Chee 225
82 O-Pee-Chee 217
83 O-Pee-Chee 287
84 O-Pee-Chee 327
86 O-Pee-Chee 186
82 opcSticker 99
83 opcSticker 295
84 opcSticker 158
86 opcSticker 184
88 PaniniSticker 47

JONES, SAM
60 opcTattoo 24
62 PostCereal 138
62 ShirriffCoin 162

JONES, SAM
22 WilliamPaterson(V89) 17
34 WWGum(V354) 31

JONES, SAMUEL POND
23 WillardsChoc.(V100) 75

JONES, STEVE
69 O-Pee-Chee 49
92 Hamilton/ClassicBest 10

JONES, TIM
90 O-Pee-Chee 533
91 O-Pee-Chee 262

JONES, TOM
90 Calgary/CMC 23
90 Calgary/ProCards 664
97 Lethbridge/Best 1

JONES, TRACY
90 FleerCdn. 607
88 Leaf 107
88 O-Pee-Chee 101
89 O-Pee-Chee 373
90 O-Pee-Chee 767
91 O-Pee-Chee 87
92 O-Pee-Chee 271
88 PaniniSticker 283
89 PaniniSticker 124

JORDAN, BAXTER
34 WWGum(V354) 75

JORDAN, BRIAN
93 O-Pee-Chee 134
94 PaniniSticker 244

JORDAN, RICKY
90 FleerCdn. 564
90 O-Pee-Chee 216
91 O-Pee-Chee 712
92 O-Pee-Chee 103
90 PaniniSticker 315
91 PaniniSticker 103

JORDAN, TIM
1912 ImperialTobacco(C46) 87

JORDAN, TIM
92 Hamilton/ClassicBest 20

JORGENSEN, MIKE
72 Dimanche/DernièreHeure
70 O-Pee-Chee 348
71 O-Pee-Chee 596
72 O-Pee-Chee 16
73 O-Pee-Chee 281
74 O-Pee-Chee 549
75 O-Pee-Chee 286
76 O-Pee-Chee 117
77 O-Pee-Chee 9
71 ProStarPostcard
71 MTL/ProStar
74 MTL/GeorgeWeston
77 MTL
77 MTL/RedpathSugar

JORGENSON, JOHN
43-47 Montréal/ParadeSportive

JORGENSEN, TERRY
93 opcPremier 106

JOSE, FELIX
90 FleerCdn. 13
90 O-Pee-Chee 238
91 O-Pee-Chee 368
92 O-Pee-Chee 105
93 O-Pee-Chee 182
94 O-Pee-Chee 191
93 opcPremier 128
93 PaniniSticker 198
94 PaniniSticker 74

JOSE, MANNY
89 London/ProCards 1385

JOSEPH, RICK
70 O-Pee-Chee 186

JOSEPHSON, DUANE
70 O-Pee-Chee 263
71 O-Pee-Chee 56

JOSHUA, VON
71 O-Pee-Chee 57
73 O-Pee-Chee 544
74 O-Pee-Chee 551
75 O-Pee-Chee 547
76 O-Pee-Chee 82

JOVA, PEDRO
94 GarciaPhoto 94

JOYNER, WALLY
88 FantasticSam's 4
90 FleerCdn. 136
87 General Mills 3
87 HostessSticker
87 Leaf 1, 252
88 Leaf 50
87 O-Pee-Chee 80
88 O-Pee-Chee 168
89 O-Pee-Chee 270
90 O-Pee-Chee 525
91 O-Pee-Chee 195
92 O-Pee-Chee 629
93 O-Pee-Chee 148
94 O-Pee-Chee 91
92 opcPremier 61
87 opcSticker 150,174,313
88 opcSticker 179,-SStar 34
89 opcSticker 183
88 PaniniSticker 40
89 PaniniSticker 291
90 PaniniSticker 31
91 PaniniSticker 180
92 PaniniSticker 5
93 PaniniSticker 103
94 PaniniSticker 75
87 Stuart Bakery 16
85 Edmonton/Cramer 2

JUDEK, JOHN
92 Vancouver/SkyBox 641

JUDEN, JEFF
90 O-Pee-Chee 164
92 O-Pee-Chee 34
93 O-Pee-Chee 309

JUDGE, JOE
23 Neilson's 21
23 WillardsChoc.(V100) 76
22 WilliamPaterson(V89) 44
33 WWGum(V353) 88

JUNCO, LAZARO
94 GarciaPhoto 12

JURAK, ED
90 Calgary/CMC 10
90 Calgary/ProCards 658

JURGES, BILL
36 WWGum(V355) 97

JUSTICE, DAVID
90 FleerCdn. 586
92 McDonald's 23
91 O-Pee-Chee 329
92 O-Pee-Chee 80
93 O-Pee-Chee 180
94 O-Pee-Chee 233, -AS 24
91 opcPremier 70
92 opcPremier 117
91 PaniniSticker 25
92 PaniniSticker 166
93 PaniniSticker 187
94 PaniniSticker 146
91 PostCdn. 12
94 PostCdn. 17

JUSTIS, WALTER
1912 ImperialTobacco(C46) 42

JUTZE, SKIP
73 O-Pee-Chee 613
74 O-Pee-Chee 328
76 O-Pee-Chee 489

K

KAAT, JIM
65 O-Pee-Chee 62
68 O-Pee-Chee 67
70 O-Pee-Chee 75
71 O-Pee-Chee 245
73 O-Pee-Chee 530
74 O-Pee-Chee 440
75 O-Pee-Chee 243
76 O-Pee-Chee 80
83 O-Pee-Chee 211,383
83 opcSticker 135,136

KAIN, MARTY
84 Edmonton/Cramer 100
85 Edmonton/Cramer 11

KAISER, JEFF
91 O-Pee-Chee 576

KALINE, AL
65 O-Pee-Chee 130
67 O-Pee-Chee 30
68 O-Pee-Chee 2,-Poster 14
71 O-Pee-Chee 180
73 O-Pee-Chee 280
74 O-Pee-Chee 215
75 O-Pee-Chee 4
60 opcTattoo 25
62 PostCereal 20
71 ProStarPostcard
62 ShirriffCoin 67

KAMIENIECKI, SCOTT
92 O-Pee-Chee 102
92 opcPremier 110

KAMM, WILLIE
22 WilliamPaterson(V89) 7
33 WWGum(V353) 68
34 WWGum(V354) 60

KARKOVICE, RON
90 O-Pee-Chee 717
91 O-Pee-Chee 568
92 O-Pee-Chee 153
93 O-Pee-Chee 198
94 O-Pee-Chee 71
93 PaniniSticker 142
88 Vancouver/CMC 15
88 Vancouver/ProCards 773

KARROS, ERIC
93 HumptyDumpty 34
92 O-Pee-Chee 194
93 O-Pee-Chee 208
92 opcPremier 63
93 opcPremier-StarPerf. 8
93 PaniniSticker 166,214
94 PaniniSticker 201

KARSAY, STEVE
94 O-Pee-Chee 11
91 TOR/Score 31
90 StCatharines/ProCards 3472

KASKO, EDDIE
70 O-Pee-Chee 489
71 O-Pee-Chee 578
72 O-Pee-Chee 218
73 O-Pee-Chee 131
62 PostCereal 119
62 ShirriffCoin 147

KAUFMANN, CURT
85 Edmonton/Cramer 20

KEALEY, STEVE
71 O-Pee-Chee 43
72 O-Pee-Chee 146
73 O-Pee-Chee 581

KEANE, JOHNNY
65 O-Pee-Chee 131

KEARNEY, BOB
85 O-Pee-Chee 386
86 O-Pee-Chee 123
87 O-Pee-Chee 73
84 opcSticker 381

KEEDY, PAT
84 Edmonton/Cramer 118
85 Edmonton/Cramer 1
86 Edmonton/ProCards

KEEFER, PAUL
89 Welland/Pucko 15

KEENAN, JAMES W.
23 WillardsChoc.(V100) 77

KEETON, RICKEY
79 Vancouver/TCMA 10

KEIFER, STEVE
85 Leaf 27

KEKICH, MIKE
70 O-Pee-Chee 536
71 O-Pee-Chee 703
72 O-Pee-Chee 138
73 O-Pee-Chee 371
74 O-Pee-Chee 199
76 O-Pee-Chee 582

KELLEHER, JOHN
21 Neilson's(V61) 87

KELLEY, DICK
66 O-Pee-Chee 84
67 O-Pee-Chee 138
70 O-Pee-Chee 474
72 O-Pee-Chee 412

KELLEY, HARRY
37 O-Pee-Chee(V300) 121

KELLEY, JACK
1912 ImperialTobacco(C46) 15

KELLEY, JOE
1912 ImperialTobacco(C46) 27

KELLEY, TOM
66 O-Pee-Chee 44
71 O-Pee-Chee 463
72 O-Pee-Chee 97

KELLNER, ALEX
53 Exhibits 64

KELLY, ERSKINE
92 Welland/ClassicBest 12
93 Welland/ClassicBest 10
93 Welland/ProCards 3373

KELLY, GEORGE
21 Neilson's(V61) 119
23 Neilson's 22
23 WillardsChoc.(V100) 78
22 WilliamPaterson(V89) 15

KELLY, PAT
70 O-Pee-Chee 57
71 O-Pee-Chee 413
72 O-Pee-Chee 326
73 O-Pee-Chee 261
74 O-Pee-Chee 46
75 O-Pee-Chee 82
76 O-Pee-Chee 212
80 O-Pee-Chee 329
92 O-Pee-Chee 612
93 O-Pee-Chee 24
94 O-Pee-Chee 156
92 opcPremier 71
92 PaniniSticker 137
93 PaniniSticker 150
94 PaniniSticker 101

KELLY, ROBERTO
90 FleerCdn. 446
92 McDonald's 4
90 O-Pee-Chee 109
91 O-Pee-Chee 11
92 O-Pee-Chee 266
93 O-Pee-Chee 79
94 O-Pee-Chee 139
92 opcPremier 83
93 opcPremier 109
89 PaniniSticker 395
90 PaniniSticker 119
91 PaniniSticker 328
92 PaniniSticker 140
93 PaniniSticker 295
94 PaniniSticker 162
91 PaniniTopFifteen 31,47

KELLY, TOM
90 O-Pee-Chee 429
91 O-Pee-Chee 201
92 O-Pee-Chee 459

KELSO, BILL
65 O-Pee-Chee 194

KEMP, STEVE
85 Leaf 100
78 O-Pee-Chee 167
79 O-Pee-Chee 97
80 O-Pee-Chee 166
81 O-Pee-Chee 152
82 O-Pee-Chee 296
83 O-Pee-Chee 260
84 O-Pee-Chee 301
85 O-Pee-Chee 120
82 opcSticker 185
83 opcSticker 50

KENDALL, FRED
73 O-Pee-Chee 221
74 O-Pee-Chee 53
75 O-Pee-Chee 332
76 O-Pee-Chee 639
77 O-Pee-Chee 213

KENNEDY, BO
92 Vancouver/ProCards 2719

KENNEDY, BOB
68 O-Pee-Chee 183

KENNEDY, JOHN
65 O-Pee-Chee 119
67 O-Pee-Chee 111
70 O-Pee-Chee 53
71 O-Pee-Chee 498
73 O-Pee-Chee 437

KENNEDY, TERRY
90 FleerCdn. 58
86 GeneralMills
85 Leaf 33
88 Leaf 99
81 O-Pee-Chee 353
82 O-Pee-Chee 65
83 O-Pee-Chee 24
84 O-Pee-Chee 166
85 O-Pee-Chee 194
86 O-Pee-Chee 230
87 O-Pee-Chee 303
88 O-Pee-Chee 180
89 O-Pee-Chee 309
90 O-Pee-Chee 372
91 O-Pee-Chee 66
92 O-Pee-Chee 253
82 opcSticker 100
83 opcSticker 293
84 opcSticker 154
85 opcSticker 148
86 opcSticker 111,152
87 opcSticker 108
88 opcStick. 161,225,-SStar 55
89 opcSticker 235
88 PaniniSticker 7,227
89 PaniniSticker 256
91 PaniniSticker 66

KENNEDY, VERNON
37 O-Pee-Chee(V300) 135

KENNEY, JERRY
70 O-Pee-Chee 219
71 O-Pee-Chee 572
72 O-Pee-Chee 158
73 O-Pee-Chee 514

KENT, JEFF
93 O-Pee-Chee 213
94 O-Pee-Chee 166
94 PaniniSticker 220
93 TOR/Donruss 41
89 StCatharines/ProCards 2091

KENT, TROY
93 Calgary/ProCards 1162

KENWORTHY, DICK
68 O-Pee-Chee 63

KEOUGH, JOE
71 O-Pee-Chee 451
72 O-Pee-Chee 133

KEOUGH, MARTY
65 O-Pee-Chee 263
62 PostCereal 69
62 ShirriffCoin 79

KEOUGH, MATT
79 O-Pee-Chee 284
80 O-Pee-Chee 74
81 O-Pee-Chee 301
82 O-Pee-Chee 87
84 O-Pee-Chee 203
82 opcSticker 225
83 opcSticker 109

KERFELD, CHARLIE
87 Leaf 195
87 O-Pee-Chee 145
88 O-Pee-Chee 392
87 opcSticker 28

KERN, JIM
75 O-Pee-Chee 621
78 O-Pee-Chee 165
79 O-Pee-Chee 297
80 O-Pee-Chee 192
81 O-Pee-Chee 197
82 O-Pee-Chee 59

KERNEY, BOB
85 opcSticker 335

KERNS, RUSS
50 WWGum(V362) 38

KERRIGAN, JOE
77 O-Pee-Chee 171
78 O-Pee-Chee 108
77 MTL
77 MTL/RedpathSugar
84 MTL
84 MTL/StuartBakery 33,38
86 MTL/ProvigoFoods

KESSINGER, DON
66 O-Pee-Chee 24
68 O-Pee-Chee 159
70 O-Pee-Chee 80,456
71 O-Pee-Chee 455
72 O-Pee-Chee 145
73 O-Pee-Chee 285
74 O-Pee-Chee 38
75 O-Pee-Chee 315
76 O-Pee-Chee 574

KESTER, RICK
71 O-Pee-Chee 494
72 O-Pee-Chee 351

KEY, JIMMY
93 Ben'sDisk 19
90 FleerCdn. 85
87 GeneralMills
88 HostessDisk 24
86 Leaf 219
87 Leaf 187
88 Leaf 67
92 McDonald's 14
85 O-Pee-Chee 193
86 O-Pee-Chee 291
87 O-Pee-Chee 29
88 O-Pee-Chee 47
89 O-Pee-Chee 229
90 O-Pee-Chee 371
91 O-Pee-Chee 741
92 O-Pee-Chee 482
93 OPC 269, -WSHero 2
93 OPC-WSChamp 8
94 O-Pee-Chee 174
91 opcPremier 71
93 opcPremier 15
86 opcSticker 191
87 opcSticker 192
88 opcSticker 190
89 opcSticker 186
88 PaniniSticker 214
89 PaniniSticker 462
90 PaniniSticker 181
91 PaniniSticker 351
95 PostCdn. 10
84 TOR/FireSafety
85 TOR/FireSafety
86 TOR/AultFoods
86 TOR/FireSafety
87 TOR/FireSafety
88 TOR
88 TOR/FireSafety
89 TOR/FireSafety
90 TOR/FireSafety
90 TOR/Hostess
90 TOR/VictoryProductions
91 TOR/FireSafety
91 TOR/Score 3,38
92 TOR/FireSafety
93 TOR/Donruss 19, WS5
93 TOR/McDonalds 19

KHALIFA, SAMMY
86 Leaf 178
86 opcSticker 127
86 opcTattoo 6
87 Vancouver/ProCards 1608

KIBBLE, JAY
84 Edmonton/Cramer 119

KIECKER, DANA
91 O-Pee-Chee 763
92 O-Pee-Chee 163

KIEFER, STEVE
86 Vancouver/ProCards

KIELY, JOHN
90 London/ProCards 1264

KIES, NORMAN
36 WWGum(V355) 120

KILDUFF, PETER J.
23 WillardsChoc.(V100) 79

KILE, DARRYL
92 O-Pee-Chee 134
94 O-Pee-Chee 176
92 opcPremier 196
94 PaniniSticker 196

KILGUS, PAUL
90 FleerCdn. 34
89 O-Pee-Chee 276
90 O-Pee-Chee 86
90 TOR/FireSafety

KILKENNY, MIKE
70 O-Pee-Chee 424
71 O-Pee-Chee 86
72 O-Pee-Chee 337
73 O-Pee-Chee 551

KILLEBREW, HARMON
65 O-Pee-Chee 3,5
66 O-Pee-Chee 120
68 O-Pee-Chee 4,6,-Poster 15
70 O-Pee-Chee 64,66,150
71 O-Pee-Chee 65,550
72 O-Pee-Chee 51,52,88
73 O-Pee-Chee 170
74 O-Pee-Chee 400
75 O-Pee-Chee 207
75 O-Pee-Chee 640
60 opcTattoo 26,76
62 PostCereal 85
71 ProStarPostcard
62 ShirriffCoin 36

KILLEFER, WILLIAM
23 WillardsChoc.(V100) 80

KIMBERLIN, KEITH
91 London/LineDrive 389
91 London/ProCards 1885

KINDALL, JERRY
62 PostCereal 191

KINDELAN, ORESTES
94 GarciaPhoto 103

KINER, RALPH
53 Exhibits 22

KING, CLYDE
75 O-Pee-Chee 589
50 WWGum(V362) 26

KING, ERIC
90 FleerCdn. 537
88 O-Pee-Chee 108
90 O-Pee-Chee 786
91 O-Pee-Chee 121
92 O-Pee-Chee 326
92 opcPremier 80
88 opcSticker 271

KING, HAL
70 O-Pee-Chee 327
71 O-Pee-Chee 88
74 O-Pee-Chee 362
36 WWGum(V355) 121

KING, JEFF
90 FleerCdn. 469
90 O-Pee-Chee 454
91 O-Pee-Chee 272
92 O-Pee-Chee 693
93 O-Pee-Chee 96
94 O-Pee-Chee 151
91 PaniniSticker 117
93 PaniniSticker 284
94 PaniniSticker 236

KING, JIM
65 O-Pee-Chee 38

KING, KEVIN
87 Edmonton/ProCards 2068
88 Edmonton/CMC 25
88 Edmonton/ProCards 573

KING, LEE (EDWARD)
21 Neilson's(V61) 92
23 Neilson's 23
23 WillardsChoc.(V100) 81

KINGERY, MIKE
88 Leaf 104
88 O-Pee-Chee 119
91 O-Pee-Chee 657
88 PaniniSticker 193
89 Calgary/CMC 20
89 Calgary/ProCards 545

KINGMAN, BRIAN
82 O-Pee-Chee 231

KINGMAN, DAVE
85 Leaf 182
72 O-Pee-Chee 147
73 O-Pee-Chee 23
74 O-Pee-Chee 610
75 O-Pee-Chee 156
76 O-Pee-Chee 40,193
77 O-Pee-Chee 98
79 O-Pee-Chee 191
80 O-Pee-Chee 127
81 O-Pee-Chee 361
82 O-Pee-Chee 276
83 O-Pee-Chee 160,161
84 O-Pee-Chee 172
85 O-Pee-Chee 123
86 O-Pee-Chee 322
87 O-Pee-Chee 266
82 opcSticker 72
83 opcSticker 11,207,259
85 opcSticker 320
86 opcSticker 167
87 opcSticker 173

KINGWOOD, TYRONE
92 LondonProCards 646
92 London/SkyBox 411

KINZER, MATT
90 FleerCdn. 652

KIPLIA, JEFF
93 Vancouver/ProCards 2610

KIPPER, BOB
90 FleerCdn. 470
90 O-Pee-Chee 441
91 O-Pee-Chee 551
92 O-Pee-Chee 64

KIRBY, CLAY
70 O-Pee-Chee 79
71 O-Pee-Chee 333
72 O-Pee-Chee 173
73 O-Pee-Chee 655
74 O-Pee-Chee 287
75 O-Pee-Chee 423
76 O-Pee-Chee 579

KIRBY, WAYNE
94 O-Pee-Chee 219, -DD 3
94 PaniniSticker 57

KIRK, THOMAS (TOM) DANIEL
52 Parkhurst 79

KIRKLAND, WILLIE
65 O-Pee-Chee 148
62 PostCdn. Cereal 41
62 ShirriffCoin 61

KIRKPATRICK, ED
66 O-Pee-Chee 102
70 O-Pee-Chee 165
71 O-Pee-Chee 299
73 O-Pee-Chee 233
74 O-Pee-Chee 262
75 O-Pee-Chee 171
76 O-Pee-Chee 294

KIRKWOOD, DON
76 O-Pee-Chee 108
79 O-Pee-Chee 334
78 TOR

KISON, BRUCE
72 O-Pee-Chee 72
73 O-Pee-Chee 141
75 O-Pee-Chee 598
76 O-Pee-Chee 161
84 O-Pee-Chee 201
84 opcSticker 235

KISSELL, GEORGE
73 O-Pee-Chee 497
74 O-Pee-Chee 236

KISSINGER, JOHN
1912 ImperialTobacco(C46) 72

KISTEN, DALE
88 Hamilton/ProCards 1728

KITTLE, HUB
73 O-Pee-Chee 624
74 O-Pee-Chee 31

KITTLE, RON
90 FleerCdn. 538
85 Leaf 210
86 Leaf 257
88 Leaf 251
84 O-Pee-Chee 373
85 O-Pee-Chee 105
86 O-Pee-Chee 288
89 O-Pee-Chee 268
90 O-Pee-Chee 79
91 O-Pee-Chee 324
84 opcSticker 382
85 opcSticker 232
86 opcSticker 289
86 opcTattoo 6
90 PaniniSticker 51
82 Edmonton/TCMA 13

KIZZIAH, DAREWN
89 StCatharines/ProCards 2076

KLAMM, TED
92 Welland/ClassicBest 14

KLAUS, BILLY
62 PostCereal 67
62 ShirriffCoin 10

KLAUS, BOBBY
65 O-Pee-Chee 227
66 O-Pee-Chee 108

KLEIN, CHUCK
34 WWGum(V354) 56
36 WWGum(V355) 13

KLESKO, RYAN
92 O-Pee-Chee 126
93 O-Pee-Chee 189
94 O-Pee-Chee 75, -HotP 9

KLIMCHOCK, LOU
70 O-Pee-Chee 247

KLIMKOWSKI, RON
71 O-Pee-Chee 28
72 O-Pee-Chee 363

KLINE, RON
65 O-Pee-Che 56
67 O-Pee-Chee 133

KLINE, STEVE
71 O-Pee-Chee 51
72 O-Pee-Chee 467
73 O-Pee-Chee 172
74 O-Pee-Chee 324
75 O-Pee-Chee 639

KLINK, JOE
91 O-Pee-Chee 553
92 O-Pee-Chee 678

KLIPSTEIN, DAVE
86 Vancouver/ProCards

KLUSZESKI, TED
73 O-Pee-Chee 296
74 O-Pee-Chee 326
62 PostCereal 82

KLUTTZ, CLYDE
50 WWGum(V362) 41

KNACKERT, BRENT
91 O-Pee-Chee 563

KNEPPER, BOB
85 Leaf 61
86 Leaf 90
87 Leaf 249
79 O-Pee-Chee 255
80 O-Pee-Chee 61
81 O-Pee-Chee 279
82 O-Pee-Chee 389
84 O-Pee-Chee 93
85 O-Pee-Chee 289
86 O-Pee-Chee 231
87 O-Pee-Chee 129
89 O-Pee-Chee 280
90 O-Pee-Chee 104
82 opcSticker 45
85 opcSticker 62
87 opcSticker 32
89 opcSticker 22,-SuperStar 63
89 PaniniSticker 82

KNICELY, ALAN
86 O-Pee-Chee 316

KNIGHT, RAY
87 Leaf 166
79 O-Pee-Chee 211
80 O-Pee-Chee 987
81 O-Pee-Chee 325
82 O-Pee-Chee 319
83 O-Pee-Chee 275
84 O-Pee-Chee 321
85 O-Pee-Chee 274
86 O-Pee-Chee 27
87 O-Pee-Chee 275
88 O-Pee-Chee 124
82 opcSticker 39
83 opcSticker 238
84 opcSticker 68
87 opcSticker 24
88 opcSticker 229
88 PaniniSticker 12

KNOBLAUCH, CHUCK
92 O-Pee-Chee 23
93 O-Pee-Chee 175
94 O-Pee-Chee 155
92 opcPremier 35
92 PaniniSticker 116
93 PaniniSticker 126
94 PaniniSticker 92
91 ScoreAllStarFanfest 10

KNORR, RANDY
93 opcPremier 25
93 TOR/Dempster's 17
93 TOR/Donruss 25
93 TOR/FireSafety
93 TOR/McDonalds 25
95 TOR/OhHenry

KNOOP, BOBBY
65 O-Pee-Chee 26
67 O-Pee-Chee 175
68 OPC-Poster 16
71 O-Pee-Chee 506

KNOTT, ERIC
97 Lethbridge/Best 24

KNOWLES, DAROLD
78 Dimanche/DernièreHeure
66 O-Pee-Chee 27
70 O-Pee-Chee 106
71 O-Pee-Chee 261
73 O-Pee-Chee 274
74 O-Pee-Chee 57
75 O-Pee-Chee 352
76 O-Pee-Chee 617
79 O-Pee-Chee 303

KNOX, JOHN
74 O-Pee-Chee 604
75 O-Pee-Chee 546
76 O-Pee-Chee 218

KNUDSEN, KURT
91 London/ProCards 2232

KNUDSON, MARK
90 FleerCdn. 327
90 O-Pee-Chee 566
91 O-Pee-Chee 267
91 PaniniSticker 211

KOBEL, KEVIN
74 O-Pee-Chee 605
75 O-Pee-Chee 337
76 O-Pee-Chee 588
79 O-Pee-Chee 6
80 O-Pee-Chee 106

KOCHER, BRADLEY
1912 ImperialTobacco(C46) 82

KOCK, BILLY
97 TOR/Sizzler 58

KOEGEL, PETE
71 O-Pee-Chee 633
72 O-Pee-Chee 14

KOEHLER, JASON
96 StCatharines/Best 14

KOENIG, MARK
33 WWGum(V353) 39

KOENIGSFELD, RON
84 Vancouver/Cramer 25

KOLP, RAY
23 WillardsChoc.(V100) 82
33 WWGum(V353) 82

KOMMINSK, BRAD
90 FleerCdn. 496
86 O-Pee-Chee 210
90 O-Pee-Chee 476

KONIECZNY, DOUG
75 O-Pee-Chee 624
76 O-Pee-Chee 602

KONUSZEWSKI, DENNIS
92 Welland/ClassicBest 13

KOONCE, CAL
65 O-Pee-Chee 34
67 O-Pee-Chee 171
70 O-Pee-Chee 521
71 O-Pee-Chee 254

KOONTZ, JIM
84 Vancouver/Cramer 45

KOOSMAN, JERRY
85 Leaf 178
86 Leaf 23

68 O-Pee-Chee 177
69 O-Pee-Chee 90
70 O-Pee-Chee 468
71 O-Pee-Chee 335
73 O-Pee-Chee 184
74 O-Pee-Chee 356
75 O-Pee-Chee 19
76 O-Pee-Chee 64
77 O-Pee-Chee 26
79 O-Pee-Chee 345
80 O-Pee-Chee 144
81 O-Pee-Chee 298
82 O-Pee-Chee 63
83 O-Pee-Chee 153
84 O-Pee-Chee 311
85 O-Pee-Chee 15
86 O-Pee-Chee 343
85 opcSticker 117

KOPACZ, GEORGE
71 O-Pee-Chee 204

KOPLITZ, HOWIE
66 O-Pee-Chee 46

KOPPE, JOE
62 ShirriffCoin 209

KORINCE, GEORGE
67 O-Pee-Chee 72

KOSCO, ANDY
69 O-Pee-Chee 139
70 O-Pee-Chee 535
71 O-Pee-Chee 746
72 O-Pee-Chee 376
74 O-Pee-Chee 34

KOSTRO, FRANK
68 O-Pee-Chee

KOTCHMAN, TOM
87 Edmonton/ProCards 2072
88 Edmonton/CMC 22
88 Edmonton/ProCards 580
89 Edmonton/CMC 25
89 Edmonton/ProCards 549

KOTES, CHRIS
91 StCatharines/ClassicBest 17
91 StCatharines/ProCards 3389

KOUFAX, SANDY
65 O-Pee-Chee 8
66 O-Pee-Chee 100
75 O-Pee-Chee 201
90 O-Pee-Chee 665
62 PostCereal 109
62 ShirriffCoin 109

KOWAR, FRANK
90 StCatharines/ProCards 3462

KRALICK, JACK
66 O-Pee-Chee 129

KRAMER, RANDY
90 FleerCdn. 471
90 O-Pee-Chee 126
89 PaniniSticker 159
90 PaniniSticker 327
92 Calgary/SkyBox 62
93 Edmonton/ProCards 1132
87 Vancouver/ProCards 1613

KRANEPOOL, ED
65 O-Pee-Chee 144
67 O-Pee-Chee 186
68 O-Pee-Chee 92
71 O-Pee-Chee 573
72 O-Pee-Chee 181,182
73 O-Pee-Chee 329
74 O-Pee-Chee 561
75 O-Pee-Chee 324
76 O-Pee-Chee 314
77 O-Pee-Chee 60
78 O-Pee-Chee 205
79 O-Pee-Chee 265
80 O-Pee-Chee 336

KRANITZ, RICK
82 Vancouver/TCMA 19

KRAUSS, TIM
84 Edmonton/Cramer 98
85 Edmonton/Cramer 17

KRAUSSE, LEW
69 O-Pee-Chee 23
70 O-Pee-Chee 233
71 O-Pee-Chee 372
73 O-Pee-Chee 566
75 O-Pee-Chee 603

KRAVEC, KEN
79 O-Pee-Chee 141
80 O-Pee-Chee 299

KREEVICH, MIKE
39 WWGum(V351B)

KREMER, RAY
34 WWGum(V354) 38

KRENCHICKI, WAYNE
86 O-Pee-Chee 81
87 O-Pee-Chee 81
86 MTL/ProvigoFoods 20

KRESS, RALPH
33 WWGum(V353) 33

KREUTER, CHAD
90 FleerCdn. 303
90 O-Pee-Chee 562
89 PaniniSticker 444

KREVOKUCH, JAMES
91 Welland/Best 5
91 Welland/ProCards 3579

KRUEGER, BILL
90 FleerCdn. 328
84 O-Pee-Chee 178
90 O-Pee-Chee 518
91 O-Pee-Chee 417
92 O-Pee-Chee 368
93 opcPremier 38

KRUG, CHRIS
66 O-Pee-Chee 166

KRUK, JOHN
90 FleerCdn. 565
87 Leaf 217
88 Leaf 176
87 O-Pee-Chee 113
88 O-Pee-Chee 32,110,G
89 O-Pee-Chee 102
90 O-Pee-Chee 469
91 O-Pee-Chee 689
92 O-Pee-Chee 30
93 O-Pee-Chee 216
94 O-Pee-Chee 257
92 opcPremier 134
93 opcPremier 76
88 PaniniSticker 325-26,403
89 PaniniSticker 200
90 PaniniSticker 310
91 PaniniSticker 242
92 PaniniSticker 270
94 PaniniSticker 3,229
87 StuartBakery 12

KRUKOW, MIKE
87 HostessSticker
87 Leaf 86
80 O-Pee-Chee 223
81 O-Pee-Chee 176
82 O-Pee-Chee 215
83 O-Pee-Chee 331
84 O-Pee-Chee 37
85 O-Pee-Chee 74
86 O-Pee-Chee 126
87 O-Pee-Chee 241
88 O-Pee-Chee 393
89 O-Pee-Chee 125
90 O-Pee-Chee 241
82 opcSticker 31
85 opcSticker 163
86 opcSticker 93
89 opcSticker 83
86 opcTattoo 8
88 PaniniSticker 417

KRUM., SANDY
97 Calgary/Best 4

KRUMM, TODD
91 London/LineDrive 390
91 London/ProCards 1875

KUBEK, TONY
65 O-Pee-Chee 65
62 PostCereal 4
62 ShirriffCoin 18

KUBIAK, TED
68 O-Pee-Chee 79
71 O-Pee-Chee 516
72 O-Pee-Chee 23
73 O-Pee-Chee 652
74 O-Pee-Chee 228
75 O-Pee-Chee 329
76 O-Pee-Chee 228

KUBSKI, GIL
81 Vancouver/TCMA 9

KUCEK, JACK
75 O-Pee-Chee 614
76 O-Pee-Chee 597

KUDER, JEFF
89 Welland/Pucko 16

KUEHL, KARL
76 O-Pee-Chee 216

KUEHN, BILL
89 Welland/Pucko 33

KUENN, HARVEY
65 O-Pee-Chee 103
73 O-Pee-Chee 646
60 opcTattoo 27
62 PostCereal 135
62 ShirriffCoin 121

KUHEL, JOE
37 O-Pee-Chee(V300) 127
34 WWGum(V354) 52
36 WWGum(V355) 63

KUIPER, DUANE
76 O-Pee-Chee 508
77 O-Pee-Chee 233
78 O-Pee-Chee 39
79 O-Pee-Chee 67
80 O-Pee-Chee 221
81 O-Pee-Chee 226
82 O-Pee-Chee 233
84 O-Pee-Chee 338
84 opcSticker 169

KUME, MIKE
52 Parkhurst 100

KUNKEL, JEFF
90 FleerCdn. 304
85 O-Pee-Chee 288
90 O-Pee-Chee 174
91 O-Pee-Chee 562
85 opcSticker 350

KUNTZ, RUSTY
82 Edmonton/TCMA 20

KUSICK, CRAIG
75 O-Pee-Chee 297
80 O-Pee-Chee 374

KUSNYER, ART
72 O-Pee-Chee 213

KUTCHER, RANDY
90 O-Pee-Chee 676

KUTZLER, JERRY
91 Vancouver/LineDrive 639
91 Vancouver/ProCards 1592

L

LAABS, CHET
50 WWGum(V362) 31

LADD, PETE
82 Vancouver/TCMA 17

LABOY, JOSE (COCO)
73 Dimanche/DernièreHeure
83 Dimanche/DernièreHeure
92 Nabisco 9
70 O-Pee-Chee 238
71 O-Pee-Chee 132
73 O-Pee-Chee 642
71 MTL/ProStar
71 MTL/LaPizzaRoyale

LACEFIELD, TIM
97 St.Catharines/Best 19

LACEY, BOB
80 O-Pee-Chee 167

LACHAPELLE, YAN
96 StCatharines/Best 15

LACHEMANN, MARCEL
71 O-Pee-Chee 84

LACHEMANN, RENE
66 O-Pee-Chee 157

LACOCK, PETE
75 O-Pee-Chee 494
76 O-Pee-Chee 101
80 O-Pee-Chee 202

LACORTE, FRANK
76 O-Pee-Chee 597
81 O-Pee-Chee 348
85 O-Pee-Chee 153

LACOSS, MIKE
90 FleerCdn. 59
80 O-Pee-Chee 111
81 O-Pee-Chee 134
90 O-Pee-Chee 53
91 O-Pee-Chee 242
88 PaniniSticker 418

LADD, JEFF
92 StCatharines/ClassicBest 18
92 StCatharines/ProCards 3389
94 StCatharines/Classic 14
94 StCatharines/ProCards 3646

LAGROW, LERRIN
71 O-Pee-Chee 39
73 O-Pee-Chee 369
74 O-Pee-Chee 433
75 O-Pee-Chee 116
76 O-Pee-Chee 138
78 O-Pee-Chee 152

LACY, LEE
85 Leaf 40
86 Leaf 104
73 O-Pee-Chee 391
74 O-Pee-Chee 658
75 O-Pee-Chee 631
76 O-Pee-Chee 99
79 O-Pee-Chee 229
83 O-Pee-Chee 69
84 O-Pee-Chee 229
86 O-Pee-Chee 226
87 O-Pee-Chee 182
84 opcSticker 138
85 opcSticker 126
86 opcSticker 229
87 opcSticker 231

LAFRANCOIS, ROGER
90 Vancouver/CMC 27
90 Vancouver/ProCards 507
91 Vancouver/LineDrive 650
91 Vancouver/ProCards 1611
92 Vancouver/ProCards 2735
92 Vancouver/SkyBox 650

LAGUE, RAYMOND
52 Laval Dairy 14

LAHOUD, JOE
69 O-Pee-Chee 189
70 O-Pee-Chee 78
71 O-Pee-Chee 622
72 O-Pee-Chee 321
73 O-Pee-Chee 212
74 O-Pee-Chee 512
75 O-Pee-Chee 317
76 O-Pee-Chee 612

LAHTI, JEFF
86 Leaf 233

LAKE, STEVE
90 FleerCdn. 560
90 O-Pee-Chee 183
91 O-Pee-Chee 661
92 O-Pee-Chee 331
81 Vancouver/TCMA 25

LAKER, TIM
93 O-Pee-Chee 276
93 opcPremier 120

LAMABE, JACK
65 O-Pee-Chee 88

LAMB, RAY
70 O-Pee-Chee 131
71 O-Pee-Chee 727
72 O-Pee-Chee 422
73 O-Pee-Chee 496

LAMONT, GENE
71 O-Pee-Chee 39
75 O-Pee-Chee 593

LAMP, DENNIS
90 FleerCdn. 280
86 Leaf 244
80 O-Pee-Chee 129
83 O-Pee-Chee 26
85 O-Pee-Chee 83
86 O-Pee-Chee 219
87 O-Pee-Chee 336
90 O-Pee-Chee 338
91 O-Pee-Chee 14
92 O-Pee-Chee 653
84 opcSticker 239
86 opcSticker 193
86 opcTattoo 12
84 TOR/FireSafety
85 TOR/FireSafety
86 TOR/AultFoods
86 TOR/FireSafety

LAMPARD, KEITH
70 O-Pee-Chee 492
71 O-Pee-Chee 728
72 O-Pee-Chee 489

LAMPE, ED
88 Hamilton/ProCards 1742

LAMPKIN, TOM
90 O-Pee-Chee 172

LANCASTER, LES
90 FleerCdn. 35
90 O-Pee-Chee 437
91 O-Pee-Chee 86
92 O-Pee-Chee 213

LANDERS, MARK
95 StCatharines/TimHortons 20

LANDESTOY, RAFAEL
81 O-Pee-Chee 326

LANDIS, BILL
68 O-Pee-Chee 189

LANDIS, JIM
66 O-Pee-Chee 128
62 PostCereal 50
62 ShirriffCoin 49

LANDREAUX, KEN
80 O-Pee-Chee 49
81 O-Pee-Chee 219
82 O-Pee-Chee 114
84 O-Pee-Chee 216
86 O-Pee-Chee 2
87 O-Pee-Chee 123
82 opcSticker 49
83 opcSticker 246
84 opcSticker 76
85 opcSticker 75

LANDRITH, HOBIE
62 ShirriffCoin 181

LANDRUM, BILL
90 FleerCdn. 472
90 O-Pee-Chee 425
91 O-Pee-Chee 595
92 O-Pee-Chee 661
92 opcPremier 68
90 PaniniSticker 326
92 MTL/Durivage 17

LANDRUM, CED
92 O-Pee-Chee 81

LANDRUM, DON
66 O-Pee-Chee 43

LANDRUM, TITO
85 O-Pee-Chee 33
86 O-Pee-Chee 171
87 O-Pee-Chee 288
84 opcSticker 14
86 opcSticker 19
86 opcTattoo 15

LANG, CHIP
77 O-Pee-Chee 216

LANGAIGNE, SELWYN
97 St.Catharines/Best 20

LANGE, DICK
74 O-Pee-Chee 429
75 O-Pee-Chee 114
76 O-Pee-Chee 176

LANGFORD, RICK
78 O-Pee-Chee 33
80 O-Pee-Chee 284
81 O-Pee-Chee 154
82 O-Pee-Chee 43
84 O-Pee-Chee 304
83 opcSticker 106

LANGSTON, MARK
90 FleerCdn. 352
85 Leaf 56
87 Leaf 55
88 Leaf 20,123
92 McDonald's 19
85 O-Pee-Chee 259
86 O-Pee-Chee 198
87 O-Pee-Chee 215
88 O-Pee-Chee 80
89 O-Pee-Chee 355
90 O-Pee-Chee 530
91 O-Pee-Chee 755
92 O-Pee-Chee 165
93 O-Pee-Chee 232
94 O-Pee-Chee 175
85 opcSticker 281,337,371
86 opcSticker 225
87 opcSticker 219
88 opcSticker 214,-SStar 63
89 opcSticker 221
88 PaniniSticker 181
89 PaniniSticker 430
90 PaniniSticker 287
91 PaniniSticker 352
92 PaniniSticker 11
93 PaniniSticker 2
94 PaniniSticker 38
87 StuartBakery 25

LANIER, HAL
65 O-Pee-Chee 118
66 O-Pee-Chee 156
67 O-Pee-Chee 4
71 O-Pee-Chee 181
73 O-Pee-Chee 479
74 O-Pee-Chee 588

LANKFORD, RAY
91 O-Pee-Chee 682
92 O-Pee-Chee 292
93 O-Pee-Chee 191
94 O-Pee-Chee 251
91 opcPremier 72
92 opcPremier 148
93 opcPremier 44
92 PaniniSticker 177
93 PaniniSticker 196
94 PaniniSticker 245
91 ScoreAllStarFanfest 1

LANSFORD, CARNEY
90 FleerCdn. 14
85 Leaf 8
86 Leaf 55
88 Leaf 195
80 O-Pee-Chee 177
81 O-Pee-Chee 245
82 O-Pee-Chee 91
83 O-Pee-Chee 318
84 O-Pee-Chee 59
85 O-Pee-Chee 327
86 O-Pee-Chee 134
87 O-Pee-Chee 69
88 O-Pee-Chee 292
89 O-Pee-Chee 47
90 O-Pee-Chee 316
91 O-Pee-Chee 502
92 O-Pee-Chee 495
82 opcSticker 2,156
83 opcSticker 32
84 opcSticker 328
85 opcSticker 330
86 opcSticker 169
87 opcSticker 171
88 opcSticker 167
89 opcSticker 170
86 opcTattoo 7
88 PaniniSticker 169
89 PaniniSticker 421
90 PaniniSticker 134
91 PaniniSticker 194
92 PaniniSticker 17
93 PaniniSticker 17
87 StuartBakery

LANSING, MIKE
93 HitTheBooks
94 O-Pee-Chee 218
93 opcPremier 82
94 PaniniSticker 212
96 MTL/Disk

LAPLANTE, MICHEL
92 Welland/ClassicBest 15

LAPOINT, DAVE
85 O-Pee-Chee 229
86 O-Pee-Chee 162
87 O-Pee-Chee 319
89 O-Pee-Chee 89
90 O-Pee-Chee 186
91 O-Pee-Chee 484
84 opcSticker 146
85 opcSticker 143
80 Vancouver/TCMA 7

LARGUSA, LEVON
92 StCatharines/ClassicBest 25
92 StCatharines/ProCards 3384

LARKER, NORM
53 Exhibits 37
62 PostCereal 113
62 ShirriffCoin 194

LARKIN, BARRY
90 FleerCdn. 423
88 Leaf 226
92 McDonald's 15
88 O-Pee-Chee 102
89 O-Pee-Chee 363
90 O-Pee-Chee 10
91 O-Pee-Chee 400,730
92 O-Pee-Chee 465
93 O-Pee-Chee 147
94 O-Pee-Chee 125
92 opcPremier 96
93 opcPremier 103
88 opcSticker 140
89 opcSticker 137,-SStar 44
88 PaniniSticker 280
89 PaniniSticker 74
90 PaniniSticker 253
91 PaniniSticker 130
92 PaniniSticker 265
93 PaniniSticker 293
94 PaniniSticker 163
91 PaniniTopFifteen 28
92 PizzaHut/DietPepsi 18
93 PostCdn. 153

LARKIN, GENE
90 FleerCdn. 379
88 O-Pee-Chee 384
89 O-Pee-Chee 318
90 O-Pee-Chee 556
91 O-Pee-Chee 102
92 O-Pee-Chee 284
88 PaniniSticker 145
89 PaniniSticker 388
91 PaniniSticker 306

LAROCHE, DAVE
71 O-Pee-Chee 174
72 O-Pee-Chee 352
73 O-Pee-Chee 426
74 O-Pee-Chee 502
75 O-Pee-Chee 258
76 O-Pee-Chee 21
77 O-Pee-Chee 61
79 O-Pee-Chee 317
83 O-Pee-Chee 333,334

LARUSSA, TONY
72 O-Pee-Chee 451
90 O-Pee-Chee 639
91 O-Pee-Chee 171
92 O-Pee-Chee 429

LARY, FRANK
65 O-Pee-Chee 127
60 opcTattoo 28
62 PostCereal 22
62 ShirriffCoin 58

LASHER, FRED
70 O-Pee-Chee 356
71 O-Pee-Chee 707

LASKEY, BILL
83 O-Pee-Chee 218
84 O-Pee-Chee 129
85 O-Pee-Chee 331
86 O-Pee-Chee 281
83 opcSticker 325
84 opcSticker 172

LASORDA, TOM
52 Exhibits 50
73 O-Pee-Chee 569
74 O-Pee-Chee 144
89 O-Pee-Chee H
90 O-Pee-Chee 669,G
91 O-Pee-Chee 789
92 O-Pee-Chee 261
52 Parkhurst 58
50 WWGum(V362) 45

LATA, TIM
89 Hamilton/Star 20

LATHAM, JOHN
89 Welland/Pucko 17

LATMAN, BARRY
67 O-Pee-Chee 28

LATTA, GREG
89 Vancouver/ProCards 574

LAU, CHARLIE
65 O-Pee-Chee 94
73 O-Pee-Chee 593

LAUDNER, TIM
90 FleerCdn. 380
87 O-Pee-Chee 392
88 O-Pee-Chee 78
89 O-Pee-Chee 239
90 O-Pee-Chee 777
83 opcSticker 93,314
88 opcSticker 278
89 opcSticker 290
88 PaniniSticker 26,27,135
89 PaniniSticker 384

LAUZERIQUE, GEORGE
70 O-Pee-Chee 41

LAVALLIERE, MIKE
90 FleerCdn. 473
88 Leaf 112
88 O-Pee-Chee 57
89 O-Pee-Chee 218
90 O-Pee-Chee 478
91 O-Pee-Chee 665
92 O-Pee-Chee 312
93 O-Pee-Chee 145
88 opcSticker 131
89 opcSticker 128,-SStar 56
88 PaniniSticker 369
89 PaniniSticker 168
90 PaniniSticker 333
91 PaniniSticker 114
92 PaniniSticker 251
93 PaniniSticker 280

LAVAN, JOHN
21 Neilson's(V61) 102
23 WillardsChoc.(V100) 83

LAVELLE, GARY
85 Leaf 114
75 O-Pee-Chee 624
76 O-Pee-Chee 105
81 O-Pee-Chee 62
82 O-Pee-Chee 209
83 O-Pee-Chee 376
84 O-Pee-Chee 145
85 O-Pee-Chee 2, -Poster 24
86 O-Pee-Chee 22
84 opcSticker 164
85 opcSticker 159
85 TOR/FireSafety
86 TOR/AultFoods
86 TOR/FireSafety
87 TOR/FireSafety

LAW, RUDY
85 Leaf 117
84 O-Pee-Chee 47
85 O-Pee-Chee 286
86 O-Pee-Chee 6
84 opcSticker 245
85 opcSticker 241
86 opcSticker 291

LAW, VANCE
90 FleerCdn. 36
86 GeneralMills
87 GeneralMills
85 Leaf 183
86 Leaf 57
83 O-Pee-Chee 98
85 O-Pee-Chee 81
86 O-Pee-Chee 99
87 O-Pee-Chee 127
88 O-Pee-Chee 346
89 O-Pee-Chee 338
90 O-Pee-Chee 287
84 opcSticker 249
85 opcSticker 242
86 opcSticker 81
89 opcSticker-SuperStar 42
88 PaniniSticker 324
89 PaniniSticker 57
86 MTL/ProvigoFoods 23

LAW, VERNON
66 O-Pee-Chee 15
60 opcTattoo 29
62 PostCereal 179

LAWLESS, TOM
90 O-Pee-Chee 49
88 opcSticker 22
89 TOR/FireSafety
90 TOR/FireSafety

LAWRENCE, CLINT
96 StCatharines/Best 16

LAWRENCE, SEAN
92 Welland/ClassicBest 16
97 Calgary/Best 15

LAWSON, ROXIE
36 WWGum(V355) 104

LAWSON, STEVE
73 O-Pee-Chee 612

LAWTON, MARCUS
90 O-Pee-Chee 302
90 Vancouver/CMC 16
90 Vancouver/ProCards 500

LAYANA, TIM
91 O-Pee-Chee 627

LAZO, DANIEL
94 GarciaPhoto 14

LAZO, PEDRO LUIS
94 GarciaPhoto 19

LAZORKO, JACK
87 Edmonton/ProCards 2062
88 Edmonton/CMC 3
88 Edmonton/ProCards 556
89 Edmonton/CMC 1
84 Vancouver/Cramer 48

LAZZERI, TONY
37 O-Pee-Chee 117
33 WWGum(V353) 31

LEA, CHARLIE
81 Dimanche/DernièreHeure
83 Dimanche/DernièreHeure
85 Leaf 21
86 Leaf 172
81 O-Pee-Chee 293
82 O-Pee-Chee 38
83 O-Pee-Chee 253

84 O-Pee-Chee 142,332
85 O-Pee-Chee 345,-Poster 10
86 O-Pee-Chee 376
84 opcSticker 98
85 opcSticker 84,182
86 opcTattoo 21
82 MTL/Hygrade
83 MTL
83 MTL/StuartBakery 23
84 MTL/StuartBakery 8

LEACH, RICK
90 FleerCdn. 305
88 Leaf 247
85 O-Pee-Chee 52
87 O-Pee-Chee 5
88 O-Pee-Chee 323
89 O-Pee-Chee 284
90 O-Pee-Chee 27
84 TOR/FireSafety
86 TOR/FireSafety
87 TOR/FireSafety
88 TOR/FireSafety

LEACH, TERRY
90 FleerCdn. 111
88 O-Pee-Chee 391
90 O-Pee-Chee 508
92 O-Pee-Chee 644

LEAL, LUIS
85 Leaf 29
81 O-Pee-Chee 238
82 O-Pee-Chee 368,-Poster 9
83 O-Pee-Chee 109
84 O-Pee-Chee 207
85 O-Pee-Chee 31
86 O-Pee-Chee 365
84 opcSticker 371
85 opcSticker 361
84 TOR/FireSafety
85 TOR/FireSafety

LEARY, TIM
90 FleerCdn. 424
89 O-Pee-Chee 249
90 O-Pee-Chee 516
91 O-Pee-Chee 161
92 O-Pee-Chee 778
89 opcSticker 62
89 PaniniSticker 99
85 Vancouver/Cramer 203

LEATHERMAN, JEFF
91 Welland/Best 17
91 Welland/ProCards 3580

LEAVELL, GREGG
91 Welland/Best 12
91 Welland/ProCards 3586

LECLAIRE, FRENCHY
1912 ImperialTobacco(C46) 3

LEDEZMA, CARLOS
87 Vancouver/ProCards 1601

LEDSMA, AARON
96 Vancouver/Best 19

LEE, BILL
79 Dimanche/DernièreHeure
80 Dimanche/DernièreHeure
92 Nabisco 1
70 O-Pee-Chee 279
71 O-Pee-Chee 58
73 O-Pee-Chee 224
74 O-Pee-Chee 118
75 O-Pee-Chee 128
76 O-Pee-Chee 396
79 O-Pee-Chee 237
80 O-Pee-Chee 53
81 O-Pee-Chee 371
82 O-Pee-Chee 323
93 MTL/McDonald's 24

LEE, BILL
36 WWGum(V355) 109

LEE, BOB
65 O-Pee-Chee 46

LEE, DEREK
94 Ottawa/ProCards 2908
92 Vancouver/ProCards 2733
92 Vancouver/SkyBox 624

LEE, JEREMY
94 StCatharines/Classic 15
94 StCatharines/ProCards 3639

LEE, LERON
70 O-Pee-Chee 96
71 O-Pee-Chee 521
72 O-Pee-Chee 238
73 O-Pee-Chee 83
74 O-Pee-Chee 651
75 O-Pee-Chee 506
76 O-Pee-Chee 487

LEE, MANNY (MANUEL)
90 FleerCdn. 86
86 O-Pee-Chee 23
87 O-Pee-Chee 289
88 O-Pee-Chee 303
89 O-Pee-Chee 371
90 O-Pee-Chee 113
91 O-Pee-Chee 297
92 O-Pee-Chee 634
93 O-Pee-Chee 320
93 O-Pee-Chee -WSChamps 9
89 PaniniSticker 468
91 PaniniSticker 337
92 PaniniSticker 28
94 PaniniSticker 129
85 TOR/FireSafety
88 TOR/FireSafety
89 TOR/FireSafety
90 TOR/FireSafety
91 TOR/FireSafety
91 TOR/Score 16
92 TOR/FireSafety
93 TOR/Donruss 8

LEE, MARK
91 O-Pee-Chee 721
92 O-Pee-Chee 384

LEE, RONNIE
53 Exhibits 51
50 WWGum(V362) 25

LEE, TERRY
92 O-Pee-Chee 262
81 Vancouver/TCMA 14

LEE, WYATT
1912 ImperialTobacco(C46) 71

LEEK, GENE
62 ShirriffCoin 82

LEEPER, DAVE
87 Vancouver/ProCards 1611

LEFEBVRE, JIM
66 O-Pee-Chee 57
69 O-Pee-Chee 140
71 O-Pee-Chee 459
72 O-Pee-Chee 369
90 O-Pee-Chee 459
91 O-Pee-Chee 699

LEFEBVRE, JOE
81 O-Pee-Chee 88

LEFFERTS, CRAIG
90 FleerCdn. 60
85 O-Pee-Chee 76
86 O-Pee-Chee 244
87 O-Pee-Chee 287
90 O-Pee-Chee 158
91 O-Pee-Chee 448

92 O-Pee-Chee 41
90 PaniniSticker 362
92 PaniniSticker 239
91 PaniniTopFifteen 84

LEFLORE, RON
80 Dimanche/DernièreHeure
75 O-Pee-Chee 628
76 O-Pee-Chee 61
77 O-Pee-Chee 167
78 O-Pee-Chee 88
79 O-Pee-Chee 348
80 O-Pee-Chee 45
81 O-Pee-Chee 104
82 O-Pee-Chee 140
83 O-Pee-Chee 297
82 opcSticker 172

LEFTWICH, PHIL
93 Vancouver/ProCards 2592

LEGER, TIM
94 Welland/Classic 12
94 Welland/ProCards 3508

LEIBOLD, HARRY L.
23 WillardsChoc.(V100) 84

LEIBERTHAL, MIKE
91 O-Pee-Chee 471

LEIBRANDT, CHARLIE
90 FleerCdn. 112
86 Leaf 171
88 Leaf 76
81 O-Pee-Chee 126
86 O-Pee-Chee 77
87 O-Pee-Chee 223
88 O-Pee-Chee 218
89 O-Pee-Chee 301
90 O-Pee-Chee 776
91 O-Pee-Chee 456
92 O-Pee-Chee 152
93 O-Pee-Chee 204
86 opcSticker 262
87 opcSticker 258
88 opcSticker 260
86 opcTattoo 1
88 PaniniSticker 100
89 PaniniSticker 351
91 PaniniSticker 27

LEIPER, DAVE
90 O-Pee-Chee 773
91 Edmonton/LineDrive 166
91 Edmonton/ProCards 1514

LEIPER, TIM
89 London/ProCards 1373
90 London/ProCards 1281

LEITER, AL
88 Leaf 43
90 O-Pee-Chee 138
91 O-Pee-Chee 233
92 O-Pee-Chee 394
89 PaniniSticker 396
90 TOR/FireSafety
91 TOR/FireSafety
91 TOR/Score 4
93 TOR/Dempster's 18
93 TOR/Donruss 34
93 TOR/FireSafety
94 TOR
95 TOR/OhHenry

LEITER, MARK
92 O-Pee-Chee 537
93 O-Pee-Chee 174
92 opcPremier 48

LEIUS, SCOTT
90 FleerCdn. 647
92 O-Pee-Chee 74
92 opcPremier 118
93 PaniniSticker 128

LEJOHN, DON
66 O-Pee-Chee 41

LEMANCZYK, DAVE
75 O-Pee-Chee 571
76 O-Pee-Chee 409
77 O-Pee-Chee 229
78 O-Pee-Chee 85
79 O-Pee-Chee 102
80 O-Pee-Chee 68
78 TOR
79 TOR/BubbleYum

LEMASTER, DENNY
69 O-Pee-Chee 96
70 O-Pee-Chee 178
71 O-Pee-Chee 636
72 O-Pee-Chee 371

LEMASTER, JOHNNIE
76 O-Pee-Chee 596
80 O-Pee-Chee 224
81 O-Pee-Chee 84
83 O-Pee-Chee 154
84 O-Pee-Chee 107
85 O-Pee-Chee 302
86 O-Pee-Chee 289
82 opcSticker 108
83 opcSticker 304
84 opcSticker 168
85 opcSticker 164

LEMBO, STEVE
53 Exhibits 36
50 WWGum(V362) 7

LEMKE, MARK
90 FleerCdn. 587
90 O-Pee-Chee 451
91 O-Pee-Chee 251
92 O-Pee-Chee 689
93 O-Pee-Chee 236
92 PaniniSticker 163
93 PaniniSticker 182

LEMON, BOB
53 Exhibits 31
71 O-Pee-Chee 91
72 O-Pee-Chee 449

LEMON, CHET
90 FleerCdn. 608
85 Leaf 77
86 Leaf 85
87 Leaf 227
88 Leaf 166
76 O-Pee-Chee 590
77 O-Pee-Chee 195
78 O-Pee-Chee 224
79 O-Pee-Chee 169
80 O-Pee-Chee 309
81 O-Pee-Chee 242
82 O-Pee-Chee 13
83 O-Pee-Chee 53
84 O-Pee-Chee 86
85 O-Pee-Chee 20
86 O-Pee-Chee 160
87 O-Pee-Chee 206
88 O-Pee-Chee 366
89 O-Pee-Chee 328
90 O-Pee-Chee 271
91 O-Pee-Chee 469
82 opcSticker 168
84 opcSticker 271
85 opcSticker 190,260
86 opcSticker 274
87 opcSticker 268
89 opcSticker 283
86 opcTattoo 10
88 PaniniSticker 96
89 PaniniSticker 344
90 PaniniSticker 77
91 PaniniSticker 292

LEMON, JIM
62 PostCereal 89
62 ShirriffCoin 9

LEMONDS, DAVE
71 O-Pee-Chee 458
72 O-Pee-Chee 413
73 O-Pee-Chee 534

LENHARDT, DON
73 O-Pee-Chee 131

LENNON, PAT
91 Calgary/LineDrive 63
91 Calgary/ProCards 528
92 Calgary/SkyBox 64

LEON, EDDIE
70 O-Pee-Chee 292
71 O-Pee-Chee 252
73 O-Pee-Chee 287
74 O-Pee-Chee 501
75 O-Pee-Chee 528

LEON, MAXIMINO
75 O-Pee-Chee 442
76 O-Pee-Chee 576

LEONARD, DENNIS
75 O-Pee-Chee 615
76 O-Pee-Chee 334
77 O-Pee-Chee 91
78 O-Pee-Chee 5,41
79 O-Pee-Chee 109
80 O-Pee-Chee 293
81 O-Pee-Chee 185
82 O-Pee-Chee 369
83 O-Pee-Chee 87
84 O-Pee-Chee 375
87 O-Pee-Chee 38
82 opcSticker 191

LEONARD, JEFFREY
90 FleerCdn. 519
85 GeneralMills
85 Leaf 92
86 Leaf 74
88 Leaf 118
85 O-Pee-Chee 132
86 O-Pee-Chee 381
87 O-Pee-Chee 280
88 O-Pee-Chee 152
89 O-Pee-Chee 160
90 O-Pee-Chee 455
91 O-Pee-Chee 55
84 opcSticker 166
85 opcSticker 161
86 opcSticker 84
87 opcSticker 90
88 opcSticker 16,86,-SStar 17
89 opcSticker 199
86 opcTattoo 15
88 PaniniSticker 245-46,427,446
90 PaniniSticker 150
87 StuartBakery 13

LEONARD, MARK
93 PaniniSticker 241

LEONHARD, DAVE
68 O-Pee-Chee 56
71 O-Pee-Chee 716

LEPLEY, JOHN
88 Hamilton/ProCards 1737

LEPPERT, DON
73 O-Pee-Chee 517
74 O-Pee-Chee 489
77 O-Pee-Chee 58
78 TOR

LERCH, RANDY
76 O-Pee-Chee 595
80 O-Pee-Chee 181

83 O-Pee-Chee 22
83 MTL/StuartBakery 23

LERSCH, BARRY
69 O-Pee-Chee 206
71 O-Pee-Chee 739
72 O-Pee-Chee 453
73 O-Pee-Chee 559
74 O-Pee-Chee 313

LESLEY, BRAD
85 Vancouver/Cramer 202

LESLIE, SAM
36 WWGum(V355) 4

LETT, JIM
97 TOR/Sizzler 23

LETTERIO, SHANE
91 Calgary/LineDrive 64
91 Calgary/ProCards 522

LEVASSEUR, TOMMY
94 Calgary/ProCards 796

LEVERETTE, GEORGE
23 Neilson's 24

LEWIS, DARREN
91 O-Pee-Chee 239
92 O-Pee-Chee 743
93 O-Pee-Chee 193
94 O-Pee-Chee 132
91 opcPremier 73
92 opcPremier 151

LEWIS, JIM
85 Calgary/Cramer 77

LEWIS, JOHN
37 O-Pee-Chee 101

LEWIS, JOHNNY
65 O-Pee-Chee 277
67 O-Pee-Chee 91
74 O-Pee-Chee 236

LEWIS, MARK
92 O-Pee-Chee 446
93 O-Pee-Chee 194
92 PaniniSticker 46
93 PaniniSticker 49

LEWIS, SCOTT
90 Edmonton/CMC 10
90 Edmonton/ProCards 516
92 Edmonton/ProCards 3537

LEWRIGHT, CLEO
52 LavalDairy 23

LEY, TERRY
72 O-Pee-Chee 506

LEYLAND, JIM
90 O-Pee-Chee 699
91 O-Pee-Chee 381
92 O-Pee-Chee 141

LEYRITZ, JIM
91 O-Pee-Chee 202
91 PaniniSticker 326

LEYSTRA, JEFF
94 StCatharines/Classic 16
94 StCatharines/ProCards 3640

LEYVA, NICK
90 O-Pee-Chee 489
91 O-Pee-Chee 141
95 TOR/OhHenry
96 TOR/OhHenry
97 TOR/Sizzler 26

LEZCANO, SIXTO
76 O-Pee-Chee 353
77 O-Pee-Chee 71
78 O-Pee-Chee 102
79 O-Pee-Chee 364
80 O-Pee-Chee 114
81 O-Pee-Chee 25
82 O-Pee-Chee 271
83 O-Pee-Chee 244
84 O-Pee-Chee 185
85 O-Pee-Chee 89
82 opcSticker 95
83 opcSticker 298

LIDDLE, STEVE
84 Edmonton/Cramer 107
85 Edmonton/Cramer 13
86 Edmonton/ProCards

LIEBRANDT, CHARLIE
93 opcPremier 116

LILLIQUIST, DEREK
90 FleerCdn. 588
90 O-Pee-Chee 282
91 O-Pee-Chee 683
93 O-Pee-Chee 211
90 PaniniSticker 223

LILLIS, BOB
74 O-Pee-Chee 31
62 ShirriffCoin 108

LIMMER, LOU
52 Parkhurst 86

LINARES, JUAN CARLOS
94 GarciaPhoto 15

LINARES, OMAR
94 GarciaPhoto 8

LINARES, RUFINO
86 Edmonton/ProCards

LIND, JOSE
90 FleerCdn. 474
88 Leaf 38
89 O-Pee-Chee 273
90 O-Pee-Chee 168
91 O-Pee-Chee 537
92 O-Pee-Chee 43
93 O-Pee-Chee 120
94 O-Pee-Chee 68
93 opcPremier 42
88 opcSticker 127
89 opcSticker 126
88 PaniniSticker 317
89 PaniniSticker 170
90 PaniniSticker 328
91 PaniniSticker 116
92 PaniniSticker 253
94 PaniniSticker 76
87 Vancouver/ProCards 1616

LINDBLAD, PAUL
68 O-Pee-Chee 127
70 O-Pee-Chee 408
71 O-Pee-Chee 658
72 O-Pee-Chee 396
73 O-Pee-Chee 306
74 O-Pee-Chee 369
75 O-Pee-Chee 278
76 O-Pee-Chee 9

LINDEMAN, JIM
87 Leaf 37
88 O-Pee-Chee 16
92 O-Pee-Chee 258

LINDSEY, BILL
88 Vancouver/CMC 16
88 Vancouver/ProCards 758

LINDSEY, TIM
91 StCatharines/ClassicBest 21
91 StCatharines/ProCards 3390

LINDSTROM, FREDDIE
34 WWGum(V354) 17
36 WWGum(V355) 65

LINTON, DOUG
33 Leaf 35
93 TOR/Donruss 35

LINTZ, LARRY
74 O-Pee-Chee 121
75 O-Pee-Chee 416
76 O-Pee-Chee 109

LINZ, PHIL
67 O-Pee-Chee 14

LINZY, FRANK
66 O-Pee-Chee 78
68 O-Pee-Chee 147
70 O-Pee-Chee 77
71 O-Pee-Chee 551
72 O-Pee-Chee 243
73 O-Pee-Chee 286

LIPON, JOHN
61 Toronto/BeeHive

LIRIANO, NELSON
90 FleerCdn. 87
90 Leaf 32
88 O-Pee-Chee 205
89 O-Pee-Chee 76
90 O-Pee-Chee 543
91 O-Pee-Chee 18
90 PaniniSticker 182
88 TOR/FireSafety
89 TOR/FireSafety
90 TOR/FireSafety

LIS, JOE
70 O-Pee-Chee 56
71 O-Pee-Chee 138
74 O-Pee-Chee 659
75 O-Pee-Chee 86

LIS, JOE (JR.)
91 StCatharines/ClassicBest 9
91 StCatharines/ProCards 3404

LISENBEE, HORACE
34 WWGum(V354) 45

LISTACH, PAT
94 O-Pee-Chee 216
93 opcPremier-StarPerf. 15
93 PaniniSticker 39,163
94 PaniniSticker 83

LITTELL, MARK
74 O-Pee-Chee 596
76 O-Pee-Chee 593

LITTLE, BRYAN
84 O-Pee-Chee 188
85 O-Pee-Chee 257
83 MTL
83 MTL/StuartBakery 24
84 MTL
84 MTL/StuartBakery 30

LITTON, GREG
90 FleerCdn. 61
90 O-Pee-Chee 66
91 O-Pee-Chee 628
92 O-Pee-Chee 238
93 Calgary/ProCards 1171

LIVINGSTONE, SCOTT
92 O-Pee-Chee 685
93 O-Pee-Chee 219
92 opcPremier 56
93 PaniniSticker 116
89 London/ProCards 1381

LIVSEY, SHAWN
92 O-Pee-Chee 124

LIZQUEL, OMAR
91 PaniniSticker 231

LLENAS, WINSTON
71 O-Pee-Chee 152
74 O-Pee-Chee 467
75 O-Pee-Chee 597
88 TOR/FireSafety
85 Edmonton/Cramer 14
86 Edmonton/ProCards

LLOYD, GRAEME
93 opcPremier 71

LOCK, DON
66 O-Pee-Chee 165
68 O-Pee-Chee 59

LOCKE, BOBBY
68 O-Pee-Chee 24

LOCKER, BOB
68 O-Pee-Chee 51
70 O-Pee-Chee 249
71 O-Pee-Chee 356
73 O-Pee-Chee 645
74 O-Pee-Chee 62
75 O-Pee-Chee 434

LOCKLEAR, GENE
75 O-Pee-Chee 13
76 O-Pee-Chee 447

LOCKMAN, WHITEY
73 O-Pee-Chee 81
74 O-Pee-Chee 354

LOCKWOOD, SKIP
70 O-Pee-Chee 499
71 O-Pee-Chee 433
72 O-Pee-Chee 118
73 O-Pee-Chee 308
74 O-Pee-Chee 532
75 O-Pee-Chee 417
76 O-Pee-Chee 166
79 O-Pee-Chee 250
80 O-Pee-Chee 295

LOFTON, KENNY
92 O-Pee-Chee 69
93 O-Pee-Chee 251
94 O-Pee-Chee 237, -AS 25
92 opcPremier 72
93 opcPremier-StarPerf. 17
93 PaniniSticker 53
94 PaniniSticker 58

LOLICH, MICKEY
67 O-Pee-Chee 88
70 O-Pee-Chee 72
71 O-Pee-Chee 71,133
72 O-Pee-Chee 94,96,450
73 O-Pee-Chee 390
74 O-Pee-Chee 166
75 O-Pee-Chee 245
76 O-Pee-Chee 3
76 O-Pee-Chee 385
71 ProStarPostcard

LOLICH, RON
71 O-Pee-Chee 458

LOLLAR, SHERM
62 PostCereal 53
62 ShirriffCoin 55

LOLLAR, TIM
85 Leaf 111
83 O-Pee-Chee 185
84 O-Pee-Chee 267
85 O-Pee-Chee 13
83 opcSticker 296
85 opcSticker 153

LOMAN, DOUG
82 Vancouver/TCMA 10
84 Vancouver/Cramer 28

LOMBARDI, ERNIE
34 WWGum(V354) 82
39 WWGum(V351B)

LOMBARDI, VICTOR (VIC)
52 Parkhurst 7

LOMBARDOZZI, STEVE
89 O-Pee-Chee 376
88 PaniniSticker 137-38,139

LONBORG, JIM
66 O-Pee-Chee 93
68 O-Pee-Chee 10,12
69 O-Pee-Chee 109
71 O-Pee-Chee 577
72 O-Pee-Chee 255
73 O-Pee-Chee 3
74 O-Pee-Chee 342
75 O-Pee-Chee 94
76 O-Pee-Chee 271
79 O-Pee-Chee 233

LONG, BILL
88 O-Pee-Chee 309
89 O-Pee-Chee 133
90 O-Pee-Chee 499
91 O-Pee-Chee 668

LONG, BOB
52 Laval Dairy 22

LONG, BOB
85 Calgary/Cramer 95

LONG, DALE
62 PostCereal 65
62 ShirriffCoin 35

LONG, DON
94 Vancouver/ProCards 1878
96 Vancouver/Best 1

LONG, STEVE
94 Edmonton/ProCards 2872

LONGAKER, SCOTT
91 Hamilton/ClassicBest 9
91 Hamilton/ProCards 4035

LONNETT, JOE
73 O-Pee-Chee 356
74 O-Pee-Chee 221

LOPAT, ED
53 Exhibits 15

LOPES, DAVE
86 Leaf 9
73 O-Pee-Chee 609
74 O-Pee-Chee 112
75 O-Pee-Chee 93
76 O-Pee-Chee 4,197
77 O-Pee-Chee 4,96
78 O-Pee-Chee 222
79 O-Pee-Chee 144
80 O-Pee-Chee 291
81 O-Pee-Chee 50
82 O-Pee-Chee 85,218,338
83 O-Pee-Chee 365
84 O-Pee-Chee 17
85 O-Pee-Chee 12
86 O-Pee-Chee 125
87 O-Pee-Chee 311
83 opcSticker 105
84 opcSticker 331
87 opcSticker 7

LOPEZ, ANGEL
94 GarciaPhoto 67

LOPEZ, AURELIO
85 Leaf 160
81 O-Pee-Chee 291
84 O-Pee-Chee 95
84 opcSticker 268
85 opcSticker 265

LOPEZ, CARLOS
78 O-Pee-Chee 219

LOPEZ, HECTOR
52 Laval Dairy 56
66 O-Pee-Chee 177

LOPEZ, JAVY
94 OPC 162,-HotProspects 7

LOPEZ, JUAN
79 Vancouver/TCMA 12

LOPEZ, LAZARO
94 GarciaPhoto 73

LOPEZ, MISAEL
94 GarciaPhoto 126

LOPEZ, LUIS
96 StCatharines/Best 17

LOPEZ, MARCELINO
66 O-Pee-Chee 155
70 O-Pee-Chee 344
71 O-Pee-Chee 137

LORANGER, BOB
52 Laval Dairy 53

LORRAINE, ANDREW
94 Vancouver/ProCards 1863

LOTT, BILLY
97 Calgary/Best 16

LOUN, DON
65 O-Pee-Chee 181

LOVELACE, VANCE
90 Calgary/CMC 7
90 Calgary/ProCards 647
91 Calgary/LineDrive 65
91 Calgary/ProCards 512
88 Edmonton/CMC 4
88 Edmonton/ProCards 557
89 Edmonton/ProCards 559

LOVIGLIO, JAY
81 Edmonton/RedRooster 23
82 Edmonton/TCMA 8

LOVITTO, JOE
73 O-Pee-Chee 276
74 O-Pee-Chee 639
75 O-Pee-Chee 36
76 O-Pee-Chee 604

LOVULLO, TOREY
89 PaniniSticker 332
94 PaniniSticker 39

LOWE, BENNY
95 StCatharines/TimHortons 4

LOWE, CHRIS
90 Hamilton/Star 14

LOWENSTEIN, JOHN
71 O-Pee-Chee 231
72 O-Pee-Chee 486
73 O-Pee-Chee 327
74 O-Pee-Chee 176
75 O-Pee-Chee 424
76 O-Pee-Chee 646
77 O-Pee-Chee 175
81 O-Pee-Chee 199
83 O-Pee-Chee 337
85 O-Pee-Chee 316
83 opcSticker 24
84 opcSticker 20,209
85 opcSticker 216

LOWERY, HARRY
53 Exhibits 29

LOWN, TURK
50 WWGum(V362) 14

LOZADA, WILLIE
82 Vancouver/TCMA 5

LUBRATICH, STEVE
84 Edmonton/Cramer 249
84 Edmonton/Cramer 112

LUCAS, FRED (RED)
34 WWGum(V354) 7

LUCAS, GARY
81 O-Pee-Chee 259
82 O-Pee-Chee 120
83 O-Pee-Chee 364
84 O-Pee-Chee 7
85 O-Pee-Chee 297
86 O-Pee-Chee 351
87 O-Pee-Chee 382
82 opcSticker 102
84 opcSticker 161
84 MTL
84 MTL/Stuart Bakery 12

LUCCHESI, FRANK
71 O-Pee-Chee 119
72 O-Pee-Chee 188
74 O-Pee-Chee 379
76 O-Pee-Chee 172

LUCERO, KEVIN
91 Hamilton/ClassicBest 4
91 Hamilton/ProCards 4036

LUDWICK, BOB
53 Exhibits 38

LUECKEN, RICK
90 FleerCdn. 113
90 O-Pee-Chee 87
85 Calgary/Cramer 98

LUGO, ANGEL
91 StCatharines/ClassicBest 23
91 StCatharines/ProCards 3391

LUGO, RAFAEL
85 Edmonton/Cramer 9

LUGO, URBANO
88 Edmonton/CMC 6
88 Edmonton/ProCards 581

LUIS, OMAR
94 GarciaPhoto 89

LUM, MIKE
70 O-Pee-Chee 367
71 O-Pee-Chee 194
73 O-Pee-Chee 266
74 O-Pee-Chee 227
75 O-Pee-Chee 154
76 O-Pee-Chee 208
79 O-Pee-Chee 286

LUMLEY, MIKE
90 London/ProCards 1265
92 London/ProCards 630
92 London/SkyBox 412

LUMPE, JERRY
66 O-Pee-Chee 161
62 PostCereal 93
62 ShirriffCoin 25

LUNA, RICHARD
93 Welland/ClassicBest 11
93 Welland/ProCards 3367

LUND, GORD (GORDY)
81 Edmonton/RedRooster 8
82 Edmonton/TCMA 22

LUNDSTEDT, TOM
74 O-Pee-Chee 603

LUPLOW, AL
66 O-Pee-Chee 188

LUQUE, ADOLFO
21 Neilson's(V61) 72
22 WilliamPaterson(V89) 9

LUSADER, SCOTT
90 O-Pee-Chee 632

LUSH, JOHN
1912 ImperialTobacco(C46) 33

LUSSIER, PAT
92 Welland/ClassicBest 17

LUTT, JEFF
93 Welland/ClassicBest 12
93 Welland/ProCards 3351

LUTZ, JOE (ROLLIN JOSEPH)
73 O-Pee-Chee 449
52 Parkhurst 74

LUZINSKI, GREG
85 Leaf 75
71 O-Pee-Chee 439
72 O-Pee-Chee 112
73 O-Pee-Chee 189
74 O-Pee-Chee 360
75 O-Pee-Chee 630
76 O-Pee-Chee 193,195,610
77 O-Pee-Chee 118
78 O-Pee-Chee 42
79 O-Pee-Chee 278
80 O-Pee-Chee 66
81 O-Pee-Chee 270
82 O-Pee-Chee 69,152
83 O-Pee-Chee 310
84 O-Pee-Chee 20
85 O-Pee-Chee 328
82 opcSticker 165
83 opcSticker 51
84 opcSticker 7,8,244
85 opcSticker 238

LYDEN, MITCH
93 Edmonton/ProCards 1139
94 Edmonton/ProCards 2877

LYDY, SCOTT
95 Edmonton/Macri

LYLE, JEFF
90 Welland/Pucko 22

LYLE, SPARKY
70 O-Pee-Chee 116
71 O-Pee-Chee 649
72 O-Pee-Chee 259
73 O-Pee-Chee 68,394
74 O-Pee-Chee 66
75 O-Pee-Chee 485
76 O-Pee-Chee 545
77 O-Pee-Chee 89
78 O-Pee-Chee 214,237
79 O-Pee-Chee 188
80 O-Pee-Chee 62
81 O-Pee-Chee 337
82 O-Pee-Chee 285
83 O-Pee-Chee 92,208

LYNCH, ED
86 O-Pee-Chee 68
87 O-Pee-Chee 16

LYNCH, JERRY
66 O-Pee-Chee 182
62 PostCereal 127
62 ShirriffCoin 198

LYNN, FRED
90 FleerCdn. 609
85 Leaf 198
86 Leaf 120
87 Leaf 9,83
88 Leaf 163
75 O-Pee-Chee 622
76 O-Pee-Chee 50,192,196
77 O-Pee-Chee 163
78 O-Pee-Chee 62
79 O-Pee-Chee 249
80 O-Pee-Chee 60
81 O-Pee-Chee 313
82 O-Pee-Chee 251,252
83 O-Pee-Chee 182,392
84 O-Pee-Chee 247
85 O-Pee-Chee 220
86 O-Pee-Chee 55
87 O-Pee-Chee 370
89 O-Pee-Chee 27
90 O-Pee-Chee 107,663,H
91 O-Pee-Chee 586
82 opcSticker 161
83 opcSticker 44,158
84 opcSticker 5,6,230
85 opcSticker 225
86 opcSticker 228
87 opcSticker 226
86 opcTattoo 8
88 PaniniSticker 15
90 PaniniSticker 73
87 StuartBakery 14

LYONS, BARRY
90 FleerCdn. 209
90 O-Pee-Chee 258

LYONS, STEVE
90 FleerCdn. 539
89 O-Pee-Chee 334
90 O-Pee-Chee 751
91 O-Pee-Chee 612
92 O-Pee-Chee 349
89 opcSticker 298
88 PaniniSticker 60
89 PaniniSticker 308
90 PaniniSticker 40

LYONS, TED
33 WWGum(V353) 7

LYTTLE, JIM
70 O-Pee-Chee 516
71 O-Pee-Chee 234
74 O-Pee-Chee 436

M

MAAS, KEVIN
90 FleerCdn. 641
91 O-Pee-Chee 4,435
92 O-Pee-Chee 710
91 opcPremier 74
93 PaniniSticker 147
91 PostCdn. 20

MABRY, JOHN
91 Hamilton/Classic Best 17
91 Hamilton/ProCards 4053

MACARTHUR, MARK
90 Hamilton/Best 21
90 Hamilton/Star 15

MACDONALD, BOB
92 O-Pee-Chee 87
92 opcPremier 152
91 TOR/Score 32
92 TOR 19
92 TOR/FireSafety 19
94 Calgary/ProCards 785

MACEY, FAUSTO
97 Vancouver/Best 19

MACFARLANE, MIKE
90 FleerCdn. 114
90 O-Pee-Chee 202
91 O-Pee-Chee 638
92 O-Pee-Chee 42
93 O-Pee-Chee 265
94 O-Pee-Chee 154
91 PaniniSticker 275
93 PaniniSticker 102
94 PaniniSticker 77

MACFAYDEN, DANNY
33 WWGum(V353) 87

MACHA, KEN
79 DimancheDernièreHeure
80 DimancheDernièreHeure
82 O-Pee-Chee 282
86 MTL/ProvigoFoods 28

MACHADO, JULIO
90 O-Pee-Chee 684
91 O-Pee-Chee 434
92 O-Pee-Chee 208

MACHADO, OSCAR
94 GarciaPhoto 79

MACIAS, OSCAR
94 GarciaPhoto 40

MACK, CONNIE (CORNELIUS)
23 WillardsChocolate(V100) 85
36 WWGum(V355) 110

MACK, QUINN
94 Calgary/ProCards 801

MACK, SHANE
88 O-Pee-Chee 283
91 O-Pee-Chee 672
92 O-Pee-Chee 164
93 O-Pee-Chee 263
92 PaniniSticker 119
93 PaniniSticker 129
94 PaniniSticker 93

MACK, TONYLYNN
85 Edmonton/Cramer 6
86 Edmonton/ProCards

MACKANIN, PETE
74 O-Pee-Chee 597
76 O-Pee-Chee 287
77 O-Pee-Chee 260
77 MTL
77 MTL/RedpathSugar

MADERA, WIL
97 Lethbridge/Best 15

MADDEN, MIKE
82 Vancouver/TCMA 14

MADDOX, ELLIOTT
71 O-Pee-Chee 11
72 O-Pee-Chee 277
73 O-Pee-Chee 658
74 O-Pee-Chee 401
75 O-Pee-Chee 113
76 O-Pee-Chee 503
79 O-Pee-Chee 28
80 O-Pee-Chee 357
81 O-Pee-Chee 299

MADDOX, GARRY
73 O-Pee-Chee 322
74 O-Pee-Chee 178
75 O-Pee-Chee 240
76 O-Pee-Chee 38
77 O-Pee-Chee 42
78 O-Pee-Chee 93
79 O-Pee-Chee 245
80 O-Pee-Chee 198
81 O-Pee-Chee 160
82 O-Pee-Chee 20
83 O-Pee-Chee 41
84 O-Pee-Chee 187
85 O-Pee-Chee 235
86 O-Pee-Chee 362
82 opcSticker 73
84 opcSticker 123
85 opcSticker 121
86 opcSticker 117
86 opcTattoo 14

MADDUX, GREG
93 Ben'sDisk 4
90 FleerCdn. 37

87 Leaf 36
88 O-Pee-Chee 361
89 O-Pee-Chee 240
90 O-Pee-Chee 715
91 O-Pee-Chee 35
92 O-Pee-Chee 580
93 O-Pee-Chee 135
94 O-Pee-Chee 101, -AS 22
93 opcPremier 126, -Star 19
88 opcSticker 59
89 opcSticker 48
89 PaniniSticker 49
90 PaniniSticker 237
91 PaniniSticker 50
92 PaniniSticker 189
93 PaniniSticker 159,164
94 PaniniSticker 147
91 PaniniTopFifteen 98
95 PostCdn. 16

MADDUX, MIKE
89 O-Pee-Chee 39
90 O-Pee-Chee 154
92 O-Pee-Chee 438
93 O-Pee-Chee 168

MADERA, LAZARO
94 GarciaPhoto 16

MADLOCK, BILL
92 Kellogg's
85 Leaf 185
86 Leaf 238
87 Leaf 120
88 Leaf 232
74 O-Pee-Chee 600
75 O-Pee-Chee 104
76 O-Pee-Chee 191,640
77 O-Pee-Chee 1,56
78 O-Pee-Chee 89
79 O-Pee-Chee 96
80 O-Pee-Chee 30
81 O-Pee-Chee 137
82 O-Pee-Chee 365
83 O-Pee-Chee 335
84 O-Pee-Chee 250
85 O-Pee-Chee 157
86 O-Pee-Chee 47
87 O-Pee-Chee 276
88 O-Pee-Chee 145
82 opcSticker 1,83
83 opcSticker 275
84 opcSticker 99,131
85 opcSticker 122
86 opcSticker 12,70
87 opcSticker 67
86 opcTattoo 19

MADRIL, MIKE
85 Edmonton/Cramer 3

MAGADAN, DAVE
90 FleerCdn. 210
88 Leaf 108
88 O-Pee-Chee 58,81
90 O-Pee-Chee 135
91 O-Pee-Chee 480
92 O-Pee-Chee 745
93 O-Pee-Chee 253
94 O-Pee-Chee 107
88 opcSticker 104
93 opcPremier 61
90 PaniniSticker 300
91 PaniniSticker 79
92 PaniniSticker 222
93 PaniniSticker 250
91 PaniniTopFifteen 3
91 PostCdn. 4

MAGALLANES, EVER
92 Vancouver/ProCards 2731
92 Vancouver/SkyBox 643

MAGNANTE, MIKE
92 O-Pee-Chee 597
92 opcPremier 57

MAGRANE, JOE
90 FleerCdn. 252
88 O-Pee-Chee 380
89 O-Pee-Chee 264
90 O-Pee-Chee 406,578
91 O-Pee-Chee 185
92 O-Pee-Chee 783
88 opcSticker 51
88 PaniniSticker 385
89 PaniniSticker 178
90 PaniniSticker 346
91 PaniniSticker 38

MAGRIA, JAVIER
89 Welland/Pucko 18

MAGUIRE, MIKE
91 Welland/Best 22
91 Welland/ProCards 3569

MAHAFFEY, ART
62 PostCereal 199
62 ShirriffCoin 112

MAHLER, RICK
90 FleerCdn. 425
86 Leaf 21
83 O-Pee-Chee 76
85 O-Pee-Chee 79
86 O-Pee-Chee 39
87 O-Pee-Chee 242
88 O-Pee-Chee 171
89 O-Pee-Chee 393
90 O-Pee-Chee 151
91 O-Pee-Chee 363
85 opcSticker 26
86 opcSticker 43
87 opcSticker 43
86 opcTattoo 11
88 PaniniSticker 239
89 PaniniSticker 35

MAHOMES, PAT
92 O-Pee-Chee 676

MAHONEY, JIM
73 O-Pee-Chee 356
74 O-Pee-Chee 221

MAILS, JOHN W.
23 WillardsChocolate(V100) 86

MAININI, MARCO
52 LavalDairy 93

MAIZE, DAVE
92 Welland/ClassicBest 18

MAKSUDIAN, MIKE
95 Edmonton/Macri
93 TOR/Donruss 39

MALANGONE, JOHN
52 LavalDairy 96

MALARKEY, WILLIAM
1912 ImperialTobacco(C46) 73

MALCHESKY, TOM
88 Hamilton/ProCards 1741

MALDONADO, CANDY
90 FleerCdn. 62
87 Leaf 216
88 Leaf 239
87 O-Pee-Chee 335
88 O-Pee-Chee 190
89 O-Pee-Chee 269
90 O-Pee-Chee 628
91 O-Pee-Chee 723
92 O-Pee-Chee 507
93 OPC 382,-WSChamp 10
93 opcPremier 83
85 opcSticker 81
87 opcSticker 94
88 opcSticker 95
89 opcSticker 89
88 PaniniSticker 428
89 PaniniSticker 221
91 PaniniSticker 220
92 PaniniSticker 31
91 TOR/Score 29
92 TOR/FireSafety
93 TOR/Donruss 9, WS4

MALDONADO, JAY
93 St.Catharines/ClassicBest 12
93 St.Catharines/ProCards 3970

MALLETTE, MALCOLM FRANCIS
52 Parkhurst 60

MALLICOAT, ROB
92 O-Pee-Chee 501

MALLON, JIM
90 Welland/Pucko 32

MALLORY, TREVOR
92 St.Catharines/ClassicBest 6
92 St.Catharines/ProCards 3385

MALONE, PAT
34 WWGum(V354) 30

MALONEY, CHRIS
90 Hamilton/Best 4
90 Hamilton/Star 27
91 Hamilton/ClassicBest 30

MALONEY, JIM
66 O-Pee-Chee 140
67 O-Pee-Chee 80
70 O-Pee-Chee 320
71 O-Pee-Chee 645

MALTZBERGER, GORDON
52 LavalDairy 36

MALZONE, FRANK
66 O-Pee-Chee 152
60 opcTattoo 30
62 PostCereal 58
62 ShirriffCoin 14

MANAHAN, ANTHONY
93 Calgary/ProCards 1172
94 Calgary/ProCards 797

MANCUSO, GUS
33 WWGum(V353) 41
36 WWGum(V355) 9
39 WWGum(V351B)

MANDIA, SAM
90 St.Catharines/ProCards 3459

MANGUAL, ANGEL
71 O-Pee-Chee 317
72 O-Pee-Chee 62
73 O-Pee-Chee 625
75 O-Pee-Chee 452

MANGUAL, PEPE
75 O-Pee-Chee 616
76 O-Pee-Chee 164

MANGUM, LEO
33 WWGum(V353) 92

MANION, CLYDE
34 WWGum(V354) 35

MANN, JIM
96 St.Catharines/Best 18

MANN, KELLY
90 FleerCdn. 642
90 O-Pee-Chee 744

MANNING, RICK
76 O-Pee-Chee 275
77 O-Pee-Chee 190
78 O-Pee-Chee 151
79 O-Pee-Chee 220
80 O-Pee-Chee 292
81 O-Pee-Chee 308
82 O-Pee-Chee 202
83 O-Pee-Chee 147
84 O-Pee-Chee 128
85 O-Pee-Chee 389
86 O-Pee-Chee 49
87 O-Pee-Chee 196
82 opcSticker 179
83 opcSticker 60
84 opcSticker 299
85 opcSticker 291

MANRIQUE, FRED
90 FleerCdn. 306
89 O-Pee-Chee 108
90 O-Pee-Chee 242
89 opcSticker 300
88 PaniniSticker 57
90 PaniniSticker 158

MANRIQUE, JUAN
94 GarciaPhoto 1

MANSER
1912 ImperialTobacco(C46) 59

MANTILLA, FELIX
65 O-Pee-Chee 29
62 ShirriffCoin 183

MANTLE, MICKEY
65 O-Pee-Chee 3,5
66 O-Pee-Chee 50,103,150
68 OPC-Poster 17
75 O-Pee-Chee 194,195,200
60 opcTattoo 31,77
62 PostCereal 5
62 ShirriffCoin 41

MANTO, JEFF
90 FleerCdn. 137
91 O-Pee-Chee 488
89 Edmonton/CMC 20
89 Edmonton/ProCards 570

MANUEL, CHUCK
70 O-Pee-Chee 194
71 O-Pee-Chee 744

MANUEL, JERRY
76 O-Pee-Chee 596

MANUSH, HEINIE
33 WWGum(V353) 47
34 WWGum(V354) 68
36 WWGum(V355) 73

MANWARING, KIRT
90 FleerCdn. 63
88 Leaf 39
90 O-Pee-Chee 678
91 O-Pee-Chee 472
92 O-Pee-Chee 726
94 O-Pee-Chee 2
89 PaniniSticker 208
93 PaniniSticker 235

MANZANILLO, RAVELO
90 Vancouver/CMC 4
90 Vancouver/ProCards 486

MARAK, PAUL
91 O-Pee-Chee 753

MARANDA, GEORGES
52 LavalDairy 5

MARANVILLE, RABBIT (WALTER J.)
21 Neilson's(V61) 90
23 Neilson's 25
23 WillardsChocolate(V100) 87
22 WilliamPaterson(V89) 42
34 WWGum(V354) 4
36 WWGum(V355) 129

MARBERRY, FREDERICK (FIRPO)
33 WWGum(V354) 8
36 WWGum(V355) 10

MARCHIO, FRANK
53 Exhibits 53

MARCHILDON, PHIL
39 WWGum(V351A)

MARCON, DAVE
90 St.Catharines/ProCards 3463

MARICHAL, JUAN
65 O-Pee-Chee 10,50
68 O-Pee-Chee 107,-Poster 18
69 O-Pee-Chee 10,-Deckle 13
70 O-Pee-Chee 67,69,210,466
71 O-Pee-Chee 325
73 O-Pee-Chee 480
74 O-Pee-Chee 330
62 PostCereal 140
71 ProStarPostcard
71 ProStarPoster

MARIS, ROGER
65 O-Pee-Chee 155
67 O-Pee-Chee 45
75 O-Pee-Chee 198,199
60 opcTattoo 32
62 PostCereal 6
62 ShirriffCoin 23

MARKELL, DUKE
52 Parkhurst 19

MARKLAND, GENE
50 WWGum Stars 37

MARKWELL, DIEGOMAR
97 St.Catharines/Best 21

MAROTTA, CHRIS
95 St.Catharines/T.Hortons 33

MARQUARD, RICHARD W.(RUBE)
23 Neilson's 26
23 WillardsChocolate(V100) 88

MARQUEZ, EDGAR
88 St.Catharines/ProCards 2025
90 St.Catharines/ProCards 3455

MARQUEZ, EDWIN
88 Edmonton/CMC 19
88 Edmonton/ProCards 575
89 Edmonton/CMC 13
89 Edmonton/ProCards 552

MARQUEZ, GONZALO
73 O-Pee-Chee 605
74 O-Pee-Chee 422

MARRERO, ORESTE
94 Ottawa/ProCards 2904

MARSHALL, CHARLIE
50 WWGumStars 35

MARSHALL, DAVE
70 O-Pee-Chee 58
71 O-Pee-Chee 259
73 O-Pee-Chee 513

MARSHALL, JIM
74 O-Pee-Chee 354
75 O-Pee-Chee 638
76 O-Pee-Chee 277

MARSHALL, MIKE
90 FleerCdn. 401
85 Leaf 12
86 Leaf 40
69 O-Pee-Chee 17
71 O-Pee-Chee 713
72 O-Pee-Chee 505
73 O-Pee-Chee 355
74 O-Pee-Chee 73,208

75 O-Pee-Chee 6,313,330
76 O-Pee-Chee 465
83 O-Pee-Chee 324
84 O-Pee-Chee 52
85 O-Pee-Chee 85
86 O-Pee-Chee 26
87 O-Pee-Chee 186
88 O-Pee-Chee 249
89 O-Pee-Chee 323
90 O-Pee-Chee 198
91 O-Pee-Chee 356
84 opcSticker 85
85 opcSticker 72
86 opcSticker 71
87 opcSticker 66
88 opcSticker 69
89 opcSticker 67
86 opcTattoo 17
88 PaniniSticker 315
89 PaniniSticker 108
90 PaniniSticker 272
87 StuartBakery 6
71 MTL/ProStar
93 MTL/McDonald's 25

MARSHALL, RANDY
91 London/LineDrive 391
91 London/ProCards 1876

MARTIN, AL
94 O-Pee-Chee 241
93 opcPremier 57

MARTIN, ANDREW
91 Hamilton/ClassicBest 11

MARTIN, BILLY
71 O-Pee-Chee 208
72 O-Pee-Chee 33,34
73 O-Pee-Chee 323
74 O-Pee-Chee 379
75 O-Pee-Chee 511
76 O-Pee-Chee 17
82 opcSticker 115
62 PostCdn. Cereal 84
62 ShirriffCoin 43

MARTIN, CHRIS
94 Ottawa/ProCards 2905

MARTIN, GREGG
89 St.Catharines/ProCards 2070

MARTIN, JARED
97 Lethbridge/Best 9

MARTIN, J.C.
66 O-Pee-Chee 47
69 O-Pee-Chee 112
70 O-Pee-Chee 488
71 O-Pee-Chee 704
73 O-Pee-Chee 552
74 O-Pee-Chee 354

MARTIN, JERRY
80 O-Pee-Chee 256
81 O-Pee-Chee 103
83 O-Pee-Chee 309

MARTIN, JON
90 Welland/Pucko 4

MARTIN, MIKE
85 Vancouver/Cramer 217

MARTIN, NORBERTO
90 Vancouver/CMC 21
90 Vancouver/ProCards 495
91 Vancouver/LineDrive 640
91 Vancouver/ProCards 1603
92 Vancouver/ProCards 2732
92 Vancouver/SkyBox 644

MARTIN, PEPPER
43-47 Montréal/ParadeSportive
33 WWGum(V353) 62

MARTIN, RENIE
81 O-Pee-Chee 266

MARTIN, VIC
86 Calgary/ProCards

MARTINES, JASON
97 Lethbridge/Best 25

MARTINEZ, ANGEL
95 TOR/OhHenry 25

MARTINEZ, BUCK
92 Nabisco 24
71 O-Pee-Chee 163
72 O-Pee-Chee 332
75 O-Pee-Chee 314
76 O-Pee-Chee 616
82 O-Pee-Chee 314
83 O-Pee-Chee 308
84 O-Pee-Chee 179
85 O-Pee-Chee 119,-Poster 13
86 O-Pee-Chee 363
84 TOR/FireSafety
85 TOR/FireSafety
86 TOR/AultFoods
86 TOR/FireSafety

MARTINEZ, CARLOS
90 FleerCdn. 540
90 O-Pee-Chee 461
91 O-Pee-Chee 156
92 O-Pee-Chee 280
91 PaniniSticke 312
89 Vancouver/CMC 17
89 Vancouver/ProCards 579

MARTINEZ, CARMELO
90 FleerCdn. 162
88 Leaf 142
85 O-Pee-Chee 365
86 O-Pee-Chee 67
87 O-Pee-Chee 348
88 O-Pee-Chee 148
89 O-Pee-Chee 33
90 O-Pee-Chee 686
91 O-Pee-Chee 779
84 opcSticker 383
85 opcSticker 157,375
86 opcSticker 109
88 opcSticker 106
88 PaniniSticker 412
89 PaniniSticker 204
93 Calgary/ProCards 1178

MARTINEZ, CHITO
92 O-Pee-Chee 479
92 opcPremier 77

MARTINEZ, DAVE
90 FleerCdn. 353
89 O-Pee-Chee 395
90 O-Pee-Chee 228
91 O-Pee-Chee 24
92 O-Pee-Chee 309
93 O-Pee-Chee 172
92 opcPremier 75
93 opcPremier 22
88 PaniniSticker 266
90 PaniniSticker 293
91 PaniniSticker 144

MARTINEZ, DENNIS
93 Ben'sDisk 5
90 FleerCdn. 354
93 HumptyDumpty 41
88 Leaf 262
92 McDonald's 16
79 O-Pee-Chee 105
80 O-Pee-Chee 2
81 O-Pee-Chee 367
|82 O-Pee-Chee 135
83 O-Pee-Chee 167
87 O-Pee-Chee 252

88 O-Pee-Chee 76
89 O-Pee-Chee 313
90 O-Pee-Chee 763
91 O-Pee-Chee 528
92 O-Pee-Chee 15
93 O-Pee-Chee 300
94 O-Pee-Chee 21
91 opcPremier 75
92 opcPremier 13
82 opcSticker 10
88 opcSticker 84
89 PaniniSticker 114
90 PaniniSticker 288
91 PaniniSticker 150
92 PaniniSticker 149,209
93 PaniniSticker 228
92 PizzaHut/DietPepsi 4
92 PostCdn. 1
92 MTL/Durivage 12
93 MTL/McDonald's 10

MARTINEZ, DOMINGO
93 TOR/Donruss 38
93 TOR/FireSafety

MARTINEZ, EDGAR
90 FleerCdn. 520
90 O-Pee-Chee 148
91 O-Pee-Chee 607
92 O-Pee-Chee 553
93 O-Pee-Chee 164
94 O-Pee-Chee 44
93 opcPremier-StarPerf. 5
89 PaniniSticker 428
91 PaniniSticker 230
92 PaniniSticker 57
93 PaniniSticker 62, 155
94 PaniniSticker 121
87 Calgary/ProCards 2309
88 Calgary/CMC 16
88 Calgary/ProCards 782

MARTINEZ, JORGE ANTONIO
94 GarciaPhoto 27

MARTINEZ, JOSE
70 O-Pee-Chee 8
71 O-Pee-Chee 712

MARTINEZ, JOSE
93 Edmonton/ProCards 1133
88 St.Catharines/ProCards 2024

MARTINEZ, MANNY
97 Calgary/Best 17

MARTINEZ, MARTY
70 O-Pee-Chee 126
71 O-Pee-Chee 602
72 O-Pee-Chee 336

MARTINEZ, PEDRO
94 O-Pee-Chee 26
94 O-Pee-Chee 41
96 MTL/Disk (x2)

MARTINEZ, RAFAEL
88 St.Catharines/ProCards 2026

MARTINEZ, RAMON
90 FleerCdn. 402
90 O-Pee-Chee 62
91 O-Pee-Chee 340
92 O-Pee-Chee 730
93 O-Pee-Chee 275
94 O-Pee-Chee 76
91 PaniniSticker 62
93 PaniniSticker 212
91 PaniniTopFifteen 58,75
92 Edmonton/ProCards 3546
93 Vancouver/ProCards 2604

MARTINEZ, ROMELIO
94 GarciaPhoto 47

MARTINEZ, SANDY
96 TOR/OhHenry
97 TOR/Sizzler 54

MARTINEZ, SILVIO
80 O-Pee-Chee 258

MARTINEZ, TED
71 O-Pee-Chee 648
73 O-Pee-Chee 161
74 O-Pee-Chee 487
75 O-Pee-Chee 637
76 O-Pee-Chee 356
79 O-Pee-Chee 59

MARTINEZ, TINO
91 O-Pee-Chee 482
92 O-Pee-Chee 481
93 O-Pee-Chee 212
91 opcPremier 76
92 opcPremier 64
93 PaniniSticker 66
94 PaniniSticker 122
90 Calgary/CMC 12
90 Calgary/ProCards 659
91 Calgary/LineDrive 66
91 Calgary/ProCards 523

MARTINEZ, TIPPY
76 O-Pee-Chee 41
77 O-Pee-Chee 254
81 O-Pee-Chee 119
83 O-Pee-Chee 263
84 O-Pee-Chee 215
85 O-Pee-Chee 247
86 O-Pee-Chee 82
87 O-Pee-Chee 269
84 opcSticker 208
85 opcSticker 200

MARTING, TIM
71 O-Pee-Chee 423

MARX, TIM
97 Calgary/Best 18

MARZANO, JOHN
88 Leaf 245
91 O-Pee-Chee 574
92 O-Pee-Chee 677

MASHKIVISH, JR.
94 Welland/Classic 13
94 Welland/ProCards 3491

MASHORE, CLYDE
71 O-Pee-Chee 376
73 O-Pee-Chee 401
71 MTL/ProStar

MASHORE, DAMON
95 Edmonton/Macri

MASOLINO, DOUG
89 Vancouver/ProCards 575

MASON, DON
71 O-Pee-Chee 548

MASON, JIM
79 Dimanche/DernièreHeure
72 O-Pee-Chee 334
73 O-Pee-Chee 458
74 O-Pee-Chee 618
75 O-Pee-Chee 136
77 O-Pee-Chee 211
80 O-Pee-Chee 259

MASON, MIKE
85 O-Pee-Chee 144
86 O-Pee-Chee 189
87 O-Pee-Chee 208
85 opcSticker 354

MASSARELLI, JOHN
94 Edmonton/ProCards 2887

MATALVO, ROB
90 St.Catharines/ProCards 3466

MATCHICK, JOHN
67 O-Pee-Chee 72

MATCHICK, TOM
68 O-Pee-Chee 113
71 O-Pee-Chee 321
73 O-Pee-Chee 631

MATHEWS, EDDIE
67 O-Pee-Chee 166
68 O-Pee-Chee 58
73 O-Pee-Chee 237
74 O-Pee-Chee 634
60 opcTattoo 33
62 PostCereal 147
62 ShirriffCoin 111

MATHEWS, GREG
90 O-Pee-Chee 209

MATHEWS, NELSON
65 O-Pee-Chee 87

MATHEWS, TERRY
94 Edmonton/ProCards 2873

MATHEWS, TIM
92 Hamilton/ClassicBest 19

MATHIAS, CARL
61 Toronto/BeeHive

MATHILE, MIKE
93 Ottawa/ProCards 2432

MATIAS, JOHN
70 O-Pee-Chee 444
71 O-Pee-Chee 546

MATLACK, JOHN
71 O-Pee-Chee 648
72 O-Pee-Chee 141
73 O-Pee-Chee 55
74 O-Pee-Chee 153
75 O-Pee-Chee 290
76 O-Pee-Chee 190
77 O-Pee-Chee 132
78 O-Pee-Chee 98
79 O-Pee-Chee 159
80 O-Pee-Chee 312
81 O-Pee-Chee 339
82 O-Pee-Chee 239

MATTHEWS, GARY
86 GeneralMills 4
85 Leaf 220
73 O-Pee-Chee 606
74 O-Pee-Chee 386
75 O-Pee-Chee 79
76 O-Pee-Chee 133
78 O-Pee-Chee 209
79 O-Pee-Chee 35
80 O-Pee-Chee 186
81 O-Pee-Chee 186
82 O-Pee-Chee 151
83 O-Pee-Chee 64
84 O-Pee-Chee 70
85 O-Pee-Chee 210
86 O-Pee-Chee 292
87 O-Pee-Chee 390
88 O-Pee-Chee 156
82 opcSticker 79
83 opcSticker 269
84 opcSticker 18,118
85 opcSticker 12,44
86 opcSticker 59
87 opcSticker 62
88 opcSticker 223
86 opcTattoo 5

MATTICK, BOBBY
80 O-Pee-Chee 300
81 O-Pee-Chee 331

MATTINGLY, DON
88 FantasticSam's 9
90 FleerCdn. 447,626,638
86 GeneralMills 1
87 GeneralMills 2
87 HostessStickers 27
85 Leaf 7
86 Leaf 103
87 Leaf 150
88 Leaf 177
84 O-Pee-Chee 8
85 O-Pee-Chee 324
86 O-Pee-Chee 180, J
87 O-Pee-Chee 229
88 O-Pee-Chee 300
89 O-Pee-Chee 26
90 O-Pee-Chee 200
91 O-Pee-Chee 100
92 O-Pee-Chee 300
93 O-Pee-Chee 103
94 O-Pee-Chee 54
91 opcPremier 77
92 opcPremier 92
93 opcPremier 46
84 opcSticker 325
85 opcSticker 171,310
86 opcSticker 296
87 opcSticker 294
88 opcSticker 3,156,299
88 opcSticker-SuperStar 35
89 opcSticker 314,-SuperStar 2
86 opcTattoo 7
88 PaniniSticker 152,154-56
88 PaniniSticker 277,430
89 PaniniSticker 404
90 PaniniSticker 125
91 PaniniSticker 324
92 PaniniSticker 135
93 PaniniSticker 154
94 PaniniSticker 102
91 PetroCanada 19
87 StuartBakery 23

MATUSZEK, LEN
84 O-Pee-Chee 275
85 O-Pee-Chee 226
85 TOR/FireSafety

MAUCH, GENE
72 Dimanche/DernièreHeure
83 Dimanche/DernièreHeure
68 O-Pee-Chee 122
70 O-Pee-Chee 442
71 O-Pee-Chee 59
72 O-Pee-Chee 276
73 O-Pee-Chee 377
74 O-Pee-Chee 531
75 O-Pee-Chee 101
76 O-Pee-Chee 556
71 MTL/LaPizzaRoyale
71 MTL/ProStar
93 MTL/McDonald's 30

MAURO, CARMEN LOUIS
53 Exhibits 47
52 Parkhurst 71

MAXVILL, DAL
65 O-Pee-Chee 78
68 O-Pee-Chee 141
70 O-Pee-Chee 503
71 O-Pee-Chee 476
72 O-Pee-Chee 206
73 O-Pee-Chee 483
74 O-Pee-Chee 358

MAXWELL, CHARLIE
62 PostCereal 25

MAY, CARLOS
70 O-Pee-Chee 18
71 O-Pee-Chee 243
72 O-Pee-Chee 525
73 O-Pee-Chee 105
74 O-Pee-Chee 195
75 O-Pee-Chee 480
76 O-Pee-Chee 110

MAY, DARRELL
97 Vancouver/Best 20

MAY, DAVE
68 O-Pee-Chee 56
69 O-Pee-Chee 113
70 O-Pee-Chee 81
71 O-Pee-Chee 493
73 O-Pee-Chee 152
74 O-Pee-Chee 12
75 O-Pee-Chee 650
76 O-Pee-Chee 281

MAY, DERRICK
90 FleerCdn. 645
91 O-Pee-Chee 288
93 O-Pee-Chee 159
94 O-Pee-Chee 40
93 PaniniSticker 209
94 PaniniSticker 154

MAY, JERRY
65 O-Pee-Chee 143
66 O-Pee-Chee 123
70 O-Pee-Chee 423
71 O-Pee-Chee 719
72 O-Pee-Chee 109
73 O-Pee-Chee 558

MAY, LEE
70 O-Pee-Chee 65,225
71 O-Pee-Chee 40
72 O-Pee-Chee 89,480
73 O-Pee-Chee 135
74 O-Pee-Chee 500
75 O-Pee-Chee 25
76 O-Pee-Chee 210
77 O-Pee-Chee 3,125
78 O-Pee-Chee 47
79 O-Pee-Chee 1
80 O-Pee-Chee 255
83 O-Pee-Chee 377,378
83 opcSticker 9

MAY, MILT
71 O-Pee-Chee 343
72 O-Pee-Chee 247
73 O-Pee-Chee 529
74 O-Pee-Chee 293
75 O-Pee-Chee 279
76 O-Pee-Chee 532
77 O-Pee-Chee 14
78 O-Pee-Chee 115
80 O-Pee-Chee 340
81 O-Pee-Chee 273
82 O-Pee-Chee 242
82 opcSticker 110
83 opcSticker 301

MAY, RUDY
78 Dimanche/DernièreHeure
70 O-Pee-Chee 203
71 O-Pee-Chee 318
73 O-Pee-Chee 102
74 O-Pee-Chee 302
75 O-Pee-Chee 321
76 O-Pee-Chee 481
79 O-Pee-Chee 318
80 O-Pee-Chee 281
81 O-Pee-Chee 179
82 O-Pee-Chee 128

MAYBERRY, JOHN C.
82 FBI BoxBottom
70 O-Pee-Chee 227
71 O-Pee-Chee 148
72 O-Pee-Chee 373
74 O-Pee-Chee 150
75 O-Pee-Chee 95
76 O-Pee-Chee 194,196,440
77 O-Pee-Chee 16
78 O-Pee-Chee 168
79 O-Pee-Chee 199
80 O-Pee-Chee 338
81 O-Pee-Chee 169,-Poster 13
82 OPC 53,382, -Poster 1
83 O-Pee-Chee 45
82 opcSticker 248
78 TOR
79 TOR/BubbleYum

MAYE, LEE
66 O-Pee-Chee 162
68 O-Pee-Chee 94
70 O-Pee-Chee 439
71 O-Pee-Chee 733
62 PostCereal 156
62 ShirriffCoin 216

MAYNARD, TOW
93 Calgary/ProCards 1179

MAYNOR, TONKA
94 Welland/Classic 14
94 Welland/ProCards 3509

MAYNE, BRENT
91 O-Pee-Chee 776
92 O-Pee-Chee 183
92 opcPremier 40

MAYO, JOHN (JACKIE)
50 WWGum Stars 36

MAYS, CARL W.
21 Neilson's(V61) 7
23 WillardsChocolate(V100) 89

MAYS, WILLIE
65 O-Pee-Chee 4,6,250
66 O-Pee-Chee 1
67 O-Pee-Chee 191
68 O-Pee-Chee 50, -Poster 19
69 O-Pee-Chee 190,-Deckle 14
70 O-Pee-Chee-Booklet 24
71 O-Pee-Chee 600
72 O-Pee-Chee 49,50
73 O-Pee-Chee 1,305
75 O-Pee-Chee 192,203
83 opcSticker 3
60 opcTattoo 34,78
62 PostCereal 142
71 Pro StarPostcard
71 ProStarPoster
62 ShirriffCoin 149

MAZEROSKI, BILL
65 O-Pee-Chee 95
70 O-Pee-Chee 440
71 O-Pee-Chee 110
73 O-Pee-Chee 517
74 O-Pee-Chee 489
62 PostCereal 170
62 ShirriffCoin 131

MAZZILLI, LEE
90 FleerCdn. 88
88 Leaf 223
78 O-Pee-Chee 26
79 O-Pee-Chee 183
80 O-Pee-Chee 11
81 O-Pee-Chee 167
82 O-Pee-Chee 243
83 O-Pee-Chee 306
84 O-Pee-Chee 225
85 O-Pee-Chee 323
86 O-Pee-Chee 373
88 O-Pee-Chee 308
90 O-Pee-Chee 721
82 opcSticker 67

MCALLISTER, LEWIS
1912 ImperialTobacco(C46) 57

MCALPIN, MIKE
88 St.Catharines/ProCards 2015
89 St.Catharines/ProCards 2093
90 St.Catharines/ProCards 3483

MCANALLY, ERNIE
72 Dimanche/DernièreHeure
71 O-Pee-Chee 376
72 O-Pee-Chee 58
73 O-Pee-Chee 484
74 O-Pee-Chee 322
75 O-Pee-Chee 318
71 ProStarPostcard
74 MTL/GeorgeWeston

MCANDREW, JIM
70 O-Pee-Chee 246
71 O-Pee-Chee 428
73 O-Pee-Chee 436

MCAULIFFE, DICK
65 O-Pee-Chee 53
67 O-Pee-Chee 170
70 O-Pee-Chee 475
71 O-Pee-Chee 3
73 O-Pee-Chee 349
74 O-Pee-Chee 495

MCBEAN, AL
65 O-Pee-Chee 25
69 O-Pee-Chee 14

MCBEAN, DOUGLAS
52 LavalDairy 71

MCBRIDE, BAKE
74 O-Pee-Chee 601
75 O-Pee-Chee 174
76 O-Pee-Chee 135
78 O-Pee-Chee 156
79 O-Pee-Chee 332
80 O-Pee-Chee 257
81 O-Pee-Chee 90
82 O-Pee-Chee 92
83 O-Pee-Chee 48
84 O-Pee-Chee 81
84 opcSticker 256

MCBRIDE, CHRIS
94 St.Catharines/Classic 1
94 St.Catharines/ProCards 3641
96 St.Catharines/Best 19

MCBRIDE, GEORGE F.
23 WillardsChocolate(V100) 90

MCBRIDE, KEN
65 O-Pee-Chee 268
62 ShirriffCoin 91

MCCABE, JOE
65 O-Pee-Chee 181

MCCAMENT, RANDY
90 FleerCdn. 64
90 O-Pee-Chee 361

MCCARDELL, ROGER
52 Laval Dairy 7

MCCARTHY, JOE
36 WWGum(V355) 53

MCCARTHY, TOM
90 FleerCdn. 541
90 O-Pee-Chee 326
89 Vancouver/CMC 4
89 Vancouver/ProCards 593

MCCARTY, DAVID
94 O-Pee-Chee 247, -DD 7

MCCARTY, TOM
1912 ImperialTobacco(C46) 89

MCCARVER, TIM
70 O-Pee-Chee 90
71 O-Pee-Chee 465
72 O-Pee-Chee 139
73 O-Pee-Chee 269
74 O-Pee-Chee 520
75 O-Pee-Chee 586
76 O-Pee-Chee 502

MCCASKILL, KIRK
90 FleerCdn. 138
87 GeneralMills 3
87 Leaf 223
87 O-Pee-Chee 194
89 O-Pee-Chee 348
90 O-Pee-Chee 215
91 O-Pee-Chee 532
92 O-Pee-Chee 301
93 O-Pee-Chee 230
87 opcSticker 181
89 opcSticker 184
92 opcPremier 60
88 PaniniSticker 36
89 PaniniSticker 285
90 PaniniSticker 37
85 Edmonton/Cramer 7

MCCATTY, STEVE
81 O-Pee-Chee 59
82 O-Pee-Chee 113
84 O-Pee-Chee 369
82 opcSticker 10,14,228
85 opcSticker 324

MCCLAIN, JOE
62 ShirriffCoin 54

MCCLELLAN, HARVEY M.
23 WillardsChocolate(V100) 91

MCCLELLAN, PAUL
92 O-Pee-Chee 424

MCCLENDON, LLOYD
90 FleerCdn. 38
90 O-Pee-Chee 337
92 O-Pee-Chee 209

MCCLOUGHAN, SCOT
92 St.Catharines/ClassicBest 20
92 St.Catharines/ProCards 3398

MCCLURE, BOB
90 FleerCdn. 139
76 O-Pee-Chee 599
81 O-Pee-Chee 156
87 O-Pee-Chee 133
88 O-Pee-Chee 313
90 O-Pee-Chee 458
91 O-Pee-Chee 84

MCCOOL, BILL
65 O-Pee-Chee 18
69 O-Pee-Chee 129
70 O-Pee-Chee 314

MCCORMICK, MIKE
66 O-Pee-Chee 118
67 O-Pee-Chee 86
68 O-Pee-Chee 9
70 O-Pee-Chee 337
71 O-Pee-Chee 438
62 PostCereal 139
62 ShirriffCoin 134

MCCOVEY, WILLIE
65 O-Pee-Chee 176
68 O-Pee-Chee 5,-Poster 20
69 O-Pee-Chee 4,6,-Deckle 15
70 O-Pee-Chee 63,65,250,450
71 O-Pee-Chee 50
72 O-Pee-Chee 280
73 O-Pee-Chee 410
74 O-Pee-Chee 250
75 O-Pee-Chee 207,450
76 O-Pee-Chee 520
78 O-Pee-Chee 185,238
79 O-Pee-Chee 107
80 O-Pee-Chee 176

62 PostCereal 131
71 ProStarPostcard
62 ShirriffCoin 142

MCCRAW, TOM
66 O-Pee-Chee 141
67 O-Pee-Chee 29
71 O-Pee-Chee 373
73 O-Pee-Chee 86
74 O-Pee-Chee 449
75 O-Pee-Chee 482

MCCRAY, RODNEY
91 O-Pee-Chee 523
91 Vancouver/LineDrive 641
91 Vancouver/ProCards 1607

MCCULLERS, LANCE
90 FleerCdn. 448
87 O-Pee-Chee 71
88 O-Pee-Chee 197
89 O-Pee-Chee 307
90 O-Pee-Chee 259
87 opcSticker 111
88 opcSticker 114
89 opcSticker 108
88 PaniniSticker 399
93 Calgary/ProCards 1163

MCCUTCHEON, GREG
88 St.Catharines/ProCards 2020
89 St.Catharines/ProCards 2094

MCDANIEL, LINDY
65 O-Pee-Chee 244
67 O-Pee-Chee 46
69 O-Pee-Chee 191
70 O-Pee-Chee 493
71 O-Pee-Chee 303
72 O-Pee-Chee 513
73 O-Pee-Chee 46
74 O-Pee-Chee 182
75 O-Pee-Chee 652
62 PostCereal 163
62 ShirriffCoin 144

MCDONALD, BEN
90 FleerCdn. 180
90 O-Pee-Chee 774
91 O-Pee-Chee 497
92 O-Pee-Chee 540
93 O-Pee-Chee 254
94 O-Pee-Chee 122
91 PaniniSticker 247
92 PaniniSticker 68

MCDONALD, BOB
93 O-Pee-Chee 131
91 TOR/Score 32
92 TOR/FireSafety
93 TOR/Donruss 36

MCDONALD, DAVE
70 O-Pee-Chee 189

MCDOUGALD, GIL
50 PalmDairies

MCDOWELL, JACK
93 Ben'sDisk 10
88 Leaf 47
89 O-Pee-Chee 143
91 O-Pee-Chee 219
92 O-Pee-Chee 11
93 O-Pee-Chee 264
94 O-Pee-Chee 173, -AS 14
89 opcSticker 302
89 PaniniSticker 302
93 PaniniSticker 134
94 PaniniSticker 8,50
89 Vancouver/ProCards 577

MCDOWELL, ODDIBE
90 FleerCdn. 589
86 Leaf 46
87 Leaf 51
88 Leaf 154
86 O-Pee-Chee 192,K
87 O-Pee-Chee 95
88 O-Pee-Chee 234
89 O-Pee-Chee 183
90 O-Pee-Chee 329
91 O-Pee-Chee 533
86 opcSticker 237,307
87 opcSticker 243
86 opcTattoo 20
88 PaniniSticker 208
89 PaniniSticker 456
90 PaniniSticker 221
92 Edmonton/SkyBox 163

MCDOWELL, ROGER
90 FleerCdn. 567
86 Leaf 248
87 Leaf 49
88 Leaf 243
86 O-Pee-Chee 139
87 O-Pee-Chee 185
88 O-Pee-Chee 355
89 O-Pee-Chee 296
90 O-Pee-Chee 625
91 O-Pee-Chee 43
92 O-Pee-Chee 713
86 opcSticker 103,312
87 opcSticker 104
88 opcSticker 100
89 opcSticker 92
86 opcTattoo 20
89 PaniniSticker 132
90 PaniniSticker 308
91 PaniniSticker 111

MCDOWELL, SAM
65 O-Pee-Chee 76
68 OPC 12,115,-Poster 21
69 O-Pee-Chee 7,11
70 O-Pee-Chee 72,469
71 O-Pee-Chee 71,150
73 O-Pee-Chee 342,511
74 O-Pee-Chee 550

MCELROY, CHUCK
90 FleerCdn. 650
92 O-Pee-Chee 727
92 opcPremier 85

MCENANEY, WILL
75 O-Pee-Chee 481
76 O-Pee-Chee 362
77 O-Pee-Chee 50
78 O-Pee-Chee 81
77 MTL
77 MTL/RedpathSugar

MCFADDEN, LEON
69 O-Pee-Chee 156

MCGAFFIGAN, ANDY
90 FleerCdn. 355
87 GeneralMills 4
87 Leaf 220
87 O-Pee-Chee 351
88 O-Pee-Chee 56
89 O-Pee-Chee 278
90 O-Pee-Chee 559
91 O-Pee-Chee 671
89 opcSticker 75
84 MTL
84 MTL/StuartBakery 34
86 MTL/ProvigoFoods, -Poster

MCGANN, DON
89 Edmonton/ProCards 560
97 Vancouver/Best 4

MCGEE, WILLIE
90 FleerCdn. 253
86 GeneralMills 4
87 GeneralMills 5
85 Leaf 125
86 Leaf 3,225
87 Leaf 113
88 Leaf 103
83 O-Pee-Chee 49
84 O-Pee-Chee 31-
85 O-Pee-Chee 57
86 O-Pee-Chee 117,L
87 O-Pee-Chee 357
88 O-Pee-Chee 160
89 O-Pee-Chee 225
90 O-Pee-Chee 285
91 O-Pee-Chee 1,380
92 O-Pee-Chee 65
93 O-Pee-Chee 210
91 opcPremier 78
83 opcSticker 147,326
84 opcSticker 141
85 opcSticker 141
86 opcSticker 45,144
87 opcSticker 48
88 opcSticker 55
89 opcSticker 36
86 opcTattoo 23
88 PaniniSticker 396
89 PaniniSticker 189
90 PaniniSticker 339
92 PaniniSticker 217
93 PaniniSticker 240
94 PaniniSticker 265
91 PaniniTopFifteen 1

MCGINLEY, JAMES
1912 ImperialTobacco(C46) 2

MCGINN, DAN
70 O-Pee-Chee 364
71 O-Pee-Chee 21
72 O-Pee-Chee 473
73 O-Pee-Chee 527
71 MTL/ProStar

MCGINNITY, JOSEPH
1912 ImperialTobacco(C46) 77

MCGLOTHEN, LYNN
73 O-Pee-Chee 114
75 O-Pee-Chee 272
76 O-Pee-Chee 478

MCGLOTHIN, EZRA MAC (PAT)
52 Parkhurst 53
50 WWGum Stars 10

MCGLOTHLIN, JIM
67 O-Pee-Chee 19
70 O-Pee-Chee 132
71 O-Pee-Chee 556
72 O-Pee-Chee 236
73 O-Pee-Chee 318
74 O-Pee-Chee 557

MCGRAW, JOHN
22 WilliamPaterson(V89) 40
23 WillardsChocolate(V100) 92

MCGRAW, TUG
66 O-Pee-Chee 124
70 O-Pee-Chee 26
71 O-Pee-Chee 618
72 O-Pee-Chee 163,164
73 O-Pee-Chee 30
74 O-Pee-Chee 265
75 O-Pee-Chee 67
76 O-Pee-Chee 565
77 O-Pee-Chee 142
79 O-Pee-Chee 176
80 O-Pee-Chee 346
82 O-Pee-Chee 250
83 O-Pee-Chee 166,187
84 O-Pee-Chee 161

MCGREGOR, SCOTT
85 Leaf 72
86 Leaf 165
87 Leaf 243
75 O-Pee-Chee 618
79 O-Pee-Chee 206
81 O-Pee-Chee 65
82 O-Pee-Chee 246,316
83 O-Pee-Chee 216
84 O-Pee-Chee 260
85 O-Pee-Chee 228
86 O-Pee-Chee 110
87 O-Pee-Chee 347
88 O-Pee-Chee 254
82 opcSticker 143
84 opcSticker 207
85 opcSticker 198
86 opcSticker 230
86 opcTattoo 6

MCGRIFF, FRED
90 Ben's/HolsumDisks 13
90 FleerCdn. 89
88 HostessDisk
93 HumptyDumpty 48
86 Leaf 28
92 McDonald's 9
88 O-Pee-Chee 395
89 O-Pee-Chee 258
90 O-Pee-Chee 295,385
91 O-Pee-Chee 140
92 O-Pee-Chee 660
93 O-Pee-Chee 255
94 O-Pee-Chee 3, -AS 13
91 opcPremier 79
92 opcPremier 166
93 opcPremier-StarPerf. 2
89 PaniniSticker 467
90 PaniniSticker 170
91 PaniniSticker 336
92 PaniniSticker 232
93 PaniniSticker 258
94 PaniniSticker 148
91 PaniniTopFifteen 16,40
87 TOR/FireSafety
88 TOR/FireSafety
89 TOR/FireSafety
90 TOR/FireSafety
90 TOR/VictoryProductions
97 TOR/Sizzler 49

MCGRIFF, TERRY
93 Edmonton/ProCards 1140

MCGUIRE, BILL
89 Calgary/CMC 21
89 Calgary/ProCards 533
90 Calgary/CMC 14
90 Calgary/ProCards 653

MCGWIRE, MARK
88 Ben's/HolsumDisks 16
88 FantasticSam's 3
90 FleerCdn. 15,638
87 Leaf 46
88 Leaf 1,194
88 O-Pee-Chee 394
89 O-Pee-Chee 70,174
90 O-Pee-Chee 690,I
91 O-Pee-Chee 270
92 O-Pee-Chee 450
93 O-Pee-Chee 201
94 O-Pee-Chee 74
92 opcPremier 99
93 opcPremier-StarPerf.16
88 opcSticker 1,164,309
88 opcSticker-SuperStar 36
89 opcSticker 151,172,-SStar 3
88 PaniniSticker 167,438
89 PaniniSticker 20,244,420
90 PaniniSticker 132,214
91 PaniniSticker 167,192
92 PaniniSticker 15
93 PaniniSticker 15
94 PaniniSticker 110
91 PaniniTopFifteen 14,23,110

MCHENRY, AUSTIN B.
23 WillardsChocolate(V100) 93

MCINNIS, JOHN
23 WillardsChocolate(V100) 94

MCINTOSH, JOE
76 O-Pee-Chee 497

MCINTOSH, TIM
90 FleerCdn. 329
91 O-Pee-Chee 561

MCKAY, DAVE
92 Nabisco 12
76 O-Pee-Chee 592
77 O-Pee-Chee 40
79 O-Pee-Chee 322

MCKECHNIE, BILL
20 MapleCrispette(V117) 25
36 WWGum(V355) 108

MCKEON, JACK
73 O-Pee-Chee 593
75 O-Pee-Chee 72
90 O-Pee-Chee 231

MCKINNEY, RICH
71 O-Pee-Chee 37
73 O-Pee-Chee 587

MCKINNON, TOM
92 O-Pee-Chee 96

MCKNIGHT, JEFF
91 O-Pee-Chee 319

MCKNIGHT, JIM
62 ShirriffCoin 199

MCLAIN, DENNY
65 O-Pee-Chee 236
68 O-Pee-Chee 40,-Poster 22
69 OPC 9,11,57,150,-Deckle 16
70 O-Pee-Chee 70,400,467
71 O-Pee-Chee 750
72 O-Pee-Chee 210
73 O-Pee-Chee 630
75 O-Pee-Chee 206

MCLAREN, JOHN
86 TOR/FireSafety
87 TOR/FireSafety
88 TOR/FireSafety
89 TOR/FireSafety
90 TOR/FireSafety

MCLAUGHLIN, BURKE
52 Parkhurst 12

MCLAUGHLIN, COLIN
89 Calgary/CMC 3
89 Calgary/ProCards 532

MCLAUGHLIN, JOEY
81 O-Pee-Chee 248
82 O-Pee-Chee 376,-Poster 8
83 O-Pee-Chee 9
84 O-Pee-Chee 11

MCLEMORE, MARK
88 Leaf 159
88 O-Pee-Chee 162
88 PaniniSticker 41

MCLEOD, KEVIN
90 Hamilton/Best 6
90 Hamilton/Star 16

MCLIN, JOE (JR.)
91 Welland/Best 13
91 Welland/ProCards 3581

MCLISH, CAL
73 O-Pee-Chee 377
74 O-Pee-Chee 531
60 opcTattoo 35

MCMAHON, DON
66 O-Pee-Chee 133
67 O-Pee-Chee 7
70 O-Pee-Chee 519
71 O-Pee-Chee 354
72 O-Pee-Chee 509
73 O-Pee-Chee 252
74 O-Pee-Chee 78

MCMANUS, MARTIN
21 Neilson's(V61) 41
33 WWGum(V353) 48

MCMICHAEL, GREG
94 O-Pee-Chee-DD 14

MCMILLAN, ROY
65 O-Pee-Chee 45
73 O-Pee-Chee 257
74 O-Pee-Chee 179
62 PostCereal 148
62 ShirriffCoin 159

MCMULLEN, KEN
67 O-Pee-Chee 47
68 O-Pee-Chee 116
70 O-Pee-Chee 420
71 O-Pee-Chee 485
73 O-Pee-Chee 196
74 O-Pee-Chee 434
75 O-Pee-Chee 473
76 O-Pee-Chee 566

MCMURTRY, CRAIG
85 Leaf 45
84 O-Pee-Chee 219
85 O-Pee-Chee 362
90 O-Pee-Chee 294
84 opcSticker 384
85 opcSticker 28
87 TOR/FireSafety

MCNAIR, ERIC
39 WWGum(V351B)

MCNALLY, DAVE
65 O-Pee-Chee 249
66 O-Pee-Chee 193
69 O-Pee-Chee 7,9
70 O-Pee-Chee 20,70
71 O-Pee-Chee 69,320
72 O-Pee-Chee 344,490
73 O-Pee-Chee 600
74 O-Pee-Chee 235
75 O-Pee-Chee 26
71 ProStarPostcard

MCNALLY, MIKE
22 WilliamPaterson(V89) 39

MCNAMARA, JOHN
73 O-Pee-Chee 252
74 O-Pee-Chee 78
75 O-Pee-Chee 146
76 O-Pee-Chee 331
91 O-Pee-Chee 549

MCNEELY, JEFF
92 O-Pee-Chee 618

MCNERTNEY, JERRY
68 O-Pee-Chee 14
70 O-Pee-Chee 158
71 O-Pee-Chee 286

MCNULTY, BILL
73 O-Pee-Chee 603

MCPHAIL, MARLIN
88 Vancouver/CMC 25
88 Vancouver/ProCards 777
89 Vancouver/CMC 15
89 Vancouver/ProCards 596
90 Vancouver/CMC 18
90 Vancouver/ProCards 501

MCQUEEN, MIKE
71 O-Pee-Chee 8
72 O-Pee-Chee 214

MCQUILLAN, HUGH
22 WilliamPaterson(V89) 14

MCQUILLEN, CARL
52 LavalDairy 59

MCRAE, BRIAN
91 O-Pee-Chee 222
92 O-Pee-Chee 659
93 O-Pee-Chee 287
94 O-Pee-Chee 245
92 opcPremier 12
92 PaniniSticker 99
93 PaniniSticker 108
94 PaniniSticker 78

MCRAE, HAL
85 Leaf 34
86 Leaf 251
71 O-Pee-Chee 177
72 O-Pee-Chee 291,292
73 O-Pee-Chee 28
74 O-Pee-Chee 563
75 O-Pee-Chee 268
76 O-Pee-Chee 72
77 O-Pee-Chee 215
79 O-Pee-Chee 306
80 O-Pee-Chee 104
81 O-Pee-Chee 295
82 O-Pee-Chee 384
83 O-Pee-Chee 25
84 O-Pee-Chee 340
85 O-Pee-Chee 284
86 O-Pee-Chee 278
87 O-Pee-Chee 246
92 O-Pee-Chee 519
83 opcSticker 19,75
84 opcSticker 278
85 opcSticker 270
86 opcTattoo 15

MCRAE, NORM
70 O-Pee-Chee 207
71 O-Pee-Chee 93

MCREYNOLDS, KEVIN
90 FleerCdn. 211
85 Leaf 43
86 Leaf 76
87 Leaf 14,214
88 Leaf 228
88 O-Pee-Chee 37
89 O-Pee-Chee 85
90 O-Pee-Chee 545
91 O-Pee-Chee 105
92 O-Pee-Chee 625
93 O-Pee-Chee 359
92 opcPremier 54
88 opcSticker 102
89 opcSticker 10,95,-SStar 51
88 PaniniSticker 346
89 PaniniSticker 139
90 PaniniSticker 305
91 PaniniSticker 83
93 PaniniSticker 107
94 PaniniSticker 79

MCWEENY, DOUGLAS
23 WillardsChocolate(V100) 95

MCWILLIAMS, LARRY
85 Leaf 247
86 Leaf 136
84 O-Pee-Chee 341
85 O-Pee-Chee 183
86 O-Pee-Chee 204
87 O-Pee-Chee 14
84 opcSticker 133
85 opcSticker 132

MEACHAM, BOBBY
85 Leaf 147
85 O-Pee-Chee 16
86 O-Pee-Chee 379
85 opcSticker 315
86 opcSticker 304

MEACHAM, RUSTY
93 O-Pee-Chee 173
90 London/ProCards 1266

MEADOWS, LOUIE
90 O-Pee-Chee 534

MEARES, PAT
94 PaniniSticker 94

MEDIAVILLA, RICH
91 Hamilton/ClassicBest 26
91 Hamilton/ProCards 4054

MEDICH, GEORGE
74 O-Pee-Chee 445
75 O-Pee-Chee 426
76 O-Pee-Chee 146
77 O-Pee-Chee 222
79 O-Pee-Chee 347
73 O-Pee-Chee 608

MEDINA, LUIS
89 PaniniSticker 315

MEDINA, ROBERT
97 St.Catharines/Best 22

MEDLINGER, IRVING
52 Parkhurst 11
50 WWGum Stars 33

MEDVIN, SCOTT
89 PaniniSticker 160

MEDWICK, JOE
36 WWGum(V355) 75

MEINERS, DOUG
93 St.Catharines/ClassicBest 13
93 St.Catharines/ProCards 3971

MEINERSHAGEN, ADAM
92 St.Catharines/ClassicBest 5
92 St.Catharines/ProCards 3386
93 St.Catharines/ClassicBest 14
93 St.Catharines/ProCards 3972

MEJIA, ROBERTO
94 O-Pee-Chee 190, -DD 2
94 PaniniSticker 177

MEJIAS, SAM
78 O-Pee-Chee 99
79 O-Pee-Chee 42
77 MTL
77 MTL/RedpathSugar

MELE, DUTCH
50 WWGum Stars 48

MELE, SAM
66 O-Pee-Chee 3

MELENDEZ, JOSE
92 O-Pee-Chee 518
92 opcPremier 139
90 Calgary/CMC 22
90 Calgary/ProCards 648

MELENDEZ, LUIS
71 O-Pee-Chee 216
73 O-Pee-Chee 47
74 O-Pee-Chee 307
75 O-Pee-Chee 353
76 O-Pee-Chee 399
88 Hamilton/ProCards 1733
90 Hamilton/Best 27
90 Hamilton/Star 26

MELHUSE, ADAM
93 St.Catharines/ClassicBest 15
93 St.Catharines/ProCards 3981

MELILLO, OSCAR
34 WWGum(V354) 94

MELTON, BILL
70 O-Pee-Chee 518
71 O-Pee-Chee 80
72 OPC 90,183,184,495
73 O-Pee-Chee 455
74 O-Pee-Chee 170
75 O-Pee-Chee 11
76 O-Pee-Chee 309
71 ProStarPostcard

MELVIN, BOB
90 FleerCdn. 181
88 O-Pee-Chee 41
89 O-Pee-Chee 329
90 O-Pee-Chee 626
91 O-Pee-Chee 249
92 O-Pee-Chee 733
88 PaniniSticker 277,278

MELVIN, SCOTT
92 Hamilton/ClassicBest 30

MENDENHALL, KIRK
92 London/ProCards 640
92 London/SkyBox 413

MENDEZ, JAVIER
94 GarciaPhoto 45

MENDEZ, SERGIO
93 Welland/ClassicBest 13
93 Welland/ProCards 3360

MENDOZA, MARIO
75 O-Pee-Chee 457
80 O-Pee-Chee 344
81 O-Pee-Chee 76
82 O-Pee-Chee 212

MENHART, PAUL
90 St.Catharines/ProCards 3464

MENKE, DENIS
68 O-Pee-Chee 184
70 O-PC 16,155,-Booklet 16
71 O-Pee-Chee 130
73 O-Pee-Chee 52
74 O-Pee-Chee 134

MENOSKY, MICHAEL
23 WillardsChocolate(V100) 96

MENOSKY, MIKE
21 Neilson's(V61) 46

MEOLA, MIKE
39 WWGum(V351A)

MEOLI, RUDI
74 O-Pee-Chee 188
75 O-Pee-Chee 533
76 O-Pee-Chee 254

MERCED, ORLANDO
92 O-Pee-Che 637
94 O-Pee-Chee 48
92 opcPremier 22
92 PaniniSticker 252
93 PaniniSticker 281
94 PaniniSticker 237
97 TOR/Sizzler 11

MERCEDES, HECTOR
89 St.Catharines/ProCards 2080

MERCEDES, LUIS
92 O-Pee-Chee 603
93 O-Pee-Chee 43

MERCHANT, ANDY
76 O-Pee-Chee 594

MERCKER, KENT
90 FleerCdn. 590
91 O-Pee-Chee 772
92 O-Pee-Chee 596

MERRIFIELD, BILL
87 Edmonton/ProCards 2074

MERRIFIELD, DOUG
86 Calgary/ProCards
88 Calgary/CMC 22
88 Calgary/ProCards 787

MERRILL, STUMP
91 O-Pee-Chee 429

MERRITT, JIM
66 O-Pee-Chee 97
68 O-Pee-Chee 64
71 O-Pee-Chee 420
74 O-Pee-Chee 318
75 O-Pee-Chee 83

MERULLO, MATT
90 FleerCdn. 542
92 O-Pee-Chee 615
92 Vancouver/ProCards 2725

MESA, GERMAN
94 GarciaPhoto 43

MESA, JOSE
91 O-Pee-Chee 512
92 O-Pee-Chee 310

MESA, VICTOR
94 GarciaPhoto 78

MESSERSMITH, ANDY
70 O-Pee-Chee 72,430
71 O-Pee-Chee 15
72 O-Pee-Chee 160
73 O-Pee-Chee 515
74 O-Pee-Chee 267
75 O-Pee-Chee 310,440
76 OPC199,201,203,305
77 O-Pee-Chee 155
78 O-Pee-Chee 79
79 O-Pee-Chee 139

METKOVICH, JOHN
52 Parkhurst 89

METRO, CHARLIE
70 O-Pee-Chee 16

METZGER, BUTCH
76 O-Pee-Chee 593

METZGER, ROGER
71 O-Pee-Chee 404
72 O-Pee-Chee 217
73 O-Pee-Chee 395
74 O-Pee-Chee 224
75 O-Pee-Chee 541
76 O-Pee-Chee 297
77 O-Pee-Chee 44
80 O-Pee-Chee 164

MEULENS, HENSLEY
90 FleerCdn. 449
90 O-Pee-Chee 83
91 O-Pee-Chee 259
92 O-Pee-Chee 154
91 opcPremier 80
91 TOR/Score 4

MEUSEL, BOB
22 WilliamPaterson(V89) 19

MEUSEL, IRISH (EMIL)
20 MapleCrispette(V117) 17
21 Neilson's(V61) 55
22 WilliamPaterson(V89) 20

MEUSEL, EMIL F.
23 WillardsChocolate(V100) 97

MEUSEL, ROBERT
23 WillardsChocolate(V100) 98

92 O-Pee-Chee 600
93 O-Pee-Chee 237
94 OPC 1, -AS 2, -TOR 2
91 opcPremier 95
92 opcPremier 141
93 opcPremier 124
82 opcSticker 200
83 opcSticker 83,139,140,156
84 opcSticker 294
86 opcSticker 203
87 opcSticker 200
88 opcSticker 194,-SStar 42
89 opcSticker 146,204,-SStar 9
86 opcTattoo 23
88 PaniniSticker 125,432
89 PaniniSticker 243,373
90 PaniniSticker 98
91 PaniniSticker 205
94 PaniniSticker 4,140
91 PetroCanada 15
94 PostCdn. 2
95 PostCdn. 3
87 StuartBakery 21
92 TOR/Dempster's 4
93 TOR
93 TOR/FireSafety
93 TOR/McDonald's 35
94 TOR
95 TOR/OhHenry
97 TOR/Sizzler 37, 48

MOLONEY, DICK
71 O-Pee-Chee 13

MONBOUQUETTE, BILL
65 O-Pee-Chee 142
69 O-Pee-Chee 64
62 ShirriffCoin 99
97 St..Catharines/Best 3

MONCHAK, AL
73 O-Pee-Chee 356
74 O-Pee-Chee 221

MONDAY, RICK
69 O-Pee-Chee 105
71 O-Pee-Chee 135
74 O-Pee-Chee 295
75 O-Pee-Chee 129
76 O-Pee-Chee 251
77 O-Pee-Chee 230
79 O-Pee-Chee 320
80 O-Pee-Chee 243
81 O-Pee-Chee 177
82 O-Pee-Chee 6
83 O-Pee-Chee 63
84 opcSticker 83

MONDESI, RAUL
94 O-Pee-Chee 199, -HotP 4

MONETTE, JACQUES
52 Laval Dairy 114

MONEY, DON
71 O-Pee-Chee 49
73 O-Pee-Chee 386
74 O-Pee-Chee 413
75 O-Pee-Chee 175
76 O-Pee-Chee 402
79 O-Pee-Chee 133
80 O-Pee-Chee 313
81 O-Pee-Chee 106
82 O-Pee-Chee 294
83 O-Pee-Chee 259

MONGE, SID
76 O-Pee-Chee 595
80 O-Pee-Chee 39
81 O-Pee-Chee 333
83 opcSticker 274

MONGOMERY, MONTY
72 O-Pee-Chee 372

MONTAGUE, JOHN
75 O-Pee-Chee 405
79 O-Pee-Chee 172

MONTALVO, RAFAEL
90 Edmonton/CMC 11
90 Edmonton/ProCards 517
91 Edmonton/LineDrive 167
91 Edmonton/ProCards 1515

MONTALVO, ROBERT
88 St.Catharines/ProCards 2021

MONTANEZ, WILLIE
71 O-Pee-Chee 138
73 O-Pee-Chee 97
74 O-Pee-Chee 515
75 O-Pee-Chee 162
76 O-Pee-Chee 181
77 O-Pee-Chee 79
78 O-Pee-Chee 43
79 O-Pee-Chee 153
80 O-Pee-Chee 119
81 O-Pee-Chee-Poster 1
81 O-Pee-Chee 63

MONTEAGUDO, AURELIO
71 O-Pee-Chee 129
72 O-Pee-Chee 458
74 O-Pee-Chee 139

MONTEFUSCO, JOHN
76 O-Pee-Chee 30,203
77 O-Pee-Chee 232
78 O-Pee-Chee 59
79 O-Pee-Chee 288
80 O-Pee-Chee 109
83 O-Pee-Chee 223
84 O-Pee-Chee 265
85 O-Pee-Chee 301
83 opcSticker 297
85 opcSticker 319

MONTELEONE, RICH
90 FleerCdn. 648
90 O-Pee-Chee 99
93 O-Pee-Chee 152
86 Calgary/ProCards
87 Calgary/ProCards 2332
88 Calgary/CMC 3
88 Calgary/ProCards 797
89 Edmonton/CMC 2
89 Edmonton/ProCards 564

MONTERO, ROBERTO
94 GarciaPhoto 96

MONTGOMERY, BOB
72 O-Pee-Chee 411
73 O-Pee-Chee 491
74 O-Pee-Chee 301
75 O-Pee-Chee 559
76 O-Pee-Chee 523
79 O-Pee-Chee 219

MONTGOMERY, JEFF
90 FleerCdn. 115
90 O-Pee-Chee 638
91 O-Pee-Chee 371
92 O-Pee-Chee 16
93 O-Pee-Chee 261
94 O-Pee-Chee 7
90 PaniniSticker 85
94 PaniniSticker 10

MONTGOMERY, MONTY
73 O-Pee-Chee 164

MONTGOMERY, REGGIE
86 Edmonton/ProCards

MONTOYO, CHARLIE
93 Ottawa/ProCards 2443

MONZON, DANNY
73 O-Pee-Chee 469
74 O-Pee-Chee 613

MONZON, JOSE
97 Vancouver/Best 22

MOON, BRAD
97 Vancouver/Best 23

MOON, WALLY
65 O-Pee-Chee 247
60 opcTattoo 36
62 ShirriffCoin 124

MOONEY, TROY
90 Welland/Pucko 23

MOONEYHAM, BILL
84 Edmonton/Cramer 110

MOORE, BALOR
71 O-Pee-Chee 747
73 O-Pee-Chee 211
74 O-Pee-Chee 453
75 O-Pee-Chee 592
79 O-Pee-Chee 122
80 O-Pee-Chee 6
78 TOR
79 TOR/BubbleYum

MOORE, BARRY
67 O-Pee-Chee 11
70 O-Pee-Chee 366

MOORE, BAYLOR
81 Vancouver/TCMA 10

MOORE, BRAD
89 O-Pee-Chee 202

MOORE, CHARLIE
74 O-Pee-Chee 604
75 O-Pee-Chee 636
76 O-Pee-Chee 116
80 O-Pee-Chee 302
81 O-Pee-Chee 237
82 O-Pee-Chee 308
84 O-Pee-Chee 138
86 O-Pee-Chee 137
87 O-Pee-Chee 93
83 opcSticker 157
84 opcSticker 301
86 opcSticker 204

MOORE, DONNIE
86 Leaf 130
85 O-Pee-Chee 61
86 O-Pee-Chee 345
87 O-Pee-Chee 115
88 O-Pee-Chee 204
86 opcSticker 182
87 opcSticker 177
86 opcTattoo 16

MOORE, JACKIE
73 O-Pee-Chee 549
74 O-Pee-Chee 379
77 O-Pee-Chee 58

MOORE, JOE
36 WWGum(V355) 8

MOORE, KELVIN
84 Vancouver/Cramer 31

MOORE, MIKE
90 FleerCdn. 16
86 Leaf 114
87 O-Pee-Chee 102
89 O-Pee-Chee 28
90 O-Pee-Chee 175
91 O-Pee-Chee 294
92 O-Pee-Chee 359
93 O-Pee-Chee 186
93 opcPremier 110
89 opcSticker 220
86 opcTattoo 2
89 PaniniSticker 431
90 PaniniSticker 136
94 PaniniSticker 66

MOORE, RANDY
34 WWGum(V354) 26

MOOSE, BOB
68 O-Pee-Chee 36
70 OPC 110,-Booklet 21
71 O-Pee-Chee 690
73 O-Pee-Chee 499
74 O-Pee-Chee 382
75 O-Pee-Chee 536
76 O-Pee-Chee 476

MORALES, ANDY
94 GarciaPhoto 41

MORALES, JERRY
70 O-Pee-Chee 262
71 O-Pee-Chee 696
73 O-Pee-Chee 268
74 O-Pee-Chee 258
75 O-Pee-Chee 282
76 O-Pee-Chee 79
78 O-Pee-Chee 23
79 O-Pee-Chee 235

MORALES, JOSE
77 Dimanche/DernièreHeure
76 O-Pee-Chee 418
77 O-Pee-Chee 90,263
78 O-Pee-Chee 63
80 O-Pee-Chee 116
77 MTL
77 MTL/RedpathSugar

MORALES, RICH
70 O-Pee-Chee 91
71 O-Pee-Chee 267
73 O-Pee-Chee 494
74 O-Pee-Chee 387
89 Calgary/CMC 24
89 Calgary/ProCards 538

MORAN, BILL
61 Toronto/BeeHive

MORAN, FRANK
88 Hamilton/ProCards 1746

MORAN, PATRICK J.
23 WillardsChocolate(V100)107

MORANDINI, MICKEY
91 O-Pee-Chee 342
92 O-Pee-Chee 587
93 O-Pee-Chee 256
91 opcPremier 83
92 PaniniSticker 243
93 PaniniSticker 271

MOREHEAD, DAVE
66 O-Pee-Chee 135
69 O-Pee-Chee 29
70 O-Pee-Chee 495
71 O-Pee-Chee 221

MOREL, RAMON
93 Welland/ClassicBest 15
93 Welland/ProCards 3352
97 Calgary/Best 19

MORELAND, KEITH
85 Leaf 197
86 Leaf 94
87 Leaf 24,77
88 Leaf 160
83 O-Pee-Chee 58
84 O-Pee-Chee 23
85 O-Pee-Chee 197
86 O-Pee-Chee 266
87 O-Pee-Chee 177
88 O-Pee-Chee 31
89 O-Pee-Chee 293
83 opcSticker 222
84 opcSticker 39
85 opcSticker 39
86 opcSticker 54

87 opcSticker 65
88 opcSticker 58
89 opcSticker 105
86 opcTattoo 12
88 PaniniSticker 263

MORELOCK, ALLEN
87 Edmonton/ProCards 2069

MORENO, ANGEL
84 Edmonton/Cramer 99

MORENO, ARMANDO
92 O-Pee-Chee 179

MORENO, JUAN CARLOS
94 GarciaPhoto 44

MORENO, MARINO
94 GarciaPhoto 109

MORENO, OMAR
79 O-Pee-Chee 321
80 O-Pee-Chee 372
81 O-Pee-Chee 213
82 O-Pee-Chee 395
84 O-Pee-Chee 16,322
82 opcSticker 81
83 opcSticker 278,332
87 opcSticker 44

MORET, ROGELIO
71 O-Pee-Chee 692
72 O-Pee-Chee 113
73 O-Pee-Chee 291
74 O-Pee-Chee 590
75 O-Pee-Chee 8
76 O-Pee-Chee 632

MORGAN, ED
34 WWGum 2

MORGAN, JOE
85 Leaf 28
65 O-Pee-Chee 16
66 O-Pee-Chee 195
68 O-Pee-Chee 144,-Poster 23
69 O-Pee-Chee 35
70 O-Pee-Chee 537
71 O-Pee-Chee 264
72 O-Pee-Chee 132
73 O-Pee-Chee 230
74 O-Pee-Chee 85
75 O-Pee-Chee 180
76 O-Pee-Chee 197,420
77 O-Pee-Chee 220
78 O-Pee-Chee 160
79 O-Pee-Chee 5
80 O-Pee-Chee 342
82 O-Pee-Chee 146,208
83 O-Pee-Chee 81,264
84 O-Pee-Chee 210
85 O-Pee-Chee 352
90 O-Pee-Chee 321
91 O-Pee-Chee 21
83 opcSticker 303
84 opcSticker 116
85 opcSticker 5,6,325

MORGAN, MIKE
90 FleerCdn. 403
84 O-Pee-Chee 6
90 O-Pee-Chee 367
91 O-Pee-Chee 631
92 O-Pee-Chee 289
93 O-Pee-Chee 209
94 O-Pee-Chee 235
92 opcPremier 180
91 PaniniSticker 63
91 PaniniTopFifteen 89
93 PaniniSticker 201

MORGAN, TOM
73 O-Pee-Chee 421
74 O-Pee-Chee 276

MORGAN, VERN
73 O-Pee-Chee 49
74 O-Pee-Chee 447

MORLAN, JOHN
75 O-Pee-Chee 651

MORLAN, MIKE
91 St.Catharines/ClassicBest 1
91 St.Catharines/ProCards 3398

MORMAN, RUSS
88 Vancouver/CMC 17
88 Vancouver/ProCards 760
89 Vancouver/CMC 16
89 Vancouver/ProCards 590

MORRIS, DANNY
69 O-Pee-Chee 99

MORRIS, HAL
90 O-Pee-Chee 236
91 O-Pee-Chee 642
92 O-Pee-Chee 773
93 O-Pee-Chee 197
94 O-Pee-Chee 153
92 PaniniSticker 262
93 PaniniSticker 291
94 PaniniSticker 165

MORRIS, JACK
93 Ben'sDisks 3
92 CSCSheet
90 FleerCdn. 610
86 GeneralMills 1
87 GeneralMills 2
93 HumptyDumpty 21
85 Leaf 142
86 Leaf 38
87 Leaf 13,135
88 Leaf 85
92 McDonald's 4
81 O-Pee-Chee 284
82 O-Pee-Chee 47,108
83 O-Pee-Chee 65
84 O-Pee-Chee 195
85 O-Pee-Chee 382
86 O-Pee-Chee 270
87 O-Pee-Chee 376
88 O-Pee-Chee 340
89 O-Pee-Chee 266
90 O-Pee-Chee 555
91 O-Pee-Chee 75
92 O-Pee-Chee 235
93 OPC 179,-WSChamp 11
91 opcPremier 84
92 opcPremier 79
82 opcSticker 10,139,183
83 opcSticker 69
84 opcSticker 263
85 opcSticker 9,15,256
86 opcSticker 268
87 opcSticker 266
88 opcSticker 268,-SStar 59
89 opcSticker 277
86 opcTattoo 11
88 PaniniSticker 85
89 PaniniSticker 334
90 PaniniSticker 76
91 PaniniSticker 296
92 PaniniSticker 122,279
93 PaniniSticker 24
92 PizzaHut/DietPepsi 6
87 StuartBakery 19
92 TOR/FireSafety
93 TOR
93 TOR/Dempter's 7
93 TOR/Donruss 20
93 TOR/FireSafety
97 TOR/Sizzler 41

MORRIS, JOHN
96 Vancouver/Best 3

MORRIS, JOHN D.
90 FleerCdn. 254
90 O-Pee-Chee 383

MORRIS, JOHN W.
69 O-Pee-Chee 111
71 O-Pee-Chee 721
75 O-Pee-Chee 577

MORRISON, JIM
87 Leaf 215
80 O-Pee-Chee 272
82 O-Pee-Chee 154
86 O-Pee-Chee 56
87 O-Pee-Chee 237
88 O-Pee-Chee 288
86 opcSticker 133
87 opcSticker 133
88 opcSticker 272
87 StuartBakery 10

MORRISON, JOHN
21 Neilson's(V61) 115
23 WillardsChocolate(V100)108

MORTON, BUBBA
67 O-Pee-Chee 79

MORTON, CARL
70 O-Pee-Chee 109
71 O-Pee-Chee 515
72 O-Pee-Chee 134
73 O-Pee-Chee 331
74 O-Pee-Chee 244
75 O-Pee-Chee 237
76 O-Pee-Chee 328
71 ProStarPostcard
71 MTL/ProStar

MORTON, JAMES LEWIS
52 Parkhurst 13

MORTON, KEVIN
92 O-Pee-Chee 724
92 opcPremier 7

MORYN, WALT
53 Exhibits 39
60 opcTattoo 37
52 Parkhurst 72

MOSEBY, LLOYD
90 FleerCdn. 90
86 GeneralMills 3
87 GeneralMills 1
88 HostessDisks
85 Leaf 143
86 Leaf 72
87 Leaf 21,105
88 Leaf 140
81 O-Pee-Chee 52,-Poster 24
82 O-Pee-Chee 223,-Poster 4
83 O-Pee-Chee 124
84 O-Pee-Chee 3,92,289
85 O-Pee-Chee 77,-Poster 19
86 O-Pee-Chee 360
87 O-Pee-Chee 21
88 O-Pee-Chee 272
89 O-Pee-Chee 113
90 O-Pee-Chee 779
91 O-Pee-Chee 632
82 opcSticker 246
83 opcSticker 130
84 opcSticker 191,365
85 opcSticker 359
86 opcSticker 195
87 opcSticker 190
88 opcSticker 189
88 opcSticker 188
86 opcTattoo 21
88 PaniniSticker 225
89 PaniniSticker 473
91 PaniniSticker 293
92 PaniniSticker 111
87 StuartBakery 28
84 TOR/FireSafety
85 TOR/FireSafety
86 TOR/AultFoods
86 TOR/FireSafety
87 TOR/FireSafety
88 TOR
88 TOR/FireSafety
89 TOR/FireSafety
90 TOR/Hostess
96 TOR/OhHenry
97 TOR/Sizzler 34
97 St.Catharines/Best 1

MOSES, GERRY
70 O-Pee-Chee 104
71 O-Pee-Chee 205
72 O-Pee-Chee 356
73 O-Pee-Chee 431
74 O-Pee-Chee 19
75 O-Pee-Chee 271

MOSES, JOHN
90 FleerCdn. 381
90 O-Pee-Chee 653
91 O-Pee-Chee 341
85 Calgary/Cramer 83
86 Calgary/ProCards
92 Calgary/ProCards 3743
92 Calgary/SkyBox 63

MOSES, WALLY
37 O-Pee-Chee(V300) 109

MOSEY, ARNOLD
39 WWGum(V351A)

MOSKAU, PAUL
78 O-Pee-Chee 181
79 O-Pee-Chee 197
81 O-Pee-Chee 358

MOSKOVICH, GEORGE ROBERT
52 Parkhurst 97

MOSSI, DON
66 O-Pee-Chee 74
60 opcTattoo 38
62 PostCereal 23

MOSTIL, JOHNNY
21 Neilson's(V61) 45
23 WillardsChocolate(V100)109

MOTA, ANDY
92 O-Pee-Chee 214

MOTA, MANNY
66 O-Pee-Chee 112
67 O-Pee-Chee 66
70 O-Pee-Chee 157
71 O-Pee-Chee 112
73 O-Pee-Chee 412
74 O-Pee-Chee 368
75 O-Pee-Chee 414
76 O-Pee-Chee 548

MOTLEY, DARRYL
85 Leaf 69
86 Leaf 95
87 O-Pee-Chee 99
85 opcSticker 276
86 opcSticker 22

MOTTON, CURT
69 O-Pee-Chee 37
70 O-Pee-Chee 261
71 O-Pee-Chee 684
72 O-Pee-Chee 393

MOULTRIE, PATRICK
93 St.Catharines/ClassicBest 16
93 St.Catharines/ProCards 3987

MOUTON, JAMES
94 O-Pee-Chee 97, -HotP 2

MOYER, JAMIE
90 FleerCdn. 307
88 O-Pee-Chee 36
89 O-Pee-Chee 171
90 O-Pee-Chee 412
91 O-Pee-Chee 138
88 opcSticker 62
89 opcSticker 53
88 PaniniSticker 255

MOYER, JIM
72 O-Pee-Chee 506

MUELLER,CLARENCE F.
23 WillardsChocolate(V100)110

MULCAHY, HUGH
52 LavalDairy 51

MUELLER, WILLIE
79 Vancouver/TCMA 23
80 Vancouver/TCMA 2
81 Vancouver/TCMA 15

MUIR, HARRY
93 St.Catharines/ClassicBest 17
93 St.Catharines/ProCards 3973

MULHOLLAND, TERRY
90 FleerCdn. 568
90 O-Pee-Chee 657
91 O-Pee-Chee 413
92 O-Pee-Chee 719
93 O-Pee-Chee 283
94 O-Pee-Chee 34
91 PaniniSticker 359
92 PaniniSticker 249
93 PaniniSticker 267

MULLANEY, JACK
52 LavalDairy 20

MULLINIKS, RANCE
90 FleerCdn. 91
86 GeneralMills 3
88 HostessDisks
85 Leaf 153
88 Leaf 204
83 O-Pee-Chee 277
84 O-Pee-Chee 19
85 O-Pee-Chee 336, -Poster 17
86 O-Pee-Chee 74
87 O-Pee-Chee 91
88 O-Pee-Chee 167
89 O-Pee-Chee 111
90 O-Pee-Chee 466
91 O-Pee-Chee 229
92 O-Pee-Chee 133
84 opcSticker 374
89 opcSticker 192
84 TOR/FireSafety
85 TOR/FireSafety
86 TOR/AultFoods
86 TOR/FireSafety
87 TOR/FireSafety
88 TOR/FireSafety
89 TOR/FireSafety
90 TOR/FireSafety
91 TOR/FireSafety
91 TOR/Score 17
92 TOR/FireSafety
93 TOR/Donruss 26

MULLINS, FRAN
81 Edmonton/RedRooster 20
82 Edmonton/TCMA 9

MUMMAU, ROB
93 St.Catharines/ClassicBest 18
93 St.Catharines/ProCards 3982

MUMPHREY, JERRY
85 Leaf 124
80 O-Pee-Chee 196
81 O-Pee-Chee 196
82 O-Pee-Chee 175
83 O-Pee-Chee 246
84 O-Pee-Chee 45
85 O-Pee-Chee 186
86 O-Pee-Chee 282
88 O-Pee-Chee 63
82 opcSticker 220
83 opcSticker 97
84 opcSticker 70
85 opcSticker 60
88 PaniniSticker 267

MUNOZ, ANTONIO
94 GarciaPhoto 98

MUNOZ, ORLANDO
94 Vancouver/ProCards 1870

MUNOZ, PEDRO
92 O-Pee-Chee 613
93 O-Pee-Chee 289
93 PaniniSticker 132
94 PaniniSticker 95

MUNSON, THURMAN
70 O-Pee-Chee 189
71 O-Pee-Chee 5
72 O-Pee-Chee 441
73 O-Pee-Chee 142
74 O-Pee-Chee 340
75 O-Pee-Chee 20
76 O-Pee-Chee 192,650
77 O-Pee-Chee 30
78 O-Pee-Chee 200
79 O-Pee-Chee 157

MURA, STEVE
83 O-Pee-Chee 24

MURAKAMI, MASANORI
65 O-Pee-Chee 282

MURCER, BOBBY
67 O-Pee-Chee 93
70 O-Pee-Chee 333,-Booklet 9
71 O-Pee-Chee 635
72 O-Pee-Chee 86
73 O-Pee-Chee 240,343
74 O-Pee-Chee 90,336
75 O-Pee-Chee 350
76 O-Pee-Chee 470
77 O-Pee-Chee 83
78 O-Pee-Chee 95
79 O-Pee-Chee 63
80 O-Pee-Chee 190
81 O-Pee-Chee 253
83 O-Pee-Chee 122,304
71 MTL/ProStar

MURILLO, RAY
81 Edmonton/RedRooster 15

MURPHY, DALE
88 FantasticSam's 13
90 FleerCdn. 591,623
85 GeneralMills 15
86 GeneralMills 5
87 GeneralMills 6
87 HostessStickers
85 Leaf 222
86 Leaf 60
87 Leaf 3,141
88 Leaf 83
79 O-Pee-Chee 15
80 O-Pee-Chee 143
81 O-Pee-Chee 118
82 O-Pee-Chee 391
83 O-Pee-Chee 21,23
84 O-Pee-Chee 150,391
85 O-Pee-Chee 320
86 O-Pee-Chee 197,M
87 O-Pee-Chee 359
88 O-Pee-Chee 90
89 O-Pee-Chee 210

90 O-Pee-Chee 750
91 O-Pee-Chee 545,J
92 O-Pee-Chee 680
91 opcPremier 85
82 opcSticker 19
83 opcSticker 160,206,211
84 opcSticker 27,180,199
85 opcSticker 22,96,177
86 opcSticker 35,145,149
87 opcSticker 36,161
88 opcSticker 45,-SuperStar 18
89 opcSticker 32
86 opcTattoo 2
88 PaniniSticker 251
89 PaniniSticker 45
90 PaniniSticker 222
91 PaniniSticker 109
92 PaniniSticker 246
91 PetroCanada 14
87 StuartBakery 2

MURPHY, DAN
90 O-Pee-Chee 649

MURPHY, DANNY
70 O-Pee-Chee 146

MURPHY, DWAYNE
90 FleerCdn. 569
85 GeneralMills 30
85 Leaf 74
81 O-Pee-Chee 341
82 O-Pee-Chee 29
83 O-Pee-Chee 184
84 O-Pee-Chee 103
86 O-Pee-Chee 8
87 O-Pee-Chee 121
88 O-Pee-Chee 334
82 opcSticker 227
83 opcSticker 107
84 opcSticker 332
85 opcSticker 323
86 opcSticker 171
87 opcSticker 170
86 opcTattoo 20
88 PaniniSticker 176

MURPHY, JEFF
92 Hamilton/ClassicBest 25

MURPHY, ROB
90 FleerCdn. 281
89 O-Pee-Chee 182
90 O-Pee-Chee 268
91 O-Pee-Chee 542
92 O-Pee-Chee 706

MURPHY, TOM
70 O-Pee-Chee 351
71 O-Pee-Chee 401
72 O-Pee-Chee 354
73 O-Pee-Chee 359
74 O-Pee-Chee 496
75 O-Pee-Chee 28
76 O-Pee-Chee 219
78 O-Pee-Chee 193
79 O-Pee-Chee 308
78 TOR

MURRAY, DALE
75 O-Pee-Chee 568
76 O-Pee-Chee 18
79 O-Pee-Chee 198
80 O-Pee-Chee 274
83 O-Pee-Chee 42
84 O-Pee-Chee 281

MURRAY, EDDIE
90 FleerCdn. 404
85 GeneralMills 14
87 GeneralMills 2
87 HostessStickers
85 Leaf 203
86 Leaf 83
87 Leaf 110
88 Leaf 172
78 O-Pee-Chee 154
79 O-Pee-Chee 338
80 O-Pee-Chee 88
81 O-Pee-Chee 39
82 O-Pee-Chee 390
83 O-Pee-Chee 141
84 O-Pee-Chee 240,291
85 O-Pee-Chee 221
86 O-Pee-Chee 30
87 O-Pee-Chee 120
88 O-Pee-Chee 4
89 O-Pee-Chee 148
90 O-Pee-Chee 305
91 O-Pee-Chee 397,590,K
92 O-Pee-Chee 780
93 O-Pee-Chee 280
94 O-Pee-Chee 184
91 opcPremier 86
92 opcPremier 193
82 opcSticker 4,6,145
83 opcSticker 29
84 opcSticker 26,194,203
85 opcSticker 196
86 opcSticker 158,227
87 opcSticker 224
88 opcSticker 11,233
89 opcSticker 238
86 opcTattoo 13
88 PaniniSticker 8,202,203,442
89 PaniniSticker 260
90 PaniniSticker 273
91 PaniniSticker 55
92 PaniniSticker 192
93 PaniniSticker 247
94 PaniniSticker 221
91 PaniniTopFifteen 2
91 PostCdn. 11
87 StuartBakery 14

MURRAY, JAMES
1912 ImperialTobacco(C46) 5

MURRAY, JED
86 Calgary/ProCards

MURRAY, JOSEPH
52 Parkhurst 99

MURRELL, IVAN
70 O-Pee-Chee 179
71 O-Pee-Chee 569
73 O-Pee-Chee 409
74 O-Pee-Chee 628

MURTAUGH, DANNY
70 O-Pee-Chee 532
71 O-Pee-Chee 437
74 O-Pee-Chee 489
75 O-Pee-Chee 304
76 O-Pee-Chee 504

MUSER, TONY
73 O-Pee-Chee 238
74 O-Pee-Chee 286
75 O-Pee-Chee 348
76 O-Pee-Chee 537
84 Vancouver/Cramer 27

MUSIAL, STAN
53 Exhibits 57
88 Leaf 263
60 opcTattoo 39,79

MUSSELMAN, JEFF
90 FleerCdn. 212
88 Leaf 234
88 O-Pee-Chee 229
89 O-Pee-Chee 362
90 O-Pee-Chee 382
88 opcSticker 308
87 TOR/FireSafety
88 TOR/FireSafety
89 TOR/FireSafety

MUSSELMAN, RON
85 TOR/FireSafety

MUSSINA, MIKE
93 Ben'sDisks 13
93 HumptyDumpty 2
92 O-Pee-Chee 242
93 O-Pee-Chee 21
94 O-Pee-Chee 82
92 opcPremier 87
93 PaniniSticker 69
94 PaniniSticker 21

MUTIS, JEFF
93 opcPremier 122

MYATT, GLENN
33 WWGum(V353) 10
36 WWGum(V355) 26

MYER, BUDDY
37 O-Pee-Chee(V300) 114
33 WWGum(V353) 78
36 WWGum(V355) 132

MYERS, ED
86 Vancouver/ProCards

MYERS, GREG
90 O-Pee-Chee 438
91 O-Pee-Chee 599
92 O-Pee-Chee 203
93 O-Pee-Chee 241
91 PaniniSticker 346
94 PaniniSticker 40
89 TOR/FireSafety
90 TOR/FireSafety
91 TOR/FireSfety
91 TOR/Score 12
92 TOR/FireSafety
93 TOR/Donruss 42

MYERS, JERRY
52 LavalDairy 35

MYERS, RANDY
91 Ben's/HolsumDisks 8
93 Ben'sDisks 9
98 HitTheBooks
87 Leaf 29
89 O-Pee-Chee 104
90 O-Pee-Chee 105
91 O-Pee-Chee 780
92 O-Pee-Chee 24
93 O-Pee-Chee 215
94 O-Pee-Chee 119
92 opcPremier 104
93 opcPremier 33
89 opcSticker 97,-SuperStar 66
89 PaniniSticker 135
90 PaniniSticker 307
91 PaniniSticker 135
94 PaniniSticker 16,155
91 PaniniTopFifteen 82

MYLLYKANGAS, LAURI
36 WWGum(V355) 82

N

NABHOLZ, CHRIS
93 HitTheBooks
93 HumptyDumpty 40
91 O-Pee-Chee 197
92 O-Pee-Chee 32
93 O-Pee-Chee 315
91 opcPremier 87
92 opcPremier 26
92 MTL/Durivage 13

NABOA, JUNIOR
91 O-Pee-Chee 182
92 opcPremier 187

NAEHRING, TIM
91 O-Pee-Chee 702
92 O-Pee-Chee 758
93 O-Pee-Chee 304
91 opcPremier 88
92 opcPremier 37
91 ScoreAllStarFanfest 5

NAGELSON, RUSS
70 O-Pee-Chee 7
71 O-Pee-Chee 708

NAGO, GARRETT
85 Vancouver/Cramer 223

NAGY, CHARLES
91 O-Pee-Chee 466
92 O-Pee-Chee 299
93 O-Pee-Chee 278
94 O-Pee-Chee 254
92 opcPremier 138
93 PaniniSticker 46
94 PaniniSticker 59
91 ScoreAllStarFanfest 8

NAGY, MIKE
70 O-Pee-Chee 39
71 O-Pee-Chee 363
72 O-Pee-Chee 488

NAHORODNY, BILL
80 O-Pee-Chee 286

NANTEL, PIERRE
52 LavalDairy 97

NAPOLEON, DAN
66 O-Pee-Chee 87

NARRON, JERRY
81 O-Pee-Chee 249
87 Calgary/ProCards 2329

NARUM, LES
65 O-Pee-Chee 86

NASH, COTTON
71 O-Pee-Chee 391

NASH, JIM
67 O-Pee-Chee 90
70 O-Pee-Chee 171
71 O-Pee-Chee 306
72 O-Pee-Chee 401
73 O-Pee-Chee 509

NATAL, BOB
93 Edmonton/ProCards 1141
94 Edmonton/ProCards 2878

NATTRESS, NATTY
1912 ImperialTobacco(C46) 8

NAVARRO, JAIME
90 FleerCdn. 331
91 O-Pee-Chee 548
92 O-Pee-Chee 222
93 O-Pee-Chee 247
94 O-Pee-Chee 14
93 PaniniSticker 35

NAYLOR, ROLIENE
23 Neilson's 28

NEAGLE, DENNY
92 O-Pee-Chee 592
92 opcPremier 165

NEAL, CHARLIE
60 opcTattoo 40
62 PostCereal 102
62 ShirriffCoin 102

NEALE, A. EARLE
23 WillardsChocolate(V100)111

NEEDLE, CHAD
96 St.Catharines/Best 21

NEEL, TROY
94 O-Pee-Chee 249
93 opcPremier 85
94 PaniniSticker 111

NEFF, MARTY
91 Welland/Best 16
91 Welland/ProCards 3588

NEHF, ART
2 1Neilson's 93
22 WilliamPaterson(V89) 41

NEGRAY, RON
61 Toronto/BeeHive

NEIBAUER, GARY
70 O-Pee-Chee 384
71 O-Pee-Chee 668
72 O-Pee-Chee 149

NEID, DAVID
93 opcPremier 107

NEIDLINGER, JIM
91 O-Pee-Chee 39

NELSON, DAVE
70 O-Pee-Chee 112
71 O-Pee-Chee 241
73 O-Pee-Chee 111
74 O-Pee-Chee 355
75 O-Pee-Chee 435
76 O-Pee-Chee 535

NELSON, ERIK
89 Welland/Pucko 19

NELSON, GENE
90 FleerCdn. 17
86 Leaf 245
90 O-Pee-Chee 726
91 O-Pee-Chee 316
92 O-Pee-Chee 62

NELSON, GLENN R. (SPIKE)
52 Parkhurst 61

NELSON, JAMIE
89 Edmonton/CMC 19
89 Edmonton/ProCards 569
84 Vancouver/Cramer 43
85 Vancouver/Cramer 221

NELSON, JIM
71 O-Pee-Chee 298

NELSON, MEL
69 O-Pee-Chee 181

NELSON, RICKY
84 opcSticker 347
85 Calgary/Cramer 91
86 Calgary/ProCards

NELSON, ROB
91 Vancouver/LineDrive 642
91 Vancouver/ProCards 1604

NELSON, ROCKY
53 Exhibits 49

NELSON, ROGER
71 O-Pee-Chee 581
73 O-Pee-Chee 251
74 O-Pee-Chee 491
75 O-Pee-Chee 572

NEN, DICK
66 O-Pee-Chee 149

NETTLES, GRAIG
86 General Mills 5
85 Leaf 177
69 O-Pee-Chee 99
70 O-Pee-Chee 491
71 O-Pee-Chee 324
73 O-Pee-Chee 498
74 O-Pee-Chee 251
75 O-Pee-Chee 160
76 O-Pee-Chee 169
77 O-Pee-Chee 2,217

78 O-Pee-Chee 10
79 O-Pee-Chee 240
80 O-Pee-Chee 359
81 O-Pee-Chee 365
82 O-Pee-Chee 21,62
83 O-Pee-Chee 207,293
84 O-Pee-Chee 175
85 O-Pee-Chee 35
86 O-Pee-Chee 151
87 O-Pee-Chee 205
82 opcSticker 215
83 opcSticker 13
84 opcSticker 326
85 opcSticker 155
86 opcSticker 106
86 opcTattoo 7

NETTLES, JIM
71 O-Pee-Chee 74
72 O-Pee-Chee 131
73 O-Pee-Chee 358
75 O-Pee-Chee 497

NETTLES, MORRIS
75 O-Pee-Chee 632
76 O-Pee-Chee 434

NEWBY, MIKE
90 Hamilton/Best 11
90 Hamilton/Star 17

NEWCOMBE, DON
53 Exhibits 16
75 O-Pee-Chee 194
60 opcTattoo 41

NEWFIELD, MARC
91 O-Pee-Chee 529
94 Calgary/ProCards 802

NEWHAUSER, DON
74 O-Pee-Chee 33

NEWHOUSER, HAL
53 Exhibits 12

NEWLIN, JIM
92 Calgary/ProCards 3728
92 Calgary/SkyBox 72

NEWMAN, AL
90 FleerCdn. 382
87 O-Pee-Chee 323
90 O-Pee-Chee 19
91 O-Pee-Chee 749
92 O-Pee-Chee 146
90 PaniniSticker 110
91 PaniniSticker 301
86 MTL/ProvigoFoods 18

NEWMAN, FRED
65 O-Pee-Chee 101

NEWMAN, JEFF
79 O-Pee-Chee 319
80 O-Pee-Chee 18

NEWMAN, RANDY
86 Calgary/ProCards

NEWMAN, RAY
73 O-Pee-Chee 568

NEWSOM, BUCK
37 O-Pee-Chee(V300) 139

NEWSON, WARREN
92 O-Pee-Chee 355
92 opcPremier 76
91 Vancouver/LineDrive 643
91 Vancouver/ProCards 1608

NICHOLS, CARL
91 O-Pee-Chee 119

NICHOLS, REID
86 Leaf 224
88 O-Pee-Chee 261

NICHOLS, ROD
90 FleerCdn. 497
90 O-Pee-Chee 108
92 O-Pee-Chee 586

NICHOLSON, DAVE
65 O-Pee-Chee 183
67 O-Pee-Chee 113

NICOSIA, STEVE
81 O-Pee-Chee 212

NIED, DAVID
93 HumptyDumpty 30
93 O-Pee-Chee 49
94 O-Pee-Chee 208

NIEDENFUER, TOM
86 Leaf 186
87 Leaf 204
85 O-Pee-Chee 281
87 O-Pee-Chee 43
88 O-Pee-Chee 242
89 O-Pee-Chee 14
90 O-Pee-Chee 306
85 opcSticker 80
88 opcSticker 232
89 opcSticker 236
89 PaniniSticker 254

NIEKRO, JOE
85 Leaf 189
86 Leaf 243
69 O-Pee-Chee 43
70 O-Pee-Chee 508
71 O-Pee-Chee 695
72 O-Pee-Chee 216
73 O-Pee-Chee 585
74 O-Pee-Chee 504
75 O-Pee-Chee 595
76 O-Pee-Chee 273
80 O-Pee-Chee 226
81 O-Pee-Chee 102
82 O-Pee-Chee 74
83 O-Pee-Chee 221
84 O-Pee-Chee 384
85 O-Pee-Chee 295
86 O-Pee-Chee 135
88 O-Pee-Chee 233
83 opcSticker 240
84 opcSticker 69
85 opcSticker 69

NIEKRO, PHIL
92 Kellogg's 3
85 Leaf 138
86 Leaf 243
87 Leaf 181
66 O-Pee-Chee 28
68 O-Pee-Chee 7
70 O-Pee-Chee 69,160
71 O-Pee-Chee 30
73 O-Pee-Chee 503
74 O-Pee-Chee 29
75 O-Pee-Chee 130,310
76 O-Pee-Chee 435
77 O-Pee-Chee 43
78 O-Pee-Chee 6,155
79 O-Pee-Chee 313
80 O-Pee-Chee 130
81 O-Pee-Chee 201
82 O-Pee-Chee 185
83 O-Pee-Chee 94,316
84 O-Pee-Chee 29
85 O-Pee-Chee 40
86 O-Pee-Chee 246
87 O-Pee-Chee 6
82 opcSticker 20
83 opcSticker 218
84 opcSticker 31
85 opcSticker 309
86 opcSticker 7
86 opcTattoo 8

NIELSEN, JERRY
93 Vancouver/ProCards 2593

NIETO, TOM
85 O-Pee-Chee 294
87 O-Pee-Chee 124

NIEVES, JUAN
87 O-Pee-Chee 79
88 O-Pee-Chee 104
90 O-Pee-Chee 467
88 PaniniSticker 117,431

NIEVES, JUAN
97 St.Catharines/Best 24

NIEVES, MELVIN
93 O-Pee-Chee 246

NILSSON, DAVE
92 O-Pee-Chee 58
93 O-Pee-Chee 272
94 PaniniSticker 84

NIPPER, AL
87 O-Pee-Chee 64

NISCHWITZ, RON
66 O-Pee-Chee 38

NIXON, DONELL
90 FleerCdn. 66
90 O-Pee-Chee 658
87 Calgary/ProCards 2327
88 Calgary/CMC 11

NIXON, OTIS
90 FleerCdn. 356
96 HitTheBooks
97 HitTheBooks
89 O-Pee-Chee 54
90 O-Pee-Chee 252
91 O-Pee-Chee 58
92 O-Pee-Chee 340
93 O-Pee-Chee 271
94 O-Pee-Chee 88
91 opcPremier 89
91 PaniniSticker 152
93 PaniniSticker 186
96 TOR/OhHenry
97 TOR/Sizzler 16

NIXON, RUSS
65 O-Pee-Chee 162
90 O-Pee-Chee 171
84 MTL
84 MTL/Stuart Bakery 38

NOBOA, JUNIOR
88 Edmonton/ProCards 564

NOCE, PAUL
89 Calgary/CMC 16
89 Calgary/ProCards 539

NOKES, MATT
90 FleerCdn. 611
88 Leaf 60
88 O-Pee-Chee 266
89 O-Pee-Chee 116
90 O-Pee-Chee 131
91 O-Pee-Chee 336
92 O-Pee-Chee 748
93 O-Pee-Chee 177
88 opcStick. 269,311,-SStar 56
89 opcSticker 280
88 PaniniSticker 88
89 PaniniSticker 339
92 PaniniSticker 134
93 PaniniSticker 146

NOLAN, DARIN
91 St.Catharines/ClassicBest 22
91 St.Catharines/ProCards 3394

NOLAN, GARY
68 O-Pee-Chee 196
70 O-Pee-Chee 484
71 O-Pee-Chee 75
72 O-Pee-Chee 475
73 O-Pee-Chee 260
74 O-Pee-Chee 277
75 O-Pee-Chee 562
76 O-Pee-Chee 444
77 O-Pee-Chee 70

NOLAN, JOE
81 O-Pee-Chee 149

NOLD, DICK
68 O-Pee-Chee 96

NOLES, DICKIE
83 O-Pee-Chee 99
85 O-Pee-Chee 149

NORDBROOK, TIM
76 O-Pee-Chee 252
78 O-Pee-Chee 139
79 Vancouver/TCMA 6
80 Vancouver/TCMA 10

NORDHAGEN, WAYNE
80 O-Pee-Chee 253
82 O-Pee-Chee 139
83 O-Pee-Chee 47

NOREN, IRV
73 O-Pee-Chee 179

NORMAN, DAN
83 O-Pee-Chee 237
82 MTL/Hygrade

NORMAN, FRED
80 Dimanche/DernièreHeure
70 O-Pee-Chee 427
71 O-Pee-Chee 348
72 O-Pee-Chee 194
73 O-Pee-Chee 32
74 O-Pee-Chee 581
75 O-Pee-Chee 396
76 O-Pee-Chee 609
77 O-Pee-Chee 181
79 O-Pee-Chee 20
80 O-Pee-Chee 362
81 O-Pee-Chee 183

NORMAN, NELSON
80 O-Pee-Chee 270

NORMAN, RUSS
94 Edmonton/ProCards 2880

NORRIS, BEN
97 Lethbridge/Best 26

NORRIS, MIKE
76 O-Pee-Chee 653
81 O-Pee-Chee 55
82 O-Pee-Chee 370
83 O-Pee-Chee 276
84 O-Pee-Chee 49
82 opcSticker 222

NORTH, BILL
73 O-Pee-Chee 234
74 O-Pee-Chee 345
75 O-Pee-Chee 121,309
76 O-Pee-Chee 33
77 O-Pee-Chee 4,106
79 O-Pee-Chee 351
80 O-Pee-Chee 213
81 O-Pee-Chee 47

NORTHEY, SCOTT
70 O-Pee-Chee 241
71 O-Pee-Chee 633

NORTHRUP, JIM
65 O-Pee-Chee 259
68 O-Pee-Chee 78
69 O-Pee-Chee 3
70 O-Pee-Chee 177
71 O-Pee-Chee 265
72 O-Pee-Chee 408
73 O-Pee-Chee 168
74 O-Pee-Chee 266
75 O-Pee-Chee 641

NOSEK, RANDY
89 London/ProCards 1377

NOSSEK, JOE
66 O-Pee-Chee 22
69 O-Pee-Chee 143
73 O-Pee-Chee 646

NOTTEBART, DON
66 O-Pee-Chee 21
68 O-Pee-Chee 171

NOVICK, WALTER ED.
52 Parkhurst 77

NOVOSEL, FRANK
52 Laval Dairy 102

NUNEZ, ABRAHAM
96 St.Catharines/Best 22

NUNEZ, EDWIN (ED)
86 Leaf 66
86 O-Pee-Chee 364
88 O-Pee-Chee 258
90 O-Pee-Chee 586
91 O-Pee-Chee 106
92 O-Pee-Chee 352
86 opcSticker 223
88 opcSticker 216
86 opcTattoo 8
88 PaniniSticker 182

NUNEZ, JOSE
88 O-Pee-Chee 28
87 TOR/FireSafety 25
89 TOR/FireSafety 25
92 Calgary/SkyBox 65

NUÑEZ, VLADIMIR
94 GarciaPhoto 56

NUTTLE, JAMISON
93 Welland/ClassicBest 16
93 Welland/ProCards 3353

NUXHALL, JOE
67 O-Pee-Chee 44

NYE, RICH
69 O-Pee-Chee 88
70 O-Pee-Chee 139
71 MTL/LaPizzaRoyale

NYMAN, CHRIS
81 Edmonton/RedRooster 7
82 Edmonton/TCMA 5

NYMAN, GERRY
69 O-Pee-Chee 173
71 O-Pee-Chee 656

NYMAN, JERRY
90 Welland/Pucko 33
91 Welland/ProCards 3592

NYMAN, NYLS
75 O-Pee-Chee 619
76 O-Pee-Chee 258

OATES, JOHNNY
72 O-Pee-Chee 474
73 O-Pee-Chee 9
74 O-Pee-Chee 183
75 O-Pee-Chee 319
76 O-Pee-Chee 62
92 O-Pee-Chee 579

OBANDO, SHERMAN
93 opcPremier 63

OBERKFELL, KEN
90 FleerCdn. 67
85 Leaf 141

87 Leaf 171
81 O-Pee-Chee 32
82 O-Pee-Chee 121
83 O-Pee-Chee 206
84 O-Pee-Chee 102
85 O-Pee-Chee 307
86 O-Pee-Chee 334
87 O-Pee-Chee 1
88 O-Pee-Chee 67
89 O-Pee-Chee 97
90 O-Pee-Chee 488
91 O-Pee-Chee 286
82 opcSticker 89
83 opcSticker 287
84 opcSticker 148
85 opcSticker 32
86 opcSticker 38
87 opcSticker 38
88 opcSticker 37
88 PaniniSticker 244
92 Edmonton/ProCards 3547

O'BRIEN, BOB
72 O-Pee-Chee 198

O'BRIEN, CHARLIE
90 FleerCdn. 332
97 HitTheBooks
90 O-Pee-Chee 106
91 O-Pee-Chee 442
92 O-Pee-Chee 56
96 TOR/OhHenry
97 TOR/Sizzler 15
86 Vancouver/ProCards

O'BRIEN, JOHN
91 Hamilton/ClassicBest 18
91 Hamilton/ProCards 4047

O'BRIEN, PETE
90 FleerCdn. 498
87 HostessSticker 30
85 Leaf 201
87 Leaf 186
88 Leaf 132
84 O-Pee-Chee 71
85 O-Pee-Chee 196
86 O-Pee-Chee 328
87 O-Pee-Chee 17
88 O-Pee-Chee 381
89 O-Pee-Chee 314
90 O-Pee-Chee 265
91 O-Pee-Chee 585
92 O-Pee-Chee 455
84 opcSticker 357
85 opcSticker 344
86 opcSticker 236
87 opcSticker 239
88 opcSticker 240
89 opcSticker 248
86 opcTattoo 19
88 PaniniSticker 200
89 PaniniSticker 452
90 PaniniSticker 55
91 PaniniSticker 228
92 PaniniSticker 55
93 PaniniSticker 59
87 StuartBakery 26

O'BRIEN, SYD
70 O-Pee-Chee 163
71 O-Pee-Chee 561
72 O-Pee-Chee 289

OCHOA, JORGE
94 GarciaPhoto 114

O'CONNELL, DANNY
50 PalmDairies
62 ShirriffCoin 221

O'CONNER, JACK
86 Calgary/ProCards

O'CONNOR, JAMES
91 St.Catharines/ClassicBest 14

O'DELL, BILLY
67 O-Pee-Chee 162

ODOM, JOHN
69 O-Pee-Chee 195
70 O-Pee-Chee 55
71 O-Pee-Chee 523
73 O-Pee-Chee 315
74 O-Pee-Chee 461
75 O-Pee-Chee 69
76 O-Pee-Chee 651

O'DONOGHUE, JOHN
65 O-Pee-Chee 71
67 O-Pee-Chee 127
70 O-Pee-Chee 441
71 O-Pee-Chee 743
71 MTL/LaPizzaRoyale
71 MTL/ProStar

O'DOUL, LEFTY
33 WWGum(V353) 58

OESCHGER, JOE
21 Neilson's(V61) 98
23 WillardsChocolate(V100)112
22 WilliamPaterson(V89) 6

OESTER, RON
86 Leaf 78
81 O-Pee-Chee 21
82 O-Pee-Chee 34
83 O-Pee-Chee 269
84 O-Pee-Chee 99
85 O-Pee-Chee 314
86 O-Pee-Chee 264
87 O-Pee-Chee 172
88 O-Pee-Chee 17
90 O-Pee-Chee 492
83 opcSticker 230
84 opcSticker 53
85 opcSticker 54
86 opcSticker 138
87 opcSticker 141
88 opcSticker 144

O'FARRELL, BOB
21 Neilson's(V61) 76
23 WillardsChocolate(V100)113
33 WWGum(V353) 34
36 WWGum(V355) 115

OFFERMAN, JOSE
91 O-Pee-Chee 587
92 O-Pee-Chee 493
93 O-Pee-Chee 299
94 O-Pee-Chee 104
91 opcPremier 90
92 opcPremier 123
93 PaniniSticker 216
94 PaniniSticker 202

OFFICE, ROWLAND
75 O-Pee-Chee 262
76 O-Pee-Chee 256
79 O-Pee-Chee 62
81 O-Pee-Chee 319
82 O-Pee-Chee 165

OGAWA, KUNI
79 Vancouver/TCMA 15

OGLIVIE, BEN
85 Leaf 123
86 Leaf 199
73 O-Pee-Chee 388
75 O-Pee-Chee 344
76 O-Pee-Chee 659
77 O-Pee-Chee 236
81 O-Pee-Chee 340
82 O-Pee-Chee 280
83 O-Pee-Chee 91
84 O-Pee-Chee 190
85 O-Pee-Chee 332
86 O-Pee-Chee 372
82 opcSticker 197
83 opcSticker 82
84 opcSticker 296
85 opcSticker 292
86 opcSticker 200
86 opcTattoo 24
97 Calgary/Best 2

O'HALLORAN, GREG
89 St.Catharines/ProCards 2079

O'HARA, WILLIAM
1912 ImperialTobacco(C46) 1

OJEDA, BOB
87 Leaf 94
84 O-Pee-Chee 162
85 O-Pee-Chee 329
86 O-Pee-Chee 11
87 O-Pee-Chee 83
89 O-Pee-Chee 333
90 O-Pee-Chee 207
91 O-Pee-Chee 601
92 O-Pee-Chee 123
91 opcPremier 91
87 opcSticker 99

OJEDA, MIGUEL
94 Welland/Classic 21
94 Welland/ProCards 3499

OLANDER, JIM
92 O-Pee-Chee 7

OLDHAM, JOHN C.
23 WillardsChocolate(V100)114

OLERUD, JOHN
96 HitTheBooks
93 HumptyDumpty 19
91 O-Pee-Chee 92,168
92 O-Pee-Chee 777
93 OPC 188,-WSChamp 12
94 OPC 130, -AS 16, -TOR 5
93 opcPremier 52
91 PaniniSticker 348
92 PaniniSticker 25
93 PaniniSticker 26
94 PaniniSticker 55,141
91 PostCdn. 17
95 PostCdn. 4
90 TOR/FireSafety
91 TOR/FireSafety
91 TOR/Score 18
92 TOR/FireSafety
93 TOR
93 TOR/Dempster's 10, WS6
93 TOR/Donruss 10
93 TOR/FireSafety
93 TOR/McDonald's 27
94 TOR
95 TOR/OhHenry
96 TOR/OhHenry
97 TOR/Sizzler 48

OLIN, STEVE
90 FleerCdn. 499
90 O-Pee-Chee 433
91 O-Pee-Chee 696
92 O-Pee-Chee 559

OLIVA, TONY
65 O-Pee-Cee 1
67 O-Pee-Chee 50
68 O-Pee-Chee 165,-Poster 24
69 O-Pee-Chee 1
70 OPC 63,510,-Booklet 8
71 O-Pee-Chee 61,290
72 O-Pee-Chee 86,400
73 O-Pee-Chee 80
74 O-Pee-Chee 190
75 O-Pee-Chee 325
76 O-Pee-Chee 35

OLIVARES, OMAR
91 O-Pee-Chee 271
92 O-Pee-Chee 193
92 opcPremier 38

OLIVER, AL
83 Dimanche/DernièreHeure
85 Leaf 67
92 Nabisco 21
69 O-Pee-Chee 82
70 O-Pee-Chee 166
71 O-Pee-Chee 388
73 O-Pee-Chee 225
74 O-Pee-Chee 52
75 O-Pee-Chee 555
76 O-Pee-Chee 620
77 O-Pee-Chee 203
78 O-Pee-Chee 97
79 O-Pee-Chee 204
80 O-Pee-Chee 136
81 O-Pee-Chee 70
82 O-Pee-Chee 22,326
83 O-Pee-Chee 5,111,206,311
84 O-Pee-Chee 307,332
85 O-Pee-Chee 130
86 O-Pee-Chee 114
82 opcSticker 239
83 opcSticker 174,205,251
84 opcSticker 87
85 opcSticker 118
86 opcSticker 14
82 MTL/Hygrade
83 MTL
83 MTL/StuartBakery
93 MTL/McDonald's 16

OLIVER, BOB
71 O-Pee-Chee 470
72 O-Pee-Chee 57
73 O-Pee-Chee 289
74 O-Pee-Chee 243
75 O-Pee-Chee 657

OLIVER, GENE
65 O-Pee-Chee 106
67 O-Pee-Chee 18

OLIVER, JOE
90 FleerCdn. 426
90 O-Pee-Chee 668
91 O-Pee-Chee 517
92 O-Pee-Chee 304
93 O-Pee-Chee 260
94 O-Pee-Chee 189
91 PaniniSticker 126
92 PaniniSticker 261
93 PaniniSticker 290
94 PaniniSticker 166

OLIVER, NATE
65 O-Pee-Chee 59
68 O-Pee-Chee 124
70 O-Pee-Chee 223

OLIVER, SCOTT
85 Edmonton/Cramer 5

OLIVER, TOM
36 WWGum(V355) 119

OLIVERAS, FRANCISCO
91 O-Pee-Chee 52

OLIVERAS, MAX
90 Edmonton/CMC 2
90 Edmonton/ProCards 531
91 Edmonton/LineDrive 174
91 Edmonton/ProCards 1531
92 Edmonton/ProCards 3553
92 Edmonton/SkyBox 174
93 Vancouver/ProCards 2613

OLIVERIO, STEVE
89 Calgary/CMC 4
89 Calgary/ProCards 543

OLIVO, MIKE
70 O-Pee-Chee 381

OLLN, STEVE
93 O-Pee-Chee 349

OLLOM, JIM
67 O-Pee-Chee 137
68 O-Pee-Chee 91

OLLVARES, OMAR
93 O-Pee-Chee 206

OLSEN, JOHN
52 LavalDairy 113

OLSEN, RICH
81 Vancouver/TCMA 13
82 Vancouver/TCMA 15
80 Vancouver/TCMA 22

OLSON, AL
88 Edmonton/ProCards 584

OLSON, GREG
91 O-Pee-Chee 673
92 O-Pee-Chee 39
93 O-Pee-Chee 296
91 PaniniSticker 18
92 PaniniSticker 161
93 PaniniSticker 180
91 PetroCanada 2

OLSON, GREGG
90 Ben's/HolsumDisk 20
93 Ben'sDisk 17
90 FleerCdn. 184
90 O-Pee-Chee 655
91 O-Pee-Chee 10
92 O-Pee-Chee 350
93 O-Pee-Chee 281
91 opcPremier 93
92 opcPremier 101
90 PaniniSticker 2
91 PaniniSticker 18,248
92 PaniniSticker 72
91 PaniniTopFifteen 88

OLSON, IVAN M.
23 WillardsChocolate(V100)115

O'MALLEY, TOM
90 O-Pee-Chee 504
91 O-Pee-Chee 257
84 opcSticker 170

O'NEIL, GEORGE M.
23 WillardsChocolate(V100)116

O'NEILL, PAUL
90 FleerCdn. 427
89 O-Pee-Chee 187
90 O-Pee-Chee 332
91 O-Pee-Chee 122
92 O-Pee-Chee 61
93 O-Pee-Chee 218
94 O-Pee-Chee 229
93 opcPremier 14
89 PaniniSticker 77
90 PaniniSticker 245
91 PaniniSticker 133
92 PaniniSticker 266
93 PaniniSticker 151
94 PaniniSticker 103
95 PostCdn. 7

O'NEILL, STEVE
21 Neilson's(V61) 22
23 Neilson's 29
23 WillardsChocolate(V100)117
36 WWGum(V355) 67

ONTIVEROS, STEVE
74 O-Pee-Chee 598
75 O-Pee-Chee 483
76 O-Pee-Chee 284
79 O-Pee-Chee 150
80 O-Pee-Chee 268

OQUENDO, JOSE
90 FleerCdn. 255
84 O-Pee-Chee 208
89 O-Pee-Chee 69
90 O-Pee-Chee 645
91 O-Pee-Chee 343
92 O-Pee-Chee 723
84 opcSticker 112
89 PaniniSticker 184
90 PaniniSticker 341
91 PaniniSticker 32
92 PaniniSticker 173

O'RILEY, DON
71 O-Pee-Chee 679

OROSCO, JESSE
85 Leaf 22
87 Leaf 175
90 FleerCdn. 500
84 O-Pee-Chee 54,396
85 O-Pee-Chee 250
86 O-Pee-Chee 182
87 O-Pee-Chee 148
90 O-Pee-Chee 636
91 O-Pee-Chee 346
92 O-Pee-Chee 79
84 opcSticker 104
85 opcSticker 101
86 opcTattoo 5

O'ROUKE, FRANK
34 WWGum 43

ORR, JIMMY
52 Laval Dairy 42

ORSINO, JOHNNY
66 O-Pee-Chee 77

ORSULAK, JOE
90 FleerCdn. 185
86 Leaf 218
90 O-Pee-Chee 212
91 O-Pee-Chee 521
92 O-Pee-Chee 325
93 O-Pee-Chee 303
93 opcPremier 55
86 opcSticker 132
87 opcSticker 132
89 PaniniSticker 263
90 PaniniSticker 5
91 PaniniSticker 246
92 PaniniSticker 71
93 PaniniSticker 77

ORTA, JORGE
85 Leaf 226
86 Leaf 205
73 O-Pee-Chee 194
74 O-Pee-Chee 376
75 O-Pee-Chee 184
76 O-Pee-Chee 560
78 O-Pee-Chee 77
79 O-Pee-Chee 333
81 O-Pee-Chee 222
82 O-Pee-Chee 26
84 O-Pee-Chee 312
86 O-Pee-Chee 44
87 O-Pee-Chee 63
82 opcSticker 175
85 opcSticker 273

ORTEGA, PHIL
65 O-Pee-Chee 152

ORTIZ, JAVIER
92 O-Pee-Chee 362

ORTIZ, JUNIOR
90 FleerCdn. 475
90 O-Pee-Chee 322
91 O-Pee-Chee 72
92 O-Pee-Chee 617
84 opcSticker 114
88 PaniniSticker 309,310

ORTON, JOHN
90 FleerCdn. 647
91 O-Pee-Chee 176
92 O-Pee-Chee 398
92 Edmonton/SkyBox 155

OSBORN, DAN
74 O-Pee-Chee 489
76 O-Pee-Chee 282

OSBORNE, DONOVAN
93 O-Pee-Chee 248
93 PaniniSticker 199
90 Hamilton/Best 1

OSINSKI, DAN
65 O-Pee-Chee 223
66 O-Pee-Chee 168

OSTEEN, CLAUDE
68 O-Pee-Chee 9
70 O-Pee-Chee 260
71 O-Pee-Chee 10
72 O-Pee-Chee 297,298
73 O-Pee-Chee 490
74 O-Pee-Chee 42
75 O-Pee-Chee 453
76 O-Pee-Chee 488

OSUNA, AL
91 O-Pee-Chee 149
92 O-Pee-Chee 614
92 opcPremier 121

OTIS, AMOS
69 O-Pee-Chee 31
70 O-Pee-Chee 354
71 O-Pee-Chee 610
72 O-Pee-Chee 10
73 O-Pee-Chee 510
74 O-Pee-Chee 65,337
75 O-Pee-Chee 198,520
76 O-Pee-Chee 510
77 O-Pee-Chee 141
78 O-Pee-Chee 16
79 O-Pee-Chee 185
80 O-Pee-Chee 72
81 O-Pee-Chee 288
82 O-Pee-Chee 162,350
83 O-Pee-Chee 75
84 O-Pee-Chee 53
82 opcSticker 194
83 opcSticker 72

O'TOOLE, DENNIS
73 O-Pee-Chee 604

O'TOOLE, JIM
65 O-Pee-Chee 60
62 PostCereal 126

OTT, ED
76 O-Pee-Chee 594
78 O-Pee-Chee 161
79 O-Pee-Chee 289
80 O-Pee-Chee 200
81 O-Pee-Chee 246
82 O-Pee-Chee 225
84 Edmonton/Cramer 120

OTT, MEL
39 WWGum(V351B)

OTTEN, JIM
75 O-Pee-Chee 624

OTTO, DAVE
92 O-Pee-Chee 499

OUELLETTE, PHIL
88 Calgary/CMC 12
88 Calgary/ProCards 801

OWCHINKO, BOB
79 O-Pee-Chee 257
80 O-Pee-Chee 44

OWEN, FRECK
36 WWGum(V355) 69

OWEN, SPIKE
90 FleerCdn. 357
85 Leaf 167
87 Leaf 87
86 O-Pee-Chee 248
88 O-Pee-Chee 188
90 O-Pee-Chee 674
91 O-Pee-Chee 372
92 O-Pee-Chee 443
93 O-Pee-Chee 327
93 opcPremier 8
84 opcSticker 349
85 opcSticker 339
86 opcSticker 224
88 PaniniSticker 30
90 PaniniSticker 285
91 PaniniSticker 142
92 PaniniSticker 205
92 MTL/Durivage 14

OWENS, BRAD
92 Hamilton/ClassicBest 28

OWENS, JIM
73 O-Pee-Chee 624

OYLER, RAY
65 O-Pee-Chee 259
66 O-Pee-Chee 81
69 O-Pee-Chee 178

OZARK, DANNY
73 O-Pee-Chee 486
74 O-Pee-Chee 119
75 O-Pee-Chee 46
76 O-Pee-Chee 384

P

PACHECO, ALEX
90 Welland/Pucko 24

PACHECO, ANTONIO
94 GarciaPhoto 105

PACHECO, EDEL
94 GarciaPhoto 83

PACHECO, TONY
74 O-Pee-Chee 521

PACILLO, PAT
90 Calgary/CMC 1
90 Calgary/ProCards 649

PACIOREK, JIM
85 Vancouver/Cramer 213
86 Vancouver/ProCards

PACIOREK, TOM
71 O-Pee-Chee 709
73 O-Pee-Chee 606
74 O-Pee-Chee 127
75 O-Pee-Chee 523
76 O-Pee-Chee 641
79 O-Pee-Chee 65
81 O-Pee-Chee 228
82 O-Pee-Chee 371
83 O-Pee-Chee 72
84 O-Pee-Chee 132
85 O-Pee-Chee 381
87 O-Pee-Chee 21
82 opcSticker 236
83 opcSticker 47
84 opcSticker 246

PACTWA, JOE
76 O-Pee-Chee 589

PADILLA, JUAN
94 GarciaPhoto 39

PADRO, LUIS ENRIQUE
94 GarciaPhoto 101

PAEZ, PAUL
93 Welland/ClassicBest 17

PAGAN, DAVE
75 O-Pee-Chee 648
77 O-Pee-Chee 151

PAGAN, JOSE
66 O-Pee-Chee 54
69 O-Pee-Chee 192
71 O-Pee-Chee 282
73 O-Pee-Chee 659
62 PostCereal 132
62 ShirriffCoin 200

PAGE, MITCHELL
78 O-Pee-Chee 75
79 O-Pee-Chee 147
80 O-Pee-Chee 307
82 O-Pee-Chee 178

PAGE, SATCHEL
92 HomersClassics 2

PAGLIARI, ARMANDO
88 St.Catharines/ProCards 2005
89 St.Catharines/ProCards 2092

PAGLIARONI, JIM
65 O-Pee-Chee 265
66 O-Pee-Chee 33
67 O-Pee-Chee 183
62 PostCereal 63
62 ShirriffCoin 81

PAGLIARULO, MIKE
90 FleerCdn. 163
86 Leaf 80
87 Leaf 189
86 O-Pee-Chee 327
87 O-Pee-Chee 195
88 O-Pee-Chee 109
89 O-Pee-Chee 211
90 O-Pee-Chee 63
91 O-Pee-Chee 547
92 O-Pee-Chee 721
85 opcSticker 317
87 opcSticker 300
88 opcSticker 295
89 opcSticker 311
88 PaniniSticker 156
89 PaniniSticker 406
91 PaniniSticker 93
92 PaniniSticker 117

PAGNOZZI, TOM
90 O-Pee-Chee 509
91 O-Pee-Chee 308
92 O-Pee-Chee 448
93 O-Pee-Chee 273
94 O-Pee-Chee 103
91 PaniniSticker 30
92 PaniniSticker 171
93 PaniniSticker 191
94 PaniniSticker 246

PALACIOS, REY
91 O-Pee-Chee 148

PALACIOS, VICENTE
88 Leaf 45
91 O-Pee-Chee 438
92 O-Pee-Chee 582
87 Vancouver/ProCards 1619

PALL, DONN
90 FleerCdn. 543
90 O-Pee-Chee 219
91 O-Pee-Chee 768
92 O-Pee-Chee 57
88 Vancouver/CMC 9
88 Vancouver/ProCards 759

PALMA, ADIEL
94 GarciaPhoto 87

PALMEIRO, ORLANDO
94 Vancouver/ProCards 1876
96 Vancouver/Best 20

PALMEIRO, RAFAEL
90 FleerCdn. 308
87 Leaf 43
88 O-Pee-Chee 186
89 O-Pee-Chee 310
90 O-Pee-Chee 755
91 O-Pee-Chee 295
92 O-Pee-Chee 55
93 O-Pee-Chee 171
94 O-Pee-Chee 25
89 opcSticker 47,52
88 PaniniSticker 268
89 PaniniSticker 60
90 PaniniSticker 164
91 PaniniSticker 252
92 PaniniSticker 75
93 PaniniSticker 81
94 PaniniSticker 130
91 PaniniTopFifteen 7,29

PALMER, DAVID
80 Dimanche/DernièreHeure
85 Leaf 105
80 O-Pee-Chee 21
81 O-Pee-Chee 243
82 O-Pee-Chee 292
83 O-Pee-Chee 164
85 O-Pee-Chee 211,-Poster 3
86 O-Pee-Chee 143
89 O-Pee-Chee 67
87 opcSticker 45
83 MTL
84 MTL
84 MTL/StuartBakery 23

PALMER, DEAN
92 O-Pee-Chee 567
93 O-Pee-Chee 258
94 O-Pee-Chee 152
92 opcPremier 112
92 PaniniSticker 77
93 PaniniSticker 84
94 PaniniSticker 131

PALMER, JIM
92 Kellogg's 4
66 O-Pee-Chee 126
70 O-Pee-Chee 68,449
71 O-Pee-Chee 67,570
72 O-Pee-Chee 92,270
73 O-Pee-Chee 160,341
74 O-Pee-Chee 40,206
75 O-Pee-Chee 335
76 O-Pee-Chee 200,202,450
77 O-Pee-Chee 5,80
80 O-Pee-Chee 310
82 O-Pee-Chee 80,81,210
83 O-Pee-Chee 299,328
84 O-Pee-Chee 194
82 opcSticker 146
83 opcSticker 23, 175
84 opcSticker 21,211

PALMER, LOWELL
70 O-Pee-Chee 252
71 O-Pee-Chee 554

PALONIA, LUIS
93 O-Pee-Chee 266

PAPI, STAN
78 Dimanche/DernièreHeure
79 O-Pee-Chee 344

PAPPAS, MILT
65 O-Pee-Chee 270
66 O-Pee-Chee 105
68 O-Pee-Chee 74
69 O-Pee-Chee 79
71 O-Pee-Chee 441

72 O-Pee-Chee 208
73 O-Pee-Chee 70
74 O-Pee-Chee 640
60 opcTattoo 42
62 PostCereal 34
62 ShirriffCoin 98

PAQUETTE, CRAIG
92 O-Pee-Chee 473

PAREDES, JOHNNY
89 O-Pee-Chee 367

PARENT, FREDDY
1912 ImperialTobacco(C46) 44

PARENT, MARK
90 FleerCdn. 164
90 O-Pee-Chee 749
91 O-Pee-Chee 358

PARESE, BILLY
89 St.Catharines/ProCards 2082

PARET, EDUARDO
94 GarciaPhoto 75

PARIS, KELLY
88 Vancouver/CMC 12
89 Vancouver/CMC 11
89 Vancouver/ProCards 594

PARKER, BILLY
72 O-Pee-Chee 213
73 O-Pee-Chee 354

PARKER, CLAY
90 FleerCdn. 451
90 O-Pee-Chee 511
91 O-Pee-Chee 183
92 Calgary/SkyBox 67

PARKER, DAVE
82 FBI BoxBottoms
90 FleerCdn. 18
86 GeneralMills 5
87 GeneralMills 6
85 Leaf 169
86 Leaf 135
87 Leaf 79
74 O-Pee-Chee 252
75 O-Pee-Chee 29
76 O-Pee-Chee 185
77 O-Pee-Chee 242
78 O-Pee-Chee 1,60
79 O-Pee-Chee 223
80 O-Pee-Chee 163
81 O-Pee-Chee 178
82 O-Pee-Chee 40,41,343
83 O-Pee-Chee 205
84 O-Pee-Chee 31
85 O-Pee-Chee 175
86 O-Pee-Chee 287
87 O-Pee-Chee 352
88 O-Pee-Chee 19,315
89 O-Pee-Chee 199
90 O-Pee-Chee 45,J
91 O-Pee-Chee 235
91 opcPremier 94,L
82 opcSticker 87,127
83 opcSticker 280
84 opcSticker 130
85 opcSticker 47
86 opcSticker 135
87 opcSticker 145
88 opcSticker 136
89 opcSticker 169
86 opcTattoo 9
88 PaniniSticker 277,284
89 PaniniSticker 424
91 PaniniSticker 210
87 StuartBakey 4

PARKER, HARRY
74 O-Pee-Chee 106
75 O-Pee-Chee 214

PARKER, RICK
91 O-Pee-Chee 218

PARKER, ROB
93 Calgary/ProCards 1164

PARKER, SALTY
73 O-Pee-Chee 421
74 O-Pee-Chee 276

PARKER, WES
66 O-Pee-Chee 134
70 O-Pee-Chee 5
71 O-Pee-Chee 430
72 O-Pee-Chee 265
73 O-Pee-Chee 151

PARKIN, DAVE
88 PaniniSticker 278

PARKINSON, FRANK J.
23 Neilson's 30
23 WillardsChocolate(V100)118

PARMELEE, ROY
36 WWGum(V355) 20

PARNELL, MELVIN (DUSTY)
50 PalmDairies

PARRETT, JEFF
90 FleerCdn. 570
88 O-Pee-Chee 144
89 O-Pee-Chee 176
90 O-Pee-Chee 439
91 O-Pee-Chee 56
89 opcSticker 73
90 PaniniSticker 312
86 MTL/ProvigoFoods 25

PARRISH, LANCE
90 FleerCdn. 141
86 GeneralMills 1
85 Leaf 41
86 Leaf 201
87 Leaf 107
88 Leaf 130
80 O-Pee-Chee 110
81 O-Pee-Chee 8
82 O-Pee-Chee 214
83 O-Pee-Chee 285
84 O-Pee-Chee 158
85 O-Pee-Chee 160
86 O-Pee-Chee 147
87 O-Pee-Chee 374
88 O-Pee-Chee 95
89 O-Pee-Chee 114
90 O-Pee-Chee 575
91 O-Pee-Chee 210
92 O-Pee-Chee 360
82 opcSticker 188
83 opcSticker 63,193,194
84 opcSticker 265
85 opcSticker 189,259
86 opcSticker 273
87 opcSticker 149,269
88 opcSticker 123
86 opcTattoo 23
88 PaniniSticker 355
90 PaniniSticker 38
91 PaniniSticker 179
92 PaniniSticker 4

PARRISH, LARRY
80 Dimanche/DernièreHeure
87 GeneralMills 3
85 Leaf 96
86 Leaf 1109
87 Leaf 209
88 Leaf 119
92 Nabisco 17
76 O-Pee-Chee 141
77 O-Pee-Chee 72
78 O-Pee-Chee 153
79 O-Pee-Chee 357
80 O-Pee-Chee 182
81 O-Pee-Chee 15,-Poster 4
82 O-Pee-Chee 353,-Poster 15
83 O-Pee-Chee 2
84 O-Pee-Chee 169
85 O-Pee-Chee 203
86 O-Pee-Chee 239
88 O-Pee-Chee 226
82 opcSticker 64
83 opcSticker 120
84 opcSticker 354
85 opcSticker 346
86 opcSticker 240
87 opcSticker 234
88 opcSticker 205
86 opcTattoo 19
88 PaniniSticker 205
87 StuartBakery 26
77 MTL
77 MTL/RedpathSugar
93 MTL/McDonald's 17

PARROTT, MIKE
79 O-Pee-Chee 300
97 Lethbridge/Best 2

PARSONS, BILL
72 O-Pee-Chee 281
73 O-Pee-Chee 231
74 O-Pee-Chee 574
75 O-Pee-Chee 613

PASCUAL, CAMILO
65 O-Pee-Chee 11,255
67 O-Pee-Chee 71
70 O-Pee-Chee 254
60 opcTattoo 43
62 PostCereal 91
62 ShirriffCoin 78

PASKERT, GEORGE H.
23 WillardsChocolate(V100)119

PASQUA, DAN
90 FleerCdn. 544
86 Leaf 195
87 O-Pee-Chee 74
88 O-Pee-Chee 207
89 O-Pee-Chee 74
90 O-Pee-Chee 446
91 O-Pee-Chee 364
92 O-Pee-Chee 107
87 opcSticker 297
89 opcSticker 301
88 PaniniSticker 159,313

PASQUALE, JEFF
91 Hamilton/ClassicBest 8
91 Hamilton/ProCards 4037

PASTORE, FRANK
81 O-Pee-Chee 1
83 O-Pee-Chee 119
84 O-Pee-Chee 87
85 O-Pee-Chee 292

PASZEK, JOHN
52 LavalDairy 31

PATE, BOBBY
81 O-Pee-Chee 136

PATEK, FREDDIE
70 O-Pee-Chee 94
71 O-Pee-Chee 626
73 O-Pee-Chee 334
74 O-Pee-Chee 88
75 O-Pee-Chee 48
76 O-Pee-Chee 1676
77 O-Pee-Chee 244
78 O-Pee-Chee 4,91
79 O-Pee-Chee 273
80 O-Pee-Chee 356

PATTERSON, BOB
91 O-Pee-Chee 479
92 O-Pee-Chee 263

PATTERSON, DARYL
68 O-Pee-Chee 113
69 O-Pee-Chee 101
71 O-Pee-Chee 481

PATTERSON, KEN
90 FleerCdn. 545
90 O-Pee-Chee 156
91 O-Pee-Chee 326
92 O-Pee-Chee 784
88 Vancouver/CMC 6
88 Vancouver/Cramer 208

PATTERSON, REGGIE
81 Edmonton/RedRooster 22
82 Edmonton/TCMA 15

PATTIN, MARTY
70 O-Pee-Chee 31
71 O-Pee-Chee 579
72 O-Pee-Chee 144
73 O-Pee-Chee 415
74 O-Pee-Chee 583
75 O-Pee-Chee 413
76 O-Pee-Chee 492

PAUGH, RICK
94 Welland/Classic 15
94 Welland/ProCards 3492

PAUL, MIKE
71 O-Pee-Chee 454
73 O-Pee-Chee 58
74 O-Pee-Chee 399
85 Vancouver/Cramer 208
86 Vancouver/ProCards

PAVANO, CARL
98 HitTheBooks

PAVLETICH, DON
66 O-Pee-Chee 196
68 O-Pee-Chee 108
69 O-Pee-Chee 179
70 O-Pee-Chee 504
71 O-Pee-Chee 409
72 O-Pee-Chee 359

PAWLOWSKI, JOHN
92 Edmonton/SkyBox 164
92 Edmonton/ProCards 3538
89 Vancouver/CMC 7
89 Vancouver/ProCards 595
90 Vancouver/CMC 10
90 Vancouver/ProCards 487

PAXTON, MIKE
79 O-Pee-Chee 54

PAYNE, JEFF
90 Hamilton/Best 25

PAYNE, JOE
50 WWGum Stars 15

PAZIK, MIKE
76 O-Pee-Chee 597

PEARLMAN, DAVID
93 St.Catharines/ClassicBest 18
93 St.Catharines/ProCards 3974

PEARSON, ALBIE
66 O-Pee-Chee 83
62 PostCereal 78
62 ShirriffCoin 63

PEARSON, MONTE
37 O-Pee-Chee(V300) 131
36 WWGum(V355) 114

PECK, STEVE
93 Vancouver/ProCards 2594

PECKINPAUGH, ROGER
20 MapleCrispette(V117) 23
23 WillardsChocolate(V100)120

PECOTA, BILL
91 O-Pee-Chee 754
92 O-Pee-Chee 236
92 opcPremier 149
91 PaniniSticker 277
92 PaniniSticker 96

PEDRIQUE, AL
88 opcSticker 128,304
88 PaniniSticker 375
93 Edmonton/ProCards 1144
94 Edmonton/ProCards 2881

PEGUERO, JOSE
95 St.Catharines/TimHortons 11

PEGUES, STEVE
90 London/ProCards 1282
91 London/LineDrive 393
91 London/ProCards 1891

PELKA, BRIAN
93 Welland/ClassicBest 18
93 Welland/ProCards 3354
94 Welland/Classic 16
94 Welland/ProCards 3493

PELTIER, DAN
92 O-Pee-Chee 618

PEMBERTON, RUDY
92 O-Pee-Chee 656

PENA, ALEJANDRO
90 FleerCdn. 405
85 Leaf 64
85 O-Pee-Chee 110
87 O-Pee-Chee 363
90 O-Pee-Chee 483
91 O-Pee-Chee 544
92 O-Pee-Chee 337
93 O-Pee-Chee 311
84 opcSticker 82
85 opcSticker 73

PENA, GEORGE
73 O-Pee-Chee 601

PENA, GERONIMO
91 O-Pee-Chee 636
92 O-Pee-Chee 166
93 O-Pee-Chee 238
93 PaniniSticker 193
94 PaniniSticker 247

PENA, HIPOLITO
87 Vancouver/ProCards 1615

PENA, JOSE
70 O-Pee-Chee 523
71 O-Pee-Chee 693
72 O-Pee-Chee 322

PENA, ORLANDO
74 O-Pee-Chee 393
75 O-Pee-Chee 573

PENA, ROBERTO
69 O-Pee-Chee 184
70 O-Pee-Chee 44
71 O-Pee-Chee 334

PENA, TONY
90 FleerCdn. 256
87 HostessStickers 14
85 Leaf 24
86 Leaf 58
87 Leaf 256
88 Leaf 95
83 O-Pee-Chee 133
84 O-Pee-Chee 152
85 O-Pee-Chee 358
86 O-Pee-Chee 260
87 O-Pee-Chee 60

88 O-Pee-Chee 117
89 O-Pee-Chee 94
90 O-Pee-Chee 115
91 O-Pee-Chee 375
92 O-Pee-Chee 569
93 O-Pee-Chee 316
83 opcSticker 281
84 opcSticker 129
85 opcSticker 124
86 opcSticker 125
87 opcSticker 129
88 opcSticker 52
89 opcSticker 38
86 opcTattoo 5
88 PaniniSticker 357,358,387
88 PaniniSticker 447-50
89 PaniniSticker 180
91 PaniniSticker 263
92 PaniniSticker 84
93 PaniniSticker 91
94 PaniniSticker 32

PENDLETON, JAMES EDWARD
52 Parkhurst 69

PENDLETON, TERRY
92 Ben'sDisk 14
90 FleerCdn. 257
86 Leaf 137
87 Leaf 124
88 Leaf 246
85 O-Pee-Chee 346
86 O-Pee-Chee 321
87 O-Pee-Chee 8
88 O-Pee-Chee 105
89 O-Pee-Chee 375
90 O-Pee-Chee 7254
91 O-Pee-Chee 485
92 O-Pee-Chee 115
93 O-Pee-Chee 322
94 O-Pee-Chee 38
91 opcPremier 95
92 opcPremier 195
86 opcSticker 53
87 opcSticker 54
88 opcSticker 49,-SuperStar 7
89 opcSticker 42
86 opcTattoo 17
88 PaniniSticker 392
89 PaniniSticker 185
90 PaniniSticker 337
92 PaniniSticker 148
93 PaniniSticker 184
94 PaniniSticker 149
93 PostCdn. 18

PENIGAR, C.L.
90 Vancouver/CMC 9
90 Vancouver/ProCards 502

PENNINGTON, BRAD
90 Vancouver/Best 21

PENNOCK, HERB
20 MapleCrispette(V117) 27
23 WillardsChocolate(V100)121
22 WilliamPaterson(V89) 50
34 WWGum(V354) 16

PENNYFEATHER, WILL
96 Vancouver/Best 22
89 Welland/Pucko 1

PEPITONE, JOE
65 O-Pee-Chee 245
66 O-Pee-Chee 79
68 O-Pee-Chee 195,-Poster 25
71 O-Pee-Chee 90
72 O-Pee-Chee 303,304
73 O-Pee-Chee 580

PERAZA, ALBERTO
94 GarciaPhoto 5

PERCIVAL, TROY
93 Vancouver/ProCards 2595
94 Vancouver/ProCards 1864

PERCONTE, JACK
85 Leaf 221
85 opcSticker 341
86 opcTattoo 1

PEREZ, ANTANASIO
77 MTL/RedpathSugar

PEREZ, CARLOS
96 MTL/Disk

PEREZ, EDUARDO
94 O-Pee-Chee 36
93 Vancouver/ProCards 2605

PEREZ, GIL
92 Welland/ClassicBest 19
93 Welland/ClassicBest 19
93 Welland/ProCards 3355
94 Welland/Classic 17
94 Welland/ProCards 3494

PEREZ, JULIO
81 Edmonton/RedRooster

PEREZ, MARTY
71 O-Pee-Chee 529
72 O-Pee-Chee 119
73 O-Pee-Chee 144
74 O-Pee-Chee 374
75 O-Pee-Chee 499
76 O-Pee-Chee 177
77 O-Pee-Chee 183

PEREZ, MELIDO
90 FleerCdn. 546
89 O-Pee-Chee 88
90 O-Pee-Chee 621
91 O-Pee-Chee 499
92 O-Pee-Chee 129
93 O-Pee-Chee 231
92 opcPremier 10
89 opcSticker 296
89 PaniniSticker 300
90 PaniniSticker 42
91 PaniniSticker 358
91 PaniniTopFifteen 96

PEREZ, MIGUEL
94 GarciaPhoto 124

PEREZ, MIKE
91 O-Pee-Chee 205
93 O-Pee-Chee 298

PEREZ, NESTOR
94 GarciaPhoto 30

PEREZ, OZZIE
90 Hamilton/Best 18
90 Hamilton/Star 18

PEREZ, PASCUAL
90 FleerCdn. 358
85 Leaf 55
88 Leaf 248
84 O-Pee-Chee 1
85 O-Pee-Chee 106
88 O-Pee-Chee 237
89 O-Pee-Chee 73
90 O-Pee-Chee 278
91 O-Pee-Chee 701
92 O-Pee-Chee 503
84 opcSticker 36
89 PaniniSticker 115
90 PaniniSticker 282

PEREZ, PAUL
93 Welland/ProCards 3368

PEREZ, PEDRO
94 GarciaPhoto 97

PEREZ, ROBERT
90 St.Catharines/ProCards 3456
96 TOR/OhHenry

PEREZ, TEOFILO
94 GarciaPhoto 86

PEREZ, TOMAS
95 TOR/OhHenry
97 TOR/Sizzler 56

PEREZ, TONY
86 GeneralMills 5
92 Kellogg's 5
86 Leaf 15
92 Nabisco's 7
66 O-Pee-Chee 72
68 O-Pee-Chee 130
70 O-Pee-Chee 63,380
71 O-Pee-Chee 64,66,580
72 O-Pee-Chee 80
73 O-Pee-Chee 275
74 O-Pee-Chee 230
75 O-Pee-Chee 560
76 O-Pee-Chee 195,325
77 O-Pee-Chee 135
78 O-Pee-Chee 90
79 O-Pee-Chee 261
80 O-Pee-Chee 69
81 O-Pee-Chee 231
82 O-Pee-Chee 255,256
83 O-Pee-Chee 74,355
84 O-Pee-Chee 385
85 O-Pee-Chee 212
86 O-Pee-Chee 85
82 opcSticker 152
83 opcSticker 8
84 opcSticker 126
86 opcSticker 8,142
86 opcTattoo 16
77 MTL
77 MTL/RedpathSugar

PERKINS, BRODERICK
82 O-Pee-Chee 192
83 O-Pee-Chee 292
82 opcSticker 98

PERKINS, CY
36 WWGum(V356) 24

PERKINS, RALPH
21 Neilson's(V61) 11
23 Neilson's 31
23 WillardsChocolate(V100)122

PERRANOSKI, RON
69 O-Pee-Chee 77
70 O-Pee-Chee 226
71 O-Pee-Chee 475
72 O-Pee-Chee 367

PERRY, GAYLORD
65 O-Pee-Chee 193
68 O-Pee-Chee 11,85
71 O-Pee-Chee 70,140
72 O-Pee-Chee 285
73 O-Pee-Chee 66,346,400
74 O-Pee-Chee 35
75 O-Pee-Chee 530
76 O-Pee-Chee 55,204
77 O-Pee-Chee 149
79 O-Pee-Chee 161
80 O-Pee-Chee 148
82 O-Pee-Chee 115
83 O-Pee-Chee 96,159
83 opcSticker 114

PERRY, GERALD
90 FleerCdn. 592
88 Leaf 216
89 O-Pee-Chee 130
90 O-Pee-Chee 792
91 O-Pee-Chee 384
92 O-Pee-Chee 498
89 opcSticker 33
88 PaniniSticker 242
89 PaniniSticker 40

PERRY, JIM
69 O-Pee-Chee 146
70 O-Pee-Chee 70
71 O-Pee-Chee 69,500
72 O-Pee-Chee 220,497
73 O-Pee-Chee 385
74 O-Pee-Chee 316
75 O-Pee-Chee 263
62 PostCereal 43
62 ShirriffCoin 32

PERRY, PAT
90 O-Pee-Chee 541

PERSCHKE, GREG
91 Vancouver/ProCards 1593
91 Vancouver/LineDrive 644
92 Vancouver/ProCards 2720
92 Vancouver/SkyBox 645

PERZANOWSKI, STAN
76 O-Pee-Chee 388

PESTANO, ARIEL
94 GarciaPhoto 69

PETEREK, JEFF
90 FleerCdn. 333

PETERMAN, ERNIE
95 St.Catharines/TimHortons 13

PETERS, CHRIS
93 Welland/ClassicBest 20
93 Welland/ProCards 3356

PETERS, GARY
65 O-Pee-Chee 9
66 O-Pee-Chee 111
68 O-Pee-Chee 8
69 O-Pee-Chee 34
70 O-Pee-Chee 540
71 O-Pee-Chee 225
72 O-Pee-Chee 503

PETERS, JACK
21 Neilson's(V61) 63

PETERS, REED
90 Edmonton/CMC 17
90 Edmonton/ProCards 529
91 Edmonton/LineDrive 168
91 Edmonton/ProCards 1529

PETERS, RICK
82 O-Pee-Chee 269

PETERSON, ADAM
90 O-Pee-Chee 299
91 O-Pee-Chee 559
88 Vancouver/CMC 7
88 Vancouver/ProCards 776
89 Vancouver/CMC 2
89 Vancouver/ProCards 589
90 Vancouver/CMC 2
90 Vancouver/ProCards 488

PETERSON, CAP
68 O-Pee-Chee 188

PETERSON, FRITZ
69 O-Pee-Chee 46
70 O-Pee-Chee 142
71 O-Pee-Chee 460
73 O-Pee-Chee 82
74 O-Pee-Chee 229
75 O-Pee-Chee 62
76 O-Pee-Chee 255
71 ProStarPostcard

PETERSON, ROB
89 Welland/Pucko 20
90 Welland/Pucko 18

PETRALLI, GENO
90 FleerCdn. 309
88 Leaf 241
89 O-Pee-Chee 137
90 O-Pee-Chee 706
91 O-Pee-Chee 78
92 O-Pee-Chee 409
89 opcSticker 24
89 PaniniSticker 451
90 PaniniSticker 161
91 PaniniSticker 251

PETROCELLI, RICO
65 O-Pee-Chee 74
69 O-Pee-Chee 215
70 O-Pee-Chee 457,-Booklet 2
71 O-Pee-Chee 340
72 O-Pee-Chee 30
73 O-Pee-Chee 365
74 O-Pee-Chee 609
75 O-Pee-Chee 356
76 O-Pee-Chee 445

PETRY, DAN
90 FleerCdn. 142
85 Leaf 188
86 Leaf 144
87 Leaf 228
83 O-Pee-Chee 79
84 O-Pee-Chee 147
85 O-Pee-Chee 392
86 O-Pee-Chee 216
87 O-Pee-Chee 27
90 O-Pee-Chee 363
83 opcSticker 70
84 opcSticker 269
85 opcSticker 264
86 opcSticker 270
91 PaniniSticker 295

PETTINI, JOSEPH
89 Hamilton/Star 27

PETTIPIECE, PAUL
95 St.Catharines/TimHortons 32

PETTIS, GARY
90 FleerCdn. 612
86 Leaf 84
87 Leaf 152
85 O-Pee-Chee 39
86 O-Pee-Chee 323
87 O-Pee-Chee 278
88 O-Pee-Chee 71
89 O-Pee-Chee 146
90 O-Pee-Chee 512
91 O-Pee-Chee 314
92 O-Pee-Chee 756
85 opcSticker 226
87 opcSticker 16,175
88 opcSticker 178
89 opcSticker 279
88 PaniniSticker 48
89 PaniniSticker 345
90 PaniniSticker 78
91 PaniniSticker 256
92 PaniniSticker 80
91 PaniniTopFifteen 115

PETTY, JESSE
34 WWGum(V354) 42

PEVEY, MARTY
90 O-Pee-Chee 137

PEYTON, ERIC
84 Vancouver/Cramer 41

PFEFFER, EDWARD J.
23 WillardsChocolate(V100)123

PFEIL, BOBBY
70 O-Pee-Chee 99

PHELAN, ART
1912 ImperialTobacco(C46) 35

PHELPS, EDWARD
1912 ImperialTobacco(C46) 36

PHELPS, KEN
85 Leaf 129
85 O-Pee-Chee 322
88 O-Pee-Chee 182
89 O-Pee-Chee 182
90 O-Pee-Chee 411
87 opcSticker 222

PHILLIPS, ADOLFO
66 O-Pee-Chee 32
67 O-Pee-Chee 148
71 O-Pee-Chee 418
71 MTL/LaPizzaRoyale
71 MTL/ProStar

PHILLIPS, BUBBA
62 PostCereal 39
62 ShirriffCoin 74

PHILLIPS, JASON
93 Welland/ClassicBest 21
93 Welland/ProCards 3357

PHILLIPS, J.R.
94 O-Pee-Chee 148

PHILLIPS, LEFTY
70 O-Pee-Chee 376
71 O-Pee-Chee 279

PHILLIPS, MIKE
74 O-Pee-Chee 533
75 O-Pee-Chee 642
76 O-Pee-Chee 93
82 O-Pee-Chee 263

PHILLIPS, TONY
90 FleerCdn. 19
88 O-Pee-Chee 12
90 O-Pee-Chee 702
91 O-Pee-Chee 583
92 O-Pee-Chee 319
93 O-Pee-Chee 262
94 O-Pee-Chee 192
85 opcSticker 329
88 opcSticker 165
88 PaniniSticker 168, 170, 171
91 PaniniSticker 290
93 PaniniSticker 115
94 PaniniSticker 67
94 Calgary/ProCards 786

PHOEBUS, TOM
68 O-Pee-Chee 97
69 O-Pee-Chee 185
71 O-Pee-Chee 611
72 O-Pee-Chee 477

PHOENIX, STEVE
95 Edmonton/Macri

PIATT, DOUG
92 O-Pee-Chee 526

PIAZZA, MIKE
93 O-Pee-Chee 314
94 OPC 147, -AS 9, -DD 1
93 opcPremier 26
94 PaniniSticker 203
94 Post

PICCIOLO, ROB
86 O-Pee-Chee 3

PICHARDO, HIPOLITO
93 O-Pee-Chee 390

PICINICH, VALENTINE
34 WWGum(V354) 3

PICKFORD, KEVIN
94 Welland/Classic 18
94 Welland/ProCards 3495

PICKISH, JEFF
93 Welland/ClassicBest 22
93 Welland/ProCards 3358

PICO, JEFF
90 FleerCdn. 39
90 O-Pee-Chee 613
91 O-Pee-Chee 311
89 PaniniSticker 50

PICOTA, LEN
93 Ottawa/ProCards 2433

PIEMEL, LEE
88 Hamilton/ProCards 1726

PIERCE
1912 ImperialTobacco(C46) 68
60 opcTattoo 44,80
62 PostCereal 54
62 ShirriffCoin 2

PIERCE, JACK
76 O-Pee-Chee 162

PIERCE, TONY
68 O-Pee-Chee 38

PIERRE, GABRIEL
94 GarciaPhoto 106

PIERSALL, JIM
65 O-Pee-Chee 172
62 ShirriffCoin 88

PIET, TONY
34 WWGum(V354) 63
36 WWGum(V355) 95

PIGNATANO, JOE
73 O-Pee-Chee 257
74 O-Pee-Chee 179
62 PostCereal 97
62 ShirriffCoin 45

PILLETTE, HERMAN
21 Neilson's(V61) 19

PILOTO, LUIS ENRIQUE
94 GarciaPhoto 48

PIMENTEL, WANDER
90 Hamilton/Best 16
90 Hamilton/Star 19

PINA, HORACIO
71 O-Pee-Chee 497
73 O-Pee-Chee 138
74 O-Pee-Chee 516
75 O-Pee-Chee 139

PINELLI, RALPH
21 Neilson's(V61) 78

PINIELLA, LOU
68 O-Pee-Chee 16
70 O-Pee-Chee 321
71 O-Pee-Chee 35
72 O-Pee-Chee 491
73 O-Pee-Chee 140
74 O-Pee-Chee 390
75 O-Pee-Chee 217
76 O-Pee-Chee 453
78 O-Pee-Chee 82
79 O-Pee-Chee 342
80 O-Pee-Chee 120
81 O-Pee-Chee 306
82 O-Pee-Chee 236
83 O-Pee-Chee 307
84 O-Pee-Chee 351
91 O-Pee-Chee 669
92 O-Pee-Chee 321

PINKSTON, LAL
52 Laval Dairy 62

PINO, ROLANDO
92 St.Catharines/ClassicBest 30
92 St.Catharines/ProCards 3402
93 St.Catharines/ClassicBest 26
93 St.Catharines/ProCards 3990
94 St.Catharines/Classic 29

PINSON, VADA
66 O-Pee-Chee 180
68 O-Pee-Chee 90
69 O-Pee-Chee 160
70 O-Pee-Chee 445, -Booklet 5
71 O-Pee-Chee 275
72 O-Pee-Chee 135
73 O-Pee-Chee 75
74 O-Pee-Chee 490
75 O-Pee-Chee 295
76 O-Pee-Chee 415
62 PostCereal 121
62 ShirriffCoin 118

PIPGRAS, GEORGE
33 WWGum(V353) 12

PIPP, WALLY
21 Neilson's(V61) 48
22 WilliamPaterson(V89) 45

PIPP, WALTER C.
23 WillardsChocolate(V100)124

PIRKI, GREG
92 Calgary/ProCards 3736
93 Calgary/ProCards 1173

PISCIOTTA, MARC
91 Welland/ProCards 3570

PITLOCK, SKIP
71 O-Pee-Chee 19
75 O-Pee-Chee 579

PITTENGER, CLARKE
21 Neilson's(V61) 42

PIZARRO, GERMAIN
52 Laval Dairy 78

PIZARRO, JUAN
65 O-Pee-Chee 9,125
68 O-Pee-Chee 19
71 O-Pee-Chee 647
72 O-Pee-Chee 18

PLACERES, BENIGNO
88 St.Catharines/ProCards 2009

PLANTIER, PHIL
91 O-Pee-Chee 474
92 O-Pee-Chee 782
93 O-Pee-Chee 332
94 O-Pee-Chee 65
92 opcPremier 74
93 opcPremier 10
93 PaniniSticker 99
94 PaniniSticker 258

PLEIS, BILL
65 O-Pee-Chee 122

PLESAC, DAN
90 FleerCdn. 334
88 O-Pee-Chee 317
89 O-Pee-Chee 167
90 O-Pee-Chee 490
91 O-Pee-Chee 146
92 O-Pee-Chee 303
93 O-Pee-Chee 297
87 opcSticker 201
88 opcSticker 203,-SStar 65
89 opcSticker 197
88 PaniniSticker 118
89 PaniniSticker 367
90 PaniniSticker 95
91 PaniniSticker 212
97 TOR/Sizzler

PLEWS, HERB
61 Toronto/BeeHive

PLUMMER, BILL
73 O-Pee-Chee 177
74 O-Pee-Chee 524
75 O-Pee-Chee 656
76 O-Pee-Chee 627
79 O-Pee-Chee 208
92 O-Pee-Chee 171
86 Calgary/ProCards
87 Calgary/ProCards 2312
88 Calgary/CMC 24
88 Calgary/ProCards 800

PLUNK, ERIC
90 FleerCdn. 452
89 O-Pee-Chee 141
90 O-Pee-Chee 9
91 O-Pee-Chee 786
92 O-Pee-Chee 672

POCOROBA, BIFF
76 O-Pee-Chee 103
79 O-Pee-Chee 285
80 O-Pee-Chee 73
83 O-Pee-Chee 367

PODBIELAN, CLARENCE
50 WWGum(V362) 12

PODRES, JOHNNY
73 O-Pee-Chee 12
52 Parkhurst 76
62 PostCereal 108
62 ShirriffCoin 172

POFF, JOHN
94 GarciaPhoto 2

POLANCO, FELIPE
94 Welland/Classic 19
94 Welland/ProCards 3503

POLCOVICH, KEVIN
97 Calgary/Best 20

POLE, DICK
74 O-Pee-Chee 596
75 O-Pee-Chee 513
76 O-Pee-Chee 326

POLEWSKI, STEVE
90 Welland/Pucko 7

POLIDOR, GUS
90 O-Pee-Chee 313
85 Edmonton/Cramer 12
86 Edmonton/ProCards
93 Edmonton/ProCards 1145

POLONIA, LUIS
88 Leaf 256
88 O-Pee-Chee 238
89 O-Pee-Chee 386
90 O-Pee-Chee 634
91 O-Pee-Chee 107
92 O-Pee-Chee 37
94 O-Pee-Chee 128
88 opcSticker 172
88 PaniniSticker 177
89 PaniniSticker 425
92 PaniniSticker 10
93 PaniniSticker 8
94 PaniniSticker 41

POMORSKI, JOHN
36 WWGum(V355) 92

PONCE, CARLOS
84 Vancouver/Cramer 34
85 Vancouver/Cramer 224

PONDER, CHARLES ELMER
23 WillardsChocolate(V100)125

POOLE, JIM
92 O-Pee-Chee 683

POPE, DAVE
61 Toronto/BeeHive

POPOVICH, PAUL
69 O-Pee-Chee 47
70 O-Pee-Chee 258
71 O-Pee-Chee 726
72 O-Pee-Chee 512
73 O-Pee-Chee 309
74 O-Pee-Chee 14
75 O-Pee-Chee 359

POPOWSKI, EDDIE
73 O-Pee-Chee 131
74 O-Pee-Chee 403

POQUETTE, TOM
75 O-Pee-Chee 622
77 O-Pee-Chee 66
78 O-Pee-Chee 197

PORTER, CHUCK
81 Vancouver/TCMA 2
82 Vancouver/TCMA 21
86 Vancouver/ProCards no #

PORTER, DARRELL
85 Leaf 258
72 O-Pee-Chee 162
73 O-Pee-Chee 582
74 O-Pee-Chee 194
75 O-Pee-Chee 52
76 O-Pee-Chee 645
77 O-Pee-Chee 116
78 O-Pee-Chee 66
79 O-Pee-Chee 295
80 O-Pee-Chee 188
82 O-Pee-Chee 98,348
83 O-Pee-Chee 103
84 O-Pee-Chee 285
85 O-Pee-Chee 246
86 O-Pee-Chee 84
87 O-Pee-Chee 213
82 opcSticker 93
83 opcSticker 148,149,182,183
84 ocpSticker 143
85 opcSticker140

PORTER, DICK
34 WWGum(V354) 88

PORTUGAL, MARK
90 O-Pee-Chee 253
91 O-Pee-Chee 647
92 O-Pee-Chee 114
92 O-Pee-Chee 338
93 O-Pee-Chee 318
94 O-Pee-Chee

POSADA, LEO
62 PostCereal 96
62 ShirriffCoin 62

POST, WALLY
62 PostCereal 128

POWELL, ALONZO
92 O-Pee-Chee 295
91 Calgary/LineDrive 69
91 Calgary/ProCards 529
92 Calgary/SkyBox 66

POWELL, DENNIS
87 Calgary/ProCards 2314
88 Calgary/CMC 4
88 Calgary/ProCards 796
91 Calgary/LineDrive 68
91 Calgary/ProCards 514
93 Calgary/ProCards 1165

POWELL, JOHN (BOOG)
65 O-Pee-Chee 3
66 O-Pee-Chee 167
68 O-Pee-Chee-Poster 26
69 O-Pee-Chee 15,-Deckle 17
70 O-Pee-Chee 64,410,451
71 O-Pee-Chee 63,700
72 O-Pee-Chee 250
73 O-Pee-Chee 325

74 O-Pee-Chee 460
75 O-Pee-Chee 208,625
76 O-Pee-Chee 45
71 ProStarPostcard
71 ProStarPoster

POWELL, DENNIS
90 FleerCdn. 521

POWELL, HOSKEN
79 O-Pee-Chee 346
83 O-Pee-Chee 77
82 opcSticker 206
84 Vancouver/Cramer 38

POWELL, RAYMOND
21 Neilson's(V61) 95
23 WillardsChocolate(V100)126

POWER, TED
90 FleerCdn. 258
86 O-Pee-Chee 108
88 O-Pee-Chee 236
89 O-Pee-Chee 331
90 O-Pee-Chee 59
91 O-Pee-Chee 621
85 opcSticker 50
86 opcSticker 140
88 PaniniSticker 272

POWER, VIC
66 O-Pee-Chee 192
62 PostCereal 37
62 ShirriffCoin 44

PRAPPAS, JIM
52 Laval Dairy 99

PRATS, JEAN
52 LavalDairy 27

PRATT, DERRILL B.
23 WillardsChocolate(V100)127

PRENDERGAST, JIM
50 WWGum 39

PRESLEY, JIM
90 FleerCdn. 522
86 Leaf 183
87 Leaf 23,154
86 O-Pee-Chee 228
87 O-Pee-Chee 45
88 O-Pee-Chee 285
89 O-Pee-Chee 119
90 O-Pee-Chee 346
91 O-Pee-Chee 643
86 opcSticker 219
87 opcSticker 214
88 opcSticker 217
89 opcSticker 223
86 opcTattoo 12
88 PaniniSticker 189
89 PaniniSticker 437
91 PaniniSticker 21

PRICE, AL
85 Vancouver/Cramer 225

PRICE, BRYAN
89 Calgary/CMC 9
89 Calgary/ProCards 540

PRICE, JIMMIE
67 O-Pee-Chee 123
70 O-Pee-Chee 129
71 O-Pee-Chee 444

PRICE, JOE
90 FleerCdn. 282
84 O-Pee-Chee 159
85 O-Pee-Chee 82
90 O-Pee-Chee 473
91 O-Pee-Chee 127
84 opcSticker 58
85 opcSticker 56

PRIDDY, BOB
67 O-Pee-Chee 26
71 O-Pee-Chee 147

PRIETO, ARIEL
94 GarciaPhoto 53

PRIMELLES, PABLO
94 GarciaPhoto 81

PRITCHETT, CHRIS
96 Vancouver/Best 23
97 Vancouver/Best 23

PPRUITT, JASON
92 O-Pee-Chee 246

PRYOR, GREG
80 O-Pee-Chee 91
87 O-Pee-Chee 268

PUCCINELLI, GEORGE
36 WWGum 127

PUCKETT, KIRBY
90 Ben's/HolsumDisk 17
92 Ben'sDisk
88 FantasticSam's 1
90 FleerCdn. 383,635
87 GeneralMills 3
93 HumptyDumpty 11
85 Leaf 107
86 Leaf 69
87 Leaf 19,56
88 Leaf 144
92 McDonald's 21
85 O-Pee-Chee 10
86 O-Pee-Chee 329
87 O-Pee-Chee 82
88 O-Pee-Chee 120
89 O-Pee-Chee 132
90 O-Pee-Chee 391,700
91 O-Pee-Chee 300
92 O-Pee-Chee 575
93 O-Pee-Chee 306
94 O-Pee-Chee 93, -AS 17
91 opcPremier 96
92 opcPremier 102
93 opcPremier-StarPerf. 11
85 opcSticker 307,376
86 opcSticker 285
87 opcSticker 146,274
88 opcSticker 283,-SStar 52
89 opcSticker 293,-SStar 19
86 opcTattoo 13
88 PaniniSticker 144,443,444
89 PaniniSticker 393
90 PaniniSticker 105
91 PaniniSticker 305
92 PaniniSticker 120
93 PaniniSticker 130
94 PaniniSticker 96
91 PetroCanada 17
92 PizzaHut/DietPepsi 27
91 PostCdn. 30
92 PostCdn. 17
93 PostCdn. 8
94 PostCdn. 18
95 PostCdn. 9
87 StuartBakery 22

PUGH, TIM
93 opcPremier 75

PUHL, TERRY
90 FleerCdn. 233
85 GeneralMills 17
85 Leaf 80
86 Leaf 138
80 O-Pee-Chee 82
81 O-Pee-Chee 64
82 O-Pee-Chee 277
83 O-Pee-Chee 39
84 O-Pee-Chee 383
85 O-Pee-Chee 283
86 O-Pee-Chee 161
87 O-Pee-Chee 227
90 O-Pee-Chee 494
82 opcSticker 42
83 opcSticker 239
84 opcSticker 67
85 opcSticker 67
90 PaniniSticker 256

PUIG, BENNY
94 Ottawa/ProCards 2899

PUJOLS, LUIS
83 O-Pee-Chee 112

PULEO, CHARLIE
83 O-Pee-Chee 358

PULLIAM, HARVEY
92 O-Pee-Chee 687

PUORTO, JAMIE
97 Lethbridge/Best 27

PURDIN, JOHN
69 O-Pee-Chee 161
71 O-Pee-Chee 748

PURDY, ALAN
93 Welland/ClassicBest 23

PURKEY, BOB
65 O-Pee-Chee 214
62 PostCereal 123
62 ShirriffCoin 153

PURTELL, WILLIAM
1912 ImperialTobacco(C46) 30

PUTNAM, PAT
80 O-Pee-Chee 8
81 O-Pee-Chee 30
82 O-Pee-Chee 149
84 O-Pee-Chee 226
82 opcSticker 241
84 opcSticker 339

PUTTMANN, SHANNON
94 Welland/Classic 20
94 Welland/ProCards 3496

PYTLAK, FRANK
39 WWGum(V351A)

Q

QUADE, MIKE
93 Ottawa/ProCards 2449

QUALLS, JIM
70 O-Pee-Chee 192
71 O-Pee-Chee 731

QUANTRILL, PAUL
96 TOR/OhHenry
97 TOR/Sizzler 21

QUEEN, MEL
69 O-Pee-Chee 81
71 O-Pee-Chee 736
72 O-Pee-Chee 196
96 TOR/OhHenry
97 TOR/Sizzler 27

QUERECUTO, JUAN
90 St.Catharines/ProCards 3453
92 St.Catharines/ClassicBest 4
92 St.Catharines/ProCards 3390
93 St.Catharines/ClassicBest 20
93 St.Catharines/ProCards 3978

QUILICI, FRANK
71 O-Pee-Chee 141
73 O-Pee-Chee 49
74 O-Pee-Chee 447
75 O-Pee-Chee 443

QUINLAN, CRAIG
91 St.Catharines/ClassicBest 10
91 St.Catharines/ProCards 3399

QUINLIN, TOM
93 TOR/Donruss 27
93 TOR/FireSafety

QUINN, JACK
33 WWGum(V353) 53

QUINONES, LUIS
90 FleerCdn. 428
90 O-Pee-Chee 176
91 O-Pee-Chee 581
92 O-Pee-Chee 356
94 Calgary/ProCards 798

QUINONES, RENE
80 Vancouver/TCMA 16
81 Vancouver/TCMA 18

QUINONES, REY
88 O-Pee-Chee 215,358
89 O-Pee-Chee 224,246
88 PaniniSticker 186,187,190
89 PaniniSticker 438

QUINTANA, CARLOS
90 FleerCdn. 283
90 O-Pee-Chee 18
91 O-Pee-Chee 206
92 O-Pee-Chee 127
91 PaniniSticker 85,264
92 PaniniSticker 127

QUIRE, JEREMY
97 Lethbridge/Best 10

QUIRK, JAMIE
76 O-Pee-Chee 598
91 O-Pee-Chee 132
92 O-Pee-Chee 19
88 PaniniSticker 103

QUIROS, GUS
79 Vancouver/TCMA 11
80 Vancouver/TCMA 4
81 Vancouver/TCMA 11

QUISENBERRY, DAN
90 FleerCdn. 259
86 GeneralMills 2
87 GeneralMills 3
92 Kellogg's 6
85 Leaf 6
86 Leaf 208
81 O-Pee-Chee 206
83 O-Pee-Chee 155,396
84 O-Pee-Chee 69,273
85 O-Pee-Chee 270
86 O-Pee-Chee 50
87 O-Pee-Chee 15
88 O-Pee-Chee 195
89 O-Pee-Chee 13
90 O-Pee-Chee 312
83 opcSticker 22,74,165
84 opcSticker 9,10,279,290
85 opcSticker 173,269
86 opcSticker 257
87 opcSticker 257
88 opcSticker 256
86 opcTattoo 3
88 PaniniSticker 101

R

RACKLEY, MARVIN
43-47 Montréal/ParadeSportive

RADATZ, DICK
67 O-Pee-Chee 174

RADCLIFF, RIP
37 O-Pee-Chee(V300) 125

RADER, DAVE
72 O-Pee-Chee 232
73 O-Pee-Chee 121
74 O-Pee-Chee 213
75 O-Pee-Chee 31
76 O-Pee-Chee 54
79 O-Pee-Chee 369
81 O-Pee-Chee 359

RADER, DOUG
69 O-Pee-Chee 119
70 O-Pee-Chee 355
71 O-Pee-Chee 425
73 O-Pee-Chee 76
74 O-Pee-Chee 395
75 O-Pee-Chee 165
76 O-Pee-Chee 44
78 O-Pee-Chee 166
90 O-Pee-Chee 51
91 O-Pee-Chee 231

RADINSKY, SCOTT
91 O-Pee-Chee 299
92 O-Pee-Chee 701

RADISON, DAN
88 Hamilton/ProCards 1732

RAGLAND, TOM
72 O-Pee-Chee 334
74 O-Pee-Chee 441

RAGLAND, TRACE
91 Welland/Best 14
91 Welland/ProCards 3589

RAICH, ERIC
76 O-Pee-Che 484

RAINES, TIM (ROCK)
90 Ben's/HolsumDisks 2
81 Dimanche/DernièreHeure
83 Dimanche/DernièreHeure
88 FantasticSam's 16
82 FBI BoxBottoms
90 FleerCdn. 359
86 GeneralMills 6
87 GeneralMills 5
88 HostessDisks 11
85 Leaf 218,252
86 Leaf 108
87 Leaf 149
88 Leaf 2,114,211
81 O-Pee-Chee 136
82 O-Pee-Chee 70,-Poster 17
83 O-Pee-Chee 227,352
84 O-Pee-Chee 370,390
85 O-Pee-Chee 277,-Poster 7
86 O-Pee-Chee 280
87 O-Pee-Chee 30
88 O-Pee-Chee 20
89 O-Pee-Chee 87
90 O-Pee-Chee 180
91 O-Pee-Chee 360
92 O-Pee-Chee 426
93 O-Pee-Chee 290
94 O-Pee-Chee 228
91 opcPremier 97
82 opcSticker 7,62,116
83 opcSticker 210,253
84 opcSticker 91,179,210
85 opcSticker 82,282
86 opcSticker 75
87 opcSticker 30
88 opcSticker 76
89 opcSticker 77
86 opcTattoo 17
88 PaniniSticker 325,326,330
89 PaniniSticker 125
90 PaniniSticker 283
91 PaniniSticker 143
92 PaniniSticker 131
93 PaniniSticker 140

87 StuartBakery 7
82 MTL/Hygrade
82 MTL/Zellers
83 MTL
83 MTL/StuartBakery 9
84 MTL
84 MTL/StuartBakery 20,36,37
86 MTL/ProvigoFoods
86 MTL/ProvigoFoods-Poster
93 MTL/McDonald's 6

RAINEY, CHUCK
84 O-Pee-Chee 334
84 opcSticker 47

RAJSICH, DAVE
97 Calgary/Best 3

RALEY, DAN
90 London/LineDrive 400
91 London/ProCards 1894

RAMIREX, RAFAEL
88 PaniniSticker 247

RAMIREZ, MANNY
92 O-Pee-Chee 156
94 O-Pee-Chee 121, -HotP 6

RAMIREZ, MILT
71 O-Pee-Chee 702

RAMIREZ, RAFAEL
90 FleerCdn. 234
85 Leaf 86
84 O-Pee-Chee 234
85 O-Pee-Chee 232
86 O-Pee-Chee 107
88 O-Pee-Chee 379
89 O-Pee-Chee 261
90 O-Pee-Chee 558
91 O-Pee-Chee 423
84 opcSticker 33
85 opcSticker 27
86 opcSticker 42
87 opcSticker 42
89 opcSticker 17
86 opcTattoo 11
89 PaniniSticker 90
90 PaniniSticker 266
91 PaniniSticker 10

RAMIREZ, ROBERTO
91 Welland/Best 24
91 Welland/ProCards 3571

RAMOS, ALEXANDER
94 GarciaPhoto 7

RAMOS, ROBERTO (BOBBY)
81 O-Pee-Chee 136
82 O-Pee-Chee 354
84 O-Pee-Chee 32
85 O-Pee-Chee 269
83 MTL/StuartBakery 20
84 MTL
84 MTL/StuartBakery 9
85 Edmonton/Cramer 15

RAMOS, DOMINGO
90 O-Pee-Chee 37
91 O-Pee-Chee 541

RAMOS, JOSE
89 London/ProCrads 1387
91 London/LineDrive 394
91 London/ProCards 1877
92 London/SkyBox 414

RAMOS, PEDRO
65 O-Pee-Chee 13
67 O-Pee-Chee 187

RAMOS, RAFAEL
94 GarciaPhoto 130

RAMSEY, MIKE
85 O-Pee-Chee 62

87 Edmonton/ProCards 2066
89 Edmonton/CMC 16
89 Edmonton/ProCards 561

RANDALL, BOB
80 O-Pee-Chee 90

RANDALL, JAMES
85 Edmonton/Cramer 10
87 Edmonton/ProCards 2076
88 Vancouver/CMC 20
88 Vancouver/ProCards 765

RANDALL, SAP
84 Edmonton/Cramer 101

RANDLE, LENNY
73 O-Pee-Chee 378
74 O-Pee-Chee 446
75 O-Pee-Chee 259
76 O-Pee-Chee 31
78 O-Pee-Chee 132
79 O-Pee-Chee 236
82 O-Pee-Chee 312
82 opcSticker 230

RANDOLPH, WILLIE
90 FleerCdn. 406
85 Leaf 83
86 Leaf 16
87 Leaf 58
88 Leaf 162
76 O-Pee-Chee 592
77 O-Pee-Chee 110
78 O-Pee-Chee 228
79 O-Pee-Chee 592
77 O-Pee-Chee 110
78 O-Pee-Chee 228
79 O-Pee-Chee 125
80 O-Pee-Chee 239
81 O-Pee-Chee 60
82 O-Pee-Chee 37,159,213
83 O-Pee-Chee 140
84 O-Pee-Chee 360
85 O-Pee-Chee 8
86 O-Pee-Chee 332
87 O-Pee-Chee 377
88 O-Pee-Chee 210
89 O-Pee-Chee 244
90 O-Pee-Chee 25
91 O-Pee-Chee 525
92 O-Pee-Chee 116
92 opcPremier 67
82 opcSticker 219
83 opcSticker 95
84 opcSticker 324
86 opcSticker 305
87 opcSticker 302
88 opcStick. 162,294,-SStar 37
89 opcSticker 309
86 opcTattoo 15
88 PaniniSticker 153,228
89 PaniniSticker 405
90 PaniniSticker 279
91 PaniniSticker 193
92 PaniniSticker 36

RANEW, MERRITT
66 O-Pee-Chee 62

RAPP, JOSEPH (GOLDIE)
21 Neilson's(V61) 104
23 WillardsChocolate(V100)128

RAPP, PAT
93 Edmonton/ProCards 1134

RAPP, VERN
82 Dimanche/DernièreHeure
83 MTL/StuartBakery 3

RASCHI, VIC
53 Exhibits 5

RASMUSSEN, DENNIS
90 FleerCdn. 165

85 Leaf 48
87 Leaf 260
87 O-Pee-Chee 364
89 O-Pee-Chee 32
90 O-Pee-Chee 449
91 O-Pee-Chee 774
92 O-Pee-Chee 252
87 opcSticker 303
88 opcSticker 145
89 PaniniSticker 195

RASMUSSEN, ERIC
84 O-Pee-Chee 377

RASMUSSEN, HARRY
76 O-Pee-Chee 182

RATLIFF, PAUL
70 O-Pee-Chee 267
71 O-Pee-Chee 607

RAU, DOUG
73 O-Pee-Chee 602
74 O-Pee-Chee 64
75 O-Pee-Chee 269
76 O-Pee-Chee 124
77 O-Pee-Chee 128
78 O-Pee-Chee 24
79 O-Pee-Chee 178

RAUTZHAN, LANCE
79 O-Pee-Chee 193
80 Vancouver/TCMA 9

RAWLEY, SHANE
90 FleerCdn. 384
85 Leaf 31
86 Leaf 109
87 Leaf 139
88 Leaf 13,92
79 O-Pee-Chee 30
80 O-Pee-Chee 368
81 O-Pee-Chee 51
84 O-Pee-Chee 254
85 O-Pee-Chee 169
86 O-Pee-Chee 361
87 O-Pee-Chee 239
88 O-Pee-Chee 66
89 O-Pee-Chee 24
90 O-Pee-Chee 101
86 opcSticker 123
87 opcSticker 120
88 opcSticker 121
89 opcSticker 118
88 PaniniSticker 352
87 StuartBakery 9

RAWLINGS, JOHN W.
23 WillardsChocolate(V100)129

RAY, JIM
70 O-Pee-Chee 113
71 O-Pee-Chee 242
73 O-Pee-Chee 313
74 O-Pee-Chee 458
75 O-Pee-Chee 89

RAY, JOHNNY
90 FleerCdn. 143
85 GeneralMills 19
85 Leaf 212
86 Leaf 19
87 Leaf 147
88 Leaf 260
83 O-Pee-Chee 149
84 O-Pee-Chee 323,387
85 O-Pee-Chee 96
86 O-Pee-Chee 37
87 O-Pee-Chee 291
88 O-Pee-Chee 115
89 O-Pee-Chee 109
90 O-Pee-Chee 334
91 O-Pee-Chee 273
83 opcSticker 327

84 opcSticker 134,186
85 opcSticker 130
86 opcSticker 124
87 opcSticker 135
89 opcSticker 182
86 opcTattoo 4
89 PaniniSticker 292
90 PaniniSticker 33
91 PaniniSticker 181
87 StuartBakery 10

RAY, LARRY
87 Vancouver/ProCards 1617

RAYFORD, FLOYD
86 Leaf 197

RAYMOND, CLAUDE
83 Dimanche/DernièreHeure
92 Nabisco 23
65 O-Pee-Chee 48
68 O-Pee-Chee 166
70 O-Pee-Chee 268
71 O-Pee-Chee 202,536
71 MTL/ProStar
93 MTL/McDonald's 26

READY, RANDY
90 FleerCdn. 571
88 O-Pee-Chee 151
89 O-Pee-Chee 82
90 O-Pee-Chee 356
91 O-Pee-Chee 137
92 O-Pee-Chee 63
89 opcSticker 106
88 PaniniSticker 405,406,407
89 PaniniSticker 201
90 PaniniSticker 311
91 PaniniSticker 104

REARDON, JEFF
90 FleerCdn. 385
86 GeneralMills 6
85 Leaf 126
86 Leaf 214
87 Leaf 143
81 O-Pee-Chee 79
82 O-Pee-Chee 123,-Poster 23
83 O-Pee-Chee 290
84 O-Pee-Chee 116
85 O-Pee-Chee 375,-Poster 12
86 O-Pee-Chee 35
87 O-Pee-Chee 165
88 O-Pee-Chee 99
89 O-Pee-Chee 86
90 O-Pee-Chee 235,K
91 O-Pee-Chee 605,M
92 O-Pee-Chee 3,182
93 O-Pee-Chee 342
83 opcSticker 254
84 opcSticker 89
85 opcSticker 85
86 opcSticker 76
87 opcSticker 81
88 opcSticker 14,280
89 opcSticker 8,284,-SStar 33
86 opcTattoo 22
88 PaniniSticker 133
89 PaniniSticker 382
90 PaniniSticker 108
91 PaniniSticker 272
92 PizzaHut/DietPepsi 8
82 MTL/Hygrade
83 MTL
83 MTL/StuartBakery 5
84 MTL
84 MTL/StuartBakery 13
86 MTL/ProvigoFoods
86 MTL/ProvigoFoods-Poster
93 MTL/McDonald's 11

REBERGER, FRANK
70 O-Pee-Chee 103

71 O-Pee-Chee 251
84 Edmonton/Cramer 242
85 Edmonton/Cramer 23
86 Edmonton/ProCards
87 Edmonton/ProCards 2077
96 Vancouver/Best 2

REDFIELD, JOE
88 Edmonton/CMC 20
88 Edmonton/ProCards 555

REDINGTON, TOM
92 O-Pee-Chee 473

REDMAN, TIM
88 Hamilton/ProCards 1729
89 Hamilton/Star 22

REDMOND, ANDRE
90 Welland/Pucko 25

REDMOND, WAYNE
71 O-Pee-Chee 728

REDUS, GARY
90 FleerCdn. 476
85 Leaf 47
84 O-Pee-Chee 231
85 O-Pee-Chee 146
86 O-Pee-Chee 342
87 O-Pee-Chee 42
88 O-Pee-Chee 332
89 O-Pee-Chee 281
90 O-Pee-Chee 507
91 O-Pee-Chee 771
92 O-Pee-Chee 453
84 opcSticker 52
85 opcSticker 49
87 opcSticker 119
88 PaniniSticker 64
90 PaniniSticker 331

REECE, BOB
78 Dimanche/DernièreHeure

REED, BOB
70 O-Pee-Chee 207
71 O-Pee-Chee 732

REED, HOWIE
71 O-Pee-Chee 398
71 MTL/LaPizzaRoyale
71 MTL/ProStar

REED, JEFF
90 FleerCdn. 429
88 O-Pee-Chee 176
90 O-Pee-Chee 772
91 O-Pee-Chee 419
92 O-Pee-Chee 91

REED, JERRY
90 FleerCdn. 523
90 O-Pee-Chee 247
86 Calgary/ProCards

REED, JODY
90 FleerCdn. 284
88 Leaf 41
89 O-Pee-Chee 232
90 O-Pee-Chee 96
91 O-Pee-Chee 247
92 O-Pee-Chee 598
93 O-Pee-Chee 357
93 opcPremier 115
89 PaniniSticker 268
90 PaniniSticker 25
91 PaniniSticker 265
92 PaniniSticker 86

REED, MARTY
88 Edmonton/CMC 9
88 Edmonton/ProCards 562

REED, PAT
93 Welland/ClassicBest 24
93 Welland/ProCards 3375

REED, RICK
90 FleerCdn. 477

REED, RON
68 O-Pee-Chee 76
69 O-Pee-Chee 177
70 O-Pee-Chee 546
71 O-Pee-Chee 359
73 O-Pee-Chee 72
74 O-Pee-Chee 346
75 O-Pee-Chee 81
76 O-Pee-Chee 58
79 O-Pee-Chee 84
80 O-Pee-Chee 318

REESE, CALVIN
92 O-Pee-Chee 714

REESE, HAROLD (PEEWEE)
53 Exhibits 21

REESE, JIMMIE
73 O-Pee-Chee 421
74 O-Pee-Chee 276

REESE, RICH
68 O-Pee-Chee 111
69 O-Pee-Chee 56
70 O-Pee-Chee 404
71 O-Pee-Chee 349

REGAN, PHIL
65 O-Pee-Chee 191
67 O-Pee-Chee 130
68 O-Pee-Chee 88
70 O-Pee-Chee 334
71 O-Pee-Chee 634
72 O-Pee-Chee 485
62 PostCereal 24

REIBER, FRANK
36 WWGum(V355) 111
39 WWGum(V351A)

REICHARDT, RICK
65 O-Pee-Chee 194
67 O-Pee-Chee 40
69 O-Pee-Chee 205
71 O-Pee-Chee 643

REID, SCOTT
70 O-Pee-Chee 56
71 O-Pee-Chee 439

REILLY, JOHN
94 St.Catharines/Classic 17
94 St.Catharines/ProCards 3647
95 St.Catharines/TimHortons 15

REIMER, KEVIN
90 FleerCdn. 310
91 O-Pee-Chee 304
92 O-Pee-Chee 737
93 O-Pee-Chee 284
93 opcPremier 131
93 PaniniSticker 43
94 PaniniSticker 85

REIMINK, ROBERT
91 London/LineDrive 395
91 London/ProCards 1887
92 London/ProCards 641
92 London/SkyBox 415

REISER, PETE
73 O-Pee-Chee 81

REITZ, KEN
73 O-Pee-Chee 603
74 O-Pee-Chee 372
75 O-Pee-Chee 27
76 O-Pee-Chee 603
74 O-Pee-Chee 372
75 O-Pee-Chee 27
76 O-Pee-Chee 158
79 O-Pee-Chee 307
80 O-Pee-Chee 103
81 O-Pee-Chee 316
82 O-Pee-Chee 245
82 opcSticker 26

REMLINGER, MIKE
92 Calgary/ProCards 3729
92 Calgary/SkyBox 68
93 Calgary/ProCards 1166

REMY, JERRY
76 O-Pee-Chee 229
79 O-Pee-Chee 325
80 O-Pee-Chee 85
81 O-Pee-Chee 131
82 O-Pee-Chee 25
83 O-Pee-Chee 295
84 O-Pee-Chee 58
85 O-Pee-Chee 173
82 opcSticker 132,149
83 opcSticker 33
84 opcSticker 215
85 opcSticker 218

RENDE, SAL
93 Edmonton/ProCards 1152
94 Edmonton/ProCards 2990

RENICK, RICK
70 O-Pee-Chee 93
71 O-Pee-Chee 694
72 O-Pee-Chee 459
86 MTL/ProvigoFoods 27
92 Vancouver/ProCards 2734
92 Vancouver/SkyBox 649

RENIFF, HAL
66 O-Pee-Chee 68

RENKO, STEVE
70 O-Pee-Chee 87
71 O-Pee-Chee 209
72 O-Pee-Chee 307,308
73 O-Pee-Chee 623
74 O-Pee-Chee 49
75 O-Pee-Chee 34
76 O-Pee-Chee 264
83 O-Pee-Chee 236
71 ProStarPostcard
71 MTL/ProStar
74 MTL/GeorgeWeston
93 MTL/McDonald's 27

RENTERIA, RICH
94 PaniniSticker 184

REPLOGIE, ANDY
79 Vancouver/TCMA 8
81 Vancouver/TCMA 16

REPOZ, ROGER
66 O-Pee-Chee 138
69 O-Pee-Chee 103
70 O-Pee-Chee 397
71 O-Pee-Chee 508

RETTENMUND, MERV
69 O-Pee-Chee 66
71 O-Pee-Chee 393
72 O-Pee-Chee 86,235
73 O-Pee-Chee 56
74 O-Pee-Chee 585
75 O-Pee-Chee 369
76 O-Pee-Chee 283
71 ProStarPostcard 11

RETZER, KEN
65 O-Pee-Chee 278

REUSCHEL, RICK
90 FleerCdn. 68
86 Leaf 207
88 Leaf 219
73 O-Pee-Chee 482
74 O-Pee-Chee 136
75 O-Pee-Chee 153
76 O-Pee-Chee 359
77 O-Pee-Chee 214
78 O-Pee-Chee 56
79 O-Pee-Chee 123
80 O-Pee-Chee 99
81 O-Pee-Chee 205
82 O-Pee-Chee 204
85 O-Pee-Chee 306
87 O-Pee-Chee 154
88 O-Pee-Chee 278
89 O-Pee-Chee 65
90 O-Pee-Chee 190,L
91 O-Pee-Chee 422
86 opcSticker 126
87 opcSticker 128
89 opcSticker 70
86 opcTattoo 7
89 PaniniSticker 210
90 PaniniSticker 206,370

REUSS, JERRY
90 FleerCdn. 335
70 O-Pee-Chee 96
71 O-Pee-Chee 158
73 O-Pee-Chee 446
74 O-Pee-Chee 116
75 O-Pee-Chee 124
76 O-Pee-Chee 60
77 O-Pee-Chee 97
81 O-Pee-Chee 153
82 O-Pee-Chee 278
83 O-Pee-Chee 90
84 O-Pee-Chee 170
86 O-Pee-Chee 66
87 O-Pee-Chee 373
90 O-Pee-Chee 424
82 opcSticker 56
83 opcSticker 247
84 opcSticker 81
85 opcSticker 66
86 opcSticker 236

REUTHER, DUTCH
21 Neilson's(V61) 64

REVENIG, TODD
95 Edmonton/Macri

REVERING, DAVE
79 O-Pee-Chee 113
80 O-Pee-Chee 227
81 O-Pee-Chee 57
82 O-Pee-Chee 109
83 O-Pee-Chee 291

REYES, GILBERTO
92 O-Pee-Chee 286
92 PaniniSticker 201

REYNALDO, FRANGEL
94 GarciaPhoto 127

REYNOLDS, ARCHIE
71 O-Pee-Chee 664

REYNOLDS, BOB
71 O-Pee-Chee 664
72 O-Pee-Chee 162
73 O-Pee-Chee 612
74 O-Pee-Chee 259
75 O-Pee-Chee 142

REYNOLDS, CARL
34 WWGum(V354) 12

REYNOLDS, CRAIG
86 Leaf 107
88 Leaf 205
76 O-Pee-Chee 596
79 O-Pee-Chee 251
80 O-Pee-Chee 71
81 O-Pee-Chee 12
82 O-Pee-Chee 57
85 O-Pee-Chee 156
86 O-Pee-Chee 298
87 O-Pee-Chee 298
88 O-Pee-Chee 18
90 O-Pee-Chee 637
82 opcSticker 46
85 opcSticker 65
88 PaniniSticker 297

REYNOLDS, HAROLD
90 FleerCdn. 524
88 Leaf 227
88 O-Pee-Chee 7
89 O-Pee-Chee 208
90 O-Pee-Chee 161
92 O-Pee-Chee 670
93 O-Pee-Chee 279
93 opcPremier 89
87 opcSticker 216
88 opcSticker 221
89 opcSticker 226,-SuperStar 5
88 PaniniSticker 188, 218, 219
89 PaniniSticker 436
90 PaniniSticker 144
91 PaniniSticker 229
92 PaniniSticker 56
94 PaniniSticker 22
91 PaniniTopFifteen 55, 111
86 Calgary/ProCards

REYNOLDS, KEN
71 O-Pee-Chee 664
72 O-Pee-Chee 252
73 O-Pee-Chee 638

REYNOLDS, KEVIN
92 PaniniSticker 228

REYNOLDS, R.J.
90 FleerCdn. 478
87 GeneralMills 5
86 Leaf 212
86 O-Pee-Chee 306
87 O-Pee-Chee 109
88 O-Pee-Chee 27
90 O-Pee-Chee 592
91 O-Pee-Chee 198
87 opcSticker 134
88 PaniniSticker 379
87 StuartBakery 10

REYNOLDS, TOMMIE
70 O-Pee-Chee 259
71 O-Pee-Chee 676

REYNOSO, ARMANDO
92 O-Pee-Chee 631
94 O-Pee-Chee 114

RHAWN, BOBBY
52 Parkhurst 3

RHEA, ALLEN
90 St.Catharines/ProCards 3496

RHEM, FLINT
33 WWGum(V353) 5

RHIEL, BILLY
36 WWGum(V355) 81

RHODEN, RICK
90 FleerCdn. 235
85 Leaf 63
87 Leaf 10
88 Leaf 98
75 O-Pee-Chee 618
76 O-Pee-Chee 439
77 O-Pee-Chee 57
78 O-Pee-Chee 159
79 O-Pee-Chee 66
81 O-Pee-Chee 312
83 O-Pee-Chee 181
84 O-Pee-Chee 46
85 O-Pee-Chee 53
86 O-Pee-Chee 232
87 O-Pee-Chee 365
88 O-Pee-Chee 185
89 O-Pee-Chee 18
90 O-Pee-Chee 588
82 opcSticker 82
85 opcSticker 127
86 opcSticker 130
87 opcSticker 130
88 opcSticker 298
86 opcTattoo 9
88 PaniniSticker 149
89 PaniniSticker 399

RHODES, ARTHUR
93 O-Pee-Chee 329
92 O-Pee-Chee 771
94 O-Pee-Chee 17

RHODES, KARL
91 O-Pee-Chee 516

RIBANT, DENNIS
65 O-Pee-Chee 73

RICCELLI, FRANK
74 O-Pee-Chee 599

RICE, EDGAR C.
23 WillardsChocolate(V100)130

RICE, JIM
82 FBI BoxBottoms
85 GeneralMills 12
86 GeneralMills 1
92 Kellogg's 7
85 Leaf 15
86 Leaf 146
87 Leaf 247
88 Leaf 215
75 O-Pee-Chee 616
76 O-Pee-Chee 340
77 O-Pee-Chee 62
78 O-Pee-Chee 2,163
79 O-Pee-Chee 210
80 O-Pee-Chee 112
81 O-Pee-Chee 68
82 O-Pee-Chee 366
83 O-Pee-Chee 30
84 O-Pee-Chee 184,364
85 O-Pee-Chee 150
86 O-Pee-Chee 320
87 O-Pee-Chee 146,F
88 O-Pee-Chee 61,I
89 O-Pee-Chee 245
90 O-Pee-Chee 785,M
82 opcSticker 150
83 opcSticker 37
84 opcSticker 102,189,217,200
85 opcSticker 208
86 opcSticker 161,246
87 opcSticker 17,248,F
88 opcSticker 247
89 opcSticker 256
86 opcTattoo 20
88 PaniniSticker 33

RICE, PAT
90 Calgary/CMC 4
90 Calgary/ProCards 650
91 Calgary/LineDrive 70
91 Calgary/ProCards 515
92 Calgary/ProCards 3730
92 Calgary/SkyBox 69

RICE, SAM
34 WWGum(V354) 18

RICHARD, J.R.
72 O-Pee-Chee 101
74 O-Pee-Chee 522
75 O-Pee-Chee 73
76 O-Pee-Chee 625
77 O-Pee-Chee 227
78 O-Pee-Chee 149
79 O-Pee-Chee 310

80 O-Pee-Chee 28
79 O-Pee-Chee 310
80 O-Pee-Chee 28
81 O-Pee-Chee 350
82 O-Pee-Chee 190

RICHARD, LEE
72 O-Pee-Chee 476
75 O-Pee-Chee 653
76 O-Pee-Chee 533

RICHARDS, DAVE
90 London/ProCards 1267

RICHARDS, GENE
80 O-Pee-Chee 323
81 O-Pee-Chee 171
82 O-Pee-Chee 253
83 O-Pee-Chee 7
82 opcSticker 103
83 opcSticker 294

RICHARDSON, BOBBY
65 O-Pee-Chee 115
62 PostCereal 2
62 ShirriffCoin 64

RICHARDSON, GORDON
66 O-Pee-Chee 51

RICHERT, PETE
65 O-Pee-Chee 252
66 O-Pee-Chee 95
69 O-Pee-Chee 86
71 O-Pee-Chee 273
73 O-Pee-Chee 239
74 O-Pee-Chee 348
95 Edmonton/Macri

RICHIE, ROB
90 O-Pee-Chee 146

RICHMOND, DON
50 WWGum Stars 43

RICKETTS, DAVE
68 O-Pee-Chee 46
73 O-Pee-Chee 517

RICKEY, W. BRANCH
23 WillardsChocolate(V100)131

RIDDLEBERGER, DENNY
71 O-Pee-Chee 93
73 O-Pee-Chee 157

RIDDOCH, GREG
91 O-Pee-Chee 109
92 O-Pee-Chee 351

RIDENOUR, DANA
94 Edmonton/ProCards 2875

RIDZIK, STEVE
65 O-Pee-Chee 211
61 Toronto/BeeHive

RIGHETTI, DAVE
86 GeneralMills 1
85 Leaf 219
86 Leaf 89
87 Leaf 53
88 Leaf 57
83 O-Pee-Chee 176
84 O-Pee-Chee 277
85 O-Pee-Chee 260
86 O-Pee-Chee 34
87 O-Pee-Chee 40
88 O-Pee-Chee 155
89 O-Pee-Chee 335
90 O-Pee-Chee 160
91 O-Pee-Chee 410
92 O-Pee-Chee 35
91 opcPremier 99
84 opcSticker 287,315
85 opcSticker 314
86 opcSticker 303
87 opcSticker 8,9,299
88 opcSticker 300,-SuperStar 6
89 opcSticker 307
86 opcTattoo 11
88 PaniniSticker 150
89 PaniniSticker 400
90 PaniniSticker 142
91 PaniniSticker 332
92 PaniniSticker 219

RIGHTNOWAR, RON
89 London/ProCards 1369
90 London/ProCards 1268

RIGNEY, BILL
65 O-Pee-Chee 66
69 O-Pee-Chee 182
70 O-Pee-Chee 426
71 O-Pee-Chee 532
72 O-Pee-Chee 389

RIGNEY, EMORY
21 Neilson's(V61) 17

RIJO, JOSE
93 Ben'sDisks 15
90 FleerCdn. 430
93 HumptyDumpty 29
87 Leaf 119
89 O-Pee-Chee 135
90 O-Pee-Chee 627
91 O-Pee-Chee 493
92 O-Pee-Chee 220
93 O-Pee-Chee 286
94 O-Pee-Chee 50
89 opcSticker 140
89 PaniniSticker 68
90 PaniniSticker 243
91 PaniniSticker 134
92 PaniniSticker 269
93 PaniniSticker 289
94 PaniniSticker 15,167

RILES, ERNIE
90 FleerCdn. 69
86 Leaf 161
87 Leaf 66
87 O-Pee-Chee 318
90 O-Pee-Chee 732
91 O-Pee-Chee 408
92 O-Pee-Chee 187
86 opcSticker 310
87 opcSticker 203
84 Vancouver/Cramer 35
85 Vancouver/Cramer 207
94 Vancouver/ProCards 1871

RILEY, MARQUIS
97 Vancouver/Best 24

RING, JAMES J.
21 Neilson's(V61) 120
23 WillardsChocolate(V100)132

RIOS, JUAN
70 O-Pee-Chee 89

RIPKEN, BILLY
90 FleerCdn. 186
88 Leaf 134
88 O-Pee-Chee 352
89 O-Pee-Chee 22
90 O-Pee-Chee 468
91 O-Pee-Chee 677
92 O-Pee-Chee 752
93 opcPremier 59
88 opcSticker 227
88 PaniniSticker 9
89 PaniniSticker 261
90 PaniniSticker 3
91 PaniniSticker 241
92 PaniniSticker 66
93 PaniniSticker 72

RIPKEN, CAL (JR.)
91 Ben's/HolsumDisks 20
92 Ben'sDisks 6
90 FleerCdn. 187,624,634
86 GeneralMills 1
93 HumptyDumpty 1
85 Leaf 14
86 Leaf 142
87 Leaf 98,100
92 McDonald's 1
83 O-Pee-Chee 163
84 O-Pee-Chee 2,363
85 O-Pee-Chee 30
86 O-Pee-Chee 340
87 O-Pee-Chee 312
88 O-Pee-Chee 74
89 O-Pee-Chee 250,J
90 O-Pee-Chee 8,388,N
91 O-Pee-Chee 5,150
92 O-Pee-Chee 40
93 O-Pee-Chee 352
94 O-Pee-Chee 184, -AS 15
91 opcPremier 100
92 opcPremier 137
93 opcPremier 125
83 opcSticker 26,315
84 opcSticker 197,204
85 opcSticker 185,197
86 opcSticker 159,226
87 opcSticker 151,233
88 opcStick. 160,228,-SStar 44
89 opcStick. 150,237,-SStar 11
86 opcTattoo 4
88 PaniniSticker 10,11,13,230
89 PaniniSticker 241,262
90 PaniniSticker 7,202,388
91 PaniniSticker 170,243
92 PaniniSticker 68,275
93 PaniniSticker 73
94 PaniniSticker 23
91 PetroCanada 1
92 PizzaHut/DietPepsi 17
91 PostCdn. 22
92 PostCdn. 15
93 PostCdn. 7
94 PostCdn. 13
95 PostCdn. 18
87 StuartBakery 14

RIPPELMEYER, RAY
73 O-Pee-Chee 486
74 O-Pee-Chee 119

RIPPLE, JIMMY
36 WWGum(V355) 28

RISCART, JOSE RAMON
94 GarciaPhoto 85

RISLEY, BILL
96 TOR/OhHenry
94 Calgary/ProCards 787
93 Ottawa/ProCards 2434

RITCHIE, WALLY
88 O-Pee-Chee 322

RITZ, KEVIN
90 FleerCdn. 613
90 O-Pee-Chee 237

RITZ, TREY
92 Hamilton/ClassicBest 17

RIVERA, BEN
93 O-Pee-Chee 330

RIVERA, BOMBO
77 O-Pee-Chee 54
80 O-Pee-Chee 22

RIVERA, LUIS
90 FleerCdn. 285
89 O-Pee-Chee 68,257
90 O-Pee-Chee 601
91 O-Pee-Chee 338
92 O-Pee-Chee 97
91 PaniniSticker 267
92 PaniniSticker 88
93 PaniniSticker 94

RIVERA, MAXIMO
93 Welland/ClassicBest 25
93 Welland/ProCards 3369

RIVERS, MICKEY
85 Leaf 35
72 O-Pee-Chee 272
73 O-Pee-Chee 597
74 O-Pee-Chee 76
75 O-Pee-Chee 164
76 O-Pee-Chee 85,198
77 O-Pee-Chee 69
78 O-Pee-Chee 182
79 O-Pee-Chee 24
80 O-Pee-Chee 251
81 O-Pee-Chee 145
82 O-Pee-Chee 51,356
83 O-Pee-Chee 224
84 O-Pee-Chee 269
85 O-Pee-Chee 371
82 opcSticker 243
84 opcSticker 361
85 opcSticker 355

RIXEY, EPPA
23 WillardsChocolate(V100)133
34 WWGum(V354) 32

RIZZUTO, PHIL
53 Exhibits 25

ROBBINS, DOUG
92 O-Pee-Chee 58

ROBERGE, BERT
86 O-Pee-Chee 154
86 MTL/ProvigoFoods 16

ROBERGE, JOSEPH ALBERT
50 WWGum Stars 46

ROBERTS, BIP
90 FleerCdn. 166
90 O-Pee-Chee 307
91 O-Pee-Chee 538
92 O-Pee-Chee 20
93 O-Pee-Chee 305
94 O-Pee-Chee 111
92 opcPremier 69
90 PaniniSticker 359
91 PaniniSticker 96
92 PaniniSticker 233
93 PaniniSticker 292

ROBERTS, DAVE
70 O-Pee-Chee 151
71 O-Pee-Chee 448
72 O-Pee-Chee 91,360
73 O-Pee-Chee 39,133
74 O-Pee-Chee 177,309
75 O-Pee-Chee 301,558
76 O-Pee-Chee 107,649
77 O-Pee-Chee 38,193

ROBERTS, LEON
75 O-Pee-Chee 620
76 O-Pee-Chee 292
79 O-Pee-Chee 81
80 O-Pee-Chee 266
82 O-Pee-Chee 186
83 O-Pee-Chee 89

ROBERTS, LONELL
92 St.Catharines/ClassicBest 17
92 St.Catharines/ProCards 3399

ROBERTS, ROBIN
65 O-Pee-Chee 15
60 opcTattoo 45
62 PostCereal 198

ROBERTS, SCOTT
84 Vancouver/Cramer 42
85 Vancouver/Cramer 218

ROBERTSON, ANDRE
84 O-Pee-Chee 282
83 opcSticker 316
84 opcSticker 323

ROBERTSON, BOB
68 O-Pee-Chee 36
71 O-Pee-Chee 255
72 O-Pee-Chee 429
73 O-Pee-Chee 422
74 O-Pee-Chee 540
75 O-Pee-Chee 409
76 O-Pee-Chee 449
79 O-Pee-Chee 158

ROBERTSON, CHARLES
21 Neilson's(V61) 10

ROBERTSON, DAVIS A.
23 WillardsChocolate(V100)124

ROBERTSON, JERRY
71 O-Pee-Chee 651

ROBERTSON, RICH
69 O-Pee-Chee 16
70 O-Pee-Chee 229
71 O-Pee-Chee 443

ROBERTSON, RICHARD
90 Welland/Pucko 26

ROBERTSON, ROD
92 London/ProCards 642
92 London/SkyBox 416

ROBIDOUX, BILLY JO
87 opcSticker 202

ROBINSON, ALAN
92 Hamilton/ClassicBest 21

ROBINSON, BILL
65 O-Pee-Chee 1,5
67 O-Pee-Chee 1
70 O-Pee-Chee 23
73 O-Pee-Chee 37
74 O-Pee-Chee 174
75 O-Pee-Chee 501
76 O-Pee-Chee 137
78 O-Pee-Chee 128
79 O-Pee-Chee 336
80 O-Pee-Chee 138

ROBINSON, BROOKS
65 O-Pee-Chee 150
68 O-Pee-Chee 20,-Poster 27
69 O-Pee-Chee-Deckle 18
70 O-Pee-Chee 230,455
71 O-Pee-Chee 300
72 O-Pee-Chee 498
73 O-Pee-Chee 90
74 O-Pee-Chee 160,334
75 O-Pee-Chee 50,202
76 O-Pee-Chee 95
78 O-Pee-Chee 239
62 PostCereal 29
71 ProStarPostcard
62 ShirriffCoin 40

ROBINSON, CRAIG
74 O-Pee-Chee 23
75 O-Pee-Chee 367

ROBINSON, DAVE
71 O-Pee-Chee 262

ROBINSON, DON
90 FleerCdn. 70
86 Leaf 159
81 O-Pee-Chee 168
82 O-Pee-Chee 332
83 O-Pee-Chee 44
84 O-Pee-Chee 22
85 O-Pee-Chee 129
87 O-Pee-Chee 387
90 O-Pee-Chee 217

91 O-Pee-Chee 104
92 O-Pee-Chee 373
83 opcSticker 277
88 opcSticker 94
89 opcSticker 86
89 PaniniSticker 211
91 PaniniSticker 73

ROBINSON, FLOYD
66 O-Pee-Chee 8
67 O-Pee-Chee 1,120
62 ShirriffCoin 214

ROBINSON, FRANK
65 O-Pee-Chee 120
67 O-Pee-Chee 62,100
68 O-Pee-Chee 2,4,-Poster 28
70 O-Pee-Chee 463
71 O-Pee-Chee 640
72 O-Pee-Chee 88,100
73 O-Pee-Chee 175
74 O-Pee-Chee 55
75 OPC 199,204,331,580
76 O-Pee-Chee 477
90 O-Pee-Chee 381
91 O-Pee-Chee 639
83 opcSticker 4
60 opcTattoo 46
62 PostCereal 122
71 ProStarPostcard
71 ProStarPoster
62 ShirriffCoin 165

ROBINSON, HUMBERTO
52 LavalDairy 91

ROBINSON, JACKIE
53 Exhibits 19

ROBINSON, JEFF
90 FleerCdn. 479,614
85 O-Pee-Chee 5
88 O-Pee-Chee 244
89 O-Pee-Chee 267
90 O-Pee-Chee 42,723
91 O-Pee-Chee 19,766
92 O-Pee-Chee 137
88 opcSticker 133
89 opcSticker 129
89 PaniniSticker 164,335

ROBINSON, KEVIN
88 Hamilton/ProCards 1730

ROBINSON, RON
90 FleerCdn. 431
88 O-Pee-Chee 342
89 O-Pee-Chee 16
90 O-Pee-Chee 604
91 O-Pee-Chee 313
92 O-Pee-Chee 395

ROBLES, RAFAEL
71 O-Pee-Chee 408

ROBLES, SERGIO
73 O-Pee-Chee 601
74 O-Pee-Chee 603

ROCK, ROYAL
1912 ImperialTobacco(C46) 10

RODGERS, ANDRE
62 PostCereal 185
62 ShirriffCoin 155

RODGERS, ROBERT (BUCK)
69 O-Pee-Chee 157
73 O-Pee-Chee 49
74 O-Pee-Chee 447
86 O-Pee-Chee 141
87 O-Pee-Chee 293
88 O-Pee-Chee 134
89 O-Pee-Chee 193
90 O-Pee-Chee 81
91 O-Pee-Chee 321
92 O-Pee-Chee 21
86 MTL/ProvigoFoods 3
86 MTL/ProvigoFoods-Poster
93 MTL/McDonald's 32

RODRIGUEZ, AHMED
90 Hamilton/Best 17
90 Hamilton/Star 20

RODRIGUEZ, AURELIO
70 O-Pee-Chee 228
71 O-Pee-Chee 464
72 O-Pee-Chee 319
73 O-Pee-Chee 218
74 O-Pee-Chee 72
75 O-Pee-Chee 221
76 O-Pee-Chee 267
77 O-Pee-Chee 136
78 O-Pee-Chee 64
79 O-Pee-Chee 83
80 O-Pee-Chee 245
82 O-Pee-Chee-Poster 10

RODRIGUEZ, EDUARDO
74 O-Pee-Chee 171
75 O-Pee-Chee 582
76 O-Pee-Chee 92

RODRIGUEZ, ELLIE (ELISE)
69 O-Pee-Chee 49
70 O-Pee-Chee 402
71 O-Pee-Chee 344
72 O-Pee-Chee 421
73 O-Pee-Chee 45
74 O-Pee-Chee 405
75 O-Pee-Chee 285
76 O-Pee-Chee 512

RODRIGUEZ, HENRY
92 O-Pee-Chee 656
96 MTL/Disk

RODRIGUEZ, IVAN
93 HumptyDumpty 17
92 O-Pee-Chee 78
93 O-Pee-Chee 331
94 O-Pee-Chee 87
92 opcPremier 55
92 PaniniSticker 74
93 PaniniSticker 80
94 PaniniSticker 132
81 Vancouver/TCMA 8

RODRIGUEZ, LUIS
94 Garcia Photo 113

RODRIGUEZ, LUIS
95 St.Catharines/TimHortons 14

RODRIGUEZ, MIKE
96 St.Catharines/Best 23

RODRIGUEZ, ORBE LUIS
94 GarciaPhoto 50

RODRIGUEZ, PEDRO LUIS
94 GarciaPhoto 34

RODRIGUEZ, RICH
91 O-Pee-Chee 573
92 O-Pee-Chee 462

RODRIGUEZ, RICK
89 Vancouver/CMC 8
89 Vancouver/ProCards 580

RODRIGUEZ, ROBERTO
71 O-Pee-Chee 424
91 O-Pee-Chee 688

RODRIGUEZ, RUBEN
91 London/LineDrive 396
91 London/ProCards 1881
87 Vancouver/ProCards 1620

RODRIGUEZ, ORBE LUIS
94 GarciaPhoto 50

RODRIGUEZ, RUBEN
94 GarciaPhoto 125

RODRIGUEZ, VICTOR
94 Edmonton/ProCards 2882
96 St.Catharines/Best 24

ROE, PREACHER
53 Exhibits 1
50 PalmDairies

ROEBUCK, ED
53 Exhibits 41
65 O-Pee-Chee 52

ROEBUCK, EDWARD JACK
52 Parkhurst 75

ROEDER, STEVE
90 Welland/Pucko 27
91 Welland/Best 19

ROENICKE, GARY
81 O-Pee-Chee 37
83 O-Pee-Chee 382
84 O-Pee-Chee 372
85 O-Pee-Chee 109
86 O-Pee-Chee 183
87 O-Pee-Chee 283
84 opcSticker 205
88 PaniniSticker 252

ROESLER, MIKE
90 FleerCdn. 645
90 O-Pee-Chee 203

ROETTER, RANDY
90 Calgary/CMC 25

ROFF, GENE
91 London/LineDrive 399

ROGELL, BILLY
33 WWGum(V353) 11
36 WWGum(V355) 52

ROGERS, KENNY
90 FleerCdn. 311
90 O-Pee-Chee 683
91 O-Pee-Chee 332
92 O-Pee-Chee 511
93 O-Pee-Chee 356

ROGERS, LEE
39 WWGum(V351A)

ROGERS, STEVE
77 Dimanche/DernièreHeure
80 Dimanche/DernièreHeure
82 Dimanche/DernièreHeure
83 Dimanche/DernièreHeure
82 FBI BoxBottom
85 Leaf 192
92 Nabisco 33
74 O-Pee-Chee 169
75 O-Pee-Chee 173
76 O-Pee-Chee 71
77 O-Pee-Chee 153
78 O-Pee-Chee 9
79 O-Pee-Chee 120
80 O-Pee-Chee 271
81 O-Pee-Chee 344,-Poster 9
82 O-Pee-Chee 52,-Poster 20
83 O-Pee-Chee 106,111,320
84 O-Pee-Chee 80,394
85 O-Pee-Chee 205,-Poster 11
82 opcSticker 59
83 opcSticker 208,256
84 opcSticker 88,182
85 opcSticker 89
77 MTL
77 MTL/RedpathSugar
82 MTL/Hygrade
82 MTL/Zellers
83 MTL
83 MTL/StuartBakery
84 MTL
84 MTL/StuartBakery 19
93 MTL/McDonald's 28

ROGGENDORF, KIP
93 St.Catharines/ClassicBest 21
93 St.Catharines/ProCards 3983
94 St.Catharines/Classic 28
94 St.Catharines/ProCards 3653

ROGODZINSKI, MIKE
74 O-Pee-Chee 492

ROHAN, JOHNNY
52 LavalDairy 67

ROHDE, DAVE
91 O-Pee-Chee 531

ROJAS, COOKIE
66 O-Pee-Chee 170
68 O-Pee-Chee 39
71 O-Pee-Chee 118
72 O-Pee-Chee 415
73 O-Pee-Chee 188
74 O-Pee-Chee 278
75 O-Pee-Chee 169
76 O-Pee-Chee 311

RODRIGUEZ, ORBE LUIS
94 GarciaPhoto 50

ROJAS, EDDY
94 GarciaPhoto 80

ROJAS, EUCLIDES
94 GarciaPhoto 59

ROJAS, EUSEBIO MIGUEL
94 GarciaPhoto 77

ROJAS, MEL
91 O-Pee-Chee 252
92 O-Pee-Chee 583
93 O-Pee-Chee 347
91 opcPremier 101
92 opcPremier 124
96 MTL/Disk

ROJAS, MINNIE
67 O-Pee-Chee 104

ROJAS, RENE
94 GarciaPhoto 65

ROJAS, RICKY
91 Calgary/LineDrive 71
91 Calgary/ProCards 516
92 London/ProCards 631
92 London/SkyBox 417

ROJAS, WILBERTO
90 St.Catharines/ProCards 3478

ROLAND, JIM
65 O-Pee-Chee 171
71 O-Pee-Chee 642
72 O-Pee-Chee 464

ROLFE, RED
36 WWGum(V355) 38

ROLLINGS, RUSSELL
34 WWGum(V354) 40

ROLLINS, RICH
65 O-Pee-Chee 90
67 O-Pee-Chee 98

ROMANICK, RON
86 Leaf 81
85 O-Pee-Chee 280
86 O-Pee-Chee 76
87 O-Pee-Chee 136
85 opcSticker 231
86 opcSticker 180

ROMANO, JAMES K.
52 Parkhurst 73

ROMANO, JOHNNY
65 O-Pee-Chee 17
67 O-Pee-Chee 196
62 PostCereal 42
62 ShirriffCoin 94

ROMERO, AL
85 Edmonton/Cramer 25
86 Edmonton/ProCards

ROMERO, ED
86 O-Pee-Chee 317
87 O-Pee-Chee 158
79 Vancouver/TCMA 17
80 Vancouver/TCMA 13

ROMINE, KEVIN
90 FleerCdn. 286
91 O-Pee-Chee 652

ROMMEL, EDDIE (EDWIN)
21 Neilson's(V61) 9
23 Neilson's 32
23 WillardsChocolate(V100)135

ROMO, ENRIQUE
78 O-Pee-Chee 186
79 O-Pee-Chee 281
81 O-Pee-Chee 28

ROMO, VICENTE
70 O-Pee-Chee 191
71 O-Pee-Chee 723
72 O-Pee-Chee 499
73 O-Pee-Chee 381
74 O-Pee-Chee 197
75 O-Pee-Chee 274

RONAN, MARC
90 Hamilton/Best 14

RONCA, JOE
90 Welland/Pucko 14

RONNING, ALBERT R.
53 Exhibits 56
52 Parkhurst 49

ROOD, NELSON
90 Edmonton/CMC 14
90 Edmonton/ProCards 525

ROOF, GENE
91 London/ProCards 1892

ROOF, PHIL
67 O-Pee-Chee 129
70 O-Pee-Chee 359
71 O-Pee-Chee 22
72 O-Pee-Chee 201
73 O-Pee-Chee 598
74 O-Pee-Chee 388
75 O-Pee-Chee 576
76 O-Pee-Chee 424
77 O-Pee-Chee 121

ROOKER, JIM
70 O-Pee-Chee 222
71 O-Pee-Chee 730
74 O-Pee-Chee 402
75 O-Pee-Chee 148
76 O-Pee-Chee 243
77 O-Pee-Chee 161

ROOMES, ROLANDO
90 FleerCdn. 432
90 O-Pee-Chee 364
90 PaniniSticker 254

ROONEY, MIKE
97 Lethbridge/Best 28

ROQUE, JORGE
72 O-Pee-Chee 316
73 O-Pee-Chee 606

ROSADO, FELIX
95 St.Catharines/TimHortons 23

ROSARIO, JIMMY
72 O-Pee-Chee 366

ROSE
53 Exhibits 42

ROSE, BOBBY
90 FleerCdn. 651
92 O-Pee-Chee 652
92 opcPremier 169
90 Edmonton/CMC 15
90 Edmonton/ProCards 526
91 Edmonton/LineDrive 169
91 Edmonton/ProCards 1524

ROSE, PETE
82 FBI BoxBottoms
85 Leaf 144
86 Leaf 53,209,260
87 Leaf 129
65 O-Pee-Chee 207
66 O-Pee-Chee 30
69 O-Pee-Chee 2,120
70 OPC 15,61,458,-Booklet 15
71 O-Pee-Chee 100
73 O-Pee-Chee 130
74 O-Pee-Chee 201,300,336
75 O-Pee-Chee 211,320
76 O-Pee-Chee 240
77 O-Pee-Chee 240
78 O-Pee-Chee 100,240
79 O-Pee-Chee 343
80 O-Pee-Chee 282
81 O-Pee-Chee 180
82 O-Pee-Chee 24,337,361
83 O-Pee-Chee 100,101,373
84 O-Pee-Chee 300
85 O-Pee-Chee 116
86 O-Pee-Chee 1,N
87 O-Pee-Chee 200
82 opcSticker 12,78,117
83 opcSticker 272
84 opcSticker 115
85 opcSticker 57
86 opcSticker 1,2,134
87 opcSticker 139
86 opcTattoo 6
71 ProStarPostcard
71 ProStarPoster
84 MTL
84 MTL/StuartBakery 17

ROSEBORO, JOHN
66 O-Pee-Chee 189
68 O-Pee-Chee 65
69 O-Pee-Chee 218
73 O-Pee-Chee 421
74 O-Pee-Chee 276
62 PostCereal 107
62 ShirriffCoin 133

ROSELLI, JOE
96 Vancouver/Best 24

ROSELLO, DAVE
74 O-Pee-Chee 607
76 O-Pee-Chee 546

ROSEN, AL
75 O-Pee-Chee 191

ROSENBERG, STEVE
90 FleerCdn. 547
90 O-Pee-Chee 379
88 Vancouver/CMC 3
88 Vancouver/ProCards 754
90 Vancouver/CMC 11
90 Vancouver/ProCards 489

ROSENTHAL, WAYNE
92 O-Pee-Chee 584
92 opcPremier 30

ROSS, DAN
89 London/ProCards 1361

ROSS, GARY
71 O-Pee-Chee 153
73 O-Pee-Chee 112

ROSS, MARK
87 Vancouver/ProCards 1602

ROSS, MIKE
88 Hamilton/ProCards 1727

ROSSITER, MIKE
92 O-Pee-Chee 474

ROSSY, RICO
93 opcPremier 123

ROUSH, EDDIE
20 MapleCrispette(V117) 28
23 Neilson's 33
22 WilliamPaterson(V89) 1

ROUSH, EDD J. (EDDIE)
21 Neilson's(V61) 79
23 WillardsChocolate(V100)136

ROWE, RALPH
73 O-Pee-Chee 49
74 O-Pee-Chee 447

ROWE, DON
84 Vancouver/Cramer 243

ROWE, SCHOOLBOY
37 O-Pee-Chee(V300) 134
36 WWGum(V355) 44

ROWLAND, DONNIE
89 London/ProCards 1363

ROWLAND, RICH
92 O-Pee-Chee 472
90 London/ProCards 1271

ROY, JEAN-PIERRE (FRENCHIE)
52 Parkhurst 90
43-47 Montréal/ParadeSportive

ROYSTER, JERRY
76 O-Pee-Chee 592
77 O-Pee-Chee 251
8 O-Pee-Chee 241
86 O-Pee-Chee 118
87 O-Pee-Chee 324
84 opcSticker 37

ROZEMA, DAVE
86 Leaf 154
78 O-Pee-Chee 38
79 O-Pee-Chee 12
80 O-Pee-Chee 151
84 O-Pee-Chee 133
86 O-Pee-Chee 208

ROZNOVSKY, VIC
67 O-Pee-Chee 163

RUBELING, ALBERT WILLIAM
52 Parkhurst 82

RUBY, GARY
91 Edmonton/LineDrive 175
91 Edmonton/ProCards 1532
92 Edmonton/ProCards 3554
92 Edmonton/SkyBox 175
93 Vancouver/ProCards 2614
94 Vancouver/ProCards 1879

RUDI, JOE
70 O-Pee-Chee 102
71 O-Pee-Chee 407
72 O-Pee-Chee 209
73 O-Pee-Chee 360
74 O-Pee-Chee 264
75 O-Pee-Chee 45
76 O-Pee-Chee 475
77 O-Pee-Chee 206
78 O-Pee-Chee 28
79 O-Pee-Chee 134
80 O-Pee-Chee 289
81 O-Pee-Chee 362
82 O-Pee-Chee 388

RUDOLPH, DICK
1912 ImperialTobacco(C46) 22

RUDOLPH, KEN
70 O-Pee-Chee 46
71 O-Pee-Chee 472
72 O-Pee-Chee 271
73 O-Pee-Chee 414
74 O-Pee-Chee 584
75 O-Pee-Chee 289
76 O-Pee-Chee 601

RUEBEL, MATT
91 Welland/Best 20
91 Welland/ProCards 3572

RUEL, HEROLD
23 WillardsChocolate(V100)137

RUEL, MUDDY
20 MapleCrispette(V117) 24
33 WWGum(V353) 18

RUETER, KIRK
94 O-Pee-Chee 255, -DD 8

RUFFCORN, SCOTT
92 O-Pee-Chee 36

RUFFIN, BRUCE
90 FleerCdn. 572
87 Leaf 168
88 O-Pee-Chee 268
89 O-Pee-Chee 222
90 O-Pee-Chee 22
91 O-Pee-Chee 637
92 O-Pee-Chee 307
87 opcSticker 123,312
88 opcSticker 119
89 opcSticker 122
88 PaniniSticker 353
89 PaniniSticker 148

RUFFING, RED (CHARLES)
37 O-Pee-Chee(V300) 136
34 WWGum(V354) 48

RUHLE, VERN
75 O-Pee-Chee 614
76 O-Pee-Chee 89
77 O-Pee-Chee 212

RUIZ, CHICO
66 O-Pee-Chee 159
71 O-Pee-Chee 686

RUNNELLS, TOM
92 O-Pee-Chee 51
92 MTL/Durivage

RUNNELS, PETE
60 opcTattoo 47
62 PostCereal 57
62 ShirriffCoin 47

RUPKEY, RICH
90 Hamilton/Best 12
90 Hamilton/Star 21

RUSH, LAWRENCE (LARRY)
80 Vancouver/TCMA 1
81 Vancouver/TCMA 12
82 Vancouver/TCMA 7

RUSKIN, SCOTT
91 O-Pee-Chee 589
92 O-Pee-Chee 692

RUSSELL, ALLEN
23 WillardsChocolate(V100)138

RUSSELL, BILL
85 Leaf 232
70 O-Pee-Chee 304
71 O-Pee-Chee 226
73 O-Pee-Chee 108
74 O-Pee-Chee 239
75 O-Pee-Chee 23
76 O-Pee-Chee 22
80 O-Pee-Chee 40
81 O-Pee-Chee 20
83 O-Pee-Chee 123
84 O-Pee-Chee 14
85 O-Pee-Chee 343
83 opcSticker 249
84 opcSticker 77
85 opcSticker 76

RUSSELL, JEFF
90 FleerCdn. 312,633
89 O-Pee-Chee 166
90 O-Pee-Chee 80,395
91 O-Pee-Chee 344
92 O-Pee-Chee 257
94 O-Pee-Chee 113
93 opcPremier 9
89 opcSticker 243
89 PaniniSticker 447
90 PaniniSticker 159

RUSSELL, JOHN
91 O-Pee-Chee 734

RUSSO, PAUL
92 O-Pee-Chee 473

RUTH, GEORGE HERMAN (BABE)
92 HomersClassic 1
20 MapleCrispette(V117) 8
21 Neilson's(V61) 37
23 Neilson's 34
73 O-Pee-Chee 1,474
76 O-Pee-Chee 345
83 opcSticker 2
22 WilliamPaterson(V89) 25
23 WillardsChocolate(V100)139
33 WWGum(V353) 80,93
34 WWGum(V354) 28

RUTHVEN, DICK
74 O-Pee-Chee 47
75 O-Pee-Chee 267
76 O-Pee-Chee 431
81 O-Pee-Chee 285
82 O-Pee-Chee 317
83 O-Pee-Chee 313
84 O-Pee-Chee 156
85 O-Pee-Chee 268
84 opcSticker 49

RUTKAY, GARY
52 LavalDairy 38

RYAL, MARK
86 Edmonton/ProCards
93 Edmonton/ProCards 1149

RYAN, BLONDY
34 WWGum(V354) 73

RYAN, KEN
93 opcPremier 41

RYAN, CONNIE
74 O-Pee-Chee 634

RYAN, CRAIG
79 Vancouver/TCMA 5
80 Vancouver/TCMA 15

RYAN, MIKE
69 O-Pee-Chee 28
71 O-Pee-Chee 533
72 O-Pee-Chee 324
73 O-Pee-Chee 467
74 O-Pee-Chee 564

RYAN, NOLAN
91 Ben's/HolsumDisks 19
82 FBI BoxBottoms
90 FleerCdn. 313,636
93 HumptyDumpty 16
85 Leaf 216
86 Leaf 132
87 Leaf 257
88 Leaf 77
92 McDonald's 5
68 O-Pee-Chee 177
71 O-Pee-Chee 513
73 O-Pee-Chee 67,220
74 O-Pee-Chee 20,207
75 O-Pee-Chee 5,7,312,500
76 O-Pee-Chee 330
77 O-Pee-Chee 6,65,264
78 O-Pee-Chee 6,105,241
79 O-Pee-Chee 51
80 O-Pee-Chee 303
81 O-Pee-Chee 240
82 O-Pee-Chee 90
83 O-Pee-Chee 360,361
85 O-Pee-Chee 63
86 O-Pee-Chee 100
87 O-Pee-Chee 155
88 O-Pee-Chee 250,N
89 O-Pee-Chee 366,K
90 O-Pee-Chee 1,2,3,4,5,O
91 O-Pee-Chee 1,6,N
92 O-Pee-Chee 1,4
93 O-Pee-Chee 229
91 opcPremier 102
92 opcPremier 81
93 opcPremier-StarPerf. 20
82 opcSticker 13,41
83 opcSticker 235
84 opcSticker 66
85 opcSticker 58
86 opcSticker 9,24
87 opcSticker 27
88 opcSticker 7
89 opcSticker 20
86 opcTattoo 24
88 PaniniSticker 288,435
89 PaniniSticker 83
90 PaniniSticker 160,387
91 PaniniSticker 259,354
92 PaniniSticker 82
93 PaniniSticker 87
91 PaniniTopFifteen 77
91 PetroCanada 25
91 PostCdn. 27
87 StuartBakery 5

RYAN, WILFRED P.D.
23 WillardsChocolate(V100)140

S

SABERHAGEN, BRET
90 Ben's/HolsumDisk 5
90 FleerCdn. 116
86 GeneralMills
86 Leaf 11
87 Leaf 261
88 Leaf 68
85 O-Pee-Chee 23
86 O-Pee-Chee 249,O
87 O-Pee-Chee 140
88 O-Pee-Chee 5
89 O-Pee-Chee 157
90 O-Pee-Chee 350,393
91 O-Pee-Chee 280
92 O-Pee-Chee 75
93 O-Pee-Chee 302
94 O-Pee-Chee 46
92 opcPremier 82
86 opcSticker 17,260
88 opcStick. 163,254,-SStar 60
89 opcSticker 263
86 opcTattoo 2
88 PaniniStick. 102,106-07,229
89 PaniniSticker 352

90 PaniniSticker 81
91 PaniniSticker 283
92 PaniniSticker 101
94 PaniniSticker 222
87 StuartBakery 20

SABO, CHRIS
90 FleerCdn. 433
89 O-Pee-Chee 156
90 O-Pee-Chee 737
91 O-Pee-Chee 5
92 O-Pee-Chee 485
93 O-Pee-Chee 333
94 O-Pee-Chee 136
92 opcPremier 23
89 opcSticker 142,325
89 PaniniSticker 64,262,476
90 PaniniSticker 202,248,388
91 PaniniSticker 129,160
92 PaniniSticker 264,283
93 PaniniSticker 294
94 PaniniSticker 168
91 PostCdn. 10

SADECKI, RAY
65 O-Pee-Chee 10,230
66 O-Pee-Chee 26
69 O-Pee-Chee 125
71 O-Pee-Chee 406
73 O-Pee-Chee 283
74 O-Pee-Chee 216
75 O-Pee-Chee 349

SADEK, MIKE
74 O-Pee-Chee 577
76 O-Pee-Chee 234
80 O-Pee-Chee 240

SADOWSKI, BOB
65 O-Pee-Chee 156

SAHRON, DICK
75 O-Pee-Chee 293

SAIN, JOHNNY
73 O-Pee-Chee 356
74 O-Pee-Chee 221

ST. CLAIRE, RANDY
86 Leaf 229
86 O-Pee-Chee 89
87 O-Pee-Chee 366
88 O-Pee-Chee 279
90 O-Pee-Chee 503

ST. VINCENT, CLAUDE
52 LavalDairy 94

SAKATA, LENN
91 Edmonton/LineDrive 175
91 Edmonton/ProCards 1533
92 Edmonton/ProCards 3555
92 Edmonton/SkyBox 175
79 Vancouver/TCMA 22
93 Vancouver/ProCards 2615
94 Vancouver/ProCards 1880

SALAS, MARK
86 Leaf 185
86 O-Pee-Chee 43
87 O-Pee-Chee 87
91 O-Pee-Chee 498
86 opcSticker 278,315
86 opcTattoo 17

SALAZAR, ANGEL (ARGENIS)
83 Dimanche/DernièreHeure
85 O-Pee-Chee 154
88 O-Pee-Chee 29
87 opcSticker 259
88 PaniniSticker 109
84 MTL
84 MTL/StuartBakery 31

SALAZAR, LUIS
82 O-Pee-Chee 133
83 O-Pee-Chee 156
84 O-Pee-Chee 68
89 O-Pee-Chee 122,276
90 O-Pee-Chee 378
91 O-Pee-Chee 614
88 opcSticker 276
89 PaniniSticker 342
91 PaniniSticker 45
92 PaniniSticker 184
88 St.Catharines/ProCards 2006

SALFRAN, FRANCISCO
52 LavalDairy 110

SALKELD, ROGER
90 O-Pee-Chee 44
92 O-Pee-Chee 676
92 Calgary/SkyBox 51
94 Calgary/ProCards 788

SALLEE, HARRY F.
23 WillardsChocolate(V100)141

SALMON, CHICO
65 O-Pee-Chee 105
67 O-Pee-Chee 43
69 O-Pee-Chee 62
70 O-Pee-Chee 301
71 O-Pee-Chee 249

SALMON, TIM
93 O-Pee-Chee 292
94 OPC 194, -AS 10, -DD11
93 opcPremier 37
94 PaniniSticker 42
92 Edmonton/ProCards 3551
92 Edmonton/SkyBox 165

SAMBITO, JOE
81 O-Pee-Chee 334
83 O-Pee-Chee 296
87 O-Pee-Chee 262

SAMBO, RAMON
90 Vancouver/CMC 15
90 Vancouver/ProCards 503

SAMPLE, BILLY
81 O-Pee-Chee 283
82 O-Pee-Chee 112
84 O-Pee-Chee 12
91 O-Pee-Chee 649
92 O-Pee-Chee 566
84 opcSticker 352
85 opcSticker 351
91 PaniniSticker 149
92 MTL/Durivage 3

SAMSON, WILLIAM
53 Exhibits 54
52 Parkhurst 51

SAMUEL, JUAN
90 FleerCdn. 215
85 Leaf 23
86 Leaf 196
87 Leaf 132
88 Leaf 146
85 O-Pee-Chee 265
86 O-Pee-Chee 237
87 O-Pee-Chee 255
88 O-Pee-Chee 19
89 O-Pee-Chee 372
90 O-Pee-Chee 85
91 O-Pee-Chee 645,O
92 O-Pee-Chee 315
85 opcSticker 114,369
86 opcSticker 121
87 opcSticker 125
88 opcSticker 120,-SuperStar 5
89 opcSticker 117,-SStar 37
86 opcTattoo 15
88 PaniniSticker 359
89 PaniniSticker 152
91 PaniniSticker 56
92 PaniniSticker 193
87 StuartBakery 9
96 TOR/OhHenry

SANCHEZ, ALEX
90 FleerCdn. 92
88 O-Pee-Chee 194
90 O-Pee-Chee 563
90 TOR/FireSafety
94 Calgary/ProCards 789

SANCHEZ, ANTONIO
94 GarciaPhoto 128

SANCHEZ, CELERINO
73 O-Pee-Chee 103
74 O-Pee-Chee 623

SANCHEZ, LUIS
84 O-Pee-Chee 258
85 O-Pee-Chee 42
84 opcSticker 233

SANCHEZ, OMAR
94 St.Catharines/Classic 18
94 St.Catharines/ProCards 3657
95 St.Catharines/TimHortons 25

SANCHEZ, PAUL
61 Toronto/BeeHive

SAND, HEINIE
34 WWGum(V354) 27

SANDBERG, RYNE
91 Ben's/HolsumDisk 6
92 Ben'sDisk 19
90 FleerCdn. 40,625,639
85 GeneralMills
86 GeneralMills
87 GeneralMills
87 HostessSticker
85 Leaf 1
86 Leaf 62
87 Leaf 234
88 Leaf 207
92 McDonald's 6
83 O-Pee-Chee 83
84 O-Pee-Chee 64
85 O-Pee-Chee 296
86 O-Pee-Chee 19
87 O-Pee-Chee 143
88 O-Pee-Chee 10
89 O-Pee-Chee 360
90 O-Pee-Chee 210,398,P
91 O-Pee-Chee 7,398,740
92 O-Pee-Chee 110
93 O-Pee-Chee 274
94 O-Pee-Chee 16
91 opcPremier 103
92 opcPremier 34
93 opcPremier-StarPerf. 4
83 opcSticker 328
84 opcSticker 45
85 opcSticker 34,175
86 opcSticker 55
87 opcSticker 61,156
88 opcSticker 57,147,-SStar 6
89 opcSticker 55,155,-SStar 38
86 opcTattoo 8
88 PaniniSticker 234,260
89 PaniniSticker 56
90 PaniniSticker 212,231
91 PaniniSticker 44,159
92 PaniniSticker 183,282
93 PaniniSticker 204
94 PaniniSticker 156
91 PaniniTopFifteen 9,27,34
91 PaniniTopFifteen 49,101
91 PetroCanada 4
92 PizzaHut/DietPepsi 16
92 PostCdn. 4
93 PostCdn. 14

SANDERS ANTHONY
94 St.Catharines/Classic 19
94 St.Catharines/ProCards 3658

SANDERS, DEION
90 FleerCdn. 454
90 O-Pee-Chee 61
92 O-Pee-Chee 645
93 O-Pee-Chee 372
94 O-Pee-Chee 118
92 opcPremier 91
93 opcPremier-StarPerf. 10
93 PaniniSticker 188
94 PaniniSticker 150

SANDERS, KEN
71 O-Pee-Chee 116
72 O-Pee-Chee 391
73 O-Pee-Chee 246
74 O-Pee-Chee 638
75 O-Pee-Chee 366
76 O-Pee-Chee 291

SANDERS, REGGIE
75 O-Pee-Chee 617

SANDERS, REGGIE
92 O-Pee-Chee 283
93 O-Pee-Chee 358
94 O-Pee-Chee 207
92 opcPremier 25
93 PaniniSticker 298
94 PaniniSticker 169

SANDERSON, SCOTT
90 FleerCdn. 41
85 Leaf 194
80 O-Pee-Chee 301
81 O-Pee-Chee 235,-Poster 12
82 O-Pee-Chee 7,-Poster 22
83 O-Pee-Chee 54
85 O-Pee-Chee 373
90 O-Pee-Chee 67
91 O-Pee-Chee 728
92 O-Pee-Chee 480
91 opcPremier 104
93 opcPremier 100
92 PaniniSticker 142
93 PaniniSticker 145
82 MTL/Hygrade
82 MTL/Zellers
83 MTL
83 MTL/StuartBakery 17

SANDOVAL, JHENSY
97 Lethbridge/Best 16

SANDS, CHARLIE
74 O-Pee-Chee 381
75 O-Pee-Chee 548

SANFORD, CHANCE
92 Welland/ClassicBest 20
97 Lethbridge/Best 21

SANFORD, JACK
65 O-Pee-Chee 228
66 O-Pee-Chee 23
62 PostCereal 141

SANFORD, MO
92 O-Pee-Chee 674
92 opcPremier 17

SANGUILLEN, MANNY
70 O-Pee-Chee 188
71 O-Pee-Chee 62,480
72 O-Pee-Chee 60
73 O-Pee-Chee 250
74 O-Pee-Chee 28
75 O-Pee-Chee 515
76 O-Pee-Chee 191,220
77 O-Pee-Chee 231

SANKEY, BEN
36 WWGum(V355) 84

SANTA, JEFF
97 Lethbridge/Best 29

SANTANA, ERNSTO
89 St.Catharines/ProCards 2087

SANTANA, RAFAEL
87 Leaf 167
90 O-Pee-Chee 651
86 opcSticker 102
89 opcSticker 313
88 PaniniSticker 344
89 PaniniSticker 407

SANTANGELO, F.P.
93 Ottawa/ProCards 2447
94 Ottawa/ProCards 2906

SANTIAGO, BENITO (BENNY)
90 FleerCdn. 167
97 HitTheBooks
93 HumptyDumpty 31
87 Leaf 31
88 Leaf 3,58
88 O-Pee-Chee 86
89 O-Pee-Chee 256
90 O-Pee-Chee 35
91 O-Pee-Chee 760
92 O-Pee-Chee 185
93 O-Pee-Chee 353
94 O-Pee-Chee 150
91 opcPremier 105
92 opcPremier 154
93 opcPremier 43
88 opcSticker 2,112
89 opcSticker 101,-SStar 57
88 PaniniStick. 402,405-06,433
89 PaniniSticker 199
90 PaniniSticker 213,358
91 PaniniSticker 90,157
92 PaniniSticker 231,280
94 PaniniSticker 185
91 PaniniTopFifteen 99
91 PostCdn. 13
92 PostCdn. 2
97 TOR/Sizzler 5

SANTIAGO, JOSE
68 O-Pee-Chee 123
69 O-Pee-Chee 21

SANTIESTEBAN, FRANCISCO
94 GarciaPhoto 35

SANTO, RONALD
65 O-Pee-Chee 6,110
67 O-Pee-Chee 70
68 O-Pee-Chee 5,-Poster 29
69 O-Pee-Chee 4,-Deckle 19
70 O-Pee-Chee 63,454
71 O-Pee-Chee 220
73 O-Pee-Chee 115
74 O-Pee-Chee 270,334
75 O-Pee-Chee 35
62 PostCereal 184
62 ShirriffCoin 136

SANTORINI, AL
70 O-Pee-Chee 212
71 O-Pee-Chee 467
73 O-Pee-Chee 24

SANTOVENIA, NELSON
90 FleerCdn. 360
89 O-Pee-Chee 228
90 O-Pee-Chee 614
91 O-Pee-Chee 744
92 O-Pee-Chee 732
89 opcSticker 78
89 PaniniSticker 112
90 PaniniSticker 289
92 Vancouver/ProCards 2726
92 Vancouver/SkyBox 646

SARMIENTO, MANNY
79 O-Pee-Chee 69

SASSER, MACKEY
90 FleerCdn. 216
88 Leaf 28
90 O-Pee-Chee 656
91 O-Pee-Chee 382
92 O-Pee-Chee 533
93 O-Pee-Chee 328
91 PaniniSticker 78

SATERFIELD, CORY
88 Hamilton/ProCards 1731

SATRIANO, TOM
65 O-Pee-Chee 124
69 O-Pee-Chee 78
71 O-Pee-Chee 557

SAUCIER, KEVIN
82 O-Pee-Chee 238

SAUER, HANK (HENRY)
53 Exhibits 7
75 O-Pee-Chee 190

SAUNDERS, DENNIS
71 O-Pee-Chee 423

SAUNDERS, REGGIE
74 O-Pee-Chee 600

SAVAGE, JACK
91 O-Pee-Chee 357

SAVAGE, TED
68 O-Pee-Chee 119
71 O-Pee-Chee 76

SAVERINE, BOB
67 O-Pee-Chee 27
68 O-Pee-Chee 149

SAVIOR, TROY
90 Hamilton/Best 10
90 Hamilton/Star 22

SAWATSKI, CARL
62 PostCereal 162
62 ShirriffCoin 119

SAX, STEVE
90 Ben's/HolsumDisk 16
90 FleerCdn. 455
86 GeneralMills
87 GeneralMills
85 Leaf 90
87 Leaf 26,203
88 Leaf 185
83 O-Pee-Chee 245
84 O-Pee-Chee 144
85 O-Pee-Chee 369
86 O-Pee-Chee 175
87 O-Pee-Chee 254
88 O-Pee-Chee 305
89 O-Pee-Chee 40
90 O-Pee-Chee 560
91 O-Pee-Chee 290
92 O-Pee-Chee 430
93 O-Pee-Chee 307
92 opcPremier 43
83 opcSticker 329
84 opcSticker 78
85 opcSticker 77
86 opcSticker 72
87 opcSticker 70
88 opcSticker 74
89 opcSticker 57,-SuperStar 39
86 opcTattoo 21
88 PaniniSticker 311
89 PaniniSticker 106
90 PaniniSticker 129
91 PaniniSticker 168,325
92 PaniniSticker 136
93 PaniniSticker 137
91 PaniniTopFifteen 46

SCALA, JERRY
50 WWGum(V362) 28

SCANLAN, BOB
92 O-Pee-Chee 274
93 O-Pee-Chee 325
92 opcPremier 14

SCANTLEBURY, PAT
61 Toronto/BeeHive

SCARCE, MAC
73 O-Pee-Chee 6
74 O-Pee-Chee 149
75 O-Pee-Chee 527

SCHAAL, PAUL
67 O-Pee-Chee 58
70 O-Pee-Chee 338
71 O-Pee-Chee 487
72 O-Pee-Chee 177,178
73 O-Pee-Chee 416
74 O-Pee-Chee 514

SCHACHT, AL
36 WWGum(V355) 29

SCHAEFER, JEFF
91 O-Pee-Chee 681
92 O-Pee-Chee 391
90 Calgary/ProCards 660
88 Vancouver/CMC 21
88 Vancouver/ProCards 753
89 Vancouver/CMC 24

SCHALK, RAY
20 MapleCrispette(V117) 3
22 WilliamPaterson(V89) 16

SCHALK, ROY
36 WWGum(V355) 124

SCHANG, WALLY
21 Neilson's(V61) 20
23 Neilson's 35
23 WillardsChocolate(V100)142
22 WilliamPaterson(V89) 11

SCHATTINGER, JEFF
82 Edmonton/TCMA 25

SCHATZEDER, DAN
78 Dimanche/DernièreHeure
83 Dimanche/DernièreHeure
90 FleerCdn. 236
85 Leaf 59
79 O-Pee-Chee 56
80 O-Pee-Chee 140
81 O-Pee-Chee 112
82 O-Pee-Chee 106
83 O-Pee-Chee 189
84 O-Pee-Chee 57
85 O-Pee-Chee 293
86 O-Pee-Chee 324
87 O-Pee-Chee 168
77 MTL
83 MTL
83 MTL/StuartBakery 22
84 MTL
84 MTL/StuartBakery 7
86 MTL/ProvigoFoods 12

SCHEID, RICH
93 Edmonton/ProCards 1135
94 Edmonton/ProCards 2876
91 Vancouver/LineDrive 645
91 Vancouver/Procards 1594
92 Vancouver/ProCards 2721
92 Vancouver/SkyBox 647

SCHEINBLUM, RICHIE
68 O-Pee-Chee 16
70 O-Pee-Chee 161
71 O-Pee-Chee 326
72 O-Pee-Chee 468
73 O-Pee-Chee 78
74 O-Pee-Chee 323

SCHERGER, GEORGE
73 O-Pee-Chee 296
74 O-Pee-Chee 326

SCHERMAN, FRED
71 O-Pee-Chee 316
72 O-Pee-Chee 6
73 O-Pee-Chee 660
74 O-Pee-Chee 186
75 O-Pee-Chee 252
76 O-Pee-Chee 188

SCHERRER, BILL
84 opcSticker 62

SCHILLING, CHUCK
65 O-Pee-Chee 272
66 O-Pee-Chee 6
62 PostCereal 56

SCHILLING, CURT
90 O-Pee-Chee 97
91 O-Pee-Chee 569
92 O-Pee-Chee 316
93 O-Pee-Chee 354
94 O-Pee-Chee 66
93 PaniniSticker 268
94 PaniniSticker 230

SCHIRALDI, CALVIN
90 FleerCdn. 168
87 Leaf 137
88 O-Pee-Chee 62
89 O-Pee-Chee 337
90 O-Pee-Chee 693
91 O-Pee-Chee 424
89 opcSticker 56

SCHIRM, GEORGE
1912 ImperialTobacco(C46) 29

SCHMANDT, RAYMOND H.
23 WillardsChocolate(V100)143

SCHMEES, GEORGE
50 WWGum(V362) 20

SCHMIDT, BOB
62 ShirriffCoin 179

SCHMIDT, BUTCH
1912 ImperialTobacco(C46) 12

SCHMIDT, DAVE
90 FleerCdn. 188
85 O-Pee-Chee 313
86 O-Pee-Chee 79
87 O-Pee-Chee 372
88 O-Pee-Chee 214
89 O-Pee-Chee 231
90 O-Pee-Chee 497
91 O-Pee-Chee 136
88 opcSticker 226
88 PaniniSticker 6
89 PaniniSticker 255
92 Calgary/SkyBox 70

SCHMIDT, JEFF
96 Vancouver/Best 25
97 Vancouver/Best 25

SCHMIDT, MIKE
88 FantasticSam's 19
82 FBI BoxBottoms
85 GeneralMills 23
86 GeneralMills
87 GeneralMills
87 HostessSticker
92 Kellogg's 8
85 Leaf 205
86 Leaf 51
87 Leaf 122
88 Leaf 124
73 O-Pee-Chee 615
74 O-Pee-Chee 283
75 O-Pee-Chee 70,307
76 O-Pee-Chee 193,480
77 O-Pee-Chee 2,245
78 O-Pee-Chee 225
79 O-Pee-Chee 323
80 O-Pee-Chee 141
81 O-Pee-Chee 207
82 O-Pee-Chee 100,101,339
83 O-Pee-Chee 300,301,342
84 O-Pee-Chee 361,388
85 O-Pee-Chee 67
86 O-Pee-Chee 200
87 O-Pee-Chee 396
88 O-Pee-Chee 321,O
89 O-Pee-Chee 100,L
90 O-Pee-Chee 662
82 opcSticker 3,5,74,123
83 opcSticker 10,172,270
84 opcSticker 101,117
85 opcSticker 94,111,178,193
86 opcSticker 114
87 opcSticker 116,160
88 opcSticker 9,125,149
88 opcSticker-SuperStar 8
89 opcSticker 120
86 opcTattoo 7
88 PaniniSticker 234,360,429
89 PaniniSticker 3,153
87 StuartBakery 9

SCHMIDT, WALTER
21 Neilson's(V61) 113
23 Neilson's 36

SCHNEIDER, DAN
68 O-Pee-Chee 57

SCHNEIDER, JEFF
94 St.Catharines/Classic 20
94 St.Catharines/ProCards 3642

SCHNEIDER, PAUL
87 Calgary/ProCards 2316
88 Calgary/CMC 2
88 Calgary/ProCards 793

SCHOENDIENST, ALBERT
50 PalmDairies

SCHOENDIENST, RED
66 O-Pee-Chee 76
70 O-Pee-Chee 346
71 O-Pee-Chee 239
72 O-Pee-Chee 67
73 O-Pee-Chee 497
74 O-Pee-Chee 236
75 O-Pee-Chee 246
75 O-Pee-Chee 581
62 ShirriffCoin 151

SCHOFIELD, DICK (SR.)
65 O-Pee-Chee 218
66 O-Pee-Chee 156
69 O-Pee-Chee 18
70 O-Pee-Chee 251
71 O-Pee-Chee 396

SCHOFIELD, DICK (JR.)
90 FleerCdn. 144
88 Leaf 178
86 O-Pee-Chee 311
87 O-Pee-Chee 54
89 O-Pee-Chee 286
90 O-Pee-Chee 189
91 O-Pee-Chee 736
92 O-Pee-Chee 230
93 opcPremier 129
87 opcSticker 176
88 opcSticker 177
89 opcSticker 174
88 PaniniSticker 45
89 PaniniSticker 294
91 PaniniSticker 183
92 PaniniSticker 8
93 TOR/Dempster's 23
93 TOR/FireSafety
93 TOR/McDonalds 30

SCHOOLER, MIKE
90 FleerCdn. 525
90 O-Pee-Chee 681
91 O-Pee-Chee 365
92 O-Pee-Chee 28
93 O-Pee-Chee 350
90 PaniniSticker 151
91 PaniniSticker 236
88 Calgary/CMC 9
88 Calgary/ProCards 795

SCHOUREK, PETE
92 O-Pee-Chee 287
91 opcPremier 106
92 opcPremier 58

SCHREIBER, ANDRE
52 LavalDairy 82

SCHROEDER, BILL
90 O-Pee-Chee 244
91 O-Pee-Chee 452
81 Vancouver/TCMA 3

SCHROEDER, TODD
91 Welland/Best 3
91 Welland/ProCards 3582

SCHROM, KEN
81 O-Pee-Chee 238
84 O-Pee-Chee 322
85 O-Pee-Chee 161
86 O-Pee-Chee 71
87 O-Pee-Chee 171
88 O-Pee-Chee 256
84 opcSticker 308
87 opcSticker 204

SCHU, RICK
86 O-Pee-Chee 16
89 O-Pee-Chee 352
90 O-Pee-Chee 498
86 opcSticker 122

SCHUBLE, HENRY (HEINIE)
33 WWGum(V353) 4

SCHUELER, RON
73 O-Pee-Chee 169
74 O-Pee-Chee 544
75 O-Pee-Chee 292
76 O-Pee-Chee 586

SCHULTE, JOHN
90 Welland/Pucko 9

SCHULTZ, BARNEY
65 O-Pee-Chee 28
73 O-Pee-Chee 497
74 O-Pee-Chee 236

SCHULTZ, JOE
21 Neilson's(V61) 114
23 Neilson's 37
73 O-Pee-Chee 323

SCHUMACHER, HAL
36 WWGum(V355) 23

SCHUNK, JERRY
91 TOR/Score 34

SCHURR, WAYNE
65 O-Pee-Chee 149

SCHUSTER, MARK
81 Vancouver/TCMA 5

SCHWABE, MIKE
89 London/ProCards, 1375

SCHWALL, DON
66 O-Pee-Chee 144
62 PostCereal 64
62 ShirriffCoin 210

SCHWARTZ, RANDY
67 O-Pee-Chee 33

SCIOSCIA, MIKE
90 FleerCdn. 407
85 Leaf 118
86 Leaf 87
87 Leaf 123
88 Leaf 97
82 O-Pee-Chee 173
86 O-Pee-Chee 111
87 O-Pee-Chee 144
88 O-Pee-Chee 225
89 O-Pee-Chee 7
90 O-Pee-Chee 605
91 O-Pee-Chee 305,404
92 O-Pee-Chee 13
93 O-Pee-Chee 326
85 opcSticker 79
86 opcSticker 68
87 opcSticker 73
88 opcSticker 67
89 opcSticker 58
86 opcTattoo 19
88 PaniniSticker 307
89 PaniniSticker 104
90 PaniniSticker 2776
91 PaniniSticker 54
92 PaniniSticker 191
93 PaniniSticker 213

SCONIERS, DARYL
85 O-Pee-Chee 256
88 Vancouver/CMC 22
88 Vancouver/ProCards 766

SCORE, HERB
60 opcTattoo 48

SCOTT, DARRYL
93 Vancouver/ProCards 2596

SCOTT, DON
85 Calgary/Cramer 81

SCOTT, EVERETT
23 WillardsChocolate(V100)144

SCOTT, GARY
91 opcPremier 107
91 ScoreAllStarFanfest 3

SCOTT, GEORGE
67 O-Pee-Chee 75
70 O-Pee-Chee 385
71 O-Pee-Chee 9
73 O-Pee-Chee 263
74 O-Pee-Chee 27
75 O-Pee-Chee 360
76 O-Pee-Chee 15,194,196
77 O-Pee-Chee 210
78 O-Pee-Chee 12
79 O-Pee-Chee 340

SCOTT, JOHN
75 O-Pee-Chee 616
77 O-Pee-Chee 94

SCOTT, MICKEY
73 O-Pee-Chee 553
76 O-Pee-Chee 276

SCOTT, MIKE
90 FleeerCdn. 237,636
87 GeneralMills
87 HostessSticker
86 Leaf 235
87 Leaf 18,258
88 Leaf 54
85 O-Pee-Chee 17
87 O-Pee-Chee 330
88 O-Pee-Chee 227
89 O-Pee-Chee 180
90 O-Pee-Chee 405,406
91 O-Pee-Chee 240
86 opcSticker 27
87 opcSticker 15,35
88 opcSticker 15
86 opcTattoo 23
88 PaniniSticker 233,289
89 PaniniSticker 84
90 PaniniSticker 262
91 PaniniSticker 14
91 PetroCanada 8
87 StuartBakery 5

SCOTT, PETE
34 WWGum(V354) 33

SCOTT, RODNEY
80 Dimanche/DernièreHeure
92 Nabisco 13
80 O-Pee-Chee 360
81 O-Pee-Chee 227,-Poster 2
82 O-Pee-Chee 124,-Poster 4
93 MTL/McDonald's 18

SCOTT, SHAWN
90 St.Catharines/ProCards 3480

SCOTT, TIM
96 HitTheBooks
96 MTL/DIsk

SCOTT, TONY
80 O-Pee-Chee 17
85 O-Pee-Chee 367

SCUDDER, SCOTT
90 FleerCdn. 434
90 O-Pee-Chee 553
91 O-Pee-Chee 713
92 O-Pee-Chee 48
92 opcPremier 181

SCURRY, ROD
87 O-Pee-Chee 393
88 Calgary/CMC 10
88 Calgary/ProCards 779

SEABURY, JARON
97 St.Catharines/Best 25

SEANEZ, RUDY
90 FleerCdn. 640
93 O-Pee-Chee 391

SEARAGE, RAY
90 FleerCdn. 408
90 O-Pee-Chee 84
92 Edmonton/ProCards 3539
84 Vancouver/Cramer 30
86 Vancouver/ProCards no#

SEARCY, STEVE
90 FleerCdn. 615
90 O-Pee-Chee 487
91 O-Pee-Chee 369
92 O-Pee-Chee 599

SEAVER, TOM
92 Kellogg's 9
85 Leaf 101
86 Leaf 234
87 Leaf 263
68 O-Pee-Chee 45
70 O-Pee-Chee 69,300
71 O-Pee-Chee 68,72,160
72 OPC 91,93,95,347,445,446
73 O-Pee-Chee 350
74 O-Pee-Chee 80,206,207
75 O-Pee-Chee 370
76 OPC 5,199,201,203,600
77 O-Pee-Chee 6,205
78 O-Pee-Chee 120
79 O-Pee-Chee 44
80 O-Pee-Chee 260
81 O-Pee-Chee 220
82 O-Pee-Chee 30,31,346
83 O-Pee-Chee 52,354
84 O-Pee-Chee 261
85 O-Pee-Chee 1
86 O-Pee-Chee 390
87 O-Pee-Chee 49
82 opcSticker 9,36
83 opcSticker 233
84 opcSticker 106
85 opcSticker 235
86 opcSticker 287
87 opcSticker 246
86 opcTattoo 10
71 ProStarPostcard

SEBRA, BOB
87 Leaf 213
87 O-Pee-Chee 314
88 O-Pee-Chee 93

SECRIST, REED
97 Calgary/Best 22

SEEDS, BOB
36 WWGum(V355) 27

SEELBACH, CHUCK
73 O-Pee-Chee 51
74 O-Pee-Chee 292

SEGUI, DAVID
96 HitTheBooks
91 O-Pee-Chee 724
92 O-Pee-Chee 447
92 opcPremier 153
94 PaniniSticker 24
96 MTL/Disk [x2]

SEGUI, DIEGO
65 O-Pee-Chee 197
70 O-Pee-Chee 2
71 O-Pee-Chee 67,215
73 O-Pee-Chee 383
74 O-Pee-Chee 151
75 O-Pee-Chee 232

SEGURA, JOSE
89 Vancouver/CMC 6
89 Vancouver/ProCards 591
90 Vancouver/CMC 12
90 Vancouver/ProCards 490

SEILHEIMER, RICK
82 Edmonton/TCMA 21

SEITZER, KEVIN
90 FleerCdn. 117
88 Leaf 105
88 O-Pee-Chee 275
89 O-Pee-Chee 58
90 O-Pee-Chee 435
91 O-Pee-Chee 695
92 O-Pee-Chee 577
93 O-Pee-Chee 312
92 opcPremier 27
93 opcPremier 121
88 opcSticker 261,306
89 opcSticker 264
88 PaniniSticker 108,436
89 PaniniSticker 357
90 PaniniSticker 86
91 PaniniSticker 278
93 PaniniSticker 40
94 PaniniSticker 86

SELE, AARON
92 O-Pee-Chee 504
94 O-Pee-Chee 89,-DD 17

SELKIRK, GEORGE
37 O-Pee-Chee(V300) 108
36 WWGum(V355) 11

SELLERS, JEFF
87 Leaf 158

SELLERS, RICK
92 London/ProCards 637
92 London/SkyBox 418

SELLS, DAVE
74 O-Pee-Chee 37

SELLS, GEORGE
90 Hamilton/Best 9
90 Hamilton/Star 23

SELMA, DICK
66 O-Pee-Chee 67
69 O-Pee-Chee 197
70 O-Pee-Chee 24
71 O-Pee-Chee 705
73 O-Pee-Chee 632

SEMBERA, CARROLL
67 O-Pee-Chee 136

SEMA, JOE
93 Welland/ClassicBest 26

SEMINARA, FRANK
93 O-Pee-Chee 282

SENCION, PABLO
97 St.Catharines/Best 26

SEPTIMO, FELIX
91 St.Catharines/ProCards 3409

SERNA, PAUL
85 Calgary/Cramer 79

SERVAIS, SCOTT
92 O-Pee-Chee 437
93 O-Pee-Chee 339

SERRA, ARMANDO
88 St.Catharines/ProCards 2037

SEVEREID, HENRY
21 Neilson's(V61) 25
23 WillardsChocolate(V100)145

SEVERINSEN, AL
70 O-Pee-Chee 477
71 O-Pee-Chee 747
72 O-Pee-Chee 274

SEVERNS, BILL
79 Vancouver/TCMA 21
80 Vancouver/TCMA 8

SEVERSON, RICH
71 O-Pee-Chee 103

SEWELL, JOE
20 MapleCrispette(V117) 12
21 Neilson's(V61) 12
23 WillardsChocolate(V100)146
33 WWGum(V353) 89

SEWELL, LUKE
33 WWGum(V353) 91
36 WWGum(V355) 62

SEYMOUR, CY
1912 ImperialTobacco(C46) 38

SEYMOUR, WINSTON
89 Welland/Pucko 21

SHAMSKY, ART
66 O-Pee-Chee 119
67 O-Pee-Chee 96
70 O-Pee-Chee 137
71 O-Pee-Chee 445
72 O-Pee-Chee 353

SHANAHAN, GREG
74 O-Pee-Chee 599

SHANKS, HOWARD S.
23 WillardsChocolate(V100)147

SHANNON, DAN
89 Hamilton/Star 23

SHANNON, MIKE
65 O-Pee-Chee 43
69 O-Pee-Chee 110
71 O-Pee-Chee 735

SHANNON, SCOTT
91 St.Catharines/ClassicBest 24
92 St.Catharines/ClassicBest 29
93 St.Catharines/ClassicBest 29

SHANNON, WILLIAM
52 LavalDairy 63

SHANTZ, BOBBY
75 O-Pee-Chee 190
62 ShirriffCoin 188

SHARON, DICK
74 O-Pee-Chee 48

SHARP, BILL
74 O-Pee-Chee 519
75 O-Pee-Chee 373
76 O-Pee-Chee 244

SHARPE, BAYARD
1912 ImperialTobacco(C46) 31

SHARPERSON, MIKE
90 O-Pee-Chee 117
91 O-Pee-Chee 53
92 O-Pee-Chee 627
93 O-Pee-Chee 346
93 PaniniSticker 217
87 TOR/FireSafety

SHATLEY, ANDY
96 St.Catharines/Best 25

SHAUGHNESSY, SHAG
36 WWGum(V355) 78

SHAW, BOB
73 O-Pee-Chee 646

SHAW, CURTIS
95 Edmonton/Macri
97 Calgary/Best 23

SHAW, DON
69 O-Pee-Chee 183
70 O-Pee-Chee 476
71 O-Pee-Chee 654
72 O-Pee-Chee 479

SHAW, ROBERT
1912 ImperialTobacco(C46) 83

SHAW, THEO
90 Calgary/CMC 20

SHAWKEY, BOB
21 Neilson's(V61) 39

SHCWARZ, JEFF
92 Vancouver/ProCards 2722

SHEELY, EARL
21 Neilson's(V61) 34
23 Neilson's 38
23 WillardsChocolate(V100)148

SHEETS, LARRY
90 FleerCdn. 189
88 O-Pee-Chee 327
89 O-Pee-Chee 98
90 O-Pee-Chee 708
91 O-Pee-Chee 281
86 opcSticker 308
87 opcSticker 229
88 opcSticker 230
89 opcSticker 239
86 opcTattoo 7
88 PaniniSticker 16
89 PaniniSticker 264

SHEFFIELD, GARY
90 FleerCdn. 336
90 O-Pee-Chee 718
91 O-Pee-Chee 68
92 O-Pee-Chee 695
93 O-Pee-Chee 317
94 O-Pee-Chee 45
93 opcPremier-StarPerf. 6
89 PaniniSticker 364

91 PaniniSticker 206
92 PaniniSticker 158,261
94 PaniniSticker 186
93 PostCdn. 163

SHELBY, JOHN
85 O-Pee-Chee 264
88 O-Pee-Chee 307
89 O-Pee-Chee 175
91 O-Pee-Chee 746
85 opcSticker 204
88 PaniniSticker 316
89 PaniniSticker 109

SHELDON, BOB
75 O-Pee-Chee 623
76 O-Pee-Chee 626

SHELDON, ROLAND
65 O-Pee-Chee 254
66 O-Pee-Chee 18

SHELDON, SCOTT
95 Edmonton/Macri

SHELLENBACK, JIM
70 O-Pee-Chee 389
71 O-Pee-Chee 351
74 O-Pee-Chee 657

SHERMAN, DARRELL
93 opcPremier 119

SHEPARD, LARRY
73 O-Pee-Chee 296
74 O-Pee-Chee 326

SHEPHERD, RON
87 O-Pee-Chee 117

SHERDEL, BILL
21 Neilson's(V61) 100
23 Neilson's 39

SHERIDAN, NEILL RAWLINGS
52 Parkhurst 16

SHERIDAN, PAT
90 FleerCdn. 71
86 O-Pee-Chee 240
90 O-Pee-Chee 422
84 opcSticker 286
85 opcSticker 272
88 PaniniSticker 58,59,97

SHERRILL, TIM
91 O-Pee-Chee 769

SHERRY, LARRY
62 PostCereal 111

SHERRY, NORM
78 Dimanche/DernièreHeure

SHINES, RAZOR
85 Leaf 164
86 O-Pee-Chee 132

SHINNERS, RALPH
23 WillardsChocolate(V100)149

SHIPANOFF, DAVE
86 Leaf 29
87 Edmonton/ProCards 2065

SHIPLEY, CRAIG
92 O-Pee-Chee 308
92 opcPremier 33
93 PaniniSticker 260
94 PaniniSticker 259

SHIRLEY, AL
92 O-Pee-Chee 306

SHIRLEY, BOB
80 O-Pee-Chee 248
81 O-Pee-Chee 49
82 O-Pee-Chee 33
89 St.Catharines/ProCards 2095

SHOCKER, URBAN
21 Neilson's(V61) 40
23 Neilson's 40
23 WillardsChocolate(V100)150

SHOCKLEY, COSTEN
65 O-Pee-Chee 107

SHOPAY, TOM
70 O-Pee-Chee 363
72 O-Pee-Chee 418

SHORE, RAYMOND E. "RAY"
52 Parkhurst 18

SHORT, CHRIS
68 O-Pee-Chee 7,139
70 O-Pee-Chee 270
71 O-Pee-Chee 511

SHOTTON, CRAIG
91 Welland/Best 15
91 Welland/ProCards 15
91 Welland/ClassicBest 21

SHOUSE, BRIAN
90 Welland/Pucko 28

SHOW, ERIC
90 FleerCdn. 169
85 Leaf 137
86 Leaf 111
83 O-Pee-Chee 68
84 O-Pee-Chee 238
85 O-Pee-Chee 118
86 O-Pee-Chee 209
87 O-Pee-Chee 354
89 O-Pee-Chee 147
90 O-Pee-Chee 239
91 O-Pee-Chee 613
92 O-Pee-Chee 132
83 opcSticker 330
84 opcSticker 162
85 opcSticker 156
87 opcSticker 112
88 PaniniSticker 400
89 PaniniSticker 196

SHOWALTER, BUCK
92 O-Pee-Chee 201

SHUMPERT, TERRY
91 O-Pee-Chee 322
92 O-Pee-Chee 483
91 opcPremier 108
92 PaniniSticker 95
91 ScoreAllStarFanfest 9

SIDDALL, JOE
93 Ottawa/ProCards 2439
94 Ottawa/ProCards 2901

SIEBERN, NORM
66 O-Pee-Chee 14
62 PostCereal 92
62 ShirriffCoin 85

SIEBERT, PAUL
75 O-Pee-Chee 614

SIEBERT, SONNY
65 O-Pee-Chee 96
67 O-Pee-Chee 95
68 O-Pee-Chee 8
71 O-Pee-Chee 710
72 O-Pee-Chee 290
73 O-Pee-Chee 14
74 O-Pee-Chee 548
75 O-Pee-Chee 328

SIEBLER, DWIGHT
67 O-Pee -Chee 164

SIERRA, RUBEN
90 FleerCdn. 314
87 Leaf 225
88 Leaf 206
88 O-Pee-Chee 319
89 O-Pee-Chee 53
90 O-Pee-Chee 185,390
91 O-Pee-Chee 535
92 O-Pee-Chee 700
93 O-Pee-Chee 243
94 O-Pee-Chee 195
91 opcPremier 109
92 opcPremier 66
87 opcSticker 10
88 opcSticker 234
89 opcSticker 242
88 PaniniSticker 209
89 PaniniSticker 457
90 PaniniSticker 162,203
91 PaniniSticker 257
92 PaniniSticker 798
93 PaniniSticker 21
94 PaniniSticker 112

SIEVERS, ROY
62 PostCereal 46
62 ShirriffCoin 66

SIEVERT, MARK
94 St.Catharines/Classic 21
94 St.Catharines/ProCards 3644
94 St.Catharines/ProCards 3643

SILVA, JOSE
97 Calgary/Best 24

SILVERA, CHARLIE
73 O-Pee-Chee 323
74 O-Pee-Chee 379

SILVERIO, TOM
72 O-Pee-Chee 213

SILVERMAN, AARON "ERNIE"
52 Parkhurst 2

SILVERMAN, ERIC
50 WWGum(V362) 19

SILVESTRI, KEN
73 O-Pee-Chee 237
74 O-Pee-Chee 634

SIMMONS, AL
33 WWGum(V353) 35
36 WWGum(V355) 77
39 WWGum(V351B)

SIMMONS, CURT
67 O-Pee-Chee 39
62 PostCereal 167

SIMMONS, GEORGE
1912 ImperialTobacco(C46) 75

SIMMONS, JOHN
53 Exhibits 35
52 Parkhurst 62
50 WWGum(V362) 5

SIMMONS, NELSON
88 Calgary/CMC 19
88 Calgary/ProCards 802

SIMMONS, SCOTT
91 Hamilton/ProCards 4038

SIMMONS, TED
85 Leaf 104
86 Leaf 167
88 Leaf 222
71 O-Pee-Chee 117
72 O-Pee-Chee 154
73 O-Pee-Chee 85
74 O-Pee-Chee 260
75 O-Pee-Chee 75
76 O-Pee-Chee 191,290
77 O-Pee-Chee 196
78 O-Pee-Chee 150
79 O-Pee-Chee 267
80 O-Pee-Chee 47
81 O-Pee-Chee 352
82 O-Pee-Chee 150
83 O-Pee-Chee 33,284
84 O-Pee-Chee 94,122
85 O-Pee-Chee 318
82 opcSticker 201
83 opcSticker 85
84 opcSticker 193,293
85 opcSticker 294
86 opcSticker 199
86 opcTattoo 4

SIMMS, MIKE
91 O-Pee-Chee 32
92 O-Pee-Chee 463
92 PaniniSticker 156

SIMONS, DOUG
91 opcPremier 110
92 O-Pee-Chee 82
93 Ottawa/ProCards 2435

SIMPSON, DICK
67 O-Pee-Chee 6

SIMPSON, JOE
84 Edmonton/Cramer 115

SIMPSON, SHELTON
90 Welland/Pucko 28

SIMPSON, WAYNE
71 O-Pee-Chee 68,339
73 O-Pee-Chee 428

SIMS, DUKE
66 O-Pee-Chee 169
67 O-Pee-Chee 3
70 O-Pee-Chee 275
71 O-Pee-Chee 172
72 O-Pee-Chee 63
73 O-Pee-Chee 304
74 O-Pee-Chee 398

SIMS, HARRY
52 LavalDairy 33

SINATRO, MATT
91 O-Pee-Chee 709
90 Calgary/CMC 13
90 Calgary/ProCards 654

SINGER, BILL
92 Nabisco 18
67 O-Pee-Chee 12
69 O-Pee-Chee 12
70 OPC 17,71,490,-Booklet 17
71 O-Pee-Chee 145
72 O-Pee-Chee 25
73 O-Pee-Chee 570
74 O-Pee-Chee 210
75 O-Pee-Chee 40
76 O-Pee-Chee 411
77 O-Pee-Chee 85

SINGER, TOM
90 St.Catharines/ProCards 3457

SINGLETON, DUANE
97 Vancouver/Best 26

SINGLETON, KEN
72 Dimanche/DernièreHeure
82 FBI BoxBottoms
92 Nabisco 3
71 O-Pee-Chee 16
72 O-Pee-Chee 425,426
73 O-Pee-Chee 232
74 O-Pee-Chee 25
75 O-Pee-Chee 125
76 O-Pee-Chee 175
77 O-Pee-Chee 19
78 O-Pee-Chee 80
79 O-Pee-Chee 324
80 O-Pee-Chee 178
81 O-Pee-Chee 281
82 O-Pee-Chee 2,290
83 O-Pee-Chee 85
84 O-Pee-Chee 165
85 O-Pee-Chee 326
82 opcSticker 136,144
83 opcSticker 28
84 opcSticker 206
85 opcSticker 201
71 ProStarPostcard
74 MTL/GeorgeWeston
93 MTL/McDonald's 19

SISK, DOUG
85 Leaf 187
84 O-Pee-Chee 21
85 O-Pee-Chee 315
85 opcSticker 103

SISK, TOMMIE
67 O-Pee-Chee 84
69 O-Pee-Chee 152
70 O-Pee-Chee 374

SISLER, DICK
53 Exhibits 62
65 O-Pee-Chee 158

SISLER, GEORGE
21 Neilson's(V61) 32
23 Neilson's 41
23 WillardsChocolate(V100)151
22 WilliamPaterson(V89) 4

SIZEMORE, TED
70 O-Pee-Chee 174
71 O-Pee-Chee 571
72 O-Pee-Chee 514
73 O-Pee-Chee 128
74 O-Pee-Chee 209
75 O-Pee-Chee 404
76 O-Pee-Chee 522
78 O-Pee-Chee 118
79 O-Pee-Chee 148
80 O-Pee-Chee 46

SKAFF, FRANK
52 Parkhurst 91

SKETT, WILL
96 St.Catharines/Best 26

SKJERPEN, TREVOR
94 Welland/Classic 22
94 Welland/ProCards 3497

SKIDMORE, ROE
71 O-Pee-Chee 121

SKINNER, BOB
73 O-Pee-Chee 12
74 O-Pee-Chee 489
62 PostCereal 171
62 ShirriffCoin 143

SKINNER, JOEL
90 FleerCdn. 501
89 O-Pee-Chee 127
90 O-Pee-Chee 54
91 O-Pee-Chee 783
92 O-Pee-Chee 378

SKOROCHOCKI, JOHN
82 Vancouver/TCMA 6

SKOWRON, BILL
65 O-Pee-Chee 70
62 PostCereal 1
62 ShirriffCoin 59

SKUBE, BOB
82 Vancouver/TCMA 1
85 Vancouver/Cramer 214

SKURLA, JOHN
90 Edmonton/CMC 12
90 Edmonton/ProCards 530

SLATON, JIM
73 O-Pee-Chee 628
74 O-Pee-Chee 371
75 O-Pee-Chee 281

76 O-Pee-Chee 163
77 O-Pee-Chee 29
78 O-Pee-Chee 146
80 O-Pee-Chee 10
83 O-Pee-Chee 114
84 O-Pee-Chee 104
84 opcSticker 302

SLAUGHT, DON
90 FleerCdn. 456
86 Leaf 155
85 O-Pee-Chee 159
86 O-Pee-Chee 24
87 O-Pee-Chee 308
89 O-Pee-Chee 238
90 O-Pee-Chee 26
91 O-Pee-Chee 221
92 O-Pee-Chee 524
85 opcSticker 279
86 opcSticker 243
87 opcSticker 241
89 PaniniSticker 403
94 PaniniSticker 238

SLAUGHTER, ENOS
50 PalmDairies

SLAUGHTER, GARLAND
89 Welland/Pucko 22

SLAYBACK, BILL
73 O-Pee-Chee 537

SLINE, FRED
1912 ImperialTobacco(C46) 9

SLOCUM, RON
71 O-Pee-Chee 274

SLOCUMB, HEATHCLIFF
92 O-Pee-Chee 576

SLUSARSKI, JOE
92 O-Pee-Chee 651

SLWY, JIM
82 Edmonton/TCMA 3

SMALL, AARON
95 TOR/OhHenry

SMALL, JEFF
93 Edmonton/ProCards 1146

SMALLEY, ROY (JR.)
76 O-Pee-Chee 70

SMALLEY, ROY (JR.)
86 Leaf 237
88 Leaf 233
76 O-Pee-Chee 70,657
79 O-Pee-Chee 110
80 O-Pee-Chee 296
81 O-Pee-Chee 115
82 O-Pee-Chee 197
83 O-Pee-Chee 38
84 O-Pee-Chee 305
85 O-Pee-Chee 26
86 O-Pee-Chee 156
87 O-Pee-Chee 4
82 opcSticker 207
83 opcSticker 96
85 opcSticker 237
87 opcSticker 282

SMILEY, JOHN
90 FleerCdn. 480
89 O-Pee-Chee 322
90 O-Pee-Chee 568
91 O-Pee-Chee 143
92 O-Pee-Chee 232
93 O-Pee-Chee 335
92 opcPremier 2
93 opcPremier 56
89 PaniniSticker 167
90 PaniniSticker 323

SMITH, ACKROYD
52 LavalDairy 77

SMITH, AL
62 PostCdn. Cereal 48
62 ShirriffCoin 29

SMITH, BERNIE
71 O-Pee-Chee 204

SMITH, BILL
61 Toronto/BeeHive

SMITH, BILLY
84 TOR/FireSafety
85 TOR/FireSafety
86 TOR/FireSafety
87 TOR/FireSafety
88 TOR/FireSafety

SMITH, BOB
61 Toronto/BeeHive

SMITH, BOBBY GENE
62 PostCereal 196
62 ShirriffCoin 176

SMITH, BOBBY GLEN
80 Vancouver/TCMA 5
81 Vancouver/TCMA 19

SMITH, BRICK
87 Calgary/ProCards 2320
88 Calgary/ProCards 803

SMITH, BRYN
90 FleerCdn. 361
86 GeneralMills
87 GeneralMills
85 Leaf 171
86 Leaf 174
87 Leaf 60
88 Leaf 129
82 O-Pee-Chee 118
83 O-Pee-Chee 234
84 O-Pee-Chee 77
85 O-Pee-Chee 88
86 O-Pee-Chee 299
87 O-Pee-Chee 281
88 O-Pee-Chee 161
89 O-Pee-Chee 131
90 O-Pee-Chee 352
91 O-Pee-Chee 743
92 O-Pee-Chee 31
85 opcSticker 90
86 opcSticker 79
87 opcSticker 83
86 opcTattoo 22
88 PaniniSticker 320
89 PaniniSticker 116
87 StuartBakery 8
82 MTL/Hygrade
83 MTL/StuartBakery 29
84 MTL
84 MTL/StuartBakery 21
86 MTL/ProvigoFoods 19
86 MTL/ProvigoFoods-Poster

SMITH, CHAD
92 Hamilton/ClassicBest 3

SMITH, CHARLEY
65 O-Pee-Chee 22
62 ShirriffCoin 135

SMITH, DAVE
90 FleerCdn. 238
87 Leaf 224
81 O-Pee-Chee 287
82 O-Pee-Chee 297
83 O-Pee-Chee 247
86 O-Pee-Chee 222
87 O-Pee-Chee 50
88 O-Pee-Chee 73
89 O-Pee-Chee 305
90 O-Pee-Chee 746
91 O-Pee-Chee 215
92 O-Pee-Chee 601
91 opcPremier 111
86 opcSticker 31
88 opcSticker 26
89 opcSticker 13
88 PaniniSticker 290
89 PaniniSticker 87
90 PaniniSticker 257
85 Edmonton/Cramer 16

SMITH, DAVE WAYNE
84 Edmonton/Cramer 103
86 Edmonton/ProCards no#

SMITH, DWIGHT
90 FleerCdn. 42
90 O-Pee-Chee 311
91 O-Pee-Chee 463
92 O-Pee-Chee 168
90 PaniniSticker 235
91 PaniniSticker 47
94 PaniniSticker 157

SMITH, EARL L.
23 Neilson's 42
23 WillardsChocolate(V100)152

SMITH, EARL S.
23 WillardsChocolate(V100)153

SMITH, GEORGE A.
23 WillardsChocolate(V100)154

SMITH, GREG
90 FleerCdn. 643
91 O-Pee-Chee 560

SMITH, HAL
62 PostCereal 181
62 ShirriffCoin 190

SMITH, JACK
21 Neilson's(V61) 75

SMITH, JACK
93 Calgary/ProCards 1174

SMITH, JOHN W.
23 WillardsChocolate(V100)155

SMITH, KEITH
89 Vancouver/CMC 13
89 Vancouver/ProCards 578
90 Vancouver/CMC 19
90 Vancouver/ProCards 496

SMITH, KEILAN
94 St.Catharines/Classic 22
94 St.Catharines/ProCards 3645

SMITH, LARRY
89 Welland/Pucko 31
93 Welland/ClassicBest 29
94 Welland/Classic 30
94 Welland/ProCards 3512

SMITH, LEE
90 FleerCdn. 287
86 GeneralMills
85 Leaf 128
86 Leaf 64
87 Leaf 80
84 O-Pee-Chee 176
85 O-Pee-Chee 43
86 O-Pee-Chee 355
87 O-Pee-Chee 23
88 O-Pee-Chee 240
89 O-Pee-Chee 149
90 O-Pee-Chee 495
91 O-Pee-Chee 660
92 O-Pee-Chee 565
93 O-Pee-Chee 324
92 opcPremier 190
84 opcSticker 44
85 opcSticker 41
86 opcSticker 56
87 opcSticker 56
88 opcSticker 64,-SuperStar 33
89 opcSticker 251
86 opcTattoo 1
88 PaniniSticker 256
89 PaniniSticker 272
90 PaniniSticker 14
91 PaniniSticker 39
92 PaniniSticker 179
93 PaniniSticker 160,192

SMITH, LONNIE
90 FleerCdn. 593
85 Leaf 225
86 Leaf 188
81 O-Pee-Chee 317
82 O-Pee-Chee 127
83 O-Pee-Chee 273
84 O-Pee-Chee 113
85 O-Pee-Chee 255
86 O-Pee-Chee 7
90 O-Pee-Chee 152
91 O-Pee-Chee 306
92 O-Pee-Chee 467
83 opcSticker 283
84 opcSticker 140
85 opcSticker 139
86 opcSticker 264
87 opcSticker 262
88 PaniniSticker 1111
90 PaniniSticker 227
91 PaniniSticker 24
92 PaniniSticker 168
91 PaniniTopFifteen 83

SMITH, MARK
90 Hamilton/Best 7
90 Hamilton/Star 24

SMITH, MAYO
69 O-Pee-Chee 40
70 O-Pee-Chee 313

SMITH, MIKE
90 O-Pee-Chee 249,552

SMITH, OZZIE
88 FantasticSam's
90 FleerCdn. 260
85 GeneralMills
86 GeneralMills
87 GeneralMills
93 HumptyDumpty 50
85 Leaf 60
86 Leaf 47
87 Leaf 5,108
88 Leaf 115
92 McDonald's 26
79 O-Pee-Chee 52
80 O-Pee-Chee 205
81 O-Pee-Chee 254
82 O-Pee-Chee 95
83 O-Pee-Chee 14
84 O-Pee-Chee 130
85 O-Pee-Chee 191
86 O-Pee-Chee 297
87 O-Pee-Chee 107
88 O-Pee-Chee 39
89 O-Pee-Chee 230
90 O-Pee-Chee 400,590
91 O-Pee-Chee 130
92 O-Pee-Chee 760
93 O-Pee-Chee 313
94 O-Pee-Chee 181
91 opcPremier 112
92 opcPremier 84
82 opcSticker 104
83 opcSticker 168,180,186,288
84 opcSticker 144,187
85 opcSticker 137,181
86 opcSticker 11,46,153
87 opcSticker 46,162
88 opcSticker 53
89 opcSticker 44,161
89 opcSticker-SuperStar 12,45
86 opcTattoo 16
88 PaniniSticker 235,393
89 PaniniSticker 186,235
90 PaniniSticker 206,338
91 PaniniSticker 34,161
92 PaniniSticker 175,284
93 PaniniSticker 194
94 PaniniSticker 248
91 PaniniTopFifteen 103
91 PetroCanada 18
91 PostCdn. 6
92 PizzaHut/DietPepsi 19
91 PostCdn. 8
92 PostCdn. 6
93 PostCdn. 17
87 StuartBakery 11

SMITH, PETE
90 FleerCdn. 594
89 O-Pee-Chee 388
90 O-Pee-Chee 771
91 O-Pee-Chee 383
92 O-Pee-Chee 226
93 O-Pee-Chee 222
89 opcSticker 31
89 PaniniSticker 36

SMITH, RANDY
94 St.Catharines/Classic 23
95 St.Catharines/TimHortons 8

SMITH, REGGIE
68 O-Pee-Chee 61
70 O-Pee-Chee 62,215
71 O-Pee-Chee 305
72 O-Pee-Chee 88
73 O-Pee-Chee 40
74 O-Pee-Chee 285
75 O-Pee-Chee 490
76 O-Pee-Chee 215
77 O-Pee-Chee 223
78 O-Pee-Chee 57
79 O-Pee-Chee 243
80 O-Pee-Chee 350
81 O-Pee-Chee 75
82 O-Pee-Chee 5,228
83 O-Pee-Chee 282,283
83 opcSticker 12,302

SMITH, ROY
90 FleerCdn. 386
90 O-Pee-Chee 672
91 O-Pee-Chee 503
90 PaniniSticker 107

SMITH, STEVE
94 Calgary/Procards 804

SMITH, TOM
52 Laval Dairy 70

SMITH, TOMMY
74 O-Pee-Chee 606
75 O-Pee-Chee 619
77 O-Pee-Chee 92

SMITH, TONY
1912 ImperialTobacco(C46) 32

SMITH, WILLIE
65 O-Pee-Chee 85
69 O-Pee-Chee 198
70 O-Pee-Chee 318
71 O-Pee-Chee 457

SMITH, ZANE
90 FleerCdn. 362
86 Leaf 222
86 O-Pee-Chee 167
87 O-Pee-Chee 226
88 O-Pee-Chee 297
89 O-Pee-Chee 339

90 O-Pee-Chee 48
91 O-Pee-Chee 441
92 O-Pee-Chee 345
93 O-Pee-Chee 170
88 opcSticker 40
89 opcSticker 27
88 PaniniSticker 240
93 PaniniSticker 278
94 PaniniSticker 239
91 PaniniTopFifteen 66

SMITHSON, MIKE
90 FleerCdn. 288
86 Leaf 73
85 O-Pee-Chee 359
86 O-Pee-Chee 101
87 O-Pee-Chee 225
88 O-Pee-Chee 389
90 O-Pee-Chee 188
85 opcSticker 301
86 opcSticker 282
87 opcSticker 275
86 opcTattoo 10

SMOLTZ, JOHN
93 Ben'sDisk 8
90 FleerCdn. 595
93 HumptyDumpty 27
90 O-Pee-Chee 535
91 O-Pee-Chee 157
92 O-Pee-Chee 245
93 O-Pee-Chee 364
94 O-Pee-Chee 39
90 PaniniSticker 228
91 PaniniSticker 26
94 PaniniSticker 151

SMYTHE, HARRY
36 WWGum(V355) 79

SNELL, NATE
86 Leaf 166

SNELLING, ALLEN
96 St.Catharines/Best 27

SNIDER, DUKE
62 PostCereal 114
62 ShirriffCoin 215

SNOW, J.T.
94 O-Pee-Che 55, -DD 9
93 opcPremier 70
94 PaniniSticker 43
94 Vancouver/ProCards 1872

SNYDER, BRIAN
85 Calgary/Cramer 92

SNYDER, CORY
90 FleerCdn. 502
87 Leaf 157
88 Leaf 125
87 O-Pee-Chee 192
88 O-Pee-Chee 169
89 O-Pee-Chee 80
90 O-Pee-Chee 770
91 O-Pee-Chee 323
93 O-Pee-Chee 250
87 opcSticker 213
88 opcSticker 208,-SStar 53
89 opcSticker 210
88 PaniniSticker 80
89 PaniniSticker 329
90 PaniniSticker 56
91 PaniniSticker 221
93 PaniniSticker 242
94 PaniniSticker 204

SNYDER, FRANK
21 Neilson's(V61) 94
22 WilliamPaterson(V89) 33

SNYDER, RUSS
65 O-Pee-Chee 204
69 O-Pee-Chee 201
70 O-Pee-Chee 347
71 O-Pee-Chee 653
62 ShirriffCoin 206

SODERHOLM, ERIC
73 O-Pee-Chee 577
74 O-Pee-Chee 503
75 O-Pee-Chee 54
76 O-Pee-Chee 214
78 O-Pee-Chee 21
79 O-Pee-Chee 93

SOFF, RAY
87 O-Pee-Chee 96
92 Edmonton/SkyBox 166

SOFIELD, RICK
81 O-Pee-Chee 278

SOJO, LUIS
90 O-Pee-Chee 594
91 O-Pee-Chee 26
92 O-Pee-Chee 206
93 O-Pee-Chee 338
91 opcPremeir 114
92 PaniniSticker 6
93 PaniniSticker 28
93 TOR/Dempster's 24
93 TOR/FireSafety
94 Calgary/ProCards 799
92 Edmonton/SkyBox 167

SOLAITA, TONY
79 Dimanche/DernièreHeure
75 O-Pee-Chee 389
76 O-Pee-Chee 121
80 O-Pee-Chee 212

SOLOMON, BUDDY (SOLOMON)
75 O-Pee-Chee 624
79 O-Pee-Chee 74

SOLTERS, JULIUS
34 WWGum(V354) 77

SORENSEN, LARY
79 O-Pee-Chee 152
80 O-Pee-Chee 84
82 O-Pee-Chee 136
83 O-Pee-Chee 48
84 O-Pee-Chee 286
84 opcSticker 259

SORRELL, BILL
71 O-Pee-Chee 17

SORRELL, VICTOR
33 WWGum(V353) 15
36 WWGum(V355) 21

SORRENTO, PAUL
91 O-Pee-Chee 654
92 O-Pee-Chee 546
93 PaniniSticker 55
94 PaniniSticker 60

SOSA, ELIAS
79 Dimanche/DernièreHeure
80 Dimanche/DernièreHeure
74 O-Pee-Chee 54
75 O-Pee-Chee 398
76 O-Pee-Chee 364
80 O-Pee-Chee 153
81 O-Pee-Chee 181
82 O-Pee-Chee 116

SOSA, JOSE
76 O-Pee-Chee 591

SOSA, SAMMY
90 FleerCdn. 548
90 O-Pee-Chee 692
91 O-Pee-Chee 414
92 O-Pee-Chee 94
94 O-Pee-Chee 161
92 opcPremier 120
91 Paninisticker 316
92 PaniniSticker 129
93 PaniniSticker 207
94 PaniniSticker 158

SOTO, MARIO
85 General Mills
85 Leaf 19
86 Leaf 119
87 Leaf 140
83 O-Pee-Chee 215
84 O-Pee-Chee 160
85 O-Pee-Chee 131
86 O-Pee-Chee 28
87 O-Pee-Chee 11
83 opcSticker 234
84 opcSticker 51
85 opcSticker 446
86 opcSticker 136
86 opcTattoo 12

SOTO, TOM
81 Vancouver/TCMA 23

SOUTHWORTH, BILL
23 Neilson's 43

SPADE, MATTHEW
94 Welland/Classic 23
94 Welland/ProCards 3498

SPAHN, WARREN
53 Exhibits 32
65 O-Pee-Chee 205
66 O-Pee-Chee 115
73 O-Pee-Chee 449
60 opcTattoo 49

SPAGNOLA, GLENN
89 Calgary/CMC 10
89 Calgary/ProCards 527

SPANGLER, AL
65 O-Pee-Chee 164
66 O-Pee-Chee 173
74 O-Pee-Chee 354
62 PostCereal 157
62 ShirriffCoin 196

SPARKS, GREG
92 London/ProCards 647
92 London/SkyBox 419

SPARMA, JOE
67 O-Pee-Chee 13
70 O-Pee-Chee 243

SPEAKER, TRISTRAM E.
22 WilliamPaterson(V89) 13
23 WillardsChocolate(V100)156
29 WWGum(V354) 29

SPEHR, TIM
92 O-Pee-Chee 342
96 MTL/Disk

SPEIER, CHRIS
80 Dimanche/DernièreHeure
83 Dimanche/DernièreHeure
90 FleerCdn. 72
72 O-Pee-Chee 165,166
73 O-Pee-Chee 273,345
74 O-Pee-Chee 129,335
75 O-Pee-Chee 505
76 O-Pee-Chee 630
77 O-Pee-Chee 53
78 O-Pee-Chee 232
79 O-Pee-Chee 221
80 O-Pee-Chee 168
81 O-Pee-Chee 97,-Poster 3
82 O-Pee-Chee 198
83 O-Pee-Chee 121
84 O-Pee-Chee 328
86 O-Pee-Chee 212
90 O-Pee-Chee 753
82 opcSticker 58
83 opcSticker 258
84 opcSticker 95
77 MTL
77 MTL/RedpathSugar
82 MTL/Hygrade
82 MTL/Zellers
83 MTL
83 MTL/StuartBakery 27
84 MTL
84 MTL/StuartBakery 27

SPENCE, BOB
71 O-Pee-Chee 186

SPENCER, DARYL
62 PostCereal 103
62 ShirriffCoin 178

SPENCER, EDWARD
1912 ImperialTobacco(C46) 81

SPENCER, GLENN
34 WWGum(V354) 37

SPENCER, JIM
70 O-Pee-Chee 255
71 O-Pee-Chee 78
72 O-Pee-Chee 419
73 O-Pee-Chee 319
74 O-Pee-Chee 580
75 O-Pee-Chee 387
76 O-Pee-Chee 83
77 O-Pee-Chee 46
78 O-Pee-Chee 122
79 O-Pee-Chee 315
80 O-Pee-Chee 147
81 O-Pee-Chee 209
82 O-Pee-Chee 88
82 opcSticker 223

SPENCER, TROY
52 LavalDairy 66

SPERRING, ROB
76 O-Pee-Chee 323

SPIERS, BILL
90 FleerCdn. 337
90 O-Pee-Chee 538
91 O-Pee-Chee 284
92 O-Pee-Chee 742
93 O-Pee-Chee 323
91 PaniniSticker 207
92 PaniniSticker 38
93 PaniniSticker 38

SPIEZIO, ED
67 O-Pee-Chee 127
71 O-Pee-Chee 6
72 O-Pee-Chee 504

SPIKES, CHARLIE
73 O-Pee-Chee 614
74 O-Pee-Chee 58
75 O-Pee-Chee 135
76 O-Pee-Chee 408

SPILLNER, DAN
75 O-Pee-Chee 222
76 O-Pee-Chee 557
82 O-Pee-Chee 1
83 O-Pee-Chee 278
84 O-Pee-Chee 91
83 opcSticker 59

SPINKS, SCIPIO
70 O-Pee-Chee 492
71 O-Pee-Chee 747
72 O-Pee-Chee 202
73 O-Pee-Chee 417
74 O-Pee-Chee 576

SPLITTORFF, PAUL
71 O-Pee-Chee 247
72 O-Pee-Chee 315
73 O-Pee-Chee 48
74 O-Pee-Chee 225
75 O-Pee-Chee 340
76 O-Pee-Chee 43
77 O-Pee-Chee 41
79 O-Pee-Chee 90
80 O-Pee-Chee 214
82 O-Pee-Chee 126
84 opcSticker 281

SPOHRER, AL
33 WWGum(V353) 94

SPOLJARIC, PAUL
95 TOR/OhHenry
97 TOR/Sizzler 17

SPRAGUE, EDWARD N.
72 O-Pee-Chee 121
75 O-Pee-Chee 76

SPRAGUE, ED
96 HitTheBooks
98 HitTheBooks
92 O-Pee-Chee 516
93 OPC 203, -WSHero 3
93 OPC-WSChamp 13
94 O-Pee-Chee 265, -TOR 7
91 ScoreAllStarFanfest 7
91 TOR/Score 26
93 TOR/Dempster's 8
93 TOR/Donruss 11
93 TOR/FireSafety
93 TOR/McDonalds 14,29
94 TOR
95 TOR/OhHenry
96 TOR/OhHenry
97 TOR/Sizzler 4

SPRIGGS, GEORGE
71 O-Pee-Chee 411

SPRINGER, RUSS
93 Vancouver/ProCards 2597
94 Vancouver/ProCards 1865

SPRINGER, STEVE
91 Calgary/LineDrive 72
91 Calgary/ProCards 524
89 Vancouver/CMC 12
89 Vancouver/ProCards 592

SQUIRES, MIKE
85 O-Pee-Chee 278
89 TOR/FireSafety
90 TOR/FireSafety
91 TOR/FireSafety

STAEHLE, MARV
65 O-Pee-Chee 41
66 O-Pee-Chee 164
71 O-Pee-Chee 663
71 MTL/LaPizzaRoyale

STAFFORD, BILL
65 O-Pee-Chee 281
62 PostCereal 13

STAGGS, STEVE
78 O-Pee-Chee 94

STAHL, LARRY
66 O-Pee-Chee: 107
70 O-Pee-Chee 494
71 O-Pee-Chee 711
73 O-Pee-Chee 533
74 O-Pee-Chee 507

STAHLHOEFER, LARRY
92 Welland/ClassicBest 22

STAHOVIAK, SCOTT
92 O-Pee-Chee 66

STAIGER, ROY
76 O-Pee-Chee 592

STAIRS, MATT
92 MTL/Durivage 16
93 Ottawa/ProCards 2448

STALLARD, TRACY
66 O-Pee-Chee 7

STALLER, GEORGE
73 O-Pee-Chee 136
74 O-Pee-Chee 306

STANGE, LEE
67 O-Pee-Chee 99
69 O-Pee-Chee 148
70 O-Pee-Chee 447
71 O-Pee-Chee 311
73 O-Pee-Chee 131
74 O-Pee-Chee 403

STANHOUSE, DON
77 Dimanche/DernièreHeure
73 O-Pee-Chee 352
75 O-Pee-Chee 493
77 O-Pee-Chee 63
78 O-Pee-Chee 162
81 O-Pee-Chee 24
77 MTL
77 MTL/RedpathSugar

STANICEK, PETE
89 O-Pee-Chee 317
89 opcSticker 232
89 PaniniSticker 265

STANKIEWICZ, ANDY
92 O-Pee-Chee 179
93 O-Pee-Chee 291
93 PaniniSticker 149

STANKY, EDDIE
53 Exhibits 9
67 O-Pee-Chee 81

STANLEY, BOB
90 FleerCdn. 289
79 O-Pee-Chee 314
80 O-Pee-Chee 35
81 O-Pee-Chee 296
82 O-Pee-Chee 289
83 O-Pee-Chee 242
84 O-Pee-Chee 320
85 O-Pee-Chee 204
86 O-Pee-Chee 158
87 O-Pee-Chee 175
88 O-Pee-Chee 369
84 opcSticker 220
85 opcSticker 215
86 opcSticker 253
87 opcSticker 245
89 opcSticker 258
88 PaniniSticker 23

STANLEY, FRED
72 O-Pee-Chee 59
74 O-Pee-Chee 423
75 O-Pee-Chee 503
76 O-Pee-Chee 429

STANLEY, MICKEY
68 O-Pee-Chee 129
69 O-Pee-Chee 13
70 O-Pee-Chee 383
71 O-Pee-Chee 524
72 O-Pee-Chee 385
73 O-Pee-Chee 88
74 O-Pee-Chee 530
75 O-Pee-Chee 141
76 O-Pee-Chee 483
79 O-Pee-Chee 368

STANLEY, MIKE
88 O-Pee-Chee 219
89 O-Pee-Chee 123
90 O-Pee-Chee 92
91 O-Pee-Chee 409
94 O-Pee-Chee 95
88 opcSticker 238
89 opcSticker 244
88 PaniniSticker 199
94 PaniniSticker 104

STANTON, LEROY
72 O-Pee-Chee 141
73 O-Pee-Chee 18
74 O-Pee-Chee 594
75 O-Pee-Chee 342
76 O-Pee-Chee 152
78 O-Pee-Chee 123
79 O-Pee-Chee 275

STANTON, MIKE
90 FleerCdn. 596
90 O-Pee-Chee 694
91 O-Pee-Chee 514
92 O-Pee-Chee 788
85 opcSticker 343

STAPLETON, DAVE
81 O-Pee-Chee 81
82 O-Pee-Chee 93
83 O-Pee-Chee 239
84 O-Pee-Chee 249
83 opcSticker 35
84 opcSticker 221

STARGELL, WILLIE
92 Kellogg's 10
66 O-Pee-Chee 99
67 O-Pee-Chee 149
68 O-Pee-Chee 86
70 O-Pee-Chee 470
71 O-Pee-Chee 230
72 OPC 87,88,343,447,448
73 O-Pee-Chee 370
74 O-Pee-Chee 100,202,203
75 O-Pee-Chee 100
76 O-Pee-Chee 270
77 O-Pee-Chee 25
79 O-Pee-Chee 22
80 O-Pee-Chee 319
81 O-Pee-Chee 127
82 O-Pee-Chee 188,372
82 opcSticker 85
71 ProStarPostcard
71 ProStarPoster

STARK, MATT
87 TOR/FireSafety
91 Vancouver/LineDrive 646
91 Vancouver/ProCards 1597

STARRETTE, HERM
74 O-Pee-Chee 634

STATHAM, CLIFF
52 LavalDairy 2

STATON, DAVE
92 O-Pee-Chee 126
94 O-Pee-Chee 84

STATON, TARRENCE
94 Welland/Classic 24
94 Welland/ProCards 3510

STATON, T.J.
97 Calgary/Best 25

STATZ, ARNOLD
20 MapleCrispette(V117) 16
23 WillardsChocolate(V100)157

STAUB, RUSTY
73 Dimanche/DernièreHeure
92 Nabisco 25
66 O-Pee-Chee 106
67 O-Pee-Chee 73
69 O-Pee-Chee-Deckle 20
70 O-Pee-Chee-Booklet 18
71 O-Pee-Chee 289,560
74 O-Pee-Chee 629
75 O-Pee-Chee 90
76 O-Pee-Chee 120
77 O-Pee-Chee 88
78 O-Pee-Chee 188
79 O-Pee-Chee 228
80 O-Pee-Chee 347
82 O-Pee-Chee 270
83 O-Pee-Chee 1,51
84 O-Pee-Chee 224
85 O-Pee-Chee 190
83 opcSticker 14
84 opcSticker 287
71 MTL/ProStar
71 MTL/LaPizzaRoyale
93 MTL/McDonald's 20

STEARNS, JOHN
76 O-Pee-Chee 633
79 O-Pee-Chee 280
80 O-Pee-Chee 41
81 O-Pee-Chee 255
82 O-Pee-Chee 232
83 O-Pee-Chee 212
83 opcSticker 264

STEELMON, WYLEY
97 Lethbridge/Best 11

STEIN, BILL
76 O-Pee-Chee 131
77 O-Pee-Chee 20
78 O-Pee-Chee 147
79 O-Pee-Chee 372
80 O-Pee-Chee 121
82 opcSticker 118

STEIN, RANDY
79 Vancouver/TCMA 16

STEINBACH, TERRY
90 FleerCdn. 20
87 Leaf 34
88 O-Pee-Chee 44
89 O-Pee-Chee 304
90 O-Pee-Chee 145
91 O-Pee-Chee 625
92 O-Pee-Chee 234
93 O-Pee-Chee 268
94 O-Pee-Chee 117
89 opcSticker 152,165
88 PaniniSticker 166
89 PaniniSticker 236,419
90 PaniniSticker 143,205
91 PaniniSticker 191
92 PaniniSticker 14
93 PaniniSticker 14
94 PaniniSticker 113

STEIRER, RICK
84 Edmonton/Cramer 102

STELMASZEK, RICK
73 O-Pee-Chee 601
74 O-Pee-Chee 611
75 O-Pee-Chee 338

STENGEL, CASEY
20 MapleCrispette(V117) 15
65 O-Pee-Chee 187

STENHOUSE, MIKE
85 O-Pee-Chee 282
86 O-Pee-Chee 17
84 MTL
84 MTL/StuartBakery

STENNETT, RENNIE
72 O-Pee-Chee 219
73 O-Pee-Chee 348
74 O-Pee-Chee 426
75 O-Pee-Chee 336
76 O-Pee-Chee 6,425
77 O-Pee-Chee 129
78 O-Pee-Chee 25
79 O-Pee-Chee 365
81 O-Pee-Chee 257
82 O-Pee-Chee 84

STEPHEN, BUZZ
70 O-Pee-Chee 533

STEPHENS, BRYAN
50 WWGum(V362)

STEPHENS, GENE
62 PostCereal 95
62 ShirriffCoin 56

STEPHENS, RON
91 Vancouver/LineDrive 647
91 Vancouver/ProCards 1595
92 Vancouver/ProCards 2723
92 Vancouver/SkyBox 648

STEPHENSON, EARL
72 O-Pee-Chee 61

STEPHENSON, JACKSON R.
23 WillardsChocolate(V100)158

STEPHENSON, JERRY
65 O-Pee-Chee 74
69 O-Pee-Chee 172
71 O-Pee-Chee 488

STEPHENSON, JOHN
66 O-Pee-Chee 17
68 O-Pee-Chee 83
71 O-Pee-Chee 421

STEPHENSON, PHIL
90 O-Pee-Chee 584
91 O-Pee-Chee 726

STEPHENSON, RIGGS
20 MapleCrispette(V117) 26

STEVENS, DONALD
52 LavalDairy 98

STEVENS, EDWARD
52 Parkhurst 25

STEVENS, LEE
90 FleerCdn. 145
91 O-Pee-Chee 648
92 O-Pee-Chee 702
93 PaniniSticker 9
89 Edmonton/CMC 21
89 Edmonton/ProCards 554
90 Edmonton/CMC 13
90 Edmonton/ProCards 527
91 Edmonton/ProCards 1530

STEVENSON, STEVIE
36 WWGum(V355) 128

STEVERSON, TODD
93 O-Pee-Chee-DraftPick 4

STEWART, DAVE
90 Ben's/HolsumDisks
90 FleerCdn. 21
88 Leaf 217
84 O-Pee-Chee 352
88 O-Pee-Chee 353
89 O-Pee-Chee 145
90 O-Pee-Chee 270
91 O-Pee-Chee 580
92 O-Pee-Chee 410
93 O-Pee-Chee 294
94 O-Pee-Chee 12
91 opcPremier 115
93 opcPremier 45
84 opcSticker 360
87 opcSticker 167
88 opcSticker 168
89 opcSticker 163,-SStar 27
88 PaniniSticker 164
89 PaniniSticker 415
90 PaniniSticker 141,198
91 PaniniSticker 199,355
93 PaniniSticker 29
91 PaniniTopFifteen 62,71,93
94 Post
93 TOR
93 TOR/Dempster's 14
93 TOR/FireSafety
94 TOR
94 TOR/Sizzler 47

STEWART, JIM
66 O-Pee-Chee 63
67 O-Pee-Chee 124
71 O-Pee-Chee 644
73 O-Pee-Chee 351

STEWART, SAMMY
85 Leaf 98
81 O-Pee-Chee 262
82 O-Pee-Chee 279
83 O-Pee-Chee 347
85 O-Pee-Chee 213
84 opcSticker 25
86 opcSticker 235

STEWART, SHANNON
93 O-Pee-Chee-DraftPick 2
97 TOR/Sizzler 57

STEWART, WALTER
33 WWGum(V353) 75

STIEB, DAVE
91 Ben's/HolsumDisks 18
82 FBI BoxBottoms
90 FleerCdn. 93
85 GeneralMills
86 GeneralMills
87 GeneralMills
88 HostessDisk 17
85 Leaf 54,251
86 Leaf 68
87 Leaf 72
88 Leaf 80
80 O-Pee-Chee 42
81 O-Pee-Chee 5, -Poster 22
82 O-Pee-Chee 380, -Poster 6
83 O-Pee-Chee 130,202
84 O-Pee-Chee 134,289
85 O-Pee-Chee 240,-Poster 22
86 O-Pee-Chee 353
87 O-Pee-Chee 90
88 O-Pee-Chee 153
89 O-Pee-Chee 4
90 O-Pee-Chee 320
91 O-Pee-Chee 460
92 O-Pee-Chee 535
93 O-Pee-Chee 235
91 opcPremier 116
93 opcPremier 60
82 opcSticker 250
83 opcSticker 127
84 opcSticker 358
85 opcSticker 191,356
86 opcSticker 186
88 opcSticker 191
86 opcTattoo 23
88 PaniniSticker 215
89 PaniniSticker 463
90 PaniniSticker 173
91 PaniniSticker 344,360
92 PaniniSticker 32
92 PaniniTopFifteen 64
91 PostCdn. 16
87 StuartBakery
84 TOR/FireSafety
85 TOR/FireSafety
86 TOR/AultFoods
86 TOR/FireSafety
87 TOR/FireSafety
88 TOR
88 TOR/FireSafety
89 TOR/FireSafety
90 TOR/FireSafety
90 TOR/Hostess

91 TOR/FireSafety
91 TOR/Score 5
92 TOR/FireSafety
93 TOR/Donruss 29
96 TOR/OhHenry
97 TOR/Sizzler 33

STIGMAN, LEE
81 Vancouver/TCMA 20

STILLMAN, ROYLE
76 O-Pee-Chee 594

STILLWELL, KURT
90 FleerCdn. 118
89 O-Pee-Chee 217
90 O-Pee-Chee 222
91 O-Pee-Chee 478
92 O-Pee-Chee 128
92 opcPremier 177
89 opcSticker 266
88 PaniniSticker 276
90 PaniniSticker 79
91 PaniniSticker 279
92 PaniniSticker 97
93 PaniniSticker 259

STINSON, BOB
70 O-Pee-Chee 131
71 O-Pee-Chee 594
74 O-Pee-Chee 653
75 O-Pee-Chee 471
76 O-Pee-Chee 466
79 O-Pee-Chee 126
80 O-Pee-Chee 305

STOBBS, CHUCK
62 ShirriffCoin 90

STOCK, MILTON
21 Neilson's(V61) 56
23 Neilson's 44
23 WillardsChocolate(V100)159

STOCK, WES
65 O-Pee-Chee 117
67 O-Pee-Chee 74
73 O-Pee-Chee 179

STOCKER, KEVIN
94 O-Pee-Chee 5, -DD 4
94 PaniniSticker 231

STODDARD, BOB
85 Calgary/Cramer 90

STODDARD, TIM
81 O-Pee-Chee 91
83 O-Pee-Chee 217
85 O-Pee-Chee 393
87 O-Pee-Chee 321

STONE, ERIC
91 London/LineDrive 397
91 London/ProCards 1878

STONE, GEORGE
70 O-Pee-Chee 122
71 O-Pee-Chee 507
73 O-Pee-Chee 647
74 O-Pee-Chee 397
75 O-Pee-Chee 239
76 O-Pee-Chee 567

STONE, JEFF
88 O-Pee-Chee 154
85 opcSticker 116

STONE, JOHN
34 WWGum(V354) 89

STONE, RON
70 O-Pee-Chee 218
71 O-Pee-Chee 366

STONE, STEVE
72 O-Pee-Chee 327
73 O-Pee-Chee 167
74 O-Pee-Chee 486
75 O-Pee-Chee 388
76 O-Pee-Chee 378
78 O-Pee-Chee 46
79 O-Pee-Chee 115
81 O-Pee-Chee 101

STONEMAN, BILL
72 Dimanche/DernièreHeure
83 Dimanche/DernièreHeure
92 Nabisco 29
68 O-Pee-Chee 179
69 O-Pee-Chee 67
70 O-Pee-Chee 398
71 O-Pee-Chee 266
72 O-Pee-Chee 95
73 O-Pee-Chee 254
74 O-Pee-Chee 352
71 ProStarPostcard
71 ProStarPoster
71 MTL/ProStar
74 MTL/GeorgeWeston
93 MTL/McDonald's 29

STOTTLEMYRE, MEL (SR.)
68 O-Pee-Chee 120
69 O-Pee-Chee 9, -Deckle 21
70 O-Pee-Chee 70,100
71 O-Pee-Chee 615
72 O-Pee-Chee 325,492
73 O-Pee-Chee 520
74 O-Pee-Chee 44
75 O-Pee-Chee 183
91 O-Pee-Chee 58

STOTTLEMYRE, MEL (JR.)
90 O-Pee-Chee 263

STOTTLEMYRE, TODD
90 FleerCdn. 94
89 O-Pee-Chee 237
90 O-Pee-Chee 591
91 O-Pee-Chee 348
92 O-Pee-Chee 607
93 O-Pee-Chee 244
93 O-Pee-Chee-WSChamp 14
89 PaniniSticker 460
90 PaniniSticker 172
91 PaniniSticker 349
88 TOR/FireSafety
89 TOR/FireSafety
90 TOR/FireSafety
91 TOR/FireSafety
91 TOR/Score 6
92 TOR/FireSafety
93 TOR
93 TOR/Dempster's 5
93 TOR/Donruss 21
93 TOR/FireSafety

STRAHLER, MIKE
71 O-Pee-Chee 188
72 O-Pee-Chee 198
73 O-Pee-Chee 279

STRAIN, JOE
80 O-Pee-Chee 280

STRAMPE, BOB
73 O-Pee-Chee 604

STRANGE, DOUG
90 O-Pee-Chee 641
94 PaniniSticker 133

STRAWBERRY, DARRYL
91 Ben's/HolsumDisk 1
88 FantasticSam's 17
90 FleerCdn. 217
87 GeneralMills
85 Leaf 159
86 Leaf 131
87 Leaf 4,68
88 Leaf 220
92 McDonald's 7
84 O-Pee-Chee 182
85 O-Pee-Chee 126
86 O-Pee-Chee 80
87 O-Pee-Chee 379
88 O-Pee-Chee 178,L
89 O-Pee-Chee 300
90 O-Pee-Chee 600
91 O-Pee-Chee 200,402
92 O-Pee-Chee 550
93 O-Pee-Chee 375
91 opcPremier 117
92 opcPremier 179
84 opcSticker 385
85 opcSticker 100,179
86 opcSticker 95,150
87 opcSticker 103,159
88 opcSticker 96,151,-SStar 21
89 opcSticker 98,157,-SStar 53
86 opcTattoo 18
88 PaniniStick. 236,341-42,347
89 PaniniSticker 140,231
90 PaniniSticker 302
91 PaniniSticker 85,164
92 PaniniSticker 196
93 PaniniSticker 219
94 PaniniSticker 205
91 PaniniTopFifteen 10
92 PostCdn. 7
87 StuartBakery 1

STRICKLAND, JIM
73 O-Pee-Chee 122

STRINCEVICH, NICK
50 WWGum(V362) 17

STRIPP, JOE
34 WWGum(V354) 91

STROHMAYER, JOHN
71 O-Pee-Chee 232
73 O-Pee-Chee 457
71 MTL/ProStar

STROM, BRENT
73 O-Pee-Chee 612
74 O-Pee-Chee 359
75 O-Pee-Chee 643
76 O-Pee-Chee 84

STROUD, ED
68 O-Pee-Chee 31
70 O-Pee-Chee 506
71 O-Pee-Chee 217

STROUD, RALPH
1912 ImperialTobacco(C46) 58

STUART, DICK
65 O-Pee-Chee 5,280
62 PostCereal 169
62 ShirriffCoin 120

STUBBS, FRANKLIN
88 Leaf 182
87 O-Pee-Chee 292
88 O-Pee-Chee 198
90 O-Pee-Chee 56
91 O-Pee-Chee 732
92 O-Pee-Chee 329
87 opcSticker 72
88 PaniniSticker 308
91 PaniniSticker 13
92 PaniniSticker 35
93 PaniniSticker 37

STUBING, MOOSE
84 Edmonton/Cramer 97

SUAREZ, KEN
69 O-Pee-Chee 19
70 O-Pee-Chee 209
71 O-Pee-Chee 597
72 O-Pee-Chee 483
74 O-Pee-Chee 39

SUAREZ, ROMAN
94 GarciaPhoto 31

SUCH, DICK
71 O-Pee-Chee 283

SUDAKIS, BILL
70 O-Pee-Chee 341
71 O-Pee-Chee 253
73 O-Pee-Chee 586
74 O-Pee-Chee 63
75 O-Pee-Chee 291

SUESS, KEN
52 LavalDairy 32

SULLIVAN, HAYWOOD
62 PostCereal 99

SULLIVAN, JOHN
84 TOR/FireSafety
85 TOR/FireSafety
86 TOR/FireSafety
87 TOR/FireSafety
88 TOR/FireSafety
89 TOR/FireSafety
90 TOR/FireSafety
91 TOR/FireSafety
92 TOR/FireSafety
93 TOR/FireSafety

SULLIVAN, JOHN L.
23 WillardsChocolate(V100)160

SULLIVAN, MARC
87 O-Pee-Chee 66

SUMMA, HOWARD
20 MapleCrispette(V117) 6

SUMMERS, CHAMP
76 O-Pee-Chee 299
80 O-Pee-Chee 100
81 O-Pee-Chee 27

SUNDBERG, JIM
85 Leaf 78
86 Leaf 149
75 O-Pee-Chee 567
76 O-Pee-Chee 226
77 O-Pee-Chee 185
79 O-Pee-Chee 53
80 O-Pee-Chee 276
81 O-Pee-Chee 95
82 O-Pee-Chee 335
83 O-Pee-Chee 158
84 O-Pee-Chee 251
85 O-Pee-Chee 102,286
86 O-Pee-Chee 245
87 O-Pee-Chee 190
82 opcSticker 240
83 opcSticker 126
84 opcSticker 355
86 opcSticker 15,259
87 opcSticker 256

SURHOFF, B.J.
90 FleerCdn. 338
87 Leaf 28
88 Leaf 164
88 O-Pee-Chee 174
89 O-Pee-Chee 33
90 O-Pee-Chee 696
91 O-Pee-Chee 592
92 O-Pee-Chee 718
93 O-Pee-Chee 343
94 O-Pee-Chee 197
88 opcSticker 202,-SStar 57
89 opcSticker 200
88 PaniniSticker 120
89 PaniniSticker 368
90 PaniniSticker 93
91 PaniniSticker 203
92 PaniniSticker 34
93 PaniniSticker 36
94 PaniniSticker 87
86 Vancouver/ProCards

SUTCLIFFE, RICK
90 FleerCdn. 43
85 Leaf 139
86 Leaf 122
88 Leaf 91
81 O-Pee-Chee 191
82 O-Pee-Chee 141
84 O-Pee-Chee 245
85 O-Pee-Chee 72
86 O-Pee-Chee 330
88 O-Pee-Chee 372
89 O-Pee-Chee 394
90 O-Pee-Chee 640
91 O-Pee-Chee 415
93 O-Pee-Chee 381
92 opcPremier 98
82 opcSticker 20,61
84 opcSticker 254
85 opcSticker 35,97
86 opcSticker 61
88 opcSticker 61,-SuperStar 27
89 opcSticker 52
86 opcTattoo 21
88 PaniniSticker 257
89 PaniniSticker 51
90 PaniniSticker 233

SUTHERLAND, DARRELL
66 O-Pee-Chee 191

SUTHERLAND, GARY
68 O-Pee-Chee 98
71 O-Pee-Chee 434
72 O-Pee-Chee 211
73 O-Pee-Chee 572
74 O-Pee-Chee 428
75 O-Pee-Chee 522
76 O-Pee-Chee 113
71 MTL/LaPizzaRoyale
71 MTL/ProStar

SUTHERLAND, LEO
81 Edmonton/RedRooster 14
82 Edmonton/TCMA 11

SUTTER, BRUCE
82 FBI BoxBottoms
86 GeneralMills
85 Leaf 163
86 Leaf 192
78 O-Pee-Chee 196
79 O-Pee-Chee 238
80 O-Pee-Chee 4
81 O-Pee-Chee 9
82 O-Pee-Chee 260,347
83 O-Pee-Chee 150,151,266
84 O-Pee-Chee 243
85 O-Pee-Chee 370
86 O-Pee-Chee 133
87 O-Pee-Chee 344
89 O-Pee-Chee 11,M
82 opcSticker 15,94,130
83 opcSticker
166,187,209,284
84 opcSticker 145
85 opcSticker 135,172
86 opcSticker 37
89 opcSticker 25
86 opcTattoo 10
89 PaniniSticker 39

SUTTON,
1912 ImperialTobacco(C46) 24

SUTTON, DON
85 Leaf 16
86 Leaf 236
87 Leaf 153

68 O-Pee-Chee 103
69 O-Pee-Chee 216
71 O-Pee-Chee 361
73 O-Pee-Chee 10
74 O-Pee-Chee 220
75 O-Pee-Chee 220
76 O-Pee-Chee 530
77 O-Pee-Chee 24
78 O-Pee-Chee 96
79 O-Pee-Chee 80
80 O-Pee-Chee 228
82 O-Pee-Chee 305,306
83 O-Pee-Chee 145,146
84 O-Pee-Chee 35
85 O-Pee-Chee 172
86 O-Pee-Chee 335
87 O-Pee-Chee 259,G
89 O-Pee-Chee N
84 opcSticker 300
85 opcSticker 7,8,290
87 opcSticker 183
86 opcTattoo 7
88 PaniniSticker 37

SVEUM, DALE
87 Leaf 156
88 O-Pee-Chee 81
89 O-Pee-Chee 12
90 O-Pee-Chee 739
92 O-Pee-Chee 478
87 opcSticker 309
88 op Sticker 199
89 opcSticker 206
88 PaniniSticker 126
89 PaniniSticker 374
94 Calgary/ProCards 800
85 Vancouver/Cramer 209

SWAFFORD, DEREK
94 Welland/Classic 25
94 Welland/ProCards 3505

SWAN, CRAIG
74 O-Pee-Chee 602
76 O-Pee-Chee 494
79 O-Pee-Chee 170
80 O-Pee-Chee 1
81 O-Pee-Chee 189
83 O-Pee-Chee 292
83 opcSticker 262

SWAN, RUSS
91 O-Pee-Chee 739
92 O-Pee-Chee 588
95 Edmonton/Macri

SWANSON, STAN
72 O-Pee-Chee 331

SWEENEY, MIKE
94 Vancouver/ProCards 1877

SWEET, JONATHAN
94 Welland/Classic 26
94 Welland/ProCards 3500

SWEET, RICK
79 O-Pee-Chee 341

SWIFT, BILL
90 FleerCdn. 526
89 O-Pee-Chee 198
90 O-Pee-Chee 574
91 O-Pee-Chee 276
92 O-Pee-Chee 144
93 O-Pee-Chee 277
94 O-Pee-Chee 79
92 opcPremier 133
93 PaniniSticker 234
94 PaniniSticker 266

SWINDELL, GREG
90 FleerCdn. 503
87 Leaf 32
88 Leaf 158
88 O-Pee-Chee 22
89 O-Pee-Chee 315
90 O-Pee-Chee 595
91 O-Pee-Chee 445
92 O-Pee-Chee 735
93 O-Pee-Chee 392
94 O-Pee-Chee 157
92 opcPremier 44
93 opcPremier 86
88 PaniniSticker 70
89 PaniniSticker 320
90 PaniniSticker 59
92 PaniniSticker 52

SWINGLE, LEO RUSSEL (RUSS)
52 Parkhurst 94

SWINGLE, PAUL
93 Vancouver/ProCards 2598
96 Vancouver/Best 26

SWISHER, STEVE
75 O-Pee-Chee 63
76 O-Pee-Chee 173
77 O-Pee-Chee 23

SWOBODA, RON
66 O-Pee-Chee 35
67 O-Pee-Chee 186
68 O-Pee-Chee 114
70 O-Pee-Chee 431
71 O-Pee-Chee 665
72 O-Pee-Chee 8
73 O-Pee-Chee 314

SYKES, JAMIE
97 Lethbridge/Best 17

SZOTKIEWICZ, KEN
71 O-Pee-Chee 749

T

TABACHECK, MARTY
50 WWGum(V362) 23

TABARES, CARLOS
94 GarciaPhoto 49

TABLER, PAT
90 FleerCdn. 119
87 GeneralMills
85 Leaf 76
86 Leaf 52
87 Leaf 182
85 O-Pee-Chee 158
86 O-Pee-Chee 66
87 O-Pee-Chee 77
88 O-Pee-Chee 230
89 O-Pee-Chee 56
90 O-Pee-Chee 727
91 O-Pee-Chee 433
92 O-Pee-Chee 333
93 O-Pee-Chee 270
91 opcPremier 118
86 opcTattoo 8
88 PaniniSticker 81
89 PaniniSticker 359
87 StuartBakery 18
91 TOR/FireSafety
91 TOR/Score 19
92 TOR/FireSafety
93 TOR/Donruss 12

TALBOT, FRED
65 O-Pee-Chee 58
70 O-Pee-Chee 287

TABOR, JAMES
39 WWGum(V351B)

TAMARGO, JOHN
80 Dimanche/DernièreHeure
80 O-Pee-Chee 351
81 O-Pee-Chee 35

TAMAYO, OSMANI
94 GarciaPhoto 120

TAMULIS, VITO
36 WWGum(V355) 101

TANANA, FRANK
90 FleerCdn. 616
85 Leaf 9
86 Leaf 241
74 O-Pee-Chee 605
75 O-Pee-Chee 16
76 O-Pee-Chee 204,490
77 O-Pee-Chee 105
78 O-Pee-Chee 7,65
79 O-Pee-Chee 274
80 O-Pee-Chee 57
81 O-Pee-Chee 369
82 O-Pee-Chee 4
84 O-Pee-Chee 276
85 O-Pee-Chee 55
86 O-Pee-Chee 124
87 O-Pee-Chee 231
88 O-Pee-Chee 177
89 O-Pee-Chee 299
90 O-Pee-Chee 343
91 O-Pee-Chee 236
92 O-Pee-Chee 458
93 O-Pee-Chee 288
85 opcSticker 348
88 opcSticker 264,275
88 PaniniSticker 86
89 PaniniSticker 336
90 PaniniSticker 72
93 PaniniSticker 120

TANDERYS, JEFF
91 Hamilton/ClassicBest 12
91 Hamilton/ProCards 4039
92 Hamilton/ClassicBest 1

TANNER, CHUCK
71 O-Pee-Chee 661
72 O-Pee-Chee 98
73 O-Pee-Chee 356
74 O-Pee-Chee 221
75 O-Pee-Chee 276
76 O-Pee-Chee 656
61 Toronto/BeeHive

TAPANI, KEVIN
90 O-Pee-Chee 227
91 O-Pee-Chee 633
92 O-Pee-Chee 313
93 O-Pee-Chee 361
94 O-Pee-Chee 247
91 PaniniSticker 307

TARTABULL, DANNY
92 Ben'sDisk 13
90 FleerCdn. 120
87 Leaf 5,190
87 O-Pee-Chee 332
88 O-Pee-Chee 211
89 O-Pee-Chee 275
90 O-Pee-Chee 540
91 O-Pee-Chee 90
92 O-Pee-Chee 145
93 O-Pee-Chee 308
94 O-Pee-Chee 8
92 opcPremier 93
87 opcSticker 223,306
88 opcSticker 257
89 opcSticker 267
88 PaniniSticker 112
89 PaniniSticker 360
90 PaniniSticker 90
91 PaniniSticker 282
92 PaniniSticker 98
93 PaniniSticker 153
94 PaniniSticker 105
85 Calgary/Cramer 94

TARTABULL, JOSE
66 O-Pee-Chee 143
67 O-Pee-Chee 56
70 O-Pee-Chee 481

TASBY, WILLIE
62 PostCereal 70
62 ShirriffCoin 21

TATE, BENNIE
36 WWGum(V355) 80

TATE, RANDY
76 O-Pee-Chee 549

TATE, STU
90 FleerCdn. 643

TATUM, JARVIS
71 O-Pee-Chee 159

TATUM, KEN
71 O-Pee-Chee 601
73 O-Pee-Chee 463

TAUBENSEE, EDDIE
92 O-Pee-Chee 427
92 opcPremier 136
93 PaniniSticker 169

TAUSSIG, DON
62 ShirriffCoin 186

TAVERAS, FRANK
74 O-Pee-Chee 607
75 O-Pee-Chee 277
76 O-Pee-Chee 36
78 O-Pee-Chee 4
79 O-Pee-Chee 79
80 O-Pee-Chee 237
81 O-Pee-Chee 343
82 O-Pee-Chee 351
82 MTL/Hygrade

TAVERAS, JOSE
97 Lethbridge/Best 12

TAYLOR, BRIEN
92 O-Pee-Chee 6

TAYLOR, CARL
70 O-Pee-Chee 76
71 O-Pee-Chee 353
73 O-Pee-Chee 99
74 O-Pee-Chee 627

TAYLOR, CHUCK
70 O-Pee-Chee 119
71 O-Pee-Chee 606
72 O-Pee-Chee 407
73 O-Pee-Chee 176
74 O-Pee-Chee 412
75 O-Pee-Chee 58

TAYLOR, DANNY
36 WWGum(V355) 72

TAYLOR, DORN
87 Vancouver/ProCards 1621

TAYLOR, GARY
91 Hamilton/ClassicBest 14
91 Hamilton/ProCards 4055

TAYLOR, HAWK
68 O-Pee-Chee 52

TAYLOR, HERB
52 LavalDairy 24

TAYLOR, JOE
52 LavalDairy 57

TAYLOR, LUTHER
1912 ImperialTobacco(C46) 41

TAYLOR, RON
92 CanadianSpiritMedallion
66 O-Pee-Chee 174
69 O-Pee-Chee 72
70 O-Pee-Chee 419
71 O-Pee-Chee 687
72 O-Pee-Chee 234

TAYLOR, SAM
62 PostCereal 189
62 ShirriffCoin 164

TAYLOR, SCOTT
97 Calgary/Best 26

TAYLOR, TERRY
87 Calgary/ProCards 2325
88 Calgary/ProCards 781
90 Calgary/CMC 5
90 Calgary/ProCards 651

TAYLOR, TEX
52 LavalDairy 28

TAYLOR, TONY
67 O-Pee-Chee 126
69 O-Pee-Chee 108
70 O-Pee-Chee 324
71 O-Pee-Chee 246
72 O-Pee-Chee 511
73 O-Pee-Chee 29
75 O-Pee-Chee 574
76 O-Pee-Chee 624
62 PostCereal 193
62 ShirriffCoin 156

TAYLOR, WADE
91 O-Pee-Chee 562
91 opcPremier 119

TAYLOR, ZACK
33 WWGum(V353) 79

TEICH, MIKE
91 Welland/Best 27
91 Welland/ProCards 3573

TEJADA, WIL
89 O-Pee-Chee 391

TEJCEK, JOHN
94 Calgary/ProCards 803

TEJERO, FAUSTO
96 Vancouver/Best 27

TEKULVE, KENT
85 Leaf 119
76 O-Pee-Chee112
80 O-Pee-Chee 297
81 O-Pee-Chee 94
82 O-Pee-Chee 281
83 O-Pee-Chee 17,18
84 O-Pee-Chee 74
85 O-Pee-Chee 125
86 O-Pee-Chee 326
87 O-Pee-Chee 86
88 O-Pee-Chee P
89 O-Pee-Chee O
84 opcSticker 132
85 opcSticker 129
87 opcSticker 118
88 PaniniSticker 354

TELFORD, ANTHONY
91 O-Pee-Chee 653

TELLERS, DAVID
90 Welland/Pucko 30

TELLMANN, TOM
84 opcSticker 297

TEMPLE, JOHNNY
60 opcTattoo 50
62 PostCereal 38
62 ShirriffCoin 52

TEMPLETON, GARRY
90 FleerCdn. 170
86 Leaf 133
87 Leaf 63
77 O-Pee-Chee 84
78 O-Pee-Chee 51
79 O-Pee-Chee 181
80 O-Pee-Chee 308
81 O-Pee-Chee 144
82 O-Pee-Chee 288
83 O-Pee-Chee 336
84 O-Pee-Chee 173
85 O-Pee-Chee 124
86 O-Pee-Chee 90
87 O-Pee-Chee 325
88 O-Pee-Chee 264
90 O-Pee-Chee 481
91 O-Pee-Chee 253
92 O-Pee-Chee 772
82 opcSticker 96
83 opcSticker 291
84 opcSticker 151
85 opcSticker 151
86 opcSticker 110
87 opcSticker 110
88 opcSticker 113
86 opcTattoo 19
88 PaniniSticker 409
89 PaniniSticker 202
90 PaniniSticker 354
91 PaniniSticker 94

TENACE, GENE
70 O-Pee-Chee 21
71 O-Pee-Chee 338
72 O-Pee-Chee 189
73 O-Pee-Chee 524
74 O-Pee-Chee 79
75 O-Pee-Chee 535
76 O-Pee-Chee 165
77 O-Pee-Chee 82
78 O-Pee-Chee 35
79 O-Pee-Chee 226
80 O-Pee-Chee 355
81 O-Pee-Chee 29
82 O-Pee-Chee 166
83 O-Pee-Chee 252
90 TOR/FireSafety
91 TOR/FireSafety
92 TOR/FireSafety
93 TOR/FireSafety
95 TOR/OhHenry
96 TOR/OhHenry
97 TOR/Sizzler 28

TEPEDINO, FRANK
71 O-Pee-Chee 342
74 O-Pee-Chee 526
75 O-Pee-Chee 9

TERPKO, JEFF
77 MTL/RedpathSugar

TERRELL, JERRY
74 O-Pee-Chee 481
75 O-Pee-Chee 654
76 O-Pee-Chee 159

TERRELL, WALT
90 FleerCdn. 457
86 Leaf 123
87 Leaf 180
85 O-Pee-Chee 287
86 O-Pee-Chee 301
87 O-Pee-Chee 72
88 O-Pee-Chee 284
90 O-Pee-Chee 611
91 O-Pee-Chee 328
92 O-Pee-Chee 722
84 opcSticker 110
85 opcSticker 109
88 PaniniSticker 87

TERRY, BILL
33 WWGum(V353) 20
34 WWGum(V354) 53
36 WWGum(V355) 7

TERRY, RALPH
66 O-Pee-Chee 109
67 O-Pee-Chee 59
62 PostCereal 10
62 ShirriffCoin 77

TERRY, SCOTT
90 FleerCdn. 261
90 O-Pee-Chee 82
91 O-Pee-Chee 539
92 O-Pee-Chee 117

TEVLIN, CREIGHTON
79 Vancouver/TCMA 23

TETTLETON, MICKEY
90 FleerCdn. 190
90 O-Pee-Chee 275
91 O-Pee-Chee 385
92 O-Pee-Chee 29
93 O-Pee-Chee 334
94 O-Pee-Chee 32
89 opcSticker 231
89 PaniniSticker 259
90 PaniniSticker 8
91 PaniniSticker 239
92 PaniniSticker 104
93 PaniniSticker 113
94 PaniniSticker 68

TEUFEL, TIM
90 FleerCdn. 218
85 Leaf 97
85 O-Pee-Chee 239
86 O-Pee-Chee 91
90 O-Pee-Chee 764
91 O-Pee-Chee 302
92 O-Pee-Chee 413
85 opcSticker 303
86 opcSticker 280
88 PaniniSticker 341,342

TEUTSCH, MARK
81 Edmonton/RedRooster

TEWKSBURY, BOB
91 O-Pee-Chee 88
92 O-Pee-Chee 623
93 O-Pee-Chee 344
94 O-Pee-Chee 217
93 PaniniSticker 190
94 PaniniSticker 249

THEOBALD, RON
72 O-Pee-Chee 77

THEODORE, GEORGE
74 O-Pee-Chee 99

THEVENOW, TOMMY
33 WWGum(V353) 36

THIBDEAU, JOHN
69 O-Pee-Chee 189

THIGPEN, BOBBY
90 FleerCdn. 549
89 O-Pee-Chee 368
90 O-Pee-Chee 255
91 O-Pee-Chee 8,255,396,420
92 O-Pee-Chee 505
93 O-Pee-Chee 336
91 opcPremier 120
89 opcSticker 305
89 PaniniSticker 303
90 PaniniSticker 50
91 PaniniSticker 320
92 PaniniSticker 132
91 PaniniTopFifteen 85
91 PostCdn. 25

THOBE, STEVEN
94 Welland/Classic 27
94 Welland/ProCards 3504

THOMAS, ANDRES
90 FleerCdn. 597
88 O-Pee-Chee 13
89 O-Pee-Chee 358
90 O-Pee-Chee 358
91 O-Pee-Chee 111
87 opcSticker 39,305
88 opcSticker 41
89 opcSticker 26
89 PaniniSticker 43
90 PaniniSticker 229

THOMAS, DERREL
72 O-Pee-Chee 457
73 O-Pee-Chee 57
74 O-Pee-Chee 518
75 O-Pee-Chee 378
76 O-Pee-Chee 493
79 O-Pee-Chee 359
80 O-Pee-Chee 9
81 O-Pee-Chee 211
85 O-Pee-Chee 317
84 MTL
84 MTL/StuartBakery 28

THOMAS, FRANK
81 Vancouver/TCMA 6
82 Vancouver/TCMA 2
84 Vancouver/Cramer 33

THOMAS, FRANK E. (BIG HURT)
92 Ben'sDisk 11
93 HumptyDumpty 6
92 McDonald's 2
90 O-Pee-Chee 414
91 O-Pee-Chee 79
92 O-Pee-Chee 555
93 O-Pee-Chee 362
94 O-Pee-Chee 127, -AS 1
91 opcPremier 121
92 opcPremier 59
93 opcPremier-StarPerf. 1
92 PaniniSticker 125
93 PaniniSticker 136
94 PaniniSticker 51
94 PostCdn. 12
95 PostCdn. 11

THOMAS, FRANK J.
65 O-Pee-Chee 123
62 PostCereal 151
62 ShirriffCoin 104

THOMAS, GEORGE
65 O-Pee-Chee 83
67 O-Pee-Chee 184
71 O-Pee-Chee 678

THOMAS, GORMAN
86 Leaf 213
74 O-Pee-Chee 288
75 O-Pee-Chee 532
76 O-Pee-Chee 139
79 O-Pee-Chee 196
80 O-Pee-Chee 327
81 O-Pee-Chee 135
82 O-Pee-Chee 324
83 O-Pee-Chee 10
84 O-Pee-Chee 146
85 O-Pee-Chee 202
86 O-Pee-Chee 347
82 opcSticker 204
83 opcSticker 84
84 opcSticker 253
86 opcSticker 16
86 opcTattoo 22

THOMAS, JIM
89 Edmonton/CMC 22
89 Edmonton/ProCards 550

THOMAS, JOHN
90 Hamilton/Best 24
90 Hamilton/Star 25

THOMAS, LEE
65 O-Pee-Chee 111

THOMAS, MARK
89 Welland/Pucko 23

THOMAS, ROY
84 opcSticker 348
85 Calgary/Cramer 82
87 Calgary/ProCards 2321

THOMAS, STAN
76 O-Pee-Chee 148

THOMAS, TROY
88 Vancouver/CMC 18
88 Vancouver/ProCards 775

THOMAS, VERN
81 Edmonton/RedRooster 9

THOMASSON, GARY
74 O-Pee-Chee 18
75 O-Pee-Chee 529
76 O-Pee-Chee 261
79 O-Pee-Chee 202
80 O-Pee-Chee 70

THOME, JIM
92 O-Pee-Chee 768

THOMPSON, CHARLIE
53 Exhibits 40
52 Parkhurst 52
50 WWGum(V362) 18

THOMPSON, DANNY
71 O-Pee-Chee 127
72 O-Pee-Chee 368
73 O-Pee-Chee 443
74 O-Pee-Chee 168
75 O-Pee-Chee 249
76 O-Pee-Chee 111

THOMPSON, JASON
86 General Mills
87 GeneralMills
85 Leaf 89
77 O-Pee-Chee 64
78 O-Pee-Chee 212
79 O-Pee-Chee 33
80 O-Pee-Chee 83
81 O-Pee-Chee 373
83 O-Pee-Chee 209
84 O-Pee-Chee 355
85 O-Pee-Chee 22
86 O-Pee-Chee
83 opcSticker 276
84 opcSticker 128
85 opcSticker 125
86 opcSticker 129
86 MTL/ProvigoFoods 15

THOMPSON, LAFAYETTE
33 WWGum(V353) 13

THOMPSON, MIKE
73 O-Pee-Chee 564
76 O-Pee-Chee 536

THOMPSON, MILT
90 FleerCdn. 262
88 O-Pee-Chee 298
89 O-Pee-Chee 128
90 O-Pee-Chee 688
91 O-Pee-Chee 63
92 O-Pee-Chee 323
93 opcPremier 74
88 PaniniSticker 363
89 PaniniSticker 157
90 PaniniSticker 345
91 PaniniSticker 36

THOMPSON, RICH
86 O-Pee-Chee 242
90 O-Pee-Chee 474
86 opcSticker 215
86 Vancouver/ProCards

THOMPSON, ROBBY
90 FleerCdn. 73
87 Leaf 64
88 Leaf 120
88 O-Pee-Chee 208
89 O-Pee-Chee 15
90 O-Pee-Chee 325
91 O-Pee-Chee 705
92 O-Pee-Chee 475
93 O-Pee-Chee 3301
94 O-Pee-Chee 20
87 opcSticker 91,307
88 opcSticker 93
89 opcSticker 87
88 PaniniSticker 423
89 PaniniSticker 215
90 PaniniSticker 371
91 PaniniSticker 68
92 PaniniSticker 213
93 PaniniSticker 237
94 PaniniSticker 267
87 StuartBakery 13

THOMPSON, RYAN
93 O-Pee-Chee 351
94 O-Pee-Chee 135
93 opcPremier 79
94 PaniniSticker 223

THOMPSON, SCOT
80 O-Pee-Chee 298
86 O-Pee-Chee 93

THOMPSON, TIM
61 Toronto/BeeHive

THOMSON, ROB
89 London/ProCards 1379

THON, DICKIE
90 FleerCdn. 573
87 Leaf 196
84 O-Pee-Chee 344
85 O-Pee-Chee 44
86 O-Pee-Chee 166
89 O-Pee-Chee 181
90 O-Pee-Chee 269
91 O-Pee-Chee 439
92 O-Pee-Chee 557
92 opcPremier 19
93 opcPremier 16
84 opcSticker 64
85 opcSticker 63
86 opcSticker 33
86 opcTattoo 1
90 PaniniSticker 318
91 PaniniSticker 106
92 PaniniSticker 245

THORMAHLEN,HERBERT E.
23 WillardsChocolate(V100)161

THORMODSGARD, PAUL
78 O-Pee-Chee 73

THORNTON, ANDRE
85 Leaf 102
86 Leaf 129
74 O-Pee-Chee 604
75 O-Pee-Chee 39
76 O-Pee-Chee 26
78 O-Pee-Chee 114
79 O-Pee-Chee 140
80 O-Pee-Chee 278
81 O-Pee-Chee 128
82 O-Pee-Chee 161

83 O-Pee-Chee 344
84 O-Pee-Chee 115
85 O-Pee-Chee 272
86 O-Pee-Chee 59
87 O-Pee-Chee 327
82 opcSticker 174
83 opcSticker 55
84 opcSticker 255
85 opcSticker 244
86 opcSticker 208
86 opcTattoo 3

THORNTON, LOU
86 O-Pee-Chee 18
85 TOR/FireSafety

THORSON, BRIAN
81 Vancouver/TCMA 7
82 Vancouver/TCMA 24

THROOP, GEORGE
76 O-Pee-Chee 591

THURMAN, GARY
90 FleerCdn. 121
88 Leaf 44
90 O-Pee-Chee 276
92 O-Pee-Chee 494
89 PaniniSticker 348

THURMOND, MARK
90 FleerCdn. 191
85 Leaf 149
85 O-Pee-Chee 236
90 O-Pee-Chee 758

THURSTON, JERREY
97 Vancouver/Best 27

TIANT, LUIS
65 O-Pee-Chee 145
69 OPC 7,9,11,-Deckle 22
70 O-Pee-Chee 231
71 O-Pee-Chee 95
73 O-Pee-Chee 65,270
74 O-Pee-Chee 167
75 O-Pee-Chee 430
76 O-Pee-Chee 130
77 O-Pee-Chee 87
78 O-Pee-Chee 124
79 O-Pee-Chee 299
80 O-Pee-Chee 19
82 O-Pee-Chee 160
83 O-Pee-Chee 179

TIBBS, JAY
90 FleerCdn. 192
87 Leaf 207
87 O-Pee-Chee 9
88 O-Pee-Chee 282
90 O-Pee-Chee 677
86 MTL/ProvigoFoods

TIDROW, DICK
72 O-Pee-Chee 506
73 O-Pee-Chee 339
74 O-Pee-Chee 231
75 O-Pee-Chee 241
76 O-Pee-Chee 248
77 O-Pee-Chee 235
79 O-Pee-Chee 37
82 O-Pee-Chee 249
82 opcSticker 27
83 opcSticker 225

TIEFENAUER, BOB
65 O-Pee-Chee 23

TIERNEY, JAMES A.
23 WillardsChocolate(V100)162

TILLMAN, BOB
65 O-Pee-Chee 222
66 O-Pee-Chee 178
67 O-Pee-Chee 36
68 O-Pee-Chee 174
71 O-Pee-Chee 244

TIMLIN, MIKE
97 HitTheBooks
92 O-Pee-Chee 108
93 O-Pee-Chee 295
91 opcPremier 122
92 opcPremier 172
91 TOR/Score 7
92 TOR/FireSafety
93 TOR/Dempster's 25
93 TOR/Donruss 22
93 TOR/McDonald's 22
93 TOR/FireSafety
95 TOR/OhHenry
96 TOR/OhHenry
97 TOR/Sizzler 19

TIMMERMAN, TOM
71 O-Pee-Chee 296
72 O-Pee-Chee 239
73 O-Pee-Chee 413
74 O-Pee-Chee 327

TINGLEY, RON
92 O-Pee-Chee 388
89 PaniniSticker 316
93 PaniniSticker 3
85 Calgary/Cramer 97
90 Edmonton/CMC 23
90 Edmonton/ProCards 520
91 Edmonton/LineDrive 171
91 Edmonton/ProCards 1519

TINSLEY, LEE
92 O-Pee-Chee 656

TISCHINSKI, TOM
70 O-Pee-Chee 379
71 O-Pee-Chee 724

TOALE, JOHN
89 London/ProCards 1365
90 London/ProCards 1283

TOBIK, DAVE
83 O-Pee-Chee 186
85 Calgary/Cramer 87

TOBIN, JOHN
21 Neilson's(V61) 2
23 WillardsChocolate(V100)163

TOCA, JORGE LUIS
94 GarciaPhoto 71

TODD, JACKSON
81 O-Pee-Chee 142
82 O-Pee-Chee 327

TODD, JIM
75 O-Pee-Chee 519
76 O-Pee-Chee 221
79 O-Pee-Chee 46

TODT, PHIL
34 WWGum(V354) 39

TOLAN, BOB
65 O-Pee-Chee 116
66 O-Pee-Chee 179
68 O-Pee-Chee 84
70 O-Pee-Chee 409
71 O-Pee-Chee 190
72 O-Pee-Chee 3
73 O-Pee-Chee 335
74 O-Pee-Chee 535
75 O-Pee-Chee 402
76 O-Pee-Chee 56

TOLENTINO, JOSE
92 O-Pee-Chee 541
97 Calgary/Best 27

TOLIVER, FRED
90 O-Pee-Chee 423

TOLLESON, WAYNE
86 Leaf 59
87 O-Pee-Chee 224
88 O-Pee-Chee 133
84 opcSticker 358
88 PaniniSticker 157

TOMLIN, DAVE
75 O-Pee-Chee 578
76 O-Pee-Chee 398

TOMLIN, RANDY
91 O-Pee-Chee 167
92 O-Pee-Chee 571
93 O-Pee-Chee 257

TOMPKINS, RON
66 O-Pee-Chee 107

TOOCH, CHUCK
91 Welland/Best 11
91 Welland/ProCards 3583
92 Welland/ClassicBest 23

TOPORCER, GEORGE
21 Neilson's(V61) 82

TORBORG, JEFF
70 O-Pee-Chee 54
71 O-Pee-Chee 314
72 O-Pee-Chee 404
73 O-Pee-Chee 154
90 O-Pee-Chee 21
91 O-Pee-Chee 609
92 O-Pee-Chee 759

TORRE, JOE
65 O-Pee-Chee 200
66 O-Pee-Chee 130
68 O-Pee-Chee-Poster 30
70 O-Pee-Chee 190
71 O-Pee-Chee 62,370
72 O-Pee-Chee 85,87,341,500
73 O-Pee-Chee 450
74 O-Pee-Chee 15
75 O-Pee-Chee 209,565
76 O-Pee-Chee 585
91 O-Pee-Chee 351
92 O-Pee-Chee 549
62 PostCereal 152
71 ProStarPostcard
62 ShirriffCoin 152

TORREALBA, PABLO
76 O-Pee-Chee 589

TORRES, HECTOR
70 O-Pee-Chee 272
71 O-Pee-Chee 558
76 O-Pee-Chee 241
91 TOR/FireSafety

TORRES, LEO
92 London/SkyBox 420

TORRES, RUSTY
72 O-Pee-Chee 124
73 O-Pee-Chee 571
74 O-Pee-Chee 499

TORRES, SALOMON
94 OPC165, -HotProspect 3

TORREZ, MIKE
72 Dimanche/DernièreHeure
68 O-Pee-Chee 162
69 O-Pee-Chee 136
70 O-Pee-Chee 312
71 O-Pee-Chee 531
73 O-Pee-Chee 77
74 O-Pee-Chee 568
75 O-Pee-Chee 254
76 O-Pee-Chee 25
77 O-Pee-Chee 144
79 O-Pee-Chee 92
80 O-Pee-Chee 236
81 O-Pee-Chee 216
82 O-Pee-Chee 312
84 O-Pee-Chee 78
82 opcSticker 151
84 opcSticker 113

TORVE, KELVIN
89 PaniniSticker 380

TOVAR, CESAR
65 O-Pee-Chee 201
70 O-Pee-Chee 25
71 O-Pee-Chee 165
72 O-Pee-Chee 275
73 O-Pee-Chee 405
74 O-Pee-Chee 538
75 O-Pee-Chee 178
76 O-Pee-Chee 246

TOWNSEND, RICHARD
92 Welland/ClassicBest 24

TRABER, JIM
90 FleerCdn. 193
89 O-Pee-Chee 124
87 opcSticker 232
89 opcSticker 233

TRABOUS, MANUEL
52 Laval Dairy 89

TRACEWSKI, DICK
65 O-Pee-Chee 279
69 O-Pee-Chee 126
73 O-Pee-Chee 323

TRAFTON, TODD
90 Vancouver/CMC 20
90 Vancouver/ProCards 497

TRAMMELL, ALAN
91 Ben's/HolsumDisk 10
88 FantasticSam's 6
90 FleerCdn. 617
85 Leaf 158
86 Leaf 101
87 Leaf 126
88 Leaf 4,167
79 O-Pee-Chee 184
80 O-Pee-Chee 123
81 O-Pee-Chee 133
82 O-Pee-Chee 381
83 O-Pee-Chee 95
84 O-Pee-Chee 88
85 O-Pee-Chee 181
86 O-Pee-Chee 130
87 O-Pee-Chee 209
88 O-Pee-Chee 320
89 O-Pee-Chee 49
90 O-Pee-Chee 440
91 O-Pee-Chee 275,389
92 O-Pee-Chee 120
93 O-Pee-Chee 360
94 O-Pee-Chee 72
91 opcPremier 123
92 opcPremier 31
82 opcSticker 181
83 opcSticker 66
84 opcSticker 266
85 opcSticker 18,21,258
86 opcSticker 267
87 opcSticker 270
88 opcSticker 273,-SStar 45
89 opcSticker 281,-SStar 12
86 opcTattoo 10
88 PaniniSticker 94,443-44
89 PaniniSticker 343
90 PaniniSticker 70
91 PaniniSticker 291
92 PaniniSticker 108
94 PaniniSticker 69
91 PaniniTopFifteen 8
87 StuartBakery 19

TRAVERS, BILL
75 O-Pee-Chee 488
76 O-Pee-Chee 573
77 O-Pee-Chee 174
79 O-Pee-Chee 106

TRAVIS, CECIL
37 O-Pee-Chee(V300)
39 WWGum(V351A)

TRAYNOR, HAROLD
20 MapleCrispette(V117) 2

TRAYNOR, PIE
76 O-Pee-Chee 343
33 WWGum(V353) 22

TREADWAY, JEFF
90 FleerCdn. 598
88 Leaf 29
89 O-Pee-Chee 61,139
90 O-Pee-Chee 486
91 O-Pee-Chee 99
89 PaniniSticker 73
90 PaniniSticker 20,218
94 PaniniSticker 61

TREBELHORN, TOM
90 O-Pee-Chee 759
91 O-Pee-Chee 459
85 Vancouver/Cramer 215

TRECHOCK, FRANK
50 WWGum(V362) 6

TRESH, TOM
68 O-Pee-Chee 69
69 O-Pee-Chee 212

TREVINO, ALEX
90 FleerCdn. 239
85 O-Pee-Chee 279
86 O-Pee-Chee 169
89 O-Pee-Chee 64
90 O-Pee-Chee 342
83 opcSticker 232
85 opcSticker 30

TRIANDOS, GUS
65 O-Pee-Chee 248
60 opcTattoo 51
62 PostCereal 33
62 ShirriffCoin 93

TRIGOURA, JORGE
94 GarciaPhoto

TRILLO, MANNY
74 O-Pee-Chee 597
75 O-Pee-Chee 617
76 O-Pee-Chee 206
77 O-Pee-Chee 158
78 O-Pee-Chee 217
79 O-Pee-Chee 337
80 O-Pee-Chee 50
81 O-Pee-Chee 368
82 O-Pee-Chee 220
83 O-Pee-Chee 73,174
84 O-Pee-Chee 180
85 O-Pee-Chee 310
86 O-Pee-Chee 142
87 O-Pee-Chee 32
82 opcSticker 76,122
83 opcSticker 141,142,268
84 opcSticker 93
86 opcSticker 88

TRIPLETT, COAKER
50 WWGum(V362) 16

TRLICEK, RICK
93 TOR/Donruss 37

TROEDSON, RICH
74 O-Pee-Chee 77

TROSKY, HAL
37 O-Pee-Chee(V300) 113
39 WWGum(V351A)

TROUT, STEVE
85 Leaf 243
81 O-Pee-Chee 364
82 O-Pee-Chee 299
84 O-Pee-Chee 151
85 O-Pee-Chee 139
86 O-Pee-Chee 384
87 O-Pee-Chee 147
82 opcSticker 169
85 opcSticker 43
86 opcSticker 57

TRUESDALE, FRED
1912 ImperialTobacco(C46) 53

TRUITT, BILL
52 LavalDairy 26

TRUJILLO, JOSE
89 Hamilton/Star 24

TRUSKY, KEN
89 Welland/Pucko 24

TSITOURIS, JOHN
65 O-Pee-Chee 221
66 O-Pee-Chee 12

TUDOR, JOHN
86 Leaf 134
88 Leaf 212
84 O-Pee-Chee 171
85 O-Pee-Chee 214
86 O-Pee-Chee 227
87 O-Pee-Chee 110
88 O-Pee-Chee 356
89 O-Pee-Chee 35
84 opcSticker 225
86 opcSticker 20,52
87 opcSticker 53
88 opcSticker 13,21
89 opcSticker 64
86 opcTattoo 12
89 PaniniSticker 100

TUHOLSKI, TOM
89 Welland/Pucko 25

TUKES, STAN
89 Hamilton/Star 25

TURANG, BRIAN
93 Calgary/ProCards 1175

TURKO, STEVE
91 Hamilton/ClassicBest 30
91 Hamilton/ProCards 4057

TURNER, CHRIS
93 Vancouver/ProCards 2602
96 Vancouver/Best 28

TURNER, JERRY
75 O-Pee-Chee 619
76 O-Pee-Chee 598

TURNER, JIM
73 O-Pee-Chee 116

TURNER, MATT
93 Edmonton/ProCards 1136

TURNER, SHANE
92 Calgary/ProCards 3741
92 Calgary/SkyBox 71
93 Calgary/ProCards 1176

TURVEY, JOE
90 Hamilton/Best 15
91 Hamilton/ClassicBest 20
91 Hamilton/ProCards 4048

TUTTLE, BILL
62 PostCereal 88
62 ShirriffCoin 87

TWITCHELL, WAYNE
71 O-Pee-Chee 692
72 O-Pee-Chee 14
73 O-Pee-Chee 227
74 O-Pee-Chee 419
75 O-Pee-Chee 326
76 O-Pee-Chee 543
78 O-Pee-Chee 189
79 O-Pee-Chee 18
77 MTL

TYRONE, JIM
74 O-Pee-Chee 598

TYSON, MIKE
74 O-Pee-Chee 655
75 O-Pee-Chee 231
76 O-Pee-Chee 86
79 O-Pee-Chee 162
80 O-Pee-Chee 252

U

UECKER, BOB
66 O-Pee-Chee 91

UHLAENDER, TED
68 O-Pee-Chee 28
69 O-Pee-Chee 194
71 O-Pee-Chee 347

UHLE, GEORGE
21 Neilson's(V61) 16
34 WWGum(V354) 22

ULACIA, LUIS
94 GarciaPhoto 76

UMBARGER, JIM
76 O-Pee-Chee 7

UNDERWOOD, PAT
80 O-Pee-Chee 358

UNDERWOOD, TOM
75 O-Pee-Chee 615
76 O-Pee-Chee 407
79 O-Pee-Chee 26
80 O-Pee-Chee 172
81 O-Pee-Chee 114
84 O-Pee-Chee 293
84 opcSticker 335
78 TOR
79 TOR/BubbleYum

UNSER, DEL
70 O-Pee-Chee 336
71 O-Pee-Chee 33
73 O-Pee-Chee 247
74 O-Pee-Chee 69
75 O-Pee-Chee 138
76 O-Pee-Chee 268
77 O-Pee-Chee 27
78 O-Pee-Chee 216
79 O-Pee-Chee 330
80 O-Pee-Chee 12
81 O-Pee-Chee 56
77 MTL
77 MTL/RedpathSugar

UPSHAW, CECIL
67 O-Pee-Chee 179
70 O-Pee-Chee 295
71 O-Pee-Chee 223
72 O-Pee-Chee 74
73 O-Pee-Chee 359
74 O-Pee-Chee 579
75 O-Pee-Chee 92

UPSHAW, WILLIE
87 GeneralMills
85 Leaf 10
86 Leaf 128
87 Leaf 231
88 Leaf 131
92 Nabisco 8
79 O-Pee-Chee 175
82 O-Pee-Chee 196
83 O-Pee-Chee 338
84 O-Pee-Chee 317
85 O-Pee-Chee 75,-Poster 14
86 O-Pee-Chee 223
87 O-Pee-Chee 245
89 O-Pee-Chee 106,241
83 opcSticker 128
84 opcSticker 363
85 opcSticker 358
86 opcSticker 188
87 opcSticker 186
89 opcSticker 185
88 PaniniSticker 217-19
89 PaniniSticker 324
78 TOR
84 TOR/FireSafety
85 TOR/FireSafety
86 TOR/AultFoods
86 TOR/FireSafety
87 TOR/FireSafety
88 TOR/FireSafety
96 TOR/OhHenry
97 TOR/Sizzler 29

URIBE, JOSE
90 FleerCdn. 74
88 Leaf 218
87 O-Pee-Chee 94
88 O-Pee-Chee 302
89 O-Pee-Chee 8
90 O-Pee-Chee 472
91 O-Pee-Chee 158
92 O-Pee-Chee 538
86 opcSticker 87
88 opcSticker 91
89 opcSticker 92
86 opcTattoo 12
88 PaniniSticker 425
89 PaniniSticker 217
90 PaniniSticker 372
91 PaniniSticker 70
92 PaniniSticker 215

USTACH, PAT
93 O-Pee-Chee 205

V

VAIL, MIKE
76 O-Pee-Chee 655
80 O-Pee-Chee 180
84 O-Pee-Chee 143
84 MTL

VALDESPINO, SANDY
65 O-Pee-Chee 201
66 O-Pee-Chee 56

VALDES, JORGE LUIS
94 GarciaPhoto 22

VALDEZ, EFRAIN
91 O-Pee-Chee 692

VALDEZ, SERGIO
90 O-Pee-Chee 199
91 O-Pee-Chee 98
93 Ottawa/ProCards 2436

VALENTIN, JOHN
93 O-Pee-Chee 220
94 PaniniSticker 33

VALENTINE, BOBBY
71 O-Pee-Chee 188
72 O-Pee-Chee 11
73 O-Pee-Chee 502
74 O-Pee-Chee 101
75 O-Pee-Chee 215
76 O-Pee-Chee 366
79 O-Pee-Chee 222
90 O-Pee-Chee 729
91 O-Pee-Chee 489
92 O-Pee-Chee 789

VALENTINE, ELLIS
77 Dimanche/DernièreHeure
80 Dimanche/DernièreHeure
76 O-Pee-Chee 590
77 O-Pee-Chee 234
78 O-Pee-Chee 45
79 O-Pee-Chee 277
80 O-Pee-Chee 206
81 O-Pee-Chee 244,-Poster 7
82 O-Pee-Chee 15
84 O-Pee-Chee 236
82 opcSticker 69
77 MTL
77 MTL/RedpathSugar
93 MTL/McDonald's 21

VALENTINE, FRED
67 O-Pee-Chee 64

VALENZUELA, FERNANDO
90 FleerCdn. 409,622
85 GeneralMills
86 GeneralMills
87 GeneralMills
87 HostessSticker
85 Leaf 184
86 Leaf 91
87 Leaf 148
88 Leaf 61
82 O-Pee-Chee 334,345
83 O-Pee-Chee 40
84 O-Pee-Chee 220
85 O-Pee-Chee 357
86 O-Pee-Chee 178,P
87 O-Pee-Chee 273
88 O-Pee-Chee 52
89 O-Pee-Chee 150
90 O-Pee-Chee 340
91 O-Pee-Chee 980
91 opcPremier 47
82 opcSticker 11,50,119
83 opcSticker 250
84 opcSticker 16
85 opcSticker 71
86 opcSticker 64
87 opcSticker 75
88 opcSticker 70,-SuperStar 30
89 opcSticker 60
86 opcTattoo 24
88 PaniniSticker 304
89 PaniniSticker 103
90 PaniniSticker 269
91 PaniniSticker 356
94 PaniniSticker 25
87 StuartBakery 6

VALERA, JULIO
91 O-Pee-Chee 504
93 O-Pee-Chee 368

VALLE, DAVE
90 FleerCdn. 527
88 O-Pee-Chee 83
90 O-Pee-Chee 76
91 O-Pee-Chee 178
92 O-Pee-Chee 294
88 opcSticker 220
88 PaniniSticker 184
90 PaniniSticker 156
91 PaniniSticker 227
92 PaniniSticker 54
93 PaniniSticker 58
94 PaniniSticker 123
86 Calgary/ProCards no#

VALLE, LAZARO
94 GarciaPhoto 52

VALLEY, CHUCK
82 Vancouver/TCMA 18

VAN BURKLEO, TY
92 Edmonton/ProCards 3548
92 Edmonton/SkyBox 169
93 Vancouver/ProCards 2606
97 Lethbridge/Best 3

VANCE, DAZZY
33 WWGum(V353) 2

VANCE, SANDY
71 O-Pee-Chee 34

VANDE BERG, ED
83 O-Pee-Chee 183
84 O-Pee-Chee 63
85 O-Pee-Chee 207
86 O-Pee-Chee 357
87 O-Pee-Chee 34
83 opcSticker 317
85 opcSticker 336
90 Calgary/CMC 8
91 Calgary/LineDrive 73
91 Calgary/ProCards 517
92 Calgary/ProCards 3731

VANDER WAL, JOHN
92 O-Pee-Chee 343
93 O-Pee-Chee 376
93 PaniniSticker 229
92 MTL/Durivage 16

VAN POPPELL, TODD
92 O-Pee-Chee 142
94 O-Pee-Chee 56
94 PaniniSticker 114

VAN SLYKE, ANDY
90 FleerCdn. 481
93 HumptyDumpty 46
88 Leaf 18,102
92 McDonald's 17
85 O-Pee-Chee 341
86 O-Pee-Chee 33
87 O-Pee-Chee 33
88 O-Pee-Chee 142
89 O-Pee-Chee 350
90 O-Pee-Chee 775
91 O-Pee-Chee 425
92 O-Pee-Chee 545
93 O-Pee-Chee 355
94 O-Pee-Chee 86
93 opcPremier 88
84 opcSticker 150
85 opcSticker 138
86 opcSticker 51
87 opcSticker 51
88 opcSticker 126
89 opcSticker 132,-SStar 54
88 PaniniSticker 380
89 PaniniSticker 173
90 PaniniSticker 324
91 PaniniSticker 121
92 PaniniSticker 257
93 PaniniSticker 285
94 PaniniSticker 240
91 PaniniTopFifteen 106
93 PostCdn. 11

VARGAS, GUILLAUME
52 LavalDairy 109

VARGAS, HECTOR
93 Ottawa/ProCards 2444

VARNEY, PETE
76 O-Pee-Chee 413

VARSHO, GARY
92 O-Pee-Chee 122
93 PaniniSticker 287

VASQUEZ, JULAIN
93 Vancouver/ProCards 2599

VATCHER, JIM
91 O-Pee-Chee 196

VAUGHAN, ARKY
36 WWGum(V355) 6

VAUGHAN, CHARLES
67 O-Pee-Chee 179

VAUGHAN, FLOYD
34 WWGum(V354) 70

VAUGHN, GREG
90 FleerCdn. 339
90 O-Pee-Chee 57
91 O-Pee-Chee 347
92 O-Pee-Chee 572
93 O-Pee-Chee 373
94 O-Pee-Chee 259
92 PaniniSticker 41
93 PaniniSticker 44
94 PaniniSticker 88

VAUGHN, JAMES L.
23 WillardsChocolate(V100)164

VAUGHN, MO
92 O-Pee-Chee 59
93 O-Pee-Chee 393
91 opcPremier 124
92 opcPremier 50
93 PaniniSticker 92
94 PaniniSticker 34

VEACH, ROBERT H.
21 Neilson's(V61) 33
23 WillardsChocolate(V100)165

VEAL, COOT
62 PostCereal 68
62 ShirriffCoin 84

VEALE, BOB
65 O-Pee-Chee 12,195
68 O-Pee-Chee 70
69 O-Pee-Chee 8
70 O-Pee-Chee 236
71 O-Pee-Chee 368
73 O-Pee-Chee 518

VEINTIDOS, JUAN
75 O-Pee-Chee 621

VELARDE, RANDY
90 O-Pee-Chee 23
91 O-Pee-Chee 379
92 O-Pee-Chee 21
93 O-Pee-Chee 337
93 PaniniSticker 148

VELEZ, OTONIEL (OTTO)
92 Nabisco 26
74 O-Pee-Chee 606
77 O-Pee-Chee 13
78 O-Pee-Chee 67
79 O-Pee-Chee 241
80 O-Pee-Chee 354
81 O-Pee-Chee 351,-Poster 23
82 O-Pee-Chee 155,-Poster 11
82 opcSticker 249
78 TOR
79 TOR/BubbleYum

VENABLE, MAX
89 Edmonton/CMC 23
89 Edmonton/ProCards 556

VENEZIA, RICH
94 Welland/Classic 28
94 Welland/ProCards 3506

VENTURA, ROBIN
90 FleerCdn. 550
93 HumptyDumpty 7
90 O-Pee-Chee 121
91 O-Pee-Chee 461
92 O-Pee-Chee 255
93 O-Pee-Chee 387
94 O-Pee-Chee 33
92 opcPremier 132
91 PaniniSticker 314
92 PaniniSticker 127
93 PaniniSticker 139
94 PaniniSticker 52

VENTURINO, PHIL
88 Edmonton/ProCards 566
88 Edmonton/CMC 8

VERBANIC, JOE
68 O-Pee-Chee 29
70 O-Pee-Chee 416

VERES, DAVE
96 HitTheBooks
96 MTL/Disk

VERES, RANDY
91 O-Pee-Chee 694

VERGEZ, JOHNNY LOUIS
36 WWGum(V355) 5

VERNON, JAMES
77 MTL/RedpathSugar

VERNON, MICKEY
53 Exhibits 59

VERNON, MICKEY
77 O-Pee-Chee 198
77 MTL
77 MTL/RedpathSugar

VERSALLES, ZOILO
65 O-Pee-Chee 157
69 O-Pee-Chee 38
70 O-Pee-Chee 365
71 O-Pee-Chee 203
62 PostCereal 86
62 ShirriffCoin 51

VERYZER, TOM
75 O-Pee-Chee 623
76 O-Pee-Chee 432
77 O-Pee-Chee 188
78 O-Pee-Chee 14
80 O-Pee-Chee 145
82 O-Pee-Chee 387

VESLING, DON
89 London/ProCards 1374
92 London/ProCards 632
92 London/SkyBox 421

VICKERS, RUBE
1912 ImperialTobacco(C46) 37

VIDMAR, DON
92 Edmonton/ProCards 3540

VIDMAR, TOM
92 Edmonton/SkyBox 170

VILLANUEVA, HECTOR
91 O-Pee-Chee 362
92 O-Pee-Chee 181
92 PaniniSticker 181

VINEYARD, DAVE
65 O-Pee-Chee 169

VIOLA, FRANK
90 FleerCdn. 219
85 Leaf 17
86 Leaf 126
87 Leaf 74
88 Leaf 94
84 O-Pee-Chee 28
85 O-Pee-Chee 266
86 O-Pee-Chee 269
87 O-Pee-Chee 310
88 O-Pee-Chee 259
89 O-Pee-Chee 120
90 O-Pee-Chee 470
91 O-Pee-Chee 60,406
92 O-Pee-Chee 510
93 O-Pee-Chee 228
94 O-Pee-Chee 88
92 opcPremier 115
84 opcSticker 312
85 opcSticker 300
86 opcSticker 284
87 opcSticker 277
88 opcSticker 25,282
89 opcStick. 153,292,-SStar 30
86 opcTattoo 18
88 PaniniSticker 134
89 PaniniSticker 237,383,475
91 PaniniSticker 87
92 PaniniSticker 229
91 PaniniTopFifteen 59,68,76

VIRDON, BILL
83 Dimanche/DernièreHeure
65 O-Pee-Chee 69
73 O-Pee-Chee 517
75 O-Pee-Chee 611
76 O-Pee-Chee 147
83 O-Pee-Chee 6
84 O-Pee-Chee 111
62 PostCereal 175
62 ShirriffCoin 168
84 MTL
83 MTL/StuartBakery 1
84 MTL/StuartBakery 2,38

VIRGIL, OSSIE (SR.)
67 O-Pee-Chee 132
77 MTL
77 MTL/RedpathSugar
90 TOR/FireSafety

VIRGIL, OZZIE (JR.)
85 Leaf 250
88 Leaf 64
85 O-Pee-Chee 103
86 O-Pee-Chee 95
87 O-Pee-Chee 183
88 O-Pee-Chee 24,291
89 O-Pee-Chee 179
85 opcSticker 110
86 opcSticker 115
88 opcSticker 36
89 opcSticker 28
88 PaniniSticker 241

VIZCAINO, JOSE
90 FleerCdn. 410
92 O-Pee-Chee 561
93 O-Pee-Chee 345
94 PaniniSticker 159

VIZQUEL, OMAR
90 FleerCdn. 528
90 O-Pee-Chee 698
91 O-Pee-Chee 298
92 O-Pee-Chee 101
93 O-Pee-Chee 379
94 O-Pee-Chee 267
92 PaniniSticker 58
93 PaniniSticker 61
94 PaniniSticker 124
89 Calgary/CMC 23
89 Calgary/ProCards 537

VOSBERG, ED
91 Edmonton/LineDrive 172
91 Edmonton/ProCards 1516

VOSMIK, JOE
36 WWGum(V355) 76
39 WWGum(V351B)

VOSS, BILL
68 O-Pee-Chee 142
70 O-Pee-Chee 326
71 O-Pee-Chee 671

VOSSLER, DAN
74 O-Pee-Chee 602

VUCKOVICH, PETE
77 O-Pee-Chee 130
78 O-Pee-Chee 157
80 O-Pee-Chee 31
81 O-Pee-Chee 193
82 O-Pee-Chee 132
83 O-Pee-Chee 375,394
84 O-Pee-Chee 313
86 O-Pee-Chee 152
82 opcSticker 10,202
83 opcSticker 86

VUKOVICH, GEORGE
85 Leaf 120
86 O-Pee-Chee 337
85 opcSticker 249
86 opcSticker 214

VUKOVICH, JOHN
73 O-Pee-Chee 451
74 O-Pee-Chee 349
75 O-Pee-Chee 602

WADDELL, TOM
86 O-Pee-Chee 86
86 opcSticker 209

WADE, JAKE
50 WWGum(V362) 3

WAGGONER, AUBREY
93 Calgary/ProCards 1180

WAGNER, GARY
66 O-Pee-Chee 151
71 O-Pee-Chee 473

WAGNER, HONUS
76 O-Pee-Chee 344

WAGNER, LEON
66 O-Pee-Chee 65
67 O-Pee-Chee 109
68 O-Pee-Chee-Poster 31
69 O-Pee-Chee 187
62 PostCereal 77
62 ShirriffCoin 57

WAGNER, MARK
80 O-Pee-Chee 13

WAGNER, PAUL
89 Welland/Pucko 26

WAINHOUSE, DAVE
92 MTL/Durivage 17

WAITS, RICK
76 O-Pee-Chee 433
78 O-Pee-Chee 191
79 O-Pee-Chee 253
80 O-Pee-Chee 94
81 O-Pee-Chee 258
82 O-Pee-Chee 142
85 Vancouver/Cramer 219

WAKAMATSU, DON
90 Vancouver/CMC 22
90 Vancouver/ProCards 491
91 Vancouver/LineDrive 648
91 Vancouver/ProCards 1598

WAKEFIELD, BILL
65 O-Pee-Chee 167

WAKEFIELD, TIM
93 Humpty Dumpty 45
93 O-Pee-Chee 227
93 PaniniSticker 279
89 Welland/Pucko 27

WALBECK, MATT
94 O-Pee-Chee 227

WALBERG, GEORGE
33 WWGum(V353) 76

WALDEN, RONNIE
91 O-Pee-Chee 596

WALEWANDER, JIM
94 Edmonton/ProCards 2883
93 Vancouver/ProCards 2607

WALK, BOB
90 FleerCdn. 482
89 O-Pee-Chee 66
90 O-Pee-Chee 754
91 O-Pee-Chee 29
92 O-Pee-Chee 486
89 opcSticker 123
93 PaniniSticker 286

WALKER, BARTIE
23 Neilson's 45

WALKER, BILL
33 WWGum(V353) 57

WALKER, CHICO
87 O-Pee-Chee 58
92 O-Pee-Chee 439
88 Edmonton/ProCards 561

WALKER, CLARENCE (TILLY)
21 Neilson's(V61) 6
23 Neilson's 46

WALKER, CLARENCE W.
23 WillardsChocolate(V100)166

WALKER, DUANE
85 Leaf 52
85 opcSticker 52

WALKER, FRED
34 WWGum(V354) 86

WALKER, GENE
93 Edmonton/ProCards 1137

WALKER, GERALD (GEE)
37 O-Pee-Chee 110
34 WWGum(V354) 81
36 WWGum(V355) 48

WALKER, GREG
90 FleerCdn. 551
87 Leaf 25
88 Leaf 86
85 O-Pee-Chee 244
86 O-Pee-Chee 123
87 O-Pee-Chee 302
88 O-Pee-Chee 286
90 O-Pee-Chee 33
85 opcSticker 236
86 opcSticker 293
87 opcSticker 291
88 opcSticker 292
88 PaniniSticker 56
89 PaniniSticker 307
90 PaniniSticker 45

WALKER, HARRY
70 O-Pee-Chee 32
71 O-Pee-Chee 312
72 O-Pee-Chee 249

WALKER, JERRY
60 opcTattoo 52,82

WALKER, JIM
88 Calgary/CMC 7
88 Calgary/ProCards 791

WALKER, LARRY
92 CanadianSpiritMedallion
90 FleerCdn. 363
93 HitTheBooks, -Poster
93 HumptyDumpty 42
90 O-Pee-Chee 757
91 O-Pee-Chee 339
92 O-Pee-Chee 531
93 O-Pee-Chee 384
94 O-Pee-Chee 253, -AS 19
93 opcPremier 39
91 PaniniSticker 145
92 PaniniSticker 206
93 PaniniSticker 231
94 PaniniSticker 213
93 PostCdn. 13

94 PostCdn. 8
92 MTL/Durivage 18
93 MTL/McDonald's 7

WALKER, LUKE
67 O-Pee-Chee 123
69 O-Pee-Chee 36
70 O-Pee-Chee 322
71 O-Pee-Chee 68,534
72 O-Pee-Chee 471
73 O-Pee-Chee 187
74 O-Pee-Chee 612
75 O-Pee-Chee 474

WALKER, MIKE
91 O-Pee-Chee 593
90 Calgary/CMC 3
90 Calgary/ProCards 652
92 Calgary/ProCards 3732
93 Calgary/ProCards 1167

WALKER, RUBE
73 O-Pee-Chee 257
74 O-Pee-Chee 179

WALKER, TOM
73 O-Pee-Chee 41
74 O-Pee-Chee 193
75 O-Pee-Chee 627
76 O-Pee-Chee 186
77 MTL

WALL, STAN
76 O-Pee-Chee 584

WALLACE, B.J.
93 O-Pee-Chee-DraftPick 1

WALLACE, MIKE
74 O-Pee-Chee 608
75 O-Pee-Chee 401

WALLACH, TIM
91 Ben's/HolsumDisk 3
81 Dimanche/DernièreHeure
90 FleerCdn. 364
86 GeneralMills
87 GeneralMills
87 HostessSticker
88 HostessDisk 7
85 Leaf 199
86 Leaf 97
87 Leaf 61
88 Leaf 193,255
82 O-Pee-Chee 191
83 O-Pee-Chee 229
84 O-Pee-Chee 232
85 O-Pee-Chee 3,-Poster 6
86 O-Pee-Chee 217
87 O-Pee-Chee 55
88 O-Pee-Chee 94
90 O-Pee-Chee 370
91 O-Pee-Chee 220
92 O-Pee-Chee 385
93 O-Pee-Chee 225
91 opcPremier 125
93 opcPremier 87
83 opcSticker 257
84 opcSticker 94
85 opcSticker 87
86 opcSticker 82
87 opcSticker 80
88 opcSticker 85,-SuperStar 9
89 opcSticker 70
86 opcTattoo 18
88 PaniniSticker 327
89 PaniniSticker 122
90 PaniniSticker 286
91 PaniniSticker 141
92 PaniniSticker 204
93 PaniniSticker 215
91 PaniniTopFifteen 102
91 PetroCanada 10
92 PizzaHut/DietPepsi
91 PostCdn. 2
92 PostCdn. 5
87 StuartBakery 7
82 MTL/Hygrade
83 MTL
83 MTL/StuartBakery 12
84 MTL
84 MTL/StuartBakery 14
86 MTL/ProvigoFoods
86 MTL/ProvigoFoods-Poster
92 MTL/Durivage 19
93 MTL/McDonald's 8

WALLING, DENNY
90 FleerCdn. 263
87 Leaf 159
88 Leaf 224
80 O-Pee-Chee 161
87 O-Pee-Chee 222
88 O-Pee-Chee 131
90 O-Pee-Chee 462
84 opcSticker 73
87 opcSticker 33
88 opcSticker 31
88 PaniniSticker 296

WALLIS, JOE
76 O-Pee-Chee 598

WALSH, DAVE
91 O-Pee-Chee 367

WALSH, JAMES
1912 ImperialTobacco(C46) 20

WALTERS, BUCKY
36 WWGum(V355) 61

WALTERS, DAN
93 PaniniSticker 257

WALTON, DANNY
70 O-Pee-Chee 134
71 O-Pee-Chee 281
73 O-Pee-Chee 516

WALTON, JEROME
90 Ben's/HolsumDisk 19
90 FleerCdn. 44
90 O-Pee-Chee 464
91 O-Pee-Chee 135
92 O-Pee-Chee 543
90 PaniniSticker 230
91 PaniniSticker 48
92 PaniniSticker 187
93 Vancouver/ProCards 2611

WALTON, JIM
73 O-Pee-Chee 646

WAMBSGANSS, BILL
20 MapleCrispette(V117) 29
21 Neilson's(V61) 31

WANER, LLOYD
33 WWGum(V353) 90

WANER, PAUL
33 WWGum(V353) 25
34 WWGum(V354) 67
36 WWGum(V355) 2

WANZ, DOUG
81 Vancouver/TCMA 3

WAPNICK, STEVE
92 Vancouver/ProCards 2724
92 Vancouver/SkyBox 627

WARD, AARON L.
23 WillardsChocolate(V100)167

WARD, CHRIS
75 O-Pee-Chee 587

WARD, COLBY
91 O-Pee-Chee 31
89 Edmonton/CMC 10
89 Edmonton/ProCards 568

WARD, DUANE
90 FleerCdn. 95
87 Leaf 45
87 O-Pee-Chee 153
88 O-Pee-Chee 128
89 O-Pee-Chee 392
90 O-Pee-Chee 28
91 O-Pee-Chee 181
92 O-Pee-Chee 365
93 OPC 310,-WSChamp 15
94 O-Pee-Chee 160
94 PaniniSticker 10
87 TOR/FireSafety
88 TOR/FireSafety
89 TOR/FireSafety
90 TOR/FireSafety
91 TOR/FireSafety
91 TOR/Score 8
92 TOR/FireSafety
93 TOR/Dempster's 11
93 TOR/Donruss 23
93 TOR/FireSafety
94 TOR
95 TOR/OhHenry
97 TOR/Sizzler 38

WARD, GARY
90 FleerCdn. 618
85 Leaf 70
86 Leaf 20
87 Leaf 177
84 O-Pee-Chee 67
85 O-Pee-Chee 84
86 O-Pee-Chee 105
87 O-Pee-Chee 218
88 O-Pee-Chee 235,303
89 O-Pee-Chee 302
90 O-Pee-Chee 679
91 O-Pee-Chee 556
83 opcSticker 92
84 opcSticker 303
85 opcSticker 353
86 opcSticker 239
87 opcSticker 235
86 opcTattoo 21
88 PaniniSticker 160
90 PaniniSticker 68
91 PaniniSticker 294

WARD, JOE
1912 ImperialTobacco(C46) 6

WARD, PETE
65 O-Pee-Chee 215
66 O-Pee-Chee 25
67 O-Pee-Chee 143
68 O-Pee-Chee 33
69 O-Pee-Chee 155
71 O-Pee-Chee 667

WARD, TURNER
91 O-Pee-Chee 555
92 TOR/FireSafety
93 TOR/Dempster's 9
93 TOR/Donruss 31
93 TOR/FireSafety
97 Calgary/Best 28

WARE, JEFF
92 O-Pee-Chee 414
96 TOR/OhHenry

WARNEKE, LONNIE
36 WWGum(V355) 100
39 WWGum(V351B)

WARNER, HARRY
77 O-Pee-Chee 58
78 TOR

WARNER, RON
91 Hamilton/ClassicBest 21
91 Hamilton/ProCards 4048

WARREN, BRIAN
92 London/ProCards 633
92 London/SkyBox 422

WARREN, MIKE
84 opcSticker 288

WARTHEN, DAN
76 O-Pee-Chee 374
77 O-Pee-Chee 99
77 MTL
77 MTL/RedpathSugar
88 Calgary/CMC 25
88 Calgary/ProCards 789
89 Calgary/CMC 25
89 Calgary/ProCards 523
90 Calgary/CMC 24
90 Calgary/ProCards 665

WARWICK, CARL
62 PostCereal 161
62 ShirriffCoin 160

WASDIN, JOHN
95 Edmonton/Macri

WASHBURN, GREG
70 O-Pee-Chee 74

WASHBURN, RAY
67 O-Pee-Chee 92
70 O-Pee-Chee 22

WASHINGTON, CLAUDELL
90 FleerCdn. 146
85 Leaf 11
86 Leaf 164
75 O-Pee-Chee 647
76 O-Pee-Chee 189
77 O-Pee-Chee 178
79 O-Pee-Chee 298
80 O-Pee-Chee 171
82 O-Pee-Chee 32
83 O-Pee-Chee 235
84 O-Pee-Chee 42
85 O-Pee-Chee 166
86 O-Pee-Chee 303
88 O-Pee-Chee 335
89 O-Pee-Chee 185
90 O-Pee-Chee 705
82 opcSticker 22
83 opcSticker 216
84 opcSticker 32
85 opcSticker 25
86 opcSticker 39
88 opcSticker 301
86 opcTattoo 17
90 PaniniSticker 30

WASHINGTON, HERB
75 O-Pee-Chee 407

WASHINGTON, RON
83 O-Pee-Chee 27
84 O-Pee-Chee 268

WASHINGTON, U. L.
81 O-Pee-Chee 26
82 O-Pee-Chee 329
83 O-Pee-Chee 67
84 O-Pee-Chee 294
85 O-Pee-Chee-Poster 4
86 O-Pee-Chee 113
84 opcSticker 282
87 Vancouver/ProCards 1622
89 Welland/Pucko 30

WASINGER, MARK
91 Edmonton/LineDrive 173
91 Edmonton/ProCards 1525
92 Edmonton/ProCards 3549
92 Edmonton/SkyBox 171

WASLEWSKI, GARY
71 O-Pee-Chee 277
72 O-Pee-Chee 108

WATHAN, JOHN
81 O-Pee-Chee 157
82 O-Pee-Chee 383
83 O-Pee-Chee 289
84 O-Pee-Chee 72
90 O-Pee-Chee 789
91 O-Pee-Chee 291
82 opcSticker 192
83 opcSticker 78,195,196
84 opcSticker 284

WATKINS, BOB
70 O-Pee-Chee 227

WATKINS, DAVE
70 O-Pee-Chee 168

WATLINGTON, JULIUS NEAL
52 Parkhurst 83

WATSON, ALLEN
92 O-Pee-Chee 654
94 O-Pee-Chee 15, -DD 16
91 Hamilton/ClassicBest 7
91 Hamilton/ProCards 4040

WATSON, BOB
70 O-Pee-Chee 407
71 O-Pee-Chee 222
72 O-Pee-Chee 355
73 O-Pee-Chee 110
74 O-Pee-Chee 370
75 O-Pee-Chee 227
76 O-Pee-Chee 20
78 O-Pee-Chee 107
79 O-Pee-Chee 60
80 O-Pee-Chee 250
81 O-Pee-Chee 208
82 O-Pee-Chee 275
85 O-Pee-Chee 51

WATSON, JOHN
22 WilliamPaterson(V89) 8

WATT, EDDIE
68 O-Pee-Chee 186
70 O-Pee-Chee 497
71 O-Pee-Chee 122
72 O-Pee-Chee 128
73 O-Pee-Chee 362
74 O-Pee-Chee 534
75 O-Pee-Chee 374

WATT, GORD
97 Lethbridge/Best 4

WATTERS, MIKE
87 Calgary/ProCards 2310
88 Calgary/CMC 23
88 Calgary/ProCards 798

WATTS, RICK
86 Vancouver/ProCards

WATYCHOWICS, STANLEY
52 Laval Dairy 64

WAY, RON
89 Welland/Pucko 28

WAYNE, GARY
90 FleerCdn. 387
90 O-Pee-Chee 348
91 O-Pee-Chee 207

WEATHERS, DAVE
91 TOR/Score 35
93 TOR/Donruss 43
93 Edmonton/ProCards 1138

WEAVER, EARL
70 O-Pee-Chee 148
71 O-Pee-Chee 477
72 O-Pee-Chee 323
73 O-Pee-Chee 136
74 O-Pee-Chee 306
75 O-Pee-Chee 117
76 O-Pee-Chee 73

91 ScoreAllStarFanfest 6
91 TOR/FireSafety

WHITFIELD, FRED
65 O-Pee-Chee 283
66 O-Pee-Chee 88
68 O-Pee-Chee 133

WHITFIELD, TERRY
75 O-Pee-Chee 622
76 O-Pee-Chee 590
79 O-Pee-Chee 309
80 O-Pee-Chee 361

WHITMER, JOE
85 Calgary/Cramer 99
86 Calgary/ProCards no#

WHITMORE, DARRELL
93 Edmonton/ProCards 1150
94 Edmonton/ProCards 2888

WHITSON, EDDIE
90 FleerCdn. 171
81 O-Pee-Chee 336
85 O-Pee-Chee 98
86 O-Pee-Chee 15
88 O-Pee-Chee 330
89 O-Pee-Chee 21
90 O-Pee-Chee 618
91 O-Pee-Chee 481
92 O-Pee-Chee 228
85 opcSticker 152
86 opcSticker 301
88 opcSticker 107
88 PaniniSticker 401
90 PaniniSticker 347
91 PaniniSticker 98
91 PaniniTopFifteen 67

WHITT, ERNIE
90 FleerCdn. 97
86 GeneralMills
87 GeneralMills
87 HostessSticker
88 HostessDisk
85 Leaf 181
86 Leaf 217
87 Leaf 69
88 Leaf 250
92 Nabisco 34
81 O-Pee-Chee 282, -Poster 20
82 O-Pee-Chee 19,-Poster 3
83 O-Pee-Chee 302
84 O-Pee-Chee 106
85 O-Pee-Chee 128
86 O-Pee-Chee 136
87 O-Pee-Chee 221
88 O-Pee-Chee 79
89 O-Pee-Chee 289
90 O-Pee-Chee 742
91 O-Pee-Chee 492
82 opcSticker 247
83 opcSticker 131
84 opcSticker 373
88 opcSticker 187
88 PaniniSticker 216
87 StuartBakery 28
84 TOR/FireSafety
85 TOR/FireSafety
86 TOR/AultFoods
86 TOR/FireSafety
87 TOR/FireSafety
88 TOR
88 TOR/FireSafety
89 TOR/FireSafety
90 TOR/Hostess
96 TOR/OhHenry
97 TOR/Sizzler 12
95 St.Catharines/TimHortons

WHITTED, GEORGE B.
23 WillardsChocolate(V100)169

WICKANDER, KEVIN
90 O-Pee-Chee 528
91 O-Pee-Chee 246

WICKER, FLOYD
71 O-Pee-Chee 97

WICKERSHAM, DAVE
65 O-Pee-Chee 9
66 O-Pee-Chee 58
67 O-Pee-Chee 112

WIDMAR, AL
84 TOR/FireSafety
85 TOR/FireSafety
86 TOR/FireSafety
87 TOR/FireSafety
88 TOR/FireSafety
89 TOR/FireSafety

WIETELMANN, WHITEY
73 O-Pee-Chee 12

WIGGINS, ALAN
85 Leaf 68
84 O-Pee-Chee 27
85 O-Pee-Chee 378
84 opcSticker 153
85 opcSticker 150

WILBORN, TED
80 O-Pee-Chee: 329

WILCOX, MILT
85 Leaf 227
71 O-Pee-Chee 164
72 O-Pee-Chee 399
73 O-Pee-Chee 134
74 O-Pee-Chee 565
75 O-Pee-Chee 14
78 O-Pee-Chee 136
80 O-Pee-Chee 204
82 opcSticker 186
85 opcSticker 10,17

WILFONG, ROB
82 O-Pee-Chee 205
86 O-Pee-Chee 393

WILHELM, HOYT
65 O-Pee-Chee 276
70 O-Pee-Chee 17
71 O-Pee-Chee 248
62 PostCereal 35

WILHELM, IRVIN K.
23 WillardsChocolate(V100)170

WILKERSON, CURT
90 FleerCdn. 46
85 O-Pee-Chee 342
86 O-Pee-Chee 279
90 O-Pee-Chee 667
91 O-Pee-Chee 142
92 O-Pee-Chee 712
85 opcSticker 349
86 opcSticker 244

WILKINS, DEAN
90 FleerCdn. 47

WILKINS, MARC
92 Welland/ClassicBest 25

WILKINS, MIKE
90 London/ProCards 1269

WILKINS, RICK
92 O-Pee-Chee 348
93 PaniniSticker 202
94 PaniniSticker 160

WILKINSON, BILL
86 Calgary/ProCards
89 Calgary/CMC 6
89 London/ProCards 1360

WILKINSON, ROY H.
23 WillardsChocolate(V100)171

WILL, BOB
62 ShirriffCoin 218

WILLARD, JERRY
85 O-Pee-Chee 142
86 O-Pee-Chee 273
94 Calgary/ProCards 794
89 Vancouver/CMC 19
89 Vancouver/ProCards 587
90 Vancouver/CMC 23
90 Vancouver/ProCards 492

WILLEY, CARLTON
62 PostCereal 155

WILLHITE, NICK
66 O-Pee-Chee 171

WILLIAMS, BERNIE
70 O-Pee-Chee 401
71 O-Pee-Chee 728
73 O-Pee-Chee 557

WILLIAMS, BERNIE
90 O-Pee-Chee 401
92 O-Pee-Chee 374
93 O-Pee-Chee 363
94 O-Pee-Chee 35
91 opcPremier 128
92 opcPremier 109
94 PaniniSticker 106

WILLIAMS, BILLY
65 O-Pee-Chee 4,220
68 O-Pee-Chee 37
69 O-Pee-Chee 4
70 O-Pee-Chee 170
71 O-Pee-Chee 64,66,350
72 O-Pee-Chee 439,440
73 O-Pee-Chee 61,200
74 O-Pee-Chee 110,338
75 O-Pee-Chee 545
76 O-Pee-Chee 525
62 ShirriffCoin 207

WILLIAMS, BRIAN
93 O-Pee-Chee 369

WILLIAMS, CHARLIE
72 O-Pee-Chee 388
75 O-Pee-Chee 449
76 O-Pee-Chee 332

WILLIAMS, CY
22 WilliamPaterson(V89) 30

WILLIAMS, DANA
90 FleerCdn. 648
90 Vancouver/CMC 24
90 Vancouver/ProCards 504

WILLIAMS, DIBRELL
34 WWGum(V354) 36

WILLIAMS, DICK
77 Dimanche/DernièreHeure
80 Dimanche/DernièreHeure
67 O-Pee-Chee 161
68 O-Pee-Chee 87
71 O-Pee-Chee 714
72 O-Pee-Chee 137
73 O-Pee-Chee 179
75 O-Pee-Chee 236
76 O-Pee-Chee 304
77 O-Pee-Chee 108
78 O-Pee-Chee 27
79 O-Pee-Chee 349
80 O-Pee-Chee 249
81 O-Pee-Chee 268
62 PostCereal 32
62 ShirriffCoin 48
77 MTL
77 MTL/RedpathSugar

WILLIAMS, EARL
71 O-Pee-Chee 52
72 O-Pee-Chee 380
73 O-Pee-Chee 504
74 O-Pee-Chee 375
75 O-Pee-Chee 97
76 O-Pee-Chee 458
77 O-Pee-Chee 252

WILLIAMS, EDDIE
88 Leaf 46

WILLIAMS, FALVIO
89 Welland/Pucko 29

WILLIAMS, FRANK
90 FleerCdn. 620
85 O-Pee-Chee 254
90 O-Pee-Chee 599
85 opcSticker 169

WILLIAMS, FRED (CY)
21 Neilson's(V61) 118
23 WillardsChocolate(V100)172

WILLIAMS, GEORGE
95 Edmonton/Macri

WILLIAMS, GERALD
92 O-Pee-Chee 656
93 O-Pee-Chee 386

WILLIAMS, JEFF
94 Calgary/ProCards 791

WILLIAMS, JIM
70 O-Pee-Chee 262
71 O-Pee-Chee 262

WILLIAMS, JIMY
87 O-Pee-Chee 279
88 O-Pee-Chee 314
89 O-Pee-Chee 381
84 TOR/FireSafety
85 TOR/FireSafety
86 TOR/FireSafety
87 TOR/FireSafety
88 TOR
88 TOR/FireSafety
89 TOR/FireSafety

WILLIAMS, KEN
88 O-Pee-Chee 92
90 O-Pee-Chee 327
91 O-Pee-Chee 274
88 opcSticker 287
88 PaniniSticker 65
90 London/ProCards 1270

WILLIAMS, KENNETH R.
21 Neilson's(V61) 52
23 WillardsChocolate(V100)173
22 WilliamPaterson(V89) 37

WILLIAMS, KENNY
91 TOR/FireSafety

WILLIAMS, MATT
90 FleerCdn. 75
90 O-Pee-Chee 41
91 O-Pee-Chee 190,399
92 O-Pee-Chee 445
93 O-Pee-Chee 348
94 O-Pee-Chee 80
92 opcPremier 144
89 PaniniSticker 218
90 PaniniSticker 366
91 PaniniSticker 69
92 PaniniSticker 214
93 PaniniSticker 239
94 PaniniSticker 268

WILLIAMS, MITCH
90 FleerCdn. 48,631
88 O-Pee-Chee 26
89 O-Pee-Chee 377
90 O-Pee-Chee 520
91 O-Pee-Chee 335
92 O-Pee-Chee 6333
93 O-Pee-Chee 226
94 O-Pee-Chee 99
89 opcSticker 247
90 PaniniSticker 232
94 PaniniSticker 232
91 PaniniTopFifteen 17

WILLIAMS, REGGIE
92 Edmonton/ProCards 3552
92 Edmonton/SkyBox 172
93 Vancouver/ProCards 2612

WILLIAMS, RICHARD
77 MTL/RedpathSugar

WILLIAMS, SHAD
96 Vancouver/Best 29
97 Vancouver/Best 29

WILLIAMS, STAN
68 O-Pee-Chee 54
69 O-Pee-Chee 118
70 O-Pee-Chee 353
71 O-Pee-Chee 638
72 O-Pee-Chee 9
62 PostCereal 115

WILLIAMS, TED
53 Exhibits 30
70 O-Pee-Chee 211
71 O-Pee-Chee 380
72 O-Pee-Chee 510
76 O-Pee-Chee 347
39 WWGum(V351A)
39 WWGum(V351B)

WILLIAMS, WALT
68 O-Pee-Chee 172
70 O-Pee-Chee 395, -Booklet 4
71 O-Pee-Chee 555
72 O-Pee-Chee 15
73 O-Pee-Chee 297
74 O-Pee-Chee 418
76 O-Pee-Chee 123

WILLIAMS, WOODY
96 HitTheBooks
95 TOR/OhHenry

WILLIAMSON, JOEL
93 Welland/ProCards 3361

WILLIAMSON, MARK
90 FleerCdn. 194
90 O-Pee-Chee 13
91 O-Pee-Chee 296
92 O-Pee-Chee 628

WILLIS, CARL
92 O-Pee-Chee 393
93 O-Pee-Chee 388
89 Edmonton/CMC 3
89 Edmonton/ProCards 567
88 Vancouver/CMC 4
88 Vancouver/ProCards 762

WILLIS, MARTY
91 London/LineDrive 398
91 London/ProCards 1879
92 London/ProCards 634
92 London/SkyBox 423

WILLIS, MIKE
77 O-Pee-Chee 103
78 O-Pee-Chee 227
79 O-Pee-Chee 366
81 O-Pee-Chee 324
78 TOR

WILLIS, RON
68 O-Pee-Chee 68

WILLOUGHBY, JIM
73 O-Pee-Chee 79
74 O-Pee-Chee 553
76 O-Pee-Chee 102

WILLS, BUMP
78 O-Pee-Chee 208
79 O-Pee-Chee 190
80 O-Pee-Chee 373
81 O-Pee-Chee 173
82 O-Pee-Chee 272
82 opcSticker 244

WILLS, FRANK
90 FleerCdn. 98
91 O-Pee-Chee 213
89 TOR/FireSafety
90 TOR/FireSafety
91 TOR/FireSafety
91 TOR/Score 10
85 Calgary/Cramer 85

WILLS, MAURY
68 O-Pee-Chee 175
69 O-Pee-Chee 45, -Deckle 23
71 O-Pee-Chee 385
72 O-Pee-Chee 437,438
75 O-Pee-Chee 200
62 PostCereal 104
62 ShirriffCoin 127

WILSON, BILLY
70 O-Pee-Chee 28
71 O-Pee-Chee 192
73 O-Pee-Chee 619

WILSON, CRAIG
91 O-Pee-Chee 566
92 O-Pee-Chee 646

WILSON, DAN
91 O-Pee-Chee 767
93 opcPremier 35

WILSON, DON
68 O-Pee-Chee 77
69 O-Pee-Chee 202
70 O-Pee-Chee 515
71 O-Pee-Chee 484
72 O-Pee-Chee 20,91
73 O-Pee-Chee 217
74 O-Pee-Chee 304
75 O-Pee-Chee 455

WILSON, EARL
65 O-Pee-Chee 42
68 O-Pee-Chee 10,160
70 O-Pee-Chee 95
71 O-Pee-Chee 301

WILSON, FRANK
52 LavalDairy 3

WILSON, GARY
92 Welland/ClassicBest 26
97 Calgary/Best 29

WILSON, GLENN
90 FleerCdn. 240
86 Leaf 160
87 Leaf 146
84 O-Pee-Chee 36
85 O-Pee-Chee 189
86 O-Pee-Chee 318
87 O-Pee-Chee 97
88 O-Pee-Chee 359
90 O-Pee-Chee 112
91 O-Pee-Chee 476
83 opcSticker 318
84 opcSticker 270
86 opcSticker 118
87 opcSticker 117
88 opcSticker 124
86 opcTattoo 9
88 PaniniSticker 357-58,364
91 PaniniSticker 11

WILSON, JEFF
97 Lethbridge/Best 30

WILSON, JIM
89 Calgary/CMC 22
89 Calgary/ProCards 536

WILSON, JIMMIE
33 WWGum(V353) 37
36 WWGum(V355) 99

WILSON, MARK
89 Hamilton/Star 26

WILSON, MOOKIE
90 FleerCdn. 99
85 Leaf 122
86 Leaf 232
87 Leaf 176
88 Leaf 249
82 O-Pee-Chee 143
83 O-Pee-Chee 55
84 O-Pee-Chee 270
85 O-Pee-Chee 11
86 O-Pee-Chee 315
87 O-Pee-Chee 84
89 O-Pee-Chee 144
90 O-Pee-Chee 182
91 O-Pee-Chee 727
92 O-Pee-Chee 436
83 opcSticker 266
84 opcSticker 108
85 opcSticker 102
86 opcTattoo 6
88 PaniniSticker 341-42,348
89 PaniniSticker 141
90 PaniniSticker 174
91 PaniniSticker 341
90 TOR/FireSafety
91 TOR/FireSafety
91 TOR/Score 24

WILSON, NIGEL
93 O-Pee-Chee 165
93 Edmonton/ProCards 1151
94 Edmonton/ProCards 2889

WILSON, SAMUEL M.
23 WillardsChocolate(V100)174

WILSON, STEVE
90 FleerCdn. 49
90 O-Pee-Chee 741
91 O-Pee-Chee 69
92 O-Pee-Chee 751

WILSON, TACK
87 Edmonton/ProCards 2070

WILSON, TREVOR
90 O-Pee-Chee 408
91 O-Pee-Chee 96
92 O-Pee-Chee 204

WILSON, WILLIE
90 FleerCdn. 123
85 Leaf 110
86 Leaf 106
87 Leaf 97
88 Leaf 189
80 O-Pee-Chee 87
81 O-Pee-Chee 360
82 O-Pee-Chee 230
83 O-Pee-Chee 16
84 O-Pee-Chee 5
85 O-Pee-Chee 6
86 O-Pee-Chee 25
87 O-Pee-Chee 367
88 O-Pee-Chee 222
89 O-Pee-Chee 168
90 O-Pee-Chee 323
91 O-Pee-Chee 208
92 O-Pee-Chee 536
93 O-Pee-Chee 370
91 opcPremier 129
93 opcPremier 53
82 opcSticker 189
83 opcSticker 15,73,161
84 opcSticker 280
85 opcSticker 277
86 opcSticker 258
87 opcSticker261
88 opcSticker 263
89 opcSticker 268
86 opcTattoo 21
88 PaniniSticker 113
89 PaniniSticker 361
87 StuartBakery 20

WILTZ, STANLEY
92 Welland/ClassicBest 27
93 Welland/ClassicBest 27
93 Welland/ProCards 3370

WINE, BOBBY
72 Dimanche/DernièreHeure
65 O-Pee-Chee 36
70 O-Pee-Chee 332
71 O-Pee-Chee 171
73 O-Pee-Chee 486
74 O-Pee-Chee 119
71 MTL/LaPizzaRoyale
71 MTL/ProStar

WINFIELD, DAVE
92 CSC Sheet
82 FBI BoxBottoms
90 FleerCdn. 458
85 GeneralMills
87 GeneralMills
93 HumptyDumpty 12
85 Leaf 127,140
86 Leaf 125
87 Leaf 20,70
88 Leaf 116
74 O-Pee-Chee 456
75 O-Pee-Chee 61
76 O-Pee-Chee 160
77 O-Pee-Chee 156
78 O-Pee-Chee 78
79 O-Pee-Chee 11
80 O-Pee-Chee 122
82 O-Pee-Chee 76,352
83 O-Pee-Chee 258
84 O-Pee-Chee 266,378
85 O-Pee-Chee 180
86 O-Pee-Chee 70
87 O-Pee-Chee 36,152,H
88 O-Pee-Chee 89
89 O-Pee-Chee 260,P
90 O-Pee-Chee 380
91 O-Pee-Chee 630
92 O-Pee-Chee 5,792
93 OPC 371, -WSHero 4
93 OPC-WSChamp 17
94 O-Pee-Chee 53
91 opcPremier 130
92 opcPremier 150
93 opcPremier 28
82 opcSticker 137
83 opcSticker 99
84 opcSticker 190,319
85 opcSticker 186
86 opcSticker 160,298
87 opcSticker 298
88 opcSticker159,302,-SStar 54
89 opcStick. 149,315,-SStar 20
86 opcTattoo 1
88 PaniniSticker 161,231
89 PaniniSticker 240,409
91 PaniniSticker 184
94 PaniniSticker 97
91 PetroCanada 5
92 PizzaHut/DietPepsi
91 PostCdn. 28
87 StuartBakery 23
92 TOR/FireSafety
93 TOR/Donruss 14, WS7
97 TOR/Sizzler 43

WINGO, IVEY B.
23 WillardsChocolate(V100)175

WINGO, IVY
20 MapleCrispette(V117) 14
21 Neilson's(V61) 83

WINKLES, BOBBY
73 O-Pee-Chee 421
74 O-Pee-Chee 276
86 MTL/ProvigoFoods 14

WINN, JIM
88 O-Pee-Chee 388
88 opcSticker 288

WINNINGHAM, HERMAN
90 FleerCdn. 435
88 HostessDisk 4
86 Leaf 153
88 Leaf 242
85 O-Pee-Chee-Poster 8
86 O-Pee-Chee 129
87 O-Pee-Chee 141
88 O-Pee-Chee 216
90 O-Pee-Chee 94
91 O-Pee-Chee 204
92 O-Pee-Chee 547
86 opcSticker 83
88 opcSticker 83
88 PaniniSticker 332
86 MTL/ProvigoFoods 22

WINSTON, DARRIN
94 Ottawa/ProCards 2900

WINTERS, MATT
90 FleerCdn. 124

WISE, RICK
67 O-Pee-Chee 37
69 O-Pee-Chee 188
71 O-Pee-Chee 598
72 O-Pee-Chee 43,44,345
73 O-Pee-Chee 364
74 O-Pee-Chee 84,339
75 O-Pee-Chee 56
76 O-Pee-Chee 170
79 O-Pee-Chee 127
80 O-Pee-Chee 370
81 O-Pee-Chee 274

WISHNEVSKI, MIKE
87 Calgary/ProCards 2324
88 Calgary/CMC 20
88 Calgary/ProCards 783

WISNASKI, LEN
52 LavalDairy 44

WITT, BOBBY
90 FleerCdn. 315
87 Leaf 112
89 O-Pee-Chee 38
90 O-Pee-Chee 166
91 O-Pee-Chee 27
92 O-Pee-Chee 675
88 PaniniSticker 198
89 PaniniSticker 448
91 PaniniSticker 260
91 PaniniTopFifteen 78

WITT, LAWTON W.
23 WillardsChocolate(V100)176

WITT, MIKE
90 FleerCdn. 148
85 Leaf 46
86 Leaf 112
87 Leaf 111
88 Leaf 49
85 O-Pee-Chee 309
87 O-Pee-Chee 92
88 O-Pee-Chee 270
89 O-Pee-Chee 190
90 O-Pee-Chee 650
91 O-Pee-Chee 536
92 O-Pee-Chee 357
85 opcSticker 195,227
87 opcSticker 179
88 opcSticker 174
89 opcSticker 176
88 PaniniSticker 38
89 PaniniSticker 286
87 StuartBakery 16

WOCKENFUSS, JOHNNY
76 O-Pee-Chee 13
82 O-Pee-Chee 46
83 opcSticker 64
84 opcSticker 274

WOHLERS, MARK
92 O-Pee-Chee 703
93 O-Pee-Chee 7

WOHLFORD, JIM
83 Dimanche/DernièreHeure
85 Leaf 82
73 O-Pee-Chee 611
74 O-Pee-Chee 407
75 O-Pee-Chee 144
76 O-Pee-Chee 286
84 O-Pee-Chee 253
85 O-Pee-Chee 4
86 O-Pee-Chee 344
87 O-Pee-Chee 169
83 MTL/StuartBakery 21
84 MTL
84 MTL/StuartBakery 24
86 MTL/ProvigoFoods 6

WOJCIECHOWSKI, STEVE
95 Edmonton/Macri

WOJNA, EDWARD
88 Vancouver/CMC 5
88 Vancouver/ProCards 756

WOLF, STEVE
92 London/ProCards 635

WOLF, WALLY
70 O-Pee-Chee 74

WOLFF, MICHAEL
96 Vancouver/Best 30
97 Vancouver/Best 30

WOMACK, DOOLEY
67 O-Pee-Chee 77

WOMACK, TONY
91 Welland/Best 2
91 Welland/ProCards 3584

WOOD, JAKE
62 PostCereal 15
62 ShirriffCoin 83

WOOD JASON
95 Edmonton/Macri

WOOD, JOE
23 WillardsChocolate(V100)177

WOOD, TED
92 O-Pee-Chee 358
94 Ottawa/ProCards 2910

WOOD, WILBUR
69 O-Pee-Chee 123
70 O-Pee-Chee 342
71 O-Pee-Chee 436
72 O-Pee-Chee 92,94,342
73 O-Pee-Chee 66,150
74 O-Pee-Chee 120,205
75 O-Pee-Chee 110
76 O-Pee-Chee 368
79 O-Pee-Chee 108

WOODALL, LAWRENCE
21 Neilson's(V61) 21

WOODARD, MIKE
88 Vancouver/CMC 14
88 Vancouver/ProCards 767

WOODARDS, ORLANDO
97 St.Catharines/Best 29

WOODESHICK, HAL
65 O-Pee-Chee 179

WOODLING, GENE
60 opcTattoo 54
50 PalmDairies
62 PostCereal 71
62 ShirriffCoin 96

WOODS, ALVIS (AL)
92 Nabisco 4
77 O-Pee-Chee 256
78 O-Pee-Chee 175
79 O-Pee-Chee 85
80 O-Pee-Chee 230
81 O-Pee-Chee 165,-Poster 17
82 O-Pee-Chee 49, -Poster 5
83 O-Pee-Chee 59
78 TOR
79 TOR/BubbleYum 20

WOODS, GARY
85 Leaf 49
77 O-Pee-Chee 22
78 O-Pee-Chee 13

WOODS, RON
72 Dimanche/DernièreHeure
70 O-Pee-Chee 253
71 O-Pee-Chee 514
72 O-Pee-Chee 82
73 O-Pee-Chee 531
74 O-Pee-Chee 377

WOODS, TYRONE
94 Ottawa/ProCards 2911

WOODSON, DICK
70 O-Pee-Chee 479
71 O-Pee-Chee 586
73 O-Pee-Chee 98
74 O-Pee-Chee 586

WOODSON, KERRY
92 Calgary/ProCards 3733

WOODSON, TRACY
90 Vancouver/CMC 25
90 Vancouver/ProCards 498

WOODWARD, WOODY
66 O-Pee-Chee 49
69 O-Pee-Chee 142
70 O-Pee-Chee 296
71 O-Pee-Chee 496

WORRELL, TODD
90 FleerCdn. 264
87 Leaf 218
88 Leaf 229
87 O-Pee-Chee 67
88 O-Pee-Chee 135
89 O-Pee-Chee 291
90 O-Pee-Chee 95
93 O-Pee-Chee 374
93 opcPremier 62
87 opcSticker 11,12,55,310
88 opcSticker 54
88 PaniniSticker 386
89 PaniniSticker 179
90 PaniniSticker 340

WORTHAM, RICH
80 O-Pee-Chee 261

WORTHINGTON, AL
65 O-Pee-Chee 216
66 O-Pee-Chee 181
73 O-Pee-Chee 49

WORTHINGTON, CRAIG
90 FleerCdn. 195
90 O-Pee-Chee 521
91 O-Pee-Chee 73
92 O-Pee-Chee 397
89 PaniniSticker 252
90 PaniniSticker 11
91 PaniniSticker 242

WOYT, BORIS
50 WWGum(V362) 29

WRIGHT, CLYDE
70 O-Pee-Chee 543
71 O-Pee-Chee 67,240
72 O-Pee-Chee 55
73 O-Pee-Chee 373
74 O-Pee-Chee 525
75 O-Pee-Chee 408
76 O-Pee-Chee 559

WRIGHT, GEORGE
84 O-Pee-Chee 314
85 O-Pee-Chee 387
83 opcSticker 124
84 opcSticker 353

WRIGHT, GLENN
33 WWGum(V353) 77

WRIGHT, JIM
79 O-Pee-Chee 180

WRIGHT, KEN
71 O-Pee-Chee 504
73 O-Pee-Chee 578

WRIGHT, MEL
73 O-Pee-Chee 517
83 MTL/StuartBakery 25

WRIGHT, RON
97 Calgary/Best 30

WRIGHTSTONE, RUSSELL
21 Neilson's(V61) 16

WRONA, RICK
90 O-Pee-Chee 187

WYNEGAR, BUTCH
85 Leaf 165
86 Leaf 147
77 O-Pee-Chee 176
78 O-Pee-Chee 104
79 O-Pee-Chee 214
80 O-Pee-Chee 159
81 O-Pee-Chee 61
82 O-Pee-Chee 222
83 O-Pee-Chee 379
84 O-Pee-Chee 123
85 O-Pee-Chee 28
86 O-Pee-Chee 235
87 O-Pee-Chee 203
82 opcSticker 208
83 opcSticker 101
84 opcSticker 321
85 opcSticker 316
86 opcSticker 299

WYNN, EARLY
60 opcTattoo 55
62 PostCereal 55
62 ShirriffCoin 97

WYNN, JIM
65 O-Pee-Chee 257
68 O-Pee-Chee 5
70 O-Pee-Chee 60
71 O-Pee-Chee 565
73 O-Pee-Chee 185
74 O-Pee-Chee 43
75 O-Pee-Chee 570
76 O-Pee-Chee 395

WYNNE, BILLY
71 O-Pee-Chee 718

WYNNE, MARVELL
85 Leaf 233
85 O-Pee-Chee 86
86 O-Pee-Chee 293
88 O-Pee-Chee H
90 O-Pee-Chee 256
91 O-Pee-Chee 714
84 opcSticker 135
85 opcSticker 131
86 opcSticker 128
89 opcSticker 107
89 PaniniSticker 205

YAEGER, EDWARD
52 LavalDairy 41

YAHRLING, CHARLES
62 O-Pee-Chee 48

YANES, CARLOS
94 GarciaPhoto 23

YARYAN, CLARENCE E.
23 WillardsChocolate(V100)178

YASTRZEMSKI, CARL
66 O-Pee-Chee 70
68 OPC 2,4,6,192,-Poster 32
69 OPC 1,130,-Deckle 24
70 O-Pee-Chee 10,461
71 O-Pee-Chee 61,65,530
72 O-Pee-Chee 37,38
73 O-Pee-Chee 245
75 O-Pee-Chee 205,280
76 O-Pee-Chee 230
77 O-Pee-Chee 37
78 O-Pee-Chee 137
79 O-Pee-Chee 160
80 O-Pee-Chee 365
81 O-Pee-Chee 110
82 O-Pee-Chee 72,358
83 O-Pee-Chee 4,31,126
82 opcSticker 120,155
83 opcSticker 6
62 PostCereal 61
62 ShirriffCoin 27

YASTRZEMSKI, MIKE
88 Vancouver/CMC 19
88 Vancouver/ProCards 774

YEAGER, JOSEPH
1912 ImperialTobacco(C46) 84

YEAGER, STEVE
73 O-Pee-Chee 59
74 O-Pee-Chee 593
75 O-Pee-Chee 376
76 O-Pee-Chee 515
77 O-Pee-Chee 159
79 O-Pee-Chee 31
80 O-Pee-Chee 371
81 O-Pee-Chee 318
82 O-Pee-Chee 219
83 O-Pee-Chee 261
84 O-Pee-Chee 252
85 O-Pee-Chee 148
86 O-Pee-Chee 32
87 O-Pee-Chee 258
84 opcSticker 86

YELDING, ERIC
90 O-Pee-Chee 309
91 O-Pee-Chee 59
91 PaniniSticker 12
91 PaniniTopFifteen 42

YETT, RICH
90 FleerCdn. 502
90 O-Pee-Chee 689

YORK, JIM
72 O-Pee-Chee 68
73 O-Pee-Chee 546
75 O-Pee-Chee 383
76 O-Pee-Chee 224

YORK, MIKE
91 O-Pee-Chee 508

YOST, EDDIE
73 O-Pee-Chee 257
74 O-Pee-Chee 179
62 PostCereal 76

YOST, NED
79 Vancouver/TCMA 13
80 Vancouver/TCMA 3

YOUMANS, FLOYD
87 GeneralMills
87 HostessSticker
88 HostessDisk 9
86 Leaf 210
87 Leaf 65,206
88 Leaf 66
86 O-Pee-Chee 346
87 O-Pee-Chee 105
88 O-Pee-Chee 365
89 O-Pee-Chee 91
87 opcSticker 79
88 opcSticker 82
88 PaniniSticker 321
87 StuartBakery 8
86 MTL/ProvigoFoods 24

YOUNG, ANTHONY
92 O-Pee-Chee 148
93 O-Pee-Chee 380

YOUNG, CLIFF
89 Edmonton/CMC 4
89 Edmonton/ProCards 557
90 Edmonton/CMC 1
90 Edmonton/ProCards 518
91 Edmonton/ProCards 1517
92 Edmonton/SkyBox 173

YOUNG, CURT
90 FleerCdn. 24
88 O-Pee-Chee 103
90 O-Pee-Chee 328
91 O-Pee-Chee 473
92 O-Pee-Chee 704
87 opcSticker 165
88 PaniniSticker 165

YOUNG, CY
92 HomersClassic 5
73 O-Pee-Chee 477

YOUNG, DON
66 O-Pee-Chee 139
70 O-Pee-Chee 117

YOUNG, ERIC
93 opcPremier 31
94 PaniniSticker 178

YOUNG, ERNIE
95 Edmonton/Macri

YOUNG, GERALD
90 FleerCdn. 241
88 Leaf 210
88 O-Pee-Chee 368
89 O-Pee-Chee 95
90 O-Pee-Chee 196
91 O-Pee-Chee 626
92 O-Pee-Chee 241
89 opcSticker 23
89 PaniniSticker 93
90 PaniniSticker 263

YOUNG, KEVIN
94 O-Pee-Chee 124
93 opcPremier 78
94 PaniniSticker 241
90 Welland/Pucko 8

YOUNG, MATT
84 O-Pee-Chee 235
85 O-Pee-Chee 136
86 O-Pee-Chee 284
87 O-Pee-Chee 19
88 O-Pee-Chee 367
90 O-Pee-Chee 501
91 O-Pee-Chee 108
92 O-Pee-Chee 403
84 opcSticker 386
85 opcSticker 340
86 opcSticker 220
87 opcSticker 218
88 opSticker 72
88 PaniniSticker 306

YOUNG, MICHAEL
97 St.Catharines/Best 30

YOUNG, MIKE
88 O-Pee-Chee 11
86 opcSticker 234
86 opcTattoo 11
88 PaniniSticker 17

YOUNG, PETE
93 Ottawa/ProCards 2437

YOUNG, RALPH S.
23 WillardsChocolate(V100)179

YOUNGBLOOD, JOEL
82 Dimanche/DernièreHeure
85 Leaf 152
79 O-Pee-Chee 48
80 O-Pee-Chee 194
81 O-Pee-Chee 58
82 O-Pee-Chee 189
83 O-Pee-Chee 265
84 O-Pee-Chee 303
85 O-Pee-Chee 97
86 O-Pee-Chee 177
87 O-Pee-Chee 378
82 opcSticker 65
83 opcSticker 143,144
84 opcSticker 173
85 opcSticker 168

YOUNGS, ROSS
21 Neilson's(V61) 106
23 WillardsChocolate(V100)180

YOUNT, ROBIN
90 Ben's/HolsumDisk 7
90 FleerCdn. 340
85 GeneralMills
87 GeneralMills
87 HostessSticker
85 Leaf 44
86 Leaf 13
87 Leaf 67
88 Leaf 106
92 McDonald's 12
75 O-Pee-Chee 223
76 O-Pee-Chee 316
77 O-Pee-Chee 204
78 O-Pee-Chee 29
79 O-Pee-Chee 41
80 O-Pee-Chee 139
81 O-Pee-Chee 4
82 O-Pee-Chee 237
83 O-Pee-Chee 350
84 O-Pee-Chee 10
85 O-Pee-Chee 340
86 O-Pee-Chee 144
87 O-Pee-Chee 76
88 O-Pee-Chee 165
89 O-Pee-Chee 253
90 O-Pee-Chee 290,389
91 O-Pee-Chee 575,P
92 O-Pee-Chee 90
93 O-Pee-Chee 365

CHAPTER SIX

CANADIAN-BORN PLAYERS CHECKLIST & PRICE GUIDE

CANADIAN PLAYERS

BILL ATKINSON

☐	77 MTL Expos [no#]	1.00
☐	77 MTL Expos/ RedpathSugar [no#]	1.00
☐	78 O-Pee-Chee #144	.75
☐	78 Topps #43	.75
☐	80 O-Pee-Chee #133	.50
☐	80 Topps #415	.50
☐	81 Edmonton Trappers/ RedRooster #12	1.00
☐	83 Appleton Foxes/Fritsch #19	1.50

DEREK AUCOIN

☐	90 Jamestown Expos/ Pucko #13	1.00
☐	96 Bowman #356	.75
☐	96 Bowman(Foil) #356	1.00
☐	96 MTL Expos/ Disk [no#]	.50
☐	97 FleerUltra #226	.25
☐	97 FleerUltra (Gold Medallion) #226	.50
☐	97 FleerUltra (PlatinumMedallion) #226	8.00
☐	97 PacificPrism-GemsOfTheDiamond #GD166	.25

JOHN BALAZ

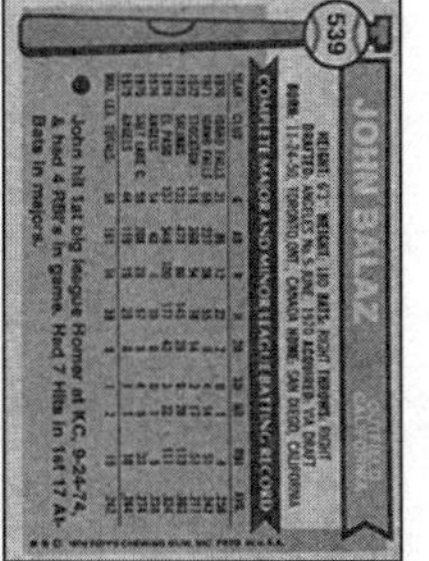

☐	75 SaltLakeCity Gullls/ Caruso #3	2.00
☐	76 O-Pee-Chee #539	1.00
☐	76 Topps #539	1.00

RENO BERTOIA

☐	58 Topps #232	15.00
☐	59 Topps #84	10.00
☐	60 Topps #297	8.00
☐	61 Topps #392	8.00

DENIS BOUCHER

☐	88 MyrtleBeach Blue Jays/ ProCards #1168	.75
☐	89 Dunedin Blue Jays/ Star [no#]	.25
☐	90 Dunedin Blue Jays/ Star 2	.25
☐	91 Bowman #29	.25
☐	91 Donruss Rookies #45	.25
☐	91 OPC Premier #13	.25
☐	90 Syracuse Chiefs/MerchantsBank [no#]	.50
☐	91 TOR Blue Jays/ FireSafety [no#]	.50
☐	91 UpperDeck #761	.25
☐	92 Colorado Springs SkySox/ SkyBox 78	.25
☐	92 Donruss #604	.25
☐	92 SkyBoxAAA #35	.25
☐	92 ToppsStadiumClub #773	.25
☐	93 O-Pee-Chee #22	.25
☐	93 Donruss #755	.25
☐	93 Fleer #405	.25
☐	93 Topps #541	.25
☐	93 Topps(Gold) #541	.50
☐	94 O-Pee-Chee #236	.25
☐	94 Topps #164	.25
☐	94 Topps(Gold) #164	.50
☐	94 ToppsFinest #294	1.00
☐	94 ToppsFinest(Refractor) #294	6.00
☐	94 ToppsStadiumClub #545	.25
☐	94 ToppsStadiumClub(Members Only) #545	1.00
☐	94 ToppsStadiumClub(Rainbow) #545	.50
☐	94 ToppsStadiumClub(First Day Issue) #545	3.00
☐	94 UpperDeck Collector'sChoice #541	.25
☐	94 UD Collector'sChoice(Silver Signature) #541	.50
☐	94 UD Collector'sChoice(Gold Signature) #541	3.00

TED BOWSFIELD

☐	59 Topps #236	8.00
☐	60 Topps #382	8.00
☐	61 Topps #216	8.00
☐	62 Topps #369	10.00
☐	63 Topps #339	10.00
☐	64 Topps #447	12.00

RICH BUTLER

☐	98 Topps #468	.25
☐	98 Topps(Minted In Springfield) #468	1.00
☐	98 ToppsChrome #468	.50
☐	98 ToppsChrome(Refractor) #468	8.00

ROB BUTLER

☐	91 St.Catharines Blue Jays/ ProCards #3406	.75
☐	92 Bowman #603	.75
☐	92 ClassicBest #89	.25
☐	92 ProCards #174	.25
☐	93 ClassicBest #45	.25
☐	93 ClassicBest Gold #86	.25
☐	93 Syracuse Blue Jays/ FleerProCards #1009	.50
☐	94 O-Pee-Chee #232	.25
☐	94 Pacific #635	.25
☐	94 Score Rookies&Traded #RT12	.25
☐	94 Score Rookies&Traded(Gold Rush) #RT12	.50
☐	94 Select #12	.25
☐	93 Syracuse Blue Jays/ FleerProCards #1009	.50
☐	94 ToppsFinest #313	1.00
☐	94 ToppsFinest(Refractor) #313	6.00
☐	94 UpperDeck #176	.25
☐	94 UpperDeck(Electric Diamond) #176	.50
☐	94 UpperDeck Collector'sChoice #71	.25
☐	94 UD Collector'sChoice(Silver Signature) #71	.50
☐	94 UD Collector'sChoice(Gold Signature) #71	3.00
☐	95 Pacific #438	.25
☐	95 Topps #116	.25

STEVE CHARLES

☐	96 St. Catharines Stompers/ Best #6	.75

REGGIE CLEVELAND

☐	70 Topps #716	15.00
☐	71 O-Pee-Chee #216	4.00
☐	71 Topps #2163	3.50
☐	72 O-Pee-Chee #375	3.50
☐	72 Topps #375	3.00
☐	73 O-Pee-Chee #104	2.00
☐	73 Topps #104	1.50
☐	74 O-Pee-Chee #175	2.00
☐	74 Topps #175	1.00
☐	74 Topps Traded #175T	1.00
☐	75 O-Pee-Chee #32	1.50
☐	75 Topps #32	1.00
☐	75 Topps Mini #32	2.00
☐	76 O-Pee-Chee #419	1.00
☐	76 Topps #419	1.00
☐	77 O-Pee-Chee #111	.75
☐	77 Topps #613	.75
☐	78 Topps #105	.75
☐	78 Topps/ BurgerKing #10	1.00
☐	79 O-Pee-Chee #103	.50
☐	79 Topps #209	.50
☐	80 Topps #394	.59
☐	81 Donruss #206	.35
☐	81 Fleer #523	.35
☐	81 Topps #576	.35
☐	82 Donruss #456	.35
☐	82 Fleer #137	.35
☐	82 Topps #737	.35

RHÉAL CORMIER

☐	91 Bowman #396	.25
☐	92 Bowman #473	.50
☐	92 Donruss #712	.25

☐	92 Fleer Update #119	.25
☐	92 Leaf #469	.25
☐	92 O-Pee-Chee #346	.25
☐	92 Topps #346	.25
☐	92 Topps(Gold) #346	.50
☐	92 Topps Mini #346	.25
☐	92 Topps MLDebut'91 #40	.25
☐	92 ToppsStadiumClub #506	.25
☐	92 UpperDeck #574	.25
☐	93 Ben'sDisk #20	1.25
☐	93 Donruss #228	.25
☐	93 Fleer #124	.25
☐	93 FleerUltra #462	.25
☐	93 Leaf #209	.25
☐	93 O-Pee-Chee #34	.25
☐	93 Pinnacle #360	.25
☐	93 STL Cardinals/ Police [no#]	.50
☐	93 Score #371	.25
☐	93 Topps #149	.25
☐	93 Topps(Gold) #149	.50
☐	93 ToppsStadiumClub #15	.25
☐	93 ToppsStadiumClub (Members Only) #15	1.00
☐	93 ToppsStadiumClub(First Day Issue) #15	3.00
☐	93 UpperDeck #79	.25
☐	94 Donruss #622	.25
☐	94 Flair #224	.50
☐	94 Fleer #630	.25
☐	94 Leaf #110	.25
☐	94 Pacific #587	.25
☐	94 STL Cardinals/ Police [no#]	.50
☐	94 Topps #594	.25
☐	94 Topps(Gold) #594	.50
☐	94 ToppsFinest #248	1.00
☐	94 ToppsFinest(Refractor) #248	6.00
☐	94 ToppsStadiumClub #437	.25
☐	94 ToppsStadiumClub(Rainbow) #437	.50
☐	94 ToppsStadiumClub(Members Only) #437	1.00
☐	94 ToppsStadiumClub(First Day Issue) #437	3.00
☐	94 UpperDeck #422	.25
☐	94 UpperDeck(Electric Diamond) #422	.50
☐	94 UpperDeck Collector'sChoice #481	.25
☐	94 UD Collector'sChoice(Silver Signature) #481	.50
☐	94 UD Collector'sChoice(Gold Signature) #481	3.00
☐	95 Donruss #352	.25
☐	95 Donruss(Press Proof) #352	3.00
☐	95 Fleer #495	.25
☐	95 Leaf #304	.25
☐	95 Topps #138	.25
☐	95 Topps Traded #30T	.25
☐	95 UpperDeck Collector'sChoice #572T	.35
☐	96 Donruss #97	.25
☐	96 Donruss(Press Proof) #97	3.00
☐	96 LeafSignatureSeries-Autograph(Bronze)	6.00
☐	96 LeafSignatureSeries-Autograph(Silver)	8.00
☐	96 LeafSignatureSeries-Autograph(Gold)	12.00
☐	96 MTL Expos/ Disk [no#]	.50
☐	96 UpperDeck Collector'sChoice #61	.25
☐	96 UD Collector'sChoice(Silver Signature) #61	.35
☐	96 UD Collector'sChoice(Gold Signature) #61	1.50
☐	97 FleerUltra #467	.25
☐	97 FleerUltra (Gold Medallion) #371	.50
☐	97 FleerUltra (Platinum Medallion) #371	8.00
☐	97 Topps #467	.25

BARRY CORT

☐	78 Spokane Indians/ Cramer #18	1.50
☐	79 Holyoke Millars/ TCMA #26	1.50
☐	80 Holyoke Millars/ TCMA #4	1.50

PETE CRAIG

☐	65 Topps #466 (w/Dick Nen)	15.00
☐	66 O-Pee-Chee #11 (w/Brant Alyea)	4.00
☐	66 Topps #11 (w/Brant Alyea)	3.00
☐	67 Topps #459 (w/Dick Bosman)	12.00

KEN CROSBY

☐	76 O-Pee-Chee #593 (w/)	1.00
☐	76 Topps #593 (w/)	1.00

DEREK DEMPSTER

☐	96 Bowman #140	1.50
☐	96 Bowman(Foil) #140	2.00

JASON DICKSON

☐	95 SP MinorLeague #28	1.50
☐	96 Bowman #219	6.00
☐	96 Bowman(Foil) #219	8.00
☐	96 Vancouver Canadians/ Best #9	6.00
☐	97 Bowman #79	1.25
☐	97 Bowman(Foil) #79	4.00

- ☐ 97 Bowman'sBest #105 — 1.50
- ☐ 97 Bowman'sBest(Refractor) #79 — 8.00
- ☐ 97 Bowman'sBest(Atomic Refractor) #79 — 15.00
- ☐ 97 DonrussSig.Series-Autograph [no#] — 15.00
- ☐ 97 Donruss Update #371 — .35
- ☐ 97 Donruss Update(Press Proof) #371 — 4.00
- ☐ 97 Donruss Update(Press Proof Gold, #/500) #371 — 15.00
- ☐ 97 Donruss TeamSets #11 — .50
- ☐ 97 Fleer #37 — .50
- ☐ 97 Fleer(Tiffany) #37 — 10.00
- ☐ 97 FleerUltra #451 — .50
- ☐ 97 FleerUltra(Gold Medallion) #451 — 1.00
- ☐ 97 FleerUltra(Platinum Medallion, #/100) #451 — 20.00
- ☐ 97 FleerUltra-GoldenProspects #7 — .75
- ☐ 97 Limited(Counterparts) #52 (w/Randy Johnson) — 2.00
- ☐ 97 Limited(Counterparts, Ltd. Exposure) #52 (w/) — 20.00
- ☐ 97 Limited(Double Team) #198 (w/Darin Erstad) — 8.00
- ☐ 97 Limited(Double Team, Ltd. Exposure) #198 (w/) — 50.00
- ☐ 97 Pinnacle #134 — .50
- ☐ 97 Pinnacle(Museum Collection) #134 — 4.00
- ☐ 97 Pinnacle(Artist's Proof) #134 — 15.00
- ☐ 97 PinnacleCertified #124 — 1.00
- ☐ 97 PinnacleCertified(Certified Red) #124 — 6.00
- ☐ 97 PinnacleCertified(Mirror Red) #124 — 25.00
- ☐ 97 PinnacleCertified(Mirror Blue) #124 — 50.00
- ☐ 97 PinnacleCertified(Mirror Gold) #124 — 150.00

A single PinnacleCertified "Mirror Black" card also exists.

- ☐ 97 PinnacleNew #158 — .50
- ☐ 97 PinnacleNew(Museum Collection) #158 — 4.00
- ☐ 97 PinnacleNew(Red Artist's Proof) #158 — 8.00

Eight "1of1" PinnacleNew "Authentic Press Plates" also exist.

- ☐ 97 PinnacleXPress #130 — .35
- ☐ 97 PinnacleXPress(Men Of Summer) #130 — 3.00
- ☐ 97 PinnacleTotallyCertified(Platinum Red) #124 — 3.00
- ☐ 97 PinnacleTotallyCertified(Platinum Blue) #124 — 6.00
- ☐ 97 PinnacleTotallyCertified(Platinum Gold) #124 — 175.00
- ☐ 97 Score #475 — .35
- ☐ 97 Score(Showcase Series) #475 — 1.50
- ☐ 97 Score(Artist'sProof) #475 — 6.00
- ☐ 97 Select #117 — .50
- ☐ 97 Select(Company) #117 — 2.00
- ☐ 97 Select(Registered Gold) #117 — 4.00
- ☐ 97 Select(Artist's Proof) #117 — 10.00
- ☐ 97 SportsIllustrated #5 — .50
- ☐ 97 SportsIllustrated(Extra Edition, #/500) — 8.00
- ☐ 97 SP #14 — .75
- ☐ 97 ToppsStars #91 — .50
- ☐ 97 ToppsStars(Always Mint) #91 — 4.00
- ☐ 97 UpperDeck Collector'sChoice #254 — .35
- ☐ 98 CircaThunder #70 — .50
- ☐ 98 CircaThunder(Rave, #/150) #70 — 20.00
- ☐ 98 CircaThunder(SuperRave, #/25) #70 — 150.00
- ☐ 98 Donruss #15 — .35
- ☐ 98 Donruss(Press Proof) #15 — 4.00
- ☐ 98 Donruss(Press Proof Gold, #/500) #15 — 10.00
- ☐ 98 Donruss Crusade(Green, #/250) — 20.00
- ☐ 98 Donruss Crusade(Purple, #/100) — 30.00
- ☐ 98 Donruss Crusade(Red, #/25) — 150.00
- ☐ 98 DonrussPreferred(Grandstand) #122 — .50
- ☐ 98 DonrussPreferred(Preferred Seating) #122 — 4.00
- ☐ 98 FleerTradition #84 — .50
- ☐ 98 FleerTradition-Vintage'63 #1 — .75
- ☐ 98 FleerTradition-Vintage'63(Classic, #/63) #1 — 50.00
- ☐ 98 FleerTradition-RookieSensations #3RS — 4.00
- ☐ 98 Leaf #141 — .50
- ☐ 98 Leaf(Bronze-X) #141 — 4.00
- ☐ 98 Leaf(X-Axis Die-Cut) #141 — 15.00
- ☐ 98 LeafFractalMaterials(#/3999) #141 — 3.00
- ☐ 98 LeafFractalMaterials(Plastic, #ed 201-3250) #141 — 4.00
- ☐ 98 LeafFractalMaterials(X Die-Cut, #ed 1-200) #141 — 30.00
- ☐ 98 LeafFractalMaterials(Z2 Axis, #/20) #141 — 175.00
- ☐ 98 MetalUniverse #130 — .50
- ☐ 98 MetalUniverse(PreciousMetals, #/50) #130 — 40.00
- ☐ 98 Pacific #3 — .35
- ☐ 98 Pacific(Silver) #3 — .75
- ☐ 98 Pacific(Red) #3 — .75
- ☐ 98 Pacific(Platinum Blue) #3 — 30.00
- ☐ 98 Score #100 — .35
- ☐ 98 Score(ShowcaseSeries) #100 — 1.00
- ☐ 98 Score(Artist's Proof) #100 — 4.00
- ☐ 98 Sports Illustrated #30 — .35
- ☐ 98 Sports Illustrated(Extra Edition, #/250) #30 — 12.00
- ☐ 98 SI: Then&Now #75 — .50
- ☐ 98 SI: Then&Now(Extra Edition, #/500) #75 — 8.00
- ☐ 98 StadiumClub #15 — .50
- ☐ 98 StadiumClub(First Day Issue, #/200) #15 — 15.00
- ☐ 98 StadiumClub(One of a Kind, #/150) #15 — 20.00
- ☐ 98 Topps #129 — .35
- ☐ 98 Topps(Minted in Cooperstown) #129 — 2.00
- ☐ 98 ToppsChrome #129 — 1.50
- ☐ 98 ToppsChrome(Refractor) #129 — 12.00
- ☐ 98 ToppsFinest #46 — .75
- ☐ 98 ToppsFinest(No Protector) #46 — 1.50
- ☐ 98 ToppsFinest(Refractor) #46 — 6.00
- ☐ 98 ToppsFinest(No Protector Refractor) #46 — 8.00
- ☐ 98 Ultra #186 — .50
- ☐ 98 Ultra(Gold Medallion) #186 — 1.00
- ☐ 98 Ultra(Platinum, #/100) #186 — 30.00

One "1of1" Ultra Masterpiece card also exists.

- ☐ 98 Ultra-BackToTheFuture #13 — 2.00
- ☐ 98 UpperDeck #21 — .50
- ☐ 98 UD-BlueChipProspects #BC3 — 10.00
- ☐ 98 UD Collector's Choice #24 — .35
- ☐ 98 UDCC-StarQuest(SpecialDelivery) #SQ3 — .50

ROB DUCEY

- ☐ 86 Ventura Gulls/ ProCards [no#] — 1.00
- ☐ 87 Syracuse Chiefs/ProCards #19 — 1.00
- ☐ 87 TOR Blue Jays/ FireSafety [no#] — .50
- ☐ 88 Fleer #107 — .25
- ☐ 88 Fleer(Glossy) #107 — .50
- ☐ 88 O-Pee-Chee #106 — .25
- ☐ 88 Score #629 — .25
- ☐ 88 Syracuse Chiefs/CMC #14 — .75
- ☐ 88 Syracuse Chiefs/ProCards #825 — .75
- ☐ 88 Topps #438 — .25
- ☐ 88 Topps(Tiffany) #438 — .50
- ☐ 88 TOR Blue Jays/ FireSafety — .50
- ☐ 89 O-Pee-Chee #203 — .25
- ☐ 89 PaniniSticker #459 — .25
- ☐ 89 Topps #203 — .25
- ☐ 89 Topps(Tiffany) #203 — .50

☐	89 TOR Blue Jays/ FireSafety	.50
☐	89 UpperDeck #721	.25
☐	90 CMC #347	.25
☐	90 O-Pee-Chee #619	.25
☐	90 ProCards AAA #364	.25
☐	90 Syracuse Chiefs/CMC #21	.25
☐	90 Syracuse Chiefs/MerchantsBank [no#]	.50
☐	90 Syracuse Chiefs/ProCards #584	.25
☐	90 Topps #619	.25
☐	90 Topps(Tiffany) #619	.50
☐	90 UpperDeck #464	.25
☐	91 Donruss #705	.25
☐	91 LineDrive AAA #502	.25
☐	91 O-Pee-Chee #101	.25
☐	91 Score #821	.25
☐	90 Syracuse Chiefs/LineDrive #502	.25
☐	90 Syracuse Chiefs/MerchantsBank [no#]	.50
☐	90 Syracuse Chiefs/ProCards #2492	.25
☐	91 Topps #101	.25
☐	91 Topps(Tiffany) #101	.50
☐	91 Topps DesertShield #101	3.00
☐	91 Topps Mini #101	.25
☐	91 ToppsStadiumClub #374	.25
☐	91 TOR Blue Jays/ FireSafety	.50
☐	91 TOR Blue Jays/ Score #22	.50
☐	92 Donruss #466	.25
☐	92 Fleer #328	.25
☐	92 O-Pee-Chee #739	.25
☐	92 ProCards #163	.25
☐	92 Topps #739	.25
☐	92 Topps(Gold) #739	.50
☐	92 Topps Mini #739	.25
☐	92 ToppsStadiumClub #422	.25
☐	92 TOR Blue Jays/ FireSafety	.50
☐	93 Donruss #489	.25
☐	93 O-Pee-Chee #55	.25
☐	93 Topps #293	.25
☐	93 Topps(Gold) #293	.50
☐	93 ToppsStadiumClub #69	.25
☐	93 ToppsStadiumClub(First Day Issue) #69	3.00
☐	93 TOR Blue Jays/ Donruss #40	.50
☐	94 Topps #618	.25
☐	94 Topps(Gold) #618	.50

BLAINE FORTIN

☐	96 St.Catharines Stompers/ Best #8	.75

DICK FOWLER

☐	49 Bowman #171	85.00
☐	50 Bowman #214	25.00
☐	52 Bowman #190	25.00
☐	52 Topps #210	55.00

DOUG FROBEL

☐	81 Buffalo Bisons/ TCMA #22	1.00
☐	82 Portland Beavers/ TCMA #20	1.00
☐	84 Donruss #38	1.00
☐	84 Topps #264	.35
☐	84 Topps(Tiffany) #264	1.00
☐	84 Topps(Nestle) #264	.75
☐	85 Fleer #464	.25
☐	85 opcSticker #128	.25
☐	85 Topps #587	.25
☐	85 Topps(Tiffany) #587	.50
☐	85 ToppsSticker #128	.25

MIKE GARDINER

☐	90 Best #262	.25
☐	90 Williamsport Bills/ Best #6	.25
☐	90 Williamsport Bills/ ProCards #1052	.25
☐	91 Donruss #417	.25
☐	90 ProCards A and AA	.25
☐	91 Donruss Rookies #46	.25
☐	91 PaniniTopFifteenSticker #91	.25
☐	91 Pawtucket Red Sox/ LineDrive #355	.25
☐	91 Pawtucket RedSox/ ProCards #31	.25
☐	91 Score #721	.25
☐	91 Topps MLDebut'90 #52	.25
☐	91 UpperDeck #14	.25
☐	92 Donruss #290	.25
☐	92 Leaf #482	.25
☐	92 Leaf(Black Gold) #482	.50
☐	92 O-Pee-Chee #694	.25
☐	92 Pinnacle #505	.25
☐	92 Topps #694	.25
☐	92 Topps(Gold) #694	.50
☐	92 Topps Mini #694	.25
☐	92 ToppsStadiumClub #732	.25
☐	92 UpperDeck #588	.25
☐	93 Fleer #558	.25
☐	93 FleerUltra #414	.25
☐	93 Topps #241	.25

	Card	Price
☐	93 Topps(Gold) #241	.50
☐	93 UpperDeck #640	.25
☐	94 Fleer Update #U-44	.25
☐	94 ToppsStadiumClub #474	.25
☐	94 ToppsStadiumClub (Members Only) #474	1.00
☐	94 ToppsStadiumClub(Rainbow) #474	.50
☐	94 ToppsStadiumClub(First Day Issue) #474	3.00
☐	95 Fleer #52	.25
☐	95 Topps #97	.25

GLEN GORBOUS

	Card	Price
☐	56 Topps #174	20.00

TIM HARKNESS

	Card	Price
☐	62 Topps #404	10.00
☐	63 Topps #436	10.00
☐	64 Topps #57	6.00

BILL HARRIS

	Card	Price
☐	60 Topps #128	8.00

JEFF HEATH

	Card	Price
☐	49 Bowman #169	85.00

JOHN HILLER

	Card	Price
☐	66 Topps #209	4.00
☐	68 Topps #307	3.00
☐	69 Topps #642	6.00
☐	70 O-Pee-Chee #12	3.00
☐	70 Topps #12	2.50
☐	71 O-Pee-Chee #629	10.00
☐	71 Topps #629	8.00
☐	73 O-Pee-Chee #448	5.00
☐	73 Topps #448	4.00
☐	74 O-Pee-Chee #24	2.50
☐	74 O-Pee-Chee #208 (w/Marshall)	2.00
☐	74 Topps #24	1.50
☐	74 Topps #208 (w/Marshall)	1.50
☐	75 O-Pee-Chee #415	2.00
☐	75 Topps #415	2.00
☐	75 Topps Mini #415	2.50
☐	76 O-Pee-Chee #37	1.50
☐	76 Topps #37	1.50
☐	77 O-Pee-Chee #257	.75
☐	77 Topps #595	.75
☐	78 Topps #258	.50
☐	79 O-Pee-Chee #71	.50
☐	79 Topps #151	.50
☐	80 O-Pee-Chee #229	.50
☐	80 Topps #614	.50

BOB HOOPER

	Card	Price
☐	51 Bowman #33	30.00
☐	52 Bowman #10	25.00
☐	53 Topps #84	20.00
☐	54 Bowman #4	20.00
☐	55 Bowman #271	25.00
☐	91 ToppsArchives '53 #84	.35

VINCE HORSMAN

	Card	Price
☐	87 MyrtleBeach BlueJays/ProCards #1440	1.00
☐	90 Dunedin BlueJays/Star [no#]	.25
☐	92 Donruss Rookies #53	.25
☐	92 Fleer Update #49	.25
☐	92 Leaf #487	.25
☐	92 Leaf(Black Gold) #487	.50
☐	92 Pinnacle #524	.25
☐	92 ProCards #164	.25
☐	92 Score Traded #106T	.25
☐	92 Topps Traded #53T	.25
☐	92 Topps Traded(Gold) #53T	.50
☐	92 Topps MLDebut'91 #81	.25
☐	92 ToppsStadiumClub #637	.25
☐	93 Donruss #347	.25
☐	93 Fleer #295	.25
☐	93 FleerUltra #259	.25
☐	93 Score #406	.25
☐	93 Select #316	.25
☐	93 Topps #263	.25
☐	93 Topps(Gold) #263	.50
☐	93 ToppsStadiumClub #256	.25
☐	93 ToppsStadiumClub(First Day Issue) #256	3.00
☐	93 ToppsStadiumClub(Members Only) #256	1.00

PETE HOY

- ☐ 90 WinterHaven RedSox/ Star #11 .25
- ☐ 91 NewBritain RedSox/ LineDrive #464 .25
- ☐ 92 Bowman #292 .35
- ☐ 92 Donruss Rookies #56 .25
- ☐ 92 FleerUltra #315 .25
- ☐ 92 Leaf #515 .25
- ☐ 92 Leaf(Black Gold) #515 .50
- ☐ 92 Pinnacle #526 .25
- ☐ 93 Score #230 .25

FERGUSON JENKINS

- ☐ 66 Topps #254 110.00
- ☐ 67 CHICubs/The Pro's Pizza [no#] 600.00
- ☐ 67 Topps #333 25.00
- ☐ 68 O-Pee-Chee #9 (w/Bunning, McCormick, Osteen) 8.00
- ☐ 68 O-Pee-Chee #11 (w/Bunning, Perry) 8.00
- ☐ 68 Topps #9 (w/Bunning, McCormick, Osteen) 6.00
- ☐ 68 Topps #11 (w/Bunning, Perry) 6.00
- ☐ 68 Topps #410 12.00
- ☐ 69 CHICubs/6"x9" [no#] 12.00
- ☐ 69 CHICubs/7"x83/4" Colour [n0# 8.00
- ☐ 69 O-Pee-Chee #10 (w/Marichal, Gibson) 12.00
- ☐ 69 O-Pee-Chee #12 (w/Gibson, Singer) 12.00
- ☐ 69 Topps #10 (w/Marichal, Gibson) 10.00
- ☐ 69 Topps #12 (w/Gibson, Singer) 10.00
- ☐ 69 Topps #640 25.00
- ☐ 70 O-Pee-Chee #69 (w/Seaver,P.Niekro,Marichal) 8.00
- ☐ 70 O-Pee-Chee #71 (w/Gibson,Singer) 8.00
- ☐ 70 O-Pee-Chee #240 12.00
- ☐ 70 Topps #69 (w/Seaver,P.Niekro,Marichal) 6.00
- ☐ 70 Topps #71 (w/Gibson,Singer) 6.00
- ☐ 70 Topps #240 10.00
- ☐ 71 O-Pee-Chee #70 (w/Gibson,Perry) 10.00
- ☐ 71 O-Pee-Chee #72 (w/Seaver,Gibson) 10.00
- ☐ 71 O-Pee-Chee #280 12.00
- ☐ 71 Topps #70 (w/Gibson,Perry) 8.00
- ☐ 71 Topps #72 (w/Seaver,Gibson) 8.00
- ☐ 71 Topps #280 9.00
- ☐ 72CHICubs/11"x14" Caricatures [no#] 4.00
- ☐ 72 CHICubs/41/4"x7" [no#] 5.00
- ☐ 72 O-Pee-Chee #93 (w/Carlton,Downing,Seaver) 5.00
- ☐ 72 O-Pee-Chee #95 (w/Seaver,Stoneman) 5.00
- ☐ 72 O-Pee-Chee #410 12.00
- ☐ 72 ProStar Postcard [no#] 15.00
- ☐ 72 ProStar Poster [no#] 30.00
- ☐ 72 Topps #93 (w/Carlton,Downing,Seaver) 4.00
- ☐ 72 Topps #95 (w/Seaver,Stoneman) 4.00
- ☐ 72 Topps #410 9.00
- ☐ 73 O-Pee-Chee #180 8.50
- ☐ 73 Topps #180 6.00
- ☐ 74 O-Pee-Chee #87 6.50
- ☐ 74 Topps #87 4.50
- ☐ 75 O-Pee-Chee #60 4.00
- ☐ 75 O-Pee-Chee #310 (w/Hunter,Messersmith) 3.00
- ☐ 75 Topps #60 4.00
- ☐ 75 Topps #310 (w/Hunter,Messersmith) 3.00
- ☐ 75 Topps Mini #60 6.00
- ☐ 75 Topps Mini #310 (w/Hunter,Messersmith) 4.00
- ☐ 76 O-Pee-Chee #250 4.00
- ☐ 76 Topps #250 4.00
- ☐ 76 Topps Traded #250T 4.00
- ☐ 77 Kellogg's 3-D #3 4.00
- ☐ 77 O-Pee-Chee #187 3.25
- ☐ 77 Topps #430 3.00
- ☐ 78 Topps #720 2.00
- ☐ 78 Topps/ BurgerKing #8 6.00
- ☐ 79 Topps #544 2.00
- ☐ 80 Kellogg's 3-D #47 3.00
- ☐ 80 O-Pee-Chee #203 2.00
- ☐ 80 Topps #390 2.00
- ☐ 81 Fleer #622 1.00
- ☐ 81 Fleer-Stickers #84 1.00
- ☐ 81 Topps #158 1.00
- ☐ 82 CHI Cubs/ Red Lobster [no#] 12.00
- ☐ 82 Donruss #643 1.00
- ☐ 82 Fleer #320 1.00
- ☐ 82 O-Pee-Chee #137 1.00
- ☐ 82 Topps #624 1.00
- ☐ 82 Topps Traded #49T 3.00
- ☐ 83 CHI Cubs/ Thorn Apple Valley [no#] 5.00
- ☐ 83 Donruss #300 1.00
- ☐ 83 Fleer #498 1.00
- ☐ 83 Fleer-Stickers #130 1.00
- ☐ 83 O-Pee-Chee #230 1.00
- ☐ 83 O-Pee-Chee #231 .75
- ☐ 83 opcSticker #224 .50
- ☐ 83 Topps #51 (w/ Leon Durham) .75
- ☐ 83 Topps #230 1.00
- ☐ 83 Topps #231 .75
- ☐ 83 ToppsSticker #224 .50
- ☐ 84 Donruss #189 4.00
- ☐ 84 Donruss-Champions(3.5"x5") #33 .75
- ☐ 84 Fleer #494 1.00
- ☐ 84 O-Pee-Chee #343 .75
- ☐ 84 opcSticker #48 .50
- ☐ 84 Topps #456 (w/ Keith Moreland) .50
- ☐ 84 Topps #483 .75
- ☐ 84 Topps #706 (w/ Carlton Seaver) .75
- ☐ 84 Topps(Tiffany) #456 (w/ Keith Moreland) 1.50
- ☐ 84 Topps(Tiffany) #483 3.00
- ☐ 84 Topps(Tiffany) #706 (w/ Carlton Seaver) 2.50
- ☐ 84 Topps(Nestle) #456 (W/ Keith Moreland) 1.00
- ☐ 84 Topps(Nestle) #483 2.00
- ☐ 84 Topps(Nestle) #706 (w/ Carlton Seaver) 1.50
- ☐ 84 ToppsSticker #48 .50
- ☐ 89 Pacific SeniorLeague #29 .50
- ☐ 91 CHI Cubs/ Vine Line #15 3.00

☐	91 UpperDeck-HeroesOfBaseball #H3	6.00
☐	91 UpperDeck-HeroesOfBaseball (Autograph) #H3	65.00
☐	93 UpperDeck All-TimeHeroes #74	.50
☐	94 UpperDeck All-TimeHeroes #97	.50
☐	98 SI: Then&Now #12	.75
☐	98 SI: Then&Now(Extra Edition #/500) #12	12.00
☐	98 SI: Then&Now-GreatShots #16	.50

MIKE JOHNSON

☐	97 Bowman #314	1.50
☐	97 Bowman(Foil) #314	2.00

MIKE KILKENNY

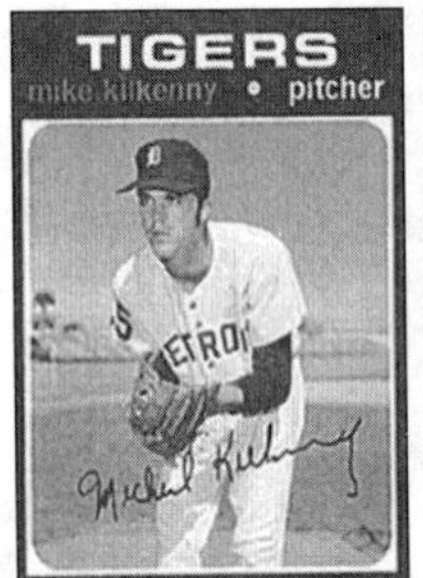

☐	69 Topps #544 (w/Ron Ward)	4.00
☐	70 O-Pee-Chee #424	4.00
☐	70 Topps #424	3.50
☐	71 O-Pee-Chee #86	4.00
☐	71 Topps #86	3.50
☐	72 O-Pee-Chee #337	3.50
☐	72 Topps #337	3.00
☐	73 O-Pee-Chee #551	8.00
☐	73 Topps #551	6.00

DANNY KLASSEN

☐	96 Bowman #328	2.00
☐	96 Bowman(Foil) #328	3.00
☐	97 Bowman #395	.50
☐	97 Bowman(Foil) #395	.75

GEORGE KORINCE

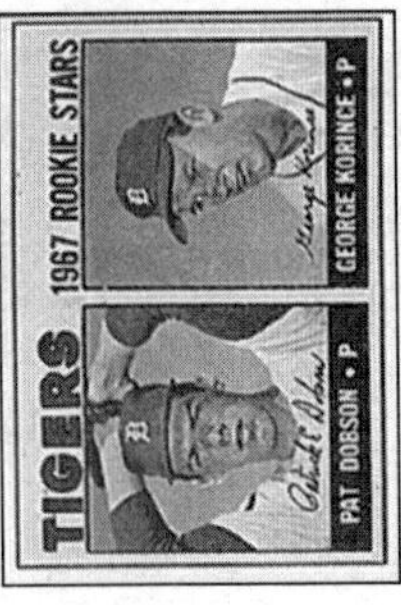

☐	67 OPC #72 (w/J.Matchick), Err. (photo Ike Brown)	4.00
☐	67 Topps #72 (w/J.Matchick), Err. (photo Ike Brown)	3.00
☐	67 Topps #526 (w/Pat Dobson)	10.00

MIKE KUSIEWICZ

☐	95 Asheville Tourists [no#]	2.00
☐	96 Bowman #113	1.50
☐	96 Bowman(Foil) #113	2.00
☐	96 NewHaven Ravens/ Best 16	2.00

YAN LACHAPELLE

☐	96 St.Catharines Stomers/ Best #15	.75

LARRY LANDRETH

☐	78 Topps #701	.75

ANDY LAWRENCE

☐	85 LyncchburgMets/TCMA #22	1.00
☐	86 JacksonMets/TCMA #16	1.00
☐	87 Jacksonville Expos/ ProCards #435	.75
☐	88 Jacksonville Expos/ Best #19	.75
☐	88 Jacksonville Expos/ ProCards #972	.75

CLINT LAWRENCE

☐	96 St.Catharines Stompers/ Best #16	.75

DICK LINES

- ☐ 67 Topps #273 4.00
- ☐ 68 Topps #291 3.50

RICK LISI

- ☐ 76 Asheville Tourists/ TCMA #7 2.50
- ☐ 79 Tulsa Drillers/ TCMA #14 1.50
- ☐ 80 Charlston Charlies/ TCMA #9 1.50
- ☐ 82 Rochester RedWings/ TCMA #14 1.50
- ☐ 83 Rochester RedWings/ TCMA #21 1.50

MIKE LUMLEY

- ☐ 90 LondonTigers/ ProCards #1265 .25
- ☐ 92 LondonTigers/ ProCards #630 .25
- ☐ 92 LondonTigers/ SkyBox #412 .25
- ☐ 93 Toledo Tigers #1653 .25

KEN MACKENZIE

- ☐ 60 Topps #534 25.00
- ☐ 61 Topps #496 12.00
- ☐ 62 Topps #421 10.00
- ☐ 63 Topps #393 10.00

SCOTT MANN

- ☐ 86 WestPalmBeachExpos/ProCards [no#] 1.00
- ☐ 87 Jacksonville Expos/ ProCards #436 1.00
- ☐ 88 Jacksonville Expos/ ProCards #964 .75

GEORGES MARANDA

- ☐ 52 LaPatrie [no#] 25.00
- ☐ 52 LavalDairy #5 30.00
- ☐ 60 Topps #479 12.00

PHIL MARCHILDON

- ☐ 49 Bowman #187 85.00

MATT MAYSEY

- ☐ 91 Harrisburg Senators/ LineDrive #264 .25
- ☐ 92 Indianapolis Indians/ FleerProCards #1855 .25
- ☐ 92 Indianapolis Indians/ SkyBox #187 .25
- ☐ 93 NewOrleans Zephyrs/ FleerProCards #968 .25
- ☐ 94 Score #610 .25
- ☐ 94 Score (Gold Rush) #610 .50

KIRK MCCASKILL

☐	83 RedwoodPioneers/TCMA #19	4.00
☐	85 EdmontonTrappers/Cramer #7	2.00
☐	86 CAL Angels/ Smokey #5	.75
☐	86 Donruss #474	.50
☐	86 Fleer #163	.50
☐	86 Topps #628	.35
☐	86 Topps(Tiffany) #628	1.00
☐	87 CAL Angels/ Smokey #5	.50
☐	87 Donruss #381	.25
☐	87 Fleer #88	.25
☐	87 Fleer(Glossy) #88	.50
☐	87 Fleer GameWinners #27	.25
☐	87 Fleer HottestStars #29	.25
☐	87 Fleer Mini #67	.25
☐	87 Fleer Stickers #75	.25
☐	87 GeneralMills Booklet(A.L. West, w/others) [no#]	8.00
☐	87 Leaf #223	.25
☐	87 O-Pee-Chee #194	.25
☐	87 opcSticker #181	.25
☐	87 Sportflics #127	.35
☐	87 Topps #194	.25
☐	87 Topps(Tiffany) #194	.50
☐	87 ToppsSticker #181	.25
☐	88 CAL Angels/ Smokey #12	.50
☐	88 Donruss #381	.25
☐	88 Fleer #496	.25
☐	88 Fleer(Glossy) #496	.50
☐	88 PaniniSticker #36	.25
☐	88 Score #552	.25
☐	88 Sportflics #78	.35
☐	88 StartingLineUp GameCard [no#]	.50
☐	88 Topps #16	.25
☐	88 Topps(Tiffany) #16	.50
☐	88 Topps Big #168	.25
☐	89 Donruss #136	.25
☐	89 Fleer #483	.25
☐	89 Fleer(Glossy) #483	.50
☐	89 O-Pee-Chee #348	.25
☐	89 opcSticker #184	.25
☐	89 PaniniSticker #285	.25
☐	89 Score #181	.25
☐	89 Topps #421	.25
☐	89 Topps(Tiffany) #421	.50
☐	89 Topps Big #149	.25
☐	89 ToppsSticker #184	.25
☐	89 UpperDeck #223	.25
☐	90 CAL Angels/ Smokey #11	.50
☐	90 Donruss #170	.25
☐	90 Fleer #138	.25
☐	90 Fleer("Ptd in Canada") #138	.75
☐	90 O-Pee-Chee #215	.25
☐	90 PaniniSticker #37	.25
☐	90 Score #217	.25
☐	90 Topps #215	.25
☐	90 Topps(Tiffany) #215	.50
☐	90 UpperDeck #506	.25
☐	91 CAL Angels/ Smokey #10	.50
☐	91 Donruss #637	.25
☐	91 DonrussStudio #28	.25
☐	91 Fleer #319	.25
☐	91 O-Pee-Chee #532	.25
☐	91 Score #590	.25
☐	91 Topps #532	.25
☐	91 Topps(Tiffany) #532	.50
☐	91 Topps DesertShield #532	3.00
☐	91 Topps Mini #532	.25
☐	91 ToppsStadiumClub #313	.25
☐	91 UpperDeck #539	.25
☐	92 Bowman #2	.25
☐	92 Donruss #340	.25
☐	92 DonrussStudio #155	.25
☐	92 Fleer #64	.25
☐	92 FleerUltra #338	.25
☐	92 Leaf #517	.25
☐	92 Leaf(Black Gold) #517	.50
☐	92 O-Pee-Chee #301	.25
☐	92 OPC Premier #60	.25
☐	92 Pinnacle #391	.25
☐	92 Topps #301	.25
☐	92 Topps(Gold) #301	.50
☐	92 Topps Mini #301	.25
☐	92 ToppsStadiumClub #688	.25
☐	92 UpperDeck #128	.25
☐	92 Topps Traded #69T	.25
☐	92 Topps Traded(Gold) #69T	.50
☐	92 UpperDeck #722	.25
☐	93 Donruss #227	.25
☐	93 Fleer #206	.25
☐	93 FleerUltra #535	.25
☐	93 Leaf #151	.25
☐	93 O-Pee-Chee #230	.25
☐	93 Pinnacle #560	.25
☐	93 Score #469	.25
☐	93 Select #387	.25
☐	93 Topps #175	.25
☐	93 Topps(Gold) #175	.50
☐	93 ToppsStadiumClub #166	.25
☐	93 ToppsStadiumClub(First Day Issue) #166	3.00
☐	93 ToppsStadiumClub(Members Only) #166	1.00
☐	93 TriplePlay #82	.25
☐	93 UpperDeck #608	.25
☐	94 Donruss #540	.25
☐	94 Flair #34	.50
☐	94 Fleer #88	.25
☐	94 FleerUltra #37	.25
☐	94 Pacific #133	.25
☐	94 Topps #724	.25
☐	95 Donruss #425	.25
☐	95 Fleer #125	.25
☐	95 FleerUltra #32	.25
☐	95 Score #544	.25
☐	95 Score(Gold Rush) #544	.50
☐	95 Score(Platinum) #544	1.00
☐	96 Fleer #73	.25
☐	96 Fleer(Tiffany) #73	.50

DAVE MCKAY

☐	75 Tacoma Twins/ KMMO #2	2.50
☐	76 O-Pee-Chee #592 (w/Randolph, Royster, Staiger)	6.00
☐	76 Tacoma Twins/ DairyQueen [no#]	2.50
☐	76 Topps #592 (w/Randolph, Royster, Staiger)	6.00
☐	77 O-Pee-Chee #40	.75
☐	77 Topps #377	.75
☐	79 O-Pee-Chee #322	.50
☐	79 Topps #608	.50
☐	81 Donruss #350	.35
☐	81 Fleer #526	.35
☐	81 Topps #461	.35
☐	82 Donruss #391	.35
☐	82 Fleer #100	.35
☐	82 Topps #534	.35
☐	83 Donruss #213	.35
☐	83 Fleer #392	.35
☐	83 Topps #47	.35
☐	92 Nabisco #12	.50

DAVE PAGAN

☐	74 SyracuseChiefs 4"x5"	3.00
☐	75 O-Pee-Chee #648	2.00
☐	75 SyracuseChiefs	3.00
☐	75 TCMA InternationalLeague All-Star #9	2.00
☐	75 Topps #648	2.00
☐	75 Topps Mini #648	2.50
☐	77 O-Pee-Chee #151	.75
☐	77 Topps #508	.75

RON PICHE

☐	61 Topps #61	8.00
☐	62 Topps #582	30.00
☐	63 Topps #179	8.00
☐	65 Topps #464	15.00

GORDY PLADSON

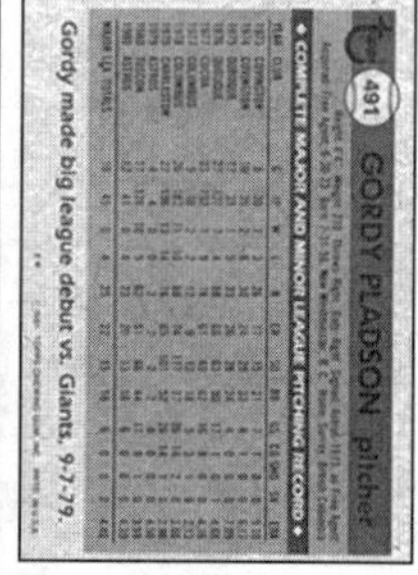

☐	75 Dubuque Packers/ TCMA #23	3.00
☐	76 Dubuque Packers/ TCMA [no#]	2.00
☐	77 Cocoa Astros/ TCMA [no#]	2.00
☐	79 Charleston Charlies/ TCMA #13	1.00
☐	80 Tuscon Toros/ TCMA #18	1.00
☐	81 Topps #491	.50
☐	81 Tuscon Toros/ TCMA #18	1.00
☐	83 Tuscon Toros/ TCMA #7	1.00

TERRY PUHL

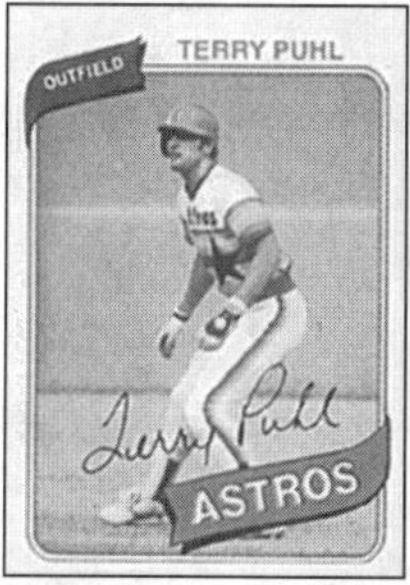

☐	75 Dubuque Packers/ TCMA #2	10.00
☐	78 Topps #553	2.00
☐	78 Topps/ Burger King #19	4.00
☐	79 Topps #617	.75
☐	80 O-Pee-Chee #82	.75
☐	80 Topps #147	.75

☐ 81 Donruss #24 .50
☐ 81 Fleer #62 .50
☐ 81 Topps #411 .75
☐ 82 Donruss #370 .50
☐ 82 Fleer #223 .50
☐ 82 O-Pee-Chee #277 .50
☐ 82 opcSticker #42 .50
☐ 82 Topps #277 .50
☐ 82 ToppsSticker #42 .50
☐ 83 Donruss #167 .35
☐ 83 Fleer #148 .35
☐ 83 O-Pee-Chee #39 .35
☐ 83 opcSticker #239 .35
☐ 83 Topps #39 .35
☐ 83 ToppsSticker #239 .35
☐ 84 Donruss #476 .75
☐ 84 Fleer #235 .50
☐ 84 HOU Astros/ Mother's Cookies #10 .75
☐ 84 opcSticker #67 .25
☐ 84 Topps #383 .35
☐ 84 Topps(Tiffany) #383 1.00
☐ 84 Topps(Nestle) #383 .75
☐ 84 ToppsSticker #67 .25
☐ 85 Donruss #426 .35
☐ 85 Fleer #356 .35
☐ 85 GeneralMills StickerPanel (w/R.Jackson) [no#] 4.00
☐ 85 HOU Astros/ Mother's Cookies #7 .75
☐ 85 Leaf #180 .35
☐ 85 O-Pee-Chee #283 .35
☐ 85 opcSticker #67 [w/253E, Camacho] .25
☐ 85 Topps #613 .35
☐ 85 Topps(Tiffany) #613 1.00
☐ 85 ToppsSticker #67 [w/253E, Camacho] .25
☐ 86 Donruss #206 .35
☐ 86 Fleer #308 .35
☐ 86 HOU Astros/ Mother's Cookies #16 .75
☐ 86 HOU Astros/ Police #21 .75
☐ 86 Leaf #138 .50
☐ 86 O-Pee-Chee #161 .25
☐ 86 Topps #763 .25
☐ 86 Topps (Tiffany) #763 .75
☐ 87 Donruss #431 .25
☐ 87 Fleer #65 .25
☐ 87 Fleer(Glossy) #65 .50
☐ 87 HOU Astros/ Mother's Cookies #7 .75
☐ 87 HOU Astros/ Police #15 .75
☐ 87 O-Pee-Chee #227 .25
☐ 87 Topps #693 .25
☐ 87 Topps(Tiffany) #693 .50
☐ 88 Donruss #533 .25
☐ 88 Fleer Update #U-90 .25
☐ 88 Fleer Update(Glossy) #U-90 .50
☐ 88 HOU Astros/ Mother's Cookies #7 .75
☐ 88 HOU Astros/ Police #17 .75
☐ 88 Score #282 .25
☐ 88 StartingLineUp GameCard [no#] .50
☐ 88 Topps #587 .25
☐ 88 Topps(Tiffany) #587 .50
☐ 89 Donruss #472 .25
☐ 89 Fleer #364 .25
☐ 89 Fleer(Glossy) #364 .50
☐ 89 HOU Astros/ HSE&Lennox #22 .50
☐ 89 HOU Astros/ Mother's Cookies #6 .50
☐ 89 HOU Astros/ Smokey [no#] .50
☐ 89 Score #567 .25
☐ 89 Topps #119 .25
☐ 89 Topps(Tiffany) #119 .50
☐ 90 Donruss #354 .25
☐ 90 Fleer #233 .25
☐ 90 HOU Astros/ HSE&Lennox [no#] .50
☐ 90 HOU Astros/ Mother's Cookies #9 .50
☐ 90 O-Pee-Chee #494 .25
☐ 90 PaniniSticker #256 .25
☐ 90 Score #473 .25
☐ 90 Topps #494 .25
☐ 90 Topps(Tiffany) #494 .50
☐ 90 UpperDeck #201 .25

PAUL QUANTRILL

☐ 90 Winter Haven Red Sox/ Star #21 .25
☐ 91 New Britain Red Sox/ LineDrive #469 .25
☐ 91 New Britain Red Sox/ ProCards #351 .25
☐ 92 Bowman #23 .50
☐ 92 Pawtucket Red Sox/ FleerProCards #921 .50
☐ 92 Pawtucket Red Sox/ SkyBox #363 .50
☐ 92 SkyBox AAA #165 .25
☐ 93 Donruss #327 .25
☐ 93 Fleer #181 .25
☐ 93 FleerUltra #155 .25
☐ 93 Leaf #544 .25
☐ 93 Pinnacle #175 .25
☐ 93 Score #221 .25
☐ 93 Topps #528 .25
☐ 93 Topps(Gold) #528 .50
☐ 94 Donruss #644 .25
☐ 94 Fleer #38 .25
☐ 94 Fleer Update #U-169 .25
☐ 94 FleerUltra #317 .25
☐ 94 Pacific #63 .25
☐ 94 Score #583 .25
☐ 94 Topps #417 .25
☐ 94 Topps(Gold) #417 .50
☐ 95 Fleer Update #U-124 .25
☐ 95 Topps Traded #127T .25
☐ 95 ToppsStadiumClub #577 .25
☐ 95 ToppsStadiumClub (MembersOnly) #577 1.00
☐ 95 ToppsStadiumClub(WorldSeries) #577 1.00
☐ 96 Donruss #348 .25
☐ 96 Donruss(Press Proof) #348 3.00
☐ 96 Flair(Silver) #191 .75
☐ 96 Flair(Gold) #191 .75
☐ 96 Fleer #281 .25
☐ 96 Fleer(Tiffany) #281 .50
☐ 96 Fleer Update #U-101 .25
☐ 96 Fleer Update(Tiffany) #U-101 .50
☐ 96 FleerUltra #258 .25
☐ 96 FleerUltra #435 .25
☐ 96 FleerUltra(Gold Medallion) #258 .50
☐ 96 FleerUltra(Gold Medallion) #435 .50
☐ 96 LeafSignatureSeriesExtended-Autograph [no#] 6.00
☐ 96 Pacific #158 .25
☐ 96 TOR Blue Jays/ OhHenry [no#] .50

☐	97 TOR Blue Jays/ Sizzler #21	.75
☐	98 Pacific #226	.25
☐	98 Pacific(Redr) #226	.50
☐	98 Pacific(Silver) #226	.50
☐	98 Pacific(Platinum Blue) #226	20.00

CLAUDE RAYMOND

☐	63 Topps #519	30.00
☐	64 Topps #504	12.00
☐	65 O-Pee-Chee #48	5.00
☐	65 Topps #48	4.00
☐	66 Topps #586	40.00
☐	67 Topps #364	5.00
☐	68 O-Pee-Chee #166	4.00
☐	68 Topps #166	3.00
☐	69 Topps #446	3.00
☐	70 O-Pee-Chee #268	4.00
☐	70 Topps #268	3.50
☐	71 O-Pee-Chee #536	8.00
☐	71 Topps #536	6.00
☐	83 Dimanche/DernièreHeure Photo [no#] (w/)	3.00
☐	92 Nabisco #23	.50
☐	93 MTL Expos/ McDonald's #26	.35

KEVIN REIMER

☐	86 SalemRedBirds/ProCards [no#]	1.50
☐	87 PortCharlotteRangers/ProCards #96	1.00
☐	89 Fleer #641	.25
☐	89 Fleer(Glossy) #641	.50
☐	90 CMC #169	.25
☐	90 Fleer #310	.25
☐	90 Fleer(Ptd. in Canada) #310	.50
☐	90 ProCards AAA #692	.25
☐	91 Donruss #80	.25
☐	91 Fleer #298	.25
☐	91 O-Pee-Chee #304	.25
☐	91 Score #836	.25
☐	91 Topps #304	.25
☐	91 Topps(Tiffany) #304	.50
☐	91 Topps DesertShield #304	3.00
☐	91 Topps Mini #304	.25
☐	91 UpperDeck #494	.25
☐	92 Donruss #251	.25
☐	92 Fleer #315	.25
☐	92 FleerUltra #444	.25
☐	92 Leaf #93	.25
☐	92 Leaf(Black Gold) #93	.50
☐	92 O-Pee-Chee #737	.25
☐	92 Pinnacle #340	.25
☐	92 Topps #737	.25
☐	92 Topps(Gold) #737	.50
☐	92 Topps Mini #737	.25
☐	92 ToppsStadiumClub #57	.25
☐	93 O-Pee-Chee #284	.25
☐	93 OPC Premier #131	.25
☐	93 PaniniSticker #43	.25
☐	94 PaniniSticker #85	.25
☐	93 Flair #228	.75
☐	93 Fleer #326	.25
☐	93 Fleer FinalEdition #F-232	.25
☐	93 FleerUltra #576	.25
☐	93 Leaf #377	.25
☐	93 Pinnacle #531	.25
☐	93 Select Rookie&Traded #101T	.25
☐	93 Topps #87	.25
☐	93 Topps(Gold) #87	.50
☐	93 UpperDeck #578	.25
☐	93 UpperDeckSP #69	.50
☐	94 Donruss #233	.25
☐	94 Fleer #189	.25
☐	94 FleerUltra #82	.25
☐	94 Score #477	.25
☐	94 Score(Gold Rush) #477	.50
☐	94 Topps #585	.25
☐	94 Topps(Gold) #585	.50
☐	94 UpperDeck Collector'sChoice #237	.25
☐	94 UD Collector'sChoice(Silver Signature) #237	.50
☐	94 UD Collector'sChoice(Gold Signature) #237	3.00

CHRIS REITSMA

☐	97 Bowman #219	1.50
☐	97 Bowman(Foil) #219	2.00
☐	97 Topps #273 (w/Josh Garrett)	.50

SHERRY ROBERTSON

☐	50 Bowman #161	25.00
☐	51 Bowman #95	30.00

JOHN RUTHERFORD

☐	52 Topps #320	300.00
☐	53 Topps #137	20.00
☐	91 Topps Archives'53 #137	.35
☐	95 Topps DodgersArchives #48	.50

DAVE SHIPANOFF

☐	84 SyracuseChiefs/TCMA #26	1.50
☐	85 PortlandBeavers/Cramer #28	1.00
☐	86 Donruss #31	.25
☐	86 Fleer #452	.50
☐	86 Leaf #29	.25
☐	86 PortlandBeavers/ProCards [no#]	1.00
☐	87 Edmonton Trappers/ ProCards #2065	1.00

PAUL SPOLJARIC

☐	93 Bowman #279	.75
☐	93 ClassicBest #118	.25
☐	93 ClassicBest #130	.25
☐	93 FleerExcel #245	.25
☐	94 Bowman #581	.25
☐	94 FleerUltra #439	.25
☐	94 LeafLimitedRookies #69	.75
☐	94 Pinnacle #539	.25
☐	94 Pinnacle(Museum Collection) #539	1.50
☐	94 Pinnacle(Artist's Proof) #539	4.00
☐	94 Score Rookie&Traded #RT137	.25
☐	94 Score Rookie&Traded(Gold Rush) #RT137	.50
☐	94 Topps #776 (w/Domingo Cedeno)	.25
☐	94 Topps(Gold) #776 (w/Domingo Cedeno)	.50
☐	94 UpperDeck #26	.25
☐	94 UpperDeck(Electric Diamond) #26	.50
☐	94 UpperDeck Collector'sChoice #668	.25
☐	94 UD Collector'sChoice(Silver Signature) #668	.50
☐	94 UD Collector'sChoice(Gold Signature) #668	2.00
☐	94 UpperDeck MinorLeague #149	.25
☐	95 Score #308	.25
☐	95 Score(Gold Rush) #308	.50
☐	95 Score(Platinum) #308	1.00
☐	95 Topps #644 (w/Angel Martinez)	.25
☐	95 TOR Blue Jays/ OhHenry [no#]	.50
☐	97 TOR Blue Jays/ Sizzler #17	.75

MATT STAIRS

☐	89 JamestownExpos/ ProCards #2141	5.00
☐	90 West Palm Beach Expos/ Star #23	.75
☐	91 Harrisburg Senators/ LineDrive #271	.75
☐	91 Harrisburg Senators/ ProCards #637	.75
☐	91 LineDrive AA #271	.75
☐	92 Bowman #434	2.00
☐	92 Bowman #602	1.50
☐	92 DonrussRookies #112	.50
☐	92 IndianapolisIndians/SkyBox #195	.50
☐	92 Leaf-GoldRookie #BC8	.75
☐	92 MTL Expos/ Durivage #16	6.00
☐	92 Pinnacle #583	.50
☐	92 Pinnacle-Rookies #28	.50
☐	92 ProCards #259	.50
☐	92 SkyBox AA #293	.35
☐	92 SkyBox AAA #94	.35
☐	92 Topps Traded #110T	.50
☐	92 Topps Traded(Gold) #110T	.75
☐	92 UpperDeck #786	.50
☐	93 Donruss #460	.35
☐	93 OttawaLynx/FleerProCards #2448	2.00
☐	93 Score #232	.35
☐	93 Select #327	.35
☐	96 LeafSignatureSeriesExtended-Autograph [no#]	10.00
☐	97 Pacific #176	.35
☐	97 Pacific(Light Blue) #176	.75
☐	97 Pacific(Silver) #176	25.00
☐	98 Donruss #50	.35
☐	98 Donruss(Press Proof) #50	4.00
☐	98 Donruss(Press Proof Gold, #/500) #50	10.00
☐	98 FleerTradition #180	.50
☐	98 Leaf #25	.50
☐	98 Leaf(Bronze-X) #25	4.00
☐	98 Leaf(X-Axis Die-Cut) #25	15.00
☐	98 LeafFractalMaterials(#/3999) #25	3.00
☐	98 LeafFractalMaterials(Plastic, #ed 201-3250) #25	4.00
☐	98 LeafFractalMaterials(X Die-Cut, #ed 1-200) #25	30.00
☐	98 LeafFractalMaterials(Z2 Axis, #/20) #25	150.00
☐	98 MetalUniverse #173	.50
☐	98 MetalUniverse(PreciousMetals, #/50) #173	35.00
☐	98 Pacific #174	.35
☐	98 Pacific(Silver) #174	.75
☐	98 Pacific(Red) #174	.75
☐	98 Pacific(Platinum Blue) #174	25.00
☐	98 Pinnacle #107	.50
☐	98 Pinnacle(Museum Collection) #107	4.00

☐ 98 Pinnacle(Artist's Proof) #107 8.00
Eight "1of1" PinnacleNew "Authentic Press Plates" also exist.
☐ 98 Sports Illustrated #106 .35
☐ 98 Sports Illustrated(Extra Edition, #/250) #106 12.00
☐ 98 Sports Illustrated-MiniPosters #OD21 .35
☐ 98 StadiumClub #268 .50
☐ 98 StadiumClub(First Day) #268 15.00
☐ 98 StadiumClub(One of a Kind) #268 20.00
☐ 98 Topps #16 .35
☐ 98 Topps(Minted in Cooperstown) #16 2.00
☐ 98 ToppsChrome #16 1.50
☐ 98 ToppsChrome(Refractor) #16 12.00
☐ 98 Ultra #16 .50
☐ 98 Ultra(Gold Medallion) #16 1.00
☐ 98 Ultra(Platinum, #/100) #16 25.00
One "1of1" Ultra "Masterpiece" card also exists.
☐ 98 UpperDeck #470 .50
☐ 98 UD Collector's Choice #195 .35

RON TAYLOR

☐ 62 Topps #591 (w/ McDowell, Nischwitz, Quirk, Redatz) 90.00
☐ 63 Topps #208 10.00
☐ 64 Topps #183 8.00
☐ 65 Topps #568 20.00
☐ 66 O-Pee-Chee #174 6.00
☐ 66 Topps #174 5.00
☐ 67 Topps #606 20.00
☐ 68 Topps #421 3.50
☐ 69 Topps #72 3.00
☐ 70 O-Pee-Chee #419 4.00
☐ 70 Topps #419 3.00
☐ 71 O-Pee-Chee #687 25.00
☐ 71 Topps #687 20.00
☐ 72 O-Pee-Chee #234 3.00
☐ 72 Topps #234 2.50

DAVE WAINHOUSE

☐ 89 Bowman #358 .35
☐ 89 Bowman(Tiffany) #358 .50
☐ 91 Harrisburg Senators/ LineDrive #272 .25
☐ 91 Harrisburg Senators/ ProCards #627 .25
☐ 92 FleerUltra #524 .25
☐ 92 IndianapolisIndians/SkyBox #197 .35
☐ 92 IndianapolisIndians/FleerProCards #1860 .35
☐ 92 MTL Expos/ Durivage #17 4.00
☐ 92 ProCards #260 .25
☐ 92 SkyBox AAA #95 .25
☐ 92 Topps MLDebut'91 #177 .25
☐ 92 ToppsStadiumClub #885 .25
☐ 93 FleerExcel #64 .25
☐ 93 Fleer FinalEdition #F-276 .25
☐ 93 FleerUltra #626 .25

LARRY WALKER

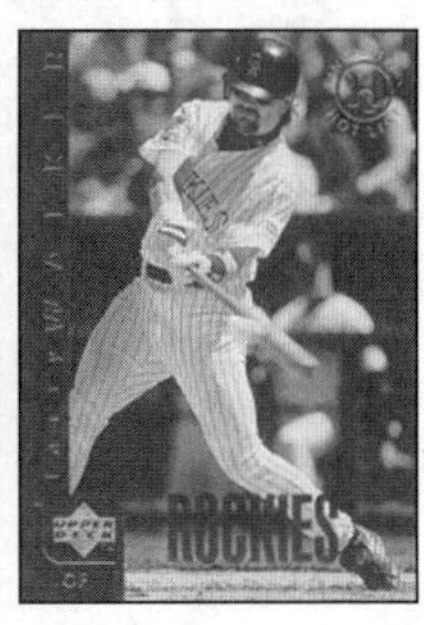

☐ 85 Utica Blue Sox/ TCMA #16 50.00
☐ 86 Burlington Expos/ ProCards [no#] 30.00
☐ 87 Jacksonville Expos/ ProCards #429 25.00
☐ 87 Southern League All-Stars #8 6.00
☐ 89 Indianapolis Indians/ CMC #23 8.00
☐ 89 Indianapolis Indians/ ProCards #1239 6.00
☐ 90 Bowman #117 1.50
☐ 90 Bowman(Tiffany) #117 6.00
☐ 90 Donruss #578 1.50
☐ 90 Fleer #363 1.50
☐ 90 Fleer("PTD in Canada") #363 3.50
☐ 90 Fleer-SoaringStars #3 8.00
☐ 90 Leaf #325 15.00
☐ 90 O-Pee-Chee #757 2.00
☐ 90 Score #631 1.50
☐ 90 Topps #757 2.00
☐ 90 Topps(Tiffany) #757 6.00
☐ 90 Topps MLDebut'89 #133 2.00
☐ 90 UpperDeck #466 3.00
☐ 90 UpperDeck #702 (w/DeShields,Grissom) 1.00
☐ 91 BaseballCardsMag. (66 Topps style card) #11 (w/) 1.00
☐ 91 Bowman #442 .75
☐ 91 Donruss #359 .75
☐ 91 Fleer #250 .75
☐ 91 Leaf #241 1.00
☐ 91 O-Pee-Chee #339 1.00
☐ 91 PaniniSticker #145 .75
☐ 91 Score #241 .75
☐ 91 Topps #339 1.00
☐ 91 Topps(Tiffany) #339 3.00
☐ 91 Topps DesertShield #339 25.00
☐ 91 Topps Mini #339 1.00
☐ 91 ToppsStadiumClub #93 2.00
☐ 91 UpperDeck #536 1.00
☐ 92 Bowman #648 2.00
☐ 92 Donruss #259 .75
☐ 92 Fleer #493 .75
☐ 92 FleerUltra #525 .75
☐ 92 Leaf #201 .75
☐ 92 Leaf(Black Gold) #201 2.50
☐ 92 MTL Expos/ Durivage #18 10.00
☐ 92 O-Pee-Chee #531 1.00
☐ 92 PaniniSticker #206 .75
☐ 92 Pinnacle #194 .75
☐ 92 Score #199 .75
☐ 92 Score-ImpactPlayers #29 2.00
☐ 92 Topps #531 1.00
☐ 92 Topps(Gold) #531 4.00
☐ 92 Topps Mini #531 1.00
☐ 92 ToppsStadiumClub #256 .75
☐ 92 ToppsStadiumClub MurphyStadiumSet #94 .75
☐ 92 TriplePlay #89 .75
☐ 92 UpperDeck #249 .75
☐ 93 Bowman #100 1.50

☐	93 Classic #97	.75
☐	93 Donruss Preview #6	5.00
☐	93 Donruss #540	.50
☐	93 Donruss-DiamondKing #DK6	3.00
☐	93 Donruss-TheEliteSeries #30	30.00
☐	93 Donruss-LongballLeaders #LL18	5.00
☐	93 Donruss-MVPs #9	2.00
☐	93 Flair #87	2.00
☐	93 Fleer #81	.50
☐	93 Fleer #715	.50
☐	93 Fleer-AllStar #NL6	3.00
☐	93 FleerUltra #71	.50
☐	93 FleerUltra-AllStars #8	2.00
☐	93 FleerUltra-AwardWinners #9	2.00
☐	93 Hostess #30	.75
☐	93 HumptyDumpty #42	1.50
☐	93 KennerStartingLineUp Figurine	18.00
☐	93 Leaf #392	.75
☐	93 MTL Expos/ McDonald's #7	3.00
☐	93 O-Pee-Chee #384	.50
☐	93 OPC Premier #39	.50
☐	93 PaniniSticker #231	.50
☐	93 Pinnacle #3	.50
☐	93 Pinnacle #299 (w/Mike Bossy)	.50
☐	93 Pinnacle-Slugfest #13	2.50
☐	93 Pinnacle-TeamPinnacle #10 (w/J.Carter)	8.00
☐	93 PostCanadian #13	3.00
☐	93 Score #95	.50
☐	93 Score-TheFranchise #20	6.00
☐	93 Select #27	.50
☐	93 Studio #123	.50
☐	93 Topps #95	.50
☐	93 Topps #406 (w/Kirby Puckett)	.50
☐	93 Topps(Gold) #95	2.00
☐	93 Topps(Gold) #406 (w/Kirby Puckett)	2.00
☐	93 Topps-BlackGold #22	1.00
☐	93 ToppsFinest #97	6.00
☐	93 ToppsFinest(Refractor) #97	325.00
☐	93 ToppsFinest(Jumbo) #97	15.00
☐	93 ToppsStadiumClub #299	.75
☐	93 ToppsStadiumClub #320	.75
☐	93 ToppsStadiumClub(First Day Issue) #299	18.00
☐	93 ToppsStadiumClub(First Day Issue) #320	18.00
☐	93 ToppsStadiumClub(Members Only) #299	5.00
☐	93 ToppsStadiumClub(Members Only) #320	5.00
☐	93 ToppsStadiumClub-MasterPhoto #24	1.50
☐	93 ToppsStadiumClub-MasterPhoto(5"x7") #24	1.50
☐	93 TriplePlay #42	.50
☐	93 TriplePlay-ActionBaseball 6	.75
☐	93 UpperDeck #144	.50
☐	93 UpperDeck #481 (w/)	.50
☐	93 UpperDeck-HomeRunHeroes #HR16	1.50
☐	93 UpperDeck-TripleCrown #TC10	3.00
☐	93 UpperDeck FunPack #98	.50
☐	93 UpperDeckSP #107	2.00
☐	94 Bowman #500	1.00
☐	94 Bowman'sBest(Red) #76	1.50
☐	94 Bowman'sBest(Red Refractor) #76	15.00
☐	94 Denny's #28	3.00
☐	94 Donruss #371	.75
☐	94 Donruss(Special Edition) #371	2.00
☐	94 Flair #404	1.50
☐	94 Feer #554	.75
☐	94 FleerExtraBases #412	.75
☐	94 FleerUltra #526	.75
☐	94 FU-AwardWinners #17	1.50
☐	94 Leaf #397	.75
☐	94 Leaf-CleanUpCrew #1	10.00
☐	94 LeafLimited #127	3.00
☐	94 O-Pee-Chee #253	.75
☐	94 OPC-AllStar #19	.75
☐	94 OPC-AllStar(5"x7") #19	1.50
☐	94 Pacific #392	.75
☐	94 PaniniSticker #213	.75
☐	94 Pinnacle #310	.75
☐	94 Pinnacle(Museum Collection) #310	6.00
☐	94 Pinnacle(Artist's Proof) #310	15.00
☐	94 Score #376	.75
☐	94 Score(Gold Rush) #376	2.00
☐	94 Score-DreamTeam #9	8.00
☐	94 Score-GoldStars #27	8.00
☐	94 Select #18	.75
☐	94 Select-Skills #SK9	10.00
☐	94 SP #86	1.00
☐	94 SP(Die-Cut) #86	2.00
☐	94 Sportflics #77	1.00
☐	94 Studio #80	.75
☐	94 Topps #230	.75
☐	94 Topps(Gold) #230	2.00
☐	94 ToppsFinest #216	4.00
☐	94 ToppsFinest(Refractor) #216	25.00
☐	94 ToppsStadiumClub #280	.75
☐	94 ToppsStadiumClub(Rainbow) #280	3.00
☐	94 ToppsStadiumClub(First Day Issue) #280	12.00
☐	94 ToppsStadiumClub(Members Only) #280	5.00
☐	94 TriplePlay #99	.75
☐	94 UpperDeck #274	.50
☐	94 UpperDeck #370	.75
☐	94 UpperDeck(Electric Diamond) #274	2.00
☐	94 UpperDeck(Electric Diamond) #370	3.00
☐	94 UpperDeck Collector'sChoice #286	.75
☐	94 UD Collector'sChoice(Silver Signature) #286	2.00
☐	94 UD Collector'sChoice(Gold Signature) #286	20.00
☐	94 UpperDeck FunPack #136	.75
☐	95 Bowman #290	2.00
☐	95 Bowman'sBest(Red) #63	2.00
☐	95 Bowman'sBest(Red Refractor) #63	15.00
☐	95 COL Rockies/ Police [no#]	3.00
☐	95 Donruss #492	1.00
☐	95 Donruss(Press Proof) #492	18.00
☐	95 Flair #348	1.50
☐	95 Fleer #361	1.00
☐	95 Fleer Update #U-171	1.00
☐	95 FleerUltra #409	1.00
☐	95 Leaf #305	1.00
☐	95 LeafLimited #91	2.00
☐	95 LeafLimited(Gold) #10	2.00
☐	95 LeafLimited-BatPatrol #4	2.00
☐	95 Pacific #273	.75
☐	95 Pacific-GoldPrism #30	6.50
☐	95 PacificPrism #89	4.00
☐	95 PaniniSticker #75	.75
☐	95 Pinnacle #372	1.00
☐	95 Pinnacle(Museum Collection) #372	6.00
☐	95 Pinnacle(Artist's Proof) #372	18.00
☐	95 PinnacleUC3 #90	1.00
☐	95 PinnacleUC3 #145	.75
☐	95 PinnacleUC3(Artist's Proof) #90	18.00
☐	95 PinnacleUC3(Artist's Proof) #145	12.00
☐	95 PinnacleZenith #67	1.50
☐	95 PinnacleZenith-ZTeam #11	15.00
☐	95 Score #346	.75
☐	95 Score(Gold Rush) #346	3.00
☐	95 Score(Platinum) #346	6.00
☐	95 Score-HallOfGold #HG71	3.00
☐	95 Score Trade'Em #346T	1.00
☐	95 Score Trade'Em HallOfGold #HGT71	4.00
☐	95 ScoreSummit #45	1.00

☐	95 ScoreSummit(Nth Degree) #45	8.00
☐	95 Select #224	.75
☐	95 Select(Artist's Proof) #224	20.00
☐	95 SelectCertified(Sample) #89	1.50
☐	95 SelectCertified #89	1.50
☐	95 SelectCertified(Mirror Gold) #89	12.00
☐	95 SkyBox E-Motion #126	1.50
☐	95 SP #50	1.00
☐	95 SP(Silver) #50	2.00
☐	95 SP-PlatinumPower #7	2.00
☐	95 SPChampionshipSeries #39	1.00
☐	95 SPChampionshipSeries #42	1.50
☐	95 SPChampionshipSeries(Die-Cut) #39	2.50
☐	95 SPChampionshipSeries(Die-Cut) #42	4.00
☐	95 Sportflics #139	1.00
☐	95 Sportflics(Artist's Proof) #139	12.00
☐	95 Studio #58	1.50
☐	95 Topps #422	1.00
☐	95 Topps(Cyberstats) #221	2.50
☐	95 ToppsTraded #20T	1.00
☐	95 ToppsBazooka #120	.75
☐	95 ToppsFinest #215	2.50
☐	95 ToppsFinest #274	2.50
☐	95 ToppsFinest(Refractor) #215	50.00
☐	95 ToppsFinest(Refractor) #274	50.00
☐	95 ToppsStadiumClub #148	1.00
☐	95 ToppsStadiumClub #618	1.00
☐	95 ToppsStadiumClub(First Day Issue) #148	12.00
☐	95 ToppsStadiumClub(World Series) #148	2.00
☐	95 ToppsStadiumClub(World Series) #618	2.00
☐	95 ToppsStadiumClub(Members Only) #148	5.00
☐	95 ToppsStadiumClub(Members Only) #618	5.00
☐	95 ToppsStadiumClub(Virtual Reality) #77	2.00
☐	95 ToppsStadiumClub(Virtual Reality Members) #77	4.00
☐	95 ToppsStadiumClub-CrunchTime #10	3.00
☐	95 ToppsStadiumClub-SuperSkills #SS15	5.00
☐	95 UpperDeck #82	1.00
☐	95 UpperDeck #415	3.00
☐	95 UD(Electric Diamond) #82	3.00
☐	95 UD(Electric Diamond) #415	3.00
☐	95 UD(Electric Diamond Gold) #82	15.00
☐	95 UD(Electric Diamond Gold) #415	15.00
☐	95 UpperDeck #SE4	2.00
☐	95 UpperDeck(Gold) #SE4	20.00
☐	95 UpperDeck-PredictorSeries #R34	3.00
☐	95 UpperDeck-PredictorSeries #R47	3.00
☐	95 UpperDeck-PredictorSeries(Gold) #R34	.75
☐	95 UpperDeck-PredictorSeries(Gold) #R47	.75
☐	95 UpperDeck Collector'sChoice #238	.75
☐	95 UD Collector'sChoice(Silver Signature) #238	2.00
☐	95 UD Collector'sChoice(Gold Signature) #238	10.00
☐	95 UpperDeck Collector'sChoice #TC1	3.50
☐	95 UpperDeck Collector'sChoice #579T	1.00
☐	95 UpperDeck Collector'sChoiceSE #96	.75
☐	95 UD Collector'sChoiceSE(Silver Signature) #96	2.00
☐	95 UD Collector'sChoiceSE(Gold Signature) #96	15.00
☐	96 Bowman #17	2.00
☐	96 Bowman(Foil) #17	4.00
☐	96 Bowman-Bowman'sBestPreview #BBP21	4.00
☐	96 B-Bowman'sBestPreview(Refractor) #BBP21	6.00
☐	96 B-Bowman'sBestPreview(Atomic Ref.) #BBP21	12.00
☐	96 Bowman'sBest #83	2.00
☐	96 Bowman'sBest(Refractor) #83	12.00
☐	96 Bowman'sBest(Atomic Refractor) #83	50.00
☐	96 Bowman'sBest-MirrorImage #5 (w/)	6.00
☐	96 Bowman'sBest-MirrorImage(Refractor) #5 (w/)	8.00
☐	96 Bowman'sBest-MirrorImage(Atomic Ref.) #5 (w/)	15.00
☐	96 Circa #124	1.00
☐	96 Circa(Rave, #/150) #124	50.00
☐	96 Donruss #342	1.00
☐	96 Donruss(PressProof) #342	12.00
☐	96 Donruss-DiamondKing #11	12.00
☐	96 Donruss-LongBallLeaders #7	18.00
☐	96 Flair(Silver) #253	2.00
☐	96 Flair(Gold) #253	2.00
☐	96 Fleer #377	1.00
☐	96 Fleer(Tiffany) #377	4.00
☐	96 Fleer Rockies Team #16	2.00
☐	96 FleerUltra #194	1.00
☐	96 FleerUltra(GoldMedallion) #194	3.00
☐	96 FleerUltra-PowerPlus #11	5.00
☐	96 KennerStartingLineUp Figurine	15.00
☐	96 Leaf #63	1.00
☐	96 Leaf(Bronze Press Proof) #63	8.00
☐	96 Leaf(Silver Press Proof) #63	15.00
☐	96 Leaf(Gold Press Proof) #63	30.00
☐	96 LeafLimited #86	2.00
☐	96 LeafLimited(Limited Gold) #86	20.00
☐	96 LeafPreferred #80	1.00
☐	96 LeafPreferred(Press Proof) #80	25.00
☐	96 LeafPreferred-LeafSteel #37	3.00
☐	96 LeafPreferred-LeafSteel(Gold) #37	25.00
☐	96 LeafSignature #77	1.50
☐	96 LeafSignature(Gold Press Proof) #77	15.00
☐	96 LeafSignature(Platinum Press Proof) #77	50.00
☐	96 LeafStudio #78	.75
☐	96 LeafStudio(Bronze Press Proof) #78	6.00
☐	96 LeafStudio(Gold Press Proof) #78	25.00
☐	96 LeafStudio(Silver Press Proof) #78	60.00
☐	96 MetalUniverse #159	1.00
☐	96 MetalUniverse(Platinum) #159	3.00
☐	96 Pacific #65	.75
☐	96 PacificPrisms #P-140	3.00
☐	96 PacificPrisms(Gold) #P-140	10.00
☐	96 PacificPrisms-FenceBusters #FB20	10.00
☐	96 PaniniSticker #86	.75
☐	96 Pinnacle #150	.75
☐	96 Pinnacle #219	1.00
☐	96 Pinnacle(Foil) #219	1.50
☐	96 Pinnacle(Starburst) #77	4.00
☐	96 Pinnacle(Starburst) #119	6.00
☐	96 Pinnacle(Artist's Proof) #77	8.00
☐	96 Pinnacle(Artist's Proof) #119	12.00
☐	96 Pinnacle-Power #19	6.00
☐	96 PinnacleAficionado #68	2.00
☐	96 PinnacleAficionado #152	1.00
☐	96 PinnacleAficionado(Artist's Proof) #68	35.00
☐	96 PinnacleAficionado(Artist's Proof) #152	18.00
☐	96 PinnacleSummit #61	1.00
☐	96 PinnacleSummit(Above and Beyond) #61	8.00
☐	96 PinnacleSummit(Artist's Proof) #61	25.00
☐	96 PinnacleSummit(Foil) #61	1.50
☐	96 PinnacleZenith #57	1.50
☐	96 PinnacleZenith(Artist's Proof) #57	25.00
☐	96 PinnacleZenith-Mozaics #12 (w/)	6.00
☐	96 Score #13	.75
☐	96 Score #374	.50
☐	96 Score(Dugout Collection) #13	2.00
☐	96 Score(Artist's Proof) #13	8.00
☐	96 Score-AllStar #17	5.00
☐	96 Score-TitanicTaters #13	5.00
☐	96 Score-GoldStars #27	3.00
☐	96 Score-NumbersGame #20	3.00
☐	96 Score-Reflextions #9 (w/Andre Dawson)	8.00
☐	96 Select #98	.75
☐	96 Select(Artist's Proof) #98	15.00
☐	96 Select-TeamNucleus #4 (w/)	4.00
☐	96 SelectCertified #85	1.50

	Card	Price
☐	96 SelectCertified(Certified Red) #85	8.00
☐	96 SelectCertified(Artist's Proof) #85	25.00
☐	96 SelectCertified(Certified Blue) #85	40.00
☐	96 SelectCertified(Mirror Red) #85	75.00
☐	96 SelectCertified(Mirror Blue) #85	150.00
☐	96 SelectCertified(Mirror Gold) #85	400.00
☐	96 SkyBox E-Motion XL #178	2.00
☐	96 SP #80	1.50
☐	96 Sportflics #72	1.00
☐	96 Sportflics #114	.75
☐	96 Sportflics(Artist's Proof) #72	15.00
☐	96 Sportflics(Artist's Proof) #114	8.00
☐	96 Sportflics-PowerSurge #18	8.00
☐	96 SP^{X} #23	2.50
☐	96 SP^{X}(Gold) #23	8.00
☐	96 Topps #5	.50
☐	96 Topps #363	.75
☐	96 Topps(PowerBooster) #5	5.00
☐	96 Topps-ProFiles #NL10	2.00
☐	96 ToppsBazooka #26	.75
☐	96 ToppsChrome #5	1.25
☐	96 ToppsChrome #147	2.00
☐	96 ToppsChrome(Refractor) #5	18.00
☐	96 ToppsChrome(Refractor) #147	30.00
☐	96 ToppsFinest(Silver) #13	6.00
☐	96 ToppsFinest(Silver) #302	6.00
☐	96 ToppsFinest(Silver Refractor) #13	25.00
☐	96 ToppsFinest(Silver Refractor) #302	25.00
☐	96 ToppsGallery #179	2.00
☐	96 ToppsGallery(Private Issue) #179	15.00
☐	96 ToppsLaser #112	3.00
☐	96 ToppsLaser-PowerCuts #16	10.00
☐	96 ToppsStadiumClub #319	1.00
☐	96 ToppsStadiumClub-ExtremePlayer(Bronze)	4.00
☐	96 ToppsStadiumClub-ExtremePlayer(Silver)	6.00
☐	96 ToppsStadiumClub-ExtremePlayer(Gold)	10.00
☐	96 ToppsStadiumClub-PowerStreak #PS11	6.00
☐	96 UpperDeck #60	1.00
☐	96 UpperDeck #421	.75
☐	96 UpperDeck-PowerDriven #PD19	6.00
☐	96 UpperDeck-PredictorSeries #R36	3.00
☐	96 UpperDeck-PredictorSeries(Gold) #R36	.75
☐	96 UpperDeck Collector'sChoice #326	.50
☐	96 UpperDeck Collector'sChoice #540	.75
☐	96 UpperDeck Collector'sChoice #753 (w/)	.50
☐	96 UD Collector'sChoice(Silver Signature) #326	1.00
☐	96 UD Collector'sChoice(Silver Signature) #540	2.00
☐	96 UD Collector'sChoice(Silver Signature) #753 (w/)	1.00
☐	96 UD Collector'sChoice(Gold Signature) #326	6.00
☐	96 UD Collector'sChoice(Gold Signature) #540	12.00
☐	96 UD Collector'sChoice(Gold Signature) #753 (w/)	6.00
☐	96 UD CC-YouCrashTheGame(6-24) #CG16	1.00
☐	96 UD CC-YouCrashTheGame(7-18) #CG16	1.00
☐	96 UD CC-YouCrashTheGame(9-27) #CG16	1.00
☐	96 UD CC-YouCrashTheGame(6-24, Gold) #CG16	4.00
☐	96 UD CC-YouCrashTheGame(7-18, Gold) #CG16	4.00
☐	96 UD CC-YouCrashTheGame(9-27, Gold) #CG16	4.00
☐	96 UD CC-YouMakeThePlay(Strikeout) #43	.75
☐	96 UD CC-YouMakeThePlay(Walk) #43	.75
☐	96 UD CC-YouMakeThePlay(Strikeout, Gold) #43	8.00
☐	96 UD CC-YouMakeThePlay(Walk, Gold) #43	8.00
☐	97 Bowman #275	2.00
☐	97 Bowman(Foil) #275	4.00
☐	97 Bowman'sBest #67	2.50
☐	97 Bowman'sBest(Refractor) #67	15.00
☐	97 Bowman'sBest(AtomicRefractor) #67	30.00
☐	97 Bowman'sBest-Bowman'sInternationalBest #BBI7	4.00
☐	97 BB-Bowman'sInternationalBest(Refractor) #BBI7	6.00
☐	97 BB-Bowman'sInternationalBest(Atomic Ref.) #BBI7	12.00
☐	97 Circa #377	1.00
☐	97 Circa(Rave, #/150) #377	50.00
☐	97 Donruss #48	.75
☐	97 Donruss(Press Proof) #48	8.00
☐	97 Donruss(Press Proof Gold, #/500) #48	30.00
☐	97 Donruss-Armed&Dangerous(#/5000) #7	8.00
☐	97 Donruss Update #410	.75
☐	97 Donruss Update(Press Proof) #410	8.00
☐	97 Donruss Update(Press Proof Gold, #/500) #410	30.00
☐	97 DonrussStudio #105	1.00
☐	97 DonrussStudio(Press Proof) #105	8.00
☐	97 DonrussStudio(Press Proof Gold) #105	25.00
☐	97 Donruss TeamSets #92	1.00
☐	97 FlairShowcase(Row 2) #76	2.50
☐	97 FlairShowcase(Row 1) #76	3.00
☐	97 FlairShowcase(Row 0) #76	15.00
☐	97 FlairShowcase(Legacy Row 2, #/100) #76	100.00
☐	97 FlairShowcase(Legacy Row 1, #/100) #76	100.00
☐	97 FlairShowcase(Legacy Row 0, #/100) #76	100.00
	Three "1of1" FlairShowcase Masterpiece cards also exist.	
☐	97 Fleer #319	1.00
☐	97 Fleer(Tiffany) #319	25.00
☐	97 FleerUltra #320	1.00
☐	97 FleerUltra(Gold Medallion) #320	3.00
☐	97 FleerUltra(Platinum Medallion) #320	50.00
☐	97 Leaf #238	1.00
☐	97 Leaf #385	.50
☐	97 Leaf(Fractal Matrix Gold-X) #238	25.00
☐	97 Leaf(Fractal Matrix Bronze-Y) #385	6.00
☐	97 Leaf(Fractal Matrix Z-Axis Die-Cut) #238	60.00
☐	97 Leaf(Fractal Matrix Y-Axis Die-Cut) #385	40.00
☐	97 Limited(Counterparts) #113 (w/Rusty Greer)	2.00
☐	97 Limited(Counterparts, Ltd. Exposure) #113 (w/)	20.00
☐	97 Limited(Double Team) #87 (w/Eric Young)	8.00
☐	97 Limited(Double Team, Ltd. Exposure) #87 (w/)	50.00
☐	97 Limited(Unlimited) #126 (w/Mike Cameron)	20.00
☐	97 Limited(Unlimited, Ltd. Exposure) #126 (w/)	120.00
☐	97 Limited(Star Factor) #169	25.00
☐	97 Limited(Star Factor, Ltd. Exposure) #169	150.00
☐	97 Limited-FabricOfTheGame(Star, #/750) #28	20.00
☐	97 MetalUniverse #76	1.00
☐	97 Pacific #291	.75
☐	97 Pacific(Light Blue) #291	4.00
☐	97 Pacific(Silver) #291	60.00
☐	97 Pinnacle-PassportToMajors #24	10.00
☐	97 PinnacleNew #9	1.00
☐	97 PinnacleNew(Museum Collection) #9	8.00
☐	97 PinnacleNew(Red Artist's Proof) #9	18.00
	Eight "1of1" PinnacleNew "Authentic Press Plates" also exist.	
☐	97 PinnacleXPress #1	.75
☐	97 PinnacleXPress #138	.50
☐	97 PinnacleXPress(Men Of Summer) #1	8.00
☐	97 PinnacleXPress(Men Of Summer) #138	5.00
☐	97 PinnacleXPress-MeltingPot #4	25.00
☐	97 PinnacleXPress-SwingForTheFences #31	1.50
☐	97 PinnacleXPress-SwingForTheFences(Upgrade) #31	8.00
☐	97 PinnacleCertified #24	2.00
☐	97 PinnacleCertified(Certified Red) #24	12.00
☐	97 PinnacleCertified(Mirror Red) #24	50.00
☐	97 PinnacleCertified(Mirror Blue) #24	100.00
☐	97 PinnacleCertified(Mirror Gold) #24	300.00
	A single PinnacleCertified "Mirror Black" card also exists.	
☐	97 PinnacleInside #114	1.00
☐	97 PinnacleInside(Club Edition) #114	8.00
☐	97 PinnacleInside(Diamond Edition) #114	80.00
☐	97 PinnacleTotallyCertified(Platinum Red) #24	6.00
☐	97 PinnacleTotallyCertified(Platinum Blue) #24	12.00
☐	97 PinnacleTotallyCertified(Platinum Gold) #24	350.00
☐	97 Score #176	.75

	Card	Price
☐	97 Score(Showcase Series) #176	3.50
☐	97 Score(Artist'sProof) #176	12.00
☐	97 Score(Premium Stock) #176	1.25
☐	97 Score Rockies Team Set #8	2.00
☐	97 Score(Platinum) Rockies Team Set #8	6.00
☐	97 Score(Premier Club) Rockies Team Set #8	30.00
☐	97 Select #97	1.00
☐	97 Select(Company) #97	4.00
☐	97 Select(Registered Gold) #97	8.00
☐	97 Select(Artist's Proof) #97	25.00
☐	97 SP # 67	1.50
☐	97 SPx #25	2.00
☐	97 SPx(Steel) #25	3.50
☐	97 SPx(Bronze) #25	5.00
☐	97 SPx(Silver) #25	8.00
☐	97 SPx(Gold) #25	15.00
☐	97 SPx(Grand Finale) #25	140.00
☐	97 SportsIllustrated #111	1.00
☐	97 SportsIllustrated(Extra Edition, #/500) #111	25.00
☐	97 Topps #461	.75
☐	97 ToppsChrome #162	2.50
☐	97 ToppsChrome(Refractor) #162	25.00
☐	97 ToppsFinest(Silver) #106	6.00
☐	97 ToppsFinest(Silver Embossed) #106	10.00
☐	97 ToppsFinest(Silver Refractor) #106	30.00
☐	97 ToppsFinest(Silver Embossed Refractor) #106	100.00
☐	97 ToppsFinest(Gold) #335	20.00
☐	97 ToppsFinest(Gold Embossed) #335	30.00
☐	97 ToppsFinest(Gold Refractor) #335	80.00
☐	97 ToppsFinest(Gold Embossed Ref. Die-Cut) #335	275.00
☐	97 ToppsGallery #72	1.50
☐	97 ToppsGallery(Player'sPrivate Issue, #/250) #72	30.00
☐	97 ToppsScreenplays-Premium [no#]	20.00
☐	97 ToppsStadiumClub #251	1.00
☐	97 ToppsStadiumClub(Matrix) #251	8.00
☐	97 ToppsStars #1	1.00
☐	97 ToppsStars(Always Mint) #1	10.00
☐	97 ToppsStars-'97AllStars #AS13	15.00
☐	97 ToppsStars-AllStarMemories #ASM9	6.00
☐	97 Ultimate Line-Up [no#]	1.00
☐	97 UpperDeck #182	1.00
☐	97 UpperDeck Collector'sChoice #98	.75
☐	97 UD Collector'sChoice-BigShots #6	2.50
☐	97 UD Collector'sChoice-BigShots(Gold) #6	10.00
☐	97 Zenith #11	1.50
☐	97 Zenith-ZTeam #2	30.00
☐	98 Bowman #23	2.00
☐	98 Bowman(International Foil) #23	4.00
☐	98 CircaThunder #275	1.00
☐	98 CircaThunder(Rave, #/150) #275	50.00
☐	98 CircaThunder(SuperRave, #/25) #275	300.00
☐	98 CircaThunder-Boss #20	2.00
☐	98 CircaThunder-QuickStrike #12	2.00
☐	98 CircaThunder-RaveReviews #15	25.00
☐	98 CircaThunder-ThunderBoomers #12	15.00
☐	98 Donruss #33	.75
☐	98 Donruss #166	.50
☐	98 Donruss(Press Proof) #33	8.00
☐	98 Donruss(Press Proof) #166	5.00
☐	98 Donruss(Press Proof Gold, #/500) #33	30.00
☐	98 Donruss(Press Proof Gold, #/500) #166	20.00
☐	98 D-LongBallLeaders #23	8.00
☐	98 D-ProductionLine(PowerIndex, #/1172) #17	25.00
☐	98 D-ProductionLine(Slugging) #11	35.00
☐	98 Donruss Crusade(Green, #/250) #67	75.00
☐	98 Donruss Crusade(Purple, #/100) #67	100.00
☐	98 Donruss Crusade(Red, #/25) #67	300.00
☐	98 DonrussElite #28	1.00
☐	98 DonrussElite #149	.50
☐	98 DonrussElite(Aspirations) #28	15.00
☐	98 DonrussElite(Aspirations) #149	8.00
☐	98 DonrussElite(Status, #/100) #28	75.00
☐	98 DonrussElite(Status, #/100) #149	40.00
☐	98 DonrussElite-Craftsmen(#/3500) #29	10.00
☐	98 DonrussElite-MasterCraftsmen(#/100) #29	80.00
☐	98 DonrussPreferred(Club Level) #26	12.00
☐	98 DonrussPreferred(Mezzanine) #189	6.00
☐	98 DonrussPreferred(Preferred Seating) #26	40.00
☐	98 DonrussPreferred(Preferred Seating) #189	20.00
☐	98 D.Pref.-GreatExpectations(#ed 301-3000) #3 (w/)	15.00
☐	98 D.Pref.-GreatExpect.(Die-Cut, #ed 1-300) #3 (w/)	40.00
☐	98 DonrussPreferred-TitleWave(#/1997) #3	12.00
☐	98 D.Pref. Green TinPack #22 (opened)	1.00
☐	98 D.Pref. Silver TinPack(#/999) #22 (opened)	6.00
☐	98 D.Pref. Green TinBox(#/999) #22 (opened)	6.00
☐	98 D.Pref. Gold TinBox(#/199) #22 (opened)	15.00
☐	98 FleerTradition #33	1.00
☐	98 FleerTradition-Vintage'63 #22	1.50
☐	98 FleerTradition-Vintage'63(Classic, #/63) #22	125.00
☐	98 FleerTradition-DiamondStandouts #20DS	2.50
☐	98 FleerTradition-LumberCompany #15LC	6.00
☐	98 FleerTradition-PowerGame #20PG	8.00
☐	98 FleerTradition-Zone #15Z	20.00
☐	98 Leaf #114	1.00
☐	98 Leaf #154	3.50
☐	98 Leaf(Gold-Z) #114	20.00
☐	98 Leaf(Silver-X) #154	25.00
☐	98 Leaf(Z-Axis Die-Cut) #114	50.00
☐	98 Leaf(X-Axis Die-Cut) #154	30.00
☐	98 Leaf-StateRepresentatives(#/5000) #14	6.00
☐	98 Leaf-StatisticalStandouts(#ed 251-2500) #19	18.00
☐	98 Leaf-Stat.Standouts(Die-Cut, #ed 1-250) #19	50.00
☐	98 LeafFractalMaterials(#/3999) #114	6.00
☐	98 LeafFractalMaterials(#/3999) #154	5.00
☐	98 LeafFractalMaterials(Plastic, #ed 201-3250) #154	7.50
☐	98 LeafFractalMaterials(Wood, #ed 201-250) #114	175.00
☐	98 LeafFractalMaterials(X Die-Cut, #ed 1-200) #114	60.00
☐	98 LeafFractalMaterials(X Die-Cut, #ed 1-200) #154	50.00
☐	98 LeafFractalMaterials(Z2 Axis, #/20) #114	400.00
☐	98 LeafFractalMaterials(Z2 Axis, #/20) #154	350.00
☐	98 MetalUniverse #61	1.00
☐	98 MetalUniverse #217	.50
☐	98 MetalUniverse(PreciousMetals, #/50) #61	100.00
☐	98 MetalUniverse(PreciousMetals, #/50) #217	60.00
☐	98 MetalUniverse-AllStar Video Game Sweepstakes Form	.10
☐	98 Pacific #290	.75
☐	98 Pacific(Silver) #290	3.50
☐	98 Pacific(Red) #290	3.50
☐	98 Pacific(Platinum Blue) #290	60.00
☐	98 Pacific-Cramer'sChoice #5	50.00
☐	98 Pacific-GoldCrown #14	10.00
☐	98 Pacific-HomeRunHitters #11	15.00
☐	98 Pacific-InTheCage #8	20.00
☐	98 PacificInvincible #94	3.00
☐	98 PacificInvincible #150	1.75
☐	98 PacificInvincible(Silver) #94	9.00
☐	98 PacificInvincible(Silver) #150	5.00
☐	98 PacificInvincible(Platinum Blue) #94	45.00
☐	98 PacificInvincible(Platinum Blue) #150	25.00
☐	98 Pcfc.Invincible-Cramer's(Green, #/99) #5	100.00
☐	98 Pcfc.Invincible-Cramer's(Drk.Blue, #/80) #5	110.00
☐	98 Pcfc.Invincible-Cramer's(Lgt.Blue, #/50) #5	150.00
☐	98 Pcfc.Invincible-Cramer's(Red, #/25) #5	300.00
☐	98 Pcfc.Invincible-Cramer's(Gold, #/15) #5	500.00
☐	98 Pcfc.Invincible-Cramer's(Purple, #/10) #5	600.00
☐	98 Pcfc.Invincible-InterleaguePlayers #11N	15.00
☐	98 Pcfc.Invincible-MomentsInTime #6	30.00
☐	98 Pcfc.Invincible-Photoengravings #5	8.00

- ☐ 98 Pcfc.Invincible-GemsOfTheDiamond #148 1.00
- ☐ 98 Pinnacle #13 1.00
  Eight "1of1" Pinnacle "Authentic Press Plates" also exist.
- ☐ 98 Pinnacle #190 .75
  Eight "1of1" Pinnacle "Authentic Press Plates" also exist.
- ☐ 98 Pinnacle #198 (w/) 1.00
  Eight "1of1" Pinnacle "Authentic Press Plates" also exist.
- ☐ 98 Pinnacle(Home Stats) #13 1.00
- ☐ 98 Pinnacle(Away Stats) #13 1.00
- ☐ 98 Pinnacle(Museum Collection) #13 10.00
- ☐ 98 Pinnacle(Artist's Proof) #13 20.00
- ☐ 98 Pinnacle(Jumbo Power Pack) #9 1.00
- ☐ 98 Pinnacle(Jumbo Power Pack) #21 1.00
- ☐ 98 Pinnacle-Hit It Here #1 1.00
  Eight "1of1" PinnacleNew "Authentic Press Plates" also exist.
- ☐ 98 Pinnacle-Spellbound 8.00
  Eight "1of1" PinnacleNew "Authentic Press Plates" also exist.
- ☐ 98 PinnacleInside #33 1.00
- ☐ 98 PinnacleInside(Club Edition) #33 8.00
- ☐ 98 PinnacleInside(Diamond Edition) #33 80.00
- ☐ 98 PinnacleInside-StandUpGuy 10a (w/Bichette) 1.50
- ☐ 98 PinnacleInside Can #20 4.00
- ☐ 98 PinnacleInside Gold Can #20 15.00
- ☐ 98 PinnacleMint(Die-Cut Card) #24 .50
- ☐ 98 PinnacleMint(Bronze Team Card) #24 1.00
- ☐ 98 PinnacleMint(Silver Team Card) #24 5.00
- ☐ 98 PinnacleMint(Gold Team Card) #24 10.00
- ☐ 98 PinnacleMint(Brass Medallion) #24 1.00
- ☐ 98 PinnacleMint(Nickel-Silver Medallion) #24 8.00
- ☐ 98 PinnacleMint(Noted Nickel Medallion) #24 15.00
- ☐ 98 P.Mint(Gold Artist's Proof Medallion, #/250) #24 40.00
- ☐ 98 P.Mint(Solid Silver Medallion) #24 80.00
  One "1of1" PinnacleMint "Solid Gold" medallion also exists.
- ☐ 98 PinnacleMint-MintGems(Card) #2 8.00
- ☐ 98 P.Mint-MintGems(Oversized Medallion) #2 8.00
- ☐ 98 Score #13 .75
- ☐ 98 Score(ShowcaseSeries) #13 1.50
- ☐ 98 Score(Artist's Proof) #13 8.00
- ☐ 98 Sports Illustrated #123 .75
- ☐ 98 Sports Illustrated(Extra Edition, #/250) #123 .35
- ☐ 98 Sports Illustrated-MiniPosters #OD10 .50
- ☐ 98 SI: Then&Now #138 1.00
- ☐ 98 SI: Then&Now(Extra Edition, #/500) #138 25.00
- ☐ 98 StadiumClub #163 1.00
- ☐ 98 StadiumClub(First Day Issue, #/200) #163 40.00
- ☐ 98 StadiumClub(One of a Kind, #/150) #163 50.00
  Four "1of1" StadiumClub "Authentic Press Plates" also exist.
- ☐ 98 StadiumClub-BowmanPreview #BP5 4.00
- ☐ 98 StadiumClub-NeverCompromise #NC13 5.00
- ☐ 98 StadiumClub-Triumvirate #T7C 8.00
- ☐ 98 StadiumClub-Triumvirate(Luminescent) #T7C 15.00
- ☐ 98 StadiumClub-Triumvirate(Illuminator) #T7C 30.00
- ☐ 98 StadiumClub-CoSigners(Aut.) #CS13 500.00
- ☐ 98 StadiumClub-CoSigners(Aut.) #CS16 150.00
- ☐ 98 StadiumClub-CoSigners(Aut.) #CS17 100.00
- ☐ 98 Topps #2 .75
- ☐ 98 Topps #482 (w/Juan Gonzalez) .50
- ☐ 98 Topps(Minted in Cooperstown) #2 4.50
- ☐ 98 Topps(Minted in Cooperstown) #482 (w/J.Gonzalez) 3.00
- ☐ 98 Topps-CloutNine #C9 8.00
- ☐ 98 Topps-FocalPoint #PF7 5.00
- ☐ 98 Topps-InterleagueFinest #ILM9 5.00
- ☐ 98 Topps-InterleagueFinest(Refractor) #ILM9 10.00
- ☐ 98 Topps-MysteryFinest(Bordered) #M14 5.00
- ☐ 98 Topps-MysteryFinest(Bordered Refractor) #M14 10.00
- ☐ 98 Topps-MysteryFinest(Borderless) #M14 12.00
- ☐ 98 Topps-MysteryFinest(Borderless Refractor) #M14 20.00
- ☐ 98 ToppsChrome #2 3.00
- ☐ 98 ToppsChrome(Refractor) #2 30.00
- ☐ 98 ToppsFinest #1 1.50
- ☐ 98 ToppsFinest(No Protector) #1 5.00
- ☐ 98 ToppsFinest(Refractor) #1 15.00
- ☐ 98 ToppsFinest(No Protector Refractor) #1 30.00
- ☐ 98 ToppsFinest-Centurions(#/500) #C17 35.00
- ☐ 98 ToppsFinest-Centurions(Refractor, #/75) #C17 140.00
- ☐ 98 ToppsFinest-MysteryFinest #M31 (w/J.Gonzalez) 30.00
- ☐ 98 ToppsFinest-MysteryFinest #M35 (W/Galarraga) 20.00
- ☐ 98 ToppsFinest-MysteryFinest #M36 (w/C.Jones) 50.00
- ☐ 98 ToppsFinest-MysteryFinest #M37 25.00
- ☐ 98 ToppsFinest-MysteryFinest(Refractor) #M31 (w/) 60.00
- ☐ 98 ToppsFinest-MysteryFinest(Refractor) #M35 (w/) 40.00
- ☐ 98 ToppsFinest-MysteryFinest(Refractor) #M36 (w/) 100.00
- ☐ 98 ToppsFinest-MysteryFinest(Refractor) #M37 50.00
- ☐ 98 ToppsFinest-PowerZone #P16 12.00
- ☐ 98 ToppsStarsN'Steel #43 5.00
- ☐ 98 ToppsStarsN'Steel(Gold) #43 20.00
- ☐ 98 ToppsStarsN'Steel(Holographic) #43 50.00
- ☐ 98 Ultra #90 1.00
- ☐ 98 Ultra(Gold Medallion) #90 3.00
- ☐ 98 Ultra(Platinum, #/100) #90 100.00
  One "1of1" Ultra "Masterpiece" card also exists.
- ☐ 98 UpperDeck #11 .75
- ☐ 98 UpperDeck #355 1.00
- ☐ 98 UpperDeck #456 1.00
- ☐ 98 UD-AmazingGreats #AG6 15.00
- ☐ 98 UD-AmazingGreats(Die-Cut, #/250) #AG6 45.00
- ☐ 98 UD-ClearlyDominant(#/250) #CD26 50.00
- ☐ 98 UD-NationalPride #NP2 8.00
- ☐ 98 UD-TapeMeasureTitans #4 8.00
- ☐ 98 UD-10thAnniversaryPreview #52 2.00
- ☐ 98 UDCC-EvolutionRevolution #ER9 2.50
- ☐ 98 UDCC-StarQuest(SuperStars) #SQ86 15.00
- ☐ 98 UDCC-SuperStickUm's #21 1.00
- ☐ 98 Zenith #1 2.50
- ☐ 98 Zenith(Z-Silver) #1 10.00
- ☐ 98 Zenith(Z-Gold, #/100) #1 100.00
- ☐ 98 Zenith-5"x7" #Z42 2.50
- ☐ 98 Zenith-5"x7"(Impulse) #Z42 10.00
- ☐ 98 Zenith-5"x7"(Gold Impulse, #/100) #Z42 100.00

PETE WARD

- ☐ 63 Topps #324 10.00
- ☐ 64 Topps #85 8.00
- ☐ 65 O-Pee-Chee #215 10.00
- ☐ 65 Topps #215 4.00
- ☐ 66 O-Pee-Chee #25 5.00
- ☐ 66 Topps #25 4.00
- ☐ 67 O-Pee-Chee #143 5.00
- ☐ 67 Topps #143 4.00
- ☐ 67 Topps #436 10.00
- ☐ 68 O-Pee-Chee #33 4.00
- ☐ 68 Topps #33 3.00

- ☐ 69 O-Pee-Chee #155 4.00
- ☐ 69 Topps #155 3.50
- ☐ 70 Topps #659 15.00
- ☐ 71 O-Pee-Chee #667 15.00
- ☐ 71 Topps #667 12.00

NIGEL WILSON

- ☐ 92 Bowman #228 .75
- ☐ 92 KnoxvilleBlueJays/FleerProCards #3005 .35
- ☐ 92 Knoxville Blue Jays/ SkyBox #397 .35
- ☐ 92 ProCards #169 .25
- ☐ 92 SkyBox AA #168 .25
- ☐ 92 UpperDeck MinorLeague #286 .25
- ☐ 93 Bowman #316 .25
- ☐ 93 Bowman #351 .25
- ☐ 93 Edmonton Trappers/ ProCards #1151 .25
- ☐ 93 Flair-WaveOfTheFuture #19 (D.Whitmore's card) 1.50
- ☐ 93 Flair-WaveOfTheFuture #20 1.50
- ☐ 93 Fleer #431 .25
- ☐ 93 FleerExcel #247 .25
- ☐ 93 Fleer FinalEdition #F-75 .25
- ☐ 93 FleerUltra #388 .25
- ☐ 93 FIA Marlins/ Publix [no#] .50
- ☐ 93 Leaf-GoldLeafRookie #R16 1.50
- ☐ 93 O-Pee-Chee #165 .25
- ☐ 93 Topps #426 .25
- ☐ 93 Topps(Gold) #426 .50
- ☐ 93 ToppsStadiumClub #720 .25
- ☐ 93 ToppsStadiumClub(First Day Issue) #720 3.00
- ☐ 93 ToppsStadiumClub(MembersOnly) #720 1.00
- ☐ 93 ToppsStadiumClub-FirstMarlinsDraftPick 2.00
- ☐ 93 ToppsStadiumClub(Marlins Team) #1 .50
- ☐ 93 UpperDeck #825 .25
- ☐ 94 Classic #106 .25
- ☐ 94 Donruss #537 .25
- ☐ 94 Edmonton Trappers/ ProCards #2889 .25
- ☐ 94 Leaf #76 .25
- ☐ 94 Pinnacle #240 .25
- ☐ 94 Pinnacle(Museum Collection) #240 1.50
- ☐ 94 Pinnacle(Artist's Proof) #240 4.00
- ☐ 94 Pinnacle-RookieTeamPinnacle #8 (w/Newfield) 7.00
- ☐ 94 Score #639 .25
- ☐ 94 Score(Gold Rush) #639 .50
- ☐ 94 Score-BoysOfSummer #35 3.00
- ☐ 94 Sportflics #158 .35
- ☐ 94 Topps #341 .25
- ☐ 94 Topps(Gold) #341 .50
- ☐ 94 UpperDeck #103 .25
- ☐ 94 UpperDeck(Electric Diamond) #103 .50
- ☐ 94 UpperDeck FunPack #30 .25
- ☐ 94 UpperDeck Collector'sChoice #301 .25
- ☐ 94 UD Collector'sChoice(Silver Signature) #301 .50
- ☐ 94 UD Collector'sChoice(Gold Signature) #301 3.00
- ☐ 95 Topps #506 .25
- ☐ 96 Pinnacle #186 .25

STEVE WILSON

- ☐ 86 TulsaDrillers #10 1.50
- ☐ 87 Port CharlotteRangers/ProCards #10 1.00
- ☐ 88 Tulsa Drillers #8 .75
- ☐ 89 Bowman #280 .25
- ☐ 89 Bowman(Tiffany) #280 .50
- ☐ 89 CHI Cubs/ Marathon [no#] .50
- ☐ 89 DonrussRookies #10 .25
- ☐ 89 Fleer #640 .25
- ☐ 89 Fleer(Glossy) #640 .50
- ☐ 89 Fleer Update #U-82 .25
- ☐ 89 UpperDeck #799 .25
- ☐ 90 Bowman #23 .25
- ☐ 90 Bowman(Tiffany) #23 .50
- ☐ 90 CHI Cubs/ Marathon [no#] .50
- ☐ 90 Donruss #394 .25
- ☐ 90 Fleer #49 .25
- ☐ 90 Fleer("PTD in Canada") #49 .50
- ☐ 90 Leaf #420 .25
- ☐ 90 O-Pee-Chee #741 .25
- ☐ 90 Score #531 .25
- ☐ 90 Topps #741 .25
- ☐ 90 Topps(Tiffany) #741 .50
- ☐ 90 UpperDeck #341 .25
- ☐ 91 Donruss #519 .25
- ☐ 91 Fleer #440 .25
- ☐ 91 O-Pee-Chee #69 .25
- ☐ 91 Score #306 .25
- ☐ 91 Topps #69 .25
- ☐ 91 Topps(Tiffany) #69 .50
- ☐ 91 Topps DesertShield #69 3.00
- ☐ 91 Topps Mini #69 .25
- ☐ 91 UpperDeck #493 .25
- ☐ 92 Donruss #710 .25
- ☐ 92 DonrussStudio #59 .25
- ☐ 92 FleerUltra #510 .25
- ☐ 92 Leaf #161 .25
- ☐ 92 Leaf(Black Gold) #161 .50
- ☐ 92 L.A. Dodgers/ Mother'sCookies #27 .50
- ☐ 92 O-Pee-Chee #751 .25
- ☐ 92 Topps #751 .25
- ☐ 92 Topps(Gold) #751 .50
- ☐ 92 Topps Mini #751 .25
- ☐ 92 ToppsStadiumClub #626 .25
- ☐ 93 Fleer #456 .25
- ☐ 93 Leaf #145 .25
- ☐ 93 Topps #133 .25
- ☐ 93 Topps(Gold) #133 .50
- ☐ 94 Fleer #529 .25

JOE YOUNG

- ☐ 95 St.Catharines Stompers/ TimHortons #2 1.00

APPENDIX

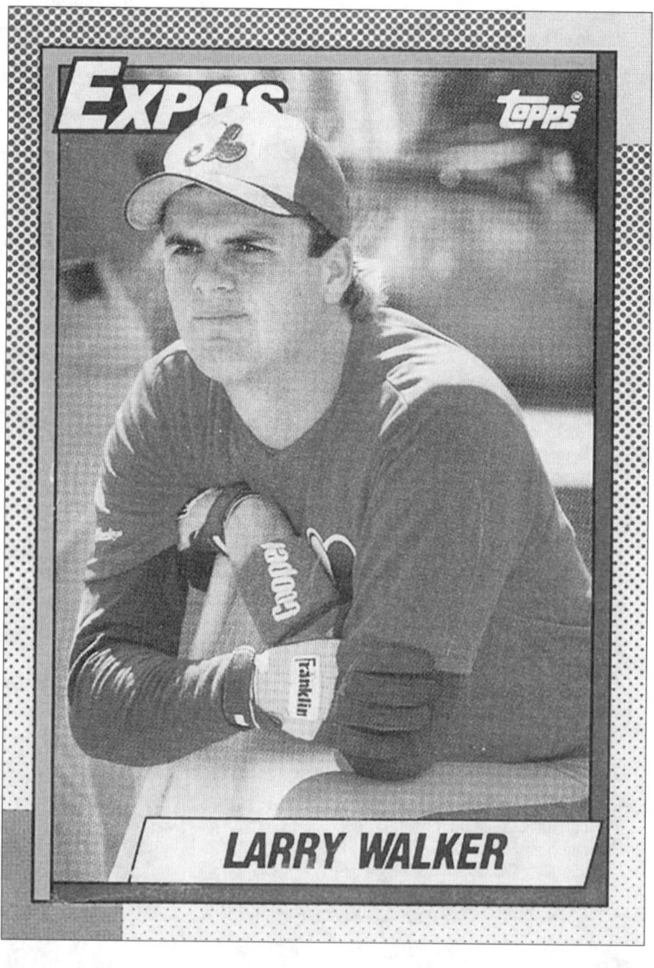

GLOSSARY OF TERMS AND ABBREVIATIONS

ACC	American Card Catalogue coding system. Candy and gum card sets are noted with a "V" (ie. V117 Maple Crispette) while cigarette cards are noted with a "C" (ie. C46 Imperial Tobacco).
A.L.	American League
Ana.	Anaheim Angels
AS	All-Star
ATG	All-Time Great
Atl.	Atlanta Braves
AW	Award Winners
Bal.	Baltimore Orioles
Bos.	Boston Red Sox
Brand Name	A card set's name. The name is most often found on the face of the card.
Cal.	California Angels
Cdn.	Canada
Chi.-N.L.	Chicago Cubs
Chi.-A.L.	Chicago White Sox
CL	Checklist
Cin.	Cincinnati Reds
Cle.	Cleveland Indians
Col.	Colorado Rockies
Det.	Detroit Tigers
DT	Dream Team
Error (Err.)	Error cards include misspellings, mistaken photos and wrong bios. Each card's error is listed in brackets after the card.
Fla.	Florida Marlins
GM	General Manager
HL	Highlight
HOF	Hall of Fame
Hou.	Houston Astros
K.C.	Kansas City Royals
L.A.	Los Angeles Dodgers
LC	Last Card
LL	League Leader(s)
Mil.	Milwaukee Brewers
Min.	Minnesota Twins
MLB	Major League Baseball
Mtl.	Montréal Expos
MVP	Most Valuable Player
N.L.	National League
No #	No number on card
NYG.	New York Giants
NYM.	New York Mets
NYG.	New York Giants
Oak.	Oakland Athletics
Pha.	Philadelphia Phillies
Pgh.	Pittsburgh Pirates
RC	Rookie Card. A player's first appearance in a regular issued MLB licensed card set. A player's rookie card can be from one year only and must be in a set featuring current MLB players. Retrospective, minor league, college, draft pick and international sets do not have rookie cards. Insert/chase cards (including parallel sets), regional, food and other oddball set cards are also not recognized as rookie cards. A player can have only one rookie card from each brand set. The player's regular card in a set is considered his rookie card. Draft pick subset cards may be classified as rookie cards. A player's rookie card may or may not be from the same year as their actual MLB rookie season. A player does not have rookie cards in every set from his given rookie card year. Cards identified with "Rookie" or "Rookie Card" by the company are not necessarily true rookie cards. Not every player has a rookie card; some players have only one rookie card while others may have as many as ten or more.
RB	Record Breaker
Sea.	Seattle Mariners
S.D.	San Diego Padres
S.F.	San Francisco Giants
Stl.	St. Louis Cardinals
TC	Team Card or Checklist
TL	Team Leader(s)
Tor.	Toronto Blue Jays
Wsh.	Washington Senators
WS	World Series
w/	with
XCX	Cameo appearance. Another player is shown visibly on someone else's card.
/b	Card Back

ALPHABETICAL DIRECTORY OF CARD ISSUERS

MAJOR LEAGUE BASEBALL

AMERICAN LEAGUE:

Toronto Blue Jays
One Blue Jays Way, Suite 3200,
Toronto, ON, Canada M5V 1J1
(416) 341-1000, Fax (416) 341-1250
E-Mail: bluejays@bluejays.ca

Anaheim Angels
PO Box 2000,
Anaheim, CA 92803, USA
(714) 940-2000, Fax (714) 940-2205

Baltimore Orioles
333 West Camden Street,
Baltimore, MD 21201, USA
(410) 685-9800, Fax (410) 547-6272

Boston Red Sox
Fenway Park, 4 Yawkey Way,
Boston, MA 02215, USA
(617) 267-9440, Fax (617) 236-6797,
E-Mail: www.redsox.com

Chicago White Sox
333 West 35th Street,
Chicago, IL 60616, USA
(312) 674-1000, Fax (312) 674-5116,
E-Mail: www.chisox.com

Cleveland Indians
Jacobs Field, 2401 Ontario Street,
Cleveland, OH 44115, USA
(216) 420-4200, Fax (216) 420-4396

Detroit Tigers
Tiger Stadium, 2121 Trumbull Avenue,
Detroit, MI 48216, USA
(313) 962-4000, Fax (313) 965-2138

Kansas City Royals
PO Box 419969,
Kansas City, MO 64141, USA
(816) 921-2200, Fax (816) 921-5775

Milwaukee Brewers
PO Box 3099,
Milwaukee, WI 53201, USA
(414) 933-4114, Fax (414) 933-7323,
E-Mail: www.milwaukeebrewers.com

Minnesota Twins
34 Kirby Puckett Place,
Minneapolis, MN 55415, USA
(612) 375-1366.
E-Mail: www.mntwins.com

New York Yankees
Yankee Stadium,
161st Street and River Avenue,
Bronx, NY 10451, USA
(718) 293-4300, Fax (718) 293-8431

Oakland Athletics
7677 Oakport Street, Suite 200,
Oakland, CA 94621, USA
(510) 638-4900, Fax (510) 568-3770,
E-Mail: www.oaklandathletics.com

Seattle Mariners
83 South King Street,
Seattle, WA 98104, USA
(206) 628-3555, Fax (206) 628-3340,
E-Mail: http://www.mariners.org

Tampa Bay Devil Rays
Tropicana Field, One Tropicana Drive,
St. Petersburg, FL 33705, USA
(813) 825-3137, Fax (813) 825-3300

Texas Rangers
PO Box 90111,
Arlington, TX 76004, USA
(817) 273-5222, Fax (817) 273-5206,
E-Mail: www.texasrangers.com

MAJOR LEAGUE BASEBALL

NATIONAL LEAGUE:

Montreal Expos
PO Box 500, Station M,
Montreal, QC, Canada H1V 3P2
(514) 253-3434, Fax (514) 253-8282

Arizona Diamondbacks
PO Box 2095,
Phoenix, AZ 85001, USA
(602) 514-8500, Fax (602) 514-8599,
E-Mail: www.azdiamondbacks.com

Atlanta Braves
PO Box 4064,
Atlanta, GA 30302, USA
(404) 522-7630, Fax (404) 614-1391

Chicago Cubs
Wrigley Field, 1060 West Addison Street,
Chicago, IL 60613, USA
(773) 404-2827, Fax (773) 404-4129

Cincinnati Reds
100 Cinergy Field,
Cincinnati, OH 45202, USA
(513) 421-4510, Fax (513) 421-7342

Colorado Rockies
PO Box 120,
Denver, CO 80201, USA
(303) 292-0200, Fax (303) 312-2319

Florida Marlins
Pro Player Stadium, 2267 NW 199th Street,
Miami, FL 33056, USA
(305) 626-7400, Fax (305) 626-7428,
E-Mail: http://www.flamarlins.com

Houston Astros
PO Box 288,
Houston, TX 77001, USA
(713) 799-9500, Fax (713) 799-9562,
E-Mail: www.astros.com

Los Angeles Dodgers
1000 Elysian Park Avenue,
Lost Angeles, CA 90012, USA
(213) 224-1500, Fax (213) 224-1269

New York Mets
123-01 Roosevelt Avenue,
Flushing, NY 11368, USA
(718) 507-6387, Fax (718) 565-6395

Philadelphia Phillies
PO Box 7575,
Philadelphia, PA 19101, USA
(215) 463-6000, Fax (215) 389-3050

Pittsburgh Pirates
PO Box 7000,
Pittsburgh, PA 15212, USA
(412) 323-5000, Fax (412) 323-9133

St. Louis Cardinals
250 Stadium Plaza,
St. Louis, MO 63102, USA
(314) 421-3060, Fax (314) 425-0640,
E-Mail: www.stlcardinals.com

San Diego Padres
8880 Rio San Diego Drive,
San Diego, CA 92112, USA
(619) 881-6500, Fax (619) 497-5454

San Francisco Giants
3 Com Park at Candlestick Point,
San Francisco, CA 94124, USA
(415) 468-3700, Fax (415) 467-0485,
E-Mail: www.sfgiants.com

THE WORLD SERIES CHAMPIONS

1903-1997

YEAR	N.L. TEAM	A.L. TEAM	WINNER	GAME
1903	Pittsburgh Pirates	Boston Pilgrims	**PILGRIMS**	5-3
1904	No Series			
1905	New York Giants	Philadelphia Athletics	**GIANTS**	4-1
1906	Chicago Cubs	Chicago White Sox	**WHITE SOX**	4-2
1907	Chicago Cubs	Detroit Tigers	**CUBS**	4-0
1908	Chicago Cubs	Detroit Tigers	**CUBS**	4-1
1909	Pittsburgh Pirates	Detroit Tigers	**PIRATES**	4-3
1910	Chicago Cubs	Philadelphia Athletics	**ATHLETICS**	4-1
1911	New York Giants	Philadelphia Athletics	**ATHLETICS**	4-2
1912	New York Giants	Boston Red Sox	**RED SOX**	4-3
1913	New York Giants	Philadelphia Athletics	**ATHLETICS**	4-1
1914	Boston Braves	Philadelphia Athletics	**BRAVES**	4-0
1915	Philadelphia Phillies	Boston Red Sox	**RED SOX**	4-1
1916	Brooklyn Robins	Boston Red Sox	**RED SOX**	4-1
1917	New York Giants	Chicago White Sox	**WHITE SOX**	4-2
1918	Chicago Cubs	Boston Red Sox	**RED SOX**	4-2
1919	Cincinnati Reds	Chicago White Sox	**REDS**	5-3
1920	Brooklyn Robins	Cleveland Indians	**INDIANS**	5-2
1921	New York Giants	New York Yankees	**GIANTS**	5-3
1922	New York Giants	New York Yankees	**GIANTS**	4-0
1923	New York Giants	New York Yankees	**YANKEES**	4-2
1924	New York Giants	Washington Senators	**SENATORS**	4-3
1925	Pittsburgh Pirates	Washington Senators	**PIRATES**	4-3
1926	St. Louis Cardinals	New York Yankees	**CARDINALS**	4-3
1927	Pittsburgh Pirates	New York Yankees	**YANKEES**	4-0
1928	St. Louis Cardinals	New York Yankees	**YANKEES**	4-0
1929	Chicago Cubs	Philadelphia Athletics	**ATHLETICS**	4-1
1930	St. Louis Cardinals	Philadelphia Athletics	**ATHLETICS**	4-2
1931	St. Louis Cardinals	Philadelphia Athletics	**CARDINALS**	4-3
1932	Chicago Cubs	New York Yankees	**YANKEES**	4-0
1933	New York Giants	Washington Senators	**GIANTS**	4-1
1934	St. Louis Cardinals	Detroit Tigers	**CARDINALS**	4-3
1935	Chicago Cubs	Detroit Tigers	**TIGERS**	4-2
1936	New York Giants	New York Yankees	**YANKEES**	4-2
1937	New York Giants	New York Yankees	**YANKEES**	4-1
1938	Chicago Cubs	New York Yankees	**YANKEES**	4-0
1939	Cincinnati Reds	New York Yankees	**YANKEES**	4-0
1940	Cincinnati Reds	Detroit Tigers	**REDS**	4-3
1941	Brooklyn Dodgers	New York Yankees	**YANKEES**	4-1
1942	St. Louis Cardinals	New York Yankees	**CARDINALS**	4-1
1943	St. Louis Cardinals	New York Yankees	**YANKEES**	4-1
1944	St. Louis Cardinals	St. Louis Browns	**CARDINALS**	4-2

YEAR	N.L. TEAM	A.L. TEAM	WINNER	GAME
1945	Chicago Cubs	Detroit Tigers	TIGERS	4-3
1946	St. Louis Cardinals	Boston Red Sox	CARDINALS	4-3
1947	Brooklyn Dodgers	New York Yankees	YANKEES	4-3
1948	Boston Braves	Cleveland Indians	INDIANS	4-2
1949	Brooklyn Dodgers	New York Yankees	YANKEES	4-1
1950	Philadelphia Phillies	New York Yankees	YANKEES	4-0
1951	New York Giants	New York Yankees	YANKEES	4-2
1952	Brooklyn Dodgers	New York Yankees	YANKEES	4-3
1953	Brooklyn Dodgers	New York Yankees	YANKEES	4-2
1954	New York Giants	Cleveland Indians	GIANTS	4-0
1955	Brooklyn Dodgers	New York Yankees	DODGERS	4-3
1956	Brooklyn Dodgers	New York Yankees	YANKEES	4-3
1957	Milwaukee Braves	New York Yankees	BRAVES	4-3
1958	Milwaukee Braves	New York Yankees	YANKEES	4-3
1959	Los Angeles Dodgers	Chicago White Sox	DODGERS	4-2
1960	Pittsburgh Pirates	New York Yankees	PIRATES	4-3
1961	Cincinnati Reds	New York Yankees	YANKEES	4-1
1962	San Francisco Giants	New York Yankees	YANKEES	4-3
1963	Los Angeles Dodgers	New York Yankees	DODGERS	4-0
1964	St. Louis Cardinals	New York Yankees	CARDINALS	4-3
1965	Los Angeles Dodgers	Minnesota Twins	DODGERS	4-3
1966	Los Angeles Dodgers	Baltimore Orioles	ORIOLES	4-0
1967	St. Louis Cardinals	Boston Red Sox	CARDINALS	4-3
1968	St. Louis Cardinals	Detroit Tigers	TIGERS	4-3
1969	New York Mets	Baltimore Orioles	METS	4-1
1970	Cincinnati Reds	Baltimore Orioles	ORIOLES	4-1
1971	Pittsburgh Pirates	Baltimore Orioles	PIRATES	4-3
1972	Cincinnati Reds	Oakland Athletics	ATHLETICS	4-3
1973	New York Mets	Oakland Athletics	ATHLETICS	4-3
1974	Los Angeles Dodgers	Oakland Athletics	ATHLETICS	4-1
1975	Cincinnati Reds	Boston Red Sox	REDS	4-3
1976	Cincinnati Reds	New York Yankees	REDS	4-0
1977	Los Angeles Dodgers	New York Yankees	YANKEES	4-2
1978	Los Angeles Dodgers	New York Yankees	YANKEES	4-2
1979	Pittsburgh Pirates	Baltimore Orioles	PIRATES	4-3
1980	Philadelphia Phillies	Kansas City Royals	PHILLIES	4-2
1981	Los Angeles Dodgers	New York Yankees	DODGERS	4-2
1982	St. Louis Cardinals	Milwaukee Brewers	CARDINAL	4-3
1983	Philadelphia Phillies	Baltimore Orioles	ORIOLES	4-1
1984	San Diego Padres	Detroit Tigers	TIGERS	4-1
1985	St. Louis Cardinals	Kansas City Royals	ROYALS	4-3
1986	New York Mets	Boston Red Sox	METS	4-3
1987	St. Louis Cardinals	Minnesota Twins	TWINS	4-3
1988	Los Angeles Dodgers	Oakland Athletics	DODGERS	4-1
1989	San Francisco Giants	Oakland Athletics	ATHLETICS	4-0
1990	Cincinnati Reds	Oakland Athletics	REDS	4-0
1991	Atlanta Braves	Minnesota Twins	TWINS	4-3
1992	Atlanta Braves	Toronto Blue Jays	BLUE JAYS	4-2
1993	Philadelphia Phillies	Toronto Blue Jays	BLUE JAYS	4-2
1994	No Series			
1995	Atlanta Braves	Cleveland Indians	BRAVES	4-2
1996	Atlanta Braves	New York Yankees	YANKEES	4-2
1997	Florida Marlins	Cleveland Indians	MARLINS	4-3

CANADIAN MAJOR LEAGUE BASEBALL PLAYERS

Name	Birth Date / Place	1st MLB Year	Position	Teams
Alexander, Robert Som.	August 7, 1922, Vancouver, BC	1955	P	Cleveland
Atkinson, Bill	October 4, 1954, Chatham, ON	1976	P	Montréal
Bahr, Edson Garfield	October 16, 1919, Rouleau, QC	1946	P	Pittsburgh
Balaz, John	November 24, 1950, Toronto, ON	1974	OF	California
Barton, Vicent	February 1, 1908, Edmonton, AB	1931	OF	Chicago Cubs
Bertoia, Reno	January 8, 1935	1953	IF	Minnesota, Kansas City
Biasetti, Hank	January 14, 1922, Beano, Italy	1949	1b	Philadelphia Athletics
Boucher, Denis	March 7, 1968, Montréal, QC	1991	P	Toronto, Cleveland, Montréal
Bowsfield, Ted	January 10, 1936, Vernon, BC	1958	P	Boston, Cleveland, Los Angeles, Kansas City
Burgess, Thomas Roland	September 1, 1927, London, ON	1954	1b	St. Louis Browns, California
Butler, Rob	April 10, 1970, Toronto, ON	1993	OF	Toronto
Buxton, Ralph Stanley	June 7, 1911, Weybutn, SK	1938	P	Philadelphia Athletics, New York Yankees
Calvert, Paul Leo Emile	October 6, 1917, Montréal, QC	1942	P	Washington, Detroit
Clarke, Jay Justin	December 15, 1882, Amherstburg, ON	1905	C	Cleveland, Detroit, St.Louis Browns, Philadelphia
Cleveland, Reggie	May 23, 1948, Swift Current, SK	1969	P	St. Louis, Boston, Texas, Milwaukee
Cockman, James	April 16, 1873, Guelph, ON	1905	3b	New York Yankees
Collins, Charles		1884	2b/SS	
Colman, Frank Lloyd	March 2, 1919, London, ON	1942	OF/1b	Pittsburgh, New York Yankees
Congalto, William Millar	January 24, 1875, Guelph, ON	1902	OF	Chicago Cubs, Cleveland, Boston
Cook, Earl Davis	December 10, 1908, Stouffville, ON	1941	P	Detroit
Cormier, Rheal	April 23, 1967, Moncton, N.B.	1991	P	St. Louis
Cort, Barry Lee	April 15, 1956, Toronto, ON	1944	P	
Craig, Pete	July 7, 1940, LaSalle, ON	1964	P	Washington
Crosby, Ken	December 16, 1947, New Denver, BC	1975	P	Chicago Cubs
Currie, Clarence F.	December 30, 1878, Glencoe	1902	P	Chicago Cubs
Daly, Thomas Daniel	December 12, 1891, St. John, NB	1913	C/OF	Chicago White Sox, Cleveland, Chicago Cubs
Daviault, Raymond, J	May 27, 1934, Montreal, QC	1962	P	New York Mets
Dee, Maurice Leo	October 4, 1889, Halifax, NS	1915	SS	St. Louis Browns
Demarris, Fred		1890	P	
Doyle, John A.		1882	SS/OF	
Dickson, Jason	March 30, 1973, London, ON	1996	P	Anaheim
Ducey, Rob	May 24, 1965, Toronto, ON	1987	OF	Toronto, Texas
Dugas, Augustin J.	March 24, 1907, St. Jean-de-Matha, QC	1930	OF/1b	Pittsburgh, Philadelphia, Washington
Dunn, Stephen		1884	1b/3b	
Emslie, Robert Daniel		1883	P	
Erautt, Joseph Michael	September 1, 1921, Vibank, SK	1950	C	Chicago White Sox
Fisher, Harry Devereaux	January 3, 1926, Newbury, ON	1951	P	Pittsburgh
Ford, Eugene Wyman	April 16, 1881, Milton, ON	1905	P	Detroit
Ford, Russell William	April 25, 1883, Brandon, MB	1909	P	New York Yankees, Buffalo
Fowler, Dick	March 30, 1921, Toronto, ON	1941	P	Philadelphia
Frisk, Emil		1899	P/OF	
Frobel, Doug	June 6, 1959, Ottawa, ON	1982	OF	Pittsburgh, Montréal, Cleveland
Gardner, Alexander		1884	C	
Gardiner, Mike	November 19, 1965, Sarnia, ON	1990	P	Seattle, Boston, Montréal, Detroit
Gibson, George C.	July 22, 1880, London, ON	1905	C	Pittsburgh, New York Mets, Chicago Cubs
Gladu, Roland E	May 10, 1911, Montreal, QC	1944	3b/OF	Boston Braves
Gorbous, Glen	July 8, 1930, Drumheller, AB	1955	OF	Cincinatti, Philadelphia
Graney, John G.	June 10, 1886, St. Thomas, ON	1908	P/OF	Cleveland
Hanifin, Patrick James		1897	OF/2b	
Handrahan, James Vernon	Nov. 27, 1938, Charlottetown, PEI	1964	P	Kansas City
Hardy, David Alexander	??, 1877, Toronto, ON	1902	P	Chicago Cubs
Harkness, Tim	December 23, 1937, Lachine, QC	1961	1b	Los Angeles, New York
Harris, Bill	December 3, 1931, Duguayville, NB	1957	P	Brooklyn, Los Angeles

Name	Birth Date / Place	1st MLB Year	Position	Teams
Harrison, Thomas James	January 18, 1945, Trail, BC	1965	P	Kansas City
Heath, Jeff	April 1, 1915, Fort William, ON	1936	OF	Cleveland, Washington, St. Louis, Boston
Hiller, John	April 8, 1943, Toronto, ON	1965	P	Detroit
Hodgson, Paul J.D.	April 14, 1960, Montréal, QC	1980	OF	Toronto
Hooper, Bob	May 30, 1922, Leamington, ON	1950	P	Philadelphia, Cleveland, Cincinatti
Horsman, Vince	March 3, 1967, Halifax, N.S	1991	P	Toronto, Oakland
Hoy, Pete	June 29, 1966, Brockville, ON	1992	P	Boston
Hulen, Bill		1896	SS/OF	
Humphries, John H.		1883	C/OF	
Hunter, William Robert		1884	C	
Irvin, Arthur Albert		1880	SS	
Irwin, John		1882	SS/3b	
Jenkins, Fergie	December 13, 1943, Chatham, ON	1965	P	Philadelphia, Chicago, Texas, Boston
Johnson, Abraham		1893	SS/2b	
Jones, Michael		1890	P	
Jones, William Dennis	April 8, 1887, Hartland, NB	1911	OF/1b	Boston Braves
Judd, Thomas Wm. Oscar	February 14, 1908, Rebecca	1941	P	Boston, Philadelphia
Kellum, Winford Ansley	April 11, 1876, Waterford, ON	1901	P	Boston, Cincinatti, St. Louis
Kerr, John Melville	May 22, 1903, Souris	1925	PR	Chicago Cubs
Kilkenny, Mike	April 11, 1945, Bradford, ON	1969	P	Detroit, Oakland, San Diego, Cleveland
Knight, Joseph William		1884	P/OF	
Knowles, James		1884	IF	
Korince, George	January 10, 1946, Ottawa, ON	1966	P	Detroit
Krakauskas, Joseph Victor	March 28, 1915, Montréal, QC	1937	P	Washington, Cleveland
Kyle, Andrew Ewing	October 29, 1889, Toronto, ON	1912	OF	Cincinatti
LaForest, Byron, J.	April 18, 1917, Edmonton, AB	1945	OF/3b	Boston
Lake, Frederick Lovett		1891	C	
Landreth, Larry	March 11, 1955, Stratford, ON	1976	P	Montréal
Lawrence, James Ross	February 12, 1939, Hamilton, ON	1963	IF	Cleveland
Law, Ronald David	March 14, 1946, Hamilton, ON	1969	P	Cleveland
Lepine, Louis Joseph	September 5, 1876, Montréal, QC	1902	OF	Detroit
Lines, Dick	August 17, 1938, Montréal, QC	1966	P	Washington
Lisi, Ricardo Patrick E.	March 17, 1956, Halifax, NS	1981	OF	Texas
Long, Nelson	September 28, 1876, Burlington, ON	1902	P	Boston Braves
Lyons, Patrick Jerry		1890		
MacKenzie, Eric Hugh	August 29, 1932, Glendon, AB	1955	C	Kansas City
MacKenzie, Ken	March 10, 1934, Gore Bay, ON	1960	P	Milwaukee, New York, St. Louis, San Francisco, Houston
Maranda, Georges	January 15, 1932, Levis, QC	1950	P	San Francisco, Minnesota
Marchildon, Phil	Nov. 25, 1913, Penatanguishene, ON	1940	P	Philadelphia, Boston
Maysey, Matt	January 8, 1967, Hamilton, ON	1992	P	Montréal, Milwaukee
McCabe, Ralph Herbert	October 21, 1918, Napanee, ON	1946	P	Cleveland
McCaskill, Kirk	April 9, 1961, Kapuskasing, ON	1985	P	California, Chicago
McGovern, Arthur John	February 27, 1882, St. John, NB	1905	C	Boston
McKay, Dave	March 14, 1950, Vancouver, BC	1975	IF	Minnesota, Toronto, Oakland
McLean, John	July 18, 1881, Fredericton, NB	1901	C	Boston, Chicago Cubs, St. Louis, New York Mets
Mead, Charles Richard	April 9, 1921, Vermilion, AB	1943	OF	New York Mets
Mensor, Ed	November 7, 1888, Woodville, ON	1912	IF/OF	Pittsburgh
Miller, Roy Oscard	February 4, 1883, Chatham, ON	1910	OF	Chicago Cubs, Boston Braves, Philadelphia
Mountjoy, Billy		1891	2b	
O'Brien, John J.		1891	2b	
O'Connor, Daniel C.		1890	1b	
O'Hara, Wm. Alexander	August 14, 1883, Toronto, ON	1909	OF	St. Louis
O'Neill, Frederick James		1887	OF	
O'Neill, James Edward		1883	P/OF	
O'Neill, John William	January 22, 1880, St. John, NB	1904	OF	Boston, Washington, Chicago White Sox
O'Neill, Joseph Henry	February 20, 1897, Ridgetown, ON	1922	P	Philadelphia
O'Rourke, James Francis	November 28, 1891, Hamilton, ON	1912	IF	Boston Braves, Brooklyn, Washington, Boston Red Sox, Detroit, St. Louis Browns
Osbourne, Frederick W		1890		
Ostrosser, Brian Leonard	June 17, 1949, Hamilton, ON	1973	SS	New York Mets
Owens, Frank Walter	January 26, 1886, Toronto, ON	1905	C	Boston, Chicago White Sox, Brooklyn, Baltimore
Oxley, Henry Havelock		1884	C	

Name	Birth Date / Place	1st MLB Year	Position	Teams
Pagan, Dave	September 15, 1949, Nipawin, SK	1973	P	New York Yankees, Baltimore, Seattle, Pittsburgh
Phillips, William B.		1879	1b	
Piche, Ron	May 22, 1935, Verdun, QC	1960	P	Milwaukee, California, St. Louis
Pinnance, Edward D.	September 22, 1879, Walpole I., ON	1903	P	Philadelphia
Pladson, Gord	July 31, 1956, New Westminster, BC	1979	P	Houston
Puhl, Terry	July 8, 1956, Melville, SK	1977	OF	Houston, Kansas
Quantrill, Paul	November 3, 1968, Port Hope, ON	1992	P	Boston
Randall, Newton J.	February 3, 1880, New Lowell, ON	1907	OF	Chicago Cubs, Boston Braves
Raymond, Claude	May 7, 1937, St. Jean, QC	1959	P	Chicago, Milwaukee, Houston, Atlanta, Montréal
Reid, Wm. Alexander		1883	IF/OF	
Reimer, Kevin	June 28, 1964, Enderby, BC	1988	OF	Texas, Milwaukee
Richardson, Arthur L.		1884	IF	
Riley, James Norman	May 25, 1895, Bayfield	1921	2b	St. Louis, Washington
Robertson, Sherry	January 1, 1919, Montréal, QC	1940	OF	Washington, Philadelphia
Rosen, Goodwin George	August 28, 1912, Toronto, ON	1937	OF	Brooklyn, New York Mets
Ross, Ernest Bertram	March 31, 1880, Toronto, ON	1902	P	Baltimore
Rowan, David	December 6, 1882, Elora, ON	1911	1b	St.Louis Browns
Roy, Jean-Pierre	June 26, 1920, Montreal, QC	1946	P	Brooklyn
Rutherford, John	May 5, 1925, Belleville, ON	1952	P	Brooklyn
Selkirk, George Alexander	January 4, 1908, Huntsville, ON	1934	OF	New York Yankees
Shank, Harvey Tillman	July 29, 1946, Toronto, ON	1970	P	California
Shields, Vincent William	November 18, 1900, Fredericton, NB	1924	P	St. Louis Browns
Shipanoff, Dave	November 13, 1959, Edmonton, AB	1985	P	Philadelphia
Siddall, Joe	October 25, 1967, Windsor, ON	1993	C	Montréal, Florida
Sincock, Herbert Sylvester	September 8, 1887, Barkerville, BC	1908	P	Cincinatti
Sketchley, Harry Clement	March 30, 1919, Virden, MB	1942	OF	Chicago White Sox
Smith, Charles Marvin		1880	IF	
Snyder, Frank C.		1898	C	
Somers, William		1889	OF	
Stairs, Matt	February 27, 1969	1985	OF	Montréal, Boston, Oakland
Steele, Robert Wesley	March 29, 1894, Cassbum	1916	P	St. Louis, Pittsburgh, N.Y. Mets
Taylor, Ron	December 13, 1937, Toronto, ON	1962	P	Cleveland, St. Louis, Houston, New York, San Diego
Thompson, John		1882	P	
Upham, John	December 29, 1941, Windsor, ON	1967	P	Chicago
Van Brabant, Camille Oscar	September 28, 1926, Kingsville, ON	1954	P	Philadelphia, Kansas City
Wainhouse, Dave	November 7, 1967, Toronto, ON	1991	P	Montréal
Walker, George A.		1888	P	
Walker, Larry	December 1, 1966, Maple Ridge, BC	1989	OF	Montreal, Col.
Ward, Pete	July 26, 1939, Montreal, QC	1962	IF/OF	Baltimore, Chicago, New York
Watkins, William Henry		1884	IF	
Webber, Joseph E.		1884	IF	
Wilkie, Aldon J.	October 31, 1914, Zealandia, SK	1941	P	Pittsburgh
Wilson, Nigel	January 12, 1970, Ajax, ON	1993	OF	Florida
Wilson, Steve	December 13, 1964, Victoria, BC	1988	P	Texas, Chicago White Sox, New York Yankees
Wingo, Edmund Armand	October 8, 1895, Ste. Anne	1920	C	Phildaelphia
Wood, Fred S.		1884	C/OF	
Wood, Peter Burke		1885	P	

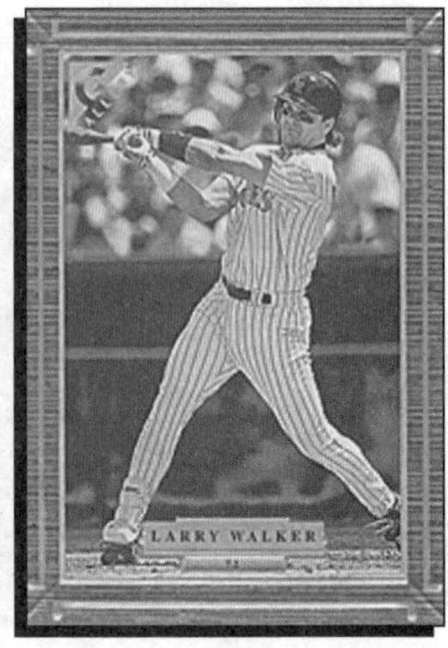

Books on Militaria and Numismatics

The Charlton Standard Catalogue of Canadian Government Paper Money, 11th Edition

Over 300 years of Canadian paper money. This new edition illustrates and prices all Canadian government paper money from the French colonial issues of 1685 to the current Bank of Canada notes. Army bills, provincial issues, municipal notes, Province of Canada bills, Dominion of Canada issues, special serial numbers and paper money errors are all included.
328 pages; 5-1/2" x 8-1/2"; softcover;
$19.95 Cdn. ($17.95 U.S.)

The Charlton Standard Catalogue of Canadian Colonial Tokens, 3rd Edition

A complete guide to the tokens used in Canada between 1794 and 1867. The tokens of Upper Canada, Lower Canada, Prince Edward Island, Nova Scotia, New Brunswick and Newfoundland are all listed and illustrated here, including Canadian blacksmith tokens. Each token is priced and described, including its composition, measurements, date and reference number.
272 pages; 5-1/2" x 8-1/2"; softcover;
$24.95 Cdn. ($19.95 U.S.)

The Charlton Standard Catalogue of Canadian Communion Tokens, First Edition

Over 130 years of Canadian communion tokens. From 1770 to the early 1900s, all tokens from Canada West, Canada East and the Maritimes are described, illustrated and priced in this handy catalogue. Also included are communion tokens from Canadian churches in the Caribbean and stock tokens. An introduction provides a history of the use of communion tokens.
288 pages; 5-1/2" x 8-1/2"; softcover;
$19.95 Cdn. ($17.95 U.S.)

The Charlton Standard Catalogue of Canadian Tire Cash Bonus Coupons, 2nd Edition, Ross Irwin

The latest in collectibles. Two hundred gas bar and store coupons produced by Canadian Tire since 1958 are described, illustrated and priced in three grades. This catalogue also includes a history of the Canadian Tire Corporation and information on the printing and grading of coupons.
72 pages; 5-1/2" x 8-1/2"; softcover;
$14.95 Cdn. ($11.95 U.S.)

The Charlton Canadian Numismatic Library – 1998

The Charlton Standard Catalogue of Government Paper Money, 10th edition and *The Charlton Standard Catalogue of Canadian Coins*, 52nd edition both on one CD-Rom. A zoom-in function allows the viewer to closely examine bank notes. The Full Text Retrieval search engine makes it simple to quickly find the coin, note or topic of your choice. A cut and paste feature allows you to easily update the spreadsheet you currently use to manage your collection.
$24.95 Cdn. ($19.95 U.S.)

The Charlton Standard Catalogue of Canadian Coins, 53rd Edition

No other coin catalogue offers so much! It illustrates, describes and prices the entire range of Canadian commercial and commemorative coins from the 1600s to the present. The historical background of each series is provided, as well as a general introduction to Canadian numismatics.
336 pages; 5-1/2" x 8-1/2"; softcover;
$12.95 Cdn. ($9.95 U.S.)

The 1999 Charlton Coin Guide, 38th Edition

An essential guide for pricing your collection. This catalogue lists, illustrates and prices all Canadian, Newfoundland and Maritime coinage, as well as Canadian medals, tokens and paper money. Also included are collector issues, Olympic coins and foreign gold coins.
120 pages; 5-1/2" x 8-1/2"; softcover;
$4.95 Cdn. ($3.95 U.S.)

The Charlton Standard Catalogue of Canadian Bank Notes, 3rd Edition

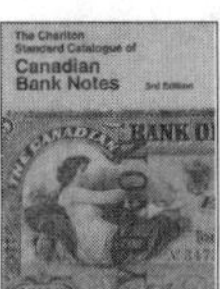

More information than in any other book of Canadian bank notes. All the bank notes produced in Canada since the 1800s are in this one easy-to-use, illustrated reference. For this edition a team of numismatic experts has expanded the data and updated the prices.
550 pages; 8-1/2" x 11"; softcover;
$59.95 Cdn. ($45.95 U.S.)

The Charlton Standard Catalogue of First World War Canadian Infantry Badges, 2nd Edition, W.K. Cross

Five times more badges than the first edition! Use this guide to easily determine the value of the cap, collar and shoulder insignia of Canada's World War I infantry. The manufacturers and the composition of the badges are listed, and the insignia are illustrated throughout. Histories of the battalions are provided, as well as background information for the collector.
432 pages; 5-1/2" x 8-1/2"; softcover;
$24.95 Cdn. ($19.95 U.S.)

The Charlton Standard Catalogue of First World War Canadian Corps Badges, 1st Edition, W.K. Cross

The only reference book of its kind! This unique catalogue lists, illustrates, describes and prices all the cap, collar and shoulder insignia of Canada's World War I corps battalions. It also features the history of many of the battalions and background information for the collector of military badges.
300 pages; 5-1/2" x 8-1/2"; softcover;
$24.95 Cdn. ($19.95 U.S.)

FOR COMPLETE ORDERING INFORMATION CONTACT US

✦ www.charltonpress.com ✦ e-mail: chpress@charltonpress.com

✦ Tel.: 1-800-442-6042 ✦ Fax: 1-800-442-1542

The Charlton Press 2040 Yonge Street, Suite 208, Toronto, Ontario, Canada M4S 1Z9